Cemetery Records of Lincoln - Moore Counties Tennessee

Compiled by:

Helen C. & Timothy R. Marsh

Southern Historical Press, Inc.
Greenville, South Carolina
1996

Copyright © 1983 by:
Marsh Historical Publications
Shelbyville, Tennessee

Copyright © Transfered 1996 to:
Southern Historical Press, Inc.
Greenville, South Carolina

All rights reserved. No part of this publication may be reproduced, stored in a retrieval system or transmitted in any form or by any means without the prior permission of the publisher.

Please Direct All Correspondence & Orders To:

Southern Historical Press, Inc.
P.O. Box 1267
375 West Broad Street
Greenville, S.C. 29602-1267

ISBN # 0-89308-234-1

Printed in the United States of America

CONTENTS

DEDICATION	iv
SYMBOLS AND ABBREVIATIONS	iv
INTRODUCTION	v
* LINCOLN COUNTY CEMETERY INDEX	vi, vii, viii, ix
* MOORE COUNTY CEMETERY INDEX	x
* LINCOLN-MOORE QUADRANGLE OVERLAY MAP	xi
* LINCOLN COUNTY CEMETERIES	1-357
* MOORE COUNTY CEMETERIES	358-439
BELLEVILLE QUADRANGLE	1-20, 358
BOONSHILL QUADRANGLE	21-49
BOONEVILLE QUADRANGLE	50-58, 359-395
CORNERSVILLE QUADRANGLE	59
CUMBERLAND SPRINGS QUADRANGLE (NOW LYNCHBURG EAST)	359-427
DELLROSE QUADRANGLE	60-85
FAYETTEVILLE QUADRANGLE	86-164
FLINTVILLE QUADRANGLE	165-191
FRANKEWING QUADRANGLE	192-213
HUNTLAND QUADRANGLE	214-227
LINCOLN QUADRANGLE	227-261
LOIS QUADRANGLE	427-439
MULBERRY QUADRANGLE	261-291, 439
PETERSBURG QUADRANGLE	291-325
TAFT QUADRANGLE	326-357
* NAME INDEX	440-452

—DEDICATION—

    This book is dedicated to the thousands of deceased citizens of Lincoln and Moore Counties, many early and prominent settlers, many relatively unknown, a number of Soldiers and Patriots of the American Revolution all sharing a common bond of being regrettably listed in this publication as: unmarked, name unknown, fieldstones with no inscriptions. We equally dedicate this book to the following for their encouragement and support, to our children, Marsha J. Markiewicz and Leslie D. Marsh, grandchildren Melissa M. and Timothy James Edwards, mothers Mrs. Vertna Braden Crawford and Mrs. Blanche Mathis Marsh and to the cherished memory of our fathers, Mr. Henry Clark Crawford and Mr. Richard Austin Marsh.

★★

SYMBOLS

* - Taken from newspapers.
** - Taken from Court Records.
*** - Taken from various family records.
F.S. - fieldstone.
TM - Temporary marker.
SOR - Soldier of The American Revolution.
Editors Note: The distances given in the cemetery locations are approximate air miles as taken from USGS Maps and road miles may differ. Detailed Quadrangle Maps as listed in this publication may be purchased from The Tennessee Valley Authority, Chattanooga, Tennessee or from the U. S. Geological Survey, Arlington, Virginia.

INTRODUCTION

    We are pleased to present this revised and combined edition of Lincoln-Moore County Cemetery Records, in the hope that it will prove helpful to all who are interested in the final resting place of the loved ones, friends and ancestors.

    For a period of five years while in quest of the lost cemeteries in Lincoln and Moore Counties, we were chased by belligerent bulls, dogs and goats, and encountered snakes and numerous varments, waded creeks and muddy branches, crawled through brush, poison ivy, briers and dense vegetation. We have walked many miles, ridden tractors and wagons, in the search. Many times after much walking and fence climbing we were distressed to find a few unmarked graves in an unnamed family cemetery, also many times we were exhilarated to find the marked grave of Pioneer Settlers who had contributed much to the growth and development of Lincoln and Moore Counties.

    Many of the old family cemeteries have completely disappeared to make way for cultivation. It was amazing to hear over and over again the story of how so many of the old family graveyards were destroyed by tenants or hired hands without the knowledge of the owner, of course, and if the owner did admit to it, well ......
"It was probably just an old Indian Graveyard".

    It seems the quickest way to deface and destroy a cemetery is to "put it in pasture". Cattle in a cemetery can do more damage in a few short weeks than years of exposure to the elements and vegetation.

    We can only wish that more of the old graves had been marked with inscribed markers. We realize the lack of finances, in so many cases, was the reason that commercial markers were not erected but a thoughtful descendant or friend with only a hammer and chisel, by inscribing a few words on a native limestone or slate rock could have contributed so much to this branch of genealogy and history.

    We have inspected each and every fieldstone for any visable sign of inscriptions, initials or dates and when so found copied and included in this publication. A number of readers will find that the dates on some of the markers do not correspond with the dates recorded in the family records. We must remember that many times the markers were erected years after the deceased were buried and the lapse of time made errors common, also, the stone cutter was subject to human errors. Those entries taken from newspaper obituary notices were also subject to error. Often the names or initials of the deceased and or survivors were listed incorrectly and occasionally the name of the cemetery was listed in error.

    The names of many of the Family Cemeteries is utter confusion in itself, having changed names time and time again down through the years. Quite often a cemetery will bear a name that has no relationship to the persons buried there.

    We have, to the best of our ability, tried to locate and record all the cemeteries in Lincoln and Moore Counties. We realize we have probably missed a few of them.

    The separate cemetery records we published of the two counties some years ago are now out of print, and as a large area of Moore County was originally part of Lincoln until 1872, we have now included the cemeteries in both counties in this revised edition. A few additions that have been received by the compilers after the first publications, have been included in this edition. No attempt has been made to update and include all the burials that have occured after the publication of the first books as this would have been an impossible undertaking.

    It is our earnest desire that this publication may be a significant contribution to a part of Lincoln and Moore County History and may benefit the present as well as future generations.

Helen C Marsh
Timothy R Marsh
1983

LINCOLN CEMETERY INDEX

ABERNATHY	351
ALEXANDER	97, 98
ALLSUP	193
ANDERSON	68
ARMSTRONG-COLE	14
ARMSTRONG-MOORE	93
ARMSTRONG-SORRELLS	13
ARNOLD	214
ASHBY	94, 95
ASHBY-WARDEN-GROCE	18
ASHBY	104
ASHBY	18
ASHBY-TURNER	104
ASHBY-WAID	261
ASHWORTH	247
AUSTIN	85
BAGGERLY	352
BARNES	31, 32
BATES	347
BAXTER	189
BEARDEN	354
BEARD	227
BEASLEY	193
BEAVERS-MOORE	184, 185
BENSON	166
BETHEL	36-39
BEVERLY	260
BLAIR	354, 355
BLAKE	301, 302
BLANCHE	74-82
BLEDSOE	2
BLEDSOE	69
BOONEVILLE	51-57
BOONSHILL-OLD SALEM	21-25
BOSTIC	169
BRADY	272
BRADY	278
BRAY	182
BRIGHT-HASTINGS	326
BROWNS CHAPEL-PLEASANT HILL	185-189
BROYLES	275
BRUCE	61
BRYAN-HOVIS	334, 335
BUCHANAN-McCOLLUM	100, 101
BUCHANAN	101
BUCHANAN-McELROY	106
BUCHANAN	106, 107
BUCHANAN	300
BUCHANAN	301
BUCHANAN	277
BUNTLEY	94
BUNTLEY	94
BURNS	275
BUTLER	334
CALDWELL	21
CAMPBELL	179-181
CAMPBELL	263
CAMPER	247
CAPTAIN SMITH	27
CARPENTER	351
CARPENTER	351
CARTER-STEPHENS	283
CARY	39
CEMETERY	39, 62, 63, 68, 99, 107, 113, 165, 171, 182, 196, 200, 204, 236, 242, 246, 261, 275, 283, 286, 301, 326, 347, 353
CENTER POINT	301
CHAMP-WARD	287, 288
CHAPMAN	302
CHILDS	26
CHILDRESS	29
CHITWOOD-MARTIN	28
CLARKE	21
CLARKE	26
CLIFT-WADE	99
COLE	351
COLE	352
COLE-ARMSTRONG	14
COLE-WILEY	15, 16
COLLIER	302
COLTER	19, 20
COLTER-DOLLINS	14, 15
COMMONS	28
COMMUNITY	214
COMMUNITY	228
CONCORD CHURCH	16, 17
CONGER	96
COPELAND	286, 287
CORDER-McCULLOCK	228
CORPIER	74
COWAN	107
CRANE	12
CRABTREE	303
CRAWFORD	27
CRAWFORD	102
CREASON	18
CROSS	74
CUMBERLAND PRESBYTERIAN CHURCH	304
CUNNINGHAM	104
CUNNINGHAM	113
DAMERON	220, 221
DANIEL	303
DAVES	102
DAVIS	59
DAVIS	192
DAVIS	242
DAVIS	250
DERRICK	26
DICKEY	40
DOLLINS-COLTER	14, 15
DUNLAP	326
EASTLAND-HOPKINS	183
ELORA	215, 219
EWING	68
FANNING	166
FANNING	288
FARRAR	60
FERGASON-THORNTON	16
FERGUSON	85
FIFE-GIVENS	327
FIRST PRESBYTERIAN CHURCH (OLD CITY)	108-112
FLINTVILLE	171-179
FLYNT	250
FORD	35

LINCOLN CEMETERY INDEX

FOSTER	2-5
FRANKLIN	84, 85
FREEMAN	5
FREEMAN	5
FULLERTON	40
GAGE	57
GATLIN	84
GATTIS	272-273
GEORGE-HOBBS	60
GEORGE-SMALL	15
GEORGE	61
GEORGE	94
GEORGE	201
GIBSON	1
GIBSON	101-102
GILBERT	8, 9
GILES	92
GILL	197, 198
GIVENS-FIFE	327
GOLDEN	166
GRAY-TAYLOR	165
GRAY	168
GREEN	114
GREER	10
GREGORY-HOVIS	198
GREGORY	278
GRILLS-KOONCE	229
GROCE-WARDEN-ASHBY	18
GROCE	20
GUM SPRING	169, 170
GUNTER	195
HAIRSTON	227
HALBERT	33, 34
HALL	14
HAMILTON	39
HANCOCK	247
HANKS	241
HARKINS	7, 8
HARRIS	100
HARRIS	167
HARRIS	241
HARRIS-JEAN	167
HASTINGS-BRIGHT	326
HAYES	59
HEDGEPETH	198
HENDERSON	246
HEREFORD	199, 200
HESTER	9
HESTER	182
HICKORY HILL	5, 6
HIGGINS-WHITAKER	98
HIGGINS	102
HOBBS-GEORGE	60
HOLMAN	214
HOLMAN	262
HOPKINS-EASTLAND	183
HOVIS-BRYAN	334, 335
HOVIS-GREGORY	198
HOWARD	275
HOWARD	286
HUDSON	297, 298
HULSEY	105
HUNTER	99
HUNTER	168
ISOM	97
ISOM	303
JACOBS-TURNEY	298
JACKSON	17
JARED	285
JEAN-HARRIS	167
JEAN	167
JOHNSON-WARDEN	95
JOHNSON	199
JOHNSTON	57
KEITH-WARDEN	96
KELSO-McGEE-McCARTNEY	229
KELSO (Old Section)	278-283
KENNEDY-THOMISON	103, 104
KENT	28
KILPATRICK	183
KILPATRICK	189, 190
KIMES	86
KING	8
KIRKLAND CHAPEL	348-350
KOONCE-GRILLS	229
LAND-SIMMS	259, 260
LAND	261
LANDESS	12
LANE	18
LAY	35
LEBANON CHURCH	40-49
LEE	194
LEONARD	167
LINCOLN	251-259
LOGAN	57
LOVETT	193
LOYD	274
MACEDONIA	243-246
MAJOR	62
MALONE	70-74
MANSFIELD	17
MARSH	305
MARTIN-CHITWOOD	28
MARY'S GROVE	350, 351
MEAD	276
MEDIUM	291-297
MELSON-WASHBURN	10, 11
MELTON	193
MERRELL	69
MERRITT	324
METCALF	60
MILAM	353
MORGAN	190, 191
MORGAN	276
Mt. MORIAH	262, 263
MOORE-ARMSTRONG	93
MOORE-BEAVERS	184, 185
MOORE	58
MOORE	263, 264
MOORES CHAPEL	283
MOOREHEAD	284
MOYERS	350, 351
MULBERRY	264-271
MUSE-STEPHENSON	5

LINCOLN CEMETERY INDEX

McADAMS	1, 2
McBURG	194, 195
McCLELLAN	165
McCARTNEY-McGEE-KELSO	229
McCLURE	286
McCOLLUM-BUCHANAN	100, 101
McCULLOCK-CORDER	228
McDANIEL	21
McDANIEL MEETING HOUSE	106
McDANIEL	242
McDANIEL-PARKS	276, 277
McELROY-BUCHANAN	106
McEWEN	324, 325
McFERRIN	346, 347
McGEE	20
McGEE-McCARTNEY-KELSO	229
McGEE	262
McLEAN	49
McNEAL	184
NEELY	353
NEW GROVE	63-68
NICHOLS	2
NOLES	273, 274
NORRIS	112
OLD	9
OLD ORCHARD-PETERSBURG	305-324
OLD SALEM-BOONSHILL	21-25
PAMPLIN	96
PAMPLIN	96
PAMPLIN	106
PARKER	98
PARKS-McDANIEL	276, 277
PARKS	105
PARK	213
PATTERSON	61, 62
PATTERSON	185
PETERSBURG-OLD ORCHARD	305, 324
PETTY	357
PHAGAN	3
PHILLIPS	8
PIGG	298, 299
PIGG	300
PITTS	93
PITTS	326
PITTS	327
PITTS	336
PITTS	336
PITTS	336
PLEASANT GROVE	236-241
PLEASANT HILL-BROWNS CHAPEL	185-189
PORCH	29
PREDESTINED PRIMATIVE CHURCH	82
PROSPECT CHURCH	233-235
PROSPERITY CHURCH	336-346
PRYOR	167
PRYOR	250
PYLANT	13
RAMBO	195
RAMSEY	49
RATLIFF	284
RAWLS	326, 327
REDD	1
REES	50
RENEGAR	273
RENEGAR	276
RENFROW	13
RHEA	114
ROBERTSON	220
ROBINSON	352
ROBISON	195
ROCKY SPRINGS	219, 220
RODEN	192
ROGERS	243
ROPER	83
ROSE HILL	114-164
ROUTT-WELLS	227, 228
ROWLAND HILL	232, 233
RUSSELL	119
RUTLEDGE	50
SANDLIN	327-334
SANDLIN	347
SCOTT	284
SHADY GROVE	221-227
SHARP	102
SHELTON	283
SHERRELL	85
SHILOH	201-204
SHOFNER	58
SHULL	99
SILVESTER	60
SIMMS	184
SIMMS-LAND	259, 260
SLATER	112
SMALL-GEORGE	15
SMALL	15
SMITH	192
SMITH	197
SMITH	168
SMITH	228
SMITH	241
SMITH	69, 70
SNODDY	166
SOLOMON	113
SOLOMON	276
SORRELLS-ARMSTRONG	13
SORRELLS	1
SOUTHWORTH	182
STATE LINE	247-250
STEPHENS	36
STEPHENSON-MUSE	5
STEPHENS-CARTER	283
STEWART CREEK	229-232
STILES	214
STILES	288-290
STONE	12
STONE	13
STONE	62, 63
STONE	98, 99
SUGG	34
SULSER	351
SULLIVAN	17
SULLIVAN	28
SULLIVAN	263
SUMNER	59
SWINEBROAD	196
SWAN CREEK CHURCH	30

LINCOLN CEMETERY INDEX

TAYLOR-GRAY 165	WARD-CHAMP 287, 288
TAYLOR 165	WARDEN-GROCE-ASHBY 18
TAYLOR 168	WARDEN-JOHNSON 95
THOMAS 14	WARDEN-KEITH 96
THOMISON-KENNEDY 103, 104	WARREN 170
THOMISON 228	WARREN 277
THORNTON-FERGASON 16	WASHBURN-MELSON 10, 11
THORPE 197	WEBB 278
TIPPS 273	WELCH 325
TOWRY 260	WELLS-ROUTT 227, 228
TOWRY 242	WELLS 196
TRAVIS 250	WHITAKER 263
TURNER-ASHBY 104	WHITAKER 272
TULEY 303, 304	WHITAKER 291
TURNEY 30	WHITAKER 108
TURNEY-JACOBS 298	WHITAKER 35
	WHITAKER-HIGGINS 98
UNITY 86-92	WHITE 84
	WHITE 275
	WHITWORTH 181
WADE-CLIFT 99	WICKS 183
WAGGONER 20	WILES 50
WAID 11	WILEY-COLE 15, 16
WAID-ASHBY 261	WILSON 32, 33
WAKEFIELD 303	WILSON 195, 196
WALKER 105	WOODROOF 114
WALKER 106	WRIGHTS 205-213
WALKER 242	
	YOUNG 62
	ZIMMERMAN 35

MOORE CEMETERY INDEX

ALLEN	359
BAXTER	359
BAXTER	395
BEAN	427
BEAN	427
BENNETT	395
BENNETT	396
BETHEL	396
BOBO	396
BRANDON	427, 428
BRAZIER	439
BROWN	359
BUCKEYE	359
BUCKEYE-WAGGONER	392-395
CEMETERY	359
CHARITY	359-362
COBLE	428
COPELAND	428
COX	362
COUNTY LINE	396-398
COUSER	399
CRESON	362
DANCE	399
DANIEL	362
DAWDY	363
EATON	363
EDEN	363
EVANS	428
EVINS	429
FRAME	429, 430
GATTIS	363
GOWAN	364
GRAMMER-WAGGONER	400
GRABLE	430
GRAY (DAVID)	430
GRAY (JOHN)	431
HICKS	364
HIGHVIEW	364-366
HOOVER GROVE	400-402
HURRICANE CHURCH	403-407
JENKINS	431
LOIS	431-433
LYNCHBURG (CITY)	366-388

MARTIN	388
MENNONITE BROTHERHOOD	388
MOOREHEAD	433
MOTLOW	388
McNATT	388
NEECE	389
OAK GROVE	433, 434
PEARSON	389
PIONEER	407, 408
PLEASANT HILL	434
PLEASANT HILL CHURCH	408-413
POLLOCK	413
PORTER	434
PORTER-SHELTON	436
PRICE	413
PROSSER	358
PROSSER	358
RABY	391
RAYSVILLE CHURCH	413
REED	434, 435
RUDD	391
SAWYER	417
SCIVALLY	436
SHELTON-PORTER	436
SNOW	436
SMITH	439
SMITH CHAPEL	418-423
TIPPS	436
TRAVIS	436
TURKEY CREEK CHURCH	423-425
UNION CHURCH	437

****

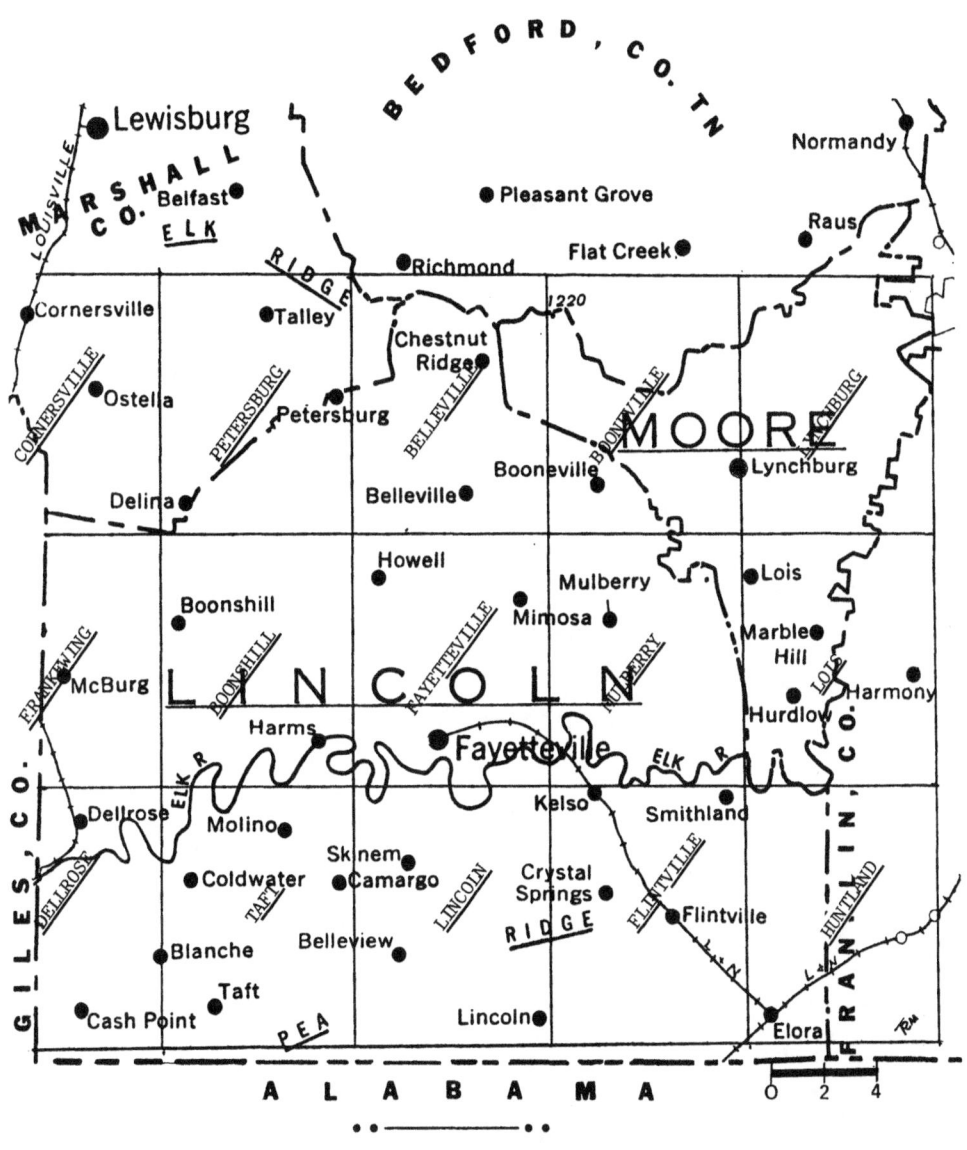

LINCOLN--MOORE QUADRANGLE MAP

BELLEVILLE QUADRANGLE

SORRELL CEMETERY

LOCATION: Three and one-half miles NE of Petersburg, Tennessee, near Bedford, Marshall County lines, near Hannah Gap.

Thomas Sorrells, his wife and child are buried here. ***

* *

GIBSON CEMETERY

LOCATION: Three and one-half miles NE of Petersburg, Tennessee, at Hannah Gap on east side of Hannah Gap-Petersburg road.

Josiah B. Gibson
Dec 18, 1819
Sep 7, 1856

Thomas Gibson
Jul 12, 1791
Dec 19, 1869
&
Mahala C. Gibson
Aug 10, 1795
Jul 2, 1861

John T. Smith
1804-1846

Tennie Smith
1885-1961

Loue V. Gibson
Jul 25, 1859
Feb 13, 1913

Mahalie C. Gibson
Oct 10, 1850
Apr 16, 1936

E. A. Gibson
(no dates)

Jessie Gibson
1889-1952

5 unmarked graves.

Thomas Gibson
Dec 6, 1819
Sep 5, 1892

M. J. Gibson
Apr 20, 1865
Jul 15, 1866
Age: 1y, 2m, 25d.

Nathan F. Gibson
Jul 28, 1821
Sep 14, 1870
Age: 46y, 1m, 17d.

Thomas W. Gibson
Aug 18, 1854
May 17, 1913

Emily E. Gibson
Feb 10, 1857
Apr 5, 1925

Elizabeth Gibson
Aug 6, 1827
Jun 23, 1899

Nathan F. Gibson
Jul 28, 1863
Jul 31, 1910

* *

REDD CEMETERY

LOCATION: Four and one half miles NE of Petersburg, Tennessee, on the south side of Chestnut Ridge, one-fourth mile off Foster Hollow Road.

James S. Redd
Dec   1821
Oct   1890
&
Mary A. Redd
        1823
Nov 3, 1905

A. D. Marsh
Apr 7, 1824
Nov 9, 1875
&
Sarah E. Marsh
Dec 16, 1827
Mar 9, 1899

John T. Marsh
Nov 29, 1849
Mar 18, 1874

T. D. Redd
Oct 28, 1862
Nov 8, 1862

James M. Marsh
Dec 15, 1858
Dec 23, 1863

M. E. Redd
Dec 26, 1858
Aug 15, 1859

A. C. Redd
Mar 5, 1849
Jul 27, 1865

Ora D. Redd
Nov 29, 1891
Sep 7, 1893

E. S. Redd
Oct 7, 1863
Oct 14, 1865

G. M. Redd
Mar 28, 1852
Aug 30, 1897

* *

McADAMS CEMETERY

LOCATION: Three and one-half miles NE of Petersburg, Tennessee, on east side of Hannah Gap-Petersburg Road.

Annie B., daughter of
W. C. & M. J. Greer
Aug 7, 1896
Oct 19, 1897

Infant Son of
W. F. & M. V. Gibson
Mar 9, 1909
Dec 20, 1907
(dates could be reversed)

Margaret W. McAdams
Jan 18, 1815
Aug 17, 1847

J. J. McAdams
Nov 2, 1828
Jul 5, 1837

BELLEVILLE QUADRANGLE

Henrietta A. McAdams
Jul 20, 1831
Oct 29, 1853

Johnnie, Son of
J. W. & R. E. McAdams
Nov 19, 1895
Jul 5, 1897

John B., Infant Son of
J. C. & M. J. McAdams
Nov 27, 1853
Dec 12, 1854

John McAdams
Sep 22, 1788
Apr 18, 1870

Henreta McAdams
Jun 13, 1789
Aug 17, 1855

M. M. McAdams
Mar 7, 1832
Sep 18, 1902

J. I. McAdams
Mar 15, 1827
Nov 25, 1893

M. J. McAdams
Jul 20, 1851
Jul 6, 1903

Callie, Daughter of
S. F. & C. D. Morris
Feb 29, 1878
Oct 22, 1893

Sarah E. Patterson
Aug 23, 1856
(no date)

Several unmarked graves.

Arthur Carol Simmons
Aug 17, 1880
Jul 31, 1930
&
Mary Modena Simmons
Jul 3, 1881
Jun 29, 1932

J. C. Patton
Sep 24, 1838
(no date)

* *

NICHOLS CEMETERY

LOCATION: Three and one-half miles NE of Petersburg, Tennessee, on east side of Hannah Gap-Petersburg Road, and south of Hannah Gap Church.

Parson
Green W. Nichols
Jun 21, 1821
Jun 14, 1880

W. H. Nichols
Mar 17, 1829
Jan 18, 1900
&
Nancy J. Nichols
Mar 11, 1842
May 18, 1910

M. J. (Martha J.), wife of
W. W. Gilbert
Jan 25, 1819
Jul 25, 1879

Several unmarked graves.

Cheriby
(fieldstone-no dates)

* *

BLEDSOE CEMETERY

LOCATION: Three and one-half miles NE of Petersburg, Tennessee, one-fourth mile east of Hannah Gap-Petersburg Road and south of Hannah Gap Church.

Horace, Son of
H. H. & Fannie Bledsoe
Jun 8, 1877
Aug 11, 1881

Delia, Daughter of
H. H. & Fannie Bledsoe
Oct 29, 1861
Aug 29, 1864

Infant of
H. H. & Fannie Bledsoe
Jul 29, 1863
Aug 3, 1863

Other unmarked graves.

* *

FOSTER CEMETERY

LOCATION: Four and one-half miles NE of Petersburg, Tennessee, in Foster Hollow and east of Foster Hollow Road.

Bessie Bledsoe
Sep 13, 1892
Mar 19, 1908

B. D. Bledsoe
Jul 3, 1860
Feb 10, 1906
& wife
Theo Foster Bledsoe
May 29, 1864
May 24, 1896

John R. Foster
Sep 22, 1827
Oct 11, 1897

Mary E., wife of
J. R. Foster
Apr 22, 1832
Nov 13, 1905

Moses Calvin, Infant Son of
John R. & Mary E. Foster
Nov 19, 1859
Oct 12, 1869

Peneta Penora, Infant Dau of
John R. & Mary E. Foster
Mar 19, 1858
Nov 10, 1858

Lee Hensley
1872-1954

J. D. Bledsoe
Died Oct 15, 1894
Age: 68 years

J. M. Nichols
May 3, 1859
Aug 28, 1882

Sarah Muse
Mar 25, 1824
May 11, 1862

Infant Daughter of
P. & R. E. Melson
B&D Nov 3, 1874

J. C., Son of
P. & R. E. Melson
Jan 27, 1881
Feb 3, 1881

Infant Son of
J. R. & M. F. Muse
B&D Sep 1871

S. L. Nichols
Feb 11, 1879
Mar 17, 1879

Tama Lambert
Died Jan 24, 1872
Age: 78ym, 10m, 16d.

Mariah Lambert
Died Jan 20, 1892
Age: 71 years

Elvira Lambert
Aug 15, 1844
Aug 21, 1860

N. E. Nichols
Feb 8, 1860
May 11, 1861

Darthula Nichols
May 21, 1875
May 25, 1875

BELLEVILLE QUADRANGLE

S. L. Nichols
Feb 11, 1879
Mar 17, 1879

J. M. Nichols
May 3, 1859
Aug 28, 1882

Johnie Nichols
Sep 28, 1888
Mar 22, 1890

Briggs Nichols
Jun   1836
Dec 27, 1891
&
Ailcy Nichols
Oct 31, 1837
Nov 11, 1910

Infant of
C. E. & M. L. Barham
B&D May 28, 1902

Ma--an Bonner
1855-1930

Hattie B. Nichols
May 13, 1895
Oct 3, 1895

Mary C. Bonner
May 7, 1882
Oct 28, 1891

W. H. Foster
Aug 22, 1829
Sep 7, 1904

Martha C. Foster
Nov 8, 1829
Nov 6, 1916

M. W., daughter of
W. H. & Mary Foster
Jun 21, 1861
May 15, 1866

Mary Foster, wife of
W. H. Foster
Jul 4, 1827
Apr 19, 1866

Infant Son of
W. H. & Mary Foster
B&D Apr 9, 1866

Henry C., Son of
H. C. & N. S. Lambert
Aug 31, 1875
Jan 5, 1876

R. A. Foster
     1835
May 1, 1861

Alice Foster
     1826
Jun 1, 1861

A. M. Foster
1851-1862

S. J. Foster
1846-1863

J. L. Foster
Feb 28, 1803
Apr 9, 1871

Nancy, wife of
Jas. L. Foster
Dec 23, 1802
Jan 2, 1867

Samuel B. Morrison
Aug 29, 1855
Sep 26, 1876

Ollie Bartlett
Oct 26, 1876
Mar 3, 1915

Infant Son of
E. H. & Allie Bartlett
B&D Feb 15, 1917

Ezella, wife of
Tom Shaddy
Aug 11, 1878
Jun 26, 1907

J. B. Bartlette
Jan 12, 1851
Jan 30, 1928

Elvira Bartlett
Jul 8, 1852
Nov 22, 1895

Horace Bartlette
Aug 11, 1880
May 11, 1881

_____ Bartlett
--- --, --05
died 1948
(Thompson F. Home)

Willis H. Foster
1871-19(no date)
&
Maggie M. Foster
1881-1943

Horace Bartlett
(no dates)

J. W. Foster
Dec 31, 1839
Aug 22, 1901

M. J. Foster
Aug 15, 1837
Nov 16, 1896

2 Infant Sons of
T. J. & A. B. Burns
B&D Jul 3, 1883

Infant Son of
T. J. & A. B. Burns
B&D Oct 7, 1882

Callie E., Daughter of
T. J. & A. B. Burns
Feb 7, 1880
Jun 4, 1882

J. O., Son of
T. J. & A. B. Burns
Jun 7, 1878
Oct 1, 1878

Infant Son of
T. J. & A. B. Burns
B&D Sep 11, 1876

Nancy J., wife of
T. W. Jones
Dec 28, 1860
Oct 24, 1888

Allie, Son of
G. M. & S. E. Redd
Apr 1, 1889
Jan 15, 1913

Bettie Wagster, wife of
G. M. Redd
1853-1943

W. C. Wagster
Jul 7, 1832
Feb 5, 1900

Mary A., wife of
W. C. Wagster
Aug 4, 1835
Jul 29, 1894

William H. Wagster
Feb 10, 1877
Aug 10, 1908

R. A. Wagster
Nov 6, 1854
Jun 17, 1930
&
Nancy R. Foster
Jan 15, 1858
1941

David Wagster
Dec 18, 1858
Jun 17, 1931

Mollie, wife of
David Wagster
Feb 18, 1858
Feb 16, 1923

A. L., Son of
J. A. & F. A. Foster
May 3, 1899
Jul 8, 1899

Cora May Heath
Oct 27, 1898
Nov 30, 1906

S. N. L.
Feb 1, 1879
Apr 5, 1879

N. L. F.
(no dates)

L. B. Foster
Apr 14, 1866
May 9, 1895

Lucy Foster
Died July 15, 1893
Age: 23y, 11m, 13d.

Peter Foster
Feb 23, 1844
(no date)
&
Sarah Foster
Feb 15, 1842
Oct 17, 1903

John Carey Burns
1887-1958
(Gowen-Smith FH)

L. O. Nichols
Dec 1, 1871
Jan 13, 1933
(Sailor Memorial)

Gothie A., wife of
L. O. Nichols
Dec 31, 1867
May 19, 1907

Maggie Nichols
Nov 10, 1914
Nov --, 1914

Winnie C., Daughter of
L. O. & M. D. Nichols
Apr 19, 1909
Aug 5, 1909

G. R. Raney
Sep 6, 1835
Sep 8, 1900

Rose, wife of
J. L. Lovett
May 14, 1875
Aug 9, 1912

J. R. Nichols
1866-1936
&
Ella Nichols
1874-1938

John S., Son of
J. L. & Rose Lovett
Sep 6, 1905
Jul 31, 1909

Ben F. Nichols
May 21, 1875
Apr 15, 1963
&
Mattie F. Nichols
Apr 29, 1877
Dec 4, 1961

P. R. Wagster
Mar 1870 - Feb 1925

BELLEVILLE QUADRANGLE

M. J., wife of
T. L. Foster
Aug 2, 1873
May 15, 1901

Infant Son of
J. W. & M. C. Foster
Jan 26, 1896
Jan 28, 1896

Minnie C., wife of
J. W. Foster
Dec 21, 1878
Feb 1, 1896

Infant Daughter of
J. M. & M. A. Lambert
B&D Jan 12, 1899

Annie O., Daughter of
J. M. & M. A. Lambert
Mar 1, 1898
Apr 7, 1898

Annie Noland
1887-1935

Mary Frances Bledsoe
1910-1911

Annie Bell Bledsoe
Feb 4, 1904
Sep 29, 1962

Frances Bledsoe
1910-1911
(Could be same as above)

John A. Bledsoe
1862-1943
&
Nora Bledsoe
1881-1959

William Leonard King
Mar 24, 1917
Sep 10, 1968
&
Peggy L. King
Apr 17, 1916

Infant of
J. H. & L. J. Greer
B&D Dec 25, 1911

Sarah E., Daughter of
G. L. & Jessie E. Redd
Nov 10, 1914
Nov 12, 1915

Robert T. King
1919-1937

Eley Hue Nunley
Alabama
Pvt Co A, 39 US Vol Inf
Jul 23, 1879
Nov 11, 1954

Annie E. Foster
Jul 13, 1895
Nov 29, 1895

T. A. Foster
Died Oct 12, 1895
Age: 36 years

J. R. Foster
Died Apr 1, 1895
Age: 38 years

G. W. Moore
Dec 7, 1862
Dec 20, 1925

J. A., wife of
G. W. Moore
Apr 20, 1874
Apr 20, 1902

Infant Daughter of
G. W. & J. A. Moore
B&D Sep 18, 1895

Finnis Moore
Dec 14, 1891
Oct 29, 1908

Bettie, wife of
Joe Shaddy
1875-1911

Verna M., Daughter of
Joe & Bettie Shaddy
Oct 14, 1894
Nov 1, 1898

Charles Edward Beck
Aug 18, 1916
Nov 13, 1927

Annie Lucile Beck
May 2, 1911
May 16, 1926

J. R. Wagster
Apr 2, 1864
Oct 3, 1928

Lonnie L. Wagster
Aug 5, 1903
Aug 19, 1923

A. E. Redd
1860-1935
&
Emma E. Redd
1866-19(no date)

Lillard "Did" Redd
Aug 4, 1891
Dec 18, 1963

Hermine Russell
Aug 8, 1923
Nov 18, 1925

Agnes Ermine, wife of
Andrew H. Beck
Jul 26, 1888
Nov 24, 1919

C. W. Freeman
Jan 24, 1876
Nov 12, 1905

Nettie L. Freeman
Oct 6, 1873
Aug 21, 1905

F. V. Freeman
Apr 24, 1854
Apr 16, 1909

A. M. Freeman
Feb 20, 1849
May 31, 1899

N. M. Freeman
Aug 17, 1893
Nov 3, 1895

A. E. Freeman
Jul 26, 1884
Oct 6, 1885

Mattie B. Bartlett
1859-1954

Loyd Bartlett
Jun 25, 1902
Feb 21, 1930

W. S. Graham
1863-1928

Sarah J. Graham
1871-1941

B. Graham
Oct 28, 1908
Dec 20, 1903

William H. Nichols
1862-19(no date)
&
Docia Ann Nichols
1867-1941

Stanley T. Nichols
Oct 16, 1896
Jan 4, 1953
&
Willie D. Nichols
Mar 31, 1900

Infant of S. T. &
Willie Nichols
B&D Jun 18, 1922

Several unmarked graves.

Infant Son of
H. A. & D. E. Foster
B&D Jul 18, 1910

Isaac Morton
Aug 9, 1842
(no date)
&
Nancy Morton
Jan 8, 1842
Aug 24, 1910

James P. Greer
1867-1934

Mary E. Greer
1875-1949

Peter Melson
Oct 22, 1833
Aug 9, 1911

Lillie, wife of
T. L. Melson
Oct 26, 1887
Jan 1, 1918

Felix, Son of
T. L. & Lillie Melson
Sep 18, 1910
Oct 9, 1910

W. T. Bledsoe
Aug 25, 1875
Mar 31, 1911

Ella Bledsoe
1879-1966
(Davis-Ralston FH)

S. J. F.
(no dates)

M. A. W.
(no dates)

A. C.
(no dates)

Laura C. King
1915-1916

Billy Logan McGee
1929-1929

Ada Lee Nunley
Dec 9, 1890
Feb 28, 1959

Otha King
Sep 16, 1882
Jan 3, 1923

J. R. King
1919-1936
&
H. N. King
1915-1934

BELLEVILLE QUADRANGLE

Mrs. S. C.*, wife of James R. Foster Died Jul 25, 1891 Age: 39 years	Mr. Marion Bonner* Died Jul 7, 1918 Age: 72 years	Mrs. W. R. Foster* Died Aug 21, 1899 Age: 50 years	Several unmarked graves.

* *

FREEMAN CEMETERY

LOCATION: Five miles NE of Petersburg, Tennessee, on top of high hill, west of Helton Hollow.

Abner Freeman and other members of his family are buried here. Only three graves, marked by native fieldstones, no inscriptions. ***

* *

FREEMAN CEMETERY

LOCATION: Five miles NE of Petersburg, Tennessee on Chestnut Ridge-Bledsoe Road.

Mary Ann, wife of P. H. Freeman Mar 29, 1852 Feb 2, 1875 & Pleasant H. Freeman Sept 25, 1851 Jun 29, 1915 & Nacy C., wife of P. H. Freeman Aug 24, 1859 Jan 2, 1921	Johnye Lee, Daughter of P. H. & N. C. Freeman Sep 10, 1898 Nov 17, 1920 Lillian Irene, wife of Rev. George H. Freeman Jan 7, 1882 Aug 23, 1917 2 graves open (moved)	W. W. Reese May 20, 1807 Mar 8, 1899 & wife Mary Jane Reese Jan 19, 1826 Jan 12, 1862	George William, Son of G. H. & Irene Freeman May 15, 1901 May --, 1902 Virginia Clare, Daughter of George H. & Irene Freeman Sep 24, 1911 Jul 30, 1914

* *

MUSE-STEPHENSON CEMETERY

LOCATION: One-fourth mile N of Bledsoe, Chestnut Ridge Road, on Foster Hollow Branch.

Clarron Raney Jan 14, 1853 Jan 15, 1911 Della E., wife of J. J. Muse Apr 21, 1870 Jun 12, 1894	W. P. Raney Sep 13, 1828 Apr 22, 1922	Oscar Muse 1870-1956 & Fannie Muse 1868-1945	Sarah Stephenson Died Dec 1, 1843 Age: 67 years

* *

HICKORY HILL CEMETERY

LOCATION: On Chestnut Ridge, at Hickory Hill Church, Bedford County line.

William Lairmore Mills 1902-1970 Rowlin T. Clifford 1913-1968 (Howell-Thompson FH) Keneth Dale Rogers B&D Feb 16, 1963	Rickey Rogers B&D Oct 31, 1959 & twin Vickey Rogers Oct 31, 1959 Nov 1, 1959 Jack Howard 1904-1964	Leonard Prosser, Son of J. L. & H. A. Graham B&D Nov 16, 1926 Leonard Graham Aug 9, 1891 Jan 21, 1933 & Hattie P. Graham Oct 21, 1893 ------------	James Oliver Graham Tennessee Tec 5 US Army, W W II Nov 8, 1917 Aug 27, 1969 Aaron Edward Bledsoe Tennessee Pvt 105, Coast ARTY BN (AA) WW II Mar 29, 1910 Jun 8, 1963

BELLEVILLE QUADRANGLE

Hoyt W. Bledsoe
1916-1969
(Gowen-Smith FH)

Arlene Bledsoe
Jun 18, 1922
Jan 21, 1923

Ebbie E. Bledsoe
Dec 31, 1874
Sep 16, 1954

Pete Phillips
Jul 10, 1882
May 31, 1963
&
Fannie P. Phillips
Sep 13, 1886

Mother Coope
(no dates)

Albert E. Coope
Jan 10, 1892
Jul 10, 1922

Emma Hazlewood Powell
Aug 14, 1889

Oliver D. Powell
1889-1939

Elsie Viola Powell
1909-1920

Leland A. Powell
1923-1940

R. W. Powell
Tennessee
Pvt AT Co 13 Inf, WW II
Jan 17, 1924
Sep 25, 1960

R. C. Coope
Jul 1, 1915
Oct 23, 1922

Davy Cleek
Jun 15, 1880

&
Rebecca Cleek
Sep 16, 1878
Aug 16, 1965

Robert, Infant of
D. C. & Beckie Cleek
Jun 9, 1918
Jun 14, 1918

James Isaac Casteel
Died 1905
(no age given)
&
Henrietta Steelman Casteel
Died 1905
(no age given)

Little Nell, Daughter of
C. T. & M. C. Holley
May 26, 1906
Oct 27, 1907

Gertrude Clifford Warren
Oct 14, 1881
Apr 2, 1966

Charlie C., Son of
J. D. & M. J. Holley
Jan 21, 1891
Jan 5, 1892

William C. Powell
1881-19(no date)
&
Viola Clifford Powell
1888-1946

John W. Smith
Jul 14, 1844
Feb 12, 1917
&
Mary A. Smith
Feb 21, 1844
Oct 20, 1905

Drucilla, wife of
Abner Freeman
Jan 10, 1820
Aug 2, 1892

Joel Steelman
1831-Nov 1, 1904

L. C., wife of
Joel Steelman
Jun 9, 1836
Nov 28, 1894

Perry G. Steelman
Sep 2, 1888
Dec 28, 1896

Mattie Steelman
Nov 19, 1864
Nov 19, 1904

William B. Freeman Steelman
Feb 22, 1886
Apr 1, 1907

Agatha, Daughter of
J. A. & Maggie Steelman
Mar 31, 1920
Nov 6, 1920

D. G. Burrow
Apr 29, 1911
Aug 7, 1911

Joel Estella Burrow
Dec 31, 1891
Aug 15, 1912

Several unmarked graves.

Maggie Woosley Steelman
Jun 14, 1877
Nov 29, 1946

J. A. Steelman
1861-1949
(Raby FH)

Susan Grammer
(no dates)

George Grammer
(no dates)

Herman Prosser
(no dates)

Lewis Prosser
(no dates)

Newsom Prosser
(no dates)

Horace Raby
(no dates)

Polly Prosser
(no dates)

Grover Prosser
(no dates)

Mary Prosser
(no dates)

Milton Marler
1859-1946

Nettie Marler
1859-1937

Horace A. Marler
Jul 3, 1884
Jul 9, 1906

Fred L. Murray
Nov 30, 1909
Apr 16, 1939

Mary B. Murray
1889-1963
(Howell-Thompson FH)

George _. Murray
Died Apr 16, 1959(?)

D. H. Murray
May 27, 1832
Jun 11, 1905

M. C. Murray
Nov 19, 1862
Aug 6, 1902

G. W. Murray
Died Dec 12, 1895
Age: 72 years
&
Charity Murray
Died Feb 19, 1896
Age: 70 years

J. M. Bledsoe
Feb 15, 1859
Jan 19, 1897

Rollie A., Daughter of
J. T. & M. J. Phillips
Mar 11, 1897
Nov 16, 1898

Earnest, Son of
J. T. & M. J. Phillips
Jun 30, 1904
Nov 24, 1904

Eunice L. Phillips
Jul 15, 1893
Jul 14, 1914

Hillsman Bledsoe
Mar 11, 1844
May 11, 1910

Matilda Bledsoe
1869-1931

Ganell, Daughter of
M. F. & S. F. Bledsoe
Jun 6, 1894
Dec 15, 1898

John T. Phillips
Oct 20, 1867
Mar 17, 1932
&
M. Josie Phillips
Apr 5, 1869
     1939
(R. H. Beasley FH)

Mrs. Sallie Bledsoe
1871-1950
(Thompson FH)

L. P. Savage
May 16, 1850
Aug 26, 1943
&
Martha J. Bledsoe Savage
Sep 4, 1855
Jul 1, 1922

Mary Ann Savage
Apr 15, 1848
Feb 23, 1916

BELLEVILLE QUADRANGLE

PHILLIPS CEMETERY

LOCATION: A short distance north of Chestnut Ridge store on west side of highway 231.

Peter Phillips, Sr.
1839-1915

Lucy E. Phillips
Aug 28, 1841
Jun 10, 1895

Charles Phillips
Dec   1875
Sep 10, 1902

Lennie Phillips
1875-1951

Polly Phillips
May 10, 1880
Mar 7, 1894

Mary A. Melson
Aug 6, 1817
May 19, 1885
Age: 67y, 9m.

* *

HARKINS CEMETERY

LOCATION: Four and one-half miles east of Petersburg, Tennessee, on south side of Petersburg-Chestnut Ridge Road.

James Wright
Jan 25, 1815
Oct 26, 1893

Mrs. Rebecca Wright
Feb 8, 1818
Apr 23, 1901

E. Flack
Apr 5, 1771
Aug 16, 1852

Susan A. Harkins,
wife of Alvis Flack
Feb 4, 1823
May 26, 1897

Thomas, Son of
A. & Susan Flack
Feb 21, 1846
Jul 14, 1852

Margaret P. Harkins,
wife of William Sorrells
Aug 16, 1813
Sep   1841

Susan E., wife of
W. G. Freeman
Jun 2, 1839
Feb 28, 1865

R. J., Son of
W. B. & Susan E. Freeman
Feb 6, 1865
Feb 9, 1865

Fannie E. Sorrells,
wife of J. L. Holly
Jan 17, 1865
Apr 26, 1909

Sue May, Daughter of
J. L. & F. E. Holly
Aug 9, 1891
Nov 18, 1897

Infant Son of
W. T. & M. R. Sorrells
Apr 7, 1870
Apr 8, 1870

M. J. Harkins
Mar 25, 1841
Jan 1, 1878

Infant Daughter of
T. M. & C. E. Harkins
B&D Aug 9, 1875

Infant Son of
T. M. & C. E. Harkins
Mar 7, 1884
Apr 26, 1884

O. R., Son of
T. M. Harkins
Dec 12, 1870
Jan 4, 1885

T. M. Harkins
Oct 10, 1825
Mar 13, 1892

"Billie"
W. T. Sorrells, Jr.
May 20, 1863
Oct 29, 1905

W. T. Sorrells
Jun 20, 1841
Oct 2, 1898

Golie F., Son of
W. T. & M. F. Sorrells
Jan 21, 1886
Jul 29, 1886

Ida, Daughter of
W. T. & M. R. Sorrells
Jul 31, 1867
Oct 5, 1867

Martha R., wife of
W. T. Sorrells
Feb 10, 1842
Sep 15, 1883

Pearl M., Daughter of
W. T. & M. R. Sorrells
Sep 7, 1881
Jul 21, 1882

William Sorrells
1810-Sep 10, 1857

Isham Sorrells
Mar 6, 1816
Apr 30, 1881

E. M. Sorrells
Apr 12, 1851
Dec 17, 1884

Henry N., Son of
N. & E. H. Sorrells
Mar 29, 1886
Mar 6, 1888

Nancy G. Sorrells, wife of
J. G. Ferguson
May 20, 1848
Mar 26, 1889

R. E. Lee, Son of
J. G. & N. G. Ferguson
Aug 1, 1867
Dec 31, 1892

J. H. Graham
1852-1936

Elenora Holly, wife of
J. H. Graham
Jun 9, 1861
Mar 10, 1896

Ellen M. Holley
Died Mar 19, 1892
Age: 68 years.

Willie J., Son of
O. E. & S. P. King
May 31, 1898
Dec 11, 1898

Girtie, Daughter of
Isham & Fanny Sorrells
Feb 6, 1884
Oct 22, 1891

M. R., wife of
B. G. Morton
May 8, 1863
Jun 19, 1898

I. S. Sorrells
Dec 16, 1853
May 24, 1914
&
Eliza F. Graham, wife of
I. S. Sorrells
Jul 1, 1849
Apr 12, 1926

W. A. Gilbert
May 28, 1839
Aug 8, 1893

J. E. Womble
Sep 3, 1875
Feb 9, 1909

Mary J. Cothrum
Feb 2, 1856
Dec 31, 1901

Evaline Burns
(no dates)

L. M. Cothrum
1861-1913

James T. Bagley
Jul 6, 1906
Mar 12, 1929

Dorothy, Daughter of
E. J. & Inda Bagley
Jul 29, 1921
Jun 29, 1923

Willie E. Sorrells
1889-1937

Mrs. N. J. Sorrells
1866-1943

B. Sorrells
1865-19(no date)

Infant Son of
G. F. & N. J. Sorrells
Mar 14, 1900
Mar 15, 1900

BELLEVILLE QUADRANGLE

J. M. Sorrells
Jul 14, 1836
Feb 16, 1904
&
M. A. Sorrells
Mar 20, 1836
(no date)

Alonzo Cothran *
Died Dec 30, 1911
Age: 30 years

Mattie E., wife of
J. C. Conwell
Apr 4, 1861
Jul 14, 1904

John,* Son of
G. W. Cowan
Died May 31, 1891
Age: 21 years

Many unmarked graves.

Ida, wife of
J. F. Hess
Apr 3, 1884
Sep 8, 1906

John G. Ferguson *
Died Aug 4, 1899
Age: 58 years

William T. Harkins *
Died Oct 29, 1905
Age: 38 years.

Mrs. Margaret Harkins *
Died Jan 24, 1888
Age: 76 years

Mrs. Margaret Judson *,
Widow of J. W. Waid
Sep 10, 1857 (Born)
Mrd Dec 1, 1881
Died May 18, 1915

* *

KING CEMETERY

LOCATION: Four and one-half miles east of Petersburg, Tennessee, on south side of Petersburg-Chestnut Ridge Road, near Haskins Cemetery.

William Noah Bonner
Feb 5, 1845
May 1, 1872

Mahala Bonner
Jan 26, 1814
Feb 27, 1891

J. W. Bonner
Feb 4, 1851
Oct 19, 1884

James M. Barham
Oct 11, 1827
Aug 5, 1890
Age: 63y, 9m, 25d.

Mary J., wife of
J. M. Barham
Mar 5, 1834
Jun 6, 186_ (broken)

J. P. Gammill   and
1839-1882

Mrs. Ada Hess *
Died Sep 8, 1906
Age: (no age given)

Mrs. Sarah King *
Died Jan 15, 1894
Age: 65 years.

Nancy C., wife of
F. M. Bonner
Sep 7, 1853
Jun 28, 1877

L. C. Barham
Dec 24, 1876
Nov 1, 1881

Charlie, Son of
W. A. & M. L. King
Aug 11, 1896
Jun 26, 1899

Infant Daughter of
W. A. & M. L. King
B&D Oct 7, 1884

S. J. King
Sep 13, 1858
Oct 23, 1872

T. E. Gammill   and
1839-1911

Mrs. Martha Jane,* wife of
W. M. Duncan
Died Apr 12, 1896
Age: 42y, 1m, 11d.

Many unmarked graves.

A. J. King
Sep 8, 1813
Jul 3, 1871

I. E., wife of
A. J. King
Mar 10, 1822
Oct 19, 1906

J. A. Barham
Dec 4, 1855
Mar 31, 1893

Infant of
S. A. & Blanch Wells
B&D Dec 15, 1914

Infant Sons of
Ulric & Lizzie Wells
B&D Jan 2, 1913

M. E. Gammill
1876-1899

Mrs. Oliver Coldwell,*
Died Feb 18, 1904
Age: 60y, 24d.

Moses C. Freeman *
Died Aug 7, 1893
Age: 60 years

Ada, Daughter of
J. J. & E. J. Delk
Jul 18, 1875
Aug 11, 1875

Eliza J. King,
wife of J. J. Delk
Jun 3, 1846
Jul 26, 1875

Alice King, wife of
N. T. Wells
Mar 2, 1861
Sep 24, 1894

Newt Wells
1867-1936

Ruric Wells
May 24, 1884
Oct 3, 1914

Mamie Diola,* Daughter of
James & Hannah C. Wade
Died Sep 27, 1893
Age: 3y, 10m.

Willie J.,* Son of
A. E. & S. P. King
Died Dec 11, 1893
Age: 6m.

* *

GILBERT CEMETERY

LOCATION: One-half mile east of Bledsoe on south of Bledsoe-Chestnut Ridge Road.

D. A. Gilbert
Jan 6, 1821
Feb 19, 1903

Lucreta Gilbert
Died Mar 24, 1893
Aged: 72y, 5m, 17d.

Henry H. Gilbert
Apr 12, 1855
Jul 7, 1865

Sarah A. Gilbert
Jan   1818
Dec   1863

Rezin A. Gilbert
Feb   1842
Aug   1857

Estil, Daughter of
P. C. & Ella Gilbert
Nov 9, 1879
Sep 6, 1884

Willie, Son of
P. C. & Ella Gilbert
Aug 21, 1885
Sep 12, 1888

Felix, Son of
P. C. & Ella Gilbert
May 5, 1895
Dec 26, 1898

BELLEVILLE QUADRANGLE

M. A. Burns
Jul 15, 1853
Nov 7, 1890

Rissie L., Daughter of
C. & Elizabeth Dyer
Feb 21, 1869
Sep 11, 1887

John H., Son of
Columbus & Lizzie Dyer
Mar 21, 1873
Jul 18, 1874

Nancy J. Dyer
born Jul 14, 1837
married R. Dyer
Jun 29, 1851
died Sep 27, 1883

Fieldstone
1851

Fieldstone
18-- U.S.

Fieldstone
1864

Approximately 15 graves with
fieldstones, no inscriptions.

****

HESTER CEMETERY

LOCATION: Two and one-half miles NE of Petersburg, Tennessee, in Wells Hollow.

Mary E. B. Woodard
Aug 29, 1821
Jun --, ---- (broken)

Fannie McAdams
Jan 13, 1845
Aug 20, 1893

Many unmarked graves.

Margaret M., Daughter of
E. G. G. & M. L. Beanland
Feb 28, 1841
Dec 27, 1845

Samuel Scott
Sep 20, 1808
Feb 6, 1874
&
Elizabeth Ryalls Scott
Dec 26, 1804
1875

Jas. R. Hester
Oct 10, 1793
Dec --, ---- (broken)

Elizabeth S., wife of
Jas. R. Hester
--- --, 1803
--- --, 187- (broken)

Mrs. S. A. Hester
Nov 18, 1837
May 8, 1908

Bernard Hester
Apr 13, 1886
Jun 13, 1907

****

OLD CEMETERY

LOCATION: Three miles NE of Petersburg, Tennessee on west side of Hannah Gap-Petersburg Road.

Gusta Old
Jun 17, 1805
Jul 3, 1833

Mary, Daughter of
W. M. & Nancy Old
Jul 3, 1819
Jul 13, 1840

(marker broken)
Aug 1833

Nancy E. Old
Dec 28, 1837
Aug 29, 1858

John Old
Jan 25, 1776
Jul 24, 1853

Nancy Old
Aug 26, 1776
Nov 30, 1860

Catharine V. Old
Jan 16, 1840
Aug 9, 1858

John C. Old
Nov 24, 1844
Nov 12, 1884
&
Isabella, wife of
John C. Old
Jul 3, 1852
Aug 31, 1885

Mattie A., wife of
W. R. Loving
Aug 2, 1847
Jul 17, 1885

William L. Old
Sep 3, 1850
Aug 11, 1870

One marker deteriorated

Sallie E. Old
Apr 22, 1853
Mar 12, 1869

W. M. Old
Sep 18, 1809
Nov 24, 1854
&
E. A. Old
Dec 25, 1812
Nov 1, 1887

Roy C., Son of
J. C. & Belle Old
Jan 18, 1881
Mar 12, 1882
Age: 1y, 1m, 24d.

****

BELLEVILLE QUADRANGLE

GREER CEMETERY

LOCATION: Two and one-half miles east of Petersburg, Tennessee, north of Petersburg-Chestnut Ridge Road and west of Hannah Gap Road.

"Here lyeth the body of Joseph Greer, he was while living an example of everything distinguished. He died on the 23 day of February 1831, in the 77th year of his age. Lamented by all who knew him."
    Metal Plaque

King's Mountain Messenger Joseph Greer carried the message of the Victory at King's Mountain to the Continental Congress at Philadelphia, thereby turning the tide of the Revolution.
    DAR Marker

Mary Ann Harmon, beloved wife of Joseph Greer
Died Dec 31, 1857
Age: 70 years

George Lewis Wilson, Son of Joseph and Mary Ann Greer
Oct 18, 1830
Aug 27, 1850
Aged: 19y, 8m, 9d.

NOTE: Joseph Greer settled here in 1806.

Col. James M. Dyer
Feb 2, 1813
Oct 18, 1889
&
Martha B. Dyer
Dec 11, 1813
Oct 8, 1874

Hariet J., wife of Stephen Ellis
Dec 22, 1808
Aug 24, 1854

Many unmarked graves.

* *

WASHBURN-MELSON CEMETERY

LOCATION: Two and one-half miles north of Belleville, Tennessee on Chestnut Ridge, east side of highway 231.

Benjamin Franklin Melson
Jun 26, 1857
Sep 10, 1934

Martha Melson
Jun 26, 1854
Nov 22, 1934

Willie Gray Melson
Sep 12, 1890
Sep 28, 1950

J. E. Bolles
Feb 18, 1845
Apr 4, 1926
&
Annie E. Washburn Bolles
May 11, 1852
Jan 3, 1924

Mary Washburn
Jun 26, 1854
Aug 25, 1930

Ernest F. Bolles
Nov 13, 1887
Oct 7, 1918

J. A. Bolles
Jan 5, 1879
Jan 29, 1898

Iva Lillian, Daughter of R. L. & Annie Bolles
May 24, 1907
Nov 5, 1909

John Gray Washburn
Sep 5, 1847
Jul 7, 1871

Abrom Washburn
Jan 17, 1817
Nov 5, 1894

Sarah M., wife of A. Washburn
Jun 5, 1816
Mar 15, 1882
Age: 65y, 9m, 10d.

J. M. Bagley
Jun 30, 1844
Apr 2, 1910

Susan Bagley
Jan 7, 1843
Jan 23, 1912

G. W. Smith
Aug 8, 1850
May 29, 1929

Bettie Hale, wife of G. W. Smith
May 30, 1848
Jan 13, 1929

Effie M., wife of J. R. Warren
Aug 13, 1880
Feb 23, 1915

John B. Smith
Jul 23, 1884
Dec 27, 1921

William Isham Smith
Jan 23, 1869
Oct 19, 1931

Sarah Ardena Lawson Smith
Apr 11, 1875
Nov 14, 1937

Robert L. Brown
Jun 15, 1926
Jul 14, 1963

Marion J. Brown
Dec 26, 1872
Jan 7, 1938

W. S. Gibson
Apr 23, 1915
Jul 19, 1959

George O. Gibson
Jun 2, 1910
Jan 12, 1962
&
Ocie M. Gibson
Jun 28, 1908

Roe Hale
1866-1937
&
Vonia Hale
1870-1939

J. T. Shelton
1896-1941

Arthur, Son of J. H. & F. J. Pack   Age: 7 months

Benny Jim Gipson
Nov 13, 1940
Jan 28, 1941

James R. Gibson
---- - 1951

Corrie Gibson
1873-1942

Harvey Fulton Smith
Jul 8, 1879
Jan 11, 1964

Addie Thomas Smith
Aug 9, 1880
May 18, 1939

P. G. Smith
Nov 15, 1857
Aug 17, 1926
&
N. C. Smith
Nov 10, 1859
Jul 4, 1920

Infant Son of Mr. & Mrs. C. F. Smith
B&D Jul 24, 1933

John F. Gibson
Mar 25, 1876
June 21, 1952

Birdia Laws Gibson
1877-1934

BELLEVILLE QUADRANGLE

Infant of
J. F. & Birdia Gibson
May 1, 1915

Infant of
J. F. & Birdia Gibson
Oct 12, 1912

Infant of
J. H. & Birdia Gibson
Mar 18, 1908

Thomas F. Gibson
Nov 9, 1903
Sep 19, 1904

Earl, son of
H. F. & Addie Smith
Oct 5, 1899
Apr 3, 1900

Henry Brown
1864-1938

Emma Brown
1863-1938

William Walter Stout
Jul 23, 1899
Feb 9, 1964

Oliver Leonard Caldwell
Died Mar 11, 1969
Age: 41 years (TM)

Mrs. Lida J. Ortner,*
Died Mar 18, 1917
Age: 72y, 3m.

Dock Brown
May 13, 1887
Sep 15, 1897

Henry Lee Gibson
Apr 8, 1933
May 29, 1933

William Thomas Hale
Aug 23, 1867
Mar 3, 1956
&
Nora Alice Hale
Feb 24, 1868
May 20, 1912

Jordan H. Rives
1886-1968
&
Patsey M. Rives
1903-

Martha J. Brown
Feb 2, 1873
Sep 15, 1921

Mary Etta Bradford
May 22, 1884
May 12, 1960

Mary Brown
1874-1943

Ida May,* Daughter of
J. R. & Cora Gibson
Died Feb 4, 1900
Age: 3y, 5m.

Rufus Franklin Laws
Feb 22, 1846
Jan 12, 1883
&
Judith Ann Smith Laws
Feb 16, 1853
Jan 22, 1924

Ella, wife of
M. J. Brown
Feb 28, 1875
Mar 3, 1900

Mattie Lou Brown Laws
Apr 4, 1885
Apr 18, 1904

Walter B. Laws
Feb 3, 1882
Mar 5, 1933

Maggie Smith
1884-1936

Oliver Smith
Nov 24, 1880
Apr 29, 1926

Jimmie L. Gibson Fenner
Jul 6, 1903

&
William Mitchel Fenner
Oct 25, 1894
Jul 30, 1953

Several unmarked graves.

Bettie Ortner
1883-1940

Infant Daughter of
Mr. & Mrs. J. J. Smith
1923

Virginia Sue Smith
Aug 8, 1927
Sep 18, 1929

William Washington Smith
Apr 23, 1878
Jan 13, 1951

Emma Bell Laws Smith
Jul 21, 1879
Aug 6, 1944

Infants of
J. W. & Flora M. Andrews
(no dates)

Mack Gibson
1941-1945

Lucy Gibson
1909-1947

Vickie Gail Fenner
---- - 1959 (date gone)

Mickey Jane Fenner
1960-1960

* *

WAID CEMETERY

LOCATION: Two and one-hald miles NNE of Belleville, Tennessee, on east side of Stoneborough Road.

E. F. Waid
Jun 15, 1822
May 17, 1906
&
S. F. Waid
Jun 1, 1864
(no date)

Caroline F. Waid
Nov 29, 1822
Jul 7, 1885

Weston F. Waid, son of
Elijah F. & C. F. Waid
Feb 18, 1856
Nov 24, 1868

Mrs. Rena,* wife of
William Waid
Died Apr 23, 1916
Age: 26y, 9m, 14d.

Mary J. Creson
Jul 29, 1853
Sep 25, 1870

J. F. Waid
Sep 1, 1858
Feb 7, 1892
"He came to his death by
being drown in R--- Fork
Creek in Jackson County,
Alabama."

Isham Waid
1861-1927
&
Ella S. Waid
1860-1947

Ottie S. Wade
1921

Infant Daughters of
I. C. & L. J. Waid
Mar 31, 1893
Mar 31, 1898

William T. Waid
1876-1933

Larence Bickley Waid
Died May 20, 1967
Age: 59 years

Rebecca E. Waid
Mar 13, 1876
Dec 11, 1905

Jessie Isham Waid
Aug 8, 1883
Mar 20, 1904
&
George Philander Waid
Aug 3, 1880
Dec 21, 1904

John C. Waid
1843-1931
&
Margarette Waid
1848-1935

Elijah F. Wade
Jul 29, 1873
May 11, 1906

Catharine Caldonia Waid
Dec 31, 1877
Mar 27, 1933

* *

BELLEVILLE QUADRANGLE

STONE CEMETERY

LOCATION: Two miles NNE of Belleville, Tennessee on east side of Stoneborough Road.

Micajah Stone May 31, 1775 Oct 7, 1827	Sarah Stone Mar 16, 1783 Mar 27, 1837 Many unmarked graves.	Martha D. Birds, Daughter of Micajah & Sarah Stone Apr 2, 1821 Mar 3, 1844	Near by are buried three Infants, children of Micajah & Sarah Stone

* *

LANDESS CEMETERY

LOCATION: Two miles NNE of Belleville, Tennessee on west side of Stoneborough Road, on west side of creek.

Mary Maud, Daughter of W. J. & M. B. Landess Sep 14, 1880 Jan 27, 1884 Age: 3y, 4m, 13d.	Our Little Gracie, Daughter of J. T. & M. R. Goodrich Oct 6, 1873 Apr 30, 1876	John Landess Nov 18, 1799 Sep 9, 1876	Charles S. Landess Feb 4, 1857 Jun 11, 1908 about 600 feet NW of main house.
E. S. N. Bobo Nov 19, 1828 Mar 11, 1898 & Eva Grace Landess, wife of E. S. N. Bobo Dec 28, 1834 Oct 20, 1904	Mary Lucile Goodrich Jun 14, 1870 Oct 24, 1891 Lucy,* Daughter of Henry & Hattie Taylor Died Mar 16, 1900 Age: 2 years.	Mary H., wife of John Landess Oct 18, 1815 Jan 12, 1891 Many unmarked graves.	

* *

CRANE CEMETERY

LOCATION: Two miles NNE of Belleville, Tennessee on west side of Stoneborough Road and on west side of creek.

Elijah F. Crane Nov 21, 1867 Apr 22, 1897	Susan G. Sorrells born Oct 22, 1833 married T. R. W. Crane Sep 15, 1853 died Mar 12, 1889	Felix G. Crane Private Co H 41st Rgt U. S. V. (Vol.) born Feb 13, 1880 died Jul 16, 1900	Mable Dee, Daughter of H. I. & M. B. Crane Feb 19, 1904 Jul 11, 1905
Ann, wife of John Crane Died Dec 23, 1872 Age: about 86 years	T. R. W. Crane Apr 29, 1825 Nov 30, 1905	at Angeles, Phillipine Islands, brought home, buried Sep 27, 1900.	Charlie M. Crane Jan 21, 1875 Nov 11, 1878
Mattie J., Only Daughter of T. B. W. & S. G. Crane Jul 19, 1870 Dec 14, 1878	J. W. Crane May 7, 1855 Mar 11, 1910	Martha E., wife of J. W. Crane Nov 24, 1856 Oct 26, 1917	Robert Crane Nov 21, 1883 Sep 29, 1907
Eva Leah, wife of J. T. Crane Nov 22, 1870 Sep 19, 1961			

* *

BELLEVILLE QUADRANGLE

PYLANT CEMETERY

LOCATION: Two miles NW of Belleville, Tennessee on Union Branch.

Drusilla A., wife of W. G. Pylant Feb 24, 1836 Aug 19, 1883	Penina Sorrell Dec 19, 1825 May 9, 1907	Marion Pylant Sep 28, 1840 May 14, 1864 C.S.A.	Sam Pylant Jun 26, 1864 May 20, 1893
Margaret Pylant Mar 7, 1801 Sep 12, 1880 (She was a Renfrow, wife of Pinkney Pylant)	Lydia E. Pylant Sep 7, 1834 Oct 17, 1867 Edith Swindle Feb 3, 1782 Dec 1, 1868	James Crawford Pylant Feb 23, 1835 Oct 18, 1908 several unmarked graves	J. L. Pylant (John Lee) Feb 23, 1830 Jul 11, 1896

* *

RENFROW CEMETERY

LOCATION: Two miles NW of Belleville, Tennessee on Cold Spring Road.

James F. Renfrow Jun 20, 1815 Aug 12, 1901 & Esther Renfrow Jun 15, 1820 Mar 4, 1908	Zettie Dyer, Daughter of Mr. & Mrs. J. M. Renfrow Apr 24, 1894 Oct 22, 1894	Paralee J., wife of H. C. Sorrells Feb 23, 1856 Mar 20, 1889	Several unmarked graves.

* *

STONE CEMETERY

LOCATION: Two miles NW of Belleville, Tennessee on Union Branch.

Luther C., Son of M. A. & L. J. Prosser Mar 7, 1867 Jul 6, 1895	J. W. Sherwood Sep 26, 1855 Sep 14, 1898	Mary, wife of John Whitworth Apr 9, 1805 Jul 25, 1879	John Cole Aug 17, 1795 Jun 10, 1844
H. M. Epps May 4, 1821 Dec 9, 1877	J. M., Son of J. W. & M. C. Sherwood Jul 25, 1875 Mar 28, 1885	Mary F., Daughter of H. C. & E. M. Whitworth Dec 9, 1873 Dec 4, 1881	Nancy, wife of John Cole Sep 9, 1796 Apr 24, 1870
Hopey J. Epps Jan 16, 1853 Sep 21, 1867	Mary _____ (name gone) 1856-1885	Mary E., Daughter of F. M. & Delila Cole Jan 28, 1871 Dec 11, 1871	E. C., Daughter of E. A. & L. E. Cole Jul 21, 1873 Nov 13, 1875

* *

ARMSTRONG-SORRELLS CEMETERY

LOCATION: Two miles WNW of Belleville, Tennessee, near junction of Cold Spring and Union Branch Roads.

Willie, Son of J. M. & M. A. Sorrells Oct 11, 1873 Mar 18, 1876	Armstrong family are buried here.*** Many unmarked graves.

* *

BELLEVILLE QUADRANGLE

HALL CEMETERY

LOCATION: Three miles south of Petersburg, Tennessee, east of Highway 431.

George R., Son of S. C. & E. M. Flynt Jul 19, 1840 Feb 2, 1847	George Hall Jan 11, 1780 May 28, 1862 Age: 82y, 1m, 20d.	Arthur B. Thornton Sep 22, 1868 Sep 6, 1875	D. B. Thornton Jun 15, 1834 Feb 18, 1882 & Martha Phenton Thornton
John R., Son of S. C. & E. M. Flynt Jun 4, 1849 Mar -9, 1850	Rachel L., Consort of Josiah Norwood Mar 31, 1803 (broken and in ground about 4 inches under a big root)	Lillie, Daughter of John M. & Anna Thornton Mar 23, 1877 Nov 28, 1877 B. A. Thornton Sep 22, 1868 Sep 6, 1875	Jun 28, 1837 May 4, 1899 & Santy Thornton Apr 11, 1880 Sep 17, 1883
Many unmarked graves.			

* *

THOMAS CEMETERY

LOCATION: Two and one-half miles west of Belleville, Tennessee on Gingerbread Creek.

Thomas J. Fox 1843-1878 & Margaret F. Fox 1841-1880	William Thomas 1790-Oct 3, 1877 Rebecca, wife of William Thomas Jul 7, 1797 Oct 17, 1867	John A. Thomas May 28, 1851 Mar 15, 1863 George W. Thomas Nov 16, 1856 May 28, 1874	E. T. Thomas Mar 1, 1819 Apr 6, 1903 Jane, wife of E. T. Thomas born Oct 19, 1823 married Apr 13, 1843 died Jun 5, 1883
Penelope Thomas Apr 22, 1838 Mar 29, 1853	Elizabeth Thomas Aug 27, 1822 Apr 28, 1829	Hugh E. Thomas Jan 2, 1855 Feb 25, 1876	Edwin T. Thomas Aug 11, 1862 Dec 29, 1876
Eliza Jane Thomas Oct 7, 1827 Nov 16, 1841	Many unmarked graves.		

* *

ARMSTRONG-COLE CEMETERY

LOCATION: One and one-half miles west of Belleville, Tennessee on Union Hollow Road.

J. W. Armstrong Apr 30, 1827 Feb 1, 1908	Jackson Armstrong Aug 30, 1872 Oct 10, 1909	Johnnie C. Cole Aug 11, 1891 Jul 24, 1899	5 unmarked graves.
N. J. Armstrong Aug 30, 1833 Jul 12, 1901		J. F. C. & C. A. Cole (no dates)	

* *

COLTER-DOLLINS CEMETERY

LOCATION: One and one-half miles west of Belleville, Tennessee on Union Hollow Road.

Miles M. Dollins Nov 13, 1818 Dec 17, 1878	Rufus M. Colter Aug 6, 1864 Jun 7, 1865	Hugh A. Dollins Mar 5, 1800 Oct 17, 1836	Minos A. Cannon Dec 18, 1846 May 30, 1871
Margaret J. Colter May 1824 Jul 8, 1868	Rufus H. Colter Mar 9, 1861 Mar 21, 1862	Infant Daughter of H. & Margaret J. Colter Dec 16, 1852 Dec 19, 1852	
A. E. Dollins died Jun 27, 1874 (no age)			Many unmarked graves.

BELLEVILLE QUADRANGLE

Presley Dollins, a
Revolutionary Soldier,
probably buried here.

Joel M. Dollins *
died May 7, 1894
Age: 82 years.

Mrs. Polly Dolline *
died Aug 30, 1877
age: 83 years

* * * * * * * * * * * * * * * * * * ** * * * * * * * * * * *

SMALL-GEORGE CEMETERY

LOCATION: One mile SW of Belleville, Tennessee and west of Highway 231.

J. M. George
Mar 7, 1816
Dec 4, 1891
Age: 75y, 8m, 27d.

Susan V., Daughter of
J. B. & M. E. Dooley
died Dec 30, 1867
Age: 21y, 11m, 19d.

Mrs. Belle Orrick McGee
May 12, 1862
Jan 30, 1893

Many unmarked graves.

Amanda M. Orrick
Apr 22, 1836
Nov 25, 1912

Mary E. Reussell
May 15, 1823
Jan 13, 1908
Age: 84 years

John R., Son of
Ather & Mary G. Washburn
Oct 25, 1851
Jun 11, 1853

Frank,* Son of
J. T. & Fannie Orrick
Died Sep 20, 1891
Age: 18 years.

Rubin Washburn
died Mar 19, 1844
Age: 64 years.

Susanna Washburn
May 3, 1795
Jun 14, 1841

Louiza Jane Washburn, wife of
James L. Thomson
Dec 20, 1828
Jan 18, 1918

Mr. William Orrick *
Died Feb 23, 1903
Age 79y, 10m.
Married Amanda Wright
Aug 11, 1861

Miss Louisa Victoria Orrick*
Died Nov 23, 1894
Age 22y, 2m.

Arthur Dudley, A Soldier
of the Revolution, is
buried here.
(Observer: Mar 5, 1910)

Miss Dillie Orrick *
Died Nov 10, 1907
Age: 41 years.

Thomas George *
Died Jul 16, 1888
Age: 86 years.

Mary,* wife of
Thomas George
died Aug 20, 1888
Age: 69 years.

* *

SMALL CEMETERY

LOCATION: One and one-half miles SW of Belleville, Tennessee on Highway 231.

Pina Jarman, wife of
George Small
(no dates)

George Small
Oct 11, 1787
Dec 17, 1879
"A Soldier under Jackson
in the War of 1812".

Naomi M. Steede, 2nd wife of
George Small
(no dates)

15 graves with fieldstones, no inscriptions.

W. H. Wright
Feb 4, 1848
Apr 3, 1914

Louisa Wright
1856-1931

George W. Wright
Apr 8, 1828
Dec 4, 1899

Elizabeth, wife of
G. W. Wright
Aug 15, 1830
Mar 1, 1894

* *

WILEY-COLE CEMETERY

LOCATION: One-half mile NW of Belleville, Tennessee in Ashby Hollow.

Minnie Cole, wife of
L. Bell
Oct 21, 1872
Nov 6, 1914

James D. Cole
Feb 9, 1781
May 3, 1853
"He was many years a
Minister (broken)".
(C. P. Church)

J. W. Cole
Aug 11, 1851
Sep 15, 1884

W. A. Patterson
1859-1935
&
Elizabeth Patterson
Apr 10, 1836
Sep 15, 1884

N. B. C.(footstone)
Broken headstone:
Died Jul 8, 1852
In 26th year of her age.

T. H. Fuller
Jul 14, 1849
Oct 17, 1890

Mary H., Daughter of
Jeff M. & Ann O. Stone
Mar 16, 1859
Jul 12, 1872

Emma F., Daughter of
Jeff M. & Ann O. Stone
Mar 23, 1855
Nov 1, 1861

Sallie A., Daughter of
Jeff M. & Ann O. Stone
Apr 21, 1849
Nov 4, 1861

John D. Cole
Sep 29, 1860
Apr 4, 1898

Walter F. Stone
Oct 22, 1864
Feb 26, 1892

Arthur A., Son of
Jas. W. & Mary Stone
Oct 15, 1881
Jan 8, 1882

BELLEVILLE QUADRANGLE

Owen, Son of
P. & V. H. Himebaugh
B&D Jan 31, 1875

Frank, Son of
P. & V. H. Himebaugh
B&D Sep 2, 1873

Gracy E., Daughter of
P. & J. L. Himebaugh
Aged: 1y, 4m.

Luther H. Wiley
Oct 10, 1829
Feb 24, 1892

Cathaline Dallis,*
Daughter of Mr. and Mrs.
Bob Buntley
Died Mar 5, 1902

W. H. Wright *
Died Apr 3, 1914
Age: 63 years.

William F. Cole *
Died Feb 22, 1893
Age: 72 years.

Joe C. Parks
1840-1911

William H. Ashby
May 28, 1830
Mar 16, 1912

Ellen E., wife of
W. H. Ashby
Mar 9, 1840
Apr 5, 1910

Eliza Dallas, Daughter of
W. H. & E. E. Ashby
Mar 13, 1876
Mar 2, 1894

John Laws *
Died Aug 12, 1905
Age: 52 years

Infant Son * of
R. S. Pamplin & wife
B&D Feb 4, 1903

Mrs. Esther,* Wife of
W. F. Cole
Died Jul 16, 1888
Age: 50y, 5m, 23d.

Hugh D. Wright
Dec 25, 1844
Aug 20, 1920
&
Amanda E. Wright
Dec 2, 1847
Aug 7, 1901

Wright Hall Ashby
Apr 14, 1895
Nov 8, 1895

Beulah E. Ashby
Sep 17, 1870
Jan 1, 1907

Harry,* Son of
W. S. & Susie Swain
Died Sep 7, 1897

James M. Bell *
Died May 17, 1891
Age: 75 years
Last of family of
Rev. John Bell.

Many unmarked graves.

J. B. Laws
1880-1950
(Raby FH)

G. G. Laws
1891-1948
(Raby FH)

Ed. J. Laws
1885-1952

Wife of
Abe McKinney
Age: 75 years

Lee,* Child of
Dave & Mary Laws
Died Feb 22, 1892

Charlie,* Son of
Dave Laws
Died Oct 14, 1892
Age: 9 years.

* *

FERGASON-THORNTON CEMETERY

LOCATION: North end of village of Belleville, Tennessee.

Dr. W. T. Fergason
1840-1914
C.S.A.

Iva J. Fergason
Oct 14, 1840
May 16, 1928

Allen E. Thornton
Jun 27, 1878
Mar 2, 1937

Lucile Fergason, wife of
Allen Thornton
1881-1907

Robert Allen Thornton
Jul 20, 1905
Jun 20, 1906

Elizabeth M. Fergason
1869-1871

Robert,* Son of
John Fergason
Died: Dec 30, 1892
Age: 28 years.

Mary Neely
Sep 14, 1850
Mar 23, 1931

Mrs. Nancy,* wife of
J. C. Fergason
Died Mar 26, 1889
Age: 40 years.

* *

CONCORD CHURCH CEMETERY

LOCATION: One and one-half miles NE of Belleville, Tennessee, between Highway 231 and Stoneborough Road.

J. Pybas
Dead-1917
(no age given)

W. M. Buntley
Dec 25, 1826
Apr 17, 1891

William Cunningham
Dec 18, 1824
May 20, 1879

Noah Cunningham
Jun 29, 1831
Sep 10, 1855

John Cunningham
Apr 3, 1800
Dec 5, 1869
&
Polly, wife of
John Cunningham
Feb 14, 1800
Feb 17, 1872

Peter Cunningham
Sep 13, 1820
Jun 6, 1889

Abriham Cunningham
May 7, 1823
Jul 28, 1846

J. W., Son of
John & Polly Cunningham
Oct 26, 1828
Aug 23, 1833

B. W., Daughter of
J. W. & Repha Cunningham
Jul 22, 1861
Apr 19, 1872

Sarah B., wife of
J. A. Lane
Jan 31, 1863
May 21, 1899

Fannie E., married
J. W. Duncan
May 5, 1878
born Mar 22, 1860
died Sep 1, 1901
Daughter of William &
Elizabeth Faulkner

Elizabeth Bandy, married
William Faulkner
born Aug 21, 1821
died Aug 27, 1877
married Sep 18, 1842
(Vault)

BELLEVILLE QUADRANGLE

Another Vault type next to Elizabeth Faulkner (no inscription)

Mary, wife of
Robert Faulkner
Died Sep 1, 1901
Age: 80 years.
"Robert, I am waiting for you."

Robert Faulkner
Oct   1819
May 10, 1905
"Well I'm here."

John E. Milstead
Aug 27, 1840
May 1, 1856

William C. Milstead
Died Sep 7, 1859
Age: 6m.

Ruthie, wife of
George Milstead
May 20, 1819
May 4, 1861

George Milstead
Jan 25, 1818
Feb 24, 1892

Sallie, wife of
George Milstead
Died Nov 25, 1888
Age: about 66 years.

W. B. McKenzie
Died Dec 17, 1901
Age: 68 years
& wife
Nannie L. McKenzie
Died Jan 3, 1903
Age: 34 years.

Regina K., wife of
D. A. McGee
Mar 25, 1859
Sep 22, 1893

George L. Shields
Aug 25, 1896
Sep 8, 1917

Mary Fannie, Daughter of
T. B. & Mattie Shields
Mar 5, 1899
May 6, 1920

Ollie G. Shields
May 27, 1889
Aug 21, 1914

T. B. Shields
Dec 22, 1858
May 10, 1920

Mattie Shields
Jan 25, 1863
Sep 21, 1930

E. J. Jackson, wife of
I. V. Forrester
Dec 27, 1835
Aug 24, 1897

Reuben E. Warren
1915-1916

M. C. Ingle
Feb 15, 1845
Dec 27, 1905

W. H. Ingle
(no dates)

William H., Son of
J. A. & S. V. Miles
Died Oct 6, 1899
Age: 6d.

W. A. Johnson *
married 1868 to
Mary E. Lineberger
Died Nov 7, 1897
Age: 50 years.

Infant * of
D. L. & Lizzie McKenzie
Died Jun 30, 1895
(no age given)

Andrew J. Buntley
Died Jul 1, 1915
Age: 55y, 4m, 7d.

Mrs. Evaline Partain *
Died Jan 10, 1900
Age: 78 years.

Geneva Cunningham *
Died Aug 25, 1903
Age: 3m.

Miss Madaline Street *
Died Oct 23, 1887
Age: 50 years.

John McKenzie *
Died Nov 19, 1887
Age: 40 years.
"A Native of Scotland."

Mrs. Nancy,* wife of
William Buntley &
Daughter of
Isaac Forrester
Jan 11, 1828
Apr 17, 1916

Mrs. William Shields *
Died Nov 24, 1916
Age: 48 years.

William Faulkner *
Died Sep 13, 1893
Age: 76 years.

Many unmarked graves.

* *

MANSFIELD CEMETERY

LOCATION: Two and one-half miles NE of Belleville, Tennessee near the forks of Belleville-Booneville Road and Lane Branch Road.

Garnett Mansfield
Oct 1, 1839
Nov 8, 1914

Nancy Ashby, wife of
Garnett Mansfield
Dec 28, 1848
Nov 25, 1908

Mrs. J. G. Mansfield
1835-1919

J. G. Mansfield
(dates illegible)

John W. Mansfield
Oct 9, 1876
Jan 2, 1928

Miss Mary Lou,*
Daughter of J. C. Mills
Died Aug 6, 1907
Age: 22 years.

* *

SULLIVAN CEMETERY

LOCATION: Two and three-fourth miles NE of Belleville, Tennessee on Belleville-Booneville Road.

Several graves with no markers.

* *

JACKSON CEMETERY

LOCATION: Two and three-fourth miles NE of Belleville, Tennessee on Belleville-Booneville Road.

Old Jackson Family buried here, no markers.
* *

BELLEVILLE QUADRANGLE

ASHBY-WARDEN-GROCE CEMETERY

LOCATION: Two and one-half miles NE of Belleville, Tennessee in Creson Hollow.

Alexander Ashby May 9, 1800 Dec 29, 1846	Martin V. Groce Sep 25, 1837 Aug 16, 1906	Mary Ann Groce Dec 30, 1829 Jan 24, 1875	Mary C., wife of John Warden (no dates)
Lavinia, wife of Alexander Ashby Jul 28, 1805 Oct 8, 1873	Mary F., Daughter of M. V. & M. Groce Jul 21, 1862 Oct 8, 1872	John Warden Apr 22, 1826 Jun 28, 1904	Rachel,* 1st wife of John Warden (no dates)
N. A. Ashby 1814-1858	L. W. Groce Apr 11, 1811 Jul 9, 1866	Martha A. E., wife of John Warden Dec 24, 1835 Jun 30, 1880	Many fieldstones with no inscriptions. Cemetery in very bad condition.

* *

LANE CEMETERY

LOCATION: One and one-half miles east of Belleville, Tennessee on Lane Branch.

Fieldstones with no inscriptions.

* *

ASHBY CEMETERY

LOCATION: Two and one-half miles SE of Belleville, Tennessee near Stoney Point Church.

Halafax Ashby Died Feb 3, 1875 Age: 65 years.	J. R. Ashby Nov 27, 1835 Oct 17, 1897	James A., Husband of Ruthie Steelman Apr 29, 1864 Apr 14, 1888	Robert C., Son of J. A. & Ruthie Steelman Mar 24, 1886 Nov 29, 1895
Eliza J. Ashby Apr 14, 1807 Oct 17, 1873	Elizabeth, wife of J. R. Ashby Dec 28, 1842 May 22, 1884	J. W. Ashby Jun 27, 1870 Oct 18, 1897	J. R., Son of J. A. & Ruthie Steelman Aug 13, 1887 Aug 18, 1888
Susie,* Wife of J. H. Duncan Died Aug 19, 1898 Age: 89 years.	Duncan Plot with fieldstones, no inscriptions.		

* *

CREASON CEMETERY

LOCATION: Two and one half miles east of Belleville, Tennessee near Stoney Point Church, joining the Ashby Cemetery.

G. M. D. Creason Mar 16, 1844 Sep 8, 1922	Willie D., Son of G. M. D. & P. E. Creason Jul 22, 1889 Jul 29, 1889	Mary Rebecca, Daughter of G. M. D. & Prudence Creason Sep 29, 1877 Jan 13, 1894	Pearlie Evaline, Daughter of Robert & Lucy Creason Mar 22, 1904 Jul 25, 1905
Prudence E. Creason Feb 28, 1857 Aug 3, 1889	Mattie R. Creason Jul 1, 1886 Jul 28, 1887	Dora A., wife of G. M. D. Creason May 22, 1870 Sep 17, 1897	Mrs. Rebecca Creason * Died Feb 24, 1891 Age: about 77 years.
Clifford Newton Ashby Sep 5, 1881 Feb 15, 1923	Ula May, Daughter of G. M. D. Creason Jul 15, 1897 Aug 31, 1897	Permelia C. Creason Jul 12, 1870 Dec 31, 1889	

* *

BELLEVILLE QUADRANGLE

COLTER CEMETERY

LOCATION: Three miles SE of Belleville, Tennessee, east of Lane Branch.

Emlie Steelman
Feb 27, 1823
Jun 3, 1903

America _____(broken)
born Sep --, ----(broken)
died Apr 5, 1893
(footstone: A. B.)

W. H. Brown
Jun 20, 1835
Dec 25, 1905

Mary Margaret Brown
May 25, 1838
Nov 9, 1924

Mary G., Daughter of
W. H. & C. S. Brown
Jul 21, 1914
Dec 30, 1915

Willie O. Brown
Jul 25, 1874
Oct 31, 1903

Mary, wife of
B. M. Brown
Feb 7, 1877
Nob 6, 1918

Sarah Harden Brown
Dec 5, 1865
Aug 2, 1888

Martha D. Brown, wife of
T. P. Noblitt
Mar 29, 1882
Jul 26, 1919

William D. Brown
Jan 15, 1833
Apr 12, 1892

Will Sullivan *
Died Jun 10, 1905
Age: 26 years.

William Franklin Steelman *
Died Aug 19, 1916
Age: 21 years.

Melissa Cordelia,*
Daughter of J. W. &
Julia Brown
Died Jul 1, 1897
Age: 1y, 3m, 16d.

John Brown *
Died Nov 27, 1899
Age: 27 years.

Child of John Boaz *
Died Aug 8, 1877
Age: about 1 year.

Walter E., Son of
John C. & M. E. Brown
Dec 29, 1870
Nov 21, 1874

James E., Son of
H. F. & Elvira Hudson
Jun 28, 1856
Nov 13, 1878
Age: 22y, 4m, 15d.

Rebecca Ann, Daughter of
E. & E. L. Lane
May 29, 1865
Nov 7, 1876
Age: 11y, 5m, 8d.

H. R. Brown
Jul 12, 1854
Jan 18, 1879

Beuna Vista, wife of
Henry R. Brown
Jul 3, 1854
Nov 17, 1896

Emily Brown
1825-Jun 30, 1890

A. M. Brown
Sep 27, 1832
Sep 1, 1899

Rossie L. Forrester
Dec 18, 1900
Feb 19, 1901
&
Infant Daughter
B&D Apr 30, 1902
Children of Mr. and Mrs.
Felix Forrester

Luella,* Daughter of
J. H. & Mary Edmondson
Died Jan 10, 1894
Age: 19 years.

Mrs. Mary,* wife of
A. F. Smith
Died May 10, 1894
Age: 20 years.

Mrs. William McAfee *
Died Dec 19, 1905
Age: 30 years.

Edward Brown *
Died Nov 8, 1897
Age: 21 years.

W. J. Brown *
Died Oct 22, 1902
Age: 49 years.

F. M. Colter
1835-1912
&
Martha M. Colter
1831-1890
&
Francis Lee Colter
1865-1888
&
Infant Son of
Albert & Mary E. Colter
Dec 5, 1891

Will O. Lane
Jan 11, 1868
Jan 10, 1894

Infants of
Will O. & Myrtle Lane
Died 1892 & 1894

Eli Lane
1838-(no date)
&
Elvira Lane
1840-1920

H. A. Stealman
Oct 7, 1826
Feb 3, 1875

Lula Edna, wife of
Ada Warden
Mar 1, 1879
Jun 1, 1900

Sidnie E., wife of
J. C. Edmison
Feb 13, 1861
Jun 7, 1898

Miss Rebecca McGee *
Died Nov 25, 1902
Age: 23 years.

Eugene,* Son of
J. W. & Willie Jordon
(no dates)

Josie,* Daughter of
Oliver & Maggie Smith
Died Oct 31, 1903
Age: 2 years.

Mrs. Mollie McGee *
Died Jun 14, 1892
Age: 72 years.

Infant * of
Mr. & Mrs. T. A. McGee
Died Dec 17, 1915

Gladys,* Daughter of
Mr. & Mrs. Wade Brown
Died Dec 31, 1915
Age: 1y, 4m.

Hampton Sims
Jul 3, 1810
Feb 27, 1896

Mary A. Sims
Dec 3, 1807
Jun 22, 1869

Elberta Edmonson
Dec 17, 1898
Jul 12, 1916
&
Effie Edmonson
Jan 20, 1880
Dec 15, 1917

Jimmie Edmison
Mar 30, 1877
Nov 4, 1900

Mrs. Rena Brown *
Died Jul 7, 1903
Age: 39 years.

Mrs. Margaret,* wife of
Hardy H. Colter
married Feb 1890
Died Aug 9, 1897
Age: 71 years.

Mattie,* Daughter of
Mr. & Mrs. William
Steelman
Died Nov 16, 1905
Age: 5y, 2m.

P. A. Keith *
Died Jan 3, 1893
Age: 45 years.

Robert,* Son of
J. A. & Mary Hasty
Died Sep 20, 1893
Age: 18 years.

Infant * of
Mr. Vol Roe
Died Nov 4, 1894
Age: 6m.

Child * of
William & Annie Steelman
Died Mar 6, 1907
Age: 10m.

Jacob McGee *
Died Apr 16, 1911
Age: 65y, 10m.

Mrs. Groce *
Died Jun 30, 1912
Age: (no age given)

BELLEVILLE QUADRANGLE

Joe Pamplin *
Died Dec 1, 1912
Age: 64 years.
C.S.A., 41st Tenn Regt.

Willie,* Son of
Lige Brown
Died Jun 20, 1903
Age: 13 years.

Infant * of
E. L. & Elizabeth McGehee
Died Jan 8, 1895
Age: 5m.

Mrs. James Brown *
Died Mar 19, 1913
Age: 67 years.

Mrs. Pharaoh Moore *
Died Aug 12, 1913
Age: 39 years.
Daughter of John W. Boaz

Clara,* Daughter of
E. L. & Elizabeth McGehee
Died Jan 5, 1896
(no age given)

Andrew Buntley
Died Nov 5, 1900
Age: 74 years.

Mrs. Martha,* wife of
G. W. J. Brown
Died Jul 27, 1891
Age: 38 years.

Many unmarked graves.

Willie,* Son of
Lisle & Lizzie McGhee
Died May 10, 1900
Age: 4 years.

Miss Louella Renolds *
Died Jan 20, 1891
Age: 25 years.

* *

GROCE CEMETERY

LOCATION: Three and one-fourth miles SE of Belleville, Tennessee, west of Gimlet Branch.

Cincinatia, wife of
John Groce
Jan 13, 1815
Jan 13, 1903

John Groce
Feb 20, 1815
Jan 10, 1858

William Groce
Jan 18, 1840
Feb 16, 1865

Martha Groce, wife of
George Tiller
Jul 28, 1844
Nov 10, 1871

Peter Groce
Dec 14, 1841
Aug 20, 1852
&
Nancy Groce
Sep 25, 1853
Jun 3, 1861

George W. Groce
1872-1936

Ethel,* Daughter of
Rev. Allen Rozier
Died Sep 10, 1896
Age: 3y, 7m.

Thomas Groce
May 16, 1838
Apr 14, 1924

Susan, wife of
Thomas Groce
Dec 20, 1848
(no date)

Mary M., wife of
Thomas Groce
Feb 16, 1840
Aug 26, 1869

Mrs. John Groce *
Died Oct 8, 1916
Age: 33 years.

James C., Son of
Susan & Thomas Groce
Jul 5, 1887
Apr 2, 1888

Sarah R., Daughter of
Thomas & Mary Groce
Apr 20, 1866

Mrs. Martha V.,* widow of
Miram Groce
Died Feb 17, 1911
Age: 70 years.

Several unmarked graves.

* *

McGEE CEMETERY

LOCATION: Three miles south of Stoney Point Church on Gimlet Branch.

John McGee
Jun 13, 1817
Apr 23, 1882

Several unmarked graves.

* *

WAGGONER CEMETERY

LOCATION: Three miles south of Stoney Point Church on Gimlet Branch.

John W. Bedwell
Aug 23, 1870
Nov 3, 1908
&
Fannie E. Bedwell
Nov 17, 1873
Nov 9, 1959

Annie May Bedwell
Apr 22, 1903
Jun 23, 1905

Jim Pearson
Aug 26, 1926
(adult grave)

Fannie, Daughter of
V. W. & N. E. Moore
Jul 4, 1894
Oct 4, 1894

Carl Ray Waggoner
1933-1935
&
Helen June Waggoner
1938 (no date)

Alexander Waggoner
May 20, 1835
Nov 23, 1903

Mary Waggoner
May 20, 1835
Mar 25, 1911

Bettiean Waggoner
Jan 20, 1857
Sep 15, 1872

George Waggoner
May 29, 1871
Sep 5, 1872

Henry Waggoner
Feb 1, 1869
Sep 14, 1875

Several fieldstones, no inscriptions.

* *

BOONSHILL QUADRANGLE

CALDWELL CEMETERY

LOCATION: One mile south of Delina, two and one-half miles north of Boonshill.

Samuel Caldwell
May 21, 1817
Aug 5, 1883
Age: 66y, 4m, 24d.

Mary J. Caldwell
Jul 15, 1859
Sep 21, 1875
Age: 16y, 1m, 6d.

3 or 4 unmarked graves.

* *

McDANIEL CEMETERY

LOCATION: Two miles NE of Boonshill on east side of Boonshill-Petersburg Road.

A. W. March
Nov 17, 1827
Aug 12, 1862

L. Ann, wife of
A. W. March
May 23, 1837
Mar 25, 1913

Loucile, Daughter of
J. S. & R. L. March
Nov 14, 1882
Nov 16, 1889

John McDaniel
May 18, 1803
Oct 17, 1861

Mary H., wife of
John McDaniel
Nov 11, 1810
Jul 2, 1891

Edgar Sugg, Son of
J. B. & S. A. Marshall
Oct 6, 1866
Aug 26, 1867

W. F. McDaniel
Aug 15, 1832
Nov 22, 1893

Mary E., wife of
W. F. McDaniel
Feb 23, 1838
Sep 25, 1879

Maggie Frank, Daughter of
J. B. & S. A. Marshall
1871-1879

John R. Marshall *
Died Feb 27, 1905
Age: 66 years.
C.S.A.
Married Josie McDaniel
Dec 12, 1872

Josie Marshall *
Died May 7, 1907
Age: 63 years.

3 graves with fieldstones, no inscriptions.

* *

CLARKE CEMETERY

LOCATION: Two and five-tenths miles NE of Boonshill, east side of Boonshill-Petersburg Road.

Capt. John Clarke
Mar 25, 1781
Dec 24, 1863

Martha Moore, wife of
Capt. John Clarke
Apr   1784
Mar 23, 1862
Age: 77y, 11m.

Joseph M., Son of
Capt. John Clarke
Aug 18, 1811
Jul   1841
Age: 29y, 11m.

Joanah Josephine, Daughter
of Capt. John Clarke
Feb   1823
Jul 6, 1844

Thomas W. Clarke
Nov 16, 1820
Oct 22, 1895
&
Mary E. Clarke
Oct 23, 1824
Aug 24, 1894

Louisa M., wife of
Rev. A. H. Bishop
Nov 22, 1818
Aug 18, 1881

Mary March
Jul 5, 1872
Sep 28, 1873

James Alfred, Son of
A. G. & S. C. March
Feb 3, 1881
May 25, 1885

G. L. Cathey
Jan 17, 1831
Jun 16, 1864

Mary Ida, Daughter of
G. L. & E. C. Cathey
Jul 27, 1855
Sep 28, 1859

William A. Cathey
Oct 30, 1828
May 26, 1849

Cyrus Cathey
Nov 11, 1803
Jan 5, 1843

William L., Son of
W. F. & D. A. Swiney
Feb 9, 1871
Jul 9, 1883

Margaret B. Clarke,
wife of Jonas L. Keith
Jul 3, 1817
Jun 2, 1884

William Olliver
Mar 22, 1788
Jul 26, 1857

J. T. Russell
Jul 27, 1827
Apr 4, 1909
& Wife
Emma Russell
Nov 1, 1837
Apr 10, 1885

Virgil A., Son of
L. E. & A. A. Wilson
Sep 18, 1882
Mar 24, 1883

Alice A., wife of
L. E. Wilson
Jan 19, 1858
Feb 13, 1883
Age: 25y, 24d.

Several unmarked graves.

* *

BOONSHILL-OLD SALEM CEMETERY

LOCATION: At Boonshill, behind the Cumberland Presbyterian Church.

BOONSHILL QUADRANGLE

Elizabeth Clark
Aug 14, 1809
Dec 25, 1847

Nancy E. Turner, wife of
J. W. Turner & Daughter of
R. T. & Lucy Collins
Oct 31, 1857
Dec 12, 1906
Age: 49y, 1m, 12d.

W. D. R. (Ruth)
(footstone)

C. H. R. (Ruth)
(footstone)

Elizabeth Ruth
Jun 18, 1813
Jan 4, 1875

H. Wilse Gunter
1841-1925
&
Lou C. Gunter
1845-1929

William Carral Childress
Mar 6, 1849
Jun 23, 1928
& wife
Sarah Elizabeth Clark
              Childress
May 24, 1854
Apr 11, 1927

Alvis Mayes Childress
Tennessee
Pvt Co A 161 Inf WW I
Aug 4, 1888
Jul 3, 1965

J. L. A. (Abbott)
(no dates)

S. M. A. (Abbott)
(no dates)

N. A. (Abbott)
(no dates)

L. J. A. (Abbott)
(no dates)

Fleming Abbott
(no dates)

J. R. Gunter
Jun 7, 1830
Feb 3, 1875
&
M. E. Gunter
Feb 3, 1838
Oct 24, 1895

Gunter
(no dates)

Martin A. Wisener
Mar 17, 1835
Jul 3, 1860

A. C. (Clark)
(footstone)

W. Clark
(footstone)

E. Clark
(footstone)

James W. Turner
Oct 3, 1844
Dec 31, 1913

Infant Son of
J. R. & Ilene Jones
B&D Mar 10, 1920

Infant Daughter of
J. R. & Ilene Jones
B&D Sep 5, 1918

W. R. Oldham
1839-1925

Sithey J. Clark, wife of
W. R. Oldham
Jun 26, 1839
Sep 20, 1895

Martha M. Clark
1849-1937

F. A. Jenkins
(child - no dates)

David B. Smith
Died Sep 1, 1875
Age: 62 years

David Owen
Jun   1804
---   1860

M. S. (Smith)
(no dates)

E. Smith
(no dates)

John Wood
Oct 13, 1808
Oct 1, 1869

Jane J. Wood
Jan 25, 1824
Jun 20, 1854

George W. Sawyers
born in Virginia
Apr 5, 1805
May 14, 1883

Eliza Sawyers
Oct 25, 1825
Jul 1, 1854

Infant of G. W. Sawyers
(no dates)

William L. Sawyers
Mar 1, 1854
Jul 6, 1854

Lizzie T. Gunter
(no dates)

R. T. Collins
Dec 15, 1831
Feb 1, 1916

Lucy, wife of
R. T. Collins & Daughter of
James & Elizabeth Clark
Died Jun 2, 1910
Age: 79y, 3m, 12d.

G. W. Clark
Aug 5, 1856
Mar 11, 1904

Mary F., wife of
G. W. Clark
Jan 14, 1847
Feb 26, 1916

James H. Wilson
1921-1953
&
Ilene Wilson
Sep 21, 1901
Feb 8, 1936

Mary Jo Mangrum
1950

Ronald Watson
1928

Nell Wilson
1933-1939

W. C. Cathcart
Jul 25, 1855
Oct 27, 1910

Mary J. Cathcart
1854-1947

Mary Russell Wood
1816-1896

S. E. Douster, wife of
Phillip Holman
Apr 27, 1834
Dec 4, 1907

Bob Walker, Son of
W. A. & Anna E. Summers
Oct 27, 1877
Dec 1, 1877

H. Oglesby (child)
(no dates)

W. H. O. (child)
(no dates)

M. S.
(no dates, fieldstone)

Amanda Wall
1866-1936

Mrs. Lee Clark
1880-1945

George Buford, Son of
L. P. & Maggie Clark
Jul 27, 1901
Jan 7, 1913

Jonnie B. Clark
1908-1922

L. P. Clark
1874-1932

J. M. Owen
Apr 13, 1849
Dec 13, 1873

Rebecca, wife of
J. M. Owen
Nov 26, 1842
Jan 17, 1872

John N. Owen
Jan 29, 1819
Mar 22, 1873
Age: 54y, 1m, 23d.

Nancy R., wife of
John N. Owen
Aug 15, 1820
Feb 13, 1873
Age: 53y, 6m, 12d.

Tippie J., wife of
Pinkney Owen
Jun 11, 1869
May 9, 1917

Pinkney Owen
1869-1940

Joshua Williams
Jan 21, 1867
Aug 19, 1911

Matilda J. Thompson
1853-1897

Infants of
Mr. & Mrs. R. F. Scott
B&D Jul 16, 1915
born Dec 31, 1926
Jan 3, 1927

Robert Lee, Son of
H. D. & Mary Smith
Jul 10, 1883
Sep 3, 1883

Louella, Daughter of
P. & T. Owen
Sep 26, 1896
Nov 6, 1896

John Wood Templeton
1862-1926

Nancy Cary Templeton
1869-1942

BOONSHILL QUADRANGLE

H. C. Templeton
(no dates)

Father
A. S. Templeton
Feb 16, 1814
Jun 6, 1898
&
Mother
M. I. Templeton
Nov 22, 1833
Feb 22, 1901

Infant Son of
W. O. & M. E. Rambo
Jan 14, 1918
Jan 16, 1918

W. W. Erwin
1846-1913

Mary Elizza Templeton Erwin
1861-1934

Addie Wood Erwin
Mar 30, 1853
Apr 30, 1894
&
Our Boys
Woody & Harris
(no dates)

Thomas B(easley) Hobbs
Feb 16, 1836
Jan 5, 1891

Hariet Hobbs
1847-1933

Astor Hobbs
(no dates)

Charly W. Hobbs
1870-1938
&
Lessie M. Hobbs
1879-1937

J. A. Clark
Jul 20, 1834
(no date)
&
Mary E. Clark
Dec 11, 1832
Aug 30, 1911

Amanda Clark McDaniel
1860-1929

Adelia, wife of
J. W. Minatree
Dec 18, 1862
Oct 13, 1885

Rev. William James
Mar 30, 1860
Jan 30, 1924

J. L. Brannon
1896-1943

L. C. Roden
Mar 30, 1844
Apr 25, 1919
&
Margaret A. Roden
Feb 17, 1848
Dec 3, 1918

J. Thomas Roden
Jun 18, 1879
Apr 29, 1922

Callie Roden
1858-1932

Bonnie Roden
Mar 29, 1890
May 16, 1928

Carrie Bell Roden ***
1882-1911

Thomas J. Roden ***
Dec 30, 1846
Jun 24, 1924

Rebecca Jane Roden ***
Feb 27, 1853
Dec 25, 1887

*** info by Haskel Roden

M. I. L.
(no dates)

Annie Myrtle Lineberger
Nov 20, 1889
Sep 10, 1916

Maggie Lee Lineberger
wife of J. L. Lineberger
Apr 21, 1879
Apr 2, 1914

Samie, wife of
L. P. Ables
May 25, 1860
May 19, 1913

J. L. Lineberger
1872-1943

Eunice May, Daughter of
J. L. & Maggie Lee
        Lineberger
Sep 19, 1900
Jul 7, 1913

D. A. Hunter
Feb 14, 1849
May 28, 1913

Fannie, wife of
D. A. Hunter
Feb 21, 1853
Apr 3, 1916

William Allen Smith
1928-1929

Henry Hopper
Apr 14, 1869
died   1967

Mary E. Hopper
wife of H. M. Hopper
1875-1952

Lydye E. Hopper, wife of
H. M. Hopper
Feb 10, 1869
Aug 6, 1917

Jimmie Hopper
Feb 7, 1902
Nov 10, 1918

A. H. Turney
Dec 22, 1842
Feb 16, 1914

Mary C., wife of
A. H. Turney
Apr 6, 1843
Mar 10, 1903

John L. Turney
1877-1945

R. H. Hughey
Oct 20, 1835
Jan 13, 1904

Sarah Hughey
Jun 27, 1837
Feb 5, 1915

Mary Ann Owen
Sep 25, 1833
May 18, 1873

A. G. Bearden
Jun 15, 1848
Mar 6, 1925

S. A., wife of
A. G. Bearden
Jul 5, 1860
Oct 2, 1896

S. J., wife of
E. M. Clark
Apr 14, 1853
Mar 31, 1889

M. E. "Dick" Whitaker
1849-1923
&
Ida Wood Whitaker
1856-1927

Infant Whitaker
(no dates)

Addie Sue Whitaker
1888-1891

Ida Wood Whitaker
1898-1898

Will H. Gunter
1834-1916
&
Mary S. Gunter
1872-1949

Casper Isper Hopper
Dec 18, 1850
Sep 25, 1928
&
Mattie L. Smith Hopper
Mar 31, 1869
Dec 19, 1959

Mattie S. Gunter
1902

John M. Ramsey
Jul 19, 1858
Jan 1, 1922
&
Elizabeth Ramsey
Sep 2, 1861
Jul 5, 1946

Josie D., Daughter of
J. M. & C. E. Ramsey
Apr 19, 1891
Jul 10, 1902

W. G. Campbell
Jun 10, 1831
Feb 2, 1901
& wife
Elizabeth Campbell
May 10, 1829
(no date)

Leonard, Son of
D. S. & Della Campbell
Jun 20, 1910
Jul 5, 1910

Ervin, Son of
D. S. & Della Campbell
Jun 9, 1900
Jul 14, 1918

D. S. Campbell
Apr 14, 1864
(no date)
& wife
Della E. Pamplin Campbell
Oct 26, 1866
Mar 2, 1919

Martha L. Clift
Feb 27, 1833
Sep 7, 1889
Age: 51y, 6m, 10d.

John H. Smith
Jun 10, 1847
Apr 5, 1917

M. A. Smith
Mar 20, 1851
Jan 23, 1933

BOONSHILL QUADRANGLE

Hattie Bearden, wife of
W. S. Johnson
Jun 20, 1882
Dec 16, 1911

W. S. Johnson
Apr 17, 1882
Apr 12, 1952

Sallie Mae Clark, wife of
W. S. Johnson
1898-1944

Emeline Owen
May 28, 1826
Feb 9, 1909

Margaret B. Owen
Mar 4, 1825
Mar 19, 1901

Julia A. Owen
Sep 9, 1822
Sep 17, 1903

Loyd Frezell, Son of
J. A. & M. E. Dodd
Apr 5, 1910
May 29, 1911

Frank W. Bearden
1843-1921

Hattie Barnes Bearden
1889-1952
&
Sam Walker Bearden
1886-1953
&
Jeffie Harrison Bearden
1889-1910

M. A., wife of
F. W. Bearden
Feb 21, 1863
May 28, 1907

Virgie Lee, Daughter of
M. A. & F. W. Bearden
May 16, 1894
Jun 25, 1894

Hugh Broadrick
Mar 17, 1866
Oct 2, 1918

A. Broadrick
Mar 11, 1864
Aug 30, 1914

Sarah Broadrick
Jan 1, 1855
Sep 1, 1917

D. Broadrick
Oct 22, 1827
Oct 20, 1909
& wife
Harriett Broadrick
Jun 12, 1832
Feb 13, 1901

R. S. "Bob" Hughey
Jan 22, 1872
Mar 16, 1913
&
Lillie S. Carden Hughey
Jan 13, 1883

Edner Luceil, Daughter of
J. W. & Lucy Gatlin
Feb 18, 1914
Oct 21, 1917

John W. Gatlin
Dec 8, 1871
Oct 27, 1958
&
Lucy Ables Gatlin
Nov 22, 1879
Jul 31, 1967

Gladys M. Tucker
Aug 30, 1928
Aug 1, 1931
&
Mary Ada Tucker
May 17, 1923
Aug 15, 1941
&
Eleanor L. Tucker
Apr 11, 1925
May 12, 1942

Charles D. Tucker
(on Mil marker: C.V.)
Tennessee
Pvt Co H 117 Inf WW I
Dec 26, 1895
Mar 10, 1954
&
Annie Mae Tucker
Jun 27, 1902

Eva Jane Collins
Mar 18, 1866
Apr 26, 1950

Roy Richardson
Sep 22, 1916

&
Edith Richardson
Jan 2, 1921
May 13, 1966

James T. Jones
Sep 5, 1859
Apr 20, 1936

Beulah Clendon, Daughter of
J. R. & Ilene Jones
Jul 11, 1922
Sep 22, 1922

W. S. Crane
1885-1960
&
Annie T. Crane
1887-1952

Emma Hamlin
Dec 17, 1873
Jul 29, 192- (broken)

Myrtle, wife of
Tilman Williams
Dec 6, 1883
Jun 10, 1912

Harrison Henry Barnes
1883-1964
&
Annie Johnson Barnes
1885-1917

James Thomas Sanders
1868-1948

N. D. Scott
Oct 22, 1865
Mar 6, 1945

Lillie M. Scott
Oct 5, 1885
Jan 24, 1963

Shuler Scott
Mar 29, 1900
Aug 27, 1918

James L., Son of
B. A. & N. C. Clark
Aug 9, 1874
Mar 1, 1887

B. A. Clark
Mar 28, 1841
Mar 6, 1916
&
N. C. Clark
Sep 5, 1850
Mar 10, 1940

W. Sam Cathey
Jan 4, 1896
Jan 9, 1965
&
Beulah R. Cathey
May 2, 1896

W. M. Cathey
Jul 23, 1858
May 17, 1917

M. L. Cathey
Jul 3, 1865
Aug 22, 1903

Eliza Cathey Flautt
Mar 14, 1833
Jul 7, 1905

J. Frank Watt
Nov 18, 1849
Mar 14, 1922
&
O. Glem Watt
Jul 14, 1852
Nov 17, 1909

Ross C. Erwin
Aug 10, 1880
Aug 6, 1931

Mary E., wife of
R. C. Erwin
Apr 27, 1887
Feb 23, 1923

Robert F. Scott
1885-1966
&
Hester F. Scott
1890-

Baby Barnes
Son of E. S. &
Carrie Barnes
B&D Aug 24, 1915

Robert H. Cunningham
1856-1942
&
I. Myra Cunningham
1852-1940

Claudia M., Daughter of
R. H. & I. E(M).
Cunningham
Oct 9, 1882
Mar 31, 1904
Age: 21y, 5m, 22d.

W. Enoch Cunningham
1874-19 (no date)
&
Ida May Cunningham
1874-1946

J. Hurley Johnson
1893-1951
&
Minnie N. Johnson
1897-19

Infant of
J. H. & Minnie Johnson
Mar 6, 1920

Joe L. Johnson
Sep 17, 1870
Aug 14, 1948
&
Fannie S. Johnson
Mar 9, 1874
(no date)

Hiram Johnson
Oct 7, 1896
Oct 22, 1923

Joe B. Johnson
1895-1951
&
Mary L. Johnson
1898-

Wiley W. Spray
1902-1954
&
Lena R. Spray
1900-

BOONSHILL QUADRANGLE

James P. Smith
Dec 21, 1887
Jan 24, 1919

Elizabeth Jane Smith
Nov 28, 1844
Jun 21, 1917

J. M. Coble
1873-1925
&
Lizzie Coble
1872-1955

James Buell Coggin
Feb 22, 1929
Jan 13, 1936

Infant Son of
Mr. & Mrs. Woodrow Coble
Feb 11, 1941
Feb 15, 1941

Ellen Coble Hardiman
Apr 24, 1929
Sep 25, 1929

Willie Bell Erwin
Oct 28, 1876
Jan 10, 1936

Donald Thompson
Aug 31, 1937
Feb 10, 1961

Owen Edward Riemer
Apr 2, 1943
Dec 31, 1944

Mary E. Sowell
Mar 14, 1869
Apr 8, 1964

Roy Gilbert Fitzsimmons
Died Feb 2, 1968
age: 55 years.

J. B. Collins
Aug 13, 1856
Aug 25, 1937

Adella, wife of
J. B. Collins
Nov 16, 1866
Dec 10, 1929

Galon Lee Bryant
Apr 24, 1901
Nov 7, 1964

Infant * of
Mr. & Mrs. W. R. Crain
Died Aug 31, 1905
(no age given)

Thomas,* Son of
Robert & Sarah Hughey
Died Dec 17, 1893
Age: 19 years.

K. L. Hamlin *
Died Mar 7, 1916, Age 59y.

Joe Wood Whitaker
Mar 15, 1884
Mar 29, 1959

Elizabeth Ross Whitaker
1882-1962

Thomas J. Whitaker
1886-
&
Ruby Barnes Whitaker
1890-1958

Alfred Paul Ramsey
Dec 15, 1884
Oct 2, 1953
&
Allie Mae Ramsey
Jan 6, 1889

Sallie Hughey Wright
Mar 22, 1878
Mar 3, 1962

James H. Wright
May 16, 1857
Oct 12, 1934

Dixie Clark Wright
Nov 9, 1872
Apr 1, 1947

Ruby, Daughter of
J. H. & D. M. Wright
May 26, 1897
Feb 17, 1920

Marion A. Wright
1894-1940

Kate Caldwell Wright
Jan 6, 1893
Jun 4, 1933

Marvin H. Wright, Jr.
Nov 13, 1929
Nov 16, 1929

Albert Wright Wilson
1884-1959
&
Edith Ranck Wilson
1887-

Alexander,* Son of
Mr. & Mrs. Fate Porch
Died Feb 5, 1898
Age: 3 years

Susie,* Daughter of
Mr. & Mrs. James Griffin
Died Jun 12, 1909
Age: 7y, 10m.

Mrs. S. E.,*
married Philip Coleman 1864
Died Dec 4, 1907
Age: 73 years.

J. M. Campbell
May 18, 1867
Jun 16, 1917

Sally A., wife of
J. A. Campbell
Jun 20, 1872
Jan 17, 1910

J. Irby Gunter
Jan 5, 1878
Mar 5, 1969

S. Jesse McAfee
1874-1960

Attice McAfee
1884-1948

James F. McAfee
1909-1962

Elizabeth McAfee
1913-1964

C. Ernest Clark
Jul 2, 1876
Oct 22, 1934
& wife
Ora George Clark
Nov 24, 1887
Mar 4, 1969

Eva Clark Wilson
Feb 4, 1874
Nov 19, 1951

Lizzie L. Clark
Oct 13, 1872
May 14, 1950

W. Loyd Sowell
1885-1957
&
Fannie J. Sowell
1890-

Shields L. Wilson
Jan 18, 1884
Feb 21, 1912

Rebecca L. Wilson
Sep 3, 1890
Apr 17, 1907

Marion C. Wilson, M.D.
Apr 5, 1886
Sep 13, 1958

W. B. Campbell *
Died Feb 2, 1901
Age: 71 years

Marion,* Daughter of
Mr. & Mrs. C. W. Hamlin
Died Oct 10, 1904
Age: 19m.

Mrs. J. T. (Dell Malls),
wife of John Turner
of Bradshaw, died Nov 17, 1902
Age: 30y, 8m.

Henry A. Arney
1878-1967
&
Eula R. Arney
1880-1949

J. Herbert Arney
Feb 12, 1903

&
Daisy C. Arney
Mar 24, 1904

W. Claiborn Crabtree
Oct 7, 1888
Apr 29, 1966
&
Sallie Will G. Crabtree
Apr 23, 1908

William Henry Glenn
Oct 25, 1877
Feb 15, 1958

Maggie Lou March Glenn
Apr 18, 1877
Mar 14, 1947

Maggie May Glenn
Apr 19, 1876
Nov 26, 1950

Sarah Glenn
Nov 30, 1839
Mar 22, 1926

Emma Glenn, wife of
J. W. Mooney
Sep 15, 1874
Dec 23, 1916

George W. Glenn
Jun 22, 1841
Feb 10, 1911

Addison B. Wilson
Sep 29, 1858
Jun 9, 1931

Mary White Wilson
Sep 16, 1860
Sep 5, 1918

Mrs. Smith *, wife of
Dave Smith
Died Jun 12, 1892
Age: 43 years.

Mrs. Sallie,* wife of
James Clark
Died May 4, 1895
Age: 64 years.

Edward Hughey *
Died Sep 2, 1899
Age: 29y, 10m.

Hugh Broadrick *
Died Aug 22, 1914
Age: 48 years.

BOONSHILL QUADRANGLE

CLARKE CEMETERY

LOCATION: One-half mile east of Hughey, south side of old Boonshill-Fayetteville road, on high hill.

Joseph H. Clarke
Oct 29, 1807
May 17, 1904
(married Dec 8, 1838)
&
Jane E. (Massey) Clarke
May 17, 1819
Aug 28, 1857

W. R. Bledsoe
Aug 12, 1823
Apr 15, 1904
&
E. J. Bledsoe
Apr 16, 1823
Nov 13, 1904

Mrs. Hens Cunningham *
Died Dec 15, 1911
Age: 53 years.

About 20 graves marked with fieldstones, no inscriptions.

Charles Cunningham
Mar 6, 1834
Feb 19, 1905
(married Jul 9, 1857)
&
Sarah E. Cunningham
1836-Jul 4, 1901

Robert Cunningham
Oct 9, 1803
Oct 25, 1878

Nancy J. Cunningham
Sep 19, 1868
Apr 14, 1891

Jimmie Bearden Cunningham
Jan 14, 1862
Dec 15, 1911

C. H. Cunningham
Nov 28, 1863
Nov 1, 1905

Maggie A. Cunningham
Nov 28, 1865
Nov 6, 1906

Joseph A. Edmison(Edmondson)
Jan 29, 1846   (2nd marker)
Jul 28, 1919
(married Dec 20, 1866)

Robert E. Edmison (Edmondson)
Feb 15, 1815
Nov 22, 1860
&
Sophia M. Edmison (Edmondson)
Dec 27, 1816
Jan 2, 1890
(married Jul 31, 1839)

Joseph A. Edmison(Edmondson)
Jan 29, 1846
Jul 28, 1919
(married Dec 20, 1866)
&
Nancy C.(Cunningham) Edmison(Edmondson)
May 11, 1836
Jun 26, 1881

Emily C. Edmison
Jun 19, 1828
Jul 12, 1916
Age: 88 years.

L. A. Smith
Apr 11, 1855
Aug 7, 1898
&
Tabitha Smith
1855-1934

* *

CHILDS CEMETERY

LOCATION: One-fourth mile north of old Sulpher Springs. One and ine-half miles NE of Hughey, in woods.

H. T. Childs
Jul 18, 1841
Dec 15, 1920

Sallie C. Taylor, wife of
H. T. Childs
Sep 19, 1845
Jan 13, 1900

Dora Whitaker, wife of
H. T. Childs
May 9, 1856
May 18, 1916
Age: 60y, 9m.

Bessie, Daughter of
H. T. & S. C. Childs
May 10, 1880
Feb 27, 1881
Age: 9m, 17d.

T. W. Childs
Aug 23, 1846
Apr 4, 1872

Many unmarked graves.

Rev. Thomas Childs
Mar 9, 1796
Aug 17, 1872

Sally, wife of
Thomas Childs
Jun 29, 1808
Oct 19, 1883

Lula May, Daughter of
J. B. & W. G. Posey
Jul 5, 1909
Jan 21, 1910

Narsie J. Daniel, wife of
Jas. T. Webb
Died Feb 9, 1902
Age: 75y, 1m, 14d.

C. V. Webb
Apr 15, 1853

* *

DERRICK CEMETERY

LOCATION: One mile west of Howell, north side of Howell-Sulpher Springs Road.

William B. Derrick
Jul 29, 1861
Apr 25, 1896

Mrs. Eliza Derrick
1864-1945

Leon C. Derrick
1889-1937

* *

BOONSHILL QUADRANGLE

CAPTAIN SMITH CEMETERY

LOCATION: Three-fourth mile west of Howell on west side of Cane Creek.

Sylvester F., 3rd Son of
Isaac & Ida Southworth
Born in Lincoln Co., Tenn.
Oct 16, 1826
Died in Lincoln Co., Tenn.
Nov 18, 1841, from the
accidental felling of a
tree on himself on that day.
Aged: 15y, 1m, 2d.
"He died and made no sign,
we know in whom we trust."
(marker broken)

Ida, Consort of
Isaac Southworth and
daughter of William &
Phebe Smith
Born in Davidson Co., Tenn.
Jan 12, 1799
Died in Lincoln Co., Tenn.
Mar 25, 1854
Aged: 55y, 2m, 13d.
(marker broken)

Captain William Smith *
"A Soldier of the Revolution"
Died Sept 1839
  and   wife
Phebe Smith

Richard Southworth,* Son of
Isaac Southworth
Died Apr 7, 1853
Age: about 22 years.

Randolph Quarles ***
and
Jemima Quarles Porter
are buried here.

Alberd Buchanan
   "Col'rd"
Dec 12, 1819
Apr 8, 1881

Many unmarked graves.

* *

CRAWFORD CEMETERY

LOCATION: One mile SW of Howell, on west side of March Mill Road. "Old Capt. Billy Crawford Place".

Titus, Son of
William & Rachel Crawford
Apr 13, 1803
Oct 8, 1818

Marietta, Daughter of
William & Nancy R.
Crawford
Apr 7, 1853
Mar 12, 1870
Age: 16y, 7m, 5d.

William Crawford
(born Augusta Co., VA)
Feb 14, 1780
Mar 7, 1859

Rachel (Titus), wife of
William Crawford
Aug 19, 1782
Jun 18, 1841

Nancy R., wife of
William Crawford
1814-Aug 6, 1868
Age: 54y, 2m, 13d.

Maggie Ellen Crawford
Jan 30, 1881
Oct 2, 1883

Mrs. Odell Tigert Mauldin
Died Feb 7, 1910
Age: 19 years.

Abner Gaines Sawyers ***
Jul 13, 1802
Aug 11, 1875

Evaline Sawyers ***
Mar 12, 1806
Aug 21, 1850

George G. Crawford
Jan 10, 1846
Sep 6, 1896
   &
Ellen B. Crawford
May 29, 1846
Nov 16, 1908

Rachel (Sawyers), wife of
William Crawford
(born Virginia)
Died Sep 4, 1821
Age: 70 years.
"Leaving 5 sons & 4
daughters to mourn her loss".

William A., Son of
William A. & Martha B.
Crawford
Sep 22, 1842
Jul 21, 1843

William Duvergne Crawford
May 22, 1886
Nov 17, 1905

Margaret L., Daughter of
A. P. & A. B. Taylor
Jan 24, 1902
Nov 10, 1904

Beatrice M. Clark
May 10, 1896
Mar 12, 1910

R. E. Sawyers ***
Mar 7, 1825
Oct 3, 1833

N. A. Sawyers ***
Oct 26, 1826
Oct 5, 1833

R. T., Daughter of
David & Rebecca Buchanan
Apr 1, 1822
Dec 22, 1822

Infant Son of
David & Rebecca Buchanan
B&D Nov 26, 1823

A. J., Son of
David & Rebecca Buchanan
Nov 27, 1829
Sep 16, 1848

David W., Son of
James & Louisa Harris
Dec 19, 1842
Jul 22, 1843

Rev. J. B. Tigert
Jan 10, 1829
Jun 14, 1904
   & wife
M. A. Tigert
(Margaret Ann)
Aug 17, 1844
May 6, 1885

_____, Son of
_____ & Rebecca Henderson
(no dates & broken)

W. C. Sawyers ***
Sep 30, 1828
Oct 5, 1833

J. D. Sawyers ***
Sep 14, 1830
Oct 10, 1833

NOTE: The four children ***
are children of
A. G. & Evaline Sawyers

George H., Son of
J. B. & M. A. Tigert
Jun 26, 1870
Sep 30, 1890
Age: 20 years

Belle G., Daughter of
J. B. & M. A. Tigert
Dec 8, 1863
Dec 5, 1880
Age: 17 years.

William C., Son of
J. B. & M. A. Tigert
B&D Sep 12, 1861

A. G. Dickey
Jul 10, 1810
Apr   1863

Eliza Dickey
Jun 9, 1811
Nov 17, 1887

Martha E. Dickey
Apr 12, 1839
May 8, 1903

Rachel S. Hampton ***
Aug 30, 1807
Jun 30, 1848

Sally S. Eastland ***
May 2, 1825
May 12, 1850

Many unmarked graves.

* *

BOONSHILL QUADRANGLE

MARTIN-CHITWOOD CEMETERY

LOCATION: One mile SE of Sulpher Springs, west side of Egam-Sulpher Springs Road.

Francis Chitwood Mar 10, 1813 Aug 12, 1896	Elizabeth Martin Sep 16, 1823 Aug 20, 1841	Sarah B. Martin Nov 23, 1828 Aug 16, 1841	Mary M.,* Widow of Anderson Martin Died Feb 21, 1900 Age: 80 years.
William Chitwood * Oct 15, 1809 Jun 22, 1863	(Senior residents says that Ben. F. Clark & wife are buried here.)	Several fieldstones with no inscriptions.	

* *

KENT CEMETERY

LOCATION: One mile north of Egam, east side of Egam-Sulpher Springs Road, top of high hill.

A. R. L., wife of
R. W. Kent
Aug 11, 1844
Jul 18, 1875

(March Family buried here)

Several unmarked graves.

* *

JOSEPH COMMONS CEMETERY

LOCATION: One-fourth mile west of Egam, north side of road inside rock wall.

Joseph Commons *
Died Feb 26, 1858
(no age given)

Inside stone wall are 2 or 3
graves with no inscriptions.

* *

SULLIVAN CEMETERY

LOCATION: One mile south of Hughey and north of Highway 64.

R. P. McWhorter Sep 3, 1854 Feb 13, 1936	B. F. Nerren Feb 2, 1823 Mar 9, 1902	N. G. Sullivan Aug 17, 1823 Nov 6, 1900	H. H. Sullivan Oct 27, 1852 Oct 14, 1917 & wife
Minerva Jane, wife of R. P. McWhorter Feb 14, 1849 (no date) Age: 88y, 2m, 8d.	Elizabeth W., wife of B. F. Nerren Feb 9, 1828 Sep 10, 1903	Margaret E. Mauldin, wife of N. G. Sullivan Jan 28, 1836 Dec 30, 1899	Jane M. Sullivan Died Apr 17, 1876 Age: 27 years.
R. W. West 1850-1927 & wife Lizzie West Feb 5, 1850 Aug 17, 1905	William A. West Sep 11, 1870 Apr 21, 1906	Maggie Sullivan Mar 31, 1870 Aug 8, 1898	Thomas G., Son of H. H. & A. E. Sullivan Jan 31, 1884 Aug 7, 1887
NOTE: Margaret E. Sullivan* Died Jan 30, 1900 NOT 1899	Newton C. Sullivan 1863-1935 & Nannie Curry Sullivan 1870-19	Octavia, wife of R. B. Collins Mar 27, 1872 Aug 19, 1898	A. H. Sullivan Dec 12, 1867 Jan 14, 1937
Many unmarked graves.	Jessie B.,* Infant of Ben Sullivan Died Apr 10, 1906 Age: 3m, 20d.	Widow * of Neil Sullivan Died March 1890 Age: 90 years.	Mrs. Lydia McAfee * Died Jun 16, 1898 Age: 81y, 9m, 27d.

* *

BOONSHILL QUADRANGLE

PORCH CEMETERY

LOCATION: One mile SSW of Hughey and north of Highway 64.

Phebe
(fieldstone)

W. H. C. Gowen
(fieldstone, no inscription)

William H. Porch
Died Sep 1870
(fieldstone)

Several unmarked graves.

* *

CHILDRESS CEMETERY

LOCATION: One and one-half miles SE of Boonshill and south of Highway 64 at old Childress brick house.

E. A. Barnes
1848-1932

Minerva Owen, wife of
E. A. Barnes
Apr 6, 1854
Oct 5, 1914

Susan T. Barnes, wife of
W. B. Nerren
Jul 5, 1875
Apr 18, 1904

W. L.
(footstone, no inscription)

Amanda M., wife of
W. H. Gunter
Sep 1, 1847
Jul 19, 1877

J. R. L. Edminson
Sep 1, 1874
Nov 12, 1875

H. T., Son of
T. J. & E. J. Lemond
Jul 17, 1860
Sep 20, 1889
Age: 20y, 2m, 3d.

Sarah C. Brady
Feb 12, 1850
Nov 22, 1893
&
C. Pointer Brady
1870-1949
Buried at Oteco, NY

Mark C. Brady
1848-1882
Buried at Sardis, Miss.

T. S. Johnson *
Died Sep 24, 1906
Age: 61 years

Mrs. Susan A., Widow of
M. L. Owen
Died Aug 26, 1891
Age: 75 years.

Jerome B. Brady
32nd Tenn. Inf.
C.S.A.

Reps O. Childress
Apr 5, 1775
Sep 3, 1826
Age: 51y, 4m, 27d.
&
Mary, wife of
R. O. Childress
Died Nov 14, 1815
(no age given)
&
Sarah Childress
Oct 4, 1787
Mar 17, 1856

Harriet Childress
Jan 12, 1823
Feb 15, 1823
Age: 1m, 3d.
&
Emiline R. Childress
Dec 18, 1825
Jun 24, 1830
Age: 4y, 6m, 6d.

Mark Childress
May 9, 1866
Oct 15, 1941

Marion F. Childress
Mar 3, 1863
May 1, 1949

Plaque:
"Ave Atque Vole
The Childress Name
M. F.(Marion) & D. L.(Mark)
These two bachelor brothers
lived together in the
ancient home nearby for
more than half a century.
Marion was prominent as a
Magistrate, Financier &
Banker; Mark was an out-
standing farmer, stockman
& sportsman. Each
successful, a compliment to
the other; both charitable,
honorable men, a credit to
their Community, and to the
name they wore with pride."

Infant Son of
Rufus M. & Mary C. Childress
B&D Jan 13, 183-(broken)

William H. Childress
Died Sep 15, 1840
Age: 25y, 6m, 9d.
"Leaving a wife & 3 children"

Rebecca B., Consort of
Alexander Smith & daughter
of Reps O. & Sarah Childress
Jun 19, 1819
Sep 25, 1838

Dr. G. B. Lester
Sep 25, 1821
Nov 13, 1894

R. S. C. Lester
May 27, 1838
Mar 11, 1901

Eliza J. Hutchison
Jan 23, 1852
Aug 21, 1906

Katherine Brady Patton
Sep 8, 1903
Dec 1, 1966

Elizabeth Hitchens Brady
Sep 18, 1871
Jun 27, 1967

John Marion, Son of
Mark C. & Sarah Childress
Brady
Aug 6, 1873
Apr 8, 1960

Cresa, wife of
J. R. Cunningham
Feb 15, 1887
Apr 13, 1909

Mary A., wife of
A. B. Edminson
Sep 9, 1842
Jun 28, 1907

James O. Childress
May 16, 1824
Sep 23, 1841
Age: 16y, 4m, 7d.
&
Amanda Childress
(information gone)

Martha A., wife of
Thomas F. Lindsay
Nov 22, 1852
Jun 3, 1881

Lou B. Childress
Jun 2, 1857
Jun 27, 1858
&
Osburn Childress
Jun 12, 1859
Jul 1, 1859
&
Mary E. Childress
Jan 28, 1861
Jan 27, 1862
&
Marion Childress
Aug 21, 1821
Oct 24, 1883

Amanda R. Childress
Feb 4, 1828
Mar 13, 1905

Virginia N., Daughter of
Alexander & Mary C. Smith
Oct 11, 1846
Jun 13, 1847

A. J. Smith *
Died Sep 24, 1905
Age: 61 years.

Andrew B. Edmiston *
Died Jun 22, 1910
Age: 67 years.
C.S.A.

* *

BOONSHILL QUADRANGLE

SWAN CREEK CHURCH CEMETERY

LOCATION: Across Swan Creek from Swan Creek Presbyterian Church, one and one-half miles south of Taylortown.

R. W. Bearden
Feb 14, 1838
Nov 23, 1907
&
N. J. Bearden
Dec 12, 1847
Feb 9, 1920

Mary E. Bearden
Dec 18, 1842
Jul 28, 1895

R. O. Bearden
Feb 9, 1877
Sep 27, 1941

Jacob A. Arney
Oct 15, 1882
Apr 19, 1902

Zoray M., wife of
D. W. Arney
Sep 7, 1852
Jun 31, 1891

Lutie Davis
Feb 13, 1849
Apr 22, 1912

Nancy Watt
Oct 8, 1811
Oct 28, 1865

E. J. Watt
Feb 1861
Oct 1862

Ruth Bearden ***
Died Apr 28, 1918

A. N. McDaniel ***
Died Nov 3, 1919

E. S. Bearden *
Died Mar 1, 1877
Age: 71 years.

Infant * of
J. M. & S. A. Campbell
Died Sep 3, 1898
(no age given)

W. A. Cunningham
Oct 11, 1842
Nov 27, 1913

James H., Son of
W. A. & M. Cunningham
Mar 18, 1880
Jun 7, 1904

Charles H. Cunningham
May 12, 1832
Feb 14, 1909

Sarah N., wife of
C. H. Cunningham
Mar 26, 1833
Apr 28, 1874

Mary B., Daughter of
S. M. & M. L. Cunningham
Nov 11, 1900
Sep 21, 1901

Nancy E. Cunningham
Jun 16, 1841
Jun 16, 1911

Bedford Forest Cunningham
Jun 9, 1902
Nov 15, 1922
"Erected by Shipmates of
U.S.S. Tennessee."

Edgar,* Son of
T. P. Cunningham
Died Sep 24, 1899
Age: 2 years.

Miss Jessie Cunningham *
Died Jun 7, 1904
Age: 24 years.

Miss Cunningham *, Daughter
of Charles Cunningham
Died Apr 14, 1891
Age: 23 years.

Roger Kilmartin *
Died Feb 20, 1875
Age: about 45 years.

Many unmarked graves.

Cecil Thorne Cunningham
Kansas
Engineman 2/c
Sep 19, 1927

John Randall, Son of
G. E. & J. I. Cunningham
Died Sep 29, 1901
Age: 13m, 16d.

J. W. Cunningham
Jul 3, 1805
Apr 14, 1889

Eliza Cunningham
Jun 12, 1808
Jan 17, 1898

J. L. Denham
Died Jul 16, 1870
Age: about 75 years
"Served in the War of 1812".

Esther Denham
Jun 3, 1806
Oct 5, 1889

J. W. Denham
Oct 22, 1841
Sep 12, 1842

Mrs. Maggie,* Wife of
T. B. Jones & Daughter of
S. N. Cunningham
Died Oct 25, 1896
Age: 30 years.

Mrs. Elizabeth Whorley *
Died Oct 13, 1897
Age: 92 years

Thomas Cunningham *
Died Jul 9, 1916
Age: about 46 years.

Mrs. Mary Elizabeth,* wife of
Moses Calvin Storey &
Daughter of
Lewis & Mary Shipp
born in Lincoln Co., Tenn.
Nov 23, 1832
married Dec 23, 1856
died Jan 13, 1916
Age: 83y, 1m, 26d.

H. R. Hamilton
Jan 26, 1810
Jun 28, 1854

John Thomas, Son of
H. R. & M. C. Hamilton
Jun 14, 1853
Jul 7, 1853

Hugh Reed, Son of
H. R. & M. C. Hamilton
Jun 15, 1854
Oct 24, 1854

Maggie, wife of
T. B. Jones
Mar 15, 1888
Oct 25, 1896

Celia Story
Jun 22, 1820
Feb 4, 1895

J. P. Sorrow
Apr 5, 1850
Apr 30, 1898

Lizzie, Daughter of
J. P. & L. P. Sorrow
Died Apr 14, 1890
Age: 13y, 6m.

Carlton Aster,* Son of
H. A. Arney
Died Aug 11, 1902
Age: 14 years.

Mrs. L. C.,* Widow of
M. M. Story
Died Oct 10, 1898
Age: 61 years.

Mrs. Addie,* wife of
C. I. Hopper
married 1875
Died Nov 7, 1897
Age: 45y, 6m.

Infant Son * of
Joe Guy
Died Jul 19, 1890
Age: 2 years.

* *

TURNEY CEMETERY

LOCATION: Two miles SE of Boonshill on south side of Barnes Road.

Henry Turney
--- 28, 1787
Jun 21, 1850
Age: 63y, 5m, 23d.

Luisa C. Turney
Apr 14, 1819
Jul 7, 1854
Age: 35y, 2m, 23d.

Nancy W. Tucker
Mar 1, 1820
Oct 6, 1886
(4 graves marked with no information)

Infant Babe of
C. G. & Nancy W. Tucker
(no dates)

* *

BOONSHILL QUADRANGLE

BARNES CEMETERY

LOCATION: Two miles SE of Boonshill on north side of Barnes Road. "John Barnes Home".

H. T. Barnes
Nov 26, 1852
Dec 6, 1932
&
Mary E. Barnes
Feb 4, 1852
Jan 12, 1934

Abraham Barnes ***
(fieldstone)
Mar 28, 1795
Dec 25, 1882
married Nov 21, 1814

Catharine Rider Barnes ***
Died Mar 15, 1873
(no age given)

Henry J. Barnes
Mar 24, 1824
Jul 15, 1891

Nancy S. Barnes
Feb 8, 1831
Jul 19, 1867

Louisa A. Barnes
Nov 5, 1833
Apr 27, 1877

Infant Son of
R. F. & N. C. Williamson
Mar 28, 1896

J. A. Barnes
1859-1943

Julia F., wife of
J. A. Barnes
Nov 5, 1865
May 20, 1894

Rebecka Barnes
Died Apr 5, 1869
(no age given)

Francis M. Barnes
Dec 13, 1835
May 30, 1914

Amanda A. Barnes
Apr 13, 1842
Apr 30, 1909

Twin Daughters of
Charles E. & Lizzie Tucker
Barnes
B&D 1906

Esther Barnes
Jun 23, 1882
Sep 6, 1889

John M. Tucker and
Apr 7, 1872
Aug 11, 1946

J. H.(Joe Henry) Barnes
Jan 28, 1855
Jan 21, 1913

Cannie Barnes
1858-1950

Thomas L. Owen
1872-1950
&
Sarah L. Owen
1879-1959

Henderson Barnes
Died Sep 7, 1909
Age: 82y, 1m, 3d.

(Mrs.) P. A. Barnes
Died Oct 18, 1910
Age: 83y, 4m, 7d.

Estella, Daughter of
J. W. & B. S. Barnes
May 16, 1882
Apr 12, 1894

Rufus M., Son of
H. & P. A. Barnes
Nov 5, 1866
May 21, 1867
Age: 6m, 16d.

L. E. Ramsey
Apr 12, 1854
May 22, 1925

Martha Ann Barnes Ramsey
1861-1938

Sam M., Son of
L. E. & M. A. Ramsey
Jul 4, 1882
Jun 29, 1896

Lucy A., Daughter of
R. D. & F. E. Collins
Sep 11, 1911
Nov 5, 1913

Robert David Collins
Aug 4, 1887
Apr 18, 1919
&
Effie Barnes Collins
Nov 5, 1885
Jun 19, 1967

R. D., Jr., Son of
R. D. & F. E. Collins
Sep 4, 1919
Nov 25, 1926

Louella Barnes Tucker
Aug 7, 1876
Apr 16, 1931

John W. Barnes
Dec 15, 1856
Jun 21, 1884
Age: 27y, 6m, 6d.

B. S., wife of
J. W. Barnes
Nov 28, 1856
Jan 24, 1892

Ernest M. Barnes
May 28, 1878
Sep 14, 1879

John T. Barnes
Sep 9, 1876
Jul 9, 1878

Eli Barnes
Sep 30, 1815
Dec 7, 1884

Talitha Barnes
1812-1858

Ellen, wife of
Eli Barnes
Dec 13, 1823
Mar 23, 1888

Henry W. Barnes
1848-1925

Louisa C. Barnes
Oct 3, 1842
Sep 26, 1929

Clyde G. Williamson
Aug 3, 1907
Jun 29, 1928

Jennie B., wife of
C. G. Williamson
Mar 1, 1899
Mar 26, 1921

R. F. Williamson
Sep 8, 1860
Sep 26, 1913

Nannie Catharine Barnes
Williamson
Oct 26, 1867
Aug 2, 1942

Melvin C. Williamson
Jan 8, 1890
Dec 5, 1910
C.S.A.

Thomas M. Barnes
1851-1930
&
Addie Barnes
1854-1911

Margaret J. Barnes, wife
of J. W. Turner
Mar 22, 1844
Aug 16, 1889

Nancie A., Daughter of
J. W. & M. J. Turner
Sep 11, 1869
Oct 26, 1873

D.(Decator) Barnes
Dec 21, 1829
Jul 29, 1904

Margarette J., wife of
Decator Barnes
Mar 5, 1831
Jun 25, 1900

M. E., wife of
T. W. Harrison
May 10, 1856
Jan 19, 1922

D. Z. Barnes
Apr 2, 1824
Jul 22, 1900
&
R. C. Barnes
Aug 6, 1821
Feb 14, 1893

Tom Rudd
Apr 17, 1886
Feb 13, 1966
&
Margaret B. Rudd
Aug 1, 1888
Jan 6, 1958

J. H. Rudd
Apr 24, 1913
Jul 26, 1914

Mollie D., wife of
J. O. Collins
Dec 1, 1895
Oct 15, 1916

N. T. Tucker
1870-1930
&
Ila B. Tucker
1880-1958

Thomas W. Barnes
May 18, 1894
Oct 14, 1967
&
Laura May Barnes
Sep 28, 1900
Jul 2, 1974

Horace Winfred, Son of
C. M. & C. L. Owen
Apr 21, 1919
Mar 3, 1920

BOONSHILL QUADRANGLE

Father
William A. Owen
1868-1950
&
Mother
Catherine Barnes Owen
1863-1947

Vallie M. Owen
Jan 4, 1894
Apr 25, 1921

Rebecca L. Owen
Dec 31, 1895
May 22, 1917

John Owen Cunningham
Mar 7, 1926
Oct 1, 1928

Sheeley Smith
1882-1938

J. Odie Collins
James Odie Collins
Tennessee
Pvt Co H 327 Inf WW I
Jan 21, 1889
Mar 3, 1967
&
Clara S. Collins
May 29, 1902

Cellie Robert Williamson
Nov 14, 1903
Jun 15, 1947

Charlie E. Barnes
1874-1952
&
Lizzie T. Barnes
1878-1960

Mattie C. Barnes
Dec 30, 1923
Jan 10, 1924

Nerlean Collins
May 9, 1928
Jun 12, 1932

Wade W., Son of
J. H. & M. E. Smith
Jun 28, 1914
May 8, 1916

J. Hiram Smith
1878-1947
&
Ella H. Smith
1881-1962

Maxie May Noah Smith
Aug 8, 1915
Dec 27, 1936

Earl C. White
1894-1965
&
Bertha P. White
1901-1939

T. C. Wilson
Feb 27, 1876
Mar 5, 1947
&
Addie Lou Wilson
Oct 30, 1899

Edward C. Barnes
California
S/Sgt Btry A, 70 Fld Arty Bn
W W II
Feb 14, 1906
Sep 4, 1959

Pleas H. Barnes
Nov 15, 1902

&
Lorene P. Barnes
Nov 4, 1904

Abraham M. Barnes
Aug 27, 1858
Feb 3, 1933
&
Fannie Ann Barnes
Jan 1, 1868
Apr 26, 1947

Sam Collins
1855-1932
&
Alice Collins
1863-1944

Mary J. Minatree
1860-1941

Henry Edgar Minatree
Jan 12, 1896
Jul 31, 1961

James Overton Harris
Died Jan 2, 1969
Age: 77y, 10m, 23d.

James Archie Harris
Jul 12, 1863
May 30, 1947
&
Lucy Jane Edmison Harris
Nov 13, 1867
Nov 27, 1929

T. N. Thompson
Dec 14, 1861
Jan 16, 1925
& wife
Rachel Allison Thompson
Feb 8, 1860
Jun 19, 1934

Baby Daughter Barnes
B&D Jan 27, 1928

Several unmarked graves.

Willie G. Collins
1891-1960
&
Nina T. Collins
1899-1937

Amy Kimball Smith
Apr 24, 1966

Robert F. Milliken
1870-1946
&
Etta L. Milliken
1871-1962

John M. Milliken
Jul 18, 1898

&
Dillia A. Milliken
Feb 14, 1907
Jan 31, 1969

Mary Arlene Massey
May 4, 1928
Nov 8, 1968

Maxie H. Barnes
1880-1952
&
Hattie E. Barnes
1886-19

John D. Barnes
Oct 31, 1911

&
Sara Askins Barnes
Oct 30, 1922

Richard L. Williamson
Alabama
Tec 5 240 General Hosp.
WW II
Mar 23, 1917
Jan 19, 1964

* *

WILSON CEMETERY

LOCATION: North of Wyatt Creek, one and one-fourth miles NNE of East Cyruston. (In cow pasture)

Robert W. Wilson
Jun 23, 1830
Jan 31, 1891
&
Mary E. Wilson
May 4, 1829
Apr 27, 1893

James A., Son of
R. W. & Mary E. Wilson
Sep 14, 1865
Sep 26, 1865

Sallie A., Daughter of
R. W. & Mary E. Wilson
Aug 6, 1863
Oct 14, 1864

Eva J., Daughter of
R. W. & Mary E. Wilson
Aug 30, 1861
Aug 19, 1869

W. A. Hughey
Nov 27, 1857
May 17, 1885

T. A. Hughey
Dec 20, 1864
Feb 26, 1872

Ann Blair
Feb 23, 1804
Jan 24, 1886

Allen Taylor
Mar 12, 1809
Dec 30, 1887

Archibald McClurkin
Feb 14, 1810
Jan 11, 1876

T. W. (Wilson)
Died 1815
(fieldstone)

E. W. (Wilson)
Died 1816
(fieldstone)

William D. Hughes
Died Sep 6, 1838
(no age given)

Mary A. Hughes
Died Nov 9, 1837
(no age given)

E. W. (Wilson)
Died 1809
(fieldstone)

B. W. (Wilson)
Died 1815
(fieldstone)

BOONSHILL QUADRANGLE

A. B.   (Blair)
1815
(fieldstone)

W. B.   (Blair)
1831
(fieldstone)

Eliza, Consort of
James Wilson
Jul 18, 1803
Oct 27, 1866
Age: 63y, 3m, 9d.

William Blair
Jun 11, 1809
Sep 9, 1841

Ada McCown
Sep 22, 1868
Dec 30, 1868

Sarah J. Strain
Dec 21, 1833
Apr 7, 1884

Robert Wilson
May 29, 1778
Nov 9, 1841

Hannah B., wife of
Robert Wilson
Nov 19, 1795
Mar 21, 1881

J. A. Wyatt
Departed 1829

Mrs. Mary Milligan *
Died Mar 4, 1905
Age: 81 years.

Miss Margaret Jane Millikin*
Died Aug 6, 1899
Age: 72 years.

Bethshery, wife of
Mathew Wilson
Mar 30, 1796
Jun 6, 1841

Matthew T. Wilson
Sep 4, 1826
Feb 13, 1866

Elvira J., wife of
M. T. Wilson
Aug 6, 1824
Jul 16, 1848

Robert E., Son of
M. T. & E. J. Wilson
Apr 25, 1848
May 1, 1848

Washington Wilson
Dec 6, 1796
Mar 6, 1875
    & wife
Mary Wilson
1806-Jul 31, 1854

Clinton Wilson
Jul 29, 1813
Apr 12, 1885

James P., Son of
J. B. & Hanna B. Conner
Sep 20, 1818
Mar 7, 1838

John Fullerton
May 1785
Oct 1864
Age: 79y, 4m, _d.

Margaret Fullerton
Jun 19, 1793
Nov 28, 1880

Jane F. Cathey
Feb 12, 1837
Jan 17, 1885

Oscur E., Son of
A. & E. S. Laseby
Sep 14, 1873
Jun 28, 1874

E. E. Hamilton
Feb 20, 1835
Jul 6, 1870

William Wyatt
Nov 10, 1802
Dec 30, 1880

Sarah, wife of
William Wyatt
Sep 21, 1804
Apr 2, 1884

Sarah A., Daughter of
William & Sarah Wyatt
Jul 18, 1846
Feb 5, 1858

Richard T., Son of
William & Sarah Wyatt
Jul 31, 1839
Sep 26, 1841

Jennie Wyatt
Jun 1, 1807
Jun 8, 1895

John B. K., Son of
William & Sarah Wyatt
Jun 18, 1835
Jul 10, 1853

Badly desecrated by cows.

Many unmarked graves.

Jane Wyatt, Consort of
Richard Wyatt was born
Oct 6, A.D. 1767 and
departed this life
June 3rd 1852.
Age: 84y, 7m, 27d.
(Vault type)

1 Large Vault beside
Jane Wyatt

M. D.
1818
(fieldstone)

J. H.
1812
(fieldstone)

Martha Hamilton
Died Aug 5, 1872
Age: 19 years.

William C. Hamilton
Jan 10, 1802
Aug 30, 1839

David M. Hamilton
May 7, 1809
Sep 24, 1845

Elizabeth J., wife of
D. M. Hamilton
Feb 22, 1813
Jul 27, 1888
Age: 75y, 5m, 5d.

Marker
1773 (no information)

E. S. Wilson
Died Jun 14, 1899
Age: 63y, 11m.
C.S.A. under
Capt. Newt Davis Co.

* *

HALBERT CEMETERY

LOCATION: One and one-half miles SSE of Swan Creek Presbyterian Church, east of main road, one-half mile north of Cyruston, on "Old Halbert Farm."

Andrew Smart
Jan   1841
Mar 2, 1920

Mary Ann Smart
Feb 14, 1855
May 18, 1933

John Lee Smart
Oct 22, 1897
Oct 14, 1918

John S., Son of
S. S. & D. L. Smart
Apr 11, 1922
(date gone)

Mary Beatrice, Daughter of
S. S. & D. L. Smart
Apr 8, 1918
Nov 21, 1918

Mintie Carpenter
May 1, 1870
Nov 14, 1918

Christopher Thomas Smart
Mar 18, 1886
Mar 2, 1902
       &
Pink Smart
Jul 22, 1878
Oct 1, 1904

Dr. T. N. Jenkins
Jun 16, 1862
Jan 6, 1913
       &
Nannie H. Jenkins
Oct 29, 1867
Jun 1, 1943

Dr. P. W. Halbert
Jul 17, 1844
Apr 4, 1907

Sallie E. Halbert
Sep 11, 1844
May 31, 1932

James C. Halbert
Feb 23, 1838
Dec 23, 1915

Fannie E. Halbert
Jan 7, 1841
Oct 19, 1915

John T. Halbert
Aug 5, 1841
May 30, 1866

Van Buren Harwell
Apr 15, 1872
Nov 8, 1918

BOONSHILL QUADRANGLE

Pleasant Halbert
born in Williamson Co., TN
Sep 16, 1811
Oct 1, 1895

Nancy Halbert
Nov 16, 1810
Aug 5, 1850

Martha V., wife of
Pleasant Halbert
Sep 15, 1827
Aug 4, 1897

Buck Smart *
Died Mar 9, 1901
Age: 17 years.

Halbert, Son of
S. M. & E. N. Clayton
Jan 8, 1880
Sep 21, 1882

Monroe, Son of
S. M. & E. N. Clayton
Aug 18, 1870
Aug 22, 1870

Naomi, wife of
S. M. Clayton
May 15, 1845
Aug 25, 1886

Mrs. Cynthia,* wife of
George Dempsy
Died Dec 30, 1906
Age: Old age

James A. Yowell
Sep 20, 1808
(date in ground)

John T. Clayton
Jul 4, 1871
Oct 30, 1891

Martha E., wife of
Dr. J. E. Yowell
Sep 25, 1834
Sep 11, 1890

Clifford Tucker *
Died Apr 12, 1904
Age: 23 years.

Maggie Clayton
Apr 14, 1875
Mar 7, 1892

Willie, wife of
M. J. Farrar
Oct 16, 1859
Jul 7, 1909

Nannie E., wife of
T. L. Hicks
Jul 8, 1887
May 6, 1912

Will Cox *
Died May 1906
Age: 76y, 6m.
married Nancy Richmond
Nov 20, 1896

* *

SUGG CEMETERY

LOCATION: At Cyruston near Church.

Mamie, daughter of
Dr. W. L. & S. J. Moores
Dec 31, 1887
Dec 21, 1889

Dr. W. L. Moores
Oct 13, 1842
Jul 6, 1896

Sallie J., wife of
Dr. W. L. Moores
Jul 5, 1844
Jun 2, 1899

William Hay, Jr., Son of
W. H. & Lela Sugg
Dec 13, 1911
Oct 25, 1913

Margaret E. Sugg
Jul 17, 1870
Jul 3, 1886

Sarah Ann, Consort of
H. H. Sugg
Jun 24, 1836
Dec 31, 1855
"Leaving a father, a
stepmother & six brothers
to mourn their loss."

Henry H. Sugg
Feb 28, 1831
Feb 25, 1907
& wife
Sallie E. (Yowell) Sugg
Jan 30, 1837
Feb 27, 1907

L. D. Sugg
Died Sep 24, 1910
Age: 84 years.

Margaret Sugg
Jul 9, 1836
Dec 7, 1895

Douglas Sugg
Oct 29, 1856
Jul 3, 1897

Mag Ellen, Daughter of
D. & M. W. Sugg
May 8, 1886
Jan 16, 1891

Nancy T. Sugg
Aug 23, 1872
Sep 19, 1889

Cullen E. Sugg
Mar 25, 1799
Sep   1849
"Leaving a wife, 6 sons &
1 daughter, a brother &
3 sisters".

Sidney C. Sugg
May 15, 1802
Feb 13, 1885

Cullen E. Sugg, Jr.
May 20, 1836
Jul 18, 1853

George A., Son of
Cullen E. & Sidney C. Sugg
Jan 11, 1824
Apr 21, 1845
"Leaving 6 brothers &
1 sister."

Vernia Sugg
Jan 20, 1875
Nov 19, 1880

Cullen E. Sugg
May 2, 1859
Jun 4, 1885

Mary E. Sugg
Aug 23, 1863
Jan 10, 1884

L. S., Daughter of
W. C. & M. S. Sugg
Aug 29, 1859
May 16, 1860

J. D., Son of
W. G. & M. S. Sugg
Apr 16, 1863
Jun 17, 1867

Julius H. Sugg
Dec 16, 1833
Aug 12, 1855

Kate E. Sugg, wife of
J. K. Whitaker
Oct 6, 1862
May 22, 1895

Mrs. Kate,* wife of
Polk Whitaker & Daughter of
H. H. Sugg
Died Jul 21, 1895
Age: (not given)

Several unmarked graves.

L. H., Son of
W. C. & M. S. Sugg
Mar 1, 1878
Mar 3, 1888

William Conrad Sugg
Aug 19, 1828
Jan 23, 1901
&
Mary Sue Sugg
Sep 21, 1841
Jun 6, 1898
married Sep 23, 1858

Hon. W. W. Wilson
born Apr 26, 1821
married M. A. Whitehead
Oct 5, 1848
died Sep 29, 1897

Minerva A., wife of
W. W. Wilson
Mar 19, 1829
Oct 21, 1911

Eliza H. Wilson
Sep 26, 1801
Sep 25, 1874

Thomas Jefferson Sugg
Nov 16, 1838
Feb 21, 1911
Age: 72y, 3m, 5d.

Sarah,* Daughter of
H. H. Sugg
Died Sep 9, 1895
Age: 25 years.
"Sister to E. L. Sugg".

* *

BOONSHILL QUADRANGLE

ZIMMERMAN CEMETERY

LOCATION: One mile SW of East Cyruston, behind a barn in a hog lot, on Cunningham Branch.

Corp. Hugh L. Zimmerman Co K 1 Tenn Inf C.S.A.	W. F. Zimmerman Died Dec 22, 1873 Age: 73 years	H. H. Moseley Sep 15, 1837 Feb 28, 1901	Robert Hatton,* Son of Hugh & O. T. Zimmerman Jul 30, 1881 Oct 16, 1895
Mrs. Orlena Hughey,* wife of H. L. Zimmerman Died Apr 12, 1894 Age: (not given)	Elizabeth R., wife of W. F. Zimmerman Died Dec 10, 1875 Age: 61 years.	Mrs. Zimmerman,* wife of H. L. Zimmerman Died Feb 19, 1879 Age: 30 years.	W. W. Zimmerman * Died Feb 16, 1899 Age: 24 years.

Several unmarked graves, badly destroyed by hogs.

* *

WHITAKER CEMETERY

LOCATION: One mile SW of East Cyruston, east of main road, on hill.

Thomas H. Whitaker Apr 23, 1823 Aug 10, 1897 & Elizabeth Whitaker Oct 5, 1819 Nov 30, 1880	Elizabeth L. Whitaker Jan 7, 1853 May 6, 1862 & Louella Whitaker Nov 29, 1860 Apr 29, 1862	James K. Moores Feb 19, 1833 May 31, 1892 Bessie R., wife of John T. Moores Jan 28, 1876 Mar 4, 1896	Jas. Astor Moores Oct 27, 1874 Oct 9, 1894 Dora Moores Oldham Jan 1840 May 1925

About 25 unmarked graves.

* *

FORD CEMETERY

LOCATION: One-half mile SSW of Pearl City on old Sumner farm, side of lane to house.

Nannie J., wife of Hezekiah Ford Nov 3, 1841 Jul 7, 1881 Age: 39y, 8m, 4d.	Harry Clinton, Son of Hezekiah & Nannie Ford Feb 15, 1881 Oct 23, 1881	Many unmarked graves, and many fieldstones with no inscriptions.

* *

LAY CEMETERY

LOCATION: One and one-half miles NNE of Pearl City in forks of Pearl City and East Cyruston roads, on hill.

William Lay Feb 19, 1777 Dec 15, 1855 Edith Lay Jun 11, 1786 Apr 27, 1873 Gideon Lay Apr 1, 1811 Mar 22, 1894 Many unmarked graves.	James L. Fullerton Aug 30, 1857 Oct 13, 1876 Mary P. Fullerton Mar 14, 1816 May 3, 1873 Susannah, Consort of P. M. Wright Apr 13, 1813 Apr 8, 1852 "Mother of 6 children."	John O. Edmaston Jun 23, 1850 Apr 13, 1906 & Sallie, wife of J. O. Edmiaston Apr 10, 1862 Jul 6, 1932 Lizzie Edmondson * Died Jan 26, 1902 Age: (not given)	Samuel C., Son of W. E. & M. E. Turley Jun 13, 1868 Aug 6, 1868 (broken) Infant Son of W. E. & M. E. Turley B&D (broken away) Miss Kate,* Daughter of Mrs. Elizabeth Edmondson Died Apr 10, 1880 Age: 23 years.

* *

BOONSHILL QUADRANGLE

STEPHENS CEMETERY

LOCATION: Three-fourth mile SE of Pearl City in open field.

This is the Old William
Stephens Homeplace.
He died 1859.

Signs of several graves.

Mary A., ---- of
T--- Pitts
Sep 8, 1834
Mar 1, 1869
Age: 35y, 5m, 25d.
(only marker left in cemetery)

* *

PHAGAN CEMETERY

LOCATION: One mile SW of Lebanon Church and located in the woods.

John H. Bradford
Nov 6, 1846
Jul 1, 1868
Age: 21y, 7m, 25d.

Jane Phagan
Died 1866
Age: 70 years.

J. P. Phagan *
Died Nov 12, 1896
Age: (not given)
Left a wife & 3 children.

P. T. Phagan
Oct --, 1826
Jun 19, 1867

Cassina J., Daughter of
P. T. & M. A. Phagan
Feb 22, 1853
Feb 19, 1878
Age: 24y, 11m, 27d.

Babe
Ella M. Phagan
Age: 9m, 8d.
(no dates)

Mary E. Phagan
(no dates, rock vault)

Mrs. Emma,* wife of
Jeff Kintchen
Died Apr 7, 1892
Age: 20 years.

Agnes Dickey
Mar 1, 1799
Jul 31, 1866
Age: 67y, 5m.
Mike Sullivan, stone cutter.

1 Adult Rock Vault
(no inscription)

1 Fieldstone
(no inscription)

* *

BETHEL CEMETERY

LOCATION: Once the location of Old Bethel A. R. P. Church, one and one-half miles south of Fairview and two miles NW of Harms.

Joseph Askins
Jul 1, 1768
Apr 7, 1872
Age: 93y, 6m, 6d.
(NOTE: checked out twice
 believe incorrect, Eds.)

Mrs. S. A., Consort of
Joseph Askins
Aug 14, 1811
Feb 10, 1862

Infant Daughter of
Joseph & Mrs. Askins
(no dates)

Infant Son of
Joseph & Susannah Askins
(no dates)

Infant Daughter of
Joseph & Mrs. Askins
(no dates)

Cornelia, Daughter of
W. S. & J. A. Murphey
(no dates)

Deford Family
Eleonora Deford Sumners
1857-1886 (mrd:Dec 24,1877
to L. D. Sumners)

J. H. Askins
Sep 26, 1834
Feb 16, 1835

Mary Hamilton
Jun 22, 1816
May 7, 1838

1 Vault Type (child)
(no inscription)

Peter Hamilton
1785-Dec 27, 1861
Age: 76 years.

Mrs. Jane Hamilton
1777-Jan 14, 1850
Age: 73 years.

Nancy E., daughter of
H. C. & M. A. Gault
Jun 10, 1847
Oct 19, 1848

Vault:(Name gone)
1787-Sep 2, 1845
Age: 61y, 5m, 24d.

John M., Son of John W. &
Marthy J. Glegg
Sep 1840

Here lies the body of
S. M. L. & Mary Coffe's Son
May 24, 1833

Glegg Vault
(inscription gone)

Sallie A., wife of
G. W. Newton
Jun 28, 1827
Jul 20, 1899

Dr. A. A. Tate
Apr 25, 1818
May 27, 1860
& wife
L. A. Tate
Jan 6, 1826
Sep 5, 1856

Lou Andrew, Son of
W. V. & R. K. Tate
Mar 19, 1870
Sep 25, 1872

James L. Tate
Sep 11, 1827
Dec 17, 1859
Age: 32y, 10m, 6d.

Turza Ann B. Jacobs
Jul 14, 1823
Jan 12, 1852
Age: 28y, 3m, 28d.

Samuel Tate
May 6, 1799
Oct 16, 1848
Age: 49y, 5m, 12d.

Mary J. Tate
Feb 21, 1802
Aug 26, 1866
Age: 63y, 6m, 3d.

Elizabeth Hamilton
Mar 6, 1807
Feb 8, 1863

Infant Son of
S. P. & S. J. Hamilton
(no dates)

Infant Daughter of
R. A. & M. J. Hamilton
Died Oct 2, 1865
(no age given)

W. B. Hamilton
Jun 1, 1833
Dec 5, 1862
Age: 29y, 6m, 5d.

BOONSHILL QUADRANGLE

Robert G. Hamilton
Jun 27, 1838
Oct 18, 1855
Age: 17y, 3m, 22d.

Peter G. McMullen
Sep 28, 1795
Mar 24, 1876
&
Sarah H. McMullen
Dec 25, 1793
Aug 28, 1864

Archibald McMullen
Died Mar 10, 1850
Age: 91 years

P. S. McMullen
May 16, 1831
Oct 12, 1838

J. W. McMullen
Sep 9, 1833
Sep 13, 1834

H. B. Taylor
Jan 3, 1838
Aug 26, 1859

Lucinda J. Taylor
Oct 6, 1868
Apr 17, 1881

Henry Taylor
Jan 14, 1768
Jul 27, 1848

Mary Taylor
Apr 2, 1768
Dec 26, 1862

Henry Taylor, Jr.
Jun 24, 1810
Sep 4, 1855

Amanda, mother of
Dr. F. H. Gault
Dec 5, 1841
Mar 25, 1893

James H. Kidd
Nov 7, 1818
Sep 2, 1898
& wife
Manica Kidd
Jul 4, 1826
Apr 12, 1869
Age: 42y, 9m, 8d.

Hiram Reese
Nov 8, 1806
Mar 29, 1873

James Davis Reese
Jun 27, 1861
May 13, 1874

Maj. John R. Toole
Mar 27, 1811
Sep 13, 1885
Age: 74y, 5m, 17d.

Matilda, wife of
Maj. J. R. Toole
Jun 9, 1813
May 18, 1902

Susan G. Toole
Died Jun 20, 1895
Age: about 52 years.

G. A. Reese
Mar 15, 1833
Apr 14, 1919
& wife
Sarah Reese
Feb 24, 1830
Oct 14, 1882
Age: 51y, 4m, 10d.
& Daughter
Idora J. J. Reese
May 22, 1859
Apr 11, 1884
Age: 24y, 11m, 11d.

Infant of
J. E. & D. W. Jobe
May 13, 1916

P. Y. Jobe
Feb 28, 1856
Jun 10, 1915

Sarah May, Daughter of
W. B. & S. T. English
Aug 11, 1884
Oct 10, 1884

Willie English
1874-1946

Robert H. Tate
Dec 1, 1847
Sep 9, 1905

Elgie Jobe
Mar 23, 1903
Jun 28, 1904

Isom G. Barnes
Feb 1, 1861
May 12, 1913

Isabella J. Barnes
Dec 10, 1849
Mar 4, 1915

George W. White
Mar 11, 1869
Oct 7, 1897
&
Alice E. White
Mar 8, 1871
Nov 18, 1903
&
Frank White
Nov 2, 1896
Sep 25, 1897

Hiram, Son of
P. S. & S. D. Gunter
Mar 30, 1889
Jun 3, 1890

Infant Son of
J. H. & M. A. Anderson
B&D Feb 23, 1896

William A., Son of
R. A. & S. E. Anderson
Sep 29, 1880
Jul 14, 1881

R. A. Anderson
Feb 3, 1843
Apr 2, 1922
&
Nancie T. Anderson
Mar 6, 1859
Sep 26, 1944

Sarah E., Daughter of
William Kidd & wife of
R. Anderson
Sep 29, 1846
Oct 27, 1881

George Kidd
May 18, 1809
Jan 6, 1883
Age: 73y, 7m, 18d.

Martha N., wife of
George Kidd
Jun 1809
Jun 26, 1889

M. Fannie, wife of
J. B. Kidd
Aug 26, 1855
Nov 27, 1876
Age: 21y, 2m, 21d.

H. C. Gault
Nov 20, 1820
Dec 12, 1901

Mary A. Gault
Nov 20, 1822
Sep --, 1879 (day gone)

Samuel Cleghorn
Nov 19, 1795
Dec 3, 1883
& wife
Mary Cleghorn
Mar 28, 1792
Sep 23, 1879
Age: 87y, 5m, 25d.

Mary E. C. Milliken
Feb 10, 1866
Feb 19, 1886

Margaret Milliken
Apr 9, 1860
Jun 11, 1880

Pinkney A. Milliken
Jun 7, 1861
May 3, 1875

John H. Milliken
Jun 7, 1832
May 28, 1872

Drucellar A. Anderson,
wife of J. H. Milliken
Dec 14, 1835
May 19, 1867

John Anderson
Aug 29, 1813
Jan 22, 1889

Margaret Anderson
Jun 15, 1804
Sep 4, 1877

Pinkney W. Anderson
Apr 11, 1840
Mar 8, 1862

Nancy F. Love, wife of
R. A. Anderson
Mar 24, 1854
Apr 21, 1872

John G. Anderson
Oct 19, 1840
Aug 2, 1867

J. A. Powell
1869-1944

Lizzie Dickey, wife of
J. A. Powell
Dec 12, 1870
Sep 1, 1915

John S. Dickey
Apr 25, 1825
Nov 8, 1877
&
Elizabeth B. Dickey
Apr 2, 1829
Feb 25, 1904

R. K. Dickey
Apr 13, 1867
Sep 18, 1904

John K. Dickey
Jun 24, 1883
Jan 2, 1885

Charlie B. Dickey
May 22, 1891
Jul 18, 1898

W. M. Kidd
1856-1933
&
Mary Dickey Kidd
1856-1935

BOONSHILL QUADRANGLE

A. L. Anderson
Jun 21, 1821
Feb 24, 1896

Elizabeth G. Fullerton,
wife of
A. L. Anderson
May 25, 1817
May 10, 1898

J. H. Anderson
Jun 1, 1842
Dec 8, 1861

M. D. Anderson
Oct 18, 1850
Dec 1, 1861

Mary A. Spence
Mar 2, 1816
Mar 1, 1851

Margaret J., Daughter of
J. L. & M. A. Spence
Aug 5, 1850
Dec 8, 1850

Archible Kidd
Mar 22, 1781
Dec 24, 1860
Age: 79y, 7m, 2d.

Elizabeth, wife of
Archible Kidd
1779-Jun 27, 1872
Age: about 93 years.

Sarah J., wife of
S. P. Hamilton
Aug 18, 1842
May 8, 1869

Martha L., wife of
S. P. Hamilton
Feb 13, 1851
Jul 16, 1871

J. P. Hamilton
Nov 19, 1844
Jun 29, 1920

Sarah D. Hamilton
Oct 25, 1847
Jan 25, 1898

P. L. Coleman
Mar 21, 1879
Mar 30, 1880

V. B. Coleman
Feb 18, 1881
Apr 27, 1883

Martha O.(Ora) Newton
1926-
&
Robert E. Newton
1925-1963

Infant Newton, Son
Feb 7, 1946

Infant Daughter of
J. H. & M. Kidd
Nov 20, 1864
Aged: 3 days

Mary, Daughter of
H. B. & E. J. McCown
Jan 24, 1865
Jul 22, 1865
Age: 5m, 28d.

Eliza J., wife of
H. B. McGown
Jun 3, 1838
Aug 7, 1868
Age: 30y, 1m, 7d.

R. H., Son of
R. A. & M. J. Hamilton
Oct 21, 1850
Jun 11, 1880

W. A. Hamilton
Mar 18, 1853
Mar 29, 1925

Robert A. Hamilton
Sep 26, 1814
Jun 2, 1887
Age: 72y, 8m, 6d.

Mary Jane, wife of
Robert A. Hamilton
Jan 16, 1825
Mar 8, 1874

Mary O., wife of
B. M. Hopper & Daughter of
R. A. & M. J. Hamilton
Nov 19, 1847
Jul 17, 1873

Lulah, Daughter of
B. M. & M. O. Hopper
Aug 7, 1872
May 3, 1873

William H. Coleman
Mar 17, 1851
Nov 4, 1937

Mary A. Doggs, wife of
W. H. Coleman
Mar 6, 1855
Nov 27, 1924

James Coleman
Died Apr 16, 1888
(no age given)

J. B. Coleman
Nov 1, 1886
Jan 30, 1887

S. A. Coleman
Jan 11, 1874
Mar 8, 1876

Infant Son of
A. F. & Iva B. Carter
Aug 22, 1901

William Kidd
Jan 4, 1814
Nov 5, 1876

Margaret Phagan, wife of
William Kidd
Apr 16, 1819
Jul 12, 1891

W. H. Kidd
Nov 2, 1851
Feb 25, 1890
Age: 38y, 3m, 23d.

Willie E. H., Son of
W. H. & Dollie Kidd
Oct 23, 1889
Dec 6, 1889

Lester E., Son of
J. W. & A. J. Wilson
Feb 11, 1855
Sep 22, 1885
Age: 28y, 7m, 11d.

Cavelean J., wife of
L. E. Wilson
Nov 11, 1855
Apr 7, 1881
Age: 25y, 4m, 26d.

J. T. Kidd
Aug 24, 1844
Nov 3, 1911

M. A. Galloway, wife of
J. T. Kidd
Nov 24, 1848
Feb 25, 1916

William H. McCown
Jan 6, 1839
Dec 26, 1865
Age: 25y, 11m, 20d.

Sarah A., Consort of
William H. McCown
Jan 20, 1842
Aug 27, 1862
Age: 20y, 7m, 7d.

Mary McCown
1874
Aged: 68 years.

Albert Lee Newton
Mar 2, 1896
Dec 23, 1941

George Newton
Sep 22, 1874
Jun 21, 1934

Lucy Newton
Dec 26, 1894
Jul 11, 1931

Ada, wife of
G. G. Newton
Died Nov 18, 1909
Age: 30 years.

Minnie Henley, wife of
H. T. Anderson
Jun 18, 1893
Sep 16, 1918

T. A. Wilson
Jul 12, 1845
Aug 9, 1922

Lucy, wife of
T. A. Wilson
May 16, 1844
Jan 19, 1902
&
Alice, Daughter of
T. A. & Lucy Wilson
May 3, 1869
Aug 6, 1901

Lucy Eva, wife of
P. G. Hamilton
Oct 3, 1864
Mar 11, 1899
Daughter of
E. S. & C. Bearden

Maggie E. Wright,
wife of
P. G. Hamilton
Dec 25, 1870
Apr 18, 1895

Minnie L. West, wife of
P. G. Hamilton
Jul 15, 1868
Jun 24, 1889

Infant Daughter of
Ellis & Ida Hamilton
May 29, 1902

Elise, Daughter of
Ellis & Ida Hamilton
Sep 14, 1899
Nov 2, 1901

Thomas H. Gault
Sep 9, 1884
Jan 3, 1952
&
Maggie L. Gault
Feb 19, 1880
Mar 20, 1926

Frank Gault
Died 1918 (no age given)
&
Mack Gault
Died Jan 1910 (no age)
&
Elizabeth Porter Gault
Died Oct 31, 1890
(no age given)
&
John W. Gault
Died 1922 (no age)

Samuel W. Gleghorn
Died Aug 5, 1908
Age: 76 years.

BOONSHILL QUADRANGLE

Mrs. Maggie,* wife of
James Sanders
Died Jul 20, 1907
Age: 62 years.

W. G. Newton *
Died Nov 27, 1903
Age: 66y, 8m, 9d.
married Eliza Coleman
in 1866

Mrs. Hannah,* Widow of
George Coleman
Died Aug 19, 1896
Age: 79 years.

W. F. Wakefield *
Died Apr 18, 1914
Age: 59 years.

Mrs. Lizzie,* wife of
John Gaunt
Died Oct 31, 1896
Age: (no age given)

J. A. Boggs *
Died Jul 1, 1901
Age: 78 years

Infant * of
Joe & Lizzie Rowell
Died Feb 5, 1906
(no age given)

Mrs. Polly Harwell *
Died May 26, 1895
Age: 80 years.

Mrs. Gleghorn,* wife of
Andrew C. Gleghorn
Died Oct 15, 1874
Age: 50 years.

Mrs. Sarah S.,* Widow of
Samuel W. Gleghorn
Died Jan 23, 1909
Age: 67 years. Left 3 Sons
and 2 Daughters.

Mrs. Nancy P.,* wife of
John H. Jobe
Died Dec 2, 1896
Age: (no age given)

Mrs. Lizzie Jackson,* wife
of B. L. Anderson
Died Dec 2, 1895
Age: 24 years.

Archie B. Webb *
Died Mar 29, 1905
Age: 54 years.

Clara,* wife of
Travis Newton
Died Feb 12, 1890
Age: 87 years.

Travis Newton *
Died Nov 24, 1890
Age: 80 years.

G. W. "Dock" Newton *
Died Mar 24, 1911
Age: 71 years. Left no
family.

Willie Alma,* Daughter of
Mr. & Mrs. G. C. Newton
Died Nov 4, 1916
Age: (no age given)

Mary C. Touchstone *
Died Nov 29, 1903
Age: 2y, 8m.

Many unmarked graves.

George Coleman *
Died Oct 21, 1891
Age: 75 years.

John Coleman *
Died Feb 24, 1893
Age: 70 years.

Mrs. Mary,* wife of
Samuel Gleghorn
Died Sep 22, 1879
Age: 87 years.

Sam Milliken *
Died Oct 24, 1900
Age: 33 years.

Mrs. William Perry *
Died Aug 14, 1912
Age: 54y, 7m.

Elizabeth Ann Newton *
Died Jan 6, 1901
Age: 61 years.

NOTE: Joseph Askins' Will
was made in 1872 and
proven in 1872.

* *

CARY CEMETERY

LOCATION: Three fourth mile SW of Egam on side of hill and south of Highway 64.

Margaret Cary
Feb 2, 1817
Aug 2, 1892

James H. Cary
Aug 15, 1824
Apr 12, 1901

John Cary
Sep 21, 1821
Mar 31, 1886

James J. Tate
Mar 25, 1820
Jan 21, 1892

Isabel Cary, wife of
J. J. Tate
May 9, 1819
Jul 8, 1888

Mrs. Fannie,* wife of
A. W. Cary
Died Apr 1, 1896
Age: 25y, 6m, 24d.

Robert Cary **
born in Ireland
in 1781
died 1869
& wife
Sarah Blair Cary **
(both are said to be
buried here.)

* *

CEMETERY

LOCATION: On bank of Union Camp Ground Branch, on north side of old road.

Two graves, no markers.

* *

HAMILTON CEMETERY

William G. Hamilton
May 24, 1807
Dec 23, 1853

C. T., wife of
William G. Hamilton
Aug 25, 1809
Sep 12, 1852

Charles B., Son of
William & Julia Timmons
Dec 1, 1843
Feb 8, 1863

NOTE: 2 unmarked graves of
Thomas H. McGaugh and wife
Catherine are said to be
buried here. This cemetery
is located on the old
Thomas McGaugh homeplace,
he located here in 1816.
He was son of William McGaugh,
a native of Ireland. ***

* *

BOONSHILL QUADRANGLE

DICKEY CEMETERY

LOCATION: Three fourth mile NE of Harms on north side of Harms-Fayetteville Road, near junction of Harms-Union Camp Ground roads.

Ephraim Dickey *** Died 1840 (A soldier of the Revolution)	Elizabeth,*** wife of Ephraim Dickey (no dates)	No markers in this cemetery.	Several unmarked graves.

* *

FULLERTON CEMETERY

LOCATION: Located near the mouth of Pitts Bend of Elk River, One and one-half miles ESE of Harms.

Robert Fullerton May 16, 1806 Dec 20, 1872	John Calhoun Died Oct 21, 1821 Age: 57y, 1d.	NOTE: There may have been other graves, but all signs are gone. Eds.

* *

LEBANON CHURCH CEMETERY

LOCATION: At Old Lebanon Church, north of Molina.

NOTE: Right Side of Drive.

Ovid L. Kidd 1880-1959 & Irene M. Kidd 1883-	Ina Louise Hamilton Aug 20, 1903 Mar 3, 1934	M. N. Caughran, wife of P. C. Askins Feb 21, 1856 Oct 25, 1897	B. W. Templeton, Sr. Nov 20, 1887 -------------- & Vallie Templeton
Elizabeth Marie Wiley Mar 2, 1919 Sep 25, 1960	J. Kenneth Hamilton Jan 23, 1881 Jan 9, 1905	Infant Daughter of W. H. & S. O. Caughran Dec 1, 1876 Dec 7, 1876	Sep 28, 1888 Mar 26, 1917 & Olevia Templeton
Edward D. Beddingfield 1888-1960 & Myrtle May Beddingfield 1890-1959	David B. Hamilton Feb 4, 1841 Jan 8, 1923 & Mary C. Hamilton Apr 1, 1842 Dec 10, 1889	Willie Davis, Son of W. H. & S. O. Caughran Sep 12, 1886 Dec 6, 1886	Jun 18, 1883 Sep 30, 1965 Martha A., Daughter of D. M. & E. J. Hamilton Jan 2, 1834 Jul 18, 1888
Judy Carol Sisk Jan 16, 1949 May 5, 1949	R. D. Williams Tennessee Sp 3 USNR WW II Aug 16, 1916 Mar 24, 1963	Florence, Daughter of W. H. & Tina Caughran Sep 13, 1893 Aug 17, 1894	Mollie Hamilton, Daughter of J. O. Montgomery Oct 5, 1861 Jun 24, 1894
Thomas Fletcher Newton Aug 23, 1875 Jun 23, 1948 & Amelia J. Ables Newton Mar 29, 1887 Jun 19, 1974	Robert D. Williams, Jr. Tennessee Cpl Co E 7 Mar 3 Mar Div Vietnam PH Mar 16, 1944 Feb 26, 1966	Sallie O., wife of W. H. Caughran Jun --, 1852 Sep 10, 1888 David L. Askins Mar 17, 1853 Aug 17, 1935	William Hamilton Apr 25, 1836 Jul 22, 1910 W. P. Gallaway Jan 29, 1851 Jan 2, 1918
John F. Hamilton Nov 6, 1866 Jan 12, 1909	Eva O., Daughter of P. C. & M. N. Askins Jun 19, 1873 Sep 21, 1895	& Elvira Askins Feb 23, 1859 Dec 10, 1906	& Martha J. Gallaway Dec 7, 1854 Jul 13, 1904
Roy D. Hamilton Jul 22, 1876 Jun 18, 1905 & Lilla M. Hamilton Jan 9, 1877 Nov 20, 1947	Minnie L., Daughter of P. C. & M. N. Askins Sep 5, 1883 Nov 2, 1893	& Daughter Delia S. Askins Apr 17, 1878 Sep 10, 1895	Charlie C., Son of W. P. & M. J. Gallaway Died Aug 29, 1910 Age: 18y, 9m.

BOONSHILL QUADRANGLE

Mrs. L. E. McCown
Apr 5, 1829
Jun 12, 1907

Robert McKinley Drennan
Oct 3, 1863
Mar 24, 1935

Iva H. Caughran, wife of
R. M. Drennan
Jul 11, 1860
Aug 8, 1902

Vallie Odell, Daughter of
R. M. & I. H. Drennan
Feb 3, 1890
Sep 20, 1892

Allie Pearl, Daughter of
R. M. & I. H. Drennan
Mar 21, 1888
Jun 24, 1889

William T. Drennan
1892-1946

Sallie Ann Wiley
Dec 1, 1823
Dec 10, 1906

Elizabeth J., Daughter of
George & M. N. Kidd
Dec 10, 1837
Dec 25, 1913

Olevia, Daughter of
J. L. & M. T. Caughran
Apr 10, 1861
Nov 12, 1882

J. L. Caughran
Nov 21, 1837
Oct 17, 1892

M. T. "Pollie" Wiley, wife
of J. L. Caughran
Died Feb 28, 1899
Age: 72y, 1m, 15d.

T. W. Caughran
Dec 16, 1853
Oct 19, 1894

Amanda J., wife of
T. W. Caughran
May 19, 1856
Jul 30, 1893

E. A. Caughran
Jun 6, 1874
Aug 13, 1895

C. W. Caughran
Oct 9, 1879
Oct 12, 1930
&
Lou Galloway Caughran
Jan 18, 1885

L. J. Wiley
Jan 16, 1833
Oct 31, 1887

M. J. Wiley
Mar 3, 1848
Apr 23, 1928

Kate E. Wiley
1881-1955

Alton C. Wiley
1904-1938

John H. Wiley
1876-1949
&
Addie E. Wiley
1881-1945

Dwight A. Wiley
Jan 14, 1885
Mar 22, 1949

Edith R. Wiley
Jun 26, 1886
Mar 12, 1967

John T. Phagan
1856-1895
&
Mary Phagan Dickey
1862-1950

Wyndol Smith Phagan
Infant of W. O. &
Burnice Phagan
May 6, 1913
Sep 1, 1913

Delia P., Daughter of
J. T. & M. E. Phagan
Jun 18, 1888
Jul 7, 1888

James P. Phagan
Jan 3, 1865
Mar 9, 1887

Mary J., wife of
G. E. York
Jan 7, 1831
Sep 1, 1887

Knox T. McCown
1881-1950
&
Mary Lowe McCown
1888-1962

H. B. McCown
Jan 18, 1834
Dec 18, 1897
&
Finecia J. McCown
Aug 23, 1840
Nov 14, 1899

Joseph I. McCown
Sep 13, 1810
Jan 17, 1896

Laura Ida, wife of
John R. Storment
Feb 6, 1853
May 2, 1880

Martha Neila, Daughter of
J. R. & L. I. Storment
Nov 15, 1878
Jul 6, 1879

James Walter, Son of
J. & S. F. Damron
Jul 3, 1889
Sep 8, 1889

Lee Stewart
1867-1938

W. Ebb Stewart
1862-1930
&
Maggie McAdams Stewart
1864-1948

Arthur Carroll West
Died May 14, 1970
Age: 78y, 15d.
(Higgins FH)

Ben F. Myers
1876-1958

Clarence M. Lewter
Jun 26, 1906

&
Aileene P. Lewter
Jul 19, 1909

Hugh Caughran
Jun 30, 1871
Dec 30, 1922

Robert Drennon
1799-1883
& wife
Martha Wiley Drennon
1800-1878
&
James J. C. Drennon
1842-1880
& wife
France Dale Drennon
1849-1950

Mrs. H. B., wife of
Rev. A. B. Coleman
Jan 5, 1840
Dec 10, 1883

Samuel Cramsie
Aug 1, 1846
Nov 3, 1904

Mamie Griffis Wilbanks
1882-1926

Alice, Daughter of
A. J. & M. A. Griffis
Apr 4, 1877
Jun 4, 1890

A. J. Griffis
Dec 9, 1847
Aug 27, 1927
&
M. A. Griffis
Feb 18, 1860
Apr 24, 1935

Martha Griffis
1859-1935

Rebecca Evans
Jul 11, 1822
Nov 29, 1902

Oscar S. Taylor
Dec 3, 1869
Sep 6, 1900

Tom L. Abbott
1886-1924
&
Beulah M. Abbott
1893-19

Clayton Abbott
1912-1933

Wilfred Jackson Lewter
B&D Mar 16, 1912

J. O. Lewter
Died Jan 3, 1910
(no age given)
& wife
Hattie L. Drennan Lewter
Feb 7, 1869
Dec 12, 1912

M. L., Daughter of
J. O. & H. L. Lewter
Mar 21, 1890
Jul 14, 1892

Orman B. Taylor
Apr 29, 1861
Sep 28, 1890

Fannie Elizabeth Taylor
Jan 16, 1863
Mar 28, 1947

Maggie A. Harris, wife of
A. P. Taylor
Oct 17, 1869
Feb 27, 1891

Catharine M., wife of
Henry Taylor
May 20, 1807
Jan 31, 1892

S. H. Taylor
Sep 21, 1829
Aug 30, 1885

Samuel H. Taylor
Apr 27, 1834
Nov 7, 1900

BOONSHILL QUADRANGLE

Archie C., Son of
S. H. & L. V. Taylor
Feb 10, 1873
Aug 26, 1887

Maria, wife of
Robert Brown
Nov 12, 1838
Apr 27, 1883

S. E. Parker
1881-1932
&
Epsey Parker
1881-19

Robert H. Askins
Feb 8, 1837
Nov 2, 1894
&
Nannie D. Askins
Oct 9, 1845
Jun 15, 1918

Albert M. Askins
Oct 13, 1865
Sep 5, 1940
&
Olevia E. Askins
Aug 28, 1876

Mabel Askins Rawls
1901-1925
&
Infant Son
1925

Karah Askins
Daughter of
A. M. & L. Askins
B&D Jun 9, 1900

R. Worth, Son of
J. F. & S. H. Montgomery
May 18, 1875
Aug 30, 1896

Janie, Daughter of
Joseph & Susan Montgomery
Aug 22, 1880
May 28, 1909

Thomas J., Son of
Joseph & Susan Montgomery
Dec 7, 1868
Sep 5, 1890

Joseph F. Montgomery
Jan 6, 1838
Apr 10, 1913

Susan H., wife of
J. F. Montgomery
Apr 6, 1845
May 8, 1887

Johnny, Son of
William & Sallie Ables
Dec 29, 1888
Sep 13, 1891

William Ables
Nov 5, 1864
Oct 18, 1921

Sallie Sisk, wife of
William Ables
Feb 2, 1869
Mar 23, 1923

Robert Lee Ables
Jan 22, 1909
Oct 19, 1937

John H. Harms, Sr.
born in Leer, Germany
Mar 8, 1823
Dec 6, 1886

Teda G., wife of
John H. Harms, Sr.
born in Dornum, Germany
Sep 11, 1822
Jul 21, 1892

Infant Son of
Henry & Eva Harms
Apr 17, 1888
Jun 15, 1888

Infant Daughter of
Henry & Eva Harms
B&D Jul 24, 1886

John Henry Harms
Jul 1856
Dec 1912

W. R. Wyatt
May 2, 1844
Jan 28, 1931
& wife
Sallie L. Wyatt
Jan 23, 1845
Jul 14, 1886
&
Sarah Adelia Wyatt
Nov 25, 1866
Dec 18, 1924
&
Mary Elizabeth Wyatt
Apr 8, 1869
May 8, 1956

Silas Dean Judia
May 1, 1873
Aug 7, 1953
&
Allie Farrar Judia
Jan 8, 1880
Sep 3, 1956

W. P. Lindsay
Oct 9, 1825
Oct 19, 1901

Sarah A., wife of
W. P. Lindsay
Dec 18, 1841
Mar 8, 1886

Josie Sheffield, wife of
W. P. Lindsay
Sep 16, 1848
Jun 12, 1929

T. Clark, Son of
W. P. & Josie Lindsay
Nov 28, 1892
Oct 5, 1895

Mary Lynn, Daughter of
H. H. & Sarah Hamilton
Feb 13, 1936
Feb 15, 1936

John L. Henderson
1869-1957
&
Lula P. Henderson
1877-1962

J. A. Hathcock
Mar 29, 1853
Sep 8, 1898

Susan D., wife of
J. A. Hathcock
May 22, 1855
Mar 21, 1893

W. J. Galloway
Nov 13, 1818
Dec 24, 1892

Mrs. M. A., wife of
W. J. Galloway
Sep 14, 1828
Jul 13, 1899

S. E. Galloway
Oct 22, 1858
Jul 11, 1931

Lora T. Galloway Good, wife
of S. E. Galloway
Oct 7, 1883
Apr 1, 1957

John W. Lindsay
Jun 7, 1861
Sep 19, 1947
&
Louanna Kidd Lindsay
Jul 13, 1870
Aug 3, 1942

Robert W. McCown
1872-1949
&
Mattie T. McCown
1876-1946

Jane McCormick, wife of
James Wiley
born in Abbeville Co., S.C.
Oct 15, 1809
Dec 7, 1887

Thomas K., Son of
J. H. & E. C. Thompson
Feb 3, 1869
drowned in Elk River
Jul 12, 1886

Jacob H. Thompson
born in Newberry Co., S.C.
Aug 14, 1844
Oct 20, 1887

Elvira Catharine Thompson
Apr 8, 1843
Sep 3, 1909

William Lewis Fife
1854-1898
&
Lula Clark Fife
1868-1895

Clark, Son of
W. L. & L. B. Fife
Jun 28, 1893
Jun 26, 1895

James Knox, Son of
W. L. & L. B. Fife
Aug 5, 1889
Mar 7, 1898

J. Rhea Thompson
1905-1954
&
J. Henry Thompson
1877-1937
&
Ermie F. Thompson
1878-1955
&
Joe Farrar Thompson
1909-1936
&
Russell F. Thompson
1902-1904

Henry Owen Thompson
Tennessee
Com U S Navy WW II
Oct 23, 1921
Apr 6, 1945

Lucile Caughran
Aug 13, 1914
Nov 16, 1914

Mildred Ophelia Farrar
Nov 14, 1889
Apr 10, 1906
&
Emma Lucy Farrar
Oct 13, 1887
Apr 14, 1906

Dr. J. P. Farrar
Sep 5, 1858
Jun 13, 1930
&
Zayda S. Farrar
Oct 7, 1855
Sep 20, 1936

BOONSHILL QUADRANGLE

John Young Toon
1887-1942
&
Icie Nora Toon
1887-1968

J. A. Isom
Jan 20, 1846
Oct 8, 1916

Robert Taylor, Son of
J. A. & D. A. Isom
Died Nov 2, 1910
Age: 4y, 2m.

Infant Sons of
C. W. & R. L. Caughran
B&D Aug 5, 1908

Infant Son of
E. J. & Christine Davis
1942

William B. Gentry
Died Apr 22, 1970
Age: 45y, 10m, 22d.

Infant Son of
C. H. & L. M. Sheffield
1916

William A. Sheffield
1852-1944
&
Ella L. Sheffield
1859-1942

John W. Neece
Sep 24, 1866
Feb 27, 1912
&
Laura V. Neece
May 18, 1874
Apr 11, 1943

J. R. Thompson
Sep 12, 1870
Mar 13, 1919
&
Emma Abbott Thompson
Oct 3, 1876
Feb 27, 1920

Lorna L. Thompson
1896-1920

Willis Forbes Thompson
Mar 30, 1909
Apr 22, 1911

William Thomas McDaniel
Jan 18, 1845
Feb 27, 1923
&
France Lauderdale McDaniel
Dec 5, 1843
Apr 19, 1923

Alva Hugh Eddins
Dec 18, 1867
Aug 19, 1912

Fannie Lucile Eddins
Jan 24, 1894
Mar 12, 1898

Children of
B. B. & Maggie L. Wyatt
Robert Orr Wyatt
Died Dec 19, 1896
Age: 6m, 16d.
&
Maggie Lou Wyatt
Died Aug 20, 1897
Age: 3y, 8m, 20d.

B. B. Wyatt
Jul 4, 1852
(no here)
&
Maggie L. Wyatt
Apr 9, 1858
Jun 19, 1901

Charles Thomas Reese
1899-1960

Lorena Reece
Jun 11, 1903
Jan --, 1911

Mance Reece
Mar 5, 1865
Sep 27, 1916

Fannie Thompson, wife of
Mance Reece
Jul 22, 1876
Aug 27, 1916

Emett R. Mathis
1889-1945
&
Martha Pearl Abbott Mathis
1891-

Cleadous Marvin Mathis
Sep 14, 1913
Dec 9, 1963

B. T. Thompson
Aug 18, 1886
Dec 29, 1944
&
Anna Thompson
Nov 4, 1887
Nov 4, 1947

Carlton S. Thompson
1916

Bob Abbott
Feb 18, 1866
Aug 3, 1920

Annie Thompson Abbott
Jan 5, 1876
Aug 18, 1963

Furnie Abbott
May 19, 1904
Dec 5, 1969

Flora Abbott, wife of
Leander Rogers
Jan 9, 1901
Jul 14, 1926

Girtie, Daughter of
A. J. & Susie Harwell
Aug 13, 1896
Apr 10, 1917

Margarett Abbott
1916-1917

Laura Reese Abbott
1888-1922

Piccola Abbott
1911-1929

James C. Abbott
1885-1947

Carl T. Phagan
1883-1959
&
Annie Lou Phagan
1886-1962

Charles Thomas, Son of
C. T. & A. L. Phagan
Jul 28, 1911
Aug 6, 1915

Alene, Daughter of
C. T. & Ada Phagan
Oct 13, 1906
Dec 5, 1921

John L. Hill
Aug 27, 1870
Aug 19, 1941

Beulah Ables Epps
Feb 15, 1896
May 30, 1955

J. Tom Winsett
1870-1938
&
Connie Winsett
1870-19

W. E. Winsett
1895-1968
&
Allie B. Winsett
1903-

James C. Vaughn
1873-1968
(Brown FH)

Susie Mary Jane Vaughn
Jul 22, 1877
Apr 19, 1936

Margarett Vaughn
Sep 13, 1895
Mar 20, 1917

Mary Elizabeth Lewter
Nov 13, 1927
Jun 15, 1930

James Alton Jacobs
Jun 25, 1919
Dec 10, 1919

Grady S. Jacobs
(no dates)

Frank E. Jacobs
(no dates)

Emma B. West
(no dates)

R. H. West
1867-1944

Walter Mills
1850-1935

Susie Mills
Died 1932
(no age given)

L. C. Vaughn
Mar 3, 1939
Sep 10, 1939

Robert Lee Brown
Jan 3, 1910
Oct 4, 1958

Sisters
Emma Clark
Jul 6, 1874

&
Sallie Maddox
Jan 10, 1872
Jul 14, 1955

Billy T. Coleman
1916-1958
(Gallant FH)

B. L. Beech
1877-1949
(Raby FH)

Kenneth Mitchell
Jun 12, 1904
(no date)
&
Mary H. Mitchell
Aug 28, 1912

Mary Alice Mitchell
1940

Fred L. Thompson
Feb 16, 1907
Jul 4, 1943

Baby Ben Stanley Brewer
1955

BOONSHILL QUADRANGLE

L. F. Webb
1902-1938

Maggie Lou Webb
1872-1959

Thurman Bradford
1929-1931

Selma Winsett
Feb 25, 1911
Jan 11, 1921

H. L. Webb
1860-1943

NOTE: Left Side of Drive.

Joe Ables
Feb 1, 1888
Nov 9, 1951
&
Pearl Ables
Sep 17, 1886
Oct 31, 1962

Thomas McDill
Sep 4, 1811
Jun 19, 1877

Rebecca J., wife of
J. L. Wilson
Oct 12, 1854
Dec 7, 1893

J. C. West
Jun 4, 1832
Dec 28, 1897

Elizabeth Hill, wife of
Thomas McDill
Feb 2, 1821
Jan 30, 1911

J. P. Stewart
Aug 4, 1832
Jan 23, 1911
&
Elizabeth Marsh Stewart
Sep 3, 1869
Jan 9, 1935

Elizabeth J., wife of
J. C. West
Aug 23, 1839
Feb 15, 1916

Olas N. Abbott
Died Dec 14, 1970
(no age given)
&
Mrs. Gladys Abbott
Died Jun 3, 1974
Age: 62 years.

Thomas W. McCown
Jun 22, 1847
Feb 17, 1925
&
Margaret L. McCown
Nov 2, 1848
Jan 24, 1918

Al. R. West
1873-1900
&
Alice R. West
1875-1949

Ronald L. Mitchell
Aug 7, 1945
Dec 24, 1952

Archie I. J., Daughter of
J. P. & N. E. Stewart
Nov 7, 1907
Jul 1, 1908

John C. West
May 5, 1871
May 12, 1930
&
Nancy Etta West
Jan 31, 1879
Jun 10, 1948

Maggie J., Daughter of
T. W. & L. E. McCown
Apr 22, 1876
Mar 1, 1899

Karl Ralph, Son of
J. P. & H. E. Stewart
Jul 14, 1897
Nov 5, 1897

Willie W. Webb
1897-1966
&
Willie Gertrude Webb
1887-1963

Clarence G. McCown
1889-1942

H. Pearson
Jun 15, 1877
(no date)

R. T., Son of
J. C. & N. E. West
Apr 24, 1895
Died at Camp Sevier
Feb 13, 1918

Lofton P. Gault
May 27, 1912
Jul 28, 1965
&
Ruth T. Gault
Jul 30, 1921

J. H. Kennedy
Nov 8, 1847
Apr 23, 1923
&
Savannah C. Kennedy
Dec 14, 1851
Aug 8, 1918

R. C. Pearson
1846-1925

Ruby J. Hall
Apr 28, 1860
Dec 30, 1905

Beulah C., Daughter of
John & Etta West
Sep 22, 1909
Apr 18, 1912

Roy L. Shelton
May 5, 1916

&
E. Irene Shelton
Apr 7, 1920

John H., Son of
J. H. & S. C. Kennedy
Mar 14, 1878
Sep 15, 1879

Ida Belle West
Sep 7, 1913
Apr 18, 1940

Martha Knox
1835-1895

W. H. Kennedy
May 29, 1874
May 28, 1916

Lillie Ann Myers
Oct 16, 1907
Oct 15, 1918

James D. Hays
Aug 13, 1815
Jun 3, 1895
&
Rebecca Hays
Oct 15, 1821
Mar 4, 1894

Elvire Wright, Jr.
1963-1963
(Gallant FH)

Joe M. Kennedy
1894-1924

Elcie, Son of
B. D. & A. L. Bailey
Dec 18, 1896
Jan 12, 1897

Stoney Turman Henderson
May 17, 1944
Jun 19, 1969
&
Virgie Lee Henderson
Oct 20, 1948
(no date)

Lawrence B. Sandlin
Jan 12, 1895
Jan 29, 1967
&
Vallie W. Sandlin
Nov 1, 1896

Mrs. P. A. Boggs
Nov 12, 1847
Feb 14, 1915

Ranie, Son of
B. D. & A. L. Bailey
Feb 22, 1894
Jun 21, 1894

Sgt. Pleasant L. Boggs
Co G 4 Penn Inf C.S.A.
Oct 12, 1841
Jan 9, 1917

Billy Joe Henderson
Feb 13, 1935
Mar 20, 1955

W. D. Rawls
Aug 8, 1862
Aug 18, 1900

P. O. West
Aug 29, 1862
Oct 20, 1909

John L. Reese
1903-1968
&
Lillian Reese
1909-

G. C. Dunman
(no dates)

Moses E., Son of
J. L. & R. J. Wilson
Jan 18, 1882
Oct 16, 1893

I. J., Wife of
P. O. West
Aug 26, 1871
Feb 27, 1895

M. D. Abbott
&
O. L. Abbott (no dates)

BOONSHILL QUADRANGLE

Boyce E. Wilson
Mar 1, 1890
Oct 11, 1917
&
Mattie Wilson West
Jul 7, 1890
Apr 27, 1968

Mary A. Caughran
Died Jun 24, 1894
Age: 74 years

Albert Sisk
Aug 17, 1909

&
Josephine Abbott Sisk
Apr 1, 1917
Nov 17, 1968

Miss Mamie E. Dale
"Author of Willie Selvilles
Missions & other stories"
Daughter of
Rev. W. T. & Mrs. L. J.
Dale
Sep 21, 1878
Mar 17, 1901
&
Miss Pearl G., Daughter of
Rev. W. T. & Mrs. L. J.
Dale
Feb 26, 1886
Aug 10, 1903
&
Mrs. L. J., wife of
Rev. W. T. Dale, D.D.
Jun 25, 1848
Jun 6, 1895

John Cornelius Galloway
1877-1896
&
Daisy Mai Galloway
1880-1887

W. C. Galloway
1854-1890
&
Loucretia Ann Galloway
1850-1927

James H. Dale
1847-1921
&
Mary E. Dale
1853-1935

Rosalie Emma, Daughter of
James H. & Mary E. Dale
Feb 1, 1876
Mar 11, 1877

John Dale
Aug 30, 1808
Jun 13, 1885

Elizabeth A., wife of
John Dale
Feb 1, 1822
Jan 14, 1883

Calvin Dale
Jul 4, 1846
Apr 22, 1921

L. L., wife of
Calvin Dale
Jun 19, 1858
Sep 15, 1887

Elizabeth, wife of
Calvin Dale
Feb 8, 1866
Dec 8, 1943

Dale
(no other information)

Dale
(no other information)

Dale
(no other information)

Kathie Sue, Daughter of
Mr. & Mrs. O. M. Dale
1949

H. P. Caughran
Feb 26, 1849
May 22, 1914

Catharine C., wife of
H. P. Caughran
Feb 19, 1852
Dec 4, 1892

Mary S., Daughter of
H. P. & C. C. Caughran
Jul 16, 1877
Jun 19, 1911

Lula Bradford
1869-1931

W. H. Bradford
Aug 3, 1869
Apr 20, 1924

Mary Jane, wife of
W. H. Bradford
Jan 8, 1874
May 21, 1895

Eugene, Son of
W. H. & M. J. Bradford
Sep 4, 1891
Jun 20, 1895

Annie Abbott
1876-1963

E. R. Mathis
1889-1945

Thomas B. Abbott
Oct 11, 1840
Dec 30, 1920

Lousendia Bradford, wife of
T. B. Bradford
Oct 17, 1842
Oct 15, 1893

J. R. Bradford
Feb 28, 1832
Oct 26, 1895

Laura E. Dickey, wife of
J. R. Bradford
Died Jun 2, 1920
Age: 80 years.

Annetta Ruth Sanders
1903-1923

Elma May Sanders
Aug 27, 1888
Nov 9, 1912

W. C. Sanders
Jan 19, 1859
Jul 22, 1908

M. J., wife of
W. C. Sanders
Mar 2, 1866
May 29, 1893

Miney Y. Dickey, wife of
W. C. Sanders
Apr 1, 1874
Feb 20, 1903

J. Y., Son of
W. C. & M. J. Sanders
May 1, 1892
Jun 14, 1894

Newton J. Dickey
1858-1930

Emma E. Dickey
1871-1946

Russell A., Son of
N. J. & E. E. Dickey
Died Aug 25, 1910
Age: 4y, 8m, 2d.

Paul Williams, Son of
Newton J. & Emma E. Dickey
May 12, 1908
Aug 25, 1909

Martha J., wife of
W. F. Holland
1862-1894

Annie Dema Hill
Dec 26, 1875
Aug 26, 1957

J. B. Hill
Jun 9, 1873
Jan 16, 1930

Infant of
J. B. & A. D. Hill
Oct 18, 1906
Oct 21, 1906

Donnie White
B&D Jun 1, 1954

Infant of
W. F. & M. J. Holland
(no dates)

James Hill
Died Jan 17, 1889
Age: about 63 years.
& wife
Mary Hill
Aug 6, 1836
Oct 18, 1893

Aunt Jane
(no dates)

Florence Hill
1874-1938

James C. Eddings
Aug 1, 1887
Oct 8, 1962
&
Laura M. Eddings
Dec 20, 1889

Nancy J. Hill
Mar 16, 1883
Apr 17, 1913

Mary L., Daughter of
J. S. & F. J. Hill
Oct 12, 1868
Aug 30, 1881

Infant Daughter of
N. J. & E. E. Dickey
Feb 6, 1892
Feb 7, 1892

William Marvin, Son of
N. J. & E. E. Dickey
Oct 6, 1900
Feb 25, 1903

James S. Hill
Sep 4, 1847
Apr 1, 1915
&
Francis J. Hill
Jan 4, 1853
(no date)

Dothia Ford Dickey
1859-1886

J. N. Dickey
Jan 17, 1830
--- --, 1887(1897)
(broken)

Mary H., wife of
Jasper Dickey
Jan 27, 1840
Nov 2, 188-(broken off)

Pheby E., wife of
Jasper Dickey
Aug 25, 1834
Mar 23, 1879

BOONSHILL QUADRANGLE

John C. Lincoln
Jan 10, 1845
May 20, 1922

Ira H. Lincoln
1870-1946
&
Fannie Askins Lincoln
1869-1954

William O. Phagan
Sep 8, 1889
Mar 28, 1952
&
Bernice Smith Phagan
Oct 28, 1886

Helen Louise Phagan
Aug 13, 1914

Hugh T. Kennedy
Feb 28, 1824
Aug 16, 1894

Jane B. Kennedy
Feb 25, 1824
May 6, 1896

James P. Kennedy
Aug 28, 1851
Sep 20, 1895

Mary E. Kennedy
Aug 27, 1861
Sep 26, 1895

Margie Fay, Daughter of
H. F. & B. B. Kennedy
Apr 8, 1900
Oct 12, 1901

W. H. Taylor
Sep 5, 1829
Feb 26, 1913

Mary J., wife of
W. H. Taylor
Jul 9, 1826
May 24, 1887

R. C. Waite
Dec 27, 1865
Apr 29, 1909
&
Myrtle D. Waite
Sep 27, 1874
Aug 22, 1904

W. J. Abbott
1854-1928

Sarah Thomas, Daughter of
T. P. & Elnorah Thornton
Aug 20, 1897
Mar 24, 1904

Jennie Cad., Daughter of
T. J. & Elnorah Thornton
Nov 28, 1888
Jul 5, 1891

Elnorah Thornton
Nov 9, 1855
Dec 23, 1938

T. J. Thornton
Aug 26, 1857
Jan 21, 1899

A. M. English
Aug 18, 1813
Aug 13, 1901

Sarah, wife of
A. M. English
Aug 17, 1821
Jun 15, 1897

A. C. Beech
1892-1941

Herbert Clarence, Son of
T. F. & E. E. Beech
Sep 6, 1897
Jun 27, 1898

Earl Cameron, Son of
T. F. & E. E. Beech
Jun 19, 1894
May 12, 1896

Eliza E., wife of
Thomas Beech
1859-1936

E. L., Son of
L. M. & L. J. Smith
Jun 27, 1893
Sep 21, 1900

H. H. Beech
Dec 25, 1844
Mar 5, 1917

Livinia Jane, wife of
H. H. Beech
May 8, 1845
Mar 3, 1920

Willie N. Gautney
May 21, 1910

&
Elizabeth Frances Gautney
Oct 15, 1910
Jul 1, 1967

S. S. McCown
Feb 2, 1837
Jun 13, 1896
&
M. J. McCown
Sep 15, 1842
May 30, 1929

Wilson J., Son of
S. S. & M. J. McCown
Aug 31, 1882
Jan 4, 1885

Infant Daughter of
W. L. & M. H. Kilpatrick
B&D May 17, 1885

Mosby Fulton
1866-1940

Mary H. Fulton
1865-1940

Earl C. Workman
1883-1951
&
Frances C. Workman
1897-19(no date)

John C. McCown
Sep 18, 1856
Aug 14, 1940

Martha C., wife of
J. C. McCown
Apr 13, 1856
Aug 20, 1894
&
Joe, son of
J. C. & M. C. McCown
Jun 2, 1887
Feb 28, 1888

Lawrence McCown
Aug 17, 1902
Jul 4, 1920

Cora E. Welch, wife of
J. C. McCown
Aug 23, 1867
Aug 13, 1900

N. Waite
Sep 10, 1841
Jan 8, 1909

Melvina Jane Waite
Jun 15, 1841
Sep 21, 1936

Annie M. Waite
May 4, 1869
Nov 4, 1900

Elyda M. Waite
Jul 8, 1873
Apr 25, 1923

John F. Clark
Oct 28, 1846
Jul 3, 1911

Mary J. McFerrin, wife of
J. F. Clark
Sep 23, 1843
Dec 10, 1895

Louiza Jane Galloway,
wife of J. F. Clark
Oct 29, 1854
Jul 20, 1920

J. K. Clark
Oct 9, 1866
Apr 16, 1928
&
Mattie Clark
Jun 9, 1872

James W. Wilson
May 5, 1832
Sep 30, 1904
&
Agnes J. Wilson
Nov 12, 1834
Mar 3, 1905

William Vinton Wilson
Dec 1, 1903
Apr 1, 1966
&
Lila Massey Wilson
Dec 30, 1916
Jul 31, 1942

J. Robert Wilson
Sep 10, 1865
Sep 10, 1939
&
Boonie H.(Holland) Wilson
Jan 7, 1877
Nov 30, 1969

Ada M., wife of
L. Richardson
Jul 30, 1872
Jun 15, 1897

Infant Son of
S. H. & I. C. Galloway
Aug 12, 1895
Aug 19, 1895

Davis Lee Gault
May 2, 1863
Jun 10, 1937

Martha Stewart Gault
Dec 21, 1870
Oct 28, 1950

Cleveland S., wife of
R. H. Askins
Oct 8, 1884
Sep 22, 1913

Maloy D. Bradley
Jun 4, 1904
May 3, 1969
&
Lena Louise T. Bradley
Nov 12, 1904

John H. Bradford
1858-1920

BOONSHILL QUADRANGLE

Green F. Bradford
1873-1938
&
Clemon T. Bradford
1873-1962

A. Lonnie Bradley
Jul 20, 1868
Jun 20, 1909
&
Jennie Idella Bradley
Feb 24, 1876
Nov 28, 1963

C. H. Ford
Sep 16, 1902
May 27, 1914

Celia M. Ford
Oct 9, 1879
May 26, 1902

James C. Dunman
Oct 26, 1874
Dec 20, 1944
&
Icie B. Dunman
May 8, 1876

Sam McCool
Tennessee
W.A.G.R. Sup Co 117 Inf
WW I
Feb 6, 1893
Apr 28, 1969

Henry Rogers
Jun 7, 1858
Feb 24, 1939

Victoria Rogers
Mar 26, 1854
Aug 26, 1937

J. C. Rogers
May 8, 1894
Mar 7, 1911

Lavina McDaniel
Jun 18, 1819
Mar 19, 1908

J. B. Kidd
Aug 17, 1847
Feb 23, 1919
&
Joannah Kidd
Nov 26, 1860
Sep 20, 1926

W. Thomas Kidd
Sep 21, 1876
Aug 8, 1890
&
J. Lowery Kidd
May 23, 1888
Oct 26, 1910

John Albert Kidd
Apr 23, 1886
Apr 30, 1964
&
Mary Katharine Rhea Kidd
Aug 10, 1889
Jul 23, 1916
&
Tommie Alease Elmore
Nov 17, 1895
Oct 25, 1956

Joe Lowery Kidd
1925-1940

Jack Spray
Aug 25, 1870
Sep 10, 1942

Ida Rogers Spray
Oct 28, 1876
Feb 10, 1966

Johnnie Floy Bates
Jun 27, 1907
May 24, 1909

William Floyd Thompson
1910-1951

Robert Warren Thompson
Aug 3, 1914

&
Bobbie Evelyn Thompson
Nov 2, 1915
Sep 8, 1966

John Mills
May 13, 1835
Jun 27, 1903

Margret J. Mills
Died Mar 2, 1928
Age: 82 years.

Eli Dunman
(no dates)

Nancy C., wife of
Eli Dunman
Oct 13, 1852
Jul 9, 1918

Mattie Sue, Daughter of
Eli & N. C. Dunman
Died Sep 23, 1897
Age: 3y, 7m.

Malah Louise A., wife of
Lewis Askins
1912-1940

Rena Amanda, Daughter of
J. L. & E. A. Caughran
Nov 24, 1896
Jan 16, 1897

James Earl Askins
Aug 8, 1884
Oct 29, 1969
&
Bettie Pitts Askins
Feb 5, 1885
May 13, 1965

John L. Stewart
Jan 23, 1877
Dec 2, 1926

Cora Price, wife of
John L. Stewart
1887-1920

Son of
J. L. & E. C. Caughran
Oct 31, 1902
Dec 23, 1903

Mabel Clare Caughran
1898-1899

Infant Daughter of
J. L. & E. C. Caughran
Feb 7, 1901
Mar 27, 1901

W. S. Dickey
Aug 28, 1862
Feb 25, 1935

Mollie, wife of
W. S. Dickey
Dec 25, 1871
Dec 27, 1898

Jennie Bruce, wife of
W. S. Dickey
Apr 20, 1872
Jan 11, 1906
&
Infant of
W. S. & Jennie Dickey
(no dates)

Maggie Mai Smith
Dec 14, 1890
Mar 12, 1916

O. W. Smith
Mar 20, 1914
Mar 14, 1915

Neil, Son of
E. J. & L. O. Askins
Aug 8, 1907
Jan 26, 1908

R. A. Ables
May 17, 1862
Dec 11, 1912
&
Mary Ables
Feb 10, 1854
Apr 26, 1947

S. G. Ables
Sep 11, 1884
Feb 27, 1899

Evelyn Bledsoe, Daughter
of Roy & Gertrude Ables
B&D Dec 7, 1937

Mary E., Daughter of
W. T. & Jennie Ables
B&D Aug 28, 1909

William Thomas Ables
Oct 2, 1882
Apr 17, 1966
&
Lucy Fanning Ables
Nov 18, 1901
Jan 31, 1963

Jennie Ables
Feb 18, 1884
Dec 22, 1923

Elizabeth Webb, wife of
Daniel Sisk
Oct 25, 1839
Dec 28, 1921

Robert H. Edmison
Sep 11, 1874
Jun 11, 1930

Ella Collins, wife of
R. H. Edmison
Jul 13, 1871
Mar 22, 1919

F. E. Jacobs
Jan 26, 1871
Nov 18, 1951

Helen Fay Vaughn
Died Jan 25, 1843
(no age given)

Elmer Lee West
Apr 30, 1909
Mar 3, 1961

Katie Hazel West
Sep 25, 1909
Aug 27, 1959

Eugene W. Campbell
1902-19
&
Lula West Campbell
1905-1935

Charles Shelby Edmison
Sep 9, 1900
Feb 10, 1951

Maggie Luella Edmison
Jul 14, 1901
Jan 2, 1929

Mary Frances, Daughter of
C. S. & Maggie Edmison
B&D May 2, 1923

BOONSHILL QUADRANGLE

R. M. Campbell
Aug 6, 1870
Sep 24, 1918

Fannie Good, wife of
R. M. Campbell
Jan 10, 1879
Sep 23, 1923

Ernie D. West
Aug 3, 1909
Jul 6, 1961
&
Martha Varden West
Aug 30, 1909

J. M. West
May 26, 1875
Feb 28, 1965

Cordelia Bryan, wife of
J. M. West
Apr 10, 1876
Oct 27, 1921

Johnie B., Son of
J. M. & Delia West
Jan 10, 1917
Jan 19, 1917

Thomas Ogle
Feb 28, 1852
Dec 23, 1918
&
Caroline Ogle
Feb 5, 1870
Sep 19, 1935

Raleigh Lee West
Nov 3, 1877
Jul 15, 1922

Olevia J. West
Sep 7, 1883
Dec 5, 1953

Motha May, Daughter of
W. L. & Mattie Berryman
Aug 3, 1905
Oct 28, 1914

Anderson Berryman
Jun 13, 1844
Nov 7, 1924
&
Anliza Waldrep Berryman
May 5, 1845
Dec 13, 1924

Infant Daughter of
W. A. & Ethel Waldrep
B&D May 2, 1914

Alexander Waldrep
Aug 13, 1888
Aug 3, 1915

James Bradford
1917-1942

Robert A. Bradford
1895-1934

O. Wood
Feb 2, 1847
May 23, 1912
&
Eliza Reagin Wood
Nov 13, 1848
May 3, 1922

Jeneva Allene, Daughter of
D. L. & M. U. Askins
Oct 24, 1902
Sep 6, 1911

Infant Son of
D. L. & M. U. Askins
B&D May 23, 1900

Una, wife of
Dennie L. Askins
Feb 28, 1879
Jul 8, 1918

Lawrence, Son of
D. S. & N. E. Hamilton
May 6, 1898
Jun 16, 1900

Infant Daughter of
W. P. & W. T. Sumners
B&D Jul 11, 1911

W. J. Mathis
1880-1945

Emma Mathis
Apr 29, 1875
Jun 10, 1919

Willie Mathis
May 28, 1908
Oct 5, 1911

Mrs. W. J. Mathis
1887-1947

Clara B. Adles (Ables ?)
1896-1939

Jane Montgomery
Apr 16, 1834
Aug 12, 1919

Joe A. Montgomery
Apr 26, 1877
Feb 16, 1956

Ollie C. Fanning
Apr 14, 1898
Oct 16, 1945
&
Della Sue Fanning
Aug 24, 1900

Margaret Louanner Askins
May 16, 1923
Sep 13, 1926

Infant Son of
J. W. Manley & Mattie
Louella Askins
(no dates)

J. W. Manley Askins
Feb 27, 1900
Apr 4, 1965
&
Mattie Louella Askins
May 5, 1903
Apr 6, 1969

John W. "Gus" Gray
1912-1942
&
Sue McAlister Gray

Henry Clay, Son of
H. R. & M. F. McAlister
Apr 8, 1913
Jul 20, 1927

Audrey May McAlister
1897-1954

Henry Robert McAlister
Dec 20, 1874
Sep 30, 1942
&
Martha Askins McAlister
May 1, 1871
Feb 6, 1952

Joseph Elgie Askins
Mar 9, 1902
May 21, 1966
&
Tennie Sue Ables Askins
Dec 27, 1901
Oct 25, 1928

Della Adeline Ables
Mar 16, 1897

Dock G. Brazelton
Oct 2, 1891

&
Lena S. Brazelton
Nov 8, 1894
Jan 22, 1948

Infant Daughter of
Dock & Lena Brazelton
1927

Presley C. Harwell
1874-1952
&
Willie S. Harwell
1883-1958

Granny Lucy F. Boling
1870-1956

C. B. Waite
(no dates)

J. H. McBride
1880-1944
&
Emma McBride
1877-19(no date)

John P. Mathis
1880-1938
&
Janie B. Mathis
1883-1964

Columbus G. Abbott
1890-1954
&
Birdie M. Abbott
1890-1963

Infant Daughter of
Mr. & Mrs. C. G. Abbott
1936

David Jerome Abbott
Apr 19, 1963
Apr 20, 1963

John W. Dunman
1876-1961
&
Pearl Dunman
1880-1939

Roy R. Dunman
Aug 16, 1905
Apr 1, 1957

Robert L. Roland
Jun 5, 1898
Jan 19, 1966
&
Annie Ray Roland
May 8, 1905

Henry R. Sumners
Apr 20, 1884
Feb 5, 1952

Mattie R. Sumners
Jan 19, 1893
Sep 14, 1963

Lillie Lawson, wife of
H. R. Sumners
Apr 4, 1886
Feb 26, 1921

J. M. Sumners
1848-19(no date)
&
Louisa Sumners
1858-1935

Andrew L. Reese
Oct 21, 1906
May 28, 1969

BOONSHILL QUADRANGLE

Mrs. Willie Reese
1909-1930

W. H. Reese
Dec 25, 1929
Jun 14, 1930

Louise Sumners
1859-1935

Mrs. John Roland
1878-1933

Lawrence P. Roland
1898-1940

Vester, Son of
T. B. & L. M. Roland
Oct 18, 1905
Feb 6, 1920

Mrs. Mary,* wife of
William Lowe
Died Feb 1, 1892
Age: 21 years.

Infant * of
S. B. & Jennie Billions
Died Sep 6, 1908
Age: 5m.

Mary Edna R. Stone
Sep 15, 1910
(only date on stone)

John E. Roland
Jan 1, 1878
Jul 15, 1948
&
Mary Ann Roland
Aug 8, 1878
Mar 13, 1933
married 1897

Robert Roland
Nov 17, 1850
Jul 2, 1921
&
Lucy Nda Pendergraft Roland
Nov 17, 1853
(no date)

Peter A. Dale, Sr. *
Died Apr 17, 1894
Age: 84 years.
married Mary G. Phagan
about 1843, who survives.

Mrs. Janie,* wife of
Joe Wyatt & Daughter of
J. F. Montgomery
Died May 28, 1909
Age: 26 years.

Edward Lee McCool
Tennessee
Pfc Co E 119 Inf, WW I
Dec 5, 1890
Sep 9, 1968
&
Jennie Lee McCool
Mar 10, 1898

Thomas Roland
Sep 19, 1850
Aug 13, 1923
&
Mattie Roland
Aug 5, 1856
Dec 16, 1929

Mack Roland
Died Apr 1, 1931
Age: 54 years.

Miss Sallie Ann Wiley *
Died Dec 10, 1906
Age: 75 years.

Several unmarked graves.

Mrs. Ida Brazelton Shaw
Died Dec 8, 1968
Age: 81 years.
(Frost FH)

Brown Shaw
Died Feb 18, 1968
Age: 84 years.
(Ralston FH)

Ila Fanning Simms
(no dates)

B. M. Fanning
Feb 23, 1862
Feb 16, 1939
&
Mattie Fanning
May 4, 1861
Mar 12, 1936

Erskin,* Son of
I. W. & N. E. Perry
Died Nov 15, 1899
Age: 22y, 1m.

* *

McLEAN CEMETERY

LOCATION: One-half mile SE of Hughey on south side of Old Fayetteville Road.

About 25 graves with fieldstones, no inscriptions.

* *

RAMSEY CEMETERY

LOCATION: One mile SE of Hughey on south side of Old Fayetteville Road.

John Ramsey, his wife and other members of his family are said to be buried here.

NOTE: No signs of this cemetery remain. Eds.

* *

BOONEVILLE QUADRANGLE

REES CEMETERY

LOCATION: Two and one-half miles NW of Booneville, head of Polecat Hollow at the Moore County line.

John Rees
May 26, 1770
Mar 8, 1863

Nancy Rees
Feb 12, 1772
Aug 9, 1853

Jordan Rees
Jun 18, 1805
Nov 16, 1881

Martha, wife of
Jordan Rees
Nov 7, 1806
Oct 25, 1887

C. H. Rives
Oct 17, 1814
Jul 3, 1853

Charlotte, wife of
C. H. Rives
Feb 16, 1814
Dec 31, 1873

Permelia, wife of
J. T. Rives
Sep 5, 1850
Apr 30, 1884

Bettie, Daughter of
J. T. & P. T. Rives
May 9, 1874
Jul 13, 1876

B. H., Son of
J. T. & P. T. Rives
Nov 25, 1876
Jul 23, 1888

Many unmarked graves.

Nancy, Daughter of
C. H. & C. T. Rives
Jun 11, 1837
Jul 4, 1855

Hudson, Son of
John & Nancy Rees
Apr 18, 1811
Nov 19, 1828

W. H. Rees
Aug 22, 1816
May 12, 1875

Mary M., wife of
W. H. Rees
Apr 17, 1820
Jun 19, 1874

Nancy, Daughter of
W. H. & M. M. Rees
Sep 1, 1847
Oct 10, 1853

Isaac, Son of
W. H. & M. M. Rees
Jun 12, 1853
May 31, 1860

Infant of
J. T. & P. T. Rives
B&D Dec 17, 1881

Mattie, Daughter of
J. T. & P. T. Rives
Aug 22, 1872
Jul 15, 1888

Mrs. Fannie Lou Rives *
Died Dec 12, 1907
Age: 32 years.

Mary, Daughter of
W. H. & M. M. Rees
Mar 11, 1859
Jun 7, 1859

L. W. Davidson
Jul 8, 1837
Jun 25, 1892

Mary, wife of
C. W. Davidson
(could be L. W. Davidson)
Oct 7, 1854
Nov 6, 1877

Challie, Son of
L. W. & R. A. Davidson
Nov 25, 1868
Dec 16, 1868

Fannie B., wife of
H. H. Neece
Dec 2, 1838
Sep 29, 1879

Addie, Daughter of
H. H. & F. B. Neece
Jan 15, 1876
Aug 7, 1876

Nancy, Daughter of
J. T. & P. T. Rives
Jul 2, 1883
Jul 13, 1888

Permelia, Daughter of
J. T. & M. C. Rives
Feb 4, 1837
Jul 29, ----
(stone deep in ground)

J. J. Rives
Dec 1, 1847
Jun 14, 1901
& wife
Ruth P. Milstead Rives
May 11, 1848
Mar 11, 1926

Mary, Daughter of
J. J. & R. P. Rives
Oct 13, 1880
Jun 1, 1884

Agnes, Daughter of
J. J. & R. P. Rives
Oct 22, 1888
Oct 16, 1891

Josie, Daughter of
J. J. & R. P. Rives
Sep 1, 1875
Jan 16, 1891

Sarah Milstead, wife of
E. B. Raby
Died Oct 26, 1911
Age: 66 years.

Nancy A., Daughter of
Jno. & E. C. Steelman
Jun 20, 1882
(date on stone is deep
in ground)

Mrs. Adeline,* Widow of
Louis Davidson
Died Apr 10, 1917
Age: 76 years.

Willis May Davidson *
Died Jun 13, 1899
Age: 18 years.

* *

RUTLEDGE CEMETERY

LOCATION: Two miles WNW of Booneville on ridge west of head of Martin Hollow.

Rutledge, Creason and others are said to be buried here.

Several graves with no markers.

* *

WILES CEMETERY

LOCATION: One and three-fourth miles WNW of Booneville on ridge west of head of Martin Hollow.

Hannah Emma Wiles
1845-1925

2 graves with the above is
located within an iron fence.

Mrs. Sylvania,* wife of
Thomas Raby & Daughter of
Charles Wiles
Died Aug 10, 1890
Age: 41 years.

Charles Wiles *
Died Jul 1, 1890
Age: 74 years.

Sallie,* Daughter of
S. P. Wiles
Died Sep 2, 1898
Age: 14 years.

* *

BOONEVILLE QUADRANGLE

BOONEVILLE CEMETERY

LOCATION: At Booneville, Tennessee.

NOTE: Colored section across the fence from main cemetery.

Celia Bailey 1807-1897	Jake Reese 1849-1930 & Emily Reese 1851-1943	Arthur Reese 1894-1969 William Reese 1884-1960	Oscar H. McGee 1904-1969 M. L. McGee (no dates)
John B. Phelps Mar 10, 1924 Aug 24, 1930	Jimmie L. Reese 1888-1940	William Stone 1845-1931	& L. B. McGee (no dates)
Walton H. Phelps 1871-1946 & Annie Phelps 1878-	Hugh Reese, Sr. 1879-1958 Calvin Reece 1895-1914	Vivia Stone 1852-1932 John A., Son of Jake & Emily Reese Oct 26, 1900	& A. McGee (no dates) & M. McGee
Tom Phelps 1879-1928	Henderson Reese 1880-1929	Oct 15, 1920 Jasp. D., Son of	(no dates) A. G.
	Mary Reese 1882-1926	Jake & Emily Reese Mar 15, 1893 Aug 24, 1925	(no dates)
Several unmarked graves.			

NOTE: Main Section of Booneville Cemetery

Fred J. Goosby Jun 14, 1890 Mar 29, 1968 & Rena Goosby Aug 4, 1894 ------------	Elvy Mae Adams Feb 19, 1922 Oct 9, 1964 Robert Lee Shields 1891-1966 & Aileene Collier Shields 1910-	Mary Louise, Daughter of N. F. & Laura B. Boone Oct 4, 1911 Jun 10, 1913 W. H. Steelman Sep 23, 1893 Jan 3, 1955 &	Nathan Boone Apr 24, 1830 Nov 21, 1898 Orpha J. Boone Nov 19, 1834 May 17, 1922 Military Marker
Willie Boon McAfee Apr 15, 1904 Jan 15, 1965 & Elsie Moore McAfee Aug 6, 1907 ------------	Jesse A. Shields Mar 5, 1895 Aug 14, 1963 & Annie E. Shields Nov 3, 1896 ------------	Isabell S. Steelman Apr 3, 1894 ------------ Albert C. Boone Aug 27, 1905 Jan 8, 1933	Sterling Samuel Boone May 16, 1925 Sep 23, 1944 "An American loyal to his Country, even unto death."
Frank F. Corder Mar 1, 1891 Jan 1, 1965 & Etta Prince Corder Jun 4, 1886 ------------	Lonnie B. Thomas Dec 1, 1910 ------------ & May King Thomas May 8, 1906 ------------	David Wilson Boone Aug 21, 1918 Sep 7, 1937 Frances Boone Jan 8, 1914 Mar 20, 1943	Clara Mai B. Edwards Sep 16, 1909 Jan 14, 1950 George David Mathis Feb 24, 1908 Sep 24, 1952 &
Clyde Lee Pitts Died Jan 25, 1969 Age: 56 years (TM) Mrs. Varie Pitts 1888-1940	Mattie Raby Apr 27, 1884 Dec 18, 1967 Estill Woodard Jan 6, 1903	Helen June Faulkner 1935-1937 Dr. W. G. Commons Oct 15, 1823 Jan 19, 1891 & wife	Lena Faulkner Mathis Feb 17, 1906 Feb 17, 1951 Raby Steelman Dec 29, 1906 ------------
Velma Cox Died Sep 2, 1964 (no age given) William Ray Burns Jul 21, 1928 Apr 24, 1955	Jun 6, 1964 Nathan Forrest Boone Feb 4, 1870 Dec 13, 1926	Mary M. Boone Commons Jul 31, 1824 married Nov 5, 1845 died Mar 8, 1892 Infant Son of Nathan & Laura Boone	& Nannie Woodard Steelman Jun 30, 1907 May 18, 1953 Anna Thomas Gatlin Sep 7, 1938
Richard Glen Burns Aug 5, 1966 Aug 6, 1966		1904	Sep 25, 1959

BOONEVILLE QUADRANGLE

Clarence Pitts Ashby
Jul 5, 1887
Feb 14, 1959
&
Elma Hart Ashby
Dec 13, 1887
Oct 6, 1960

Ella Ashby Helms
Jan 24, 1870
Feb 4, 1962

Randy Neil Ward
Tennessee
Sp 4 Co C, 35 Inf, 4th
Inf Div., Vietnam PH
May 9, 1947
Jan 27, 1968

William Dickson Faulkner
Mar 25, 1890
Mar 15, 1966
&
Vivian Solomon Faulkner
Feb 23, 1901

W. C. Faulkner
Mar 24, 1852
Apr 10, 1935
&
Annie M. Faulkner
Feb 5, 1856
Jan 26, 1950

T. V. Faulkner
Feb 26, 1895

Eva Lena Collins
Dec 11, 1899
Jun 21, 1935

Samuel Boone
Oct 6, 1801
Mar 23, 1860
&
Cynthia Boone
Apr 20, 1802
Jul 8, 1891

Maude Boone
Jan 14, 1859
May 10, 1862

Albert Henderson Boone
Jun 26, 1866
Oct 2, 1879

Sterling Samuel Boone
Jan 9, 1862
Feb 17, 1882

Dr. D. J. Noblitt
Apr 16, 1838(6)
Jan 25, 1899
&
Kate Noblitt
Aug 5, 1832
Feb 18, 1905

S. A., wife of
A. Noblitt
Jul 5, 1814
Nov 24, 1892

William Collins, Son of
T. V. & Eva Lena Faulkner
Jun 3, 1924
Aug 15, 1924

Lucy A. Dunn, wife of
Clarence Partain
Aug 29, 1887
Feb 20, 1912

B. M. Dunn
Jan 19, 1862
(no date)
& wife
Mary L. Milstead Dunn
Apr 25, 1857
Jan 2, 1928

W. G. Forrester
Feb 26, 1867
Oct 16, 1888

Dr. J. T. Graham
1854-1936
&
Leona Noblitt Graham
1861-1938

Annie Boone Graham
Oct 11, 1893
Apr 10, 1921

Inez Graham
May 24, 1895
Aug 19, 1919

David W., Son of
J. T. & Leona Graham
Jul 14, 1888
Feb 1, 1891

Felix W., Son of
D. B. & M. S. Waggoner
Oct 8, 1904
Sep 27, 1911

Nora M., Daughter of
M. A. & G. S. Conwell
Jun 10, 1881
Aug 1, 1895

Fannie Mae Raby
Oct 13, 1904
Jul 2, 1925

Charles W. Raby
1877-1951
&
Pearl R. Raby
1883-1967

Thomas S. Raby
1852-1927
&
Margaret M. Raby
1860-1925

Helen Ruth Raby
Nov 12, 1939
Jun 8, 1949

Infant Son of
Bobby & Marilyn Faulkner
1954

C. A. "Alex" Ashby
Jun 20, 1874
Jul 2, 1957
&
May Faulkner Ashby
Aug 30, 1884

L. Raby McNatt
Died Jan 6, 1968
Age: 79 years
(1889-1968 on TM)
&
Matalou McNatt
1894-

Donna Rae Faulkner
Nov 28, 1949
Jul 17, 1950

Jim Creson
Apr 1, 1879
May 4, 1947
&
Pearl Wagster Creson
Nov 8, 1886
Jun 27, 1962

Walter Brad Cates
Sep 19, 1894
Nov 8, 1961
&
Ozelle B. Cates
Jun 1, 1899

James E. Bartlett
1870-1953
&
Etta Mae Bartlett
1872-1952

James W. Moore
Aug 22, 1909
Aug 30, 1963
&
Lena V. Moore
May 10, 1909

James W. Campbell
1908-1945
&
Evelyn P. Campbell
1908-

Clarence D. Partain
1885-1964
&
Corrie F. Partain
1892-

Trall Terrell McCurdy
Jan 6, 1886
Jul 18, 1925
&
Ezella Rives McCurdy
Aug 25, 1889

Joel R. Martin
Feb 7, 1925
Jun 20, 1925

Ben Berry Waggoner
Jul 3, 1874
Oct 19, 1959
&
Susie Ashby Waggoner
Sep 5, 1881
Jan 26, 1963

Homer Cowden Norman
Jul 8, 1917
Apr 17, 1925
&
Homer Lawson Norman
Jun 22, 1889

Clara Boone Cates
Oct 8, 1891

John T. Faulkner
Feb 13, 1878
Aug 8, 1938
&
E. Beulah Faulkner
Jan 1, 1878
Apr 23, 1939

J. T., Son of
J. T. & E. B. Faulkner
Nov 27, 1910
Apr 29, 1923

Judith, Daughter of
J. T. & E. B. Faulkner
Jan 18, 1918
Nov 15, 1919

Annie B., Daughter of
J. T. & E. B. Faulkner
Aug 22, 1913
Jan 2, 1915

Francis O., Son of
J. T. & E. B. Faulkner
Dec 14, 1916
Apr 2, 1918

Felix Waggoner
Oct 8, 1872
May 27, 1902

J. J. Waggoner
Jan 6, 1850
Oct 20, 1901
&
Lou V. Waggoner
Mar 1, 1850
(no date)

BOONEVILLE QUADRANGLE

Robert Lee Ingle
Jun 30, 1865
Oct 25, 1882

Emma Susan Ingle
Oct 9, 1857
Sep 1, 1878

Benjamin B. Ingle
C.S.A.
Sgt Tenn Cav.
Jan 2, 1830
Jan 13, 1900

Martha Ann Ingle
Nov 24, 1833
Feb 10, 1908

J. W. Ingle
Jun 16, 1856
Jun 10, 1897

Ellis C. Woosley
Jan 4, 1878
Sep 8, 1951
&
Mollie C. Woosley
May 26, 1872
Feb 26, 1948

Mertie, Daughter of
J. P. & M. E. Woosley
Died Sep 13, 1894
Age: 12 years.

Clara Lee Ingle
Oct 14, 1862
Sep 17, 1912

Bernice Allen, wife of
Christopher C. Ingle
Jul 15, 1874
Nov 28, 1958

Christopher C. Ingle
Jan 20, 1862
Feb 3, 1924

Mary Bell Woosley, wife of
Christopher C. Ingle
Feb 15, 1866
Dec 2, 1899

Harry Miller
1883-1944
&
Kate Miller
1892-1966

Thomas A. Corder
1861-1936
&
Mattie Hasty Corder
1871-1896

W. E. Woosley
Dec 16, 1860
Nov 9, 1893

James T. Pylant, D.V.M.
Apr 28, 1853
Nov 18, 1935
&
Maggie W. Pylant
Sep 30, 1860
May 10, 1933

Ella Elizabeth Martin
B&D Mar 17, 1900

Jimmie Wilson, Son of
G. C. & J. E. Martin
Dec 24, 1878
Jul 30, 1888

James P. Woosley
Dec 16, 1837
Jun 30, 1887
&
Mary E. Woosley
Nov 20, 1840
Feb 9, 1921

Thomas J. Carriger
Nov 5, 1812
Jul 28, 1855
&
Susan Carriger
May 10, 1814
Mar 13, 1879

Infant Son of
James M. Brown
1857

James M. Brown
Mar 5, 1833
Jun 22, 1857

Britian Felps
1770-Jul 16, 1847
&
Susan Ann Felps
1781-Oct 9, 1859

Christiana Elizabeth
Carriger
Dec 17, 1840
Sep 3, 1849

Polly Ann Carriger
Dec 7, 1839
Sep 14, 1849

Finetta Carriger
Oct 13, 1832
Sep 18, 1849

Margarett Carriger
Mar 7, 1834
Sep 21, 1849

Sarah Carriger
Jul 5, 1847
Sep 17, 1868

Infant Daughter of
B. F. & M. J. Carriger
Jan 2, 1893
&
Infant Son of
B. F. & M. J. Carriger
Nov 28, 1895

Margaret Elizabeth, wife of
T. B. Felps
Jun 1, 1865
Apr 4, 1889

Ezekiel Felps
Mar 3, 1815
Jul 2, 1880
Age: 65y, 3m, 29d.

Marvia Felps
Dec 13, 1821
Oct 11, 1884
Age: 62y, 9m, 29d.

David E., Son of
E. & M. Felps
Nov 22, 1848
Dec --, 1849 (broken)

Infant Son of
E. & M. Felps
B&D Oct 22, 1861

Felps
B&D Feb 23, 1853

J. N., Son of
J. N. & Caroline Felps
Feb 23, 1853
Jun 23, 1854

J. N. Felps
Jul 24, ----
--- --, ----
(broken & in ground deep)

Thomas B. Phelps
1854-1932
&
Margret E. Phelps
1865-1889

B. F. Martin
Oct 28, 1843
May 27, 1921
&
Mattie J. Martin
May 1, 1844
Jun 2, 1933

Katie Martin
Aug 5, 1869
Dec 24, 1902

Frank D. Martin
Feb 16, 1868
Jan 9, 1919

Lucie E., Daughter of
B. F. & M. J. Martin
Jul 24, 1877
Oct 7, 1882

"Sisters"
Bettie Martin Frost
Feb 4, 1873
Nov 22, 1940
&
Callie Martin
Jun 9, 1871
Apr 17, 1941

Thomas Felps
Jul 4, 1810
Jun 23, 1888

Susan Jane Felps
(no dates, broken)

Thomas B., Son of
Mr. & Mrs. Thomas Felps
Age: 2 years.
(no dates)

Christian Carriger
May 18, 1810
Nov 29, 1888
& wife
Elizabeth Rowe Carriger
Jan 15, 1811
Nov 3, 1892

Jim H. Cox
1903-1952
&
Edna P. Cox
1908-

Col. David C. Boone
Nov 15, 1834
Jan 27, 1901

Fannie Boone Childs
1838-1915

Sallie Boone, wife of
T. M. Hudson
Mar 31, 1828
Mar 24, 1898
&
Samuel B., Son of
T. M. & Sallie Hudson
Oct 6, 1857
Mar 31, 1895

T. P. Noblitt
Dec 11, 1855
Jul 1, 1911

James Warden
1853-1940

Abraham Noblitt
Feb 12, 1859
Jun 27, 1909

BOONEVILLE QUADRANGLE

Lina, Daughter of
L. J. & A. H. Noblitt
Sep 16, 1878
Nov 8, 1893

J. M. Thompson
(no dates)

Sally Thompson
(no dates)

A. B. Thompson
(no dates)

Nancy Thompson
1838-1852

Ola Thompson
(no dates)

Henry H. Dunn
Mar 1, 1832
Jul 25, 1919

Avrilia, wife of
Henry H. Dunn
Aug 18, 1832
Jul 30, 1894

Newman Dunn
Sep 14, 1866
Sep 12, 1933

Press. O. Faulkner
1866-1948
&
Ella D. Faulkner
1869-1933

Bessie Elaine, Daughter of
T. E. & S. T. Campbell
Jun 24, 1917
Feb 17, 1918

William Jackson Goosby
Jun 2, 1860
Apr 3, 1934
&
Cyntha Emaline Goosby
Feb 14, 1873
Mar 13, 1953

Bob Carroll
1885-1931

Carrie Warden Carroll
1889-1962

Clara B. Carroll
Dec 5, 1910
Apr 22, 1914

Andrew Johnson Phelps
Dec 13, 1853
Jun 18, 1922
&
Lucinda Womack Phelps
Jul 7, 1864
Oct 14, 1927

J. F. Wiseman
Feb 12, 1839
May 14, 1919

Mary L. Wiseman
Jan 3, 1848
Feb 15, 1921

G. W. Felps
Jan 11, 1846
Jan 10, 1912

Robert L. Millard
1881-1950
&
Burdah Millard
1885-

William E. Martin
1866-1950

Infant Daughter of
H. B. & S. E. Parks
May 10, 1896
May 15, 1896

H. B. Parks
1848-1932
&
Elizabeth Parks
1856-1910

Lucy P. Link
Dec 15, 1882
Aug 11, 1960

James M. Bearden
1867-1942
&
Ida O. Bearden
1873-1946

Rollie R. Bearden
Tenn. Sgt Co M, 326 Inf
WW I
May 9, 1893
Feb 23, 1953

George C. Martin
1854-1925
&
Ella W. Martin
1862-1950

Berry B. Wagoner
Nov 7, 1893

&
Ethel M. Wagoner
Dec 7, 1889
May 17, 1968

Julia, wife of
E. E. Reagor
Nov 28, 1878
Feb 29, 1904

Hasty, Son of
E. E. & J. M. Reagor
(no dates)

A. A. Hasty
1875-1911
&
Minnie O. Hasty
1875-1954

James A. Hasty
1904-1912
&
Annie E. Hasty
1909-1910

Walden Martin
1881-1962
&
Minnie Martin
1887-

Claude J. Terry
1884-1926

W. W. Terry
1858-1930
&
Callie Felps Terry
1858-1912

E. M. McClure
Nov 2, 1839

&
Susan C. McClure
Jan 9, 1836
Jun 28, 1907
"Joined the Primative
Baptist Church 1876."

B. F. Carriger
1842-1928
&
Pollie Carriger
1854-(no date)

Robert L. Edmison
Nov 18, 1885
Sep 1, 1928

Candace Bailey
1847-1941
&
Lida Bailey
1851-1940

W. H. "Buck" Cannon
1902-1931

A. H. Rozar
Jul 30, 1860
Jun 29, 1927

Montie Rozar
Jul 4, 1865
Oct 9, 1934

Peyton Rutledge
Jun 8, 1894
Jul 5, 1946

Jack Russell
1869-1947
&
Fannie Russell
1870-1927

P. L. Bryant
Apr 1, 1863
(no date)
&
Margaret Sullivan Bryant
1868-Oct 18, 1934

C. T. Cates
Oct 29, 1867
Nov 28, 1937
&
Lou F. McGee Cates
Mar 8, 1870
May 2, 1927

J. F. Faulkner
Feb 4, 1855
May 31, 1935
&
Tennie Faulkner
Feb 7, 1850
Feb 26, 1940

Robert T. Moore
Nov 24, 1886
Nov 21, 1953

Jesse Mae Faulkner,
wife of
B. T. Moore
Mar 24, 1898
Jun 9, 1931

Clifton Oniel, Son of
B. T. & J. M. Moore
Apr 9, 1917
Oct 6, 1917

Walter Johnston
Jul 31, 1877
Sep 3, 1930
&
May Gill Johnston
May 20, 1892
Nov 11, 1964

William T. Gill
Mar 1, 1887
Aug 29, 1930

Permelia E. Gill
Apr 4, 1851
Mar 10, 1928

Tennie E. Faulkner,
wife of A. D. Creson
Oct 12, 1903
Apr 13, 1929

Arthur Van Saun
1893-
&
May G. Van Saun
1890-

BOONEVILLE QUADRANGLE

I. D. Carroll
Apr 1, 1883
Apr 3, 1926
&
Mary E. Carroll
Mar 16, 1880
Jan 21, 1941

Dr. J. R. Carroll
Feb 11, 1843
Apr 3, 1926
&
Dillie Carroll
Dec 6, 1868
Aug 30, 1960

John Alston Johnston
Aug 11, 1879
Apr 4, 1947
&
Sarah Jane Moore, wife of
Stephen Johnston
Mar 13, 1841
Jun 21, 1917

Walter Higgins Johnston
B&D Apr 24, 1950

P. M. Gill
Oct 15, 1856
Nov 3, 1951
&
Denie Raby Gill
Jan 3, 1867
Jan 8, 1929

Nat S. Forester
Jun 11, 1834
Jan 27, 1917
& wife
Margarett Forester
Feb 29, 1845
Oct 27, 1918

Joel T. Rives
Jun 8, 1850
Nov 2, 1932
&
Katherine Rives
Sep 17, 1857
Apr 15, 1941

J. A. Hasty
May 4, 1838
Feb 10, 1912

Mary Warden Hasty
Feb 14, 1848
Oct 24, 1923

Mother
Helda M. Pitts
Jul 10, 1923

& Daughter
Lynda R. Pitts
Nov 27, 1941
Sep 3, 1965

John W. Groce
Sep 22, 1873
Nov 12, 1957
&
Ruby B. Groce
Jan 10, 1900

James A. Rives
1879-1952
&
Mattie B. Rives
1884-1946

Marion G. Mansfield
1873-1961
&
Lillie Mansfield
1883-1965

George M. Rives
1877-1958
&
Mattie May Rives
1882-1950

Walter N. Reagor
1878-1949
&
Mamie M. Reagor
1880-1966

Henry H. Clark
Nov 9, 1885
Apr 1, 1949
&
Oda F. Clark
Sep 15, 1889

Lilburn H. Clark
Aug 11, 1924
Jun 8, 1956

Hayes Bartlett
1877-1964
&
Betty Bartlett
1879-1964

Edna S. Moore
Jan 6, 1890
Jul 28, 1956

Ode Moore
Dec 9, 1887
Feb 20, 1961

Wendy Lynn Moore
Jan 25, 1967
Apr 22, 1967

Frank G. Moore
1929-Nov 7, 1955

Johnnie A. Moore
Nov 26, 1919
Nov 27, 1955
&
Elvie Moore
Jun 1, 1930
Nov 26, 1955

Guy & Elle Moore
Jun 23, 1943
&
Elvylen Moore
--- 19, 1943

William O. Smith
1870-1954
&
Nora Smith
1883-1957

Isom Richardson
1897-1966
&
Pearl Richardson
1896-1940

Joanne Rives
Jul 16, 1943
Oct 13, 1943

Jim N. Wiles
1878-1946
&
Nannie G. Wiles
1882-

Birdie McGee Cates
Mar 13, 1891

John J. McGee
May 23, 1901
Nov 1, 1955

T. A. Faulkner
1881-1946
&
Fannie Faulkner
1882-

Hollis G. Logan
1909-
&
Ruth A. Logan
1914-

Milton S. Rozar
Jul 31, 1889

&
Clara G. Rozar
May 12, 1889
Dec 13, 1966

Birdie Smith
1876-1935
&
Sallie L. Smith
1869-1948

Wilson M. Smith
Jul 28, 1848
Dec 29, 1918

Bettie Bailey, wife of
Wilson M. Smith
Sep 20, 1848
Oct 5, 1923

Carroll Creson
Tennessee
Pvt 105 field Signal Bn.
WW I
Feb 11, 1889
Nov 10, 1954

Ben G. Creson
1891-1936

James F. Creson
1838-1920
&
Mary F. Creson
1859-1925

Frank A. Thomison Hoots
1859-1940
married 1879
&
Richard T. Hoots
1858-1936

Albert E. Phelps
1885-1957
&
Pauline H. Phelps
1887-1917

Grady Odell Smith
1904-1960

Infant Son of
Odell & Ernie Smith
1928-1928

Joe H. Lane
Jan 10, 1867
Dec 7, 1933
&
Maude P. Lane
Mar 5, 1871
Jul 22, 1935

Robert Creson
1876-1957
&
Lucy B. Creson
1879-1961

Will Martin Groce
1883-1965
&
Sally A. Groce
1884-1938
&
Mattie E. Groce
1874-1962
&
Susan A. Groce
1848-1939

Ben F. Sullivan
Oct 16, 1871
Jul 31, 1946

Elix Waggoner
1856-1947
&
Venie Waggoner
1854-1964

Rufus F. Cates
Mar 13, 1889
Jul 15, 1952

Mary Willie McGee
Mar 25, 1877
Dec 21, 1963

Son
Danny Ray Blankenship
1965-1965

Billie Dixon Logan
Sep 6, 1890
Mar 22, 1965
&
Mary Crockett Logan
Sep 4, 1895

D. Ernest Gowan
Feb 4, 1910
Apr 15, 1950

Henry M. Mansfield
1865-1938
&
Anna E. Mansfield
1878-1965

Homer M. Ashby
Dec 10, 1876
May 17, 1953
&
Ida Faulkner Ashby
Mar 30, 1882

Andrew Britt Faulkner
1875-1945
&
Laura Edmison Faulkner
1881-

Mary B. Gowan
1865-1938

A. B. Gowan
Aug 10, 1865
May 11, 1945
&
Ophia Faulkner Gowan
Apr 14, 1880
Aug 15, 1938

"Son"
Berry C. Gowan
Nov 8, 1894
Mar 5, 1930

E. G. Lane
1870-1941

Iva Mable Bedwell
Sep 11, 1912
Aug 12, 1918

John W. Ashby
1897-1966
&
Lona Young Ashby
1893-

Charles E. Park
Jul 1, 1886
Mar 22, 1958
&
Cathleen H. Park
Oct 24, 1899

Ross B. Phelps
Jan 20, 1884
Sep 27, 1951

Andrew J. Martin
Aug 25, 1881
Oct 21, 1954
&
Mabel S. Martin
Aug 31, 1895

Sallie B. Phelps
Jan 2, 1889
Aug 3, 1963

Holland B. Phelps
1916-1930

Gladys Phelps
Nov 25, 1910
Sep 24, 1939

Billie Creson
1890-1929
&
Florence Creson
1900-

Billie Jackson, Son of
Mr. & Mrs. Billie Creson
Mar 10, 1923
Mar 16, 1923

James Marvin Creson
Tennessee
A2C 354 FTR Intcp Sq A.F.
Apr 21, 1928
Dec 15, 1955

Wilse G. Steelman
1869-1932
&
Kate Waid Steelman
1869-1936

Eulas E. Thomas
Dec 8, 1918

&
Altha G. Thomas
Feb 20, 1920
Nov 19, 1968

Vernon Waggoner
Dec 29, 1901

&
Nannie Gill Waggoner
Nov 19, 1902

James Boone Steelman
Tennessee
Pvt U.S.Army, WW I
Jan 22, 1896
Sep 30, 1961

May Terry Steelman
1904-1966

Buddie Edward Wilson
Steelman
Oct 21, 1922
Jan 17, 1939

Isom Ward Steelman
Oct 25, 1898
Apr 28, 1968

Edward F. Johnson
May 30, 1868
Apr 13, 1947
&
Mary Terry Johnson
Nov 3, 1879
Mar 1, 1958

Patricia Sue, Infant of
Farris & Vivian Allen
1944-1944

Jean Mayre & Terry
Jul 16, 1966

David M. Edgeman
Dec 1, 1901
Jul 3, 1960

Jerry Ray, Son of
Don & Nell Wilkes
Dec 18, 1955

Travis B. Smith
1874-1956
&
Ozelle R. Smith
1887-1952

Roscoe Creson
Sep 7, 1893

&
Florence Rives Creson
May 17, 1896
Dec 25, 1960

Edward Creson
Sep 10, 1897
Aug 13, 1968
&
Laura Clift Creson
May 19, 1960

Ollie J. Price
1887-1962
&
Ulma I. Price
1897-

Donnie B. Smith
1865-1938

Edward Creson
Tennessee
Pfc Co E 119 Inf, WW I
Sep 10, 1897
Aug 13, 1968

Joseph M. Wilkes
1868-1947
&
Nancie J. Wilkes
1867-1938

John L. Thomas
1886-
&
Callie R. Thomas
1888-1938

Johnnie Haynie
1898-1958
&
Mary W. Haynie
1902-

Nannie Cox
1871-1953

George L. Thomas
Jun 21, 1907

&
Effie Shields Thomas
May 19, 1904
Mar 16, 1964

Tommie Groce
Aug 3, 1880
Aug 22, 1961
&
Myrtle Groce
Sep 7, 1884
Jun 3, 1952

Dave F. Buntley
Mar 6, 1887
Jan 10, 1961
&
Viola W. Buntley
May 7, 1889

Claude Groce
1912-1965
&
Ruth Waggoner Groce
1922-

Harold S. Tucker
1917-1934

John Henry Bateman
1888-1946

John A. Bateman
1865-1935
&
Annie E. Bateman
1860-1935

BOONEVILLE QUADRANGLE

Lillian Smith Tucker
Dec 31, 1895
Oct 10, 1948

A. R. "Dick" Rorax
1869-(no date)
&
Lou F. Rorax
1874-1949

Mrs. M. W. Phelps *
Died Feb 27, 1908
Age: 88 years
married T. Phelps in 1842

Pearlie,* Daughter of
Mr. & Mrs. Robert Creason
Died Aug 24, 1905
Age: (not given)

Miss Sallie Thompson
Died Apr 16, 1900
Age: 20 years.

William Jackson Goosby
Jun 2, 1860
Apr 3, 1934
&
Cynthia Emaline Goosby
Feb 14, 1873
Apr 13, 1953

Marion,* Daughter of
Mr. & Mrs. C. W. Hamlin
Died Oct 10, 1904
Age: 19m.

Clara,* Daughter of
Mr. & Mrs. Robert Carroll
Died Apr 22, 1914
Age: 3y, 6m.

Forney,* Son of
S. D. & Minnie Fuller
Died Jul 6, 1899
Age: 16m.

William C. Steelman
1861-1937
&
Annie Brown Steelman
1866-1942

John Stacy *
Died Apr 2, 1898
Age: 35 years.

Cora,* wife of
W. G. Forrester
Died Apr 9, 1892
Age: 23 years.

Leonard Ingle,* Son of
J. H. & Maud Lane
Died Jul 9, 1900
Age: 1y, 1m, 13d.

Several unmarked graves.

Bessie Groce Cannon
Nov 15, 1908
Jul 27, 1938

J. R. Ashby *
Nov 7, 1835
Oct 17, 1897
Age: 61y, 11m, 20d.

Mrs. Martha,* wife of
Dr. W. D. Frost
Died Sep 21, 1874
Age: (not given)

Mrs. Mattie Dunn *
Died May 2, 1902
Age: 37y, 4m, 22d.

J. W.,* Son of
J. R. Ashby
Jun 27, 1870
Oct 18, 1897
Age: 27y, 3m, 21d.

* *

GAGE CEMETERY

LOCATION: Three-fourth mile SSW of Buckeye Church, west side of Buckeye Creek at Moore County line.

Informed sources states that Aaron D. Gage, a Soldier of the Revolution is buried here.

Other families buried her are: The wife of James Wood, Thomisons and others.

All native fieldstones removed years ago, no markers remain.

* *

LOGAN CEMETERY

LOCATION: One mile SW of Booneville, west side of Buckeye Creek.

R. B. Logan
1848-1923

R. K., wife of
R. B. Logan
1854-(no date)

Sallie, Daughter of
R. B. & R. K. Logan
Sep 1, 1875
Jun 27, 1888

4 or 5 unmarked graves.

* *

JOHNSTON CEMETERY

LOCATION: One mile SW of Booneville, three-fourth mile south of main Waggoner Hill Road.

Descendants said that
Howell Johnston, born
May 26, 1793 and his wife
Orpha, born Dec 13, 1796
are buried here.

10 graves with fieldstones
and no inscriptions. Rock
fence enclosure.

Stephen Johnston *
Sep 5, 1832
Jun 25, 1910

Martha Bright Johnston *
1841-1877

* *

BOONEVILLE QUADRANGLE

MOORE CEMETERY

LOCATION: Two and one-half miles SW of Booneville on Gimlet Creek, in forks of road.

Arreva McGee, wife of
W. J. Moore
Feb 19, 1855
Aug   1881

Malessa Moore
1856-1936

Susie Hudson, wife of
A. B. Cowan
Mar 26, 1865
Jul 8, 1900
"Also her infant Son by her side."

Infant Daughter of
A. B. & Susie Cowan
Oct 8, 1895
Oct 10, 1895

Olla Hudson
Mar 20, 1876
Sep 5, 1885

Several unmarked graves.

* *

SHOFNER CEMETERY

LOCATION: One and one-half miles south of Booneville on west side of main road.

J. H. Shofner
Dec 18, 1811
Mar 11, 1886
&
Nancy Logan, wife of
J. H. Shofner
May 31, 1816
Apr 15, 1904

William G. Shofner
Aug 27, 1877
Nov 3, 1878
&
Nancy Shofner
Mar 27, 1875
Sep 23, 1876

Newton M. Shofner
Jun 31, 1843
Jan 26, 1863

(name missing) McNatt
Aug 9, 1890
Mar 31, 1909

Mary A. Rutledge, wife of
James C. Shofner
Sep 1, 1846
Nov 27, 1888

Several unmarked graves.

* *

CORNERSVILLE QUADRANGLE

HAYES CEMETERY

LOCATION: Three miles WSW of Delina on hill in forks of Delina-Red Oak roads.

Thomas W. Hayes May 3, 1794 Nov 5, 1866 & Mrs. Hayes 1802-Dec 27, 1865	Commodore P. Hayes Sep 22, 1825 Dec 23, 1867	Curran D. Benson Sep 10, 1820 Aug 20, 1868 Marcissa E., wife of Curran D. Benson Apr 4, 1828 Apr 17, 1890	3 or 4 unmarked graves. NOTE: All markers are on ground, in pasture.

* *

DAVIS CEMETERY

LOCATION: Three miles WSW of Delina, south of Delina-Cornersville road, on Haskel Roden Farm.

N. C. Davis Feb 5, 1827 Jul 30, 1865	William A. Davis *** Died 1834, also, wife Mary Davis buried here.	4 unmarked graves.

* *

SUMNER CEMETERY

LOCATION: Two and one-half miles WSW of Delina on Red Oak-Delina road, on north side of road.

Thomas Sumners 1805-(no date) Elizabeth, wife of Thomas Sumners 1810-(no date) Annie D., wife of Thomas Sumners Jul 12, 1845 Apr 2, 1924	Adam G. Sumners Apr 15, 1835 Dec 7, 1900 Sally Sumners born about 1807 Died (no date) 25 graves with markers and no inscriptions.	Mary P. Brady Dec 12, 1842 Sep 12, 1902 W. M. Brady Jan 10, 1835 Jan 23, 189-(date gone) Loucinda Brady Feb 25, 1822 Dec 18, 1905	J. F. Coble Jan 25, 1849 Mar 8, 1889 Everette Davis Died Apr 6, 1924 Age:(not given, child) Telar S., Daughter of O. W. & S. L. Strane Jun 5, 1891 Oct 1892

* *

DELLROSE QUADRANGLE

SILVESTER CEMETERY

LOCATION: Three fourth mile NNW of Dellrose on top of hill, northeast side of McBurg road.

Peninah Silvester Oct 20, 1812 Apr 21, 1858	John C. Silvester May 8, 1861 Sep 3, 1864	W. B. Silvester Jun 6, 1853 Mar 21, 1856	G. W. Silvester Feb 9, 1849 Feb 23, 1849

Several unmarked graves.

* *

GEORGE-HOBBS CEMETERY

LOCATION: One mile NE of Dellrose and one-fourth mile SW of Shilo Methodist E. Church.

D. J. George Mar 6, 1849 Dec 26, 1932	Hattie George Rutherford Nov 20, 1855 Nov 15, 1920	William George Feb 8, 1795 Nov 23, 1862	W. P. A. George Oct 30, 1817 Feb 7, 1888 &
Nancy E., wife of D. J. George Apr 10, 1853 Jul 11, 1888	Renther B., Daughter of J. B. & Addie Cheatham May 25, 1885 Nov 3, 1885	Margaret George Jan 18, 1796 Jul 12, 1866	Elizabeth George Nov 4, 1818 Dec 9, 1875
Maggie, Daughter of D. J. & N. E. George Mar 3, 1875 Aug 25, 1897	Sarah, Consort of Needam George born in South Carolina, Union Dist. Feb 12, 1796 Died Jun 29, 1850 (by her son, J. H. G.)	3 old Rock Slab Vaults side by side, no inscriptions. Old Sand Stone Footmarker has: C. P.	Nathaniel Hobbs Jul 17, 1827 Jul 21, 1885
Ernest, Son of D. J. & F. A. George Sep 16, 1894 Aug 12, 1905		D. F. Hobbs born in North Carolina Jul 25, 1820 died at Clardyville, Tenn. Jan 2, 1899	Margaret B. Hobbs May 10, 1831 Jan 22, 1893
F. A., wife of D. J. George Dec 18, 1858 Feb 22, 1912	Jessie W. Hobbs Oct 13, 1822 Jun 19, 1898		Pleasant Hobbs Apr 4, 1844 Nov 30, 1915
--lah ------ 1867-1868	Eliza Hobbs Died Jul 5, 1905 Age: 81y, 2m.	Sarah A. Hobbs born in Lincoln Co., Tenn. Oct 23, 1823 Died May 29, 1900	Laura G., wife of Pleasant Hobbs Feb 13, 1854 Oct 12, 1887

Several unmarked graves.

* *

METCALF CEMETERY

LOCATION: One-fourth mile east of Shilo Methodist E. Church on side of hill, east side of main road.

Mary Jane, wife of
William H. Metcalf
Jan 24, 1822
Aug 20, 1863

1 grave, fieldstone, no inscription.

* *

FARRAR CEMETERY

LOCATION: One mile SE of Shilo Methodist E. Church near Old Clardyville.

Nancy Caroline, Consort of Daniel Farer Jan 20, 1822 Jul 18, 1852 Age: 30y, 5m, 28d. "The Mother of 6 children." Joseph Farrar * Died Apr 29, 1890, Age: abt 83	John Farrar * A Soldier of the Revolution, born in England 1750, came to America 1770. Served in Virginia 5 years under George Washington. Settled in S.C. Came to Lincoln Co., Tenn.	1810, on land owned by Ples. Hobbs, 14 miles west of Fayetteville. Died 1830. Buried at Old Homeplace. Sent to Newspaper 1909 by Great Grand Son, J. R. Abernathy

* *

DELLROSE QUADRANGLE

BRUCE CEMETERY

LOCATION: One fourth mile north of New Dellrose in pasture.

Large Vault with part inscription: Rev. Bruce, erected by the Virginia Conference. Rev. Philip Bruce Dec 25, 1755 May 10, 1826 "A Soldier of the Revolution" (One of the first circuit riders of the Methodist Church.)	Joel Bruce * Oct 12, 1820 Died 1884 Caroline,* wife of Wormly R. Bruce Died Jan 7, 1846 Age: 34 years. Several gravestones, many have been destroyed or taken away. Other names were: Cothrans & Mitchells.	Phillip Bruce * Died Apr 13, 1888 Age: 37 years. Mother * & Brother *, (Joel Bruce, Sr.) of Rev. Philip Bruce buried here, no dates.

* *

GEORGE CEMETERY

LOCATION: Three fourth mile SW of Dellrose between main road and Elk River.

F. A. George Oct 14, 1827 Jan 11, 1907 Elizabeth J., wife of F. A. George Jun 3, 1833 Nov 22, 1905	Joseph F. George Jan 8, 1864 Apr 16, 1940 Viola E. George Mar 10, 1877 Jul 21, 1905 Several unmarked graves.	Infant Daughter of H. K. & C. George Dec 2, 1897 Dec 4, 1897 R. J. N. (Nelson) Died May 1875 (no age given)	Theo E. Jones Jan 14, 1878 Aug 20, 1945 James M. Young Died Sep 2, 1906 Age: 73 years.

* *

PATTERSON CEMETERY

LOCATION: One and one-half miles SW of Dellrose and west of O'Neal Branch, on dead-end road.

Elnor Obediance, Daughter of J. G. & E. F. McGuire Oct 30, 1899 Apr 11, 1900 E. F., wife of J. G. McGuire Nov 22, 1879 Dec 7, 1899 William K. Whitaker Dec 8, 1900 May 25, 1918 Nelia B. Stevenson 1858-1938 W. B. Stevenson Jan 24, 1856 Feb 26, 1919 Pearl M., Daughter of W. B. & Nelia B. Stevenson Sep 13, 1888 Feb 12, 1903 Martha E., wife of Joseph L. Sherrell Jul 4, 1830 Apr 24, 1862 Age: 31y, 9m, 20d.	W. S. Patterson Jun 21, 1859 Dec 16, 1893 & Annie Sue Patterson Jun 24, 1886 Jan 30, 1894 & Burnice Arrene Patterson May 9, 1889 Nov 9, 1890 "Annie & Burnice are the children of W. S. & B. V. Patterson." Mary L., wife of N. Smith Nov 1, 1836 May 4, 1870 Note: There are 14 graves all inside rock fence with Mary L. Smith, no inscriptions. Rachael Eugenie, Daughter of J. L. & M. E. Sherrell Jul 2, 1855 Feb 14, 1856 Age: 7m, 12d.	Infant Daughter of M. L. & Maggie L. Patterson May 10, 1885 May 14, 1885 J. L., Son of N. & M. L. Smith Dec 18, 1866 Jun 26, 1886 Lieut. L. M. Patterson of the Confederate Army Apr 23, 1832 was killed at the Battle of Shilo Apr 8, 1862 D. S. Patterson Mar 3, 1823 Apr 4, 1862 Elizabeth, wife of John Hobbs Died Dec 24, 1888 Age: (broken) David L., Son of A. A. & M. H. Sherrell Died Mar 29, 1843 Age: 13d.	Mrs. E. R. Cheatham, born Dec 19, 1817 married D. S. Patterson Dec 23, 1844 died Aug 20, 1888 (W. F.) Patterson (child, broken) E. F. Patterson Aug 8, 1848 --- --, 1866 (broken) Henderson Patterson 1853-1917 Frank Cheatham Gibbs Died Mar 1869 Age: 4 years. & Amanda C. Cheatham Gibbs Died Oct 2, 1881 Age: 44 years. W. N. Gibbs Died Feb 3, 1880 Age: 46 years.

DELLROSE QUADRANGLE

Emmett R., Son of
J. L. & M. E. Sherrell
Apr 19, 1853
Jun 4, 1879

Mrs. Tildie Holland *
Died Jun 19, 1905
Age: 77y, 7d.

W. B. Patterson
Feb 18, 1821
Oct 2, 1841

D. L. Patterson *
Died Jan 15, 1917
Age: 64 years.

Violette M. Patterson
1834-Feb 6, 1894
&
James H. Patterson
1st Lieut. Co A 44 Regt
Tenn Inf C.S.A.

Many unmarked graves.

* *

MAJOR CEMETERY

LOCATION: Two miles SSE of New Dellrose, west of O'Neal Branch on dead-end road.

"Father"
E. D. McGuire
Jan 5, 1875
Feb 2, 1893

"Mother"
E. F. McGuire
Apr 28, 1877
Feb 3, 1893

Infant of
J. M. & Anna O'Neal
Mar 25, 1888
Apr 30, 1888

Anna, wife of
J. M. O'Neal
1867-Apr 15, 1888

F. M., wife of
J. M. O'Neal
Jan 2, 1861
Dec 24, 1885

M. S. Paysinger, wife of
J. W. O'Neal
Jun 18, 1861
Aug 7, 1930

J. W. O'Neal
1857-1942

Jessie A. O'Neal
Jun 28, 1890
May 24, 1922

John W. McAfee
Jun 22, 1872
Jul 8, 1873

Eddie Ross, Daughter of
J. W. & M. S. O'Neal
Jul 23, 1900
Feb 28, 1919

E. M., Son of
J. M. & F. M. O'Neal
Jan 10, 1885
Dec 5, 1885

Nealy Bell, Daughter of
J. M. & M. J. Conine
May 20, 1888
Oct 31, 1889

William Emmett, Son of
J. M. & M. J. Conine
Sep 30, 1879
Nov 6, 1893

L. E. Paysinger
Jan 25, 1876
Feb 10, 1876
&
W. S. Paysinger
Jan 13, 1879
Oct 25, 1879
&
Gussie Paysinger
Jul 1, 1884
Jan 23, 1885

W. P. Paysinger
Jul 9, 1848 (Jul 5)
Aug 29, 1891
& wife
Eliza Roper Paysinger
Sep 14, 1850
May 19, 1917

Adaline, wife of
T. A. Paysinger
Dec 29, 1824
Mar 29, 1914

Many unmarked graves.

* *

YOUNG CEMETERY

LOCATION: One-fourth mile east of Wheelerton near Giles Co. line.

No markers.

* *

CEMETERY

LOCATION: One and one-half miles SE of Dellrose in Cheatham Bend of Elk River.

No markers remain.

* *

STONE CEMETERY

LOCATION: One and one-half miles SE of Dellrose on west Bluff of Elk River.

Connie E. Oneal
Mar 27, 1891
Jan 26, 1916

J. H. George
Aug 22, 1852
Jan 23, 1925

Tommie George
Dec 3, 1866
Jan 25, 1939

Alto George Post
Jun 3, 1897
Jan 26, 1924

DELLROSE QUADRANGLE

Vasgar George
Jan 17, 1892
Oct 16, 1932

James Stone
Col'd
Apr 15, 1853
Feb 22, 1888

Lydia Dobbins
Dec 25, 1871
Feb 23, 1916

D. C. Sherrell
Oct 10, 1851
Sep 2, 1919
&
Mary E. Sherrell
Jan 1, 1862
Jun 8, 1935

William E. McCoy
1842-1927
&
Eleanor McCoy
1845-1917

Harold Hereford,* Son of
Mr. & Mrs. Oce Strain
Died Feb 21, 1908
Age: 10 years.

Mrs. Maggie Dollar *
Died Aug 29, 1907
Age: (not given)

Many unmarked graves.

Thomas J. Stone
Aug 7, 1806
Apr 13, 1874

Mary E., wife of
Thomas A.(?) Stone
May 16, 1819
Jul 17, 1883
Age: 64y, 2m, 1d.

Ann Madora, Daughter of
T. J. & A. Stone
Dec 29, 1844
Apr 26, 1872
Age: 27y, 3m, 27d.

Benjamin Scoggin Stone
Jun 15, 1849
Oct 23, 1892
&
Violet Ann Stone
Dec 13, 1856
May 4, 1918

E. R.(Roy), Son of
Dr. B. S. & V. A. Stone
Oct 2, 1876
Jun 13, 1894

James P. Dollar *
Died Sep 8, 1917
Age: 76 years
C.S.A.

Grady,* Son of
J. P. & Sarah A. Dollar
Died Nov 7, 1899
Age: 12y, 10m.

Mary Martha, Daughter of
William & M. Simms
Dec 13, 1841
Apr 4, 1873
(stone by J. T. Canterbery,
  Pulaski, Tenn.)

Martha J., Daughter of
Dr. A. L. Glaze
Jun 18, 1842
May 2, 1886

Lilla, Daughter of
Dr. A. L. & M. J. Glaze
Jul 31, 1867
Jun 19, 1887

Morris Stone, Son of
C. G. & M. V. Welch
Sep 9, 1898
Apr 22, 1899

Infant Son of
C. G. & M. V. Welch
B&D May 19, 1900

Thomas A. Eagin
Dec 14, 1867
Jul 23, 1906

Infant * of
Howard H. Stone
Died Feb 21, 1908
Age: (not given)

Annie Lou Glaze
Nov 12, 1876
Aug 2, 1892

Infant Son
Solon, Son of
A. L. & Ophelia Glaze
Sep 5, 1895
Nov 11, 1895

W. R. Bowers
May 2, 1866
Jan 23, 1891

B. A. Sherrell
1862-1941

Anna Sherrell
1866-1945

Mamie Lee, Daughter of
Dr. B. A. & Anna Sherrell
Nov 18, 1895
Jun 27, 1896

Virginia Belle, Daughter
of Dr. B. A. & Anna Belle
Sherrell
Mar 24, 1889
Jul 9, 1902
Age: 13y, 3m, 15d.

Emmett Randolph,* Son of
Dr. Joseph Sherrell
Died Jun 4, 1879
Age: 26y, 1m, 15d.

* *

CEMETERY

LOCATION: Three fourth mile NNW of Hobbs Bridge and east of
Cheatham Bend, in field.

About 10 graves, some with fieldstones with no inscriptions.

* *

NEW GROVE CHURCH CEMETERY (Old Nebo)

LOCATION: Two miles NW of Blanch and north of Kelly Creek.

Wilk M. Corbin
1882-
&
Lola E. Corbin
1886-1968

Hilliard L. Corbin
1914-1921

D. W. Corbin
Nov 14, 1845
Nov 1, 1922

T. A. Corbin
1883-1914

  Helum children:
  Topsy, 1885-1896
  Sammy, 1892-1898
  Infant, (no dates)

Thomas A. Corbin
1884-1941
&
Annie Bell Corbin
1898-Mar 5, 1949
Age: 59y, 2m, 23d.

W. H. Emerson
Jan 31, 1888
Dec 23, 1953

Lou V. Emerson
Mar 9, 1888
Dec 23, 1928

Bryan W. Emmerson
1861-1902

Doris Joan Thomas
Oct 21, 1932
Oct 25, 1932

"Baby"
Flora Leona Thompson
Jun 16, 1910
Oct 30, 1910

Mary Lois, Daughter of
Clarence & Edna May
Dec 7, 1924
Jun 11, 1926

Jeff W. Helums
Feb 22, 1854-Apr 27, 1932
&
Catherine Helums
Jun 13, 1863-Jul 31, 1931

John Floyd Holt
Jun 4, 1893
May 7, 1930
&
Ona Mai Turner Holt
Feb 4, 1900
May 7, 1930

Thurman Monroe, Son of
O. R. & S. B. Snow
Nov 12, 1919
Nov 13, 1919

Emit Snow
1875-1923

DELLROSE QUADRANGLE

Violet A. Hawkins
Mar 1, 1869
Jan 14, 1911

Infant of
R. E. & V. A. Hawkins
(no dates)

Ruff Vickers
1844-1920

Willie Vickers
1900-1902

_____ Lewter
1881-1948

Emmer L. Vickers
1872-1929

Sollom Vickers
1909-1929

Martha Vickers
1872-1931

Silas B. Vickers, Jr.
1939

Juanita Vickers
1937-1938

George Vickers
1905-1931

Eleanor Mallory
1872-1942

James W. McGee
1926-

Smith Davis
1854-1919
&
Nannie Davis
1851-1928

Sally Malone Hawkins
Mar 4, 1878
Mar 12, 1914

Euin Hawkins
Feb 1914
Sep 1914

P. T. Malone
1874-1942

Lula Mitchell, wife of
P. T. Malone
Aug 6, 1875
Sep 27, 1900

Brantlet, wife of
P. T. Malone
Dec 4, 1885
Aug 13, 1916

Grover P., Son of
P. T. & S. B. Malone
Oct 3, 1913
Mar 29, 1914

Sarah E., wife of
B. F. Malone
Mar 9, 1844
Jul 29, 1922

Brave Polly
1866-1949

Annie Polly
1861-1934

John Polly
Nov   1892
Nov 22, 1917

J. B. Polly
Died Aug 22, 1936
(TM)

W. H. Polly
Died Feb 11, 1897
(no date)

N. E. C(G).
1893
(fieldstone)

Armatha, Daughter of
C. N. & W. C. Dollar
Sep 9, 1884
Nov 14, 1890

J. W. Keen
(no dates, fieldstone)

W. H. Keen
(no dates, fieldstone)

Miss Sarah Smith
Jan 12, 1838
Jan 15, 1911
&
J. F. Smith
Aug 1, 1835
(no date)
&
Nancy Smith, wife of
J. J. Vickers
May 11, 1834
Aug 27, 1888

L. L. Smith
Jul 7, 1815
(no date)
&
Annie Smith
Feb 11, 1859
Jul 19, 1923

Sealey C., wife of
Thomas Writch
Died Oct 17, 1914
(no date)

Stacy A. Tiller
1844-1914
&
W. B. Tiller
1837-1914
&
Elizabeth Tiller
1865-1927
&
The Knox Baby
&
Susan A. Tiller
1869-1892
&
W. R. Tiller
1872-1903
&
Annie B. Tiller
1902-1913

Auther Maddox
1889-Sep 14, 1918

Nancy Walker, Daughter of
William Freeman & wife of
F. M. Walker
Jul 10, 1865
Jul 11, 1906

James Wilson Hall
Dec 18, 1849
Jul 4, 1933

Mary Ann Hicks, wife of
J. W. Hall
Nov 26, 1875
Aug 16, 1912

Victoria Hall
Sep 20, 1906
Oct 18, 1906
&
David Cowan Hall
Jan 9, 1898
Mar 24, 1910
&
Theodore Hall
Jun 15, 1903
Dec 10, 1912
&
Nora Belle Hall
Jan 8, 1896
Feb 25, 1917

Emma Myrtle Hall
Nov 5, 1891
May 2, 1938

Joe Holt
1867-1938

Sarah Holt
1872-1957

Joe Holt
1936-1939

Mary J. Holt
1931-1935

Crella Holt
1905-1943

Solon Holt
Jan 16, 1909
Jan 19, 1963

S. L. Bryant
Died Nov 26, 1901
Age: 52 years.

Thomas B. Campbell
1870-1934
&
Eliza L. Campbell
1863-19(no date)

Zeno H. Grubbs
Mar 29, 1843
Feb 28, 1905

Susan E. Bledsoe, wife of
Z. H. Grubbs
Mar 2, 1846
Sep 10, 1907

Ellen C., wife of
W. H. Grubbs &
Daughter of
Elisha & Nancy Abernathy
Sep 10, 1810
Feb 28, 1866

Eliza J., wife of
J. F. Byers &
Daughter of
W. H. & E. C. Grubbs
Sep 20, 1831
Mar 2, 1863

M. A. Grubbs
1862-1919

Anson R. Marshall
Feb 1, 1858
Mar 5, 1922
&
Sara Francis Green Marshall
Jul 6, 1860
Aug 31, 1938

William J. Marshall
May 19, 1883

&
Margaret Lou Boggs Marshall
Jul 23, 1886
May 2, 1969

C. E. Brock
Nov 13, 1830
Jul 9, 1901

W. W. Grubbs
1875-1928

Jeff H. Grubbs
1907-1920

DELLROSE QUADRANGLE

Janice Ellen Grubbs
Apr 5, 1949

H. Dalton Grubbs, Sr.
1918-1967

James Harvey Mitchell
Feb 8, 1880
Nov 16, 1956

Eva Thompson Mitchell
Jul 4, 1882
Jun 17, 1966

D. B. Mitchell
1914-1969

Clint Snow
1887-1968

Nervie Ratley
1869-1937

Loyd R. Steadman
1901-1968
&
Drucilla Steadman
1904-

W. Vernon Lewter
Mar 19, 1901
Feb 26, 1955
&
Mary Lewter
Feb 10, 1903

Dennis W. Luna
Aug 2, 1880

&
Pearl L. Vickers Luna
Nov 6, 1882
Feb 4, 1950

J. F. Steadman
Apr 8, 1867
Jan 4, 1959
&
Lula Steadman
Feb 9, 1879
Sep 17, 1912

Herbert Steadman
Jul 25, 1905
Jan 3, 1913

Viney, wife of
J. F. Steadman
May 22, 1865
Oct 8, 1901

Brown Holland
1907-1935

Dennis Thompson
1952-1957

Dannie Thompson
1954-1954

Ed Thompson
1893-
&
Nannie B. Thompson
1899-1967

Fronie _____
(all information gone)

Jesse H. Steadman
1892-1920

W. A. Thompson
1862-1928
&
Nerva Thompson
1864-1937

W. P. Lewter
Apr 8, 1852
May 16, 1928

Frances Lewter
1872-1940

Elijah Dollar
Died 1884
(fieldstone)

Emmet L. Vickers
Oct 22, 1887
Dec 30, 1943
&
Dovie Vickers
May 7, 1889
Dec 4, 1922

Carroll Commons
Mar 10, 1829
Nov 21, 1909
& wife
Elizabeth W. Commons
Jun 5, 1842
(no date)

Lue Slayton
Mar 15, 1854
Nov 6, 1915

Horace L. Slayton
1872-1946
&
Mary G. Slayton
1877-

Son
Hilton Slaton
1922-1923

Mable Slaton
1910-1923

W. C. Mitchell
1872-1951

Hughey Edward, Son of
B. H. & Bertha Gulley
Aug 7, 1907
Nov 20, 1907

James Wiley Gulley
Jun 23, 1866
Sep 4, 1944

Lucy Goolsby
1866-1939

W. A. Hall
1866-1941
&
Eliza Hall
1871-19(no date)

Annie Cathleen, Daughter of
W. A. & E. J. Hall
Jun 1, 1912
Dec 3, 1914

Infant of
E. T. & G. G. Fite
B&D Jun 27, 1916

Mary Stratton
(no dates)

Carl, Son of
E. M. & F. E. Hicklen
Jan 15, 1905
Jan 27, 1908

Edna, Daughter of
E. M. & F. E. Hicklen
Aug 21, 1901
Sep 21, 1902

Bunyon, Son of
E. M. & F. E. Hicklen
Aug 12, 1907
Apr 17, 1917

Fannie, wife of
E. M. Hicklen
Apr 18, 1869
Dec 1, 1912

Annie _____ (name gone)
Aug 7, 1842
Aug   1922

Riley Sanders
Nov 1, 1876
Dec 17, 1902

Anderson, Son of
Riley & Addie Sanders
Oct 17, 1902
Jan 29, 1908

F. A. Sanders
May 3, 1853
Mar 30, 1912

Cicero Corbin
1900-1943

Emma Corbin
1867-1937

Bobby Corbin (child)
(no dates)

Raymond Corbin (child)
(no dates)

Jude Corbin, Sr.
Nov 25, 1889
May 22, 1965
&
Ethel Corbin
May 5, 1896

Charles Corbin
1880-1951

Raymond Corbin
1892-1930

Everett Corbin
1889-1956

J. H. Thompson
1856-1939

Mary Thompson
1877-1955

Joe Smith
(no dates, TM)

R. A. Marshall
Feb 14, 1880
Oct 1, 1942

Tom Jones
1887-1963

Alvin Jones, Jr.
1943-1944

Alvin Jones
1916-1959

Will Ayers
1871-1939 (TM)

Mary J. Ayers
1885-1953

Mr. Sherrell Ayers
Died May 27, 1969
Age: 64y, 9m, 29d. (TM)

John D. Gordon
Jul 11, 1892
Sep 23, 1965
&
Sallie B. Gordon
Oct 27, 1895

Thomas Goolsby
1888-1964

Billie Malone
Mar 15, 1888
Jul 15, 1949
&
Mae Malone
May 23, 1888
Apr 7, 1944

DELLROSE QUADRANGLE

D. J. Moore
1874-1946
&
Ella L. Moore
1887-19

James Moore
Aug 3, 1949
Sep 13, 1962

Sam Polley
Apr 1, 1882
Apr 5, 1954

Andy Brown
Jan 15, 1886
Dec 25, 1964
&
Lida Brown
Nov 19, 1892

Linda Fay Brown
(no dates, child)

Carol Sue Patterson
1961-1962

Roberta Brown
1943-1944

John Elbert Wilbanks
1952-1956

Nannie Grubbs
1869-1939

W. C. Grubbs
1908-1952

Fannie Lock
1896-1966

Danny Wray Thompson
1954

C. L. Thompson
1932-1933

Roy Polly
1874-1951

Pearl Polly
1883-1963

John R. Hicklen
1888-1928

J. W. Bryant
Feb 29, 1916
Oct 17, 1917

Oliver Walker
1884-1921
&
Nannie Walker
1886-(no date)

F. B. Wherly
(no dates)

Jim Carter
1876-1941
& wife
Sadie Carter
1915-1951

Vanuel Holland
Mar 29, 1912
Apr 27, 1912
&
W. O. Holland
Oct 21, 1882
Dec 2, 1951

Hattie Lewter Holland
Dec 15, 1886
Dec 9, 1945

W. H. Wynne
Mar 1, 1858
May 24, 1931
&
M. F. Wynne
Feb 7, 1860
(no date)

Lemmie Colas Wynne
Mar 5, 1893
Sep 10, 1945
&
Flossie Mae Wynne
Oct 28, 1895

Roe Landas Steadman
1868-19(no date)
&
Lucenda Bell Steadman
1880-1937

Betty Ann Walker
1944

W. Cull Ellis
1884-1957
&
Annie L. Ellis
1885-1922

James Beech Ellis
Tennessee
Pfc Air Corps, WW II
Jan 6, 1922
Sep 25, 1945

John W. Lewter
Oct 14, 1896
Dec 20, 1967
&
Mary E. Lewter
Oct 10, 1899

J. W. Lewter, Jr.
1923-1953
&
Annie Mae Lewter
1933-

Floyd C. Lewter
May 1, 1892
Nov 2, 1948
&
Annie B. Lewter
Nov 19, 1898

Esker "Babe" Mitchell
Jul 7, 1906
Jan 20, 1962
&
Ada Lucy Mitchell
May 2, 1915

J. Marvin Holt
Sep 27, 1917
Jan 29, 1967
&
Virgie L. Holt
Dec 22, 1917

Ella Hardin
1864-1932

John W. Whitman
Apr 16, 1888
Jun 20, 1967
&
Georgia E. Whitman
Nov 20, 1888

John Willard, Son of
Georgia & J. W. Whitman
Jul 14, 1921
Sep 28, 1922

Mary Alice Whitman
Sep 18, 1869
Aug 28, 1917

Susie Paples (Peoples)
Sep 18, 1846
Mar 28, 1922

Charlie Peoples
1877-1956

Nelta Peoples
1883-(no date)

Doris Billons
1935-1960

Vera Owema Billons
1938-1940

Mary Billions
1881-1956

Thomas F. Morton
Feb 9, 1939
Jul 27, 1965
&
Josephine C. Morton
Dec 10, 1936

Joanie Maxine Cowan
May 19, 1962
Jan 3, 1963

Nancy Alma Pitts
1902-1961

Mavoline Woodalf
1930-1954

Mary Martha Williams
1943-1960

Robert Pool
Jun 3, 1933
Feb 14, 1955

Mrs. W. M. Pool
1854-1935

Nathan Pool
1896-1950

J. C. Maddox
Apr 8, 1811
Sep 11, 1901
& wife
Jimmie Shands Maddox
Mar 5, 1801
Nov 16, 1902
Age: 101 years.

William J. McCown
Jan 9, 1866
May 5, 1928

Rachel E. McCown
May 14, 1866
Aug 31, 1901

Fred R., Son of
W. J. & Rachel E. McCown
May 24, 1900
Sep 27, 1900

Early Percy, Son of
S. W. & M. J. Turner
Aug 22, 1886
Aug 7, 1888

Ike Tosh
1884-1964
&
Lois Tosh
1895-1966

Fred D. Marshall
1884-1933
&
Addie M. Marshall
1893-

Henry F. Malone
1871-1944
&
Mary J. Malone
1874-1944

Dora Slayton Davis
Sep 13, 1918
Apr 20, 1969

DELLROSE QUADRANGLE

Nancy Ivey
1881-1949

Cathey Franklin
Died Nov 1958
(no age given)

Maudie Lock
1908-1967

Pat Mullins
1872-1958

Lena Mullins
1888-1939

Theo W. Slayton
1881-1968
&
Dee M. Slayton
1875-1944

Howard Slayton
Mar 16, 1903
Feb 28, 1959
&
Dell Slayton
Mar 23, 1903

Phillis D. Slayton
5/57

Katherine Slayton
1925-1937

Will T. Slayton
1935-1936
(The above two are
 brother & sister)

Martha R. Mitchell
1946-1947

Effie J. Dempsey
1948-1952

Earl Jordan
1895-1961

Elbert Jordan
1917-1946

Datesy May Holland
Swinford
Feb 22, 1895
Jan 7, 1929

Cal J. Holland
1868-1929
&
Lillie J. Holland
1877-1936

Brown Holland
1907-1935

W. Wayne Holland
May 10, 1936
Jun 14, 1938

Claude Howard Hall
1937-1939

Bettie Jo Jester
Oct 21, 1932
Mar 30, 1936

Lummy C. Jester
Mar 23, 1890
Apr 14, 1961
&
Viola S. Jester
Jan 28, 1897
----
married Dec 25, 1918

Robert K. Mitchell
May 20, 1916

&
Nellie L. Mitchell
Jul 23, 1910
Oct 15, 1965

Martha Ruth Mitchell
1946-1947

John T. Buffaloe
Mar 17, 1883
Mar 1, 1958
&
Ona Jester Buffaloe
May 20, 1882

E. L. Jester
Nov 17, 1884
Dec 4, 1959
&
Lillie T. Jester
Jul 8, 1884
Feb 27, 1963

William Leon Jester
Nov 28, 1921
Aug 4, 1927

Bessie T. Cooper
1900-

Claude Sanders
Jul 19, 1897
Jun 27, 1953
&
Estelle Sanders
Dec 20, 1897

Arnie D. Minor
Oct 1, 1886
Sep 22, 1964
&
Ellen R. Minor
Jan 6, 1899

Coy L. Minor
1888-19
&
Monroe Minor
1884-1950

Anna Jester
1879-1966

Tera Shand
Jul 21, 1862
Sep 12, 1926

W. T. Thompson
Mar 23, 1850
Jan 27, 1929

Mary L. Thompson
Aug 12, 1857
Aug 31, 1939

Mary Thompson
1885-1957

Tom Jester
1852-1915
&
Elizabeth Jester
1861-1906

Joe Jester
1892-1969

W. B. Slayton
1887-1926
&
Emma Slayton
1903-1931

Joe R. Minor
Jun 23, 1858
Dec 1, 1939
&
Sarah A. Minor
Feb 15, 1859
May 28, 1935

Stepens
(no dates, fieldstone)

Charlie Minor
Dec 7, 1888
Oct 15, 1891

Minor
(no dates, fieldstone)

Minor
(no dates, fieldstone)

John J. Jester
Sep 17, 1882
Jan 4, 1919

B. D. Jester
Oct 14, 1885
Sep 8, 1938

Mary Alice Moran
Feb 14, 1877
Apr 3, 1931

Ida Mitchell
1878-1909

Infant * of Mr. & Mrs.
Joe Smith
Died Oct 31, 1910 (no age)

G. W. Dunn
Feb 28, 1852
Sep 11, 1909
& wife
Martha Dunn
Feb 4, 1858
Nov 9, 1910

Nettie Evans
1862-1936

W. T. Minor
May 1, 1874
Aug 9, 1930

Julia Minor
1876-1939

T. O. Knox
(no dates)
(Pulaski FH)

Ben H. Hardin
Aug 31, 1883
Feb 9, 1951
&
Lena L. Hardin
Feb 22, 1882

Mary B. Hardin
1842-1927

Jim Hardin
1914

Rufus Hardin
1862-1909

Charlie Hardin
(no dates)

Infant of
Mr. & Mrs. Tom Hardin
(no dates)

Edna Hardin
(no dates)

Loggie Hardin
(no dates)

Thomas Frank Jester
1886-1957
&
Fannie Phillips Jester
1888-

Annie Cornelia Jester
1913-1919

Miss Jennie Smith *
died at the home of her
Uncle, Esq. J. F. Smith,
Oct 23, 1910
Age: 45 years.

A. C. James *
Died Jan 22, 1896
Age: 75y, 9m, 21d.

DELLROSE QUADRANGLE

Ida Pure Murrah *
Died Aug 15, 1905
Age: 22 years.

Mrs. Catharine,* wife of
Denham Bills
Died Oct 10, 1902
Age: 70 years.

R. T. Thompson *
Died Jun 14, 1904
Age: 52 years.

Mrs. Mary E.,* wife of
J. R. McCool
Died Mar 8, 1900
Age: 50 years.

* *

CEMETERY

LOCATION: Three fourth mile SE of Kelly Creek Church on the north side of Baugh road on side of hill.

Herbert B. Hamilton
May 4, 1899
Jun 18, 1900

T. B.
(no dates, fieldstone)

J. B.
(no dates, fieldstone)

F. B.
(no dates, fieldstone)

Several unmarked graves.

S. B.
(no dates, fieldstone)

K. Y.
(no dates, fieldstone)

X. Y.
(no dates, fieldstone)

Members of the Hoosier family are buried here.

* *

ANDERSON CEMETERY

LOCATION: One-half mile south of Kelly Creek Church and south of Baugh road and Kellys Creek, on hill.

Thomas J. Anderson
Mar 14, 1805
Feb 15, 1858

2 graves with fieldstones, no inscriptions.

* *

EWING CEMETERY

LOCATION: In the forks of New Grove-Baugh Roads, north side of Kelly Creek, on Philpot Farm.

Joshua Ewing
Oct 16, 1773
Jun 27, 1847

Mary, wife of
Joshua Ewing
Jul 12, 1788
Oct 8, 1864

W. D. Ewing
Nov 27, 1812
Jul 12, 1853

Mary E., Daughter of
R. C. & Rebecca J. Ewing
Nov 16, 1856
Oct 6, 1858

J. K. P. Wallace
Co E 8th Tenn.
Sep 24, 1840
Oct 9, 1903
   C.S.A.

About 20 unmarked graves.

James Porter Ewing, M.D.
Aug 6, 1829
Mar 31, 1856

Rebecca Jane Ewing
Nov 23, 1825
Oct 18, 1866

John M. Ewing
Nov 15, 1818
Sep 26, 1852

George G. Ewing
Jan 24, 1852
Mar 15, 1853

Franklin Philpott
Died Apr 17, 1909
Age: 78y, 7m.
     &
Druzilla J. Philpott
Died Jul 27, 1902
Age: 78y, 1m, 18d.

F. E., wife of
T. P. Paysinger
Apr 25, 1848
Nov 30, 1870

W. B. E.
(no dates, fieldstone)

Elizabeth, wife of
Rev. Robert D. Hardin &
Daughter of
Joshua & Mary Ewing
Jun 11, 1822
Apr 12, 1855

Mary Alice, Daughter of
Rev. Robert D. & Eliza M.
Hardin
Jul 11, 1854
May 25, 1855

Hugh E., Son of
J. B. & E. P. Morell
1854-1860
     &
Fannie, Daughter of
J. B. & E. P. Murell
1851-1857

H. E. M.
(no dates, fieldstone)

M. F. M.
(no dates, fieldstone)

Fines H. Brown
Jun 3, 1834
Feb 17, 1862

Margaret E. Brown
Jun 11, 1841
Aug 12, 1861

Mariah Ann Brown
Feb 25, 1839
Aug 24, 1857

Joshua D. Brown
Aug 17, 1804
Jul 3, 1852

Mary E. Brown
Oct 31, 1831
Jul 12, 1854

Ellanor, wife of
J. D. Brown & Daughter of
J. & M. Ewing
Oct 13, 1806
Oct 1, 1845

* *

DELLROSE QUADRANGLE

MERRELL CEMETERY

LOCATION: At the forks of Old Blanch-Kelly Creek Roads on the north side of Kelly Creek.

George Reed Apr 3, 1810 Jun 17, 1893 Cyntha C., wife of George Reed Dec 11, 1820 Jun 24, 1891	J. S. Merrell Mar 8, 1839 Mar 23, 1914 & wife Louisa J. Merrell Jul 22, 1843 married Dec 11, 1860 died Aug 29, 1900	Mollie B., Daughter of J. S. & L. J. Merrell Jun 20, 1875 May 17, 1891 Martha E., wife of A. J. Smith Aug 2, 1862 Oct 19, 1879	Infant Son of P. L. & C. J. Hall Dec 10, 1893 Feb 28, 1894 Several unmarked graves.

* *

BLEDSOE CEMETERY

LOCATION: One and three-fourth miles NW of Cash Point at the head of Bledsoe Hollow in the woods.

H. M. Bledsoe
Feb 26, 1813
Feb 19, 1877
   & wife
Matilda Bledsoe
Apr 12, 1820
Mar 26, 1860
 	
R. L. Bledsoe
Jan 27, 1880
Jun 8, 1901
	S. W. Bledsoe
	Dec 30, 1818
	Nov 18, 1856
	   & wife
	M. N., wife of
	S. W. Bledsoe & E. McKiney
	Feb 11, 1823
	Apr 1, 1900
		W. C. Burford
		Jul 23, 1812
		Nov 17, 1889
		&
		Mary M., wife of
		W. C. Burford
		Aug 6, 1816
		Dec 12, 1885
		
		Infant Son of
		L. J. & Mary E. Bledsoe
		Feb 23, 1875
		Feb 27, 1875
			Mary E., wife of
			L. J. Bledsoe
			May 11, 1852
			Feb 18, 1900
			
			Francies E., wife of
			L. J. Bledsoe
			Jan 12, 1844
			Oct 18, 1873
			
			Infant Son of
			L. J. & Mary E. Bledsoe
			(no dates)

* *

SMITH CEMETERY

LOCATION: Two miles NW of Cash Point on the Giles County line.

J. P. Whaley Aug 25, 1865 Jan 23, 1900 & J. M. Whaley Jan 18, 1888 Jul 7, 1889 Simeon Whitt Dec 2, 1857 Nov 10, 1897 Minnie V., wife of S. E. Whitt Sep 13, 1863 Oct 1, 1890 L. M. Whitt Jun 26, 1879 Sep 22, 1895 (broken) Eliza A., wife of S. E. Whitt Feb 15, 1860 Jan 23, 1885 S. P. Smith Oct 24, 1847 Mar 20, 1893	Ephraim D. Whitt Apr 19, 1820 Mar 5, 1888 Sallie, wife of Ephraim D. Whitt Died Feb 17, 1898 Age: (no age given) E. A. Whitt Nov 27, 1861 Apr 9, 1884 married Jul 10, 1879 Infant Daughter of Bob & Ruth Whitt B&D Jul 8, 1916 (no name) C.S.A. Star Marker 1861-1865 Deo. Vindice J. E. Bolton Mar 12, 1852 Jul 6, 1923	Delany Bolton Jan 21, 1826 Sep 19, 1900 & Richard Bolton Jun 23, 1847 Jul 17, 1891 W. S. Bolton Feb 20, 1844 Jun 26, 1911 J. S. Matlock Sep 25, 1825 Oct 2, 1887 & wife Adaline Matlock Apr 12, 1833 Aug 11, 1918 J. H. Lewter Oct 14, 1836 Mar 28, 1918 Nancy A., wife of J. H. Lewter Feb 3, 1834 Jan 17, 1921	M. C. Lewter Apr 6, 1843 Feb 23, 1917 W. J. Rodgers Mar 15, 1338 Oct 18, 1895 Martin Buckner Rodgers May 10, 1863 Oct 12, 1886 O. C. Smith Apr 25, 1846 Apr 4, 1895 W. M. Smith May 10, 1847 Jun 9, 1919 R. C. Smith Jun 1, 1810 Mar 13, 1884 Nancy, wife of R. C. Smith Jan 1, 1805 Dec 23, 1889

DELLROSE QUADRANGLE

A. W. Matlock
Feb 24, 1866
Mar 2, 1930

S. M. Moore
Mar 7, 1862
Apr 11, 1906

Simeon Whitt
Dec 2, 1857
Nov 10, 1897

Florence B. Whitt
Jul 1, 1890
Mar 5, 1891

Mrs. Mattie,* wife of
James Luna & Daughter of
W. J. McAlister
Died Feb 13, 1908
Age: 33 years.

J. P. Whaley
Aug 25, 1865
Jan 23, 1900
&
J. M. Whaley
Jan 18, 1838
Jul 7, 1889

Many unmarked graves.

Laura Ada,* Daughter of
W. R. Rodgers
Died Sep 6, 1895
Age: 18 years.

Ada,* Daughter of
W. J. Rodgers, dec'd
Died Oct 26, 1895
Age: 18 years.

* *

MALONE CEMETERY

LOCATION: One and three-fourth miles NW of Cash Point.

Minnie L., Daughter of
G. W. & M. J. Whitt
Dec 26, 1897
Jan 5, 1903

Lawrence S., Son of
A. R. & R. Currin
Oct 16, 1914
Mar 23, 1915

John C. Campbell
Feb 12, 1854
Sep 3, 1923
&
Jane Campbell
Dec 25, 1862
Jul 14, 1962

Hugh M. Campbell
May 2, 1889
Dec 15, 1926

James Glen Wilson
Jan 9, 1924
May 29, 1927

James Wilson
Jan 1, 1883
Feb 13, 1932

Thomas Dillard, Son of
J. T. & Mary Smith
Jun 15, 1919
Sep 7, 1920

Myra Smith
Feb 2, 1915
Jul 30, 1915
&
Marvis Smith
Feb 24, 1918
Mar 8, 1918

4 graves, Smith
Children of
D. W. & E. P. Smith
(no dates)

Dee Wilson Smith
Jan 27, 1885
Dec 5, 1943
&
Emma Pearl Smith
Jul 26, 1888
Jul 17, 1947

Thomas L. Smith
Nov 22, 1929
Nov 17, 1964

Thomas L. Price
Dec 25, 1891
Aug 14, 1943

Synthia J. Smith
Mar 26, 1886
Mar 28, 1942

Namogene Price
1934-1936

Knox R. Price
Sep 23, 1894
Mar 30, 1929

W. C. Malone
1906-1939
&
Ada Malone
1907-1944

Nina Mae Price
Nov 22, 1900
Aug 4, 1939

A. W. C.
(no dates, fieldstone)

A. Jasper Broadway
Sep 25, 1854
Aug 20, 1927
&
Sarah Jane Broadway
Jan 15, 1857
Mar 21, 1924

Fannie Rogers
Dec 4, 1856
Aug 23, 1944

Aline, wife of
Otha Dunnavant
Feb 21, 1912
Oct 20, 1931

A. W. George
Mar 12, 1878
Sep 24, 1926

E. Alice George
Sep 23, 1881
Jul 25, 1968

Infant Son of
Paul & Pearl Mitchell
Jan 15, 1918
Jan 17, 1918

Horace L. Whitt
1873-1942
&
Beulah D. Whitt
1873-1933

Infant Son of
H. L. & Beulah Whitt
B&D May 12, 1917

Mahlon, Son of
Mr. & Mrs. H. L. Whitt
Dec 18, 1906
Jul 26, 1929

A. J. Whitt
May 6, 1875
Nov 26, 1933
&
D. M. Whitt
Aug 24, 1884

Sallie Smith
1848-1918

Sherman Whitt
May 13, 1900
Jul 2, 1924

Alma Ozelle Whitt
Mar 9, 1902
Apr 17, 1928

Elsie, Son of
A. J. & D. M. Whitt
Jan 6, 1913
Sep 16, 1913

G. S. Whitt
1864-1940

Ada C. Whitt
1869-1914

James A., Son of
W. R. & G. T. Campbell
Feb 15, 1916
Jun 7, 1917

W. H. Broadway
Jul 17, 1878
Apr 21, 1921

Ida M. Broadway
Apr 29, 1876
Nov 27, 1946

Flossie L., Daughter of
W. H. & I. M. Broadway
Aug 5, 1911
Feb 2, 1913

Willard Spencer Rogers
1909

George A. Holman
1874-1921
&
Mary Jane Holman
1888-1934

Laban, Son of
G. A. & M. J. Holman
Feb 21, 1906
Sep 9, 1909

DELLROSE QUADRANGLE

Samie L. George
Jun 16, 1902
Jul 26, 1933

James M. George
Apr 23, 1915
May 22, 1916

Amy A. Merrill
Jul 20, 1832
May 9, 1902

Henry L. Lewter
Oct 19, 1855
Feb 20, 1942
&
Calline Lewter
May 31, 1859
Jan 20, 1936

Infant Son of
G. S. & Ada A. Whitt
Nov 10, 1901

Purine Beatrice, Daughter of
G. S. & A. A. Whitt
Jul 21, 1898
Nov 14, 1899

John W. Whitt
Jan 1, 1816
Aug 4, 1899

Mary, wife of
John W. Whitt
Oct 11, 1830
Oct 17, 1912

James Hargrove
Aug 15, 1876
Oct 29, 1902

Bettie Hargrove, wife of
J. T. Hamilton
Aug 12, 1865
Apr 15, 1905

Elizabeth, Daughter of
M. L. & Effie Whitt
Mar 8, 1914
Mar 16, 1914

H. T. Bolton
May 7, 1858
Apr 14, 1943

Sallie Hargrove, wife of
H. T. Bolton
Jan 7, 1871
Aug 18, 1908
&
Charlie A. Bolton
Feb 28, 1906
Apr 22, 1927

Alice Brown
Aug 17, 1856
Feb 10, 1934

William Austin
1872-1944

Flora Austin
1876-1947

J. A. Hargrove
Jan 31, 1844
Jul 2, 1919

Dora H. Griffin
Mar 7, 1876
Nov 30, 1928

Infants of
A. R. & J. M. Merrell
Apr 9, 1889
Vera M.
Died Apr 18, 1889

Hermann Ray, Son of
A. R. & J. M. Merrell
Died Jan 31, 1890
Age: 1m, 20d.

Joe Stacy Merrell
Jan 3, 1884
Jun 18, 1884

Infant Son of
G. W. & M. C. Merrell
Aug 5, 1873
Aug 14, 1873

Martha C. Smith
Aug 19, 1855
Feb 24, 1882

Infant Daughter of
G. W. & M. C. Merrell
Oct 27, 1866
Nov 11, 1866

Garrett Merrell
1798-Dec 22, 1865

Rebecca E., wife of
F. F. Tilery
Mar 17, 1858
Apr 7, 1876

Ollive, wife of
Garrett Merrell
1800-1849

Louisa F., wife of
N. Smith
Nov 1, 1833
May 13, 1862

Susan A., Daughter of
N. & L. F. Smith
Nov 11, 1858
Dec 2, 1868

Susan, wife of
John R. Carter
Nov 10, 1837
Jul 4, 1862

Nancy, Consort of
Joseph Roper
Feb 15, 1823
married Feb 15, 1844
Jun 30, 1852

Mrs. C. S. Fisk
1867-1937

J. J. & J. S., Sons of
J. J. Malone
Jan 7, 1884
Jan 11, 1884
Age: 4 days old

Jack Malone
1897-1949

Martha, Daughter of
J. J. Malone
Jul 15, 1881
Mar 3, 1883

Malinda E., wife of
J. C. Malone
Mar 14, 1824
Apr 7, 1884

E. D. T. (Infant)
1896 (fieldstone)

Infant
1901 (fieldstone)

J. E. Malone
Aug 9, 1845
Sep 27, 1902

Martha Blackshire, wife of
J. E. Malone
Dec 2, 1844
Jan 21, 1924

Edd Thornton
1872-1914
&
Sallie Malone Thornton
1873-1938

Frances T. Davis
Jul 14, 1892
Jan 15, 1916

Mary Ida, Daughter of
J. C. & M. W. Malone
Oct 12, 1898
Jan 6, 1899

John Calvin, Son of
J. C. & M. W. Malone
Jun 8, 1900
Oct 15, 1902

Infant Son of
J. C. & M. W. Malone
Jan 3, 1903
Jan 17, 1903

Emma Sue, Daughter of
J. C. & M. W. Malone
Sep 27, 1914
Nov 28, 1914

J. C., Jr., Son of
J. C. & M. W. Malone
Mar 9, 1922
Jul 21, 1922

J. C. Malone
Nov 3, 1876
Jan 9, 1943
&
Mary Willie Malone
Sep 13, 1878
(no date)

Bettie J. Armstrong
1834-1918

Vernon S. Thornton
Feb 15, 1929
Mar 21, 1929

Bettie Dean Thornton
May 18, 1939
May 13, 1951

Foster S. Thornton
Jan 23, 1901

&
Zellie Thornton
Feb 12, 1900
Oct 2, 1965

R. L. Lewter
Dec 11, 1880
Dec 18, 1918

Millie Malone Lewter
Feb 6, 1882
Aug 9, 1962

T. J. Lewter
Apr 22, 1884
Jun 22, 1942

Mary E. Malone, wife of
T. J. Lewter
1864-1939

J. E. Malone
1884-1949

J. G. Fowler
Jun 27, 1844
Dec 15, 1900
&
Eliza E. Fowler
Jan 13, 1848
May 29, 1899

George D., Son of
T. J. G. & Eliza E. Fowler
Jul 25, 1866
Oct 20, 1883

Calvin Brice Reeves
1889-1962
&
Mattie Mitchell Reeves
1892-1948

DELLROSE QUADRANGLE

John D. Collins
1921-1934

Estell Collins
1895-1922

Amanda M., wife of
Henry Hamilton
Jun 4, 1843
Jan 2, 1904

Son of
J. D. & E. Hamilton
Jan 27, 1902
Mar 27, 1902

Myrtle Odell, Daughter of
J. D. & E. Hamilton
Feb 2, 1903
Dec 12, 1903

Grodon Holman
1881-1940

Emma Holman
1877-1948

Ruby Holman
1921-1941

Josephine Holman
1940-1942

Robert, Son of
J. H. & C. M. Elliott
Nov 8, 1914
Dec 13, 1917

Robert Windel, Son of
O. F. & C. B. Ferguson
Sep 21, 1909
Jan 16, 1912

James H. Hobb
Oct 13, 1934
Sep 9, 1957
&
Deverle Smith Hobb
Oct 11, 1939

Luther J. Roper
1886-1952
&
Vinnie L. Roper
1884-1933

Mary Lena Dotson
Apr 5, 1894
Apr 3, 1957

C. M. Burns
1881-1959

Zella Burns
1921-1923

Elizabeth Tribble
1874-1946

Mary M. Mitchell, wife of
L. T. Bradford
Mar 12, 1857
(date gone)

Jake Bradford
1882-1952

Ola Toone
1899-1939

Jesse A. Mitchell
Mar 7, 1892
Feb 2, 1928

Garland Vickers
1911-1954
&
Dimple Vickers
1913-19

A. T. Vickers
1867-1940

Bettie Vickers
1872-1949

G. W. Vickers
1910-1954

Jessie Allen Collins
1904-
&
Carrie Thornton Collins
1905-1942

Rachel Collins
Mar 29, 1860
Apr 23, 1943

William E. Elmore
Jan 20, 1915
Aug 13, 1944

William Levon, Son of
W. E. & Miriam Elmore
Aug 31, 1936
Sep 13, 1936

Gilbert R., Son of
G. G. & Rosie Malone
Nov 22, 1932
Nov 28, 1932

Tom P. Vickers
1904-1946
&
Katie Lou Vickers
1909-

James Calvin, Son of
R. D. Malone
Oct 6, 1879
Feb 1, 1893

Jack Malone
1897-1949

George Jones
1859-1929

Oscar Dale Billions
Aug 5, 1928
Aug 6, 1928

Lewis Hargrave
Jun 10, 1874
Jan 16, 1943
&
Jennie Hargrave
Jun 27, 1875
Jul 24, 1922

Maxine Hargrave
Mar 13, 1919
Oct 19, 1933

A. W. Lewter
Apr 24, 1882
Jul 18, 1934

Nealy, Daughter of
A. W. & Esta Lewter
Aug 3, 1923
Dec 21, 1924

Doris Irene Lewter
Mar 29, 1926
Oct 7, 1926

Martin Eugene Lewter
Died Dec 1, 1867
Age: 57 years.

Lizzie Sims
1890-1955

Andrew Lewter
Mar 5, 1876
Aug 5, 1948
&
Nancy Ann Lewter
Oct 27, 1874
Mar 15, 1918

Earnest K. Smith
1910-1954
&
Etolia I. Smith
1911-

Delna Smith O'Neal
1903-1926

S. E., Jr., Son of
S. E. & Alma Hall
Sep 21, 1928

R. A. Smith
Sep 2, 1910
Dec 26, 1911

Infant Son of
W. F. & E. M. Smith
Aug 5, 1903

Lonza L. Smith
Dec 11, 1897
May 26, 1900

H. B. "Bud" Merrell
1860-1883

J. M. Smith
Feb 25, 1869
Jan 28, 1962

Ada Smith
Aug 20, 1874
May 28, 1909

Mary Mitchell
1923-1923

Jean Mitchell
1933-1933

John D. Smith
Jul 1, 1905

&
Myrtle Virginia Smith
Aug 5, 1909
Jul 16, 1968

Mattie Smith
1881-1958

Raymond Smith
1913-1952

Charlie Smith
1872-1940

W. C., Son of
W. P. & J. B. Smith
Sep 4, 1905
Mar 18, 1907

Charlie Smith
1872-1940
&
Belle Smith
1878-19

Nelson Smith
Jan 6, 1839
May 9, 1924
&
M. J. Smith
Jul 6, 1840
(no date)

Infant of
Mr. & Mrs. Edward Teeples
Aug 2, 1929

Ida, wife of
J. F. Lewter
Sep 14, 1895
Mar 14, 1920

Frank Smith
1875-
&
Lizzie Smith
1878-1961

Harvell Smith
Oct 12, 1909
Apr 30, 1910

Melvin Smith
Sep 4, 1905
Dec 2, 1907

DELLROSE QUADRANGLE

Bessie Jones
1904-1928

Linda Jones
Died Jul 15, 1926
Age: 75 years.

Marjorie Lou Jones
Jan 8, 1930
Jul 5, 1933

Virginia Muriel Jones
Jul 8, 1931
Aug 30, 1934

Hershel Medley
1910-1935

T. D. Griffin
1881-1951

Emma Griffin
1888-1957

D. Lynn Dugger
Sep 8, 1968
Dec 29, 1968

James Anderson
Alabama
WW I
Oct 11, 1895
Jul 9, 1948

Betty Anderson
Aug 2, 1884
Dec 9, 1967

Buck Lewter
1863-1955

Clara Sue Lewter
1870-1940

G. W. Merrell
Aug 2, 1843
Dec 26, 1918
&
M. C. A. Merrell
Aug 1, 1839
May 22, 1923

A. R. Merrell
Oct 27, 1866
Aug 22, 1924
&
Mrs. A. R. Merrell
Jul 22, 1867
Aug 30, 1956

Perry L. Hall
Oct 4, 1858
Jul 2, 1927
&
Cynthia J. Hall
Mar 22, 1865
May 6, 1930

Grady B. Hall
1908-1909

John W. Austin
Mar 19, 1908
Apr 26, 1924

Freda Margaret Austin
Jan 17, 1932
Mar 5, 1933

Arsena Austin
1918-1935

Allie Dee Sanderson
Mar 30, 1888
Sep 9, 1930
&
Elizabeth Sanderson
Aug 28, 1894
(no date)

J. D. Sanderson
May 8, 1857
Feb 8, 1926
&
M. A. Sanderson
Nov 14, 1857
Dec 27, 1937

Mirrow June Todd
Oct 25, 1938
Feb 28, 1941

Nathan Merrell
Dec 31, 1892
Dec 22, 1958

Ethel Smith Merrell
Nov 21, 1892
Sep 7, 1939

Stacy Reed, Son of
N. G. & M. E. Merrell
Jul 12, 1915
Feb 3, 1917

Infant Daughter of
N. M. & Ethel Merrell
Oct 13, 1919

Martha Sisk
1920

J. C. Heard
1895-1964

Cordie B. Heard
1894-

Nina D. Thompson
Nov 2, 1873
Jun 6, 1951

Lorene Heard
1919-1953

Darthra Louise, Daughter of
A. W. & Mattie Chandler
Feb 8, 1922
Mar 27, 1923

W. W. Ferguson
Dec 4, 1823
Nov 29, 1911
& wife
Margaret Ferguson
Jan 1, 1834
Nov 29, 1913

Hattie, wife of
J. Robert Smith
Oct 23, 1893
Feb 5, 1916

James Robert Smith
Jan 3, 1861
Jun 12, 1911

Sara Lou Tisha Smith
Aug 16, 1859
Sep 1, 1938

Evelyn, Daughter of
Bunyan & Amye Anderson Smith
Oct 1, 1913
Aug 11, 1914

W. F. Smith
Feb 3, 1841
Dec 6, 1938
&
Myria M. Smith
Jul 8, 1841
Oct 26, 1926

M. P., Daughter of
W. F. & M. M. Smith
Aug 30, 1880
Aug 14, 1896

A. J., Son of
W. F. & M. M. Smith
Jan 4, 1871
Mar 5, 1894

M. F., Son of
W. F. & M. M. Smith
Apr 15, 1878
Mar 1, 1894

William D. Mullins
1865-1924
&
Dora E. Mullins
1866-1956

Margaret F. Treece
Oct 30, 1934
Jun 13, 1937

Alma M., Daughter of
Mr. & Mrs. A. H. Treece
Aug 31, 1926
Dec 31, 1928

Will Collins
1886-1965

Annie B. Collins
1901-1953

Infant Son (Smith)
Died Oct 27, 1865
Age: 1 week.

Lula E. Smith
Died Dec 23, 1879
Age: 3y, 2m, 16d.

Nathan F. Smith
Died Mar 5, 1883
Age: 3m, 1d.

J. D. Ferguson
Jun 27, 1862
Jul 17, 1893

M. P. Ferguson
Sep 18, 1866
Mar 4, 1894

R. W. Ferguson
Oct 25, 1886
Mar 7, 1894

Trudelle, Daughter of
J. R. & M. L. Smith
Died Sep 1, 1895
Age: 13y, 8m, 27d.

John S. Ferguson
1869-1936
&
Janie Ferguson
1870-19(no date)

C. S. Ferguson
Sep 13, 1867
(no date)
&
Louisiana Ferguson
Aug 12, 1867
Oct 28, 1936
&
Nina Bell Ferguson
1908-1938

W. Elbert Mullins
Mar 11, 1904
Apr 29, 1957
&
Mary Jane Mullins
Apr 30, 1910
Mar 22, 1960

Clayton D. Mullins
1934-

Charles D. Mullins
1932

Thurman Wilson Smith
Apr 16, 1911
Jul 27, 1939

James Cletice Collins
May 28, 1934
Jan 20, 1945

DELLROSE QUADRANGLE

James Marion, Son of
R. W. & Velma Chandler
Apr 22, 1919
Sep 31, 1919

Albert L. Scott
1890-1963

Rev. H. Con Smith
1850-1923
&
Harriett C. Smith
1852-1923

Many unmarked graves.

William A. Smith
Jun 15, 1856
Oct 15, 1938
&
Susan C. Smith
Oct 7, 1861
May 3, 1937

John E. Malone
Feb 13, 1884
May 5, 1949
&
Beatrice S. Malone
Feb 29, 1882
(no date)

* *

CORPIER CEMETERY

LOCATION: One and one-fourth miles NW of Cash Point on south side of road.

A. L. Corpier
Mar 4, 1844
Jan 23, 1900

Mary M., Wife of
A. L. Corpier
Sep 18, 1857
Apr 22, 1904

John H. Corpier
Aug 28, 1876
Jan 14, 1946

Lura Moore Parks
Died Aug 31, 1962
Age: 71y, 10m, 15d.

Emmitt O. Smith
Jun 22, 1876
Apr 18, 1957
&
Fannie P. Smith
Dec 28, 1881
Jan 4, 1957

W. Lamacie, Son of
E. O. & F. P. Smith
Jan 21, 1913
Jan 1, 1914

3 unmarked graves.

* *

CROSS CEMETERY

LOCATION: One and one-half miles SW of Blanch and three-fourth mile north of Ardmore Highway.

Lou Hargrave
1879-1960
&
B. A. Hargrave
1861-1936
&
Alice Hargrave
1866-1900

Callie A. Z. Hargrave
Dec 6, 1918
Jun 7, 1925

Lofton Hargrave
Oct 17, 1902
Aug 5, 1903

Infant Daughter of
B. A. & N. L. Hargrave
Jun 22, 1901
Jul 9, 1901

Infant Son of
B. A. & A. A. Hargrave
Sep 8, 1885

Emmer E. Hargrave
Jul 12, 1883
Aug 13, 1884

F. C. Cross
1884-1957
&
Georgia Cross
1886-1930

Lucile, Daughter of
Mr. & Mrs. F. C. Cross
B&D Mar 23, 1907

R. C. Cross
1837-1938

Several unmarked graves.

Brackin Roper
Jan 31, 1800
Sep 25, 1866

Emmoline Roper
Jun 21, 1826
Sep 21, 1914

Carl C. Cross
Jan 20, 1896
Apr 27, 1963
&
Willie B. Cross
Sep 25, 1897
Mar 31, 1958

Herbert Ray Cross
1940-1943

Hilda Murrell, Daughter of
C. C. & W. B. Cross
Dec 21, 1920
Sep 15, 1922

F. M. Cross
Jan 20, 1842
Mar 20, 1897

Permilla F., wife of
F. M. Cross
Oct 17, 1846
Nov 13, 1915

Mathew Cross
Mar 23, 1869
Feb 14, 1895

Ellen, Daughter of
M. & L. Cross
Feb 10, 1894
May 4, 1895

Lillie May Bond
Aug 15, 1906
Dec 13, 1931
&
Infant Bond
B&D Nov 14, 1922

* *

BLANCHE CEMETERY (Old Section)

LOCATION: At Blanche, Tennessee.

G. M. Riley
Dec 21, 1849
Jan 22, 1926

Margaret R., wife of
G. M. Riley
Sep 27, 1850
Dec 18, 1900

Lois Riley
Aug 21, 1876
Nov 26, 1941

Bertha, Daughter of
J. W. & M. E. Stovall
Mar 11, 1900
Aug 10, 1902

Florence, Daughter of
J. W. & M. E. Stovall
Feb 27, 1898
Oct 1, 1901

Wesley Stovall
Jan 15, 1912
Sep 29, 1929

Mary Olevie Stovall
Oct 23, 1872
Oct 14, 1900

DELLROSE QUADRANGLE

John J. Stovall
Jun 28, 1861
Sep 29, 1926

Myrtle Stovall
Jul 23, 1878
Apr 20, 1939

James Billings
Co K 13 Tenn Cav
   C.S.A.

M. G., wife of
J. M. Billions
Jan 8, 1849
Oct 25, 1899

C. C. Faulkinberry
Oct 12, 1855
May 21, 1923

Sarah E. Caple, wife of
C. C. Faulkinberry
Jan 19, 1853
Feb 20, 1928

Andrew Bryce, Son of
C. C. & S. E. Faulkinberry
Aug 3, 1890
Dec 12, 1892

Jacob Faulkinberry
Nov 6, 1809
Nob 6, 1872

Rebekah Faulkinberry
May 16, 1801
Mar 13, 1889

J. M. Faulkinberry
Mar 19, 1855
Mar 22, 1920

Infant Children of
J. M. Faulkinberry
"Here we lie in a roe".

W. Marion Williams
Jun 15, 1828
Oct 1, 1876

Jane E., wife of
W. M. Williams
Oct 27, 1827
Mar 16, 1889

John R. Franklin
Sep 18, 1849
Aug 20, 1883

Z. T. Faulkinberry
May 18, 1846
May 18, 1892
Age: 46 years.

Claude B. Brock
Oct 31, 1880
May 7, 1935

W. R. Faulkinberry
Nov 8, 1831
Jun 15, 1912

Jane, wife of
W. R. Faulkinberry
Sep 19, 1828
Jun 17, 1896

Elizabeth Hicklen
Nov 20, 1844
Feb 14, 1910

Howard B. Stalcup
Jun 15, 1908
Oct 17, 1925

Newton Combs
Dec 30, 1824
Jun 7, 1892

J. N. Combs
Aug 10, 1862
Aug 8, 1921

Lucinda F. Combs
Mar 7, 1887
Jan 18, 1904

J. Y. McDaniel
Feb 21, 1840
Oct 13, 1906
&
Mary J. McDaniel
Mar 31, 1843
Oct 23, 1883

Lidia Smith
Oct 12, 1821
Oct 15, 1887

Lillie Dale Hinton
Aug 25, 1880
Oct 5, 1946

Florence V., Daughter of
L. R(S). & M. V. Freeman
Aug 1, 1866
Oct 14, 1887

Dr. L. S. Freeman
Jun 12, 1834
Aug 12, 1903

Margaret V., wife of
Dr. L. S. Freeman
Mar 28, 1834
Jul 19, 1898

Nancy Bates
1833-1915

Illie H., wife of
Rev. W. J. Brown
Jan 1, 1836
Apr 13, 1889

Infant Sons of
John & Minnie Faulkinberry
B&D Jan 4, 1901

Mary V. Brock Porter
Oct 9, 1883
Nov 26, 1967

Myrtle Brock
Feb 4, 1882
Jul 19, 1928

Dr. B. B. Brock
Jun 12, 1851
Aug 9, 1922

Mary L., wife of
Dr. B. B. Brock
Sep 9, 1854
Jan 13, 1891

Nannie, wife of
B. B. Brock
Jul 17, 1863
Feb 14, 1939

Infant Son of
C. B. & Mary L. Brock
B&D Jun 26, 1914

Infant Son of
Dr. B. B. & M. L. Brock
B&D Jan 10, 1891

Infant Daughter of
J. M. J. & F. M. Faulkinberry
B&D Aug 17, 1905

Dr. S. J. McLaughlin
Apr 13, 1852
Nov 27, 1889

M. G. Bryan
Dec 2, 1860
Nov 10, 1927
&
Mary E. Poole Bryan
Dec 19, 1874
May 18, 1936

J. H. Locke
Mar 26, 1865
Sep 24, 1950
&
Viria Locke
Apr 27, 1859
Mar 15, 1926

J. E. Locke
1859-1939

Lawrence E. Locke
Alabama
Pvt U.S.Army   WW I
Jan 19, 1895
Apr 30, 1962

Mrs. Flora _____(name gone)
Died Apr --, --- (date gone)
Age: 73 years.
(Ralston FH)

E. E. Clem
Dec 9, 1859
Nov 16, 1897

Lula Faulkinberry, wife of
E. E. Clem
Aug 24, 1876
Oct 27, 1900

John A. Poole
Apr 29, 1840
Aug 16, 1927
&
Martha J. Poole
Dec 27, 1845
Dec 14, 1909

William A. Poole
Jan 14, 1876
Aug 10, 1895

Father
J. T. Griffin
1864-1943
&
Mother
Nancy A. Griffin
1854-1905
& Daughter
Myrtle L. Griffin
1882-1893

Katie B. Jobe
Sep 29, 1890
Nov 17, 1892
&
Annie S. Jobe
Apr 10, 1902
Jun 8, 1903

William T. Franklin,
Father of
Bennie R. Franklin
Sep 26, 1852
Jun 6, 1900

Mary Susan, wife of
G. L. Putman
Oct 4, 1861
Oct 31, 1898

Palatine B., Daughter of
G. L. & M. S. Putman
Died Nov 22, 1898
Age: 1m, 10d.

Ida Mae George
Nov 9, 1866
Dec 25, 1947

W. L. Rhodes
1852-1936
&
Nancy Rhodes
1856-1935

Nancy May, Daughter of
F. J. & Retha Dever
Jun 30, 1898
Aug 26, 1899

DELLROSE QUADRANGLE

Hardy McCown
1847-1925
&
Delia McCown
1849-1898

Walter J. Owens
1870-1942
&
Lula M. Owens
1873-1956

Rev. William D. Owen
1899-

Mary M. Owen
1899-

M. B. McLemore
Died Jun 9, 1911
Age: 78y, 9m.
& wife
Iris B. D. Winsett McLemore
Nov 18, 1827
(no date)

Eudela, Daughter of
M. B. & S. R. McLemore
Jul 7, 1907
Feb 2, 1912

Brice McLemore
1865-1928
&
Sallie McLemore
1875-1956

Richard H. McLemore
Jun 11, 1859
May 1, 1924
&
Ellie L. McLemore
May 2, 1871
Nov 19, 1939

Estella Pearl, Daughter of
R. H. & L. E. McLemore
Jul 2, 1899
Feb 28, 1915

Deray E., Daughter of
R. H. & L. E. McLemore
Aug 4, 1894
Aug 21, 1897

Jimmie Anderson Coats
May 25, 1896
Sep 26, 1899
&
Eddie Lee Coats
May 30, 1885
Jun 6, 1887
"Sons of J. J. &
Millie Coats".

Jessie J. Coats
1861-1917
&
N. Willie Coats
1866-1939

Judie, Daughter of
J. B. & S. E. Coats
Feb 13, 1869
Apr 27, 1877

Lewis Coats
Nov 22, 1819
May 6, 1903
"erected by Mrs. D. A.
 Sparkman."

Mary, wife of
Lewis Coats
Died Oct 20, 1899
Age: 75 years.

Tennie, Daughter of
Lewis & Mary Coats
Feb 15, 1866
Mar 2, 1894
Age: 28y, 15d.

William E. Simms
Oct 14, 1811
Apr 11, 1887

Malinda G., wife of
William E. Simms
Aug 21, 1816
Mar 24, 1896

Susan H., wife of
C. T. Simms
Jan 4, 1844
Feb 13, 1880

Margaret J., wife of
G. W. Johnson
Jan 12, 1851
Aug 22, 1920

Flora Bessie, Daughter of
H. H. & W. B. Smith
Nov 19, 1886
Sep 11, 1887

Lizzie Klugh, Daughter of
H. H. & W. B. Smith
Aug 28, 1885
Oct 27, 1887

Mary, Daughter of
H. H. & W. B. Smith
Dec 25, 1891
Mar 8, 1910

Cora May Smith
Jul 11, 1880
Nov 14, 1920

George M. Smith
Nov 4, 1871
May 16, 1948

Nola Smith
Sep 9, 1889

Evelyn McLemore Hosse
Sep 2, 1916
Dec 9, 1949

Fred, Son of
G. M. & Cora Smith
Aug 8, 1914
Apr 2, 1920

Infant Son of
G. M. & Cora Smith
Aug 8, 1914
Apr 2, 1920

Infant Son of
G. M. & Cora Smith
Nov 12, 1901
Nov 15, 1901

Nellie, Daughter of
G. M. & Cora Smith
Sep 20, 1908
Sep 23, 1909

Prof. J. A. Holland
Mar 1, 1836
Mar 17, 1907
Age: 71y, 16d.

Ella E. Dunnavant, wife of
J. A. Holland
Nov 11, 1845
May 20, 1897

J. Bunyan Holland
Dec 10, 1874
Jul 9, 1893

M. C. Forbes
Mar 20, 1827
Jan 30, 1883

E. Jane, wife of
M. C. Forbes
Sep 4, 1826
Dec 24, 1895

William Petty Forbes
1851-1914
&
Ella Philpot Forbes
1853-1939

Hallena L. Blair
18-- - 1914 (date gone)

Maggie E., Daughter of
J. H. & H. L. Blair
Died Jun 1, 1883
Age: 1y, 8m.

W. T. Blair
1870-1941

Eula Blair
1874-1940

John F. Steadman
1874-1933

Mollie Steadman
1870-1952

H. E. Dunnavant
Jul 23, 1820
Professed Religion,1861
Died Feb 23, 1889

Lucinda, wife of
H. E. Dunnavant
Jan 18, 1820
Feb 11, 1904

W. S. Woodard
Jul 19, 1849
Mar 8, 1926

Annie, wife of
W. S. Woodard
Nov 19, 1849
May 21, 1893

Laura, wife of
W. S. Woodard
Dec 7, 1849
Mar 10, 1926

Sarah B. Woodard
Sep 22, 1882
Dec 9, 1958

Ada L. Woodard
Apr 28, 1877
Feb 13, 1965

Moses Clark Woodard
Aug 9, 1868
Sep 10, 1947

Lizzie, wife of
M. C. Woodard
Oct 17, 1873
Oct 11, 1904

W. L. Woodard
Aug 15, 1876
Oct 21, 1917

Lula A. Woodard
1883-1966

Infant Daughter of
W. L. & L. A. Woodard
B&D Feb 19, 1905

James Robert Billions
1871-1924
&
Susie Mae Billions
1873-1918

Cleveland McLemore
Nov 14, 1892
Dec 17, 1962
&
Winnie McLemore
Nov 26, 1897

Elizabeth, Daughter of
J. C. & Winnie McLemore
Nov 6, 1935
Jan 10, 1936

DELLROSE QUADRANGLE

Elaine McLemore Shearron
Oct 8, 1927
Jun 17, 1955

O. G. Smith
1848-1927

Kate V. McDonald, wife of
O. G. Smith
Feb 4, 1868
Jun 2, 1903

Anna Lee, Daughter of
O. G. & Kate Smith
Aug 15, 1899
Nov 28, 1913

Eliza A. Boyce McDonald
1835-1920

C. B. McDonald
1860-1928

Ina Ferguson Wilson
1880-1954

John W., Son of
T. L. & S. E. Ferguson
Jun 24, 1891
Jul 27, 1891

Sarah E., wife of
T. L. Ferguson & Daughter
of J. H. & N. J. Coats
Jul 18, 1857
Oct 26, 1891

T. L. Ferguson
Jun 28, 1857
Feb 3, 1936
&
Lou E. Ferguson
Dec 18, 1875
Mar 27, 1939

Ralph H., Son of
T. L. & S. E. Ferguson
Feb 27, 1889
Jan 14, 1892

Mary E., Daughter of
T. L. & Edie Ferguson
Jun 12, 1893
Jun 25, 1893

Edie F., wife of
T. L. Ferguson & Daughter
of Isaac & Annie Whitt
Jan 4, 1870
Jul 4, 1893

Infant Son of
T. L. & L. E. Ferguson
B&D Feb 14, 1896

Annie Myrl, Daughter of
Mr. & Mrs. T. L. Ferfuson
Nov 21, 1898
Jan 8, 1913

Carl, Son of
T. L. & L. E. Ferguson
Aug 21, 1901
Feb 19, 1918

Fleet, Son of
T. L. & L. E. Ferguson
Jun 2, 1916
Feb 12, 1918

David McCann Taft
Aug 29, 1831
Oct 18, 1910

Francis A. Tafts
Feb 7, 1839
May 7, 1907

P. C. Carpenter
Mar 26, 1852
May 19, 1918

Martha J. Martin, wife of
P. C. Carpenter
Apr 4, 1855
May 1, 1913

Hugh Rawls
Jan 12, 1882
Oct 5, 1963
&
Alma Twitty Rawls
Jul 24, 1885

D. C. Rawls
May 5, 1843
Jan 23, 1917
&
Martha A. McCann Rawls
May 15, 1846
Dec 3, 1923

Martha N., wife of
Whitfield Twitty
May 20, 1810
Jul 4, 1889

John W. Rawls
Dec 22, 1869
Dec 31, 1920

Virgie Twitty, wife of
John W. Rawls
Dec 22, 1874
Nov 9, 1915
 and her children:
Polly, Clay, Fred & Mary.

Mary Rawls
Dec 22, 1901
Nov 16, 1959

Margaret E. Johnson
(no dates)

Cecile Sue Sulser
B&D Jul 12, 1935

Marietta Sulser
B&D Mar 2, 1934

W. W. Twitty
Nov 8, 1848
Oct 7, 1917

Sarah A. E., wife of
W. W. Twitty
Oct 19, 1847
Jan 5, 1883

Annie, wife of
W. W. Twitty
Mar 14, 1856
Aug 18, 1894

Mary L. McDonald, wife of
W. W. Twitty
Nov 23, 1838
Nov 7, 1908

Ellen C., wife of
W. W. Twitty
1870-1936

Pinckney Twitty
Jan 13, 1831
Dec 18, 1888

Mattie F. Thompson, wife of
Pinckney L. Twitty
Jan 15, 1853
Dec 25, 1910

Mary Alice, wife of
T. W. Twitty
Jan 7, 1885
Nov 3, 1906

Alice Rober, wife of
T. W. Twitty & G. S. Whitt
1882-1958

Thomas W., Son of
P. L. & M. F. Twitty
Aug 20, 1880
Jan 1, 1910

Katie M., Daughter of
T. W. & Alice Twitty
Oct 30, 1909
Oct 5, 1912

Horace B. Twitty, Jr.
Jan 9, 1927

Vallie Maude Twitty
Feb 14, 1887
Nov 25, 1899

Mary D. Philpot
Mar 5, 1948
Feb 3, 1954

W. F. Philpot
Jun 22, 1868
Jun 6, 1932
&
Mary Sue Philpot
Sep 25, 1882
Feb 10, 1931

Mattie J. Smith, Daughter
of W. W. & S. A. Twitty
Dec 22, 1871
Apr 28, 1909

Infant Daughter of
W. W. & S. A. Twitty
(no dates)

Charlie G., Son of
W. W. & S. A. Twitty
Jul 18, 1880
Aug 18, 1889

Nellie, Daughter of
T. G. & A. C. Watson
Sep 9, 1896
Jul 9, 1897

S. E. Poston
May 19, 1818
Mar 1, 1895

Mary, wife of
S. E. Poston
Jan 23, 1821
Sep 22, 1897

Dennis Washington Burgess
Jan 26, 1857
Apr 7, 1929

Sarah E. Burgess
Mar 27, 1862
Jan 29, 1928

Nancy E., wife of
John Burgess
Aug 11, 1827
Feb 29, 1908

T. N. Burgess
Jan 27, 1876
Mar 30, 1901

W. W. McDaniel
Oct 12, 1831
May 15, 1903

Susie K. Carpenter, wife
of W. W. McDaniel
Mar 6, 1839
May 6, 1911

Infant Daughter of
W. O. & S. L. McDaniel
B&D Dec 19, 1903

Nellie, Daughter of
W. O. & S. L. McDaniel
Feb 25, 1897
Nov 9, 1904

Warren O. McDaniel
1859-1929
&
Louella Milliken McDaniel
1868-1962

DELLROSE QUADRANGLE

Joel H. Thompson
May 26, 1859
Dec 22, 1927
& Wife
Sarah E. Pepper Thompson
Dec 15, 1862
(no date)

A. D. Cole
Apr 25, 1879
Dec 3, 1940

Maude Thompson, wife of
A. D. Cole
Aug 1, 1887
Mar 18, 1926

Mattie Pearl, Daughter of
J. H. & S. E. Thompson
Dec 8, 1901
Jul 19, 1909

J. Bryson Sanders
Nov 26, 1870
Jan 24, 1905
&
Mary Sanders Cathcart
Feb 13, 1877
Feb 26, 1921

Walter B. McDaniel
Oct 29, 1872
Apr 10, 1926

Vergie, wife of
Walter B. McDaniel
Oct 6, 1831
Nov 29, 1899

Stella, Daughter of
Walter B. & Vergie McDaniel
Jul 31, 1899
Dec 3, 1905

Kate Vickers McDaniel
1878-1936

Bertha B., wife of
J. M. Robertson
Died Feb 23, 1912
Age: 23 years.

Father
_____ Bowling
1852-1931
&
Mother
M. F. B. (Bowling)
1855-1902

Byrum Blair
1875-1940
&
Nora Blair
1880-(no date)

Madeline Blair
May 10, 1905
Aug 14, 1956

Dovie Blair
1915-1919

Morten Blair
1908-1911

Mary Blair
1904-1905

J. W. Williams, M.D.
1864-1934

Pinkney Alphonso Twitty
Aug 25, 1870
Jan 25, 1957

Griffie M., wife of
P. A. Twitty
Aug 23, 1866
Aug 22, 1922

Lydia H., wife of
P. A. Twitty
May 26, 1883
Jul 3, 1968

D. W. Byers
Nov 12, 1846
Jun 30, 1932

L. V. Byers
Aug 27, 1852
Jul 18, 1923

Charles B. Mitchell
185-(4)-1937

Hunter H. Christian
Nov 30, 1865
Aug 30, 1911

A. D. Flanagan
1862-1915
&
Sarah E. Flanagan
1867-1952

Frank P. Colbert
Sep 22, 1858
Apr 11, 1941
&
Bettie Colbert
Dec 15, 1866
May 29, 1944

James L. Stalcup
1856-1941
&
Margaret E. Stalcup
1865-1937

D. W. Buchanan
Nov 20, 1854
Nov 30, 1920

Mattie Buchanan
1857-1952

John Sidney Maddox
Sep 24, 1876
Mar 1, 1948

Berthie Marvin Maddox
Aug 17, 1878
Oct 5, 1959

Nathan Smith
1835-1910
&
Mary A. Smith
1844-1913

James J. Maddox
Feb 5, 1837
Jun 7, 1906

Mattie Maddox
Jul 3, 1855
Sep 18, 1927

Elizabeth Riley
May 2, 1816
May 12, 1900

Lewis Jefferson Anderson
1854-1945
&
Sarah Maddox Anderson
1854-1918

J. L. Maddox
Jan 14, 1844
Jan 16, 1910

Mercy Forbs
Mar 11, 1793
Nov 18, 1862

Mrs. Sarah Catharine Gatlin
Oct 8, 1839
Aug 16, 1894
"erected by her Son,
J. S. Simmons'.

Infant of
R. W. & A. C. Turner
May 16, 1873
May 21, 1873

Robert W. Turner
Oct 23, 1852
Jun 20, 1873

J. N. Turner
Nov 4, 1824
Dec   1865
&
Elizabeth Turner
Aug 27, 1824
Feb 12, 1895

B. R. McAnn
Mar 27, 1870
Oct 17, 1889

John W., Son of
J. J. & S. F. McAnn
Died Dec 4, 1882
Age: 18y, 10m, 23d.

Lottie, Daughter of
J. J. & S. F. McAnn
Died Nov 8, 1882
Age: 5m, 2d.

Emma B., Daughter of
J. J. & S. F. McAnn
Died Aug 10, 1881
Age: 10m, 28d.

J. F., Son of
J. J. McAnn
Nov 11, 1859
Dec 21, 1861

James J. McAnn
Dec 20, 1837
Nov 2, 1900
&
Sarah F. McAnn
Jan 3, 1844
Jun 27, 1924

Mariah B. Philpot
1809-May 29, 1898

William W. Turner
1855-1935
&
Elizabeth C. Turner
1862-1931

Robert F. Turner
1905-1929

W. Tooney Turner
1894-1948

Margaret R. Smith
1858-1909

Irene Smith
Jul 4, 1827
Nov 26, 1905

Joe Lester Smith
Dec 30, 1892
Jul 22, 1893

Mary Dell Smith
Oct 13, 1894
Jul 13, 1895

Annie K. Buffaloe
1888-1918

Hannah
"Our Old Black Mammy"
(no dates)

Oliver P. Taft
1862-1942
&
Margaret C. Taft
1876-1935

Daniel W. Taft
Dec 24, 1861
Oct 30, 1946

DELLROSE QUADRANGLE

Jane Carpenter
1844-1929

F. R. Wallace
Aug 31, 1843
Nov 16, 1926

M. J., wife of
F. R. Wallace
Sep 8, 1856
Mar 23, 1929

Martha J. Johnson, wife of
M. D. Hutchinson
Nov 24, 1847
Jul 12, 1886

Sarah A. Watkins, wife of
J. R. Johnson
Oct 14, 1827
Aug 23, 1898

J. F. Byers
Mar 3, 1837
Jan 17, 1880

A. E., wife of
James F. Byers &
Daughter of
R. H. & M. A. Grantland
Mar 2, 1848
Jan 28, 1873

Joe F. Byers
Jun 9, 1850
Oct 14, 1881

Lillian, Daughter of
B. L. & C. B. Coats
May 3, 1885
May 20, 1893

B. L. Coats
Dec 28, 1855
Mar 25, 1895

Cornelia B., wife of
B. L. Coats
Aug 3, 1858
Jan 13, 1889

Ben Lewis, Son of
Mr. & Mrs. B. L. Coats
Jun 8, 1895
Aug 2, 1895

Dave A. Tucker
Sep 25, 1861
Nov 15, 1921

Cordie Woodard Tucker
Aug 17, 1870
Aug 16, 1946

Coy Mitchell
1878-1959

May Mitchell
1888-1941

Annie Belle Mitchell
1894-1964

F. R. Mitchell
Jun 1, 1853
Jan 5, 1923

Sallie Carter Mitchell
1861-1945

Cornelius Rainey
1878-1945
&
Maude Rainey
1878-1953

H. H. Smith
1858-1950

Willie Smith
1860-1957

Rheubin F. Smith
1889-1936

J. L. Maddox
1853-1921

Mary Jane Maddox
1859-1936

Joseph C. Gleghorn
1881-1941
&
Lizzie Gleghorn
1878-1947

R. Vickers
Dec 9, 1849
Nov 14, 1921

Sarah E., wife of
R. Vickers
Oct 27, 1855
Nov 28, 1908

Frank W. Vickers
1881-1950
&
Mammie B. Vickers
1887-1949

J. B. Vickers
1879-1930

J. P. Vickers
1845-1905
&
Eliza Ann Vickers
1850-1925

John Howard, Son of
J. H. & N. J. Coats
Jan 3, 1880
Jun 28, 1897

Bettie, Daughter of
J. H. & N. J. Coats
Mar 3, 1871
May 29, 1892

Mattie E., Daughter of
B. L. & Ella E. Ferguson
Dec 25, 1887
Feb 5, 1889

Infant of
B. L. & Ella E. Ferguson
Nov 17, 1888
Nov 18, 1888

Ella E., wife of
B. L. Ferguson
Aug 30, 1866
Nov 27, 1888

W. M. Byers
Jan 18, 1810
Feb 12, 1888

Malena, wife of
W. M. Byers
Apr 18, 1819
married Mar 1, 1836
Died Feb 26, 1900

William M., Son of
James F. & E. J. Byers
Nov 10, 1859
Aug 28, 1871

Edward J. Byers
1846-1894
&
Sarrah Francis Stewart Byers
1854-1927

Warner W., Son of
J. A. & Jennie V. Allison
Aug 17, 1891
Aug 18, 1913

Infant Daughter of
E. J. & S. F. Byers
Aug 10, 1887
Aug 15, 1887

Infant of
J. W. & M. F. Bland
B&D May 29, 1886

Eustacie E., Daughter of
J. W. & M. F. Bland
Jun 13, 1887
Jun 17, 1888

Mollie F., wife of
J. W. Bland
Apr 13, 1864
Aug 1, 1888

Cornelia A., Daughter of
J. H. & N. J. Coats
Apr 26, 1869
Jun 1897

Thomas J., Son of
J. H. & N. J. Coats
Dec 2, 1859
Jan 31, 1890

J. H. Coats
Apr 18, 1831
May 17, 1905

Mary J., wife of
J. H. Coats & Daughter of
B. F. & Edney Hargrove
Oct 28, 1836
Jun 17, 1891

John W. Carpenter
1869-1949
&
Lizzie Carpenter
1849-1932

Dr. John C. Coats
Dec 15, 1853
Jul 30, 1905
&
Alice E. Coats
1858-1936

S. T. Farrar
Feb 3, 1833
Apr 17, 1911

Delia O., wife of
S. T. Farrar, Mother
of Mary D. C. Farrar &
Daughter of
A. & M. Bearden
Dec 13, 1840
Jul 9, 1876

William F. Holland
1854-1906
&
Mannie C. Holland
1874-1908

B. F. Whitt
Jan 22, 1866
Oct 24, 1912

Ida Elizabeth, wife of
B. F. Whitt
Nov 4, 1875
Jun 7, 1951

William R. Bryant
Feb 10, 1860
Jun 28, 1917

Exie C. Bryant
Mar 13, 1866
Mar 10, 1939

J. E. Watson
1857-1921

Delia Watson
1868-1947

John Carl Watson
1893-1962

Annie Lee Watson
1896-19

Mary Lee Watson
1898-1944

DELLROSE QUADRANGLE

Andrew Ulysses Puckett
Dec 19, 1868
Oct 28, 1941
&
Mattie Poole Puckett
Sep 10, 1872
Aug 31, 1964

Joseph Philpott
Mar 4, 1831
Oct 19, 1907

W. N. Hemphill
Oct 17, 1844
Dec 18, 1905

Susan N. Chesser, wife of
W. N. Hemphill
Aug 13, 1865
Feb 27, 1920

R. H. Ferguson
1895-1969

Mamie V. Tallent, wife of
Roy Ferguson
Dec 31, 1895
Dec 24, 1918

J. W. Barham
Jul 3, 1859
Feb 20, 1942
& Wife
Icie H. Bleadsoe Barham
Apr 5, 1851
Jul 3, 1917

Verna Evelyn, Daughter of
J. W. & Icie H. Barham
Jul 24, 1894
Aug 6, 1927

Fred L. Watson
1885-1955
&
Lucy B. Watson
1887-

Melba Belle, Daughter of
F. L. & L. B. Watson
Nov 17, 1922
Jan 29, 1927

W. L. McAnn
Sep 7, 1827
Oct 29, 1912
& Wife
Mary J. Rawls McAnn
Nov 3, 1832
Jul 29, 1921

G. W. Puckett
Feb 25, 1811
May 30, 1888

Martha, wife of
G. W. Puckett
Mar 29, 1829
Mar 15, 1880

Clide Bouldin
Dec 14, 1881
Feb 4, 1887

Maud Bouldin
May 10, 1887
Jan 4, 1897

Minnie May Downing
Aug 9, 1863
May 31, 1879

L. H. Rawls
Apr 1, 1809
May 10, 1873
&
Sarah A. Rawls
Jan 15, 1814
Jun 13, 1890
"Their children:
M. J. Rawls
J. J. Rawls
H. S. Rawls
W. A. Rawls
W. J. Rawls
D. C. Rawls
R. H. Rawls
W. L. Rawls
A. A. Rawls
F. R. Rawls
H. B. Rawls
R. M. Rawls
N. A. Leatherwood."

A. A. Rawls
Jun 12, 1850
Feb 26, 1908

Annie, wife of
A. A. Rawls
Mar 25, 1856
Feb 19, 1901

J. J. Rawls
Aug 24, 1834
Jun 11, 1909

Madeleine, wife of
John J. Rawls
Mar 1, 1834
Feb 31, 1926

Samuel G. Riley
Jul 28, 1813
Oct 23, 1898

Nancy J., wife of
Samuel G. Riley
Jun 27, 1815
Mar 20, 1852

Clarience B., Son of
F. R. & Jessie Rawls
Age: 11y, 7m, 15d.
(no dates)

Birdie, only Daughter of
F. R. & J. M. Rawls
Jul 15, 1884
Jan 19, 1905

Dr. F. R. Rawls
Apr 1, 1855
Apr 26, 1910
& wife
Jessie Lovless Rawls
Aug 19, 1858
(no date)

Thomas A. Rawls
1873-1951
&
Mary E. Rawls
1876-1940

Infant Daughter of
T. A. & Mary E. Rawls
Aug 6, 1909
Aug 8, 1909

Infant Daughter of
T. A. & Mary E. Rawls
1910

Infant Son of
T. A. & Mary E. Rawls
1904

Paul W. Rawls
Nov 23, 1888
Nov 1, 1915

Thomas Mitchell
Dec 25, 1866
Nov 8, 1907
&
Nora Mitchell
Dec 6, 1864
Aug 23, 1929

Ona Mitchell, wife of
Rosco Hasten
Aug 28, 1890
Oct 26, 1914

J. H. Reynolds
Died Mar 7, 1911
Age: 69 years.

Parthenia Bearden, wife of
J. H. Reynolds
Apr 4, 1845
Sep 14, 1919

S. Odie Bland
1857-1935
&
Lula E. Bland
1868-1954

Arthur D. Maddox
Nov 19, 1883
Dec 28, 1922

Andrew Addison McDaniel
1866-1948

Betty Hutchinson McDaniel
1872-1961

James L. Mitchell
Jan 2, 1876
Jan 21, 1933

Idella Brown, wife of
James L. Mitchell
Aug 16, 1879
Jul 18, 1913

Mary Tillery Merrell
Mar 15, 1854
Feb 10, 1932

B. S.
(footstone)

J. L. Bishop
Aug 19, 1843
Apr 19, 1937

Sara E. Cooper, wife of
J. L. Bishop
Jul 2, 1844
Dec 1, 1895

Sallie Sheffield Bishop
May 6, 1871
Jul 11, 1926

Harry F. Colbert
Nov 16, 1891
Aug 6, 1892

Charley, Son of
E. L. & M. S. Hatchett
Feb 13, 1896
Oct 30, 1900

Lillian, Daughter of
E. L. & M. S. Hatchett
Aug 16, 1894
Mar 25, 1895

Duran S-----
was born Jul 12, 1853
& died Jul 17, 1882
(slate rock)

Sgt. M. A. Malone
Co H 8 Ala Inf
C.S.A.

James Rufus Winford
Feb 16, 1872
Jul 11, 1922
&
Martha Jane Winford
Apr 17, 1879
Jan 11, 1964

A. C. Young
Apr 15, 1889
Jan 10, 1913

Lucy Sanders
1882-1947

Luther L. Sanders
1882-1964
&
Flora E. Sanders
1884-

DELLROSE QUADRANGLE

Clay R. Smith
Dec 22, 1908
Jul 1, 1964
&
Mary E. Smith
Mar 30, 1889
Sep 1, 1963

Vinson Mullens
Apr 29, 1816
Dec 31, 1891

Mary Mullens
May 4, 1813
Mar 1, 1895

Cora A. Smith
Oct 8, 1894
Oct 4, 1904

Wade G. Hardin
Tennessee
Sgt 559 field Arty Bn
WW II
Dec 24, 1910
Jul 5, 1944

Joseph Beaty Hardin
Feb 23, 1877
Jan 29, 1916
&
Mollie Jester Hardin
Jan 14, 1877
Dec 21, 1949

Loranza R. Staton
Jan 30, 1861
Apr 19, 1904

Sarah A. Staton
Aug 31, 1867
Aug 26, 1918

Bonnie E. Staton, wife of
A. W. Rogers
Feb 21, 1890
Apr 21, 1919

Emanuel Carpenter
Mar 4, 1836
Nov 3, 1906
& wife
Isabelle E. McCalla
Carpenter
Jul 4, 1842
Feb 3, 1915

Leroy L. Cole
Dec 23, 1876
May 30, 1950
&
Fannie C. Cole
Apr 7, 1881
(no date)

Vashtye Crawford
Jan 28, 1881
Oct 1, 1928

Otie T. Pepper
Aug 17, 1881
Sep 26, 1928

John C. Pepper
Nov 26, 1864
Nov 11, 1939

Chloe Bell Corder, wife of
John C. Pepper
Aug 19, 1871
Dec 3, 1927
married Dec 6, 1900

John J. Neaves
1848-1918

Joanna Neaves
1858-1927

W. A. Robertson
Sep 27, 1850
Jul 10, 1938
&
Delitha Ann Noah Robertson
Feb 9, 1850
Jun 29, 1925

Mabe E., Daughter of
W. A. & D. A. Robertson
Aug 26, 1871
Sep 9, 1897

Annie R., Daughter of
R. M. & A. L. Henderson
Oct 21, 1899
Oct 29, 1904

Pleas A. Robertson
1866-1914
&
Mollie J. Robertson
1874-1936

Millie Mullens
1813-Dec 23, 1890

Willey M. Marshall, wife of
J. W. Kebnell
Dec 3, 1853
Jul 6, 1891

Thomas D. Beverly
Apr 27, 1890
Oct 10, 1911

James A. Jones
Jul 20, 1866
Sep 18, 1952
&
Elizabeth R. Jones
Aug 2, 1874
Aug 4, 1950

James R. Jones
May 2, 1890
Died in service in France
Oct 11, 1918
Co C 144 Inf.

George Sulser
Sep 4, 1877
Feb 23, 1968
&
Bertha Sulser
Jun 6, 1889
Oct 4, 1967

William Francis Berryhill
1873-1953

Minnie Mae Berryhill
Aug 25, 1877
Nov 22, 1959

J. N. Jones
Oct 1, 1836
Nov 1, 1907

Jane Jones
Mar 17, 1837
Oct 13, 1890

Andrew Jones
1872-1956

Harvey M. Taft
Jun 28, 1840
Nov 17, 1916
&
Elizabeth Taft
Jul 27, 1844
Mar 23, 1918

William Taft
Jan 5, 1833
Jan 20, 1915

Mollie, Daughter of
William & M. I. Taft
Nov 18, 1867
May 9, 1905

Joe D. Bolander
Dec 5, 1887
May 17, 1921

Lizzie Taft Bolander
Sep 29, 1859
Aug 28, 1922

Walter E. Gary
Nov 13, 1869
Sep 27, 1902

Little Diemer, Infant of
W. E. & M. E. Gary
Dec 21, 1897
Jan 9, 1898

Joseph A. Graves
Aug 16, 1864
Nov 16, 1953
&
Sarah B. Graves
Dec 4, 1877
Jul 1, 1959

Robert & Gatlin, Sons of
J. L. & M. L. Graves
(no dates)

James A. Jones
Aug 24, 1880
Dec 20, 1957
&
Katie Rainey Jones
Jun 19, 1879
(no date)

Martha Jane, wife of
J. B. Rainey
Jan 4, 1859
Apr 26, 1902

Theodore Rainey
1885-1932
&
Bertha M. Rainey
1890-1962

Eugene Gibbs
Apr 4, 1874
Sep 24, 1900

Sidney Payne
1884-1917

Ernest R. Franklin
1882-1953
&
Virgie M. Franklin
1892-1929

Charles Ordway Woodfin
Sep 24, 1878
Jan 9, 1929
&
Fanny Ola Woodfin
Apr 18, 1880
Jul 21, 1951

J. E. Webster
1850-1910

N. E. Webster
1849-1913

James Webster
1888-1927

Joe W. Webster
1880-1963

Jim Lemmons
1865-1949
&
Mary F. Lemmons
1875-1947
&
Marvin Lemmons
1930-1947

Jim H. Lemons
1865-1950

Jim Boldin
1881-1928
&
Erie Boldin
1878-1941

Mollie Mary Bates
1871-1951

DELLROSE QUADRANGLE

Albert F. Baird
Mar 11, 1874
Apr 4, 1952
&
Emma D. Baird
May 8, 1884
Sep 17, 1958

Miss Evelyn Maddox
Died Feb 16, 1970
Age: 57 years.

F. M. Downing
1842-1930

Carl E. Downing
Alabama
Pvt 167 Inf 42 Div
Sep 10, 1932

Many unmarked graves.

T. P. Downing
1868-1945

Lizzie Downing
1875-1947

John Thomas *
Died Sep 23, 1908
Age: 30y, 15d.
Married Lucinda Poole

Son * of
John Danley
Died Feb 13, 1897
Age: (no age given)

Neil P. Brown *
Died Feb 27, 1908
Age: about 48 years.

* *

PREDESTIONED PRIMITIVE CHURCH CEMETERY

LOCATION: One and one-half miles SW of Blanche at Kelly Creek Church on Ardmore Highway.

James K. Leatherwood
Jul 28, 1839
Oct 18, 1900
& wife
Bethenie J. Leatherwood
Aug 16, 1838
Aug 7, 1893

Emma Bell Leatherwood
Jan 18, 1866
Sep 7, 1891

Benjamin S. Leatherwood
Apr 1, 1873
Oct 3, 1891

James S. Leatherwood
Dec 23, 1874
Sep 25, 1891

William T. Leatherwood
Nov 13, 1867
Aug 23, 1893

Sara Ida, Daughter of
M. N. & N. A. Rowell
Jul 21, 1872
Oct 18, 1873

S. A., wife of
T. M. Barnett
Jan 25, 1833
Jan 5, 1903

Samuel Bond
Dec 7, 1803
Aug 19, 1892

Elizabeth Bond
Nov 24, 1809
Feb 3, 1901

Lou R., wife of
G. W. Bond
Feb 9, 1846
Jun 26, 1909

S. Edwards
(no dates, fieldstone)

William R. Martin
Sep 11, 1811
Jan 10, 1891

Mary J. Nance, wife of
William R. Martin
Jan 22, 1821
Oct 4, 1883

------a Jordan
Feb 22, 17--
Jun --, ----
Age: 4- (almost illegible)

William D. Walker
Jan 2, 1835
Sep 16, 1855
Age: 20y, 8m, 14d.

Sarah A. Walker
Dec 17, 1839
Dec 24, 1844

S. F. Leatherwood
Jun 17, 1842
Aug 11, 1839

Infant Son of
J. & F. Leatherwood
B&D Aug 18, 1855

Infant Son of
J. & F. Leatherwood
B&D Aug 27, 1850
&
Infant Son of
J. & F. Leatherwood
Dec 12, 1839

Infant Daughter of
J. & F. Leatherwood
B&D Aug 10, 1856

Oliver B., Son of
J. & F. Leatherwood
Aug 27, ----
J-- --, ---- (info. gone)

William M. Leatherwood
Dec 11, 1836
Oct 4, 1837

Mother
W. L. F.
(no dates, fieldstone)

John H. Dollar
Aug 17, 1873
Sep 8, 1874
&
Alvis Dollar
Mar 8, 1880
Nov 6, 1881
"Children of C. N. & W. C. Dollar."

William Beard *
Died May 1907
Age: (not given)
Buried by his wife & child.

Nannie Johnson *
Died Dec 1893
Age: no age given)
All family is dead, buried by her mother.

Zadock Hanks Walker ***
buried here,
1798-1878

*** Family Records.

Note: Once called Kelly's Creek church.

DELLROSE QUADRANGLE

ROPER CEMETERY

LOCATION: One and one-half mile SW of Blanche at Kelly Creek Church on the Ardmore Highway.

Ed. Whitt
1865-1934
&
Ella Whitt
1880-1932

Flet E. Bryant
1845-1915

Dollie H. Bryant
1867-1913

Flossie B. Lewter
1891-1914

Florence B. Lewter
1895-1917

William E. Curtis
Mar 11, 1909

&
Valeria C. Curtis
Aug 7, 1912
Jul 4, 1966

Mrs. G. A. Bolin
May 28, 1862
Jul 1, 1910

Louvicie Cross
Jun 21, 1870
Oct 24, 1946

J. B. Roper
Aug 18, 1846
Feb 13, 1919

Sarah Edwards, wife of
J. B. Roper
Jan 22, 1850
Sep 19, 1919

Maud, Daughter of
J. B. & Sarah Roper
Jun 22, 1878
Jul 17, 1902

Acy Roper
Apr 18, 1877
Sep 3, 1930

Minervy L., wife of
Asa Roper
Jan 16, 1878
May 15, 1908

Minnie M., Daughter of
Acy & M. L. Roper
Aug 31, 1915
Jul 31, 1917

L. P., wife of
Asa Roper
Jan 21, 1883
Jun 23, 1900

James T. Roper
Nov 25, 1844
May 31, 1917

George Sterling, Son of
J. T. Roper
Jun 4, 1887
Jul 6, 1889

William, Son of
J. T. Roper
Feb 19, 1872
Jul 1, 1892

Joseph, Son of
J. T. & M. J. Roper
Dec 1, 1873
Jun 12, 1902

Margrett J. Roper
Jul 26, 1847
Nov 30, 1913

G. A. Roper
Oct 19, 1882
Mar 18, 1929
&
Beatrice Roper
May 25, 1883
Feb 22, 1929

Virginia B., Daughter of
G. A. & Beatrice Roper
Apr 24, 1917
Apr 29, 1917

Alice Roper
1919-1950

Birten H. Roper
Jun 10, 1883
Mar 18, 1959

Della F., wife of
B. H. Roper
Mar 28, 1883
Nov 26, 1958

Willie B. Roper
Apr 25, 1911
Dec 24, 1931

Rosa Lee Roper
Nov 20, 1915
Dec 21, 1932

John H. Roper
Dec 10, 1854
Aug 30, 1893

Alice, wife of
John H. Roper
(no dates)

Elzie Newman Roper
Aug 19, 1905
Apr 18, 1907

G. T. Roper
Jan 18, 1841
Jul 7, 1900

E. J., wife of
G. T. Roper
Jan 16, 1843
Feb 8, 1904

Joseph F., Son of
W. J. & M. J. Edwards
Aug 25, 1875
Jan 25, 1887

W. J. Edwards
Apr 25, 1845
Jul 22, 1927

M. J. Roper, wife of
W. J. Edwards
Aug 27, 1844
Feb 8, 1914

Donnie Roper Hargrove
Jul 14, 1854
Nov 8, 1925

Sarah J. Edwards, wife of
W. R. Hargraves
Jun 23, 1865
Dec 7, 1892

Lonnie T. Roper
Mar 5, 1890
Jul 18, 1893

Ollie D. Roper
Jan 27, 1878
Jan 6, 1896

Donnie B. Roper
Mar 5, 1890
Mar 22, 1895

William N. Roper
Mar 10, 1857
Feb 25, 1893

Annie Viola Roper
1884-1885

Lolie L. Miny Roper
Dec 12, 1880
Dec   1881

Lillie Leona Roper
Apr 7, 1879
Jan 19, 1880

L. H.
(fieldstone)

M. H.
(fieldstone)

W. E.
(fieldstone)

J. E.
(fieldstone)

L. J. B.
(fieldstone)

Joseph Roper
1812-Aug 8, 1862

M. J. V.
(fieldstone)

M. R.
(fieldstone)

S. E. Barnett
Jun 26, 1847
Aug 26, 1876

Mrs. A. E. Barnett
Aug 5, 1850
May 10, 1874

Milly Ann, Infant of
J. B. & Sarah Roper
B&D Aug 24, 1873

John E. Tillery
Aug 15, 1887
Feb 27, 1963
&
Lula M. Tillery
Mar 9, 1890

J. Curby Tillery
Sep 5, 1916
Feb 26, 1917

Infant Son of
William & Daisy Tillery
Jun 11, 1935
Jul 3, 1935

Lucy Bean
1861-1923

Mary G., Daughter of
G. T. & E. J. Roper
Dec 2, 1874
Dec 1, 1905

Infant of
C. W. & Mary Baird
B&D Jan 2, 1896

DELLROSE QUADRANGLE

Thomas Wayne, Son of
Thomas & Ruby Roper
Aug 1, 1938
Aug 2, 1938

Mattie Caperton
Feb 25, 1876
Jan 1, 1943

John Caperton
Aug 29, 1866
Nov 28, 1949

Eliza Caperton
Aug 17, 1868
Sep 29, 1935

Berry Beddingfield
Nov 3, 1903
Mar 20, 1966

Alice R. J., Daughter of
W. T. & M. F. Beddingfield
(dates illegible)

William T. Beddingfield
1861-1931
&
Melissa F. Beddingfield
1866-1939

Ida O. Beddingfield
Jun 21, 1891
Sep 22, 1960

Elbert L. Ivy
Sep 26,---- (date gone)
Aug 17, 1883

N. A. Wallace Ivy
Feb 12, 1865
Apr 29, 1884

Saddie Mae Lewter
1893-1916

Several unmarked graves.

* *

GATLIN CEMETERY

LOCATION: One-fourth mile south of Cash Point on east side of road.

J. W. Gatlin
Jul 1, 1840
Mar 5, 1900

Lucy Ann, wife of
J. W. Gatlin
Feb 28, 1836
Mar 21, 1918

E. S. A. Gatlin
Oct 7, 1875
Dec 11, 1876

Infant Daughter of
Y. N. & Rhoda Gatlin
B&D Dec 15, 1901

Y. N. Gatlin
Oct 20, 1873
May 8, 1953

Rhoda, wife of
Y. N. Gatlin
Oct 19, 1875
Jan 2, 1902

Lucinda Gatlin
Jun 15, 1798
Dec 18, 1883

Lena E. Gatlin
Jan 29, 1882
Aug 23, 1965

* *

WHITE CEMETERY

LOCATION: One-half mile SW of Cash Point on the south side of Ardmore Highway.

Ira A. White
Apr 1, 1842
Jul 18, 1923

Charllota F., wife of
Ira A. White
Oct 1, 1847
Nov 21, 1924

Lenora, Daughter of
Ira A. & C. F. White
Sep 19, 1884
Oct 31, 1885

W. W. White
Feb 17, 1878
Jan 28, 1928

O. B. Matlock
Dec 12, 1881
Mar 22, 1922

Paul L., Son of
O. B. & Lula Matlock
Oct 8, 1916
Apr 20, 1918

Infant Daughter of
O. B. & Lula Matlock
B&D Oct 5, 1910

Albert B. Matlock
Aug 23, 1906
Jul 7, 1932

* *

FRANKLIN CEMETERY

LOCATION: One mile south of Cash Point on the west side of road.

Mary Franklin
1878-1952

America, wife of
J. M. Shannon
Apr 21, 1856
Jun 26, 1876
   & Their Daughter
Mary A. Shannon
Apr 16, 1876
Jun 15, 1876

Cordelia Massey
Mar 5, 1869
Mar 25, 1943

Edward Willis Holman
Died Jan 21, 193-(gone)
Age: 57y, 6m, 30d.

Fannie E. Holman
1877-1934

Marvin Franklin
Jan 6, 1905
Jan 9, 1923

Pearl Franklin
Oct 19, 1903
Nov 5, 1903

Garland Franklin
Feb 9, 1906
Jan 10, 1908

Atlas Franklin
Nov 22, 1878
Aug 2, 1952
&
Willie A. Franklin
Mar 28, 1872
Aug 31, 1932

J. W. Franklin
1877-1958

Minnie Ann Franklin
Jun 3, 1885
Oct 25, 1920

Daniel W. Franklin
Aug 20, 1912
Mar 4, 1944

Albert M. Franklin
Aug 31, 1904
Oct 27, 1925

DELLROSE QUADRANGLE

C. Thomas Franklin
Mar 17, 1882
Oct 17, 1924
&
Pearl H. Franklin
May 8, 1880
----
married Dec 17, 1902

J. T. Franklin
Jul 15, 1878
Jul 13, 1923

Oda Franklin
Sep 8, 1909
Feb 6, 1914

Sam Woods
Oct 20, 1863
Aug 16, 1936
Age: 73 years

Betty Woods
1877-1937

Infant of
E. D. & E. M. Lewter
B&D May 20, 1928

Silvie K. Solomon
Nov 5, 1926
Jan 3, 1928

A. C. Solomon
Apr 14, 1928
Apr 4, 1929

Lonnie Solomon
1903-1947

Auburn M. Campbell
Aug 27, 1897
Feb 27, 1929

Lawrence Griffin
1931-1939

* *

AUSTIN CEMETERY

LOCATION: Two miles SW of Cash Point on Ardmore Highway.

Alex Austin
Mar 4, 1864
Nov 23, 1934

Maggie R. Austin
May 10, 1872
Jan 30, 1953

C. H. "Pete" Austin
Oct 6, 1896
Sep 3, 1951

* *

SHERRELL CEMETERY

LOCATION: Two and one-half miles west of Coldwater, off Dellrose Road on Hall Road. Data copied by Clarence Griffin and Martha and Bobby Lewter in January 1973.

Uty Sherrell
Oct 14, 1783
Jul 16, 1852

Mary, wife of
Uty Sherrell
Oct 31, 1787
Jul 8, 1845

William Sidney Sherrell
Jun 6, 1822
Dec 13, 1872

Several graves marked with fieldstones, no dates or inscriptions.

Gidion Lay, Son of
J. T. & M. H. Rowell
Nov 3, 1879
Jan 5, 1880

Warren P., Son of
John A. & Louisa Jane Hill
Jun 29, 1834
Jun 14, 1847

* *

FERGUSON CEMETERY

LOCATION: One-half mile NE of Kelley's Creek Baptist Church. Contributed by Mr. Russell O'Neal.

Infant Son of
W. W. & M. F. Ferguson
May 8, 1876
Dec 6, 1876

Marget T., Daughter of
J. H. & F. A. Ferguson
Dec 4, 1872
Aug 26, 1894

Johnie S. Ferguson
Nov 23, 1889
Nov 24, 1889
&
Della J. Ferguson
Oct 8, 1891
Dec 18, 1891
Children of
J. S. & S. J. Ferguson

Margret L., Daughter of
C. S. & Lou Ferguson
Jan 24, 1896
Mar 7, 1896

Hubert J., Son of
C. S. & Lou Ferguson
Apr 29, 1894
Dec 7, 1894

Florence E., Daughter of
C. S. & Lou Ferguson
Jan 20, 1891
Mar 7, 1891

* *

FAYETTEVILLE QUADRANGLE

KIMES CEMETERY

LOCATION: One and one-half miles NE of Howell, one-fourth mile east of Old Unity Church and Cemetery.

John Kimes
Jan 18, 1798
Oct 8, 1851
&
Margaret, wife of
John Kimes
Jun 29, 1820
Jan 28, 1873

Eliza Ann, the Darling wife
of John Patterson
Nov 23, 1818
Feb 8, 1846

12 to 15 graves with
fieldstones, no inscriptions.

* *

UNITY CEMETERY

LOCATION: One and one-fourth miles NE of Howell at the site of Old Unity Presbyterian Church.

Mary E.(Elizabeth) Cole
Jun 27, 1824
Jun 20, 1855
"Leaving a Husband & 4
  children." (Ezra Cole,
  married Sep 28, 1848)

Joseph McMillen
May 25, 1784
Feb 5, 1859
&
Rachel, wife of
Joseph McMillen
Dec 6, 1792
Jun 28, 1865

Francis McMillen
Sep 14, 1829
Nov 25, 1856

N. D. Crawford
Sep 24, 1830
Age: 18 months.

Dr. Alexander Rosborough
Oct 7, 1763
Jun 10, 1845

John Beatie
1763-Aug 1, 1849
"Leaving 5 sons & 1
  daughter."
&
Anna, wife of
John Beatie
Died Oct 19, 1840
Who left Husband, 6 sons
& 3 daughters.
Age: 62 years.

Sarah E., Daughter of
John & Anna Beatie
Oct 15, 1817
Oct 8, 1841
Age: 24 years.

G. W. C. Edmiston
Nov 18, 1785 in
Washington Co., Virginia
Died Jul 10, 1847
&
Elizabeth Edmiston
Oct 16, 1791 in
Washington Co., Virginia
Died May 6, 1839
Age: 47y, 6m, 20d.
(G. W. C. Edmiston married
  Sally Dobbins Nov 16, 1842)

Ann Edmiston
Died Apr 24, 1842
Age: 45 years.

Rosanah M. Smith
Jan 22, 1811
Mar 20, 1843
"Leaving a Husband & 1 Son."

Dr. N. A. Smith
Died Dec 31, 1862
Age: 29 years.
"By Unity Lodge # 84, I.O.O.F."

Alex McCallum
born Oct 1768 in
Cantire, Scotland
died Jan 28, 1844
Age: 76 years.

Lilburn Shugart of
Washington Co., Virginia
Died Sep 30, 1841
Age: 24y, 8m, 19d.

Isabel J. Clark
Died Nov 5, 1843
Age: 7y, 2m, 23d.

Infant Daughter of
S. A. M. & Emily Hart
Mar 19, 1851
Jul 5, 1851

William McClellan
Jul 11, 1775
Sep 7, 1852

Caroline M. McClellan
Jan 28, 1776
Jul 11, 1852

Henry Davis
Oct 9, 1804
May 26, 1843
"Left a wife & 1 Son &
  1 Daughter."

Joseph H. Greer
Jun 18, 1828
Sep 19, 1858
(Married Mary M. Edmiston,
  Sep 26, 1847)

John, Son of
J. I. & Anna Beatie
Sep 2, 1844
Oct 22, 1846

Ruth A. Toole
Feb 28, 1819
Oct 16, 1911

Mrs. S. L. J., Consort of
S. M. Slaughter & Daughter
of G. W. C. & Elizabeth
Edmiston
Aug 23, 1832
Dec 13, 1855

S. A. M. Hart
Oct 10, 1815
Jul 19, 1854

Emily G. (Motlow), wife of
S. A. M. Hart
Nov 18, 1819
Sep 7, 1884
(married Feb 28, 1839)

Catharine, wife of
T. L. Williamson
Apr 23, 1830
Jan 14, 1891

John H. Williamson
Sep 13, 1855
Jan 28, 1863

Martha A. E. & Mary C.
Williamson
born Sep 29, 1866
Mary C. Died Dec 10, 1866
Martha A. E. Died
Oct 19, 1866

Arthur D., Son of
James R. & Catharine Toole
Born in Lincoln Co., Tenn.
Dec 10, 1829
Died Jan 27, 1848

James R. Toole
born in Knoxville, Tenn.
Apr 18, 1787
died in Lincoln Co., Tenn.
Jul 2, 1850

Catharine, Consort of
James R. Toole
born in York Dist., S.C.
Jul 30, 1789
died in Lincoln Co., Tenn.
Nov 22, 1850

Henry Kimes
Who died Apr 12, 1854
Age: 58y, 2m, 12d.

Eleanor H. Kimes
Sep 13, 1799
Sep 15, 1856

H. M. Kimes
Died Apr 8, 1854
Age: 20y, 3d.

D. J. Kimes
Died Aug 8, 1854
Age: 22y, 11d.

FAYETTEVILLE QUADRANGLE

James J. Hines
Mar 23, 1813
Apr 14, 1879

Elizabeth Toole, wife of
James J. Hines
Mar 11, 1817
Jun 11, 1903

Martha Elizabeth Hines
Aug 16, 1841
May 25, 1897

Betsy Jane Hines
Jul 26, 1877
Feb 19, 1920

James T. Hines
Oct 23, 1837
Jul 17, 1906

Mary Zimmerman, wife of
James T. Hines
Feb 21, 1849
Feb 25, 1923
(married Oct 23, 1873)

Nancy Ruth Hines
Jan 9, 1879
Sep 9, 1937

William G. Hines
1851-1909

Mary Kate Hines
1841-1925

Charles O. Kimes
1882-1936

Mary C. Kimes
1887-1912

Charles T. Kimes
Mar 23, 1912
Jun 20, 1912

John Kimes
Jun 13, 1822
Apr 20, 1906
&
Louisa (Allison) Kimes
Feb 11, 1843
(no date)

L. J.(McAdams), wife of
John Kimes, Jr.
Sep 12, 1827
Jul 27, 1878

Mary Ade, wife of
John K. Kimes, Jr.
Feb 21, 1829
May 20, 1872
"Leaving 2 children."

Mary A., wife of
John Kimes, Jr.
Nov 20, 1829
Oct 2, 1868
"Leaving 10 children."

Lucy L., Daughter of
John & Mary A. Kimes
May 30, 1867
Died the same year, 1867

David J., Son of
John & Mary A. Kimes
Feb 16, 1863
Mar 31, 1864

John A., Son of
John & Mary A. Kimes
Sep 16, 1860
Mar 26, 1864

Infant Son of
John & Mary A. Kimes
B&D 1866

Nathaniel Millard
Dec 13, 1821
Feb 3, 1886
&
Minerva S., wife of
Than Millard
Apr 1819
Feb 12, 1903

Thomas Millard
Apr 23, 1828
May 27, 1896

Infant Son of
W. A. & M. A. Millard
Still born Feb 1, 1878

W. A. Millard
Jan 25, 1836
Dec 17, 1913
& wife
Mary A. Beatie Millard
Jan 13, 1846
Aug 6, 1900

Maggie D., Daughter of
W. A. & M. A. Millard
Jan 16, 1876
Jul 5, 1877

Infant Son of
W. A. & M. A. Millard
B&D Nov 3, 1874

Robert Zadock Beatie
Sep 26, 1855
Feb 6, 1859

David M. Beatie
May 3, 1813
Feb 20, 1881

Mary Beatie
Sep 22, 1823
Oct 18, 1862

Charles B. Patton
born in Rockingham Co., Va.
Sep 5, 1794
(date broken away)

A. M. Beatie
Nov 25, 1822
Sep 6, 1889
Age: 67y, 9m, 11d.

Joe Beatie
May 12, 1823
Nov 29, 1905

Jane Stewart, wife of
Alexander Rosborough
Jul 26, 1786
Sep 3, 1877

Harriet Ellen, wife of
W. M. Rosborough & Daughter
of William & Rebecca Thomas
Jan 1, 1831
Jul 23, 1889

W. M. Rosborough
Died Mar 7, 1909
Age: 81y, 8m, 21d.
Co C Tenn Reg 4th Div.

James L. Kimes
1879-1965
& wife
Carrie L. Kimes
1879-1930

Jonas S. March
1864-1935
&
Mary T. March
1873-1949

Mary Thomas March
Jul 11, 1907
Jul 28, 1923

William Thomas, Son of
Joe & Mary March
Nov 18, 1899
Oct 7, 1900

John D., Son of
Joe & Mary March
Jan 20, 1903
Sep 4, 1908
Age: 5y, 7m, 14d.

George C. Thomas
1861-1922

Elizabeth Barbara, Daughter
of W. L. & E. B. Thomas
Jul 31, 1869
Dec 12, 1890

Harriet Rebecca, Daughter of
William L. & Elizabeth
Thomas
Mar 25, 1860
Feb 19, 1940

William L. Thomas
Apr 16, 1829
Jul 16, 1905
& wife
Elizabeth D. Clark Thomas
Apr 25, 1828
Jan 24, 1900

George W. Thomas
Jan 5, 1836
Jul 27, 1906
&
Lucinda Thomas
Feb 17, 1837
Oct 30, 1913

Grover C. Prosser
Apr 15, 1883
Jun 30, 1942
&
Myrtle K. Prosser
May 4, 1884
1967

George W. Poindexter
Jun 8, 1841
Nov 25, 1889

T. N. McMillen
1868-1940
&
Mecca McMillen
1875-19

John D. Roseborough
1880-1951
&
Susie E. Roseborough
1874-1937

J. W. Roseborough
Jan 8, 1856
Aug 22, 1904
& wife
Margaret Fannie Roseborough
Jul 18, 1859
Jul 27, 1885
Age: 26y, 9d.

Robert D. McMillen
Aug 17, 1822
Jul 7, 1895
& wife
Mary J. McMillen
Dec 13, 1833
Jan 14, 1878

Robert Harris, Infant of
Mr. & Mrs. J. W. Hulsey
Feb 1, 1904
Feb 21, 1904

Mary Agnes, Infant of
J. W. & M. L. Hulsey
Oct 5, 1899
Oct 25, 1899

FAYETTEVILLE QUADRANGLE

Charles S. Clark
Jul 4, 1852
Aug 2, 1902
&
Margaret M. Patton Clark
Jun 27, 1822
Feb 14, 1900

James B. Wright
Dec 3, 1804
Feb 10, 1872

Julia B., wife of
James B. Wright
Nov 21, 1804
Feb 5, 1879

A. F. Patton
Dec 22, 1829
Nov 12, 1903
& wife
Mary Patton
Jan 1, 1846
Apr 16, 1903

James Fulton, Son of
Abe & Maggie Winsett
Died Jun 19, 1902
Age: 4m, 8d.

Lanard Patton, Son of
Abe & Maggie Winsett
Jun 23, 1903
Mar 3, 1904

Mary Church
1891-1931

Roy, Son of
T. J. & S. F. Sawyers
Aug 11, 1919
Nov 1, 1920

Frank, Son of
T. J. & S. F. Sawyers
Jun 13, 1918
Jul 29, 1918

Nannie Laura Sawyers
Nov 8, 1915
Nov 14, 1914(5)

Ben T. Armstrong
1884-1936
&
Martha E. Armstrong
1886-1946

W. Tom Adcox
1886-
&
Annie A. Adcox
1896-1960
&
Junior B. Adcox
1929-1948
&
Cecil Shelton Adcox
1947-
&
Irene Adcox
1919-1927

Joe C. Posey
Mar 10, 1884
Dec 19, 1962
&
Leeuna Posey
Oct 22, 1886

Little Maud Brown
Mar 8, 1924
Mar 3, 1928

Iv-- Brown
---- - 1934 (gone)

Mrs. Jim Posey
1903-1937

D. J. Hines
Mar 13, 1841
Jul 28, 1867
Age: 26y, 4m, 15d.

W. B. Beatie
Aug   1810
Sep 21, 1882

James Watson
born in England
Feb 3, 1820
Oct 7, 1891
Age: 71y, 8m, 4d.

Martha J. Watson
"Grandmother"
(no dates)

Joe E. Thomas
Dec 13, 1871
Sep 11, 1951

Ida E., wife of
Joe E. Thomas
Jan 10, 1877
Nov 17, 1909

Mattie Moore Thomas
Jan 2, 1885
Aug 29, 1947

Robert Matt Buchanan
Tenn Cpl 6th Inf WW I PH
Aug 4, 1891
Jan 16, 1951

Fannie Daves Buchanan
Nov 12, 1897
Dec 18, 1934

Robert Matt Buchanan
1854-1933
&
Ida Smith Buchanan
1863-1950

Edd Eakes
1890-1957

Dovie, wife of
R. H. Eaks
Mar 28, 1865
Nov 20, 1892

Grace Lee, Daughter of
Dovie & R. H. Eaks
Mar 11, 1892
Oct 8, 1892

P. L. T.
(no dates, fieldstone)

Nancy A., wife of
James Epps
Sep 16, 1808
May 6, 1884

James Epps
Mar 28, 1836
Dec 15, 1919
& wife
Addie Epps
Oct 6, 1845
Jan --, 1890

Bettie Epps
Oct 2, 1863
May 11, 1887

Infant Daughter of
C. M. & Nannie Conaway
Aug 17, 1914

Lois Kent, wife of
J. D. Epps
Mar 3, 1887
Sep 22, 1931

Oliver N. Short
Mar 14, 1886

&
Olivia C. Short
Dec 25, 1883
Oct 22, 1968
Age: 84y, 9m, 27d.

John J. Short
Nov 19, 1836
Jun 12, 1898
&
Mary A. Short
Dec 8, 1845
May 12, 1910

Lafayette E., Son of
J. J. & M. A. Short
Jul 22, 1888
Oct 1, 1888

H. B. Talley
Dec 10, 1842
Feb 16, 1929

Mary I., wife of
H. B. Talley
Jun 13, 1850
Sep 26, 1913

E. J. Talley
Dec 8, 1845
Jul 13, 1902

N. W. George
Feb 17, 1857
(not buried here, see below)
& wife
Ellen George
Jan 2, 1862
Jun 2, 1887
& wife
Maggie Scott George
Jun 23, 1871
Oct 19, 1892

N. W. George
1857-1937
&
Sina A. George
1870-1943

Campbell F. Edmiston
Died Sep 21, 1868
Age: 46 years.

Elizabeth Buchanan, wife
of C. F. Edmiston
Sep 27, 1831
Jan 9, 1897

John C. Edmiston
May 24, 1851
Sep 2, 1868

James S(H). Edmiston
185-- - 1929 (broken)

Virginia Beatie
Died Sep 24, 1926
(no age given)

Lavoid, Son of
J. C. & L. E. Epps
Oct 19, 1899
Nov 14, 1912

Thomas H., Son of
G. W. C. & Elizabeth
Edmiston
(dates broken away)

John S. Edmiston
Feb 28, 1815
Sep 23, 1888

Margrette E., wife of
John S. Edmiston
Jan 18, 1833
Mar 2, 1903

J. J. Cummins
Apr 22, 1842
Mar 17, 1906
&
H. Fannie Cummins
Feb 14, 1843
Apr 1, 1919

John Walker Scott
1866-1927
&
Dollie Armstrong Scott
1870-1902

FAYETTEVILLE QUADRANGLE

James B. Armstrong
Feb 14, 1828
May 1, 1901
&
Elizabeth J. Armstrong
Feb 4, 1835
Jul 29, 1917

J. Hinkle Moore
May 9, 1849
Jan 23, 1928
&
Nancy Whitaker Moore
Sep 30, 1853
Mar 6, 1914

Mollie Moore
1850-1935

Carrie Lou Ella, Daughter
of Joe S. & Louisa Hines
Apr 2, 1869
Aug 9, 1900

Joe S. Hines
Apr 9, 1843
Jan 1, 1921
& wife
Louisa Pylant Hines
Apr 13, 1847
Oct 3, 1917

Walter J. Hines
Aug 31, 1866
Jul 24, 1936

Rose Emma Hines
Jan 11, 1877
Aug 17, 1949

Dr. T. H. Clark
Jul 27, 1840
Dec 22, 1899

Jane B., wife of
T. H. Clark
Aug 19, 1838
Jan 18, 1916

Mattieal, Daughter of
J. W. & Maggie Orrick
Jul 31, 1878
Sep 9, 1884

J. W. Orrick
1852-Oct 10, 1908
Age: 57y, 6m, 9d.
&
Maggie W. Orrick
1854-1927

Ellen Orrick
1864-1942

Lucile, Daughter of
J. W. & M. J. Orrick
Jun 18, 1888
Oct 22, 1889

Thomas G. Wade
1823-1911
&
Mary E., wife of
Rufus Chapman
1827-1907

William D. Wade
1829-(no date)
& wife
Louisa J. Wade
1826-1892

Henry Wade
1867-1934
&
Mary E. Wade
1879-1966

John Armstrong
1875-1948
&
Sophia Armstrong
1881-1945

Calvin Leroy Armstrong
Mar 29, 1918
Jan 26, 1919
&
Malvin Leroy Armstrong
Mar 29, 1918
Oct 25, 1918

E. H. Conwell
Jan 21, 1836
Dec 15, 1907

Susan White Conwell
Dec 6, 1846
Jan 12, 1920

Addie Leota, Daughter of
W. M. & N. J. Armstrong
Jul 25, 1898
Sep 26, 1907

A. B. Armstrong
1881-1938

Bryant, Son of
C. L. & Jennie Forest
Jun 14, 1896
Nov 18, 1898

Joel T. Armstrong
1859-1940
&
J. Sophia Armstrong
1858-1934

Elizabeth Armstrong
1846-1913
&
Minnie Louisa Armstrong
1882-1968
Age: 86 years.
&
Mary D. Moore
1851-1926

William B. Hudson
1840-1917
&
Alice T. Hudson
1861-1937

Will M. Haselwood
1868-1950
&
Mollie F. Haselwood
1878-1965

Joe Martin Hazelwood
Jun 27, 1914
May 13, 1918

John N. Epps
Mar 27, 1841
Aug 25, 1929
&
Florence C. Epps
Nov 1, 1849
Feb 5, 1938

James S., Son of
J. N. & Florence Epps
Sep 1, 1882
Mar 6, 1914

Joel M. Harris
Jan 29, 1868
Jul 19, 1897

W. S. Harris
Mar 18, 1833
Feb 17, 1897

Mamie, Daughter of
W. A. & E. E. Hopper
Aug 18, 1894
Jun 28, 1896

James L. Armstrong
Feb 27, 1871
May 9, 1944

Mary F., wife of
J. L. Armstrong
Jul 3, 1871
Aug 7, 1918

Anna M., wife of
A. C. Long
Oct 10, 1875
Feb 10, 1911

Preston Long
Dec 18, 1901
Dec 19, 1901

Mary Bessie Morrison
Feb 27, 1896
Oct 4, 1899

David N. Taylor
May 6, 1858
Jan 12, 1892

Luther H. Gambill
Nov 2, 1879
Mar 28, 1900

Emma McRady, Daughter of
G. N. & R. C. Gambill
Feb 19, 1890
Aug 19, 1894

Charlie G., Son of
G. N. & R. C. Gambill
Sep 14, 1886
Feb 1, 1890

Lula E., Daughter of
G. N. & R. C. Gambill
Jan 2, 1885
Sep 9, 1885

Cora M., Daughter of
G. N. & R. C. Gambill
May 21, 1879
Oct 6, 1888

George Gambill
Aug 13, 1853
Jul 8, 1923
&
Ruth Reavis Gambill
Mar 23, 1849
Jul 4, 1930

Alexander Thane
Apr --, 1817
Mar --, 1884

T. J. Gamble
(no dates)

Mrs. T. J. Gamble
(no dates)

John F. Price
Jun 14, 1832
Jun 26, 1883
Age: 51y, 12d.

Mary M. Price
Nov 4, 1833
Aug 5, 1909

Beulah Erlene, Daughter of
J. N. & Elizabeth Price
Jul 29, 1904
Jul 17, 1905

W. F., Son of
J. W. & M. F. Gambrill
Oct 2, 1899
Oct 14, 1899

Jennie, Daughter of
J. W. & M. F. Gambrill
Sep 23, 1888
Aug 3, 1896

J. W. Gambrill
Dec 24, 1857
Dec 23, 1902

M. R. J., wife of
J. W. Gambrill
Jun 8, 1856
Jul 27, 1896

FAYETTEVILLE QUADRANGLE

Twin Daughters of
J. W. & M. R. Gambrell
Jun 11, 1880
Jun 18, 1880

Ellen Nora Walker
1865-1944

Matilda P., wife of
H. M. Pirtle
Nov 26, 1867
Nov 10, 1886

Susan, wife of
John M. Scot
Jan 29, 1842
Apr 18, 1883

James L. Tate
May 29, 1836
Jun 30, 1902

Rachel Myers Tate
Aug 29, 1834
Apr 31, 1919

J. B. George
Mar 13, 1855
Aug 28, 1931
& wife
Delitha Tate George
Jan 29, 1860
May 8, 1925

J. Edgar George
Dec 2, 1881
Sep 20, 1899

Polly George
Died Aug 19, 1883
Age: 67 years.

Thomas George
Nov 17, 1803
Jul 13, 1888

James W. George
1879-1920

Floyd George
Dec 21, 1909
Apr 1, 1917

Ruth George
1916-1920

Ellen George
1911-1920

Samuel Jahue Tate
Jul 26, 1858
Nov 20, 1912

Rosa B. Conrad, wife of
Eld. W. A. Pinkstaff
Dec 17, 1877
Oct 2, 1924

Emaly G. Pylant
Apr 3, 1832
Jun 18, 1896

Edd Wood
1887-1962
&
Edna B. Wood
1888-1932

Neil G. Smith
Nov 22, 1872
May 12, 1932
&
Edna Clayton Smith
Mar 17, 1877
Nov 4, 1962

Charlie F. Smith
Jan 23, 1869
Apr 7, 1923
&
Mollie Boaz Smith
Mar 9, 1873
May 12, 1946

Thomas W. Smith, Sr.
Jan 28, 1842
Jul 28, 1919
&
Cynthia B. Thomas Smith
Jan 9, 1834
Dec 9, 1919

Hugh Thomas
Jan 7, 1824
Mar 19, 1899
Age: 75 years.

Cynthia Millard, wife of
Hugh Thomas
Sep 23, 1829
May 13, 1907

Lizzie Thomas
1862-1934
&
Cora Thomas
1867-1928

Infant Daughter of
Mr. & Mrs. M. L. Thomas
B&D Jan 23, 1900

H. H. Colter
Feb 8, 1829
Mar 29, 1910
"Mexican & Confederate
 Veteran."

Annie Holman, Daughter of
W. D. & Josie White
Feb 15, 1893
Jul 29, 1895

Willie B., Son of
W. N. & R. B. Thomas
Aug 28, 1897
Jun 25, 1899

Infants of
Joe & Ida Thomas
B&D Sep 22, 1899
B&D Sep 12, 1900

Children of
W. N. & R. B. Thomas
Flora Rosborough Thomas
Nov 18, 1895
Jul 11, 1896
&
Eugene Logan Thomas
Sep 17, 1883
Aug 2, 1896

William N. Thomas
1863-1936
&
Barbara C. Thomas
1865-1933

Maggie Lou Thomas, wife of
James Castleman
1886-1957

James B. Talley
Nov 22, 1863
Nov 25, 1950
&
Maggie B. Talley
Oct 19, 1880
Feb 26, 1939

Allie B., Son of
J. B. & L. I. Talley
Nov 13, 1887
Jan 7, 1912

Laura I. Ellis, wife of
J. B. Talley
Jan 6, 1868
Apr 22, 1909

Luciel, Daughter of
J. B. & L. I. Talley
Dec 14, 1896
Feb 11, 1916

Infant Daughter of
J. L. & M. F. Scott
Mar 16, 1912
Mar 31, 1912

J. A. Daves
Jan 6, 1859
Jul 3, 1897

Mrs. Nell Turney Daves
Died Jul 2, 1974
Age: 70 years.

George W. Thomas
1879-1951
&
Naomi Giles Thomas
1889-19

Wiley B. Ellis
Sep 20, 1841
Jul 19, 1926
&
Lou Chitwood Ellis
May 16, 1847
Dec 12, 1932

Ellis M. Scott
Feb 10, 1845
Jan 31, 1913
& wife
Margaret Scott
Jun 28, 1849
Oct 9, 1914

John J. Daves
Sep 21, 1856
Apr 1, 1931

Mary C. Daves
Nov 26, 1862
Apr 30, 1925

Madie Thomas, wife of
W. R. Daves
Dec 21, 1890
Sep 2, 1914

James W. Daves
Sep 17, 1881
Apr 18, 1936

William Roy Daves
Jul 24, 1885
Oct 31, 1943

Bessie Daves Simms
Nov 22, 1898
Aug 19, 1956

John C. Daves
Pvt N.G. Co 6 Inf WW I
Jul 20, 1892
Aug 9, 1943

Myrtle Pitts
1886-1963

Mike W. Bryant
Aug 3, 1901
May 22, 1968
&
Marjorie S. Bryant
Oct 5, 1904

Married Nov 12, 1925

Mark L. Thomas
1871-1936

Elizabeth Thomas
1881-1951

Jackson Haynie
Jun 8, 1870
Oct 11, 1951

Nancy A. Hanks, wife of
T. J. Haynie
Mar 20, 1871
Jun 27, 1928

Daniel Isaac Haynie
Died Mar 12, 1911
Age:(Not given)

FAYETTEVILLE QUADRANGLE

Samuel Haynie
Oct 5, 1832
Aug 21, 1916

Anna Haynie
Jun 24, 1832
Nov 7, 1914

S. J. Haynie
Sep 29, 1861
Oct 12, 1941

Anna Lou, Daughter of
Samuel & Anna Haynie
Apr 10, 1873
Nov 15, 1898
Age: 25y, 7m, 5d.

R. T. Moore
1852-1925

Lou R. Thomas, wife of
R. T. Moore
Nov 27, 1860
Mar 8, 1917

Walter L. Moore
Sep 17, 1887
Mar 4, 1948
&
Nell L. Moore
Aug 9, 1888
Mar 4, 1962

Bobby Glen Moore
Jan 12, 1938
Jun 17, 1948

Children of
J. L. & Mary L. Moore
Ruth Moore
1915-1923
&
Dan Moore
1918

Daniel F. Moore
Sep 1, 1844
Sep 24, 1915

Fannie A. Moore
Mar 19, 1845
Nov 14, 1931

Lizzie Moore Wade
Dec 8, 1874
Oct 16, 1896

James L. Moore
Dec 18, 1872
Jun 27, 1951
&
Mary L. Moore
Jan 27, 1879

Rufus Earl Welch
Sep 19, 1887
Aug 17, 1952
&
Maudie Ervin Welch
Dec 11, 1886
Jun 1, 1960

Rufus O. Welch
Tennessee
Pfc 263rd Fld Arty
Bn 26 Inf Div WW II
Apr 8, 1917
Nov 15, 1944

Jack Sawyers
Jan 13, 1904
Dec 16, 1935

Charlie G. Sawyers
Tennessee
Tec 5, 9201 Tech S.V.C.Unite
WW II
Apr 18, 1912
Apr 12, 1951

George Sawyers
Jul 1, 1874
Oct 10, 1938

Leoda Sawyers
Sep 1, 1882
Jul 18, 1965

Isaac Tate
Oct   1870
Jan   1940
& wife
Leona Tate
Dec 15, 1862
Feb 17, 1925

M. L. Brown, wife of
I. C. Tate
Apr 3, 1873
Jan 14, 1904

Son of
J. C. & Erby T. Lyons
Jul 11, 1913

Martin V. Brown
Oct 26, 1837
Dec 10, 1901

Martha Ann Brown
1848-1920

Sallie J. Riley
Jun 13, 1850
Sep 17, 1904

S. Green Riley
Apr 25, 1883
May 12, 1905

Allen Summerford
Aug 6, 1882
Oct 7, 1904

David A. Summerford
May 14, 1859
Feb 12, 1925

Nannie D. Summerford
Nov 3, 1850
Apr 19, 1941

Albert D. Summerford
May 26, 1893
Jan 27, 1916

John Edgar Thomas
Dec 18, 1905
Jan 8, 1906

Walter C. Thomas
Jul 21, 1872
Mar 6, 1940

Letsie C. Thomas
Feb 27, 1872
Jun 21, 1937

Mrs. Ann Moore
1850-1934

Edd Johnson Cashion
Died Oct 28, 1910
Age: 37y, 2m, 15d.

Caldonia Cashion
Aug 28, 1873
Apr 27, 1918

Richard W. Cashion
Mar 20, 1851
Nov 23, 1916
&
Mary Eliza Johnson Cashion
Feb 24, 1854
Aug 22, 1916

Frank, Son of
J. E. & Sallie Posey
Jan 6, 1889
Jan 15, 1916

Myrtle Lee, Daughter of
Mr. & Mrs. G. W. Powell
Jun 28, 1894
Aug 6, 1896

S. M. Jordan
1853-1914

Tabitha, wife of
S. M. Jordan
(no dates)

William F. Crabtree
1854-1940

Mrs. William F. Crabtree
1872-1939

Wiley W. Smith
Jul 19, 1869
Sep 26, 1904

Thomas H. Smith
1861-1940
&
Mollie Fox
1855-1942
"Brother & Sister."

George W., Son of
Abe & Lucy Summerford
Jan 22, 1843
Aug 26, 1869

Francis Ellanor, wife of
George G. Crawford
Jun 16, 1855
Dec 21, 1872
&
Fannie Etta, Daughter of
G. G. & F. E. Crawford
Dec 15, 1872
Aug 9, 1873

Claiborne S. Clark
May 25, 1839
(Date cemented into base)

Sue E., wife of
C. S. Clark
Aug 5, 1846
Feb 16, 1903

Rebecca M., wife of
Joe Roe
Feb 1, 1834
Feb 25, 1907

Mary D., Daughter of
C. S. & S. E. Clark
Jun 24, 1880
Jan 27, 1888

Martha H., Daughter of
C. S. & S. E. Clark
Sep 30, 1875
Aug 30, 1889

William S. Clark
Oct 17, 1870
Oct 1, 1941
&
Fannie B. Clark
Jan 16, 1885

Thomas A. Boaz
Dec 16, 1843
Apr 8, 1918
& wife
Leatha Ann Thomison Boaz
Sep 18, 1848
(no date)

Rufe Bryant
1866-1947
&
Callie Bryant
1868-1939

FAYETTEVILLE QUADRANGLE

Francis S., wife of
S. R. Brown
Aug 3, 1828
Jul 12, 1895

Samuel R. Brown
Jan 4, 1826
Mar 17, 1899

Lavina A. Brown
Dec 1, 1847
Mar 17, 1900

William E. Bryant
1858-1937
&
Gertrude C. Bryant
1863-1941

Samuel H. Turney
1873-1937

Pearl Turney
1871-1957

Ada Clift Scott
1874-1940

Joe D. Beatie
Apr 1, 1884
Jan 16, 1916

Maggie Lee Childs
Jun 26, 1871
Oct 19, 1892

John B. Beatie
May 26, 1851
Oct 10, 1890

Earl Beatie
Mar 27, 1890
1892

Wrightie Beatie
Jun   1884
       1889

E. G. Johnson
Jan 4, 1818
Dec 15, 1831
&
Sarah Ann Johnson
Jun 21, 1823
Aug 8, 1879

William Clark
born in Washington Co., Va.
Dec 18, 1792
Jun 28, 1870

Harriet, wife of
William Clark
born in Washington Co., Va.
Dec 14, 1802
Apr 14, 1891

Mammie May, Daughter of
W. F. & M. A. Hamilton
Died Feb 28, 1876
Age: 9 days.

J. L. Clark
Feb 4, 1830
Jun 27, 1871

Susan R., wife of
James L. Clark
Jan 11, 1832
Sep 24, 1899

Walter L. Clark
Jun 27, 1876
Aug 6, 1877

Marion Clark
Mar 3, 1878
Nov 28, 1879

Infant Son of
W. T. & Fannie Clark
Sep 17, 1879

David Crawford Clark
Died May 2, 1969
Age: 81y, 4m, 14d.

W. T. Clark
May 26, 1853
Jan 8, 1916
& wife
Fannie Harris Clark
Apr 1, 1856
Dec 14, 1892

Lilburn W. Clark
May 9, 1881
May 25, 1961

Margaret, wife of
L. L. Clark
Sep 27, 1831
Feb 25, 1905

Lilburn L. Clark
born in Washington Co., Va.
Feb 6, 1825
Sep 28, 1881

Hattie F., wife of
J. T. Monday
Oct 3, 1857
Jul 19, 1903

J. T. Monday
Dec 14, 1849
Nov 3, 1910

Sally Tallman
Jul 8, 1826
Jan 9, 1888

J. H. Tallman
Died Aug 4, 1893
Age: about 75 years.

D. F. Tallman
1850-1927

William Henry, Son of
D. F. & M. Tallman
Jul 16, 1888
Jan 27, 1905

Sarah Allen Summerford
Died Apr 11, 1913
Age: 80y, 1m.

Sophia Summerford
Oct 14, 1869
Nov 16, 1893

Irene Summerford
Jul 4, 1867
Aug 13, 1891

William Summerford
May 30, 1862
(date broken away)

A. L. Summerford
Aug 29, 1864
Nov 23, 1888

A. C. Smith
Feb 12, 1840
May 27, 1909

Ameralle Buchanan, wife of
A. C. Smith
Jun 20, 1848
(no date)

Fannie Lou, Daughter of
A. C. & S. A. Smith
Nov 19, 1885
Jul 24, 1896
&
Infant Son of
A. C. & S. A. Smith
Jan 2, 1880
Mar 3, 1880

A. T. Smith
Dec 19, 1796
Jun 15, 1879

Mary B., wife of
A. T. Smith
May   1808
Dec 19, 1877

Kate M. Summerford
Sep 16, 1859
Jul 31, 1880

Meck, wife of
W. P. Bledsoe
Nov 22, 1850
Mar 14, 1880
Age: 29y, 3m, 22d.

Lillian L., child of
W. & M. A. Bledsoe
Aug 8, 1874
Feb 5, 1875

Jennie, Daughter of
Thomas & M. J. Hampton
Dec 10, 1868
Jun 10, 1875

Alford M. Hampton
May 28, 1852
Oct 25, 1876

P. R. Jenkins
1863-1934

Jennie Jenkins
1854-1937

Mary A., Daughter of
W. F. & M. A. Hamilton
Jul 8, 1877
Aug 19, 1878

Thomas Hampton
Oct 29, 1815
Apr 29, 1905

Martha J., wife of
Thomas Hampton
Feb 14, 1826
Jul 21, 1883

Emma Hampton
1859-1936

Lacy Dee Conwell
Sep 2, 1879
Sep 12, 1906

Clay Rosborough
1858-1927
&
Effie Rosborough
1861-1946

Fannie Rosborough
1888-1962
&
Mary Rosborough
1885-1941

James M. Scott
1857-(no date)
&
Maggie Eaks Scott
1855-1936

Jane George, wife of
William Eaks
Jul 22, 1829
Aug 10, 1904
Age: 75 years.

William Neely Eaks
Apr 26, 1833
Jan 11, 1903

Mary Eaks
Nov 4, 1853
Jun 16, 1896

Thomas Eaks
Oct 3, 1871
Jun 22, 1895
Age: 22y, 8m, 19d.

James E. Hazlett
Tennessee
Pvt 17 Co 157 Depot Brig.
WW I
Sep 16, 1893
Oct 21, 1952

FAYETTEVILLE QUADRANGLE

Legrand Hazlett
Aug 9, 1851
Feb 22, 1916
&
Annette Hazlett
May 25, 1854
(no date)

Lillie B., Daughter of
M. S. & J. M. Scott
Aug 9, 1889
May 26, 1896
&
Ewing, Son of
M. S. & J. M. Scott
Aug 21, 1883
Jun 5, 1896

William Leonard, Son of
W. A. & Lonie Moore
Jun 3, 1905
Aug 28, 1905

James McNeill
Aug 24, 1827
Oct 14, 1905
& wife
Sallie McNeill
Jun 25, 1835
(no date)

W. A. McNeill
Jan 4, 1859
Aug 4, 1887

Joseph Epps *
Died Jan 8, 1892
Age: 42 years.

W. A. Patton *
Died Dec 6, 1896
Age: 71 years.

H. M. Pirtle *
Died Jun 10, 1909
Age: 62 years.
C.S.A.

Miss Netta A. Jenkins *
Died Nov 23, 1916
Age: 60y, 6d.

_____ Nichols
1874-1946 (name gone)
&
Ruby Nichols
1869-1936

James A., Son of
T. O. Hazlett
Sep 19, 1895
Sep 4, 1930

J. G. Chapman
1864-1942
&
Alice McNeill Chapman
1866-1911

W. A. McNeill
Jan 4, 1859
Aug 4, 1887
&
James McNeill
Sep 1, 1864
Aug 11, 1905

Ida P. McNeill, wife of
T. O. Hazlett
Apr 12, 1863
Oct 4, 1894

T. O. Hazlett
Nov 7, 1864
(no date)
& wife
Lillian Hazlett
Oct 3, 1859
Aug 17, 1932

James Smith *
Died Nov 14, 1893
Age: 19 years.

George Newman,* Son of
James & Ida Tallman
Died Apr 7, 1897
Age: 13m.

Nellie,* Daughter of
Mr. & Mrs. Frank Ayers
Died Feb 7, 1914
Age: 5y, 7m.
"Burned to death."

Marvin Earl Bryant
Jun 25, 1894
Aug 15, 1955
&
Mary Lou Hazlett Bryant
Apr 12, 1900
Sep 13, 1947

Sallie May, Daughter of
T. O. & Lillian Hazlett
B&D 1896

C. C. Armstrong
1893-1940

Grace Young Davidson
1898-1957

William H. Young
1860-1929
&
Willie M. Young
1857-1936

Infant Daughter of
W. H. & Willie Young
B&D 1902

Infant Son of
W. H. & Willie Young
B&D 1904

Sister
Alline Young
1895-1947

Mrs. Rebecca Ann Scott *
Died Aug 8, 1902
Age: 33y, 11m.

Samuel,* Son of
T. S. & Alice Haynie
Died Mar 12, 1911
Age: 5y, 20d.

Leonard Potent,* Son of
Mr. & Mrs. Abe Winsett
Jun 25, 1903
Mar 3, 1904

Many unmarked graves.

George T. Eshman
Oct 3, 1853
Dec 23, 1924
& wife
Lorena Taylor Eshman
Feb 2, 1864
(no date)

Henry F. Steelman
1864-1946
&
Rosa F. Steelman
1869-1944

Miss Effie Clift
1868-1938

Infant * of
John Beaty
Died Jun 30, 1891
Age: 15m.

Infant * of
John & Mollie Daves
Died Oct 7, 1896
Age: (not given)

Mrs. Rosa May,* wife of
James Moore
Died Jul 15, 1917
Age: 32 years.

Mrs. Nancy Virginia
Sawyers * died at a
Daughter's, Mrs.
Thomas Deal on
Jul 28, 1917
Age: 61 years.

Mrs. Lavinia A. Brown *
Died Mar 17, 1906
Age: 57y, 3m, 16d.

James E. Johnson *
Died Aug 6, 1903
Age: 75y, 10m.

Rev. John Conrad *
Died Feb 3, 1916
Age: 83 years.
Born in Illinois.

* *

GILES CEMETERY

LOCATION: Two miles NE of Howell in Giles Hollow and three-fourth mile west of Highway 231.

Thomas H. Giles
May 21, 1816
May 28, 1892

Dorothy Giles
Aug 17, 1821
Dec 8, 1893

S. L. Giles
Apr 12, 1862
Aug 8, 1900

Dollie G. Giles
Feb 18, 1865
Oct 26, 1889

Mrs. Ursula,* wife of N. C.
Harris & Daughter of Thomas
H. Giles, Dec'd. Died Jun 5,
1897, Age 46y. Mrd 1875.

Sallie A. Giles
Dec 25, 1856
Apr 17, 1894

C. M. Giles
Oct 4, 1853
Feb 13, 1899

C. H. Harris
Nov 20, 1875
Mar 14, 1898

J. U., wife of
N. C. Harris
Aug 10, 1851
Jun 5, 1897

T. F., Daughter of
N. C. & J. U. Harris
Mar 13, 1892
Jun 17, 1902

* *

FAYETTEVILLE QUADRANGLE

ARMSTRONG-MOORE CEMETERY

LOCATION: Two miles south of Belleville and east of Highway 231 on hill.

Mary Elise Armstrong
Jan 29, 1907
Jun 18, 1910

Andrew Moore
Aug 1, 1806
Sep 5, 1854

Rachel Moore
Sep 28, 1810
Jun 26, 1893

W. N. Moore
Dec 10, 1817
Nov 2, 1875
  & wife
Martha Moore
Dec 18, 1822
Sep 10, 1892

George T. Armstrong *
Died Feb 21, 1903
Age: 75 years.

Mrs. Dollie Corder *
Died Feb 19, 1903
Age: 47 years.
Married Perry Corder in 1880.

Son * of
Mr. & Mrs. Isaac Perry
Died Jul 27, 1909
Age: 2y, 7m.

F. F. Steed *
Died Oct 28, 1899
Age: 71 years.
Married in 1858 to
Mary Tucker

Emma Lou,* Daughter of
F. F. & Mary Steed
Died May 24, 1899
Age: 21 years.

Hugh Moore
Sep 7, 1812
Dec 5, 1872
Age: 60y, 16d.

"Our Mother"
Margaret H., wife of
John H. Moore
Apr 18, 1813
May 3, 1882
Age: 69y, 15d.

C. F. Moore
Sep 28, 1850
Dec 5, 1881
Age: 31y, 2m, 7d.

Nancy Moore
Mar 2, 1833
Jun 15, 1918

James A. McGee *
Died Apr 5, 1903
Age: 28 years.

Miss Mary Sawyers *
Jul 3, 1903
Age: 26 years.

Lee Sanders,* Son of
Mr. & Mrs. Ike Perry
Died Jan 29, 1904
Age: 13m.

William Dempsey *
Died Sep 4, 1911
Age: (not given)

David Ross,* Son of
D. F. & Caroline Moore
Died Sep 22, 1895
Age: 10y, 9m.

J. P. Hudson
Mar 6, 1844
Aug 22, 1909

Estelle P. Clark
(no dates)

Cynthia Smith
(no dates)

Lee Perry
(no dates)

Tommy Perry
(no dates)

William Perry
(no dates)

Eddie E. Reese
Jan 14, 1887
Jun 15, 1912

Mrs. Elizabeth Armstrong *
Died Apr 23, 1905
Age: 72 years.

Mrs. Lou,* wife of
Silas Bradford
Died Apr 14, 1896
Age: 39 years.

Newton Pearson *
Died Jul 13, 1915
Age: 84 years.

Mrs. Elizabeth,* widow of
James B. Hudson
Died Aug 30, 1892
Age: 82 years.

many unmarked graves.

NOTE: The following 4 graves are located across the old road.

Eliza, wife of
W. E. Moore
Died Feb 2, 1896
Age: 72 years.

Mary D., wife of
W. E. Moore
Sep 12, 1851
(no date)

Infant Daughter of
Edward & Martha Summerford
Jan 24, 1848
Mar 10, 1848

Eliza, Daughter of
Edward & Martha Summerford
Feb 9, 1854
Nov 8, 18--(gone)

John H. Moore *
Died Oct 15, 1897
Age: 82 years.
Married 1837 to
Margaret H. Armstrong

Mrs. Charlotie,* wife of
Thomas Armstrong & Daughter
of James & Elizabeth
Crane.
Died Jun 7, 1896
Age: 79 years.

Martha Fannie Moore *
Died Sep 14, 1897
Age: 43y, 5m, 17d.

* *

PITTS CEMETERY

LOCATION: Two and one-fourth miles SW of Belleville on Hungry Branch, on Rutledge Hill Road.

Sarah, wife of
B. Pitts
Apr 4, 1824
Oct 28, 1891
married Jul 4, 1849

Bryant, Son of
W. H. & Rena Ladd
Died Jun 22, 1890
Age: 2y, 10m, 5d.

About 10 graves with fieldstones, no inscriptions.

* *

FAYETTEVILLE QUADRANGLE

BUNTLEY CEMETERY

LOCATION: Two miles NW of Mimosa on Hungry Branch Road.

Wade Hampton Brown
1879-1957
&
Cynthia Groce Brown
1881-1954
 	
2 unmarked infant graves.
	Robert Haggard Isom
	May 14, 1858
	Jul 12, 1940
	&
	Sarah Ann Buntley Isom
	Dec 21, 1859
	Dec 20, 1932
		George C. Buntley
		Jun 29, 1859
		Nov 23, 1898
		&
		Mary Etta Buntley
		Nov 11, 1863
		Feb 19, 1948
			Vickey Jan & Vivian Ann
			Cashion
			   Oct 13, 1966
			
			Patricia Lynn, Daughter of
			J. V. & Grace Buntley
			   Dec 24, 1935
			
			Rossia L., Daughter of
			Dave & Ola Buntley
			   Jun 28, 1914

* *

BUNTLEY CEMETERY

LOCATION: One and three-fourth miles NW of Mimosa on Hungry Branch Road.

Jacob B. Buntley Jan 6, 1831 Sep 29, 1887 & Elizabeth Buntley Dec 4, 1830 Aug 27, 1888	William M. Buntley Nov 17, 1863 Nov 20, 1938 Sallie Warden, wife of W. M. Buntley 1867-1935	Jacob H., Son of J. M. & Mary M. Geowen May 6, 1883 Nov 1883 Louisa M. Mills Died Feb 13, 1851 Age: (not given)	George,* Son of Jake & C. H. Buntley Died Mar 31, 1897 Age: 1y, 3m, 15d. About 8 graves with fieldstones, no inscriptions.

* *

GEORGE CEMETERY

LOCATION: One and one-fourth miles NW of Mimosa on Hungry Hollow Road.

James O. George Feb 4, 1875 May 24, 1893 Leola George Aug 17, 1879 Apr 14, 1903 James H. Rutledge 1848-1947 Mrs. J. H. Rutledge 1852-1934 Mrs. Nannie Lane * Died Feb 17, 1918 Age: 33 years.	P. O. George Aug 1821 Dec 1894 P. E., wife of P. O. George Nov 27, 1839 Jun 17, 1892 Annie Bell Edmondson * Died Jun 22, 1895 Age: 15 years. James H. Edmondson * Died Dec 6, 1907 Age: 57 years. Married Mary Jane Rutledge Oct 12, 1872 Many unmarked graves.	Philipp Pamplin B&D 1897 Charlie Pamplin B&D 1898 Horace Pamplin B&D 1905 Alfred Alexander,* Son of J. H. Edmondson Died Apr 24, 1898 Age: 20y, 26d. James M. George * Died Feb 21, 1900 Age: 23 years.	Myrtle Lane Died about 1969, early Age: 98/99 years. J. Deimer Pamplin Oct 9, 1874 Dec 29, 1931 & May Pamplin Oct 3, 1877 ----------- Mrs. Mary Jane,* wife of J. H. Edmiston Died Apr 18, 1899 Age: 57y, 20d. Ivy Edmondson * Died Mar 29, 1901 Age: 17y, 5m, 24d.

* *

ASHBY CEMETERY

LOCATION: One mile north of Mimosa on west side of road.

Jessee M. Bedwell Mar 15, 1851 Sep 19, 1885	G. B. Bedwell Feb 15, 1847 Jan 25, 1893	Infant of Joel A. & Ellie Pitts Died Dec 22, 1897 Age: (not given)	Joel A. Pitts Nov 18, 1837 Apr 26, 1902

FAYETTEVILLE QUADRANGLE

Peter G. Ashby
Feb 12, 1821
Dec 10, 1857
&
Mary J. Ashby
Mar 31, 1828
Aug 3, 1889

Ada Bedwell Waid
Oct 29, 1876
Apr 13, 1901

Charlie Warden
1872-
&
Maggie Warden
1869-1945

Many unmarked graves.

E. W. Ashby
Sep 25, 1835
Mar 30, 1912

Cyntha E. Ashby
Mar 22, 1840
Dec 3, 1886

Flora Belle, wife of
J. M. Warden
Sep 26, 1863
Aug 8, 1899

Brother
David F. Warden
(dates are deep in ground)

Malissie M. Warden
Dec 31, 1858
Apr 16, 1892

H. M. Largen
Jul 20, 1836
Nov 13, 1904

Mary Ann Sims Keith Largen
May 6, 1839
Jan 12, 1912

Thomas D. Sims
Feb 13, 1850
Jul 29, 1925

Ann Sims
1856-1936

Mable,* Daughter of
Mr. & Mrs. E. Bedwell
burned to death
Jun 30, 1918
Age: 6 years.

H. L. Brown
1903-1934

Lucy Ann Brown
1907-1941

W. A. Pitts
Sep 11, 1812
Nov 4, 1889

Mary Pitts
Jan 12, 1807
Sep 30, 1890

Mrs. Julia Ann,* wife of
William Forrester
Died Feb 18, 1908
Age: (not given)

* *

JOHNSON-WARDEN CEMETERY

LOCATION: One-half mile north of Mimosa on west side of road.

Allen Hanks
1869-1947
(Raby FH)

I. J. Hanks
Nov 19, 1835
Sep 23, 1912

Nancy J. Hanks
Oct 16, 1832
Aug 1, 1891

John T. Pamplin
Nov 30, 1841
Feb 1, 1907

Sallie Pamplin
Sep 27, 1871
Nov 14, 1891

Robert G. Haynie
Mar 16, 1864
Sep 4, 1900
&
Fannie L. Haynie
May 3, 1866
Aug 23, 1942

L. A. E. Smith
Apr 13, 1851
Jun 10, 1852

Bernice O., Son of
N. C. & Mary Lane
Nov 19, 1894
Mar 15, 1901

John Lane
Dec 7, 1862
Feb 9, 1893
NOTE: John Lane's wife
may be buried here also
as his large marker is
on the ground and the
inscription cannot be
read.

Mrs. S. A. E. Whitworth *
Died May 25, 1900
Age: 62y, 8m, 20d.

Gertrude,* Daughter of
G. W. & Sallie Lane
Died Apr 23, 1906
Age: 18 years.

Adrian Nathi,* Daughter of
J. C. & Lillian Isom
Died 1897
Age: 6y, 14d.

Several unmarked graves.

Several fieldstones,
no inscriptions.

NOTE: According to information
supplied by David P. Johnson
of Montgomery, Alabama, that
three of the unmarked graves
are:

Angus Johnson
1790-Mar 14, 1861

Lucy Isom Johnson
1795-Apr 11, 1877

James Madison Johnson
Aug 10, 1836
Sep 10, 1894

NOTE: The following two are
supplied by Lilly May Pamplin
of Salt Lake City, Utah.

McCager Armstead Pamplin
born Halifax Co., Va.
1805, died 1863.

Mrs. Lavina Frances, wife of
McCager Pamplin
born in Halifax Co., Va.
Died Mar 12, 1893
Age: 87y, 3m, 12d.

Miss Ada Rebecca Lane *
Died Jan 16, 1904
Age: (not given)

Mrs. Sarah Holman Lane *
Died Dec 8, 1913
Age: 65 years.

W. A. Parks *
Died Aug 8, 1905
Age: 82 years.

Mrs. Sarah Pamplin *
Died May 13, 1900
Age: 35y, 8m.

Mrs. Nancy D. Pamplin *
Died Jul 2, 1900
Age: 68y, 1m, 3d.

John Pamplin *
Died Jan 12, 1910
Age: 70 years.

Mrs. Caroline,* wife of
John T. Pamplin
Died Jan 27, 1917
Age: 67 years.

* *

FAYETTEVILLE QUADRANGLE

WARDEN-KEITH CEMETERY

LOCATION: Two miles North of Mimosa, west of Lane Branch Road on side of hill.

J. S. Keith Jun 10, 1831 (no other date)	William R. Warden Feb 14, 1852 Sep 13, 1852	Prudence E. Warden Nov 10, 1827 Oct 5, ---- (broken)	Susie Pearl Warden * Died Dec 31, 1902 Age: 3y, 11m, 19d.
Infant * of Mr. & Mrs. Henry Brown Died Feb 7, 1903 Age: 2 days.	Jessie May Warden * Died Oct 14, 1907 Age: 16 years.	Mrs. Mary,* widow of Harden Warden Died Jun 30, 1900 Age: 72 years.	Infant * of Albert Tucker Died Jun 5, 1901 Age: (not given)
	George W. Mills Died May 7, 1907 Age: 58y, 5m, 9d.	About 20 fieldstones with no inscriptions.	

* *

PAMPLIN CEMETERY

LOCATION: Three-fourth mile NNW of Mimosa in Toddy Hollow.

L. P. (footstone) Ella Pamplin *** Nov 1, 1875 Mar 1, 1896	Andrew Jackson Pamplin *** Dec 19, 1838 Nov 23, 1895 & Mary Etta Victoria Pamplin Oct 23, 1856 Nov 23, 1886	Leoda Pamplin *** Apr 23, 1880 Oct 23, 1881 Etta Pamplin *** Dec 5, 1876 Feb 25, 1892	Ella Bell Pamplin *** Jan 5, 1896 Apr 23, 1896 Several graves with fieldstones, no inscriptions.

*** According to information in the Book "Scamps of Bucksnort" by Lily May Pamplin.

* *

PAMPLIN CEMETERY

LOCATION: One-fourth mile NNW of Mimosa.

Some of the early Pamplins are said to be buried here.

10 to 12 graves with fieldstones, no inscriptions.

* *

CONGER CEMETERY

LOCATION: One-half mile east of Mimosa and east of main road.

Mary Conger Nov 15, 1782 Mar 4, 1857	Felix H. Conger Dec 14, 1812 Nov 4, 1834 "Remember men as you pass by, As you are now, so once was I. As I am now, so you must be prepared for death and follow me."	Henry Moores Oct 9, 1744 Feb 1, 1811 "A Soldier of the Revolution." Jane Brown Moore Feb 25, 1800 Dec 25, 1858	Major John Moore Oct 9, 1777 Oct 29, 1844 Jane Moores Oct 24, 1777 Jul 25, 1840
Matilda Conger Apr 16, 1807 Oct 23, 1812			
"Montie" Montene Conger Oct 21, 1860 Sep 27, 1862	Delila L. Conger Aug 11, 1805 Oct 11, 1837	Ellison R. Hines Dec 9, 1833 Jan 30, 1853	Eli Moore Mar 29, 1793 Aug 17, 1855
Sion M. Conger May 7, 1810 Jan 27, 1874	Isaac Conger Nov 8, 1779 Mar 30, 1847 Several unmarked graves.	Henry Moores, Son of W. & S. Whitaker Jun 4, 1836 in Fairfield District, S. C. Died Sep 9, 1837	Mrs. Finnetta Moore Jul 12, 1807 Dec 19, 1834

* *

FAYETTEVILLE QUADRANGLE

ISOM CEMETERY

LOCATION: One-half mile SSE of Mimosa and east of main road.

G. F. Isom
Apr 14, 1825
May 12, 1907
&
Cyntha C. Isom
Oct 13, 1839
Mar 2, 1902

Mrs. Mary Jane,* wife of
W. C. Warden
Died Jul 18, 1893
Age: 40 years.

John W. Isom
Dec 14, 1873
Feb 28, 1894

James Isom
Nov 25, 1789
Apr 12, 1874

Several unmarked graves.

W. C. Warden *
Died Jan 22, 1922
Age: 56 years.

William T. Isom
Oct 15, 1875
Sep 23, 1877

John Gordon,* Son of
Mr. & Mrs. L. A. Isom
Died Mar 17, 1916
Age: (not given)

William Homer,* Son of
W. C. & Jane Warden
Died Jan 1, 1895
Age: 13y, 5m.

Jesse J.,* Son of
Mr. & Mrs. James Isom
Died Dec 20, 1897
Age: 4m.

Mrs. Elizabeth Smith *
Died Jun 27, 1896
Age: 73 years.

* *

ALEXANDER CEMETERY

LOCATION: One and one-fourth miles SW of Mimosa near Possum Hollow.

Lewis M. Fleming
Mar 21, 1828
Oct 25, 1857

Rachel Salina, wife of
Lewis M. Fleming
Sep 1, 1833
Jan 8, 1887

John Oliver, Son of
J. W. & S. R. Boaz
Oct 11, 1876
Sep 7, 1877

Grover Largen, Son of
J. W. & S. R. Boaz
Jan 1, 1893
Feb 8, 1895

Fletcher, Son of
T. A. & L. A. Boaz
Feb 17, 1869
Nov 7, 1879

Tera Boaz, wife of
P. F. Moore
Jul 4, 1874
Aug 12, 1913

Marietta, wife of
H. I. Marrs, & Daughter of
F. M. & C. E. Pamplin
born Feb 16, 18--
died (date gone, broken)

M. B. Pamplin
Jul 3, 1865
Jul 28, 1888

William L. Alexander *
Died Apr 13, 1896
Age: 68y, 25d.
Brother to George J. &
H. H. Alexander.

Sam Little
(footstone has S. L., headstone missing)

Jane, wife of
Sam Little
Jan 7, 1821
Aug 15, 1897

B. G. Little
Aug 23, 1852
Mar 9, 1899

Emma Oldham, wife of
B. G. Little
Sep 17, 1855
Nov 3, 1922

Mary M., wife of
S. H. Little
Aug 28, 1850
Apr 7, 1899

Fannie V., wife of
R. M. Lane
Mar 22, 1872
Mar 1, 1893

J. E. Mills
Dec 12, 1844
Feb 22, 1904

William V. Tate
born in S. C.
May 9, 1825
Feb 13, 1899

Ruth K., wife of
W. V. Tate
Jan 15, 1827
Nov 13, 1890

Willie Vance, Son of
W. V. & R. K. Tate
Sep 20, 1867
May 30, 1887

Charles H., Son of
W. V. & R. K. Tate
Jan 1, 1875
Feb 17, 1914

Mollie Ruth, Daughter of
W. V. & R. K. Tate
Jun 1, 1872
Aug 16, 1889

Samuel Woodruff Tate
Mar 15, 1858
Jul 4, 1929
Age: 66y, 3m, 8d.

James Tillman, Son of
H. H. & L. A. Alexander
Dec 13, 1871
Dec 17, 1887

Martha C., wife of
A. J. McClain & Daughter of
S. S. Alexander
Mar 5, 1849
Jun 19, 1875

S. S. Alexander
born in Williamson Co., Tenn.
May 5, 1806
died in Lincoln Co., Tenn.
Jun 13, 1881

Mary M., wife of
S. S. Alexander
Nov 9, 1809
Jan 31, 1881
Married Nov 8, 1827

R. X., wife of
W. W. Alexander
Oct 1, 1827
Jun 12, 1892

Smith Alexander, Son of
W. V. & R. K. Tate
Jun 17, 1862
Apr 7, 1886

W. W., Son of
S. S. & M. M. Alexander
Mar 19, 1832
Oct 25, 1878

J. R. Badgett
born in Knox Co., Tenn.
Jul 14, 1836
Dec 10, 1880

Amanda Alexander, wife of
J. R. Badgett
Jul 25, 1853
Jul 19, 1929

Infant Daughter of
A. J. & M. C. McLain
Jun 14, 1875
Jun 17, 1875

Delia Alexander, Daughter
of A. J. & Delia McLain
Jun 14, 1875
Jun 28, 1876

Homer D., Son of
J. G. & Kate Jacobs
Died Jan 29, 1880
Age: 6y, 16d.

Margaret Warden Alexander
Died Jan 31, 1926
Age: 76 years.
Erected by Jack Alexander

Woodruff,* Son of
W. L. Alexander
Died Dec 7, 1878
Age: 21 years.

FAYETTEVILLE QUADRANGLE

Mrs. Marietta,* wife of
H. I. Marrs & Daughter of
F. M. Pamplin
Died Apr 10, 1896
Age: 24 years.
Married 1890

William M. Boaz *
Died Nov 18, 1916
Age: 70y, 18d.
C.S.A. 44th Tenn Regt
"Left wife, 4 Daughters &
2 Sons."

Mrs. Susie Alexander *
Died Sep 9, 1897
Age: 36 years.

Mrs. Eliza Boaz *
Died Apr 12, 1917
Age: 28 years.
"Left 3 Sisters &
2 Brothers".

Mrs. William Boaz *
Died Jul 19, 1915
Age: 33 years

Mrs. Cynthia,* widow of
F. M. Pamplin
Died at Daughter, Mrs.
Rebecca Elkins of Grove,
Oklahoma on
Feb 13, 1917
Age: 74 years.
"Left 1 Son, Rufe."

Miss Sallie Boaz *
Died Dec 22, 1903
Age: 83 years.

Several unmarked graves.

Mrs. Lu V.,* wife of
H. L. Smith & Daughter of
E. A. Isom
Died Jun 27, 1890
Age: 24 years.

John Hoots *
Died Nov 25, 1893
Age: 67 years.

Mrs. Mattie L.,* wife of
T. B. Pitts & Daughter of
William E. Bradford
Apr 23, 1854
Oct 22, 1891

* *

PARKER CEMETERY

LOCATION: One and three-fourth miles WNW of Mimosa on top of Tonie Stone Ridge.

Jahue Parker
Mar 4, 1861
Jun 11, 187- (broken)

Mrs. Maria,* wife of
J. L. Parker
Died May 14, 1897
Age: 45 years.

Martha Parker
Nov 22, 1826
Oct 22, 1883

Mrs. Elizabeth,* wife of
A. A. Parker
Died May 20, 1899
Age: 39 years.

William Thomas Parker *
Died Jan 6, 1907
Age: 49 years.

Several unmarked graves.

Mary Ida,* Daughter of
A. A. & Elizabeth Parker
Died Apr 29, 1899
Age: 15y, 9m, 15d.

* *

WHITAKER-HIGGINS CEMETERY

LOCATION: Three miles south of Belleville on east side of Highway 231.

John A. Higgins
Dec 25, 1810
Oct 4, 1835
Age: 24y, 9m, 10d.

James Higgins
Oct 11, 1772
Apr 13, 1858

Nancy, wife of
James Higgins
Died 30 Mar 1825
Age: 30 years.

Sarah W., wife of
James Higgins
Sep 23, 1788
Jun 22, 1857

George Whitaker
Jun 13, 1812
Jun 17, 1900
&
Ann J. Whitaker
1829-1865

William R. Whitaker
Aug 12, 1855
Aug 17, 1891

John J. Whitaker
Nov 15, 1850
Nov 28, 1901

Several unmarked graves.

Jessie R. Childers
Oct 15, 1850
Dec 20, 1875

George Leftwich, Son of
John J. & May E. Whitaker
Oct 29, 1889
Oct 29, 1889

Infant Son of
George & A. J. Whitaker
(no dates)

H. R. Whitaker
Sep 25, 1857
Jul 24, 1901
&
Pink Rhea Whitaker
Aug 11, 1850
Dec 23, 1937

Miss Janie Whitaker,*
Daughter of
Mrs. May Etta Mansfield
Died Jul 30, 1915
Age: 22 years.

* *

STONE CEMETERY

LOCATION: Three and one-half miles south of Belleville at Norris Creek, on west side of Highway 231.

Elizabeth, wife of
M. R. Sherrell
Died Oct 4, 1848
Age: 29 years.

Little Frank, Son of
H. G. & F. A. Higgins
Died Mar 29, 1876
Age: 21m, 23d.

L. L. Stone
Sep 5, 1803
May 12, 1872
Married May 21, 1830

Julia Ann Stone
Oct 22, 1836
Jan 7, 1860

FAYETTEVILLE QUADRANGLE

Mrs. Nancy Tucker *
Died Jun 28, 1892
Age: 68 years.

Boone Shull *
Died Jan 14, 1902
Age: 85 years.

* *

SHULL CEMETERY

LOCATION: Three and one-half miles south of Belleville on west side of Highway 231 at Norris Creek.

Sarah L., wife of
D. B. Shull
Nov 17, 1826
Oct 19, 1891
NOTE: This stone is on ground, possible inscription on reverse side.

Miss Fannie Shull *
Died Mar 24, 1910
Age: (not given)

1 large Rock Vault, no inscription.

* *

CEMETERY

LOCATION: Four miles south of Belleville on west side of Highway 231, and four miles north of Fayetteville.

20 or more fieldstones, no inscriptions.

NOTE: First Settler on this land was William Edmiston, Esq.

* *

HUNTER CEMETERY

LOCATION: Four miles north of Fayetteville on the east side of Highway 231 and east side of Norris Creek on high hill.

Reubin Hunter
Nov 4, 176-
Jul 15, 1833

About 25 graves with
fieldstones, no inscription.

A. Branson
Died 1831
(no age given)

M. Branson
Died 1843
(no age given)

E. Branson
Died 1843
(no age given)

Branson
Died 1836
(no age given)

Sarah Davis
Died Jul 28, 1839
(no age given)

Lucinda Davis
Apr 21, 1811
Aug 4, 1840

* *

WADE-CLIFT CEMETERY

LOCATION: One mile ESE of Howell and west of Daves Hollow Road.

J. C. & H. C.
(footmarkers)

William Moffett
Jan 23, 1820
Mar 16, 1898
  & wife
Susan E. Moffett
Jun 23, 1824
May 28, 1902

About 10 graves with fieldstones, no inscriptions.

James F. Moffett
Feb 17, 1844
Aug 11, 1862

S. A. W.
(fieldstone, no dates)

Louisa J., wife of
W. D. Wade
Jan 5, 1826
Jan 23, 1896

Alfred W. Smith
Dec 4, 1826
Oct 18, 1890
  &
Nancy A. Smith
Jan 8, 1829
Jul 17, 1903
  &
Sarah E. Smith
Dec 20, 1860
Oct 5, 1861

J. K. Clift *
Died Nov 21, 1898
Age: 71 years.

Mrs. Elizabeth Taylor,*
wife of Joe K. Clift
Jun 2, 1845
Sep 22, 1905

A. P. Clift *
Died Oct 16, 1898
Age: 67 years.

* *

FAYETTEVILLE QUADRANGLE

HARRIS CEMETERY

LOCATION: One-fourth mile east of Howell, north side of Daves Hollow Road.

William Harris
1785-1820

Jane M. Harris
1792-1885

Howell Harris
Nov 13, 1813
Mar 24, 1881

Joel M. Harris
Sep 22, 1811
Oct 10, 1878
Age: 67y, 18d.
&
Tabitha D. Harris
Nov 5, 1812
Aug 20, 1872
Age: 59y, 2m, 15d.

Newton Cannon Harris
1850-1903

Thomas Howell Harris
Mar 1, 1839
Sep 19, 1907
&
Mary Campbell Harris
1843-1882

Joel M. Harris
1848-1914
&
Lucy Lee Harris
1855-1919

Alton J. Harris
Jun 14, 1887
Mar 23, 1925
&
Esther R. Harris
Nov 13, 1893
Nov 12, 1964

Sadie Bell, Daughter of
J. M. & L. L. Harris
Nov 11, 1879
Nov 25, 1879

Mary C. Harris
"Annie Harris"
1868-1946

Ernest Harris
1881-1957
&
Cora Harris
1888-

William C. Harris
1885-1923

Alice M. Harris
1855-1929

Daisy Lorance Harris
1879-1962

Elenor Harris
1912-

William Robert Crawford
Nov 3, 1869
Sep 2, 1936

Mary E., Daughter of
M. G. & W. R. Crawford
Jun 22, 1894
Sep 2, 1895

Infant Son of
W. R. & M. G. Crawford
(no dates)

Joseph Warren Crawford
"Memorial"
Sep 17, 1847
Jan 31, 1871
Buried in Georgia.

Preston T. Rhodes, M.D.
1863-1938
&
Mable W. Rhodes
1866-1942

Mary Elizabeth Rhodes
Oct 9, 1897
Sep 2, 1960

Olgia, Son of
Mr. & Mrs. Rufus Bryant
May 3, 1903
May 21, 1903

F. T., Daughter of
T. B. & N. J. Bryant
Jun 21, 1862
Sep 7, 1864

Squire Pickle
Died Oct 2, 1895
Age: 80 years.
&
Martha B. Pickle
Sep 22, 1811
Apr 21, 1860

John Ward
1873-1947
&
Sarah Ward
1891-1928

Abigail Ward
Mar 10, 1844
Feb 2, 1872

Mary Beatie Ward
Dec 21, 1881
Feb 3, 1920

Joseph Warren,*** Son of
W. R. & M. G. Crawford
Nov 5, 1895
Jul 11, 1897

*** Crawford Family Records.

Several unmarked graves.

Elizabeth Satterfield,
wife of
J. D. & A. H. March
1869-1943

Dr. B. M. Satterfield
Dec 10, 1834
Jun 17, 1869
&
Frances Harris Satterfield Ward
May 4, 1844
Mar 27, 1921
&
John F. Ward
Jan 20, 1839
Jul 26, 1904

Infant Sons of
J. D. & Elizabeth March
B&D 1898

Benjamin S., Son of
J. D. & Elizabeth March
1899-1926

Isaac B. Halbert
1858-1937
&
Laura S. Halbert
1867-1943

Ward K. Halbert
Nov 27, 1891
Sep 17, 1946

* *

BUCHANAN-McCOLLUM CEMETERY

LOCATION: One-half mile west of Howell on "Old S. S. Buchanan Farm."

Samuel S. Buchanan and
Mar 23, 1796 in Davidson
Co., Tenn.
Jan 20, 1873 in Lincoln
Co., Tenn.

Mary, wife of
S. S. Buchanan
born Sep 10, 1793
Rockingham Co., N. C.
died Feb 24, 1868 in
Lincoln Co., Tenn.

Andrew J., Son of
S. S. & Mary Buchanan
Oct 18, 1822
Oct 22, 1881

Pheoby T., wife of
T. W. Buchanan
Sep 20, 1819
Jan 27, 1898

FAYETTEVILLE QUADRANGLE

John Pryor Buchanan
1841-1915

Mary Elizabeth, wife of
J. P. Buchanan
Oct 18, 1846
Aug 4, 1883

Alex J. McCollum
Oct 25, 1825
Feb 10, 1902
&
Mary A., wife of
Alex McCollum
Nov 22, 1833
Feb 16, 1913

Nancy Emma Buchanan
1850-1914

Eugene P. Buchanan
May 6, 1881
Aug 15, 1896

William P. Moore
Jan 22, 1822
Aug 8, 1890
& wife
Margaret Moore
Jun 22, 1829
Jun 5, 1883

M. H. Caughran
May 7, 1829
Jan 20, 1898
&
Julia Caughran
Mar 22, 1831
Nov 27, 1900

Elizabeth A., wife of
J. M. Buchanan
Jun 3, 1820
Mar 4, 1890
&
J. M. Buchanan
Son of S. S. & Mary Buchanan
May 4, 1817
May 30, 1888
Age: 71y, 26d.

Margaret E., wife of
N. W. Cowden
Jan 6, 1855
Mar 4, 1890

William S., Son of
William P. & Margaret Moore
Dec 19, 1850
Dec 26, 1928

Mrs. Amanda Buchanan *
Died May 24, 1899
Age: 78 years.

Mary E. C., wife of
N. W. Cowden
Jul 14, 1846
Dec 25, 1887

John S., Son of
J. M. & E. A. Buchanan
Aug 11, 1849
Dec 8, 1874

Emily Louisa, Daughter of
J. M. & E. A. Buchanan
Jun 28, 1843
Jan 13, 1863

S. S. McCollum
Jul 22, 1867
Oct 7, 1894

William, Son of
Mary & A. J. McCollum
1885-1923

Eddie, Son of
W. S. & M. E. Martin
Mar 4, 1874
Jul 8, 1875

Miss Annie McCollum *
Died Dec 25, 1898
Age: (not given)

Ollie Buchanan
Mar 8, 1879
Aug 29, 1895
&
Dernia Buchanan
Nov 30, 1881
Jul 11, 1899

Hubert, Son of
T. N. & V. I. Moore
Oct 7, 1884
Oct 12, 1884

Floura, Daughter of
T. N. & V. I. Moore
Jun 27, 1873
Jul 7, 1873

A. G. Martin
Dec 31, 1820
Mar 11, 1882
&
Louisa, 1st wife of
A. G. Martin
Jun 10, 1825
Apr 19, 1861
&
Margaret E., wife of
A. G. Martin
Jan 25, 1821
Aug 16, 1867

* *

BUCHANAN CEMETERY

LOCATION: One-half mile south of Howell on "Old Dave Buchanan Place".

David Buchanan
born in Rockbridge Co., Va.
Aug 30, 1764
Aug 26, 1844
Age: 80 years.

Margaret, wife of
David Buchanan
born in Rockbridge Co., Va.
Mar 1765
Nov 11, 1851

William S., 2nd Son of
Samuel & Mary Buchanan
born in Lincoln Co., Tenn.
Dec 15, 1818
Nov 22, 1855

David R., 3rd Son of
Samuel & Mary Buchanan
1820-1828

Newton M., 5th Son of
Samuel & Mary Buchanan
born in Lincoln Co., Tenn.
Apr 26, 1821
Jan 18, 1849

Joshua Gibson
(of Rockingham Co., N.C.)
(no dates)

Infant Son of
William P. & Margaret Moor
Died 1849

Several unmarked graves.

* *

GIBSON CEMETERY

LOCATION: One and one-fourth miles SSW of Howell, one-half mile north of Clayton Lane in pasture, known as "Old John Gibson Place."

John Gibson
(Soldier of the Revolution)
Sep 16, 1760
May 14, 1844
Age: 84 years.

Margaret, wife of
John Gibson
Apr 24, 1770
Oct 31, 1848
Age: 78 years.

Felix Grundy Gibson
Dec 7, 1803
Aug 21, 1851

Minerva Clayton, wife of
Felix G. Gibson
Nov 1, 1813
(no date)

NOTE: John & Margaret Gibson are natives of Rockingham Co., N. C.

Minerva Josephine, Daughter of
Felix & Minerva Gibson
Mar 9, 1847
Jan 26, 1848

Child of
Felix & Minerva Gibson
1848

Ed. Note: Located SW of Old Pioneer Gibson Camp Ground.

Niedham Gibson
Oct 25, 1865
May 28, 1879

Rev. A. G. Gibson*
A pioneer Cumberland
Presbyterian Preacher.
1800-1854

FAYETTEVILLE QUADRANGLE

Emaline, wife of
Niedham George
May 10, 1816
Aug 21, 1871

Child of
William P. Warren
Jul 25, 1846
Nov 5, 1847
Age: 15m, 10d.

* *

CRAWFORD CEMETERY

LOCATION: One and one-half miles SSW of Howell at the end of Clayton Lane on the north side of lane.

John Crawford
(born in Augusta Co., Va.)
Mar 27, 1775
Sep 17, 1847

Margaret, wife of
Dr. T. U. Stephenson
Feb 8, 1822
Feb 4, 1853
Married Apr 11, 1844

Susan E. Stephenson
Dec 1, 1848
Oct 28, 1871

Thomas Middleton Crawford *
Oct 15, 1825
Jul 11, 1845

John Crawford ***
1818-1856

Sarah Bradshaw
Mar 16, 1795
Nov 29, 1871

Margaret Buchanan Crawford ***
Dec 3, 1777
Mar 14, 1816

*** Family Records.

Mary J. Cowen
Jul 4, 1848
Aug 21, 1871

Joanna Crawford ***
Oct 12, 1814
Oct 19, 1828

Several unmarked graves.

* *

DAVES CEMETERY

LOCATION: Three miles north of Fayetteville on the east side of Highway 231.

Eddie Conwell
Dec 29, 1866
Oct 24, 1899

Mary M. Conwell Clark
Jun 23, 1867
Jan 25, 1916

W. T. Clark *
Died Jan 1916
(no age given)

James C. Daves
Jun 1, 1829
May 6, 1875

Margarette M. Daves
Dec 28, 1827
Jul 20, 1896

Rosa Lee Conwell *
Died Nov 18, 1905
Age: 17 years.

Mary Daves
Jan 8, 1815
Sep 1888

Sallie Lou Conwell,*
Daughter of
Mrs. Molly Clark
Died Oct 9, 1905
Age: 9 years.

Infant Son of
J. J. & M. C. Daves
Sep 30, 1896
Oct 7, 1896

Anna Lena, Daughter of
J. J. & M. C. Daves
Jan 26, 1884
Sep 20, 1884

* *

SHARP CEMETERY

LOCATION: Three miles north of Fayetteville on the west side of Highway 231.

Mrs. Nancy S., Consort of
William R. Gracy
Sep 29, 1808
Mar 11, 1862

Adlia Sharp
Feb 16, 1779
Jul 9, 1826

Alice R., wife of
Adlia Sharp
Aug 29, 1785
Nov 20, 1850

Asbery Sharp
Feb 2, 1811
Jul 25, 1818

Walter B. Sharp
Mar 1, 1807
Nov 4, 1834

Benjamine F. Sharp
Nov 22, 1821
Oct 7, 1855

* *

HIGGINS CEMETERY

LOCATION: Three and one-half miles north of Fayetteville on west side of Highway 231.

O. W. Higgins
Sep 17, 1801
Apr 25, 1865

Fannie H., wife of
O. W. Higgins
Sep 26, 1804
Dec 20, 1872

3 or 4 fieldstones,
no inscriptions.

* *

FAYETTEVILLE QUADRANGLE

KENNEDY-THOMISON CEMETERY

LOCATION: Two and one-half miles north of Fayetteville on the east side of Highway 231.

Robert Warden
Sep 29, 1855
Mar 23, 1911

Daniel Warden
Jun 3, 1828
May 31, 1905

Sallie Landess, wife of
Daniel Warden
Dec 8, 1837
Nov 16, 1895
"Joined the Primitive
Baptist Church 1870."

Mary, wife of
Daniel Warden
Nov 19, 1835
Apr 21, 1891
"Joined the Primitive
Baptist Church Oct 1856."

Holman Frost, Son of
J. W. & K. E. Warden
Mar 26, 1882
Mar 25, 1893

Travis A. Warden
Sep 8, 1853
Mar 18, 1899

Fannie, wife of
J. E. Broadaway
Feb 18, 1854
Dec 1, 1907

Son of
G. R. & Julia Ann Cowan
B&D Sep 9, 1855

Infant Son of
H. & E. Thomison
Died Monday Aug 1, 1837
(no age given)

Infant Daughter of
H. & J. C. Thomison
Died Friday Oct 10, 1834
(no age given)

Mrs. Buenavista,* wife of
John Hill
Died Feb 19, 1898
Age: 49 years.

Mrs. Martha,* widow of
Jordan Rees
Died Oct 25, 1887
Age: 80 years.

Mrs. Amelia A.,* wife of
Jasper Jean
Died Dec 16, 1879
Age: 22 years.

Cora Ann Gray
Jun 25, 1872
Jan 7, 1877

Elizabeth, wife of
J. W. Jean
Oct 12, 1833
Mar 30, 1902

M. Sparks
of Georgia
A Confederate Soldier
Died Feb 1862

Blunt W. Grigsby
Jan 13, 1846
Aug 12, 1867

James R. Cunningham
1883-1951
&
Lola Cunningham
1893-1938

J. W. Cunningham
1912-1934

W. H. Jones
Jun 29, 1841
Aug 17, 1912

Caroline Little, wife of
W. H. Jones
Feb 28, 1850
Jan 16, 1935

Sarah A. Thomison
Dec 29, 1828
Jun 24, 1843

A. L. McK.
(footmarker)

F. M. Anderson
Apr 14, 1835
Jan 22, 1863

Martha E., wife of
J. J. Gammill & Daughter of
A. & M. Anderson
Oct 26, 1835
Jan 12, 1873

Mrs. William Anderson *
Died Nov 28, 1907
Age: 83 years.

James Walter,* Son of
W. R. & Jennie Boaz
Died Sep 18, 1901
Age: 14m.

Mrs. Ida,* wife of
George J. Alexander & Daughter
of Hugh Thomison
Died Jul 2, 1887
Age: 40 years.

Samuel Lee, Son of
W. H. & M. C. Jones
Aug 27, 1866
Sep 30, 1880

Mary L. K. Jewell
Mar 12, 1840
Mar 7, 1854
Age: 13y, 11m, 26d.

Mary M. Kercheval
Feb 14, 1799
Nov 29, 1854

David Newsom
May 29, 1817
Jun 5, 1815
NOTE: There is an error on
the dates.

Sarah M. Conaway
Dec 25, 1801
Feb 20, 1854
Age: 52y, 1m, 20d.

Robert Campbell Kennedy
Aug 25, 1761
Feb 25, 1815
&
Esther Edmiston Kennedy
Apr 13, 1766
Aug 16, 1823
&
Sally Buchanan Kennedy
Aug 1, 1806
Jul 25, 1818

William Carroll Thomison
Jun 18, 1838
Feb 9, 1854
Age: 15y, 7m, 22d.

Sallie F. Thomison
Feb 24, 1849
Mar 6, 1871

Amos Anderson
Aug 22, 1809
Jul 28, 1875

Malinda, wife of
Amos Anderson
May 6, 1801
Dec 8, 1884
Age: 83y, 7m, 2d.

Mrs. Ann Woodard *
Died Sep 12, 1891
Age: 55 years.
"Sister to M. H. Conaway."

Wiley H. Jean *
Died Apr 9, 1911
Age: 73y, 5m, 17d.

Bettie E. Jenkins, wife of
B. F. Renfro
Jun 15, 1863
Jun 7, 1913
On reverse side of stone:
"She was the sunshine of
our home."

Hugh Thomison, Sr.
Jul 11, 1805
Sep 19, 1878
&
Jane C., Consort, 1st wife
of Hugh Thomison, Sr.
May 13, 1808
Nov 10, 1831
&
Elizabeth, 2nd wife of
Hugh Thomison, Sr.
Dec 14, 1814
Jul 3, 1895

Martha Jane, wife of
Willis Blankenship &
Daughter of
Hugh & Jane C. Thomison
Nov 15, 1830
Oct 2, 1859

Elizabeth C. Thomison
Nov 23, 1832
Aug 2, 1853
Age: 20y, 8m, 21d.

Susie Thomison
Oct 13, 1861
Nov 6, 1883

James Z., Son of
Z. & Mary E. Motlow
Sep 7, 1880
Aug 28, 1892

William M. Anderson
Oct 6, 1832
Jul 25, 1905

Jane C. Anderson
Jan 12, 1834
Nov 28, 1907

Vila Knox,* Daughter of
Mr. & Mrs. R. S. Grigby
Died Apr 1, 1892
Age: 6m.

Rush S.,* Son of
R. S. Grigsby
Died Jan 25, 1898
Age: 11 years.

Gilbert G. Grigsby *
Died Feb 14, 1898
Age: 63 years.
"Brother to R. S. Grigsby."

FAYETTEVILLE QUADRANGLE

Mary Iva,* Daughter of
Nathan Warden
Died Jan 4, 1904
Age: 16 years.

Thomas H. Holland *
Died Jun 9, 1905
Age: 88 years.

Miss Sarah Wiley *
Died Jun 22, 1891
Age: 82 years.

Mrs. Norris Hurlston *
Died Apr 16, 1906
Age: 35 years.
Left Husband and 8 children.

Arch L. Conoway *
Died Jun 17, 1910
Age: 68 years. C.S.A.

Lucy Frances Grigsby *
Died Dec 18, 1897
Age: 10m, 26d.

Mrs. Fernetta Chick *
Died Feb 22, 1904
Age: 68 years.

Infant * of
Mr. & Mrs. S. C. Caudle
Died Jul 2, 1900
Age: (not given)

Green B. Evans ***
1834-May 19, 1893
& wife
Julia Ann McCandlis Evans
Died 1926 (no age given)

Daniel Willard,* Son of
S. C. & S. E. Caudle
Died Nov 11, 1896
Age: (not given)

Bessie,* Daughter of
Mr. & Mrs. S. Caudle
Died Feb 24, 1899
Age: (not given)

*** Family Records.

* *

ASHBY-TURNER CEMETERY

LOCATION: Two and one-half miles NE of Fayetteville and one-fourth mile west of Mimosa Road.

C. T. K.
Feb 12, 1893
A-- 7, 1894
(chipped away)

Ida A., wife of
B. A. Ashby
May 9, 1862
Nov 22, 1891

E. S. Yant, wife of
J. P. Keith
Nov 7, 1837
Apr 8, 1910

Dr. C. D. Curlee
Nov 20, 1852
Jun 9, 1900
&
Grave, with TM marker gone.

** Court Records.

John H. Curlee
Sep 29, 1883
Jan 9, 1884

Turner, Son of
C. D. & Mourning Curlee
Jul 9, 1888
Nov 26, 1890

Hugh Thomison **
Died May 27, 1911
Age: 59 years.

Mourning Turner, wife of
Dr. C. D. Curlee
Apr 4, 1856
Sep 2, 1924

Earl Ward McCullough *
Died at his grandmother,
Mrs. Mourning T. Curlee
Jun 9, 1915
Age: 14 years.

* *

CUNNINGHAM CEMETERY

LOCATION: North end of Creson Addition, Fayetteville.

George Cunningham
Died Mar 5, 1836
Age: 49y, 8m, 26d.

M. C. (fieldstone)
Nov 27, 1824
Dec 20, 1824

Col. J.(Joseph) Hester
Age: 49 years.
(no dates on old sand stone)

M. A. H. (Mary Hester)
(no dates, fieldstone)

E. Jinkins
Died November
Age: 39 years
(no dates)

1 Vault type with no info.

(no name)
Died Aug 1, 1823
Age: 1y, 7m, 8d.

Several unmarked graves.

* *

ASHBY CEMETERY

LOCATION: 2 miles NE of Fayetteville and one-fourth mile west of Old Mulberry Road.

Ernie B., Son of
J. W. & E. N. Ashby
Oct 31, 1890
Dec 1, 1890

Infant of
J. J. & S. C. Cole
Died Mar 11, 1888

Burney C., Son of
J. W. & E. N. Ashby
Oct 31, 1890
Nov 12, 1890

Joel G. Pitts
Feb 24, 1842
May 8, 1884

Ella Pitts, wife of
J. W. Ashby
Feb 15, 1872
Jan 1, 1897

Infant Son of
W. T. & Tennie Davis
B&D Jul 27, 1887

* *

FAYETTEVILLE QUADRANGLE

HULSEY CEMETERY

LOCATION: One mile NE of junction of Mulberry Road and Highway 64 and one-fourth mile east of Mulberry Road.

W. J. Hulsey Sep 24, 1825 Jul 12, 1896 & Sarah A. Hulsey Sep 12, 1830 Aug 22, 1901	John W. Hulsey Sep 20, 1851 Jul 23, 1938 Julia E., wife of J. W. Hulsey Aug 4, 1855 Jul 10, 1895	James K. Polk, Son of G. D. & Sallie Hulsey Aug 3, 1860 Oct 16, 1863 Emma, Daughter of W. J. & S. A. Hulsey Died Sep 20, 1890 Age: 17y, 3d.	Miss Freddie, Daughter of John W. & Julia Hulsey Jun 10, 1881 Mar 6, 1924 Julia Gracie Hulsey Oct 4, 1891 Apr 6, 1896
Eliza C. Reece Jun 2, 1814 Mar 21, 1880 Age: 65y, 9m, 14d.	Nancy C. Brewer * Died Apr 9, 1892 Age: 57 years.	27 unmarked graves.	

* *

WALKER CEMETERY

LOCATION: Two miles NNE of junction of Mulberry Road and Highway 64, one-fourth mile west of Mulberry Road.

Benjamin W. D. Harden Jun 16, 1824 Sep 24, 1851	Annie Stone May 15, 1872 Feb 3, 1911	Mary F. Walker Mar 13, 1850 May 28, 1920	Mattie Walker Aug 23, 1876 Dec 11, 1906
Moses Harden May 8, 1772 Oct 24, 1849	Eld. E. W. Walker Jun 15, 1836 Jan 29, 1901	Ima Walker Jan 3, 1880 Aug 27, 1940	Mary J. Walker Oct 14, 1904 Oct 21, 1905
	Infant Son of Mr. & Mrs. J. M. Walker Dec 1, 1901 Dec 3, 1901	Several unmarked graves.	

* *

PARKS CEMETERY

LOCATION: Two and one-half miles NE of junction of Mulberry Road and Highway 64 on west side of Mulberry Road on side of hill.

Woodroof Parks Feb 27, 1799 May 11, 1870	Woodroof Parks Mar 29, 1855 Apr 10, 1876	William Parks Aug 16, 1785 Dec 23, 1863 & Mary C. Parks Apr 15, 1795 Nov 19, 1840	Riley Washington Pitts Jul 2, 1851 Apr 4, 1857 "Father" Henry P. Pitts Sep 2, 1811 Jul 2, 1869
Dovey Parks Sep 25, 1815 Oct 21, 1873	Jennie B. Pitts Sep 8, 1857 Jun 6, 1877		
	Several unmarked graves.		"Mother" --- --, 1825 Sep 1, 1913 (broken)

* *

FAYETTEVILLE QUADRANGLE

McDANIEL MEETING HOUSE CEMETERY

LOCATION: At the site of Old Meetinghouse on the north side of Providence Road and about three miles NE of Fayetteville.

Land for McDaniel Meeting House, Methodist Episcopal and Graveyard was given by Fielding McDaniel in 1828. One acre and 8 sq. poles. Information from Court Records.

Fielding McDaniel ***
1781-1840
   & wife
Lucy Baker McDaniel
1783-1839

Other members of his family are said to be buried here.

8 or 10 graves with fieldstones, no inscriptions.

* *

WALKER CEMETERY

LOCATION: North side of Providence Road, about three miles NE of Fayetteville.

N. P. Walker
Sep 8, 1790
May 13, 1846   Other graves, unmarked.

* *

PAMPLIN CEMETERY

LOCATION: One-half mile NE of junction of Mulberry Road and Highway 64.

H. J. Pamplin
Aug 11, 1832
Jul 13, 1912

Mary E., wife of
H. J. Pamplin
Jan 23, 1841
Mar 16, 1898

* *

BUCHANAN-McELROY CEMETERY

LOCATION: Four miles NW of Fayetteville and one-half mile NE of Old Boonshill Road.

Sarah Buchanan
Feb 3, 1823
Jul 2, 1850

Mattie A. McElroy, wife of
J. L. Buchanan
Feb 13, 1859
Jul 17, 1895

William N.,* Son of
Jasper Ellis
Died May 26, 1894
Age: 38 years.

John L. Buchanan *
Died 1928
Age: 77 years.

Amanda A. Smith, wife of
R. G. McElroy
May 17, 1836
Jul 23, 1895

Mary A., Daughter of
R. G. & A. A. McElroy
May 15, 1856
Sep 9, 1858

Rufus C. McElroy *
Died May 7, 1910
Age: 82 years.
C.S.A.

This Cemetery is located on the Old Micajah McElroy Estate. Court Records.

Archey, Son of
J. L. & Mattie Buchanan
born Aug 18, 1880
died (no date)

Emma J. Eddins
May 15, 1878
Oct 4, 1878

James R. McElroy *
Died Aug 12, 1909
Age: 40 years.

Daughter * of
William Ellis
Died Jul 11, 1890
Age: 1 year.

Mrs. Mollie McElroy
1873-1950

Con McElroy
1857-1933

S. S. "Brooks" Smith *
Died Sep 16, 1915
Age: 86y, 8m, 8d.

Infant * of
Mr. & Mrs. Con McElroy
Died Oct 13, 1915
Age: (not given)

* *

BUCHANAN CEMETERY

LOCATION: Two and one-half miles NNW of Fayetteville on a high hill about one-half mile west of 431.

FAYETTEVILLE QUADRANGLE

John Buchanan
born in Washington Co., Va.
1778-1856
&
Hannah Buchanan
Oct 27, 1780
Feb 10, 1861

Emily, wife of
Pleasant Halbert
Jul 10, 1814
Feb 9, 1868

David Buchanan
Sep 29, 1802
Mar 19, 1872
&
Rebecca Buchanan
Dec 28, 1866

Elizabeth Flyn
1840-1868

Francis M., wife of
John A. Gracy
1835-1869

Milton Buchanan
Jan 30, 1809
May 25, 1899
& wife
Araminta Buchanan
Jan 18, 1821
Apr 12, 1867

Andrew Buchanan
Dec 7, 1855
Jul 11, 1857

Sarah Emaline Buchanan
Jul 28, 1842
Jun 19, 1863

Andrew Moor
1791-1827

Ellis Moor
(no dates)

Pat. Mc.
Mar 26, 1922

Elizabeth, wife of
Ruben Woodard
Aug 27, 1802
Apr 26, 1849

Orphan E. Bumpas
Mar 6, 1844
Oct 26, 1858

Marcus Marrs
1841-1914
&
Clayton Marrs
1884-1902
&
Clarence Marrs
1837-1894

Minnie Marrs
1880-1887

_____, Consort of
Andrew Kiness
1791-1827

Susan B. Bayles
Died Nov 6, 1886
Age: 52 years.

Bird H., Son of
William & E. P. Woodard
B&D Oct 14, 1859

William L. Woodard
Mar 1, 1866
Sep 25, 1867

Robert Buchanan **
(no dates)

** Court Records. This
cemetery is on the old
Robert Buchanan place.

* *

CEMETERY

LOCATION: One and one-half miles NW of Fayetteville and east of Old Boonshill Road.

Several fieldstones, no inscriptions.

* *

COWAN CEMETERY

LOCATION: One mile NW of Fayetteville on side of hill, east of Old Boonshill Road.

John C. Cowan
Mar 13, 1847
Jan 7, 1880
"A Consistant Member of
the Methodist E. Church."

Andrew J. Cowan
Feb 14, 1849
Dec 27, 1891

Son *** of
Harvey C. & Agnes Barker
McDaniel Cowan
(no dates)

Charles Barker McDaniel ***
May 15, 1819
Oct 27, 1882
Age: 65y, 5m.

John,* Son of
C. B. McDaniel
Died Nov 7, 1878
Age: 25 years.

Jane M. Cowan ***
1813-1818

Dialtha Cowan ***
1818-1820
(Jane M. & Dialtha are sisters
of Harvey C. Cowan)

Nancy Louise Wakefield,***
wife of
Charles B. McDaniel
Mar 22, 1820
Jan 6, 1867

James A.,* Son of
Sarah & C. B. McDaniel
Died Feb 8, 1882
Age: 11m, 20d.

Agnes B. McDaniel Cowan ***
Mar 29, 1814
Nov 24, 1881
Wife of Harvey C. Cowan.

Harvey C. Cowan ***
Nov 15, 1809
Jan 13, 1892

Sarah Elizabeth McDaniel ***
Feb 22, 1848
Oct 11, 1854

James Cowan ***
1844-1861

*** Family Records of
Mr. J. C. Cowan.

* *

FAYETTEVILLE QUADRANGLE

WHITAKER CEMETERY

LOCATION: Two miles west of Public Square of Fayetteville on the north side of Highway 64.

This cemetery was located on the Benjamin Whitaker place and he is said to be buried here.

Several graves with no markers.

ED'S NOTE: Located near the Old Blue Spring, the site camp of the Edmiston Company Land Survey Party in the Spring of 1784 and across the highway from site of Early Residential Court House.

* *

FIRST PRESBYTERIAN CHURCH-OLD CITY CEMETERY

LOCATION: One block east of the Public Square in Fayetteville.

William M. Smith
Jul 10, 1813
Mar 23, 1878

Frances Smith
Jul 29, 1787
Feb 21, 1868
"A Soldier of 1812 with Gen. Jackson at Battle of New Orleans, 1815."

Fannie Gray, wife of
Frances Smith
Sep 5, 1782
Sep 7, 1871

Jno. Clarke, Jr.
Apr 13, 1811
Sep 12, 1858

Mrs. Eliza C., wife of
John Clarke
Aug 18, 1826
Aug 28, 1854
To the Memory of her Son
Jan 30, 1852
Jan 31, 1852

Capt. J. D. Scott
Co C 41st Tenn Regt
1826-1884
    & wife
Laura A. Scott
Died Mar 27, 1919
Age: (not given)
    & Son
Thomas Scott
1850-1860

Luctus P., Youngest Son of
James & Nancy Bright
Dec 1, 1832
May 28, 1841

Mary Selina, Daughter of
James R. & Priscilla M.
Bright
Died Aug 5, 1849
Age: 10m, 26d.

James Bright
Born in Botetourt Co., Va.
Jun 16, 1782
Feb 24, 1871
"Was a Pioneer to Lincoln Co. filled the office of deputy surveyor, Gen. Commissioner of the State to run and mark the boundary line between Tenn. & Ky; Commissioner of the U. S. to locate and value the reservation lands in the Creek Nation; first Clerk of the Circuit Court of Lincoln Co., Clerk and Master of the Chancery Court. His life was without reproach, his death truimphant in Christian faith."

Nancy, wife of
James Bright & Daughter of
John & Mary Morgan
Born in Sumner Co., Tenn.
Jan 19, 1786
Married in Lincoln Co., Tenn.
Feb 9, 1813
Died Nov 5, 1856

John M. Bright
Feb 20, 1817
Oct 10, 1911
"Noted Scholar, Orator & Lawyer, L.L.D., Statesman."

Belle Buckner, 3rd wife of
John M. Bright
Sep 7, 1835
Sep 7, 1917
Age: 82 years.

Zurilda Buckner Bright
(2nd wife of John M. Bright)
Jan 2, 1831
Nov 10, 1877

Judith Campbell, wife of
John M. Bright (1st wife)
Jul 25, 1820
Dec 24, 1855

Margaret, Relict of
Matthew Martin & Daughter of
James & Nancy Bright
Nov 13, 1813
Aug 22, 1860
Married Mar 27, 1834

Marion Drake
Mar 20, 1853
Aug 10, 1853

Martha Rebecca Douglas,
Mother of Edwin Henry, Hugh
Bright, Lee, Byrd, Mary
Margaret Douglas.
Born in Fayetteville, Tenn.
Jun 8, 1819
Died at Harrisburg, Pa.
Jul 10, 1848

Mary A. Drake
Jun 8, 1819
Apr 13, 1853

J. W. F.
    &
R. F.
(no dates)

Ebenezer Hill
Oct 14, 1791
May 16, 1875
    &
Mary T. Hill
Feb 26, 1799
Apr 19, 1871

"Sister"
Katie H. Hill
Dec 22, 1835
Jul 15, 1861

Martha Jorden, Daughter of
W. H. & M. M. Moores
Nov 4, 1850
Dec 13, 1854

Mrs. Avarilla Boone
Jun 15, 1836
Aug 3, 1854

Mrs. Malinda Porterfield,
wife of
Rev. William D. Chadick
Born in Memphis, Tenn.
Mar 19, 1821
Died Fayetteville, Tenn.
Nov 14, 1848

James Russell
Apr 7, 1769
Oct 30, 1842
    & wife
Mary Russell
Oct 8, 1783
Dec 18, 1847
    &
Sophronia M., wife of
T. A. Owen
Jul 11, 1819
Dec 23, 1847

Christiana J. Russell
Mar 3, 1816
Mar 28, 1845

General T. A. Owen
Dec 15, 1808
Jul 1, 1855
Age: 46y, 6m, 16d.
    &
_____, Daughter of
T. A. & Sophronia Owen
Apr   1847
Dec   1854
Age: 6 years.

Henry Robertson
Aug 13, 1786
Aug 28, 1844

Elizabeth Robertson
Oct 22, 1792
Jul 30, 1856
    &
Richard I. J. Robertson
Dec 30, 1823
Oct 4, 1834

FAYETTEVILLE QUADRANGLE

Joel Commons ***
Nov 30, 1791
Mar 21, 1870
(marker now gone)

Joel C. Commons
Died Feb 8, 1831
Age: 3 years.

Sarah E., wife of
Joseph Scott
Died Jan 17, 1848
Age: 30y, 11m, 21d.

Garland B. Miller
May 8, 1816
Jul 4, 1860

Woods S. Miller
Feb 28, 1850
Oct 7, 1851
&
Mourning S. Miller
Sep 1, 1854
Sep 4, 1855

Mary S. Farrar
Died Mar 30, 1830
(no age given)

Eliza Ann, Daughter of
A. T. & E. W. Nicks
Died Sep 5, 1838
Age: 1y, 8m, 25d.

Charles Boyles
Dec 17, ----
Jul 24, 1840
(stone broken)

Mary Boyles
Died Aug 9, 1819
Age: (not given)

Elisha Bagley
Feb 10, 1776
May 21, 1858
Age: 82y, 3m, 10d.

Sarah, wife of
Elisha Bagley
May 23, 1780
Jan 2, 1830

Elisha M. Gordin
Nov 12, 1822
Jun 20, 1842

Mary Elizabeth Lacky
Died Mar 10, 1839
Age: 15y, 10m, 12d.
Also her Infant Daughter
Mary Ellen Lacky
May 26, 1839
Age: 2m, 6d.

John R. Boyles
Dec 4, 1826
Mar 26, 1860

Pauline Boyles
Feb 27, 1831
Aug 17, 1842

John S., Son of
J. T. & Louisa Gorden
Died Sep 20, 1847
Age: 1y, 3m, 20d.

Robert Ball, Son of
John & Louisa Gordon
May 13, 1863
Jun 27, 1863

John O. Griffis
Aug 29, 1802
Dec 30, 1812

Miss Josephine Miles
Nov 3, 1838
Jun 24, 1864

Mary Frances, Daughter of
William & Lucy R. Bonner
Born Fayetteville, Tenn.
Oct 25, 1830
Died Jul 19, 1837
Age: 6y, 8m, 21d.

Samuel Fulton
Died Aug 7, 1843
Age: 76 years.

Margaret C. Fulton
Died Mar 17, 1838
Age: 60 years.

Samuel E. Gilliland
Mar 17, 1799
Aug 29, 1860

Eliza Gilliland
Died Aug 6, 1836
(no age given)

Mary S. Gilliland
Died Jul 12, 1833
(no age given)

Infant Daughter of
M. H. & A. F. Bonner
B&D Jan 7, 1840

John T. Morgan
Born in Armagh, Ireland
Jan 8, 1790
Died May 26, 1855
"A Member of Union Chapter
18 Royal Arch Masons".
&
Eleanor P. Zivley, wife of
John T. Morgan
Sep 19, 1812
Jul 1, 1881

Elijah R. Morgan
1849-1892

Francis L. Morgan
1835-1846

Catharine R. Morgan
1834-1834

Permelia A. Morgan
1845-1847

Permelia Ziveley
1797-1856

Mary E. Morgan
1842-1867

Peter M. Ro--
Oct 26, 1803
Jan 3, 1813

Samuel S. Holding, Jr.
Died Dec 9, 1838 (child)
Age: (not given)

Benjamin Lewis, Son of
John & Rosea G. Lanier
Apr 9, 1837
Nov 5, 1839

Calvin, Son of
A. & H. Bradshaw
Died Oct 11, 1833
Age: 6m, 20d.

Susan O. Hansell, 2nd wife of
S. H. McCord
1829-May 19, 1870
Age: 41 years.

Caroline W. Hansell, 1st wife
of S. H. McCord
Jul 21, 1815
Dec 15, 1860
Age: 51 years.

Benjamin Wear, died
Oct 5, 1838 in the 66 year
of his age.

Frances E. Franklin
Oct 28, 1797
Aug 6, 1868

Fanny Ross, wife of
Dr. Robert Franklin
Nov   1832
Sep 10, 1911

Frances R. Carloss
Apr 21, 1841
Dec 7, 1855

Robert A. Franklin
Oct 15, 1860
Apr 20, 1870

Robert H., Son of
James & Fannie Franklin
May 13, 1833
Jan 8, 1890

Elvira H. Holding
Died Jul 28, 1837
Age: (not given)

Willie H. King
Feb 2, 1861
Apr 1, 1861

Kizer Alexander
Feb 10, 1779
May 20, 1856

James I. Kincannon
Feb 22, 1813
Dec 31, 1833

Hugh A. Kincannon
Oct 12, 1804
Aug 11, 1832

Little Frank, Son of
G. F. & J. A. Smith
Mar 19, 1853
Oct 24, 1857

Lettitia, wife of
Barnett Metcalfe
Born near Lexington, KY.
Jan 1, 1792
Died Mar 29, 1865

Susan, wife of
James G. Woods
Sep 13, 1824
Nov 28, 1865
Age: 41 years.

Brice Fleming, Son of
J. T. & Susie Boaz
Oct 16, 1892
Nov 10, 1892

Archie, Son of
J. H. C. & Nannie Woods
May 18, 1878
Apr 16, 1898

William Neeld
May 17, 1787
Aug 16, 1858

James H. Cobb
Jun 10, 1805
Mar 14, 1860
&
Martha J. Cobb
May 24, 1802
--- 27, 1875 (broken)
1st married to
Joseph Boyce
Jun 7, 1820

FAYETTEVILLE QUADRANGLE

John V. McKinney
(marker under slab,
 information gone,
 footstone: J. V. McK.)

Polly McKinney
Died Oct 4, 1820
Age: 6 years.
&
Lucinda Jane McKinney
Died Nov 26, 182-(broken)
Age: 2y, 8-.
Daughters of
John V. & Ann McKinney

Richard C., Son of
E. J. & R. R. McKinney
Jan 10, 1837
Jun 12, 1838
Age: 1y, 4m, 26d.

Dr. Charles McKinney
Aug 18, 1788
Jan 5, 1864
&
Mrs. Mary A. McKinney
Oct 5, 1790
Mar 25, 1863

W. M. Dickson
Jan 20, 1824
Aug 12, 1840

John R. Hague
Died Jun 30, 1869
Age: (not given)
 & his wife
My beloved sister
Maggie McGhie Hague
who rests in Elwood, Texas
where she fell asleep
Oct 14, 1881.

Col. James Fulton
was born Dec 18, A. D. 1792
and departed this life
Feb 15 A.D. 1856
&
Mary Fulton
Oct 19, 1806
Feb 28, 1856

Little Sadie, Sarah Ada
Wallace
Oct 27, 1871
Sep 30, 1873
&
Little Willie,
William Wallace
Dec 27, 1863
Jul 12, 1865
Children of
N. O. & M. E. Wallace

John S. Fulton
Mar 31, 1828
Died from wounds received in
front of Petersburg, Va.
Jul 4, 1864
&
Robert Fulton
Jun 1843
Died from wounds received
at Battle of Chicamauga
Oct 2, 1863

J. M. Alford
Co G 1st Tenn
C.S.A.

John T. Greer
Age: 32 years.
(no dates)

Lucinda D. Greer
Aug 30, 1802
Aug 30, 1867

Samuel J. Isaacs
A Worthy M. Mason, erected
by Jackson Lodge 68, A. Y. M.
Dec 31, 1818
Jun 1, 1853

Thomas B. Wilson
Sep 20, 1826
Sep 13, 1859

Susan C., Consort of
James R. Chilcoat
Jan 7, 1816
Jul 25, 1856
Age: 40y, 6m, 18d.

Susan Chilcoat
Feb 26, 1814
Mar 1, 1884

L. R., Son of
L. E. & N. N. Tucker
Jul 1, 1835
Dec 22, 1852
Age: 17y, 5m, 21d.

John Alexander Hamilton
Aug 16, 1832
Aug 27, 1865

Mary E. Hunter
Sep 1, 1838
Mar 13, 1857

Thomas Sherod Hunter
Mar 3, 1857
Jul 6, 1857

Liberty B. Hobbs
Dec 8, 1826
May 8, 1852

William T. Moyers
Sep 16, 1827
Jan 19, 1892
 & wife
Martha J. Moyers
Sep 23, 1837
Aug 23, 1891

Curtis B., Son of
W. T. & M. J. Moyers
Oct 20, 1874
Dec 14, 1893

John W., Son of
W. T. & M. J. Moyers
Nov 3, 1854
Dec 15, 1857

Christie C., Daughter of
W. T. & M. J. Moyers
Apr 29, 1860
Oct 7, 1868

"Twins"
Ada Moyers & Ida Moyers
Apr 28, 1856
Jun 26, 1856
Children of
W. T. & M. J. Moyers

Felix B., Son of
W. T. & M. J. Moyers
Feb 5, 1865
Oct 29, 1866

Eliza M. Russell
Jun 22, 1846
Jun 11, 1860

Frank Burrough
1844-1864
C.S.A.

Infant Daughter of
Hardy C. & Sarah T. Holman
Died Sep 5, 1852
Age: 1y, 3m, 18d.

John Goodrich
Aug 20, 1807
Nov 23, 1857

Mildred, wife of
John Goodrich
Nov 20, 1803
Dec 8, 1872

Ann, wife of
John C. Goodrich
Jan 2, 1832
Sep 3, 1862

John R. Massey
1864
"A Confederate Martyr"

George Waddle
Mar 12, 1842
Died in Dalton, Ga.
Oct 11, 1864
 & Brother
William A. Waddle
Feb 12, 1840
Died in Richmond, Va.
Aug 6, 1862
 & Sister
Rebecca Waddle, wife of
A. J. Renegar
Dec 13, 1848
Jan 2, 1878
&
John Sant, Son of
A. J. & R. W. Renegar
Mar 13, 1874
Apr 27, 1882

NOTE: The following are
 on the left side
 of the Church.

James Conway, Son of
Dr. T. B. Banister of
Amelia Co., Va.
May 8, 1819
Oct 9, 1855
"The End of Pilgrimage"

Maria, Consort of
James Muntz
Died Aug 2, 1861
Age: 29 years.
 Also
Her Son Michael
born Mar 11, 1861
died Mar 15, 1861

John N., Son of
C. B. & E. G. Worsham
Born Nov
Died Mar 8, 1837

Mrs. Mary A. E. Boyd
Jan 16, 1831
Jun 9, 1881

Mrs. Nancy A. Fleming
Daughter of
William & Nancy Neeld
Nov 17, 1830
Dec 12, 1860

H. C., Son of
John Burke
Jun 16, 1815
Dec 6, 1851

Mary, A Servant of
John R. Massey

Reubin, A faithful servant
of John R. Massey
Aug 21, 1832
Jan 30, 1860

David, Servant of
John R. Massey

FAYETTEVILLE QUADRANGLE

America, wife of
A. M. McDonald
Died Apr 15, 1856
Age: about 35 years.

Margaret E. G., Daughter
of William L. & Nancy G.
Berry
Jan 11, 1835
Oct 3, 1836

William C., Son of
C. B. & E. G. Worsham
Feb 11, 1833
Jun 26, 1836

Sarah Wallace Neeld
1822-1857

James Irwin Neeld
1823-1864
A Confederate Vet.

Margaret, wife of
John Gray
Died Feb 16, 1841
Age: 37 years.

Albert, Son of
S. J. & J. I. Neeld
Jan 24, 1857
Feb 17, 1857

Benjamin W. D. Carty
Apr 21, 1799
Jun 14, 1854

James S. Gough
Davis Co., KY
Co A. (broken)
Died Feb 15, 1862
Age: 22 years.

Martha Gillespie
Apr 16, 1825
Nov 29, 1840

William Bright
Oct 20, 1780
Oct 21, 1818

William L. Carty
Died Apr 8, 1857
Age: 26 years.

Bethiah L. Edmondson
1821-1865

Emmaline Koonce, wife of
William M. Smith
Died Jun 19, 1854
Age: (not given)
"Mother of Hugh D. Smith"

J. W. Steele
Apr 10, 1817
Dec 10, 1878
&
Mary J. Steele
Mar 9, 1822
May 5, 1863

Martha J. Winn
Oct 12, 1814
Jul 13, 1854

(W). L. Rowzee
Apr 11, 1818
Feb 24, 1851

Madison Rowzee
A Master Mason, Member of
Jackson Lodge # 68 F & A.M.
Jan 13, 1812
--- --, 1854

Samuel Edmondson
of Calhoun Lodge # 26 I.O.O.F.
Jul 28, 1827
Jun 14, 1854
&
Margaret F.(Robinson), wife
of Samuel Edmondson
Aug 27, 1833
Jul 11, 1854
& Only Child
William C. Edmondson
Oct 4, 1853
Jun 13, 1854

Mary Ann, wife of
G. M. Steele
Nov 6, 1813
Jun 7, 1854

Jane M. Reed
Died Dec 17, 1858
Age: (not given)

Harry M. Smith
Jan 13, 1854
Sep 12, 1862

Harmon Cummins
Oct 8, 1799
May 2, 1865

Dorcas Cummins
Jul 15, 1804
Jun 29, 1890

Many unmarked graves.

U. Z. Diemer
Mar 21, 1833
Sep 22, 1858

James D. Grisard
Oct 11, 1817
Mar 6, 1866

William Redding, Son of
J. D. & M. A. Grisard
(no dates)

Mary B. Kercheval
Died Sep 20, 1858
Age: 27 years.
& Her children
James B. Kercheval
Died Mar 1854
Age: (not given)
&
Margaret B. Kercheval
Died Feb 1854
Age: (not given)
&
W. Kercheval
Died Jun 1857
Age: (not given)

Lizzie, Consort of
W. D. Yant
May 31, 1839
Aug 3, 1859
&
Mary A., Daughter of
Harmon & Durcas Cummins
Apr 7, 1827
Apr 11, 1866

On Memorial Bronze Plaque

Mason, Son of
George A. & Mary E. Wilson
Died Oct 9, 1833
Age: 1y, 1m, 9d.

William J. Gant
Jul 15, 1837
Feb 1, 1843

Mary J. Gant
1817-1844

Keturah Katherine, Only
Child of Agnes & A. A.
Kincannon
May 20, 1825
May 29, 1860

Catherine W. Kincannon
Jul 1, 1815
Apr 13, 1831

William J. Garner
1813-1830

Elizabeth J. Todd
Nov 11, 1829
Nov 21, 1843

John Todd
Died Feb 13, 1829
Age: 83 years.

Susan Todd
Died Mar 24, 1834
Age: 30 years.

Sarah Lorela Roberts
Apr 24, 1835
Sep 9, 1864

Infant Daughter of
John & Elizabeth Baggett
Age: 8 days
(no dates)

Jane Ramsey
Dec 3, 1811
Nov 16, 1833

Infant Son of
J. M. Goodrich
(no dates)

Grave, name unknown

Grave, name unknown

Louisa E., Consort of
H. Douglas
Jul 6, 1819
Feb 29, 1844

Grave, name unknown

Grave, name unknown

Henrietta Sawyer Carpenter
Died Aug 30, 1859
Age: 43 years.

Richard H. Boyd
Dec 4, 1811
May 27, 1827

Grave, name unknown

Graves from 21 to 26
names unknown.

Mrs. Henrietta Sawyer
Oct 31, 1819
Aug 23, 1859
Married Sep 7, 1839

William H. Boyd
Dec 27, 1831
Sep 16, 1838

Grave, name unknown

Grave, name unknown

Peggy Bright
Died Sep 22, 1821
Age: 33 years.

Henry Moyers
Died Jul 1833
Age: (not given)

Graves 33 & 34,
names unknown

FAYETTEVILLE QUADRANGLE

Mary L. Gullet
Died Jun 27, 1833
Age: (not given)

Mrs. Priscilla Manley,*
Widow of
James R. Bright
born in Murfreesboro, N. C.
Died Apr 29, 1893
Buried beside of
James R. Bright.

Feraby Moyers
Died Mar 5, 1837
Age: 33 years.

Mala,* Child of
W. A. & Sina Webb
Died May 14, 1896
Age: 1y, 7m.

Grave, name unknown

Grave, name unknown

Mrs. Mary A. McNelley *
Born in Fayetteville, Tenn.
& Daughter of
Dr. Charles McKinney
Died in Chattanooga, Tenn.
May 17, 1893
Age: 67 years.

C. C. S.
(no dates)

Stones once stood for:

Alexander Peterson Smith
Dec 19, 1796
Jun 15, 1879
&
Mary V. Smith
1803-1877

Isaac Short
Mar 6, 1817
Jan 11, 1860

Many unmarked graves.

Many stones have been removed.

NOTE: Newspaper lists of Confederate Graves:

John M. Alfred	James R. Bright
James R. Chilcoat	W. R. Franch
Col. John S. Fulton	Robert Fulton
Dr. Robert H. Franklin	John T. Greer
W. T. Moyers	John R. Massey
James I. Neeld	Capt. J. D. Scott
W. A. Waddle	George Waddle
John W. Martin (KY Regt.)	J. S. Gough (KY Regt.)
Dr. W. W. McNelly	John V. McKinney
F. M. Fleming	Frank Burrough

* *

SLATER CEMETERY

LOCATION: Once located at Franklin and Campbell Streets in Fayetteville.

In 1915,* One marker remained with the inscription:
Elizabeth L. Slater
Departed this life
Jun 1, 1815
Age: 10m.

Cornelius Slater **
owned this lot. He died 1833.

** Court Records.

NOTE: At one time this graveyard had a number of visable graves. No sighn of graves now.

* *

EZEKIEL NORRIS CEMETERY

LOCATION: Located at the corner of Goodlett and Elk Streets in Fayetteville.

This was the Family Graveyard of Ezekiel Norris, First Settler of Fayetteville in 1806. The graveyard was located to the rear of the Norris House. The Cumberland Presbyterian Church erected in 1829, joining the cemetery on the north east. This graveyard was used for a time as a Church Graveyard. The dimension of the Cemetery was 60 Sq. ft. This information is found in Court Records.

Ezekiel Norris
Died Aug 17, 1828

Mrs. Norris
Died Nov 16, 1827
(no age)

Henry, Son of
Ezekiel Norris
Died young (no dates)

No signs of this cemetery remains.

* *

FAYETTEVILLE QUADRANGLE

CEMETERY

LOCATION: One-half mile SW of Fayetteville, back of the County Garage and north of the Molina Road.

Marj Liaceah
(no dates)

Only one stone remain in this cemetery.

Joel Mullins ***
(no dates)
& wife
Mrs. Joel Mullins
Died Mar 14, 1875
Age: 36 years.

*** Family Records.

* *

SOLOMON CEMETERY

LOCATION: One mile east of Fayetteville and one-fourth mile south of Highway 64.

William Solomon
Jul 9, 1785
Jun 30, 1845

Harty Solomon
Sep 22, 1791
Aug 23, 1851

William B. Solomon
Jan 18, 1850
Jan 9, 1852

Harriet H. Solomon
Mar 11, 1820
Jun 23, 1852

Lucinda C. M. Solomon
Mar 23, 1822
Feb 5, 1852

Elizabeth Harrison
Oct 27, 1787
May 22, 1855

Mary Louisa, Consort of
Joel R. Reese
Nov 28, 1823
Nov 7, 1849

3 graves with fieldstones, no inscriptions.

* *

CEMETERY

LOCATION: Four miles east of Fayetteville, south of Highway 64 near Old Chennault Ford.

Several graves, fieldstones, no inscriptions.

NOTE: Court Records mentions this cemetery as early as 1812.

* *

CUNNINGHAM CEMETERY

LOCATION: Two and one-hald miles east of Fayetteville and south of Old Chennault Ford Road.

Alfred Lay
Mar 1, 1866
Jun 28, 1884

Katie H. Jones
Died May 1909
Age: 44 years.

NOTE: This was on the Griffith Cunningham Property. Info from Court Records.

Edman G. Jones
May 23, 1823
Feb 2, 1899

Mary E. Demasters, wife of
Edman G. Jones
Jun 25, 1831
Apr   1884

Griffith B. Cunningham *
Died Feb 19, 1855
Age: 25 years.

Several unmarked graves.

Emma Florence _____
(all other info gone)

William Morrison *
Died Oct 1, 1895
Age: 90 years.

Griffith Cunningham *
Died Jul 2, 1867
Age: about 80 years.

Mrs. Sarah,* wife of
Griffith Cunningham
Died Mar 22, 1852
Age: 60 years.

NOTE: Informed sources says that John R. Jones, A Revolutionary Soldier, was buried here.
John Jones *
Died Dec 23, 1831
Age: (not given)
& wife
Mary Jones
(no dates)

* *

FAYETTEVILLE QUADRANGLE

WOODROOF CEMETERY

LOCATION: Two and one-half miles east of Fayetteville and south of Old Chennault Ford Road, one-half mile north of Elk River.

Jesse Woodroof
"A Revolutionary Soldier
who died on the 13th of
Oct. A.D. 1826."
Age: 60 years.

5 unmarked graves.

* *

RHEA CEMETERY

LOCATION: One and one-half miles ENE of Fayetteville, between Highway 64 and Old Mulberry Road.

John Rhea
Feb 23, 1776
Feb 5, 1839 in the
68 year of his age.

Sally Rhea
Dec 24, 1776
Aug 19, 1847

B. M. G. Rhea
Sep 20, 1818
Jul 10, 1852

Several unmarked graves.

W. B. Rhea
May 20, 1814
Feb 27, 1861

Nancy Rhea
Nov 29, 1818
Aug 20, 1865

Elizabeth, Daughter of
W. B. & N. Rhea
Nov 14, 1834
Oct 17, 1835

Ann G., Daughter of
W. B. & N. Rhea
Feb 27, 1843
Oct 26, 1845

Sarah H., Daughter of
W. B. & N. Rhea
Apr 30, 1836
Jul 31, 1853

Susan M., Consort of
W. G. Solomon
Sep 12, 1820
Sep 3, 1853

J. B. Rhea
Nov 23, 1848
Jul 15, 1871

Lizzie Rhea
Sep 5, 1855
May 8, 1861

S. A. Broyles
Apr 11, 1816
Aug 27, 1859

* *

GREEN CEMETERY

LOCATION: Two miles SE of Fayetteville on the north side of Elk River at Eldad Bridge.

James Green
Dec 25, 1840
Oct 17, 1917
&
Hettie Green
Nov 18, 1850
Nov 18, 1915

2 or more unmarked graves.

* *

ROSE HILL CEMETERY

LOCATION: In NW Fayetteville.

Ola M. Askinson
Mar 29, 1876
Sep 30, 1940

Isabella V. Atkinson
1844-1925

Mahlon C. Atkinson
1840-1913

W. S. Atkinson
1868-1900

Jimmie, Son of
M. C. & A. I. V. Atkinson
Apr 3, 1873
Jul 1, 1874

Robert W. Ashby
Jan 24, 1897
Mar 25, 1942

Catharine T. Ashby
Jul 27, 1896
Feb 1, 1870

Dr. J. M. Anderson
Oct 19, 1837
Dec 13, 1925
&
Amanda H. Anderson
Apr 25, 1842
Jul 29, 1919

Carlee Allen
Jul 4, 1875
Mar 21, 1964

Belle Allen
Dec 16, 1872
Oct 7, 1960

Mary Gleghorn, wife of
R. H. Askins
Jul 5, 1875
Dec 27, 1919

Ross H. Askins
1886-1947
&
Vela T. Askins
1897-

Harmon H. Alexander
Jan 15, 1841
Dec 2, 1921

L. Arrena Alexander
Nov 4, 1846
Dec 12, 1918

FAYETTEVILLE QUADRANGLE

Allie Mae Srong Alexander
(no dates)

W. Smith Alexander
Apr 20, 1878
May 2, 1961

R. Douglas Alexander
B&D Nov 30, 1925

Wanda C. Alexander
Feb 12, 1911
Nov 7, 1944

William Roy Askins
May 19, 1929
Nov 1, 1931

William Manley Askins
May 30, 1866
Oct 23, 1939
&
Nancy J. Baker Askins
Jul 15, 1868
Dec 28, 1939

Leonerdous Almore Archer
May 31, 1894
Apr 29, 1971

Delia May, wife of
L. A. Archer & Daughter of
J. C. & Cora Milstead
Feb 1, 1897
Apr 6, 1926

J. N. Ashby
Apr 3, 1874
Dec 3, 1945
&
Grace M. Ashby
Jan 26, 1898
(no date)

Travis D. Ashby
1847-1896
&
Nancy J. Ashby
1852-1923

M. F., Daughter of
T. O. & N. J. Ashby
Sep 23, 1877
May 20, 1881

H. B. Alexander
(Harman Bartlett)
Aug 9, 1874
Nov 2, 1963
&
Louella Roach, wife of
Harman Bartlett Alexander
(no dates)

Etoile Moore Alexander
Mar 2, 1881
Dec 6, 1966

L. Woodruff Alexander
May 5, 1880
Mar 19, 1943

Benjamin G. Alford
Jan 3, 1842
May 23, 1904

J. H. F. Anderson
Nov 30, 1871
Mar 18, 1939

Alice Kidd Anderson
Sep 27, 1873
Feb 4, 1943

Mary Anderson
Jan 10, 1905
Aug 19, 1926

Addie Ashby
Jan 21, 1856
Mar 21, 1893

Ashby
(no dates)

Bettie Anthony
1836-1908

George J. Alexander
Nov 9, 1838
Feb 20, 1915
&
Cecil Olga, Daughter of
George J. & Ida M. Alexander
May 30, 1879
Apr 21, 1909

William G. Anderson
1872-1939
&
Bertha L. Anderson
1881-1965

Deimer C. Anderson
Feb 28, 1874
May 16, 1954
&
Flossie R. Anderson
Apr 13, 1884
Jul 1, 1955

H. Knox Askins
Sep 30, 1903
May 9, 1965
&
Alverne B. Askins
Jan 31, 1906

Horace K. Alexander
Tennessee
1st Lt. Medical Corp, WW I
Oct 2, 1885
Jul 15, 1958

Mamie Kidd Askins
Mar 12, 1887
(no date)

Dennie Louis Askins
Feb 14, 1877
Jan 17, 1959

Alma Hicks Askins
Mar 1, 1878
Jan 3, 1961

W. G. Adkins
41st Tenn. C.S.A.
Aug 25, 1820
Jul 30, 1892
&
Mary E. Adkins
Dec 31, 1835
Aug 30, 1897
&
John S. Adkins
Nov 3, 1867
Jun 12, 1910

Goria Rees, wife of
James L. Anderson
1924-1948

Sara Cornelia Elizabeth,
Daughter of
J. A. & S. M. E. Albright
Feb 11, 1873
Feb 24, 1880

James Rudy Montgomery, Son of
J. A. & S. M. E. Albright
Aug 14, 1877
Oct 27, 1877

Susanna Jane, Daughter of
J. A. & S. M. E. Albright
Feb 23, 1861
Mar 24, 1874

William M. Alexander
Jul 24, 1816
Sep 9, 1881

John S. Alexander
Dec 5, 1838
Sep 16, 1920
& wife
Florinda H. Smith Alexander
May 18, 1845
May 24, 1887

Edward Lee Allen
1836-1877

R. Cecil Allen
Dec 5, 1900
Feb 24, 1969

Cornelius Allen
May 5, 1811
Apr 14, 1872
& wife
Mary C. Allen
1820-1884

Lucile P. Allen
Mar 21, 1901

Lytle G. Anderson
Died Dec 26, 1898
Age: (not given)

A. M. Anderson
Died Apr 15, 1886
Age: (not given)

M. A. Akin
Died Jul 11, 1877
Age: 62 years.

D. L. Anderson
Dec 7, 1839
Dec 7, 1923
&
M. E. Anderson
Aug 4, 1842
May 27, 1917

W. W. Alexander
Died Feb 27, 1907
Age: 54 years.

W. S. Alexander
Dec 22, 1836
Nov 19, 1914

Sina L. Alexander
Jun 18, 1868
May 31, 1909

Willie Renegar Archer
1891-1955

Roy Askins
Jul 3, 1877
Mar 1, 1958

Nora Askins
Aug 10, 1881
Oct 20, 1950

Hayden Askins
May 11, 1900
Feb 23, 1948

Anna Diemer Adams
Apr 9, 1845
Jul 23, 1928

P. C. Askins
Sep 22, 1849
Oct 3, 1929
&
Sallie E. Askins
Dec 17, 1858
Sep 14, 1922

Irene Ogle Abbott
Jul 16, 1902
Mar 18, 1950

Homer C. Askins
Apr 12, 1915
Aug 29, 1939

Worth Askins
Oct 13, 1911
Feb 20, 1951

FAYETTEVILLE QUADRANGLE

Charles H. Askins
Sep 29, 1920
Sep 23, 1922
&
Rubie L. Askins
May 20, 1923
Dec 31, 1923
&
Elgie J. Askins
Apr 30, 1880
Jan 15, 1953
&
Lizzie Clark Askins
Jan 20, 1881
Jun 25, 1933

Harry Stiles Ashby
Jan 11, 1902
Nov 14, 1917

Bessie Motlow Ashby
Nov 4, 1904

Marilyn Stiles Ashby
Jan 11, 1934

Retha Strong Ashby
Dec 30, 1884
Oct 30, 1959

Sam Ashby
Apr 9, 1867
Dec 6, 1942

May Koonce Ashby
Mar 5, 1876
Oct 18, 1905

William Edd Brown
Sep 24, 1891
Sep 5, 1918

Alease Bedwell Boggs
Jan 30, 1922
Mar 4, 1966

Mittie Moore, wife of
E. F. Benderman
Feb 24, 1884
Jan 26, 1918

Ernest Bond
Sep 15, 1876
Sep 26, 1913
& wife
Fannie Bond
Sep 20, 1872
Oct 10, 1918

Josephine Carrigan Bond
1847-1920

Moses W. Broadway
Dec 9, 1880
Jul 25, 1932
&
Ava Ashby Broadway
Jul 4, 1888

Elizabeth Mai Broadway
Dec 12, 1912
Dec 21, 1916

Jo Reba Bordinaro
Mar 8, 1945
Dec 17, 1958
(picture)

William Henry Buntley
1891-1944
&
Donia McGee Buntley
1895-1970
(Tullahoma FH)

C. W. Bonner
1866-1937
&
Mattie Hicks Bonner
1865-1947

J. B. Barnes
Jul 12, 1933
Apr 26, 1969
&
Infant Daughter,
Jeannie Rene Barnes
B&D Feb 17, 1967

Marty Ray Barnes
2 days
196?
(Higgins FH)

Ernest Patrick Barnes
Oct 6, 1936
Oct 28, 1936

Robert Lee Barnes, Sr.
Sep 7, 1895

&
Jennie Askins Barnes
Oct 20, 1897
Sep 10, 1961

Rob L. Burns
1907-19
&
Lucile Burns
1907-19

Oliver Barnes
1858-1945
&
Frances Barnes
1852-1914

Beulah M. Barnes
1889-1936

Edd A. Bartlett
Tennessee
Pvt 316 MG Bn 81 Div
Died Jan 11, 1937
(no age given)

Mary Allie Bartlett
Jul 2, 1884
Apr 5, 1942

Henry Williamson Bonner
1865-1920

Rev. R. S. Brown
Feb 15, 1858
Jul 1, 1939

Sadie Smith Brown
Aug 5, 1862
Dec 2, 1937

Moses M. Bunn
Dec 27, 1852
Jan 31, 1924
&
Josie Bunn
Jun 24, 1873
Oct 21, 1922

Eld. J. R. Bradley
Sep 3, 1846
Sep 9, 1923

Mary E.(nee Liles), wife of
Eld. J. R. Bradley
Jan 28, 1848
Apr 4, 1911

Eliza B., Daughter of
G. B. & M. M. Broyles
1868-1870

Catharine Boyles
Nov 9, 1871
Aug 18, 1934

George B. Boyles
Dec 22, 1833
Jan 27, 1897
& wife
Margaret Boyles
Sep 14, 1838
Dec 18, 1916

Margaret (Boyles)
Died Mar 9, 1966
Age: (not given)

Margarett, Daughter of
G. H. & E. S. Boyles
Jul 17, 1891
Aug 22, 1892

E. A. B.(Boyles)
(no dates)

Edgar (Broyles)
(no dates, child)

J. W. Barnett
Died Oct 20, 1922
Age: (not given)

Julia C., wife of
J. W. Barnett
Dec 31, 1849
Jul 20, 1881

Tom Bigham
Jun 30, 1893
Aug 7, 1969

Maude Ruth Bigham
Sep 6, 1902

Bessie Bedwell
May 8, 1888
Aug 16, 1954

George F. Bell
Jan 14, 1887
Dec 24, 1922

Roy C. Bercheen
1884-1958

Sarah M. Bercheen
Dec 14, 1891
Jun 28, 1965

Charles F. Bercheen
1911-1939

Maurelle, Daughter of
Roy & Sarah Bercheen
Mar 31, 1914
Oct 5, 1921

W. E. "Jack" Bearden
1878-1966

Phoebe Barrett Bowen
1875-1933

Charlie C., Son of
Jas. & M. A. Barrett
Died Jul 19, 1899
Age: 15y, 6m.

Iva Smith Buntley
1897-1932

Otha Brents
1856-1924
&
Maude Brents
1864-1945

David Thomas Buchanan
Aug 4, 1887
Oct 29, 1964

William Diemer Bunn
Dec 22, 1905
Sep 30, 1963

Virginia Crick Bunn
Feb 17, 1909

Wilma Janice Bunn
Dec 3, 1937
Jul 1, 1938

Edna R., Daughter of
S. E. & Marie Battson
May 15, 1899
Nov 26, 1900
&
Infant Son, Battson
B&D Jan 18, 1903

James Barrett
Nov 10, 1846
Jul 25, 1928

Mary A., wife of
Jas. Barnett
Nov 6, 1848
May 12, 1893

Sue Alice Barrett
Dec 29, 1878
Mar 9, 1963

T. Beth Bailey
Died 1942
Age: (not given)

James M. Barnes
Tennessee
Pfc Btry A 113 Fa Bn WW II
Oct 18, 1920
Dec 15, 1966

Sarah Ables, wife of
J. M. Barnes
Feb 12, 1894
Aug 25, 1929
 & Daughter
Mary Frances Barnes
Apr 18, 1914
Mar 25, 1935

Albert G. H. Brandon
Feb 22, 1832
Apr 23, 1911
&
Sue E. Brandon
Apr 15, 1853
Mar 11, 1937

John Moffett Brandon
Jul 27, 1836
Jun 2, 1958

Allison G. Buckner, D.D.S.
Nov 22, 1874
Dec 15, 1963

Clare Barnett Buckner
Feb 8, 1875
Mar 13, 1947

Julia Mai Buckner
Mar 19, 1893
Apr 2, 1918

Allison G. Buckner
Apr 29, 1903
Dec 12, 1923

Lila Hovis Briggs
Sep 2, 1885
Jan 30, 1961

Clara Taylor Boaz
1897-1938

Jean W. Boaz
May 28, 1895
Jul 23, 1926

William Rufus Boaz
May 19, 1866
Sep 4, 1943

Virginia Jean, wife of
W. R. Boaz
Oct 4, 1863
Feb 11, 1933

H. D. Boaz
1848-1931

J. H. Blair
1835-1895

Essie Holland, wife of
W. B. Burns
Dec. 1868
(no other dates)

Jake Buntley
1860-1940

Corina Hoots Buntley
1863-1924

John Isaac Buntley
Tennessee
WAGR 1 Bn Trench Arty CAC
WW I
Jan 28, 1887
May 30, 1961

J. A. Blakemore
1856-1926
 & wife
Ada Blakemore
1855-1899

Mrs. John A. Bintzler
Died Sep 14, 1970
Age: (not given)
(Higgins FH)

Robertson Wright Boyce
Feb 18, 1882
Aug 31, 1882

John W. Boaz
Apr 25, 1842
Jul 29, 1917
&
Sue R. Boaz
May 3, 1866
Jan 5, 1919

Hosea A. Broyles
Jan 8, 1887
Oct 21, 1957

Frank Horton Broyles
Feb 18, 1919
Mar 8, 1919

Stanley W. Bingham
SK2c U.S.C.G.R.
Oct 21, 1912
Jun 4, 1943

Kitty R. Alexander Bingham
Dec 28, 1909

Ephraim Bouldin
Aug 10, 1828
Jul 10, 1893
Age: 64 years, 11m.

Nora Fanning, wife of
E. J. Brook
Mar 28, 1887
Mar 20, 1921

John W. Brown
1876-1943
&
Mary V. Brown
1880-1960

Thomas Cannon Brown
Dec 24, 1908
Jun 22, 1939

Sue Maude Brown
Feb 17, 1904
Nov 1, 1964

Sadie Rambo, wife of
Robert F. Buchanan
1886-1919

J. D. Buchanan
Aug 12, 1844
Jan 9, 1914
&
Mary E. Buchanan
Dec 23, 1845
Jan 1, 1928

Goodner Buchanan
May 6, 1875
May 9, 1947
&
Josie C. Buchanan
Feb 26, 1872
Oct 6, 1946

John Thomas Buchanan
1887-1966

Lona Wakefield Buchanan
1893-1951

Thomas Pickle Bryant
Sep 19, 1890
Oct 13, 1960

Ora Buchanan Bryant
Sep 27, 1891
Mar 25, 1937

Lucy Jones Benjamin
Aug 10, 1883
Aug 29, 1963

John Milton Buntley
May 10, 1856
Jul 25, 1923
&
Annie Barnes Buntley
Dec 27, 1881
(no date)

Rev. John F. Beasley
1860-1928

Sallie Higgins Beasley
1864-1910

Frances B. Beasley
1936

Russell H. Beasley
1887-1963

Viola W. Bidwell
Nov 17, 1883
Sep 15, 1913

Almeda Flora Ousley, wife
of Gordon Bradshaw
Died Mar 2, 1897
Age: 25y, 7m, 26d.

David Thomas Buchanan, Jr.
Jan 26, 1912
Jan 29, 1912

Willa Diemer, wife of
E. E. Brossard
Jul 3, 1872
Apr 7, 1906

James Fletcher Bogle
Texas
Cpl 448 Bomb Gp AAF WW II
Mar 31, 1919
Aug 27, 1953

Annie Kerr Bogle
1889-1956

Samuel S. Benson
Sep 15, 1873
Jan 3, 1960
&
Nancy Ella Benson
Jul 6, 1874
Mar 23, 1958

Ollie W. Baites, Jr.
1908-1910

Ollie W. Baites
1881-1937

Henry Knox Bryson
1851-1933
&
Nettie M. Bryson
1875-1917
&
Cecil Bryson
1905-1938

FAYETTEVILLE QUADRANGLE

Joseph Tully Buchanan
1885-1962

Fannie Neece Buchanan
1893-

Stacie Maie Jean Barnes
May 26, 1906
Feb 10, 1944

Evelyn Jane Bates
1930-1931

Charles N. Bates
1873-1957
&
Ethel W. Bates
1877-1946

Infant Son of
Charles & Ethel Bates
(no dates)

Willie Bates Bunn
Nov 18, 1898
Oct 13, 1918

Marilou Palmer Brooks
Mar 4, 1932
Jul 29, 1969

Homer T. Blankenship
1912-1937

Ada Sweeney Brown
Aug 16, 1893
Jan 26, 1970

Robert Carey Barnes
Sep 21, 1884
May 9, 1964
&
Lucy McDaniel Barnes
Jan 18, 1886
Jan 19, 1953

James T. Beddingfield
1883-1962

Minnie Lou Beddingfield
1878-1935

James W. Bell
1895-1923

Mattie Barrett, wife of
John W. Bell
1871-1967

John W. Bell
1867-1923

Cornice Allen Barnette,
Mother of
Elaine Largen
1871-1933

David Mitchell Bright
1866-1940

James H. Burnam
1838-1906

Victoria Fulton, wife of
James H. Burnam
1840-1911

Mary, wife of
James H. Burnam
1835-1870

Alfred F. Burnam
B&D 1874
&
Bennet Burnam
1882-1883

Samuel Alston Bright
1863-1940

Mathew M. Bright
1860-1942

Virginia Burnam, wife of
Mathew M. Bright
(no dates)

W. W. Blake
1858-1938

George Washington Blake
1822-1885

Eliza Hansell McCord Blake
1837-1906

Thomas Bearden
1883-1934

Ellis Miller Bearden
1890-(no date)

Alfred Woods Bearden
1879-1892

Mattie Miles Bearden
1877-1893

Matt Marshall Bearden
1847-1906

Susan Woods Bearden
1853-1934

Octavia W. Baber
1874-1946

William Bonner, Jr.
Jul 14, 1837
Dec 21, 1891

Jennie, wife of
William Bonner, Jr.
Sep 30, 1840
Nov 12, 1870

William Bonner
Oct 7, 1793
Sep 20, 1879
& wife
Lucy R. Bonner
Jan 19, 1808
Oct 3, 1862
&
Infant Son, (Bonner)
Nov 28, 1828
Dec 12, 1828
&
William Henry Bonner
Jun 10, 1836
Jul 2, 1836

Eva L. Young Brents
May 26, 1859
May 8, 1883
Married to A. C. Brents
Mar 21, 1878

Frank Edward, Son of
A. C. & E. L. Brents
Oct 28, 1870
May 13, 1880

A. O. Battle
Mar 22, 1848
Oct 28, 1878
&
Allen Overion Battle
Died Apr 13, 1878
Age: 5m.

M. L. Hayes, wife of
J. J. Blakemore
May 28, 1822
May 9, 1887

Mary Eliza W., Daughter of
M. H. & A. F. Bonner
Aug 9, 1845
Dec 6, 1848

Henry Jones, Son of
M. H. & A. F. Bonner
Nov 16, 1843
Jan 10, 1856

David Robertson, Son of
M. H. & A. F. Bonner
Oct 17, 1859
Jul 14, 1878

Dr. Moses H. Bonner
Born in Granville Co., N.C.
Feb 25, 1806
Died in Fayetteville, Tenn.
Feb 17, 1880
& wife
Ann Faliah Bonner
Jan 2, 1822
Jun 26, 1889

Eleanora Bonner
Died Oct 16, 1913
Age: (not given)

Elizabeth Shores,
Daughter of
M. H. & A. F. Bonner
1852-1930

Mary Bright
Died Jan 24, 1961
Age: (not given)

Willis Collins Bright
Mar 17, 1844
Nov 22, 1887

John Bramlitt Bright
Jun 10, 1872
Apr 9, 1941

Anna Bramlitt Bright
Aug 2, 1849
Apr 26, 1941

J. Clark Bright
Co K 8th Tenn.
C.S.A.

Mattie Gardner Bright
Jan 23, 1853
Sep 15, 1876

Hunter Bryson Blakely, D.D.
Jan 6, 1862
Sep 20, 1945
&
Susan Marshall Blakely
Dec 10, 1865
Jul 29, 1937

James Morgan Blake
Oct 31, 1854
Feb 3, 1923
&
Ellis Woods Blake
1862-1938

Ernest Bates
1901-1933

Christopher C. Boyd
Apr 8, 1824
Jan 11, 1900

J. B. Bevils
Dec 28, 1857
Mar 2, 1936

Gracie Lee Bruce
1879-1896

Marcia Brandon Bradford
May 10, 1880
Jul 5, 1960

Mrs. Ethel Easley Buchanan
1892-Sep 8, 1970

FAYETTEVILLE QUADRANGLE

Angus G. Brandon
May 14, 1890

&
Leela Boaz Brandon
Apr 26, 1892
Sep 23, 1970

R. H. C. Bagley
Mar 1, 1806
Nov 6, 1878

Mrs. E. B., wife of
R. H. C. Bagley
Jan 5, 1815
Jan 10, 1900

Sarah Frances Bagley
Jul 15, 1836
Dec 30, 1908

James H. Bell
Apr 17, 1837
Dec 14, 1879

Sarah Fisher Bell
Feb 11, 1839
Jan 7, 1881

Ella Houston Bell
Mar 24, 1858
Jan 14, 1911

Octa A. Bell
Nov 30, 1873
Jul 10, 1930

Hugh M. Burras
1907-1941

Bettie Rodgers Bryant
Jun 10, 1880
Sep 24, 1894

Walter Jasper Bunn
Jun 29, 1876
(no date)
&
Bettie Brown Bunn
Feb 28, 1879
Sep 20, 1939

George Davis Bunn
Mar 24, 1903
Sep 18, 1903

John W. Bunn
Apr 5, 1864
Jun 20, 1930

John A. Bunn
Aug 8, 1834
Sep 22, 1912
& wife
Eleanor E. Bunn
Aug 2, 1839
Sep 16, 1883

William M. Buchanan
1907-1929

John L. Buchanan, Jr.
Sep 16, 1881
Sep 4, 1947
&
Minnie D. Buchanan
Feb 3, 1885

Katheryne F., wife of
J. L. Buchanan, Jr.
Sep 2, 1887
Jan 17, 1913

Allen Boaz
Oct 21, 1889
Feb 15, 1968
&
Mamie Boaz
Sep 19, 1895

Jennie A., Daughter of
C. & Mary Allen & wife of
J. A. Boaz
Nov 3, 1861
Aug 18, 1918
&
J. A. Boaz
Oct 28, 1845
Feb 7, 1931

Lee A. Boaz
Jan 2, 1882
Sep 15, 1883

Doris Boaz
1922-1935

Grace Boaz
1913-1969

James L. Boaz
1883-1955
&
Egera W. Boaz
1889-1970

Wallace Boaz
1920-1936

Horace W. Boaz
1896-1967
&
Pearl E. Boaz
1901-

Martha Buchanan
Feb 24, 1875
Mar 9, 1941

Thomas McClellan, Son of
F. G. & Kate Buchanan
Apr 2, 1879
Apr 22, 1905

Major Felix G. Buchanan
Mar 23, 1838
Mar 16, 1907
   C.S.A.

Kate McClellan, wife of
Felix G. Buchanan
Jul 10, 1848
Jun 7, 1931

Andrew Buchanan
Nov 12, 1783
Nov 20, 1868
"Buried in cemetery at
Homestead."
&
Bethiah Line White Buchanan
Aug 7, 1784
May 20, 1883

Andrew Buchanan
Feb 3, 1877
Jan 7, 1956

Malema Higgins Buchanan
Aug 12, 1882
Aug 27, 1963

Robert F. Buchanan
Feb 20, 1886
Sep 14, 1959

Sue Ella Morgan, wife of
W. D. Brooks
Oct 10, 1869
Jul 21, 1894

James Warren Bagley
Tennessee
Lieut-Colonel Corps of Engrs
Oct 31, 1881
Feb 19, 1947
&
Agnes Stevens Bagley
Dec 13, 1887
Mar 29, 1968

Thomas O. Bagley
Mar 21, 1845
Jun 14, 1909
&
Ellen Colville Bagley
Mar 9, 1856
Apr 13, 1926

Charles Frank Bagley
Nov 27, 1884
Sep 30, 1947

William P. Bell
1865-1932

Paris O. Bell
(no dates)

Ben Roy Bell
(no dates)

Letitia Metcalfe Bell
(no dates)

Tom Bagley
Mar 3, 1879
Nov 16, 1947
&
Daisy Pitts Bagley
Apr 22, 1881
Dec 29, 1954

Martha Suzanne, Daughter of
Tom & Daisy Bagley
Aug 16, 1908
Dec 17, 1909

Charles Boyles Bagley
May 1, 1843
Dec 1, 1935
&
Margaret Ann Warren Bagley
Jul 2, 1848
Dec 19, 1935

W. Greenfield Bagley
(no dates)

Margaret Bagley
Died 1918
Age: 6 days.

Sam C. Bagley
Jan 22, 1882
Jun 18, 1902

Ethel Bagley
(no dates)

Robert H. C. Bagley
(no dates)

Amanda Murrell Bagley
(no dates)

John T. Boaz
1867-1938
&
Susie Woods Boaz
1869-1942

Hardy W. Bailey
1876-1956
&
Nina C. Bailey
1879-1960

Miss Annie D. Burgess
Died Oct 18, 1971
Age: 90y, 11m, 13d.
(Higgins FH)

Daniel W. Bills
1855-1909
&
Josephine C. Bills
1858-1938

H. C. Barz
Apr 9, 1858
Feb 12, 1923

FAYETTEVILLE QUADRANGLE

Carl J. Browson
Virginia
S Sgt 499 Base Unit AAF
WW II
Mar 14, 1916
Jun 6, 1969

Emma F. Burgess
Feb 22, 1842
Apr 14, 1906

W. B. Burgess
Jun 8, 1850
Apr 9, 1919

John F. Broadaway
1875-1958
&
Collie W. Broadaway
1878-1959

Maud Brown
Aug 2, 1877
Dec 11, 1920

Sam M. Brogan
1862-1927

Myrtle D. Brogan
1871-1946

Clifford M. Brogan
1893-1917

Edwin J. Brogan
1905-1923

Ralph H. Brogan
1896-1897

Paul J. Brogan
1907-1918

Josie C. Beavers
Mar 16, 1847
Jan 4, 1923

Polly Beavers
Jun 21, 1829
Jan 1, 1909

Dr. E. K. Blair
1867-1929

Sarah J. Blair
1835-1918

Lavania D. Blair
1865-1943

Reuben M. Blair
1897-1963

Marjorie Bell
Nov 17, 1920
Apr 13, 1922

Mala Kelso Cunningham
Sep 2, 1866
Sep 16, 1948

O. E. Cashion
Aug 29, 1887

&
Allie Bryant Cashion
Jun 23, 1883
Jan 19, 1918

Nauvie Johnson Clark
Oct 1, 1882
Sep 12, 1966

Mitchel M. Clark
Mar 12, 1883
Jan 1, 1930

Annie Sloan Clark
Jun 10, 1884
Feb 27, 1954

Claude E. Clark
Jan 10, 1885
Sep 6, 1910

Thomas B. Clark
Jun 24, 1861
Apr 25, 1929

Mollie E., wife of
Thomas B. Clark
Mar 21, 1852
May 6, 1926

Cornelius F. Coleman
Feb 5, 1893

&
Susie R. Coleman
May 20, 1897
May 6, 1955

J. W. Clark
Dec 27, 1858
Jul 11, 1925

Lula S., wife of
J. W. Clark
Sep 8, 1865
Oct 12, 1915

William Jackson Cambron, D.D.
PHD.
1866-1936
&
Lillian Amonette Cambron
1873-1955

Edna Stedman Cole
Sep 13, 1874
Apr 4, 1959

William Fleming Cole
Jun 30, 1873
Apr 17, 1961

Jesse Crick
1880-1947
&
Gauda Crick
1892-1938

Archie B. Caughran
1917-19
&
Wilma Louise Caughran
1920-1936

John A. Caudle
Tennessee
MOM M2 U.S.N.R. WW II
Jun 15, 1906
Sep 27, 1969
Married Dec 24, 1930
&
Cullum Ward Caudle
Jul 22, 1911

Charles J. Caudle
Sep 16, 1932
Mar 11, 1934

Miss A. E. Cashion
1873-1944

Raymond E. Capley
1905-1951

Samuel Warren Carmack
1871-1964

Susan Halbert Carmack
1874-1971

S. W. Carmack
Forrest's Escort
C.S.A.

Robert Lecky Cunningham
Dec 13, 1861
May 20, 1928

Robert Kelso, Son of
R. L. & M. K. Cunningham
Died 1893
Age: 22m.

Francis Kelso Cunningham
Jul 4, 1905
May 6, 1908

Hamilton E. Carter
1911-1966
&
Irene T. Carter
1911-

Paul Craig
Nov 17, 1874
Aug 14, 1954
&
Ida Ann Cline Craig
Feb 12, 1874
Oct 22, 1928

Will T. Clark
1882-1953
&
Beulah L. Clark
1890-19

Hiram Carrigan
1815-1891

Frances Carrigan
1817-1901

William R. Carrigan
Oct 7, 1837
Nov 22, 1911

J. C. Carrigan
1835-1900

F. H. Carrigan
1836-1900

Dr. C. A. Crunk
Aug 1, 1831
Jan 29, 1918

Mrs. Elizabeth G. Friend,
wife of
Dr. C. A. Crunk
Died Sep 8, 1902
Age: (not given)

Mrs. Minie Crunk
Died 1903
Age: 42 years.

Dr. W. F. Crunk
(no dates)

Willie, Son of
W. T. & L. Cowan
Died May 7, 1898
Age: 2m.

Mollie Vance, wife of
W. T. Cowan
Aug 5, 1859
May 3, 1893
"Member of C. P. Church."

Murrell Roach Cloyd
Oct 26, 1898
Nov 8, 1953

Robert Lee Caldwell
Feb 4, 1858
Mar 12, 1935
&
Elizabeth Bagley Caldwell
Jun 2, 1876
Oct 9, 1962
&
Alton Eugene Caldwell
1901-
&
Winifred Caldwell
1909-

George G., Son of
B. J. & S. K. Chafin
Dec 11, 1870
Aug 12, 1889

Roscoe Ewing, Son of
B. J. & S. K. Chafin
born Friday Jul 4, 1873
died Friday Aug 11, 1876

Father
Christopher Chafin
(no dates)
&
Mother
Bessie Chafin
(no dates)
&
Miss Mag Chafin
Age: 72 years
(no dates)

T. Cordie Croney
Jul 20, 1890
Mar 18, 1962
&
Martha M. Croney
Nov 21, 1890

Y. Curlee
1885-1948
&
Mattie White Curlee
1890-19

Paul B. Curlee
1882-1940

Edna Farrar Clark
Dec 4, 1883
Jan 8, 1955

Lottie Eley Cothrum
Feb 3, 1901
Dec 13, 1921

James T. Caldwell
1866-1914

Ozelle Small Caldwell
Aug 30, 1872
Feb 13, 1950

Robert M. Caldwell
1895-1938

William T. Cathcart
Co F
82 Indiana Inf.

Oliver H. Carroll
Jun 11, 1897
Aug 8, 1947

Mollie E. Carroll
Aug 5, 1874
Jun 6, 1927

Dixie Montean Conger
Oct 23, 1897
May 30, 1893

Charles P. Conger
B&D Jun 1, 1901

Ola Shofner, wife of
R. A. Conger
May 27, 1870
Oct 7, 1923

Robert Alonzo Conger
Mar 13, 1869
Feb 27, 1951

Sallie Morgan, wife of
R. A. Conger
Feb 19, 1880
Mar 17, 1961

John L. Collier
Oct 11, 1888
Jan 18, 1959

Eileen Faulkner Collier
Oct 13, 1901
Jul 4, 1963

Isom Collier
Nov 14, 1863
Feb 13, 1939

Callie Waid, wife of
I. J. Collier
Jun 29, 1867
May 24, 1918

William J. Collier
1891-1948

John Wilson Cunningham
Jan 25, 1867
Nov 18, 1953
&
Mattie Boaz Cunningham
May 18, 1873
Sep 22, 1957

Alma Lee, Daughter of
J. W. & Mattie Cunningham
Nov 10, 1895
Mar 7, 1922

Georgia L. Cunningham
1903-1941

J. E., Son of
James & Arrepha Cunningham
Mar 22, 1871
Nov 24, 1875
Age: 4y, 8m, 2d.

Jas. Cunningham
Jan 25, 1847
Nov 23, 1927

Arepha Roe Cunningham
Nov 9, 1847
Dec 6, 1933

F. Edgar Cunningham
Jun 29, 1882
Feb 25, 1955

P. Lon Cunningham
Jan 1, 1880
Jun 27, 1953

John B. Cunningham
Dec 25, 1860
Oct 20, 1929
&
Mollie H. Cunningham
Jan 24, 1870
Jan 28, 1940

George D. Cunningham
Jan 4, 1877
Oct 8, 1955
&
Josephine Cunningham
Aug 20, 1898

Lewis H. Cunningham
Tennessee
Pvt U. S. Army
Aug 19, 1929
Jan 8, 1956

Jas. B. Cheatham
1862-1937
&
Addie Hobbs Cheatham
1864-1939

Joseph Leslie Cheatham
1883-1948

James D. Currin
May 3, 1870
Jul 4, 1953
&
Pearl B. Currin
May 14, 1900
Apr 25, 1971

William Forrest Caughran
Jan 2, 1895
Jan 17, 1965

W. H. Caughran
1850-1931

Tinie Ashby Caughran
1860-1954

Ettie A. McDill Caughran
Mar 23, 1876
Apr 21, 1950

Nellie A. Caughran
Sep 4, 1903
Jan 20, 1923

W. H. Cashion
Sep 10, 1841
Mar 24, 1917
&
Elizabeth M. Cashion
Feb 20, 1843
Jan 21, 1940

Mary Anderson Carter
1884-1913

George Farrar Carter
1879-1945

Ervan F. Cunningham
Feb 16, 1878
Nov 19, 1929
&
Annie L. Fanning, wife of
Ervan F. Cunningham
Feb 11, 1890
Apr 6, 1938

Jim D. Cunningham
1869-1942
&
Sallie E. Cunningham
1867-1937

Alexander F. Carter
1889-1961

Mary Lou Hayes Carter
1889-1968

Catharine Parks, Relict of
Joseph Cashion
Mar 14, 1828
Jun 3, 1896

William R. Cashion
Feb 21, 1854
Feb 19, 1913
& his wife
Mattie E. Cashion
Feb 4, 1862
Jul 5, 1926

William Conrad
1870-1943

Kate Jean Conger
Jan 16, 1876
Nov 24, 1930

Gladys Carpenter
1899-1930

William Morgan Conaway
Feb 13, 1892

Married Aug 7, 1913
Mary Bell Harris Conaway
Feb 24, 1888
Jun 8, 1968

William Corder
1877-1940

Hurley W. Clark
1891-1953
&
Bessie T. Clark
1893-

John H. Cummins
Jul 28, 1847
May 1, 1935

Pricilla, wife of
J. H. Cummins
Feb 25, 1895 (died)
Age: 37 years.

FAYETTEVILLE QUADRANGLE

Charlie B., Son of
J. H. & L. G. Cummins
Sep 30, 1884
Oct 7, 1890

Laura G., wife of
J. H. Cummins
Died Jun 1, 1893
Age: (not given)

Nancy Catharine Davis,
wife of John Cary
Jun 20, 1850
Mar 12, 1928

Kate Cary
Sep 22, 1879
May 19, 1963

James Robert Childers
1876-1924

Beatrice Prosser, wife of
J. R. Childers
Dec 20, 1874
Jun 7, 1919

Roberta Childers
1906-1926

James J. Crane
1883-1919

Cora R. Crane
1884-1962

I. S. Crane
1860-1925

Bettie Washburn Crane
1859-1917

William Guy Cowan
Feb 16, 1872
Sep 24, 1955

Myra McGuire Cowan
Jul 22, 1881
Apr 29, 1939

Samuel R. Cramsie
1871-1943
&
Minnie B. Cramsie
1875-1926
&
Laura Pitts Cramsie
1908-1943

Neeley D. Crawford
1894-1956

Mary Ivah Crawford
May 24, 1919
Feb 5, 1946

Julia Elizabeth, Daughter of
Mr. & Mrs. George R. Cowan
(no dates)

George Robert Cowan
Died Aug 15, 1918
Age: 50 years.

Johnnie Kathlen Cowan
McClellan
Aug 24, 1879
Aug 31, 1957

James Hugh Cowan
Sep 22, 1850
Feb 10, 1927
&
Ida Cashion Cowan
Apr 20, 1859
Jan 4, 1945

Julia Catherine Cowan
Sep 26, 1888
Dec 7, 1956

Paul A. Cramsie
1874-1920
&
Affie H. Cramsie
1875-1943

Emma A. Chick
B&D Jan 23, 1921

R. B. Collins
1862-1929

Beulah Cunningham
1892-1953

W. E. Cunningham
1889-1935

Richard M. Coleman
Tennessee
2 Lt. 56 Fd Arty 19 Div
Died Jun 20, 1941

Reubin M. Carter
Dec 2, 1860
Apr 20, 1937

Martha J. Carter
Jul 21, 1859
May 7, 1939

Basha M. Carter
Apr 2, 1884
Oct 11, 1969

Hugh J. Cummins
Jun 28, 1869
Jan 1, 1951

Mary Moore Cummins
Dec 19, 1865
Mar 27, 1942

Robert L. Clift
1865-1941
&
Clara C. Clift
1875-1928

McDonald Creson
Apr 17, 1873
Sep 15, 1958

James A. Craig
Mar 28, 1876
Oct 30, 1951

George Barnard Creson
Mar 27, 1878
Jan 7, 1964
&
Annie Phelps Creson
Mar 1, 1887
Jan 20, 1962
&
Serena Kincaid
In memory of Mother
Serena Creson and Infant Son
Carroll.

W. W. Christian
Age: 31 years.
(no dates)

William Daisy Cunningham
1879-1952
&
Willie Harbin Cunningham
1901-

Ruth Twitty Cunningham
Aug 17, 1894
Jun 15, 1924

W. C. Chick
1896-1933

John Edgar Chick
Oct 28, 1907
Mar 11, 1948

W. W. Crawley
1891-1918
Gunner in U.S.A. Service
6 years.

Charles Henry Conger
Oct 7, 1866
Nov 30, 1911

Sion Ilaff Conger
Dec 22, 1861
Dec 27, 1933

Willie Malon Conger
Jul 7, 1866
Jan 30, 1937

Beall Norton, wife of
S. M. Conger
Jul 16, 1836
May 26, 1911

Sion Moores Conger
Mar 7, 1810
Jan 27, 1874

Dixie L. Conger, Sr.
Feb 20, 1864
Apr 4, 1952

Mary Shofner, wife of
Dixie L. Conger, Sr.
Sep 5, 1879
Apr 11, 1969

R. W. (Wiley) Cunningham
May 28, 1863
Dec 26, 1918
& wife
Dela Gunter Cunningham
Oct 8, 1864
Aug 26, 1914

Antonio Conaway
1854-1927

Lizzie Conaway
1855-1938

Charles F. Clark
1871-1922

Lena Conway Clark
1881-1959

Emma Jones Conaway
1883-1962

Lucy Hinkle Conaway
1885-1907

A. B. Cowan
1847-1933

William C. Cowan
1864-1926

George R. Cowan
1820-1905

Julia A. Cowan
1827-1907

Elizabeth Cowan
1857-1930

Mary A. Cowan
1860-1952

Frank W. Carter
1850-1904

S. J. Carter
(no dates)

McRady "Mac" Crabtree
Jan 12, 1919
Dec 29, 1967
&
Agnes B. Crabtree
Jan 4, 1913

William S. Clayton
Mar 2, 1873
Jul 15, 1967
&
Elizabeth B. Clayton
Jun 24, 1886
Oct.12, 1982

Stephen Monroe Clayton
Mar 5, 1850
Nov 11, 1923
&
Martha Conger Clayton
Jan 8, 1844
May 12, 1927

Chesley Monroe Colston
1854-1914
&
Mary Jane Colston
1857-1914

John Willis Carter, Jr.
Mar 26, 1926

Sara Sumners Carter
Apr 17, 1928
Jan 7, 1970

Mildred Rodes Kinningham
(Cinningham)
Oct 12, 1811
Feb 8, 1885

Nelson P. Carter
1847-1917
&
Orra Lee Smith Carter
1855-1938

N. P. Carter, Jr.
1878-1934

James C. Carter
Dec 7, 1807
Mar 27, 1881
Age: 73y, 3m, 20d.
&
Nancy G. Carter
Jul 1, 1812
Jun 8, 1886
Age: 73y, 11m, 7d.

Capt. Davis W. Clark
1st Tenn Regt C.S.A.
1835-1880

Addison B. Carter
Died Feb 9, 1872
Age: 34y, 2m, 22d.

Calvin D. Curlee
Pfc U. S. Army
WW I
Oct 8, 1893
Mar 2, 1949

T. M. Clayton
Mar 14, 1855
Nov 12, 1886

William E. Clark
Mar 28, 1871
Jul 3, 1871
&
Infant Son
B&D Jun 6, 1869
&
Infant Son
Dec 28, 1866
Jan 7, 1867
&
Infant Daughter
B&D Mar 13, 1868

Elmer Ross Caughran
1885-1966
&
Rose Higgins Caughran
1887-1961

Infant Coston
1895

Dr. C. C. Carpenter
Nov 28, 1860
May 12, 1926

Alice Lindsay, wife of
Dr. C. C. Carpenter
Oct 19, 1865
Dec 19, 1925

Alice C. McKay
Died Jan 5, 1918
Age: (not given)

Mrs. Lucy B. Cooper,
Daughter of Dr. M. H. &
Ann F. Bonner at whose feet
she lies buried. Wife of
Edmund Cooper
Jan 31, 1848
May 16, 1909

John R. Crowder
Nov 1, 1884
Mar 17, 1960
&
Velia B. Crowder
Feb 15, 1891

Mary, Daughter of
J. R. & V. B. Crowder
Feb 11, 1911
Oct 18, 1924

Austin Couch
1882-1947
&
Bernice Couch
1885-

Dr. D. W. Christian
Nov 6, 1817
Mar 9, 1880

James Cashion
Jul 29, 1828
May 22, 1892
C.S.A.

J. E. Caldwell
Died Sep 5, 1889
Age: 69 years.
&
Claude, Son of
J. E. & A. F. Caldwell
Died May 25, 1890
Age: 23 years.

Thomas Yeates Caldwell
(no dates)

Amanda Frances Caldwell
1838-1921

Thomas S. Caldwell
1790-1879

W. K. Caldwell
1879-1935

Andrew J. Carloss
Born in Chatham Co., N.C.
Oct 27, 1815
Married Jul 30, 1839
Died Apr 1, 1895
&
Mary Ann, Daughter of
James & Fannie F. Franklin
& wife of
Andrew Jackson Carloss
Aug 16, 1821
Jan 15, 1892

Robertson Clarke
May 6, 1849
Oct 2, 1879

W. R. Carter, Sr.
Nov 18, 1850
Dec 28, 1928

Ida B. Carter
May 18, 1860
Oct 27, 1951

John W. Carter
Feb 20, 1892
Nov 1, 1957

Beulah Carter
Jun 11, 1883
Jan 4, 1929

James William Couch
Tennessee
Pfc 571 MP Escort, Guard Co.
WW II
Jun 11, 1919
Nov 11, 1967

Frances Boaz Couch
1924-1965

Thomas Carver
1847-1929

Robert L. Crawford
1868-1944
&
Karah A. Crawford
1874-1959

Alice S. Caldwell
Jan 4, 1879

J. E. "Bert" Caldwell
Sep 21, 1870
Oct 18, 1938

Callie Stephenson, wife of
C. F. Clark
Jan 30, 1871
Nov 29, 1906

Walter Davis Clark
Jun 20, 1872
Aug 23, 1898

Mary McGee, wife of
F. S. Clark
Sep 2, 1841
Aug 17, 1904

Charles McKinney Cummins
Jul 28, 1847
May 7, 1904
&
Margaret Moore Cummins
Mar 7, 1868
Dec 5, 1955

Fred Augusta Caughran
May 1, 1904
Dec 14, 1934

Horton Lee Caughran
Nov 5, 1882
Sep 28, 1926

Kate Pitts, wife of
H. L. Caughran
Nov 15, 1879
Nov 13, 1918

Robert F. Cunningham
Jun 6, 1907

&
Viola M. Cunningham
Jan 10, 1915

Clinton S. Colgrove
1846-1926
&
Blanche Colgrove
1852-1912

Celia Colgrove
1831-1908

Infant Son of
Rev. & Mrs. T. G. Carter
Oct 20, 1925

Arch Cashion
1837-1915

Mrs. Arch Cashion
1847-1919

FAYETTEVILLE QUADRANGLE

Robert L. Caughran
Feb 6, 1887
Jan 25, 1930

Elizabeth Moore, wife of
Robert L. Caughran
Aug 5, 1887
Nov 27, 1923

John L. Caughran
Apr 29, 1863
Feb 22, 1929

Delia Pitts, wife of
John L. Caughran
May 12, 1865
Sep 3, 1935

Clay C. Caughran
May 26, 1892
Aug 24, 1924

Elizabeth Ann Campbell
Oct 17, 1860
May 3, 1934

John W. Campbell
Tennessee
Pfc Corps of Mil Police
WW II
Jul 14, 1898
Apr 12, 1965

W. F. Cannon, M.D.
1869-1941

Sophia Rice Cannon
1879-1943

J. H. Clardy
Apr 27, 1858
Apr 19, 1932

Emma Blair Clardy
Jan 8, 1871
Mar 9, 1954

Mary Clardy
Oct 21, 1897
Aug 3, 1907

Pleas Sheffield Clardy
Sep 24, 1894

Ozella Sumners Clardy
Nov 17, 1894

Martha Jane Colter, wife
of M. A. Cannon
1851-1910

J. Frank Cannon
1844-1919

M. Jane Cannon
1835-1919

William A. Carter
Sep 25, 1882
Oct 15, 1911

A. F. Carter
Feb 3, 1856
Sep 22, 1929

Iva B. Carter
Mar 21, 1862
Mar 10, 1935

Robert James Carter
Sep 11, 1884
May 1, 1958

Gertrude McCown Carter
Feb 22, 1884
Sep 22, 1919

James Nelson, Infant Son of
R. J. & Gertrude Carter
B&D Mar 15, 1918

Andrew Franklin Collins
May 17, 1865
Oct 10, 1937

Mary Katherine Collins
Jul 18, 1870
Dec 24, 1942

Joe Pleasant Collins
Nov 4, 1904

Sarah Lee Kane Collins
Nov 12, 1907
Apr 8, 1960

William J. Capley
1873-1942

Ozella Capley
1886-1960

Elizabeth Ray Crabtree
Jan 23, 1937
Aug 20, 1957

Infant Son of
H. L. & K. P. Caughran
B&D Aug 30, 1910

J. H. DeHaven
1853-1900
&
Laura Janson DeHaven
1861-1924

Nell Woodard Dowdy
Mar 26, 1907
Oct 27, 1968

John E. Dunn
Nov 9, 1900
Jun 29, 1967

Juanita S. Dunn
Apr 27, 1915

Max Dodson
1901-1936
&
Lorene Dodson
---- - ----

Robert Melven Donovan
Nov 19, 1906
Jun 17, 1935

Eddie Dunivan
Jul 6, 1900

&
Ethel Dunivan
Sep 8, 1902

Henry J. Donovan
Aug 15, 1881
Apr 26, 1959
&
Cordelia Donovan
Feb 25, 1876
Apr 4, 1943

Betty Gleen Dunivan
Oct 6, 1935
Jun 9, 1940

Jack Dunivan
1855-1937

Ellen Dunivan
1865-1936

William C. Dale
1874-1958

Lillie E. Dale
1881-1969

Infant Son of
Mr. & Mrs. W. C. Dale
B&D Apr 16, 1902

Nathan B. Dozier
1881-1932
&
Elise L. Dozier
1883-1946

Dozier Baby Boy
(no dates)

E. B. Davis, Sr.
Aug 2, 1870
Oct 30, 1933

Leota Pearl Davis
Nov 25, 1872
Jun 25, 1941

John T. Dean
1888-1928

Sallie Anderson Dean
1862-1957

Mason Henry Daly
Jun 14, 1898
Mar 19, 1967
&
Ethel Coble Daly
Jul 3, 1908

John C. Drennan
1871-1948

Olivia Prosser Drennan
1889-1942

Martha Boaz Dobbins
1917-1962

C. W. Durham
Oct 21, 1870
Jun 17, 1950

Nannie Ashby, wife of
C. W. Durham
May 1, 1872
May 27, 1911

John W. Durham
1831-1904
&
Mary Collier Durham
1841-1912

Mattie Durham
Dec 13, 1871
May 24, 1960

Annie D. Durham
May 4, 1883

John A. Downing
May 22, 1858
Mar 22, 1928

Russell Glenn Davis
Tennessee
2nd Lt. FA CEN OFF TNG SCH
WW I
Jul 5, 1897
Aug 6, 1964

Manley Ray, Son of
J. M. & Ola Dillworth
Oct 16, 1915
Jan 31, 1918

Florence Milhous Davis
Oct 3, 1869
Jan 7, 1932

Margaret Shaw Denwiddie
Sep 27, 1882
Jun 6, 1969

Tafy Tula Hobbs Davenport
1889-1925

FAYETTEVILLE QUADRANGLE

D. S. Dyer
Feb 25, 1852
Nov 29, 1911
&
Susa Dyer
Jan 18, 1840
Nov 21, 1919

Sgt Thomas E. Dobbins
Co I 32 Tenn Inf
C.S.A.

J. B. Derrick
Sep 10, 1831
Nov 7, 1906
&
Martha Derrick
1843-1912

T. E. Dryden
1841-1912

Ann Dryden
1848-1929

H. E. Dryden
1875-1934

Martha M. Dryden
1877-1953

J. H. Dooley
Sep 19, 1858
Jun 19, 1925

Margaret Ladd Dooley
Mar 28, 1865
Jun 21, 1948

Robert Hiller Dryden
Feb 10, 1901
Apr 10, 1971
&
Addie Lee Pitts Dryden
Nov 30, 1901
(no date)

William Houston Douthat
Jan 7, 1891
Apr 27, 1929

James A. Davis
Aug 11, 1893
May 7, 1971

Elia Mai Scott, wife of
James A. Davis
1900-

Carrie Johnson, wife of
J. F. Darnell
Mar 7, 1887
Jun 25, 1909

Susan M. Martin, wife of
Sidney L. Diemer
Apr 6, 1852
Oct 21, 1899
Married Aug 16, 1871

John Clem, Son of
Sidney L. & Susan M. Diemer
Dec 25, 1877
Jun 13, 1921

Sidney Burnitt Diemer
May 15, 1891
Aug 24, 1949

Pressley Dunn
1863-1948
&
Nancy Dunn
1867-1955

Dr. J. W. Davis
1863-1902
&
Annie M. Davis
1871-1935

Beulah Benton Davis
Jan 27, 1866
Nov 21, 1941

Robert E. Downing
1866-1947
&
Mattie L. Downing
1867-1946

Eddie Stowe, Son of
D. J. & Nellie Dimoch
Born in Charleston, S. C.
Mar 6, 1875
Died in Fayetteville, Tenn.
Oct 21, 1876

Albert Fulton Davidson
Died Oct 8, 1893
Age: 5m.

Robert Emmett Davidson
Died Mar 14, 1915
Age: 65 years.

Hallie Mayhew Davidson
Died Jan 16, 1949
Age: 82 years.

Robert Emmett Davidson
Sep 4, 1890
Jan 26, 1965

Virginia R. Davidson
Feb 1, 1892
Dec 17, 1958

James M. Davidson
Oct 16, 1888
Feb 9, 1944

Jennie Davidson
Died Apr 14, 1920
Age: (not given)

Fannie Davidson
Died Dec 19, 1919
Age: (not given)

Mary Margaret Davidson
(no dates)

James Davidson
(no dates)

Isham P. Dismukes
Apr 19, 1832
Sep 14, 1875
&
Virginia Fulton Dismukes
Apr 12, 1839
May 6, 1915

A. C. Dunn
1855-(no date)
&
Mary Dunn
1861-1925

"Dunn Sisters"
Mattie Dickey
1888-1946
&
Pearl Martin
1891-1972
&
Annie C. Dunn
1897-1966

Katie Dunn, wife of
John Daniels
Dec 10, 1882
Mar 10, 1923

Collier M. Dyer
1869-1930
&
M. Ella Dyer
1879-1925

Clement A. Diemer, Jr.
1859-1904

David Wyly Diemer
1869-1921

C. L. Diemer
1863-1939

John Caldwell Diemer
Feb 2, 1862
May 7, 1945
&
Exie Ann Hines Diemer
Jul 8, 1884
Feb 22, 1969

Dr. Joe. Dinwiddie
Feb 29, 1832
Nov 15, 1906

Ann M. Dinwiddie
1845-1928

L. A. Dinwiddie
1871-1943

J. B. Drake
Jan   1839
Mar 22, 1873

Mary A., Daughter of
J. B. & Mattie Drake
May 6, 1862
     1873

Mannon M. Dean
Dec 21, 1840
Feb 8, 1909
&
Ida E. Dean
Jun 30, 1853
Jun 2, 1926

Richard R. Dean
Jun 30, 1877
Dec 31, 1957

James H. Dean
1873-1888
&
Hugh A. Dean
1879-1888
&
Lucy N. Dean
1889-1896

Kate Caldwell, wife of
P. H. Dietz
1859-1903

Clement Alexander Diemer
Nov 13, 1821
Oct 13, 1907
"Dr. Diemer practiced
medicine in Fayetteville
44 years."
&
Rebecca Jane Greer Diemer
1832-Dec 1, 1903

Douglas B. Diemer
1902-1961

Eliza D. Diemer
Sep 21, 1805
Jul 6, 1873

C. A. Dowda
Co A 35th Ga.
C.S.A.

William Bluford Davidson
Jul 1, 1862
Feb 23, 1931
&
Pearl Johnson Davidson
Dec 16, 1883
Jul 2, 1943

Rebecca Davidson
Aug 12, 1898
Mar 20, 1936

R. S. Douthat
(no dates)
& wife
Mary Annie Douthat
Died Jun 20, 1899
Age: (not given)

David G. Douthat
Nov 22, 1853
Jul 12, 1902

Susie B. Douthat
Dec 5, 1855
Aug 12, 1921

Dr. M. T. Dyer
1869-1938

Rev. L. F. Dickens
1868-1937

Robert D. Dryden
1871-1932

A. M. Daniel
1875-1930
&
Frances E. Daniel
1877-1938

W. J. Davidson
Aug 31, 1863
Jun 9, 1919

Elizabeth A. Davidson
Nov 26, 1829
Aug 7, 1893

W. J. Davidson
Feb 1, 1836
Jul 30, 1891

Harry Davidson
Feb 13, 1871
Oct 2, 1883

Susie, wife of
George S. Davidson
Aug 10, 1875
Mar 4, 1898

John Davis
1901-1935

Nora Davis
1877-1943

Sam W. Davis
Aug 19, 1883
Jan 11, 1919

J. F. Davis
Nov 25, 1844
May 3, 1901

Doc Davis
1871-1965

James H. Dodson
1930-1931

T. Hawley Dodson
1896-
&
Elizabeth Warden Dodson
1895-1958

Billy M. Downing
Tennessee
Tec 5 U. S. Army WW II
Feb 3, 1916
Aug 10, 1969

P. A. Deford
Jun 27, 1855
Jun 25, 1938
&
Mary E. Deford
May 28, 1851
Mar 21, 1930

J. H. Deford
Dec 5, 1827
Aug 19, 1917
&
M. S. Deford
Mar 15, 1835
Mar 31, 1925

Eliza Beavers Downing
Apr 30, 1875
Apr 27, 1951

Morgan M. Downing
Jan 14, 1869
Feb 15, 1917

Wesley A. Dickson
1898-1971

Mattie Lee Dickson
Jun 21, 1902
Jan 3, 1913

William G. Dunivan
1890-1943
&
Bessie H. Dunivan
1894-1931

Marvin Daves
1907-1917

Benjamin Daves
1863-1939
&
Elizabeth Daves
1870-1926

Deward Alvin Daves
1909-1954

A. Jackson Eslick
1867-1937
&
Maggie Baxter Eslick
1868-1951

Mary C. Englman
Sep 1833 - Sep 1908
&
Martha Englman
May 1862 - Jun 1908

Frank W. Eakes
Pvt 1st Class
Born Mar 11, 1901
Killed by accident in Line
of Duty at Neuwied, Germany
Nov 24, 1920

W. A. Eakes
1862-1930

A. K. Edmondson
1838-1912

Jane Edmondson
1836-1914

Charles Goodrich Elliott
Nov 6, 1916
Nov 5, 1919

John F. Edmondson
Feb 22, 1853
Jun 12, 1916

Anna Lovina Downing, wife of
John F. Edmondson
Feb 3, 1865
Oct 7, 1963

Charles K., Son of
Mr. & Mrs. Charles B.
Edmondson
Mar 11, 1916
Jul 15, 1917

Infant Daughter of
Mr. & Mrs. John F. Edmondson
Dec 4, 1955

C. W. Eley
1875-1943

Cordelia Edwards
1893-1918

E. A. Evans
1868-1944

Mrs. E. A. Evans
1872-1931

Ellen Rebecca, Daughter of
Earl & Laura Evans
May 3, 1909
Jul 7, 1910

T. O. Evans
1861-1933

Morgan R. Eslick
Dec 28, 1882
Jan 17, 1968

Walter R. Eslick
Jul 20, 1874
Mar 29, 1912

W. A. Ellis
1873-1950

Minnie Jarvis Ellis
1877-1939

Morgan S. Eslick
Apr 27, 1840
Sep 23, 1923
&
Julia Steele Eslick
Jun 7, 1853
Jan 2, 1935
&
Kimble K. Eslick
May 29, 1885
Mar 16, 1954 (TM)

Macie Morton Eley
Died Oct 10, 1971
Age: 72 years.
(Ralston FH)

John M. Eslick
Nov 19, 1892

&
Roxie C. Eslick
Sep 17, 1890

John Marvin Eslick
Apr 16, 1916
May 8, 1916

Martha J. Eakin
Feb 16, 1829
Oct 24, 1907

Hugh McMillain Eakin
1837-1922
&
Eliza Anderson Eakin
1839-1918

John McNeal Eakin
Aug 20, 1877
Jul 3, 1967

Mary E. Wright, wife of
J. M. Eakin
Jan 14, 1881
May 7, 1912

Houston Endsley
Died Sep 2, 1969
Age: 55y, 11m, 16d.
(Higgins FH)

Leroy W. Erwin
1882-1944

Katie B. Erwin
1881-1919

James Polk Edwards
Aug 4, 1839
May 26, 1920

Lucy, wife of
J. P. Edwards
1859-Sep 9, 1901

Bettie Warren, wife of
J. P. Edwards
Oct 29, 1846
Jul 28, 1899

William Owen Edwards
Jul 9, 1876
Apr 11, 1962

Sidney Edmiston
1872-1919

Austin Eslick
Aug 20, 1825
Mar 23, 1904
&
Ann Cashion Eslick
Sep 27, 1823
Apr 27, 1902

Robert Hargis Elmore
1905-1969
&
Amy Meeks Elmore
1908-

Betty Lane Edwards
Sep 1, 1948
Sep 2, 1948

Jackson Z. Easley
1890-1958

Mellie Reep Easley
1863-1941

Robert A. Easley
1863-1927

Fannie Moores Evans
1928

Nancy Forrester
1851-1930

Dr. C. E. French
Died Sep 21, 1892
Age: 47 years.

Robert G., Son of
S. T. & Maggie B. Freeman
Jul 28, 1904
Aug 2, 1906

Infant Daughter of
S. T. & Maggie B. Freeman
Nov 24, 1905
Nov 25, 1905

William Feeney
Oct 16, 1874
Oct 11, 1904

James W. Feeney
Mar 20, 1869
Mar 15, 1940

Roy Feeney
Nov 25, 1876
Jan 1, 1903

Sallie Bruce, wife of
Capt. J. R. Feeney
Died Jun 20, 1884
Age: (not given)

Capt. J. R. Feeney
May 11, 1842
Jan 14, 1917
Co C 41st Tenn. C.S.A.
&
Celista Edwards, wife of
J. R. Feeney
Died Jun 3, 1879
Age: 31 years.

Ola Feeney
Died Dec 5, 1873
Age: 11m 9d.
&
Lou May Feeney
Died Dec 2, 1872
Age: 1y, 9m, 6d.
Children of J. R. &
Celista Feeney.

Bert Feeney
Died Nov 25, 1884
Age: 5y, 8m.

Robert T. Feeney
Oct 13, 1812
Jun 26, 1895
&
Martha A. Feeney
Dec 22, 1822
Aug 21, 1904

Pearl Feeney
Died Sep 5, 1877
Age: 9y, 4m, 26d.

Ann A. Feeney
Born in Philadelphia, Penn.
Aug 23, 1790
Jan 17, 1871
Age: 80y, 4m, 20d.

John Marks, Son of
J. M. & Mollie Johnson
Feeney
1893

Minnie Feeney
Jan 11, 1860
Dec 24, 1937

Baby Feeney
(no dates)

Merle Feeney
Died Jun 28, 1883
Age: (not given)

Allen Feeney
Died Jul 6, 1883
Age: (not given)

Robert Earl Feeney
Jun 17, 1867
Aug 21, 1958

Edgar Feeney
Died 1971 or 1972
Age: (illegible)
(Higgins FH)

Anne Bagley Feeney
Dec 5, 1874
May 17, 1958

Mary Jane McKnight Feeney
Jan 10, 1909
Jan 21, 1950

Alma E., wife of
Dr. B. E. Franklin
Sep 24, 1887
Aug 17, 1939

Robert Lee Farrer III
Died Oct 24, 1971
Age: 45 years. (Ralston FH)

John E. Fanning
Nov 3, 1881
Jan 16, 1953

Henderson Fanning
Sep 21, 1859
Feb 28, 1920

Sarah E. Burgess, wife of
H. Fanning
May 17, 1858
Nov 5, 1940

Mayme Fanning
Jan 22, 1884
Jun 8, 1969

Nathan Boon Foster
Dec 4, 1899
Dec 8, 1961

Gladys Foster
1895-1935

George Lee Forrest
1860-1958

Jennie Long Forrest
1870-1932

Jack Farrar
1832-1942

Dayse H.(Haslett) Farrar
1886-1970

John H. Foster
1870-Sep 21, 1920

William Rogers Few
Aug 18, 1907
Jul 14, 1953

Fred Fleming
1901-1940

S. W. Fleming
1855-1929

Sallie W. Fleming
1868-1950

Mary Fleming
1894-1910

W. B. Freeman
Aug 29, 1839
Oct 12, 1912

Catherine Prosser, wife of
W. B. Freeman
May 29, 1853
Sep 9, 1925

Alf S. Fulton
Sep 9, 1824
Nov 2, 1879

Laura Fulton
Jul 9, 1837
Oct 4, 1899

Francis P. Fulton
1830-1885
&
Martha E. Fulton
1835-1909

Benny Wayne Finn
1951
(Wilson FH)

Mollie Lou, Daughter of
J. A. & M. D. Formwalt
Died Apr 11, 1874
Age: 1y, 11m, 11d.

D. M. Formwalt
(no dates)

J. A. Formwalt
(no dates)

W. W. Formwalt
May 10, 1819
Mar 27, 1878

Mrs. Mary Formwalt
Feb 14, 1821
Jan 20, 1884

Ida Orrick, wife of
J. A. Formwalt
1869-1947

Robert Fulton
Died Aug 7, 1948
Age: (not given)
&
Maude Allen Fulton
Died Dec 21, 1933
Age: (not given)

Hugh Francis
1852-1942

Sallie Goodrich, wife of
Hugh Francis
Nov 29, 1856
Sep 16, 1883
Married May 13, 1880

Margaret Smith, wife of
Hugh Francis
1864-1942

FAYETTEVILLE QUADRANGLE

Robbie, Daughter of
R. G. & Lucy Fullerton
Jul 8, 1873
Feb 8, 1892

Robert Farquharson
Sep 14, 1814
Sep 26, 1869
&
Sarah Adelaide Farquharson
Jun 16, 1834
Feb 21, 1923
& Their children:
Robert Farquharson, Jr.
Jun 1, 1859
Sep 29, 1891
&
John Francis Farquharson
Jul 4, 1865
Apr 19, 1871
&
James Charles Farquharson
Dec 21, 1867
Nov 4, 1869

William Arthur Fowler
Dec 6, 1876
Oct 9, 1933
& wife
Anna Goodrich Fowler
Mar 8, 1876
Dec 23, 1947

Martha Christiana Fowler
Jan 30, 1915
Mar 6, 1915

Eugenia Wright Feeney
Dec 3, 1866
Aug 14, 1909

Baby Feeney
(no dates)

Robert Lee Farrer
Jan 20, 1895
Nov 1, 1956
&
Mary McClain Farrer
Dec 1, 1894

Cyril Francis, Son of
J. M. & M. M. Feeney
Jul 12, 1895
Mar 8, 1908

Ella Hamilton, wife of
Charles J. Formwalt
Apr 25, 1875
May 17, 1905
&
Charles J. Formwalt
Aug 31, 1915

Daris Marie Franklin
Apr 22, 1929
Jul 11, 1930

O. D. Evans
1830-1897
Co C 41st Tenn. C.S.A.
& wife
Sarah Ellen Wilson Evans
1841-1880
& Son
Carl Clark Evans
1872-1873
& Infant
Birdie Evans
1896
& Daughter
Jim Eva Evans
1878-1907
&
W. D. Evans
1866-1911

John William Farrar
1876-1950
&
Maud W. Farrar
1879-1958

Anna Lee Farrar
1906-1966

Rev. J. T. Farrar
Aug 13, 1844
Nov 20, 1928
&
Sarah L. Fullerton Farrar
May 29, 1842
Aug 22, 1910

Bettye Towry Farrar
Sep 25, 1937
Dec 27, 1941

James Pierce Farrar
Jun 22, 1880
May 9, 1954

Robert R. Farrar
Tennessee
Sgt 56 FTR Control Sq AAF
WW II
Aug 6, 1916
May 14, 1971

Infant Son (Farrar)
May 23, 1923
May 26, 1923

Infant Daughter (Farrar)
B&D May 5, 1914

Infant Daughter (Farrar)
Jun 17, 1913
Jun 19, 1913

Lucy Waggoner Gore
Sep 21, 1874
Sep 10, 1901

Lemuel Harrison George
1875-1958

Herbert Hicks Gray
Feb 16, 1887
Jun 5, 1947

Staley E. Gray
Tennessee
Pvt Btry C 113 field Arty
WW I
Jan 31, 1891
Jun 3, 1956

Kathleen Gray
Mar 12, 1910
Aug 15, 1958

Thomas S. Gleghorn
Oct 15, 1871
Jul 25, 1916

Samuel W. Gleghorn
Feb 20, 1832
Aug 5, 1908
&
Sarah S. Gleghorn
Oct 30, 1841
Jan 22, 1909

Samuel Moses Gleghorn
Jul 5, 1875
Aug 6, 1913

Chalmers A. Gleghorn
Jan 25, 1868
Apr 6, 1945

Martha E. Gleghorn
Oct 14, 1877
Oct 19, 1955

Marion Timothy Gowder
1900-1957

Callie Bunn, wife of
C. L. Grammer
1900-Jun 27, 1926

Margaret George
Sep 29, 1830
Jan 17, 1911

Carrie Bell Greer
1861-1929

John Jacob Greer
1824-1912

Eliza Bell Walker, wife of
J. J. Greer
Jan 16, 1831
Nov 22, 1898

Mary Kate Greer
1869-1911

Sarah Hall Green
Sep 20, 1824
Nov 12, 1892

Virginia B. Gordon
Mar 8, 1848
May 19, 1885

Sue A. Gordon
Feb 4, 1858
Aug 5, 1879

John T. Gordon
Mar 7, 1852
Jun 2, 1886

Edgar D. Gray
1883-1922
&
Mattie Florence Gray
1887-1972

O. P. Gray
May 27, 1858
Mar 1, 1913
& wife
Lizzie Gray
Oct 7, 1864
May 12, 1935

Lillian F., Daughter of
E. D. & M. F. Gray
Jun 15, 1912
Apr 5, 1913

T. S. Gunter
1858-1934
&
Sussie Sullivan Gunter
1860-1945

I. W. Grizzard
1861-1895

J. H. Gregory
1851-1920

Susan D. Gregory
1857=1930

Julius Elbert Green
Dec 21, 1905
May 24, 1962

E. Oliver Green
1870-1923

Jessie Neeld, wife of
Elbert Oliver Green
Jan 24, 1871
Aug 13, 1963

Marion James Gray
1902-1961

S. H. Galloway
Jun 19, 1873
May 3, 1926
& wife
Iva C. Askins Galloway
Jun 19, 1873
Apr 7, 1922

Myrtle Alsup Galloway
1881-1952

J. B. Gordon
Aug 25, 1847
Jul 22, 1929

M. E. Gordon
Jul 18, 1846
Apr 30, 1918

William Carroll Gotcher
S/Sgt 320 Sqd 90 Bomber
Group B
Died in service of his
Country in Guinea
Apr 26, 1914
Dec 1, 1943

William C. Gotcher
Nov 30, 1889
Mar 30, 1958

Lora Sanders Gotcher
Sep 25, 1886
Jan 20, 1968

I. C. Galloway
1874-1963

Harley V. Gaskill
Apr 21, 1860
Jul 30, 1913

Clyde W. Galloway
Jul 17, 1883
Dec 21, 1956

Lyda K. Galloway
1882-

Frank C. Galloway
Tennessee
Co B 3 Inf Repl Regt, WW I
Aug 19, 1887
Aug 21, 1956

Tishie Grider
(no dates)

Henry Grider
(no dates)

Sarah Grider
(no dates)

R. E. "Pete" Grills
Feb 15, 1905
Mar 5, 1970
&
Clarice O. Grills
Apr 21, 1912

Lillie Caughran Galloway
1873-1946

Floyd Goosby
1893-1971
&
Jennie Goosby
1900-

Robert E. "Bob" Grills, Jr.
Jan 9, 1927
Aug 4, 1970
&
Annabelle N. Grills
May 1, 1930

O. J. "Boss" Grills
Jan 5, 1891
Oct 10, 1928
& wife
Willie Wood Grills
Aug 20, 1885
(no date)

Owen H. Grills
Tenn Sup Sgt 161 Inf 41 Div
WW I
Sep 19, 1896
Feb 2, 1950

William Boone Grills
Mar 9, 1867
Dec 18, 1941
&
Susie Taylor Grills
Dec 10, 1869
Jan 28, 1933

Virginia Gattis
Feb 22, 1900
Jun 26, 1903

Lucile, Daughter of
D. M. & V. Gattis
Jun 7, 1893
Jul 22, 1893

John Griffis
1850-1921

Elizabeth Byers Griffis
1855-1920

Benjamin M. Glass
Died Mar 11, 1909
Age: 34 years.

Robert Wilson Gant
1879-1961

Mabel K. Gant
1882-1929

Paul Wilson Gant
1907-1963

Robert E. Galloway
1865-1934
&
Dollie P. Galloway
1870-1942

Willie Holland White, wife
of Cecil A. Green
Oct 30, 1893
Jun 12, 1942

Robert Brown Galloway
Aug 29, 1886
Jun 15, 1930
&
Nancy Irene Galloway
Jul 12, 1891
Nov 2, 1941

Robert Lewis Galloway
Sep 25, 1923
Mar 28, 1936

James Pressley Galloway
Jun 9, 1920
Jun 13, 1936

Betty D. Gray
Jul 13, 1940
Dec 23, 1940

Jennie L. Gray
1941-1941

Hence Goodrich Gray
1916-1929

William Davidson Gray
1874-1946
&
Birdie Norman Gray
1884-(no date)

Helen Merritt Givens
Jul 28, 1895
Jul 8, 1939

Henry Barbee, Son of
H. M. & S. B. Guynn
B&D May 1, 1911

J. P. Gray
1855-1937

Mrs. Era Gray
1860-1900

Jonathan Gilliland
Mar 25, 1871
Mar 5, 1874

James Moores Gray
Tennessee
GM2 U. S. Navy   WW II
Feb 4, 1926
Jul 29, 1970

Robert W. Gray
Tennessee
1st Lt. 119th Inf WW I
Jan 28, 1886
Feb 2, 1954

Col. N. J. George
1839-1919
"Soldier"

Thomas J. Gray, Jr.
1889-1891

Mark H. Gray
1853-1919

Mattie F., wife of
Mark H. Gray
Died Sep 22, 1889
Age: 29y, 1m, 16d.

Myrtle Wilson Gray
Jul 12, 1869
Feb 1, 1957

Robert H. Gray
Apr 6, 1854
Apr 23, 1939

John O. Gray
Dec 5, 1855
Dec 25, 1883

Capt. T. J. Gray
Apr 25, 1831
Oct 9, 1887

Lucy N., wife of
Capt. T. J. Gray
Aug 21, 1830
Oct 7, 1907

Clark Gattis
May 17, 1896
Sep 11, 1969
&
Bernice F. Gattis
Jan 16, 1898
Oct 26, 1971

George Clarke Goodrich
Dec 9, 1866
Jan 23, 1924

Mildred Rodes Goodrich
Oct 18, 1866
Mar 11, 1953

Clark Goodrich
Nov 12, 1895
Mar 28, 1893

George Jones Goodrich
1840-1902
(Sculptured picture)
&
Sallie H., wife of
George J. Goodrich
(no dates)

James F. Goodrich
May 27, 1844
Dec 7, 1878
&
Sallie A. Goodrich
Jun 29, 1846
May 17, 1887

Goodrich Infant
1877

FAYETTEVILLE QUADRANGLE

George, Son of
John & Ann F. Goodrich
Sep 3, 1875
Jan 27, 1936
&
Virge Bagley, wife of
George Goodrich &
Daughter of
T. O. & Ellen C. Bagley
Nov 2, 1877

Virge, Daughter of
George & Virge Goodrich
Jun 17, 1902
Jun 18, 1903

Colville Bagley, Son of
George & Virge B. Goodrich
Dec 8, 1897
Dec 26, 1946

John C. Goodrich
Oct 21, 1836
Feb 3, 1886
& wife
Ann F. Goodrich
Jun 17, 1846
Jan 24, 1922

Robert Feeney, Son of
J. C. & A. F. Goodrich
Apr 16, 1871
Jul 24, 1876

William Knight, Son of
James & Omagh Goodrich
Jul 20, 1929
Jul 23, 1929

James Clarence Goodrich
1879-1931

Omagh Knight Goodrich
1891-1966

Mattie Lizzie, Daughter of
J. Y. & M. E. Gill
Jan 25, 1873
Dec 8, 1877

Robert H. Gill
1885-1949

Lloyd Collins, Son of
W. A. & M. A. Gill
Jun 14, 1879
Apr 17, 1880

William A. Gill
1850-1894
&
Mattie A. Gill
1852-1918

Fredrick Charles Gill
Nov 22, 1877
Nov 21, 1909

Frank M. Gray
1874-1929

Perry N. Gillespie
1862-1892

Trousdale Gillespie
Died 1878
Age 5 years.

Frank Gillespie
1855-1902

Jessie Cage Gillespie
1871-1899

John Field Gillespie
1831-1912
Married in 1854
C.S.A.
&
Adeline Newman Gillespie
1833-1919

James Gillespie
1878-1938

Eleanor Molloy Gillespie
1867-1948

Henry Austin Gillespie
1870-1904

J. C. Goodrich
May 14, 1867
Nov 1, 1923
&
Ida B. Goodrich
Jan 1869
Dec 1944

William B. Goodrich
Jul 13, 1901
Feb 15, 1937

John C. Goodrich
Jan 20, 1896
Dec 22, 1965

Lyda Lee Goodrich
Dec 10, 1894
Sep 2, 1964

H. P. George
1836-1931

Sue M. George
1848-1937

C. R. George
1876-1929

Mrs. Lola Talley George
Died Aug 18, 1970
Age: 81y, 10m.

Dr. C. L. Goodrich
Jul 27, 1878
Nov 19, 1963

Mrs. C. L. Goodrich
Mar 4, 1880
May 14, 1959

Charles Stokes Goodrich
Apr 30, 1902
May 18, 1913

John T. Goodrich
Jun 20, 1844
Feb 2, 1917
&
Mary L. Goodrich
1844-1934

John B. Goodrich
1872-1894
&
Kate W. Goodrich
1871-1946

James P. Gray
Co E 8th Tenn.
C.S.A.

Crawford Franklin Groce
1903-1962

Allen Groce
1906-1947

Udo I. Griffin
Jan 26, 1907
Feb 17, 1958

Kathleen C. Griffin
Jul 30, 1903

James Davis Gray
Jul 12, 1905
May 20, 1968
&
Hattie Emma Gray
Dec 9, 1912

Charles W. Gunter
Apr 3, 1871
Feb 23, 1965

Lee Ella Gunter
Oct 23, 1887
Jan 24, 1917

Lula Elizabeth Gunter
Aug 9, 1869
Jun 22, 1906

Lizie Gary
Jan 28, 1891
Oct 6, 1913

William M., Son of
W. E. & L. L. Gary
Feb 18, 1912
Nov 25, 1912

Mattie Lake Gammon
1889-1942

Ida Gordon
Oct 7, 1956

W. C. Griswell, M.D.
1831-1909

Martha Cannon, wife of
W. C. Griswell
1841-1918

Lee E. Goodrich
Mar 5, 1889
Feb 26, 1910

Elizabeth Dollins, wife
of W. C. Goodrich
Dec 20, 1846
Feb 17, 1909

W. Thomas Glazier
1868-1950
&
V. Victoria Glazier
1870-1943

Saddie Stewart, wife of
L. H. George
1874-1935

Henry C. Harris
Jun 25, 1852
Nov 13, 1935
&
Mary Wallace Harris
Jun 14, 1862
Aug 10, 1958

Infant Son of
Wallace & Eunice Harris
Aug 17, 1913
Aug 18, 1913
&
Thomas M. Harris
May 15, 1911
Mar 20, 1969

J. T. Hastings
Jul 30, 1856
Feb 22, 1930
&
S. E. Hastings
Feb 25, 1866
Mar 30, 1942

William K. Hamilton
May 27, 1870
Mar 23, 1954
&
Lillian Lee Hamilton
Sep 26, 1870
Sep 11, 1953

Margaret J., Daughter of
Mr. & Mrs. W. K. Hamilton
June 1912

Vera M. Hendrix
Nov 14, 1892
May 12, 1943

George Franklin Howard
1869-1952
&
Mary Frances Howard
1877-1957

FAYETTEVILLE QUADRANGLE

Lizzie Gordon, wife of
J. W. Hall
Jul 25, 1854
Apr 18, 1886

Saidee Gordon, Daughter of
J. W. & Lizzie Hall
Jul 21, 1883
Jul 31, 1883

Myrtle Farrar Harwell
1879-1968

Robert E. Harwell
May 31, 1871
Dec 9, 1934
&
Sarah A. Harwell
Jan 26, 1873
Mar 17, 1938

Lenamay, Daughter of
J. T. & S. E. Hastings
Jul 23, 1901
Nov 15, 1915

Infant Son of
Earl & Lillian Hereford
Oct 1, 1921

Infant Son of
Earl & Lillian Hereford
Oct 10, 1916

Ruth, Daughter of
Earl & Lillian Hereford
Feb 6, 1914
Feb 7, 1914

Laura Caldwell Hulsey
1864-1944
&
William F. Hulsey
1854-1943
&
Maria Blakemore Hulsey
1851-1895

W. R. Harris
1895-(no date)
&
Estella Harris
1896-1935

Robert C. Harris
1929-1931

Peter Garvin Hamilton
Jun 24, 1856
Jul 19, 1946
&
Margaret Katharine Hamilton
Apr 17, 1872
Jun 7, 1935

Alvie Hastings
1888-1935
&
Vera Hastings
1898-

Norris C. Hastings
Nov 9, 1886
Oct 30, 1964
&
Nettie M. Hastings
Aug 10, 1892
Mar 17, 1961

Mamie Pamplin Hoots
(no dates)

Son of
Mamie Evans Hoots
(no dates)

Clarence Hoots
Sep 20, 1897

&
Mamie Evans Hoots
Nov 27, 1899
Nov 18, 1919

James M. Harris
Apr 1, 1846
Dec 9, 1921
&
Nancy H. Stephenson Harris
Oct 26, 1850
Feb 10, 1935

John W. Harris
Feb 24, 1886
Jun 4, 1974

Flora Harris Eshman
1890-1921

Roy Peter Himebaugh
Feb 26, 1880
Mar 14, 1954

Annie L. Renegar Himebaugh
Jan 4, 1884
Oct 16, 1961

Virginia Higgins Himebaugh
(no dates, Infant)

R. P. and R. W. Himebaugh
(no dates, Infants)

Leroy Himebaugh
(no dates, Infant)

A. J. Himebaugh
(no dates, Infant)

Charlie Walter Hasty
Nov 10, 1867
May 21, 1949
&
Estella George Hasty
Jun 1, 1868
Feb 15, 1917

Mary F. Hasty
Nov 17, 1899

Charlie T. Hasty
Nov 29, 1896
Jun 30, 1969

Fred S. Hamilton
1897-1940

Dunkin Hunter
1890-1923

Lizzie Price, wife of
A. H. Harbin
Nov 14, 1879
Oct 1, 1903

George W. Harbin
1861-1938
&
Dora Price Harbin
1870-1949

H. C. Higgins
May 2, 1846
Jan 7, 1915

Ellis Rhodes Henson
Dec 31, 1894
Oct 19, 1966

Annette Moore Henson
Aug 11, 1894

James Harding Hopper
Jul 17, 1853
Nov 3, 1914

Theo M. Hereford
1883-1932

Nan Caldwell, wife of
T. M. Hereford
1889-1926

Rebecca Hereford
1915-1932

James E. Hereford
1879-1931

Thomas Owen Hatcher
Jun 25, 1937
Apr 24, 1939

Adolphus H. Hatcher
Dec 9, 1851
Jul 15, 1954

Annie Swanson Hatcher
Jun 12, 1861
Apr 13, 1929

W. L. Hatcher
1848-1930

William J. Hill
1839-1917

Emily Hill, wife of
Dr. J. E. Houch
Nov 1, 1828
Mar 30, 1892

Dazie M. Hill
1823-1891(?)

J. B. Hill
1833-1887

Aggie Bearden Hill
1849-1886

John Henson
Apr 22, 1869
Feb 25, 1944
&
Annie Henson
Jun 9, 1869
Dec 10, 1959

James R. Henson
Mar 20, 1833
Aug 23, 1889
& wife
Saluda Ann Henson
Aug 13, 1842
Apr 30, 1905

J. N. Hamilton
Mar 28, 1869
Married to
Emma B. McLaughlin
on Apr 4, 1894
Died Feb 9, 1910

Henry Kelso Holman
1853-1909

Martha McPhail Holman
1861-1936

Ruth Rutledge Holman
1897-1917

McPhail, Son of
H. K. & Martha Holman
Mar 18, 1884
Mar 14, 1887

Thomas S. Holland
1880-1941

R. T. Holland
Apr 25, 1835
Jul 12, 1915
& wife
Margaret Craig Holland
Dec 13, 1845
Mar 30, 1922

Susan Holland
Died Oct 17, 1884
Age: (gone)

Infant Daughter of
R. T. & M. D. Holland
May 16, 1883
Jun 12, 1883

FAYETTEVILLE QUADRANGLE

Buford R. Hickson
1916-1953

Smith G. Hines
Dec 10, 1871
May 30, 1956
&
Laura C. Pitts Hines
Mar 3, 1885
Oct 8, 1957

John Calvin Hampton
Mar 9, 1889
Jan 28, 1948

John C., III, Son of
John & Bessie Hooper
Nov 23, 1915
Sep 7, 1941

Bessie Lynn Conger, wife
of John C. Hooper, Jr.
Nov 4, 1893
Apr 13, 1940

A. H.
(no dates, marker)

John Edward Howe
1840-1913

Ellen Gray Howe
1843-1920

Mamie McFerrin Howe
1887-

William Emerson Howe
1880-(no date)

Wade Hampton
1881-1936

Anne B. Hampton
1889-1944

Mary Morgan Hampton
Jul 9, 1904
Jun 9, 1915
Age: 10y, 11m.

Cyril Francis Hereford
Mar 30, 1863
Nov 9, 1950

Sara Boyce Hereford
Jul 15, 1874
May 2, 1965

William Raymond Harwell, Sr.
Oct 22, 1900
Oct 25, 1958

Evelyn Wilson Harwell
Jan 18, 1908

Martha Halbert Harwell
Jan 15, 1876
Jan 27, 1971

Oscar A. Hamilton
Mar 3, 1859
Jan 29, 1945
&
Iva Lindsay Hamilton
Sep 13, 1863
Nov 25, 1932

D. P. Holman
Jan 11, 1821
Dec 19, 1896
& wife
Mary Anderson Holman
born in Howard Co., Mo.
Feb 7, 1822
died in Fayetteville, Tenn.
Feb 15, 1893

Belinda Michelle Hall
Feb 22, 1962
Oct 1, 1963

Frank B. Hamilton
May 9, 1883
Feb 26, 1908

Mildred L., Daughter of
Frank & Alice Hamilton
Sep 10, 1906
Sep 7, 1907

James Robert Hancock
1854-1930
&
Caroline Gillespie Hancock
1859-1916

Robert Ott Hancock
Private 334th AERO Squadron
U.S.A.
1896-1918
"Died in Service of his
Country, buried in
Brookwood, England."

Howard Thomas Hancock
1882-1904

Winfield Cleveland Hancock
1884-1907

Rufus Gillespie Hancock
1885-1911

Rev. M. K. Harwell
1882-1966

William Raymond, Jr., Son
of Raymond & Evelyn Harwell
B&D May 17, 1940

Bobbie Miller Higgins
1863-1936

Mrs. W. F. Higgins
1893-1932

Lizzie C. Kimbrough, wife of
J. H. Holman
Mar 21, 1840
Jul 2, 1900

Col. J. H. Holman
1836-1910

Elizabeth Haynes Holman
1860-1917

Dick Allen Hobbs
1858-1901

Mary Elizabeth Hobbs
1864-1955

Baby Hobbs
(no dates)

Dr. T. P. Holman
Mar 3, 1834
Jul 17, 1925

Silena Moore, wife of
Dr. T. P. Holman
Jul 9, 1850
Sep 18, 1915
"President of Tennessee
W.C.T.U. from 1899 to 1915".

Neil Dow Holman
Feb 27, 1888
Jun 7, 1953

Burke E. Holman
May 4, 1876
Aug 28, 1958

Ethel T.(?) Holman
Nov 4, 1881
Jan 25, 1970

Gladys Holman
Nov 16, 1909
May 1, 1917

Charles Richard Howard
1908-1970

Russell E. Haislip
1916-1963

John B. Harris
Mar 15, 1846
Feb 25, 1918
&
Mary E. Harris
Oct 3, 1846
Apr 25, 1926

Allen Marvin Hester
Jun 1, 1879
May 1, 1915

John J. Hines
Died Jun 1, 1971
Age: 92 years.
(Ralston)

Albert Fulton Hines
Dec 6, 1901
May 7, 1961

Ola Pitts Hines
Apr 17, 1882
Nov 25, 1949

Raymond F. Hardin
Oct 25, 1902
Apr 7, 1938

Samuel Franklin Harding
Jun 2, 1875
Jun 17, 1958

Sarah Stovall Harding
Oct 5, 1870
Jan 15, 1946

Margaret Humphreys
"Widow of a C.S.A."
(no dates)

Edward Swanson Hatcher
1889-1948

Elise Newsom Hatcher
1895-1966

Phillip Holly
Aug 5, 1927

W. A. Hampton
Oct 6, 1872
Jan 12, 1919

Jennie Knox Hester
Oct 20, 1840
Mar 17, 1911

Hiram E. Harris
1831-1947

Dovie Beavers Harris
1880-1968

James Kelso Hobbs
May 8, 1908
Apr 24, 1948

David Franklin Hobbs
Aug 14, 1876
Jun 2, 1933

Mary Kelso, wife of
D. F. Hobbs
1879-1923

Mary E. Hobbs
1873-(date illegible)

Mary Park Hendrix
Feb 20, 1900
Dec 21, 1950

George W. Higgins
1831-1897
&
Susan C. Higgins
1842-1909

FAYETTEVILLE QUADRANGLE

Owen Halbert Higgins
1866-1947

Fannie Higgins
1869-1959

Gene Higgins
Mar 11, 1901
Nov 9, 1915

Fannie Owen Higgins
Feb 5, 1906
Jan 24, 1910

E. J. Higgins
May 7, 1853
Feb 16, 1909

Addie Woodard Higgins
Oct 27, 1853
Jul 12, 1917

Infant of
Carl & Julia Higgins
(no dates)

Carl Fulton Higgins
1878-1963

Julia Renegar Higgins
1884-1963

Joseph C. Higgins
1872-1946

Mary Hill Higgins
1871-1958

Hiram Clay Higgins
1876-1955
& wife
Died Jun 4, 1974
Age: 93 years

Frances Hill
1937-1939

John M. Hart
Jan 12, 1859
Jun 26, 1938
&
Mary A. Hart
Aug 21, 1870
(no date)

David Samuel Hamilton
Jun 24, 1871
Dec 7, 1946

Nancy McFerrin Hamilton
Mar 3, 1870
Mar 3, 1948

Herbert Terrall Hamilton
Nov 1, 1900
Sep 28, 1917

James Lawrence Hamilton
May 6, 1898
Jun 15, 1900
"Buried at Lebanon Cemetery"

Mack Hamilton
1900-1953

David Knox Hamilton
Mar 14, 1859
Feb 25, 1934

Agnes McCown, wife of
D. K. Hamilton
Oct 14, 1864
Dec 11, 1921

Mary Keeling Hunter
1896-1964

Willa S. Hancock
May 3, 1926
Dec 20, 1964

Joseph Newell Hines
1885-1929

Theo Harris
May 14, 1861
Oct 10, 1911
& wife
Mary K. Harris
Nov 25, 1862
Feb 12, 1938

Theo Harris
Died Dec 5, 1893
Age: 80 years
& wife
Eliza E. Wells Harris
Died Aug 19, 1883
Age: 54 years

Ed Harris
1883-1944
&
Sallie Francis Harris
1883-1956

Stacia Hicks
Apr 13, 1857
Oct 11, 1937

Joe Haley
Apr 3, 1889
Feb 21, 1957

Scott Dayne Harris
Tennessee
S2C USNRF WW I
Dec 25, 1892
Jul 26, 1946

Elizabeth Warren Harris
Apr 28, 1929
Mar 31, 1936

Sunolia Vaughn, wife of
George E. Harter
Toledo, Ohio & Daughter of
James S. & Katherine Vaughn
Apr 7, 1888
Mar 7, 1930
"DAR Past Regent"

Dr. O. R. Hatcher
Aug 30, 1846
Aug 23, 1896

Mary E. Hatcher
Sep 7, 1849
Nov 4, 1925

Robert A. Hatcher
Jun 19, 1877
Jul 6, 1878
&
Clara P. Hatcher
Jan 12, 1875
Aug 14, 1875
&
Walter W. Hatcher
Nov 20, 1873
Nov 27, 1873

Carl T. Harms
Mar 25, 1862
Apr 21, 1924

Bessie, wife of
Carl T. Harms
May 27, 1867
Jul 9, 1913

Charles Henry Harms
Jun 29, 1894
Aug 15, 1957

Joseph Rose Hiller
Mar 29, 1871
Jun 15, 1939
&
Roberta Waddle Hiller
Dec 3, 1876
Jun 21, 1949

Joseph R. Hiller, Jr.
Aug 11, 1900
Nov 7, 1903

George Jackson Henley
husband of
Rachel Morris Henley
Jan 28, 1905
Jul 25, 1954

Elder James W. Holman
Mar 1, 1812
Feb 21, 1892
& wife
Jean Holman
Apr 27, 1810
Sep 5, 1888

R. M. Holman
Jul 25, 1840
Aug 8, 1883

Colonel D. W. Holman
Oct 2, 1832
Sep 22, 1885
Age: 52y, 11m, 20d.
& wife
Fannie Landess Holman
Oct 22, 1843
Nov 23, 1923

Roy L. Holman
Aug 17, 1874
Sep 27, 1948

Mary Holman
Nov 17, 1882
Jun 5, 1883

Florence Landess, Daughter
of James W. &
Mamie E. Holman
Dec 18, 1913
Mar 14, 1916

Our Baby Holman
(no dates)

Mamie Landess, Daughter of
James W. & Mamie E. Holman
Apr 16, 1918
Mar 22, 1938

James Wilson Holman
May 12, 1876
Apr 25, 1961
&
Mamie Elder Holman
Jul 31, 1880
Oct 5, 1960

Daniel Wilson Holman
Died Nov 18, 1970
Age: 85y, 11d.
(Higgins FH)

John Thomas Hart
Sep 11, 1894
Apr 30, 1959

Hattie Rodes Hart
Mar 12, 1899
May 29, 1964

Fred L. Hovis
1894-1951
&
Nellie C. Hovis
1898-

Mrs. Mary Hoots
Died 1946
(no age given)

Rev. George Horne
born in Wythe Co., Va.
Aug 9, 1795
died Fayetteville, Tenn.
May 27, 1868

Newton Fleming Hancock
Sep 7, 1866
Dec 5, 1959
&
Martha Newman Hancock
Nov 20, 1868
Jul 26, 1946

133

FAYETTEVILLE QUADRANGLE

J. B. Hays
Apr 22, 1850
Mar 9, 1925

Minnie Brandon, Wife of
J. B. Hays
Dec 15, 1877
Apr 7, 1938

John O. Hatcher
Apr 12, 1862
Nov 27, 1879

Edwin, Son of
B. M. & S. F. Hatcher
Sep 19, 1874
Sep 9, 1875

B. M. Hatcher
Died Jul 11, 1893
Age: 74 years.
& wife
Susanah F. Hatcher
Died Sep 9, 1883
Age: 54 years

Eugene N., Son of
W. D. & S. J. Holman
Jan 18, 1868
Oct 10, 1879

Samuel Hamilton
1871-1946

Minnie Hamilton
1873-1950

Mary Edith Smith Houchin
1902-1932

Robbie Reese, Daughter of
A. N. & Elnora Hughey
Oct 9, 1891
Dec 22, 1907

Alonzo N. Hughey
Jun 29, 1852
Nov 28, 1905

Elnora Reese, wife of
Alonzo N. Hughey
Jul 17, 1862
Jul 27, 1901

John Robert Hamilton
1858-1947

Lenna Bunn Hamilton
1890-1960

Fannie McElroy Hamilton
1869-1915

Edith Kathleen Hamilton
1904-1914

Glenn Greer Hamilton
Jan 21, 1907
Jul 23, 1907

Ralph Hamilton
Nov 27, 1902
Nov 30, 1902

Davis, Son of
J. R. & F. F. Hamilton
B&D Jul 10, 1900

Mattie Hilliard
1858-1945

Harvey Hoots
1856-1930
&
Sue Hoots
1859-1929

Tom B. Henderson
1871-1952
&
Maggie N. Henderson
1877-1956

Annie Sue Henderson
1897-1919

Addie Henderson
1873-1964

Bass L. H. Henderson
1841-1924
&
Susan E. Henderson
1840-1927

Dr. William S. Harwell
1875-1928
&
Ida Lineberger Harwell
1883-1924

H. S. Hoots
1884-1927

Lewis J. Hoots
1915-1943

Eddie, Son of
R. A. & L. E. Holman
B&D Mar 9, 1874

James M. Henson
1863-1936
&
Mamie Price Henson
1879-1962

A. D. Harbin, Sr.
Sep 29, 1883
Dec 19, 1944

Annie L. Harbin
Feb 28, 1887
May 15, 1944

Infant Daughter of
A. D. & Annie L. Harbin
(no dates)

S. P. Hamilton
Dec 17, 1839
Dec 11, 1911
&
Josie Hamilton
1856-1917

Lillie Lee Hamilton
1868-1950

J. A. Henderson
Dec 4, 1847
Jun 30, 1901
& wife
Lucretia Hathcock Henderson
Jul 30, 1854
Feb 1, 1934

J. B. Hamilton
1829-1912

Henrietta Hamilton
1838-1913

Evans G. Hamilton
1873-1906

James C. Halbert, Jr.
Dec 7, 1880
Apr 21, 1913
& wife
Gertrude Murphy Halbert
Nov 11, 1880
Mar 23, 1921

David Cowan Hall
Feb 1, 1819
Oct 26, 1897
"Buried in Hall Family
Cemetery in NW part of
Lincoln County, Tenn."
&
David Cowan Hall, Jr.
Apr 1, 1862
Dec 27, 1867
"Buried in the Bethany
Presbyterian Church Cemetery
Giles, Co., Tenn."
&
Mary Ann McLaurine Hall
Jan 7, 1834
Jun 2, 1904
"Buried beneath this stone."
&
Children of David Cowan Hall
& Mary Ann McLaurine Hall:
William McLaurine Hall,
David Cowan Hall, Mary Ann
Hall, Rossie E. Hall, Tommie
Belle Hall and David Hall.
&
Mary Ann Hall Fleming
Jan 14, 1864
Dec 28, 1885
"Buried in Presbyterian
Church Cemetery near
Bloomingdale, Fla."

Relda Hays
Sep 14, 1853
Apr 19, 1927

Grace Carter Hastings
Jan 18, 1888
Mar 10, 1935

William T. Hovis
Dec 4, 1917
Mar 11, 1934

Alma Jobe Hovis
Aug 22, 1895

Robert H. Hovis
Aug 27, 1889
May 12, 1962

Mary Ann Hovis
Aug 4, 1856
Feb 19, 1932

Elzie Hamlin
Feb 21, 1899
Jul 16, 1924

Jack E. Hamlin
Tennessee
Sp3 U. S. Army
Jan 11, 1937
Mar 27, 1967

J. W. Hamlin
Apr 10, 1869
(no date)
&
Rena Hamlin
Dec 25, 1865
May 10, 1929

Jack M. Hamlin
Died Jan 4, 1972
Age: 79y, 10m, 12d.
(Higgins FH)

Diemer Isom
Nov 10, 1867
Sep 22, 1952
&
Molly Mills Isom
Apr 24, 1871
Apr 12, 1953

Charles L. Ingle
Jul 9, 1859
May 16, 1933

Mannie Warren, wife of
Charles L. Ingle
Dec 28, 1870
May 22, 1908

Margaret Warren, Daughter
of Roy & Zelpha Ingle
Jul 30, 1929
Nov 10, 1938

FAYETTEVILLE QUADRANGLE

Richard Bond Isom
Sep 1908
Jun 1927

Louise Metcalf Isom
1879-1970

Fannie Neil, wife of
C. S. Ivie
Sep 3, 1862
Jul 12, 1890

Infant Son of
C. S. & Fannie Neil Ivie
B&D Jun 8, 1888

Eddie Woods, wife of
C. A. Isom
Mar 10, 1876
Jan 4, 1912

C. A. Isom
1871-1935

Guy Woods, Son of
C. A. & Eddie Isom
Sep 29, 1902
May 17, 1904

Elizabeth Wherry Janson
1820-1912

Homer D. Jacobs
1874-1880
&
Everett G. Jacobs
1878-1881
&
Chapman D. Jacobs
1880-1883

Fannie E. Moore Johnson
Sep 17, 1892
Jan 11, 1933

Elizabeth Lamb, Daughter of
R. B. & E. L. Jean
May 18, 1910
May 24, 1911

Rev. John M. Jordan
1844-1916
&
Mary P. Jordan
1844-1919

Charlie C. James
(no dates)

Terah H. James
(no dates)

Joel J. Jones
1858-1927

Mollie Goodrich, wife of
Joel J. Jones
1859-1928

Laurence Rains Jones
1901-1951

Sarah F., wife of
Joel J. Jones
Apr 11, 1826
Dec 1, 1873

Elizabeth Lamb Jean
1885-1965

Ray J. Jean, Sr.
1884-1946

Ray B. Jean, Jr.
1907-1934

Edith Edna, Daughter of
G. W. & F. N. Johnson
Jul 3, 1889
Apr 24, 1899
&
Charlie, Son of
G. W. & F. N. Johnson
Sep 10, 1895
Oct 22, 1896

George R. Jenkins
Died Sep 4, 1887
Age: (not given)
&
Marcis Clark, wife of
George R. Jenkins
Died Jun 26, 1902
Age: (not given)

Rev. J. C. Jones
Oct 9, 1859
Nov 23, 1896

Massey Goodrich Jones
1881-1937

Adaline Hancock Jones
1887-1957

Elisha Parks Johnson
Nov 2, 1868
Aug 25, 1952

Blanche Warden, wife of
E. P. Johnson
Dec 15, 1883
Apr 12, 1919

E. P., Jr., Son of
E. P. & Irene Johnson
May 2, 1927
Nov 13, 1927

William Milton Jones
1865-1958

Jennie Merrell Jones
1869-1899

George W. Jean
Oct 20, 1870
Sep 29, 1923

Charles H. Johnston
Dec 8, 1866
May 13, 1938
&
Sallie E. Johnston
Aug 27, 1877
Jul 15, 1971

George L. Johnson
1864-1937

Fannie Johnson
Mar 11, 1875
May 8, 1957

J. Alex Johnson
Died Oct 15, 1949
Age: (not given)

Anna W., wife of
J. A. Johnson
Died Oct 14, 1922
Age: (not given)

Angus D. Johnson
May 13, 1829
Oct 29, 1917
&
Elizabeth Alexander Johnson
Jun 26, 1834
Jun 12, 1910

S. S. Johnson
Oct 5, 1877
May 31, 1932

Claude C. Jennings
Mar 26, 1870
Oct 6, 1950
&
Belle Pickett Jennings
Sep 22, 1872
Jan 11, 1956

Elizabeth Gossom Jennings
Feb 3, 1911
Jun 3, 1953

James C. Jennings
Mar 22, 1861
Apr 13, 1945

Joe Dan Johnson
Jul 20, 1935
Oct 15, 1968
Tennessee
1st Lt. 82 Aviation Bn.

William A. Johnson
Dec 7, 1840
Sep 1, 1903

Mary Johnson
1855-1934

Willie E. Johnson
Feb 2, 1880
Nov 16, 1893

Charlie Johnson
1894-1968

Idella Johnson
1923-

Mack Johnson
1847-1911

Elvira Johnson
1855-1949

Susie Johnson
1888-1963

W. M. H. Jean
Oct 21, 1850
Dec 25, 1919
&
M. C. Jean
Dec 10, 1862
(no date)

Starling J. Jean
Apr 10, 1876
Jul 15, 1938
&
Gertie Smith Jean
May 12, 1886
Sep 23, 1933

Leo, Son of
S. J. & Gertrude Jean
Jun 8, 1915
Mar 6, 1924

Caroline Malone Jennings
Nov 23, 1860
Aug 31, 1910

Nellie Mai Jones
1899-1949

Amos W. Judd
Feb 27, 1846
Apr 27, 1929

Carrie McPhail, wife of
Amos W. Judd
Jan 21, 1857
May 9, 1888

Amos W. Judd
Jun 29, 1885
Jun 5, 1886

Carrie May Judd
May 29, 1887
Dec 31, 1963

Ida Eakin Judd
Feb 13, 1863
Apr 23, 1946

Ray B. Jean
1884-1946
(Thompson FH)

FAYETTEVILLE QUADRANGLE

Edward M. Johnson
1848-1892

Mollie Alexander Johnson
1856-1787

George W. Jones
Born in King & Queen Co.,
Va. Mar 15, 1806
Moved to Lincoln Co., Tenn.
1821
Died in Fayetteville
Nov 14, 1884

Estill G. Jones
1895-1917

Mary M. Wilson, wife of
C. N. Jones
Sep 23, 1865
Jul 25, 1899

James D. Jean
Mar 17, 1868
Nov 20, 1910

Angus Johnson
Apr 2, 1844
Dec 5, 1897
& wife
Nannie Renegar Johnson
Dec 27, 1860
Mar 3, 1939

Robert H. Johnson
1892-1911

Eliza Johnson
1887-1889

Baby Johnson
B&D 1879

Jackson Renegar Johnson
1848-1882

Infant Son of
W. R. & Lizzie Johnson
B&D Jul 21, 1907

W. C. Jones
Aug 25, 1842
Jan 23, 1908
C.S.A.

Mary C. Jones
Mar 10, 1858
Jun 9, 1929

John M. Jones
Mar 15, 1884
Dec 17, 1927

Mary Arena Jones
Nov 25, 1882
Dec 30, 1882

William A. Jones
Apr 11, 1880
Jan 16, 1955

Earle Hopkins Jones
1882-1958

Horace M. Jones
1878-1968
&
Margueritt F. Jones
1886-1961

Charlie Jones
Jul 7, 1850
Sep 14, 1928

Cordie Moores, wife of
Charlie Jones
Oct 6, 1846
Dec 29, 1920

Carol Jones
Mar 25, 1949
Mar 28, 1949

Jane Nelson Jerome
Apr 23, 1923
Mar 13, 1945

John Alexander Jean
Jan 7, 1858
May 13, 1918

Thomas A. Jean
Aug 26, 1836
Oct 8, 1916

Martha Emily, wife of
T. A. Jean
Dec 21, 1829
Jan 6, 1907

Martha Johnston
1935

Jane Johnston
1946

George A. Jarvis
1875-1951

Willie Mai Jarvis
1876-1927

"A Soldier"
Homer L., Son of
Mack & Melverna Jean
Aug 14, 1893
Nov 10, 1917

S. L. Jobe
1892-1953

Leno M. Jobe
1892-1956

Mary M. Jobe
1862-1951

W. B. Jobe
1871-1952

J. Bryson Jobe
Aug 23, 1897
Feb 22, 1920

Claude Johnson
1880-1925

Mable Johnson
1878-1917

Virginia Johnson
1917-1917

Minnie L. Johnson
1889-1950

George Koonce, Jr.
1911-1936

Joe Mullins Koonce, Sr.
1930-1963

Allen M. Koonce
Dec 25, 1905
Nov 3, 1967

George Murphy Koonce, Sr.
1871-1946

Lucy Beavers Koonce
1877-1952

Phil Murray Koonce
Tennessee
Pvt 803 Ordnance Co. WW II
May 13, 1900
Jan 6, 1966

Thomas Benton Kelso
Sep 2, 1898
Feb 2, 1969

Lucile Jarratt Kelso
Mar 20, 1900
Nov 29, 1968

Robert Donald Kelso
Jun 26, 1896
Apr 2, 1955

Francis Marion Kelso
Lieut 44 Tenn Reg
Confederate Soldier, C.S.A.
1842-1907
&
Bobbie Strong, wife of
F. M. Kelso
1843-1889

W. D. Koonce
Dec 28, 1857
Mar 17, 1925

Josie, wife of
W. D. Koonce
Sep 17, 1851
Jan 23, 1903

Sam R. Kirkland
1896-1966

Jennie Mai Koonce
(no dates)

Eld. John V. Kirkland
Jan 9, 1857
Apr 23, 1918
& wife
Minnie Martin Kirkland
Oct 17, 1869
Sep 12, 1939

John D. Kelso
Feb 25, 1865
Dec 18, 1927

Carrie Small, wife of
John D. Kelso
Jan 9, 1875
Nov 5, 1957
(DAR Marked)

James Kirkpatrick
1825-1877
&
Josephine B. Kirkpatrick
1833-1870

William Kirkpatrick
1857-1880
"Requiescat in pace."

John P. Kent
Sep 5, 1827
Apr 6, 1912
&
Rutha K. Kent
Oct 22, 1843
Dec 13, 1910

Hugh E. Kirby
1885-1892

Homer M. Kirby
1883-1902

Milton C., Son of
I. W. & Dorcas H. Kirby
Dec 12, 1893 (died)
Age: 3y, 2m.

Lou Hamilton Kennedy
Apr 4, 1871
Dec 24, 1962

Mamie L. Patrick, wife
of E. H. Kennedy
Nov 23, 1886
Mar 19, 1920

TM: (no name on marker)
(no dates)
(Higgins FH, could be
E. H. Kennedy)

Richard McFarland Kirby
1873-1954

Lillie Wiley Kirby
1874-1960

FAYETTEVILLE QUADRANGLE

Newt J. Kelso
1885-1949

Rebecca Kelso
Dec 6, 19 (no other date)
Dec 11, 19 (no other date)

Ervie Lee Kent
Nov 16, 1899
Mar 25, 1957
&
Susie May Kent
Dec 17, 1903
Dec 30, 1932

James Fletcher Kerr
1852-1929

Anna Darnall Kerr
1869-1916

Dona Neely Kerr
1860-1894

Alline, Daughter of
J. F. & M. D. Kerr
Jan 18, 1887
Nov 3, 1887

Calvin Lee Kerr
1899-1900

Bruce Clark Kerr
1883-1959

Robert Harris Kerr
1907-1934

J. P., Son of
S. N. & M. A. Kent
Nov 15, 1908
Jan 18, 1911

Lela May Kent
1910-1931

F. M. Kent
1863-1928

C. E. Kent
1912

Samuel N. Kent
Sep 14, 1875
Jul 2, 1952
&
Martha A. Kent
Sep 1, 1879
Oct 23, 1917

J. B. Keeling
Died Jan 1, 1888
Age: 59 years.

Elizabeth, wife of
J. B. Keeling
Mar 16, 1835
Apr 29, 1907

Marjorie Frances Pitts, wife
of Herbert L. Krauss
Feb 4, 1919
Oct 8, 1968

A. D. Kelso
May 9, 1839
Dec 22, 1901
"Confederate Soldier,
1861-1865."

Virginia Chilcoat, wife of
A. D. Kelso
Mar 16, 1846
Sep 20, 1925

Don Kelso
1875-1928

William Marion Kelso
May 12, 1889
Mar 27, 1904

Baby Kelso
B&D Apr 14, 1922
&
Evelyn Joyce Kelso
May 4, 1926
Sep 22, 1928

Frank B. Kelso
Oct 29, 1871
Jun 24, 1958

Birdie Koonce Kelso
Jan 31, 1873
Dec 25, 1944

William Kidd
Feb 26, 1916
Oct 5, 1931

G. E. Kidd
Jun 20, 1884
Mar 3, 1930

Josephine Kidd
Nov 22, 1905
Mar 21, 1928

Dr. R. C. Kennedy
Apr 12, 1856
Apr 21, 1917

Mary Ann Kennedy
Mar 6, 1855
Jul 17, 1930

Dr. M. A. Keeling
1850-1900

Emma Johnston Keeling
1860-1927

Sara Bernice Keeling
1884-1958

Robert E. Koonce
Apr 26, 1907
Jun 26, 1930

Delia, wife of
W. D. Koonce
Jul 7, 1869
Aug 8, 1919

James C. Kelso
Jun 30, 1830
Nov 22, 1905
&
Elizabeth Strong Kelso
Jan 13, 1841
Aug 9, 1927

Jefferson, Son of
J. C. & Lizzie Kelso
May 17, 1870
May 20, 1890

William Joseph Knight
1857-1925

Mary Blackwell Knight
1869-1943

Rodger Kilmartin
Native of the County Clare,
Ireland
1830-Feb 19, 1875

R. M. Koonce
1847-1920

Mary S. Koonce
1846-1929

Rose Lee Koonce
1883-1951

James E. Kelso
Jan 16, 1873
Apr 25, 1874
&
Henry Kelso
Jul 30, 1878
Sep 7, 1878
Children of
J. C. & Lizzie Kelso

Rossie Hall Kilgore
Mar 5, 1869
Feb 5, 1925

Belle Koonce
Jan 16, 1860
Jul 22, 1930

Abel A. Lineberger
Mar 31, 1848
Dec 24, 1938

Mattie Porch Lineberger
Jan 30, 1871
Apr 2, 1947

William Cowan Lineberger
May 14, 1909
Nov 3, 1965

William J. Landess
1914-1933

W. J. Landess
1852-1932

May Boone Landess
1856-1949

William M. Landess
Tennessee
2nd Lt FA RES WW I
Sep 13, 1888
Jan 27, 1964

Clement Deimer Lamb
Oct 20, 1892
Sep 12, 1964
&
Lila Motlow Lamb

William Bonner Lamb, Jr.
1882-1939
&
Martha Hancock Lamb
1889-1960

William Bonner Lamb, III
1913-1936

William Bonner Lamb
Jan 5, 1858
Dec 28, 1933
&
Josephine Deimer Lamb
Oct 21, 1857
Jan 23, 1945

Stonewall J. Little
Aug 27, 1877
Jan 2, 1952

Jimmie McGuire Lamb
Oct 18, 1866
Feb 12, 1940

James T. Laten
1891-1961

Marcella H. Laten
1898-1958

Ollie P. Laten
1867-1937

Joshua T. Laten
1864-1937

Albert C. Landess
1889-1917

John H. Landess
1849-1912
&
Bettie Shofner Landess
1850-1932

FAYETTEVILLE QUADRANGLE

Robert Terry Landess
1875-1939

Infant Son of
T. D. & Ora Lasater
Sep 1, 1893
Sep 2, 1893

Johnny O., Son of
T. D. & Ora Lasater
Died Nov 21, 1892
Age: 6m, 14d.

Mrs. Nettie Conger Landess
(no dates)
(Higgins FH)

Joel Jones, Son of
W. & Kate Lloyd
Mar 12, 1882
--- --, 1882 (broken)

John W. Lloyd
Oct 3, 1843
Mar 9, 1904
& wife
Kate Jones Lloyd
Mar 31, 1852
Jul 22, 1940

Mary Lloyd
Dec 17, 1886

Sarah Lloyd
Feb 15, 1892
May 8, 1962

Sumner H. Lloyd
Apr 11, 1884
Jun 5, 1950

Nannie Lasater
1850-1929

Grace Davidson Lasater
1897-1898

Robert Louis Lasater
1863-1956
&
Lucy Landess Lasater
1872-1958

Elizabeth Anderson Landess
1882-1955

Eugene Shofner Landess
1879-1957

Nelle Rives Ladd
1878-1946

Hattie H. Lindsay
1867-1926

Maud C. Lindsay
1880-1914

Henry T. Landsay
1875-1947

Arthur Pressley Lindsay
Jun 29, 1890
Aug 24, 1951

Pearl Taylor Lindsay
Jul 30, 1885
Sep 18, 1962

Marge Gaskill Lane
1885-1942

Son of
A. R. & Loreing Lotts
Sep 10, 1928
Sep 11, 1928

Alice, wife of
J. A. Lumpkin
Died Jul 29, 1888
Age: 32 years.

Ruby Lumpkin
1880-1897
&
Pearl Lumpkin
1880-1950

"UDC"
Liza H. Lumpkin
1861-1901

Annie Warden Lawler
Oct 5, 1877
May 19, 1964

Wiley E. Lindsay, M.D.
Aug 8, 1883
Dec 13, 1944

Ella Scott Lindsay
May 17, 1883
Jun 18, 1935

W. H. Ladd
Feb 8, 1860
Jan 16, 1920

Rena Pitts Ladd
Mar 8, 1861
May 2, 1939

Robert Hancock Lamb, Jr.
Apr 11, 1947
May 2, 1970
Age: 23y, 22d.

Thomas Harry Lindsay
Dec 21, 1930

Harry H. Lindsay
1892-1952

Anna L. Lindsay
1868-1942

J. H. Lindsay
1868-1944

Lillie Hayes, wife of
J. Clyde Lindsay
1899-1946

Harvey A. Lackey
Aug 12, 1891
Apr 28, 1971

Emma D. Lackey
Nov 30, 1895

James Ernest Laws
Jul 28, 1886
May 7, 1965
&
Lizzie Wright Laws
Dec 9, 1886
Jun 5, 1949

John Bonner Laws
Jul 15, 1878
Jul 31, 1945

Helen Josephine Laws
Jun 19, 1911
Sep 14, 1968

Sara "Sally" Neece Laws
1871-1913

Will T. Laws
Nov 19, 1870
Sep 11, 1939

Margaret Sumners Wilson
Lindsay
1880-1960

W. T. Lauderdale
Apr 25, 1829
Feb 7, 1900
Freeman's Battery, C.S.A.

Josephine Lauderdale
Dec 24, 1848
Dec 2, 1932

Robert L. Lindsay
Oct 29, 1885
Jan 18, 1942

Lillie K. Lindsay
Feb 26, 1887
Jan 21, 1970

Margaret A. E., wife of
W. T. Lauderdale
Aug 17, 1833
Oct 24, 1885

Lizzie, Daughter of
W. T. & M. A. E. Lauderdale
Aug 10, 1866
Nov 16, 1871

Samuel Lauderdale
May 5, 1804
Oct 14, 1870

Elizabeth Lauderdale
Feb 3, 1804
Jul 31, 1877

Willie Adolphus Lane
Jul 30, 1880
Dec 1, 1957
&
Mary Lou Boaz Lane
Oct 10, 1886
Feb 10, 1967

Joel Levy
1884-1939

Robert Andrew Largen
Mar 16, 1887
Jan 19, 1963

Phil, Son of
Andy & Elaine Largen
1938-1938

Bobbie, Son of
Andy & Elaine Largen
Jun 3, 1927
Aug 11, 1927

T. C. Largen
1852-1930

Rachel Ann Largen
Sep 9, 1860
Jul 30, 1946

James B. Lamb
Feb 20, 1822
Jan 2, 1894
&
Elizabeth Bonner Lamb
Dec 20, 1832
Aug 14, 1882

Lucy Lamb
Sep 19, 1859
Sep 12, 1870

Tilman James Lamb
Aug 15, 1868
Jul 1, 1918
&
Eva Stone Lamb
Aug 20, 1868
Jan 13, 1937

Morton Carloss Lamb
Nov 30, 1860
Jan 25, 1903

McGuire, Son of
H. C. & Jimmie Lamb
Dec 20, 1882
Jul 23, 1889

Thomas C. Little
Died 1933 (no age)

Agnes G. Little
Died 1911 (no age)

John G. Little
1887-1888

Goodrich, Son of
T. C. & Agnes Little
Oct 26, 1877
Mar 14, 1878

Ida E. Little
Died 1937 (no age)

Katherine Murray Landess
1885-1936

John Boone Landess
1883-1961

Isaac N. Lane
1857-1938

Kate Jones Lane
1874-

Rufus Marion Lane
Apr 20, 1862
Jun 3, 1945
&
Mary Lou Lane
Jun 20, 1877
Oct 11, 1954

Mary, wife of
E. R. Lusk
Oct 26, 1849
Jul 14, 1878

Maggie Douthat Lamb
Feb 21, 1881
May 22, 1929

William M. Luna
May 20, 1882
Jul 22, 1941

Mary E. Roach, wife of
M. R. Luna
Mar 8, 1851
Dec 18, 1920

James Adolphus Luna
1870-1952
&
Elnora Cowley Luna
1874-1956

James Thomas Leming
Jul 29, 1874
Dec 1, 1950
&
Ada Byrd Leming
Apr 8, 1879
Mar 6, 1957

Corp. Erroll W. Lineberger
Dec 25, 1893
Sep 29, 1918
Killed in action
Co E 119 Inf

Michael M. Lineberger
Jan 6, 1853
Dec 16, 1950
&
Martha M. Lineberger
Feb 1, 1854
Apr 23, 1918

Ann R. Lineberger
May 29, 1829
Apr 30, 1904

Edmund D. Lineberger
Oct 26, 1879
May 7, 1955

John William Lauderdale
1838-1921

Willie Lauderdale
Oct 19, 1855
Aug 29, 1943

Ann, wife of
J. W. Lauderdale
Died May 12, 1887
Age: (not given)

W. R. Locker
1866-1943
&
Ella Locker
1871-1943

Fannie Moores Light
Jan 31, 1842
Apr 29, 1900

Wesley Light
1844-1921

J. A. Lane
1859-1936

Pinkie Lane
1875-1937

John Lewis, Son of
J. W. & Willie Lauderdale
Feb 13, 1891
Jan 31, 1892

Annie L. Lauderdale
Jun 27, 1895
Jul 27, 1961

William Oliver Largen
Aug 21, 1882
Jun 29, 1959

Ora Simms Largen
Aug 31, 1890
Jul 5, 1931

Jimmie Lane
1897-1941

Miss Delia Lane
Died Sep 12, 1952
Age: 82y, 11m, 2d.
(Higgins FH)

John M. Lindsay
1910-1950

William Virgil Lindsay
1878-1957

Nellie May Lindsay
1876-1937

Charles R. Lindsay
1906-1966
&
Edith M. Lindsay
1905-

William S. Lindsay
1903-1958
&
Wilma L. Lindsay
1904-1955

Lewis D. Lane
1914-1957

Napoleon Lane
1870-1950

Mary Fannie Lane
1871-1955

William T. Luna
Oct 16, 1878
Sep 11, 1955

Emma Tate Luna
May 7, 1884
Feb 3, 1921

Lucy Milhous Legg
May 25, 1873
Jun 8, 1960

John Landess McKenzie
1880-1951

Daisy DeHaven McKenzie
1905-1907

Frank O. McCord
Jan 14, 1839
Aug 19, 1895

J. W. Madden
Dec 5, 1893
Feb 19, 1900

Harry Wright Moyer
Nov 2, 1897
Oct 15, 1917

Jacob Edward Moyer
May 9, 1872
Aug 3, 1916

Pearl Wright Moyer
Sep 11, 1878
Oct 6, 1964

Carrie Pointer McKinney
Died Sep 11, 1968
Age: 92 years.
(Ralston FH)

C. F. McKinney
1865-1933

James D. McKinney
1862-1936

Tennie Little, wife of
J. D. McKinney
1873-1918

Charles C. McKinney
1828-1910
&
Ellen Dennis McKinney
1837-1910

J. E. Malone
1890-1955
&
Molly W. Malone
1883-(no date)

J. F. Madden
Nov 17, 1869
Jun 3, 1925

Ethel McWaters Madden
Nov 25, 1872
Feb 5, 1960

Mary F. Menefee
1856-1924

James P. McNatt
Dec 27, 1914
Oct 1, 1938

Mrs. J. B. McNatt
Oct 1, 1876
May 13, 1965

J. B. McNatt, Sr.
Apr 20, 1874
Feb 8, 1962

Marvin McCullough
1913-1938

Samuel W. McCullough
1881-1936

Nannie B. McCullough
1874-1940

Janie London Muse
Mar 21, 1890
Jan 3, 1970

Lewis Brown Marks
1906-1969

Mabel Bass Marks
1903-

FAYETTEVILLE QUADRANGLE

(Albert) Vincent Marrs
Apr 15, 1908
Jun 21, 1974
&
Vivian Marrs
Sep 8, 1914

Julia Marrs
Jan 13, 1908
Oct 23, 1933

Baxter Marrs
1937-1937

Mrs. Maggie McCullough
Buchanan
Died Sep 2, 1968
Age: 91y, 11m, 4d.
(Higgins FH)

Samuel McCullough
1818-1904
&
Fannie McCullough
1852-1937

W. D. McKenzie
May 20, 1869
Feb 3, 1901

Bridget Lohan, wife of
John McKenzie
born in Roscommon, Ireland
Jan 6, 1839
Jan 26, 1916

W. W. McClellan
Sep 13, 1843
Sep 6, 1917
"He was a Confederate
Soldier"
&
Margaret E. McClellan
Aug 20, 1849
Dec 22, 1931

Eliza Pearl, Daughter of
W. W. & M. E. McClellan
Dec 17, 1885
Aug 26, 1901
Baptised Sep 1, 1899

Nannie Lou S. Miller
Feb 20, 1887
Feb 6, 1945

Walter D. Matlock
1882-1952

Iva B. Matlock
1885-1962

Leona Matlock
1880-1930

A. L. Matlock
1854-1928

Frances Motlow
1853-(no date)

Addie Anderson, wife of
W. B. Moore
Feb 9, 1869
May 24, 1896

Marion Boone March
1858-1939
&
Mary Boone March
1864-1962

Madison F. McClusky
1878-1945
&
Covie P. McClusky
1887-1946

Thomas W. Moores
Pfc Hq Sp TRP 70 Inf Div
WW II
Feb 13, 1910
Sep 28, 1954

Mary Eliza, Daughter of
J. L. & Lizzie McWhirter
Age: 6m, 14d.
(no dates)

T. W. Mitchell
1874-1945
&
Sallie A. Mitchell
1876-1940

Joseph J. Martin
Feb 16, 1848
Apr 29, 1922

Cynthia C. Martin
Mar 30, 1855
Feb 23, 1917

Robert Tom, Son of
B. W. & M. V. Mockbee
Died Feb 5, 1891
Age: 8m, 14d.

Eeulah H. Russell, Daughter
of A. M. & Emma McLaughlin
Age: 8m, 16d.
(no dates)

A. M. McLaughlin
1854-1916

Emma McLaughlin
1860-1953

Robert Taylor McLaughlin
1893-1967

J. M. McLaughlin
1885-1929

Laura Hobbs McLaughlin
1887-1944

S. H. Muse
1882-1936

Dr. Calvin B. McGuire
Jul 1, 1831
Mar 25, 1906
&
Elizabeth P. Green McGuire
Oct 15, 1843
Jan 20, 1900

Frank F. McGuire
May 20, 1871
Jan 28, 1900

Elsa Drennan Martin
Nov 17, 1936

Isaac M. Morton
1881-19(no date)
&
Beuna M. Morton
1886-1933

George Washington Morton
Mar 10, 1847
Jun 13, 1903
&
Elizabeth Young Morton
Jan 25, 1850
Sep 8, 1932

Paul Tuley McKnight
1905-1965

Andrew Clinton McKnight
1869-1944

Alzora Tuley McKnight
1871-1940

Bennett Cecil McKnight
1898-1940

Lola M. McKnight
1892-1955

Rufus McKinney
Feb 27, 1863
Oct 19, 1960
&
Eula Pack McKinney
Oct 28, 1873
Dec 1, 1934

Joseph Braden McClusky
1883-1935

Robert C. McEwen
1879-1959
&
Viola H. McEwen
1882-1977

Clarence G. Moyers
1898-1955

Vivian, Infant of
Mr. & Mrs. E. E. McNeal
1948

Rosie Motlow
1932-1941

Cyrus Lenuel Moores
Oct 29, 1901
Aug 26, 1954

Jean Moores
Jan 18, 1935
Aug 6, 1955

H. Lon Moore
1850-1918
(Lincoln County Court Clerk)

Sue E. Moore
1861-1950

Fuller D. Moore
Feb 2, 1894
Mar 20, 1945

Carolyn Mills Moore
Aug 18, 1896
Dec 27, 1958

Lee, Son of
H. L. & Sue E. Moore
Feb 17, 1886
Jul 14, 1899

Charles D. Moore
Feb 9, 1948
Feb 11, 1948

Ira G. McCalla
1876-1943

Madie H. McCalla
1874-1947

Thomas Benton Mills
1850-1935
&
Rose Emma Jones Mills
1870-1943

Fannie K. Mills
Jul 17, 1881
Jul 6, 1905

Henry C. Mills
Apr 8, 1879
Dec 24, 1900

William H. Mills
Dec 26, 1883
Nov 23, 1900

Elizabeth Mills
1852-1892

Reuben McDonald
1937

_____ McDonald
_____-1927
(information gone)

Roy Alexander Moyers
Died Oct 7, 1970
Age: 76y, 7m, 16d.
(Higgins FH)

FAYETTEVILLE QUADRANGLE

John Knox Moore
1888-1939
&
Lula Freeman Moore
1888-1966

Smith Morgan
May 10, 1807
Mar 17, 1891
&
Abigail Morgan
Nov 27, 1810
Feb 28, 1888

Mary J. Morgan
Feb 26, 1836
1895
&
Martha A. Morgan
Feb 26, 1836
Mar 17, 1899

Eliza C., wife of
J. P. Morrison
May 16, 1846
Aug 7, 1873

Mayme Su Medearis
1901-1967

Leland D. Medearis
1901-1941

Lucy A. Medearis
1863-1948

W. D. Medearis
1856-1931

Maggie Wright Motlow
Feb 4, 1878
Mar 3, 1925

Bertha L. Hamilton McFerrin
1898-1964

W. T. McCown
Oct 7, 1866
Jan 29, 1951

Frank McCown
1886-1888

Agnes Ralston McCown
Jul 17, 1872
Jul 29, 1944

George E. Marr
1876-1925
&
Tennie Howe Marr
1873-1957

Samuel Hamilton McDill
Oct 31, 1854
Sep 23, 1914

Emma Taylor, wife of
S. H. McDill
Jun 9, 1857
Feb 16, 1945

Floyd S. Moore
1885-1964

Robert L. Moore
1852-1936

Lucy S. Moore
1856-1939

Pearl Mai Moore
1890-1960

Holman C. Milhous
1885-1918

Emily Hill Milhous
1882-1967

William A. Milhous
1843-1925

Sue Holman Milhous
1848-1916

Nora B. Moore
Sep 3, 1881
Mar 12, 1967

Infant Son of
John V. & Helen P. Matthews
Jan 27, 1955

Joseph A. Moore
Dec 5, 1874
Feb 14, 1957

Atlee Moore
Dec 14, 1891
Oct 29, 1965
&
Cassie Moore
Jun 12, 1895

James Robert, Son of
Charles W. & Ruth C. Morgan
Jul 28, 1943
Sep 28, 1968

Floyd A. McCown
Nov 18, 1885
Jun 2, 1960

Mamie, wife of
Floyd McCown
Nov 14, 1888
Apr 6, 1922

H. J. Moore
Nov 28, 1858
Apr 6, 1926

Mollie Green Moore
Jul 5, 1863
Aug 23, 1929

Horton Moore
Nov 15, 1895
Feb 5, 1930

Archie Lee Mills
Dec 16, 1899
Aug 17, 1961
&
Mildred Pack Mills
Jan 6, 1910

C. Minze Moore
1879-1934

J. A. McCollum
1870-1918

Elizabeth Jones McCollum
1864-1919

Annie McCollum
1901-1918

Walton S. McWilliams
Oct 23, 1850
Mar 3, 1904
&
Alice B. McWilliams
Dec 31, 1854
Oct 4, 1928

Ora Goodner, wife of
J. M. McWilliams
Feb 6, 1880
Jan 15, 1917

Norsisa Monday
1836-1926
&
Minnie Monday
1845-1924

W. C. Martin
1834-Jan 19, 1910

John P. Marrs
Jan 12, 1869
Jan 31, 1950

Minnie Lee, wife of
J. P. Marrs
Mar 25, 1878
Feb 22, 1918

John A. Moore
Jun 8, 1848
Jan 26, 1932

Ezella Moore
Sep 4, 1852
Apr 26, 1918

W. Milton Moore
Sep 9, 1882
Jun 14, 1964

Ophelia S. Moore
Oct 10, 1885
Jul 1, 1971

Fanny Lynne Holman, wife of
J. E. Marsh
1882-1920

J. C. McFerrin
1880-1957

Sallie Caughran McFerrin
1883-1939

Lillian Kirby Mansfield
1907-1934

Homer T. McCown
Jun 12, 1879
Jun 8, 1946

Bess Small McCown
Aug 30, 1881
Jan 3, 1960

T. Jarman McCown
Apr 1, 1910
Jan 24, 1949

John James Morgan
Feb 25, 1910
Feb 17, 1915

Gladys Marie Morgan
Jun 23, 1914
Jun 9, 1917

George McGuire Morgan
Jul 1, 1883
May 4, 1914

Beulah Morgan Martin
Aug 30, 1887
Mar 30, 1953

Clell Homer McKinney, Sr.
Jun 17, 1890
Dec 8, 1960

Laura L. Terry, wife of
Felix W. McDaniel
1868-1964

Neda McPhail
1862-1936

Polk Grills Morgan
1894-1969
&
Marjorie Ruth Morgan
1914-
&
Max Grills Morgan
1912-1953

Guy J. McLaughlin
1886-1953

J. B. McLaughlin
1856-1914

Della McLaughlin
1870-1938

Guy J. McLaughlin, Jr.
Lieutenant US AAF
Oct 13, 1921
Missing in action
Jul 19, 1943

FAYETTEVILLE QUADRANGLE

Lofton V. Maddox
Tennessee
2nd Lt. Field Arty WW I
Nov 16, 1891
Oct 25, 1962

J. H. Morris
1834-1932

Houston M. McBay
1890-1929
&
Jean McBay
1894-

George McBay
1880-1962
&
Hattie McBay
1885-1941

James E. McCown
Jan 8, 1869
Jan 25, 1940

J. C. Milstead
Mar 12, 1911
Nov 14, 1945

John C. Milstead
Feb 20, 1875
Sep 2, 1925

Cora S. Milstead
Aug 5, 1879
Dec 12, 1967

Dorothy Moores
1918

Mary Elizabeth Moores
1912-1922

William Collier Moores
1884-1926

Ruth Moores
Jun 1915
Nov 1922

James A. Moores
Jun 3, 1871
Mar 9, 1950

Mrs. J. A. Moores
Died Jun 14, 1971
Age: 98y, 11m, 15d.
(Higgins FH)

Horton Lamb Moores
Jul 6, 1903
Jul 27, 1971

William A. Mills
Feb 11, 1875
Sep 5, 1942
&
Maggie Alma Mills
Jul 23, 1880
Oct 29, 1946

Una Collins Mills
Dec 28, 1907
Oct 22, 1928

Julia Ann Swing Mills
1907-1947

H. V. McKinney
Sep 29, 1858
Sep 30, 1928
&
Elizabeth McKinney
1871-1963

J. Horace McKinney
Nov 30, 1863
Aug 19, 1936

Zula Johnson McKinney
Aug 22, 1870
Jul 16, 1931

Pvt Raymond McKinney
Dec 23, 1894
Died in Paignton, England
Sep 29, 1918

Horace Roy McKinney
Dec 23, 1894
Jan 15, 1943

John Carl Moore, Sr.
Oct 4, 1890
Apr 4, 1961
&
Julia Flynt Moore
Aug 24, 1895

Robert Moyers
1930-1931

Duncan A. McClellan
Texas
Pvt 3rd Calvery
Aug 7, 1940

Elizabeth A. McNatt
1869-1923

Earl Moore
1895-1936

Mollie A. Moore
1855-1936

Boone Moore
1887-1929

Elizabeth Curlee, wife of
Boone Moore
1891-1949

John M. Moore
1895-1945

Nancy Elizabeth Moore
Jul 24, 1963
Jul 26, 1963

Martha Belle Moore
1933-1964

David J. Millard
1881-1941

Bertie Millard
1888-1949

Andy J. Mills
Aug 6, 1871
Jul 27, 1927
&
Mattie H. Mills
May 15, 1877
(no date)

Pvt Elgie D. Mills
Co E 119th Inf
Sep 6, 1897
Killed in action in France
Oct 13, 1918

George W. Marsh
1880-1959

Daisy M. Marsh
1886-1982

Infant Son of
George W. & Daisy Marsh
1927

Thomas L. Merritt
1860-1939
&
Lillie A. Merritt
1862-1928

Virginia Martin
1913-1932

Mrs. H. C. Martin
1858-1911

Floyd C. Moore
May 11, 1898
Jul 2, 1968
&
Susie Mae D. Moore
May 17, 1902

Floyd A. Marrs
Feb 16, 1877
Jul 10, 1948

Isaac Marrs
Feb 13, 1846
Jan 26, 1920
&
Mary L. Marrs
May 8, 1849
(no date)

Julia Ann McElroy
Mar 3, 1883
Aug 23, 1910

James William Moyers
Tennessee
Sgt Co E 119 Inf WW I
May 1, 1894
Jul 17, 1953

William McCullough
Jul 22, 1899
Sep 30, 1918
&
Ward McCullough
Mar 21, 1901
Jun 9, 1915

Robert L. Moyers
1867-1946

Alice H. Moyers
1869-1958

Cora, wife of
Fred Marshall
Feb 4, 1885
Mar 26, 1913

Florence Moyers
Jun 22, 1888
Jan 24, 1913

William H. Moyers
Jan 8, 1883
Aug 29, 1960
&
Sallie Moyers
Nov 3, 1888
Aug 21, 1966

James Henry Mitchell
Apr 16, 1941
Jun 27, 1971

Roy Ashby Moyers
Oct 10, 1899
Nov 7, 1900

Hardy W. Moyers
Dec 4, 1869
Dec 19, 1949

Ellie A. Ashby Moyers
Feb 22, 1872
Jan 29, 1957

Raymond H. Moyers
Oct 27, 1902
Sep 22, 1971

John A. McPhail
Nov 19, 1817
May 2, 1862
& wife
Mary E. Gilliland McPhail
Jul 13, 1824
Jun 30, 1889
& Son
Samuel G. McPhail
Jan 26, 1847
May 18, 1864

Carrie Martain
Oct 14, 1876
May 5, 1882

James Medley
1888-1941

FAYETTEVILLE QUADRANGLE

Everett J. Medley
Aug 5, 1910
Dec 4, 1969
(picture)

Hugh McGaha
Born on County Deery,
Ireland
1790-(broken)

S. J. McGaha
Born in Charlotte, N.C.
Oct 10, 1836
Sep 7, 1919

William S. Morgan
Jun 4, 1858
Mar 9, 1941
&
Fannie Bonner Morgan
Jul 31, 1863
Nov 6, 1927

James Edward Morgan
Jan 27, 1856
Oct 6, 1876
&
Elizabeth Polk Morgan
Oct 28, 1871
Aug 3, 1887

Rebecca March
1856-1934

Miss Lizzie March
1838-1936

Gussie McG.(no other name)
Gussie
Carlotta
Garlotta
(no dates)

William H. McGown
May 10, 1863
Oct 31, 1888
Age: 25y, 5m, 21d.

James H. McDaniel
1861-1929

Sara Wright McDaniel
1867-1945

Marvin Wright, Son of
J. H. & Sallie McDaniel
Dec 27, 1891
Jun 30, 1900

J. M. Metcalfe
(no dates)

F. C. Metcalfe
(no dates)

Miss Felicia Metcalfe
1835-Nov 27, 1969
Age: 63y, 10m, 29d.

Jessie E. Moore
Feb 4, 1877
Aug 5, 1952
&
Gracie C. Moore
Oct 19, 1882
Oct 5, 1964

Criss Mills
1860-1928
&
Ida Mills
1872-1953

Emma M., wife of
R. M. Martin
Oct 29, 1888
Dec 25, 1914

Richard O. Mitchell
1876-1963
&
Lucy R. Mitchell
1896-1954

Charles Moore Matlock
Tennessee
Sgt 345 base Unit AAF WW II
Sep 6, 1920
Oct 30, 1962

C. H. Matlock
1873-1935

Newton Wilson Mansfield
Aug 23, 1878
Nov 15, 1949
&
Lou Dunn Mansfield
May 16, 1885
Dec 21, 1960

Dorothy Marie, Daughter of
N. W. & F. L. Mansfield
Oct 26, 1920
Jun 7, 1922

Luther L. Meeks
1875-1949
&
Gussie W. Meeks
1879-1965

J. Jackson Moyers
1888-1937

William C. Marrs
Jan 6, 1890
Dec 10, 1954

James Harold McDaniel
1901-1948

William Warner Morris
Feb 14, 1880
Sep 29, 1963

Mary Benton Woodard, wife of
William Warner Morris
Jan 28, 1882
Jul 4, 1948

James Allen Morris
Apr 7, 1902
Dec 9, 1960

David Johnston McMillen, Son
of Joan Y. & Frank V.
McMillen
Feb 15, 1957
Jul 14, 1960

Alice Christine McKay
Jan 5, 1918
Mar 24, 1934

Phillip T. Murray
1891-1912

Rachel Murray
1887-1922

Philip T. Murray
1826-1886

Donna E. Murray
1860-1940

Kate J., wife of
P. T. Murray
Jun 29, 1840
Mar 16, 1876

Mathew Murray
1894-
&
Mary Murray
1862-1894

Rachel McKinney
Oct 23, 1898
Jun 20, 1900

W. B. Martin
Nov 19, 1823
Mar 8, 1905
&
Eliza M. Martin
Jan 3, 1851
Oct 25, 1901

E. C. McLaughlin
Dec 6, 1831
Jun 26, 1877

Sarah Caldwell McLaughlin
Feb 14, 1836
Nov 8, 1914

Joseph Bunyan Markham
Jul 20, 1893
Aug 28, 1965

Fred Walker, Son of
J. B. & E. H. Markham
Feb 26, 1922
Jul 16, 1924

William Campbell, Son of
Rufe & Louisa A. Campbell
Moorehead
Died Sep 1882
(no age given)

F. R. Moorhead
Sep 27, 1847
Oct 5, 1884
& wife
Delia Alexander Moorhead
Jan 27, 1847
May 9, 1883

W. M. McCown
Sep 11, 1841
Jan 16, 1915

Charles C. McDaniel
Feb 17, 1853
Mar 20, 1922

James Dennis McKinney
Apr 27, 1903
Jul 27, 1958

Capt. Rane McKinney
Co E 8th Tenn.
C.S.A.

J. A. McClain
Dec 15, 1847
Dec 16, 1924
&
Emma Wood McClain
Jul 20, 1854
Jul 22, 1917

M. B. McClain
Apr 11, 1892
Jan 20, 1919

Mildred W. McClain
Nov 5, 1918
Nov 29, 1918

3 Infants of
J. A. & Emma McClain

Lucy Ann McClain
1858-1940

A. C. McClain
Aug 8, 1816
Apr 24, 1890

Hannah M. Reynolds, wife
of A. C. McClain
Mar 26, 1817
Jul 12, 1884

Marcus Marrs
1841-1914
&
Sara Marrs
1846-1928

Bessie Birch, Oldest
child of L. E. & C. A.
McGhia, Fell asleep on
Advent Sunday Morning
Nov 28, in Cleveland,
East Tenn. & was laid
to rest beside her
beloved Mother
Nov 30, 1880.

W. A. Miles
Aug 19, 1837
Dec 12, 1905
& wife
Mattie Woods Miles
Sep 28, 1844
Dec 28, 1897

Mrs. Mary Woods Miller
Nov 8, 1850
Jun 25, 1921

Bessie Dunivan Montgomery
Oct 16, 1885
Jul 30, 1968

M. Ed Muse
Jun 14, 1880
Sep 12, 1949
&
Annie L. Jones Muse
Sep 17, 1888
Jul 10, 1963

Elizabeth N. McKeove
Dec 22, 1833
Mar 26, 1879

J. T. McCauly
Freeman's Btry
  C.S.A.

Col. C. A. McDaniel
Nov 23, 1823
Jul 15, 1896

Margaret Buchanan, wife of
Col. C. A. McDaniel
Nov 4, 1831
May 27, 1903

William McDaniel
Died Feb 27, 1922
Age: 78 years.
(no marker)Freeman's Btry.

Feldin C. McDaniel
Jul 22, 1866
Sep 6, 1926

Andrew C. McDaniel
Jan 14, 1862
Dec 20, 1932

Summers Curlee, wife of
A. C. McDaniel
Dec 3, 1880
Jul 1, 1910

Charles Grier Moore
Died Feb 12, 1970
Age: 77y, 8m, 11d.
(Higgins FH)

James Neeld, Son of
J. A. & Eva Moores
Sep 23, 1898
Dec 11, 1898

Joe S. Mullins
Apr 9, 1888
Mar 15, 1948

Annie W. Mullins
Feb 15, 1895
Mar 30, 1969

Thomas Isaac Marrs, Sr.
1878-1953
&
Laura Boaz Marrs
1879-1920

Sarah T., wife of
Roy F. Moore
Jan 31, 1895
Nov 25, 1933

Luther C. Moore
Mar 22, 1896
Oct 28, 1926

Andy Moore
Feb 15, 1855
Mar 14, 1937
&
Elizabeth Moore
Dec 31, 1860
Sep 10, 1937

William Moyers
1884-1925

Samuel Henry Moyers
Jun 25, 1851
Mar 14, 1952

Dan A. Moyers
1863-1912
&
Jennie V. Moyers
1869-1948

George W. Moyers
Sep 9, 1868
Mar 20, 1889

Georgianna, wife of
John V. Moyers
Jun 30, 1838
Feb 7, 1891

John V. Moyers
Jun 20, 1821
May 18, 1884

Erskine E. Mitchell
1884-1954
&
Flossie K. Mitchell
1882-1965

Benjamin W. Mills
Apr 4, 1869
Jan 26, 1961
&
Kate Sugg Mills
Dec 29, 1877
Jun 26, 1941

Martha L. McDaniel
Feb 11, 1872
Aug 30, 1964

J. M. McWilliams, M.D.
Oct 17, 1877
Feb 2, 1957

Hallie Neel McWilliams
Jul 31, 1892
Jul 9, 1963

Henry McGee
Aug 3, 1859
Feb 9, 1927

Vina Lane McGee
Feb 9, 1865
Mar 14, 1947

John J. Morgan
Dec 23, 1837
Dec 23, 1892

Sallie L. Stone, wife of
John J. Morgan
Oct 26, 1839
Mar 27, 1913

Francis, Son of
J. J. & L. L. Morgan
Sep 13, 1878
Aug 24, 1879

Ed L. McElroy
1861-1923

Mary E. McElroy
1866-1934

Clyde McElroy
1864-1936
&
Fannie Marrs McElroy
1874-19(no date)

Sherrod J., Son of
S. G. & L. A. McElroy
Jul 15, 1853
Jun 24, 1883

S. G. McElroy
May 17, 1826
Jul 7, 1907
& wife
Lucy Ann McElroy
Apr 26, 1831
Nov 18, 1903

M. L. McElroy
Apr 9, 1828
May 21, 1901
&
Mattie V. McElroy
Jul 22, 1843
Nov 2, 1897

Arthur A. McElroy
1879-1915

John C. McMillen
1870-1951
&
Lem B. McMillen
1882-1956

W. H. Moores
Aug 6, 1818
May 7, 1884

Margaret M., Consort of
W. H. Moores
Jun 1, 1818
Apr 22, 1874

Mary Mertilla, Daughter
of Henry Moores
Nov 21, 1878
Nov 7, 1893

Isaac Baxter Marr
1882-1947
&
Minnie Pogue Marr
1884-

Lou, wife of
David S. McElroy
Jun 2, 1852
Mar 26, 1880

Sallie Will Moores
Mar 21, 1894
Oct 11, 1903

Cordelia Hovis Moores
Mar 18, 1871
Mar 27, 1928

Cyrus Sugg Moores
Jul 16, 1869
Jul 16, 1943

Edna Moores
Jan 9, 1879
Aug 12, 1956

Clarence L. Mason, Sr.
Alabama
Pvt Co A 551st ACFT Wing Bn
WW II
Nov 21, 1898
May 16, 1956

Robert B. Mason
May 24, 1901
Sep 15, 1903

James H. Mason
Dec 27, 1909
Oct 9, 1911

Robert L. Mason
Jun 6, 1860
Apr 30, 1943

Laura L. Mason
Mar 24, 1870
Jun 7, 1948

J. P. McGee
Co D 41st Tenn Regt C.S.A.
Sep 13, 1844
Oct 1, 1896

W. R. McGee
Jul 2, 1868
Jun 15, 1918

J. M. Moyers
Jan 17, 1858
Mar 3, 1928

Lizzie Moyers
1875-1942

Ada S. Moyers
Dec 2, 1891
Jul 23, 1956

Infant Daughter of
J. M. & Lizzie Moyers
Sep 13, 1905
Sep 15, 1905

William T. McCown
Feb 3, 1904
May 26, 1971

James Orvis Murphy
Aug 23, 1884
Jun 17, 1968
&
Vernia Wilson Murphy
Oct 28, 1883
Mar 11, 1938

T. P. Murphy
Oct 23, 1855
Apr 11, 1932
& wife
Bettie Murphy
Oct 6, 1857
Jul 13, 1910

Jennie Mai Pitts, wife of
Charles L. Moore
Mar 14, 1883
Jul 12, 1922

Maria Louisa McLaurine
Aug 27, 1827
Sep 21, 1912

John S. McPhail
1886-1926

Harry G. Murphy
Mar 11, 1886
Nov 23, 1921

Mary Gaines Murphy
Jan 1, 1856
Jul 18, 1944

Paul S. Marquess
Mar 30, 1911
Nov 21, 1967

William B. Montgomery
1871-1953

Mary L. Montgomery
1886-1969
(on TM marker it has
Mary L. Armstrong
Montgomery)

John D. Neeld
Nov 15, 1845
Dec 22, 1881

Howard M. McFerrin
1893-
&
Clemma C. McFerrin
1895-1964

William B. McCown
1883-1952
&
Frances S. McCown
1910-

R. T. Moore
1839-1929

M. J. Moore
1845-1929

Arline Ballard McFerrin
1921-1966

Rubie Lenna McFerrin
1915-1917

R. C. Marshall
1876-1942

Dizzie S. Marshall
Aug 14, 1881
Apr 29, 1951

John W. Neece
1892-1936

William Sanford Noles
1873-1948
&
Eula Marrs Noles
1865-1955

Elizabeth Kidd Noles
1905-1937

Raymond T. Newman, Jr.
Michigan
Pvt U. S. Army WW II
Jul 23, 1924
Nov 26, 1962

Raymond T. Newman
Mar 23, 1901
Sep 9, 1948

Thomas P. Naylor
Aug 22, 1865
Mar 2, 1889

Pleasant O. H. Nevill
Apr 29, 1874
May 9, 1902

Annie Lee Nevill
Feb 6, 1879
Apr 9, 1958

Dr. B. C. Newman
Died May 21, 1886
Age: (no age given)

Mary Dade Nored
1852-1939

Cornie L. Nevill
Dec 3, 1896
Jan 29, 1964
&
Minnie R. Nevill
Jun 1, 1897

Clyde O. Nevill
Jun 21, 1899
Oct 27, 1965

Infant Daughter of
Clyde & Lila R. Nevill
Aug 28, 1923

H. Nevill
Oct 20, 1843
Feb 2, 1920

Madora Nevill
Nov 15, 1845
May 21, 1910

Johnie O., Son of
H. & M. P. Nevill
Apr 24, 1876
Dec 18, 1883

Henderson Overby Newsom
1869-1940
&
Mannie Alford Newsom
1871-1946

William Granville Newsom
Apr 20, 1899
Aug 18, 1899

J. W. Newsom
Jan 31, 1836
Jan 8, 1892
&
Sarah C. Newsom
Mar 29, 1840
Oct 31, 1899

Robert L. Newsom
1871-1940

Artie S. Reeves, wife of
E. H. Newsom
Nov 11, 1869
Jan 12, 1899

J. L. Newsom
Jul 5, 1861
Dec 3, 1906
&
J. L. Newsom, Jr.
Dec 7, 1901
Aug 11, 1922

Mattie Hanks Norman
May 10, 1863
Sep 26, 1923

Carolyn Newman
1870-1925

Laura Noah
Jul 11, 1911-Mar 25, 1914

Paul D. Norman
Jul 8, 1898
Apr 16, 1935

Mabel G. Norman
Feb 20, 1900

John D. Nichols
Sep 18, 1857
Nov 6, 1930

Hattie Jackson, wife of
John D. Nichols
Feb 3, 1861
Feb 14, 1962

Edgar B. Newsom
Dec 7, 1897
Jul 30, 1959

Martha Dale Newsom
1924-1925

Joel H. Neece
1863-1922

Dorsey V. Neece
Tennessee
Mus 3 Cl HQ Co 51 Inf
6 Div WW I
Dec 5, 1889
Nov 14, 1952

Charles J. Neece
1886-1914

Mary E. Neece
1864-1941

William Neece
1833-1902

Martha Neece
1835-1928

Berry Owen Neece
1876-1946

Orrie P. Neece
1879-1931

Ruby Neece
1903-1903

E. B. Noles
1891-1970
&
Amanda E. Noles
1892-1969

James W. Newman
Born in Staunton, Va.
Feb 8, 1832
Died Fayetteville, Tenn.
Dec 26, 1885
&
Sarah M. Newman
Born in Knoxville, Tenn.
Jul 23, 1835
Died Fayetteville, Tenn.
Feb 8, 1916

FAYETTEVILLE QUADRANGLE

George Horne Newman
1858-1929
&
Pauline Anderson Newman
1864-1949

Amanda, Daughter of
George N. & Pauline Newman
Oct 3, 1905
Nov 5, 1905

Dennie C. Noblin
1880-1955
&
Laila D. Noblin
1882-1957

Dr. Boone Edgar Noblitt
1866-1922

Elizabeth Sullivan Noblitt
1875-1945

Carr Mankin Noblitt
1900-1917

Boone Little Noblitt
1905-1965

David John Noblitt
1895-1947

George Wiley Neel
May 7, 1872
Oct 29, 1952 (picture)
&
Nina Neel   (picture)
Dec 26, 1876
Nov 13, 1955

Saidee M. Noah
Jul 16, 1885
(no date)

Thomas A. Noah
Dec 29, 1872
Jun 6, 1940

Albert Sloan, Son of
R. O. & L. S. Nelson
Jun 9, 1925
Aug 3, 1927

Lorene Sloan Nelson
1899-1935

J. Malcolm Newman
1901-1952

John M. Newman
Mar 17, 1876
Jun 25, 1947

Ora Bell Newman
Jan 26, 1874
Jun 8, 1943

James Milton Newman
Born in Jefferson Co., Tenn.
Oct 23, 1849
Jan 31, 1914

Mrs. Mary Semirah Newman
Jan 14, 1853
May 4, 1909

Thomas E. Norman
Mar 8, 1922
Feb 17, 1970

Pearl Norman
Sep 5, 1899
May 24, 1924

W. R. Noah
Oct 16, 1844
Dec 21, 1921
&
S. E. Noah
Oct 14, 1846
Sep 26, 1928

Edd Lee Noah
1875-1939
&
Nancy Ellie Noah
1878-1936

Robert M. D. Nelson
Mar 22, 1898
Aug 27, 1923

Elizabeth Brown, wife of
O. W. Pack
Died Nov 7, 1917
Age: 49 years.

Thomas D. Pitts
1849-1928

M. Annie Pitts
1856-1927

William R. Pack
Mar 17, 1882

&
Bertha G. Pack
Jun 30, 1885
Aug 9, 1966

Wesley W. Porter
May 11, 1878
Jun 26, 1947

Robert Franklin Pitts
Aug 4, 1866
Feb 25, 1936

Thomas Earl Pack
B&D Sep 9, 1938

Helen, Daughter of
Marvin & Hazel Pack
May 19, 1935
Jun 13, 1937

Joe Parks
1840-1911
&
Sally Wiley Parks
1856-1942
&
Luther Wiley
1829-1892
&
Knox Wiley
1887-1933
&
Joe Wiley
1890-1948
&
Horace Wiley
1885-1963
(all above on one stone)

Bernnie Perry
1901-1936

Hiram B. Partain
1851-1935
&
Eliza E. King Partain
1852-1935

B. C. Partain
1882-1968
&
Mary F. Lane Partain
1887-1952

Eloise Percy, wife of
Ernest M. Pigg
Jun 30, 1921
Feb 27, 1945

Henry Phillips
1879-1958

Lucy Smith Phillips
1894-1960

Henry Thomas Phillips
B&D 1935

Oscar W. Pack
1870-1952

Frances Perry
Sep 12, 1917
Jun 16, 1934

Lyda Bagley Payton
Dec 5, 1874
Mar 10, 1964

Dr. Thomas Alexander Patrick
1883-1954
&
Ruth Thomas Patrick

Roberta Brown Putman
Jun 29, 1886
Oct 25, 1942

Mrs. O. T. Putman
1886-1942

Otto W. Pope
1892-1945

Madeline B. Pope
1892-1956

R. L. "Bob" Patton
Nov 22, 1882
Nov 6, 1964
&
Bettie Raby Patton
Aug 9, 1898

James Elliot Poindexter
Dec 3, 1848
Aug 3, 1920
(Clerk & Master of Lincoln
 County, Tenn.)
&
Mary Thomas Poindexter
Dec 11, 1866
Sep 2, 1887

Grace, Daughter of
J. E. & Mary Poindexter
(no dates)

Laura Wright Pitts
Died Jan 25, 1957
Age: (no age given)

William Hodges Pitts
Died Dec 9, 1956
Age: (no age given)

S. Thornton Peake
1884-1971
&
Rachel Barrett Peake
1888-1966

Robert F. Pope
1898-1943

Edward Pope, Jr.
1890-1890
&
Edwina Mary Pope
1894-1894

Amelia Speer Pope
1866-1934

Carly Amalie Pope
1896-1897

Edward Pope
1846-1924

Sidney B. Patton
South Carolina
Pvt 27 Co 157 Depot Brig
WW I
Aug 10, 1892
Jul 6, 1966

Kate Parks
Feb 4, 1902
Aug 6, 1939

FAYETTEVILLE QUADRANGLE

John Morgan Pearson
1883-1961

Olga McKnight Pearson
1894-19

R. C. Pearson
May 4, 1851
(no date)
& wife
Mary J. Pearson
May 5, 1851
Feb 10, 1914

J. C. Paryear
1889-1923

Willie, Son of
N. A. & M. S. Pearson
Feb 28, 1884
Sep 7, 1884

Edwin Warren Parrill
1878-1970

Mae Helen Parrill
1884-1950

Josephine Parrill
Mar 22, 1882
Jul 17, 1883

Thomas J. Price
Sep 22, 1840
Nov 15, 1882
&
Sarah K. Price
Nov 22, 1840
May 31, 1901

Samuel B. Price
Oct 24, 1870
Dec 8, 1891

William F. Price
Apr 23, 1872
Feb 21, 1905

Annie Petty
1872-1928
"By Everygirls Bible Class
Washington, D.C."

Gertie Petty
1870-1936

_. L. Petty
Died Feb 1967
Age: 85y, 7m, 26d.

Rufus S. Pamplin
1868-1948
&
Willie E. Pamplin
1863-1945

J. Mack Pamplin
1867-1954
&
Ruhanah Pamplin
1873-1957

Elmer Lee Pamplin
Tennessee
Sgt 1 Cl Q.M.Corps
Died Nov 30, 1941
Age: (not given)

Pinkney Lee Pylant
Nov 4, 1863
Dec 1, 1939

Sallie Hines Pylant
Oct 16, 1881
Dec 13, 1962
"W.C.T.U."

Winnie Elizabeth Ford, wife
of John Lee Pylant
Aug 4, 1882
Aug 13, 1920

Edgar W. Pylant
Mar 24, 1886
Sep 3, 1961

Jimmie D., wife of
H. C. Pylant
Oct 3, 1884
Nov 6, 1913

William W. Pylant
1856-1939
&
Idora Pylant
1860-1933

Andrew, Son of
W. W. & Idora Pylant
Jan 30, 1883
Oct 30, 1904

Effie Mai, Daughter of
W. W. & Idora Pylant
Mar 10, 1891
Aug 5, 1907

H. H. Pitts
1860-19(date gone)
(Beasley FH)

Josephine Diemer Pitts
Jul 23, 1885
Aug 22, 1968

Angie Tate Pack
1866-1927

J. T. Phagan
1860-1932

Lizzie Parkinson Phagan
1862-19(no date)

Frances Brock, wife of
Frank Porter
Sep 8, 1913
Nov 3, 1935

Mattie Lou, wife of
W. J. Partin
1888-1927

T. P. Pitts
Jul 28, 1858
May 16, 1940

Sallie Bryan Pitts
Aug 1, 1864
Jun 9, 1947

W. Roy Pylant
1888-1937

Enos W. Pitts
Aug 18, 1852
Jan 13, 1916
& wife
Emily Renegar Pitts
Dec 31, 1921
Feb 12, 1921

William Woodruff Pitts
Mar 19, 1877
Jun 5, 1953

John F. Pitts, Sr.
Mar 27, 1877
Mar 3, 1948

Rees H. Pitts
1874-1953

Laura W., wife of
Rees H. Pitts
1878-1943

Robert H. Pitts
Sep 6, 1842
Jun 7, 1927

Johnie J. Prosser
Oct 16, 1860
Jan 12, 1946
&
Fannie E. Prosser
Jan 4, 1854
Feb 12, 1929

Roy W. Prosser
Pvt Co E 119 Inf
Feb 22, 1896
Was killed in Battle at France
Sep 29, 1918
&
Mary Ella Prosser
Feb 16, 1862
(no date)

Sallie A. Posey
Jan 19, 1869
Nov 30, 1955

W. B. Posey
Dec 17, 1904
Oct 22, 1965

Thelma Faulkner Posey
Jul 28, 1906

Joseph Patton
Tennessee
Sgt Fa
Died Oct 19, 1938
Age: 62y, 4m, 15d.

Elizabeth Hamilton Patton
Nov 27, 1885
Jan 3, 1953

Susie Brossard Pearce
Aug 25, 1893
Jun 27, 1914

James I. Pearce
Aug 28, 1855
Jul 16, 1927
&
Mary L. Pearce
Mar 14, 1856
Jan 7, 1929

Emily J., wife of
Dr. M. J. Price
Dec 26, 1842
Mar 16, 1903

Joel Parks
Jun 7, 1837
Oct 9, 1916
C.S.A.

Mary Renegar, wife of
Joel Parks
Oct 3, 1850
Nov 19, 1925

Frank Parks
Sep 14, 1891
Mar 5, 1929

"Parks Brothers"
Aaron T. Parks
Oct 28, 1853
Nov 2, 1901
&
William C. Parks
Jan 19, 1852
Nov 11, 1901
&
Joel D. Parks
Jun 9, 1850
Nov 9, 1931
&
Emma Puckett Parks
Apr 3, 1872
May 1, 1934

Sallie Parks
May 11, 1881
Sep 29, 1946

Eliphas Monroe Parkinson
Sep 2, 1861
Jun 2, 1941

Olevia Sloan Parkinson
Mar 31, 1862
Jul 31, 1944

FAYETTEVILLE QUADRANGLE

Lillian Gertrude Parkinson
Jan 16, 1890
Mar 20, 1969

Archie Brown Parkinson
Jan 1, 1900
Jul 26, 1966

Mary Laws Parkinson
Dec 14, 1904

E. P. Pitts
Dec 7, 1888
Aug 3, 1953

Martha P. Pitts
Feb 7, 1855
Jul 31, 1922

Green F. Pitts
Mar 17, 1853
Sep 19, 1917

Robert F. Pitts
1885-1924

Matilda C.(Clark) Pitts
1887-1971 (Mar 11)

Alfred Houston, Son of
Mr. & Mrs. Rees H. Pitts
Aug 12, 1908
Jul 7, 1909

James O. Phagan
Dec 23, 1886
May 26, 1961

Matilda G. Phagan
Jan 25, 1891
Jan 19, 1971

Laura E., wife of
A. W. Pitts
Sep 10, 1884
May 25, 1925

Melba Posey
1930-1934

James D. Posey
1892-1955
&
Willie W. Posey
1893-

Carl Lee Parks
Died Aug 7, 1971
Age: 45 years.
(Ralston FH)

J. B. Pigg
1916-1934

Mildred L. Parks
1898-1903

Parks Daughter
1897

Joe Brazier Parks
Jul 25, 1869
Nov 8, 1955

Lucy Little Parks
Apr 10, 1872
Sep 6, 1946

John Mack Pack
May 4, 1890
Dec 10, 1969
&
Edith Hines Pack
May 27, 1892
Oct 31, 1926
&
Mabel Simmons Pack
Oct 27, 1895

Alfred Parker
Tennessee
Pvt 1st Cl 119 Inf 30 Div PH
Died Sep 3, 1940
Age: (not given)
&
Mattie Ann Parker
Jan 22, 1888
May 7, 1964

Frank Payne
Kentucky
SFC 306 Aux RMT Depot
QMC WW I
Jul 9, 1883
Mar 28, 1950

William Peach
1809-1898

Mary, Consort of
Alex Philpott
Dec 19, 1813
Jul 6, 1880
Age: 66y, 6m, 17d.

J. B. Prosser
May 30, 1869
Apr 30, 1909

Arthur Austin Philips
(no dates)

Thelma Lee Payne
Oct 6, 1915
Feb 27, 1938

Eugenia Puckette
1931-1936

Iva Parker
1888-1946

Rufus Knox Pitts
Aug 27, 1888
Nov 25, 1953
&
Inez Puckette Pitts
Sep 22, 1888

T. I. Pitts
Mar 16, 1860
Sep 25, 1905

Mary Sue Kerr Pitts
Jan 18, 1898

F. A. Pitts
Nov 5, 1853
Feb 20, 1905
& wife
M. F. Pitts
Dec 12, 1858
Aug 8, 1922

Ollie Polk Pitts
Mar 7, 1882
Jan 1, 1939

Eaphrim W. Pitts
1857-1939

Will Pitts
1882-1935
&
Nova Pitts
1881-

R. A. Pitts
1864-1942

Etta P. Pitts
1870-1955

John Loyd Pitts
Mar 25, 1894
Oct 2, 1971

Edna E. Pitts
Sep 25, 1894
Jul 22, 1907

Edna M. Pitts
1857-1941

W. A. E. Pitts
Feb 25, 1847
Jul 21, 1907

Parthenia Pitts
1860-1934

Julie E., wife of
J. H. Pollock
Oct 17, 1888
Feb 7, 1917

Maudie I., Daughter of
J. H. & J. E. Pollock
Sep 11, 1914
Oct 22, 1914

Albert H. A., Son of
J. H. & J. E. Pollock
May 5, 1916
Sep 22, 1916

Dell S. Patterson
Feb 26, 1866
Jul 16, 1946

Raymond Anderson Pitts
Nov 13, 1916
Feb 22, 1970

Geraldine Carter Pitts
Sep 8, 1918

Minnie Dickson Pike
1877-1950

Flossie Purtle
1908-1942

Younger R. Pitts
1889-1954

Susie McCown Pitts
1893-1948

Joe Wesley Pitts
1924-1936

Charlie Hartson Quimby
Born at Shelbyville, Tenn.
Jun 11, 1857
Sep 18, 1897

Mrs. W. A. Quimby
1867-1932

Sarah Isabella Quimby
1901-1961

E. Conway Richardson
1856-1936
&
Myrtle Sullivan Richardson
1866-1958

Jack Richardson
1931-1933

Kenneth O. Richardson, Sr.
Mar 18, 1896
Jan 9, 1968
&
Grace Taylor Richardson
Jul 23, 1900

James W. Rhea
1868-1937
&
Martha S. Rhea
1875-1953

W. D. Rudd
1895-1950

Laura E., wife of
W. T. Rudd
Apr 19, 1866
May 27, 1927

Marvin Rhodes
1930-1935

Nolan Renfro
Nov 24, 1884
Jan 21, 1932

FAYETTEVILLE QUADRANGLE

Garland M. Ross
Aug 28, 1875
Sep 14, 1943

William T. Ross
1840-1894
&
Anna W. Ross
1851-1883

Robert C. Ross
Jun 2, 1872
Sep 5, 1928
&
Nannie S. Ross
Nov 3, 1892

Felix S. Rhea
Sep 1, 1885
Dec 7, 1931
&
Lilly E. Rhea
Mar 12, 1891
Aug 7, 1933

William Henry Reese
Jul 17, 1880
Jul 18, 1932
&
Johnnie McNatt Reese
Apr 22, 1879
Oct 29, 1952

Ben T. Roach
1843-1902
&
Adaline Roach
1849-1901

William Rufus Roach
Sep 6, 1872
Feb 25, 1934

Girtie D., wife of
M. R. Roach
Nov 11, 1877
Jul 30, 1905

Ethel Lee Rouse
Died May 10, 1970
Age: 70y, 5m, 11d.
(Rudder FH, Stevenson, AL)

T. R. Ramsey
Oct 11, 1824
Dec 11, 1912
& wife
Jane Ramsey
Nov 19, 1827
Sep 21, 1890

G. A. Ramsey
Nov 6, 1865
Oct 5, 1892

M. L. Ramsey
Jun 21, 1883
May 17, 1916

S. B. Ramsey
May 24, 1849
(no date)
& wife
Sallie Belle Renegar Ramsey
Jan 14, 1854
Jul 5, 1929

Freddie Jackson, Son of
S. B. & Belle Ramsey
May 24, 1875
Aug 13, 1877

Daniel L. Ready
1876-1943
&
Mary E. Moore Ready
1881-1968

William Shannon Ready
Died Dec 15, 1971
Age: 67 years.
(Ralston FH)

Charlotte Ready
Mar 4, 1923
Oct 8, 1923

Fred Rawls
Feb 15, 1899
Feb 17, 1954

C. R. Rives
Oct 7, 1882
Feb 13, 1922

Tom Wright Rives
May 30, 1886
Jul 15, 1948

Ruth Rives
B&D Nov 1, 1920

Frank L. Rives
May 20, 1906
Feb 7, 1934

Joe Conley Roach
(no dates)

Joseph J. Roach
(no dates)

Victoria J. Roach
(no dates)

Kate Smith, wife of
J. M. Robertson
1861-1913

J. H. Redd
Apr 19, 1867
Oct 18, 1907

Frank C. Renegar
1880-1938

Agnes Robertson
Sep 21, 1847
Sep 10, 1913

Mary Alice Bryan, wife of
J. W. Rawls
1859-1915

Elizabeth Ann Rives
Aug 23, 1887
Oct 15, 1913

Eliza J. Dollins, wife of
N. S. B. Rives
Mar 19, 1850
Jun 28, 1918

Will N. Rives
1879-1941

Joel M. Rives
1890-1946
&
Gladys Rives
1901-

R. H. L. Rambo
1863-1941

Mary Frances Rambo
1865-1943

Joe Bennett Rambo, Sr.
Jul 14, 1898
Dec 7, 1970

James Lee Robison
Jan 15, 1895
Dec 24, 1970

Mary Agnes Robison
Oct 24, 1900
Aug 7, 1967

Prof. H. H. Robison
Dec 25, 1861
Dec 12, 1937

Ida Wylie Robison
Aug 26, 1873
Apr 24, 1955

A. K. Reese
1877-1916

Mollie, wife of
J. K. Raby
(no dates)

Rosanna Stone, wife of
Iverson T. Rodes
1879-1942

John C. Ray
Oct 23, 1853
Jul 28, 1888

Jack Renegar
Dec 10, 1886
Aug 8, 1962

Clara Terry Renegar
May 25, 1888
Apr 5, 1965

Ezella Prosser Richardson
1873-1947

John E. Routt
Sep 10, 1861
Dec 26, 1931

Emma J. Routt
Dec 4, 1864
Mar 4, 1948

Mary Lou, Daughter of
J. E. & E. S. Routt
Aug 21, 1894
Mar 30, 1895

William Edward, Son of
J. E. & Emma S. Routt
Mar 18, 1897
Jul 2, 1898

Mrs. Mournnin L. Carter,
wife of F. M. Ramsey
May 22, 1858
Jul 6, 1920

E. Winford Reynolds
1924-1938

Berry P. Raby, Sr.
Died Jan 30, 1971
Age: (not given)
(Higgins FH)

H. R. Ramsey
Aug 25, 1866
(no date)
&
Emma Ramsey
Sep 2, 1868
Feb 9, 1929

Willie Ramsey
Dec 4, 1901
Aug 24, 1949

Berry P. Raby, Sr.
1876-1938

Gertrude Bobo Raby
Jan 8, 1883
Feb 6, 1943

Rachel M. Raby
1907-1941

Harold B. Raby
1914-1938

Estelle N. Raby
1909-1947

Joe Eggleston Raby
Tennessee
S/1 U.S.N.R. WW II
Oct 30, 1909
Aug 24, 1969

Infant of
Frank & Ruth Rambo
(no dates)

Frank D. Rambo
Sep 4, 1888
Sep 4, 1961

Ruth Pitts Rambo
Sep 2, 1895
Oct 28, 1954

Oscar L. Ralston
Oct 24, 1875
Aug 3, 1916

Jay H. Ralston
Sep 1, 1862
Apr 26, 1930

James David Ralston
Aug 3, 1867
Dec 4, 1940
&
Jessie Jones Ralston
Oct 27, 1877
Mar 2, 1933

James McNeil Ralston
Oct 3, 1908
Nov 6, 1935

William Ralston
Dec 31, 1824
Sep 3, 1914

Agnes Finney Ralston
Apr 20, 1837
Apr 13, 1912

T. F. Ralston
Nov 24, 1863
Aug 16, 1914

Columbia Ralston
Jul 4, 1873
Sep 14, 1877

Joseph Guy Ralston
Feb 10, 1869
Aug 15, 1877

William Ralston
1861-1935
&
Beulah M. Ralston
1866-1936

Mary Ralston
Sep 11, 1865
Jun 26, 1942

McNeil Ralston
Dec 30, 1878
Jan 23, 1960

Kathryn Ralston
1911-1919

A. J. Renegar
Sep 3, 1848
May 6, 1923
&
Mattie Cown Renegar
May 4, 1853
Aug 31, 1932

C. W. Riegger
1881-1921

Charles William Richardson
Sep 6, 1881
Jul 20, 1971

Charles Michell Reed
Sep 9, 1938
Sep 10, 1938

Susie Kelso Ralston
Feb 15, 1882
Mar 6, 1937

Robert M. Rawls
1875-1918

Elizabeth K. Rawls
1875-1947

Charles Kelso Rawls
1898-1959

Will Hickman Rees
1878-1962

Ella Whittaker Rees
1856-1935

R. Adolphus Rees
1850-1941

Hal Bynum Rees
1898-1918
"USMC"

Whittaker Reynolds Rees
1960

Muriel Rees
Jul 5, 1901
Aug 27, 1905

H. Newton Rees
1883-1964

E. Collier Rees
1880-1967

Bess Mathis Rees
1880-1958

Little Dick, Son of
R. A. & E. W. Rees
Nov 29, 1886
Aug 25, 1887
Age: 8m, 27d.

J. C. Rogers
Died Jan 31, 1846
Age: 30 years.
&
E. J. Rogers
1826-1888

Mrs. T. A. Renegar
1845-1933

Erwin E. Reynolds
1901-1934

John T. Reynolds
1870-1956

Louisa Daniel, wife of
Samuel Rutledge
1829-1925

Robert Frank Rutledge
1858-1942

Sarah Howard Rutledge
1860-1944

J. Fred Ray
Feb 24, 1889
Jul 11, 1961

Laura May, Daughter of
W. G. & Laura E. Rodes
Feb 10, 1900
Jul 1, 1901

Arthur S. Rodes
Mar 27, 1871
Jan 9, 1918

Thomas Miller Rodes
Sep 15, 1861
Sep 5, 1952

Iverson T. Rodes
Jan 19, 1838
Sep 14, 1895
& wife
Emma I. Rodes
Oct 21, 1839
Mar 24, 1880

Iverson Twyam Rodes
Sep 17, 1873
May 29, 1959

John Butler Rutledge
Jun 19, 1872
Jun 3, 1950
&
Corinne Carter Rutledge
Mar 16, 1876
Apr 26, 1960

Ivie Neil, Son of
J. E. & Mamie L. Rodes
Jun 12, 1890
Aug 16, 1891

Infant Daughter of
J. E. & Mamie L. Rodes
B&D Feb 17, 1892

Mamie, wife of
J. E. Rodes
Died Jun 1, 1892
Age: 25y, 7m, 14d.

Henry Ernest Rodes
Feb 2, 1876
Jun 28, 1964
&
Mary Battle Rodes
Mar 3, 1879
Mar 15, 1949

Thomas M. & James E.,
Sons of Henry E. &
Mary B. Rodes
Dec 28, 1914
Jun 7, 1916

H. E. Rodes
(no dates)

Annie Lee Dinwiddie,
wife of
Thomas M. Rodes
Jun 13, 1867
May 14, 1891

Marguerite P. Ramsey
Apr 3, 1914
Jul 12, 1967

Mary, Daughter of
Henry & Elizabeth Robertson
May 6, 1811
Mar 8, 1889

George E. Ruth
1869-1936

Alleine, Daughter of
A. D. & Jennie Ruth
Died Jan 27, 1882
Age: 9m, 10d.

H. Knox Rives
1871-1914

Caddie Yates Rives
1876-1953

C. D. "Doug" Reese
1907-1939
&
Ruth Adams Reese
1904-

C. G. Ramsey
Mar 29, 1868
Mar 7, 1913

Ella Ramsey
Jul 5, 1863
Sep 7, 1890

Martha A. Ramsey
Mar 17, 1837
Sep 5, 1902

B. F. Ramsey
Born in North Carolina
Jul 19, 1822
Jul 5, 1872
Age: 49y, 11m, 16d.

Elizabeth Johnson, wife of
W. R. Roach
Sep 10, 1880
Jul 11, 1916

J. Y. Reynolds
1846-1916
&
Margaret B. Reynolds
1852-1940

Emma Bunn Rodgers
Apr 4, 1860
Jan 23, 1935

Joseph V. Roe
1870-1939

Sarah J., wife of
Madison Rowzee
Died May 26, 1891
Age: 63 years.

Annie Hoodrich Raby,
Daughter of
J. T. & Mary L. Goodrich
Jan 12, 1876
Jan 15, 1923

Myrtle Randolph
Jul 6, 1880
Aug 12, 1952

Nelson Carter Rutledge
Aug 18, 1893
Feb 22, 1966

Mary Moores Rutledge
Aug 18, 1898
Feb 25, 1965

Thomas Eric Reed
Tennessee
S2 U. S. Navy WW I
Aug 23, 1897
Jul 26, 1950

Lillian Formwalt Reed
Jun 19, 1898
Aug 18, 1958

John H. Rees, Jr.
1885-1920

Ernest Rees
Apr 11, 1876
May 25, 1951

Beatrice Milhous Rees
Dec 16, 1881
Apr 30, 1965

Evalyn Thomison, wife of
J. T. Rennolds
1888-1918

G. W. Renegar
Jul 13, 1855
Apr 5, 1936
&
Maranda Durham Renegar
Aug 8, 1853
Feb 25, 1902

Maxie Swiney Roach
May 1, 1865
Apr 9, 1950

Claiborn M. Roach
Apr 22, 1849
Nov 11, 1911

John H. Rees
1851-1913

Mary E. Rees
1851-1911

Jack Russell
1861-1924
&
Cora Russell
1859-1927

Lifus O. Reynolds
May 26, 1886
Aug 12, 1969
&
Sallie P. Reynolds
Aug 5, 1386

L. W. Reynolds
1882-1957
&
Lucy Reynolds
1880-1950

Elizabeth Rucker
1848-1929
&
Susan C. Rucker
1881-1961

Joel C. Rucker
1879-1938

Oliver A. Ready, Sr.
Feb 26, 1888
May 2, 1969

Sarah E. Partain, wife of
O. A. Ready
Nov 14, 1889
Mar 18, 1922

Beeye Farrell, wife of
O. A. Ready
Apr 2, 1895
Apr 9, 1943

Myra Massey, wife of
O. A. Ready
May 8, 1912
Mar 28, 1968

Marian, Infant of
Mr. & Mrs. O. A. Ready
B&D Sep 13, 1938

Holden Moores "Ty" Rice
Dec 1, 1893
Mar 8, 1962

Sarah Hammond Rice
Sep 9, 1852
Mar 11, 1917

Ariadnie, wife of
George Rice
Aug 28, 1885
Mar 3, 1920

Mary J. Rubert
Sep 22, 1905
Mar 9, 1966

W. U. S. (footstone)
(Headstone broken, with
 only date 1877)

Mollie Lee Childs, wife of
T. W. Swanner
1875-1912

Temple B. "Stub" Stubblefield, Jr.
Apr 15, 1920
Jan 17, 1939

Myrtle Nix Stubblefield
Mar 13, 1884
Mar 30, 1969

Temple Brooks Stubblefield
Jul 1, 1883
Oct 29, 1966

John Albert Snoddy
Aug 6, 1864
Dec 11, 1937

Mary Renegar Snoddy
Mar 22, 1869
Mar 15, 1948

William Hurley Stedman
Jun 11, 1870
Nov 26, 1936
&
Mattie Neece Stedman
Nov 30, 1871
(no date)

Rachel C. Spencer
1875-1934

Clyde Sweeney
Oct 26, 1907
Feb 18, 1938

John Landess Stone
Oct 13, 1890

&
Margaret Trigg Stone
Jun 28, 1884
Sep 26, 1959

Frances Stone
1923-1936

Ida L. Stone
Jun 10, 1865
Dec 1, 1949

John W. Scott
Age: 82 years
(no dates)
&
Luella K. Scott

Lawrence W. Sloan
Tennessee
T/Sgt U.S.Air Force
WW II
Jun 7, 1915
Jan 2, 1967

Lawrence W. Sloan
Sep 6, 1892
Mar 13, 1935

S. D. Smith
Jun 15, 1878
Dec 28, 1912

Mary Eva Renfro Shelton
May 25, 1898
Aug 30, 1969

M. L. Simmons
May 27, 1863
Aug 5, 1930
&
S. M. Simmons
Sep 22, 1864
Dec 30, 1931

George G. Street
Sep 30, 1880
Mar 24, 1947

Robert Lafayette Smith
Feb 3, 1889
Oct 14, 1950

Thelma Ward Smith
Nov 29, 1904

C. M. Short
Jul 31, 1852
(no date)
&
Ella Blakemore Short
Apr 13, 1855
Feb 12, 1915

Mary, Daughter of
C. M. & Ella Short
Aug 1, 1880
Nov 26, 1881

Susie, Daughter of
C. M. & Ella Short
Dec 17, 1892
Dec 10, 1896

FAYETTEVILLE QUADRANGLE

Eugene Stewart
1878-1953

Annie B. Stewart
1882-1939

Henry C. Spray
Mar 6, 1878
Sep 28, 1951
&
Lizzie H. Spray
Oct 27, 1884
May 4, 1969

Malcolm Alvie Spray
Nov 10, 1915
Sep 30, 1933

Homer R. Spray
Nov 7, 1907
Aug 3, 1968
&
Mildred S. Spray
Aug 12, 1914

Conrad H. Spray
May 27, 1913
Aug 20, 1969

Thomas S. Spencer
Mar 20, 1881
May 17, 1964
&
Rachel Lou Spencer
Feb 14, 1875
Mar 24, 1934

Herman E. Stewart
1888-1933

Jack L. Smith
Dec 11, 1849
Nov 9, 1929
&
Mattie Lathum Smith
Apr 24, 1869
(no date)

Adella, wife of
J. L. Smith
Jun 19, 1858
Sep 4, 1895

Bernice Scott Smith
Apr 16, 1895
Apr 6, 1927

J. P., Son of
J. L. & M. L. Smith
May 2, 1909
Jun 2, 1909

Matt Riley Smith
1882-1940
&
Nina Lee Smith
1885-1946

T. W. Smith
Mar 28, 1868
Mar 3, 1940
&
Lelia Smith
Aug 30, 1870
Jul 26, 1932

William Stewart Snell
May 29, 1921
Dec 13, 1923

Bobby Lewis Stocstill
Oct 19, 1931
Apr 13, 1964

George W. Stocstill
1885-1939

Ova Lee Stocstill
Oct 27, 1887
Apr 1, 1933

Estill Stocstill
1915-1951

Earl Simmons
1882-(no date)
&
Ada L. Simmons
1893-1935

Elcie Smith
1901-1941
(Higgins FH)

Lula A. Smith
1879-1941

Jesse E. Smith
1878-1944

Robert Lee, Son of
A. J. & Alice Spencer
Sep 4, 1894
May 6, 1922
"He served in the U.S. Navy
during the World War I."

A. J. Spencer
Oct 26, 1867
Nov 5, 1952
&
Alice Spencer
Apr 10, 1865
Jan 22, 1957

William M. Spencer
Jul 30, 1890
Jan 19, 1961
&
Nellie Irene Spencer
Jul 10, 1897
Sep 5, 1965

Burrell Smith
Oct 2, 1876
Mar 22, 1906

N. P. Smith
Jun 16, 1846
Aug 15, 1901
& wife
Emily M. Smith
Aug 15, 1832
Dec 17, 1921

W. J. Smith
May 13, 1864
Apr 19, 1942
&
Birdie Koonce Smith
May 6, 1877
Nov 16, 1941

Nolan Fenton, Son of
R. C. & Dovie Smith
Dec 23, 1915
Feb 3, 1916

Wiley B. Stocstill
Feb 12, 1870
Jun 15, 1932

Margaret Clark Stephenson
Sep 20, 1910
May 17, 1954

Jeff M. Stone
1823-1905
&
Ann O. Stone
1830-1915

William J. Stone
1857-1934
(A Shriner)

Eleanor Gabard Stone
1861-1939

Jessie M. Chappin, wife of
G. C. Sweeney
May 9, 1904
Dec 2, 1923

James W. Smith
Oct 4, 1840
Apr 29, 1891

W. J. Stubblefield
1870-1949

Clyde E. Sweesy
Dec 3, 1918

&
Sarah Eley Sweesy
Jan 9, 1926
Jul 12, 1963

Robert J. Small
Apr 11, 1843
Aug 25, 1914
&
Alice Shofner Small
Apr 27, 1853
Jun 5, 1945

A. A. Stone
May 17, 1885
Mar 29, 1925

Mary B. Stone
Jul 18, 1887
Dec 19, 1956

Aaron P. Street
1889-1942
&
Lillie B. Street
1889-Aug 3, 1971
Age: 81y, 9m, 26d.

John F. Sweeney
Dec 11, 1873
Nov 17, 1939

Maye B. Sweeney
Jun 30, 1880
Nov 21, 1966

Clarence Steelman
Jan 10, 1900
Jan 19, 1929

Eugene Forrest Shofner
Sep 25, 1878
Jun 8, 1960
&
Margaret Hill Shofner
Sep 12, 1879
Jan 13, 1951

Mary E. Thornton, wife of
L. J. Swiney
Nov 1, 1847
Mar 5, 1922

Mary B. Shelton
Feb 2, 1843
Married to Jas. R. Shelton
Sep 27, 1868
Sep 23, 1871

Martha M., wife of
Alfred Smith
Feb 11, 1807
Aug 14, 1879
&
Alice Smith
Feb 4, 1848
Sep 18, 1876

Icenora Smith
Aug 25, 1845
Aug 13, 1894

Era Bicknell, wife of
Arthur Smith
Jan 25, 1895
Jan 19, 1929

Sylvia Christine Spurlock
Mar 5, 1946
Oct 16, 1964

FAYETTEVILLE QUADRANGLE

Robert R. Smith
Oct 23, 1907
Apr 22, 1965

Willie Eslick Chockley
Mar 15, 1890
Apr 17, 1970

J. T. Sloan
Feb 10, 1855
Feb 9, 1924
&
Mary T. Sloan
Jan 11, 1857
Mar 13, 1930

Annie Stone
Dec 11, 1900
Jun 27, 1920

C. L. Stone
Apr 19, 1868
Jun 21, 1961
&
Lou Ella Stone
Oct 11, 1873
Dec 24, 1939

R. P. Smith
1861-1922

Naomi Sugg
1860-1948

Arthur Smith
  ? -1835
(Date gone)

Nancy L. Smith
1862-1916

John Preston Smith
Mar 26, 1886
Apr 18, 1962

J. A. "Lon" Stewart
Sep 7, 1869
Jul 11, 1941

Mary Lou Stewart

Hattie B. Pylant Sowell
Jun 17, 1878
Dec 27, 1958

W. M. Shaw
18??-1899(illegible)

Mildred L. Shaw
1856-1937

Henry C. Sorrells
1865-1923
&
Fannie Sorrells
1869-(no date)

N. A. Sorrells
Mar 21, 1857
Apr 19, 1926

Susie, wife of
N. A. Sorrells
Jul 15, 1863
Jun 20, 1906

Sarah M. Sanders
Mar 9, 1903
Sep 20, 1956

David R. Scott
1853-1944
&
Laura E. Scott
1859-1948

Clara Irene Scott
1892-1969

Louvenia Wilson, wife of
Jodie G. Stewart
May 25, 1885
Jul 6, 1919

William D. Sims
1841-1927
&
Cynthia E. Sims
1847-1920

Laura L. Sims
1870-1949

Lucy I. Sims
1877-1956

F. Ira Sims
1875-1933

William H. Sims
1872-1938

G. C. Smith
1835-1946

Thomas Day Sugg
May 28, 1880
Nov 15, 1958

Alma Patterson Sugg
Jun 7, 1882
Feb 17, 1971

Day Sugg
Sep 20, 1910
Oct 8, 1953

J. D. Sugg, Jr.
1893-1964

Mary McRady Sugg
1900-1967

J. D. Sugg
1861-1920

Sallie H. Sugg
1874-1968

C. M. Smith
1866-1945
(Higgins FH)

Mrs. Lum Smith
1863-1932

Lewis Edward Strong
1917-1946

Lucille Terry, wife of
Lewis E. Strong
1912-1947

Mary Smith Saunders
Apr 23, 1889
Nov 23, 1953

Mary A. Strong
Jun 15, 1905
May 23, 1923

A. F. "Buddy" Smith
1868-1950
&
Ruthie P. Smith
1867-1926

Rufus Nat Smith
Tennessee
Pvt 114 M.G. Bn 30 Div
Died Sep 25, 1938
Age: (not given)

Edwin E. Stone
Aug 5, 1874
Feb 11, 1900

Frank Stone
1898-1959

Berry Boone Stone
1871-1910

Margaret Hester Stone
1872-1944

Infant Sons of
B. B. & Maggie Stone
1902

James D. Stone
Dec 25, 1838
Nov 24, 1923
&
Susan A. Stone
Jun 7, 1844
Jul 29, 1906

Sallie Moore, wife of
Edwin M. Sherrell
1865-1910

Henery S., Daughter of
John F. & F. M. Baxter &
wife of J. R. Shelton
Jun 26, 1872
Aug 13, 1914

John R. Shelton
1871-1949
&
Burlie S. Shelton
1892-

Arthur Welsley Smith
Dec 23, 1869
Apr 16, 1956
&
Sarah Glass Smith
Aug 3, 1872
Dec 6, 1962

William Lawrence Smith
Mar 20, 1897
Jul 1, 1907

Helen Marie Shelton
1931-1931

Nora Brown Shelton
1898-1918

James C., Son of
R. L. & Sallie Stewmon
B&D Aug 8, 1969

Nancy Shaw
1853-1943

Sugg Shaw
Apr 8, 1888
(no date)
&
Beulah Shaw
Jul 31, 1891
(no date)

Clarence Shaw
Nov 12, 1913
Mar 25, 1930

John L. Scott
Aug 18, 1869
Oct 29, 1954
& wife
Mollie F. Thomas Scott
1875-1924

Lillie A. McAfee, wife of
John L. Scott
1882-1959

Roy Scott
Jun 27, 1904
Aug 22, 1967

C. M. Solomon
1873-1931

Willa Bobo Solomon
1876-1948

James Elmer Smith
1892-1953

Samuel W. Sloan
1882-1955
(Cremated)

FAYETTEVILLE QUADRANGLE

W. J. Smith
Aug 15, 1855
Sep 25, 1926

Lucy Ann Smith
Jan 15, 1863
Jun 20, 1950

Burnie D. Smith
Mar 23, 1893
Aug 17, 1920

Rufe T. Scott
Aug 28, 1878
Mar 21, 1956

Eulah Hamilton Scott
Jun 18, 1876
Feb 15, 1943

Robert Thomas Smith
1859-1938

Nancy Emma Smith
1871-1938

Rufas Ira Smith
1891-1928

William M. Smith
Feb 7, 1889
Jun 29, 1956
&
Pearl Rudd Smith
Sep 4, 1889

Noah C. Steelman
Nov 1, 1866
Jan 12, 1940
&
Emma R. Steelman
Dec 7, 1872
Jun 18, 1941

Pvt 1st Class
James D. Steelman
Co E 119th Inf
Born Mar 2, 1898
Killed in action at
Bellicourt, Hindenburg Line
Sep 29, 1918

Fletcher Steelman
1867-1928
&
Lizzie Steelman
Dec 9, 1871
Jan 27, 1908

Lizzie D., Daughter of
F. & L. Steelman
Jan 26, 1908
Mar 4, 1908

Connie Steelman
1897-1933

A. H. Smith
Mar 18, 1853
Oct 16, 1899

Garland Stewart
1875-1937
&
Ella Mae Stewart
(no dates)

Edd C. Shofner
Sep 8, 1875
Aug 12, 1964
&
Flora C. Shofner
Jul 29, 1885
Jan 13, 1971

A. Boone Shofner
1873-1944

W. E. Smith
Feb 3, 1883
Feb 23, 1950

George M. Smith
Nov 17, 1873
Oct 9, 1952

Edna S. Smith
Sep 28, 1879
Jul 10, 1944

Thomas E. Shipp
Died Jul 10, 1943
Age: (not given)

Mrs. A. E. Shipp
(no dates)

A. E. Shipp
(no dates)

Mrs. E. L. Shipp
(no dates)

J. C. Storey
Jan 27, 1884
Mar 14, 1941

Lexia A. Storey
Feb 24, 1891
Feb 15, 1951

Clyde Stubblefield
Nov 23, 1888
May 12, 1958
&
Dorris Stubblefield
Mar 17, 1890

Coleman M. Stevenson
1893-1930
&
Agnes Stevenson
1893-

R. L. Smith
Oct 14, 1883
Aug 30, 1905

Robert D. Smith, Sr.
May 14, 1918
May 17, 1967

James Stubblefield
1882-1927

Cora Stubblefield
1882-

Thomas D. Sumners
Jan 16, 1854
Mar 15, 1939

Lucy S. Sumners
Dec 16, 1871
Nov 21, 1961

Robert F. Sumners
Oct 24, 1934
Jun 19, 1935

Joseph Lawson Stone
Jan 22, 1882
Aug 30, 1947

Eleanor Harwell Stone
Jun 9, 1896
Jan 9, 1969

Collins Bright Smith
Tennessee
Pvt Inf WW I
Oct 13, 1889
Mar 31, 1965
&
Zula Warden Smith
Oct 10, 1891
Dec 8, 1961

Ethel, Daughter of
Morgan & Lizzie Sandlin
Dec 14, 1895
Jul 26, 1900

Morgan, Son of
Morgan & Lizzie Sandlin
Feb 2, 1900
Nov 2, 1900

Infant Son of
Morgan & Lizzie Sandlin
Aug 17, 1897
Sep 17, 1897

Judith Ann Steelman
B&D Nov 2, 1946

Frances Marie Steelman
Apr 3, 1924
Oct 16, 1929

Infant Daughter of
Webb & Judith Shofner
(no dates)

Frank Nathaniel Stowers
1878-1932

Dora Crawley Stowers
1885-1957

Harry Rees Strong
Apr 23, 1871
Nov 7, 1957

Nena Carter Strong
Aug 31, 1875
Apr 1, 1957

John C. Stephenson
Jan 22, 1845
Nov 11, 1908
&
Amanda E. Stephenson
Nov 13, 1850
Jun 4, 1924
& Son
Crawford Stephenson
Jan 5, 1882
May 29, 1952

Dr. T. U. Stephenson
Nov 15, 1813
Aug 13, 1901
& wife
Mary R. Stephenson
Dec 27, 1815
Oct 27, 1905

W. L. Shofner
Forrests Escort, C.S.A.
Sep 3, 1838
Feb 28, 1927
&
Lilly Lynn Powers Shofner
May 15, 1847
Jan 16, 1924

William J. Stegall
Oct 11, 1886
Oct 14, 1960

Fannie Stegall
1857-1953

Ewing B. Stegall
1851-1924

Clarence (Stegall ?)
Our Darling
Jul 2, 1883
Age: 6 years.

Thomas J. Scott
1883-1956

Clara Stegall Scott
1883-1960

John Alford Stegall
1880-1949
&
Harriette Andrews Stegall
1896-1951

W. W. Stegall
1856-1890

Malvina Temple Stegall
1832-1859
&
William J. Stegall
1823-1903
&
Florence Magnolia Stegall
1848-1936

FAYETTEVILLE QUADRANGLE

D. M. Sanders, Sr.
Sep 26, 1846
Dec 4, 1925

Tillie Scott Sanders
Aug 12, 1866
Feb 18, 1955

Octa Spurlock
1884-1941

Tommie Lucille Smith
1917-1966

Dorothy Smith
1924-1934

William Medearis Smith
Oct 16, 1878
Aug 18, 1956

John Wilson Sullivan
1877-1950

Jennie Love Renegar Sullivan
1880-1938

Smith
(no dates)

Wiley B. Stogstill
Sep 12, 1870
Jun 15, 1932

Bright Solomon
1877-1947
&
Myrtle Solomon
1887-1970

E. D. Strong
1849-1919

Sallie Strong
1849-1894

C. T. Simms
Oct 19, 1845
Apr 13, 1923
&
Mary E. Simms
Nov 10, 1848
Dec 19, 1925

Daisy Webb Stone
1887-1950

Ervin Hart Stone
Jan 1, 1917
Jun 16, 1918
(picture)

Ervin H. Stone
1894-1956

Robert Samuel Solomon
1902-1908

Irene Woodard, wife of
B. B. Smythe
Aug 14, 1872
Feb 1, 1906

W. Ed Smith
Sep 28, 1870
Aug 9, 1944
&
Ola Mai Ellis Smith
May 2, 1879
Jan 6, 1962

D. P. Shackleford
May 4, 1832
Mar 12, 1875
& wife
Aletha Young Shackleford
Sep 21, 1838
Oct 21, 1875

Ella A. South
Died Mar 7, 1876
Age: 7 years.

James B. Smith
Sep 12, 1850
Jul 30, 1878

Otey Smith
Sep 3, 1869
Aug 22, 1870
&
Harry Smith
Jul 6, 1872
Sep 1, 1872
"Children of
George F. & J. A. Smith."

George F. Smith
Jan 3, 1826
Jun 8, 1900

Judith A. Smith
Apr 23, 1829
Mar 12, 1905

William A. Steele
Aug 1, 1860
Apr 19, 1882

Martha P. Greer, wife of
Galenus M. Steele
Apr 18, 1830
May 22, 1911

George Stonebreaker
Born at Lancaster, Penn.
Nov 5, 1792
Died at Fayetteville, Tenn.
Apr 28, 1869
& wife
Martha Yates Stonebreaker
Born in Barren Co., KY.
Feb 16, 1805
Died Fayetteville, Tenn.
Jul 30, 1882

Martha Ellen Sullivan
Died 1939
Age: (not given)
(Higgins FH)

Oscar E. Stewart
Jul 16, 1876
Aug 27, 1953
&
Ida C. Stewart
Mar 17, 1876
Mar 21, 1939
&
Arthur T. Stewart
Jul 16, 1876
Oct 19, 1944
&
Bessie Lee Stewart
Aug 1, 1886

(Twin brothers married
sisters)

Marvin M., Son of
A. T. & Bessie Stewart
Sep 4, 1908
Sep 17, 1919
(picture)

Martha J. Short
Oct 9, 1824
Jun 3, 1871
&
Susan F. Short
Apr 16, 1843
Oct 23, 1876

George J. Stonebraker
Aug 4, 1842
Feb 15, 1905
&
Lettie Renegar Stonebraker
Feb 1, 1844
Jan 19, 1904

Hugh D. Smith
Feb 24, 1852
Jun 26, 1921
& wife
Fannie Medearis Smith
Nov 11, 1858
Mar 18, 1881

Fannie, Daughter of
Hugh D. & Fannie Smith
Mar 8, 1881
Aug 28, 1882

Dorothy Smith
1942

Laura Jane Smith
1956

Hugh Lauderdale Smith
May 31, 1919
Jul 6, 1965

Lucy Neeld Smith
Feb 16, 1852
Sep 29, 1947

C. C. Stubblefield
Jul 7, 1920
May 19, 1966

Clifton C. Stubblefield
1877-1930
&
Bessie C. Stubblefield
1886-(no date)

Fee Smith
1871-1940
&
Donnie Smith
1877-1946

Charles Wayne Smith
1915-1930

Aussy, Son of
J. G. & L. C. Stonebraker
(no dates)

Sarah M. Stonebraker
Aug 14, 1882
Sep 14, 1896

E. L. Shipp
Nov 26, 1879
Mar 6, 1940

Maud Hoots, wife of
E. L. Shipp
Died Apr 12, 1913
Age: 29y, 4m, 10d.

Roy Gardner Swindell
Tennessee
Capt. Inftry 86 Div
Died Jul 10, 1939
Age: (not given)

Sarah Martin Swindell
Mar 27, 1889
Jun 3, 1959

John Lauderdale Swindell
Oct 13, 1928
Mar 4, 1948

Jessie M. Smith
Aug 20, 1897

&
Cardene H. Smith
Dec 3, 1896

Rufus Clay Smith
Aug 13, 1869
Dec 8, 1948

Mattie S. Smith
Aug 7, 1869
Sep 2, 1949

Walter A. Smith
1869-1935

Mattie Childs Smith
1872-1959

FAYETTEVILLE QUADRANGLE

Porter Albert Stowers
1880-1951
&
Alice Parks Stowers
1889-1969

George C. Simmons
Apr 11, 1864
Oct 31, 1936

Cora Locker Simmons
Mar 10, 1876
Apr 30, 1936

E. H. Simmons
1873-1923

Dena Simmons
Mar 21, 1894
Sep 18, 1920

James Henry Smith
Nov 18, 1853
Aug 16, 1900
&
Willie Ann Smith
Jan 26, 1857
Mar 23, 1903

James Robert Smith
Oct 6, 1879
Nov 20, 1936
&
Stella Taylor Smith
Apr 29, 1887
Mar 10, 1968

Julian Benjamin Simpson
Feb 21, 1885
Dec 25, 1950

Addie Little Moores Simpson
Jul 14, 1895
Feb 22, 1953

Frank J. Spencer, Jr.
1915-1927

Frank J. Spencer
1891-1949

Ada L. Spencer
1891-1926

John Lee Smith
Sep 26, 1891
Apr 23, 1960
&
Josephine Erwin Smith
Dec 2, 1890

Ollie Askins, wife of
A. L. Sloan
Nov 15, 1874
Sep 18, 1909

J. R. Stephenson
1860-1934

Cordie H. Stephenson
1861-1945

Harriette Stephenson
1890-1970

Ernest R. Stephenson
1883-1956

Daniel Kelly Shofner
Oct 7, 1865
Jul 28, 1951

Tommie Hall Shofner
Jan 20, 1872
Jan 5, 1949

Margaret S. Schoenberger
1914-1948

William Hay Sugg
1880-1932
&
Lela Woodard Sugg
1885-1963

Myrtle Iva, wife of
Paul B. Smith
Dec 27, 1896
Mar 20, 1923

Florence Harms Strong
1896-1947

Tom G. Strong
1888-1932

Laurine Blair Strong
1895-1917

Louis C. Strong
1849-1920

Ella Smith Strong
1854-1960

Robert L. Stewman
Tennessee
Pvt 110 guard Co ASC WW I
Mar 12, 1894
Jun 15, 1962

George W. Stewman
Jun   1851
Jan 4, 1920
&
Ella Stewman
Died May 1870
Age: (not given)

J. D. Stewman
1899-1944

Herbert Stone Sherrell
Dec 18, 1887
Jun 10, 1948

Josie Stewman Shelton
Oct 10, 1897
Oct 16, 1957
&
Lonnie Rufus Shelton
Feb 14, 1892
Apr 16, 1964
&
Laura Reynolds Shelton
Oct 27, 1888
Jun 2, 1921

Finetta Deford Sherrell
Jul 22, 1890
Jul 19, 1971

B. W. Sherrell
1866-1935

J. W. Sherrell
Jan 16, 1864
Dec 3, 1946

Vick Sugg, wife of
J. W. Sherrell
Sep 21, 1872
Apr 11, 1938
Married Dec 23, 1903

Permelia T. Sherrell
1835-1917

Sue Twitty Smith
Died Jan 20, 1972
Age: 80y, 8m.
(Higgins FH)

Richard F. Taylor
Tennessee
Pvt U.S. Army, WW I
Oct 15, 1892
Apr 26, 1969

Julia E. Lackey, wife of
Fleet W. Taylor
Nov 5, 1887
Apr 19, 1921

Nannie Trigg
May 5, 1861
Dec 29, 1948

Fannie Trigg
1866-1948

Ernest Ashbury Thompson
Jul 4, 1885
Mar 17, 1956

Mary Ward Thompson
Aug 23, 1896

Sugg, Son of
Thomas & Siddie Thomison
Jul 5, 1888
Nov 21, 1888

Lemuel, Son of
Thomas & Siddie Thomison
Nov 6, 1894
Jun 23, 1895

Tom Thomison
Apr 26, 1847
Aug 31, 1906
&
Siddie Sugg Thomison
Jun 10, 1866
Dec 9, 1950

John Thomison
1857-1924

Iolman Thomison
Sep 15, 1889
Mar 6, 1960

John F. Taylor
1858-1937
&
Mattie A. Taylor
1863-1943

George P. Thomas
May 14, 1872
Feb 26, 1934
&
Maudie Newsom Thomas
Aug 1, 1883
Jun 14, 1937

Felix Thompson
Oct 8, 1923
Mar 18, 1966

Lucille Thompson
Jul 31, 1930
Sep 4, 1932

George W. Thompson
Feb 8, 1888
Jan 10, 1945

Onia L. Thompson
Mar 13, 1890

Robert D. Thornton
Feb 14, 1892
Feb 12, 1962
&
Angel Lee Bates Thornton
Jan 19, 1894
Feb 16, 1939

James S. Tuley
1880-1937

Lucy P. Tuley
1886-1965

William Tate
1885-1941
&
Virgie W. Tate
1888-19(broken)

FAYETTEVILLE QUADRANGLE

Abidnego S. Thomas
Jun 16, 1841
Jan 14, 1903
&
Jennie Thomas
1852-1913

Josie Atkins, wife of
S. M. Teel
Oct 16, 1855
Apr 5, 1893

James M. Thornton
Apr 21, 1822
Aug 20, 1889

Lucinda, wife of
J. M. Thornton
Died Jan 21, 1887
Age: 60 years.

R. B. Thornton
Nov 11, 1854
Aug 22, 1889
& wife
Tommie Z. Davis Thornton
Jul 13, 1859
Aug 31, 1889

Jimmie Bell, Daughter of
R. B. & T. Z. Thornton
Age: 10m.
(no dates)

Thomas H., Son of
J. M. & Lucinda Thornton
Jan 27, 1858
Nov 11, 1881

Robert D. Thornton
1855-1923

Mary Ellen Thornton
1851-1929

Elizabeth Thornton
Feb 28, 1902
Aug 2, 1903
&
Homer Thornton
Apr 16, 1889
Dec 2, 1889
"Children of
R. L. & M. Thornton."

James N. Thomas
1917-1919

William C. Thomas
1910-1919

Hattie Buntley Towry
Sep 12, 1900
Sep 10, 1969

Thomas Mahlon Thornton
1881-1938
&
Mary Robertson Thornton
1885-1945

Joan Thornbrough
Jun 16, 1933
May 6, 1935

Buford L. Tucker, Sr.
Jun 20, 1893
Feb 6, 1954

Lara E. Tucker
Mar 26, 1897
Dec 8, 1966

Jennings Thompson
Mar 11, 1905
Oct 5, 1967

Rev. David Tucker
Died Nov 1896
Age: About 70 years.

Samuel D. Tate
Tennessee
Pfc 114 Field Arty Bn WW II
Dec 1, 1899
Mar 20, 1950

R. S. Terry
1882-1929

Susie Irvin Terry
1882-1961

Infant Terry
(no dates)

E. S. Terry
1844-1924

Henry Clay Tucker
Feb 16, 1856
Sep 13, 1917

Thomas Newton Towery
1879-1943
&
Lula Davidson Towery
1888-1946

Charlie C. Thompson
Mar 30, 1888
Feb 11, 1970

H. L. Thomas
1864-1923

Mattie Thomas
1873-1956

Sarah Francis Templeton
Feb 25, 1917
Mar 2, 1959

Pearl W. Templeton
Jul 17, 1896
Feb 27, 1933

Wiley M. Templeton
1866-1941
&
Florence V. Templeton
1866-1956

P. L. Thornton
Feb 4, 1851
Dec 1, 1926

Maggie E., wife of
P. L. Thornton
Sep 12, 1855
Sep 29, 1921

Hugh Kirby Thornton
Aug 15, 1879
Dec 18, 1949

Lena R. Johnson, wife of
Kirby Thornton
Dec 4, 1882
Feb 5, 1922

W. Adrain Taylor
1884-1940
&
Ada Bell Taylor
1881-1918

Infant of
W. A. & Ada Taylor
Jul 9, 1915

"Aunt Fan"
Fannie Waddle, wife of
S. A. Tomlinson
1845-1923

D. A. Templeton, Sr.
Sep 13, 1900
Jun 3, 1955

Dick A. Templeton, Jr.
Apr 2, 1923

J. P. Thomison
1863-1917

Mary Anthony Thomison
1878-1969

Martha Thomison
1906-1910

William M. Templeton
Tennessee
Capt. Signal Corps
Nov 25, 1929
Apr 4, 1961

Herley M. Templeton
Mar 22, 1889
Jul 15, 1962

Mamie Lindsay Templeton
Aug 11, 1889
Mar 22, 1945

Infant Son of
Templeton
May 26, 1927
May 29, 1927

Mamie Elizabeth Templeton
1920-1921

Charlie Tucker
1884-1944

Walter C. Taylor
1879-1937

Clara A. Taylor
1876-1934

Howard H. Taylor
Mar 5, 1897
Dec 2, 1899

Leona Thomison
1910-1934

Hugh Thomison
1852-1911

Willie Thomison
1858-1931

Dee Thomison
1886-1918

Staten Thomison
1889-1960

S. C. Tigert
1914-1964

Joan Stegall Tucker
Aug 12, 1916
Nov 28, 1937
&
Jas. Rogers Tucker
Nov 28, 1937

F. P. Taylor
Sep 19, 1851
Married Ada Fulton
Dec 7, 1881
Died May 2, 1888
Age: 36 years.

William L. Turley
Nov 25, 1869
Aug 11, 1951

Lillie G. Turley
Sep 21, 1871
Oct 30, 1960

W. E. Turley
Dec 28, 1833
Jan 21, 1893

Margaret E. Turley
Oct 29, 1835
Jul 3, 1906

William E. Turley
Feb 19, 1899
Jul 21, 1940

Henry H. Taylor
Mar 15, 1872
Nov 3, 1942
&
Hattie P. Taylor
Oct 1, 1876
Apr 24, 1928

Robert P. Tate
1872-1951
&
Ella Marrs Tate
1879-1960

James Davidson Tilman
1841-1916
C.S.A. 1861-65
Col. 41st Tenn Regt
Ent 1863. Col. of 3rd
Tenn. Consolidated,
Composed of the remnants
of ten Regiments, 1865,
elected State Senator
1873, 1893 & 1901. U. S.
Minister to Ecquador 1895-
98.
& wife
Frances Bonner Tilman
1841-1921

Nell Payne Tripp
Jan 7, 1891
Feb 11, 1948

Emma D. Dean, wife of
Charles Taylor
May 30, 1875
Jul 5, 1942

A. J. Toon
Feb 7, 1815
Apr 10, 1905
& wife
Susan Toon
Mar 15, 1824
Nov 14, 1874
& Daughter
Mary F. Toon
Apr 3, 1844
Jul 13, 1854
& Daughter
Susan M. Toon
Mar 16, 1846
Jul 25, 1891

William M. Todd
Feb 28, 1832
Feb 24, 1889

Mary Old Todd
Feb 11, 1834
Sep 29, 1903

Davis Benton Thornton
Aug 27, 1884
Mar 5, 1955
&
Lucy Bagley Thornton
Nov 13, 1890

Martin Vance Tate
Jul 7, 1955

Gertrude Martin Tate
May 7, 1916

Joyce Ann Tate
Apr 4, 1935

Charles Wisbert Tryling
Aug 9, 1921
Oct 29, 1921

William Bucy Trigg
1894-1925

Malcolm Lee Tate
Jun 1, 1903

Robert Donald Tate
Jun 7, 1936

Mayme Boaz Tate
Feb 8, 1885
Jun 15, 1965

Curtis Lee Tate
Mar 18, 1879
Jul 29, 1958

Ira J. Trantham
Apr 26, 1879
Jan 5, 1907

Bradley K., Son of
J. B. & D. M. Thomison
Dec 26, 1883
Feb 14, 1902

James H. Thomison
1869-1937

Capt. J. B. Turney
Oct 4, 1831
Mar 19, 1909
Co K 1st Tenn Regt
Con. Vols
& wife
Mary J. Turney
Feb 6, 1837
Jan 25, 1920
&
L. K. Taylor
Nov 17, 1866
May 27, 1912
& wife
Ida F. Taylor
Mar 23, 1871
Sep 9, 1904

Mary Frances, Daughter of
L. K. & Ida Taylor
Jul 27, 1904
Oct 4, 1904

J. B. Thomison
1843-1904
Co K 8th Tenn. C.S.A.
&
Delia Kimbrough Thomison
1845-1928

Infant Son of
H. H. & E. K. Thomison
(no dates)

Freeman Tom
1877-1931
&
Mary Tom
1875-(no date)

Fenor L. Tribble
Oct 14, 1895
Jul 28, 1922

Irene J. Thomison
1872-1971

William C. Thomison
1871-1959

Estelle Thomison
1907-1909

Dr. L. W. "Kirk" Taylor
Jan 12, 1845
Nov 3, 1922

Lilla Taylor
Jul 2, 1873
Apr 23, 1939

Floyd D. Thompson
Tennessee
Pvt Co A 131 Engrs WW I
Jul 3, 1895
Mar 15, 1971

Bessie Ora Thompson
Died Jul 14, 1971
Age: 66 years.
(Gallant FH)

Robert H. Terry, Sr.
1872-1942

Nannie Lucile Motlow,
wife of
R. H. Terry, Sr.
1871-1938

Lillian Merritt Tureman
Jun 4, 1891
Sep 17, 1956

William G. Tipps
Jul 13, 1879
Dec 1, 1959
&
Lulu Mae M. Tipps
Mar 1, 1886
Nov 24, 1967

Mabel Tipps
Apr 15, 1923
Apr 16, 1923

Belle C. Vickers
1862-1938

Jacob Vance
(Crypt, 3 Vaults)
1877

John, Second Son of
J. S. & K. S. Vaughn
Mar 11, 1882
Jan 27, 1912

Bernice S., Oldest Son of
J. S. & K. S. Vaughn
Jan 26, 1881
Mar 16, 1903

Floyd Vaughn
Age: 6y, 7m.
(no dates)

R. A. Vining
Apr 21, 1846
Jan 25, 1910
&
Elizabeth L. Vining
May 7, 1845
Mar 29, 1916

Emma Vining
Oct 13, 1876
Oct 13, 1876
&
Callie Henry Vining
Jun 13, 1882
Jul 5, 1883
"Daughters of
R. A. & Lizzie Vining."

William C. Vickers
Dec 24, 1875
Jul 3, 1929

Pearl E. Vickers
Nov 25, 1876
Feb 2, 1957

Lt. William C. Whitaker
May 6, 1888
Dec 24, 1918

Mary Addie Whitaker
Jul 25, 1867
Feb 7, 1957

James C. Whitaker
Sep 2, 1891
Apr 14, 1892

Harold Lee, Son of
C. E. & Buna Wells
Jul 5, 1918
Nov 12, 1919

James McDaniel Waggoner
Jul 2, 1850
Apr 19, 1930

Josephine Janson Waggoner
Apr 7, 1855
Nov 1, 1917

Nora E. Waggoner
Mar 16, 1880
Sep 27, 1891

FAYETTEVILLE QUADRANGLE

Annie Alzy Waggoner
Aug 28, 1878
Jun 26, 1950

James Walter Waggoner, Jr.
1918-1935

N. Odell Wallace
Nov 9, 1823
Sep 22, 1918
&
Margaret E. Wallace
Jul 3, 1834
Aug 30, 1903

Robert Gray, Son of
C. T. & Gussie Wallace
Dec 24, 1893
Aug 20, 1899

M. L. Waggoner
Dec 27, 1852
Jul 7, 1900

Mattie Waggoner
Feb 14, 1856
Jan 6, 1892

Andrew M. Waggoner
Aug 9, 1888
Nov 18, 1910

Flora Pitts Warden
1885-1929

H. B. Webb
Apr 10, 1887
Feb 28, 1922

Jack Webb
1911-1956

Minnie Webb
1888-(no date)

Joe, Son of
J. E. & M. H. Webb
Aug 20, 1917
Mar 17, 1918

James S. Woodard
Tennessee
Tec 5 24 Cav Recon Trp
24 Inf Div, WW II
Sep 10, 1909
Mar 8, 1952

Samuel N. Woodard
Aug 29, 1872
Jan 31, 1918
& wife
Bertha Menefee Woodard
May 31, 1881
Jun 28, 1969

Jane Wilson
1872-1939

James K. Wakefield, Jr.
Died Sep 8, 1970
Age: 55y, 7m, 4d.
(Higgins FH)

John E. Woodard
1885-1962
&
Emma R. Woodard
1885-(no date)

Luther Wiley
1829-1892
&
Knox Wiley
1887-1933
&
Joe Wiley
1890-1948
&
Horace Wiley
1885-1963
(See Parks)

Margarette Louise Widner
Sep 13, 1913
Dec 4, 1953

John Knox Widner
Jan 17, 1891
Jan 19, 1933
&
Dovie Talent Widner
Jul 27, 1894
Feb 12, 1961

Jeff C. Ward
1865-1938
&
Emma Solomon Ward
1869-1948

William T. Wells
May 18, 1869
Mar 21, 1946
&
Elizabeth Lamb Wells
Dec 31, 1871
Jun 22, 1938

Bernard Martin Welch
Nov 24, 1887
Apr 18, 1961
&
Elizabeth McCown Welch
Jan 8, 1888

Robert A. Welch
Feb 23, 1877
Dec 3, 1953
&
Nora C. Welch
Dec 6, 1882
Oct 13, 1935

James J. White
1854-1924
&
Eliza J. White
1860-1938

Frances Belle White
Nov 7, 1912
Jan 7, 1914

Alvie L. White
Jan 7, 1893
Mar 12, 1967
&
Mattie L. White
Oct 26, 1890

Margarett A. Wyatt
Apr 20, 1832
Aug 18, 1916

I. B. Whitaker
1855-1931
&
Mary Lou Whitaker
1859-1943

Virginia Whitaker
1842-1932

J. Fielden, Son of
I. B. & M. L. Whitaker
Jan 31, 1892
Sep 25, 1896

Ambie Lee, Daughter of
I. B. & M. L. Whitaker
Feb 7, 1879
May 7, 1880

J. Mark Whitaker
1885-1949
&
Ida Harris Whitaker
1892-1932

Rev. R. M. Woodard
Dec 19, 1829
Sep 12, 1909

Nancy A., wife of
R. M. Woodard
May 10, 1831
Feb 3, 1893

John M. West
Apr 5, 1845
Aug 2, 1900

A. J. Warren
Jan 22, 1866
Jan 26, 1938
&
Mary M. Thomas Warren
Nov 21, 1867
Mar 2, 1942

W. H. Watkins
Oct 27, 1850
May 23, 1934

Jane Watkins
1848-1936

James Norman Waggoner
Jun 25, 1932
Jun 16, 1935

Martha Howe Weller
1871-1959

Zachariah McCree Wilson
Feb 23, 1865
Jun 28, 1945
&
Mattie Susan Wilson
Jun 23, 1866
Aug 17, 1915

Mrs. George Wells
1875-1954
(Beasley FH)

Maude Pearson Wells
1875-1954

William D. White
1863-1942
&
Josephine White
1856-1933

Mrs. Eliza White
1865-1937

Frank French, Son of
T. M. & Gennie F. Wilson
May 22, 1892
Sep 15, 1893

Mollie Parrill Wade
Oct 9, 1859
Apr 12, 1935

William B. Wilson
Mar 11, 1883
Jun 10, 1910

James B. Wilson
Oct 18, 1886
Sep 2, 1901

Lillian B. Wilson
Apr 22, 1860
Nov 8, 1930

William H. Wilson
Feb 8, 1858
Jan 12, 1924

Horace Lee Wilson
Jul 12, 1873
Mar 1, 1925

Robert M. Wilson
Jun 14, 1849
Sep 27, 1904

John Knight Williams
Feb 28, 1853
Nov 6, 1926
&
Mary Kerchavel McKinney
Williams
Mar 12, 1855
Aug 25, 1940

Henry W. Wright
1884-1952
&
Lucy Wright
1884-1960

FAYETTEVILLE QUADRANGLE

Z. H. Waggoner
Feb 2, 1864
Mar 30, 1925

Mrs. Z. H. Waggoner
Dec 11, 1867
Nov 4, 1908

Clara Peschau, Daughter of
J. L. & Sallie Waggoner
Mar 2, 1880
Sep 10, 1882

Samuel Waggoner
Dec 31, 1891
Mar 18, 1900

Judith Ann, Daughter of
Abednego & Margaret
Williams
Nov 7, 1923
May 5, 1939

Margaret C., wife of
Abednego Williams
Mar 16, 1884
Jun 4, 1948

Josephine Wilson
May 3, 1873
Nov 5, 1936

Elder J. G. Woods
Feb 1, 1823
Oct 19, 1895

Mary Ann, Daughter of
J. G. & S. J. Woods
Aug 11, 1857
Jun 30, 1880

Belle Feeney Woods
Oct 31, 1854
Aug 31, 1942

W. E. Woods
Died Mar 23, 1889
Age: 37y, 9m, 14d.

Daisie Woods
Died Jul 19, 1876
Age: 4y, 8m, 11d.

Lewis Colyar Woodard
Dec 7, 1897

&
Pearl Snowden Woodard
Nov 9, 1898
Dec 8, 1967

John R. Woodard
1855-1914
   & wife
Rosa Feeney Woodard
1857-1902

Horace Blakely Warren
1888-1947

Clinton Robertson Wallace
Jul 12, 1899
Jun 12, 1958

Jennie Robertson Wallace
Dec 31, 1870
Oct 20, 1962

Robert McKinney Wallace, Sr.
Jun 2, 1858
Feb 18, 1946

Nathaniel Odell Wallace
1860-1937

Lester G. Wagster
1889-1950

Mattie E. Wagster
1887-

Lucian J. Warren
1863-1920
   & wife
Lucy Kelso Warren
1867-1952

Mary Wade Pulley, wife of
N. O. Wallace
Died Mar 13, 1948
Age: (not given)

Emma B. Whitaker
Sep 2, 1882
Jul 1, 1965

McDaniel Whitaker
Died Sep 17, 1971
Age: 90 years
(Ralston FH)

Charles M. White
1890-1935

Lucy McDaniel Fullerton
Wilson
Apr 28, 1850
(no date)

William Columbus Ward
Mar 15, 1915
Dec 4, 1967
&
Anna Katherine Ward
Feb 11, 1918
Dec 4, 1967

Benjamin Columbus Ward
Jul 3, 1894
Jun 27, 1970
&
Annie Kate Ward
Sep 18, 1894

Tom J. Wiley
Oct 28, 1878
Jul 6, 1942

John White Wilson
Feb 24, 1882
May 18, 1964
&
Lucy Clark Wilson
Feb 16, 1882

Robert M. Woodard
1878-1938
&
Maude Rawls Woodard
1881-1956

Ernest Tillman Warden
Feb 26, 1888
Jul 30, 1952
&
Lillian Rowlett Warden
Aug 21, 1892

Raymond A. Williams
Aug 29, 1897

&
Alberta J. Williams
Sep 1, 1914

J. Benjamin Williams
1861-1937
&
Leona Sims Williams
1868-1941

Kate C. Wiley
Sep 16, 1881
Jan 16, 1944

Dr. J. M. Wyatt
Sep 24, 1848
Apr 11, 1932

Alice McDill, wife of
Dr. J. M. Wyatt
May 15, 1860
May 18, 1925

Hurley T. Wyatt
Jul 9, 1880
Jan 13, 1953

Lemuel D. Wilson
1836-1924

Edward L. Wilson
1859-1942
&
Ethel M. Wilson
1858-1916

Ethel Wilson
Jun 6, 1901
Feb 8, 1958

Dianne Wilson
1948

Dr. R. L. Whitaker
1890-1944

Marietta Whitaker
1863-1939

J. Iliff Warden
Jul 7, 1890

&
Mattie Lou J. Warden
Nov 5, 1897

Nancy Warden
May 31, 1893

Horace E. Warden
Nov 29, 1895

Mary Iva Warden
Feb 5, 1888
Jan 15, 1904

Nathan M. Warden
Apr 9, 1860
Mar 27, 1944

Cordelia Warden
Sep 13, 1860
Jan 12, 1940

Thomas Jefferson White,
Father of Willie Holland
Green
Aug 3, 1848
Apr 22, 1900

T. Wyman
1900

Cleo A., Daughter of
J. P. & A. Woodard
Apr 8, 1864
Feb 6, 1908
&
Mollie, Daughter of
J. P. & A. Woodard
Jul 9, 1860
May 30, 1911
&
Mrs. Annie, wife of
J. P. Woodard
Oct 5, 1831
Sep 12, 1891
&
J. P. Woodard
(Stone face down on ground)

R. H. Woodard
May 1, 1896

&
Ilar P. Woodard
Jan 2, 1901
Apr 9, 1969

FAYETTEVILLE QUADRANGLE

F. W. Wegold
Feb 17, 1852
Nov 2, 1914

Emma Esther Wegold
1860-1925

J. Frank Woodard
1874-1930

Mayme G. Woodard
1877-1953

J. Gray Woodard
1871-1954

Attie Mae Woodard
1871-1934

J. Matt West
Mar 31, 1837

Effie Park West
Sep 16, 1893
Nov 14, 1970

J. W. Warden
Jul 31, 1850
Jun 8, 1930
&
Kizzie E. Warden
Aug 9, 1857
Jul 25, 1930

James W. Warden
Feb 18, 1886
Oct 9, 1943

Annie Joyce Wright
1886-1936

Eldridge B. Wright
1878-1949

Mary Lou Wright Whorley
1879-1925

Jennie Belle Joyce Wright
Died May 2, 1968
Age: 78y, 6m, 3d.
(Higgins FH)

Joybelle Joyce Wright
1889-1968

John T. Wright
1887-

George E. Wright
1855-1938

Amanda Davis Wright
1859-1949

Albert, Son of
W. J. & Jennie Warden
Dec 3, 1900
Feb 14, 1909

William James Warden
Nov 1, 1861
May 7, 1948
&
Jennie Johnson Warden
Aug 23, 1866
Jun 18, 1953

Daniel Warden
1875-1932 (broken)

Edward Waddle
Aug 1, 1884
Jan 19, 1925

John R. Waddle
Apr 4, 1882
Mar 28, 1912

Frank M. Waddle
Apr 24, 1889
Jul 14, 1924

William Waddle
Jan 29, 1886
Jan 22, 1893

John S. Waddle
Dec 3, 1851
Sep 6, 1909

Mollie H. Waddle
Dec 10, 1855
May 28, 1928

John S. Waddle
Born in Mecklenburg Co., N.C.
Dec 17, 1810
Nov 28, 1885

Nancy Shanks, wife of
John S. Waddle
Born in Orange Co., N.C.
Sep 11, 1813
Jan 12, 1888

John R. Williams
Jan 20, 1881
May 27, 1961
&
Lula E. Williams
Jul 29, 1888
Sep 13, 1959

Kermit Winford
1908-1935

William Franklin Winford
Jan 23, 1907
Jul 29, 1932

Henry B. Warren
1872-1940

Emma Warren
1876-1947

Thomas Lavert Woods
1881-1946

Ellis Warren
1899-1965
&
Vera Warren
1901-

Joseph L. Wells
1896-1958
&
Alberta Riegger Wells
1884-1969

Harmon H. Wilson
1870-1943

W. C. Weiss
1943

Lula Myrtle Weiss
Mar 16, 1890
Apr 21, 1928

Clifford M. Welsh
May 6, 1910
Feb 26, 1963
&
Ada A. Welsh
Mar 10, 1911

Joe Hayes Whittaker
Jun 28, 1917
Nov 28, 1938

Annie H. Whittaker
Dec 21, 1891
Jan 31, 1948

Joe C. Whittaker
Aug 20, 1885
Jan 5, 1961

James R. Whittaker
Apr 5, 1927
Jul 16, 1957

Polly Ann Whittaker
Jun 3, 1954
Jul 16, 1967

James B. Wood
Jul 31, 1855
Jan 27, 1920
& wife
Dora Thomason Wood
Jul 28, 1864
(no date)

W. D. Wells
1868-1907

Jim M. Ward
Dec 10, 1889
Jan 14, 1957
&
Ena D. Ward
Feb 10, 1892

Albert A. Wright
Oct 16, 1844
Jul 28, 1907
"Freeman's Battery".
&
Anna McPhail Wright
Apr 4, 1850
May 1, 1902

John McPhail Wright
1874-1933

Mary Bagley, wife of
John McPhail Wright
1877-1960

Louis D. Wiley
Nov 27, 1827
Dec 16, 1884
"S.C.I. of C.S.A."

Laura Lizzie, Daughter
of L. B. & Josephine Wiley
Oct 31, 1877
Jan 5, 1882

Ovid T. Wiley
Sep 23, 1875
Mar 9, 1920

Jennie G. Wiley
Jan 21, 1879
Feb 18, 1959

Charles S. Wilson
Mar 11, 1868
Jun 29, 1924
&
Agnes Whitaker Wilson
Jan 11, 1869
(no date)

Clarence S. Wilson
1835-1904

Charles S. Wilson
Jul 29, 1835
Nov 28, 1904
& wife
Mary E. Lauderdale Wilson
Oct 18, 1840
Mar 8, 1890

Fannie, Daughter of
C. S. & M. E. Wilson
Jul 10, 1872
Aug 4, 1888

M. E. Wilson
1840-1896

Robert Wilson, Son of
W. K. & Beulah Woodard
Nov 17, 1889
Apr 28, 1892

William Clarence Woodard
Aug 3, 1899
Jun 4, 1900

FAYETTEVILLE QUADRANGLE

W. K. Woodard
Aug 12, 1859
Dec 12, 1924

Beulah Woodard
May 26, 1865
Jul 31, 1933

Andrew J. Wright
Mar 28, 1838
Aug 9, 1898
& wife
Sara J. Wright
Feb 6, 1831
Aug 19, 1897
& Daughter
Mary Sue Wright
Aug 23, 1861
Jul 4, 1888

Alice E., Daughter of
A. J. & S. J. Wright
Aug 16, 1859
Sep 18, 1874

James L. Woodard
Nov 16, 1843
Dec 5, 1910
&
Emma Bradshaw Woodard
Aug 17, 1847
May 23, 1914

Mary Ellen S. White
Jul 15, 1879
Feb 8, 1953

Wilkes Conway Webb
Mar 23, 1904
Jul 19, 1904

Moses Bonner Webb
Jun 27, 1868
Aug 16, 1914

Franklin H. Webb
1850-1918

Eugenia Lillie Webb
1854-1928

Charles M. Webb
1863-1945

Mattie L. Webb
1866-1933

Charles M. Webb
1885-1951

Minnie F. Webb
Dec 14, 1895
Dec 19, 1958

Ottie Isom Waid
May 17, 1894
Sep 21, 1933

Jim Waid
Oct 30, 1899

&
Ola Waid
Dec 25, 1904
Jul 20, 1964

Charles Waddle
Aug 20, 1848
May 5, 1918
& wife
Lou May Waddle
Oct 28, 1857
Oct 22, 1884
Married Oct 28, 1873

Charles Waddle
Dec 31, 1883
Jan 14, 1945

William Thomas Waddle
1874-1933
&
Annie Craug Waddle
1873-1927

Horace Thurston Whittaker
Jan 24, 1872
Nov 13, 1944

Bonnie McAdams Whittaker
Jul 18, 1882
Mar 17, 1949

Betty McAdams, Daughter of
H. T. & B. M. Whittaker
Aug 24, 1905
Sep 14, 1905

Ann Epps, widow of
Thomas B. Grantland
(no dayes, no marker)

Cornelia Grantland Whittaker
1832-1900

Robert Nelson Whittaker
1822-1903

Agnes Wyatt
1891-1969

Ben Burgess Wyatt
1852-1927
&
Minnie Harms Wyatt
1859-1928

John M. Warden
Aug 1, 1862
Jul 6, 1927

Gothie Ellis, wife of
John M. Warden
Nov 15, 1869
Oct 7, 1949

A. B. Woodard, Jr.
Aug 24, 1885
Sep 19, 1887

Andrew B. Woodard
Sep 8, 1851
May 25, 1907
&
Maude Lowery Woodard
Mar 29, 1856
May 24, 1930

Evelyn, Daughter of
M. W. & Ida Woodard
1894-1915

R. S. Woodard
Jan 16, 1821
May 14, 1877

Mary McKinney, Relict of
R. S. Woodard
Aug 14, 1824
Nov 10, 1897

Wells
"Our Baby Boys"
(no dates)

Mamie Neil Wells
Nov 4, 1895
Jul 27, 1904

Henry Williams
Died 1962
Age: (not given)

Agnes Little Williams
Died 1958
Age: (not given)

Mary White, Daughter of
W. N. & M. B. Wright
Died Nov 8, 1877
Age: 8 years.
&
Mamie Wright
(no dates)

Matthew R. Wright
1867-1943
(West FH)

William N. Wright
Jul 16, 1831
Jun 10, 1899
&
Mary Buchanan Wright
May 23, 1834
Nov 17, 1912

Annie E. Dinwiddie Waddell
Mar 16, 1901
May 19, 1963

Annie Myrtle Warren
Mar 11, 1870
Jan 25, 1872

W. N. Wright, Jr.
Sep 17, 1861
Oct 11, 1921
& wife
Blanche Bonner Wright
Mar 14, 1862
May 9, 1895

Andrew Buchanan Wright
Dec 12, 1857
Sep 12, 1939

Lila Redman, wife of
Andrew B. Wright
Jan 17, 1866
Jul 21, 1936

Katherine Moore, Daughter
of Andrew B. &
Lila R. Wright
Aug 8, 1900
Dec 6, 1906

James Holland Wright
Jul 12, 1859
Oct 31, 1950

Willa McCord, wife of
Holland Wright
1859-1932

Rev. Jas. H. Warren
Oct 31, 1849
Nov 27, 1890
&
Lucy Ransom Warren
May 7, 1863
Jan 19, 1900

Robert Paul, Son of
R. D. & M. G. Warren
Sep 27, 1879
Apr 7, 1892

May Gibson, wife of
R. D. Warren
Jun 6, 1858
Aug 25, 1889

Benedict Warren
(no dates)

James Eris Warren
1889-1940
"American Legion No. 42"

Fulton Morgan Wilson
Dec 2, 1876
Apr 14, 1948
&
Judith Bright Wilson
Oct 28, 1879
Feb 19, 1965

Kate Fulton Wilson
Mar 16, 1851
Jul 20, 1879

FAYETTEVILLE QUADRANGLE

Kate Fulton Wilson
Mar 16, 1851
Jul 20, 1879

Little Rogers Wilson
(no dates)

James Madison Wilson
1848-1899
C.S.A.

John L. Waggoner
Aug 23, 1872
Mar 20, 1920

Mrs. J. L. Waggoner
1872-1945

J. B. Wilson, Sr.
1834-1907

Mahulda Ann, wife of
J. B. Wilson
Jul 9, 1837
Aug 31, 1875

William O. Wilson
Sep 3, 1857
Mar 16, 1878

Mollie B., wife of
W. O. Wilson
Oct 18, 1858
Jan 20, 1884

M. W. Woodard
1846-1916
&
Ida L. Hatcher Woodard
1854-1921

Sallie Davis, Daughter of
M. W. & I. L. Woodard
Feb 24, 1892
Aug 15, 1892

Lucy Early, Daughter of
M. W. & I. L. Woodard
Aug 16, 1887
Nov 28, 1889

Joseph William Winsett
Tenn Cox Swain U.S.N.
Died Nov 18, 1937
Age: (not given)

America J. Whittaker
1850-1932

Anne R. Whittaker
1884-1962

Lizzie, Daughter of
W. H. & America J.
Whittaker
Apr 8, 1878
Jul 20, 1879

Infant Son of
Henry & Martha Wright
B&D Dec 7, 1944

Eulysse Perry Wilks
Oct 11, 1878
Dec 19, 1948
&
Flora Reynolds Wilkes
May 26, 1885
Aug 23, 1971
Age: 86y, 2m, 27d.

Union A. Wilson
May 2, 1813
Sep 26, 1875
&
Rebecca Wilson
Jan 17, 1826
Jul 5, 1904

Jennie Bell Whitaker
(no dates)

Susan, wife of
Capt. Benjamin Whitaker
Died Apr 23, 1895
Age: 87 years.

Hildrethe Wells
Apr 10, 1838
Mar 14, 1873

William H., Son of
Mr. & Mrs. Hildreth Wells
Died Mar 28, 1909
Age: 38y, 4m, 3d.

Andrew Jackson Waggoner, Jr.
1924

Andrew Jackson Waggoner
Jan 4, 1890
Mar 27, 1955
&
Mamie W. Waggoner
Oct 19, 1889
Apr 26, 1953

D. J. Whittington
Mar 31, 1818
Jun 11, 1880

W. B. Wood
Feb 4, 1857
Apr 11, 1910

Lennie Wood
1868-1964 (TM)

Infant Son of
Oliver & Ethel Waid
B&D Sep 6, 1909

Marion Waid
Died Oct 6, 1910
Age: 34y, 2m, 12d.

Virginia F. Waid
1924-1929

Susan Fannie Wade
Jun 1, 1864
Feb 26, 1920

Ethel Herron Wade
1887-1953

Oliver Waid
Nov 10, 1880
1953
&
F. M. Waid
Sep 19, 1845
1920
&
Martha R. Waid (nee Rives)
Jul 20, 1843
1912
&
Charles R. Waid
Jun 1, 1872
1954
&
Elijah M. Waid
Jul 24, 1876
Sep 6, 1910
&
W. D. Waid
Jul 6, 1867
(no date)
&
J. A. Waid
Sep 3, 1878
(no date)
&
Joel B. Waid
Mar 30, 1869
(no date)

Willie A. Lane Warden
Dec 5, 1862
Mar 18, 1904

Clyde Warden
Aug 14, 1905
May 23, 1906

Sarah Warden
Jan 15, 1908
Mar 13, 1908

Billy Winston Warden
Feb 10, 1918
Sep 14, 1918

J. H. C. Woods
Sep 26, 1844
Sep 21, 1909
C.S.A.

Nannie Woods
Apr 9, 1843
Aug 23, 1928

Green Edward Warden
Jan 11, 1865
May 31, 1919

Elma Lane Warden
Mar 5, 1877
Aug 26, 1953

I.(Ike) M. Williamson
1874-1940
(Higgins FH)

Sam T. Williamson
Dec 3, 1874
Feb 10, 1906

E. Clayton Wilson
Nov 30, 1892
Feb 16, 1954
&
Cathey M. Wilson
Jun 28, 1892
Feb 7, 1965

Leonard L. Warren
1911-

Ezella M. Warren
1916-

Lee A. Warren
1887-1961

Nora A. Warren
1891-

Harlan Widner
1886-1945

Mary Jean Widner
May 15, 1868
Jul 22, 1953

T. Everette White
Feb 11, 1883
(no date)
&
Lista Jean White
Sep 1, 1890
Apr 15, 1952

Otha Lee Woods
Sep 11, 1885
Oct 4, 1958
&
Mary Brazier Woods
Oct 30, 1893
Mar 22, 1925

Mrs. Mary Yarbrough
Oct 6, 1845
Oct 24, 1900

Billy Drain Young
1924-1926

Belle V. Young
Apr 1, 1859
Jun 22, 1930

B. V. Yates
Died Jun 29, 1894
Age: 24 years.
&
Hattie B. Yates
Oct 9, 1871
Jul 22, 1901

Infant of
Mr. & Mrs. H. Yearwood
1938

FAYETTEVILLE QUADRANGLE

Hoyle E. Yearwood
Alabama
Sgt base Hosp 69 WW I
Feb 5, 1896
Mar 1, 1963

Dr. A. L. Yearwood
1869-1945

Gail Irene Young
Jul 6, 1954
Aug 5, 1954

John William Young, Jr.
1883-1936

Sue Pitts Young
1883-1952

Virgil C. Yearwood
Mar 27, 1881
Jul 5, 1962

Ena Freeman Yearwood
Mar 25, 1888
Apr 4, 1951

William Lee Yearwood
Feb 23, 1910
Dec 29, 1950

Virgil Clarence Yearwood
Jul 18, 1912
May 23, 1914

Matilda Young
May 5, 1822
Mar 19, 1892

William Yates
(no dates)

Sara Jane Yates
1837-1921

* *

Note: Rose Hill cemetery was dedicated July 2, 1870

FLINTVILLE QUADRANGLE

McCLELLAN CEMETERY

LOCATION: One-half mile SW of Kelso on top of high hill, west of Corder Cross Roads road.

W. A. McClellan Oct 28, 1821 Nov 9, 1873 John G. McClellan Feb 8, 1814 Apr 14, 1864 Thomas McClellan Jul 26, 1851 Aug 25, 1868	Joseph D. McClellan Dec 19, 1827 Aug 26, 1898 & Mary A. McClellan Sep 5, 1830 Jul 18, 1906	Jacob Stonebraker Born in Fredrick Co., Maryland Jun 25, 1795 Dec 22, 1864 Mahala McCartney, wife of Jacob Stonebraker Jun 27, 1808 May 27, 1878	Martha Y., Consort of J. Hill Southworth Born May 28, 1837 in Fayetteville, Tenn. Died Feb 27, 1860 Age: 22y, 8m, 28d. Few unmarked graves.

* *

TAYLOR-GRAY CEMETERY

LOCATION: One-half mile south of Kelso in forks of Corder Cross Road and Brighton Road.

Mariah, wife of   Susan, wife of
James B. Taylor   L. M. Gray
Mar 4, 1805   Died Jun 9, 1869
Jul 24, 1856   Age: 50 years.

Mrs. Puss Dobbs Norman ***
(no dates)

*** Family Records of   About 50 unmarked graves.
James Norman.

* *

TAYLOR CEMETERY

LOCATION: Two miles SW of Kelso on Lucy Memorial-Pleasant Grove Church road.

Thomas Taylor
Born 1824
Died about 85 years of age.   Only one grave.

* *

CEMETERY

LOCATION: One and one-half miles SE of Kelso on east side of Brighton Road.

No markers remain.

* *

CEMETERY

LOCATION: One and one-fourth miles SE of Kelso and one-fourth mile NE of Brighton Road.

No markers remain.

* *

FLINTVILLE QUADRANGLE

SNODDY CEMETERY

LOCATION: One and one-half miles SE of Kelso and one-fourth mile south of Highway 64.

Infant Son of
John & Mary Snoddy
Mar 24, 1909
Mar 25, 1909

John A., Son of
John & Mary Snoddy
Feb 8, 1900
Jun 18, 1901

Others buried here with no markers with inscriptions are: Bensons, Jennings, Ples & Frances Crawford Snoddy, Martha White and David Snoddy **
1786-1858

Christopher Columbus
Snoddy **
1868-1900

This Cemetery was Old Rocky Point Church Community Graveyard.

Roy Fulton,* Son of
Mr. & Mrs. Clay Street
Jul 10, 1905

Maggie Snoddy *
Died Aug 13, 1906
Age: 25y, 7m, 19d.

Nancy Purvis,** wife of
David Snoddy
(no dates)

John Snoddy **
1824-Dec 26, 1903
   & wife
Mary Elizabeth Weddington
Snoddy **
Died Jan 26, 1918
Age: (not given)

William Benson *
Died Oct 30, 1893
Age: 80 years.

Mrs. C. C. Snoddy *
Died Sep 4, 1900
Age: 32 years.

Mrs. Jennie,* wife of
Thomas Leatherwood
Died Feb 18, 1916
Age: 30 years.

David A. Snoddy **
1860-1900

John Snoddy *
Died Dec 26, 1903
Age: 79y, 8m.

William Snoddy *
Died May 3, 1898
Age: 18 years.

Mrs. Mary Eliza Snoddy *
Died Jan 26, 1918
Age: 75y, 5m, 13d.

About 50 unmarked graves.

' ** Court & Family Records.

* *

FANNING CEMETERY

LOCATION: One and three-fourth miles SE of Kelso on south side of Brighton Road.

Mahaley Fanning
1800-Feb 14, 1856   Only one grave.

* *

GOLDEN CEMETERY

LOCATION: Two miles SE of Kelso and south side of Brighton Road.

2 Golden Children
(no dates)

* *

BENSON CEMETERY

LOCATION: Two and one-half miles SE of Kelso, top of Big-Cut.

W. D. Benson
Feb 19, 1837
Aug 16, 1897

Louisa J., wife of
W. D. Benson
Jan 10, 1840
Aug 3, 1908

Robert C., Son of
Mr. & Mrs. R. F. Benson
Jun 21, 1908
Jul 17, 1908

W. D. Benson
Oct 2, 1875
Sep 9, 1899

R. A. Benson
Died Jun 9, 1898
Age: 26 years.

Mary Alda Little
Jan 4, 1890
Dec 26, 1890

Infant Daughter of
N. O. & Eliza Little
B&D Jun 25, 1885

* *

FLINTVILLE QUADRANGLE

LEONARD CEMETERY

LOCATION: Two and one-fourth miles SE of Kelso, top of Big Cut.

This Graveyard has now disappeared but had several graves with a fence around it.

Local information states that this was the Old Jeff Leonard Graveyard and that he was a Soldier in C.S.A.

* *

PRYOR CEMETERY

LOCATION: Two and one-half miles SE of Kelso between Rail Road and Brighton Road.

Old Nathan Pryor *** Graveyard.

Pryors and Edwards families are buried here.***

*** Family Records.

Several fieldstones with no inscriptions.

* *

JEAN CEMETERY

LOCATION: Three miles SE of Kelso and west of Brighton Road.

No signs remain of this graveyard today. Many of Old Taylors, Jeans, Cashions and others are buried here.

Mrs. Done,* wife of Plenton Jean
Died Jul 2, 1896
Age: 40 years.

David Jean *
Died Jan 6, 1878
(born 1794 Stokes Co., N.C.
War Record of 1812)

Dr. Temple Taylor ***
1782-1852
&
Jane White Olliphant Taylor
(no dates)

Henry C. Taylor ***
1810-1875
&
Nancy Cashion Taylor
1815-1882

William Y. Taylor ***
(no dates)

Lucy Womack Taylor ***
1840-1900

H. P. Womack *
married Rintha Berry
in 1870
Died Mar 2, 1898
Age: 53 years.

* *

HARRIS-JEAN CEMETERY

LOCATION: Three miles SE of Kelso and west of Brighton Road.

Eliza A. Harris
Nov 19, 1858
Apr 30, 1890

Thomas J. Jean
Sep 16, 1861
Mar 23, 1900

W. L. Jean
May 28, 1864
Oct 9, 1899

Elizabeth D., Daughter of
W. N. & E. A. Harris
Jul 26, 1886
Dec 12, 1904

* *

HARRIS CEMETERY

LOCATION: Two and three-fourth miles SE of Kelso on east side of Brighton Road, bottom of hill.

Thomas H. Harris
Jun 7, 1872
Nov 3, 1915

Susan Tabitha Harris
Jul 1, 1871
Sep 20, 1909
Age: 38y, 2m, 28d.

Margaret M. Harris
Aug 17, 1874
Jul 26, 1896
Age: 21y, 11m, 9d.

Alice B. Harris
Apr 16, 1860
Aug 5, 1893
Age: 33y, 5m, 15d.

Other unmarked graves.

Julia A., wife of
David L. Harris
Jan 29, 1838
Mar 24, 1870

D. L. H. (David L. Harris)
(footstone)
Tombstone buried in ground.

Maud F.,* Daughter of
David L. & Sarah Harris
Died Jul 26, 1896
Age: 20 years.

Sarah J. Bray, wife of
David L. Harris
Nov 9, 1841
Jan 8, 1920

Alice,** wife of
Rev. B. C. Goodwin &
Daughter of
Mr. & Mrs. David L. Harris
Born Mar 16, 1860
Married Jan 1890
Died Aug 5, 1893

** Court Records

* *

FLINTVILLE QUADRANGLE

HUNTER CEMETERY

LOCATION: One and one half miles WSW of Smithland, one mile east of Big Cut curve of Highway 64.

"Father" and A. J. Hunter 1854-1892	"Daughter" Roxie Hunter 1885-1887	George P. Hunter and 1811-1887	Cincinnata Howard Hunter 1825-1885

* *

SMITH CEMETERY

LOCATION: West bank of Lincoln Lake at Smithland.

W. H. Smith Apr 16, 1831 Oct 14, 1912 Manda E., wife of W. H. Smith Mar 10, 1833 May 22, 1901 Sarah, wife of Hance Hunter Mar 5, 1771 Nov 5, 1855	Richard Smith Died Sep 1855 Age: 55y, 9m. & Elizabeth Smith Died Oct 1850 Age: 53y, 6m. William Faulkner Died Apr 10, 1870 Age: 73 years Many fieldstones, no inscriptions.	Ethel, wife of John Simmons Mar 1, 1883 Jun 5, 1909 & Donel Simmons Feb 13, 1909 Jun 6, 1909 Richard Smith Jan 8, 1827 Aug 23, 1911 (Marker on ground, footstone: M. E. S.)	Mrs. Eliza,* wife of Richard Smith Married Feb 25, 1847 Died May 20, 1898 Age: 67y, 9m, 2d. Wilson F. Smith * Died Dec 30, 1897 Age: 74y, 1m, 27d. Brother to Richard Smith. 10 old Rock Vaults, no inscriptions.

* *

TAYLOR CEMETERY

LOCATION: One fourth mile east of Smithland, "Judge Taylor Crawford Place."

James H. Taylor Apr 11, 1822 Oct 18, 1879 & Martha, wife of J. H. Taylor Apr 16, 1828 Apr 17, 1881 Bertie Elizabeth, Daughter of J. R. & M. A. Taylor Apr 24, 1878 Nov 8, 1879 Malinda Arnold, *** 1st wife of Jarred Simmons 1808-(no death date)	W. B. Faulkner Nov 22, 1835 May 7, 1901 Charlotte, wife of W. B. Faulkner Nov 24, 1832 Nov 24, 1877 Age: 45 years. William A., Son of W. B. & Charlotte Faulkner Oct 17, 1877 Aug 14, 1892 Jarred Simmons *** 1803-1884	W. C. Jennings Jun 20, 1805 Jul 21, 1893 Melissa, wife of W. C. Jennings Jun 18, 1810 Sep 26, 1884 James Knox, Son of W. Y. & Annie Taylor Aug 3, 1889 Sep 12, 1899	Dr. M. A. Keeling * Died Jul 3, 1901 Age: 51y, 6m, 13d. Jarred S. Taylor * Born Apr 29, 1847 Married Mar 9, 1871 Mollie McLaughlin Died Jul 12, 1898 Harriet A., * wife of W. B. Faulkner Mar 25, 1854 Sep 1, 1896

* *

GRAY CEMETERY

LOCATION: One mile NNE of Gum Springs.

J. D. Gray Apr 4, 1823 May 21, 1904 & wife Elizabeth Gray Mar 22, 1829 Sep 11, 1900	Brice P. Gray Jan 16, 1821 Aug 12, 1902 Octavis Gray 1868-1931	Terrell, Son of G. A. & H. B. Gattis Aug 14, 1897 Feb 24, 1909	Mr. W. R. Gattis * Died Apr 19, 1891 Age: 28 years. 2 unmarked graves.

* *

FLINTVILLE QUADRANGLE

BOSTICK CEMETERY

LOCATION: One mile south of Smithland, one and one-half miles north of State Fish Hatchery, on east side of road.

A. C. Bostick
Born Feb 21, 1836
Son of Berrie & Sophia
Bostick
Married Malinda Simmons
Feb 17, 1864
Married Titia Gattis
Feb 5, 1891
Died Jun 14, 1924

Malinda Simmons, Daughter of
Jarred & M. A. Simmons &
wife of A. C. Bostick
Born Dec 3, 1847
Married Feb 17, 1864
Died Jul 19, 1890

Omoa, Daughter of
A. C. & Malinda Bostick
May 27, 1890
Jul 29, 1890

L. O. Bostick
Aug 12, 1872
Apr 13, 1908
Killed by fallen tree,
Son of A. C. & Malinda
Bostick(Daughter of Jarred
Simmons).

A. C. J. F., Son of
A. C. & Malinda Bostick
Oct 30, 1880
Jul 29, 1883

Flora Bostick
Daughter of A. C. &
Malinda Bostick
Born Sep 24, 1883
Married A. B. Bostick
May 29, 1901
Died Mar 25, 1904

Clara Bostick Dickey
Sep 1, 1886
Jul 28, 1959

* *

GUM SPRINGS CEMETERY

Esther A. Gray
Jan 8, 1864
Jun 18, 1864

William H. Copeland
Sep 25, 1880
Dec 8, 1882?
&
Mary E. Copeland
Jun 30, 1889
Jul 7, 1889
Children of
J. M. & M. J. Copeland.

Infant of
H. C. Cown
(no dates, fieldstone)

Nancy J., Daughter of
J. H. & M. A. Hardin
Feb 18, 1871
Jul 22, 1873

Ebenezer F. McDaniel
Jun 11, 1830
May 19, 1834

A. C. Counts
1899-1899

H. Bray
(no dates, fieldstone)

T. L. Pickett
Sep 25, 1880

K. E. T.
Died Dec 5, 1919
Age: (not given)

John F. Luttrell
Jun 25, 1853
Mar 5, 1905

Elmer C. Luttrell
Dec 13, 1896
Jan 7, 1897

Rhoda Luttrell
Mar 25, 1885
Jun 4, 1914

Thornton Luttrell
Mar 3, 1822
Aug 12, 1902
Age: 80y, 5m, 9d.

Elizabeth Luttrell
Sep 18, 1832
Jan 10, 1907
Married Oct 29, 1846

William Orr
Jul 4, 1813
Nov 21, 1871
Age: 58y, 4m, 17d.

Terissa, wife of
William Orr
Mar 11, 1819
Feb 2, 1890
Age: 70y, 11m, 13d.

N. E. Cown
Feb 4, 1882

W. M. Gattis
Oct 23, 1826
Jun 18, 1894
&
M. J. Gattis
Sep 25, 1822
Oct 5, 1917

C. F. G.
(no dates, fieldstone)

Infant Daughter of
W. N. & Ada L. Gattis
B&D Dec 17, 1900

Walter Jackson, Son of
D. B. & M. J. Gattis
Apr 15, 1881
Jan 13, 1898

Felix Norman
1867-1941

Mary E. Norman
1845-1929

Althis L. Bennett
1878-1945
&
Etta C. Bennett
1888-1954

Horace Bennett
1910-1937

Ola May Bennett
Nov 3, 1908
Nov 12, 1908

Ambrose Bennett
Co H 1st Tenn Inf
C.S.A.

Virginia Hall, wife of
A. Bennett
Died Oct 30, 1912
Age: 72 years.

John T. Bennett
1881-1936

A. M. Bennett, Jr.
Sep 3, 1876
Apr 18, 1956
&
Maymie B. Bennett
Jul 6, 1893

Crick Brooks
(no dates)

Raybon Johnson
B&D 1937

John A. Johnson
1909-1941

Roy Warren
1947-1965

Dorothy L. Warren
Feb 12, 1936
Apr 19, 1936

Charley C. Bradley
Mar 17, 1885
Oct 20, 1952
&
Crickett A. Bradley
Dec 5, 1894

John William Arnold
Dec 2, 1867
Jan 23, 1939
&
Patsy Bennett Arnold
Apr 2, 1870
Aug 3, 1925

John L. Johnson
1879-1944
&
Ova Bennett Johnson
1887-1966

Joseph E. Johnson
Feb 24, 1915
Jan 13, 1956

J. M. Cagle
B&D Jul 8, 1947

George W. Cahela
1899-1944
&
M. Leola Cahela
1900-1949

R. L. Smith
1908-1947

Alta Mae Wilburn
1914-1958

FLINTVILLE QUADRANGLE

Jesse Edgar Pickett
Died Apr 3, 1969
Age: 90y, 3m, 6d.
&
Emerline Higby Pickett
Nov 30, 1890
Apr 28, 1963

Mrs. Lizzie Noe
1882-1938

Herbert A. Sisk
Aug 25, 1901
Feb 6, 1961

Jerry R. Lewis
Died Apr 30, 1964
Age: (not given)

William W. Johnson
1853-1932
&
Sarah J. Johnson
1865-1910
&
Rezina J. Johnson
1865-1901

Mattie C. Johnson
Aug 6, 1882
Jan 1, 1929

Guy Rexford Speck
Died Aug 8, 1962
Age: (not given)

Roy L. Hill
1915-1968
&
Mary E. Hill
1920-

Mrs. Elizabeth Eslick *
Died Feb 25, 1916
Age: 92y, 4m, 29d.

Mrs. Parthenia Barker *
Died Feb 13, 1898
Age: 73y, 4m, 6d.

Dock Simmons
(no dates)

Annie Simmons
Jan 25, 1883
May 3, 1949

John Simmons
1870-1958

Eddie Simmons
Mar 14, 1904
Jan 26, 1928

George W. Simmons
1872-1937
&
Mattie R. Simmons
1877-1956

Baby Griffin
Died Oct 1958
Age: (not given)

Mildred Carter
(no dates)

Jake Griffin
1878-1954

Synthia Griffin
(no dates)

M. W. Carter
Aug 20, 1844
May 14, 1919

Floyd Talbert Hill
Died May 29, 1967
Age: (not given)

Jessie Cambron, * Son of
Edgar Pickett
Died May 29, 1905
Age: 11 days.

Mrs. Nancy J. Brooks *
Died Jul 30, 1916
Age: 50y, 10m.

John Cuzzort
Feb 14, 1866
May 15, 1940

John R. Cuzzort
1866-1940
&
Susie Y. Cuzzort
1875-1952

John Pitcock
Oct 25, 1839
Mar 25, 1919
&
S. E. Pitcock
Nov 10, 1850
Apr 28, 1931

Elbert Pitcock
1902-1938

Roy Overton Pitcock, Jr.
1946-1964

Florence Payne
Jul 20, 1901
Mar 21, 1963

Herbert T. Russell
Jul 27, 1904
Dec 10, 1965

Infant of
H. T. & Monnie Russell
Died Sep 28, 1929
Age: (not given)

J. O.,* Son of
W. H. & Belle Barker
Died Jul 19, 1900
Age: 1y, 10m.

Miss Millie Cashion *
Died Jan 25, 1894
Age: 70 years.

Jacob Griffin *
Died May 2, 1906
Age: 97 years.
Married Lucy Pate in 1892

Mattie E. Tucker
1870-1955

Lesley Sherrell
1910-1949

Ann Sherrell
1871-1950

W. H. Sherrell
1879-1939

L. T. S. (Sherrell)
(no dates, fieldstone)

William Richard Bryant
Jan 10, 1879

&
Rachel Fanning Bryant
Aug 7, 1878
Mar 10, 1953

PFC James G. Hentz
1930-1951
Killed in 25th Div in
Korea, 35th Inf
Sep 15, 1930
Jul 6, 1951

Dorothy J. Hentz
1942-1947

Hiram William Metcalf
1854-1942
&
Mary Austell Shelton Metcalf
1869-1952

Mrs. Millie,* wife of
Jeff Leonard
Died Feb 22, 1898
Age: 59y, 11m, 23d.

Mrs. Lettie,* wife of
James Smith
Died Apr 14, 1916
Age: 50y, 8m, 6d.

Many unmarked graves.

* *

WARREN CEMETERY

LOCATION: At State Fish Hatchery, in Warren Hollow.

James H. Warren
May 15, 1844
Jun 27, 1897
&
Eliza H. Warren
Mar 11, 1850
Sep 14, 1900

Susie Warren
Sep 17, 1879
Jan 30, 1897

Infant * of Mr. & Mrs.
J. H. Warren, died Aug 13,
1907, One of twins, Age 1 y.

Mary, wife of
Henry Warren
1821-Jan 3, 1892

Henry Warren *
Died Jul 22, 1895
Age: 81y, 5m, 20d
Married Mary Bright
Oct 8, 1840
"Founder of Oregon Cotton
Factory."

John, Son of
Henry & Mary Warren
Feb 23, 1852
Feb 26, 1852

Emma, Daughter of
Henry & Mary Warren
Sep 16, 1853
Nov 29, 1861

Mrs. Martha Matthew Warren *
Died Dec 23, 1899
Age: 52 years.

James E. Warren *
Died Feb 1, 1909
Age: 25 years
Brother to Henry Warren
of Texas.

Charlie Warren *
Died Dec 23, 1899
Age: 52 years
Married Martha L. Matthews
Dec 3, 1863

* *

FLINTVILLE QUADRANGLE

CEMETERY

LOCATION: At Flintville, back of Cumberland Presbyterian Church.

3 or 4 graves, no markers.

* *

FLINTVILLE CEMETERY

Thomas Abner Luttrell
Sep 21, 1850
Jun 1, 1934

Elizabeth B. Luttrell
May 2, 1859
Apr 6, 1916

Unevista Luttrell
B&D Aug 28, 1875
&
Infant Son
B&D Sep 13, 1876
Children of
T. A. & E. B. Luttrell

Inda U., Daughter of
T. A. & E. B. Luttrell
Jan 7, 1883
Oct 3, 1884

Cecil, Son of
T. A. & E. B. Luttrell
May 6, 1888
Sep 28, 1893

Infant Daughter of
T. A. & E. B. Luttrell
B&D Apr 27, 1902

Wilsie P., Son of
J. W. & Rebecca Cunningham
Feb 22, 1895
Sep 29, 1918
First Class Private
Co E 119 Inftry 30 Div
AEF. "His body sleeps in France."

Willie M. Cunningham
Tennessee
Pfc Co E 119 Inf WW I PH
Feb 22, 1895
Mar 23, 1960

James W. Cunningham
Aug 6, 1879
Nov 22, 1908

Maggie May, Daughter of
J. W. & Rebecca Cunningham
Oct 31, 1884
Aug 31, 1893

John W. Cunningham
Apr 15, 1855
Nov 10, 1934

Rebecca Land, wife of
J. W. Cunningham
Jun 6, 1857
Aug 11, 1934

Nancy R. Howell, wife of
Perry Land
Died Oct 21, 1868
Age: 40 years.

Joel Parks, Son of
J. W. & E. J. Cooper
Sep 29, 1876
Nov 10, 1876

Joel Cunningham
Aug 18, 1829
Oct 24, 1873

Susan E. Cunningham
Apr 8, 1836
Apr 11, 1904

Estelle E., Daughter of
J. M. & S. E. Harmening
Jun 9, 1871
Jun 6, 1874

James Manley Harmening
Dec 4, 1885
(no date)
&
Susan Estelle Harmening
May 11, 1889
Oct 2, 1961

J. R. Cole
Sep 2, 1853
Nov 19, 1919

Ruth G. Allen
Jun 22, 1928
May 31, 1929

George W. Young
1875-1963
(Gallant FH)

Laura B. Young, Daughter of
J. D. & S. A. Bryant
May 25, 1889
Apr 19, 1899

Gordan Lipscomb, Son of
Thomas M. & Ella Harrell
Died Aug 16, 1885
Age: 4m, 22d.

Earl C. Gray
May 24, 1890
Aug 26, 1918

Lulen S. Gray
Dec 1, 1891
Oct 30, 1919

Saphronia C. Mann
Aug 17, 1845
Aug 13, 1930

Thomas P. Shirey
Apr 8, 1859
Oct 6, 1947
&
Beulah Mann Shirey
Jul 31, 1867
Nov 9, 1953

Mary N., Daughter of
Drury M. & Martha Mims
Nov 22, 1866
Apr 4, 1933

Herbert V., Son of
Mary Mims
Feb 24, 1890
Feb 7, 1907

Letitia, Daughter of
D. M. & M. M. Mims
Feb 25, 1865
Apr 30, 1894

Drury M. Mims
Mar 10, 1835
Apr 29, 1903
&
Martha M. Mims
May 21, 1837
Jan 1, 1910

William Wisener
Oct 11, 1848
Feb 11, 1886

Nancy N. Wisener
Jul 26, 1812
Aug 18, 1890

Robert E. Noles
Apr 19, 1881
Aug 26, 1941
&
Kate W. Noles
May 1, 1876
Oct 15, 1957

Robert J., Son of
R. E. & Kate Noles
Aug 14, 1913
Jan 14, 1919

William C. Sims
Mar 1, 1879
Jul 19, 1966

Mildred M. Sims
Oct 28, 1902
Nov 17, 1948

Arthur R. Sims
Jun 24, 1900
Aug 10, 1920

Sallie Corder Bryant
Mar 31, 1874
Dec 24, 1951

Ida Bell Corder
Jun 23, 1871
May 27, 1955

John A. Corder
Oct 20, 1841
May 18, 1901

Hannah E. Corder
Apr 31, 1847
Feb 5, 1930

Dr. Jas. A. Collett
Dec 12, 1839
Mar 25, 1877

Mary B., wife of
Roy Ferguson
Sep 11, 1896
Nov 17, 1915

John M. Franklin
Jan 9, 1849
Jan 12, 1917
&
Mary H. Franklin
Jan 22, 1858
Apr 14, 1935

R. P. (Patterson)
(footstone)

E. P. (Patterson)
(footstone)

Rebecca A. Lewis, wife of
S. I. Patterson
Dec 2, 1847
Oct 26, 1906

FLINTVILLE QUADRANGLE

Robert A., Son of
J. C. & S. N. M. Patterson
Oct 4, 1885
Sep 14, 1886

Franklin P. Copeland
Jun 12, 1856
Mar 5, 1940
&
M. Ella Copeland
Sep 24, 1862
Mar 18, 1938

Mrs. R. N. O'Neal
1868-1930

Andy Stiles
Dec 28, 1890
Aug   1897

William G. Knowles
(dates broken away)

Francis E. Knowles
Sep 22, 1832
Mar 5, 1908

John E. Knowles
Dec 28, 1863
Dec 11, 1910

Lula B. Bryson
Jun 1867
Apr 1938

Louisa Ward
Died Feb 17, 1918
Age: (not given)

H. L. Brown
Nov 27, 1858
Mar 20, 1913

J. N. Brown

    & wife
Willie Brown
Jul 29, 1884
Aug 20, 1920

Dewitt, Son of
J. C. & L. E. Rich
Dec 13, 1896
Jul 24, 1917

J. W. Henson
Oct 22, 1861
Apr 18, 1917

Adie E. Eslick
Oct 12, 1880
May 18, 1944
&
Eunice C. Eslick
Apr 14, 1897

Alta Pauline Franklin
May 27, 1899
May 19, 1901

Richard Marr
Mar 9, 1839
Sep 13, 1905

Mary Marr
Mar 5, 1850
Jun 4, 1933

Infant Son of
Mr. & Mrs. W. J. Marr
(no dates)

Jack Farrar
Oct 22, 1924
Aug 5, 1935

Elvie, Son of
W. S. & Susie Harbin
Nov 3, 1902
Sep 30, 1919

Mattie Kathleen, Daughter of
J. W. & Emma Eslick
Jan 28, 1912
Mar 6, 1912

Eugene Bates
1920-1921

E. W. Bates
1922-1927

Margie Blankenship
Mar 7, 1924
Mar 11, 1927

J. C. Holt
Jan 7, 1928
Apr 11, 1938

Martha Mitchell Graham
1875-1953

James Mitchell
Jul 29, 1871
Sep 25, 1905

Sanford, Son of
James & Ellis Mitchell
Aug 18, 1897
Dec 20, 1912

Ellen Deneva George Cowan
Oct 27, 1883
Oct 26, 1915

J. M. M. George
Jan 22, 1848
Jun 24, 1899
&
Mary E. George
Oct 19, 1853
Jan 23, 1926

Henry A. Bryant
May 4, 1861
Feb 19, 1899

William J. Bryant
Dec 14, 1836
Jan 31, 1907

A. J. Summers
Dec 7, 1829
Sep 15, 1902

Elizabeth S., wife of
A. J. Summers
Apr 30, 1833
Feb 27, 1901
Age: 67y, 9m, 27d.

Alice C. Noe
1872-1899

Lee R. Noe
1862-1927

Lonie Noe
1870-1911

Mary J., wife of
Rev. H. S. Blair
Jan 3, 1833
Nov 13, 1909

Columbus C., Son of
Rev. H. S. & Mary J. Blair
Feb 2, 1882
Jan 27, 1904

Clarence Theodore Mullikin
Feb 28, 1906
Nov 3, 1905

Thomas A. Mullikin
Tennessee
Sgt 17 Inf
Jun 16, 1909

James Robert Mason
Oct 18, 1879
Apr 1, 1939
&
Maymie R. Mason
Aug 21, 1882
Jan   1970

Robert Morris Mason
B&D Apr 11, 1940

Andrew G. Yost
Nov 4, 1852
Sep 22, 1929
&
Lillie B. Yost
Aug 9, 1860
Dec 25, 1915

Oscar Barcley Counts
Apr 5, 1875
Aug 31, 1917
&
Ellie Shrader Counts
Oct 22, 1882
Jun 6, 1957

C. Tipton Layman
1852-1926
&
Sarah E. Layman
1856-1904

George W. Counts
Mar 13, 1848
Sep 10, 1903

Eliza A. Counts
Mar 10, 1852
Oct 31, 1921

Evelyn Mildred Hudson
Oct 28, 1923
Sep 18, 1960

Alford F. Hudson
Jun 19, 1868
Nov 13, 1894
&
Josie C. Hudson
Mar 9, 1874
Jul 23, 1960

A. J. Malone
Oct 21, 1837
Nov 14, 1897

N. A. M. (Malone)
(no dates, fieldstone)

Thomas G. Hester
May 7, 1842
Feb 22, 1906
&
Fannie E. Hester
Sep 15, 1843
Apr 25, 1904

E. J. Cambron
Oct 8, 1841
Jan 16, 1914
&
Martha H. Usry Cambron
Dec 16, 1845
Mar 4, 1918

E. L. Kilpatrick
1877-1946

Ellen Brooks Kilpatrick
(no dates)

Charles Kelley
Apr 24, 1812
Feb 3, 1900

Lucy E., wife of
Charles Kelley
Sep 14, 1817
Mar 23, 1895

Robert E., Son of
H. A. & L. M. Bryant
May 23, 1895
Jun 9, 1896

Ada Bell, wife of
W. A. Taylor
Died Jan 13, 1908
Age: 27 years.

FLINTVILLE QUADRANGLE

J. M. Cambron
Dec 12, 1868
Aug 3, 1918
&
Cora M. Cambron
May 26, 1869
Jun 5, 1948

Nattie Ruth, Daughter of
J. M. & Cora M. Cambron
Oct 1, 1889
Oct 5, 1889

Erroll J., Son of
E. J. & Lou Eva Cambron
Apr 4, 1919
Apr 6, 1919

F. Capley
Mar 15, 1842
Apr 11, 1912

Sarah E. Capley
Jan 22, 1857
Jul 14, 1921

J. U. Capley
Jul 26, 1875
Feb 21, 1913

O. G. Capley
Jan 16, 1885
Jan 12, 1918

Rufus W. Stiles
Jan 15, 1861
Jul 5, 1929
&
Mattie Knoles Stiles
Apr 7, 1859
Sep 23, 1915

H. Arthur Durham
Tennessee
Pvt 14 U.S. Volunteer Inf
Feb 2, 1875
Oct 17, 1944
&
M. Ola Durham
Oct 8, 1885
Jun 19, 1967

E. M. Luttrell
Nov 13, 1877
Mar 6, 1925

Fannie, wife of
E. M. Luttrell
Jan 15, 1879
Aug 26, 1941

Infant Son of
E. M. & Fannie Luttrell
B&D Sep 28, 1904

J. D. Bryant
Oct 19, 1839
Apr 30, 1926

Mrs. Susan A., wife of
J. D. Bryant
Oct 27, 1844
Apr 12, 1909

Daisey D. Honey, Daughter of
J. D. & S. A. Bryant
May 21, 1882
Sep 18, 1918

Jimmie Cashion Bryant
Oct 3, 1884
Oct 11, 1965
&
Walter Clark Bryant
May 21, 1878
Apr 12, 1964

Charlie Thomas Bryant
Jan 26, 1870
Feb 9, 1937

James M. Stewart
Aug 8, 1851
Mar 22, 1916

Sarah J., wife of
James M. Stewart
Aug 17, 1850
Jun 18, 1913

Elizabeth Stewart
Dec 12, 1827
Dec 16, 1901

George M. Stewart
Apr 3, 1882
Feb 17, 1941
&
Joseph E. Stewart
Apr 28, 1885
Feb 10, 1940

James Reed Stewart
1906-1954
&
Eva Leona Stewart
1903-

Earnest Jessie, Infant of
J. R. & V. E. Stewart
Sep 26, 1904
Jan 4, 1905

Jesse J. Stewart
Jun 10, 1875
May 3, 1949
&
Eva J. Stewart
Feb 12, 1874
Feb 4, 1944

Ollie J., wife of
C. L. Swindell & Daughter of
Mr. & Mrs. Henry Shrader
Died Sep 16, 1911
Age: 22 years.

Frank E., Son of
H. & M. J. Shrader
Jan 25, 1877
Jan 1, 1899

Henry Shrader
Oct 8, 1851
Was killed by a fall of
a tree, May 23, 1894

Jane Whitt
1858-1936

Ulysis B., Son of
H. & M. J. Shrader
Mar 11, 1891
Jul 21, 1900

Marshall W., Son of
H. & M. J. Shrader
Jun 3, 1879
Aug 4, 1900

G. T. Counts
Apr 10, 1848
Jun 15, 1911

Pluma B. Goodman, wife of
J. J. Smith
Mar 12, 1893
Jul 27, 1916

Simon Goodman
Died Jun 13, 1903
Age: about 55 years.

Maggie I. Goodman
Jan 5, 1881
Jul 22, 1893

William A. Bruce
Nov 11, 1891
Dec 12, 1956

Ora Eliza Ann Bruce
1893-1936

Mary Evelyn Bruce
Dec 10, 1917
Feb 25, 1943

J. Walter Bruce
1878-1967
&
Gertrude B. Bruce
1876-1932

Carrie Bruce Currey
1899-1924

George W. Bruce
1858-1924
&
Frances Anne Bruce
1857-1933

Jessie M. Williamson
Sep 25, 1906
Sep 2, 1920

Walter J. Dan Sheppard
1872-1965
(Gallant FH)

Lizzie T. Sheppard
1879-1953
(Wilson FH)

Mattie E., wife of
W. J. Shepard
Dec 6, 1885
Feb 20, 1911

Clyde N. Shepard
Mar 4, 1910
Jul 13, 1910

J. J. Shepard
Jan 24, 1868
Apr 2, 1926

Martha E. Shepard
Sep 27, 1865
Jul 26, 1939

William Shepard
Mar 9, 1812
Jan 8, 1897

Elizabeth A. B., wife of
William Shepard
Apr 30, 1833
Apr 5, 1884

Leiler B., wife of
R. L. Shepard
Aug 31, 1864
Mar 20, 1893

Leiler, Daughter of
R. L. & L. B. Shepard
Jun 16, 1892
Sep 13, 1893

Ruby, Daughter of
R. L. & A. G. Shepard
Jan 10, 1900
Sep 18, 1907

W. D. Hawkins
Jul 1, 1846
Sep 13, 1907

Laura A. Hawkins
Jun 7, 1855
Aug 6, 1907

Willie, Son of
W. D. & Laura Hawkins
Dec 2, 1884
Jan 25, 1890

Riley Simmons
May 6, 1887
Sep 4, 1926
&
Belle Cox Simmons
Oct 15, 1889
(no date)

FLINTVILLE QUADRANGLE

Mr. Jid Simmons
Died 1945
Age: (not given)
(Gallant FH)

Mrs. Alice Simmons
Died 1923
Age: (not given)
(Gallant FH)

Kate Simmons
1913-1929

Ella Simmons
1876-1949
(Raby FH)

Mary E. George
1860-1949
(Raby FH)

Hubbert Marrs
May 28, 1868
Dec 2, 1942

Hannah Deaily
Died Feb 15, 1927
Age: 99 years.

Bettie Ann, wife of
John Fowler
Mar 8, 1870
Dec 5, 1936

Z. B. Langford
1861-1927

Rose Anna B. Langford
Nov 11, 1864
Dec 5, 1944

Cornelia Frances Faulkner
1870-1963

Infant of
R. P. & Lorena Faulkner
B&D Sep 25, 1928

Mack Smith
1855-1929

Cal Collins
1888-19
&
Ola E. Collins
1897-1946

Bascom Holmes
Dec 1, 1913
Mar 2, 1930
"Killed in car wreck".

Arthur A. Holmes
1877-1952
&
Ada C. Holmes
1892-1966

Troy Halcomb
1914-1948

Walter B. Holmes
1879-1963
&
Toxanna J. Holmes
1881-1969

Lorena Frances Wright
Died Mar 6, 1969
Age: 88 years.
(Gallant FH)

Dorothy Rooks
1850-1929

Francis Y. Taylor
1891-1934
&
Minnie A. Taylor
1890-1948

Frank Odem
1905-1951

William L. McDonald
May 16, 1875
Jul 12, 1948
&
Edna Jean McDonald
Nov 27, 1889
Jan 24, 1964

Essie Moorehead
1902-1936

Wiley S. Pitts
1863-1930
& wife
Addie E. McNatt Pitts
1868-1948

William A. Stiles
Oct 29, 1882
Jul 18, 1949
&
Clemmie A. Stiles
Jan 11, 1885
Nov 16, 1968

Ethel Counts Bingham
1907-1926

Lige M. Counts
Dec 10, 1912
Sep 1, 1959
&
Avis S. Counts
Jan 19, 1921

Rev. J. D. Counts
1877-1943
&
Bettie B. Counts
1880-1949

Horace M. Counts
1901-1962
&
Mammie C. Counts
1906-

Clarice Halcomb Whitfield
1920-1968

Rev. F. M. Copeland
1859-1945
&
Susan S. Copeland
1862-1942

Jesse F. Copeland
1900-1965
&
Jessie M. Copeland
1901-

John M. Gammon
Jan 12, 1901

&
Lela E. Gammon
Jul 31, 1895

Daniel Walter Pruett
Sep 16, 1889
Dec 7, 1949
&
Avierilla Frances Pruett
Dec 3, 1891
1970

Linda M. Pruett
Nov 22, 1937
Nov 28, 1937

James C. Hudgins
Mar 24, 1883
Jul 16, 1958
&
Myrtle C. Hudgins
Oct 9, 1888
Sep 17, 1942

Shelby Tom Williamson
Jan 20, 1933
Apr 5, 1956

Jennie E. Braden
Oct 14, 1878
Dec 23, 1956

Henry C. Crawford
Dec 25, 1897
Nov 29, 1953
&
Vertna M. Crawford
Mar 31, 1902
Mar 29, 1990

Homer W. Luttrell
Feb 19, 1894
Jan 2, 1981
&
Margaret E. Luttrell
Oct 30, 1899

Harold Wayne Colbert
Sep 12, 1934
Jan 22, 1955

Nellie Sue Brown
Dec 7, 1935
Dec 12, 1935

Rufus A. Armstrong
1893-1968
&
Bessie B. Armstrong
1906-

George Armstrong
Feb 22, 1929
Jul 25, 1930

Ruby W. Simmons
1899-

James David Luttrell
Jan 4, 1932
Jan 7, 1932
&
Jaunita Luttrell
Jan 4, 1932
Jan 4, 1932
&
Geneva Luttrell
B&D Jan 4, 1932

Larry O. Luttrell
Oct 7, 1914

Roy R. Luttrell
1880-1959
&
Hallie A. Luttrell
1895-

Dewey Wayne Luttrell
B&D Feb 9, 1950

Anthony Luttrell
(no dates, TM)

Howard E. Benson
Italy
Tec 5 473 Inf WW II
Aug 8, 1921
Apr 21, 1945

Jesse B. Benson
1895-1966
(Moore-Cortner FH)

Doshie Benson
1895-1942

Lytle B. Grizzell
1929-1935

Sarah Ann, wife of
J. M. Hatley
Apr 2, 1862
Apr 19, 1938

Thomas Holt
Tennessee
Pfc U. S. Army
Jul 7, 1904
May 3, 1961

FLINTVILLE QUADRANGLE

William I. Reed
Nov 18, 1867
Aug 29, 1938
&
Anah M. V. Reed
Sep 8, 1870
Sep 14, 1944

Harvey H. Reed
Nov 16, 1902
Oct 28, 1929

Infant of
H. H. & E. B. Reed
(no dates)

Infant Daughter of
Mr. & Mrs. John E. Smith
B&D Jun 16, 1927

John E. Smith
Aug 27, 1892
Nov 5, 1957
&
Lola H. Smith
Jul 13, 1897
Feb 4, 1960

Thomas Aubrey Smith
Killed on Cebu Island in
the Phillipines
Apr 5, 1945
While in the Service of
his Country, Holder of the
Bronze Star Metal
Tennessee
Staff Agt 182 Inf WW II
Born May 29, 1923

Huey O. Cook
Oct 25, 1916
Aug 25, 1935

Robert D. Cook
May 6, 1896
Oct 23, 1965
&
Emma Wooten Cook
Oct 22, 1898
Jun 16, 1938

Jesse B. Bryant
1900-1959
&
Battie B. Bryant
1911-

Charles Bryant
B&D May 4, 1941

Hosea L. Harris
Apr 20, 1889
Sep 6, 1928
&
Alda May Norman Harris
Aug 28, 1892

William N. Harris
Mar 10, 1858
Jun 26, 1939

Mary Harris
1864-1940

Joe Lee Harris
Jun   1883
Mar 27, 1921

Nancy W. Bradford
1898-1926
(TM)

Linda K. Simmons
B&D Jun 15, 1943
(TM)

W. Lafayette Whitworth
Tennessee
Cpl 15 MC Bn 5 Div
Died Jan 1, 1944
Age: (not given
Born 1894
&
Pearl P. Whitworth
1905-

James S(Steve) Caldwell
Nov 6, 1954
Aug 18, 1959

Rose Marie Caldwell
B&D Sep 19, 1951

P. D. Warren
1887-(no date)
&
Ida B. Warren
1888-1945

Thomas Newt Copeland
Tennessee
Pvt Field Arty
Born 1880
Died Apr 3, 1938

Edward Harrold, Son of
Mr. & Mrs. J. H. Raines
Sep 13, 1927
Oct 11, 1928

J. A. Fisher
1903-1948

A. S. W. Benson
1858-1943

Lucy Benson
1860-1934

John W. Benson
Tennessee
Pvt 1 Cl 325 Inf 82 Div
Died Jun 7, 1935

William D. Benson
1884-1959
&
O. Beatrice Benson
1895-

Mrs. L. H. Anderson
1880-1932

Doyle L. Shubert
Jun 22, 1928
Jul 29, 1929
&
Robert G. Shubert
Jan 21, 1920
Jul 18, 1945
"Killed in Action in
WW II."

J. R. Simmons
1934-1935

Robert G. Winn
Aug 16, 1868
Dec 8, 1942
&
Emma C. Winn
May 4, 1873
Jul 15, 1952

Dennis L. Barker
Oct 2, 1933
Sep 13, 1934

Helen E. Barker
Jul 4, 1931
Aug 4, 1932

Robert L. Ray
Dec 9, 1894
May 18, 1969
&
Louise Ray
Jun 26, 1906

Vallie Evans
1878-1964

Alex Evans
1876-1937

George H. Counts, Sr.
Feb 1, 1880
Oct 29, 1965
&
Florence L. Counts
Mar 6, 1882
Mar 28, 1963

Jimmie C. Simmons
Tennessee
A2C U. S. Air Force
May 23, 1942
Jul 9, 1966

Horace Lee Simmons
Died Nov 3, 1968
Age: 64 years.
(Ralston FH)

Mrs. H. L. Simmons
1905-1947

Kenneth Edward Wells
Sep 19, 1945
Mar 20, 1946

W. W. Wells
Jan 24, 1897

&
Avie D. Wells
May 1, 1897
Feb 8, 1956

Luther R. Wells
1886-1946
&
Lula E. Wells
1890-1947

George T. Foster
1895-1961
&
Alma G. Foster
1895-19

Roy Wells
Died Apr 27, 1970
Age: 57 or 58 years.

John L. Pruett
Oct 31, 1881
Sep 11, 1938
&
Mary L. Pruett
Feb 25, 1882
Apr 12, 1958

Ethridge L. Pruett
Mar 25, 1907
Jul 19, 1938

Arthur Roper
Oct 15, 1885
Mar 26, 1954
&
Sarah Roper
Oct 4, 1883
Dec 26, 1938

Joel F. Cranford
Mar 20, 1890

&
Claudie P. Cranford
Feb 15, 1895
Aug 9, 1969

Beauman F. Cranford
Aug 19, 1920
Jun 15, 1937

Jewet J. Cranford
Cox U. S. N.
Killed in Action, buried
at sea.
Born Aug 31, 1924
Died Jan 21, 1945

Britton F. Tucker
Oct 14, 1871
Mar 21, 1961
&
Kittie F. Tucker
Mar 12, 1880
Jul 23, 1958

FLINTVILLE QUADRANGLE

Beatrice Gay Brown
1915-1938

Beulah Brown
1892-1963

Jesse Harvey Brown
1932-1950

L. C. Brown
1887-1949
(Raby FH)

Wilson Holman Copeland
1876-1938
&
Sallie Spencer Copeland
1885-1969

Maude M., wife of
Charlie Fowler
Jan 19, 1897
Jan 27, 1936

John L. Smith
Feb 12, 1879
Dec 16, 1936
&
Nora M. Smith
Jun 1, 1895
Nov 14, 1931

Theron O. G. Allen
Tennessee
Pvt 1 Cl 29 Inf 17 Div
Born 1905
Died Nov 22, 1941

John M. Allen
May 12, 1862
Sep 2, 1939
&
Mary Alma Allen
1886-1931

Mrs. John Snow
1906-1929

Hugh F. Spencer
1832-1945
&
Ella Snow Spencer
1888-1947

H. H. Snow
May 25, 1859
Jul 30, 1927
&
Emma E. Copeland
Feb 5, 1867
Jan 1, 1948

Thurston Myrick
1902-1959
&
Lyda Ruth Myrick
1897-(1982)

Drewy Tribble Myrick
Sep 26, 1871
(no date)
&
Mary Ann Myrick
Feb 28, 1873
Apr 27, 1935

John M. Fuller
1875-1931

Mary E. "Mollie" Fuller
1870-1951

Wylie A. Sims
1869-1934
&
Josie Morgan Sims
1871-1957

Herbert L. Shrader
Dec 5, 1901
Dec 27, 1968
&
Gladys S. Shrader
Dec 23, 1909

Jr. R. Sims
1919-1946

J. T. "Jep" Sims
1861-1931
&
Anna L. Sims
1878-1945

Artie Eugene, Infant of
J. T. & Anna Sims
Dec 14, 1919
Mar 28, 1924

Mary J., Infant of
J. C. & L. V. Sims
Feb 25, 1923
Feb 13, 1924

L. Hugh Gilliam
1869-1924

Ann Nix Gilliam
1889-1948

Rettie McLaughlin, wife of
L. P. Gilliam
1846-1934

William P. Gilliam
1868-1945

Margaret McLaughlin
1862-1936

W. H. Barker
1871-1957
&
Ida Belle Barker
1876-1953

John C. Evans
Jul 11, 1869
Apr 28, 1938
&
Sallie F. Evans
Jul 21, 1872
Apr 21, 1953

May Groover Ennies
Jul 13, 1905
Apr 7, 1936

James O. Teal
Oct 11, 1892
Nov 7, 1936

Melba Ruth Pursley Flynn
1934-1960

Nancy Ann Lee
1948-1950
(Wilson FH)

J. P. Lee
Jan 1, 1904
May 10, 1966
&
Ola Mae Lee
Jul 29, 1909

I. B., wife of
T. C. Lee
Jan 20, 1919
Jul 24, 1938

Jackie Lou Lee
Aug 10, 1942
Sep 27, 1942

Joe D. Carlisle
1881-1952
&
Sallie W. Carlisle
1887-1952

Jerry Carlisle
Oct 25, 1943
Jan 1, 1944

Joe E. Carlisle
Oct 2, 1922
Mar 28, 1934

William Henry Harmening
1889-1954
&
Nora Myrick Harmening
1897-1947

Jim W. Ferguson
1900-1949

Mattie Gibson Watson
Mar 25, 1874
Jul 30, 1947

James Bailey Hester
1863-1941

Hoyt Nathaniel Frasier
Alabama
BM1 U. S. N. R. WW II
Aug 20, 1910
May 27, 1968
&
Louise Weir Frasier
Feb 25, 1914

Married Nov 12, 1932

William Hugh Weir
Feb 25, 1872
Apr 25, 1940
&
Ida Haynie Weir
Feb 18, 1888

B. O. Taylor
1881-1944
&
Mary C. Taylor
1875-1940

John J. Ferguson
1938-1939

John P. Bryant
1867-(no date)
&
Jennie Bryant
1866-1940

D. W. Currey
Mar 26, 1941
Mar 28, 1941

Henry Marr
1874-(no date)
&
Kate Marr
1878-1952

Margaret Ann Marr
Mar 6, 1957
Jun 3, 1961

Joseph W. Glassco
1900-1958

Joe Wheeler Glassco
Alabama
F 1 U. S. Navy, WW II
&
Ola L. Glassco
1911-

Barbara Loreta Glassco
1902-1942

Zach E. Lee
Oct 28, 1880
(no date)
&
Lonnie H. Lee
Aug 2, 1885
Jun 13, 1964

Irene Taylor
1915-1955

FLINTVILLE QUADRANGLE

Ernest Copeland
Jan 20, 1909
Jul 20, 1969
&
Daisy D. Copeland
Oct 25, 1912

Lon Copeland
1873-1960
&
Victoria Ann D. Copeland
1875-1962

Wincie Angela Pendergrass
1895-1952

Brenda Dell Stiles
1941

Alice Marie Todd
B&D Aug 8, 1941

Infant of
Mr. & Mrs. N. H. Warren
Apr 30, 1941
May 2, 1941

Linda & Jene, Infants of
Mr. & Mrs. E. C. Crumbley
Apr 1, 1941

Sarah Gray
Jun 9, 1855
Sep 4, 1950

Hannah Gattis
Sep 19, 1871
Nov 22, 1949

John N. Brown
1891-1956

Jessie S. Brown
1906-

W. G. Alexander
1871-1929

H. F. Durham
Nov 28, 1842
Jul 4, 1931
&
Elizabeth Smith Durham
Feb 23, 1844
Jan 20, 1926

V. L. Durham
1885-1953
(Wilson FH)

Raymond Howard Durham
Oct 1, 1909
Jan 3, 1945

Rena Durham Pepper
1875-1957
(Gallant FH)

Andrew Jackson Copeland
May 30, 1888
Mar 21, 1966
&
Annie Mary Pickett Copeland
Jul 30, 1888
Jul 19, 1930

Hugh McCoen Screws
Jul 19, 1934
Jul 21, 1934

Homer Lee Screws
May 25, 1937
May 27, 1937

John Young
1879-1943
&
Myrtle Young
1880-1957

Luvenia, wife of
J. C. Wells
Feb 1, 1894
Mar 14, 1925

Joe Thomas Counts
Tennessee
Sp 4 HQ & HQ Co 187 Inf
Jul 11, 1939
Feb 10, 1960
(picture)

Mary M., Daughter of
W. C. & Celiah Bonner
Apr 25, 1925
Jun 27, 1927

John W. Burden
Nov 26, 1852
Nov 27, 1941

Amanda P. Green, wife of
J. W. Burden
Nov 8, 1856
Dec 28, 1925

Ollie Burden
Jun 5, 1880
Oct 22, 1950

Ludie Willie Crumbley
Oct 24, 1888
Oct 20, 1923
&
Bessie White Crumbley
Jul 8, 1894
Oct 29, 1960

Jerry Crumbley
Mar 5, 1947
Apr 10, 1965
(picture)

Infant Daughters of
Mr. & Mrs. John L. Crumbley
(no dates)

John L. Crumbley
Jun 7, 1917
Jun 7, 1963
&
Edna M. Crumbley
Apr 30, 1923

Paul Patrick
Apr 24, 1924
Apr 13, 1941

William Wiley Currey
1856-1943
&
Amanda Catharine Currey
1861-1923

Willie A. Currey
Alabama
Pvt HQ Co 71 Engrs WW I
Aug 13, 1887
Jul 3, 1955

Jesse Otto Currey
1886-1936

W. B. Syler
Sep 22, 1875
Jan 9, 1926
&
Mollie Copeland Syler
Jun 28, 1881
Feb 18, 1939

James Lee Langford
Oct 1, 1914

James Nathan Langford
Oct 3, 1890
1970

Birtie Counts Langford
Jun 7, 1891
Apr 18, 1969

Phillip R. Odem
Nov 20, 1862
Nov 30, 1925
&
Mary J. Odem
Aug 16, 1868
Oct 18, 1935

Ernest Odem
Dec 18, 1905
Sep 2, 1926

Grover Bennett
1913-1946

Tillman Young
1888-1966
&
Ethel Young
1895-

Ada Pigg
1910-
&
Ida Pigg
(Twins)

John Clayborn Pigg
1874-1965
&
Emma Golden Pigg
1898-1954

Carrie Edna Pigg
1906-

Demie Lucile Pigg
1898-1955

W. A. Shields
Sep 26, 1886
Dec 29, 1948

Maggie R. Shields
Mar 2, 1894
May 15, 1963

M. Frank Currey
1880-1955

Belle Currey
1888-1963

Roy E. Currey
1912-1954

Jerry M. Shubert
1941-1955

Fannie Laura Bynum
Died Sep 20, 1969
Age: 68 years.
(Gallant FH)

Joe Norman
1886-1961
Tennessee
Pvt Co E 119 Inf WW I PH
Jul 17, 1885
Mar 2, 1961
&
Lula F. Norman
1887-1959

John P. Groover
1870-1959
&
Charlsie W. Groover
1879-1966

James Roger Harbin
1956-1957
(Gallant FH)

Warner B. Marty
1895-1958
&
Emma Lou Marty
1900-

Sam Whitworth
Tennessee
Sgt Co B 118 Inf WW I
Feb 5, 1891
Jun 16, 1965

FLINTVILLE QUADRANGLE

Dall Cuzzort
Jul 16, 1900
Dec 2, 1950
&
Pauline Cuzzort
Nov 9, 1907

Phillis Ann Counts
1952
(Wilson FH)

Kerry Ronald Clevenger
1953-1953

Oscar Theo Hoots
Oct 28, 1893
Mar 7, 1961

Troy Wynn
Aug 18, 1937
Jun 16, 1949

Charles Hite Snow
Jul 28, 1892
Mar 22, 1964
&
Fairy Ophellia McGehee Snow
Oct 23, 1896

Married May 17, 1914

Toney Marty
Mar 27, 1889
Jun 23, 1963
&
Lettie Marty
Sep 29, 1895

Married Mar 9, 1919

Raymond Hann Andrews
B&D May 27, 1963
(Gallant FH)

Patrick B. Reynolds
Apr 27, 1883
May 15, 1961
&
Maggie E. Reynolds
May 3, 1886

Reuben Coy Reynolds
Apr 9, 1912
Jun 14, 1944
"He made the supreme
sacrifice on Normandy
Beach, France, WW II
Tennessee
Pvt 22 Inf 4 Div.

Homer B. Carlisle
1919-1957
&
Sarah L. Carlisle
1928-

Infant Thomas D. Carlisle
1946

Fred B. Carlisle
Oct 27, 1955
Oct 31, 1955
(Gallant FH)

Ben Marshall Barnett
Mar 20, 1939
Jan 12, 1946

James Timothy Counts
Oct 26, 1961
Mar 6, 1968

Lee W. Daniel
Jul 29, 1919
May 10, 1966
&
Mattie Shields Daniel
Oct 26, 1919

Henry T. "Heck" Rutledge
Tennessee
Sgt 285 Co MP WW I
Oct 7, 1895
May 28, 1965
&
Elizabeth Spray Rutledge
Jan 22, 1922

W. A. "Bill" Rutledge
Feb 12, 1903
Jul 25, 1959
&
Ruby Lee S. Rutledge
Mar 16, 1917

Katrina L. Rutledge
Died Oct 21, 1963
Age: (not given)
&
Infant Son
Died Jul 28, 1962
Age: (not given)

George W. Rutledge
Oct 30, 1907
Apr 19, 1957
&
Clara V. Rutledge
Apr 3, 1916

Oliver D. Smith
1882-1968
&
Myrtle W. Smith
1885-

Judith Fay, Infant Daughter
of Mr. & Mrs. Fred T. Smith
May 21, 1948

Steve Wayne Campbell
Died Nov 18, 1966
Age: 2 days.
(Higgins FH)

Dewey C. Hazelwood
1900-1961
&
Queenie B. Hazelwood
1907-

Walter B. George
Nov 14, 1890

&
Bessie Whitworth George
Oct 12, 1895
Jun 10, 1959

Joe Denis Simmons
Tennessee
RCT U.S.Army
Jul 17, 1941
Mar 26, 1968
&
Margaret Simmons
Jun 15, 1947

J. "Newt" Mason
1873-1954
&
Janie K. Mason
1873-1965

Ollie W. Pitts
Oct 12, 1892
Jan 9, 1950
&
Denever Pitts
Oct 13, 1897

Will Harbin
May 4, 1877
Apr 29, 1958
&
Narcissa Harbin
Jan 15, 1887
Jun 10, 1959

Ruby Irene Gattis
Nov 11, 1908
Apr 16, 1969

Solon McClellan Fite
1865-1951

Mrs. Flossie Marie McCreless
Died Jan 6, 1969
Age: 52 years.
(Gallant FH)

Melvin Wiley Pitts
Sep 3, 1918
Jan 2, 1956

Ira Bervon McCreless
Oct 8, 1914
Nov 6, 1960

Winnie Geraldine Luttrell,
Daughter of Mr. & Mrs.
Gilbert McGehee
Sep 24, 1931
Apr 2, 1962

Lewis S. Shubert
Jul 28, 1890
Jun 17, 1961
&
Lou J. Shubert
Aug 27, 1892
Aug 25, 1966

Mark Shubert
Jan 18, 1954
Jan 19, 1954

Stanley Wayne Counts
B&D Aug 25, 1954

James F. Gibson
Jul 5, 1926
Sep 25, 1963
&
Dorothy S. Gibson
May 28, 1931

Mrs. Frank Christa
May 29, 1883
Apr 4, 1956

Linda Kay Thompson
1967

Raymond E. Pruett
Dec 14, 1911
Jun 24, 1955
&
Gertrude L. Pruett
May 21, 1915

Menton C. Todd
May 13, 1895

&
Lou Alice Todd
Oct 26, 1890
Mar 5, 1962
Married Dec 3, 1911

Garland Coolidge Cranford
1921-1958

William B. Cuzzort
Jul 21, 1912
Mar 25, 1963
&
Opha R. Cuzzort
Jul 24, 1919

Teresa Kay Hill
Oct 28, 1956
Mar 21, 1961

Althea Langford
1890-1963

Hubert Harold Gray
1913-1958
(Gallant FH)

Mrs. Retsy Helm
1905-1962

FLINTVILLE QUADRANGLE

Joe E. Amason
Apr 5, 1931
Dec 10, 1963

Tammy Carol Hunt
Jul 4, 1966

H. O. Speck
1904-1963
(Gallant FH)

Branda Pamela Sullivan
1959-1962(?)/63

Raymond H. Harris
Apr 12, 1919

&
Mildred A. Harris
Sep 30, 1926
Feb 14, 1970

Mrs. Rosie Bell Bates
Died Dec 22, 1968
Age: 57y, 9m, 19d.
(Gallant FH)

Vell G. Winn
Died May 19, 1970
Age: 72 years
(Gallant FH)

Mrs. Pauline Reynolds Smith
Died Mar 21, 1969
Age: 55 years.
(Gallant FH)

Donald A. Counts
Feb 20, 1937
Jul 21, 1968

Mrs. Ollie Odell *
Died Aug 11, 1903
Age: 24y, 4m.

Mamie Ethel,* Daughter of
Mr. & Mrs. Ottie Cowan
Died Feb 15, 1906
Age: 8y, 4m, 23d.

Nolen Clarence Sullenger *
Died Oct 21, 1906
Age: 5m.

John Young *
Died Apr 21, 1892
Age: 50 years

Infant * of
Mr. & Mrs. Robin Husch
B&D Apr 2, 1908

Claude George *
Died Aug 2, 1915
Age: 34 years.

Infant * of
Mr. & Mrs. S. S. Harris
Died Dec 29, 1916
(no age given)

Marion Frances,* Daughter
of Mr. & Mrs. V. W. Wine
Died Sep 5, 1917
Age: 7y, 8m, 11d.

Charles Weiss
Died Jul 27, 1915
Age: 65 years.
Native of Germany

Miss Martha Cothran *
Died Jul 8, 1914
Age: 75 years.

Mrs. Alexander *
Died Nov 7, 1892
Age: 59 years.

Mrs. Nancy,* wife of
R. A. Stevenson
Died Nov 28, 1898
Age: 70y, 9m.

Mrs. Jane Clark,* wife of
W. R. Oldham
Died Sep 20, 1895
Age: 55 years.

A. D.,* Son of
W. R. Stiles
Died Aug 24, 1896
Age: 6 years.

W. J. Bryant *
Died Feb 31, 1907
Age: 70 years.

Richard J.,* Son of
John & Bettie Ann Fowler
Died Oct 21, 1909
Age: 2m.

Rachel,* Daughter of
Oscar Counts
Died Jun 24, 1916
Age: 18m.

J. M. Shelton *
Died Nov 27, 1897
Age: 56 years.

Infant * of
J. M. Cambron
Died Oct 4, 1899
Age: 4 days.

Ellen Brooks Kilpatrick *
Died Dec 1, 1899
Age: 24y, 9m, 18d.

Mrs. Susan Crawford *
Died Oct 5, 1915
Age: 53 years.

W. P. Preston *
Died Dec 23, 1916
Age: 43y, 9m, 12d.

Mamie,* Daughter of
John & Belle Ann Fowler
Died Apr 9, 1907
Age 2 weeks.

Many unmarked graves.

* *

CAMPBELL CEMETERY

LOCATION: One and one-fourth miles south of Corders Cross
Roads on the east side of New Hope Road.

Cora Mae Andrews, wife of
Roy Fitch
Aug 16, 1917
Jul 11, 1954

Rhoda Jane, Daughter of
Roy & Cora Mae Fitch
Jun 22, 1954
Jan 5, 1955

Edd E. Bradford
1886-1946
&
Lucy M. Bradford
1894-1968

Marion T. Pitts
1889-1953
&
Maie T. Pitts
1892-

Infant Son of
Marion & Maie Pitts
Nov 5, 1911
Nov 15, 1911

Kathleen Shelton
Apr 6, 1913
Dec 6, 1936

Charlie Shelton
Jul 5, 1939
May 10, 1969

Martha Lou Fitch Bradford
Dec 26, 1853
Dec 16, 1918

Uncle
Ark D. Bradford
Mar 5, 1878
Aug 27, 1959

William Tom Jackson
Alabama
Pvt U. S. Army WW I
Mar 12, 1894
Oct 11, 1959

Jennie Helm
1902-1940

Joe Steve Street
Apr 24, 1958
Dec 1, 1958

Blanche Bradford Drennan
Sep 15, 1917
Jan 25, 1943

Willard J. Bradford
Tennessee
TEC 5 U. S. Army WW II
Jul 27, 1912
Mar 31, 1969

Paul Richard Smith
B&D Jul 26, 1961
&
Patrick Royal Smith
Jul 26, 1961
Aug 12, 1961

Florence Middleton
Nov 9, 1863
Jan 11,(no year given)

Della Smith Morrow
Oct 20, 1886
Sep 19, 1955

Mae Bryant
Jun 2, 1898
Dec 29, 1930

Ronald Wayne Gault
Aug 3, 1948

FLINTVILLE QUADRANGLE

George W. Rudd
Jul 3, 1864
Dec 17, 1943

Martha Elizabeth, wife of
G. W. Rudd
Jul 13, 1865
Mar 19, 1935

William Carl Gulley
Aug 23, 1884

&
Retta Norman Gulley
Jul 26, 1894
Nov 12, 1950

George W. Norman
1871-1941
&
Kate Norman
1872-1949

Allean Corder
Mar 19, 1924
Jan 13, 1929

John Jacob Corder
Nov 11, 1892
Feb 10, 1967
&
Martha Norman Corder
Feb 25, 1900
Nov 10, 1962

Jewell, Infant of
E. N. & Cora Jean
B&D Feb 17, 1921

Luther S. Halcomb
1897-1964

S. P., wife of
M. N. Renegar
Nov 30, 1865
Jun 9, 1897

E. C., wife of
M. N. Renegar
Nov 25, 1853
May 16, 1890

Billy Joe, Son of
Glenn & Johnie Mae Tucker
Feb 6, 1941

Clayton W. Tucker
1888-
&
Sallie E. Tucker
1891-1957

Lon Tucker
1886-1966

George Petty
Tennessee
Pvt 6th Inf 5th Div
Sep 3, 1930

Mary E. Petty
1856-1932

W. A. Petty
1858-1934

Eddie L. Taylor
1872-1944

Roy Tillmon Taylor
Jan 8, 1896
Aug 22, 1965
&
Bessie Taylor
Apr 16, 1895

Eugene Taylor
Tennessee
Pvt Co E 384 Inf   WW I
Jan 28, 1900
Jun 27, 1963

Carl A. Taylor
Tennessee
Tec 5 U.S.A. Bsm PH WW II
Oct 16, 1922
Apr 13, 1950

Nell Christine Taylor
Jan 19, 1923
Jul 16, 1924

J. _. Taylor
1938-1939

T. W. Taylor
1842-1923

B. G. Corder
1841-1915

Ruth R., wife of
B. G. Corder
Jun 10, 1845
Jun 29, 1905

Claud Benson
1877-1948
&
Mary Benson
1882-1946

Garland Benson
1905-1947

Mrs. Mattie Benson Malone
Died Jun 7, 1968
Age: 52y, 9m, 10d.

Walter Frank Jean
Jun 18, 1891
Jun 16, 1912

Allene Corder
1924-1929

Matthew M. Corder
Oct 24, 1886
Sep 15, 1947

Izzie V. Norman, wife of
M. M. Corder
Jan 13, 1891
Apr 18, 1917

Missouria, wife of
J. T. Corder
Dec 23, 1853
Jun 25, 1895

J. T. Corder
Dec 24, 1848
May 25, 1931

Martha V. Corder
Feb 13, 1874
Sep 2, 1958

Octa Belle Corder
Oct 1, 1897
Apr 17, 1963
&
Aldia L. Jean
Dec 29, 1890
Jan 3, 1970

E. Beasley Jean
Aug 1, 1885
Mar 11, 1967

Rosa Frame Brewer
Oct 21, 1906
Jan 29, 1966

Will Petty
Jun 19, 1877
May 16, 1958
&
Josie Petty
Apr 17, 1878
Apr 17, 1957

Warner D. Baxter
1943

J. D. Corder
Sep 8, 1852
Jun 4, 1904
&
Julia Corder
Feb 12, 1856
Nov 4, 1928

Sarah McClure, wife of
Jacob B. Corder
May 30, 1829
Jul 8, 1915

Jacob B. Corder
Jun 13, 1815
Nov 20, 1892

James Ferrell Corder
Apr 16, 1867
Jun 6, 1942
&
Fannie Harris Corder
Jun 24, 1873
(no date)

Edgar H. Corder
1893-1897

Claudie Corder
Feb 2, 1906
Aug 5, 1938

Benjamin T. Corder
Apr 27, 1865
Nov 8, 1940
&
Nancy Benson Corder
Jan 29, 1872
Oct 31, 1965

Warner Duke, Son of
Russell & Virginia Baxter
Oct 22, 1943
Oct 30, 1943

Theo T. Corder
May 18, 1895
May 10, 1966
Tennessee
Pvt Co A 3rd Inf Repl Regt
WW I

William M. Taylor
Oct 14, 1885
May 15, 1965
&
Gertrude Taylor
May 21, 1886
Aug 5, 1962

William L., Son of
W. M. & Gertrude Taylor
Mar 2, 1919
Mar 27, 1923

Jerry Frank, Son of
Elmer & Muriel Taylor
Dec 10, 1938
Jun 28, 1939

A. J.(Andrew Jackson)Taylor
Mar 30, 1861
Jul 28, 1944
& wife
Ruthie L. Corder Taylor
Apr 1, 1863
Jul 23, 1900

Elsie Mae Corder, wife of
A. J. Taylor
(no dates)

Clara O., Daughter of
A. J. & R. L. Taylor
Sep 21, 1892
Dec 4, 1892

James William Seaton
Sep 5, 1871

&
Florence R. Taylor Seaton
Jul 28, 1870
Oct 30, 1950

Horace W. Seaton
Feb 4, 1897
Dec 19, 1907

Clarence F. Seaton
May 23, 1899
Feb 12, 1904

FLINTVILLE QUADRANGLE

Mary L. Seaton
Aug 23, 1901
Jan 12, 1902

A. F. Seaton
Jan 10, 1843
Sep 10, 1919
&
Mary Ann Seaton
Jul 29, 1851

Jennie Koonce, wife of
J. T. Fitch
Aug 18, 1882
Mar 1, 1933

Horace Macculic
Apr 4, 1880
Sep 10, 1909

Sarah Benson McCullock
Died Mar 20, 1926
Age: 90 years.

Robert Frame
May 12, 1877
Apr 14, 1936
&
Monnie Frame
Jan 6, 1875
Feb 1, 1940

Netta Sue, Daughter of
S. S. & L. M. Harris
Dec 8, 1916
Dec 28, 1916

William Byrd Tucker
Sep 18, 1893
Apr 25, 1949

Estil Cowan Tucker
Feb 10, 1903
Sep 27, 1944

John Taylor *
Died Apr 27, 1917
Age: 49 years.

John McBay
Died Dec 28, 1946
Age: (not given)

George A. McCullough
Jul 13, 1908
Mar 18, 1909

Arleva McBay, wife of
Sam McBay
Died May 15, 1910
Age: 65 years
&
Fannie, Daughter of
S. & A. McBay
Died Aug 1, 1904
Age: 26 years.

Edith Mai Lackey
Dec 20, 1922
Oct 11, 1927

P. R. Powell
Oct 12, 1840
Feb 14, 1923

Lizzie Street, wife of
P. R. Powell
May 2, 1868
Oct 10, 1933

Maggie Dobbs, wife of
P. R. Powell
Jun 19, 1845
Jun 18, 1913

Malcolm Bledsoe
Nov 1925
Jun 1928

John Robert Pirtle
Aug 18, 1941
Oct 17, 1970

Ovie Blair Graham
Died Jan 4, 1971
Age: 55 years.
(Gallant FH)

Infant * of
William & Sallie Ashby
Died May 23, 1896
Age: (not given)

Infant of
Parvin & Mai Bledsoe
Oct 31, 1911

John Allen Malone
Mar 24, 1860
Oct 20, 1941

Lucy Ray Malone
Sep 26, 1869
Jan 10, 1936

Mattie Ozell Malone
Dec 21, 1900
Jun 29, 1909

Frances Cox Ray
Jan 13, 1833
Jan --, 1905

Mahala Ray
Jul 8, 1853
Mar 29, 1939

Asa Street
Mar 29, 1835
May 23, 1916

Martha Themmon, wife of
Asa Street
May 2, 1837
Apr 5, 1922

Alvie Street
1919-1937

Eddie Street
1878-1936

David Pitts
1884-1957

Lillie Mae Pitts
1886-1965

Ed N. Taylor *
Died Apr 28, 1903
Age: 22 years.

Several unmarked graves.

Street
(no dates)

Street
(no dates)

Street
(no dates)

Street
(no dates)

Street
(no dates)

Street
(no dates)

Street
(no dates)

Horace Land
1933-1938

Paul W. Land
1936-1936

Granville Counts
Feb 3, 1938
Mar 6, 1938

Carolyn Tucker
Nov 1937
Jun 1938

Tom R. Patterson
1873-1960

Myrtle Patterson
Oct 25, 1884
Feb 16, 1937

Mrs. Ineeda T. Cotner
Jul 28, 1922
Jul 28, 1970

H. Revis * of
Crystal Springs
Died Jan 20, 1904
Age: 83 years.

* *

WHITWORTH CEMETERY

LOCATION: One and one-half miles NNE of New Hope on east side of main road.

M. L., wife of
R. L. Whitworth
Jan 18, 1837
Apr 16, 1885   3 unmarked graves.

* *

FLINTVILLE QUADRANGLE

BRAY CEMETERY

LOCATION: One and one-half miles NNE of New Hope on east side of main road.

Richard N. Bray Sep 6, 1854 Nov 21, 1887	Ann Bray Nov 22, 1849 Jan 19, 1884	Sarah Bray Died Oct 13, 1889 Age: 74 years.	Charlotte Bray Oct 30, 1844 Mar 29, 1880

Mrs. Charlotte Bray *
Died Oct 12, 1889
Age: 60 years.   1 unmarked grave.

* *

CEMETERY

LOCATION: One and one-half mile NE of New Hope, south side of Stewart Chapel Road.

5 graves with no markers.

* *

SOUTHWORTH CEMETERY

LOCATION: One mile NNE of New Hope, east side of Corder Cross Roads road.

L. B. (no dates, fieldstone) S. B. (no dates, fieldstone) J. B. (no dates, fieldstone) Martha A., wife of E. G. Walker May 1, 1817 Feb 11, 1879 "Erected by her son Jas. R. Walker". Edward G. Walker Jun 18, 1817 Jan 21, 1892 Age: 75y, 7m. "Erected by Son Jas. R. Walker". Miss Nancy J. Woodall * Died Sep 6, 1901 Age: 55 years.	Sarah Cordealy Walker May 18, 1849 May 25, 1876 Age: 27y, 7d. J. M. Shelton Feb 11, 1842 Nov 20, 1897 J. J. Woodall Aug 10, 1825 Jul 11, 1896 Sarah Ann Woodall Jul 24, 1823 Apr 16, 1899 Mrs. Hunter * Died Dec 12, 1907 Age: 78 years. Tate Gray * Died Oct 25, 1897 Age: 51y, 8m, 13d. NOTE: Old Isaac Southworth Academy was near here in 1840.	R. A. C. Stevenson * Died Sep 23, 1899 Age: 85 years. Married Nancy Jean in 1852 Mrs. Josie Langford * Died May 24, 1897 Age: 37 years. Charles Berrier * A Soldier of the Revolution Died 1850 Age: (not given) Miss Cora Stevenson * Died May 23, 1900 Age: 20 years. Bray's are said to be buried here. Susan Shasteen,* Daughter of John & Sarah Shasteen Died Jul 26, 1896 Age: 4y, 5m, 18d.	W. M. Young * Died Feb 2, 1896 Age: 61 years. Married 1860 to Mahailey Woodall Mrs. Jane Stevenson * Died Oct 21, 1897 Age: 47 years. Mrs. Mary E. Shelton * Died Jul 3, 1902 Age: 50y, 10m, 27d. Mrs. Delia,* wife of John A. Woodall Died Jan 2, 1899 Age: 76 years. Johnnie,* Son of Will & Josephine Langford Died Mar 21, 1894 Age: 2 years. Many old fieldstones.

* ****

HESTER CEMETERY

LOCATION: Three fourth mile NNW of New Hope, south side of road.

E. L. Hester Born 1841 Died Nov 12, 1907 Infant grave (no dates) W. H. Stevenson * Died Jul 23, 1890 Age: 77 years.	Tom Kerbo 1861-1914 Laura Kerbo 1875-1907 Mrs. Mildred Hester * Died Oct 12, 1912 Age: 87 years.	Jesse J. Stevenson (Esq.) 41 Tenn. Inf.(Feb 6, 1839)* C.S.A. (Jul 27, 1917) Gracey Thelma,* Daughter of Mr. & Mrs. Stephen Bynum Died Jul 1, 1906 Age: 7 years.	R. S. Stevenson Oct 1, 1866 Sep 3, 1930 & Mattie Stevenson Feb 12, 1870 1948

* *

FLINTVILLE QUADRANGLE

HOPKINS-EASTLAND CEMETERY

LOCATION: One fourth mile NNE of New Hope on west side of road.

Z. G. Ivey
Jul 22, 1849
Jul 7, 1927
& wife
Mary J. Stevenson Ivey
Jul 25, 1853
Jan 2, 1937

Fannie Ivey Kilpatrick
1880-1918

NOTE: Informed sources say that the Hopkins and Eslick Families are buried here. This was part of the old Samuel Hopkins' Estate.

Mrs. Zack Ivey
1853-1937 (old marker)

Robert J. Ivey
1877-1932

Henry Pitts
Jan 17, 1900
Dec 17, 1903

Infant * of
W. S. & Addie Pitts
B&D Feb 3, 1905

Bertha,* Daughter of
Mayhew & Mattie Smith
Died Jan 8, 1899
Age: 2 years.

David Lee Smith
Co C 41 Tenn Inf
C.S.A.

Oscar Bates
1833-1942

Birdie Bates
1884-1945

Hoyt A., son of
J. O. & Bertie Bates
Oct 3, 1907
Feb 20, 1908

Miss Sallie Smith *
Died Jul 15, 1899
Age: 75 years.

Dr. Thomas Eastland *
Died 1881
Age: (not given)

Mrs. Susan E.,* wife of
William Stevenson
Died Nov 7, 1892
Age: 22 years.

D. T. Eastland *
Died Apr 30, 1897
Age: 52 years.

Mrs. Florinda Hopkins,*
wife of
Dr. Thomas Eastland
Died Jul 11, 1889
Age: 65 years.

* *

WICKS CEMETERY

LOCATION: One and one fourth miles NE of New Hope on the south side of a lane.

Gabe D. Wicks
1850-1939

Lucy A. Crawford, wife of
G. A. Wicks
Jan 29, 1855
Jan 30, 1912

Charles Edward Wicks
1878-1948

John A. Wicks **
Oct 7, 1801
Jan 15, 1876
&
Catherine Wicks **
Jun 8, 1811
Feb 23, 1869

F. S. Clark *
Died Feb 6, 1908
Age: 69 years.

Roy L. Wicks
Dec 20, 1881
Feb 5, 1908

Charles T. Wicks
Jan 12, 1853
Sep 8, 1927
&
Ermine C. Wicks
May 31, 1854
(no date)

Ozella Cowan **
1910-1974

Lila Cowan Brooks **
1910-1973

** Mr. & Mrs. Fred Brown
Fayetteville, Tenn.

Mrs. Mahala Wicks
Died Apr 24, 1887
Age: 70 years.

David Luther Smith
Nov 5, 1877
Jun 1, 1964
&
Cora E. Wicks Smith
Sep 3, 1878
Jun 18, 1964

Kattie Smith
Oct 23, 1877
Jul 17, 1903

Dolly Wicks Haney **
Sep 2, 1894
Mar 8, 1973

Elsie Flentory Haney **
Aug 6, 1895
Jan 2, 1982

Many unmarked graves.

Ora Cowan Eslick
1904-1955

Elsie Lena Haney
Jul 3, 1926
Aug 28, 1926

James T. Cowan
1877-1919

Delia Wicks Cowan
1883-1955

Infant Sons ** of
James T. & Delia Cowan
(no dates)

Infant Son * of
J. T. Cowan
Died May 12, 1918

Mrs. Kate,* wife of
J. T. Smith
Died Jul 17, 1908
Age: 30 years.

* ** * * * * *

KILPATRICK CEMETERY

LOCATION: Two miles SW of Flintville, west side of the Lincoln Road.

E. R. Kilpatrick *
Died May 3, 1899
Age: 76 years.

10 to 12 unmarked graves.
(According to informed sources the last persons to be buried here, about 1890 were the Kilpatricks.)

* *

FLINTVILLE QUADRANGLE

McNEAL CEMETERY

LOCATION: One and one half miles east of New Hope, south of Flint River.

Mrs. Texie P.; wife of
John E. Crawford
Died May 28, 1896
Age: 39y, 2m, 20d.

John Henry,* Son of
John E. & Texa Crawford
Died Aug 20, 1881
Age: 9m.

James McNeal *
Died Feb 7, 1879
Age: 67y, 9m.

4 or 5 graves with fieldstones, no insc.

* *

SIMMS CEMETERY

LOCATION: One mile SE of New Hope, north side of Flintville-Lincoln Road.

Benjamin Simms
Oct 20, 1776
Sep 6, 1855
& wife
Elizabeth Simms
Sep 10, 1786
Jul 30, 1852

ED NOTE: Progenitor of the Simms Family in this area.

* *

BEAVERS-MOORE CEMETERY

LOCATION: One mile SSE of New Hope, west side of Flintville-Lincoln Road.

Jasper Lee Hearlston
May 23, 1968
Mar 19, 1969

Armon Ray Hearlston
Dec 27, 1924
Feb 14, 1926

Jasper G. Hearlston
Tennessee
Pvt 1 Cl 119 Inf 30 Div
Apr 28, 1930
(James Hearlston
1897-1930)

James J. Towry
1873-1945

Mattie Towry
1879-1904

Agnes Towry
Jul 20, 1888
Oct 25, 1969

Robert Lee Newgent
Jan 6, 1892

&
Bertha Mae Newgent
Aug 21, 1897
Feb 10, 1968

Mary Newgent
(no dates)

Baby Newgent
(no dates)

A. R. Newgent
1938-1940

Altie Newgent
(no dates)

Eva Nell Horton
1925-1952
(Wilson FH)

Eddie Lee Horton
1948-1950
(Raby FH)

Bryson C. Cowan
1885-1946
&
Mary E. Cowan
1890-19(no date)

Billy Newgent
Died Dec 6, ----(gone)
(TM)

Lou Ella Newgent
1895-1966
(Gallant FH)

J. M. Jetton
Apr 17, 1856
Jul 27, 1884

P. E. Purdy
Sep 12, 1854
Aug 11, 1890

Leamon Robison
1920-1922

M. J. Kennedy
Jul 25, 1825
Jul 16, 1894

Ezekiel Kennedy
Mar 11, 1819
Mar 12, 1895

Martha, wife of
E. Kennedy
May 24, 1832
Apr 26, 1888

Shields Kennedy
Feb 9, 1892
Aug 24, 1893

Henry F. Smith
Nov 14, 1854
Nov 16, 1924

Myrtle Smith
Mar 18, 1885
Jan 13, 1919

Wanda Mae Mason
Apr 2, 1916
Feb 19, 1938

William M. Golden
Tennessee
PFC 410 Inf 103 Inf Div WW II
Oct 2, 1921
Jan 26, 1945

Charlie Golden
1889-1970
(Moore-Cortner FH)

William Amos Beavers
(TM: 1902-1937)
Died Nov 27, 1937
Age: 35y, 9m, 24d.

Velma Lee Golden
May 28, 1934
Apr 20, 1936

John M. Towry
Jan 3, 1876
Feb 24, 1952

Ella M. Towry
Jun 22, 1884
Sep 7, 1934

Winford, Son of
J. M. & Ella Towry
Jan 9, 1923
Jun 11, 1923

Ray Bert "Burton" Towry
Tennessee
Pfc SVC Btry 169 FA Bn
WW II B.S.M.
Sep 28, 1912
Sep 21, 1964

J. S. Hearlston
1862-1935

J. A. Smith
1924-1969

Sherley L. White
Aug 17, 1950
Oct 2, 1950

FLINTVILLE QUADRANGLE

Asa C. Cowan
Tennessee
Pvt 157 Depot Brig
Died Mar 30, 1939
(no age given)

Lesley Cowan
1905-1937

Horace Cowan
Tennessee
Pvt 318 MG Bn 81 Div
Died Jul 21, 1927
Age: (not given)

Carl,* Son of
Pomp & Mattie Mires
Died Jan 25, 1902
Age: 7y, 5m, 12d.

Mary Ellen,* Daughter of
J. J. & M. L. Towry
Died Sep 3, 1900
Age: 4y, 8m.

Otis Moyers *
Died Feb 1, 1918
Age: 21 years.

Woodie A. Cowan
May 5, 1902
Jan 27, 1951
&
Myrtle Cowan
Apr 26, 1907
Mar 17, 1937

Dolly Agnes Cowan
1936-1936

Nelson Cowan
1917-1936

Mrs. B. F. King *
Died Jul 1, 1894
Age: 70 years.

Albert Timothy,* Son of
Cephas & Lucinda King
Died Aug 17, 1901
Age: 10m.

Infant Daughter * of
B. J. Mires
Died Aug 17, 1916
Age: (not given)

Effie, Daughter of
Sam & Lucy Cowan
Mar 11, 1883
Mar 30, 1902

Loise H. Hall
Jun 28, 1908
Jul 3, 1942

J. Garfield Robinson
Jul 28, 1883
Oct 25, 1967
&
Claudia C. Robinson
Sep 27, 1889
Jul 12, 1967

John Nunley *
Died Jan 13, 1894
Age: 67 years.

Mrs. Eliza Beavers *
Died Jul 18, 1908
Age: 78 years.

ED NOTE: This cemetery was once known as the Kennedy Cemetery.

Eric W. Robinson
Tennessee
Cpl 456 AMPH Truck Co
WW II
May 18, 1914
May 17, 1958

Thelma Mai Cooper
Feb 20, 1933
Sep 26, 1943

Mrs. Jennie,* wife of
William Crowder
Died Jan 12, 1903
Age: 44 years.

J. K. Beavers *
Married 1860 to
Eliza Summers
Died Jul 10, 1896
Age: 70 years.

Alta,* Daughter of
Mr. & Mrs. Robert Newton
Died Oct 15, 1927
Age: 7 years.

Several unmarked graves.

* *

PATTERSON CEMETERY

LOCATION: One and one fourth miles west of Vanntown, north of Vanntown-Lincoln Road.

Infant Daughter of
A. J. & Annie E. Patterson
B&D Mar 11, 1887
Twin Sister of
Neva M. Patterson

Newton M., Son of
A. J. & Annie E. Patterson
Jun 13, 1881
Dec 19, 1885

* *

PLEASANT HILL-BROWNS CHAPEL CEMETERY

LOCATION: One mile east of Vanntown at Pleasant Hill Church. (Old Browns Chapel).

Carlton Gibson
Aug 3, 1890
Feb 1, 1963
&
Emma G. Gibson
Sep 14, 1893
(no date)

Raymond J. Stone
1903-1970
&
Wyline A. Stone
1910-1958

Dewey E. "Bud" Walden
Jul 31, 1922 (Pfc Tenn. 644
Jan 26, 1969 (TD Bn WW II)
&
Pauline W. "Polly" Walden
May 14, 1922

Albert E. McAnally
Jan 10, 1879
Mar 8, 1967
&
Mattie B. McAnally
May 7, 1881
Jul 10, 1964
Married Feb 4, 1900

Joe Rufus Wolaver
Tennessee
Pvt U. S. Army
Aug 21, 1947
Jun 22, 1969
&
Venice W. Wolaver
Nov 25, 1947

Mrs. Laura Payne Hale
Died Apr 3, 1971
Age: 81 years

Henry Hale
1885-1955

Nancy Woods
B&D Jun 27, 1965

Cynthia C. Pruitt
Aug 27, 1957
Mar 26, 1958

George T. McNeal
Sep 16, 1888
Aug 24, 1965

Martha McNeal
Jun 6, 1889
Nov 25, 1956

L. T. Gardner
1933-1953

H. D. Cummins

H. D. Cummins
Died Mar 26, 1949
Age: 92 years.

Emmett H. Echols
Tennessee
Sgt 343 Engr Gs Regt WW II
Jan 14, 1926
May 5, 1946

Emmett R. Echols
Aug 6, 1903
May 6, 1965
&
Louise H. Echols
Mar 21, 1909

Robert W. Ables
1912-
&
Maggie R. Ables
1905-

FLINTVILLE QUADRANGLE

James Clayton Sanders
Tennessee
Sfc 526 Armd Inftry Bn
Feb 16, 1928
Feb 17, 1969

J. P. Holt
B&D Jul 19, 1936
&
Ruby Edna Mae Holt
B&D Aug 27, 1935

Charles Edward Holt
Died Mar 12, 1971
Age: 39 years.
(Gallant FH)

James T. Rice
1913-1941
"Brother"
&
Amaline Gray Rice
1924-1933
&
Jim B. Rice
1859-1931
&
Eldorado Rice
1909-1927

Martha Ann, Daughter of
H. C. & Etha Vann
Mar 24, 1941
Apr 5, 1941

H. Chalmas Vann
Nov 24, 1902
Apr 11, 1964
&
Etha W. Vann
May 8, 1912

Infant Daughter of
T. J. & Estelle Powell
B&D Jul 16, 1930

Infant Daughter of
T. J. & Estelle Powell
B&D May 25, 1937

Infant Son of
T. J. & Estelle Powell
Aug 17, 1928
Aug 24, 1928

Infant Son of
John & Effie Powell
B&D Jan 25, 1934

James Benny Hambric
Mar 26, 1939
Apr 10, 1939

Lora Vann, wife of
John Powell
Oct 31, 1888
Jan 25, 1926

Infant Powell
(no dates)

Infant Powell
(no dates)

John Garland, Son of
John & Lora Powell
May 17, 1922
Apr 9, 1924

Honduras, Son of
Lee & Edna Van
Mar 12, 1924
Nov 7, 1925

Seldon Lee Vann
Jan 25, 1891
Jan 11, 1953
&
Edna Niles Vann
Jan 24, 1893
(no date)

Clyde E. Vann
Jan 27, 1909
Jun 7, 1934

John F. Vann
Jan 11, 1887
Mar 5, 1935

Infant Son of
James & Jennie Vann
B&D Apr 20, 1940

Donna Lynn Van
1948

William Aaron Vann
Jan 18, 1879
Jun 16, 1941
&
Martha Zaddie Vann
Mar 9, 1881
May 22, 1963

S. J. Earl Vann, Jr.
1953

William L. Vann
Sep 24, 1900
Mar 26, 1959
&
Rosa B. Vann
Dec 10, 1903

Jerry Wayne Clark
1959-1960

Sandra Kay Clark
(no dates)

Ruchelle Yvette Clark
1961

Lowell Wendell Jones
Dec 29, 1949
Jun 16, 1969

Anthony B. Vaughn
Mar 14, 1958
Aug 5, 1958

Lundy J. Plunkett
Apr 23, 1902
Oct 26, 1962
&
Josie A. Plunkett
Apr 13, 1899

Willie Leon Williams
Apr 28, 1914
Sep 9, 1951
&
Josie Thrasher Williams
Apr 16, 1913

John Keith Bradford
Mar 9, 1894
Feb 6, 1963
Tennessee
Cook 15 Co Coast Arty WW I
&
Hattie W. Bradford
1906-

Sherlie Woods (Infant)
Died Nov 8, 1954
(Laughlin FH, Huntsville, AL)

George W. Woods
Died Oct 14, 1970
Age: 78 years.
(Gallant FH)

Sam A. Powell
Jan 4, 1865
Mar 30, 1946

Elizabeth Ann Tunstill
Mar 26, 1947
Jun 3, 1949

James L. Worsham
Jan 22, 1923
Aug 8, 1964
&
Hilda Lackey Worsham
Dec 10, 1926

Erskine W. Worsham
1879-1953
&
Luna G. Worsham
1908-

J. C. Mearse
Tennessee
Pvt 314 Sig Const Bn
May 15, 1932
Jun 6, 1951
(picture)

Henry Fate
1856-1944

Harvey A. Mearse
Jul 4, 1934
Aug 5, 1934

Robert Lee Dye
1909-1924

C. R. Dye
1880-1954
& wife
S. B. Collins Dye
1880-1958

Cordeal Decker
Sep 18, 1921
Oct 8, 1923

James W. Terry
Dec 12, 1880
May 18, 1968
&
Elizabeth B. Terry
Feb 17, 1881

J. B. Terry
May 19, 1928
Nov 8, 1932

Sarah Speck
1859-1934

William P. Robinson
Oct 18, 1875
Dec 19, 1959

Joyce, Daughter of
Mr. & Mrs. J. A. Robinson
Oct 8, 1933
Jan 3, 1935

Pearl Robinson
1905-1925

Maude Robinson
Jun 6, 1879
Jun 16, 1919

Josephine Robinson
1903-1905

John Robinson
1918-1919

Charles A. Holt
Jun 23, 1877
Oct 23, 1950
&
Annie May Holt
May 30, 1878
Jun 27, 1929

Mark M. Caldwell
Mar 25, 1883
Nov 13, 1967

Hubert James Caldwell
Oct 15, 1911
Jan 9, 1964

A. B. Byers
Apr 12, 1865
Oct 8, 1934

FLINTVILLE QUADRANGLE

Henry Caldwell
Apr 8, 1878
Aug 19, 1955
&
Ethel Caldwell
Aug 26, 1889
Jan 6, 1958

Willie C. Caldwell
May 30, 1877
Jan 19, 1935
&
Ninnie Caldwell
Feb 12, 1877
May 31, 1934

Mayhue Smith
1872-1940
&
Mattie S. Smith
1881-1941

J. D. McCreary
1859-1933

Lev Caldwell
1893-1935

James C. Finch
Sep 26, 1890
Oct 28, 1939
&
Dollie Ann Finch
Aug 9, 1890
Dec 8, 1954

Willie Moore
1887-1939

Elias Johnson Thrasher
Apr 9, 1884
Jan 30, 1968
&
Lucy Rogers Thrasher
Sep 10, 1892
Oct 31, 1942
(TM: Lucy Thrasher
1892-1942)

Hershel V. Gardner
May 25, 1908
Oct 7, 1969
&
Belle V. Gardner
Nov 16, 1905

Infant Son of
H. V. & A. B. Gardner
B&D Oct 26, 1934

C. I. Gardner
1876-1928
&
Ola Gardner
1890-1952

Phillip Hershel Cox
Died May 12, 1971
Age: 1m.

Kelly Kimbrough
B&D Oct 20, 1962

Alesia Nanette Kimbrough
Jul 27, 1960
Dec 7, 1960

Stancil Eugene Cossey
Sep 30, 1912
Apr 24, 1948

Noah Lester Cossey
Jul 4, 1907
Jan 30, 1963

Thomas Miles Cossey
Jul 14, 1918
Nov 25, 1926

NOTE: Stancil & Thomas are Sons of Mr. & Mrs. C. F. Cossey.

Columbus F. Cossey
Jan 1, 1879
Jul 21, 1960
&
Hettie L. Cossey
May 12, 1883
Oct 27, 1953

Maud Nixon
(no dates, fieldstone)

Douglas McKelvie
1932-1932

John Franklin McKelvie
1897-1938
&
Rosie Lee McKelvie
1903-

Ray Rozal
1878-1942

John L. Whitaker
Died Feb 24, 1917
Age: 62 years
(Gallant FH)

Mrs. Ella, wife of
J. M. Golden
(no dates)

Press Williams
1898-1967

A. E. Keller
1880-1949
&
Cora E. Keller
1885-

Izzie K. Bates
1881-1960
&
Flora Webb Bates
1913-1952
"Mother & Daughter"

George N. Sanders, Sr.
1878-1954
&
Sallie T. Sanders
1878-1962

George N. Sanders, Jr.
May 25, 1921
Mar 24, 1945
(picture)

Melvin C. Sanders
Jun 30, 1907
Jul 1, 1967

Rev. L. C. Swinford
1893-1947

Odell S. Dodson
Feb 11, 1911
Feb 3, 1957

Edward Farmer
Jan 2, 1941
Jan 25, 1941

William Andrew Whitaker
1880-1957
&
Mary Emma Whitaker
1888-1966

Nannie H. McAnally
Feb 15, 1913
Jul 13, 1964
&
Jaunita McAnally
Apr 8, 1940
Oct 26, 1942

Linzy C. Tipton
1892-1955
&
Rosie I. Tipton
1894-

Joan Leniece, Daughter of
Mr. & Mrs. John E. Prater
Apr 4, 1940
Jan 25, 1941

William F. Mason
Alabama
Wagoner 142 Inf 36 Div
Died May 3, 1939
Age:(not given)

Odas V., Son of
H. W. & Rachel Cossey
May 30, 1920
Oct 5, 1923

George A. Fowler
1898-1965
&
Cora B. Fowler
1900-1949

Baby Fowler
B&D Nov 15, 1932

Mrs. Malah Jacks Jones
Died Apr 18, 1971
Age: 64 years.
(Laughlin FH, Huntsville, AL)

Father
Walter A. Winsett
1876-1955
& wife
Annie D. Winsett
1879-1900
& Mother
Nina K. Winsett
1883-1969

Sarah Aileen, Daughter of
Tom & Laura Sanders
Nov 27, 1932
Dec 29, 1935

Ferrell H. Hudson
Jul 1, 1882
Jul 28, 1965
&
Jennie Smith Hudson
Jul 14, 1884
Jun 24, 1936

Infant of
Duey & Pearl Gray
(no dates)

L. W., Son of
Duey & Pearl Gray
Aug 12, 1934
Jan 12, 1936

Pete K. Fanning
Dec 13, 1899
Oct 22, 1967
&
Laura Fanning
Nov 12, 1911
Feb 18, 1965

Blen Arnold Fanning
Jun 9, 1936
Jan 18, 1940

Bessie Fanning, wife of
Robert Farmer
Apr 13, 1904
Aug 8, 1936

Robert M. Farmer
Nov 29, 1902
Aug 10, 1964
&
Ina Lee Farmer
Jul 6, 1912

Monroe Felix Hudson
Mar 30, 1902
Aug 6, 1966
&
Beulah Winsett Hudson
Feb 17, 1906

FLINTVILLE QUADRANGLE

Madison Hudson
Dec 22, 1921
Nov 28, 1935

Velma Inez Hudson
Nov 25, 1933
Jun 17, 1935

Rufus Ray Keller
Dec 28, 1925
Mar 29, 1934

J. Calvin Hill
Apr 30, 1858
Feb 6, 1937

Felix P. George
1858-1939

Emily V. Jones Miller
Tennessee
TEC 5 WAC Corps WW II
May 26, 1905
Apr 20, 1967

Melva Nell, Daughter of
W. M. & Dora Day
Jun 24, 1933
Dec 24, 1933

Rev. J. L. Jones
1874-1953

Nancy G. Jones
Dec 3, 1938
Nov 6, 1943

Infant Son of
Jewell & Malah Jones
B&D Feb 13, 1936

Henry W. Gray
Feb 8, 1893
May 8, 1960
&
Lillie M. Gray
Sep 29, 1890

Infant of
H. W. & Lillie May Gray
(no dates)

John J. Dunston
May 11, 1848
Feb 23, 1929
&
Arminta M. Dunston
Sep 27, 1850
Sep 13, 1939

Gracie Bynum
Dec 15, 1898
Sep   1905
&
Virginia H. Bynum
Jan 1, 1880
Jan 10, 1900

Infant of
Mr. & Mrs. F. O. Bynum
1901

Mrs. D. A. Pendergrass
Jun 25, 1857
Mar 8, 1932

John W. Martin
Jul 20, 1882
Oct 7, 1966
&
Nancy M. Martin
Feb 29, 1884
Mar 15, 1971

Carlton, Son of
J. W. & Nancy Martin
Jan 23, 1914
Sep 9, 1928

Miles McGehee
Nov 30, 1869
(no date)
&
Matilda Bell McGehee
Oct 10, 1870
Dec 15, 1937

Elsie Marie, Daughter of
Howard & Flora McGehee
Feb 24, 1930
Mar 12, 1930

Infants of
B. E. & Annie McGehee
B&D Jan 10, 1922

Vera, Daughter of
E. McGehee & Wife
Jun 21, 1918
Jun 7, 1922

Royal U. Reid
1878-1948
&
Exia L. Reid
1889-19

Amanda Reid
Oct 5, 1850
Nov 19, 1937

W. H. Reid
Mar 7, 1851
May 21, 1927
&
Martha I. Reid
Oct 4, 1946
May 20, 1922

Francis Marion Farmer
Feb 5, 1868
Mar 25, 1949
&
Sarah Ellie Farmer
Mar 1, 1875
Jul 5, 1963

W. Shelton Bates
1903-
&
Lillie P. Bates
1909-1947

2 Infant graves in Brown Plot.

Jasper G. Smith
1886-1955
&
Olevia L. Smith
1886-

William Henry Sharp
Jun 25, 1895
Apr 24, 1967
&
Clara Mae Hudson Sharp
Nov 30, 1899
May 19, 1950

Jennie Pearl Panter Ray
Sep 14, 1900
Apr 25, 1961

James Panter
1866-1948
&
Mary J. Panter
1876-1940

Howard Gray
Pvt U. S. Army WW II
Jul 20, 1904
Apr 28, 1963

Samuel S. Gray
1869-1956
&
Sussie A. Gray
1869-1960

Infant of
Owen & May Gray
Given Aug 29, 1951
Taken Apr 25, 1952

Allie Powell, wife of
Otis L. Winsett
Nov 25, 1903
Apr 9, 1946

John Winsett
1926-1933

Glenn O. Winsett
Nov 1, 1908
Jul 5, 1961
&
Arva Vann Winsett
Jun 30, 1912

Melba Jean, Daughter of
G. O. & Arva Winsett
B&D Apr 1, 1933

Ermine L. Pitts, wife of
J. O. Winsett
May 11, 1886
Nov 22, 1951

Beauton, Infant of
Mr. & Mrs. C. C. McGee
B&D Jul 26, 1926

Gracie Winsett Powell
1902-1921
"& Her Infant Son, Wayne."

James O. Winsett
Mar 22, 1874
Apr 29, 1942
&
Maggie D. Winsett
Feb 16, 1877
Feb 2, 1904

Willie Stevenson
1893-1930

W. M. Stevenson
1873-1930

Sadie Baker
May 22, 1811
Feb 8, 1903

Marvin E. Winsett
Dec 24, 1887
May 22, 1959
&
Lizzie Norman Winsett
Jun 20, 1885
Aug 24, 1921

Rufus Ray Keller
Dec 28, 1925
Mar 29, 1934

John A. Winsett
Sep 24, 1847
Jan 13, 1922
&
Mary L. Winsett
Nov 5, 1849
Dec 15, 1925

A. B. Rozell
Apr 29, 1826
Jun 19, 1903

John C. Patterson
1853-1939
&
Sarah N. Patterson
1855-1934

Mary Jane, wife of
J. L. Baxter
Feb 24, 1852
Aug 20, 1898
Age: 76y, 5m, 27d.

Sarah Catharine, wife of
John A. Stiles
Aug 14, 1835
Dec 24, 1913

"My Husband"
J. T. Loyd
Died Apr 2, 1900
Age: 43y, 18d.

Infant Son Pepper
1921-1921

FLINTVILLE QUADRANGLE

Clark W. Pepper
1909-1923

Irene Pepper
1916-1922

Infant Son Pepper
1921-1921

W. Ezra Edmondson
1889-1969
&
Sarah J. Edmondson
1892-

Ralph, Son of
Mr. & Mrs. W. E. Edmondson
Jul 19, 1921
Jun 4, 1932

Miss Sadie Baker *
Died Feb 8, 1903
Age: 92y, 8m, 14d.

Mrs. Jennie Bynum *
Died Jan 10, 1900
Age: 19 years.

Paul Anthony Henderson
Died Sep 20, 1971
Age: B&D
(Ralston FH)

Charles E. Holt
Aug 22, 1931
Mar 12, 1971

Johnnie Mae Hazlewood
Apr 2, 1917
Oct 7, 1950
(picture)

Infant of
Allen & Buna Winsett
(no dates)

Joe F. Pruitt
1891-1961
(Gallant FH)

Flora Lee Pruitt
Jul 10, 1886
Jan 11, 1945

Mrs. Mary Jane Baxter
Married John L. Baxter
Apr 6, 1866
Died Aug 20, 1898
Age: 46y, 5m, 27d.

Mrs. Maud Nixon *
Married John Nixon in 1900
Died Aug 2, 1903
Age: 18 years.

Ollie F. Pitts
Jan 20, 1894
Aug 20, 1971
&
Lonie B. Pitts
Jan 26, 1895

Christopher H. Hone
Oct 9, 1884
Jul 3, 1960
&
Annie Mae Cooper Hone
Jun 17, 1886
Jun 10, 1950

Robert E. Hone
Aug 17, 1907
Mar 6, 1967

Thomas Gurley Cornelius
May 24, 1914
Mar 16, 1956
&
Jewell Manderson Cornelius
Feb 20, 1920

W. M. Stevenson *
Died Feb 6, 1899
Age: 21 years.

Son * of
Mr. & Mrs. J. H. May
Died Feb 26, 1911
Age: 4m.

Phillip Hershell Cox
Apr 13, 1971
May 12, 1971
Son of Mr. & Mrs. Randall Cox

Kinnon C. Manderson
Alabama
Pvt Oct Auto Repl Draft
WW I
Apr 22, 1897
Oct 4, 1958
&
Lula Camp Manderson
Sep 2, 1896

Otis Lee Winsett
Died Jun 4, 1974
Age: (not given)

Mrs. Annie D. Winsett *
Died Dec 6, 1900
Age: (not given)

Mrs. Maggie D. Winsett *
Married J. O. Winsett
Nov 8, 1903
Died Feb 2, 1904
Age: 26y, 11m, 16d.

Miss Cindy Lou Cris Gardner
Died Dec 15, 1971
Age: 14 years.
(Gallant FH)

Emma Lorene Stevenson *
Died Sep 28, 1906
Age: 8y, 10m.

Lee Evans *
Died Sep 4, 1916
near Lincoln
Age: 34 years.
Left 3 children.

* *

BAXTER CEMETERY

LOCATION: One and one half miles east of Vanntown, north of Hester Creek and south of Limestone Road.

Iredell Phillips
Dec 3, 1819
Oct 27, 1867

Mary Ann Vines
Jul 9, 1838
Nov 25, 1855

Alfred William Baxter *
Died May 6, 1899
Age: 66y, 5m, 21d.

Thomas Baxter *
Died Nov 15, 1873
Age: 70 years.

Jane,* wife of
Thomas Baxter
Died Nov 19, 1873
Age: (not given)

Ed NOTE: Old Hesters Creek Meeting House once stood near this cemetery.

* *

KILPATRICK CEMETERY

LOCATION: Two miles SSE of Flintville on bank of Big Huckleberry Creek, west side of Flintville-Limestone Road.

John Houston Hickson
Sep 22, 1885
Jun 5, 1963
&
Mattie Mae Hickson
Apr 22, 1892
Jan 21, 1951

Roy Hickson
Nov 17, 1912
Aug 11, 1932

Walter Hickson
Jul 23, 1915
Jan 12, 1919

Silas Hickson
B&D Dec 14, 1911

Y. T. Stiles
Feb 10, 1864
Feb 3, 1905

Leonzel, Son of
Y. T. & Emma Stiles
Oct 10, 1902
Aug 26, 1903

Hillis Baby
B&D Aug 31, 1963
(Gallant FH)

FLINTVILLE QUADRANGLE

Mariah M. Stiles
Dec 1896
Feb 1900

Lattie Cates
1900-(no date)

James Porter Kilpatrick
1881-1959
&
Florence Stiles Kilpatrick
1884-1924

Irene Greer Kilpatrick
1917-1936

John Goodwin Kilpatrick
Feb 21, 1920
Jul 2, 1953

John F. Kilpatrick
1867-1936
&
Lela I. Kilpatrick
1879-1956

5 unmarked graves.

John Wilson Thompson
Oct 18, 1918
Nov 12, 1918

James Herman Thompson
Aug 1, 1894
Dec 29, 1951
&
Sarah Kilpatrick Thompson
Sep 5, 1898

Rebecca Stewart
1869-1939
(Higgins FH)

Mary L. Turner
Feb 5, 1863
Mar 12, 1928

* *

MORGAN CEMETERY

LOCATION: Three miles SE of Flintville, north of Rail Road and one and one half miles NW of Elora.

Carl Jackson Counts
Died Jul 31, 1969
Age: 45y, 10m, 6d.
(TM)

Andrew J. Counts
Tennessee
Cpl U. S. Army WW I
Aug 8, 1893
Apr 16, 1959
&
Bessie D. Counts
1898-1961

Grat D. Davis
Sep 20, 1896
Feb 24, 1952
&
Dora A. Davis
Dec 12, 1900

Phoebe Crabtree Counts
Jun 10, 1862
Jan 25, 1957

W. G. Counts
1905-1926

H. W. Counts
1855-1918

Christine Counts
1933-1933

Arthur Milton Counts
Dec 12, 1886
May 2, 1964

Ida Counts Honey
Jan 12, 1882
Apr 2, 1958

Wilme Jean Staton
Died May 10, 1967
Age: 47y, 5m, 5d.

Edd E. Honey
Jan 9, 1887
Jan 6, 1958
&
Rebecca C. Honey
Jul 2, 1890

Avery H. Dotson
Feb 17, 1894

&
Bonnie M. Dotson
Oct 4, 1897
Apr 12, 1964

Edna W. Dotson
Jul 18, 1933
Jul 25, 1933

Infant Son
Joe Wayne Counts, Jr.
B&D Feb 19, 1963

Infant Daughter
Jenifer Jo Counts
B&D Jun 26, 1964

Margaret A. Counts
Feb 2, 1843
Jun 15, 1912

J. D. Counts
1812-1900

Nancy Counts
(no dates)

W. D. Harmening
1855-1932
&
Mary E. Harmening
1866-1934

James Crabtree
(no dates)

Aaron Benson
Apr 6, 1879
Jun 11, 1943
&
Maud Benson
Aug 6, 1883
(no date)

George W. Morgan
1876-1901

Maggie Morgan
1878-1897

Susie E. Morgan
1854-1913

Dr. W. L. Morgan
1858-1919

Millard H. Morgan
1895-1953

Ola P. Morgan
1881-1954

Walter M. Morgan
1885-1941

Mildred Louise Cartwright
(no dates, child)

Albert J. Cartwright
Pfc Btry E 113 field Arty
WW I
1888-1968
&
Geneva M. Cartwright

Nannie B. Roland
1910-1953

Marshall M. Stone
1907-1939

Walter A. Stone
Died Oct 19, 1956
Age: 79y, 6m, 15d.
(Spray FH)

J. M. Morgan
Jan 22, 1850
Oct 19, 1908
Married Julia Burchfield
Dec 3, 1903

Sam Jones Moore
Mar 17, 1904
Aug 11, 1905

Mattie Lou Moore
Dec 31, 1882
May 19, 1899

Jennie Moore
Apr 20, 1861
Jan 21, 1893

R. H. Morgan
Mar 4, 1869
May 23, 1925

W. H. Morgan
Feb 10, 1848
May 25, 1906
Age: 55y, 3m, 15d.
Erected by Rail Road
Associates.

G. W. Morgan
Apr 1, 1815
Aug 22, 1901

Louesa L., wife of
G. W. Morgan
Jul 8, 1827
Jul 17, 1892

Avery Bell Turner
May 15, 1894
Nov 15, 1961

FLINTVILLE QUADRANGLE

George W. Turner
Apr 15, 1866
Apr 1, 1928

Charity E. Turner
Apr 29, 1873
Dec 27, 1958

Will T. Waters
1873-1936
&
Sarah Ann Waters
1879-1936

Layman L. Whitfield
Aug 15, 1902

&
Gracie Whitfield
Oct 18, 1904
May 17, 1968

George David Whitfield
Apr 24, 1871
Jun 23, 1954
&
Nannie Lou Whitfield
Sep 16, 1876
Nov 26, 1930

Vernice L. Whitfield
Mar 6, 1900
Sep 11, 1902

Mrs. Elizabeth E.,* wife
of Joseph Pitcock
Died Jul 4, 1899
Age: 49y, 7m, 26d.

Thomas Hicks Whitfield
Jan 2, 1879
Sep 10, 1959

Sarah Caroline Whitfield
Mar 6, 1874
Feb 6, 1941

Ada Louise Whitfield
B&D Jan 22, 1928

William Dewvoice
Jun 25, 1917
Jan 30, 1919

Wornie Dewvoice
May 8, 1893
Jan 20, 1919

Thomas Self
Dec 8, 1934
Dec 19, 1935

B. H. Whitfield
Jul 22, 1849
Sep 29, 1936

M. A. Whitfield
Mar 25, 1845
Oct 10, 1934

Margrette E. King
Died Feb 18, 1928
Age: 75 years.

Mrs. C. A. Stone *
Married G. W. Stone in 1894
Died Mar 11, 1906
Age: 30y, 1m, 6d.

Homer Self
Feb 6, 1901
May 27, 1945
&
Virgie Self
Oct 28, 1896

Loise J. Self
Tennessee
Pfc 7 Inf 3 Div WW II
Sep 11, 1924
Aug 18, 1944

Ruby Steele
Nov 15, 1914
Aug 12, 1937

Nannie McKelvy
Aug 11, 1865
May 17, 1905

E. F. Hawkins
Dec 28, 1874
Nov 14, 1906

Julia Ann McKee
Jul 25, 1878
May 17, 1952

William Thomas McKee
Jul 22, 1936
Jul 22, 1936

Cleveland Clinton McKee
Oct 19, 1890
Mar 20, 1955

George W. Stone
Oct 27, 1872
Dec 23, 1955

M. E., wife of
G. W. Stone
Mar 20, 1867
Mar 13, 1949

C. A., wife of
G. W. Stone
Feb 5, 1876
Mar 11, 1906

John D. Stone
Dec 6, 1929
Jun 22, 1961

Arthur W. Counts
Mar 24, 1886
Dec 14, 1918

Annie L. Counts
1874-1962

David Counts * of
Flintville
Died Aug 20, 1906
Age: 89y, 5m, 20d.

N. D. Counts *
Died Oct 24, 1908
Age: 55y, 5m, 8d.

Willie,* Son of
J. M. Morgan
Jan 17, 1876
Jan 13, 1893
Age: 21y, 11m, 26d.

* *

FRANKEWING QUADRANGLE

SMITH CEMETERY

LOCATION: One fourth mile SE of Red Oak.

William Smith Jan 28, 1782 Dec 1871	D. M. Smith Oct 7, 1828 Dec 25, 1915	Lizzie May Smith Died Jul 19, 1890 Age: 23 years.	John W. Smith Aug 20, 1858 Aug 24, 1859
Jane Smith 1803-1886 Age: 83 years.	Martha Jane Smith Nov 25, 1838 Sep 14, 1910	Mary Ida Smith Died Jul 24, 1857 Age: 6m.	

* *

RODEN CEMETERY

LOCATION: One mile NE of Red Oak and north of Delina Road.

Idar Jane, Daughter of William Roden (no dates) Born before 1830 ***	William Roden *** 1798-1882 (fieldstone)	John Sumners *** 1772-1845 (fieldstone)	Several unmarked graves.
Jane,*** Daughter of John & Rebecca Sumners (no dates)	Sarah Sumners,*** wife of William Roden 1810-1869 (fieldstone)	Rebecca, *** wife of John Sumners Died 1857 (fieldstone)	*** Family Records of Haskel Roden.

* *

DAVIS CEMETERY

LOCATION: Two miles NW of Boonshill, two miles east of Red Oak and one half mile NE of Boonshill-Red Oak Road.

N. P. Davis (no dates, fieldstone)	J. B. Davis Nov 2, 1822 Mar 20, 1881 & wife	W. B. Alsup Jul 22, 1855 Oct 24, 1890	Donnie, wife of J. B. Collins Died Feb 21, 1888 Age: 26y, 22d.
J. B. Davis Died Nov 1881 Age: 32 years. (fieldstone)	Mary A. Davis May 22, 1840 May 24, 1909	Anderson Alsup Jul 16, 1809 Dec 16, 1887 &	Epp Harden Oct 1, 1822 Jan 11, 1898 Age: 77y, 3m, 10d.
M. C. E. Davis Died Jun 28, 1890 Age: 55 years. (fieldstone)	Ann E. Wilson Died Sep 7, 1877 Age: (not given) (fieldstone)	Sarah Alsup Oct 19, 1815 Jun 1, 1887	C. C. Harden Feb 17, 1828 Feb 15, 1899
J. Davis Died Jun 4, 1849 Age: (not given) (fieldstone)	J. T. Wilson Died Dec 24, 1902 Age: 86 years. (fieldstone)	Elmira Buffalo 1859-1936 J. E. Bell (no dates, fieldstone)	Leroy Wright 1854-1908
Priscilly Davis Died Jan 23, 1868 Age: (not given)	J. C. Reed Dec 13, 1820 Jul 28, 1897	C. Barrow Died Feb 3, 1890 Age: 77 years. (fieldstone)	Harriet Wright Oct 25, 1815 Aug 19, 1905
J. D. Robinson Died Oct 11, 1893 Age: 31y, 11m, 19d.	Lou Reed Aug 31, 1833 May 7, 1921	R. E. Smith Nov 2, 1886 Nov 26, 1908	Annie W. Harper 1854-1909
Thaddeus, Son of A. T. & C. M. Spivy Jul 22, 1890 Sep 24, 1891	Katie Sue Swaner Jun 4, 1891 Mar 28, 1900	P. M. (no dates, fieldstone)	Rena, wife of J. L. Moore Nov 11, 1869 Nov 6, 1902
			Many unmarked graves.

* *

FRANKEWING QUADRANGLE

BEASLEY CEMETERY

LOCATION: Two and one half miles NNW of Boonshill, one mile south of Delina on "Old Archer Beasley Place."

*** Family Records of Timothy R. Marsh

Archibald Beasley ***
1773-1850

Nancy,*** wife of
Archibald Beasley
Died between
1840-1850

Elizabeth,*** wife of
David S. Hobbs
(no dates)

____ ***, Daughter of
Archer & Nancy Beasley
(no dates)

5 graves with native fieldstones with no inscriptions.

NOTE: Archer Beasley was born in Nottoway Co., Va.

* *

LOVETT CEMETERY

LOCATION: Two and one fourth miles NNE of McBurg on Chicken Creek.

Allen Coble
Mar 14, 1817
Jan 3, 1913

Saluda A., wife of
Allen Coble
Nov 11, 1821
Nov 14, 1894

J. M. Brady
Mar 22, 1837
May 16, 1902

Mary Ann, wife of
J. M. Brady
Sep 24, 1838
Feb 5, 1925

W. M. Coble
Jan 14, 1845
Aug 18, 1899

Frances Haislip
1930-1946

Donnie, wife of
F. F. Haislip
Mar 1, 1898
Oct 19, 1930

Infant Daughter of
F. F. & Donnie Haislip
B&D May 13, 1923

Infant of
Mr. & Mrs. A. J. Lovett
Jun 29, 1903
Jul 7, 1903

Algie V. Lovett
Nov 9, 1907
Aug 6, 1923

Infant * of
M. C. & Ethel Cathcart
B&D Oct 29, 1896

A. J. Lovett
Oct 29, 1855
Jan 8, 1939

Elizabeth Jane Brady,
wife of
A. J. Lovett
Oct 16, 1864
Apr 29, 1926

Mrs. Reney Cathcart *
Died Aug 21, 1895
Age: 34 years.

* *

MELTON CEMETERY

LOCATION: One and one half miles NNW of McBurg on top of Backbone Ridge.

About 10 fieldstones with no inscriptions.
(T.V.A. map lists this cemetery as Melton Cemetery.)

* *

ALLSUP CEMETERY

LOCATION: One mile north of McBurg on east side of road.

B. M. Allsup
Feb 26, 1805
Jul 16, 1868

Margarett, wife of
B. M. Allsup
Jun 4, 1811
Nov 25, 1893

Brice D. Alsup
1888-1907

Sallie Young, wife of
J. W. Mooney
Died Feb 15, 1911
Age: 56 years.

Laura E., wife of
B. G. Allsup
Jul 31, 1860
May 16, 1893

Emmaranda, wife of
A. J. Compton
Dec 19, 1847
Mar 22, 1883

William Ross Whitaker
Nov 11, 1898
Nov 10, 1899
&
Slater Mooney Whitaker
Jun 3, 1897
Jun 7, 1898
Children of
J. K. & E. M. Whitaker

W. B. Alsup *
Died Oct 24, 1890
Age: 35 years.

Elizabeth Allsup
Feb 6, 1832
Apr 13, 1893

Jos. D. Whitaker
Sep 8, 1902
Dec 7, 1904

* *

FRANKEWING QUADRANGLE

LEE CEMETERY

LOCATION: One half mile north of McBurg on east side of road.

Court Records say this was Old Daniel Lee Estate.

Several unmarked graves.

* *

McBURG CEMETERY

LOCATION: At McBurg adjoining the church.

Sallie A. Joines
1874-1920

Mary A. Joines
1847-1912

A. Davis
Nov 16, 1844
Dec 20, 1911

Jesse Orena, wife of
J. O. Gill
1889-1913

B. A. Harwell
Aug 2, 1836
Aug 30, 1902

Elizabeth G.(C) Harwell
Jul 13, 1856
Mar 3, 1922

James A. Hatfield
Oct 4, 1812
Jan 1, 1908
&
Sarah E. Hatfield
Mar 2, 1867
May 25, 1919

John M. Moore
Apr 25, 1846
Jul 31, 1901

Little Maggie, Daughter of
J. M. & M. A. Moore
Nov 17, 1882
Sep 29, 1899

Mrs. Mary Ann,*
Married J. B. Davis
May 13, 1859
Died May 24, 1909
Age: 69 years.

Robert Lexie,* Son of
R. E. & Beatrice Davis
Died Apr 8, 1905
Age: 1y, 4m, 27d.

Mrs. Amtic,* wife of
W. C. Bryant
Died Sep 17, 1905
Age: 32 years.

Infant * Daughter of
Gus Brewer
B&D Sep 2, 1902

Luther, Son of
B. A. & E. G(C). Harwell
Feb 24, 1889
Mar 15, 1902

Sarah J., wife of
A. M. Collins
Nov 14, 1833
Jul 24, 1900

J. Frank Abbott
Dec 18, 1885
Apr 29, 1919

Maude G(C). Abbott
Jan 21, 1879
Jan 21, 1904

Sam Knox Beard
1906-1922

Brice G. Alsup
1854-1920

Emma Holt, wife of
B. G. Alsup
1869-1929

Children of
B. G. & Emma Alsup
(no dates)

W. H. Jacobs
1855-1936

Ella Jacobs
1867-19?? (illegible)

Mrs. Mollie C.,*
Married J. W. Troxler in 1883
Died Sep 5, 1897
Age: 32 years.

Mrs. Ruthie,* wife of
Robert Davis
Married 1857
Died Aug 24, 1897
Age: 81 years.

William C. Bryant *
Died Feb 8, 1908
Age: 41 years.

Infant * Son of
Mr. & Mrs. Gus Brewer
Died Feb 27, 1904
Age: 1m.

J. A. Abbott
Jul 14, 1850
Jun 4, 1904

Eliza, wife of
J. A. Abbott
Jul 21, 1851
Jun 26, 1907

S. Bettie Davis
Dec 20, 1853
Jan 22, 1904

Lula Abbott, wife of
W. B. Markham
Dec 24, 1888
Apr 11, 1909

W. C. Harwell
Dec 12, 1874
Mar 12, 1927

Fannie Josie Abbott, wife of
W. C. Harwell
Sep 21, 1876
Jul 15, 1912

Nancy A. Bass
Sep 22, 1826
Dec 23, 1899

Floyd, Son of
H. T. & C. L. Baster
Jun 23, 1908
Jul 11, 1908

Mary A., Daughter of
H. T. & C. L. Baster
Aug 8, 1900
Sep 30, 1900

Henry S., Son of
H. T. & C. L. Baster
Jul 23, 1902
Sep 30, 1902

John T., Son of
H. T. & C. L. Baster
May 12, 1906
Mar 30, 1907

Infant * Son of
Mr. & Mrs. Gus Brewer
Died Aug 27, 1908
Age:(not given)

*** Info by Haskel Roden

Mary Adell, Daughter of
W. C. & Maude Harwell
Oct 15, 1917
Jul 2, 1926

William T. Edwards
1876-19(1946)
&
Myrtle Edwards
1879-19(1946)
&
Jake V. Edwards
1881-1941

Polly Roten
(no dates) or
Mary Margaret Roden ***
1827-1910

Wesley W. Edwards
Co K 1st Tenn Inf C.S.A.
(died 1927 ***)

Martha Ann Edwards
May 19, 1839
Jul 15, 1915

James Milton
Feb 10, 1836
Feb 10, 1914
&
Susie E., wife of
James Milton
May 28, 1840
Mar 27, 1912

Mattie Sue, Daughter of
W. T. & L. V. Milton
Aug 9, 1905
Oct 7, 1910

Sam,* Son of
Mr. & Mrs. J. W. Troxler
Died Jan 15, 1897
Age: 14m, 18d.

Eugene,* Son of
Theo McCracken
Died in Fulton, KY
May 25, 1905
Age: 16 years.

Samuel McCullough *
Died Dec 14, 1904
Age: 86 years.

FRANKEWING QUADRANGLE

Mrs. Retta,* wife of
Gus Brewer
Died Jun 10, 1905
Age: 26y, 3m, 26d.

Lela Robison *
Died Oct 10, 1907
Age: 18 years.

many unmarked graves.

* *

RAMBO CEMETERY

LOCATION: At McBurg on north side of Highway 64.

William C. Rambo
1842-1922

Martha E. Rambo
Aug 5, 1876
Dec 24, 1896

Miss Dempsie Rambo *
Died Mar 11, 1898
Age: 19 years.

Mrs. Polly Rambo *
Died Jan 17, 1894
Age: 76 years.

Mrs. Emiline,* wife of
W. C. Rambo
Died Mar 21, 1897
Age: 50 years.

* *

GUNTER CEMETERY

LOCATION: One mile NE of McBurg, north of Highway 64.

John Henry Gunter
Sep 4, 1843
May 20, 1941

Menzia G. Gunter
Oct 4, 1850
May 18, 1910

William Gunter
(no dates, fieldstone)

S. A. Haislip
Jun 26, 1879
Apr 9, 1905

Laura Haislip
1882-1939

Gracie B., Daughter of
S. A. & Laura Haislip
Aug 31, 1903
Mar 20, 1904

Bertha May Gunter
May 16, 1884
Jul 29, 1909

Maggie Lee Gunter
Jan 23, 1879
Sep 17, 1927

Cleo Gunter
Sep 5, 1908
Jun 14, 1910

* *

ROBISON CEMETERY

LOCATION: On side of Ridge, north side of Highway 64 at Bowden Gap.

Mrs. Mildred,* wife of
Henry Robison
Married Jan 18, 1842
Died Oct 6, 1905
Age: 84y, 1m, 19d.

Only fieldstones with no
inscriptions.

* *

WILSON CEMETERY

LOCATION: One mile west of Boonshill, three-fourth mile NNW of Taylortown on west side of McAfee Branch.

John, Son of
J. H. & S. E. Clark
Dec 15, 1871
Jan 15, 1892

J. Porter Clark
Mar 27, 1846
Jan 4, 1898

Rebecca McClain Clark
1846-1936

Matt Wilson
(no dates)

John Clark
Aug 2, 1815
Oct 13, 1890

P. B. Clark
Jun 14, 1834
Apr 12, 1901

Byrd D. Wilson
1879-19(no date)
&
Eva W. Wilson
1874-19(no date)

Infant Children of
Matt & Maggie Wilson
Mar 10, 1897
Mar 13, 1897

Ellen, Daughter of
Matt & Maggie Wilson
Dec 19, 1895
Jan 18, 1897

Infant Children of
Matt & Maggie Wilson
B&D Dec 25, 1894

Frank, Son of
Matt & Maggie Wilson
Sep 22, 1893
Sep 25, 1893

Little Twins, Children of
Matt & Maggie Wilson
Dec 3, 1886
Dec 7, 1886

Annie Adell, Daughter of
Matt & Maggie Wilson
Jan 19, 1888
Jul 11, 1888

FRANKEWING QUADRANGLE

Shields Wilson Jul 16, 1835 Jun 15, 1899 & Mary Lou Wilson Dec 7, 1834 (no date) John H. March Feb 29, 1860 Oct 8, 1873 William H. Marshall Jun 3, 1811 Mar 1, 1880 Andrew M. Suttle Mar 1, 1845 Aug 4, 1855 Jonas S. Suttle Oct 5, 1854 Aug 12, 1855	Boon Wilson Aug 30, 1791 Dec 28, 1859 Nancy, wife of Boon Wilson Aug 2, 1792 Sep 25, 1871 Nannie M., Daughter of W. H. & Delina Marshall Feb 22, 1847 May 1, 1847 Infant Son of B. F. & F. A. Suttle Age: 6m. (no dates) Many unmarked graves.	Rebecca A., Consort of A. G. March Oct 10, 1836 Married Nov 29, 1853 Died Feb 11, 1866 Age: 29y, 4m. "She was a member of the C. P. Church." Sarah A. H., Consort of S. A. Hillyard Mar 26, 1840 Aug 25, 1866 Age: 26y, 5m. "She was a member of the C. P. Church." Miss Claudie,* Daughter of Mrs. E. S. Wilson Died Sep 24, 1907 Age: (not given)	W. B. March Mar 20, 1863 Jul 20, 1864 S. E. March Dec 26, 1857 May 13, 1873 Ben H. Marshall Jun 22, 1815 Jan 2, 1892 & wife Sarah E. Wilson March Sep 12, 1827 Jul 1, 1890 Mrs. Josie Marshall * Died May 7, 1907 Age: 63 years.

* *

WELLS CEMETERY

LOCATION: One half mile WSW of Boonshill, north of Highway 64 on south side of hill.

1 Large Rock Vault with no inscription.
7 feet high by 6 feet wide.

Arron Wells *
Died 1842
& Son
Thomas Wells
(no dates)

(Tradition is that Aaron Wells, a Pioneer of Lincoln County, died 1842, was buried here in an upright position. Also, his son, Thomas Wells is buried here.)

ED NOTE: Aaron Wells was an early, large land owner on Swan Creek near Boonshill. His widow, Mary Wells died in Marshall County, Tennessee.

* *

CEMETERY

LOCATION: One half mile WNW of Boonshill on top of hill.

Mary E., Daughter of
Andrew & Ann Wilson
Mar 3, 1828
Sep 17, 1845

Several fieldstones, no inscriptions.

* *

SWINEBROAD CEMETERY

LOCATION: One mile NW of Boonshill, south side of Red Oak Road, in the woods.

John B. Swinebroad Aug 30, 1831 Jan 11, 1847	John W. Sanders May 17, 1828 Jul 10, 1879	W. A. D. (no dates, fieldstone)	1 large Vault (no inscription)

* *

FRANKEWING QUADRANGLE

SMITH CEMETERY

LOCATION: One half mile SW of McBurg, on south side of a small branch.

Sarah G. Sutton
Feb 15, 1841
Mar 16, 1905

Willie Sutton McKnight
Aug 29, 1885
Mar 11, 1905

Jeffie P. Sutton, wife of
G. W. McKnight
Jul 27, 1861
Sep 14, 1887

G. W. Woodard
Dec 25, 1856
Aug 13, 1897

Colmore, son of
G. W. & Hortense Woodard
Dec 14, 1876
Jul 27, 1877

Infant Daughter of
Arrowsmith & Myrtle H.
Clark
B&D Jul 8, 1915

1 unmarked grave.

William G. Smith
Jul 24, 1789
Oct 6, 1840

Sarah, Consort of
William G. Smith
Died Oct 8, 1840
Age: (not given)

Maselda Rilla Smith
Jan 2, 1821
Aug 18, 1845

William Boon, son of
William P. & Martha J. Smith
B&D Feb 18, 1846

William P. Smith
Apr 21, 1825
(no date)

Martha Jane Smith
Mar 8, 1824
Oct 9, 1878

Charles Emmett Sutton
Nov 8, 1845
May 7, 1916
&
Nancy Harwell Sutton
Jun 21, 1852
Mar 24, 1904

Kelly Brown, Son of
R. E. & S. A. Harwell
Oct 28, 1894
Jul 3, 1895

Sarah Katharine, Daughter of
William S. & Nancy Harwell
Jul 30, 1844
May 13, 1848

William S. Harwell
Nov 6, 1824
Aug 15, 1885

Nancy Y., wife of
William S. Harwell
Jan 29, 1822
Jun 22, 1891

Infant child of
W. G. & E. O. Harwell
B&D Nov 20, 1892

Colmo B. Sutton
Apr 13, 1870
Jan 9, 1897

William David Sutton
Feb 25, 1872
Oct 23, 1893

Several unmarked graves.

Ella O., Daughter of
W. G. & Ella O. Harwell
Sep 17, 1883
Oct 2, 1884

W. G. Harwell
Jul 14, 1849
Jan 26, 1902

Eleanor O. Benson, wife of
W. G. Harwell
Jun 15, 1851
Sep 20, 1924

Robbie Louise Story
Dec 20, 1900
Mar 24, 1903

Samuel Eugene, Son of
R. F. & Edna Story
Feb 2, 1904
Oct 15, 1908

Jeff Davis Sutton
Sep 21, 1894
Mar 11, 1895

* *

THORPE CEMETERY

LOCATION: One mile south of McBurg on east side of Dellrose Road.

John Thorpe
Born in Virginia
Sep 14, 1808
Died in Lincoln Co., Tenn.
Nov 5, 1875
Age: 67 years.

Jose B. Thorpe
Born in Giles Co., Tenn.
Mar 29, 1850
May 9, 1879
Age: 29 years.

Nancy, wife of
John Thorpe
Aug 7, 1813
Jun 10, 1890
&
Maud J., wife of
R. P. Parker
Mar 6, 1872
Jun 24, 1897
&
Susan E., wife of
Newton Malone
Mar 17, 1835
Jul 19, 1914

James Thorpe
Born in Virginia
Apr 14, 1775
Died in Lincoln Co., Tenn.
Aug 6, 1868
Age: 93 years.

Sarah, Consort of
James Thorpe
May 29, 1776
Aug 6, 1854

Several unmarked graves.

* *

GILL CEMETERY

LOCATION: Two miles SE of McBurg on east fork of Leatherwood Creek, on top of hill in woods.

Margaret A. Braden
Sep 24, 1860
Aug 26, 1872
Age: 11y, 11m, 12d.

Alafair Robinson, wife of
J. B. Gill
Aug 12, 1818
Apr 8, 1890

Ed NOTE: Unmarked grave is next to Alafair R. Gill, probably J. B. Gill.

Mail Mattox
Jul 28, 1790
Dec 29, 1831

FRANKEWING QUADRANGLE

Sarah L., Daughter of
E. H. & M. C. Gregory
Jul 19, 1873
Apr 20, 1877

William M., Son of
E. H. & M. C. Gregory
Dec 20, 1877
Aug 3, 1898

Talitha G., wife of
John Brotherton
Feb 14, 1815
Jan 4, 1885

George Martin Bevels
Jan 18, 1844
Apr 23, 1916

Nannie Thelma, Daughter of
J. W. & M. C. Arnold
Sep 19, 1902
Aug 14, 1903

Levoy, Son of
Walter & Delia Arnold
B&D May 12, 1925

About 100 unmarked graves.

Mrs. Jane Childress *
Died Jan 4, 1893
Age: 75 years.

Jennie,* Daughter of
Mr. & Mrs. James Smith
Died Aug 14, 1895
Age: 13m.

J. H. Arnold
May 14, 1857
Jun 18, 1930

Nancy Suzana, wife of
J. H. Arnold
Nov 11, 1851
Nov 6, 1917

Mary Elizabeth Carpenter
Oct 9, 1874
Apr 18, 1891

John Britton Carpenter
Apr 5, 1880

Ella Belle Carpenter
Mar 18, 1876
Married Jul 17, 1900
Died May 7, 1905

Daisy May, Daughter of
J. M. & Myrtle Arnold
Mar 24, 1909
Jan 9, 1919

George L., Son of
S. E. & L. E. Barnes
May 25, 1909
Sep 9, 1910

Mrs. Ruthie,* widow of
Jackson Mitchell
Died Sep 30, 1897
Age: 80 years.

T. M. Beddingfield *
Died Sep 15, 1898
Age: 69 years.

J. W. Carpenter
Jul 24, 1843
Aug 8, 1929

Elzetta Taylor, wife of
J. W. Carpenter
Mar 22, 1847
Nov 15, 1910

_____ Carpenter
- 192_
(Raby FH)

Mary Carpenter
1889-1952
(Wilson FH)

Albert, Son of
O. B. R. & Nancy Carpenter
Nov 1, 1900
Sep 25, 1906

Peggie G. Harris
Mar 11, 1899
Mar 12, 1905

J. W. Gregory
Aug 12, 1867
Nov 14, 1913

Mrs. Gracy,* wife of
Sam Beddingfield
Died Jul 16, 1904
Age: 27 years.

S. M. Beddingfield *
Died Jan 16, 1918
Age: 68y, 10m, 11d.

Dr. T. G. Smith
Aug 21, 183_
___ 9, 1902 (broken)

M. V., wife of
Dr. T. G. Smith
Oct 1, 1838
Nov 24, 1919

Mecca, Daughter of
T. G. & M. V. Smith
Feb 19, 1874
Feb 5, 1896

M. C. Gregory
May 8, 1848
May 19, 1925
&
E. H. Gregory
Dec 12, 1851
Jun 9, 1925

Leonard, Son of
W. E. & S. M. Gregory
Nov 21, 1908
Dec 9, 1910

Martha A. Gregory
Died 1900
Age: 15 years.

Mrs. M. J. Coble *
Died Feb 21, 1908
Age: 55 years.

ED NOTE: Once a large
Community Burying Ground.

* *

HOVIS-GREGORY CEMETERY

LOCATION: Three miles SE of McBurg on east side of hill and
west side of main road, in Bugtussle Hollow.

Elizabeth Hovis
Died Apr 13, 1884
Age: 75 years.

S. Gregory
Jul 25, 1829
Oct 11, 1894

B. C. Debose
Apr 26, 1825
Jun 2, 1896

Several unmarked graves.

* *

HEDGEPETH CEMETERY

LOCATION: One and one fourth mile SSW of Taylortown, One
and one fourth mile west of Swan Creek Church.

A. B. Johnson *
Married Aug 6, 1868 to
Ida Hedgepeth
Died Dec 27, 1897
Age: 52 years.

No signs of this cemetery
remain today. All stones
have been removed.

* *

FRANKEWING QUADRANGLE

JOHNSON CEMETERY

LOCATION: One and one fourth miles SSW of Taylortown, one and one fourth mile west of Swan Creek Church.

No markers remain today.

* *

RUSSELL CEMETERY

LOCATION: Two and one fourth miles SSW of McBurg, west of Railroad near Giles County line, north of Bunker Hill Road, on side of hill.

Asa G. Russell
Feb 19, 1825
Sep 2, 1848
&
M. D. Russell
May 16, 1838
May 8, 1860

J. G. Russell
Sep 10, 1819
Jul 18, 1878

R. R. (fieldstone)
(no dates)

M. D. R. (fieldstone)
(no dates)

A. G. R. (fieldstone)
(no dates)

Sarah E., Daughter of
David & R. L. Russell
Oct 11, 1841
Jan 29, 1848

Robert, Son of
David & R. L. Russell
Dec 27, 1843
Jan 20, 1948

James M., Son of
D. & R. L. Russell
Mar 8, 1850
Apr 12, 1856

Permelia A., Daughter of
D. & R. L. Russell
Apr 8, 1854
Apr 20, 1856

William Kirk, Son of
J. K. & M. M. Cardin
Dec 21, 1873
Feb 21, 1878

William Merrell
Jan 24, 1817
Oct 30, 1881

George Washington Merrell
Pvt Co H 3rd Tenn Regt
Son of William &
Charlotte Merrell
Feb 25, 1843
Died at Camp Tousdale
Sep 10, 1861

Charlie May, Daughter of
R. D. & F. J. Merrell
Oct 8, 1874
Apr 20, 1877

M. D. (fieldstone)
Died 1868

H. G. D.(fieldstone)
Died 1868

M. J. D.(fieldstone)
(no dates)

1 large vault
(no inscription)

Several unmarked graves.

* *

HEREFORD CEMETERY

LOCATION: Two and one half miles SSW of McBurg, west side of Railroad, west side of Bee Spring Road, near Giles County Line.

Amanda F., wife of
J. S. Routt
Apr 12, 1857
Apr 3, 1886

Mattie Hereford
Apr 25, 1891
Mar 25, 1892
&
Eva Hereford
Sep 20, 1893
Aug 20, 1894

Josiah McCracken
Jul 8, 1811
May 5, 1856

Julia Ann McCracken
Jan 13, 1816
Jul 14, 1908
Age: 92y, 6m, 1d.

John W. McCracken
1840-1893

F. L. Ezell
May 5, 1830
Jun 6, 1897
Age: 67y, 1m, 1d.

Mary I., wife of
F. L. Ezell
May 7, 1836
Oct 19, 1908

J. L. Ezell
Feb 14, 1870
Aug 6, 1929

Mary Lou Smith Ezell
1870-1944

James Everette Ezell
Nov 26, 1901
Aug 12, 1922

Matt F. Story
1863-1934
&
Carrie A. Story
1871-1959

S. L. Curtis
Aug 16, 1862
Aug 8, 1945
&
Ella Mae Curtis
Sep 30, 1868
(no date)

Katharine Story Blunt
Jul 7, 1892
Aug 29, 1915

Margaret A. Edward, wife of
J. E. Christopher
Jul 17, 1888
Nov 19, 1912

Caladonia, Daughter of
Thomas & Mary McCracken
Aug 1, 1841
Feb 28, 1864
Age: 22y, 6m, 27d.

T. D. Curtis
Died Apr 12, 1918
Age: 67 years.

Thomas C. McCracken
Sep 4, 1801
Oct 23, 1856
Age: 51y, 3m, 19d.

Mary Williams, wife of
Thomas C. McCracken
Nov 25, 1802
Feb 17, 1867
Age: 64y, 2m, 22d.

Julia A., wife of
W. T. Woodard
Oct 6, 1860
Apr 11, 1912

Eldin H., Son of
A. S. & Nora Curtis
May 11, 1911
May 31, 1911

W. S. Curtis
Nov 14, 1823
Jun 10, 1894

FRANKEWING QUADRANGLE

M. F., wife of
W. S. Curtis
Jan 10, 1834
Sep 20, 1903

Sarah J., wife of
R. J. Curtis
Mar 3, 1845
Mar 14, 1878
&
Infant Son of
R. J. & S. J. Curtis
B&D Nov 7, 1870

Charles Mays Curtis
Feb 4, 1866
       1955
&
Martha Estella Curtis
Dec 20, 1870
Nov 5, 1938

Sally May Thorpe
Sep 14, 1900
Jun 26, 1902

Harry Thorpe
Aug 10, 1882
Jun 1, 1903

C. F. Thorpe
1836-1924
&
Amanda Thorpe
1838-1905

Ned Thorpe
Feb 6, 1905
Apr 10, 1925

S. M. Thorpe
1863-1929
&
Maggie Thorpe
1874-1961

Mrs. E. E., wife of
Thomas Curtis
Died Jan 10, 1893
Age: 67 years.

Bonnie Allen Thorpe
Sep 6, 1902
Jun 19, 1951

Mary Margaret Thorpe
(no dates)
&
Sue Gail Thorpe
(no dates)

Thomas E. Thorpe
1878-1956

John Thorpe
1912-1965

James E. Thorpe
1917-1958

Joe D. Thorpe
1895-1958
&
Sallie E. Thorpe
1903-

Colie Brown Thorpe
Tennessee
Pvt Medical Dept WW II
Mar 15, 1899
Jan 8, 1959

Sallie May, Daughter of
S. M. & M. L. Thorpe
Sep 14, 1900
Jun 26, 1902

Jasper C. Curtis
Jan 10, 1890
Feb 25, 1913

Elmo Curtis
1889-1930

Mrs. Elizabeth Thorpe *
Died Jan 24, 1891
Age: 79 years.

J. B. McCracken *
Nov 2, 1844
Jul 24, 1903
   C.S.A.

Sarah Curtis
1870-1958

George Curtis
1903-1959

Don Roger Curtis
1953-1953

Tom J. Curtis
Apr 6, 1880
Sep 25, 1960
&
Margaret E. Curtis
Apr 10, 1880
Oct 30, 1933

Garlin Curtis
1897-1939

Rev. C. C. Curtis
(dates gone)

Mrs. A. C. Curtis
1899-1948

Martha V. Curtis
Feb 14, 1867
Jan 14, 1962

Ora Harney
1885-1962

Loney Jones
1896-1964

Gertie H. Curtis
1908-1968

Mrs. Mary E. Nation
1938-1965
(London FH)

Theo Massey
1887-1955

Several unmarked graves.

Robert Strong Hereford
Jul 19, 1847
Dec 25, 1929
&
Elizabeth McCracken
Hereford
Sep 21, 1850
Jun 21, 1906

John Will Hereford
1872-1957
&
Tera M. Hereford
1880-1956

Matthew Wilson, Son of
J. W. & T. M. Hereford
Aug 25, 1915
Oct 11, 1917

J. H. Curtis
Aug 16, 1875
Aug 25, 1946
&
Anna Curtis
May 16, 1884
(no date)

Benton Smith Curtis
Nov 17, 1910
Dec 15, 1933

Mattie Sherrell Zinimon
Apr 15, 1887
Feb 15, 1912

Mrs. Alice Dyer
1905-1958
(Mayberry FH)

Price Driver
1861-1949
(Queen Ann FH)

Mollie Driver
1859-1955
(Queen Ann FH)

* *

CEMETERY

LOCATION: Two miles NNW of Dellrose, on west side of the
Dellrose-Frankewing Road.

4 or 5 graves with fieldstones, no inscriptions.

* *

FRANKEWING QUADRANGLE

GEORGE CEMETERY

LOCATION: Two miles north of Dellrose on top of Ridge between Harrison and Hames Hollows.

Eliza, wife of
O. G. Harrison
Jul 22, 1850
Mar 28, 1878

S. E., wife of
O. G. Harrison
Jul 13, 1852
Oct 12, 1899

Mollie L., Daughter of
O. G. & S. E. Harrison
Jan 21, 1889
Jun 19, 1891

Infant of
O. G. & S. E. Harrison
B&D May 20, 1884

Several unmarked graves.

Cora A., Daughter of
O. G. & E. J. Harrison
Jun 8, 1871
Aug 15, 1874

T. R., Son of
R. M. & S. E. Harrison
Dec 10, 1875
Dec 2, 1892

M. A., wife of
J. P. Mitchell
Jan 11, 1858
Apr 1, 1895

C. H. George
Jan 17, 1872
Mar 28, 1878

Cela Elerson
1785-Mar 1, 1856

James Monroe Elerson
Oct 31, 1836
Apr 22, 1854

Lucy Ann Elerson
Dec 15, 1855
Apr 23, 1858

G. E. George
Jan 17, 1856
Apr 25, 1876

Mary F. George
Jan 19, 1854
Aug 18, 1875

C. H. Hall
Born 1899
Died 1901

Abner Meax Collins
Mar 21, 1883
Sep 6, 1908

Joe John Morgan, Son of
Abner Meax & Cordelia
Collins
Nov 7, 1908
Feb 12, 1909

Eddie Wright, Son of
Abner Meax & Cordelia
Collins
Jan 24, 1905
Jun 29, 1905

Floyd, Son of
W. L. & Viola George
Jun 5, 1895
Jun 19, 1896

* *

SHILOH CEMETERY
(Old Section)

LOCATION: Shiloh Methodist Episcopal Church, one and three-fourth mile NE of Dellrose.

Infants of
W. T. & Satoka Woodard
(no dates)
(erected Nov 1912)

J. W. Woodard
Mar 9, 1843
May 1, 1917

Mary E. Woodard
Nov 21, 1845
Nov 24, 1906

Katie A. Woodard
Mar 22, 1881
Nov 5, 1881

M. O. Woodard
B&D Aug 12, 1868

M. L. A. Woodard
May 28, 1867
May 29, 1867

M. C. Woodard
Oct 10, 1816
Sep 30, 1860
&
L. C. Woodard
Dec 23, 1818
Jan 19, 1887

Baxter, Son of
R. A. & D. M. Stuart
B&D Nov 28, 1882

R. A. Stewart
Jun 3, 1852
Mar 8, 1936
&
Docia M. Stewart
Feb 28, 1855
Jun 23, 1899

Erby, Son of
M. G. & D. A. Stuart
May 20, 1876
Nov 11, 1876

Doeice M., wife of
R. P. Stewart
Feb 28, 1855
Jun 23, 1899
(Same as Docia M. Stewart)

R. A. Stewart
1853-1936
(Same as R. A. Stewart, above)

Martha Virginia, wife of
J. M. Clark
Sep 6, 1854
Mar 20, 1919

Minnie, wife of
J. O. Gill
Jun 2, 1881
Jun 4, 1908

T. J. Gill
Nov 12, 1847
Jun 13, 1878

John Hamilton
Apr 19, 1824
Jul 3, 1898

Ann Hamilton
Apr 16, 1826
Mar 17, 1912

S. C., wife of
J. H. George
Feb 28, 1856
Oct 16, 1880

John W. Farrar
Oct 22, 1853
Feb 9, 1869

Infant Daughter of
J. N. & Emma Hamilton
Oct 7, 1895
Oct 8, 1895

Nancy Jane, wife of
William H. Metcalfe
Apr 14, 1830
Apr 1, 1866

Mariah S. Bryant
Aug 23, 1865
Jun 25, 1868

Willie, Son of
W. L. & Lucinda Elerson
Sep 20, 1861
Apr 1, 1863

DeWitt Monroe, Son of
W. L. & L. Elerson
Apr 7, 1860
Sep 12, 1860

Joseph Farrar
Jun 11, 1811
Apr 29, 1890

Elizabeth Farrar
May 7, 1814
Oct 7, 1892

Henry Beal
Born in Loudon Co., VA.
Jun 1, 1801
Died in Lincoln Co., TN
Jun 1, 1863

John M. Hobbs
Born in Madison Co., Ala.
Jul 21, 1862
Died in Lincoln Co., TN
Oct 24, 1865

Mary M. Hughey
Sep 24, 1817
Feb 17, 1837
Age: 19y, 1m, 23d.

Sarah Ann Hampton
Jul 7, 1850
Nov 4, 1866
Age: 16y, 4m, 27d.

FRANKEWING QUADRANGLE

W. M. Hampton
(no dates)

William Owen
(no dates)

Nancy Owen
Feb 5, 1789
Oct 3, 1869

John Owen
Sep 18, 1821
Aug 15, 1859

John W. Douthit
Jun 21, 1816
Jun 9, 1859

Clay, Son of
W. T. & Satoka Woodard
Nov 21, 1882
Jun 6, 1885
&
Leonard, Son of
W. T. & Satoka Woodard
B&D Sep 10, 1884

John D. Harrison
Aug 22, 1861
Oct 10, 1901

J. H. Harrison
Jul 7, 1818
Apr 26, 1900
& wife
Annie Harrison
Jul 4, 1820
Mar 16, 1862

Sally, wife of
J. H. Harrison
1838-1963

G. M. Bevels
Feb 3, 1865
Mar 12, 1904
&
Herman Lee Bevils
Age: 4 months old.
(no dates)

James Buckner, Son of
E. G. & I. J. Bevels
Feb 20, 1891
Jan 30, 1892

Carrie May, Daughter of
E. G. & I. J. Bevels
Jul 16, 1886
Jul 9, 1888

Eathyle, Daughter of
E. G. & I. J. Bevels
Jan 7, 1901
May 4, 1908

Gladys, Daughter of
E. G. & I. J. Bevels
Aug 13, 1911
Jul 29, 1913

J. P. Russel
Aug 8, 1847
May 7, 1906

Martha Jane, wife of
J. P. Russel
Oct 18, 1851
Apr 28, 1887

Henry Russel
Mar   1857
Oct 12, 1889

Mable E., Daughter of
B. L. & T. M. Jean
May 17, 1899
Jan 30, 1900

Ross Dugless, Son of
B. L. & T. M. Jean
Jan 2, 1898
May 18, 1898

C. L. Brotherton
Apr 22, 1850
Aug 20, 1899

Neeter Hampton
Apr 12, 1820
Jul 27, 1882

S. M. Hampton
Jul 28, 1808
Apr 18, 1882
&
A. A. Hampton
Dec 28, 1815
Mar 30, 1877

Sarah A. Lackey
May 12, 1837
Jul 30, 1890

H. L. Hampton
Feb 2, 1842
Dec 9, 1909

Misaniah E. Hampton
Jan 21, 1847
Jun 24, 1928

George Stuart
Mar 27, 1814
Married Harriet J. Woodward
Aug 4, 1836
Died Apr 7, 1887

Harriet J. Stuart
Jun 1, 1817
Jun 9, 1905

Harriet E., Daughter of
W. F. & N. L. Tucker
Oct 11, 1870
Sep 21, 1878

Ellen Gill
1889-1964

Mary Ellen, Daughter of
Mr. & Mrs. G. A. McDaniel
Mar 22, 1909
May 4, 1909

Bunyan Gill
Dec 19, 1891
Sep 14, 1911

J. Harvey Gill
Sep 21, 1855
Mar 24, 1929

Rusia P. George, wife of
J. Harvey Gill
Feb 5, 1861
Sep 8, 1895

"Father"
W. D. Gill
May 8, 1831
Oct 1, 1871
& "Mother"
E. J. Gill
Apr 3, 1832
Sep 23, 1909

N. M., wife of
J. M. Hobbs
Aug 11, 1855
May 29, 1896

John H. Gill
Mar 1, 1857
May 5, 1903

Letitia Ross, wife of
John H. Gill
Apr 4, 1867
Oct 17, 1911

J. O. Hobbs
Dec 4, 1877
May 8, 1902

S. G. Ross
Nov 14, 1819
May 3, 1874
& wife
M. E. Ross
Aug 16, 1825
Nov 9, 1901

Ellen, Consort of
S. C. McKay & Daughter of
W. H. Rodgers, desc. of
Florence, Ala.
Feb 23, 1837
Oct 18, 1870

J. H. Mitchell
Oct 12, 1850
Oct 3, 1875

J. H. Beddingfield
Jun 11, 1844
Mar 21, 1924

V. G., Son of
T. H. & S. E. Gentry
Aug 31, 1888
Oct 25, 1891

Willie Sanders
Jul 16, 1878
Dec 8, 1911

Fannie Mae, wife of
Willie Sanders
Feb 28, 1882
Apr 2, 1963

Arthur B., Son of
T. H. & S. E. Gentry
Nov 24, 1883
May 22, 1899

James M. Sanders
Oct   1894
Nov 27, 1917
Drafted into U. S. Army
Sep 21, 1917
Died At Camp Jackson
Nov 27, 1917

T. J. Noah
Aug 16, 1842
Aug 20, 1900

Sarah F., Daughter of
T. J. & Argenia Noah
Feb 4, 1877
Oct 4, 1897

Argenia McDaniel, wife of
T. J. Noah
Mar 25, 1846
Sep 28, 1897

W. H., Son of
T. J. & Argenia Noah
Oct 5, 1878
Aug 13, 1890

W. W.
1882-1890

Lena, wife of
C. B. Beddingfield
Apr   1881
Jul 9, 1917

Milton Green Stewart
Nov 20, 1846
Mar 16, 1895
&
Theodocia A. Stewart
Oct 10, 1852
Apr 19, 1906

Mamie Stewart, wife of
Earl B. George
Jan 6, 1883
Feb 22, 1902
&
Oliver George
Jun 17, 1901
Jun 24, 1901 Cletus A.

Cletus A. Robinson
Apr 25, 1897
Feb 3, 1945

FRANKEWING QUADRANGLE

I. E. Swaner
May 22, 1856
Aug 30, 1901
   & wife
Emma F. Swaner
Sep 18, 1862
(no date)

W. S. Robinson
Apr 26, 1848
Sep 11, 1911
   & wife
Margaret A. Robinson
Jul 17, 1853
Mar 15, 1929

R. C. Robinson
Jan 7, 1885
Feb 22, 1920

Reba M. Robinson
Oct 16, 1903
Jun 17, 1906

William H. Robinson
1874-1940
&
Nora J. Robinson
1876-1949

Dr. Ben L. Jean
1871-1934
&
Tennie M. Jean
1877-19

Mildred D., Daughter of
B. L. & Tennie Jean
Nov 27, 1900
Feb 17, 1919

P. E. Farrar
Oct 22, 1850
May 2, 1917
   & wife
Amanda J. Jean Farrar
Oct 22, 1855
Oct 28, 1836

"Lizzie"
Mary E., Daughter of
P. E. & A. J. Farrar
Aug 24, 1877
Jan 21, 1897

J. Frank Smith
Jul 3, 1864
Oct 29, 1900

Ella Smith Gill, wife of
J. Frank Smith
1866-1945

Lola L., Daughter of
J. F. & Ella Smith
Dec 16, 1885
Sep 28, 1890

John H. Smith
Jan 22, 1834
Oct 31, 1905

Nancy Maria Smith
Oct 23, 1834
Aug 19, 1914

Malula, Daughter of
J. H. & M. M. Smith
Nov 4, 1868
Oct 28, 1877

Infant Son of
R. B. & E. Bryant
Aug 2, ----(date gone)
Age: 2 days old.

Tobe Sherrell
1851-1920
&
Emma Sherrell
1863-1922

Sam R. Sherrell
Feb 26, 1889
Apr 18, 1907

Garland L., Son of
Mr. & Mrs. J. S. Baxter
Sep 29, 1909
Apr 29, 1910

Willie Baxter
1831-1930

William F. Walden
1868-1940

Gennette, Daughter of
William F. & Ella Walden
May 31, 1896
Jun 26, 1898

George Turner
1880-1900

J. C. Harrison
Apr 15, 1839
Jul 19, 1915
   & wife
Virginia Frances Mitchell
Harrison
Oct 6, 1847
Sep 2, 1914

J. A. Donaldson
1874-1947

Sallie Lou, wife of
J. A. Donaldson
Jan 30, 1878
Sep 29, 1917

Mrs. Wade Hampton
Died Jan 26, 1955
Age: 53y, 10m, 10d.

Annie B. Taylor, wife of
M. Wade Hampton
Feb 5, 1881
Apr 18, 1923

W. Lawson, Son of
Wade & Anna Hampton
Feb 18, 1911
Sep 11, 1913

Robert Franklin, Son of
G. E. & V. E. Stewart
Sep 8, 1912
Nov 1, 1917

Infant of
Mr. & Mrs. J. L. Baxter
B&D Jun 3, 1899

W. D. Sanders
1877-1930
&
Minnie B. Sanders
1885-1952

William Dean, Son of
W. D. & M. B. Sanders
Apr 29, 1913
Jul 16, 1913
&
Thomas Aubrey, Son of
W. D. & M. B. Sanders
Dec 29, 1909
Apr 28, 1912

Roy Lee, Son of
Mr. & Mrs. C. M. Sanders
Feb 6, 1923
Feb 10, 1923

W. G. West
Nov 8, 1828
Feb 16, 1910

Nannie A. West
Oct 13, 1837
Sep 29, 1918

Robert M. Stewart
Aug 22, 1902
Apr 5, 1904

Elijah R. Mitchell
1870-1944
&
Nancy F. Mitchell
1872-1944

Mary E., Daughter of
E. R. & N. F. Mitchell
Aug 3, 1900
Jan 28, 1901
&
Gladys Odessa, Daughter of
E. R. & N. F. Mitchell
May 1, 1909
Nov 30, 1912

G.(C) Y. Douthit
Dec 30, 1821
May 11, 1895
&
Mary J. Douthit
Apr 9, 1831
Apr 30, 1909

Pleasant H. Story
Apr 15, 1868
Apr 5, 1899

M. G. Story
Dec 3, 1825
Aug 3, 1908
&
M. E. Story
Nov 23, 1832
Jan 18, 1916

E. J. Story
Apr   1835
Feb 16, 1898

S. G. Story
Apr   1842
Killed in Cyclone
Apr 29, 1909

E. F. Story
Jan 28, 1839
Jul 9, 1922
(picture)
&
Sarah F. Story
Dec 18, 1848
May 3, 1917
(picture)

D. C. Story
Jun 27, 1875
Aug 26, 1914

Violet, Daughter of
E. F. & S. F. Story &
wife of J. O. Gill
Mar 20, 1886
May 28, 1911

R. B."Henry" Bryant
1867-1935
&
Emma Lou Bryant
1872-(no date)

T. H. Phillips
Dec 7, 1847
Sep 26, 1911

Lillie Mai, Daughter of
J. M. & L. J. Sorrow
Jul 9, 1901
Feb 16, 1919

Johnie W. Hopper
Jun 15, 1884
Sep 20, 1906

FRANKEWING QUADRANGLE

George W. Hopper
Aug 25, 1832
May 21, 1904

Elizabeth J. Hopper
Apr 4, 1843
Sep 6, 1909

Mable Bryant
Mar 1, 1905
Feb 28, 1906
&
Lizzie Bryant
Sep 6, 1898
Jan 19, 1907
Daughters of
R. B. & E. Bryant

Belle, wife of
J. H. Mullins
Dec 24, 1884
Jul 12, 1907

Lucile, Daughter of
J. H. & Z. B. Mullins
May 22, 1907
Apr 4, 1911

Mrs. Mack Hughey *
Died Jul 17, 1906
Age: 70 years.

Gordon,* Son of
D. C. & Maggie Story
Died Mar 14, 1899
Age: (not given)

Mrs. Sarah Elizabeth Mullins*
Died Sep 14, 1904
Age: 54 years.

I. G. Wilbanks *
Died Jul 2, 1908
Age: 76 years.
C.S.A. 41st Tenn Regt
Capt. George's Co.

N. E. Bevels *
Died Jan 4, 1904
Age: 24 years.

Mrs. Nester,* wife of
Nat Hobbs & Daughter of
Mrs. Tilda Ross
Died May 29, 1894
Age: 38 years.

Virginia Two Harrison, wife
of D. W. Mullins
Dec 6, 1893
Oct 21, 1916

Robert Kelly, Son of
D. W. & V. T. Mullins
Oct 1, 1916
Jul 6, 1917

Maggie Sullivan, Daughter of
L. D. & Suisan Mullins
Jun 4, 1885
Apr 19, 1911

Viola Arnold
Mar 4, 1878
Sep 21, 1943

John F. Ross
1859-1914
&
Mary J. Ross
1870-1940

W. J. Ellis
Sep 2; 1870
Nov 11, 1914

Ellis
1900-1922

Miss Ruthie Bearden *
Died Apr 29, 1918
Age: 65 years.

Mrs. Elizabeth,* widow of
H. H. Hughey
Died Jan 6, 1907
Age: 84y, 8m, 6d.

H. H. Hughey *
Died Sep 28, 1895
Age: 81 years.

Mrs. Polly,* widow of
Peter W. Moyers
Died Aug 4, 1909
Age: 84y, 4m, 16d.

Charles Hughey *
Died Nov 26, 1890
Age: 24 years.

Talvin Cloma Ross
Nov 23, 1901
Mar 29, 1927

Lola Ross Phillips
Jan 5, 1895
Jun 22, 1932

James M. Bradley
Apr 23, 1825
(date broken away)
&
Ida Susan Bradley
May 4, 1863
(no date)

Nancy E. Perry
Aug 10, 1840
Killed in cyclone
Apr 29, 1909

James M. Perry
Dec 4, 1864
Sep 6, 1915

Leon, Son of
R. H. & Ola Meeks
Mar 14, 1910
May 12, 1911

Bertha May,* Daughter of
T. H. & Nancy Phillips
Died Nov 22, 1898
Age: 9 years.

Miss Ada Metcalf *
Died Apr 23, 1900
Age: 22 years.

P. W. Moyers *
Sep 21, 1821
Mar 28, 1898

John H. Davis *
Died Dec 15, 1910
Age: 68 years.

Mrs. Frances Cole *
Died Apr 8, 1906
Age: 57 years.

Stella,* Daughter of
Mr. & Mrs. Samuel Colston
Died Sep 4, 1904
Age: 1 year.

Jessee Day, Son of
B. W. & B. B. Willbanks
Jun 17, 1905
Dec 24, 1909

W. R. Parr
Mar 28, 1868
May 5, 1902

"Mother"
Eular Gay Parr
Sep 15, 1874
Dec 15, 1943

Madison H., Son of
C. F. & P. V. George
Oct 25, 1903
Dec 16, 1903

Several unmarked graves.

Garland,* Son of
Walter Clark
Died Mar 17, 1923
Age: (not given)

M. Monroe Nelson *
Died Mar 21, 1898
Age: 26y, 4m.

Mrs. J. M. Ellis *
Died Apr 5, 1905
Age: 66 years.

Miss Sallie Sue,*
Daughter of
Mr. & Mrs. Henry Hobbs
Died Jan 31, 1908
Age: 28 years.

Mrs. Jane Mays *
Died Nov 15, 1900
Age: 64 years.

Michael Sanders *
Died Apr 22, 1905
Age: 67 years.

Oliver,* Son of
Jackson Pearce
Died Jul 8, 1904
Age: 13 years.

E. J. Watson *
Died Apr 25, 1904
Age: 76 years.

* *

CEMETERY

LOCATION: West Cyruston.

Several fieldstones with no inscriptions.

* *

FRANKEWING QUADRANGLE

WRIGHTS CEMETERY

LOCATION: One and one half miles SW of Boonshill on the south side of Highway 64.

M. B. "Tom" Sawyers
May 22, 1894
May 30, 1958

Clellie Sawyers Speer
Jul 14, 1899
Dec 20, 1964

Colyar Paxton Sawyers
May 26, 1900
Aug 3, 1963

Mary Sawyers
Died Dec 3, 1963
Age: (not given)

George M. Hopper
Jun 5, 1879
Mar 21, 1959
&
Rebecca Lou Hopper
Feb 7, 1879
Jan 1, 1952

Eric B. Cunningham
1897-1899
&
Lena E. Cunningham
1874-1950
&
Thomas P. Cunningham
1870-1916

Harvy Lee Smith
1890-1962

Bessie Coble Smith
1894-1947

Henderson Wade
1908-
&
Lillie H. Wade
1913-
&
Bobby T. Wade
1945-

E. R. Cole
Mar 19, 1895
Feb 21, 1957
&
Velma Cole
Mar 10, 1905

Will Griffis
Jan 9, 1879
Oct 5, 1953
Age: 85y, 2m, 15d.
&
Johnnie Griffis
Jan 13, 1881
Aug 28, 1966

Herman E. Smith
May 16, 1898
Aug 25, 1957
&
Lena C. Smith
Sep 25, 1895

"Baby"
Teresa Marlene Tucker
Oct 5, 1957

Hattie Lee Reed
1920-

Robbie Lee Reed
1916-1954

Kenneth C. Reed
1913-

Willie A. Haislip
1891-1951
&
Josie B. Haislip
1894-1952

Effie Nola, Daughter of
Adron & Dorris Haislip
Apr 11, 1955

Thelma Baxter
1903-1951

James M. Arnold
Feb 1, 1882
Dec 18, 1954
&
Myrtle M. Arnold
Mar 3, 1884
Sep 6, 1951

Robert M. Melton
B&D Sep 6, 1954

Billy Milton
1865-1950
&
Mattie Milton
1877-1961

Connie Louise Mitchell
1952

B. Brown Harwell
1905-1953
&
Catharine Harwell
1907-1965

Baby Hamlin
Dec 27, 1966

John C. Jackson
1886-1956
&
Mamie L. Jackson
1885-1952

M. L. "Bud" Parr
Sep 21, 1897

&
Clara Odell Parr
Jan 5, 1900
Dec 11, 1954

Timothy Joe Gleghorn
Nov 3, 1960
Mar 2, 1966

Larry Gene Brewer
A3C U.S.A.F.
Mar 13, 1946
Dec 29, 1966

Willis M. Brewer
1900-1955
&
Florence H. Brewer
1904-1960

Alvis C. Mitchell
1893-1959
&
Lucile J. Mitchell
1900-

James O. Burns
Apr 1, 1929

&
Annie M. "Dorris" Burns
Jan 13, 1927
Apr 18, 1966

Eddie Cleveland Beddingfield
1917-Nov 4, 1968, Age: 51y
&   (TM)
Catharine Beddingfield
1919-

L. Garlon Burns
1899-1965
&
Iver L. Burns
1901-1965

Arthur D. Smith
May 26, 1876
Sep 1, 1958
&
Mary A. Smith
Apr 22, 1885

W. Frank Hobbs
Sep 10, 1876
Jun 15, 1964
&
Margaret S. Hobbs
Jul 10, 1902

George W. Ringo
1878-1955
&
Kate J. Ringo
1884-1959

Fred Douglass Mitchell
Apr 26, 1956
Feb 12, 1957

Tullie "Dick" Mitchell
Nov 25, 1903
Sep 26, 1963
    & married Jun 27, 1927
Eleanor G. Mitchell
Dec 27, 1910

Eliza Dee Pollock
Nov 15, 1894

Addie Mae Gault
Jul 20, 1896
Dec 26, 1954

J. D. Lovett
1915-1955
&
Bessie M. Lovett
1923-

W. G. Lovett
1838-1963
&
Ida Mae Lovett
1893-1954

Willie Green Davis
1871-1956
&
Annie Idora Davis
1875-1960

Charles A. Clark
Jun 12, 1898
Nov 15, 1968
&
Lorena D. Clark
Dec 6, 1900

Married Nov 15, 1923

Gay Nell Devers
Jul 20, 1959

FRANKEWING QUADRANGLE

Leonard K. Warren
Aug 11, 1908

&
Bessie L. Warren
Jun 17, 1911
Aug 7, 1962

Samuel M. Cunningham
1873-1954
&
Maggie B. Cunningham
1880-1952

Dolan Johnson
1903-1953

Charles S. Harwell
Tennessee
Pfc TRP D 15 Cav
Jul 27, 1934
Feb 26, 1965

Eddie Charles Edward Harwell
Oct 3, 1954
Feb 1, 1956

Charles C. Harwell
Feb 28, 1884

&
Nora B. Harwell
May 21, 1884
Dec 6, 1952

Estella J. Davis
1880-

Collie B. Davis
1877-1952

Mrs. Hallie Mae Harwell Fite
Died Jun 19, 1968
Age: (not given)

Bobby G. Fite
Sep 23, 1933
Dec 28, 1955

Leslie Mitchell
1867-1960
&
Zilphy Mitchell
1872-1957

John Allen Joins
1884-1950
&
Mamie Davis Joins
1884-

Gracie May Mitchell
Aug 21, 1892

Floyd Davis
1880-
&
Effie L. Davis
1882-1958

Catherine Mitchell Lanier
1913-1946

Ben W. Brewer
1896-1941
&
Wilma Brewer
1906-

Guss L. Brewer
1875-1948
&
Nannie M. Brewer
1877-1963

W. Payne Smith
1865-1952
&
Tippie F. Smith
1874-1958

O. Fred Gill
1907-1952
&
Edith B. Gill
1917-

Tom E. Gill
1901-
&
Eva Mae Gill
1907-1964

Roy Benton Birdsong
Feb 1, 1955
Feb 2, 1955

Roy H. Gatlin
Jul 30, 1894
Sep 29, 1957
&
Velma Ray Gatlin
Oct 5, 1897

Robert L. Cunningham
1908-1969
&
Ruby M. Cunningham
1915-

Randell Cunningham
Died Apr 4, 1947
Age: (not given)
&
Craig Cunningham
Died Sep 26, 1951
Age: (not given)

John M. West
1876-1945

Annie Jane Luna
May 10, 1874
Jul 6, 1959

Porter R. Smith
1902-1954
&
Cleo Smith
1902-1948

Annie Frances Coble
1927-1942

Infant Sons of
Mr. & Mrs. H. W. Tallman
(no dates)

Vic Sanders Collins
Sep 23, 1873
Jul 16, 1948

George Osborne Collins
Jul 31, 1905
Nov 14, 1955

James Elmer Clark
Tennessee
Pfc 310 Inf 78 Div WW I
Sep 8, 1896
Jan 28, 1950

Robert D. Burgess
May 14, 1927
Oct 22, 1967
&
Pauline W. Burgess
Jul 21, 1927

Woodrow Wilson Dunnavant
Tennessee
Pvt 675 Sig AW Reporting Co
WW II
Mar 3, 1920
Apr 10, 1943

Jim H. Dunnavant
Sep 12, 1884
Jun 11, 1963
&
Ella Dunnavant
May 11, 1890

Carlee J. Tallman
Tennessee
S/Sgt 313 Inf 79 Div
WW II PH
Jan 11, 1918
Jul 13, 1944

J. Herman Tallman
1893-1955

Jimmie A. Johnson
1861-1937
&
Ella C. Johnson
1867-1959

Ronald Lynn Payne
Feb 4, 1965
Jun 29, 1965

Lettie E. Prosser
Dec 11, 1903

Shirley Prosser
Tennessee
AS U.S.N.Rf. WW I
Mar 7, 1897-Dec 30, 1954

John Paul Davis
Tennessee
Pfc Co D 39 Inf 9 Inf Div
Vietnam B.S.M. &
O. L. C. - T. H.
Sep 6, 1948
Jan 11, 1969

Walter R. Davis
Jan 20, 1942
Mar 5, 1943

Jack Davis
1912-
&
Verna M. Davis
1914-1941

William E. Davis
Dec 11, 1888
Dec 24, 1960
&
Fannie M. Davis
Mar 29, 1889

J. Claud West
1880-1949
&
Eva L. West
1885-1952

Robert R. Taylor
1871-1941
&
Mary Amanda Taylor
1872-1943

Harold Leon Wright
Mar 12, 1934
Sep 28, 1947

M. Knox Ramsey
1880-1958
&
Cannie S. Ramsey
1882-1962

J. Hollie Wright
1900-1949
&
Covie E. Wright
1907-

W. T. Griffis
Jan 25, 1875
Dec 8, 1941
&
Lora Griffis
Aug 13, 1886

Leon Robinson
Oct 29, 1895
Jan 24, 1966
&
Nina Mae Robinson
Nov 16, 1899

FRANKEWING QUADRANGLE

Gil Parker
Aug 26, 1896

&
Louise O. Parker
Sep 18, 1904
Feb 5, 1962

Tommy L. Luna
Apr 9, 1942
Dec 11, 1967
&
Linda L. Luna
Sep 7, 1943

Married Nov 30, 1963

O. B. R. Carpenter
1849-1938

Dick Carpenter
1885-1956
&
Minnie R. Carpenter
1891-1950

Ermon S. Harwell
Aug 22, 1895
Nov 21, 1940
&
Alleyne A. Harwell
Dec 25, 1902

Walter Harwell
Nov 9, 1870
Jun 21, 1959
&
Josie Harwell
Feb 28, 1876
Feb 7, 1955

Ray J. Pruitt
Apr 3, 1921
Apr 21, 1969
&
Christine A. Pruitt
Jan 12, 1924

Edith Arnold
Jan 25, 1927
Jul 15, 1939

H. B. Richardson
1906-1938

William J. Richardson
Tennessee
Sp 3 Co A 41 Signal Bn
Feb 1, 1934
May 15, 1965

H. Richardson
Jul 6, 1906
Jun 4, 1938

J. T. Richardson
1883-1950

Joe F. Richardson
Tennessee
Pvt Ant-Tank Co 406 Inf WW II
Feb 3, 1905
Nov 19, 1960

John T. Richardson
Apr 13, 1917
Mar 14, 1968

Bill Richardson
Nov 14, 1873
(no date)
&
Ada Richardson
Dec 6, 1886
Aug 20, 1920

Abe H. Mitchell
Mar 15, 1893

John W. Arnold
1876-1956
&
Cora P. Arnold
1879-1948

Raymond G. Arnold
1904-1957
&
Ozelle Reed Arnold
1909-

Thomas H. Mitchell
Tennessee
Tec 5 U. S. Army WW II
Sep 20, 1915
Jun 12, 1959

Pat A. Bates
1964
&
Lee Ann Bates 1963
"Bates Children"

"Brother"
J. Tom Collins
1887-1949

"Sister"
Sarah E. Collins
Feb 21, 1882
Jul 5, 1958

James Ash Collins
1872-1946
&
Mattie Viola Collins
1879-1949

Charley M. Collins
Nov 19, 1876
Sep 7, 1954
&
Pearl B. Collins
Nov 3, 1884
Jul 8, 1959

Henry A. McKinney
Jul 15, 1860
Dec 29, 1952
&
Augusta M. McKinney
Sep 15, 1870
Oct 29, 1947

T. A. "Lon" Storey
Apr 30, 1858
(no date)
&
Ida J. Storey
May 2, 1867
May 16, 1938

Verna Partain
1896-1942

Ellen B. Gunter
1880-1957

Robert M. Porter
1892-1954
&
Mary J. Porter
1894-

James A. Harris
1944-1944

Robert Harris
1874-1954
&
Gordie Harris
1876-1935

Grover B. Gunter
1888-
&
Lucy I. Gunter
1890-1956

J. H. Wright
Nov 28, 1812
Nov 22, 1898

Annie, wife of
J. H. Wright
May 4, 1831
Jul 1, 1910

Lamenda P., wife of
Capt. J. L. Hogan
Apr 12, 1829
Apr 6, 1897
Married to G. Sanders
1869

W. N. "Bill" Brownlow
1867-1945
&
Dollie Saunders Brownlow
1873-1964
"Grand-daughter of
Jacob Wright"

Lelabel McKinney
1902-1952
&
Lillian McKinney
1897-

William A. Dunnavant
Aug 11, 1932
Dec 28, 1936
&
Lucill Dunnavant
Feb 12, 1931
Feb 24, 1931

Will Dunnavant
1890-1957
&
Della Dunnavant
1898-

N. Gary
Aug 26, 1853
May 10, 1916

Kelly Dunnavant
May 20, 1896

&
Ina P. Dunnavant
Sep 17, 1895

Albertine Halbert
Mar 10, 1837
Jul 18, 1902
&
Bell Halbert
May 20, 1852
(no date)

Holbert Howell
1902-
&
Nannie Howell
1894-1963

James Howell
1859-1929
& wife
Tinnie Carpenter Howell
1876-1949

Susie Carpenter
(no dates)

Sallie Carpenter
(no dates)

Rev. John G. York
Jul 11, 1811
Oct 1, 1868

George W. Evans
1855-1942
&
Frances C. Evans
1872-1945

Lorie Evans
(no dates)

Lucy Evans
(no dates)

May Evans
(no dates)

FRANKEWING QUADRANGLE

Rufus A. Smith
Jul 23, 1858
Jan 24, 1942
&
Mattie Smith
May 7, 1865
Oct 26, 1939

J. Edd Swanner
1883-1951
&
Fannie B. Swanner
1889-1956

Pattie Sue Brady
Jan 27, 1935
Feb 4, 1935

Alvie Lee Mitchell
1898-1959
&
Vera Mitchell
1898-

Ernest & Florence Malone
1947

William C. Hill
1921-
&
Sallie Belle Hill
1921-Mar 29, 1963
Age: 47y, 1m, 15d. (TM)

Sam Floyd Collins
Tennessee
S2 U. S. N. R. WW II
Nov 11, 1915
Jul 6, 1966
&
Grace R. Collins
Dec 16, 1920

William Burton Riner
Feb 14, 1887
Dec 16, 1959
&
Annie B. Riner
Mar 7, 1885
Oct 18, 1963

Marvin W. Parr
Jun 22, 1894
Feb 28, 1960
&
Lizzie M. Parr
Mar 11, 1896

Tully M. Reed
Apr 17, 1896   Inf 1918
-------------   WW I
&
Lela M. Reed
Jul 30, 1894

&
Charles M. Reed
Apr 27, 1921
Apr 14, 1967

Claude Milliken
1930-1966

Joseph Shaw
Aug 22, 1818
Aug 19, 1875

Nancy H., Daughter of
J. & M. L. Shaw
Jun 8, 1859
Jun 15, 1863

Horace T. Baxter
1875-1961

Nora H. Baxter
1878-1964

I. Bradley Johnson
Jan 26, 1891
May 17, 1933

Tollie Lee Summers
Dec 6, 1882
Dec 2, 1965

Laura Dixon Summers
Mar 31, 1881
Feb 24, 1968

Nora Rivers, Daughter of
I. B. & Essie B. Johnson
Oct 13, 1917
Oct 2, 1920

J. J. Summers
Apr 16, 1852
Jul 3, 1917
&
N. A. Summers
Jul 30, 1855
Jun 23, 1917

G. W. Collins
Nov 7, 1853
Jul 5, 1930
&
Amitus E. Collins
Sep 26, 1852
May 9, 1923

Albert Lee Dixon
1874-1924
&
Mary Cordelia Dixon
1881-1945

W. E. Wright
1879-1939
&
Kate Wright
1883-

Selwyn G., Son of
W. E. & Kate Wright
1917-1937

Samuel R. Luna
1874-1947
&
Sara J. Luna
1878-1949

John Alvis Collins
&
Veda Aileen Collins

Herm. Bert Johnson
Jan 21, 1919
Jan 15, 1936

Henry V. Johnson
1873-1941
&
Lillie C. Johnson
1878-

Henry V. Johnson, Jr.
Tennessee
Pfc Co G 155 Inf WW II BSM
Feb 20, 1922
Oct 20, 1956

Paul Nevills
Sep 8, 1931
Jul 8, 1933

Catherine W., wife of
L. F. Arney
Jan   1817
Mar 21, 1859

Mary, Consort of
Amos Hurley
Feb 24, 1797
Aug 17, 1853

A. W. Wright
Jan 30, 1859
Feb 6, 1889

V. C. Burt, wife of
Wright & Myers
1880-1933

R. G. Myers
1853-1933

Ethel Caldwell
1894-1937
&
Tulley M. Caldwell
1879-
&
Bruce Caldwell
1893-

Walter W. Partin
Mar 23, 1875
May 29, 1954

Elzada Dean Partin
Jun 29, 1880
Feb 15, 1939

Oscar D. Campbell
Apr 17, 1896
Jun 13, 1963
&
Katie L. Campbell
Mar 28, 1896
Nov 19, 1938

Annie Pearl Campbell
Mar 14, 1908-

Joel E. Carpenter
Oct 6, 1855
Apr 4, 1951

William T. Smith
1896-1938
&
Mary Lou Smith
1894-

Patrick Lee Samples
&
Michael Thomas Samples
July 1950

Dan W. Arney
1853-1934
&
Ella I. Arney
1867-1950

Infant Daughter of
Mr. & Mrs. B. W. Gunter
1936

Lynn Chapman
1865-1933
&
Leona Chapman
1867-1938

Mildred E. Poarch
1907-1932

Elder Stephen M. Emmons
Feb 10, 1810
Mar 15, 1886
& wife
Elizabeth Emmons
Feb 11, 1811
Jan 18, 1894

Arthur Emmons
May 13, 1893
Nov 2, 1893

James M. McAfee
Feb 7, 1838
Oct 1, 1893

Elizabeth A. McAfee
Jun 15, 1842
Aug 30, 1924

Nettie McCracken
1882-1938

Sam McCracken
1888-1939

Nora McCracken
1900-1911

Crecy Davis
Dec 15, 1860
Aug 15, 1956

A. L. Trantham
Feb 9, 1856
Dec 2, 1901

FRANKEWING QUADRANGLE

James L. Moore
Feb 2, 1867
Jul 9, 1936
& wife
Addie Moore
Feb 10, 1872
Aug 7, 1897

Madison Johnson
Mar 25, 1888
Nov 8, 1913

Ada Johnson Holly
1894-1918

Milburn C. McAfee
Nov 21, 1880
Nov 10, 1947
&
Minnie L. McAfee
Mar 17, 1885
Aug 1, 1942

Eddie West Chapman
1943-1943

Thomas M. Chapman
1922-1947

Allen B. Armstrong
Sep 13, 1904
Apr   1968
&
Sammie H. Armstrong
Jan 21, 1905

Elzie A. Smith
Jul 12, 1908
Jul 29, 1966
&
Lillian C. Smith
Mar 24, 1905

Allen Gunter
1900-1936

Edna Gunter Donahew
Aug 10, 1900

J. F. Moore
Jul 27, 1839
Jan 21, 1924
& wife
Mary E. Moore
Jan 26, 1847
Aug 31, 1915

Maggie A. Moore
May 10, 1882
Sep 18, 1900
Age: 18y, 4m, 21d.

J. H., Son of
J. F. & M. E. Moore
Jul 13, 1880
Aug 2, 1898

James Walter Emmons
Dec 31, 1887
Feb 24, 1955

Delia, Daughter of
J. C. & M. L. Brewer
Nov 2, 1900
Nov 22, 1915

Jimmie East, Son of
P. B. & Dollie Smith
(no dates)

Sarah M. Menefee
Feb 1, 1839
Nov 23, 1914

W. T. Menefee
Apr 7, 1844
Jul 23, 1914

Arthur Brewer
Feb 14, 1856
Mar 14, 1928

J. C. Brewer
Sep 6, 1848
Apr 11, 1912

Mary A. Ryals, wife of
E. Mc. Brewer
Oct 21, 1824
Mar 17, 1898

Martha Wright McKinney
Jan 6, 1834
Apr 11, 1920

Mollie L. McKinney, wife of
J. D. Hopper
Feb 13, 1853
Jan 18, 1908

Thomas Grady Hopper
Mar 5, 1893
Aug 30, 1894

Eula R., Daughter of
G. W. & L. E. Bennett
Sep 19, 1870
Oct 8, 1882

Infant Son of
G. W. & L. E. Bennett
(no dates)

Etta M., Daughter of
J. D. & M. E. Wright
Dec 14, 1872
Oct 10, 1875

Guy S. Markham, Sr.
Apr 14, 1871
Mar 8, 1950
&
Bessie Chapman Nipp Markham
Feb 2, 1882

T. Ollie Markham
Feb 6, 1889
Nov 22, 1893

Johney D., Son of
W. J. & S. E. Markham
Nov 11, 1882
Jun 21, 1885

Willie Bob, Son of
W. J. & S. E. Markham
Aug 20, 1874
May 1, 1888

W. J. Markham
Jun 8, 1850
Jun 30, 1890
&
Sallie E. Markham
Jul 21, 1850
Aug 2, 1929

Infant Sons of
Mr. & Mrs. B. W. Markham
B&D Sep 11, 1918

J. W. West
Mar 18, 1853
Aug 25, 1887
&
M. A. Sawyers West
Apr 27, 1850
Apr 14, 1899

J. N. Clark
Nov 5, 1861
Jul 19, 1945

Frank Lester Clark
Aug 7, 1903
Mar 17, 1949

Martha Ann Dunnavant
Mar 5, 1959
Jul 25, 1960

Bill Wright
1905-1964
&
Cleo Wright
1907-

Addie D. Clark
Sep 12, 1901
Sep 4, 1928

Inez Baxter, wife of
J. W. Markham
Sep 29, 1869
Jan 24, 1942

Sallie B. Braden
Jan 10, 1837
Mar 20, 1896

Mrs. G. M. Luna
Feb 12, 1829
Jan 18, 1904

J. W. Markham
May 7, 1853
May 30, 1908
&
Henretta J. Markham
Oct 2, 1858
Aug 1, 1891

R. E. Sumner
Sep 5, 1810
May 29, 1888
& wife
Mary C. Sumner
Dec 29, 1811
Dec 14, 1887

Thomas Lemuel Sawyers
Jul 11, 1951
Aug 17, 1955

Fannie D. Clark
Jun 23, 1869
Sep 3, 1928

A. B. Clark
Dec 21, 1871
Apr 7, 1940

Infant Son of
W. J. & Ada West
Apr 30, 1905
May 4, 1905

Infant Daughter of
W. J. & Ada West
(no dates)

Ruby West
Jan 2, 1901
Oct 13, 1901

Ada D. West, wife of
W. J. West
Nov 10, 1871
May 5, 1947

William Julius West
Jul 17, 1855
May 26, 1916

Mary Sue, 1st wife of
W. J. West
Aug 22, 1858
May 10, 1895

Mandy L. West
Aug 21, 1887
Sep 18, 1891

Mary J. Sawyers
Apr 23, 1889
Jun 13, 1890

William D. Sawyers
1849-1897
&
Callie B. Sawyers
1856-1938

Lem Sawyers
1881-1955

Sadie A. Sawyers
1885-1956

J. L. Sawyers
1917-1920

Thomas C. Sawyers
1865-1927
&
Fannie B. Sawyers
1876-1955

W. H. Sawyers
Oct 2, 1886
Sep 11, 1911

Ben S. Sawyers
1867-1926
&
Sallie Sawyers
1860-1929

W. P. Sawyers
Mar 16, 1826
Aug 1, 1896

Mrs. E. L., wife of
W. P. Sawyers
May 28, 1829
Jan 29, 1909

Indant Son of
R. E. & L. M. Sawyers
B&D Apr 27, 1927

Rufus E. Sawyers
Dec 27, 1851
Apr 27, 1927
&
Lillie Mae Sawyers
May 28, 1869
Sep 12, 1903

Mack Thomas Brewer
Dec 4, 1878
Mar 16, 1932
&
Maudie Mae Brewer
Feb 9, 1883
May 24, 1953

Emmett Reed
Jul 20, 1873
Feb 13, 1936
&
Silda Reed
Oct 12, 1873
Dec 13, 1955

Infant Daughter of
C. E. & S. A. Reed
Apr 24, 1907
May 1, 1907

Dallas Harwell Davis
Aug 15, 1902
Dec 14, 1957

Clifford M. Harwell
Apr 25, 1902
Apr 19, 1931

Kevin Armstrong
Mar 4, 1963
Dec 26, 1965

John W. Wright
1878-1952
&
Maggie L. Wright
1886-1945

John Henry Smith
Oct 4, 1887
Nov 17, 1954
&
Vernie Lou Smith
Apr 30, 1892
Feb 6, 1957

S. Bruce Reed
1884-1937
&
L. Pearl Reed
1892-

Allen R. West
1882-1957
&
Irene Joins West
1896-1944

O. E., Son of
J. M. & E. J. Reed
Apr 6, 1877
Oct 9, 1899

J. M. Reed
Dec 16, 1852
Aug 17, 1908

Eliza Reed
1853-1928

Mollie Dee, Daughter of
J. M. & Eliza Reed
Jan 14, 1890
Aug 17, 1908

J. C. Reed
Mar 2, 1879
Dec 5, 1918

Luther Reed
Mar 9, 1875
Apr 14, 1941
&
Edna Reed
Mar 6, 1884
Jun 17, 1963

Infant Son of
M. L. & Edna Reed
B&D Mar 24, 1917

Infant Son of
M. L. & Edna Reed
Mar 11, 1910
Mar 17, 1910

Infant Daughter of
R. E. & Vera Wright
Jun 21, 1912
Jul 14, 1912

Selmer, Daughter of
R. E. & Vera Wright
Nov 17, 1909
May 29, 1910

Emmitt Wright
1881-1946
&
Vera Wright
1885-1918

Burnice L. Robison
Mar 29, 1907
Apr 8, 1915

Levi Trantham
Aug 28, 1825
Aug 4, 1902

Henry Ingle, Son of
O. L. & Edna Robison
Mar 24, 1910
Jun 3, 1911

Ike Mitchell
1865-1931
&
Ida Mitchell
1865-1920

Morris Dalton Braden
1927-1928
&
Infant Son of
Mr. & Mrs. J. W. Braden
(no dates)

J. Henry Robison
Mar 30, 1851
Feb 21, 1923
&
Catie Robison
Jan 4, 1858
Sep 23, 1925

James B. Robison
1876-1954
&
Mona E. Robinson
1880-1937

Otis Lee Robinson
1874-1956

Fannie Edna Robinson
1877-1965

W. Kermit Robinson
Nov 30, 1905
Feb 3, 1945

Thomas A. Jackson
Nov 15, 1873
Apr 25, 1952

Annie B. Davis, wife of
T. A. Jackson
Dec 5, 1876
Jul 20, 1920
Married Mar 14, 1906

Sherry Ann Kent
May 23, 1953
Jun 15, 1958

Betty M. Kent
May 12, 1949
Jun 21, 1967

Samuel Cathcart
1880-1945
&
Grace Cathcart
1891-

Minnie Estill Story
Nov 16, 1882
Jan 27, 1963

Buford L. Hamlin
Oct 24, 1886
Oct 20, 1960
&
Minnie Ethel Hamlin
Jul 26, 1898

Luther C. Partin
Feb 25, 1902
Oct 28, 1961

William Roy Tratham
1884-1936
&
Ethel May Tratham
1891-1954

Josephine Bland
1921-1936

Betty J. Bland
1879-1961

George A. Bland
Tennessee
Cpl Btry A 317 Field Arty
WW I
Nov 26, 1889
Apr 14, 1961

P. M. Bland
Jul 26, 1845
Nov 21, 1918
&
M. V. Bland
Apr 19, 1854
(no date)

W. E. Haislip
1940

W. H. Tuley
Sep 10, 1849
Feb 12, 1917

FRANKEWING QUADRANGLE

Roe Tulley
Dec 25, 1862
Jan 22, 1942

Elmon C. Long
Jun 22, 1890
Aug 28, 1966
&
Effie Long
May 14, 1895

Sarah Frances Long
Jan 6, 1917
May 18, 1926

W. D. West
Aug 5, 1877
Jul 28, 1922
&
Bertha B. West
Dec 29, 1892
Sep 21, 1920

Robert L. West
Jun 24, 1918
Sep 4, 1919

Jonas Wilson Gilliam
Feb 13, 1878
Jun 3, 1958
&
Maudie Bland Gilliam
Sep 30, 1886
May 1, 1945

Geneva Gilliam
1918-1920

W. Cooper West
1879-1943
&
Eula J. West
1876-1951

N. Gertrude West
1906-1953

James Marion Brewer
Sep 15, 1888
Oct 3, 1963
&
Ola H. Brewer
Jan 29, 1894

James M. Owen
1879-1956
&
Laura D. Owen
1883-1963

Mavis Layerne Reed
Oct 18, 1925
Jul 17, 1926

W. O. Reed
1888-1951
&
Nettie L. Reed
1888-

Herman Lonnie Hughes
Jan 10, 1951
Jan 11, 1951

Infant Daughter of
C. L. & Besset Abbott
B&D Nov 16, 1927

R. L. Smith
1863-1941
&
Loner M. Smith
1866-1941

Shields W. Brewer
Jul 2, 1887
Jun 7, 1948
&
Maggie L. Brewer
Nov 26, 1892
Dec 27, 1958

W. Carl Brewer
Jan 14, 1923
Jun 7, 1928

James Fullenwider Collins
Dec 31, 1900
May 31, 1967

Willie L. Higgs
Tennessee
Sgt 2 MSL Bn 44 Arty
WW II ARCOM
Feb 7, 1925
May 27, 1966
&
Elizabeth A. Higgs
Dec 1, 1924

John E. Watson
1899-1959
&
Nellie O. Watson
1900-

William C. Curtis
1883-1959
&
Mildred B. Curtis
1888-1967

N. B. Abbott
Apr 17, 1838
Feb 16, 1928

Laura Scott Abbott
Feb 14, 1859
Aug 31, 1937

Leonard Abbott
Nov 15, 1896
Jun 23, 1963
&
Bessie Abbott
Apr 13, 1895
Sep 7, 1947

William E. Holley
Dec 10, 1893
Jan 8, 1963
&
Gladys F. Holley
May 28, 1910

Jim W. Braden
1891-1960
&
Effie Mae Braden
1896-1950

Floyd Braden
1896-1957
&
Bessie Braden
1899-

Sam Braden
1862-1931
&
Tippie J. Braden
1866-1946

James R. West
1909-1956

William E. Whitehead
1886-1956
&
Ora D. Whitehead
1890-

Harvey Whitehead
1883-1953

Infant Sons of
John T. & Aileen Wright
Nov 29, 1947

John B. Davis
1860-1935
&
Mattie A. Davis
1866-1936

Audie Arney
Jun 28, 1890
Oct 22, 1926

Maudie Davis Smith Harwell
1886-1963

Harvey Joins
1854-1920
&
Martha Coble Joins
1859-1941

Thomas E. Grimes
Jun 13, 1884

&
Ruby M. Grimes
Sep 16, 1904

J. D. Grimes
Jun 4, 1896
Apr 5, 1925

C. A. Grimes
Mar 18, 1861
Mar 20, 1948
&
C. O. Grimes
Nov 22, 1848
Aug 30, 1917

George M. Collins
Dec 18, 1890
Aug 17, 1947
&
Margaret T. Collins
Oct 13, 1894
Feb 26, 1915

Fred Morgan, Son of
G. M. & Margaret Collins
Sep 7, 1913
Jan 29, 1925

Donald O. Pruitt
Mar 16, 1921
Sep 22, 1961
&
Melba I. Pruitt
Jul 25, 1926

Thomas J. Holt
1876-1936
&
Susan D. Holt
1877-
&
Marshall Holt
1912-1919

John Marshall Holt
1919-1963
Tennessee
Pfc Hq Co 119 Inf
WW II   BSM
Sep 25, 1919
Nov 13, 1963
&
Susan D. Holt
1877-

W. F. Gunter
1847-1921
&
Frances Gunter
1847-(no date)

H. T. Trantham
Jan 2, 1856
May 24, 1917
&
Sarah Trantham
Feb 1, 1861
Sep 2, 1939

Sarah H. Johnson
Feb 8, 1843
May 22, 1916

FRANKEWING QUADRANGLE

Infant Son of
W. W. & Era Johnson
1923

J. T. Brady
Sep 5, 1861
Sep 28, 1912
   & wife
Mary V. Brady
Feb 27, 1859
Jan 23, 1916

T. S. Caldwell
Sep 14, 1869
Feb 12, 1943
   &
Fannie Caldwell
Dec 14, 1872
Jun 30, 1954

Eula G., Daughter of
T. S. & Anna Caldwell
Nov 5, 1894
Dec 11, 1914

William Ira Trantham
Aug 26, 1877
May 24, 1947
   & wife
Nora Trantham
Mar 1, 1880
Sep 2, 1917

Anna Smith, wife of
T. S. Caldwell
Jun 24, 1867
Jul 3, 1919

Sidney Lee West
Sep 16, 1884
Jun 1, 1957
   &
Nora P. West
Jun 16, 1891

Infant of
S. L. & Nora West
Jul 6, 1912
Jul 7, 1912

Sarah N. George, wife of
T. A. Story
Mar 12, 1857
Jul 20, 1909

Mattie Irene Davis
Jul 8, 1915
Jul 20, 1915

Joseph Tucker
1900-1922
   &
Gladys Gary Tucker
1906-1926

Tippie A., wife of
C. C. Garrett
Sep 14, 1895
May 22, 1926

Corder (fieldstone, no dates)

Tom W. Davis
Tennessee
S 2 U.S.N.R.F. WW I
Sep 24, 1898
Mar 6, 1961

J. Hardy Wright
1867-1937
   &
Cora Dean Wright
1869-1921

David L. Coggin
1904-1941
   &
Ora Lee Coggin
1901-

Lena C. Davis
Jun 22, 1900

James Robert West
Apr 16, 1882
Apr 14, 1963
   &
Estelle M. West
Jan 24, 1885
Apr 20, 1963

Infant Daughter of
Mr. & Mrs. J. R. West
B&D Jan 29, 1903

Annie West Bruce
Apr 5, 1880
Feb 8, 1919

R. L. Hollow
1846-1940

Nannie H. Hollow
Nov 13, 1872
Jul 3, 1933

A. R. Endsley
1892-1935
   &
Dena Endsley
1895-1957

Paula Robinson
Oct 1, 1958
Oct 3, 1958

Marshall L. Brady
1890-1958

Rose M. Markham
Mar 8, 1913
Nov 1, 1959

William E. Johnson
1880-1924
   &
Zada B. Johnson
1881-1947

John Lee McCracken
1867-1944
   &
Lula Raines McCracken
1881-

Billy W. Markham
Mar 7, 1887
Dec 20, 1963
   &
Mattie E. Markham
Jan 6, 1894

Rachel Dorris Markham
Nov 20, 1915
Jan 1, 1935

John C. Smith
Jan 7, 1873
Aug 6, 1966
   &
Mary E. Smith
Nov 4, 1876
Aug 3, 1966

Thomas A. McCracken
1874-1929

Lelia W. McCracken
1876-1947

Myrtle M. Collins
1897-1939

Joe White McCracken
Dec 23, 1917
Aug 20, 1934

Myrtle M. McCracken
1878-1935

J. W. McCracken
1876-1963

Kathleen H. McCracken
1896-

Floyd Lee Arnold
Tennessee
Tec 4 Medical Dept WW II
Jun 15, 1909
Apr 3, 1963

W. Emmett McLin
1898-1962
   &
Marjorie C. McLin
1917-

John W. Watson
Oct 1, 1905
Jun 26, 1963
Married Jun 26, 1926

Lorena S. Watson
Jun 4, 1903

Monte Loyd Nichols
May 28, 1965
Nov 26, 1965

John B. Davis
1860-1935
   &
Mattie A. Davis
1866-1936

Zechariah G. Hurley
The dutiful Son &
affectionate Brother,
The kind husband &
indulgent Father, the
esteemed citizen &
Pious Christian
May 23, 1827
Aug 3, 1852

F. M. Wright
Aug 10, 1823
Jul 8, 1889
Age: 65y, 10m, 29d.
   & wife
Lucinda V. Wright
Apr 10, 1825
Oct 26, 1902

Jacob Wright
Jun 2, 1804
Apr 25, 1886

W. Mc.
Jun 16, (broken)
(fieldstone)

N. Wright
Nov 3, 1778
Jun 30, 1840
Age: 61y, 6m, 27d.

G. W.
(fieldstone, no dates)

N. H.
1816
(fieldstone)

W. W.
(fieldstone, no dates)

Childress
Jan 2, 1821
Jun 1846

F. E. M.
1862

T. W. Harper
(no dates)

L. Shelton
Died Sep 5, 1848
Age: (not given)

M. M.
(no dates, fieldstone)

S. M.
(no dates, fieldstone)

M. H. H. (Harper)
Oct 3, 1802
Feb 7, 1859

A. M. E. (Emmons)
(no dates, fieldstone)

N. E.
(no dates, fieldstone)

FRANKEWING QUADRANGLE

Mrs. Lou J. Sanders *
Died Nov 9, 1921
Age: 83 years.

Jacob Wright ***
Born in Virginia
Oct 3, 1774
Died Aug 2, 1867

*** Wright Family Records.

Eld. James H. Nelson *
Died Sep 28, 1905
Age: 70y, 8m, 24d.

Ira Wilson,* Son of
Carl Trantham
Died Aug 26, 1912
Age: (not given)

F. H. Noah *
Died May 25, 1902
Age: 33y, 5m, 15d.

James Kintchem *
Died Sep 1, 1902
Age: 45 years.

Infant * of
Mr. & Mrs. Collie Davis
B&D Jan 17, 1904

Mrs. C. M. Luna *
Died Jan 18, 1904
Age: 75 years.

Infant * Son of
Mr. & Mrs. James Wright
Died Jan 31, 1904

Infant * Son of
James Braden
Died May 2, 1916

N. Gary *
Died May 10, 1916
Age: 63 years.

Marie,* Daughter of
Mr. & Mrs. G. W. Evans
Died Oct 5, 1896
Age: 5 years.

ED NOTE: This Cemetery was also once called Sawyers Graveyard.

Many unmarked graves.

* *

PARK CEMETERY

LOCATION: One and one half miles ENE of Red Oak on south side of Delina Road.

J. M. Park
Feb 19, 1808
Jan 15, 1892

Thomas Moore Park
Nov 12, 1861
May 27, 1941

Mary F. Ellis Park
May 23, 1861
Dec 15, 1901

William Hill Park
1868-1890

Claudie D. Park
1896-1911

Margaret Park
Died Mar 31, 1884
Age: about 52 years.

* *

HUNTLAND QUADRANGLE

COMMUNITY CEMETERY

LOCATION: One mile ENE of Smithland on west side of bluff at Sullenger Bend.

M. B. 1831 (fieldstone) J. B. (no dates, fieldstone)	M. W. (no dates, fieldstone) 1921 (fieldstone) (Many of the early settlers in the Smithland area are said to be buried here.)	About 150 graves with fieldstone, no inscriptions. This was part of the Old Zachariah Arnold Estate ** ** Court Records.	(John Stiles, died 1825 and wife Margaret Stiles, died 1839, also their Daughter Margaret is buried in this Cemetery.)

* *

ARNOLD CEMETERY

LOCATION: One mile east of Smithland and one fourth mile south of Sullenger Bend of Elk River.

Moses Arnold May 24, 1800 May 17, 1874 Maria, wife of T. P. Arnold 1834-Sep 5, 1859	W. B. Jennings Oct 29, 1830 Jun 28, 1892 Sarah,* wife of W. B. Jennings Died Sep 13, 1892 Age: 62 years.	William C., Son of T. P. & Maria Arnold Sep 3, 1859 Jun 8, 1860 John W. Jennings Oct 22, 1861 Jan 22, 1863	(This Cemetery is located on the Old Zachariah Arnold homeplace, he was a pioneer settler in this area.)

* *

HOLMAN CEMETERY

LOCATION: One half mile south of Sullenger Bend of Elk River on the south side of Shady Grove Road.

Joseph Allison 1801-1860	W. P. Holman Mar 3, 1811 Jul 9, 1888	Eliza, wife of W. P. Holman Jul 24, 1834 May 11, 1908	Eliza Pearl, Daughter of J. H. & M. L. Stubblefield Jul 21, 1887 Jun 18, 1888

* *

CEMETERY

LOCATION: Three fourth mile south of Sullenger Bend of Elk River on the south side of Shady Grove Road.

Several fieldstones, no inscriptions.

* *

STILES CEMETERY

LOCATION: One half mile south of Sullenger Bend of Elk River and on north side of Shady Grove Road.

Capt. Samuel Stiles Jun 17, 1821 May 12, 1905 & wife Mary Stiles Jan 11, 1817 Feb 2, 1875	W. Z. Jennings Oct 5, 1837 Mar 11, 1925 Margaret A. Jennings Nov 13, 1842 Dec 2, 1910	Cora L. Jennings Dec 27, 1866 Mar 30, 1899 Molly E. Jennings Jul 10, 1862 Mar 12, 1910	Jane, wife of William Renegar Jun 11, 1816 Dec 31, 1882 Age: 66 years.

* *

HUNTLAND QUADRANGLE

ELORA CEMETERY

LOCATION: Elora.

Huey Edward Mayes
Jul 22, 1952
May 31, 1969
(color picture)

Donnie L., Son of
A. & Sallie Hamilton
Aug 22, 1899
Mar 12, 1914

Amos Hamilton
1868-1947

Sallie Hamilton
1876-1966

W. L. Caughran
Jun 26, 1846
Oct 26, 1910

J. Collens, Son of
W. L. & Lizzie Caughran
Aug 8, 1886
Oct 9, 1918

Elbert Ross Morgan
Feb 14, 1880
Jan 10, 1948
&
Sallie Caughran Morgan
Dec 3, 1890
Nov 15, 1938

Billie Joe Morgan
Sep 16, 1930
Jul 2, 1936

Iva Lee, Infant of
E. R. & Sallie Morgan
May 3, 1924
Apr 3, 1925

Louis Baxter
Jan 26, 1911
Jan 24, 1912
&
Jewel Baxter
Sep 13, 1905
Dec 15, 1911

Walter D. Baxter
1903-1956
&
Pearl G. Baxter
1905-

U. C. "Jack" Baxter
1870-1928
&
Mary E. Baxter
1870-1959

Joseph W., Son of
U. C. & Mary Baxter
Nov 22, 1900
Feb 16, 1924

Mary Jacks Swafford
1885-1962

C. H. Jacks
1888-1955

Gen. Lee Jacks
1915-1934

Fred R. Jacks
May 2, 1923
Sep 22, 1956

John B. Gattis
1835-1960
&
Nita D. Gattis
1887-

Joseph C. Campbell
Jul 5, 1880
Jun 20, 1933

Maggie Florence Campbell
1879-1958
(Moore-Cortner FH)

Maggie Ovelee Campbell
Apr 22, 1918
Apr 25, 1918

J. B. Patrick
1860-1937
&
Etta Patrick
1863-1952

Mary Jane Caughran
Mar 24, 1848
Dec 1, 1912

Mary Ida Caughran, wife of
T. G. Yarbrough
Oct 21, 1868
Oct 31, 1951
(picture)

Ethel Pylant, wife of
C. W. Brooks
Nov 22, 1873
Sep 22, 1913

Classie Stovall
Oct 3, 1883
Jul 8, 1927
&
Melva Stovall
Oct 18, 1913
Apr 16, 1921
&
Billy Boy Stovall
Apr 2, 1925
Feb 11, 1926

H. B. "Hop" Stovall
Nov 12, 1885
May 14, 1958

Earnie C. Pylant
Dec 10, 1884
Jul 14, 1968
&
Maude K. Pylant
Feb 11, 1894
Feb 8, 1964

Nolan Pedro Pylant
Aug 10, 1908
Aug 10, 1968

Marion Arch Pylant
Mar 10, 1878

&
Dora Craig Pylant
May 28, 1882
Apr 30, 1954

Infant Daughter of
W. F. Hudson & wife
Died May 15, 1910
Age: (not given)

Sarah Rogers
Jun 27, 1835
Jan 7, 1920

Raymond Wells
Apr 7, 1903
Jun 12, 1921

James Wells
Aug 24, 1918
Jun 13, 1920

Jane, wife of
J. B. Upton
Dec 22, 1840
May 24, 1909

John McElderry
Jan 22, 1845
Dec 12, 1906

Elizabeth McElderry
1850-1915

William E. McElderry
Jul 7, 1917
Sep 3, 1950

Eugene McElderry
Ohio
Pvt Btry K 5 Regt Arty
Spanish American War
Mar 12, 1872
Jul 9, 1959

Flora, wife of
Eugene McElderry
Nov 25, 1869
Jan 8, 1909

Rebecca McElderry
Dec 22, 1887
Jun 21, 1965

Luther Owens
Sep 12, 1911
Apr 12, 1936

John O. Owens
May 23, 1880
Sep 7, 1960
&
Ezzie P. Owens
Aug 6, 1881
Nov 22, 1965

Luther F. Gattis
1875-1933
&
Maud S. Gattis
1883-

Infant of
L. F. & M. S. Gattis
B&D Feb 28, 1919

L. S. Wright
Feb 20, 1846
Jan 30, 1926
&
Amanda Wright
Mar 6, 1852
Aug 4, 1925

Stephen W. Brown
Feb 1, 1826
(no date)
&
Mary Ann L. Brown
Jul 11, 1825
Oct 16, 1906
"Cumberland Presbyterians"

Jewel, Daughter of
D. S. & Plumah Counts
Feb 12, 1916
Feb 13, 1916

G. A. Raynolds
Nov 3, 1839
(no date)
&
Martha J. Raynolds
Jun 19, 1850
Jul 1, 1905

Harry W. Raynolds
Feb 4, 1880
Oct 2, 1908

Claude C., Son of
G. M. & S. J. Pylant
Mar 10, 1887
Killed in R. R. Wreck
May 25, 1910

Clayton Pylant
Jul 30, 1895
Mar 2, 1915

HUNTLAND QUADRANGLE

Freddie B. Pylant
Sep 1, 1899
Oct 29, 1954

G. M. Pylant
Oct 10, 1847
Jan 10, 1924
&
Sallie J. Pylant
Apr 5, 1851
Oct 9, 1921

John Allen Pylant
1874-1953
&
Maggie Broughton Pylant
1879-1948

Wayne Pylant
Tennessee
Cpl 47 Inf 9 Inf Div WW II
Oct 1, 1913
Jan 11, 1949

Infant Son of
J. A. & Maggie Pylant
Oct 6, 1909
Oct 17, 1909

Infant Daughter of
Ira & May Pylant
Jan 26, 1910
Feb 2, 1910

Joel E. Patton
Mar 21, 1869
Sep 29, 1939
&
Anna E. Patton
Jun 8, 1872
Jun 17, 1941

H. C. Patton
(no dates)

P. Hamilton
(no dates)

Kudeller Hamilton
Nov 12, 1842
May 2, 1912
&
Sarah Hamilton
Jan 1, 1846
(no date)

Annie Lee, Daughter of
A. T. & M. L. Pylant
Aug 15, 1904
Jul 28, 1912

Ray Robertson
1907-1941

James Thomas Robertson
1869-1940

Delonie Robertson
1868-1939

Ralph Robertson
1907

Infant Daughter of
Eugene & Bessie Mai Kidd
B&D Mar 13, 1938

J. B. Smith
Mar 2, 1835
(no date)
&
Sarah E. Smith
Nov 2, 1844
Sep 30, 1907

Minor Smith
1880-1947
&
Bertha Smith
1870-1937

James H. Canant
Mar 4, 1824
Oct 10, 1899

Amanda A. Canant
Dec 12, 1833
Jan 11, 1916

J. H. Smith
Aug 30, 1862
Jun 3, 1951
&
Bertha Smith
Jan 13, 1868
Nov 16, 1918

William D. Cambron
Sep 30, 1877
Feb 13, 1926

Johnsie Wade Morgan
Dec 8, 1861
May 21, 1937

H. A. Smith
Oct 9, 1865
Mar 26, 1942

Mollie Parks Smith
Nov 14, 1874
Feb 10, 1949

R. K. Smith
Feb 14, 1865
Dec 1, 1939
&
Mattie Flora Smith
Feb 10, 1871
Jul 19, 1912

Leon Horton
1896-1953

James Sutton
1905-1949

Dorcas McCord, wife of
J. W. Cambron
Oct 25, 1835
Apr 22, 1910

Mary Wade, Daughter of
W. H. & W. C. Smith
May 5, 1902
Aug 26, 1908

Woodie Cambron
1874-1957

Wilson Hamilton
1868-1933

Newton L. Steele
Feb 7, 1844
Jan 3, 1911
&
Anna E. Damron Steele
1854-1938
Married Jun 10, 1874

Pearl Hamilton
Aug 30, 1876
Apr 12, 1948

Berta E. Steele
Sep 23, 1882

Thomas B. Patton
1873-1937
&
Daisy H. Patton
1881-

Matilda E. Hamilton
May 18, 1845
Jan 5, 1915

W. I. Harper
(no dates)
&
Leta Harper
(no dates)

Anna Byers
May 14, 1873
Dec 22, 1963

Stacy A. Hill (Infant)
(no dates, Gallant FH)

S. P. Jones
May 27, 1857
(no date)
&
Mira J. Jones
Jul 6, 1861
Oct 27, 1917

Fleta Jones, wife of
Fred Damron
Jan 8, 1892
Feb 11, 1912

Titia Gattis, wife of
A. C. Bostick
May 23, 1853
Nov 21, 1927

Janet Higgins
May 29, 1929
Oct 3, 1930

D. B. Gattis
Aug 26, 1845
(no date)
&
M. J. Gattis
Jun 1842
May 21, 1910

W. N. Gattis
May 31, 1878
Dec 27, 1913

Ada Wright Gattis
Feb 11, 1878
Jan 10, 1951

Infant Son of
G. W. & Emily Powell
Jan 9, 1908
Jan 16, 1908

Lillian Broughton Pylant
1875-1952

Nancy Elizabeth Horton
1881-1960

W. H. Summarell
1876-1965 (TM)

Mrs. L. Summarell
1883-1965 (TM)

Bessie Lee Morgan
Apr 16, 1894
Mar 10, 1914
&
Sarah L. Morgan
Sep 2, 1849
Jun 6, 1919

James William Craig
Dec 12, 1861
Apr 14, 1921

Mary Howard Craig
May 1862
Aug 1942

Finella Howard Griffin
1858-1944

James Howard
1860-1939
&
Sallie Howard
1864-1927

John Honea
1872-1935
&
Mary Honea
1884-1951

J. R. Honea
1888-1940

Bernie B. Higgins
1900-1965
&
Florence D. Higgins
1903-

HUNTLAND QUADRANGLE

Herman V. Daniel
1908-1938

Annie J. Daniel
1873-1937

Raymond Paul Daniel
1938-1969
(Davis-Culbertson FH)

Sammie Dotson
1866-1944
&
Laura B. Dotson
1871-1942

John F. Dotson
Jan 21, 1906
Feb 9, 1963

Otho D. Brents
1897-1943

Mamie B. Brents
1896-1964

Billy H. Jackson
Oct 12, 1956
Oct 14, 1956

James W. Jackson
Jun 18, 1958

Omo Jone Jackson
Jul 11, 1960

Lorraine R. Hoots
May 10, 1910
May 19, 1965
"L.P.N. Tenn."

Vern Mc. Ramsey
1895-1927

J. E. Ramsey
May 25, 1859
Nov 20, 1943
&
Anna M. Ramsey
Aug 12, 1859
Feb 21, 1922

James G. Ramsey
1835-1943
&
Nora B. Ramsey
1836-1922

John Kilpatrick
1931-1932

Richard Sims
1929-1945

Robert Sims
Feb 7, 1906
Dec 28, 1952
&
Mary L. Sims
Mar 16, 1904

Clarence G. Scott
1904-1939
&
Mable P. Scott
1906-

George Rufus Scott
Feb 1, 1875
Sep 27, 1965
&
Geneva B. Kidd Scott
Dec 20, 1884
Feb 21, 1946

Carl R. Scott
Jun 4, 1907
Dec 14, 1969

Vallie W. Scott
Jul 4, 1907
Oct 2, 1960

Harvey C. Jacks
Mar 1, 1893
Oct 4, 1960
&
Vivian P. Jacks
Aug 12, 1900

Lois Jacks Mills
1923-1947

Larry Ray Payne
Aug 3, 1951
Feb 16, 1952

Harlan I. Miller
1910-1957
(Moore-Cortner FH)

Arch Baud Miller
Sep 23, 1876
Aug 14, 1960

Kans Buchanan
May 25, 1876
May 16, 1958
&
Gertrude Buchanan
Jul 24, 1881
Apr 17, 1969

John Flowers
1946-1967

Ronnie Flowers
1954-1964

James N. Flowers
1952-1959
(Motlow-Moore FH)

-------------(name gone)
1875-1958 (TM)

Annie Hatley
1874-1950
(Raby FH)

John H. Griggs
Jun 19, 1892-Dec 13, 1949

Jessie, Son of
Tom & Mary Lee Moore
Dec 19, 1939
Oct 14, 1943

William T. Rigsby
1881-1959
&
Nettie Hill Rigsby
1880-1944

George McCoy
Died Apr 27, 1964
Age: (gone)
(Higgins FH)

C. D. Anderson
Jun 18, 1910

&
Lillie Anderson
Apr 10, 1925
Jul 16, 1967

Clara Louise McCoy
Died Mar 1942
Age: (gone)
(Higgins FH)

Astill McCoy
1892-1942

3 graves (McCoy)
TM, no information)

James B. Scivally
Sep 16, 1900
Dec 13, 1941

2 graves "Ross"
(no information)

Vickie L. Jones
1951-1953

Obie Dee Pack
May 3, 1883
Oct 3, 1968

Hettie Parkerson
1905-1965

Henry Ross Parkerson
Tennessee
Pfc Btry I 70 Coast Arty WW II
Apr 25, 1921
May 31, 1965

Thomas J. Parkerson
Tennessee
Cpl 43 Air Supply Sq AAF
WW II
Apr 17, 1927
Aug 22, 1962

Melry Jan Parkerson
Feb 14, 1893
Mar 10, 1955

A. C. Carter
Jun 25, 1881

&
Ellen T. Carter
Jan 27, 1877
Jun 19, 1966

G. W. Yarbrough
1880-1952

Frank McElyea
Apr 16, 1891

&
Lettie K. McElyea
Nov 14, 1892
Apr 27, 1957

Laymon Bedford White
Tennessee
Tec 4 4 Service Command
WW II
Jun 19, 1917
Aug 4, 1953

Larry Wayne Whitehead, Jr.
B&D Nov 20, 1963

Malica Carol McElyea
1960-1960

John Jones
Tennessee
Pfc Co G 26 Inf WW I PH
Mar 5, 1894
Nov 23, 1957

Lemmer Farmer
1893-19(no date)
&
Mrs. Sam Farmer
1880-1935

Sarah E. Johnson
1850-1948

Maude Hulsey
Nov 11, 1881
Mar 26, 1944

James A. Wilbanks
1846-1939
&
Elizabeth Wilbanks
1860-19(no date)

Theo Shrader
Jan 8, 1900
Dec 9, 1942

Cora J. Layman Shrader
Aug 13, 1875
Nov 10, 1966

William Caswell Shrader
Jul 14, 1866
Dec 2, 1958

HUNTLAND QUADRANGLE

Joe B. Scivally
May 25, 1888
May 18, 1955
&
Grace Nix Scivally
Jul 22, 1891

Clyde M. Scivally
Aug 8, 1909
Oct 10, 1950

Annie Jane Scivally
Jan 16, 1931
Nov 25, 1931

Benjamin Smith
Nov 30, 1848
Jan 3, 1929
&
Martha D. Smith
Jan 17, 1857
Mar 9, 1942

Alice F. Reed
1918-1947

William Thomas McGehee
1871-1949
&
Mollie Nix McGehee
1873-1961

John Thomas Byrd
Feb 2, 1887
Jul 2, 1957
&
Zenna Belle Byrd
Aug 18, 1891
Feb 10, 1958

W. C. Tucker
May 4, 1936
May 1, 1967

Evelyn I. Austin
Feb 13, 1927
Jul 6, 1968

Tissie L. Ragan Hayes
Apr 21, 1906
Nov 21, 1962

Mary Selma Couch
Feb 23, 1917
Nov 7, 1919

Samuel Newton Couch
1888-1969
&
Carrie Alice Couch
1887-1935

Maude Couch
Jul 6, 1900

Brenda Rogers Cline
1942-1964

Sandra Gayle Caldwell
May 25, 1950
May 26, 1950

Ruby Jo Garner
1912-1939

J. B. Garner
Aug 10, 1863
Feb 16, 1922

Sim L. Caldwell, Sr.
1887-1944
&
Roxie J. Caldwell
1894-1919

Daisy Caldwell
1880-1946
(Raby FH)

Stephen R. Jacks
Jul 28, 1869
Jan 14, 1959
&
Delilah F. Jacks
Oct 9, 1876
Jun 10, 1966

Henry S. Perry
1866-1939
&
Sina C. Perry
1872-1934

William E. Shelton
Aug 17, 1846
Oct 18, 1919
&
Jaala K. Shelton
Sep 13, 1852
1940

Oliver A. Shelton
Tennessee
Pvt 16 Co 152 Depot Brigade
WW I
Mar 21, 1892
Dec 14, 1957

Wiley F. Fanning
May 10, 1876
Feb 7, 1969
&
Mary Lee Fanning
Died Oct 22, 1969
Age: 89 years.

Lawson Early Hamilton
Apr 29, 1876
Jun 12, 1917

Mary Katharine, Daughter of
L. E. & Eva Hamilton
Aug 21, 1910
Oct 24, 1911

Nola E. Layman
1908-1964
(Moore FH)

Luther F. Austin
Jul 24, 1857
May 28, 1948

Martha J., wife of
L. F. Austin
Dec 9, 1857
Jul 28, 1919

Robert Scott Austin
Oct 26, 1883
Apr 11, 1948

Mrs. Mattie Mae Austin
Died May 12, 1970
Age: 87 years.
(Gallant FH)

_____(Name gone)
1877-1920

Katharine Elizabeth
Scarbrough
Apr 27, 1923
May 10, 1923

Wilma Jean Scarbrough
Mar 25, 1920
Oct 21, 1929

G. Curtis Reagan
1906-
&
A. Wilma Reagan
1919-1964

Robert C. Panter
1903-1970
&
Birdie A. Panter
1910-

Elvis C. Couch
Alabama
Sgt 11 Base Hq WW II
Jan 29; 1905
Jan 2, 1968

Ernest Craig
Jul 14, 1898

&
Emma Craig
Dec 7, 1898
Jun 16, 1963
Married Jul 4, 1920

Herman Morris
1914-1970
(Moore-Cortner FH)

Louis W. Hall
Jul 11, 1901
May 3, 1960
&
Thula Hall
Nov 14, 1902

Judie Helen Hall
Nov 1, 1952
Jun 23, 1953

Sylvester H. Hambrick
May 30, 1877
(no date)
&
Mary M. Hambrick
Aug 8, 1883
Jan 14, 1957

P. R. Young
Nov 1, 1862
Oct 13, 1927

G. D. Cates
Jul 4, 1874
Nov 22, 1928
&
Minnie Cates
Sep 24, 1877
(no date)

Jessie J. Moore
Jan 26, 1884
Jul 27, 1965
&
Ida T. Moore
Nov 6, 1880
Jul 3, 1933

B. H. Stovall
Dec 25, 1861
Dec 3, 1913

Hugh Franklin Merrell
Jan 21, 1873
Sep 28, 1955

Emma Margaret Merrell
Mar 10, 1873
Mar 1, 1927

Ernest L. Merrell
Jan 1, 1897
Nov 27, 1927

Henry W. Morgan
Died Jun 22, 1970
Age: 79 years.
(Gallant FH)

G. A. Donaldson
Sep 14, 1879
Nov 18, 1957
&
Esther L. Donaldson
Jan 23, 1894
Oct 4, 1950

Lee R. Cantrell
Mar 28, 1884
May 27, 1968
&
Lillie M. Cantrell
Jun 3, 1891

HUNTLAND QUADRANGLE

Mrs. Maggie Ann Jones
Died Sep 2, 1969
Age: 65 years.
(Gallant FH)

Lonnie M. Camp
Nov 27, 1889
Dec 15, 1947
&
Lillie M. Camp
Dec 29, 1889
Feb 29, 1940

Mrs. Christine Bryant Camp
Died Dec 8, 1966
Age: 45 years.
(Gallant FH)

James Douglas Hardin
1942-1959

George Dewey Hardin
Tennessee
Pvt Co B 383 Inf WW I
Oct 29, 1898
Jan 28, 1956

Betty Smith Hardin
Aug 11, 1900
Oct 21, 1960

James E. Hardin
1873-1947
&
Glenn Hardin
1871-1964

Robert Dawson Hardin
Aug 6, 1879

&
Ella Smith Hardin
Feb 28, 1893
May 30, 1963

Infant Children of
Minie & Gorden Harden
(no dates)

Several unmarked graves.

Pfc James Earl Daniel
Dec 5, 1930
Oct 7, 1951

Mildred Burwell Osborn
May 23, 1923
May 24, 1925

Margaret Ann Pepper
1935-1938

* *

ROCKY SPRINGS CEMETERY

LOCATION: One half mile south of Elora on hill near the Cave Spring.

William T. Patten
Co E
2 U.S. Vol Inf

I. A. Patten
(no dates)

A. W. Patten
(no dates)

Infant Son of
W. M. & Maggie E. Parker
B&D Apr 27, 1899

R. F. Hamilton
May 15, 1864
Sep 10, 1912

W. D. L. Hamilton
Jan 19, 1872
Married to Pearl Steel
Feb 7, 1900
Died Aug 24, 1901

Elisabeth Catharine Hamilton
Nov 9, 1858
Dec 2, 1876

E. L. Hamilton
(no dates)

Julia A., wife of
J. S. Hamilton
Jan 16, 1856
Dec 3, 1897

Purnie Ellison, wife of
I. N. Hamilton
Dec 20, 1875
Oct 4, 1900

Thomas G. Yarbrough
Mar 5, 1861
Mar 28, 1920

James H. Crawley
Jan 29, 1842
Jun 8, 1896

Nancy Syler, wife of
N. A. Hamilton
Nov 7, 1842
Aug 11, 1904

Millard, Son of
Marion & Arreva Raynolds
Died Jun 6, 1903
Age: 1y, 10m, 2d.

Alonzo Hamilton
Mar 9, 1840
Oct 2, 1888

Mattie A. E. Hamilton
Jan 9, 1865
Sep 19, 1884
Age: 19y, 8m, 10d.

Mary W., Daughter of
J. B. & S. E. Smith
Feb 16, 1870
Aug 14, 1892

William Guy, Son of
W. H. & W. C. Smith
Sep 22, 1899
Jun 5, 1902

Mildred D. Steele, wife of
J. P. Hamilton
Sep 26, 1845
Apr 10, 1900

Kittie, wife of
D. T. Kennedy & Daughter of
J. P. & M. D. Hamilton
May 18, 1873
Apr 3, 1905

Clarence, Son of
M. A. & Dora Pylant
Jul 17, 1904
Jan 2, 1905

Sally W. Pylant
Died Sep 27, 1888
Age: 58y, 9m, 5d.

G. A. Pylant
Died Jan 27, 1905
Age: 82y, 28d.

Infant Boys of
A. & M. E. Hamilton
Born Jul 26, 1879
One died Jul 29, 1879
Other died Aug 9, 1879

Arcola Pearl Hamilton
Feb 25, 1875
Apr 14, 1890

Jasper S. Hamilton
Nov 22, 1812
Apr 26, 1876
& wife
Martha Hamilton
Oct 5, 1817
Sep 25, 1854

Jacob Hamilton
Oct 4, 1785
Jan 26, 1852
Age: 66y, 3m, 22d.

Elizabeth Hamilton
Oct 16, 1807
Jul 17, 1881
Age: 73y, 9m, 1d.

Elise, Daughter of
Mr. & Mrs. T. G. Yarbrough
Mar 24, 1901
Mar 26, 1922

A. T. Pylant
Dec 23, 1856
Dec 14, 1905

T. Stewart
(no dates)

James E., Son of
W. C. & S. A. Stewart
Feb 1, 1873
May 30, 1890

Infant Baby of
John & Nita Gattis
B&D Feb 9, 1907

Nancy Lou, Daughter of
R. C. & M. J. Austin
Jun 7, 1872
Mar 20, 1892

P. B. Austin
Jan 18, 1868
Apr 12, 1901

John W. Walker
Apr 22, 1830
Jun 9, 1900

Augustus M. Yarbrough
Mar 22, 1820
Jun 24, 1901

Mahala J. McKee, wife of
Augustus Yarbrough
May 1, 1827
Aug 21, 1897

Charlie, Son of
T. G. & M. I. Yarbrough
Oct 21, 1906
Nov 2, 1906

HUNTLAND QUADRANGLE

James Oakley Austin *
Sep 16, 1869
Married L. D. Park
Aug 11, 1895
Died Jan 28, 1899
Age: 29y, 4m, 11d.

Mrs. Letitia,* wife of
W. C. Stewart
Died May 18, 1906
Age: 40 years.

ED NOTE: Was a Community
Graveyard.

Mrs. Jane Austin *
Died May 15, 1896 at the
residence of Son-in-law
John Williamson
Age: 65 years.

N. A. Hamilton *
Died Nov 27, 1909
Age: 76y, 11m, 7d.

Many unmarked graves.

* *

ROBERTSON CEMETERY

LOCATION: One and one half miles east of Elora and south of Highway 122.

Avery Robertson
1869-1947
&
Mollie Cambron Robertson
1858-1939

Thomas William Robertson
Mar 6, 1874
Feb 1, 1955

John F. Robertson
Oct 4, 1826
Apr 3, 1862

Many unmarked graves.

G. L. Cambron
Dec 21, 1856
Nov 21, 1883

Thomas W., Son of
G. L. & Mollie Cambron
Jul 22, 1881
May 15, 1884

James Price Cambron
Sep 1, 1883
Mar 5, 1884
&
Anna Myrtle Cambron
Mar 16, 1879
Jun 18, 1880
"Son & Daughter of
G. L. & Mollie Cambron"

Thomas Alton, Son of
E. W. & F. Robertson
Mar 5, 1905
Apr 30, 1906

Jessee M. Robertson
Sep 16, 1824
Jan 20, 1902

Willa Fay Robertson
Apr 26, 1908
Jun 3, 1909

James Mercer Robertson
Mar 19, 1914
Jun 18, 1919

Ezekiel W. Robertson
Oct 9, 1877
Feb 3, 1948
&
Celia Florence Robertson
Jan 13, 1832
(no date)

Silas Mercer Robertson
Dec 13, 1832
Oct 18, 1910
& wife
Prudence Ann Robertson
Jun 29, 1837
Aug 3, 1898

* *

DAMERON CEMETERY

LOCATION: Two miles east of Elora on south side of Highway 122.

Charlie Dameron
1859-1906
&
Anna C. Dameron
1867-1953

William Dameron
Jun 15, 1809
Aug 24, 1898
& wife
Loudemia Dameron
Jan 17, 1816
Aug 28, 1899

James H. Wakefield
Apr 14, 1836
Jan 2, 1905
Age: 68y, 8m, 19d.

Mary Dameron, wife of
J. H. Wakefield
1843-1930

Joe B., Son of
Mary & J. H. Wakefield
Dec 29, 1870
Oct 3, 1895

Nannie Mildred Birmingham
Jan 4, 1901
Jul 1, 1926

Lana Cheryl, Daughter of
Mr. & Mrs. Clyde Smith
B&D May 8, 1946

Nell, Daughter of
J. F. & L. M. Dameron
Nov 5, 1903
Sep 27, 1907

Charles Cary Dameron
Aug 19, 1902
Aug 16, 1909

John F. Dameron
1879-1959
&
Lola Myrtle Dameron
1877-1953

Lizzie Chapman, wife of
W. L. Hamilton
Jul 19, 1866
Aug 19, 1902

Sigmund, Son of
W. L. & L. Hamilton
Apr 21, 1889
Nov 28, 1892

Will Ewing, Son of
W. L. & L. Hamilton
Died Feb 1897
Age: 2 months.

Elbert R. Hamilton
Sep 12, 1866
Mar 29, 1889

Charles A. Dameron
May 12, 1929
Apr 17, 1967
&
A. Louise Dameron
May 4, 1928

William A. Reid
Feb 29, 1892
Feb 8, 1921

Etta R. Reid
1884-1960

Joe B., Son of
J. H. & E. Reeves
Mar 19, 1896
Nov 1, 1918

Martha J. Reeves
1897-1924

J. H. Reeves
Jan 15, 1858
Aug 5, 1932

Emma Reeves
Feb 7, 1866
May 7, 1944

Infant Son of
J. H. & E. L. Reeves
B&D May 12, 1906

E. M., Daughter of
J. H. & E. L. Reeves
Apr 21, 1899
Jun 12, 1903

C. B., Son of
J. H. & E. L. Reeves
Jul 28, 1889
Mar 2, 1897

M. B., Son of
J. H. & E. L. Reeves
Oct 9, 1886
Jul 12, 1890

HUNTLAND QUADRANGLE

James Cleo, Son of
Mr. & Mrs. H. C. Reeves
Sep 19, 1914
Oct 18, 1919

John Green
Dec 29, 1804
Nov 13, 1864

John C. Green
Mar 14, 1840
(Date broken away)

Celia Dameron, wife of
Thomas J. Stovall
Feb 27, 1836
Aug 29, 1870

Mary A. Hardin
Died Apr 4, 1847
Age: about 80 years.

Agatm(?) J. J. Bostick
Jan 1, 1844
Oct 20, 1852

William A. Bostick
Oct 21, 1859
Apr 8, 1860

Mrs. Jane Smith *
Widow of J. A. Smith
Died Oct 4, 1906
Age: 70 years.
"5 children"

J. F. H.
(footstone)

E. J. H.
(footstone)

Hardin H. _____
M-- --, 1876
Feb 22, 1877 (broken)

Nancy J. Crawford
Dec 1, 1849
May 10, 187? (illegible)

N. A. Bostick
Jun 15, 1819
Aug 11, 1881

Rolin L. Walker
Mar 22, 1878
Jun 7, 1879

Cyntha P. Bostick
Feb 7, 1857
Jun 29, 1879

India N. Wakefield
Aug 16, 1882
Apr 21, 1883

David Wright
Died Jul 28, 1831
Age: 45 years.

Jane Wright
Nov 20, 1786
Aug 25, 1857

Infant of
John & Mary Wakefield
B&D Jun 9, 1881

Infant of
John & Mary Wakefield
B&D Mar 4, 1876

Nancy Jane Wakefield
Feb 18, 1828
Feb 23, 1872

Clark Wakefield
Dec 4, 1874
Aug 9, 1889

Sarah C. Wakefield
Aug 4, 1889
Aug 2, 1892

James M., Son of
J. H. & M. Wakefield
Aug 29, 1862
Nov 26, 1880

J. W. Hudson
Apr 11, ----(date gone)
Aug 18, 1893

Many unmarked graves.

Margaret Ann Robertson
May 5, 1836
Aug 2, 1853

Walter W., Son of
J. A. & C. J. Smith
Jul 21, 1856
Sep 18, 1887

Ludemia, Daughter of
J. A. & Celia J. Smith
Dec 29, 1869
May 18, 1871

James Franklin Baxter
Sep 27, 1908
Jul 28, 1909
&
Gladys Baxter
Jan 29, 1899
Feb 13, 1899

John Dameron
May 3, 1839
Sep 6, 1845

James W. Dameron
May 3, 1849
Jul 7, 1852

Sister Dameron
Aug 12, 1851
Jul 2, 1852

* *

SHADY GROVE CEMETERY

LOCATION: One fourth mile north of Shady Grove and north of Happy Ridge Road.

Thomas J. Durham
Apr 16, 1860
Oct 17, 1938
&
Sarah K. Durham
Jan 21, 1869
(no date)

Smith Durham
Jan 14, 1907
Jan 3, 1923

Thomas Durham
1886-1925
&
Tennie Durham
1887-1929

Paul M. Durham
Jul 30, 1897
Jun 26, 1920

Levi Shelton Durham
May 28, 1919
Jun 5, 1919

Juanita Jane Durham
Feb 17, 1923
Mar 9, 1923

James Richard Durham
Died Feb 13, 1955
Age: 57 years
(J. C. Moore FH, Winchester)

Daisy Pate Durham
Aug 27, 1892
Mar 19, 1923

Lee Gaston Durham
1922

Lila Ruth Pickett
Sep 1, 1924
Mar 1, 1926

Wilma Evelyn Pickett
May 12, 1921
Nov 1, 1922

W. A. "Buck" Jones
Oct 26, 1877
Apr 22, 1951

Judia Emmaline Jones
Dec 29, 1877
Apr 10, 1965

Tinia Pearl Jones
Sep 1, 1904
Jul 19, 1914

Roy Cecil Jones
Mar 8, 1907
Aug 21, 1909

Infant Son of
J. B. & M. J. Derrick
Feb 9, 1872
Feb 26, 1872

Barsha E. Rogers, wife of
F. P. Bowen
Aug 20, 1883
Sep 17, 1907

Infant of
F. B. & B. E. Bowen
Sep 2, 1903
Sep 5, 1903

"Son"
Bobby Stiles
1930   Age: 4 months

Julia Rich
1879-1949

Jake Henry Hilliard
1877-Aug 1914

Benjamin F. McCormick
Feb 13, 1895
Nov 13, 1966
Tennessee Pvt 107 Guard Co
ASC WW I
&
Eunice Syler McCormick
Jan 25, 1902

HUNTLAND QUADRANGLE

William I. Syler
Nov 18, 1874
Oct 17, 1945
&
Louretta Riley Syler
Apr 26, 1874
Jun 10, 1955

Sam Ivey
Sep 16, 1867
Nov 23, 1905

Thomas P. Riley
Jul 28, 1830
Nov 8, 1907

Mary Ann, wife of
Thomas P. Riley
Dec 22, 1843
Jan 29, 1910

Thomas P. Riley, Jr.
Feb 7, 1863
Apr 14, 1930

Johanna, wife of
M. G. Arnold
Sep 12, 1869
Dec 20, 1903

Velma L., Daughter of
J. M. & B. F. Riley
Died Jul 27, 1913
Age: 8m, 8d.

Robert Leon, Son of
J. M. & B. F. Riley
Dec 23, 1908
Sep 24, 1909

James M. Riley
Dec 8, 1877
May 16, 1938
&
Beulah F. Riley
1886-Jun 25, 1959

Leon W. Harmening
Oct 25, 1922
Dec 28, 1928

Luther Estell Norman
May 29, 1883
Jan 31, 1932
&
Mary Magdalene Norman
Jan 31, 1885

Isaac Mason
1849-1936
&
Elizabeth Mason
1867-1918

William Mason
1899-1928

Robert M. Brown
May 15, 1876
Jul 31, 1898

J. W. Donaldson
Nov 29, 1852
Mar 16, 1926
& wife
Alice D. Donaldson
Oct 26, 1875
May 6, 1918

Fred Lee, Son of
R. L. & Bess Bradley
Jul 22, 1916
Dec 28, 1917

Luther E. Norman
May 29, 1882
Jan 31, 1932

W. W. Parker
Mar 10, 1829
Jun 11, 1905
&
Nancy E. Parker
Oct 29, 1829
Jun 25, 1904

James L., Son of
W. W. & Nancy E. Parker
Jun 11, 1866
Aug 3, 1890

Ules, Son of
W. B. & O. A. Bowen
Apr 26, 1888
Jul 15, 1889

John J. Norman
Jul 1, 1846
Aug 6, 1928

Daniel Keeling, Son of
J. F. & M. E. Harmening
Jan 28, 1886
Feb 7, 1886
Age: 9 days.

John William, Son of
J. F. & M. E. Harmening
Oct 5, 1881
Feb 26, 1882

John F. Harmening
Mar 4, 1847
Jun 11, 1900

Altha I., Daughter of
M. C. & S. C. Smith
Jul 20, 1883
Jan 14, 1884

William H. Lucas
Mar 8, 1798
Dec 4, 1861

Grizella Lucas
Dec 1, 1798
Nov 9, 1881

Nannie E. Talley
1859-1925

J. B. Riley
Jul 7, 1819
Apr 1, 1899

Elizabeth Riley
Feb 15, 1821
Sep 3, 1898

Robert H. Templeton
1845-1929
&
Mattie A. Templeton
1863-1956

John H. Templeton
Mar 27, 1812
Dec 2, 1877
&
James P. Templeton
Feb 19, 1840
Feb 26, 1859

Fannie F., Daughter of
R. H. & E. C. Templeton
B&D 1881

William Riley
Oct 15, 1792
Dec 27, 1872
&
Catharine Riley
Apr 1797
Sep 30, 1852

Charlott Riley
Feb 14, 1833
Jan 10, 1904

Son of
W. M. & Z. C. Rich
(no dates)

Jessee McClure
Dec 31, 1787
Feb 19, 1856

Jane McClure
Sep 14, 1794
Apr 17, 1869

James H. McClure
Jun 26, 1828
Dec 14, 1852

Joanna, Daughter of
W. M. & Z. C. Rich
Jul 8, 1863
Jun 26, 1882

Mrs. Elizabeth Ann Newman
Dec 9, 1822
Jun 7, 1857

Mary A. S. Alley
Mar 28, 1836
Aug 27, 1853

Mary Beatrice Brown, wife of
George Williams
Sep 8, 1879
Dec 6, 1910

James Couch
Dec 29, ----
Sep 7, ----(broken away)

Mary Couch
Sep 12, 1837
Oct 2, 1871

James Couch
Jul 15, 1815
Mar 22, 1889

Mary Couch
Oct 15, 1816
Feb 4, 1908

Nelson Couch
Dec 2, 1859
Aug 22, 1884

George Couch
Dec 5, 1856
Apr 19, 1909

Mary Couch
Died Oct 19, 1861
Age: 84 years.

Vind Hodge
Oct 9, 1846
May 19, 1882

Katie Edmiston
1813-1883

Martha, wife of
J. H. Foster
Sep 1816
Jun 27, 1889

James F. Foster
Died Mar 12, 1909
Age: 39y, 8m, 25d.

W. L. Norman
Died Feb 8, 1924
Age: (not given)
&
L. C. Norman
Died May 6, 1904
Age: (not given)

Pallis M., Son of
W. C. & L. S. Norman
May 6, 1871
Jun 17, 1889

Nancy I., Daughter of
W. C. & L. S. Norman
Aug 17, 1876
Aug 10, 1878

Levi Benson
Died Mar 21, 1879
Age: 65 years.
&
Susan C. Benson
Died Jul 12, 1893
Age: 68 years.

HUNTLAND QUADRANGLE

Mary J. Hall
Aug 25, 1836
Nov 30, 1902

Willie Byrd Benson
1894-1962
&
Millie Rosia Benson
1894-

Charley Benson
Oct 3, 1882
Sep 26, 1906

Lovina Benson
Mar 5, 1854
Jun 20, 1936

D. B. Benson
May 26, 1855
Sep 21, 1901

Margaret M., wife of
Dr. W. H. McLaughlin
May 18, 1822
Oct 18, 1881

Dr. W. H. McLaughlin
Nov 9, 1820
Jan 25, 1871

Henry Smith
Sep 2, 1805
Dec 25, 1883

L. P. Gilliam
Oct 29, 1840
Dec 19, 1870

Mariah, wife of
Charles Littrell
Died Apr 10, 1913
Age: 76 years.
&
Maggie, wife of
Charles Littrell
Died May 7, 1917
Age: 28 years.

S. Coope(r)
1869
(fieldstone)

Maud Lela, Daughter of
R. E. & F. E. Walker
B&D Jul 1882

Unice Catharine, wife of
J. Hamilton
Mar 29, 1834
Apr 23, 1887

Rufus K. Smith
Oct 5, 1829
Jan 5, 1862

Eular E. Gattis
Sep 26, 1876
Oct 7, 1881
(fieldstone)

W. J. Gattis
Oct 6, 1870
Nov 7, 1881

Lizzy Troop
(no dates, fieldstone)

James Luttrell
Died Sep 23, 1888
Age: 55 years.

Infant Daughter of
W. A. & M. A. Southerlan
Oct 5, 1881
Feb 21, 1882

S. F. Norman
Nov 22, 1823
Oct 22, 1890

William C. Norman
Apr 12, 1815
Sep 1, 1894

Martha Sue, Daughter of
G. W. & Pearl Lee
1925-1926

Donald D., Son of
Albert Hall
Jan 4, 1902
Jan 15, 1919

Daniel, Son of
Mr. & Mrs. Charley Parks
B&D Jan 3, 1915

Carl William, Son of
Mr. & Mrs. Charley Parks
Mar 4, 1912
Dec 30, 1913

Minnie Pearl, Daughter of
J. P. & S. J. Bryant
Jul 18, 1893
Jun 12, 1904

Wade Keith
Jan 16, 1877
Feb 1, 1909

Mollie Pruitt
1871-1941

Ader Farley
Aug 6, 1911
Jan 1, 1916

Charlie R. Grammer
1937-1941
&
Billie H. Grammer
1939-194?
Children of
W. H. & F. A. Grammer

James O. Pickett
1846-1924
&
Josephine Cambron Pickett
1859-1949

Johnson Gulley
Mar 11, 1844
(no date)
& wife
M. A. Prince Gulley
Mar 22, 1858
Nov 27, 1918
&
Jesse A. Gulley
Oct 16, 1898
Nov 18, 1923

John Drury Pate
1862-1940
&
Martha Lily Pate
1860-1936
& Daughter
Johnny Belle Pate
1895-1936

Tom Preston
Nov 14, 1886
Jul 25, 1933

Wessie Taylor
1910

Willie Taylor
1914-1917

Claudie Taylor
1928

Maudie Taylor
1928-1930

Louella Taylor
1900-1958

J. J. Taylor
1898-1946
(Raby FH)

Dal Couch
(Dates deep in ground)

Ruby Florence, Daughter of
Mr. & Mrs. Lee Norman
B&D Nov 12, 1946

Martha Jean, Daughter of
Mr. & Mrs. Lee Norman
Jun 13, 1936
Nov 8, 1941

Edith Jewel, Daughter of
Mr. & Mrs. Lee Norman
Oct 3, 1928
Oct 16, 1928

Herbert E. Norman
Dec 28, 1902
Aug 27, 1903

John J. Norman
1850-1928
&
Julia Norman
1863-1938

Fannie May Tipps, wife
of B. C. Norman
Mar 29, 1929
Age: (in ground)

W. J. Norman
Feb 21, 1876
Nov 2, 1945

Lillie Benson, wife of
W. J. Norman
Oct 2, 1877
Dec 6, 1943

John W. Norman
1869-1923

Ella Benson, wife of
W. A. Norman
Apr 12, 1879
May 3, 1918
"For many years a consist-
ant member of Baptist
Church"

Oscar L. Norman
Aug 7, 1887
Nov 26, 1944

Infant Daughter of
O. L. & M. L. Norman
B&D Jun 10, 1929

Infant Son of
O. L. & M. L. Norman
Apr 20, 1925
Apr 25, 1925

Lucile, Daughter of
O. L. & M. L. Norman
Died Jul 9, 1910
Age: 1y, 4m, 11d.

J. C. Bryant
Mar 6, 1874
Dec 26, 1953

Alice Bryant
Dec 1, 1874
Apr 5, 1904

L. E., wife of
P. I. Griffin
May 11, 1877
Aug 27, 1897

James H. Syler
Sep 14, 1857
Aug 20, 1929

Nancy A., wife of
J. H. Syler
Feb 25, 1865
Apr 26, 1910

Pallis Griffin
Aug 28, 1833
Jun 1, 1906

HUNTLAND QUADRANGLE

Elizabeth A., wife of
Pallis Griffin
Oct 25, 1833
Jun 26, 1904

Infant Daughter of
Nancy & James Syler
Jun 6, 1898
Jul 16, 1898

Margaret Ann Griffin
Dec 4, 1869
Dec 8, 1943

Robert Woodruff
Died 1936
Age: (not given)

Robert Lee Pickett
B&D Oct 24, 1931

Cecil Pickett
B&D 1934

Melda Dean Pickett
1935-1936

John Samuel Pulliam
Mar 21, 1865
(no date)
&
Linda Bryant Pulliam
Mar 11, 1865
Mar 21, 1933

J. M. Mearse
1906-1946
(Raby FH)

C. L. Mearse
1865-1941

W. M. Clay Norman
1904-1966
&
Emma E. Norman
1904-19

Nancy Caroline Tipps
Aug 15, 1870
Aug 2, 1944

Floyd Jeans
Dec 20, 1906
Apr 5, 1965
&
Pearl Jeans
May 24, 1902

Married Jun 26, 1927

Ben Williams
1886-1954
(Steed-Anderton FH)

Ambers Franklin Williams
Jun 9, 1919
Mar 24, 1954

James Manuel Jones
Dec 10, 1905
Jan 9, 1964

Dena Hall Taylor
Dec 18, 1874
May 22, 1955

Ira Clay Pickett
1878-1952
&
Eunice E. Pickett
1891-19(no date)

William F. Arnold
Nov 14, 1883
Nov 13, 1960
&
Jessie A. Arnold
Apr 13, 1891

Bedford C. Norman
(no dates)
&
Clara Jean Norman
(no dates)

J. D. Pickett
Dec 12, 1919
&
Bobbie L. Pickett
Dec 15, 1933
Jun 2, 1962

Johnny Allen Murray
Oct 18, 1946
Dec 11, 1969

Isaac Farris
1906-1966

George W. Crowell
Oct 31, 1883
Feb 5, 1966
&
Bessie H. Crowell
Nov 9, 1884
Jan 17, 1928

Mildred Crowell
1922-1965
(Gallant FH)

Ruby Hall
1917-1964
(Moore FH)

William Jean
Jan 10, 1871
Dec 7, 1955
&
Martha Jean
Aug 2, 1876
(no date)

Paula H. Mearse
1965
(Gallant FH)

Harvey Jean
Mar 6, 1910
Apr 24, 1945
&
Della Jean
Jan 22, 1904
Nov 22, 1944

Aldar Mearse
1893-1963

------ Mearse
Died --- 17, 196_
Age: 67 or 57y, 3m, 25d.
(Gallant FH)

Marie Moore
Jul 11, 1922
Oct 2, 1922

Larry Jean
Oct 16, 1945
Nov 11, 1945

Almer Speck
1876-1949
&
Bertie Keith Speck
1881-1944

John Wesley Bowen
1878-1948
&
Hattie Keith Bowen
1879-1947

Altie Speck
Dec 19, 1900
Jan 5, 1954

Baby
Walter Warren
1918-1920

Infant Son of
N. P. & Lisey Bostic(k)
B&D Dec 5, 1916

_____(Name gone)
Died Sep 19, 1920
Age: 41y, 8m.

Thomas Arnold
1938-1938

Barbara Arnold
Sep 10, 1941
Jun --, 1943

Julie Blair
1867-1931

Nellie Jane Taylor
Mar 25, 1956
Oct 12, 1956
(Gallant FH)

Jack Church
1911-1947
(Raby FH)

W. Floyd & W. Loyd Mearse
Jun 26, 1959
Jun 27, 1959

John H. Pruitt
Jul 16, 1885
May 13, 1959
&
Hannah G. Pruitt
Dec 6, 1898

James W. Pruitt
1905-1956
(Gallant FH)

John Bruce Owen
Died Jan --, ----
(Infant, date gone)

Elmer ------
(all other info gone)

Patrick Neal Bryant
B&D Apr 22, 1970
(Gallant FH)

Jodie Syler
1968
(Moore-Cortner FH)

William F. Mann
Feb 5, 1880
Feb 9, 1965
&
Sarah B. Mann
Feb 14, 1884

Married Aug 2, 1902

Infant Sons of
Mr. & Mrs. Clayton Mann
B&D Jan 4, 1955
&
Dec 8, 1947
Dec 11, 1947

William Eden Templeton
Sep 22, 1879
Jan 15, 1956
&
Orphia Speck Templeton
Sep 15, 1880
1968
(Harrison FH)

Frank Eley, Jr.
1941-1953
&
Icey Eley
1900-1952

Frank Eley
Oct 12, 1899
Dec 6, 1956

Frank H. Luttrell
Jun 26, 1904
Jun 16, 1941

HUNTLAND QUADRANGLE

Albert Taylor
1889-1953
&
Dora Taylor
1891-1967
&
Clistine Taylor
1934-1950

"Mother"
Ada L. Preston
1884-1962
& "Son"
Johnny D. Preston
1906-1952

Ida Bell George
Aug 20, 1936
Feb 13, 1953

Ida Bradley Jeans
May 20, 1889
Jan 10, 1919

Benton Jeans
Apr 11, 1884
May 8, 1959
&
Ida Harris Jeans
Dec 6, 1897
Nov 8, 1950

Coleman Mearse
1902-1963
(Gallant FH)

Mary Lou (Mearse)
Died --- --, 196-(gone)
Age: (gone)
(Ralston FH)

J. W. Walker
1925-1957

Sarah _. Walker
1944-1944

Tom W. Clark
Feb 12, 1891
Sep 24, 1942
&
Bonnie B. Clark
Nov 30, 1904

Maggie Carter
Oct 11, 1881
Nov 8, 1948

Nolgar J. Clark
Apr 14, 1896
Jun 13, 1946
&
Jennie B. Clark
Jan 10, 1902

J. M. Clark
Jul 15, 1940
Oct 30, 1940

Roy Calvin Mearse
Oct 24, 1913
Apr 12, 1962
&
Lillie Mae Mearse
Aug 18, 1914

William C., Son of
Robert Ervin &
Jennie Wakefield Walker
Dec 30, 1899
Sep 21, 1968
&
Carrie Walker, Daughter of
Otho Dillon &
Lillie Waggoner Harrison
Sep 16, 1900

Jennie Wakefield Walker Cowley
Nov 25, 1868
Mar 9, 1960

Sidney W. Walker
May 25, 1895 Pvt Co B 166
Apr 16, 1966 Inf WW I
&
Louellar Miles Walker
Dec 12, 1897
Dec 13, 1969
Married Jan 11, 1920

John W. Crouch
1881-1966
(Harrison FH)

Myrtle S. Crouch
1887-1964
(Harrison FH)

Billy Hugh Clark
May 4, 1939
May 6, 1939

Eva Fay Ballard
B&D Jan 3, 1939

Elvira Ashby
1856-1932

James Abner Jones
Mar 14, 1880
Aug 8, 1956
&
Emma Lou Alice Jones
Mar 10, 1882
May 29, 1947

Will Jones
1907-1932

Clayton Jones
1923-1924

John Jones
Jul 12, 1874
Jun 17, 1903

Mary E. Jones, wife of
W. N. Benson
Nov 17, 1877
Aug 17, 1903

W. R. Riley
1905-1941 (Same as below)

William Roy Riley
Apr 17, 1905
Aug 6, 1941
&
Ruth Hall Riley
Sep 15, 1910
(no date)

J. C. Little
Nov 20, 1850
Jun 2, 1892

Nancy Little
Feb 24, 1855
Apr 7, 1897

Mary Ann Little
Died May 7, 1884
Age: (Not given)

Harriet A., wife of
W. B. Faulkner
Mar 25, 1854
Sep 1, 1896

Sarah Maud, Daughter of
W. B. & H. A. Faulkner
Jan 13, 1885
Sep 9, 1885

Joseph Franklin Syler
Mar 14, 1866
May 20, 1921
&
Amanda Elizabeth Syler
Oct 20, 1866
Nov 30, 1902

Emma Fay Davis
Oct 6, 1936
Jan 1, 1937

Clara L. Davis
1907-1951
(Wilson FH)

Henry Lafayette Hall
Jul 10, 1877
Jul 23, 1946
&
Emma Wood Hall
Jul 10, 1878
Feb 8, 1947

Bill & Elizabeth Williams
(no dates)

John Luttrell
1862-1937

Dr. L. D. Hall, D.D.S.
May 15, 1851
Mar 28, 1936

Sallie G. Hall
Jun 27, 1869
Nov 29, 1941

Edward S. Hall
Dec 26, 1897
Jun 26, 1963
&
Ina Bryant Hall
Apr 21, 1893
Nov 17, 1956

Louise Marie Hall
Mar 22, 1929
Oct 19, 1953

Herman B. Smith
Nov 9, 1893
Apr 19, 1963
&
Odell G. Smith
Jul 9, 1913

Marilla D. George
May 23, 1861
Nov 3, 1892

Rutha Benson Keith
Aug 10, 1870
Apr 13, 1925

Katie Ethel Benson
May 29, 1902
Jun 5, 1903

M. C. Brazelton
Apr 11, 1901
Mar 3, 1963

T.
(no dates, fieldstone)

T.
(no dates, fieldstone)

Albert Arnold
1880-1955
&
Annie Arnold
1893-1957

W. Howard Arnold
Jan 17, 1913
Jul 7, 1965

Thomas S. Young
1877-1939
&
Nannie N. Young
1883-1939

Sarah N. Syler
Aug 17, 1944
Oct 20, 1944

HUNTLAND QUADRANGLE

Frank L. Syler
Dec 23, 1936
Feb 20, 1942

William Michael Syler
Jun 29, 1938
Feb 17, 1939

Sarah N. Syler
Sep 13, 1856
Jan 26, 1918

Joel Foster
Died Jan 15, 1896
Age: 75 years.

Sarah F. Foster
Died Aug 22, 1905
Age: (not given)

James Robert Syler
Aug 25, 1876
Dec 27, 1942
&
Bertha Rilla Syler
Jul 2, 1886

Wiley Wiseman
1868-1930

Fannie Wiseman
1860-1936

M. P. "Dock" Syler
1887-1947

Edith Catharine, Daughter
of C. C. & Eunice Pogue
B&D Nov 28, 1922

F. C., wife of
R. E. Walker (Same as
Sep 12, 1860 Fannie Walker
Oct 9, 1893 below.)

Bennie G., Son of
J. M. & R. E. Walker
B&D Dec 17, 1901

R. E. Walker
Nov 17, 1850
Jul 28, 1914
&
Fannie Walker
Sep 12, 1860
Oct 9, 1893

Robert H. Walker
May 29, 1884
May 13, 1941
&
Addie P. Walker
Apr 30, 1837

Hugh Kimble, Son of
R. H. & Addie Walker
May 12, 1912
Jul 19, 1914

Mary Glen, Daughter of
J. & U. C. Hamilton
Aug 23, 1877
Sep 13, 1892

Mary Holman
1827-Jan 22, 1885

Hilton Luttrell
Nov 13, 1937
Oct 9, 1954

Gracie Lee Luttrell
Dec 16, 1932
Apr 4, 1946

M. E. T.
1867
(fieldstone)

G. W. Bradley
1892-1936

Roxie Arnold Bradley
1890-1968
(Moore-Cortner FH)

Ace M. Bradley
1857-1932
&
Nara S. Bradley
1859-1937

Beatrice Davis
1901-1940

William Roy, Son of
J. H. & Nancy Jean
Feb 28, 1916
Dec 25, 1917

Infant Daughter of
J. H. & Nancy Jean
1902

Thelma, Daughter of
J. H. & Nancy Jean
Aug 28, 1913
Mar 31, 1922

James Henry Jean
Aug 6, 1875
Oct 11, 1962
&
Nancy Bradley Jean
Feb 3, 1883
Jun 11, 1950

A. M. Bradley
1857-1932

Mrs. Nora Bradley
1859-1937

Nancy A. Bolin
Jun 28, 1844
Feb 15, 1912

Mrs. Annie Harris *
Died Nov 14, 1893
Age: 55 years.

Donnie McClure, wife of
J. W. Brown
Feb 17, 1878
Feb 23, 1907

Jessie R., Daughter of
J. S. & R. S. McClure
Aug 22, 1876
Apr 25, 1897

Josie D., Daughter of
S. E. & D. R. McClure
Nov 4, 1892
Feb 18, 1893

Davis B. McClure
Oct 5, 1861
Jul 9, 1893
&
Salina E. McClure
Nov 28, 1858
Apr 19, 1919

Jessee S. McClure
May 4, 1826
Feb 5, 1886
&
Rutha S. McClure
Nov 16, 1837
Mar 25, 1907

Wade M. Rogers
Sep 26, 1848
Apr 7, 1926
&
Mattie A. Rogers
Nov 23, 1854
(no date)

Mattie E. Smith
Sep 20, 1873
Feb 3, 1887

Beulah J. Rogers
Nov 14, 1874
Jan 29, 1897

Daisy M., Daughter of
W. M. & M. Rogers
May 15, 1881
Jun 27, 1888

Horrace S., Son of
W. M. & M. Rogers
Nov --, 1876
Jul 10, 1883

Moses G. Arnold
Jul 12, 1877
Oct 14, 1958
&
Lou Bradley Arnold
Oct 10, 1881
Feb 10, 1943

Several unmarked graves.

Frank Brooks *
Died Apr 24, 1900
Age: 52 years.

Robert,* Son of
Mr. & Mrs. H. T. Duff
Died Dec 27, 1905
Age: 9 months.

Mrs. Elmira,*
Married Austin Keller
Jul 15, 1877
Died Jan 28, 1906
Age: 62 years.

Mrs. H. T. Duff *
Married H. T. Duff
Jul 26, 1896
Died Jan 25, 1906
Age: 29y, 9m, 16d.

E. D. Harmening *
Died Apr 22, 1894
Age: 82 years.

Sarah,* Daughter of
W. R. & Jane Smith
Died Sep 21, 1897
Age: 2 years.

Mrs. Elizabeth Langston *
Died May 21, 1916
Age: 86 years.
Left a Husband who is
88 years old and feeble.

John D. "Nappy" Taylor *
Died Jul 5, 1916
Age: 90y, 27d.
C.S.A. Left a wife,
a Son & a Daughter.

Mrs. Nancy,* wife of
W. J. Cambron
Died Oct 29, 1916
Age: 81 years.
Left an aged husband
almost blind, 1 Son &
3 Daughters.

Miss Mattie Harmening *
Died Oct 17, 1907
Age: 24y, 8m, 24d.

Elisha Griffin *
Died Oct 11, 1908
Age: (not given)
Died by accident, left
wife & 5 children.

Son * of
Jake Wiseman
Died Jul 26, 1909
Age: 14 years.

Effie,* Daughter of
Arch & Josie Mearse
Died Oct 13, 1909
Age: 6 years.

Mrs. Mary,* wife of
Moses Brady
Died Dec 31, 1909
Age: 89 years.

HUNTLAND-LINCOLN QUADRANGLE

Mack,* Son of
W. F. & Nannie Smith
Died Jul 27, 1914
Age: 20 years.

Mrs. Dora Ann Sutherland *
Born Feb 4, 1876
Married John T. Sutherland
Died Aug 26, 1903

* *

HAIRSTON CEMETERY

LOCATION: Three miles SW of Fayetteville on the southwest bank of Morgan Bend of Elk River.

R. P. Hairston
Jan 22, 1847
Apr 10, 1884

Margaret, Mother of
M. M. Hairston, Sr.
Died Nov 16, 1862
Age: 77 years.

Infant Daughter of
M. M. & M. P. Hairston
B&D Apr 1, 1857

Many unmarked graves.

M. M. Hairston
Oct 7, 1809
May 22, 1891

Martha P., wife of
M. M. Hairston
Feb 1, 1817
Apr 8, 1857

M. M., Son of
M. M. & M. P. Hairston
Aug 18, 1850
Aug 29, 1862

Wife,* of John Askins
Died Sep 26, 1895
Age: 20y, 1m, 25d.

C. V. _., wife of
W. H. Hairston
Jul 28, 1827
Nov 6, 1862

Willie E. Askins
May 5, 1893
Jan 20, 1894

J. N. Cannon
Nov 4, 1837
Jun 30, 1895

Infant * of
John & Lizzie Adkins(Askins)
Died Aug 13, 1898
Age: (not given)

Mrs. B(P)arthenia
McCullough
Died Nov 1879
Age: about 72 years.

Infant Son of
R. & F. Jean
B&D Jul 27, 1905

Julia B., wife of
B. F. Marshall
Died Feb 12, 1892
Age: 43 years.

* *

BEARD CEMETERY

LOCATION: Between Camp Dunroamin and Highway 241 near the junction of Liberty Road.

Duncan Beard
(no dates)
&
Wife (no name)
(no dates)

Only two graves.

* *

ROUTT-WELLS CEMETERY

LOCATION: King Subdivision, east side of Highway 241 and one fourth mile south of Liberty Road.

Thomas A. Beard
Aug 9, 1871
Dec 17, 1890

Mary Eliza, Daughter of
Theo & E. E. Harris
Died Jun 12, 1856
Age: 8 years.

Mrs. Julia,* widow of
S. G. Beard
Died Oct 13, 1901
Age: 71 years.

Mrs. M. M. Downing *
Died Sep 12, 1902
Age: 64 years.
Widow of Daniel B. Downing.

Mary J., wife of
J. R. Routt
Died Jun 14, 1889
Age: 55 years

Mary A. Routt
Jun 9, 1896
Jan 5, 1905

Mr. Isaac Porter *
Jul 8, 1817
Dec 26, 1891
Age: 75 years.

Mrs. Josie Scott *
Daughter of
John Colbert
Died Mar 5, 1896
Age: 19 years.

Martha E. Bearden
Sep 26, 1831
Oct 2, 1858

D. B. Downing
Feb 15, 1835
Nov 6, 1881

Several unmarked graves.

Miss Mary Beard *
Died Sep 11, 1902
Age: 36 years.

Benjamin Rowe *
Soldier of Revolution
1758-1849

Mrs. Amanda Wells *
Died Jan 17, 1923
Age: 89 years.

Payton Wells
Nov 20, 1786
Mar 16, 1864

Rufus P. Wells
Oct 12, 1844
Aug 14, 1874

Benjamin Porter *
"Soldier of Revolution"
1763-1828

Mrs. Emily,* wife of
I. S. Porter
Died Mar 8, 1893
Age: 76 years.

Mrs. Joan M. Brock *
Died Nov 3, 1892
Age: 25 years.
Daughter of Newton Wells,
dec'd & widow of J.C.Brock.

LINCOLN QUADRANGLE

Rufus N. Koonce *
Died Dec 16, 1893
Age: 45 years.

Joseph Nicholas Gray ***
Died about 1860

S. G. Beard *
Died Oct 2, 1898
Age: 71 years.
Married Julia McKinney

*** Bob Allen Gray Records

Thomas,* Son of
Samuel Beard
Died Dec 1889
Age: 18 years.

Mary P.,* Relict of
Payton Wells, dec'd
Died Sep 30, 1877
Age: about 73 years

* *

SMITH CEMETERY

LOCATION: Three fourth mile south of Camp Dunroamin on west side of Highway 64 in forks of Old Wells Hill Road and Highway 241.

W. R. Smith
Jul 20, 1838
May 31, 1896

Martha Koonce Smith
1843-1901

*** By Bob Allen Gray

Infant Daughter *** of
O. P. & Elizabeth Bell Smith
Gray
(no dates)

Infant Daughter *** of
J. P. & Era Hicks Gray
(no dates)

* *

OLD COMMUNITY CEMETERY

LOCATION: At Liberty, on west bank of Stewart Creek and one fourth mile NE of Liberty School.

John Beard
Oct 25, 1805
Apr 7, 1845

Sarah M. McClellan
Mar 19, 1801
Nov 5, 1850

ED NOTE: Local Senior residents say that some of the early "Howells" are buried here with no markers. About 150 graves or more, no markers. Stewarts Creek Baptist Church, which was active in the 1830's, was located near this cemetery.

* *

THOMISON CEMETERY

LOCATION: Two miles SW of Kelso, three fourth mile east of Lee Creek on west side of hill in woods.

Col. John Thomison
Son of Elisha Thomison
Nov 22, 1806
Feb 1, 1841
Age: 35 years.

Elisha Thomison *
Died Dec 1, 1853
Age: (not given)

5 Rock Vaults, no inscriptions
5 graves with fieldstones, no inscriptions.

* *

CORDER-McCULLOCK CEMETERY

LOCATION: Two miles NNE of Howell Hill and one mile east of Stewart Creek Community.

T. S. Corder
(no dates)

C. J. Corder
(no dates)

M. J. Corder
(no dates)

Eady Honey
Nov 9, 1832
1884

J. R. Lackey
(no dates)

3 large Vaults
(no dates or inscriptions)

Miss Denie,* Daughter of
Mat Corder
Died Jul 24, 1892
Age: 15 years.

Samuel Gray *
Died Apr 5, 1912
Age: 68 years.

Mr. _____ Bryant *
Died Aug 14, 1893
Age: 83 years.

Britton Wicks *
Died Apr 4, 1891
Age: 73 years.

Mrs. Sarah A.,* wife of
Wesley Gray
Died Jul 24, 1897
Age: 35 years.

J. C. Corder *
Died Apr 12, 1897
Age: 78 years.
Married Jane Stephenson

* *

LINCOLN QUADRANGLE

GRILLS-KOONCE CEMETERY

LOCATION: One and one half miles NE of Howell Hill and one mile ESE of Stewart Creek Community.

William L. Grills Mar 17, 1831 Sep 27, 1906	Dillana Grills Apr 8, 1840 Dec 30, 1895	John N. Smith Dec 25, 1816 Aug 19, 1859	W. I. Grills * Father of W. B. Grills Died Sep 27, 1906 Age: 75 years.
John Smith *** (Schmidt) Aug 7, 1792 Jan 10, 1849	Margaret A.,*** Daughter of John Nicholas & Nancy Bains Smith	Mrs. Nancy,* widow of John N. Smith Died Feb 11, 1893 Age: 86 years. Died at the residence of her Son W. R. Smith.	Nepoleon Polk Koonce *** (no dates) & wife Emily Brown Koonce (no dates)
Nancy F. Adams,*** wife of John Schmidt	ED NOTE: This was once Old Koonce Farm. *** By Bob Allen Gray	About 75 unmarked graves.	

* *

McGEE-McCARTNEY-KELSO CEMETERY

LOCATION: In the Stewart Creek Community, two miles SE of Liberty on west side of Lincoln Road.

Mrs. Letty Koonce Jul 27, 1801 Oct 15, 1868	Andrew McCartney Died Aug 13, 1846 Age: 76 years.	William McGee Feb 1, 1805 Nov 4, 1853	Children of J. W. & N. G. Steelman 3 markers: Born Jun 6, 1884 Died: 2 died Jun 7, 1884 1 died Jun 8, 1884
Jefferson Kelso Jan 8, 1806 Jun 17, 1871	Sarah, wife of A. McCartney Died --- 12, 1846 Age: (not given)	Martha, Consort of William McGee Aug 25, 1802 Nov 10, 1857	Alice A. Hudgins Mar 8, 1853 May 6, 1876
Margaret M., wife of Jefferson Kelso Mar 6, 1810 Apr 17, 1877	Sarah McCartney Jan 3, 1815 Jun 20, 1840	Infant Daughter of J. M. & L. J. Routte Sep 14, 1859 Sep 26, 1859	ED NOTE: Members of the Dodson family is said to be buried here.
Margaret L., Daughter of N. & J. Kelso Jul 4, 1870 Aug 10, 1870	Robert McCartney Dec 5, 1831 Aug 21, 1841	Phillip Koonce Soldier of Revolution Died Feb 2, 1841 is said to be buried here.	J. P. Gray * Died Nov 20, 1893 Age: 24 years.
Infant Daughter of N. P. & M. D. Koonce B&D Mar 24, 1874	I. W. Williamson * Died Jan 3, 1907 Age: 27 years.	Helen Dennis Koonce *** 1836-1874	*** By Bob Allen Gray
Nancy Dodson McGee Koonce*** Widow of Phillip Koonce Mar 14, 1782 Oct 23, 1853	George Koonce *** Husband of Lettie McGee Koonce Died 1846 Age: about 46 years.	Several unmarked graves.	

* *

STEWART CREEK CEMETERY

LOCATION: One and one fourth miles west of Stewart Creek Community in Bugger Hollow.

F. M. Koonce Feb 8, 1866 Mar 7, 1894 Age: 28y, 7d. & wife Mary V. Koonce Sep 17, 1872 Dec 17, 1893	Mr. W. R. Walker 1861-1937 Mary A., wife of W. R. Walker Apr 29, 1854 May 12, 1894	W. J. Ventress Jun 27, 1848 Feb 18, 1912 & Mary F. Ventress May 30, 1845 Jan 8, 1932	Needham Koonce Jul 11, 1806 Feb 16, 1874 & wife Burrdottie Koonce Jan 21, 1811 Nov 17, 1884
Ollie Lawson Moore Apr 17, 1899 Sep 17, 1899	Loma A., wife of A. T. Stewart Jun 14, 1878 Dec 5, 1904	Jane Honey, wife of W. R. Locker Died 1893 Age: (not given)	Theophilus Koonce Feb 21, 1839 Dec 20, 1853

LINCOLN QUADRANGLE

John Patrick
Aug 2, 1808
Mar 23, 1883
&
Mary Patrick
Nov 15, 1810
Sep 9, 1901

Mary J. Patrick
Oct 2, 1833
Nov 11, 1917

H. C. Patrick
Feb 13, 1870
Aug 25, 1891

John F. Patrick
Jan 9, 1856
Jan 26, 1877

Eva L. Patrick
May 10, 1872
Aug 21, 1878

Mary Jane Patrick
Feb 19, 1858
Feb 10, 1862

James Locker
Jun 17, 1806
Jun 25, 1858
&
Rebecca Locker
May 28, 1811
Sep 4, 1884

E. P. Locker
Oct 27, 1874
Jan 31, 1893

J. W. Price
Apr 13, 1863
May 23, 1906

Susan Ann Price
May 4, 1837
Feb 26, 1908

Lonzy F. Price
1891-1946
&
Flora Towry Price
1891-1960

Coradelia Price
Sep 20, 1870
Aug 11, 1954

Jordan, Son of
J. W. & C. D. Price
1838-1889

Robert Flint
1862-1941

Y. T. Flint
Nov 4, 1838
Feb 4, 1913

Paralee Flyntt
1842-1930

Minnie Florence, wife of
J. F. Douthat
Apr 6, 1882
Sep 6, 1899

F. M. Ventress
Dec 15, 1821
Sep 6, 1901
&
Susan C. Ventress
Sep 2, 1827
Feb 22, 1902

Dale W. Marsh
Died Sep 20, 1963
Age: (not given)

Elza A. Porter
Dec 5, 1847
Aug 8, 1928
Age: 81 years.

O. A. Porter
1871-1946

Luther Lee, Son of
O. A. & Mamie Porter
Nov 7, 1917
Jan 1, 1918

Infant Daughter of
O. A. & Mamie Porter
B&D Apr 1911

Belle, wife of
A. J. Ventress
Nov 12, 1860
Jan 3, 1885

G. W. Porter
Died Nov 3, 1909
Age: 68y, 6m, 8d.

Eliza A. Porter
Dec 5, 1846
Aug 7, 1928

Elmina C., Daughter of
G. W. & E. A. Porter
Died Oct 4, 1880
Age: 3y, 5m, 24d.

Cordy I., Daughter of
G. W. & E. A. Porter
Died Oct 25, 1877
Age: 2y, 5m, 19d.

Eliza A., Daughter of
G. W. & E. A. Porter
Died Dec 8, 1874
Age: 11m, 23d.

Edgar Gray
Feb 8, 1900
Apr 1, 1901

Elizabeth M. Gray
Nov 8, 1840
Nov 11, 1917

Rebecca J. Locker George
Oct 26, 1875
Sep 30, 1928

Mattie C. Stewart
Jun 30, 1879
May 17, 1896

Blanche, wife of
H. F. Whitworth
Aug 10, 1897
Feb 27, 1920

Grover Patrick
1885-1915

Arville Patrick
1889-1925

Andrew J. Patrick
Apr 3, 1862
Jan 29, 1900
&
Sarah Elizabeth Patrick
Aug 10, 1864
1884

T. E. Patrick
Mar 4, 1866
Oct 7, 1892

W. E. Patrick
Jun 16, 1832
Sep 21, 1900

Margaret A. Patrick
Nov 28, 1832
Jan 1, 1893

G. A. Williams
Feb 9, 1849
Apr 9, 1917

Elizabeth C. Mayes
Nov 3, 1815
Jan 27, 1888

F. E., wife of
B. C. Laten
Mar 28, 1871
Sep 16, 1899

Johnathan A. Cantrell
Feb 9, 1867
Dec 16, 1894

Laura, wife of
C. R. Pickett
Aug 27, 1876
Mar 5, 1902

Dewie Laten
1900-1901

J. S. Laten
May 13, 1838
Feb 23, 1904

Margaret A. Laten
Nov 16, 1838
Jan 29, 1927

Sadie B., Daughter of
J. T. & O. P. Laten
Sep 2, 1888
Sep 9, 1889

Infant Son of
J. T. & O. P. Laten
(no dates)

Infant Twin Daughter of
J. T. & O. P. Laten
Aug 5, 1904
Aug 5, 1904

James Henderson
Dec 2, 1817
Feb 2, 1900

Infant Son of
J. P. & Delia Henderson
B&D Sep 18, 1887

Rufus Desso, Son of
J. P. & Delia Henderson
May 12, 1886
Aug 20, 1886

Mary H. Patterson
Died Sep 1, 1886
Age: (not given)

Evie, Daughter of
W. R. & M. E. Walker
Oct 6, 1898
Sep 24, 1899

Mrs. W. R. Walker
1866-1932

O. A.
(no dates)

Florence Armstrong, wife
of J. A. Warren
May 28, 1887
Apr 23, 1921

J. A. Warren
1894-1946

Winnie M. Mullins
1907-1940

Ellen Henderson
Died Dec --, 1960
Age: (illegible)
(Ralston FH)

Clifford Henderson
1899-1939

Oliver E., Son of
J. P. & Della Henderson
Nov 18, 1903
Jan 12, 1909

Julia Palmyra Smith
Jul 6, 1874
Jul 8, 1904

LINCOLN QUADRANGLE

J. P. Henderson
Dec 15, 1854
Mar 18, 1937
&
Della J. Henderson
Jan 13, 1863
Jan 30, 1922

Palmyra E. Smith
Dec 18, 1834
Dec 9, 1904

Caleb B. Smith
Mar 24, 1824
Apr 9, 1914

Leona Land Winsett
Dec 18, 1910
Apr 25, 1944

Cleveland H. Locker
1884-1968

Luther Francis Locker
Jul 13, 1879
May 13, 1921
Husband of Pearle Shook

Fenton Locker
Feb 15, 1854
Dec 23, 1922
&
Mary E. Locker
Apr 7, 1856
Sep 5, 1940

R. K. Locker
Apr 22, 1849
May 31, 1931
& wife
Alice A. Ventress Locker
Nov 13, 1856
Sep 2, 1920

Elgie, Daughter of
R. K. & Alice A. Locker
May 23, 1888
May 4, 1909

Charles N. Koonce
Sep 23, 1871
May 26, 1935

Minnie Howell Koonce
Jul 1, 1876
Nov 6, 1966

Lillie Ventress Koonce
Aug 26, 1875
Dec 11, 1904

J. M. Koonce
Jan 15, 1838
Jan 12, 1904

Glenn M. Flynt
Apr 14, 1911
Jul 28, 1938

John J. Flynt
Oct 6, 1876
Feb 9, 1947

Ada M. Porter, wife of
J. J. Flynt
Mar 16, 1882
Sep 11, 1906

Ella Koonce, wife of
John Barker
1877-Nov 29, 1912

Edna L. Flynt
1902-1940

I. S. Street
1864-1945
& wife
Annie Koonce Street
Oct 16, 1865
Dec 17, 1918

Infant Daughter of
I. S. & M. A. Street
B&D Nov 3, 1910

Theo Koonce
Pvt Co G 57 Pion Inf
Nov 20, 1895
Died in Service
Oct 14, 1918

N. P. Koonce
Co G 8 Tenn Regt C.S.A.
1829-1907

Mary Murphy,*** wife of
Needham P. Koonce
1863-1928

H. M. Koonce
Died Jan 15, 1910
Age: 73y, 11m, 15d.

Fannie Koonce
1861-1926

Mary Sue Koonce Carpenter
Oct 8, 1900
Mar 13, 1963

Infant Daughter of
Mr. & Mrs. Worthie Henderson
B&D Jan 3, 1917

Infant Twin Sons of
Charles N. & Minnie H. Koonce
1913

Frank Locker
1882-1936

Milderd Simms Locker
1894-1933

J. Hiram Locker, husband of
Faye Locker
1836-1930

Famie Lois Pickett, wife of
E. C. Locker
Dec 28, 1896
Feb 4, 1918

C. H. Locker
Mar 19, 1839
Aug 25, 1918

Mary Jane, wife of
C. H. Locker
Jun   1844
Jan 22, 1905

Leona Laten
1906-1915

Lige M. Laten
Mar 24, 1878
Mar 9, 1966
&
Viola M. Laten
Sep 3, 1879
Jun 24, 1946

Roy Laten
1893-1915

Andy M. Henderson
1856-1940
&
Louella Henderson
1861-1934

Ada Pearson Henderson
Mar 2, 1883
Jun 18, 1927

William R. Jones
Jun 11, 1857
May 2, 1928
&
Susan M. Jones
Dec 8, 1861
May 29, 1930

W. Frank Jones
Nov 2, 1881
Dec 2, 1926

Mrs. Ida Dell Henderson Jones
Died Mar 4, 1968
Age: 79y, 5m, 28d.

Roy Leonard Walker
Died Oct 30, 1965
Age: 60 years.

Hollis Walker
1929-1946

Denia Thompson
1908-1931

Samuel L. Oldham
Jan 31, 1847
Nov 7, 1917

Roy V. Gray
1902-1923

Thomas A. Moore
Mar 27, 1880
Jul 15, 1962
&
Bobbie P. Moore
Jan 15, 1884
Sep 19, 1951

Allie, Daughter of
W. H. & Ida Laten
Dec 12, 1889
Feb 29, 1908

William H. Laten
May 27, 1870
Jul 2, 1940
&
Ida Holt Laten
Sep 15, 1870
Sep 9, 1933

A. I. Laten
(no dates)

Margaret Smith Magness
Jun 1, 1869
Apr 17, 1917

Mattie Moore Marrs
Jun 30, 1869
Jun 30, 1920

Caroline Mills Moore
Jan 3, 1847
Jan 16, 1919

David F. Moore
Feb 14, 1846
Nov 16, 1928

Ethel Gray
Oct 28, 1894
Feb 8, 1942

Lela Gray
Nov 26, 1904
Jan 26, 1905

Henry E. Gray
Dec 15, 1866
May 20, 1944

Sarah M. Gray
Apr 22, 1872
Feb 18, 1953

J. W. Moore
Nov 18, 1874
Mar 23, 1942
&
E. M. Moore
Jan 23, 1876
Dec 17, 1951

Joe A. Gray
Mar 27, 1871
Aug 4, 1950
&
Lorena Porter Gray
May 9, 1872
Aug 16, 1953

LINCOLN QUADRANGLE

Infant Son of
Frank & Mossie Ventress
B&D Oct 16, 1916

J. F. Koonce
1868-1946

Infant *** of
Frank & Nadine Burton Koonce
(no dates)

Campbell Tate Koonce ***
Died Mar 20, 1902
Age: 52 years.

Dana V. Koonce ***
1868-1937

Jesse David Ventress ***
1850-1929
&
Mattie Foster Ventress ***
1860-1929

Pearl,*** Daughter of
David & Mattie Ventress
1902-1923

Mrs. Lula,* wife of
James Koonce
Jan 19, 1889
Dec 26, 1906

Jesse Leatherwood *
Died Nov 2, 1897
Age: 80 years.

Henderson Davis *
Died Aug 4, 1899
Age: 22 years.
Married 3 months before
to Mrs. Alice Honey

A. O. Moore
1883-1960
&
Mamie Moore
1894-1954

W. T. Land
Feb 20, 1854
Oct 27, 1923

Mary Tenne Koonce, wife of
W. T. Land
Dec 10, 1855
Mar 2, 1928

Rufus Green Ventress ***
Jul 13, 1864
Feb 9, 1931

Kate Grier,*** wife of
Rufus Ventress
Apr 8, 1870
Dec 13, 1961

R. A. Porter *
Died Aug 16, 1903
Age: 47y, 4m.

Mrs. Kate Porter *
Died Nov 28, 1903
Age: 43 years.

I. D. Honey *
Married Aug 15, 1883 to
Alice Hambrick
Died Feb 20, 1898
Age: 36 years.

Infant * of
Mr. & Mrs. Eli Henderson
Died Feb 4, 1909
Age: (not given)

Arthur Land
Dec 21, 1861
May 25, 1911

Royal Land
Nov 29, 1890
Nov 12, 1954
&
Ocie Carter Land
Sep 7, 1893
Dec 23, 1973

Willie R. Locker
Dec 21, 1861
Dec 4, 1933

Lila Moore Locker
May 17, 1878
Aug 20, 1950

Mrs. Nancy Duncan *
Died Nov 24, 1890
Age: 83 years.

Mrs. Martha,* wife of
Jonathan Cantrell
Died Oct 9, 1891
Age: 77 years.

Mrs. Martha Jane,* wife of
W. R. Locker
Died Apr 17, 1893
Age: 26 years.

Daughter * of
W. R. & Eliza Brown
Died Jul 9, 1899
Age: 4 years.

Many unmarked graves.

*** By Bob Allen Gray

James Polk Koonce
1888-1947

Kathleen, Daughter of
Polk & Donnie Koonce
Aug 1, 1920
Feb 4, 1928

Donnie Koonce
1900-1957

Thelma Land
1910-1933

Elvie Land
1885-1957
&
Dovie Land
1891-1973

Infant,* of
Mr. & Mrs. J. T. Laten
Died Nov 12, 1895
Age: (not given)

Mrs. Sallie,* wife of
William Hill
Died May 5, 1896
Age: 33 years.

Mrs. A. V.,* wife of
Remie McCullough
Died Nov 17, 1897
Age: 25 years.

Laura,* Daughter of
Mr. & Mrs. Tom Kerbo
Died Jun 9, 1907
Age: 12 years.

* *

ROWLAND HILL CEMETERY

LOCATION: Three fourth mile ESE of Prospect and north of Howell Hill Road.

Robert Lindsey Swinford
Mar 5, 1915
Jun 5, 1962

Mary Dollar Moore
Sep 28, 1842
Jun 4, 1931

C. Wilson Cowan
(no dates)
(Gallant FH)

Roy Cowan
1888-1963
(Gallant FH)

Mary I. Moore
1843-1931

J. Sam Moore
Jul 27, 1874
Jan 13, 1950
&
Jessie Moore
May 27, 1877
Apr 2, 1936

Hugh F. Moore
Feb 20, 1898
May 6, 1955

May Lorena Ivey Cowan
Feb 15, 1883
Feb 4, 1952

George Otie Cowan
Dec 28, 1882

Judith J. Gray
B&D Jan 14, 1966

John F. Koonce
WW I American Soldier
May 14, 1891
May 16, 1925

Fred B. Gibson
Oct 20, 1900
May 5, 1963

Jessie Smith
1869-1903
&
MaryTalent Smith
1876-1905

Mary Locker
Jan 4, 1813
Sep 15, 1883

W. M. Locker
Oct 18, 1808
Sep 3, 1876

William G. Locker
1883-1888

Elijah L. Locker
1851-1889

Martha Alice Moore Locker
Jul 28, 1862
Jun 28, 1932

Shirley Ruth Brown
Oct 17, 1942
Jul 3, 1943

Martha Frances Cowan
Aug 31, 1915
Apr 20, 1917

LINCOLN QUADRANGLE

Walter Eugene Cowan
Aug 8, 1880
Aug 6, 1965
&
Mary M. Locker Cowan
Oct 4, 1884
Feb 6, 1957

Andrew J. Talley
Feb 22, 1863
Sep 15, 1944

Ethel Oldham Talley
Oct 13, 1898

Eddie B. Talley
Aug 20, 1919
Oct 9, 1922

James Charles Oldham
1873-1927

Anna Oldham
1880-1925

Infant Son of
James & Anna Oldham
1902

Mela Tallent
Mar 20, 1862
Jul 23, 1899

W. C. Talent
Jun 21, 1889
Jul 9, 1889

Stella P. Talent
Aug 10, 1883
Oct 15, 1883

Mattie C. Talent
Dec 11, 1871
Sep 18, 1880

D. P. Roland
Jul 15, 1882
Dec 5, 1882

Tommy Wade Gibson
1963

Freddie Lee, Son of
Robert Earl & Paulette
Williams Gibson
Died Jun 16, 1967
Age: 1 day
(Gallant FH)

4 unmarked graves.

Mrs. Evaline,* wife of
O. C. Talent
Died Jul 24, 1898
Age: 49y, 3m, 4d.

Donnie,* Son of
O. C. & E. T. Talent
Died Aug 21, 1898
Age: 8 years.

David Henderson
Soldier of 1812
Died 1857
is said to be buried
here in an unmarked
grave.

* *

PROSPECT CHURCH CEMETERY

LOCATION: At Prospect Church, Park City-Howell Hill Road.

Fannie Gault
1857-1947

Fannie Hester Kerbo
Jul 19, 1858
May 14, 1947

J. W. Price
Sep 9, 1837
Jun 5, 1916

Lucille Kerbo Tucker
Jul 23, 1928
Dec 21, 1947

Bush J. Laten
1868-1951
&
Nina Hamlin Laten
1887-1967

M. A., wife of
J. M. Hambrick
Dec 1, 1860
Aug 1, 1899

J. M. Hambrick
Jul 31, 1853
Jun 12, 1917

Rufus M. McDougal
Oct 29, 1875
May 24, 1948
&
Etta W. McDougal
Oct 24, 1885

Andy Holman McDougal
1903-1951

Evelyn Nelson
1921-1946

James Blanton White
Jul 22, 1876
Feb 6, 1967
&
Minnie Simmons White
Dec 10, 1882
Nov 4, 1932

Clifford E. Payne
Sep 18, 1895
May 31, 1967
&
Sarah T. Payne
Sep 3, 1897

Frank M. Sherwood
Mar   1856
       1926
&
Maggie M. Sherwood
Jul 8, 1866
(no date)

Sherwood
1913

Roy Sherwood
1897-1915

A. J. Jean
1873-1934

Galla Jeans
(no date)

Tom Jeans
(no dates)

Meriga Jean
(no dates)

Gracie Quick
(no dates)

Quick Infant
(no dates)

Lawson Faris
1888-1912

Johnny Tucker
Aug 31, 1886
Mar 31, 1950

Martha Shelton Tucker
Died Sep 8, 1968
Age: 80y, 4m, 12d.

Alvie Henderson
1886-1949
&
Maude R. Henderson
1888-1962

Daniel Presley Tafts
Sep 12, 1878
Jan 23, 1957

Alice, wife of
D. P. Tafts
Apr 22, 1879
Jun 25, 1918

Jesse McDougal
Dec 16, 1873

&
Anna McDougal
Sep 14, 1875
Dec 21, 1947

Rufus M. Henderson
Nov 4, 1876
Sep 21, 1899

J. M. Henderson
Nov 14, 1851
Feb 26, 1891

Thomas J. Henderson
Apr 27, 1865
Sep 19, 1915

Caroline Satterfield
May 22, 1857
Sep 11, 1899

Nancy Rebecca, Daughter
of I. H. & Polly Henderson
Aug 21, 1862
Jan 2, 1915

Boby Henderson
1881-1881

Bob Henderson
1872-19(broken)

Infant Henderson
(no dates)

Henderson Infant
(no dates)

Edd Henderson
1879-1941

V. W. Satterfield
Died 1835
Age: (not given)

Francis Davis
(no dates)

N. A. Davis
1840-1921

LINCOLN QUADRANGLE

James Davis
Age: 73 years
(no dates)

Bettie A. Davis
Age: 70 years
(no dates)

Charles F. Seaton
1884-1951
&
Tishie Seaton
1883-1962

William P. Seaton
Sep 4, 1905
Aug 19, 1956

Eugene Cantrell
1901-1901

Bell Cantrell
1877-1901

Rosey Crunk
1821-1935

W. P. Crunk
1853-1934

Claudine Payne
1937-1938

Verna Cole Hunter
Jun 2, 1887
Apr 3, 1926

Diemer N. George
Dec 18, 1887
Jan 9, 1968
&
Mae Kerbo George
Oct 28, 1899

A. J. Steelman
Jul 9, 1865
Feb 12, 1948
&
Polly W. Steelman
Oct 20, 1859
Feb 14, 1944

Jennie Sullenger
Nov 20, 1849
Oct 21, 1913

Charles M. Dickey
1928-1944

A. L. Bates
Aug 3, 1818
Feb 5, 1898

Mrs. Bates
(no dates)

F. V. Hill
1879-1895

Virginia Hill
Died 1896
Age: (Not given)

Hinton Hill
Died 1902
Age: (not given)

S. M. Hill
1869-1893

A. J. Hill
1875-1896

Edwin Lyn, Son of
William & Pearl Brazelton
B&D Sep 3, 1946

Rev. G. S. Campbell
Oct 8, 1834
Oct 2, 1914
& wife
Dortha Campbell
Oct 3, 1831
Jan 9, 1895

M. L. Campbell
Mar 27, 1870
Oct 6, 1872

Ida Crunk
1887-1889

Rosie Crunk
(infant, no dates)

Rosie Crunk
(infant, no dates)

Moore
(no dates)

A. B. Moore
Wife
(no dates)

A. B. Moore
(no dates)

Infant of
E. D. & Allie Henderson
(no dates)

Infant of
E. D. & Allie Henderson
(no dates)

Infant of
E. D. & Allie Henderson
(no dates)

Infant of
E. D. & Allie Henderson
(no dates)

Eli Henderson
Mar 17, 1858
Mar 17, 1922

Mollie B., wife of
E. D. Henderson
Apr 12, 1865-Jun 5, 1904

Reeves M. Steelman
Oct 25, 1893
Aug 20, 1958
&
Allie V. Steelman
Jan 3, 1898

D. A. McDougal
Jul 21, 1849
Jul 26, 1924
& wife
Rena McDougal
Oct 17, 1850
Mar 7, 1904

Isabel McDougal
1869-1935

Jay Dellous Steelman
Jan 24, 1891
Jul 31, 1939
&
Ortha Cinthy Steelman
Oct 1, 1899

Williams
(no dates)

Williams
(no dates)

Rena Williams
1901-1908

Almeda Davis Williams
Sep 5, 1875
Sep 30, 1949

Joshway Cantrell
1874-1874

J. A. "Tobe" Simmons
1868-1942
&
Jossie Simmons
1872-1938

Gordon Reavis
Oct 18, 1926
Oct 9, 1961
&
Sybil M. Reavis
Jul 15, 1927

Married Apr 29, 1945

Leslie L. Reavis
1904-1957
&
Exie E. Reavis
1908-

Leonard E. Cassel
1912-1956
&
Della N. Cassel
1914-

Oscar A. Owens
1889-1950
&
Zula M. Owens
1891-

Roy A. Keller
1907-1949
&
Viola M. Keller
1912-

Steve Vann
Mar 17, 1890
Jun 23, 1933
&
Lillie Vann
Sep 2, 1884
Jul 4, 1936

Coy L. Crumley
1936-1938

Steelman Infant
(no dates)

Carol Ann Colbert
1938-1938

Sherman C. Colbert
1903-1960
&
Lucille H. Colbert
1905-1951

Paul Colbert
Dec 7, 1926
Dec 18, 1966
&
Christine Colbert
Oct 10, 1927

Infant Son of
Bill & Sibyl Whitaker
B&D Jun 15, 1967

John N. Whitaker
1880-1961
&
Willie I. Whitaker
1900-1968

Virginia L. Whitaker
1925-1939

John J. Howell
1867-1940

Thomas A. Patrick
1943-1944

Levy McBay
1924-1950

Kenneth Lee Ables
Died Aug 31, 1968
Age: 10 years.

LINCOLN QUADRANGLE

Alvie F. Howell
Jun 9, 1892
Jun 22, 1963

Isaac D. Hayes
1900-1941

Birdie Hayes
1906-1961

Claudie Ernest Tucker
Aug 31, 1891
Jan 11, 1946
&
Ersa Mae Tucker
Jul 16, 1891
(no date)

Lue Ellar Harris
Jan 10, 1870
Feb 16, 1946
&
Victoria Street Price
Jan 20, 1910

Michael Timothy Newbourn
1965
(Gallant FH)

Allie Cash
May 3, 1903
Jan 19, 1927

Alma Cash
1909-1939

Revie Moore
Jul 28, 1922
Nov 5, 1940

Elbert J. Moore
Oct 11, 1924
Feb 11, 1958
&
Annie Ruth Moore
Jul 1, 1928

John Edmon Thompson
Mar 12, 1877
Sep 6, 1954
&
Cassie T. Lincoln Thompson
Oct 24, 1896

Charlie V. Price
Apr 23, 1902
Apr 2, 1968
&
Margurite E. Price
Jul 4, 1910

Garland Edmon
Aug 28, 1922
Aug 5, 1942

Bessie E. Bishop
1896-1957

Rebecca Rose Ann Slagle
Mar 2, 1856
Jan 26, 1941

Minnie C. Stone
Dec 14, 1892
May 18, 1954

J. T. Cash
Apr 28, 1863
Nov 2, 1925

John Denton
1900

Mary Recard
1914

William D. Moore
Feb 24, 1870
Mar 23, 1958
&
Ezella B. Moore
Oct 8, 1872
Oct 24, 1960

Smith Holman
Jun 21, 1871
Sep 17, 1889

John Holman
Sep 24, 1824
Sep 15, 1890

Mrs. Sarah Holman
Died May 25, 1910
Age: 79 years.

Marava Moore
1875-1956

Clemmie, wife of
Marava Moore
Mar 7, 1887
Dec 12, 1925

Lonus Moore
Feb 12, 1912
Jun 29, 1913

N. M. & A. M.
(no dates)

George Bishop
Oct 27, 1853
(no date)
&
Mary Bishop
Nov 1, 1863
Sep 9, 1931

Carolyn Ann Metcalf
1947-1967

Miss Leoma Bishop
Died Feb 6, 1971
Age: 62 years.

Walter Henderson *
Died Sep 5, 1899
Age: 18 years.

Teresa Bates
Mother of
Zole & Jim Bates
Aug 13, 1859
Dec 4, 1902

Joseph T. Moore
Aug 17, 1821
Aug 19, 1895
& wife
Nancy Moore
Aug 17, 1837
Nov 15, 1926
&
Vato Moore
Oct 16, 1877
Oct 1, 1896
&
Aurora Moore
Apr 10, 1856
Jun 4, 1903

Leona Moore
Nov 3, 1868
Jun 2, 1886
&
Nannie Moore Hambrick
Jul 22, 1870
Apr 28, 1890

Gus D. Ables
Aug 27, 1900
Sep 15, 1953

Annie May Ables
Jul 8, 1900

Dana Neal
(no dates)

I. H. Neal
1855-1930

Homer Martin
1873-1934

Kenneth Martin
1920-1921

Luberta Martin
May 25, 1907
Mar 12, 1941

Eveline Burgess
1837-1894

Thomas Burgess
1835-1911

Kate Burgess
1857-1941

Infant Son * of
Thomas Burgess
Died Aug 21, 1893
Age: (not given)

Miss Edna Hutchinson *
Died Sep 18, 1899
Age: 17 years.
* *

Latson Infant
(no dates)

Latson Infant
(no dates)

Eugene Hanvey
Died Feb 3, 1930
Age: 40 years.

Fread Martin
Died Jul 2, 1935
Age: 27 years.

S. A. Camp
(no dates)

H. E. Simmons
Jul 21, 1897

&
Delma S. Simmons
Feb 7, 1897
Aug 3, 1968

Elaine Simmons
Mar 9, 1924

Francine Simmons
Sep 18, 1953
Sep 19, 1953

Mitchell H. Simmons
Aug 7, 1919
Jul 10, 1955
&
Margie Simmons
Dec 10, 1927
Jul 10, 1955

William E. Bishop
1883-1958
&
Minnie C. Bishop
1882-1944

James W. Ables, Jr.
Nov 5, 1919
Nov 5, 1967
&
Pauline C. Ables
Nov 10, 1927

James William Ables
Died Oct 19, 1970
Age: 84y, 5m.

Claude Rufus Carter
Died Feb 1, 1971
Age: 59y, 10m.

Theo,* Son of
Jones & Fannie Bishop
Died Sep 20, 1897
Age: 2 years.

Many unmarked graves.

LINCOLN QUADRANGLE

CEMETERY

LOCATION: Two and one fourth miles SW of Skinem, between Ardmore and Carmargo Roads.

Several fieldstones, no inscriptions.

* *

CEMETERY

LOCATION: Two miles SW of Skinem on the north side of Ardmore Highway.

About 20 graves with no inscriptions.

* *

PLEASANT GROVE CEMETERY

LOCATION: One mile NNW of Bellview, west of Old Huntsville Highway.

Charlie Higgins Towry
Died 1967
Age: (gone)
(Gallant FH)

Clarence E. Gray
Feb 13, 1908
Nov 15, 1967
&
Irene Gray
Sep 26, 1914
Nov 26, 1956

George McAlister
1885-
&
Pearl McAlister
1886-1939

Judith McAlister
B&D Nov 23, 1943

William Monks
1848-1931

Barbara June Harris
1933-1934

William F. Manning
Aug 31, 1876
Sep 30, 1947
&
Minnie M. Manning
Feb 24, 1883
Nov 4, 1932

Nancy L. Walker
Sep 24, 1844
Jan 15, 1918

S. D. Walker
Aug 25, 1852
Feb 13, 1925

William M. Walker
1878-1902

William Monks
Jan 16, 1847
Apr 4, 1931
&
Emely Monks
Sep 6, 1852
Aug 15, 1922

B. M. McClusky
Aug 18, 1851
Jun 10, 1908
& wife
H. W. Jones McClusky
May 8, 1855
Nov 17, 1926

Nancy A. McClusky
Nov 22, 1829
Jul 28, 1916

I. N. McClusky
Nov 25, 1853
Oct 22, 1931
& wife
Letta Stephens McClusky
Feb 8, 1853
Mar 8, 1928

Martha Victoria Moyers
Sep 1, 1956
Apr 8, 1951

David Henderson Tucker
B&D Sep 16, 1956

Edd Lee Tucker
1902-1957
&
Wilma Tucker
1926-

Joseph Bruce Quick
1882-1956
(Gallant FH)

K. Sol Colbert
Dec 27, 1891
May 15, 1966

Eugene Levi Bates
Jan 13, 1881
Jan 18, 1948
&
Lula Sisco Bates
Aug 25, 1889

Walter Levi, Son of
E. R. & Lula Bates
Nov 1, 1927
Mar 13, 1932

James Emmons McClusky
Nov 11, 1878
Dec 2, 1965
&
Mary Ella McClusky
Nov 20, 1907
Feb 8, 1908

Rose Emmie Towry, wife of
Luther Bates
Mar 8, 1889
Jan 23, 1927

Hildred I. Monks
1916-1916

Selma R. Monks
1917-1918

Burlan L. Monks
1931-1932

Loyd Henry Marshall
Mar 11, 1934
Oct 26, 1933

Exie Corene Monks
May 20, 1926
May 24, 1926

Joe Harold Billings
B&D Apr 4, 1947

Albert L. Monks
May 9, 1893

&
Exie M. Monks
Sep 9, 1897
May 27, 1926
&
Louise W. Monks
Nov 13, 1908

Clyde E. Key
Tennessee
Sp 4 Btry B 92 field Arty
Oct 24, 1938
Jul 5, 1964
(picture)

Wesley G. Phillips
1859-1936
&
Martha E. Dickey Phillips
1869-1925

Thomas A. Burton
Mar 5, 1880
Oct 13, 1934
&
Tishie Burton
Feb 18, 1884
Jul 5, 1936

Fount Jones
Alabama
Sgt 3441 Area Svc Unit
WW II
Sep 22, 1906
Mar 3, 1965

Charlie A. Owens
Dec 13, 1884
Jun 16, 1962
&
Fannie Mc. Owen
Jan 14, 1890
Sep 9, 1958

LINCOLN QUADRANGLE

Harrison Albright
Sep 17, 1857
Jan 16, 1934
&
Hettie Albright
Apr 14, 1862
Mar 24, 1940

I. H. Albright
1858-1934

Lawrence Sisco
1914-19??

May Daniel
1903-1930

Malcom D. Milner
Mar 6, 1937
Sep 13, 1958

Willard H. Milner
Alabama
Pfc 382 Inf 2 Inf Div
Korea
Oct 10, 1928
Jul 19, 1951
(picture)

Exie E. Milner
Nov 20, 1926

George Henry
Dec 25, 1891
Nov 11, 1948
&
Addie Henry
Dec 6, 1896

Exie Lorine Henry
Jan 16, 1916
Oct 12, 1919

J. H. Childress
Aug 3, 1852
Nov 7, 1928
& wife
Martha E. Phillips Childress
Aug 25, 1852
(no date)

Marion Childress
1931-1931
&
Mildred Childress
1914-1914

Henry Jackson Monks
1868-1954
&
Iva Jeffries Monks
1838-19

Thomas W. Monks
1856-1937
&
Bethina Monks
1860-1928

Emma Elmina Gray
1883-1916

Lora Margaret King Monks
Apr 9, 1887
Jan 25, 1917

Cecil Fulton Monks
Aug 1, 1909
Apr   1918

John Thomas Monks
Nov 28, 1878
Apr 10, 1922

Mary Fannie Moore Monks
Mar 16, 1892
Apr 5, 1964

Thomas Monks
1818-(no date)

Elizabeth Monks
1821-(no date)

Cyntha Monks
1842-(no date)

David Monks
1854-1924

Margaret Monks
1853-1931

Alfred F. Monks
1858-1940

Louisa Towry
1864-1932

E. M. Monks
1860-1947
(Raby FH)

Goodloe Monks
1877-1957
&
Ellie B. Monks
1878-1954

Granville E. Williams
1909-
&
Exie E. Williams
1905-1941
&
Annie Lee Williams
1907-1967

James J. Monks
Aug 5, 1883
Oct 17, 1951
&
Mary E. Monks
Jun 11, 1886

James A. Walker
1881-1936
&
Bertha Monks Walker
1886-1933

William Clark
1929-1931

Marvin P., Son of
A. M. & C. V. Monks
Jan 13, 1918
Nov 3, 1920

Ida Januita Fite
May 6, 1928
Nov 10, 1930

Henry Towry
1930-1931

Barnie B. Stephens
Jun 10, 1895
Apr 21, 1899

Oliver A. Towery, Jr.
B&D Dec 11, 1940

Naomi Towry Colbert
Oct 10, 1894
Jan 19, 1968

James W. Mullins
Tennessee
Pvt 129 Inf 33 Div
1894-Dec 22, 1931
&
Maudie L. Mullins
1901-

Roy S. Daniel
Oct 1, 1892
Oct 26, 1951

Robert B. Daniel
Aug 1940

Thomas G. Bragg
1930-1952

Icie Barnes
1891-1920

Jane Stewart
1846-1905

Rufus F. Joines
1861-1941

Wilford N. Towry
1929-1929

Evelyn Towry
1925-1946

Tillman N. Towry
May 22, 1897
Aug 11, 1957
&
Ollie V. Towry
Feb 14, 1908

Mary Bragg
1906-1935

Thomas M. Bragg
Aug 3, 1876
Mar 14, 1943
&
Mary V. Bragg
Jan 16, 1905
Oct 26, 1935

Oliver Williams
1931-1932

Daisy Williams
1906-1933

Henderson V. Williams
Died Feb 7, 1969
Age: 74y, 11m, 19d.
(Higgins FH)

Cabe Pennington
Apr 10, 1896
Nov 29, 1968

Grenville A. Towry
1871-1948

Alton W. Sisco
1904-1953
(Gallant FH)

John E. Sisco
1861-1933

Fanney Sisco
1862-1947
(Raby FH)

E. D. Graves, Jr.
Aug 17, 1925
Jul 31, 1965

Thelma Mae Graves
Mar 8, 1928
Jul 22, 1942

O. L. Abbott
1883-(no date)
&
Estella J. Abbott
1883-1957

Dallas Lee Abbott
1912-1934

Willie F. Payne
Mar 5, 1892
Dec 2, 1928

Vasco Vaughan
1882-19
&
Alma Vaughan
1882-1941

Johnnie F., Daughter of
J. K. & V. F. Williams
Mar 11, 1919
Oct 5, 1922

LINCOLN QUADRANGLE

Elder J. M. Walker
1885-1958
&
Lona S. Walker
1885-1964

Jack Walker
Sep 13, 1905
Oct 27, 1940
&
Beulah Walker
Feb 23, 1911

Mary Walker
Feb 18, 1912
Sep 26, 1927

Harry C. Gurley
Jan 12, 1908
Mar 5, 1943

Infant of
Mr. & Mrs. J. R. Gurley
Nov 8, 1910
Dec 19, 1910

J. R. Gurley
May 27, 1879
Jun 18, 1928
&
Lula Gurley
Dec 17, 1887

Martha A. Hinton
Dec 3, 1847
Jul 14, 1913

James R. Routt
Mar 1, 1834
Jun 1, 1915

William G. Seaton
Apr 18, 1841
Sep 18, 1908

Vera Stephens
1897-1899

Tom Ben Towry
Feb 16, 1869
May 2, 1930

Miss Celia A. Towry
Feb 3, 1841
May 11, 1919

M. Gussie Cole
Dec 5, 1883
Oct 3, 1962

William M. Towry
Oct 3, 1871
Jan 31, 1927
&
Mary V. Towry
Sep 12, 1861
Jun 18, 1943

H. Kelley Towry
Mar 22, 1901
Apr 27, 1930

Alton H. Reese
Sep 21, 1891
Sep 9, 1940
&
Jessie E. Reese
Feb 18, 1892

Howard, Son of
Alton & Jessie Reese
Apr 27, 1910
Jan 5, 1923

Lucile Franklin
1914-1934

Helen Fay Towry
1880-1930

Elmer Quick
1931-1932

Lessa May Quick
Sep 13, 1922
Sep 19, 1922

Rufus J. Quick
Jan 10, 1921
Apr 11, 1921

Walter J. Quick
Dec 3, 1875
Jul 22, 1945

Della Quick
Jun 25, 1879
Apr 22, 1916

Edna Quick
Jan 19, 1899
Dec 9, 1914

Mahala H. Quick
Jun 1, 1846
Jan 28, 1928

T. M. Quick
Jun 29, 1839
Jun 1, 1908

Rufus M. Towry
Mar 4, 1870
Jul 4, 1911

Eliza Gertrude Towry
Feb 19, 1878
Jun 14, 1915

D. L. Towry
1880-1949
(Raby FH)

Evelyn Towry
Jun 14, 1915
Jun 10, 1920

Jephtha Towry
Sep 17, 1837
Dec 31, 1908
&
Elvira Towry
Dec 9, 1849
Jan 2, 1930

W. B. Richardson
Jul 12, 1865
Aug 24, 1893

Benton L. Towry
Sep 25, 1849
Jun 22, 1921
&
Emmaline Towry
Mar 24, 1850
Feb 4, 1906

Elizabeth Hammons
1861-1949
(Thompson FH)

Permelia G. Towry, wife of
P. J. Green
Feb 1, 1859
Nov 17, 1901

Sarah Towry
Jun 10, 1811
Feb 15, 1903

I. J. Towry
Mar 11, 1831
Jun 26, 1898

Celia, wife of
I. J. Towry
Mar 30, 1837
Jun 29, 1883

Sidney J. Towry
Mar 9, 1876
Mar 2, 1898

Thomas E. Towry
Sep 20, 1857
Jul 29, 1903

Beatrice M., wife of
Thomas E. Towry
Jul 23, 1867
Apr 1, 1891

Victoria Towry, wife of
W. C. Tanner
Jul 31, 1861
Sep 4, 1921

Dorothy Towry Stewart
Nov 21, 1870
Apr 12, 1944

Arthur F. Towry
Tennessee
Sgt 78 Qm Training Co WW II
Jan 3, 1910
Mar 28, 1953

Herbert, Son of
A. N. & Annie L. Towry
Feb 9, 1907
Jul 27, 1907

Arthur N. Towry
Sep 9, 1831
Nov 6, 1952
&
Annie L(S). Towry
Feb 26, 1883
Mar 27, 1959

Roy Lee Beddingfield
Sep 24, 1904
May 3, 1924
(picture)

John A. Beddingfield
1877-1927

Maggie Beddingfield
1880-1949

Theo A. Wilson
Feb 8, 1908
Apr 30, 1959

Thomas Newton Jeffries
Dec 4, 1848
Jun 27, 1914
&
Lucy Ann Jeffries
May 22, 1855
Jan 26, 1918

Jack A. Childress
1859-1918
&
Kate C. Childress
1874-1907

Edna Childress, wife
of W. F. Coggins
Apr 26, 1896
Oct 6, 1918

Infant Son of
J. H. & V. O. Monks
B&D May 13, 1931

Elisha Hunter
Feb 7, 1867
Mar 23, 1945
&
Millie Jones Hunter
Dec 11, 1871
Jan 29, 1957

Edith Hopkins
Jul 10, 1928
Jul 11, 1928

_. Hunter
(no dates)

L. H.
(no dates, fieldstone)

LINCOLN QUADRANGLE

J. H. Jones
Apr 28, 1864
Jul 1, 1934
&
Lue Jones
Nov 3, 1871
(no date)

Jesse Childress
Aug 2, 1854
Jun 7, 1902
&
Belle Childress
Jul 11, 1860
Sep 27, 1936

Tilmon Towry
Nov 16, 1832
Jan 15, 1892

Nancy J. Towry
Dec 29, 1834
Jun 21, 1906

Nancy B. Towry
Jan 1, 1870
Oct 23, 1891

John H. Towry
Mar 26, 1865
Dec 4, 1878

I. L. Jones
Sep 26, 1847
Mar 29, 1910
&
Rebecca A. Jones
Mar 1, 1839
(no date)
Married Sep 26, 1871

B. F. Swinford
Age: 69 years
(no dates)

G. J., wife of
B. F. Swinford
Nov 7, 1863
Nov 13, 1917

Hamilton Towry
May 12, 1856
Jun 15, 1931
&
Hannah Stevens Towry
Jan 27, 1856
Apr 6, 1936

L. Kannie Swinford
Aug 31, 1909
Feb 13, 1919

Eliza Jane Simmons
May 29, 1847
Jun 18, 1920

A. L. Turner
Apr 28, 1881
Oct 19, 1927

W. F. Simmons (Ferrel)
Mar 26, 1872
1934
& wife
Allie Childress Simmons
Nov 23, 1880
Sep 24, 1933

Frank R. Rogers
Dec 17, 1871
Aug 2, 1961
&
Sarah Ann Rogers
Sep 24, 1862
Dec 12, 1936
"Widow of Robert McAlister"

Robert McAlister
Mar 3, 1858
Oct 3, 1892

S. J. Walker
1905-1940

Mary Walker
1912-1937

Elder Lawson M. Walker
1873-1945
&
Mattie S. Walker
1871-1942

J. B. Walker
May 21, 1926
Jun 11, 1926

Gertie May, Daughter of
L. M. & M. M. Walker
Feb 24, 1900
Jun 11, 1900

W. M. Towry
Feb 12, 1859
Jun 11, 1928
&
Emma J. Towry
Oct 11, 1866
May 11, 1939

Monnie Rene Towry
Mar 29, 1891
Jun 1, 1916

Thomas B. Tipps
Nov 9, 1843
May 11, 1907
&
Elizabeth Tipps
Nov 13, 1849
Mar 8, 1925

Arthur T. Childress
May 17, 1890
Oct 28, 1923

Clarence G. Towry, Jr.
B&D Aug 19, 1935

E. Pauline, Daughter of
Clyde & E. L. Crawford
Aug 23, 1915
Sep 5, 1917

Fred Moore
Jun 2, 1895
Feb 22, 1956
&
Leona Moore
Jun 14, 1890

George Franklin Joines
Mar 23, 1935
Jul 25, 1954

Nancy J., Daughter of
W. G. & C. A. Towry
Nov 21, 1924
Nov 17, 1925

W. G. Towry
1888-1944
& wife
Ossie M. Hopkins Towry
Feb 20, 1893
Feb 12, 1920

W. S. Towry
Dec 24, 1844
Jul 24, 1917
&
Nancy J. Towry
Jan 3, 1845
Dec 24, 1913

Elder M. J. Towry
1864-1939
&
Fanny Jane Towry
1868-1946

W. L., Son of
M. J. & J. F. Towry
B&D Oct 8, 1890

Infant of
M. J. & J. F. Towry
(no dates)

William T. Hopkins
1877-1956
&
Sallie M. Hopkins
Sep 20, 1886
Feb 6, 1911
&
Ona M. Hopkins
1891-1950

Morgan McDaniel Towry
Dec 3, 1878
Oct 2, 1883

Sherman S. Towry
1898-1943
&
Alma V. Towry
1899-19

Rufus Hopkins
1883-1937

W. H. Hopkins
Oct 3, 1852
Mar 1, 1927

Mary McDougal, wife of
W. H. Hopkins
Oct 20, 1852
Oct 16, 1899

G. H. Towry
Feb 24, 1867
Sep 16, 1939

Beatrice Hopkins, wife of
G. H. Towry
Jan 11, 1875
Sep 24, 1916

S. E. M. (Moyers or Mullins)
(no dates, fieldstone)

M. V. M.   "
(no dates, fieldstone)

_. M.   "
(no dates, fieldstone)

M.   "
(no dates, fieldstone)

Stephen Sawyer
Aug 13, 1811
Dec 8, 1896

Sallie, wife of
Stephen Sawyer
Jun 13, 1823
Jan 19, 1894

Mitt Sawyer
Mar 6, 1889
Feb 25, 1932
&
Elizabeth Sawyer
Feb 1, 1899
(no date)

Robert S., Son of
Mitt Sawyer
Jan 27, 1909
Jul 3, 1930

Infant Daughter of
Mitt & M. E. Sawyer
B&D Feb 14, 1928

J. Stephen Sawyer
1861-1944
&
Sallie D. Sawyer
1869-1941

Leavern Brown
1913-1936

Lonnie Clay Sawyer
Jan 29, 1896
Oct 25, 1942

LINCOLN QUADRANGLE

James Robert Moyers
Tennessee
Sgt Co F 29 Inf WW I
Jul 19, 1896
Jul 16, 1956
&
Maudie Lou Moyers
Feb 4, 1900

Minnie Moyers
1879-1938

Floyd H. Moyers
1929-1931

O. B. Hopkins
1877-
&
Fannie Hopkins
1877-1961

Obie Hopkins
1909-1927

W. J. Hopkins
Jan 16, 1842
Nov 18, 1919
    & wife
Martha S. Franklin Hopkins
Oct 22, 1845
Jan 7, 1924

Infant Son of
Mr. & Mrs. E. F. Hopkins
Nov 15, 1913
Jan 12, 1914

John W. Ivey
Dec 26, 1887
Nov 11, 1961

Connie May Sawyer, wife of
J. W. Ivey
Jan 29, 1896
Sep 30, 1953

Alvie Gene Underwood
B&D Jan 15, 1957

Ben F. Moyers
1904-
&
Ethel M. Moyers
1902-1958

John W. Moyers
1901-1942

Fletcher A. Williamson
Tennessee
Pfc Co E 119 Inf WW I PH
Feb 9, 1891
Aug 30, 1956

George L. Williamson
T/Sgt 5700 Air Base GPAF
Jul 17, 1914
Apr 21, 1955

Arie Jean Cates
B&D Oct 27, 1934

William A. Childress
Dec 10, 1883
Oct 11, 1964
&
Addie McAlister Childress
Nov 15, 1883
Apr 18, 1945

Henry F. Rogers
Nov 23, 1902
Sep 18, 1945
&
Lorene C. Rogers
Oct 14, 1903

Mrs. Clara Violet Hopkins
Died Dec 16, 1969
Age: 77 years.
(Gallant FH)

Henry I. Hopkins
1923-1930

Mary Williamson
1870-1932

William Mullins
Apr 11, 1872
Apr 25, 1926

Mary Mullins, wife of
W. A. Bates
Aug 17, 1871
Nov 21, 1936

W. A. Bates(or W. E. Bates)
1874-1947

Mary Mullins
Aug 17, 1843
Jun 19, 1908

J. T. Mullins
Feb 18, 1841
Apr 19, 1912

Davis S. Swinford
1877-1953
&
America Towry Swinford
1876-1941

Daisy Mae Swinford
1898-1901

Dove Eulege Swinford
1917-1920

Fanny Hopkins
Jul 4, 1875
Jul 28, 1911

Margaret, Daughter of
U. B. & Lottie Newby
Dec 15, 1928
Dec 16, 1929

J. W. McAlister
1882-19
    & Anna Spray McAlister
Jun 22, 1886
Oct 28, 1911
    &
Agnes Moore McAlister
1888-

Velma Towry
Sep 16, 1910
Jun 15, 1911

William Alex Towry
Apr 15, 1869
Feb 22, 1941
    &
Rosana Towry
Aug 28, 1874
Feb 2, 1954

J. H. Towry
Nov 27, 1871
Aug 10, 1895

John H. Hopkins
1861-1940
    &
Mary J. Hopkins
1867-1943

E. S. ?.
(no dates, fieldstone)

J. Cleve Colbert
Jun 1883
Jul 1925

J. Wiley Duncan
Aug 11, 1853
Mar 22, 1921

J. B. T. (Towry)
(no dates)

Cora Annie Towery
1885-1957

W. C. Myrick
Apr 11, 1836
(no date)
    & wife
Mary J. Myrick
May 5, 1863
Jan 23, 1925

Bufford F. Moffitt
Oct 29, 1909
Oct 25, 1930

Norman Paul Hunter
1932-1965
(picture)

W. R. Mullins
Jun 5, 1858
Sep 6, 1916

Mary J., wife of
W. R. Mullins
Oct 10, 1856
Apr 4, 1932

Emerson H. Hunter
Oct 9, 1888
May 11, 1945
&
Zela Towry Hunter
Dec 24, 1893

Maxine Hunter
1917-1935

Ophelia Hunter
1918-1932

Edward Denton ***
Aug 30, 1858
Feb 23, 1910
(Murdered)
    & Wife
Nancy Dollar Denton ***
Dec 24, 1858
Oct 3, 1912

Hiram Denton ***
1821-1887
    &
Farby Ann Ables Denton ***
1820-1881 (?)

*** By Bob Allen Gray

Infant * of
N. F. & Alice Tucker
Died Mar 30, 1901
(no age given)

G. W. Towry *
Married Mary J. Monks
in 1865
Died Mar 29, 1903
Age: 68 years.

Ulrich Tillman,* Son of
Higgins & Bedie Towry
Died Apr 3, 1903
Age: 1y, 4m.

William A.,* Son of
Thomas N. Jeffries
Died Oct 4, 1891
Age: 20y, 9m.

David Tipps *
Died Jun 25, 1894
Age: 77 years.

Thomas Monks *
Married Elizabeth Bostic
Died Oct 26, 1895
Age: 77 years.

Nancy Zenia,* Daughter of
B. L. & E. D. Towry
Died Dec 16, 1896
Age: 8y, 3m, 26d.

Emma Lou Sawyer *
Died Apr 2, 1899
Age: 9 months.

LINCOLN QUADRANGLE

Barnie Burrell,* Son of
Burrell & Sarah Stephens
Died Apr 21, 1899
Age: (not given)

Infant * of
L. H. & Milly Hunter
Died Sep 17, 1899
Age: (not given)

James T. Walker *
Married Vashie Abbott
Oct 26, 1893
Died Feb 19, 1900
Age: 25 years.

J. T. Moffatt *
Died May 25, 1914
Age: 63 years.
Left a wife and 3 Sons:
J. T., J. E., & W. O."

Mrs. M. E.,* wife of
W. A. Walker
Died Nov 27, 1907
Age: 65y, 7m, 27d.

Benjamin A. Beard *
Died Dec 8, 1911
Age: 80 years.

Mrs. Lucy,* widow of late
George Tipps
Born in Franklin Co., Tenn.
Died Jul 21, 1903
Age: 66 years.

Mrs. Lula Hopkins *
Died Oct 8, 1912
Age: (not given)

Thomas B. Tipps *
Died May 19, 1907
Age: 60 years.

Lucy,* Daughter of
George Tipps
B&D Jul 20, 1903

Mrs. William Hopkins *
Died Jan 7, 1911
Age: 32 years.

Many unmarked graves.

Mrs. Mary,* wife of
J. T. Mullins
Died Feb 19, 1908
Age: (not given)

Henry Payne *
Married Elizabeth Walker
Died Apr 21, 1908
Age: 39y, 3m, 18d.

Mrs. Margaret Moffatt *
Married J. T. Moffatt
Died May 26, 1909
Age: 65 years.

* *

HANKS CEMETERY

LOCATION: One half mile NW of Skinem.

Members of the Hanks family are buried in this cemetery.

* *

HARRIS CEMETERY

LOCATION: One half mile NNW of Skinem.

Newton F. Harris
Apr 13, 1835
Jan 5, 1892
&
Stacie J. Harris
Sep 22, 1851
Jan 18, 1931

Annie, Daughter of
N. F. & S. J. Harris
Jun 1, 1890
Nov 11, 1898

* *

SMITH CEMETERY

LOCATION: At Skinem and on the east side of Fayetteville Highway.

Lindsey B. Smith
Tennessee
Sgt 168 Inf 42 Div
Dec 17, 1934

J. Ansleum McKinney
Feb 16, 1876
Aug 28, 1897

J. P. Wallace
Jul 19, 1829
Feb 24, 1917

Ansleum Thomas, Son of
W. B. & L. J. Nicks
Sep 29, 1874
Sep 14, 1875

J. A. McKinney
Apr 24, 1844
Jul 24, 1901
& wife
Martha J. McKinney
Jul 20, 1844
Jun 31, 1914

Wiley A. Jean
1871-1945
&
Della M. Jean
1872-1937

Esq. James M. Wells *
Nov 12, 1835
Nov 2, 1916
41st Tenn Regt
C.S.A.

Dr. N. M. Jenkins
Oct 3, 1829
Jun 7, 1914
& wife
Elenora Nicks Jenkins
Jul 25, 1840
Aug 25, 1906

F. S. Clark
Jul 12, 1839
Feb 6, 1903

John H. Kay
Mar 20, 1820
Nov 3, 1898

Benjamin Franklin Smith ***
Oct 10, 1841
Jun 20, 1931

Rosa B.,*** wife of
Benjamin Franklin Smith
Feb 12, 1859
Mar 22, 1942

Wattie Franklin, ***Son of
B. F. & R. B. Smith
Jan 21, 1891
Mar 22, 1942

*** By Mrs. Robert Ivey

* *

LINCOLN QUADRANGLE

CEMETERY

LOCATION: One half mile north of Bellview on the west side of Old Huntsville Highway.

No markers remain.

* *

TOWRY CEMETERY

LOCATION: One half mile east of Bellview.

Several fieldstones, no inscriptions.	Members of the Towry family are buried here.

* *

DAVIS CEMETERY

LOCATION: Three fourth mile SE of Bellview.

James Davis (no dates)	(James Davis was a U. S. Marshall, An old Jail was located on this farm.)

* *

McDANIEL CEMETERY

LOCATION: One and one fourth mile SW of Bellview.

Henry McDaniel Feb 12, 1833 Jun 18, 1888	Angeline McDaniel Aug 17, 1832 Aug 1, 1916	(Both graves are enclosed with an iron fence.)

* *

CEMETERY

LOCATION: Three fourth mile south of Bellview on the west side of Old Huntsville Highway.

Rev. E. F. Cook Died Jan 11, 1875 Age: 25 years.	Several unmarked graves.

* *

WALKER CEMETERY

LOCATION: One mile south of Bellview on the east side of Highway.

Mary J. Phillips Apr 15, 1830 May 21, 1891	Stephen Walker Died 1858 Age: 75 years. Elizabeth S., wife of Stephen Walker Age: 78 years (no dates)	S. T. Walker 1831-1924 Julia, wife of S. T. Walker Jun 2, 1838 Jun 19, 1888	Clarissa, wife of S. T. Walker Aug 9, 1834 Feb 11, 1905

* *

LINCOLN QUADRANGLE

ROGERS CEMETERY

LOCATION: One fourth mile NW of Old Macedonia and west of Old Huntsville Highway, in pasture.

John A. Rogers Jun 1, 1861 May 14, 1910	Catharine Rogers Feb 18, 1826 Jul 4, 1888 & Martha Rogers Jan 20, 1828 Jun 30, 1908 & Peggy Rogers Oct 8, 1822 Dec 28, 1886 & Winnie Rogers Apr 18, 1824 Apr 13, 1893 & Absalam Rogers Jul 25, 1796 May 18, 1885 & wife Mildred Rogers Jun 21, 1794 Jun 19, 1854	W. W. Rogers May 25, 1830 Aug 6, 1911 Martha J., wife of W. W. Rogers Jan 4, 1836 Oct 9, 1917 Sallie Rogers Jul 3, 1867 Nov 12, 1930 Addie Rogers Jan 11, 1875 Jan 2, 1945 Several unmarked graves.	Willie F., Son of J. V. & M. E. Gill Mar 30, ---- --- --, 186-(broken) General Lee Rogers Oct 22, 1869 Mar 1, 1937 Addie Freeman, wife of G. L. Rogers Aug 25, 1870 Dec 25, 1909 Mrs. Martha Rogers * Died Jul 1, 1908 Age: 80y, 5m, 10d.
W. R. Rogers Dec 11, 1864 Nov 7, 1924			
Alvin C. Rogers Mar 15, 1907 Sep 26, 1908			
Annie L. Rogers Nov 29, 1903 Jul 20, 1904			
Infant * of John Rogers Died Sep 26, 1908 Age: 1y, 8m.			

* *

MACEDONIA CEMETERY

LOCATION: On east side of Old Huntsville Highway where the Old Macedonia M. E. Church once stood.

Albert H. Shockley 1881-1956 & Annie S. Shockley 1882-1949	George Schnetzler Dec 18, 1839 Aug 16, 1909 & Mary Jane Schnetzler 1852-1934	William L. Brazell Died Dec 21, 1967 Age: 63 years. Mildred Brazell Jul 1, 1910 Apr 15, 1937	Allie Bates 1880-1956 J. T. Bankston 1871-1948 & Sally Bankston 1872-1956
Morgan McBride Mar 8, 1924 Apr 11, 1934	Infant of Richard Rex Duncan B&D Jan 29, 1962	James H. Bankston Nov 27, 1872 Jan 16, 1924 & Lula B. Bankston Sep 4, 1882 Apr 24, 1962	Frank Bankston 1890-1937
John Wesley Porter Apr 22, 1904 Oct 23, 1924	John Vann 1895-1954		Y. Turner Hancock Jun 4, 1868 Apr 10, 1950
Edward Anderson Porter A.R.M. 2C Feb 20, 1924 Mar 18, 1944	Solon Moss 1881-1934 Lillie Moss 1885-1960	Aaron A. Rutledge Aug 30, 1889 Nov 24, 1953 & Ethel P. Rutledge Aug 14, 1896 ------------	Rev. T. J. Jones Nov 1, 1812 Mar 27, 1893
Andrew Greenfield Schnetzler Aug 1, 1877 Jan 7, 1940	Virginia Louise Helms Jan 15, 1942 Jan 20, 1942		Lucy M. Jones Jan 1, 1819 Jul 16, 1883
Floyd W. Schnetzler May 12, 1925 Dec 9, 1945	Carey Tielking Apr 21, 1940 Dec 24, 1940	J. W. Rutledge Dec 25, 1916 Nov 7, 1918	R. F. Jean 1873-1957 & Fannie M. Jean 1876-1947
W. J. Schnetzler Jun 3, 1880 Jun 24, 1952 & wife Kate Hancock Schnetzler Jan 20, 1886 Feb 19, 1935	Margaret Virginia Passon Feb 25, 1925 Mar 26, 1962 Allen Jones 1869-1932	W. D. Jones Aug 6, 1835 May 16, 1922 Elizabeth S. Jones Sep 1845 Feb 1937	Lonnie Mack, Son of R. F. & F. M. Jean Oct 6, 1896 Mar 12, 1918

LINCOLN QUADRANGLE

Gordon W. Jean
May 7, 1918
Sep 18, 1918
&
Ralph W. Jean
May 7, 1918
May 7, 1918
"Twins"

Riley Jean
Sep 15, 1876
Dec 31, 1956
&
Fannie Jean
Nov 12, 1887
Jan 18, 1966

Homer R. Jean
Sep 30, 1911
Nov 8, 1932

Nannie D. Jean
Feb 7, 1927
Nov 4, 1932

A. L. Jean
1875-1932

Thomas Edward, Son of
Mr. & Mrs. J. E. Jean
Aug 11, 1961
Oct 26, 1961

Mary E. Jean
Dec 7, 1948
Mar 14, 1965

L. B. "Poss" Gammon
Feb 6, 1892
Jul 7, 1964

Clio Taylor, wife of
L. B. Gammon
Nov 21, 1894
Mar 6, 1932

Douglas L. Gammon
Oct 10, 1939
Jan 22, 1942

W. Larry Gammon
Apr 28, 1943
Jun 21, 1962

_____ Jean
Died 195-
Age: (all info gone)

W. F. Jean
Feb 22, 1853
Sep 22, 1926

Morgan Mack Towry
Died Sep 20, 1968
Age: 80 years.

James Howard, Son of
Harry & Elizabeth Miller
B&D Mar 13, 1929

Roberta Simmons
1893-1928

T. Earla Slayton
1873-1951
&
Christina E. Slayton
1878-1946

Mable Dean Slayton
B&D Feb 9, 1947

John A. Davidson
Sep 15, 1878
Dec 31, 1920

W. F. Simmons
1880-1957
&
Mary Alice Simmons
1879-1951

Jackson Bolander
1915

Sarah L., wife of
Henry Bolander
Dec 10, 1856
Feb 4, 1883
Age: 26y, 1m, 24d.

Elizabeth Bolander
1921

William T. Walker
Nov 27, 1879
Jan 20, 1938
&
Margaret F. Walker
Feb 18, 1888
Jul 12, 1942

Tyine McG., wife of
Fred Tielking
Aug 1860
(no date)

William F. Tielking
1888-1960
&
Eula E. Tielking
1895-1958

Paul Tielking
Dec 8, 1934
Jan 4, 1935

Albert Tielking
Aug 30, 1914
Sep 6, 1914

Joan Tielking
Aug 6, 1912
Aug 12, 1912

John Tielking
Mar 6, 1918
Jul 12, 1919

Pauline Tielking
Jul 28, 1924
Nov 27, 1927

Charles Walter Tielking
Sep 7, 1882
\-\-\-\-\-\-\-\-\-\-\-\-

Lydia Rosie V. S. Tielking
Aug 5, 1887
Feb 22, 1967
Age: 79 years.

Ruby Tielking
1904-1954

Infant of
R. J. & G. I. Tielking
B&D Apr 24, 1925

Edward Tielking
1911-1914

Walter D. Tielking
Jan 30, 1936
Oct 7, 1961

Mattie Sue Porter
Sep 23, 1896
Apr 22, 1928

Luther Simmons
1888-1924

Robert E. Walker
1888-1948
&
Beadie S. Walker
1886-19(no date)

Mary Simmons
1850-1928

John Simmons
1855-1893

Mary Ann, Daughter of
Luther & Annie Simmons
B&D Mar 8, 1920

John Robert Walker
Jul 18, 1914
Nov 23, 1914

Hariston (two graves)
(no dates)

Addie Hopkins
Dec 16, 1887
Jul 30, 1922

J. M. Hopkins
Jul 4, 1844
Jun 2, 1908
&
S. T. Hopkins
Sep 16, 1853
Mar 1, 1911

Flora H. Reed
1884-1907

William Stafford
B&D Sep 21, 1935

Ida T. Porter
1875-1935

William F. Porter
1871-1947

James M. Ashworth
Jun 17, 1865
Mar 11, 1918

Sarah E. Ashworth
1868-1938

Tennie Witt, wife of
Dr. D. T. Hardin
Nov 1, 1887
Aug 8, 1907

Mary E. Witt
Aug 30, 1842
May 10, 1890

Jane Simmons
Died Jan 5, 1906
Age: 53 years.

Ethel, wife of
G. W. Simmons
Feb 17, 1853
Mar 20, 1905

George W. Simmons
Nov 5, 1859
Apr 12, 1934
& widow
Elizabeth Simmons
Feb 27, 1883
Apr 26, 1962

G. T. Simmons
Apr 3, 1917
Apr 6, 1917

Buford Simmons
1906-
&
Sallie Simmons
1906-May 19, 1963
Age: 56 years.

Infant Son of
Ed & J. L. Shockley
B&D Aug 19, 1919

Little Annie, Daughter of
J. M. & Sadie Ashworth
Apr 21, 1896
Mar 31, 1905

Margaret P., wife of
J. L. Smith
Apr 23, 1856
Oct 10, 1885

Viola Cobb Ashworth
Aug 5, 1893
Jul 3, 1925

Phillip Bryant Ashworth
Aug 17, 1916
Aug 24, 1929

LINCOLN QUADRANGLE

Chris L. Blaylock
Aug 19, 1956
Mar 23, 1969

D. B. Blaylock
1893-(no date)
&
Maggie M. Blaylock
1900-1932

Willis A. Blaylock
1833-1918

Mrs. Willie B. Blaylock
1880-1935

Willis (Blaylock)
B&D Jul 11, 1941

Geneva, Infant of
Mr. & Mrs. A. E. Blaylock
Sep 4, 1925
Nov 22, 1925

Will Haley
1868-1893

George Hunter
1874-1900

Baby
Danny Simmons
Jul 6, 1940
Feb 8, 1941

Milton M. Simmons
Dec 20, 1877
Dec 20, 1947
&
Mamie E. Simmons
Aug 8, 1877
Mar 7, 1941

Benjamin Franklin Ashworth
Mar 24, 1859
Jul 2, 1927

Evea Bell Witt
1913-1929

William M. Witt
Dec 27, 1870
Nov 19, 1933

Sarah E., wife of
William M. Witt
Nov 21, 1859
Sep 14, 1907

Rosco C. Witt
Oct 30, 1834
Feb 11, 1919

Cecil S. Phillips
1921-1923

F. N. McCown
1861-1930

Otis N. McCown
1893-1959

Julia McCown
1896-1931

Mary Ellen McCown
1931

Ferd. N. McCown
1861-1930
&
Ellen McCown
1855-1933

Robert C. Walker
1866-1938
&
Martha A. Walker
1868-1930

Andrew J. Baites
Apr 5, 1875
Dec 23, 1937
&
Ionia Cooper Baites
Jul 30, 1877
Jul 22, 1965

Lucy J., wife of
L. M. Smith
Mar 25, 1863
Dec 10, 1927

Edward Hopkins
Jan 6, 1914
Nov 8, 1941

Hezekiah Ford
Jan 5, 1832
Apr 8, 1914

Mrs. A. W. Hancock
1868-1941

Amelia Varnell, Daughter of
F. E. & S. R. Wright
B&D Jul 8, 1916

L. L. Wright
Sep 12, 1838
Dec 17, 1931
&
Julia F. Wright
Oct 22, 1850
Oct 11, 1922
&
Roy G. Wright
May 22, 1888
Sep 20, 1906

C. O. Wright
Jan 7, 1922
Oct 16, 1942
Lost in Pacific (Navy)
&
J. L. Wright
Dec 2, 1923
May 3, 1944
Lost in Atlantic (Navy)

Charles L. Wright
Apr 17, 1879
Mar 29, 1965
&
Sarah E. Wright
Sep 28, 1903

Patrick Crabtree
1890-1929
&
Lula Mae Crabtree
1890-1920
&
Lorene Crabtree
1910-1926

Ora Manley
1898-1920

Ava Manley
1876-1944

Will Manley
1872-1944

Everett E. Slayton
1901-(no date)
&
Ora May Slayton
1906-1952

Robert T. Phillips
1888-1927
&
Junie D. Phillips
1892-1957

Edward Carlton, Son of
Robert T. & Junie Phillips
Jun 10, 1914
Dec 12, 1914

J. W. King
Aug 7, 1842
Dec 7, 1908
& wife
Susanna King
Feb 3, 1843
Jan 6, 1936
&
Frances S. King
Nov 21, 1875
Dec 13, 1903
&
Ora May King
Jun 24, 1884
Mar 24, 1906

Perry J. King
& his wife
Lucy Rutledge King
& their children
Infant Son,
Perry Edsel King
Infant Son,
Malcolm Dean King
Infant Son,
Bobby Wayne King
(no dates on any of the above)

J. H. Mills
1862-1943
&
M. A. Mills
1860-1937

William Walton Hancock
B&D Feb 18, 1928

A. Walton Hancock
1872-1951

Isaiah Hancock
Mar 16, 1827
Jun 20, 1911
&
Martha E. Hancock
Jan 29, 1834
Jan 31, 1905

Clifford Jean
1890-(no date)
&
Rhoda Jean
1898-1953

Linda Ruth Dollar
Jul 3, 1950
Jan 29, 1952

Ronald Jean Dollar
B&D Jun 24, 1951

Barbara Gale Jean
Nov 1, 1950
Sep 22, 1950

Lyman Knox Hancock
Oct 2, 1909
Apr 16, 1952

Infant Boy Garland
Died Nov 11, 1968
(no last name on stone)

William E. Blaylock
Tennessee
Sgt HQ Det 5 Grand Div T.C.
WW I
Jul 14, 1889
Mar 15, 1966

Daniel B. Reeves, Sr.
Tennessee
CM 3 U.S.N.R. WW II
Dec 10, 1907
Aug 21, 1968

Kenneth Bankston
Died Aug 31, 1952?
Age: 5y, 7m, 3d.

Carrie Frances Crawford
Sep 1, 1896
Jan 26, 1910

Sallie Crawford Hancock
Nov 7, 1877
Mar 25, 1912

LINCOLN QUADRANGLE

William Blake Crawford
May 7, 1851
Dec 23, 1915
&
Mary Elizabeth Ashworth
Crawford
Mar 6, 1851
Jun 22, 1907

Blake Rufus Crawford
Jan 3, 1894
Nov 10, 1966

Sidney J. Crawford
Jul 24, 1891
Aug 23, 1960
&
Grace J. Crawford
Jan 9, 1903

Mary Anna Crawford
Jun 14, 1889

Sandra Gail Crawford
Dec 14, 1942
Jan 23, 1943

Sidney B. Hentz

&
Margaret Crawford Hentz
Died Dec 1, 1965
Age: (not given)

J. M. Pierson *
Died Feb 17, 1888
Age: 43 years.

William Ashworth *
Died Apr 24, 1892
Age: 83 years.

Charles Henry,* Son of
George & Mary Schnetzler
B&D Jul 23, 1890

Pearl May,* Daughter of
O. J. & Rosa E. Bolander
Died Dec 1891
Age: 7 months.

Miss Susan Bevel *
Died Dec 21, 1896
Age: 78 years.

Infant * of
Thomas & Maggie Walker
Died Nov 6, 1903
Age: (Not given)

Mrs. Louisa D.,* Married
John L. Washburn
Dec 24, 1874
Born Jul 30, 1852
Died Apr 5, 1875
Daughter of
Robert & Nancy Templeton.

Mrs. Martha Green*
Died Feb 14, 1901
Age: 47 years.
Married T. C. Green

Mrs. Lizzie Witt *
Died May 1, 1891
Age: 50 years.

Miss Eva A. McGeehon *
Died Jun 8, 1894
Age: 20 years.

Knox Bryson Bankston *
Died Nov 1, 1906
Age: 8y, 9m.

Mrs. Francis S. Howard *
Died Dec 13, 1903
Age: 28 years.

Mrs. Sallie M. Hancock *
Daughter of
John & Julia Rogers
Married in 1882 to
T. A. Hancock
Died Oct 26, 1890
Age: 30 years.

Many unmarked graves.

J. H. McGeehan *
Married Mary Thomas
Sep 11, 1896
Died Oct 11, 1901
Age: 64 years.

Ida,* Daughter of
Mr. & Mrs. Newton Hopkins
Died Dec 26, 1892
Age: 20 years.

Mrs. M. A. E., * wife of
J. McGeehon
Died Feb 18, 1899
Age: 29 years.

Elizabeth,* wife of
T. A. Hancock
Died Jun 15, 1903
Age: 38 years.

Mollie,* Daughter of
Rev. Charles Laxon
Died Jun 8, 1896
Age: 33 years.

Infant * of
Jim & Sarah Hopkins
Died May 14, 1897
Age: (not given)

* *

HENDERSON CEMETERY

LOCATION: Across the Highway and south of Old Macedonia.

Henry Henderson
May 27, 1825
May 31, 1895

Sarah E. Henderson
Nov 8, 1827
Aug 2, 1893

William,*** Son of
John Crawford
(no dates)

V. M., wife of
W. T. Phillips
May 1, 1859
May 8, 1896

Emma Lucy Phillips ***
Age: 17 years.
(no dates)

L. Emma Phillips
Dec 30, 1881
Apr 18, 1901

*** Family Records.

* *

CEMETERY

LOCATION: One fourth mile SE of Old Macedonia on west side of Highway.

W. C. Butler
Died Mar 5, 1864
Age: 53y, 7m, 5d.

W. A. G. Blaylock ***
Apr 14, 1814
Sep 9, 1874

About 20 unmarked graves.

*** Family Records.

* *

LINCOLN QUADRANGLE

HANCOCK CEMETERY

LOCATION: One half mile SE of Old Macedonia on the west side of Highway.

J. Newton McCluskey *
Died Oct 6, 1899
Age: 72 years.

Elizabeth M. McCluskey *
Died Oct 18, 1895
Age: 73 years.

This Cemetery has no markers.

* *

ASHWORTH CEMETERY

LOCATION: Immediately south of the junction of Old Huntsville Highway and 241 and west of 241.

(DAssie Ashworth &
another Ashworth woman are
buried here, no markers)   Only two graves, no markers.

* *

CAMPER CEMETERY

LOCATION: Immediately south of junction of Old Huntsville Highway and 241, on east side of 241.

Fieldstones, no inscriptions.

(One grave was the wife of
John Rogers, no dates)

* *

STATE LINE CEMETERY
(Old Bethesda Church & Old Section)

LOCATION: Immediately south of Tennessee State Line, on east side of 241, at M. E. Church, Church was established in 1826.

Martha Posey
Oct 4, 1833
Mar 19, 1904

William R. Posey
Nov 1, 1856
Mar 2, 1925

S. L., wife of
W. R. Posey
Jun 31, 1859
Feb 3, 1898

Eliza Hill Posey
Jun 11, 1879
May 16, 1939

Stella, Daughter of
Mr. & Mrs. W. R. Posey
B&D Jun 1, 1903

William L. Phillips
1860-1934
&
Louana Towry Phillips
1873-1942

Patt M., Son of
W. L. & Josephine Phillips
Feb 2, 1883
Jun 2, 1908

Ora Lee, Daughter of
W. L. & Louana Phillips
Apr 2, 1856
Jul 21, 1902

Leahman, Son of
W. L. & Louana Phillips
Apr 12, 1899
Apr 11, 1900

Josephine, wife of
W. L. Phillips
Apr 7, 1862
Jun 11, 1885

John J. Phillips
Feb 25, 1833
Oct 28, 1890
C.S.A.
&
Mary L. Phillips
Mar 1, 1839
Jun 28, 1891

Charles C. Vining
Jul 24, 1856
Apr 20, 1877

E. C. Kenney
Feb 1, 1876
Oct 8, 1953
& wife
Effie H. Kenney
May 13, 1875
Nov 4, 1924

G. D. Kenney
Mar 28, 1852
Mar 9, 1923

Sallie W., wife of
G. D. Kenney
1849-1910

J. W. Hannah
Jan 1, 1855
Mar 6, 1906

J. M. Kenney
Oct 25, 1813
Feb 26, 1890

Mrs. Mary Kenney
Sep 15, 1813
Jan 8, 1899

Rev. D. D. Smith
Aug 2, 1818
Jun 15, 1875

Gray Hill
1896-1952
Pvt Hq Co 166 Inf WW I

Raymond Hill
1886-1935

Jim T. Hill
Pfc 1st Class Co G
M.G. Bat
Dec 5, 1892
Killed in action near
the Medeah Farm in
France Oct 5, 1918

W. G. Hill
Feb 2, 1859
Mar 9, 1945
&
Lucindy Hill
Nov 28, 1859
Aug 14, 1941

LINCOLN QUADRANGLE

John S. Lowe
Dec 31, 1813
Jan 26, 1888

Annie Lowe
Jun 11, 1827
Dec 12, 1907

James S. Lowe
Sep 23, 1853
Aug 21, 1873

Mable Lee, Daughter of
I. H. & Exie Lowe
May 29, 1885
Sep 28, 1892

Peter S., Son of
I. H. & Exie Lowe
Dec 25, 1882
Feb 2, 1901

Isaac Henderson Lowe
Apr 19, 1844
Oct 20, 1920
&
Exine Grantland Lowe
Jul 1, 1852
May 2, 1936

A. S. Godbey
Mar 13, 1871
Sep 27, 1897

Rev. Crockett Godbey
Born May 23, 1818
in Montgomery Co., Va.
Died Sep 20, 1901
Methodist Preacher 58
years, Holston & North
Alabama Conference.

Evaline M., wife of
Rev. Crockett Godbey &
Daughter of
James R. & Rachel Forgey
of Hawkins Co., Tenn.
Died Jun 10, 1914
Age: 78 years.

James M. Gipson
May 27, 1866
Mar 21, 1941
&
Mollie J. Gipson
Sep 3, 1872
May 23, 1944

Rev. Berry Hicks Bridges
Jul 4, 1840
Jan 7, 1903

Frances E. Murphy
Apr 13, 1844
Nov 24, 1897

Thomas L. Bullard
Jan 3, 1879
Jun 14, 1888

David H. Bullard
Apr 3, 1872
Oct 24, 1901

Martha Bullard
Mar 1, 1874
Oct 7, 1898

B. F. Bullard
Jan 10, 1845
Feb 21, 1927
&
Sarah A. Newbey Bullard
Jan 24, 1842
May 2, 1915

John Henry Price
1891-1946
&
Tishie Eakes Price
1891-1957

Andrew J. Mason
Feb 14, 1868
Apr 20, 1927
&
Addie M. Mason
Jun 13, 1881
Mar 22, 1964

Virginia Ann Cotton
Mar 22, 1891
Jun 8, 1929
Daughter of
J. P. Grissom

Virginia A., wife of
R. J. Scrimsher
Sep 24, 1840
Feb 24, 1887

R. H. Grantland
Mar 4, 1824
Apr 2, 1896
& wife
Mary A. Grantland
Sep 22, 1824
Jun 22, 1904

Minnie Lee, wife of
R. V. Cantrell
Dec 18, 1876
Nov 11, 1895

Naomi S. Lewis
Nov 18, 1846
Feb 19, 1918

Allie B., Daughter of
W. C. & N. S. Lewis
Aug 7, 1881
Jan 22, 1895

O. H., Son of
W. C. & N. S. Lewis
Nov 9, 1883
Sep 18, 1907

W. H. Wimberley
Jan 28, 1861
Feb 9, 1929
& wife
Mary Snowden Wimberley
Jan 14, 1865
Jul 27, 1927

J. C. Webster
1849-1915
&
Mary E. Webster
1853-1911

Callie, Daughter of
J. C. & M. E. Webster
Died Jun 1876
Age: 6 months.

Infant Daughter of
J. C. & M. E. Webster
B&D July 1878

Minnie, wife of
A. W. Hancock & Daughter of
J. C. & M. E. Webster
1873-1907

Eliza Jenkins
Dec 24, 1813
Jun 8, 1891

Janie L. Blackwell, wife of
U. F. Posey
Mar 9, 1902
Jul 11, 1927

Sarah M., wife of
S. C. Riley
Jan 4, 1839
Aug 16, 1902

Mary Rebecca McKee Vining
1858-1936

William Baggerley McKee
1829-1896

Margaret Thompson McKee
1842-1918

John H. Poor
1845-1884
& wife
Susan R. Overton Poor
1853-1925

Samuel A. Hill
Sep 25, 1842
Dec 25, 1909

Eliza Jane, wife of
S. A. Hill
Dec 16, 1835
May 28, 1899

Zena, wife of
G. G. Cornell
Jul 1877
Dec 1911

J. M. Hill
Apr 17, 1870
Oct 6, 1926

Julia K. Hill
Mar 17, 1878
May 18, 1965

Glen G. Cornell
Jan 27, 1885
Jun 30, 1957

Annie B. Carter Cornell
Oct 29, 1890
Apr 30, 1959

Mae Cornell
Apr 10, 1875
Feb 28, 1928

R. T. Cornell
Apr 8, 1847
Nov 1, 1924
& wife
Agnes Ann Sherman Cornell
Sep 4, 1848
Jun 28, 1920
Married May 20, 1869

Mary E. Carter
Nov 29, 1856
Sep 3, 1936

Lawrence Haynes Carter
Jul 31, 1864
Dec 27, 1921
&
Lula Mae Carter
Jul 7, 1866
Mar 1, 1930

Wilburn Carter
1892-1949

Ed Carter
1894-1953

William W. Lasater
Nov 12, 1884
Aug 7, 1962
&
Rose Lee Lasater
Apr 23, 1892
(no date)

James Anderson Solters
Oct 27, 1870
Dec 30, 1943

W. F. Turner
May 7, 1876
May 1, 1939
& wife: Lula B. Turner
Sep 6, 1880
May 6, 1927

Myrtle Odell Turner
Feb 26, 1909
Aug 30, 1922

LINCOLN QUADRANGLE

John R. Record
1840-1916
"Erected by G-Grandson
James R. Record"

Talmage W. Harwell
Aug 1, 1882
Oct 3, 1918

Phillip M. Clark
Aug 5, 1851
Jul 19, 1922
&
Mary A. Clark
Dec 26, 1846
Mar 11, 1937

Albert C. Clark
Sep 1, 1875
Aug 11, 1923
&
Beulah S. Clark
Nov 1, 1884
Mar 4, 1964

F. M. Jean
Sep 2, 1821
Sep 6, 1884
"Father of Mary Ramy,
Grandfather of Marion,
Demie, Elzina & Travis
Ramy."

Elizabeth Jean
Aug 7, 1809
Feb 15, 1886
"Mother of Mary Ramy,
Grandmother of Marion,
Demie, Elzina & Travis
Ramy."

W. C. Lewis
Jan 17, 1845
Oct 21, 1895

I. D. Allen
1870-1933

Ammie Swindell Allen
1873-1944

S. H. Knowles
Apr 15, 1862
Mar 7, 1923

Frances L. Knowles
Dec 11, 1868
Apr 25, 1933

J. W. Knowles
Nov 8, 1837
Nov 24, 1912
C.S.A.

William Henry Johns
Mar 25, 1855
Sep 17, 1942

John K. Shockley
1860-1939

Mary F. Shockley
Feb 28, 1850
May 1, 1919

Jeff. Hodge
1866-1922

Martha Hodge
Jan 17, 1863
Feb 4, 1904

Irba-Dollie Hodge
Died 1904
Age: (not given)

M. J. Shockley
Dec 17, 1844
Dec 16, 1904

David Posey
1874-1960

Ida Ray Street, wife of
D. L. Posey
Jul 31, 1875
Sep 21, 1926

Virgie Gilliland
Mar 11, 1858
Dec 3, 1908

Samuel Walter Harton
Jan 23, 1875
Jul 19, 1939

Addie L. Harton
1873-1947

Rev. E. L. Pigg
Aug 12, 1873
(not buried here)
&
Juley Pigg
Mar 24, 1875
Mar 7, 1912

Elyia Pigg
1867-1947

Cynthia Fronnie Erwin
1874-1959

Eliza Knowles
Jul 7, 1845
Jul 12, 1926

Jane Knowles
Sep 11, 1841
Feb 28, 1934

T. J. Miles
1872-1961

Curtis L. Wadding
Aug 12, 1884
Aug 20, 1905

W. C. Rutledge
1861-1929
&
Donie Brown Rutledge
1870-

John P. Thomason
Jan 6, 1846
Mar 24, 1920
C.S.A.
&
Mary C. Dunafon Thomason
Sep 10, 1854
(no date)

John A. Moore
Oct 7, 1847
May 12, 1926
&
Margaret E. Stanley Moore
Mar 10, 1858
Jul 7, 1924

George Cope
1857-1927
&
Vina Cope
1876-(no date)

Delia Clementine Davis
Nov 27, 1865
Dec 8, 1943

Mary Ann Harris
1845-1930
& Son
Jim Harris
1862-1949

Bert F. Wadding
Jan 30, 1880
Sep 14, 1917

Jane E. Wadding
Nov 21, 1847
Dec 11, 1915

John W. Wadding
Sep 16, 1847
Sep 24, 1925

Emma Miles Mason
Mar 8, 1872
Jun 1, 1903

John Ernest Mason
Jul 27, 1895
Dec 7, 1935

Henry Clay Cothren
Dec 23, 1875
Apr 28, 1937
&
Beulah Turner Cothren
Apr 27, 1885
Mar 21, 1963

Mrs. W. R. Cothren
Jul 22, 1840
Mar 2, 1907

Silas L. McBride
Oct 10, 1872
Jan 31, 1969

Ovie S. McBride
Jan 13, 1871
Aug 25, 1940

T. J. Mooneyham
Mar 21, 1842
Jun 16, 1927

Moses C. Towry
Jan 25, 1853
Aug 26, 1940
&
Adelia Towry
Jul 22, 1868
Oct 14, 1923

Thomas M. Jean
1862-1943
&
Orpha R. Jean
1867-1941

Wayman A. Gooch
1875-1929
&
Almeda S. Gooch
1878-1960

Carrie Lee, wife of
W. L. Foster
May 23, 1882
Mar 22, 1907

George W. Mason
Jun 16, 1876
May 26, 1954
&
Ella Bea Mason
Dec 19, 1880
Feb 15, 1954

R. L. McCrory
1868-1955
&
Mora McCrory
1870-1928

W. Paul Collins
1845-1904
&
Hannah G. Collins
1855-1941

Andrew J. Patterson
Oct 28, 1844
Jun 6, 1925
&
Annie E. Griffin Patterson
Dec 25, 1846
Apr 18, 1918
Married Dec 1, 1864 by
John A. Moore, Esq.

LINCOLN QUADRANGLE

Benjamin A. Butler
Jun 23, 1814
Oct 31, 1896
Age: 82y, 4m.
&
Elizabeth Butler
May 11, 1820
Dec 15, 1896
Age: 76y, 7m, 15d.

Capt. Charles D. Dennis
Sep 17, 1829
Sep 12, 1906
Age: 76y, 11m, 25d.
Co E 72 Ohio Inf.

Several unmarked graves.

Richard H. Parm
Oct 30, 1854
May 15, 1916
& wife
Tommie A. Parm
Aug 13, 1868
Dec 1, 1917

W. Joe Parm
Dec 11, 1853
Dec 26, 1935

James I. Mason
1871-1933
&
Docia S. Mason
1883-1952

Sgt G. W. D. Porter
C.S.A.
Co B 44 Tenn Reg.
Aug 29, 1839
Jun 4, 1922
& wife
Mattie R. Porter
Sep 27, 1847
Apr 13, 1931

Henry A. Bobo
1871-1935
&
Edna I. Bobo
1872-1937

Henry Echols *
Died Jul 9, 1914
Age: 35 years.

Albert R. Bland
Feb 11, 1883
Dec 29, 1909
& wife
Minnie L. Smith Bland
Jun 5, 1886
Jun 24, 1915

Carl T. Bland
Jan 21, 1889
Feb 26, 1911

Polina Cole Bland
Dec 9, 1859
Jan 29, 1942

****

FLYNT CEMETERY

LOCATION: Immediately north of Alabama State Line on the east side of Lincoln-Hazelgreen Road.

Mary Davis
Jun 11, 1780
Jan 8, 1869
Age: 88y, 7m, 27d.

Several unmarked graves.

J. C. Flynt
Mar 17, 1802
Jul 19, 1838

M. C. Flynt
Dec 24, 1838
Apr 4, 1839

Mary E. Moore
Feb 22, 1831
Aug 6, 1854

Henrietta Moore
Jul 10, 1844
Dec 23, 1857

****

DAVIS CEMETERY

LOCATION: One half mile SSW of Lincoln on "Old Strang Place."

3 or 4 graves,
no markers remain.

(John Davis buried here,
Died about 1825, marker gone.
He settled here in 1822)

NOTE: Compiler remembers graves here in 1920's.

****

TRAVIS CEMETERY

LOCATION: On hill side above Cottrell Spring Branch and three-fourth mile down stream from Old Rozell's Mill.

Patton Travis
Died Aug 20, 1828
Age: 13y, 11m.

ED NOTE: This lone grave was located in 1921 by Richard A. and Blanche Marsh and 50 years later, they led the compiler back to copy the marker which is now captured in the trunk of an old cedar tree.

****

PRYOR CEMETERY

LOCATION: At Lincoln, on south side of old Goshen Road.

William Pryor &
Aug 9, 1796
Jan 14, 1864
&
Jane C. Pryor
Jan 3, 1813
Dec 22, 1882

Jennie Pryor
May 20, 1842
Jan 10, 1900
&
Mattie G. Pryor
Nov 30, 1847
Jan 17, 1913

Thomas M. Harton
Mar 1, 1834
Apr 3, 1909

Ann Harton
Aug 15, 1839
Aug 1, 1928

Flora G., Daughter of
J. B. Love
Died Oct 30, 1887
Age: 1y, 8m.

(John Pryor, early settler, said to be buried here in 1841.)

NOTE: John Pryor owned several hundred acres here in 1820. It included the Village of Lincoln.

****

LINCOLN QUADRANGLE

LINCOLN CEMETERY

LOCATION: At Lincoln, at the A. R. Presbyterian Church.

Daniel Ray Price
Dec 1, 1959
Feb 9, 1960

Janice Elaine Price
B&D May 22, 1962

Bobby Gene McKin
B&D Aug 22, 1959

John Thomas Buck
Alabama
BM3 U. S. Navy
Oct 9, 1930
Feb 2, 1958

Ed C. Shelton
1894-1964
&
Nora May Shelton
1895-1958

Billy Wayne Stewman (Pete)
Aug 29, 1941
Feb 8, 1959
(picture)

Johnny Mac Stewman
Nov 9, 1946
Nov 21, 1946

J. D. Stewman
1918-
&
Pauline Stewman
1920-1960

Robert A. Daniel
Jun 2, 1912
May 23, 1965
&
Margaret Daniel
Dec 17, 1912

Shelby L. Daniel
1888-1963
&
Lora S. Daniel
1890-1966

Teresa Ann Shelton
Apr 30, 1961
Jul 23, 1961

Cheryl Ann Key
Nov 26, 1959
Jun 30, 1961

J. D. Tielking, Jr.
Oct 27, 1924
Oct 15, 1962

Mrs. Betty Henderson Fuller
Died Nov 30, 1969
Age: 87y, 4m, 4d.
(Higgins FH)

John L. Holder
Dec 8, 1894
Apr 3, 1969
&
Susie M. Holder
Apr 7, 1897

Dillard Anthony Bates
Died Aug 3, 1969
Age: 52y, 9m, 13d.
(Higgins FH)

Paul W. Walker
Sep 18, 1969 (died)
Age: 29y, 11m, 25d.
(TM)

Henry Clay Taylor
Died May 26, 1970
Age: 75 years.
(Ralston FH)

Willie R. Spray
Aug 14, 1892
Feb 26, 1965
&
Mary J. Spray
Dec 23, 1893
Mar 21, 1968

Herman Brumitt
1911-1963

Elzina Walker Pruitt
Aug 18, 1881
Sep 11, 1968 (picture)

Annie Laura Perry
Died May 7, 1970
Age: 62 years.
(Laughlin FH, Huntsville, Alabama)

Buford Wade Eley
Tennessee
A1C U. S. Air Force Korea
Jul 22, 1931
Jun 14, 1958

Jack Hopkins
1909-1957
&
Flavia Hopkins
1910-19

Billy Gayle Hopkins
Died Nov 19, 1969
Age: 38y, 13d.
(Higgins FH)

Chester H. Pruitt, Jr.
B&D Sep 21, 1968

Theo Pruitt
Jun 25, 1899
Sep 3, 1960
&
Neva Pruitt
Jun 18, 1904

H. Clyde Shelton
1921-1951
&
Irene W. Shelton
1919-

Cleveland W. Spray
Aug 6, 1914
Nov 7, 1969
&
Gracie Lee Spray
Mar 17, 1920
Jul 9, 1957

James Clarence May
Jan 9, 1904

&
Mary Edna Owen May
Oct 17, 1906
Sep 8, 1969

Claude Warden
1883-1951
&
Anna Warden
1891-19

W. S. Warren
1872-1950
(Wilson FH)

Richard Hugh Warren
1913-1962
(Gallant FH)

Jeffrey Beech
Apr 16, 1957
Oct 18, 1958
(picture)

Infant Daughter of
Mr. & Mrs. Ernest Moore, Jr.
B&D Dec 28, 1953

Daughter of
Mr. & Mrs. Ernest Moore, Jr.
B&D Oct 18, 1957

Shirley Ruth Metcalf
Feb 17, 1947
Jul 18, 1957

Shields Rutledge
Apr 21, 1921
Mar 17, 1965

Bruce Luttrell
Oct 13, 1907
Mar 12, 1966
&
Annie Mae Luttrell
Nov 15, 1908

Roy Calvin May
Dec 6, 1909
Jan 19, 1961
&
Oma Lee Shelton May

H. A. Dempsey
1884-(no date)
&
Mrs. H. A. Dempsey
1903-1952

Wiley W. Bunn
1904-1947

Martha Elizabeth Pearson
Jul 2, 1867
Jun 28, 1958

G. O. Cothren
1870-1941

Phoebe Cothren
1934

E. Earl Quick
Jul 19, 1926
Apr 12, 1965
&
Marie King Quick
Jun 26, 1935

William Gordon Counts
Husband of
Edna Holder
Aug 24, 1924
May 28, 1952
Alabama
Pfc 1152 A. A. F. Base
Unit   WW II

Jessie T. Counts
Feb 15, 1895
Jul 3, 1963

Infant Daughters of
Jerry & Sue Hunter
B&D May 9, 1964

Joe B. Quick
Sep 26, 1901
Feb 14, 1967
&
Aline G. Quick
Sep 26, 1907

LINCOLN QUADRANGLE

John R. Shelton
Feb 25, 1889

&
Allie H. Shelton
Feb 14, 1896
Dec 16, 1962

Lynden H. Shelton
Jun 12, 1917

&
Larah D. Shelton
Nov 17, 1921
Oct 13, 1966

Lynette, Daughter of
Lynden & Larah Shelton
B&D Oct 29, 1951

Nolen Stafford
Dec 1, 1903

&
Agnes Stafford
May 11, 1903
Nov 1, 1964
Married Mar 28, 1925

Oval Howard
May 3, 1892
Feb 16, 1964
&
Connie Dee Howard
Aug 19, 1899

Richard Cothren
1898-1925

Addie Frame
Mar 22, 1893
Apr 4, 1918

Thomas Suggs
1929-1935

Harold E., Son of
J. C. & E. C. Suggs
Mar 17, 1933
Jun 3, 1934

Tillmon Bates
Aug 24, 1877
Nov 28, 1948
&
Martha Bates
Nov 11, 1887
Jun 21, 1936

John A. Bates
B&D Mar 1919

John Houston Shelton
Oct 22, 1897
Mar 2, 1923

John Blanton Shelton
1877-1964
&
Ora Hester Shelton
1882-

Mary Bafford
1879-1948

G. H. "Bob" Mires
1869-1942

Maggie Mires
1855-1931

James W. Mires
1870-1945

Leslie R. Holman
1902-1962
&
Rose W. Holman
Died Mar 28, 1967
Age: (not given)

Charlie Pruitt
Dec 26, 1919

&
Odell Pruitt
Oct 18, 1920
Dec 14, 1962

Trent Clay Towry
Jun 5, 1967
Jun 6, 1967

John Henry Hyatt
Feb 23, 1867
Jan 10, 1966

William L. Sherwood
1906-1966
&
Nellie S. Sherwood
1909-

Earnest D. Stewart
Oct 9, 1904
Jul 9, 1968

Elizabeth Williams
Jul 9, 1871
Jul 2, 1935

Edgar Williams
Jan 19, 1860
Feb 20, 1928

Ezekiel Williams
1832-Dec 9, 1898

Our Babe (no last name)
1877

William T. McCrory
1895-1946
&
Hattie M. McCrory
1889-

Mack Mansfield
1926
&
Ellis Mansfield
1915
Sons of Zach & Eula
Mansfield.

John (M.) Simpson
Born in Butler Co., Ohio
Sep 4, 1812
Nov 3, 1884
&
Martha Simpson
Born in Preble Co., Ohio
Jun 17, 1823
Aug 18, 1874
& Daughter
Margaret A. Simpson
Born in Preble Co., Ohio
Nov 14, 1846
Apr 17, 1873

Madge Howell Holt
Sep 1, 1915
Apr 5, 1959

Janice Diane, Daughter of
Charles & Janice Delap
Oct 27, 1955
Jul 19, 1957

J. Robert Stewart
Sep 7, 1872
Dec 1, 1965
&
Eula M. Stewart
Jan 8, 1883
(no date)

J. C. Stewart
Alabama
BKR 1 U. S. Navy WW II
Jul 24, 1919
Sep 2, 1951

William Harvey Graves
Tennessee
Pfc Army Air Force WW II
Feb 26, 1923
Mar 26, 1965
&
Frances B. Graves
Jan 24, 1924

Hoyte E. Sims
Sep 4, 1901
Aug 4, 1965
&
Nola L. Sims
Feb 3, 1907

James Harvey Hollis
Died May 12, 1969
Age: 34y, 6m, 11d.
(Higgins FH)

Hollis
(no dates, Gallant FH)

Hollis
(no dates, Gallant FH)

James F. Hopkins
1900-1958
&
Lila Hopkins
1898-

Theo Trenthram
Jun 8, 1905
Oct 21, 1966
&
Inez Pitts Trenthram
Oct 11, 1911

Ray E. Stevenson
Jun 12, 1926

&
Mattie M. Stevenson
Nov 8, 1924
Nov 7, 1964

J. Richard Sanders
1898-1966
&
Thelma B. Sanders
1902-

James Ramer Davis
Jan 23, 1898
Mar 15, 1970
&
Mattie S. Davis
Jan 15, 1902

Lonnie A. Burrows
1918-
&
Retha D. Burrows
1922-

James Hazel Whitaker
May 12, 1902

&
Allie Leona Whitaker
May 23, 1904
Dec 2, 1956

James R. Burrows
1921-1965
&
Frances L. Burrows
1926-

Larry A. Burrows
1880-1962
&
Mollie T. Burrows
1885-(no date)

Hampton Edward Burrows
1916-1922

Infant Daughter of
L. A. & M. N. Burrows
B&D Jul 25, 1914

M. L. Cannan
Dec 11, 1845
Jul 1, 1922

Martha I. Cannan
Nov 30, 1843
Nov 25, 1921

LINCOLN QUADRANGLE

Doshise Alice Cannon
Dec 3, 1899
Sep 19, 1936

Jennie Lue Cannon
Feb 11, 1836
Jan 17, 1929

Mrs. H. F. Cannon
1879-1936

Jerry M. Cannon
1853-1918
&
Donnie C. Cannon
1877-1961

Mike Cannon
Jul 8, 1897
Jul 13, 1954
&
Nora Mathis Cannon
Sep 7, 1896
Nov 1, 1963

Clara C. Clark
1895-1942

Willie C. Cowan
1872-1957
&
Ada T. Cowan
1875-1942

Ralph Nelson, Son of
Aron & Frances McKin
Apr 6, 1955
May 29, 1956

Philip Michael Brown
Mar 2, 1956
Aug 11, 1956

Dock P. Green
May 9, 1887
Dec 26, 1952
&
Alma Delong Green
Jun 1, 1899

F. Herbert Tucker
Aug 21, 1879
Dec 16, 1930
&
Lillie Jane Towry Tucker
Mar 3, 1883
Oct 10, 1962

Nuton G., Infant of
E. L. & Ella Bates
Oct 14, 1908
Feb 1, 1909

Ella Tucker, wife of
E. L. Bates
Sep 3, 1884
Mar 2, 1909

Holman H. Marshall
Jan 19, 1881
Jul 15, 1914

Hugh G., Son of
W. T. & N. E. Marshall
Sep 21, 1901
May 18, 1913

Elzina Marshall
Jul 6, 1893
Aug 10, 1912

Mary E. Marshall
May 7, 1885
May 25, 1900

Lucy C., wife of
W. T. Marshall
Dec 12, 1861
Oct 7, 1897

Robert A. Mansfield
Oct 12, 1830
Mar 17, 1951

Margret E., wife of
W. T. Cummins
Sep 12, 1832
Oct 18, 1896

Patrick R. Baker
Nov 15, 1871
Oct 13, 1932

Dora L. Baker
Mar 7, 1875
Sep 23, 1946

Altie Baker
Oct 9, 1907
Mar 8, 1929

M. E. Rush
Nov 23, 1868
Jul 5, 1917
&
A. C. Rush
Died Dec 31, 1908
Age: (not given)

Zach Mansfield
1849-1895
&
Julia Mansfield
1855-1924
&
Miss Jennie Porter
1851-1922

J. P. Rutledge
1890-1934

Lizzie Rutledge
1882-19

Robert McCrory
Jun 2, 1921
Jan 14, 1923

James E. English
Dec 5, 1808
Aug 9, 1886

Julia E. Ingle, wife of
John R. Smith
Oct 28, 1851
Dec 15, 1888

Joey, Son of
J. M. & Anna Quick
Dec 19, 1886
Aug 16, 1887

Anna Montgomery, wife of
John M. Quick
1865-1934

Joseph E., Son of
R. M. & M. E. Welsh
Died Feb 11, 1879
Age: 2 years.

Bernard Desso Welsh
Nov 9, 1861
Sep 15, 1887
&
Martha McDill Welsh
Feb 22, 1866
Aug 26, 1918

Ruth H. Rush
Dec 15, 1926
Dec 21, 1926

James M. Rush
Sep 27, 1927
Feb 17, 1928

Malcolm L. Rush
Mar 3, 1946
Mar 22, 1946

James W. Rush
Mar 4, 1896
Jul 6, 1961
&
Ruth T. Rush
Aug 6, 1903

Otis S. Damron
May 15, 1878
Aug 21, 1926

Amma Damron
Nov 4, 1884
Nov 3, 1969

M. F. Gautney
1853-1930

Fronie, wife of
M. F. Gautney
Jun 7, 1858
Feb 3, 1923

Ann M. Henderson
1886-1950
(Raby FH)

Charles Gautney
May 30, 1904
Nov 25, 1957
&
Sallie D. Gautney
Jul 17, 1907
May 20, 1966

Infant of
C. L. & Dee Gautney
B&D Dec 25, 1926

Beatrice Tucker
1909-1934

Walter Tucker
1906-1939(Higgins FH)

Zelma Tucker
1926-1945

Claudie Lee Tucker
Died Jul 1, 1947
Age: 67 years

Mrs. Eli M. Henderson
1879-1944

Bert Mansfield
Tennessee
Cpl Btry E 54 Arty CAC
WW I
Jul 18, 1885
Nov 4, 1965
&
Hattie Dickey Mansfield
Jan 25, 1897

Iva Mae Sanders
1871-1956
(Gallant FH)

Joe Cleveland Sanders
Died Jan 14, 1969
Age: 79 years.
(Gallant FH)

Mrs. Mae Sanders
Died May 17, 1969
Age: 73 years
(Gallant FH)

Laura Bunn
1901-1940

John Metcalf
1939-1942

Leonard Metcalf
1939-1942

Sarah Towry
1874-1942

John Maxey Wicks
1886-1944
&
Pearl Tucker Wicks
1887-1963

LINCOLN QUADRANGLE

James M. Hirlston
Sep 4, 1909
Apr 10, 1963
&
Ella Lee Hirlston
Sep 8, 1908

James E. Taylor
Apr 17, 1875
(no date)
&
Aquilla E. Taylor
Sep 1, 1873
Oct 10, 1962

Homer Wilson Spray, Jr.
1943-1944

John Amos McGee
Dec 3, 1874
Mar 18, 1944
&
Georgia Tucker McGee
Dec 17, 1878
Aug 24, 1955

Billie Reece, Son of
Reece & Villa Durham
Dec 13, 1939
Jan 11, 1946

Ernest Lee Newman
Jan 14, 1884
Feb 3, 1969
&
Mary Margaret Davidson
Newman
Apr 2, 1897
Jan 26, 1968

Zach T. Mansfield
Nov 24, 1891
Oct 29, 1956
&
Eula McCrory Mansfield
Aug 28, 1893
Jul 5, 1955

Garland Dee Towry, Husband
of Louise Castleman
Nov 1, 1908
Nov 2, 1953 (picture)

Carl Delap
Died 1970

Garland Dee Towry, Jr.
Jul 6, 1934
Dec 14, 1958
(picture)

L. V. Crabtree
1894-1955
(Gallant FH)

Annette May
Aug 27, 1951
Apr 16, 1953
(Higgins FH)

Charlie L. Crabtree
1909-1942

Garland F. Henderson
1890-1964
&
Mamie S. Henderson
1899-1969

Wiley Holbert Henderson
Mar 3, 1879
Jun 23, 1955

Nannie Moorehead, wife of
W. H. Henderson
Jul 1, 1886
Sep 10, 1950

William Jasper Noblitt
Sep 1, 1880
Nov 10, 1950
&
Maggie Lou Cowley Noblitt
Sep 29, 1880

Arthur Price
Feb 4, 1890
Apr 5, 1967

Dollie Price
Jun 18, 1905
Jun 18, 1967

James Arthur Price, Jr.
Feb 2, 1927
Jun 27, 1943

Glendon Alvin Cothren, Jr.
B&D Aug 7, 1943

Nellie Jane Cothren
B&D May 16, 1942

Sidney Johnson King, Sr.
Jul 30, 1879
Feb 12, 1965
&
Necie Elizabeth King
Feb 25, 1885
(no date)

Lt. J. W. King
U. S. N. R.
Oct 25, 1915
Jul 9, 1943

Martine M. Simms
May 1, 1922
Nov 20, 1979

John Beasley Marsh
Tennessee
CM2 U. S. N. R. WW II
Sep 1, 1911
Sep 13, 1967

Richard A. Marsh
1899-1980
&
Blanche M. Marsh
1901- 1992

Michael Goodrum Marsh
Mar 17, 1871
Oct 11, 1962
&
Lelia Beasley Marsh
Apr 28, 1876
Sep 17, 1939

Nathan Boon Cashion
Mar 14, 1874
Oct 12, 1940
&
Lucy Cashion
May 28, 1878

Nathan A. Simms
1831-1945
&
Minnie L. Simms
1884-1967

Mrs. Rossie Lee Stevenson
Died May 22, 1970
Age: 75 years.

Russell W. Shelton
Mar 2, 1884
Sep 8, 1962
&
Nora Lee Shelton
Oct 15, 1892

Andrew, Infant Son of
Will & Nora Shelton
Dec 20, 1916
Jan 6, 1918

Henry Brown
1866-1944

James Hunter
1930-1930
(Raby FH)

Arthur Ewin Hunter
Feb 24, 1885
Feb 6, 1961
&
Annie Mae Turner Hunter
Sep 3, 1888
Jan 31, 1950

Harvey C. Simms
Sep 7, 1892
May 5, 1867
&
Oma C. Simms
Jun 29, 1893

Gemella Simms
Aug 31, 1885
Dec 19, 1958

Mary Jane Hunter
Nov 16, 1851
Jan 24, 1923

J. H. Crabtree
Jul 11, 1844
Mar 16, 1918

Mrs. R.(Roena) E. Crabtree
Sep 25, 1858
Aug 28, 1937

Sam Wolaver
(no dates)

Lula H. Wolaver
(no dates)

Maud Cashion
Apr 20, 1898
Dec 20, 1901

Grace Cashion Dickey
1896-1939

Sarah E., wife of
J. E. Harbin
Nov 17, 1858
Nov 29, 1916

Jim E. Harbin
1852-1930
&
P. Com. Williamson
1874-1930

James Damron
Dec 11, 1844
Oct 9, 1914
&
Celia Damron
May 25, 1846
Dec 3, 1905

James H. Pruitt
May 1903-Aug 1951

Aaron Pruitt
May 23, 1912
Aug 23, 1896

Lillian Pruitt
Jan 21, 1919
Mar 10, 1920

Mary E. Welsh
Mar 29, 1840
Jul 19, 1920
"Teacher, Missionary &
Writer."

N. Margaret Welsh
1850-Sep 14, 1899
Daughter of
R. & N. Welsh.

Robert Welsh
Died Feb 1, 1891
Age: 81 years.
&
Nancy V. Welsh
Died Mar 10, 1894
Age: 82 years.

LINCOLN QUADRANGLE

Lillian, Daughter of
J. T. & Ella Simms
Dec 19, 1892
Jan 11, 1893

J. Thomas Simms
Mar 18, 1869
Jul 27, 1941
&
Ella M. Simms
Dec 26, 1861
May 29, 1951

G. W. Higgins Simms
Sep 22, 1866
Aug 17, 1946
&
Kate McCown Simms
Sep 23, 1873
Apr 1, 1952

H. H. McCown
Children
(no dates)

Tabitha J., wife of
William H. Bell
Died Nov 4, 1892
Age: 51y, 5m.

George Wilson Koonce
Apr 13, 1919
Nov 13, 1936

Frederick Tielking
Oct 16, 1861
Mar 22, 1935

Hellena Tielking
1872-1941

Mrs. Elizabeth E. Woodard
Sep 22, 1822
Jul 4, 1895

William A. Graves
Nov 21, 1871
Feb 20, 1929
&
Sarah Almeda Graves
Oct 6, 1876
Jul 24, 1948

Daniel O. Tucker
Feb 21, 1863
Oct 17, 1918

Elzie Pirtle
Aug 27, 1916
Apr 6, 1956
&
Thelma Pirtle
Feb 28, 1919

Earnest A. Mitcalf
May 24, 1898
Dec 14, 1951

Will R. Patrick
Apr 16, 1900
Oct 2, 1943

Mary Jane Patrick
Feb 4, 1870
Apr 3, 1955

Edgar L. Quick
1924-1954
&
Nellie R. Quick
1934

Mary Heath
1868-1952
(R. H. Beasley FH)

G. W. L. Heath
Mar 12, 1829
Nov 28, 1907
& wife
A. V. Hise Heath
Feb 21, 1834
Apr 16, 1924
Married Jan 26, 1851

Katie Heath, wife of
James Taylor
Nov 25, 1857
Mar 6, 1900

C. D. Laughlin
Sep 24, 1855
Nov 27, 1910
&
Martha Heath Laughlin
Aug 16, 1864
(no date)

Baby Laughlin
Feb 17, 1899
Feb 24, 1899

Virginia Laughlin
May 31, 1892
Sep 16, 1897

Abner B. Sullivan
Oct 19, 1866
Feb 7, 1946
&
Pallie H. Sullivan
Jun 8, 1873
Feb 24, 1937

Earl Simms
(no dates)

S. Tom Collins
1877-1961
&
Nettie Collins
1878-1966

Paul Collins
1925

Marlin Collins
1923-1925

Infant Daughter Collins
(no dates)

Janette Collins
(no dates)

S. T. Collins, Jr.
(no dates)

Malessa Henderson
Died Oct 30, 1928
Age: 80 years.

Wonneda, Daughter of
A. J. & Pearl Cobble
Mar 10, 1910
Oct 2, 1913

Roy E. Cobble
1903-1956

A. J. Cobble
1881-1932
&
Pearl H. Cobble
1886-1964

(Judge) Arthur E. Simms
1893-1961
&
Maude M. Simms
1891-1965

Infant Son of
W. O. & Ora Largen
B&D May 17, 1913

M. J. Simms
Nov 5, 1862
Dec 23, 1917

Donia Simms
1856-1940

Infant Daughter of
S. & Minnie Mitchell
B&D Nov 13, 1907

Steve Mitchell
Feb 28, 1874
Nov 3, 1923

Minnie B. Mitchell
Oct 29, 1887
Mar 5, 1936

Solomon Mitchell
Jan 20, 1841
Dec 6, 1911

Brother
Estell Stevenson
Dec 27, 1910
Jan 27, 1913
&
Sister
Nellie Stevenson
Feb 6, 1917
Oct 13, 1924

Estill Lee Stevenson
Dec 27, 1909
Jan 27, 1912

Rev. Curtis Stevenson
1889-1946
&
Viola M. Stevenson
1889-19

Marvin Wayne Hill
Oct 13, 1951
Apr 1, 1952

Rilda Birdie Hoots
Apr 9, 1898
Nov 24, 1921

Lawrence Ray Jones
Aug 18, 1947
Nov 7, 1956

Bessie Keith
1901-1959

Charles Reece Howell
Dec 2, 1881
Jul 27, 1958
&
Maud Simms Howell
Jun 23, 1889
Jan 20, 1947

Nellie L., Daughter of
C. R. & Maude Howell
Apr 1, 1917
Jul 21, 1918

Ercell W., Son of
C. R. & Maude Howell
Apr 3, 1920
Apr 28, 1924

Infant Daughter of
C. R. & Maud Howell
B&D Aug 12, 1928

Infant Son of
C. R. & Maud Howell
B&D Jul 31, 1929

Arch C. McCown
1871-1941

Mary E. McCown
1871-1916

Baby Son of
A. C. & Lizzie McCown
B&D May 12, 1904

Myrtle Dickey
1903-1930

Vera L. Dickey
Dec 24, 1907
Dec 25, 1908
&
Laura E. Dickey
Sep 24, 1906
Oct 12, 1906
Daus of Dr.& Ettie Dickey

Dr. Edward Walter Dickey
1870-1950

Ettie McCown Dickey
1870-1957

Maurice Kendle Dickey
Sep 8, 1902
Nov 15, 1963

William P. Green
Jul 8, 1845
Nov 2, 1913

Eliza Green
Oct   1849
Apr 5, 1917

Grace Cashion Dickey
1896-1939

Archie Lewis Cashion
Aug 26, 1933
Feb 4, 1934

Clarence Cashion
Apr 10, 1901
Apr 20, 1959
&
Annie Cashion
Dec 11, 1904
Oct 16, 1943

J. L. & Loulous Gillham
(Babies)
(no dates)

James Robert May
Nov 20, 1877
Sep 2, 1925
&
Daisy Dean Woods May
Oct 8, 1883
Sep 27, 1947

Ben May
Died Mar 28, 1913
Age: 92 years.

Jane Graham, wife of
Ben May
Dec   1841
Jan 30, 1919

William D. Tucker
Oct 1, 1849
Nov 12, 1920
&
Maria Josephine Felps Tucker
Apr 8, 1858
Nov 29, 1916

Ben Butler Tucker
Sep 30, 1883
Sep 17, 1967

Mary Josephine Stewart
Nov 14, 1923
May 1, 1924

Leabert H. Price
Jan 23, 1915
Nov 8, 1936

Catharine Price
Jan 22, 1920
May 10, 1924

William Thomas Price
Nov 1, 1893
Oct 20, 1921

James W. Price
Alabama
Pft 167 Inf 42 Div
Died Aug 7, 1919
(no age given)

William Milton May
Dec 11, 1875
May 6, 1936
&
Maggie Winsett May
Jul 17, 1886
Jul 14, 1944

Edna Lois May
Jan 17, 1947
Mar 19, 1947

Frank May
Jul 23, 1906
Jul 9, 1951
&
Gladys May
Apr 12, 1913

Finis Ewin Damron
Jun 20, 1881
Jan 1, 1942
&
Susie Eunice Damron
Sep 3, 1886
Dec 16, 1936

Diane McCrory
1948-1948

Minnie E. Bates
1887-1947

W. S. Endsley
1868-1944
&
Ella E. Endsley
1874-1942

Lula Frame Hazelwood
Aug 23, 1895
Apr 22, 1969

Infant Daughter of
Mr. & Mrs. Ernest Pamplin
B&D Mar 7, 1941

James Homer George
Mar 2, 1893
Nov 30, 1948
&
Annie Hazelwood George
Sep 5, 1902

William Robert Simms
1905-1937

David S. Simms
1878-1959
&
Bertha R. Simms
1882-1960

Lora Lee, Daughter of
Mr. & Mrs. J. M. May
Jun 9, 1928
Apr 6, 1941

Mack Key
1893-1963
&
Nellie Key
1903-

Earl L. Frame
Jun 20, 1910
May 27, 1965
&
Anna Lee Frame
Nov 15, 1910

Erie L. Stevenson
1895-1962
&
Robbie L. Stevenson
1894-

Nancy Margaret George
Mar 10, 1941
Mar 11, 1941

Novella George
Sep 2, 1905
Dec 31, 1951

Richard W. George
Sep 20, 1895
Jun 24, 1962
&
Dessie Cowan George
Jul 6, 1885
(no date)

Robert Walter Shelton
Dec 18, 1913
Jul 21, 1960
&
Lila Tucker Shelton

Charlie B. Tucker
1895-1944

Kenny, Son of
L. D. & Lela Tucker
Aug 30, 1950
Aug 31, 1950

L. D. Tucker
Aug 28, 1924

&
Lela M. Tucker
Oct 5, 1925
Dec 22, 1967
Married Dec 23, 1945

Emmett Towry
1906-1954
&
Elizabeth Towry
1910-

Angelia Pride (Price)
Died May 25, 1970
Age: (not given)
(Gallant FH)

John Quick
Feb 18, 1899

&
Annie May Quick
Jan 20, 1899

Ballard B. Barnett
Nov 30, 1913
Nov 16, 1957
&
Jane Barnett
Jun 22, 1911

J. Almer Shelton
Mar 24, 1895
Mar 31, 1967
&
Bertha Z. Shelton
Jul 15, 1900

Lonnie L. McPherson
1904-1942
&
Betty B. McPherson
1908-

Walter W. Bunn
1902-1968
(London FH)

Newt McPherson
1871-1954
(Gallant FH)

Lizzie McPherson
Mar 22, 1892
Jul 25, 1940

Jessie Wright
1937-1940

LINCOLN QUADRANGLE

May B. Henderson
1920-1941

Gordon W. Wolaver
Died Jun 14, 1974
Age: 75 years.

Thelma Hudson Wolaver
Oct 14, 1905
Oct 11, 1966

Louise Wolaver Tully
Jun 25, 1926
Nov 7, 1964

David Lewis Howell
Mar 6, 1955
Mar 10, 1955

Robbie Gray
Mar 9, 1939
Mar 20, 1939

Bud Tucker
1882-1935

Ross Tucker
Jan 4, 1906
Oct 2, 1966
&
Dee Tucker
Sep 16, 1910
Dec 30, 1969
Married Nov 1, 1924

Reba Joy Tucker
Jul 10, 1932
May 13, 1934

James W. Shelton
Mar 20, 1892
Oct 3, 1966
&
Ethel Mae Shelton
Sep 27, 1898
Jun 12, 1958

Aubrey E. Shelton
Jul 2, 1896
Dec 30, 1930
&
Lillian J. Sullivan Shelton
May 6, 1903
(no date)

Levoy Shelton
1925-1937

Oscar L. Tielking
Sep 18, 1906
Sep 16, 1949

Lula Moorehead
1912-1927

Wilborn F. Tucker
Mar 4, 1852
Mar 2, 1926

John Buran Tucker
Tennessee
Pvt U. S. Army WW I
Jun 14, 1889
Sep 17, 1963

J. Herbert McCown
Aug 23, 1879
Dec 14, 1943

Ethel Glass McCown
Apr 28, 1886
Feb 4, 1959

Miss Beulah Howell
Died Feb 1969
Age: 81y, 2m, 2d.
(Higgins
&
Virginia Howell

F. M. Howell
Dec 3, 1848
Sep 16, 1925
&
Rebecca Howell
Aug 28, 1852
Mar 19, 1940

Rossie
(no dates, fieldstone)

E. R. Kennaird
May 16, 1870
Jan 6, 1936

Laura A. Kennaird
Oct 4, 1868
Sep 1, 1945

J. P. McCown
Dec 25, 1830
Nov 25, 1902

Jane A. McCown
Mar 22, 1840
Jan 23, 1914

W. S. McCown, M.D.
Mar 22, 1870
Jun 18, 1923

Rossie Ina McCown
Oct 7, 1869
Nov 29, 1956

Walter Steele McCown
Apr 8, 1928
Oct 21, 1941

J. R. McCown
Aug 12, 1835
Mar 7, 1909
& wife
Keziah McCown
Feb 14, 1836
May 5, 1914

McCown Woods Simms
Mar 19, 1896
Apr 17, 1963
Age: 72y, 28d.

W. G. McCown, M.D.
May 7, 1901
May 6, 1961

Willard E. Metcalf
Aug 1, 1871
Jan 14, 1953
&
Mary A. Metcalf
May 23, 1874
Feb 28, 1928

Jessie Mae Metcalf
Sep 28, 1911
Mar 7, 1917

John Loyd Metcalf
May 29, 1916
Nov 11, 1918

Robbie Metcalf
1938-1938

Elizabeth Christine, Daughter
of W. V. & N. M. Metcalf
Aug 2, 1927
Jul 4, 1931

Willard Franklin Tucker
Feb 13, 1930
Mar 21, 1956

Ruby B. Young
Jul 30, 1899
Oct 8, 1948

Eula Mae Young
Apr 8, 1915
Apr 30, 1917

Bettie G. Young
B&D Jul 7, 1932

Aron N. McKin
1875-1952
&
Bessie Ledford McKin
1899-

Infants of
Laurence & Glennis Kerbo
B&D Oct 3, 1952

W. S. J. Clayton
Apr 8, 1863
Mar 10, 1930
&
Fannie Clayton
Oct 16, 1873
(no date)

Lebert L. Clayton
Co B 2 Tenn. Inf.
N.G.

Frank H. Towry
1893-(no date)
&
Lucy A. Towry
1884-1964

L. D. Towry
(no dates)

Henry Bee Pickett
1871-1951
&
Lou Essie Pickett
1890-1919

George Washington Pickett
Jan 2, 1843
Jul 23, 1933
&
Nancy Walker Pickett
May 8, 1847
Aug 4, 1927

Mary Jane Pickett
Mar 8, 1844
Oct 7, 1928

William G. "Will" Pickett
Dec 8, 1885
Nov 29, 1963
&
Lela Smith Pickett
Sep 14, 1893

(pictures)

Robert Earl Hopkins
Sep 12, 1930
May 12, 1932

Cecil R. Roberts
Oct 23, 1911
May 2, 1949

Z. T. Wells
Dec 22, 1874
Feb 2, 1967
&
Margaret E. Wells
Jan 20, 1877
Mar 16, 1935
&
Robert Wells
Jan 31, 1900
Jan 25, 1920

T. B. Beavers
Sep 7, 1874
Aug 4, 1933
&
Maud White Beavers
Sep 21, 1875
Oct 22, 1969

Ruby Dee Shelton
Feb 21, 1921
Feb 18, 1930

LINCOLN QUADRANGLE

Edd W. McCown
Jun 2, 1880
Aug 29, 1913

Alda C., wife of
Edd W. McCown
Jul 31, 1888
Jan 13, 1910

Sam Shelton
Aug 29, 1898

&
Ethel Shelton
Nov 19, 1901
Feb 19, 1960

Itasca Dollar Simms
1904-1922

Frank M. Howell
1895-
&
Reva Burton Howell
1900-1952

Francis B. Howell
1938

H. Oaklus Henderson
Mar 5, 1882
Sep 5, 1951
&
Gertrude Q. Henderson
Jul 25, 1884

James R. Henderson
Dec 16, 1914
Mar 7, 1935

Shields Fenton Quick
1887-1952
&
Leva Esther Quick
1898-1946

Infant of
Fent & Neva Quick
(no dates)

Infant of
Febt & Neva Quick
(no dates)

Infant of
Fent & Neva Quick
(no dates)

Stephen L. Quick
Dec 28, 1846
Aug 5, 1926
&
Mary J. Quick
Nov 17, 1858
Nov 11, 1939

J. L. Gilliland *
Died in Blair, Okla.
Jun 13, 1916
 Age: (not given)

Elmer E. Quick
Feb 3, 1892
Feb 18, 1924

Laura Q. Mansfield
Feb 9, 1883
Nov 7, 1956

Bud Sanders
Apr 8, 1833
Aug 18, 1925

Martha Jane Sanders
Aug 9, 1850
Dec 10, 1923

Rufe Moorehead
May 7, 1861
Oct 2, 1927

Willa Ward Moorehead
Nov 5, 1868
Feb 17, 1926

Infant of
W. D. & V. L. Moorehead
Apr 5, 1939
Apr 16, 1939

R. M. Welsh
Jan 8, 1836
Mar 10, 1919
&
Mary E. Welsh
Apr 15, 1840
Feb 27, 1912

Minnie J. Kennedy
1875-1918

Rose Kennedy
1878-1933

Annie Laurie Kennedy, wife
of J. W. Vaughan
1919-1943

Josie Grissom
1871-1957

George Grissom
1900-1935

John L. Grissom
1859-1929

Charles Ross Kennedy
1901-1953
&
Ola Grissom Kennedy
1902-

Clarence D. Mitchell
1904-1945

H. E. Lane
1907-1952

Rufus Pruitt
1886-1953
&
Lula Pruitt
1891-1950

James Madison Shelton
Dec 16, 1930
Jul 3, 1938

Joe A. Shelton
Dec 16, 1906
Sep 1, 1967
&
Clara H. Shelton
Sep 21, 1911

Climmie E. Hambrick
Aug 31, 1914
Mar 31, 1964
&
Effie Bain Hambrick
Oct 1, 1915

Charles Rowland
1875-1948

John T. Bain
1886-1950
&
Julia M. Bain
1886-1949

Hannah Pirtle
1888-1948
(Raby FH)

Acie Monroe Bain
Dec 6, 1889
Mar 12, 1946
&
Myra Turner Bain
Jan 28, 1893

Ezekiel Mooneyham
Feb 22, 1881
Jan 22, 1957
&
Lillie J. Mooneyham
Dec 23, 1890

Richard H. Quick
1870-1935
&
Jennie Mae Quick
1871-1933

Richard L. Quick
Jul 3, 1911
Nov 21, 1968
&
Rossie L. Quick
Jan 10, 1910

William M. Wolaver
1874-1949
&
Purnie L. Wolaver
1881-1953

Jackie L. Mills
Dec 6, 1935
Jun 29, 1941

Fred Mills
Oct 5, 1907
Jun 30, 1936

Russell N. Mills
Pfc U. S. Army WW II
Jan 29, 1925
Jun 27, 1976

Fred Rogers Mills
Jun 24, 1932
Dec 31, 1932

Lillian Stafford
Sep 5, 1927
Feb 4, 1928

Lola Dale, wife of
J. N. McCown
1897-

John Nole McCown
1881-1966

Leila, wife of
J. N. McCown
1885-1916

James W. Cunningham
Tennessee
Pvt 327 Inf 82 Div
Oct 19, 1937

Maude Shelton
1900-1931

Etta George, wife of
J. F. Shelton
Aug 11, 1878
Jan 1, 1962

Jesse F. Shelton
May 31, 1873
Apr 19, 1958

Etta Oldham, wife of
J. F. Shelton
Oct 9, 1873
Nov 14, 1932

Mrs. Fianese,* widow of
Henry McCown
Died Nov 14, 1899
Age: about 59 years.

Mrs. Minnie,* wife of
Doug Fuller
Died Jun 7, 1899
Age: 22 years.

LINCOLN QUADRANGLE

Mrs. Mitt Sawyers *
Died Jun 24, 1916
Age: 24 years
Left a Father, Husband
& 4 children.

W. M. Worldly *
Died Apr 6, 1903
Age: 69 years.

Miss Callie May *
Died Jul 26, 1917
Age: 46y, 5m, 17d.
Left 3 Brothers & 3
Sisters and a Mother.

J. O. Damron *
Died Dec 29, 1898
Age: 24 years.

Beula,* Daughter of
James & Sadie Harbin
Died Apr 16, 1899
Age: 5y, 6m.

Mrs. Sallie,* wife of
William Worley
Died Mar 25, 1897
Age: 72 years.

Child * of
Mr. & Mrs. Henry Cole
Died Sep 8, 1909
Age: 13 months.

W. Y. Lackey *
Married Maggie Corder
Died Mar 27, 1903
Age: 69 years.

Thomas M. Horton *
Married Ann Pryor
Mar 21, 1869
Died at Fisk, Ala.
of accident
Apr 3, 1909
Age: 75 years.

Mrs. Ida,* wife of
Walter Damron
Died Sep 25, 1899
Age: 27 years.

Moores,* Son of
Hunter & Bessie McCown
Died Nov 14, 1893
Age: (not given)

Several unmarked graves.

Infant * of
Mr. & Mrs. J. R. May
Died Apr 26, 1914
Age: (not given)

Loretta,* Daughter of
Mr. & Mrs. Gabe Miles
Died Apr 29, 1903
Age: 3 months.

Mrs. Lizzie,* wife of
George Fowler
Died Jul 30, 1914
Age: 28 years.
Left Husband & 2 children.

Infant * of
J. L. & Lula Gilham
Died Oct 6, 1899
Age: (not given)

Remon,* Son of
Mr. & Mrs. Leslie Manning
Died Jul 25, 1915
Age: 4 years.

ED NOTE: This Cemetery started on land owned by John Simpson who moved here from Ohio shortly after the Civil War.

Rosa Lee,* Daughter of
Frank & Julia Webb
Died Jul 24, 1900
Age: 10m, 24d.

Mrs. Noah Cooper *
Died Jan 23, 1917
Age: 68 years.

George W. Cowan *
Died Oct 24, 1916
Age: 68 years.

Willie,* Son of
Newton Tucker
B&D Oct 6, 1903

Child * of
Oscar Marshall
Died Dec 27, 1914
Age: 2½ years.

Morencis Althens A. Locker*
of Kelso
Died Jan 11, 1904
Age: 12y, 9m.

* *

SIMMS-LAND CEMETERY

LOCATION: One and one half miles west of Lincoln at the Baptist Church.

William V. D. Land
(no dates)

Polly Land
(no dates)

Mattie Simms
(no dates)

Peggy Jane Simms
Oct 7, 1860
Feb 16, 1896

William B. Simms
May 14, 1857
Nov 27, 1937

Sarah Eliza Simms
Oct 13, 1869
Aug 27, 1931

George Melvin Simms
Mar 15, 1905
Sep 25, 1905

"Our Father & Mothers"
G. W. Simms
&
M. L. Simms
&
M. A. Simms
(no dates)

"Our Babies"
J. T. & M. A. Mason
(no dates)

Mary J. Epps
Aug 8, 1842
Jul 16, 1861

1 Flat Slab Marker (Wicks)
information illegible
(no dates)

Mable Clara Simms
Jun 27, 1904
Jul   1906

E. L. E. Wicks
(no dates)

Joe Wicks, Jr.
(no dates)

Lillie R., wife of
D. F. Simms
Sep 2, 1881
Oct 22, 1908

Myrtle Johns
Jan 1923
Sep 1927

Infant Baby of
C. H. & L. A. Johns
B&D Jan 1908

Ella S. Hudson
1869-1958

Bonnie Blanch Rozell
Mar 20, 1920
Sep 18, 1924

Lee Ray Rozell
Nov 15, 1924
May 16, 1927

Darcus R. Rozell
Apr 28, 1866
Dec 18, 1936
&
Dawson H. Rozell
Aug 2, 1858
Jan 10, 1921
&
Emily C. Rozell
Apr 19, 1896

Elnora Stevenson
May 25, 1872
Aug 4, 1896

Canzora Stevenson
May 25, 1872
Oct 15, 1886

Rev. James M. Stevenson
May 12, 1827
Apr 3, 1904
&
Jala B. Stevenson
Dec 14, 1830
Mar 29, 1885

D. P. Henderson
Dec 13, 1850
Jun 25, 1921

Mary E. Henderson
Sep 16, 1821
(dates gone)

_____ Pruitt Quick
Died Oct 1867
Age: 84 years.

Lawson Quick
1879-1956

Lizzie Quick
(no dates)

Little Lee, Son of
R. H. & M. L. Quick
Sep 7, 1908
Nov 18, 1908

LINCOLN QUADRANGLE

Ray Fenton, Son of
R. H. & M. L. Quick
Apr 10, 1904
Jun 28, 1910

Roger Lee Mires
(no dates)

Theo M. Mires
1875-1941

Ella Mires
1873-1941

Lillian George
(no dates)

James Carty Stevenson
Jul 12, 1851
Oct 28, 1911
&
Ida Cornelia Smith Stevenson
Jul 20, 1873
Dec 12, 1914

Carson Oliver,* Son of
Levi & Fannie Quick
Died Feb 26, 1901
Age: (not given)

Dennie Ross,* Son of
Bunk & Sallie Shelton
Died Jun 6, 1896
Age: 9y, 4m, 20d.

Bapp Petty *
Died Sep 23, 1897
Age: 76y, 10m.

Levi Oliver Quick
Feb 13, 1873
Jun 12, 1960
&
Fannie Quick
Jan 20, 1875
Dec 27, 1928

Jack Mires
1908-1961
&
Lucy C. Mires
1918-

B. H. (Henderson)
(no dates, fieldstone)

B. S. S. (Simms)
(no dates, fieldstone)

Roy Stevenson
Died Mar 18, 1909
Age: (not given)

Mrs. Mary E. Boles *
Died Mar 3, 1901
Age: 32 years.

S. D. Miller *
Died Nov 15, 1916
Age: 54 years.
He had 6 children.

E. E. Shelton *
Died Apr 28, 1912
Age: 74 years.

Albert G. Boles
Jan 2, 1867
Feb 13, 1905
"Erected by Goshen Lodge # 39"

Thomas Pruitt
Mar 10, 1845
Feb 25, 1928
&
Betty Pruitt
Jul 2, 1849
Oct 14, 1923

Claude Stevenson
Died 1905 or 1906
Age: (not given)

Annie Stevenson
May 9, 1829
(no date)

Hughy Stevenson
(no dates)

Amie Lee Stevenson *
Died Sep 1905
Age: 5y, 4m, 12d.

J. R. Shelton *
Died Jan 2, 1915
Age: 53 years.

Many unmarked graves.

Beulah Pruitt
Jun 24, 1893
Mar 5, 1968

G. C., Son of
T. A. & E. D. Pruitt
Jun 22, 1891
Jun 16, 1898

J. P. Walker
Apr 20, 1856
Dec 7, 1916
& wife
N. M. Walker
Apr 23, 1850
Apr 24, 1891

E. E. Shelton
Jun 19, 1899
Dec 16, 1970

ED NOTE: This Cemetery
was established as the
Land Cemetery, Rev.
William Land buried
here in 1865 and his
wife Delania in 1880.

G. W. Simms *
Died Sep 7, 1893
Age: 66 years.

Mattie,* Daughter of
G. W. Simms
Died Sep 14, 1889
Age: 14 years.

* *

BEVERLY CEMETERY

LOCATION: Three fourth mile west of Lincoln on the south side of Old Goshen Road on "Old Arthur Smith Farm."

This Cemetery has been destroyed. No markers remain.

William Beverly *
Born in Maryland and came
to Lincoln Co., Tenn. in
1823-4
Married 1826
Died Jun 10, 1871
Age: 82 years.

Miss Theodocia Beverly *
Died Sep 26, 1882
Age: about 46 years.

Other members of the
Beverly family are buried here.

NOTE: Mr. Richard A. Marsh remembered markers standing here in 1920.

* *

TOWRY CEMETERY

LOCATION: One and one half miles north of Lincoln on the east side of Lincoln-Fayetteville Road.

No markers remain.

Descendants said
Dora Towry
Died about 1908
Age: 25 years.

&

Her child
(no dates)

* *

LINCOLN-MULBERRY QUADRANGLE

CEMETERY

LOCATION: Two miles north of Lincoln on the east side of Lincoln-Fayetteville Road.

No markers remain.   Years ago fieldstones were here.

* *

LAND CEMETERY

LOCATION: One half mile south of Howell Hill on the east side of Lincoln Road.

No markers remain.

* *

MULBERRY QUADRANGLE

WAID-ASHBY CEMETERY

LOCATION: Three miles NW of Mulberry Village, up Ginlet Creek on the east side.

Weston L. Waid
1834-1862
Killed in Battle of
Murfreesboro. C.S.A.

George Milstead
Apr 7, 1850
Apr 27, 1907

Lavina J. Milstead
Jul 11, 1848
Aug 6, 1905

Elijah F., Jr., Son of
E. F. & C. F. Waid
1849-1853

Infant Daughter of
E. F. & C. F. Waid
1850

F. M. Waid
1785-1871

Hannah J. Waid
1801-1849

John J. Crane
Jan 3, 1846
Feb 29, 1904

William A., Son of
J. J. & S. P. Crane
Mar 3, 1890
Mar 28, 1893

Elijah H. Conway
(no dates)

Claud Milstead
Died Sep 25, 1909
Age: 26y, 11m.

George M. D., Son of
Jonah & Sarah Moore
Oct 3, 1844
Jan 3, 1850

P. M., Son of
E. W. & M. J. Moore
Apr 27, 1861
Apr 12, 1870

Jonah Moore
Sep 15, 1803
Jul 12, 1891

Sarah, wife of
Jonah Moore
Jun 12, 1894 (died)
Age: about 82 years.

J. B. Sullivan
Jul 18, 1843
Oct 6, 1905

Bettie A. Ashby, wife of
J. B. Sullivan
Jul 7, 1840
Jul 11, 1901

Mrs. Mattie Dusenberry
1864-1933

Samuel Ashby
Jun 13, 1798
Apr 5, 1866

Rachel Ashby
Jun 24, 1795
Sep 2, 1889

William G., Son of
T. N. & E. T. Ashby
Aug 24, 1857
Sep 13, 1881

Elizabeth T., wife of
T. N. Ashby
Jan 31, 1828
Jul 8, 1904

T. L. Ashby
Husband of Ada M. Ashby
Feb 9, 1861
Sep 22, 1890

Annie Lizzie, Daughter of
T. L. & Ada Ashby
Dec 25, 1889
Mar 3, 1892

Several unmarked graves.

ED NOTE: According to information supplied by Mr. L. L. Ashby, the grave beside Elizabeth T. Ashby is the unmarked grave of T. N. Ashby.

Newton Ashby *
Died May 10, 1915
Age: 87 years.
He died at the place of his birth, left a Daughter Mrs. Dusenberry.

Hon. Morgan H. Conway *
"Member of General Assembly"
Died Sep 1, 1905
Age: 75 years.

* *

MULBERRY QUADRANGLE

McGEE CEMETERY

LOCATION: Two miles NNW of Mulberry Village, head of McGee Hollow.

J. B. McGee Dec 7, 1858 Apr 11, 1934	Tillman A. McGee May 25, 1865 Nov 23, 1940 & Mary R. McGee Mar 29, 1872 Dec 20, 1952	Abner McGee Feb 26, 1888 May 7, 1916	W. D. McGee 1866-1949
Stacy Ann, wife of J. B. McGee Feb 16, 1860 Oct 11, 1927		A. S. McGee Nov 1, 1832 Jan 15, 1891	Jane McGee 1885-1941 Elizabeth, wife of Henry Andrews Died Aug 7, 1891 Age: about 60 years.
3 Rock Vaults, no inscriptions.	Mattie McGee Faulkner 1857-1933	Sarah T. Jones Feb 28, 1848 May 24, 1884	
Many unmarked graves.	Mrs. Annie McAfee * Died May 25, 1909 Age: 28 years.	Ester Lena,* Daughter of Mr. & Mrs. John McGee Died Oct 22, 1910 Age: 21y, 9m.	Samuel Boone,* Son of Samuel Roe Died Aug 10, 1895 Age: 16m.
Kate,* Daughter of Samuel Roe Died Sep 13, 1895 Age: 8 years.			

* *

HOLMAN CEMETERY

LOCATION: Two and one fourth miles NNE of Mulberry Village, one fourth mile north of Old Mt. Moriah Church site, on west side of the Buckeye Dirt Road.

Minos Cannon Died Aug 6, 1853 Age: 56 years.	Hardy Holman Mar 17, 1774 Apr 9, 1926	Hetty K. Holman Oct 20, 1816 Mar 11, 1825	Daniel H. Holman Nov 11, 1806 Aug 26, 1827
Robert T. Holman Nov 24, 1837 Apr 6, 1862	Elizabeth Holman Nov 13, 1779 (no date)	Nancy Moore Mar 28, 1800 Jan 13, 1819	Joseph W., Son of Willis & Ann Holman Apr 7, 1849 Apr 4, 1871
Laura J. Holman Dec 13, 1844 Oct 11, 1855			

* *

MT. MORIAH CEMETERY

LOCATION: Two miles NNE of Mulberry Village on east side of the Buckeye Dirt Road.

Marker for 3 Confederate Soldiers Joe Stacy Billy Martin George Street Members of Co K 8th Tenn Regt., killed at Battle of Franklin December 1864	Joseph Roe Died May 28, 1913 Age: 96y, 8m, 15d. & Susan Roe Died Apr 29, 1879 Age: 63y, 9m, 9d.	Thomas Bailey Nov 14, 1823 Nov 12, 1898 & Amanda M. Bailey Dec 31, 1821 Sep 8, 1934	Fanny, Consort of B. H. Berry Jul 1809 Jan 13, 1842
			Henry Bateman Mar 12, 1840 Sep 14, 1899
Isaac Rutledge Sep 1, 1819 Aug 8, 1886	Eliza, wife of Edward Taylor Nov 4, 1818 Dec 30, 1883	W. K. Shofner Apr 28, 1826 Oct 23, 1830	Bettie C. Bateman Jun 27, 1844 Mar 15, 1907
S. H. Eaton Nov 20, 1821 Apr 4, 1842	Christopher Shofner Jul 25, 1789 Aug 23, 1826	Margarette E., wife of W. K. Shofner Dec 3, 1835 Nov 3, 1913	Samuel Rutledge Mar 11, 1821 Mar 1, 1884 Age: 62y, 11m, 20d.
	3 other Vaults beside Christopher Shofner.	R. A. M. (foot marker)	

MULBERRY QUADRANGLE

Hardy H., Son of
I. C. & Donnie Rutledge
Jun 26, 1879
Oct 8, 1879
Age: 3m, 12d.

David Waggoner
May 11, 1818
Sep 2, 1848

Many unmarked graves.

Many fieldstones,
no inscriptions.

Kelso Plot
2 graves within
Stone wall.

William Forrestor *
Died Jun 14, 1914
Age: 67 years.

Miss Jennie Kelso *
Died Apr 30, 1909
Age: (not given)
Buried beside her Father
and Mother.

Rebecka Pitts
Jun 21, 1816
Nov 11, 1856

R. B. Nance *
Died Sep 8, 1899
Age: 77 years

Robert Jarman Small *
Died Aug 25, 1914
Age: 71 years.
C.S.A.

Nannie (no last name)
Born 1864
(fieldstone)

William Lee,* Son of
W. A. Pitts
Died Apr 30, 1891
Age: 1y, 9m.

Rachel,* wife of
Samuel Ashby
Born in Surry Co., N.C.
Jun 24, 1796
Moved to Lincoln Co.,
Tenn. in 1821
Died Aug 1890

* *

SULLIVAN CEMETERY

LOCATION: Two and one half miles NW of Mulberry on the east
side of Hamestring Branch.

Dorris McAfee
1928-1940
(Higgins FH)

J. H. Sullivan
1853-1940

Several graves with
fieldstones, no inscriptions.

Ada Sullivan
1877-1940

Johnnie Lee,* Son of
Ben Sullivan
Died Dec 3, 1906
Age: (not given)

* *

CAMPBELL CEMETERY

LOCATION: One and one fourth miles NW of Mulberry Village
on west side of Gimlet Creek and Booneville Road.

2 Iron enclosures,
no inscriptions.

James D. Campbell ***
Died Jun 12, 1883
Age: (not given)

Mary J. Campbell ***
Died Feb 4, 1890
Age: (not given)

Mary Collins ***
Died Aug 29, 1883
Age: (not given)

Sallie Faulkner ***
Died Oct 27, 1885
Age: (not given)

*** Campbell Family Records

Several unmarked graves.

* *

WHITAKER CEMETERY

LOCATION: One mile NNW of Mulberry Village in fork of Gimlet
Creek and West Mulberry Creek.

Rock Wall around this
Cemetery.

Ann Haseltine Judson
(no dates)

Nancy S., Consort of
Thomas Whitaker
Mar 1, 1806
Sep 15, 1850

Many unmarked graves.

* *

MOORE CEMETERY

LOCATION: Three fourth mile north of Mulberry Village on
east side of West Fork of Mulberry.

William Moore
Sep 28, 1786
Mar 9, 1871
(Captain in War of 1812,
also State Senator in
1833-1837)

Sophia Moore
Aug 1825-Feb 1845

R. T. Mesia Moore
Mar 1832
1849

Artinesia Yell
Sep 1834-Jun 1853

Willie Hobb
(no dates, infant)

Archibald Y. Moore
Aug 1833
1853

S. M. Moore
(no dates, infant)

MULBERRY QUADRANGLE

Ann J. Pearson
Apr 1821-Oct 1853

Edna Pearson
(no dates, infant)

Sarah Pearson
(no dates, infant)

William, Son of
Martha Ann Pearson
(no dates)

Anna Hobb
(no dates, infant)

William Holman
1841-1862

Jane D. Holman
1822-1842

Mary Frances, Daughter of
F. W. Nicks
Born Feb 9, 1851
Age: 6m, 25d.

Margaret Ann, Daughter of
C. S. & E. M. Nicks
Feb   1854
Apr 28, 1854

Elizabeth, wife of
Col. A. S. Nicks
Jan 3, 1813
Jul 4, 1851

* *

MULBERRY CEMETERY
(Old Section)

LOCATION: One and one fourth miles NE of Mulberry Village on west side of Lynchburg Highway.

Eliza Brown
Died Jul 1, 1893
Age: 63 years

W. Flem Hazlewood
1870-1950
&
Myrtle S. Hazlewood
1880-1943

Wiley Grisard
Sep 18, 1814
Apr 1, 1849
Age: 35y, 6m, 18d.

Thomas H. Freeman
Dec 19, 1824
Jul 7, 1863

F. W. Wagoner
Aug 8, 1832
Oct 18, 1895

Birdie Bailey Thomas
Oct 1, 1866
May 6, 1940

Cullen Bailey
Aug 19, 1828
Jun 20, 1897

Catherine K. (Kimbrough)
Bailey
Mar 12, 1843
Aug 1, 1932

Saphronia H. Bailey
Jul 18, 1840
May 9, 1862
&
An Infant Son
by her side.

John Bailey
Aug   1782
Feb 20, 1858

Nancy Bailey
Aug   1788
Oct 13, 1855

Thomas W. Bailey
Died Oct 31, 1887
Age: 17y, 3m, 6d.

Lizzie H. Bailey
Mar 31, 1878
Jul 31, 1879

Cordelia, Daughter of
B. A. & M. A. Renegar
B&D Sep 16, 1879

Penelopy Bateman
Died Dec 17, 1862
Age: 86 years.

Thomas J. Neeld
Oct 30, 1843
Mar 7, 1908
&
Sarah E. Neeld
Oct 30, 1845
(no date)
NOTE: no evidence of her
being buried here.

Charles Mitchell
Feb 15, 1796
Jan 31, 1873

Mary J. Mitchell
Jul 20, 1804
May 7, 1882

M. B. Parks
1863-1936

J. H. Lloyd
May 18, 1855
May 12, 1918

Jimmie Hunter
1874-1951

Fannie, Daughter of
L. W. & M. E. Hazlewood
Aug 11, 1865
Sep 11, 1879

Ella Hazelwood
1869-1952

John W. Hazelwood
Mar 7, 1839
Apr 26, 1924

Mary Ann, wife of
J. W. Hazelwood
Aug 20, 1837
Feb 3, 1908

Ethel Holman
Sep 16, 1892
Mar 17, 1897

Ann E. Waggoner
Jun 10, 1840
Apr 13, 1928

James Jeptha Holman
Apr 26, 1860
Jun 20, 1936

Dora Jenkins Holman
Sep 10, 1861
Mar 9, 1945

Gillam G. Harris
Sep 14, 1885
Oct 19, 1918

Beulah Holman Harris
Sep 25, 1888
Nov 6, 1950

E. P. Solomon
Aug 20, 1821
Jun 18, 1899

Mary Ann, wife of
E. P. Solomon
Apr 12, 1847
Nov 4, 1929

Susie, wife of
J. T. Solomon
Dec 12, 1881
Feb 17, 1916

Eldridge & Maude, Infants of
Frank C. & Annie P. Allison
(no dates)

Jonny Jewel Smith
Dec 31, 1924
Dec 18, 1925

John Edgar Smith
Feb 15, 1891
Nov 3, 1943
&
Sarah Waggoner Smith
Apr 17, 1889

Louisa Jane, Daughter of
William & Jane Thomison
Jan 27, 1850
Sep 26, 1865

William Thomison
Feb 19, 1809
Jul 19, 1877

Jane Bailey, wife of
William Thomison
Jan 25, 1815
Nov 21, 1895
Age: 70y, 9m, 26d.

Rev. Bradley Kimbrough
Died Jun 30, 1874
Age: 74 years.

Martha W., wife of
Rev. Bradley Kimbrough
Feb 5, 1808
Mar 27, 1891

Nannie, wife of
William B. Whitaker &
Daughter of
Bradley Kimbrough
Oct 8, 1841
Oct   1866

John W. Oakley
Tennessee 1st Sgt
156 Depot Brig.
Apr 23, 1886
Jan 5, 1935

MULBERRY QUADRANGLE

F. G. Blackwell
Apr 7, 1787
Died   1857
&
Mary Blackwell
Jan 12, 1803
Died   1857

G. W. Alexander
Jul 31, 1808
Nov 22, 1874
Age: 66y, 3m, 21d.

Martha, wife of
G. W. Alexander
Died Jun 5, 1851
Age: 44y, 11m, 10d.

Emeline, wife of
C. L. McLane
Feb 12, 1814
Apr 26, 1849

John Dusenberry
Dec 26, 1777
Jun 8, 1851
Age: 74 years.

John Whitaker
Died Jun 13, 1837
Age: 77 years.

Charlie T. Freeman
1870-1947
&
Fannie B. Freeman
1871-1948

Dora Ann, Daughter of
A. J. & Sarah J. Whitaker
Sep 23, 1858
Dec 1, 1862

Margaret A., Daughter of
T. J. & Julia F. Hill
Jan 9, 1859
Jan 22, 1862

Joseph Whitaker
Sep 19, 1788
Sep 20, 1874

Martha, wife of
Joseph Whitaker
Born 1795
Died 1829

Ann W., wife of
Joseph Whitaker
Apr 27, 1795
Jun 13, 1863

Dr. O. F. Baxter
Aug 23, 1847
May 10, 1873

Alexander Franklin, Son of
T. D. & J. F. Hill
May 31, 1869
Jun 21, 1869

Julia (Hill)
(all information on stone
is illegible)

Lizzie Gertrude, Daughter of
Dr. G. W. & L. M. Jones
Oct 15, 1873
Jul 30, 1874

Paul, Son of
Dr. G. W. & L. M. Jones
Nov 2, 1880
Mar 9, 1881

Estill, Son of
Dr. G. W. & L. M. Jones
Dec 23, 1876
Mar 11, 1882

Dr. G. W. Jones
Jan 27, 1835
Mar 24, 1900

Lizzie M., wife of
Dr. G. W. Jones
Jan 12, 1842
Feb 22, 1889
Age: 47y, 1m, 10d.

Richard R. Whitaker
Jun 29, 1854
Oct 11, 1943

E. L. Whitaker
Apr 16, 1863
May 24, 1924

Mary Winn Whitaker, wife of
Capt. Sam H. Estill
Feb 23, 1844
Aug 30, 1926

Newton Whitaker
Jul 1, 1816
Aug 28, 1878
Age: 62y, 1m, 27d.

Frances Ann Whitaker
Mar 12, 1821
Aug 12, 1889
Age: 68y, 5m.

Dr. P. R. Whitaker
Oct 19, 1826
Jul 31, 1868
Age: 41y, 8m, 14d.

Eliza J., wife of
I. J. Sebastian
Jan 12, 1820
Feb 25, 1886

Eugenia Whitaker Sebastian
May 28, 1856
Dec 12, 1950

R. F., Son of
I. J. Sebastian
Dec 5, 1843
Jan 16, 1881

John C., Son of
Isaac & Eliza Sebastain
May 9, 1849
Oct 7, 1922

Zana Sebastain
Jul 3, 1885
Mar 19, 1933

Isaac J. Sebastian
Sep 4, 1808
Apr 14, 1880

W. P. Sebastian
Died Aug 7, 1912
Age: 65 years.

Oliver I. Sebastian
Dec 27, 1854
Jul 27, 1912

Mary Ellen Durham, wife of
O. I. Sebastian
Mar 3, 1861
May 3, 1938

Mary E. Sebastian
Feb 4, 1886
Apr 3, 1906

Annie Harrison
Jun 26, 1861
Dec 27, 1879

George Gray Mitchell, Jr.
1887-1905

Victor Lavoy Mitchell
1882-1898

Susie May Mitchell
1880-1925

Virginia Dusenberry Mitchell
1855-1941

George Gray Mitchell
1847-1908

Lugene Mitchel
(no dates)

Rev. T. D. Jones
Oct 30, 1832
Aug 20, 1872

Sam Rutledge
Dec 15, 1838
Sep 14, 1893

W. R. Call
Apr 22, 1834
May 30, 1911
&
Martha J. Call
Mar 10, 1837
Sep 1, 1900
& Son
George F. Call
Feb 28, 1861
Dec 24, 1879

Ike C. Rutledge
1853-1935
&
Donie Rutledge
1859-1946
&
John B. Rutledge
1896-1943

Elizabeth Crawford
Dec 8, 1803
Nov 3, 1880
Age: 76y, 10m, 25d.

Martha Frances
Infant, June 1921
(no last name)

Elma Shofner
Oct 7, 1886
Oct 3, 1933

Reuben T. Shofner
Aug 17, 1884
May 18, 1964

George F. Rutledge
1838-1948

Arch L. Caughran
1879-1947

Clara R. Caughran
1881-1947

William C. Solomon
Dec 19, 1818
Dec 9, 1880

Sallie C., wife of
W. C. Solomon
May 3, 1820
Jun 21, 1897
Age: 77y, 1m, 24d.

Sallie B. Moore
1837-1942

Kenneth Morgan, Son of
P. H. & S. M. Hampton
B&D May 17, 1918

Willie S. Hampton
Jul 1, 1900
Jan 31, 1902

MULBERRY QUADRANGLE

P. H. Hampton
Aug 31, 1863
Jun 1, 1928

Ella S. Hampton
Jan 18, 1857
Aug 24, 1916

Placie Huston Hampton
May 6, 1895
Jan 14, 1940

Martha Louise Hampton
Mar 8, 1896
Nov 6, 1960

William E. Baldwin
Oct 22, 1873
May 14, 1963

Ella H. Baldwin
Nov 29, 1869
Oct 18, 1954

J. Claud Baldwin
Jun 24, 1896
Jul 11, 1951

Mrs. Sarah J. Rhoten
Nee Moore
Nee Simpson
Apr 5, 1831
Aug 5, 1881

Wiley B. Daniel
1842-1931
 & wife
Sue E. Daniel
1847-1914

John A. Daniel
1886-1946

Dick Austin Daniel
Oct 2, 1914
Jan 26, 1920

Infant of
E. S. & V. J. Terry
Died Aug 5, 1881
Age: (not given)

James D., Son of
J. D. & Rose T. Acuff
Apr 10, 1903
Jun 22, 1904

Martha A. Elmore
Jun 19, 1819
Dec 18, 1898

Thomas M. Elmore
Mar 10, 1851
Mar 6, 1926
 &
Mattie S. Elmore
Sep 24, 1862
May 22, 1938

Lillian, Daughter of
T. M. & Mattie Elmore
Feb 3, 1884
Sep 30, 1892

Infant Son of
R. M. & L. W. Hague
Dec 15, 1884
Dec 15, 1884

Willie Massey
Aug 30, 1889
Jan 21, 1940

Lucille Perkins
Feb 26, 1892
Mar 29, 1893

Willie Renegar, Daughter of
W. H. & J. C. Perkins
Dec 12, 1896
Jun 12, 1897

J. A. D. Middleton
Jul 24, 1842(1824)
Apr 23, 1913

Cordelia Jane, wife of
J. A. D. Middleton
Jul 4, 1828
Mar 9, 1883
Age: 59y, 8m, 5d.

Tina Morgan, wife of
J. A. D. Middleton
Oct 28, 1856
May 24, 1911

Lillie May Middleton
Jun 18, 1892
Sep 29, 1893
 &
Stella Eugenia Middleton
May 17, 1893
Aug 20, 1893
Daughters of J. A. D. &
Tima M. Middleton.

William J. Goosby
Jan 31, 1924
Feb 23, 1924

Frank Wilson Hazelwood
May 27, 1898
Sep 15, 1898

Lula Solomon Hazelwood
Jan 1, 1874
Jun 2, 1898

Mary Abbie Solomon
Sep 5, 1887
Jul 20, 1909

P. S. Solomon, Sr.
Aug 10, 1834
Jul 9, 1918
 &
Mary E. Solomon
May 1, 1844
(no date)

Jessie Mac Spencer
Jul 28, 1904
Jul 5, 1909

Mitchell L. Spencer
May 8, 1866
Oct 14, 1952

Maude E. Spencer
Jan 26, 1878
Dec 16, 1959

Lemuel Milton Shofner
Aug 1, 1848
Oct 25, 1935
 &
Estelle Rochelle Shofner
Nov 22, 1852
Jan 28, 1915

Urban Shofner Small
1905-1964

Urban Shofner Small
Sep 23, 1878
Sep 11, 1953
 &
Nora Candace Small
Jul 1, 1883
May 22, 1968

Deborah Gail, Daughter of
Gene & Doris Johnson
Feb 11, 1957
Apr 23, 1957

Henry K. Johnson
Dec 24, 1854
Jun 14, 1936
 &
Sallie Dixon Johnson
Oct 24, 1856
Jul 5, 1934

Roy Eugene Tipps
Nov 11, 1886
Nov 19, 1937

C. S. Massey
Apr 26, 1846
Aug 20, 1919
 & wife
Martha Dennis Massey
May 14, 1848
Jan 1, 1928

Margaret Evans
Apr 9, 1814
Aug 15, 1891
Mother of the Massey Boys.

Hulda Massey Blackburn
Dec 19, 1879
Jun 23, 1957

Dr. W. J. Massey
Sep 17, 1869
Oct 1, 1897

Birdie A. Massey
Oct 9, 1872
Oct 9, 1956

John W. Massey
Jun 10, 1874
Jan 30, 1938
 &
Etta S. Massey
Jul 20, 1877
Jun 26, 1950

Little Webb, Son of
J. H. & M. E. Rees
Mar 31, 1889
Apr 7, 1889

W. J. H. Campbell
Apr 17, 1851
May 20, 1930

William M. Wood
May 15, 1849
Jun 12, 1942
 &
Bettie Campbell Wood
Apr 8, 1857
May 12, 1941

Annie Wood McLain
1886-1932

E. T. Parks
Aug 11, 1839
Feb 22, 1920

Mary A. Parks
Apr 28, 1843
Jun 15, 1922

Cora A. Parks
Dec 9, 1881
Jan 22, 1931

O. E. Parks
Oct 6, 1872
Jul 19, 1943

Henry B. Parks
Oct 12, 1902
Jan 14, 1927

Lillie Cashion Parks
Aug 19, 1879
Apr 20, 1920

S. O. Parks
Apr 2, 1870
Aug 1, 1938

Robert Anderson, Son of
Ben E. & Birdie Parks
Sep 12, 1903
Sep 7, 1905

Birdie Pearl, wife of
Ben E. Parks
Dec 7, 1879
Sep 23, 1905

Donie C., wife of
H. W. Pitts
Jan 8, 1858
Sep 23, 1906

MULBERRY QUADRANGLE

George B. Gattis
May 24, 1869
Mar 19, 1937
&
Ida E. Gattis
Nov 17, 1874
Jan 15, 1944

George F. Gattis
1835-1869
& wife
Susan C. Gattis
1836-1910

Lula Grace Gattis
Apr 24, 1899
May 8, 1901

Abner Bready
Oct 26, 1815
Jan 3, 1896

Julia Ann., wife of
Abner Brady
Oct 6, 1819
May 28, 1894

Abner Brady Call
1830-1964

J. W. Call
Oct 25, 1873
Nov 13, 1943

J. A. Call
1877-1916

Elizabeth, wife of
J. B. Wiseman
Sep 24, 1864
Dec 12, 1886
Mother and Infant
Daughter.

Rebeca, wife of
J. C. Spencer
Jun 26, 1857
Jun 24, 1889

James Chaney Spencer
Oct 17, 1853
Aug 1, 1939

Daniel Spencer
Jul 1, 1881
Nov 18, 1885

Alex J., Jr., Son of
A. J. & S. J. Whitaker
Jun 8, 1877
Feb 18, 1883

Charles Whitaker
1865-1941

Thomas R. Helms
Oct 26, 1868
Oct 14, 1909

Charlsie Tucker, wife of
T. W. Helms
Sep 13, 1876
Apr 16, 1902

Lucy Helms
Dec 17, 1906
Feb 23, 1903

Miss Annie McWhorter
Died Oct 8, 1968
Age: 69y, 1m, 23d.

Will McWhorter
Died 1903
(no age given)

Jane McWhorter
Died 1918
(no age given)

W. M. McWhorter
1839-1923

Walter King Hill
1865-1933

J. W. Ashby
Sep 15, 1846
(no date)
&
Mollie V. Ashby
Sep 13, 1843
Jan 15, 1905

Hardee Childress
1864-1937

Willie Wilson Childers
Feb 1, 1889
Dec 17, 1960

May Boyd, wife of
W. W. Childers
Feb 27, 1891
Nov 26, 1918

J. Edgar Hill
Oct 28, 1863
Mar 25, 1925

Ophelia Scott, wife of
Ed. Hill
Jan 11, 1868
May 2, 1895

Agatha Alice Hill
Dec 4, 1875
Jul 18, 1926

Charlie F. Newsom
1869-1939
&
Fannie H. Newsom
1870-1958
&
Julia B. Newsom
1891-1919
&
Lourie B. Newsom
1917-1919

A. J. Whitaker
Apr 30, 1833
Dec 25, 1916
& wife
Sarah J. Whitaker
Dec 18, 1835
Mar 21, 1907

William H. Whitaker
Tennessee
Sgt Infantry WW I
Nov 14, 1886
Aug 5, 1966

T. D. Hill
May 3, 1837
Dec 15, 1887
&
Julia F. Hill
Oct 20, 1837
Mar 9, 1902

Elizabeth Hill Johnson
1861-1891

Robert Eustace Johnson
1891-1892

Homer A. Spencer
Feb 11, 1893
Nov 1896

Nancy E., wife of
B. W. Tipps
Aug 6, 1867
Jun 3, 1895

Joseph F., Son of
D. H. & M. J. Call
Sep 1, 1884
Jan 12, 1887

Huldah A., Daughter of
D. H. & M. J. Call
Oct 3, 1878
Nov 5, 1899

Daniel H. Call
1836-1904
& wife
Mary J. Call
1839-1922

George E. Conner
Apr 26, 1852
Sep 5, 1925

Samuel Thomas Baldwin
1879-1959
&
Alla Louvenia Poplin Baldwin
1884-1949

Rufus Hal Baldwin
Sep 28, 1905
Apr 5, 1908

Odena W., wife of
P. F. Warren
Apr 7, 1864
Nov 29, 1915

Sarah E., wife of
W. J. Baldwin
Aug 18, 1851
Jun 20, 1893

W. T. Baldwin
Nov 3, 1838
Mar 6, 1898

Fannie M., Daughter of
W. T.(J) & S. E. Baldwin
May 31, 1888
Mar 19, 1892

Dot, wife of
Gene Jones
Jul 25, 1929
Sep 20, 1965

John Reese Jones
Jun 6, 1872
Feb 6, 1960
&
Manda Lou Jones
May 15, 1878
Jan 28, 1928

Edward C., Son of
J. R. & M. L. Jones
Jun 25, 1917
Jan 12, 1920

Mary E., wife of
J. M. Brown
Oct 21, 1870
May 27, 1900

Aaron F. Brown
Aug 22, 1896
Feb 24, 1912

Paul Ingle
Feb 29, 1812
Aug 3, 1889
&
Adlade Ingle
Jul 18, 1818
Oct 26, 1895

Mathias Waggoner
1822-1912

Catharine Waggoner
1825-1913

David Waggoner
Sep 20, 1811
Mar 26, 1892
&
Catherine Waggoner
Jun 18, 1814
Aug 4, 1893

William Polk Tolley
1839-1909

Mary Tolly Williams
1875-1938

MULBERRY QUADRANGLE

William Tolley
Born at Perryville, KY
Dec 6, 1804
Died at his residence near
Lynchburg, Tenn.
Feb 11, 1884
& wife
Mary M. Tolley
May 21, 1816
Jul 26, 1896

Eliza Tolley
1856-1915

Henry L. Tolley
1857-1904

Felix Waggoner
1820-1912
& wife
Mahulda Waggoner
1826-1894

Flossie, Daughter of
G. T. & Minnie Waggoner
1895-1912

F. L. "Fate" Waggoner
1870-1948

George T. Waggoner
Jul 31, 1860
Aug 2, 1935
&
Minnie G. Waggoner
May 25, 1865
Mar 17, 1940

James K. Raby
Apr 9, 1846
Apr 9, 1917

Laura, wife of
J. K. Raby
May 16, 1851
Aug 27, 1886

Eugene, Son of
J. K. & Laura Raby
Mar 4, 1881
Nov 16, 1882

Kalista Payne, wife of
William B. Jennings
Apr 12, 1880
May 27, 1907

Smith D., Son of
J. C. & M. H. Jennings
Oct 9, 1889
Nov 11, 1911

Clyde R. Jennings
Jun 1, 1898
Nov 14, 1901
&
John T. Jennings
Mar 1, 1893
Mar 13, 1893
Children of
J. C. & M. H. Jennings

Laura Mai, Daughter of
J. S. & L. M. Gray
Dec 13, 1903
Jan 12, 1904

Mary Cooper Caldwell
Aug 4, 1820
Feb 29, 1893

Avery Claude Blackwell
Feb 15, 1867
Dec 22, 1908
& (Reverse side)
A. C. B.(Avery Claude)
& wife
M. J. B.
Martha Jane Blackwell
Jun 21, 1844
Dec 29, 1913
&
C. F. B.
Charles Fleming Blackwell
Sep 20, 1842
Nov 9, 1923

Elizabeth C., wife of
J. N. Blackwell
Jul 21, 1831
Dec 2, 1901

R. N. Freeman
Jun 7, 1847
Jun 24, 1912
& wife
Clementine Freeman
Feb 8, 1846
Jan 28, 1915

William J. Freeman
1876-1923
&
Polly S. Freeman
1887-1967

Pauline Freeman
Died 1922
Age: 4 months.

Bettie Landers, wife of
H. F. White
1825-Feb 6, 1901
&
H. F. White
Jan 18, 1848
(no date)
&
M. S. Hill, wife of
H. F. White
Jul 26, 1868
May 21, 1910

Jessie Shadden
Age: 10 months
(no dates)
&
Florie Shadden
Age: 11 days
(no dates)
Children of
Mr. & Mrs. A. R. Shadden

James C. Shofner
Jun 5, 1845
Dec 21, 1934
& wife
Ada McMath Shofner
Sep 26, 1862
Aug 30, 1946

W. H. Whitaker
1872-1941

M. D. L. Whitaker
Aug 15, 1832
Dec 2, 1908
& wife
Mattie K. Rhea Whitaker
Dec 3, 1841
Sep 12, 1907

Helen Evelyn, Daughter of
A. A. & Helen Huff
Feb 26, 1904
Jul 6, 1905

Sallie Cooper, wife of
H. H. Cooper
Mar 10, 1861
Jan 5, 1882

Dr. Floyd Mullins
May 15, 1894
Aug 25, 1965

Flossie Melton, wife of
Floyd Mullins
Oct 22, 1895
Mar 7, 1920

Esther Mullins Baldwin
Oct 10, 1895
Dec 12, 1960

James D. Mullins
Feb 24, 1865
Jan 7, 1959
& wife
Eva Floyd Mullins
Aug 25, 1870
Feb 18, 1926

R. M. Hague
Oct 1, 1862
Sep 28, 1907

Lelia Winn, wife of
R. M. Hague
Sep 21, 1866
Aug 17, 1895

Kalista Neeld, wife of
R. M. Hague
Aug 28, 1870
Jan 3, 1918

George F. Hague
1849-1915

Nannie R. Hague
1869-1937

Rufus A. Renegar
1858-1945
&
Willie A. Renegar
1857-1936

R. A. Price
Oct 8, 1902
Nov 9, 1943

Anderson R. Whitaker
1882-1950
&
Eveline Price Whitaker
(no dates)

Nannie Pitts, wife of
J. A. Arnold
Feb 25, 1873
Jul 28, 1909

John Harry Street
Jun 28, 1880
Sep 19, 1880
&
William Rees Street
May 28, 1884
Oct 15, 1884
&
Infant Son
B&D Feb 13, 1879

John W. Street
Aug 4, 1858
Jul 16, 1890
& wife
Mattie Rees Street
Jul 21, 1854
Jun 17, 1886
Age: 31y, 10m, 26d.

Ann G., Daughter of
W. H. & Mary E. Rees Street
Mar 30, 1843
Aug 25, 1897
Age: 54y, 4m, 25d.

W. A. Waggoner
Nov 19, 1850
(no date)
& wife
Mattie Spencer Waggoner
Dec 30, 1847
May 24, 1927

Willie Lee Pitts
Jul 18, 1889
May 3, 1891

William G. Tipps
Jan 23, 1871
Jun 6, 1930
&
Sue W. Tipps
Feb 15, 1881

J. E. Brown
Nov 20, 1824
May 5, 1892
Age: 67y, 5m, 15d.

MULBERRY QUADRANGLE

Ben Newman Tucker
Dec 30, 1873
Aug 19, 1929
&
Ida Lackey Tucker
Sep 1, 1874
Aug 2, 1944

James Ross Kimes
1909-1967

Infant of
Ross & Christine Kime
1933

Martha A., wife of
T. H. Freeman
Dec 19, 1824
Jun 14, 1897

Fannie F. Mitchell
1870-19
&
Thomas W. Mitchell
1871-1948
&
Lona Mitchell
1894-1910

George W. Jones
Jan 2, 1911
Jan 5, 1911

W. A. Taylor
1887-1940
&
Jennie Mae Taylor
Dec 8, 1884
Jun 4, 1952
&
Lucile Taylor
Oct 23, 1906
Jul 25, 1956

Mattie Lee Tucker, wife of
Roy E. Tipps
Jun 13, 1893
Nov 26, 1917

W. W. Rhea
Nov 23, 1859
May 6, 1899

Sallie Rhea
Apr 1, 1851
Dec 12, 1925

Mark Rhea
1887-1940

Lelia Hague, Daughter of
M. W. & L. E. Rhea
Died Nov 5, 1909
Age: 3 days

Lizzie Rhea Marrs
1889-1949

Bob, Infant of
M. W. & L. E. Rhea
B&D Feb 19, 1911

Douglas, Son of
M. W. & L. E. Rhea
Jul 20, 1913
Nov 13, 1919

M. L. Mead
Jun 4, 1825
Jan 10, 1903

Sallie Ellen, Daughter of
R. L. & Cora Farrar
Jun 2, 1902
Sep 6, 1902

Robert E. Lee Farrar, Sr.
Jan 22, 1867
Jul 4, 1942
&
Cora Shofner Farrar
Feb 18, 1872
Sep 15, 1939

Claud W. Shofner
1870-1941
&
Allie A. Shofner
1896-1956

Lucile Farrar Holland
Apr 26, 1890
Jul 2, 1963

Thomas Percy Holland, Sr.
May 24, 1885
Mar 27, 1932

Infant Son of
T. P. & Lucile Holland
1921-1921

Dr. E. F. Holland
1867-1929

Pearl Ingram, wife of
Dr. E. F. Holland
Nov 24, 1883
Mar 2, 1963

Jennie Mae, wife of
Dr. E. F. Holland
May 11, 1875
May 31, 1904

Clarence B., Son of
Dr. E. F. & J. M. Holland
Died Apr 5, 1898
Age: 1y, 11m, 12d.

Eugene F., Son of
Dr. E. F. & J. M. Holland
May 28, 1904
Sep 3, 1904
&
Infant Daughter of
E. F. & J. M. Holland
Jul 17, 1903
Jul 28, 1903

Robert Lee Motlow
Apr 4, 1864
May 8, 1959
& wife
Huldah Daniel Motlow
Sep 30, 1872
Jan 3, 1909
& wife
Margaret Lynne Whitaker Motlow
May 1, 1883
Nov 7, 1968

Thomas White Richardson
1858-1923
&
Kate Waggoner Richardson
1873-1954
&
Martha Waggoner Richardson
1842-1936

G. W. Gattis
Dec 15, 1846
Aug 10, 1885
Age: 39y, 7m, 4d.

Mary Eliza Allen
1876-1900

J. L. Goosby
1879-1931
&
Canzada Goosby
1878-19

Bob Casey
Dec 16, 1896
Mar 6, 1926

Clifford, Son of
T. F. & Mollie M. Casey
Mar 8, 1890
Dec 3, 1913

T. F. Casey
Aug 23, 1849
Nov 29, 1919
&
Mollie M. Casey
Nov 29, 1858
Sep 3, 1923

Fannie Mae Gill
1899-1957

Berry F. Gill, Jr.
1906-1947

"Mother"
Susie Beatrice Gill
1878-1954

Barry F. Gill
1872-1936

"Father"
Jesse N. Gill
Aug 23, 1850
Dec 31, 1937

Thomas Cartwright
1930-1940
&
Eugene Cartwright
1927-1943
"Cartwright Brothers"

William S. Raby
1869-19
&
Franklin Whitaler Raby
1875-1902
&
Jennie McDowell Raby
(no dates)

Mary Holman Mitchell
Feb 2, 1855
Sep 23, 1919

Alice Mitchell
1877-1938

Clarence R. Moorehead
Jun 21, 1888
Jun 22, 1959

David R. Moorehead
1858-1931

Susan E. Waggoner, wife
of D. F. R. Moorehead
Apr 19, 1867
Dec 3, 1901

Lizzie C. Stubblefield,
wife of John F. Pitts
Sep 30, 1888
Jan 12, 1919

Joe D. Stubblefield
Aug 8, 1861
Jul 26, 1928

Mary A. Tucker, wife of
J. D. Stubblefield
Sep 1, 1856
May 29, 1925

T. H. Stubblefield
Sep 29, 1884
Dec 10, 1900

J. W. Mitchell
Feb 22, 1832
Jul 30, 1909

B. O. Brown
Nov 9, 1902
Sep 17, 1968

Overton, Son of
W. S. & J. M. Faulkner
Sep 2, 1925
Jan 28, 1937

Tom E. Campbell
Feb 13, 1898
Jan 17, 1928

MULBERRY QUADRANGLE

Bettie Buntley Norman
1885-1949

Charles Abner Norman
1887-1930

James H. Norman
1866-1947

Louisa McGee Norman
1866-1952

Joan Norman
1938

Roy E. Tucker
1883-1943
&
Stella Taylor Tucker
1889-1968
(Died Aug 25, 1968
Age: 79 years.)

David Christopher Sullivan
Aug 4, 1878
Mar 30, 1955
&
Eliza Ashby Sullivan
Dec 22, 1878
Jun 2, 1960

William H., Son of
J. B. & M. I. McLaughlin
Jul 28, 1889
Aug 5, 1889

Benjamin A. Whitaker
1856-1932
&
Sue Craig Whitaker
1861-1942
&
"Father"
H. C. Whitaker
1822-1898
&
"Mother"
Lettie L. Whitaker
1830-1885

S. J. Whitaker
1863-1888

Larkin Moore Whitaker
Jul 29, 1870
Jun 13, 1945

Louise, Daughter of
L. M. & Elizabeth Whitaker
Sep 14, 1902
Oct 12, 1909

Elizabeth Daniel Whitaker
Jun 22, 1878
Oct 14, 1940

Infant Son of
L. M. & Elizabeth Whitaker
B&D Aug 1913

Floyd Elam Farrar
1894-
&
Mary B. Parks Farrar
1896-1958

Benjamin Newton Parks
1866-1953
&
Minnie Taylor Parks
1876-1954

"Mother"
Grace Howard Lane
Aug 3, 1895
Aug 20, 1925

W. B. Taylor
Feb 11, 1838
Jun 11, 1911

Angeline D., wife of
W. B. Taylor
Oct 12, 1843
Jun 15, 1884

Mollie Rhea, 2nd wife of
W. B. Taylor
Dec 3, 1846
Feb 16, 1907

George A. Howard
1860-1932

James W. Taylor
1867-1925
&
Florena Derror Taylor
1869-1926

J. A. L. Taylor
Jul 31, 1862
Sep 2, 1927

Mary E. Hamilton, wife of
J. A. L. Taylor
Apr 3, 1862
Jul 2, 1921

Margaret Taylor
Feb 1, 1904
Feb 1, 1904
&
Sarah A. Taylor
Feb 28, 1889
Mar 7, 1889

W. H. Warren
Oct 19, 1851
Jan 23, 1919
&
Fannie E. Warren
Mar 27, 1859
Apr 24, 1909

Hattie, Daughter of
W. H. & Fannie Warren
Aug 2, 1881
Sep 8, 1882

S. A. McGeehee
Jun 6, 1846
Aug 14, 1921

Hannah C., wife of
S. A. McGeehee
Sep 22, 1844
Jun 9, 1884
Age: 39y, 9m, 6d.

Sallie R., wife of
S. A. McGeehee
Apr 15, 1857
Feb 5, 1938

Lillian T. Scott
Jun 16, 1897
Feb 3, 1967

J. J. Tucker, Sr.
1822-1896

Sarah A. Tucker
1825-1893

J. J. Tucker, Jr.
1864-1928

Laura D. Tucker
1876-1936

T. J. Allison
Sep 14, 1839
Jan 15, 1885
&
Sallie F. Allison
Dec 12, 1844
Apr 6, 1903

W. H. Derror
Mar 8, 1871
Nov 20, 1928

A. Derror
Oct 4, 1846
Dec 2, 1916
& wife
Huldah M. Derror
Mar 19, 1832
Nov 4, 1911

Jimmie V. Howard
Apr 30, 1862
Dec 22, 1921

W. H. Allison
1866-1936

Ruby Allison Fiske
1878-1956

Joe Thomas Allison
1867-1931
&
Ethleen Allison
1883-1926

Thomas Jefferson, Son of
J. T. & Ethleen Allison
Aug 30, 1904
Jul 17, 1905

Emmett Clarence Allison
1913-1967

Martin V. Riddle
Oct 23, 1836
Jun 22, 1915
&
Theresa C. Riddle
Mar 7, 1834
Jan 18, 1911

Annie Lynne Edwards
May 18, 1886
Aug 20, 1886
&
Infant Son
B&D 1888
Children of
J. P. & Bettie Warren
Edwards.

Elizabeth, wife of
Benjamin T. Rives
Oct 27, 1829
Mar 7, 1894

William B. Riddle
Feb 3, 1860
Jan 22, 1915
& wife
Cora M. Brandon Riddle
May 19, 1875
Apr 23, 1919

Jasper F. Waggoner
1856-1935

Sue McNeece Waggoner
1862-1952

Ethel V. Waggoner
1880-1946

Hence H. Waggoner
1860-1921
&
Bolan M. Waggoner
1865-1929

H. M. McNeece
Apr 17, 1833
Feb 20, 1916

David L. Brown
Apr 15, 1867
Apr 19, 1892
&
Lula J. Brown
Jun 20, 1868
May 10, 1895

Caleb C. Groves
1845-1915
&
Alma K. Groves
1879-1937
&
Lydia L. Groves
1845-1929

MULBERRY QUADRANGLE

Frank Norman
Oct 8, 1888
Jan 7, 1947
&
Annie Isom Norman
Sep 19, 1886
May 7, 1964

Sarah E., Daughter of
J. F. & M. Norman
Dec 12, 1911
Aug 11, 1912

G. C. Logan
Dec 12, 1842
Dec 20, 1899

Elizabeth C. Logan
Jun 1, 1843
May 14, 1923

Mary Earle Parks Barnes
(no dates)

Curtis Parks
1882-1931
&
Mary Lou Parks
1886-1936
&
William H. Parks
1909-1918
&
Sarah E. Parks
1918-1918

Annie Maud,* Daughter of
Frank Allison
Died Sep 15, 1902
Age: 8m, 15d.

Mrs. Jennie Renegar *
Died Aug 28, 1891
Age: 30 years.

Miss Mamie,* Daughter of
R. H. Pitts
Died Nov 11, 1871
Age: 20 years.

Hiram M. Cooper *
Died Mar 23, 1893
Age: 73y, 9m, 22d.

Miss Anna Harrison *
Died Nov 27, 1879
Age: 20 years.

Zula,* wife of
Dr. Mathew Parks &
Daughter of
T. J. Neeld & Sister of
Kalista Hague
Died Dec 27, 1914
Age: (not given)

Mrs. Margarett,* wife of
John Evans
Died Aug 15, 1891
Age: 99 years.

Nannie E. Wood
1851-1939

C. B., Son of
C. C. & N. E. Wood
Jul 26, 1883
Jul 26, 1885

C. C., Son of
C. C. & N. E. Wood
May 28, 1886
May 27, 1887

John H. Campbell
Dec 1, 1895
Feb 10, 1967
&
Della T. Campbell
Mar 29, 1890
Feb 24, 1953

Infant Son of
J. H. & D. T. Campbell
B&D Feb 12, 1925

Ruby Duff Boone Creson
Mar 15, 1875
Apr 19, 1955

Hugh L. W. Boone
Died Mar 6, 1899
Age: 59y, 3m, 19d.

John R. Webb
1885-1943

Villa L. Webb
Oct 3, 1906
Aug 11, 1958

Mary Alice Webb
1934-1936

Mrs. Mary,* wife of
Harrison Reece
Died Jun 19, 1874
Age: about 50 years.

Robert A.,* Son of
Mr. & Mrs. Ben Parks
Died Sep 8, 1905
Age: 21months.

Mary A. Caldwell,* Daughter
of Charles Mitchell, dec'd.
Born in Granville, N. C.
Aug 4, 1820
Feb 29, 1892
Age: 71y, 6m, 25d.

Miss Mary Mead *
Died Aug 10, 1891
Age: 72 years.

Emmett Allison *
Died Jul 30, 1906
Age: about 23 years.

Many unmarked graves.

R. B. Campbell
Died 1936
Age: (not given)

Nancy Campbell
Apr 16, 1860
Apr 2, 1906

James Henry Campbell
Sep 9, 1889
Apr 21, 1903

J. M. Campbell
Jan 26, 1865
Jan 6, 1932

Bettie P. Campbell
Mar 10, 1866
Feb 9, 1925

Eliza Duff
Dec 10, 1810
(gone) 1868

Alfred Fulton, Son of
J. H. C. & J. C. Duff
Died Mar 31, 1889
Age: 9y, 5m, 8d.

Douglas Spencer
Dec 7, 1936
Jul 20, 1938
&
Ruth P. Spencer
Aug 27, 1900

&
William Spencer
Sep 8, 1896

E. M. Ousley *
Mar 4, 1832
Feb 16, 1897
C.S.A.

Infant * of
Mr. & Mrs. Ray Bateman
Died Nov 25, 1916
Age: (not given)

L. W. Davidson *
Died Jun 25, 1892
Age: 55 years.

Mrs. Josie Farris *
Died Dec 17, 1899
Age: 53 years.

W. A. Wood *
Died Mar 19, 1900
Age: 77y, 6m.

Garner Craig,* Son of
B. A. & Susan Whitaker
Died Dec 28, 1890
Age: 1 week.

George W. Quarles
1878-1940
&
Margarette Quarles
1896-19

Felix Motlow
Apr 9, 1838
Sep 6, 1917
&
Nettie Josephine Motlow
Apr 12, 1846
Jan 2, 1891

J. Frank Motlow
Jun 9, 1871
Mar 29, 1906

William G. Motlow
Dec 17, 1878
Oct 12, 1911

Esther L. Pitts Bateman
Apr 21, 1878
Sep 14, 1941

J. D. Bateman, Jr.
May 7, 1910
Feb 10, 1911

Hugh Moore
Pfc Btry C 5 field Arty
Jun 29, 1909
Aug 17, 1968

Frank Ayers
1882-1957
&
Fannie Ayers
1885-1963

Mrs. Nancy M.,* wife of
G. W. Payne
Died Jun 25, 1892
Age: 42 years.

Annie Mai,* Daughter of
J. W. & V. L. Adair
Died Jul 13, 1900
Age: 7m, 13d.

Daniel Waggoner *
Died Feb 7, 1897
Age: 93 years.

John,* Son of
Berry Gill
Died Apr 1, 1914
Age: 3 years.

Mrs. Addie Lane *
Died Feb 9, 1892
Age: 74 years.
Mother of Robert Lane.

Marshall M. Caldwell *
Died Sep 9, 1899
Age: 67 years.

* *

MULBERRY QUADRANGLE

WHITAKER CEMETERY

LOCATION: Two and one fourth miles NE of Mulberry Village on the east side of East Fork of Mulberry Creek.

William Jones Osborne
Jun 3, 1860
Feb 17, 1936

Delia Whitaker, wife of
William J. Osborne
Jan 8, 1861
Jun 24, 1893

Mrs. Willie Caldwell,*
wife of Mark Whitaker
Died Oct 16, 1891
Age: 34 years.
Daughter of
M. M. Caldwell.

Mark Whitaker
Jun 19, 1806
Aug 28, 1887

Rosanna Rutledge, wife of
Mark Whitaker
Feb 29, 1812
Sep 8, 1895

America Fredonia Whitaker
1842-1877
&
James Porter Tolley
Age: 1 year.

Mark Whitaker
North Carolina
Pvt Capt. F. Lock's Regt.
Revolutionary War
1750-1842

Catherine Boone, wife of
Mark Whitaker
1760-1845

Mark L. Whitaker *
Died Oct 4, 1890
Age: 39 years.

Ruth A. Whitaker, wife of
F. P Taylor
Aug 6, 1849
Aug 22, 1877

Rebecca Amby, Daughter of
Ruth Ann Taylor
Mar 12, 1877
Sep 12, 1877

3 unmarked graves.

Slave Graveyard to the
rear of this Cemetery.

* *

BRADY CEMETERY

LOCATION: Three miles east of Mulberry Village on Gattistown Branch.

Alex Brady
Member of Co K 8th Tenn Reg.
Killed at Battle of Franklin.
Nov 30, 1864
Age: (not given)

M. A. Hill
Died Dec 28, 1880
Age: (not given, fieldstone)

Hill
(no dates, fieldstone)

* *

GATTIS CEMETERY

LOCATION: Immediately east of Gattistown.

Irene Josephine Tipps
Oct 7, 1874
Mar 9, 1907

James Hilman Gattis
Feb 2, 1906
Feb 13, 1906
&
Annie Elizabeth Gattis
Dec 26, 1893
Dec 15, 1908

Julia E., Daughter of
W. H. & M. E. Gattis
Nov 12, 1907
Jun 8, 1908

John C. Riddle
1859-1936
&
Mary F. Riddle
1855-1910

Mary Sue, Daughter of
J. E. & Amanda Owens
1911-1920

S. L Tripp
Mar 12, 1892
Dec 9, 1908

Infant of
J. A. & A. F. Tripp
(no dates)

Infant of
J. A. & A. F. Tripp
(no dates)

J. A. Tripp
Jun 6, 1857
Jul 7, 1899
&
A. F. Tripp
Feb 6, 1851
Aug 30, 1908

William W. Riddle
Dec 4, 1877
Dec 18, 1899

James N., Son of
Frank & Ida Riddle
(no dates)

Clara Ada Gattis
Oct 23, 1888
Apr 4, 1905

James Wesley Gattis
Feb 27, 1857
Jan 7, 1937

Julia Ann Gattis
Apr 12, 1861
Dec 17, 1938

Mary Tripp, wife of
J. D. Preston
May 18, 1887
May 27, 1926

Infant Daughter of
J. N. & Monnie Walker
B&D Jun 4, 1934

W. H. Tripp
1845-1930

Robert L. Owens
Aug 1, 1891
Jan 20, 1916
Age: 25y, 7m, 19d.

Sue Ella Gattis
Mar 28, 1881
Jul 28, 1922

Mary G. Duke
Dec 6, 1900
Nov 16, 1903

William Riddle
Dec 13, 1816
Feb 3, 1876

Mary C. Riddle
Nov 29, 1824
Sep 6, 1900

Mary Elizabeth Owen
Oct 28, 1878
Sep 6, 1899

C. L. Owens
Apr 7, 1881
Sep 22, 1908

Catharine Owens
1855-1934

Anna May Owens
Sep 19, 1911
Oct 23, 1911

Mary R. Owens
1890-1924

MULBERRY QUADRANGLE

Conchitia Owens
1910-1941

S. F. Owen
1912-1943

Thomas J. Miles
Jun 10, 1875
Apr 14, 1955

Ida A. Miles
Sep 24, 1878
May 4, 1906

Nannie Lee Duke
Mar 8, 1907
Aug 14, 1920

George W. Gattis
Oct 10, 1830
May 31, 1886
&
Mary Jane Gattis
Dec 18, 1833
(no date)

Charley Brown *
Died Aug 4, 1903
Age: 19 years.
Married Lula Tucker
Oct 30, 1901

Ella Gattis Tripp
Apr 10, 1867
Aug 3, 1903

George W. Tripp
Feb 6, 1894
May 8, 1918

William M. Tripp
Dec 4, 1868
Dec 29, 1906

Emily Copeland Tripp
Jul 17, 1869
Dec 16, 1951

C. Roscoe Tripp
1904-1943

Susan E., wife of
J. W. Mitchell
Jan 28, 1839
Mar 10, 1885

Many unmarked graves.

Mrs. Lula,* wife of
Charles Brown
Died Nov 9, 1903
Age: 24y, 6m, 13d.

M. Riddle
Died Dec 18, 1899
Age: 80 years.
(fieldstone, broken)

Virginia F., Daughter of
G. W. & M. J. Gattis
Sep 15, 1867
Sep 13, 1868

Laura S., Daughter of
H. L. & C. E. Brown
Sep 1, 1881
Apr 17, 1901

Cordelia E., wife of
H. L. Brown
Oct 28, 1862
Jul 14, 1888

Infant Son of
H. L. & A. M. Brown
(no dates)

Newton B. Riddle *
Died Sep 25, 1902
Age: 21 years.

Mrs. Vista Swinney *
Died Aug 19, 1902
Age: 23 years.

Mrs. Nancy Gattis *
Died Jul 11, 1894
Age: 89 years.

Miss Bartie Moore Tucker *
Died Jan 22, 1906
Age: 15 years.

Susie Tripp *
Died Oct 9, 1908
Age: (not given)

Jane Gattis *
Died Feb 1891
Age: 50 years.

Lizzie Gattis *
Died Dec 12, 1902
Age: 9 years.

Mr. William Goosby *
Died Apr 19, 1900
Age: 83 years.

* *

TIPPS CEMETERY

LOCATION: Two and one half miles ESE of Mulberry Village on south side of Crystal Ridge, head of Stephens Creek.

James Ernest Tipps
May 19, 1920
Mar 1, 1923
&
Ethel Madilene Tipps
Sep 25, 1917
Mar 14, 1920

Dudley Tipps
Jun 16, 1839
Feb 8, 1916
&
Jane R. Tipps
Dec 4, 1840
Jul 24, 1921

Emma C. Tipps
Jul 25, 1868
Oct 25, 1903

Henry H. Tipps
Mar 19, 1880
Mar 20, 1897

Davis M. Tipps
Jun 30, 1861
Jan 8, 1916

Nora F. Tipps
Jul 19, 1874
Jul 5, 1911

* *

RENEGAR CEMETERY

LOCATION: Two and one half miles SE of Mulberry Village on west side of Stephens Creek and east side of a ridge.

8 to 10 graves, fieldstones with no inscriptions.

NOTE: The Old Henry Renegar probably buried here.

* *

NOLES CEMETERY

LOCATION: Two miles SE of Mulberry Village, north of Cooper Branch, north of road leading to Crystal Ridge.

Emma Cook
1856-1931

Odie B., Son of
Guy & Myrtle Cartwright
Mar 31, 1911
Jun 14, 1911

Myrtle Cowley, wife of
J. G. Cartwright
Jul 8, 1876
Mar 5, 1911

W. A. Carter
Sep 27, 1828
Jun 21, 1902

Elizabeth M., wife of
W. A. Carter
Mar 21, 1827
Feb 5, 1902

James Darnell Carter
Oct 10, 1898
Nov 7, 1900

G. Bell Campbell
1875-1951
(Gallant FH)

Sarah Emma Campbell
1871-1957
(Gallant FH)

MULBERRY QUADRANGLE

George E. Campbell
Jan 11, 1860
Jan 13, 1920
&
Laura Campbell
Jan 22, 1857
Aug 8, 1921

G. Cleveland Campbell
1887-1932
&
Ida Pearl Miles Campbell
1882-1923

E. Josephine Ramsey, wife
of John T. Howard
Apr 28, 1859
Nov 20, 1904

Christopher B. Howard
Jun 26, 1860
May 9, 1888

J. S. Ramsey
Apr 2, 1854
Apr 10, 1917

E. G., wife of
J. S. Ramsey
Jun 16, 1857
May 24, 1901

Fannie J., Daughter of
J. S. & E. G. Ramsey
Aug 4, 1884
Sep 14, 1899

F. N. Ramsey
Jan 2, 1857
Jun 22, 1894

B. B. Ramsey
Apr 13, 1814
Jul 7, 1883

Matilda B., wife of
B. B. Ramsey
Jan 11, 1822
May 20, 1880

Mary L., wife of
T. B. Howard
May 20, 1826
Dec 8, 1907

Litty Clidy, Son of
J. P. & M. J. Howard
May 15, 1901
Oct 21, 1905

Bobby Joe Kent
Jan 4, 1938

Hugh Wilson Mansfield
Mar 9, 1869
Nov 24, 1935

Pearl Cowley, wife of
H. W. Mansfield
Dec 16, 1884
Jan 4, 1913

D. R. Sanders
1885-1937

T. C. Simmons
Oct 9, 1936
Oct 9, 1936

Rosie Nell Simmons
Apr 13, 1943
Apr 21, 1943

Shirley A. Simmons
July 1948

P. B., wife of
H. L. Womack
Jun 5, 1853
Oct 6, 1895

Several unmarked graves.

Little Clidy,* Son of
Mr. & Mrs. Jim Howard
Died Oct 21, 1905
Age: 4y, 5m, 6d.

Newman Walter Miles
Jun 30, 1873
Nov 26, 1944
&
Molly Ramsey Miles
Mar 30, 1880
Dec 28, 1938

K. E. Miles
1915-1948
(Raby FH)

Saffer E. McNeece
Jul 22, 1833
Jul 21, 1893

Malinda, Daughter of
J. A. & S. V. Miles
Died Apr 12, 1904
Age: 6 days.
&
George C., Son of
J. A. & S. V. Miles
Died Oct 7, 1910
Age: 5y, 11m, 21d.

James Arthur Miles
Sep 9, 1876
Jan 7, 1918
& wife
Sarah Violet Winfrey Miles
Sep 13, 1875
Sep 1, 1967

Bradley K. White *
Died Nov 16, 1916
Age: 73 years.

Charity,* wife of
George B. Campbell
Died Feb 15, 1902
Age: 74y, 11m, 19d.

Miss Mary Perry *
Died Mar 11, 1898
Age: 16 years.

Laura Ann Noles
Jan 5, 1873
Jan 17, 1929

B. W. Noles
May 15, 1865
Jan 30, 1913
&
Syntha Renegar Noles
Nov 16, 1887
Dec 5, 1924

Charlie J. Noles
Jan 24, 1893
Mar 13, 1912

Emma Noles
Nov 19, 1879
Aug 24, 1904

Malissie H. Noles
Sep 2, 1887
Sep 4, 1890

Katie M. Noles
Mar 2, 1889
Aug 4, 1890

Sofronia Certain *
Feb 27, 1877
Jul 23, 1901
Age: 37y, 10m, 24d.
Married Henry Cartain

Infant * of
Sophronia Certain
Died Jan 5, 1898
Age: (not given)

W. H. Certain *
Died May 26, 1917
Age: 55 years.

* *

LOYD CEMETERY

LOCATION: One and three fourth miles NE of Old Loyd's Chapel,
on west side of Stephens Creek.

E. C. Loyd
May 10, 1833
Mar 21, 1901

Mary Jane Loyd
Nov 22, 1875
May 24, 1952

R. Frank Loyd
Jun 8, 1869
Jun 15, 1912

Riley G. Loyd
Apr 21, 1859
Nov 11, 1934

George W. Loyd
Jan 30, 1862
Nov 19, 1921

Malinda Loyd *
Died May 29, 1906
Age: 87 years.

About 12 fieldstones,
no inscriptions.

Miss Lucinda Loyd *
Died Apr 4, 1903
Age: 85y, 9m.

* *

MULBERRY QUADRANGLE

WHITE CEMETERY

LOCATION: One mile NE of Old Loyd's Chapel and west side of Stephens Creek.

James Carrol White Jul 6, 1847 Aug 7, 1847	J. F. White Aug 10, 1816 Aug 2, 1852	Martha M. White May 9, 1851 Aug 13, 1852	Thomas J. White * Died Apr 22, 1900 Age: 52 years.
	Mrs. Martha V.,* widow of James F. White Died Apr 21, 1891 Age: 74y, 11m, 15d.	2 Infants of J. F. & M. V. White (no dates)	

* *

BURNS CEMETERY

LOCATION: One mile NE of Old Loyd's Chapel and on east side of Stephens Creek.

J. M. Thompson 1855-1933 Janey Thompson 1879-1936	James M., Son of W. R. & M. J. Burns Oct 23, 1854 Mar 19, 1879	Mrs. Mary J. Burns * Died Feb 18, 1909 Age: 71y, 5m, 19d.	Several fieldstones, no inscriptions.

* *

CEMETERY

LOCATION: One mile north of Old Loyd's Chapel.

No markers remain in this cemetery.

* *

HOWARD CEMETERY

LOCATION: One and one half mile south of Mulberry Village on the east side of Kelso-Mulberry Road.

Jane, wife of C. Howard Died Feb 13, 1871 Age: 63 years.	Thomas B. Howard Dec 11, 1835 Feb 25, 1882	Several unmarked graves.

* *

CEMETERY

LOCATION: At Old Cumberland Presbyterian Church in the Village of Mulberry.

Several graves, no markers.

* *

BROYLES CEMETERY

LOCATION: One fourth mile SW of Village of Mulberry.

Isaac Broyles Jul 25, 1779 Feb 15, 1842	Mary A. Broyles May 19, 1781 May 5, 1843	(Both graves are covered with a Slab type markers.)

* *

MULBERRY QUADRANGLE

MORGAN CEMETERY

LOCATION: One mile SW of Village of Mulberry, between Fayetteville Highway and West Fork of Mulberry Creek.

Capt. John Morgan **
1753-1816/17
Soldier of the American Revolution.

** Court Records.

No signs of this cemetery remain.

* *

RENEGAR CEMETERY

LOCATION: One and one half miles SW of Village of Mulberry between Fayetteville Highway and West Fork of Mulberry Creek.

Andrew Cashion Nov 2, 1812 Aug 18, 1880	Joseph W., Son of Andrew & Catharine Cashion Mar 16, 1851 Dec 25, 1856	George Renegar Mar 30, 1791 Mar 1857	G. F. Renegar Apr 25, 1821 Apr 10, 1902 Married Apr 13, 1843
Catharine Renegar, wife of Andrew Cashion Sep 16, 1817 Dec 17, 1896	George F., Son of Andrew & Catharine Cashion Dec 23, 1845 Nov 20, 1870	Ann, wife of George Renegar Oct 3, 1788 Aug 1859	Sarah, wife of G. F. Renegar Mar 31, 1818 Aug 9, 1885 Married Apr 13, 1843
Mary H., Daughter of Andrew & Catharine Cashion 1848-1860	Lucy, Daughter of W. H. & L. M. Cashion Oct 6, 1877 Oct 28, 1881	Elizabeth Renegar Jan 4, 1823 Apr 18, 1830	W. J. Parks * Died Dec 24, 1900 Age: 56 years.
Infant Daughter of W. F. & S. Renegar B&D 1847		Ann Renegar Dec 29, 1829 Apr 10, 1836	Mrs. Sarah F.,* wife of W. J. Parks Died Jul 8, 1894 Age: 40y, 4m, 21d. Sister to W. H. Cashion.
	Several unmarked graves.	Mahulda Renegar Apr 23, 1825 Apr 12, 1836	

* *

MEAD CEMETERY

LOCATION: Two and one fourth miles SW of Village of Mulberry, three fourth mile south of Fayetteville Highway # 50 on east side of lane to the Old Park Scott Homeplace.

Mary M. Mead
Aug 31, 1819
Aug 10, 1891

L. G. M. (Mead)
Died Apr 12, 18--
(stone broken)

Several unmarked graves.

* *

SOLOMON CEMETERY

LOCATION: North of Providence Road and one and one half mile west of Mulberry Creek.

Several graves, no inscriptions. Rock Fence enclosure.

* *

McDANIEL-PARKS CEMETERY

LOCATION: North side of Providence Road and one and one half mile west of Mulberry Creek.

Mattie A. Parks Dec 31, 1850 Dec 22, 1863	Lou M., wife of J. D. Ventress Jun 16, 1851 Apr 6, 1894	Jesse W. Parks * Died Jan 14, 1900 Age: 72 years. Died at his son M. B. Parks.	Mrs. Ida,* wife of W. H. Parks Died Dec 30, 1906 Age: 32 years.
J. W. P. (Parks) (footstone)			

MULBERRY QUADRANGLE

Taylor,* Son of
Mrs. Maud Crutcher
Died Jun 30, 1907
Age: 18 months.

Laura * Daughter of
Mr. & Mrs. J. D. Ventress
Died Nov 14, 1895
Age: 13y, 9m.

Nina D.,* Daughter of
J. D. Ventress
Died Sep 1, 1905
Age: (not given)

Several markers have been destroyed or missing. Cemetery is now in a cowpasture.

* *

WARREN CEMETERY

LOCATION: South side of Providence Road and immediately west of Mulberry Creek.

Henry Loyd
May 31, 1849
Mar 9, 1905

Lizzie E., Daughter of
B. & E. G. Warren
Apr 18, 1867
May 4, 1884

Sarah Caraline Warren
Jan 10, ---- (gone)
Sep 10, 1848
Age: 5y, 7m.

(Name gone)
Jan 1, 1885
Dec 31, 1885

Merrett,* Son of
Mr. & Mrs. William Moyers
Died Oct 30, 1907
Age: (not given)

Large Cemetery, many fieldstones, some Vaults destroyed by cows.

* *

BUCHANAN CEMETERY

LOCATION: One mile SE of Buchanan Crossing on the north side of Highway # 64 on "Posey Farm".

Bethiah L. Buchanan
(no dates)

Andrew Buchanan
(no dates)

Mathew Buchanan
(no dates)

Elizabeth Buchanan
(no dates)

White Buchanan
(no dates)

J. F. F.
(footstone)

Mrs. Ida McGehee *
Died Nov 30, 1898
Age: 26 years.

Mrs. Bethiah Lyne,*
wife of Andrew Buchanan
& Daughter of
Capt. William White
Born Aug 7, 1794
Died May 20, 1883
Married Feb 19, 1815

Andrew Buchanan *
Died Nov 20, 1868
Age: 87 years.

Manta Lou, Daughter of
W. M. & J. A. Groce
Mar 28, 1871
Feb 16, 1878

Mattie Payne Lynch
Jun 3, 1853
Mar 17, 1912

Iva, wife of
L. Long
Died Aug 17, 1925
Age: (not given)

Louis Long
1841-1929

Mrs. George (Jennie) Williams
Died Apr 27, 1907
Age: (not given)

Mrs. Eva Reynolds *
Died Dec 28, 1903
Age: (not given)

Nancy C., wife of
H. R. Williams
Jul 19, 1826
Jan 24, 1874

Julia M., wife of
J. M. Ward
Dec 21, 1892
Apr 21, 1913

Jane Herndon
"Colored"
Born in Virginia
Died in Lincoln Co., Tenn.
Oct 24, 1920
Age: 75 years.

Many unmarked graves.

Elizabeth Buchanan *
Died Jan 1882
Age: 67 years.

Henry Williams *
Died Apr 8, 1896
Age: 55 years.

Byrd Wilson,* Son of
Mr. & Mrs. Clay Tucker
Died Nov 21, 1914
Age: (not given)

Mrs. Victoria Williams *
Died Jun 18, 1896
Age: 58 years.

Infant * of
George & Jennie Williams
Died Jun 4, 1907
Age: (not given)

Infant * of
H. D. & Russia Hoots
Died Jul 6, 1901
Age: (not given)

Matthew Buchanan *
Died Mar 12, 1862
Age: 33 years.
C.S.A.

* *

MULBERRY QUADRANGLE

WEBB CEMETERY

LOCATION: One and one half miles NNW of Kelso and west side of Mulberry Road in the "QUARTER" of Elk River.

Sarah Frances Webb
Jun 4, 1836
Sep 2, 1850

About 30 unmarked graves. Many of the Webb Family buried in this cemetery.

* *

GREGORY CEMETERY

LOCATION: One mile NW of Kelso on west side of Railroad and on south side of Eldad Road.

Tunstall Gregory Mar 19, 1789 Apr 9, 1870	Ebenezer Hill, III Apr 8, 1826 Jun 19, 1896 &	Zanga McCartney Aug 29, 1822 Sep 13, 1880 &	A. T. McCartney Jun 21, 1856 Jan 15, 1908
Febton Gregory May 6, 1810 Aug 11, 1849 (Rock Vault)	Ruth Ann Gregory Hill Nov 14, 1827 Jul 18, 1886	Elizabeth McCartney Aug 29, 1822 Oct 7, 1882	Beulah Benton McCartney Jul 3, 1866 Jan 13, 1956
	2 Adult graves, no inscription.	1 Child Rock Vault, no inscription.	Ida Izetta McCartney Oct 15, 1859 Mar 21, 1931

* *

BRADY CEMETERY

LOCATION: One mile WNW of Kelso and one half mile south of Eldad Road.

Alex. Brady Feb 2, 1777 Nov 21, 1865 & Ruth J. Brady May 11, 1787 Oct 28, 1855	John,* Son of A. & R. Brady Mar 3, 1832 Nov 21, 1842 Infants * of Oscar & Maud Marshall Died Feb 6, 1906 Age: (not given)	T. J. M. (footmarker) About 20 graves with fieldstones, no inscriptions.

* *

KELSO CEMETERY

LOCATION: Main Cemetery at Kelso (Old Section)

Clemenzal, wife of T. C. Taylor Died Oct 24, 1911 Age: 72 years.	A. T. Renegar Jul 8, 1857 Aug 30, 1904	Susie, Daughter of R. M. & M. E. Routt Sep 22, 1901 Jun 20, 1904	Claude Solomon 1886-1969 & Callie R. Solomon 1864-1948
Bettie G. Kennedy 1873-1961	Elizabeth M., wife of A. T. Renegar Oct 23, 1860 Mar 29, 1940	John M. Routt Dec 12, 1834 Jan 15, 1904 Age: 73y, 1m, 3d.	& Rufus A. Solomon 1857-1903
James T. Gray 1837-1911 & Matilda J. Gray 1836-1894	Infant Son of John & Mary Snoddy Feb 14, 1896 Feb 18, 1896	Louisa J. Kelso, wife of J. M. Routt Oct 17, 1833 Mar 6, 1892	Rufus Lee (Solomon) 1901-1902 Edgar (Solomon) 1896-1897
William D. Gray 1869-1906	Dana Routte 1870-1934		Infant (Solomon) 1892

MULBERRY QUADRANGLE

W. D. Moorhead
Oct 22, 1813
Apr 2, 1898
Married Mariah Cunningham
Jan 3, 1839
    & wife
Mariah Moorhead
Apr 29, 1820
Jan 13, 1894

Catharine McClure Jean
Nov 27, 1827
Mar 20, 1912

Mattie F. Jean
Jul 14, 1857
Aug 21, 1933

E. M. Jean
Mar 3, 1858
Oct 13, 1902

Renel W., Son of
A. E. & D. C. Smith
Jan 20, 1875
Apr 14, 1889

Pearl Alline, Daughter of
Mr. & Mrs. G. J. Carter
Mar 2, 1896
Oct 6, 1903

George J. Carter
1860-1932

W. F. Keith
Dec 25, 1841
(no date)
&
Samantha S. Pamplin Keith
Jul 19, 1849
Nov 24, 1919
  Married Aug 18, 1864

James Leslie Keith
Sep 22, 1875
Sep 25, 1901

General Lee Taylor
Mar 23, 1863
Mar 23, 1906

Mary W., wife of
Thomas Taylor
Jan 25, 1825
Aug 8, 1890

Eliza W., Daughter of
J. H. & S. E. Taylor
Mar 31, 1875
 Sep 21, 1893

James H. Taylor
Jan 4, 1849
Jul 19, 1922

Susan Taylor
1850-1933

Clarence Goodrich, Son of
M. A. & J. F. Taylor
Dec 22, 1893-Jun 6, 1894

Milton Goodner, Son of
M. A. & J. F. Taylor
Dec 22, 1893
Mar 28, 1894

J. C. Sullenger
1874-1964

John W. Sullenger
1878-1948
&
Eevater T. Sullenger
1880-1965

Charlie Lee Sullenger
Apr 15, 1884
Jan 9, 1968
&
Adie E. Sullenger
1883-1941

Thomas B. Stubblefield
Jun 18, 1859
Jun 27, 1928
&
Mary A. Stubblefield
Oct 12, 1865
Jul 27, 1928
&
James G. Stubblefield
Jun 4, 1904
Nov 30, 1925

George W. Webb
1853-1931

Hulda Solomon Webb
(Mrs. G. W. Webb)
1855-1936

Pearl, Daughter of
G. W. & H. A. Webb &
wife of W. C. Foster
Dec 12, 1893
Dec 22, 1911

John Bennett Solomon
May 25, 1859
Apr 25, 1894
Son of J. W. &
M. A. Solomon

J. W. Solomon
Jul 16, 1830
Jul 29, 1905

Mary A. Taylor, wife of
J. W. Solomon
Nov 1, 1830
Feb 10, 1913

John V. Carter
Jan 18, 1852
Dec 30, 1896

M. E., wife of
J. V. Carter
Jun 2, 1863
Feb 28, 1890

Callie Carter Hampton
Nov 18, 1849
Apr 13, 1925

Morgan Davis Hampton, Sr.
Apr 9, 1827
Sep 2, 1904

Amanda Hampton Tarkington
Died Apr 28, 1950
Age: 66 years.

W. E. Carter
May 18, 1823
Oct 22, 1898
Age: 75y, 5m, 4d.
    & wife
Amanda Carter
Apr 1, 1829
Jun 12, 1887
Age: 57y, 2m, 12d.

Robert T., Son of
W. E. & Amanda Carter
Sep 6, 1854
Feb 14, 1877

Mannie, Daughter of
W. E. & Amanda Carter
Feb 17, 1874
Aug 1, 1893

Morgan Davis Hampton, Jr.
Sep 16, 1879
May 4, 1904

Charles Weiss
Nov 16, 1852
Aug 28, 1915
Age: 62y, 8m, 12d.
    & wife
Maggie Plemons Weiss
Jul 28, 1857
Sep 26, 1942

Carl Weiss
Died 1935
Age: (not given)

Adah Ozell, Daughter of
Charley & M. E. Weiss
Jul 22, 1893
Dec 25, 1893

E. M. Stubblefield
Jun 12, 1869
Mar 4, 1904

Lula Mae Caldwell
1909-1947

W. M. Askey
Aug 14, 1861
(no date)
&
Sallie Askey
Aug 13, 1869
Nov 2, 1917
Age: 48 years.

W. M. Williams
Jul 22, 1850
Jan 19, 1914

Ellen C. Williams
Oct 16, 1840
Nov 1, 1918

Georgie W., Son of
William & E. C. Williams
Jan 20, 1875
Jan 29, 1893

Alfred M., Son of
William & E. C. Williams
Nov 29, 1887
Aug 6, 1888

Willie D., Daughter of
W. & E. C. Williams
Feb 21, 1879
Jan 6, 1881

Alda Bell Harbin
Jan 6, 1886
Feb 3, 1890

Lillian Harbin
Sep 29, 1895
Jul 21, 1896

Margarette L. Harbin
Oct 31, 1868
Apr 29, 1927

James W. Harbin
Mar 7, 1861
Jan 9, 1919

H. D. Cowley
Feb 22, 1842
Feb 21, 1907

Sallie C. Thompson,
wife of H. D. Cowley
Aug 1, 1853
Jul 13, 1949

B. B. Thompson
Dec 9, 1839
Nov 11, 1916
    & wife
Sarah H. Cowley Thompson
Jan 25, 1852
May 23, 1918

Maggie Thompson
Sep 11, 1887
Mar 7, 1904

Sallie Thompson
Aug 11, 1884
May 26, 1903

Ellen Thompson
Apr 18, 1880
Jul 19, 1904

J. E. Pitts
Jun 6, 1875
Apr 19, 1902

MULBERRY QUADRANGLE

Clarence Kelso
Died 1859
Age: 9 months.
Son of
Mr. & Mrs. Henry Kelso

Orvel B. Thompson
1859-1948
&
Henretta Thompson
1849-1939

Nertha Largen Thompson
May 6, 1892
Mar 28, 1938
(Mrs. Ben Thompson)

Thomas J. Kelso
Jun 30, 1869
Aug 13, 1889
&
Infant
B&D Dec 2, 1887
&
Margaret M. Kelso
Jul 29, 1882
Jan 29, 1887

John P. Cowley
Jan 7, 1845
Sep 13, 1926

Susan J. Erwin, wife of
J. P. Cowley
Jun 9, 1854
Jan 8, 1921

Sarah J. Locker, wife of
J. P. Cowley
Jan 5, 1851
Apr 21, 1880

Margaret E. Nicks, wife of
Benjamin T. Cowley
Nov 17, 1820
Aug 8, 1907

Infant Daughter of
Charles & Catharine G.
Gillham
B&D May 30, 1919

Superior Goodner
Mar 13, 1813
Aug 30, 1885
Age: 70y, 5m, 17d.

Mrs. Jane E. Adair
Mar 24, 1835
Sep 1, 1894

Mrs. L. J. Goodner
Died Jul 28, 1888
Age: 53y, 5m, 29d.

Dr. D. M. Goodner
Jan 26, 1849
Aug 28, 1932

Mrs. N. R., wife of
Dr. D. M. Goodner
Jun 10, 1856
Apr 16, 1942

Ida Belle, Daughter of
D. M. & N. R. Goodner
Died Jul 28, 1882
Age: 4m, 22d.

John A. Taylor
1849-1911
& wife
Mary E. Taylor
1847-1919
&
Ella T., wife of
Dr. L. H. Gillam
1871-1909
&
Ida M. Taylor
1875-1877
&
James B. Taylor
1877-1879
&
Clyde V. Taylor
1881-1884

Matt W. Thorton
1871-1946
& wife
Alda T. Thorton
1873-1942

Matt Webb
Died Sep 13, 1904
Age: 53 years.
& wife
Minnie Johnson Webb
Died Feb 5, 1892
Age: 36 years.

George T. Webb
1842-1923

Lisa I. Webb
Mar 25, 1848
Feb 15, 1917

Gatewood Webb
Apr 28, 1796
Oct 3, 1885

H. C. Webb
Oct 3, 1853
Aug 26, 1888

Fannie Webb
Feb 28, 1848
Dec 3, 1887

Mary Pearl Dickey
B&D Mar 25, 1926

Louisa E., wife of
John M. Dickey
Oct 20, 1840
May 7, 1877

"Mother"
Mary M., wife of
James L. Dickey
(no dates)
& "Son"
John M. Dickey
Jul 3, 1864
Mar 19, 1933

Lucy Vernon, Daughter of
J. M. & Louisa E. Dickey
Jan 7, 1869
Sep 11, 1909

Samantha E., wife of
R. A. McWhorter & Daughter of
Ephraim & Eliza Dickey
Feb 7, 1850
Feb 19, 1879
Age: 29y, 12d.

Laura Voyage, Daughter of
J. J. & Elizabeth Tucker &
wife of John M. Dickey
Mar 25, 1845
May 24, 1913

John M. Dickey
Mar 18, 1840
Nov 24, 1920

Joseph T. Dickey
Aug 20, 1888
Feb 20, 1936

Fred C. Dickey
Mar 11, 1880
Jul 14, 1937

Sue Voyage Freeman
Age: 8 years.
(no dates)

Infant Son of
Mr. & Mrs. Lawson Freeman
(no dates)

Joseph Dean McClellan
Jul 27, 1870
Dec 25, 1934
&
Ella Dickey McClellan
Feb 18, 1874
Jun 22, 1955

Edward Davis Dickey
Nov 14, 1879
Jan 23, 1946

Ephraim Franklin Dickey
Oct 18, 1875
Dec 10, 1950

Edward M. Dickey
May 20, 1847
Nov 13, 1903
&
Malvina F. Dickey
Jul 22, 1849
Nov 23, 1937

Allen Marshall, Son of
E. M. & M. F. Dickey
Sep 11, 1877
Oct 2, 1880

Mrs. Malda Dickey
1849-1937

Wealthy I. Dundas
Mar 22, 1889
Jun 25, 1889

Sarah G., wife of
J. C. Lively
Died Mar 7, 1880
Age: 26y, 11m.

John M. Caldwell
Jun 1, 1844
Sep 16, 1914

Evaline, wife of
John M. Caldwell
Mar 22, 1848
Apr 24, 1885

Mary, 2nd wife of
J. M. Caldwell
Nov 23, 1867
Jan 23, 1892

Dorah Tucker Caldwell
Feb 26, 1863
Jun 16, 1934

Allie, wife of
D. S. Solomon
Feb 5, 1868
Dec 28, 1900

Mamie Frank Solomon
Aug 10, 1890
Jan 26, 1906

Ola Bird Solomon
Mar 18, 1889
Jun 6, 1892

James B. Solomon
Aug 7, 1894
Jul 8, 1897

George Alfred Britton
Apr 30, 1864
Dec 24, 1903
& wife
Laura Simmons Britton
Jul 16, 1870
Feb 14, 1925

Ester Lois Fry
Jun 22, 1895
Aug 23, 1895

Jacob Hamilton
Aug 9, 1846
Jan 11, 1914

MULBERRY QUADRANGLE

Georgie Belle Solomon
Mar 31, 1904
May 3, 1907

Gertie M. Solomon
Mar 27, 1884
Feb 20, 1963

James J. Solomon
Aug 26, 1876

Jane Franklin Simmons
Mar 29, 1882
Apr 25, 1900

Allen Solomon
Apr 1, 1878
May 11, 1913

Charlie Solomon
Nov 28, 1894
Aug 27, 1915

Delpha F. Solomon
Aug 7, 1857
Apr 11, 1918

G. W. Solomon
Oct 30, 1853
Jan 14, 1899

James Cashion
Aug 7, 1844
Sep 10, 1914
& Wife
Margaret Cashion
Oct 16, 1847
(no date)

Clara E. Cashion, wife of
F. S. Bryant
Sep 21, 1882
Feb 27, 1917

Frank S. Bryant
Jan 2, 1873
Dec 12, 1957

Alton F. Bryant
Aug 25, 1904
Oct 10, 1930

G. F. Cashion
Jan 9, 1877
Jan 9, 1926

Lula K., wife of
N. M. Flynt
Dec 14, 1868
Sep 16, 1889

Infant Son of
N. M. & L. K. Flynt
B&D Sep 16, 1889

Nannie Cecelia Imogene,
Daughter of
George B. & Madeline J.
Warren
Oct 31, 1900
May 15, 1904

George Bonner Warren
Nov 13, 1858
Nov 11, 1936
&
Madeline Jane Warren
Feb 14, 1873
Nov 18, 1936

Willis A. Warren
Jun 18, 1849
Aug 2, 1936

Della Warren
Sep 18, 1868
Oct 20, 1941
&
Nannie Warren
Apr 8, 1861
Oct 3, 1938
"Sisters"

S. A. Warren
May 2, 1824
Apr 12, 1896
& wife
Celia Pulley Warren
Feb 13, 1828
(no date)

David Elie Warren
Jun 5, 1856
Sep 4, 1906
&
Mary Georgia Warren
Nov 6, 1872
Apr 12, 1954

Daniel M. Eslick
Apr 22, 1838
Jul 24, 1883

Mary, wife of
E--- Eslick
Mar 7, 1804
Sep 2, 1879

William Harbin
Apr 16, 1879
Feb 18, 1884

Daniel J. Bradey
Mar 15, 1836
Jan 26, 1902

Mary J. McCullock, wife of
D. G. Bradey
Jul 8, 1846
Apr 7, 1917

Raymy Lee McCullough
Apr 3, 1863
May 19, 1900

Thomas Jefferson McCullough
Jan 9, 1851
Dec 11, 1889

Annie E., Daughter of
J. H. & Cora Warren
Aug 17, 1899
Oct 16, 1900

James Henry Warren
Aug 29, 1863
May 18, 1930
&
Cora Wren Warren
May 13, 1870
Sep 7, 1920

Jarred M. Simmons
1867-1899
&
Issie C. Simmons
1870-1943

Beulah S., Daughter of
M. S. & Julia Eslick
Jul 2, 1881
Sep 9, 1882

Homer Eslick
1883-1961

George S. Campbell
Feb 6, 1869
Feb 5, 1933

Infant of
G. S. & N. V. Campbell
Sep 23, ----(illegible)

Infant of
G. S. & N. C. Campbell
Nov 6, 1906

Lydie Campbell
Jul 3, 1903
Apr 10, 1904
&
Lula May Campbell
Aug 4, 1892
Dec 25, 1901
Children of G. S. &
N. V. Campbell.

William Gray
May 5, 1845
Jul 15, 1892
&
Elizabeth Gray
Oct 17, 1846
Oct 16, 1877

James Harbin
Nov 6, 1816
Jun 16, 1892

Nancy, wife of
James Harbin
May 3, 1818
Jun 31, 1904

John S. Harbin
Jul 5, 1851
Mar 5, 1926

Cora C. Moyers
Apr 4, 1873
Mar 21, 1894

Lucy A. Moyers
Jun 14, 1869
Dec 1, 1902

Frank M. Moyers
Oct 9, 1877
Feb 6, 1902

Festus, Son of
W. S. & Alice Moyers
Dec 3, 1883
Jun 25, 1888

Robert Rich
Jun 12, 1832
Nov 3, 1918
& wife
Violet Rich
May 3, 1827
Nov 16, 1905

S. F. Warren
Aug 10, 1853
Apr 1, 1902

Della Ann, wife of
S. F. Warren
Mar 2, 1870
Oct 20, 1904

Emma J., wife of
S. F. Warren
Oct 4, 1858
Mar 13, 1888

F. M. Moyers
Sep 15, 1829
Dec 6, 1902
&
America H. Moyers
Apr 9, 1839
(no date)

D. L. Pigg
Died 1946
Age: (not given)

Fannie Simmons, wife of
D. L. Pigg
Oct 11, 1875
Jun 12, 1907

Ernest Johnson, Son of
D. L. & Fannie Pigg
Aug 1, 1897
Apr 8, 1905

William Thomas Pigg
Jan 13, 1861
Apr 15, 1931
&
Mary Arvella Simmons Pigg
Aug 27, 1872
Jan 3, 1929

W. S. Pigg
Aug 16, 1838
Nov 22, 1915
&
Madiline Pigg
Feb 3, 1841
Apr 28, 1917

Infant of
W. T. & Vella Pigg
(no dates)

MULBERRY QUADRANGLE

G. W. Moyers
Jun 20, 1823
Apr 15, 1893
& wife
Salatha Eslick Moyers
Oct 21, 1821
Aug 13, 1898

Mary Franklin Moyers
(no dates)

George J. Moyers
Feb 7, 1862
Mar 29, 1937
&
Jennie T. Moyers
Mar 5, 1868
Nov 5, 1934

Rachel, Daughter of
G. J. & Jennie Moyers
May 12, 1903
Mar 24, 1913

George C. Moyers
Jul 3, 1890
Oct 24, 1891

John Simmons
Mar 1, 1840
Apr 1, 1885

Demia Simmons Hamilton
Dec 10, 1848
Jun 12, 1929

Infant Son of
A. M. & L. F. Bray
B&D Dec 4, 1889

A. M. Bray
Nov 16, 1855
Jul 6, 1915

Luvenia F. Moyers, wife
of A. M. Bray
May 31, 1863
Jun 22, 1911

Alf Harbin
1885-1958

Mamie Norman
Died Sep 30, 1903
Age: 6m, 12d.

Infant Daughter of
W. H. & M. A. Harbin
Jul 18, 1892
Aug 8, 1892

J. W. Thompson *
Died Jun 13, 1907
Age: 44 years.
Married Alice Sanders
Sep 20, 1888

Mrs. John Caldwell *
Died May 12, 1900
Age: 90y, 3m, 8d.

W. M. Norman
May 15, 1869
Apr 17, 1943

Gracie Cashion, wife of
W. M. Norman
Nov 3, 1870
Oct 12, 1927

Luther Norman
May 16, 1901
Oct 14, 1946

James E. Britton
Jun 8, 1866
Mar 7, 1906

Mattie L., wife of
L. T. Carter
Jan 10, 1880
Sep 19, 1905

Cathern, Daughter of
T. & M. L. Carter
Sep 30, 1904
Oct 12, 1905

M. C., wife of
W. L. Bray
1847-1914

Lizzie, Daughter of
W. L. & M. C. Bray
Died Oct 16, 1900
Age: 20y, 1m, 14d.

George W. L. Bray
May 24, 1858
Mar 14, 1921

Helen J. Coston, wife of
S. K. Hopkins
Dec 7, 1860
Mar 19, 1893

Helen, Daughter of
S. K. & H. J. Hopkins
Mar 12, 1893
Apr 4, 1893

Infant of
H. R. & Rose Coston
Aug 28, 1898
Aug 29, 1898

Infant Son of
Dr. H. R. & Rose Coston
B&D Jul 14, 1901

Mrs. Fannie R.,* wife of
W. A. Caldwell
Died Apr 21, 1893
Age: 30 years.

Dixie Goodner,* Son of
Ike & Mary E. Williamson
Died Sep 14, 1899
Age: 4m, 14d.

James Barbee Coston
May 1, 1872
Jan 21, 1900

J. H. Hamilton
Mar 30, 1848
Oct 19, 1901

Margaret Ann Hamilton
Jun 25, 1853
Apr 26, 1948

W. E. Thompson
Aug 22, 1853
Aug 3, 1915

John William Gammon
Sep 19, 1857
Mar 31, 1940
&
Mattie E. Minick Gammon
Mar 11, 1867
Mar 1, 1958

Taylor, Son of
J. W. & Mattie Gammon
Mar 30, 1882
Mar 11, 1902

Martha I. Gammon
Jan 9, 1834
Mar 14, 1910

Several unmarked graves.

Infant * of
Mr. & Mrs. George S. Campbell
Died Oct 6, 1906
Age: (not given)

Morgan Caughran Flynt *
Died Oct 26, 1889
Age: 26 years.

Birdie Williams *
Died Dec 10, 1890
Age: 18 years.

W. G. Gray *
Died Jul 25, 1892
Age: 58 years.

Mrs. Bettie,* wife of
Matt Webb
Died Feb 6, 1892
Age: 36 years.

Infant * of
N. O. Little
Died Dec 29, 1890
Age: 1 year.

William D. Moorhead *
Married Jan 3, 1839 to
Mariah Cunningham
Died Apr 2, 1898
Age: 86y, 5m, 11d.

Lillie Pearl Short *
Died Jul 16, 1895
Age: 9 months.

Mrs. Mary E.,* Consort of
H. B. Griffin & Daughter
of Dr. N. M. Jenkins
Died Sep 18, 1877
Age: 18y, 8m, 18d.
Married Dec 21, 1876

Willie Edna,* Daughter of
Mr. & Mrs. John Edmondson
Died Feb 11, 1916
Age: 9 years.

Son * of
Richard Benson
Died Feb 17, 1911
Age: 14 years.

Mrs. Ada,* wife of
Ed Ashworth & Daughter of
R. N. & E. C. Freeman
Died Aug 2, 1900
Age: (not given)

Son * of
Alex Harbin
Died Sep 22, 1887
Age: 13 years.

Child * of
J. T. Harbin
Died Sep 19, 1887
Age: 2 years.

Miss Gulley *
Died Nov 8, 1887
Age: 20 years.

Mr. Gulley *
Died Dec 31, 1893
Age: (not given)

Mrs. Jane E. Adair *
Died Sep 1, 1894
Age: 60 years.

John P. Cashion *
Died Aug 29, 1897
Age: 24 years.

Miss Ellie,* Daughter of
Bud Street
Died Feb 10, 1898
Age: 29 years.

John,* Son of
Mr. & Mrs. Allen Taylor
Died Nov 5, 1910
Age: 1 year.

Mrs. Elizabeth Ann,*
wife of John Caldwell
Died Feb 12, 1908
Age: 90 years.

Ora Bell,* Daughter of
Gilbert & Ellan Cashion
Died Jul 9, 1910
Age: 1y, 8m, 11d.

MULBERRY QUADRANGLE

Tommie Lee,* Son of
Willis & Callie Holder
Died Mar 21, 1896
Age: 3 years.

S. A. Warren *
Married Celia Pulley
Jun 6, 1848
Died Apr 12, 1896
Age: 72 years.

W. F. Gattis *
Died Jul 2, 1892
Age: 44y, 11m, 4d.

Mr. Anderson *
Died Jul 3, 1896
Age: 83 years.

* *

STEPHENS-CARTER CEMETERY

LOCATION: Three fourth mile SSW of Old Loyd's Chapel, on west side of Stephens Creek on side of ridge.

Robert Stephens **
Died Dec 1836
Age: (not given)
"A Revolutionary Soldier"
    & wife
Sallie Farmer Stephens
(no dates)

** Court Records.

About 25 graves with fieldstones, no inscriptions.

* *

MOORES CHAPEL CHURCH CEMETERY
(Colored)

LOCATION: Mouth of Moorehead Hollow at Dickey Bridge.

Rev. D. W. Stephens
Mar 2, 1856
May 29, 1913
    & wife
Charlotte Snoddie Stephens
Dec 25, 1849
Jan 5, 1912

Hariet Stephenson
Oct 17, 1884
Nov 11, 1914

R. F. Simmons
Jan 8, 1859
Dec 10, 1906

Nancy Taylor, wife of
Isaac Cooley
Died May 26, 1914
Age: 54 years.

Many unmarked graves.

John Vinzant
Tenn. Pfc Engineers
Died Jan 9, 1930
Age: (not given)

* *

CEMETERY

LOCATION: One mile NNE of Dickey Bridge on west side of Moorehead (or Roundtrees) Creek.

6 graves with fieldstones, no inscriptions.

* *

SHELTON CEMETERY

LOCATION: Immediately east of Loyd's Chapel on east side of Stephens Creek.

B. A. Shelton
Aug 14, 1841
Aug 24, 1912
    & wife
Mary E. Shelton
Mar 12, 1840
Mar 20, 1906
(These two graves are
buried north & south)

Infant Son * of
William & Ida Kent
Died Sep 26, 1897
Age: 1 month.

Frances A. Thompson
Mar 18, 1838
Jan 10, 1911

Mrs. Martha Thompson
Apr 19, 1869
Jun 26, 1906

Several unmarked graves.

Arthur Bates *
Died Oct 12, 1899
Age: (not given)

Saline Elen,* Daughter of
William B. Thompson
Died Feb 20, 1879
Age: 20 years.

Eddie, Son of
M. D. & F. Thompson
Died Mar 6, 1899
Age: 10y, 11m, 12d.

Aline, Daughter of
J. H. & Alda Kent
Dec 6, 1914
Jan 27, 1921

Wils. Thompson *
Died Mar 27, 1918
Age: 80 years
C.S.A.

Julia A., wife of
J. M. Dickey, Jr.
Mar 26, 1867
Oct 15, 1918
Married Jan 19, 1890

Mariah Thompson
Jun 20, 1846
Feb 28, 1900

Thomas B. Thompson
Dec 9, 1848
Mar 12, 1894

MULBERRY QUADRANGLE

Charley E.,* Son of
William Kent
Died Oct 6, 1900
Age: 5y, 9m.

Infant * of
Hence & Mattie Thompson
Died Mar 30, 1901
Age: (not given)

Willis R.,* Son of
Robert & Emily Ramsey
Died Dec 11, 1891
Age: 3y, 7m.

John L. Thompson *
Died Jun 2, 1901
Age: 64 years.

Frank David,* Daughter of
Horace & Martha Thompson
Died Jun 20, 1901
Age: 6y, 7m, 6d.

Child * of
W. H. Certain
Died Oct 16, 1893
Age: 8 months.

Infant Daughter * of
W. M. & Martha Carter
Died Mar 4, 1898

Mrs. Lucinda,* widow of
David Thompson
Died Feb 1, 1900
Age: 80 years.

Logan,* Son of
Hence & Mattie Thompson
Died Jun 26, 1901
Age: 2 years.

Eula G.,* Daughter of
Robert & Emily Ramsey
Died Dec 13, 1891
Age: 2y, 4m.

Mrs. Marie Thompson *
Died Feb 28, 1900
Age: 53y, 8m, 8d.

Mrs. Elizabeth Casaway *
Died Apr 4, 1906
Age: 81 years.

Green B. Evans *
Married 1869 to
Julia McCanless
Died May 19, 1893
Age: 59 years.

Daniel Willard,* Son of
S. C. & S. E. Caudle
Died Nov 11, 1896
Age: 4 months.

* *

RATLIFF CEMETERY

LOCATION: One and one half mile NE of Dickey Bridge of Elk River, Moorehead Hollow on west side of Creek.

J. T.(John Turley) Ratliff
May 7, 1833
Feb 11, 1898
&
Sarah P. Ratliff
Dec 29, 1841
(no date)

Thomas J.,* Son of
J. T. Ratliff
Died Jul 2, 1891
Age: 15y, 1m.

Mrs. Henrietta, Consort of
Samuel Webb
Dec 25, 1822
Oct 5, 1853
"The Mother of Margaret,
Joseph & George."
(Rock Vault)

Talvin,* Son of
John & Sarah Ratliff
Died 1891
Age: (not given)

John C. Webb *
(1800-1870)

2 concrete markers, broken
& crumbled, no inscription.

Several fieldstones,
no inscriptions.

H. A. Shelton *
Dec 4, 1884
Feb 5, 1909
Age: 62 years.
Married Mary Austin.

Mrs. Nancy,* widow of
William Ratliff
Died Oct 17, 1906
Age: 104 years.

NOTE: This Cemetery joined
the Old Hickory Grove
Church property and was
also called Hickory Grove
Cemetery.

Sam McWhorter *
Died Feb 9, 1911
Age: 85 years.

Starlie Glen,* Son of
W. H. & Bertha Ratliff
Died Aug 27, 1899
Age: 1y, 6m.

* *

MOOREHEAD CEMETERY

LOCATION: Two and one half miles NE of Dickey Bridge on west side of road.

John Moorehead ***
(no dates)

*** Family Records

Tolley Grove *
Died Mar 2, 1906
Age: 25 years.

Several unmarked graves.

* *

SCOTT CEMETERY

LOCATION: Three miles NE of Dickey Bridge on west side of Road.

All stones gone.

* *

MULBERRY QUADRANGLE

JARED CEMETERY

LOCATION: Two miles SE of Old Loyd's Chapel, access from top of Crystal Ridge, down lane to valley and cemetery.

R. F. Tucker
Aug 14, 1854
Dec 15, 1927
&
Sarah Katherine Tucker
Jan 29, 1857
Jun 24, 1927
&
Sarah Florence Tucker
Jul 20, 1883
Feb 9, 1900

William F. Fanning
1869-1940

Julia Fanning
1879-1933

N. H. "Dick" Sullenger
1859-1918
&
Laura T. Sullenger
1866-1949

T. F. Sullenger
Sep 26, 1851
Jun 10, 1916
&
M. J. Sullenger
Jan 24, 1852
(no date)

Cordelia, Daughter of
T. F. & M. J. Sullenger
Feb 10, 1870
Oct 6, 1897

George Reed *
Died Jan 10, 1908
Age: 24 years.

Mrs. Eliza E.,* wife of
W. F. Jared
Died Dec 28, 1908
Age: 40 years.

Ben Noles *
Died Jan 30, 1913
Age: 62 years.

Mrs. Mary Fanning *
Died Jun 5, 1914
Age: 80 years.

Mrs. Caroline Sullinger *
Died Apr 10, 1900
Age: 74y, 9m.

Nannie,* Daughter of
J. R. & M. M. Jared
Died Sep 17, 1899
Age: 8m, 13d.

Etta Smith, wife of
A. E. Eslick
Oct 18, 1878
Dec 3, 1928

J. L. Eslick
Apr 12, 1852
Jan 28, 1925
&
Georgeanna Eslick
Dec 2, 1851
Apr 2, 1926

Josie Sullenger Campbell
Jul 2, 1877
Sep 7, 1926

W. H. "Sul" Sullenger
May 8, 1856
Jan 3, 1922

Beulah G., Daughter of
R. B. & Alice Sullivan
Nov 17, 1900
Mar 28, 1917

R. B. Sullivan
1851-1931

Laura E. Eslick
Sep 14, 1896
Jun 27, 1906

Lizzie Eslick
Aug 30, 1879
Jun 12, 1906

Thomas C. Fanning *
Died Oct 31, 1904
Age: 80 years.
Brother to B. F. Fanning.

Anderson Tucker *
Married in 1880 to
Mattie Koonce
Died Jan 19, 1901
Age: 99y, 10m, 4d.

John Helms *
Died Sep 17, 1916
Age: 68 years.

Mrs. Cindey Thompson *
Died Mar 12, 1901
Age: 82y, 20d.

Mrs. Laura,* wife of
Nathan Smith
Died Feb 11, 1904
Age: 19 years.

Mary Ellen,* Daughter of
N. A. & Lou Reed
Died Apr 23, 1897
Age: 19y, 4m.

J. H. "Ham" Sullenger
Mar 15, 1862
Dec 6, 1921

W. H. Jared
Dec 6, 1908
Dec 9, 1910

Frank M. Faris
Feb 27, 1879
Oct 28, 1949

Elvina Carter
Jul 28, 1840
Feb 17, 1913

Nathan Smith
Died Jun 26, 1911
Age: 27 years.

Alice Mitchell, wife of
R. B. Sullivan
Jan 14, 1869
Jun 2, 1916

Nicholas Renegar
Jul 30, 1865
Oct 5, 1892

William A. Sullenger
Jan 24, 1836
Apr 16, 1909
&
Eliza S. Sullenger
Feb 14, 1843
Mar 5, 1950

Mrs. Elizabeth,* wife of
Jefferson Duke
Died Jan 16, 1894
Age: 78 years.

Louis Tucker,* Son of
P. G. Davidson
Died Feb 4, 1907
Age: about 3 years.

Nannie Perl Bryant *
Died Jun 8, 1901
Age: 1y, 6m, 6d.

Mrs. Amanda Jared *
Died Jun 4, 1901
Age: 60y, 11m, 21d.

Sandford Renegar *
Died Oct 25, 1894
Age: 67y, 5m.

Rubie Ethel,* Daughter of
P. G. Davidson
Died Jan 30, 1911
Age: 1y, 6m, 10d.

Infant of
H. D. & Betty Jared
May 19, 1918
May 20, 1918

Billy, Son of
H. D. & Betty Jared
Dec 31, 1920
Sep 14, 1921

Willie J. McGehee
Jul 3, 1866
(no date)
&
William C. McGehee
Apr 7, 1849
Jul 9, 1931

Son of
W. C. & W. J. McGehee
B&D Aug 22, 1894

James Edward Fanning
Sep 30, 1924
Aug 3, 1925

Maymie Sue Fanning
Sep 21, 1922
Mar 18, 1929

N. A. Reed
Nov 11, 1847
Jun 21, 1903

Frank Loyd *
Died Jul 15, 1912
Age: (not given)

D. B. Reed *
Died Jul 14, 1908
Age: 38y, 7m, 2d.

Mrs. Patsey Miles *
Died Jan 8, 1895
Age: 74 years.

Clifford,* Son of
Mr. & Mrs. Newton Thompson
Died Apr 29, 1909
Age: 10y, 3m.
Died by cyclone.

Lucy Sullivan *
Died Jun 19, 1901
Age: 8 years.

Mrs. Elizabeth,* wife of
William Fanning
Died Dec 8, 1903
Age: 32 years.

Mrs. Frances,* wife of
J. W. Helms
Mar 7, 1849
Jun 1, 1912

* *

MULBERRY QUADRANGLE

CEMETERY

LOCATION: One and one half NNW of Champ, on top of Crystal Ridge on south side of road.

About 10 graves, no inscriptions.

* *

McCLURE CEMETERY

LOCATION: One and one half miles north of Champ on the west side of Tuckers Creek road.

Sullenger children are buried here.	F. M. Tucker * Died Nov 26, 1907 Age: 80 years.	(F. M. Tucker's wife Nancy McClure Tucker, no dates)

Several graves, no inscriptions.

* *

HOWARD CEMETERY

LOCATION: One and one fourth miles NNE of Champ on east side of Tuckers Creek road.

W. Mack Tucker Mar 16, 1835 Feb 21, 1924 & Manda Jane Tucker Sep 23, 1842 Jan 29, 1914 Bertia James Tucker Jul 1, 1884 Jul 4, 1884	Infant Daughter of T. B. & S. T. George B&D Jan 25, 1887 Dorsey Benton George Jul 13, 1883 Jul 7, 1890 Many fieldstones with no inscriptions.	Marion Franklin, Son of M. P. & Emma Lewis Oct 11, 1916 May 20, 1922 W. F., Son of J. T. & M. Lesley Dec 7, 1883 Mar 15, 1883	Jessie A. Tucker Mar 15, 1881 Oct 7, 1894 William Mack Tucker Dec 9, 1863 Mar 17, 1888 Elizabeth Tucker Oct 23, 1861 Jan 24, 1862

* *

COPELAND CEMETERY

LOCATION: One half mile NE of Champ on the east side of Tuckers Creek and road.

Bert Lee Jennings, Jr. Tennessee Corp. U. S. Marine Corps WW I S.S. & G.S. May 1, 1898 Aug 10, 1958 & Sally Junia Franklin Jennings Feb 25, 1904 ------------ Married Sep 20, 1919 Charles Edward, Infant of R. J. & Gladys Jennings Aug 17, 1932 Oct 17, 1932 Jeff M. Copeland Sep 19, 1855 Mar 7, 1888 John F., Son of William & M. A. Copeland Dec 11, 1864 Mar 11, 1882	Ella Vester, Daughter of W. M. & M. A. Copeland Dec 23, 1868 Jun 24, 1881 James L., Son of W. M. & M. A. Copeland Dec 11, 1862 May 11, 1864 William Copeland Died Apr 1, 1890 Age: 60y, 5m, 27d. Mary Ann George, wife of William Copeland Dec 21, 1833 Jun 6, 1920 Cecil J., Son of J. M. & M. H. Franklin May 28, 1880 Jan 8, 1882	W. Ross, Son of T. N. & Myrtle Copeland Mar 8, 1911 Jul 28, 1911 Susie Jennings Spencer Mar 11, 1906 May 16, 1925 Myra T., Daughter of B. L. & Bessie Jennings B&D Jun 9, 1919 Elwyn May Jennings Jun 21, 1911 Jun 24, 1914 Thomas S. George 1791-Sep 15, 1859 Mrs. Mary, wife of Thomas S. George 1800-Aug 1870 Member of Primitive Baptist Church.	Bert Lee Jennings Jun 23, 1874 Jan 8, 1931 & Ida Copeland Jennings May 11, 1876 May 22, 1914 Robert Lee Copeland Apr 1, 1873 Oct 10, 1947 & Florence Tucker Copeland Mar 5, 1873 Apr 17, 1912 & Carl Franklin Copeland Dec 23, 1904 May 2, 1905 T. N. Copeland Dec 15, 1860 Sep 3, 1892

MULBERRY QUADRANGLE

Mrs. Parmelia,*
Married in 1863 to
W. F. Tucker
Died Dec 18, 1907
Age: 51 years.

Infant Twins of
Robert Lee & Florence
Copeland
(no dates)

Mrs. Ova Copeland *
Died Jul 26, 1902
Age: 24y, 4m, 10d.

Several unmarked graves.

* *

CHAMP-WARD CEMETERY

LOCATION: At Champ, on west side of Tuckers Creek Road.

Dan M. Young
1865-1934
&
Annis Young
1865-
&
Walker Young
1881-1952

M. E. T.
(Rock Slab, no dates)

R. T. W.
(Rock Slab, no dates)

W. G. K. (King)
(Rock Slab, no dates)

M. S. W.
(no dates)

E. D. C.
(no dates)

4 Children, Rock Slabs
(no dates)

4 Adults, Rock Slabs
(no dates)

Willie Guy Thompson
1887-1960

A. Tillman Corder
Dec 27, 1889
Nov 21, 1963
&
Neva Mai G. Corder
Jul 17, 1898
Jul 15, 1964

Etta George
1878-1955

J. Middleton Towry
Sep 16, 1884
Jan 22, 1952

Charles Lee Walker
Nov 26, 1910
Aug 28, 1954

Malcolm P. Jennings
Jan 4, 1908
Jan 20, 1935

John C. Spencer
Sep 24, 1844
Sep 4, 1903
(Rock Slab)

Martha J. Spencer
Nov 18, 1845
Jul 17, 1925
(Rock Slab)

Charlie, Son of
John C. & M. J. Spencer
Apr 14, 1877
Aug 7, 1892
(Rock Slab)

Mrs. James Waid
Died Oct 3, 1905
Age: 53 years.

Mamie Viola, Daughter of
J. T. & H. C. Waid
Nov 27, 1894
Sep 27, 1898

Bessie Tucker, wife of
Bert L. Jennings
Mar 15, 1881
Jan 16, 1957

James Luther Hayes
Jul 23, 1881
Mar 28, 1965

Bertha Hayes
1885-1946

Gilbert T. Walker
Jun 6, 1932
Jun 29, 1933

Chester Harold, Son of
Mr. & Mrs. C. H. Smith
B&D Aug 18, 1938

Dovie Hensley Walker
Nov 20, 1867
Sep 6, 1937

Rufus Y. Jennings
1863-1932

Charlie B. Jennings
Jan 5, 1903
Jan 29, 1921

Julia F., wife of
Tillman Young
1884-1916

E. C. Ward
Jun 4, 1815
Nov 5, 1891

Mary, wife of
E. C. Ward
Apr 6, 1816
Jun 2, 1892

Thomas L. Smith
1857-Dec 11, 1893

Hulda C. Smith
Jan 1, 1859
Mar 29, 1916

H. C. "Lum" Smith
Aug 15, 1888
Aug 1, 1965
&
Bettie T. Smith
Nov 15, 1893

Agatha Jewel Smith
Nov 6, 1916
Jun 27, 1920

Infant Son of
H. C. & Bettie Smith
B&D May 1, 1912

Mary S., wife of
Orlando Duke
Jan 22, 1847
Sep 9, 1880

Jessie M. Walker
Nov 13, 1877
Apr 7, 1934

Minnie C., wife of
J. E. Powers
Dec 13, 1883
Jun 3, 1962

Noah S. Ward
1853-1926
&
Nancy W. Ward
1863-1952

Noah Cecil, Son of
N. S. & Nancy Ward
Jul 16, 1900
Jul 21, 1912

E. C. Ward
Sep 3, 1866
Aug 6, 1881

W. M. Taylor
Died Sep 15, 1915
Age: 53 years.

Emma C. Taylor
Aug 24, 1843
Aug 27, 1968
(Marker has: 1943-1868)

William Jean
Jul 10, 1868
Jan 24, 1925
&
Ella Jean
Feb 21, 1876
Dec 15, 1943

Nat Taylor
1855-1946
&
Ruby Taylor
1876-1948

Arthur W. Stewman
1886-1963
&
Emma E. Stewman
1888-1955

George Ward
Dec 21, 1875
Dec 15, 1961
&
Sarah Ward
Apr 8, 1878
Feb 5, 1946

Erasmus A. Ward
1852-1924
&
Saphronia M. Ward
1855-1933

Infant Son of
Mr. & Mrs. C. L. Gunn
1921-1922

Will E. Owens
1888-1945

Annie W. Owens
1885-1963

Noah David Owens
Oct 27, 1914
Nov 9, 1918

Ward Owens
B&D Oct 18, 1911

MULBERRY QUADRANGLE

John K. Ward
Dec 27, 1840
(no date)
& wife
Rachel C. Fanning Ward
Sep 12, 1846
Aug 14, 1919

N. S. W.
(Rock Slab, no dates)

Nannie E., wife of
N. S. Ward
Dec 28, 1854
Jul 13, 1891

Sterling J., Son of
N. S. & N. E. Ward
Mar 10, 1890
Nov 17, 1891

Bobbie W. Ward
1928-1931
&
Infant Ward
1921-1921

Charlie Ward
1896-1968
(Moore-Cortner FH)

Massie O. Copeland
Jan 24, 1896
Jan 5, 1900
&
Flossie Lee Copeland
Apr 21, 1899
Jan 14, 1900

Several unmarked graves.

S. B. Binkley *
Died Jan 25, 1907
Age: 46 years.

Miss Polly Moorehead *
Died Apr 3, 1914
Age: 25 years.

George Guthrie *
Died Sep 25, 1917
Age: 25 years.

* *

FANNING CEMETERY

LOCATION: One and one fourth miles SW of Champ on the west side of Kelso Road.

Malissa A. Franklin
Died Nov 6, 1912
Age: 76 years.

Tom B. George
1875-1944
&
Etta B. George
1878-(no date)

(John Gray, a Soldier of
the Revolution probably
buried here. He died in
1836 ***)

*** Family Records.

H. M. Franklin *
Married Phoebe Fanning
in 1844
Died Nov 2, 1905
Age: 79y, 1m, 18d.

Herbert J. Thompson
1918-1930

Hal K. Franklin
1868-1945

Anna L. Franklin
1872-1911

Over 100 unmarked graves.

Miss Martha Jane George *
Died May 18, 1915
Age: 47 years.

Mrs. Phoebe Franklin *
May 30, 1839
Jan 21, 1916

James Madison,* Son of
Mr. & Mrs. Hiram Franklin
Died Oct 28, 1906
Age: (not given)

Florence Alberta, Daughter of
H. K. & A. L. Franklin
Died Jun 12, 1909
Age: 14y, 11m, 7d.

W. J. Fanning
Jul 26, 1855
Jan 28, 1920

B. M. W. (Child Vault)
(no dates)

Fannie B. Thompson *
Died Jun 10, 1906
Age: 23m, 14d.

Bartha Gattis *
Died Dec 6, 1905
Age: 10 months.

Alice,* wife of
C. T. Fanning
Died Mar 7, 1915
Age: 23 years.

Arretter, Daughter of
R. F. & S. F. Fanning
Feb 7, 1862
Apr 9, 1867

Middleton Fanning
Died Feb 1861
Age: 63 years.

Rachel, wife of
M. Fanning
Died Oct 1865
Age: 64 years.

Miss Delona,* Daughter of
W. W. Sullinger
Died Aug 29, 1917
Age: 14 years.

J. O.,* Son of
H. M. & Phoebe Franklin
Died Nov 4, 1893
Age: 26 years.

* *

STILES CEMETERY

LOCATION: Two and one half miles SW of Champ on the north bank of Elk River.

Britton F. Tucker
Aug 4, 1839
May 12, 1894
&
Mary L. Tucker
Jan 24, 1840
(no date)
Married May 8, 1862

William Cashion
Nov 18, 1827
Died at Camp Fisher, Va.
Nov 16, 1861
A Vol. of Co G 1st Tenn Reg
Army N. V. A.

Robert Nix
(no dates)

Elijah Nix
(no dates)

Jim Nix
(no dates)

Sim. Nix, Sr.
(no dates)

Allie Nick
(no dates)

Sim. Nix, Jr.
(no dates)

S. T. Nix
Nov 13, 1842
Mar 25, 1916

Eugene Walker Nix
Died Jun 15, 1900
Age: (not given)

James Otho Nix
May 9, 1902
Jun 22, 1904

William Hobson Tidwell
1904-1933

James Madison Nix
Feb 2, 1869
Jan 10, 1923
&
Cora Tucker Nix
Jan 1, 1868
Feb 19, 1957

W. M. Eslick
1872-1945

Emma Eslick
Jan 17, 1872
Oct 25, 1938

MULBERRY QUADRANGLE

Cora Copeland
(no dates)

William F. Nix
1866-1930
&
Cora Eslick Nix
1869-1896
&
Cora Tucker Nix
1873-1939

Sandy Nix
(no dates)

Pearl Nix
(no dates)

Corbine E. Nix
(no dates)

A. C. Nix
Jul 23, 1849
Oct 29, 1920
&
L. J. Hoots Nix
Oct 17, 1850
Nov 5, 1941

Rosie L., Daughter of
A. C. & L. J. Nix
Dec 13, 1874
Feb 15, 1877

John H. Bostic
1885-1965
&
Callie Lou Bostic
1882-1931

Raymond R., Son of
J. H. & C. L. Bostic
Oct 19, 1907
Oct 21, 1907

George T. Lackey
Oct 1, 1872
Jun 10, 1925

Sarah J. Lackey
Sep 23, 1826
Feb 18, 1887

Charles N. Lackey
Dec 1, 1880
Dec 23, 1934

William A. Copeland
Jul 15, 1849
Dec 10, 1942

Hannah C., wife of
W. A. Copeland
Oct 19, 1847
Sep 14, 1922

Myrtle Franklin, wife of
J. M. D. Dickey
Jul 13, 1885
Mar 7, 1917

Sallie Nix, wife of
J. M. Brown
Mar 13, 1876
Sep 23, 1915

Martin L. Dickey
Nov 4, 1852
Jan 30, 1926

Sarah J. Nix, wife of
M. L. Dickey
Jan 4, 1848
Sep 16, 1903

William H. R., Son of
M. L. & S. J. Dickey
Feb 23, 1878
Nov 18, 1899

James A., Son of
M. L. & S. J. Dickey
Apr 25, 1876
Dec 13, 1880

Cassey N., Daughter of
M. L. & S. J. Dickey
Feb 24, 1874
Jul 6, 1874

Emit Alton Tucker
Aug 1, 1896
Feb 27, 1898

S. J. Lackey
Died 1887
Age: (not given)

R. P. Lackey
Aug 31, 1838
Nov 21, 1928
&
Eliza J. Lackey
Dec 7, 1856
May 1, 1910

Infant of
R. P. & E. J. Lackey
(no dates)

Infant of
R. P. & E. J. Lackey
(no dates)

John Wesley Franklin
Aug 29, 1823
Dec 17, 1919
&
Delphia Ann Franklin
Jul 7, 1839
Jan 5, 1920

John M. D. Dickey
Jan 23, 1883
Nov 30, 1955

Sallie W. Dickey
Dec 24, 1888
Mar 28, 1964

William J. Simmons
1872-1946
&
Maggie Nix Simmons
1875-1958

Infant Son of
W. J. & M. L. D. Simmons
B&D Apr 7, 1912

Temple B. Lackey
Feb 14, 1829
May 27, 1889

Elizabeth, wife of
T. B. Lackey
Sep 22, 1834
Jul 13, 1892

Ruthie J., Daughter of
T. B. & Elizabeth Lackey
Feb 19, 1855
Sep 15, 1856

William Y., Son of
T. B. & Elizabeth Lackey
Sep 1, 1853
Sep 30, 1854

James, Son of
J. A. & Elizabeth Taylor
May 13, 1841
Apr 22, 1862

John A. Taylor
Nov 30, 1809
Apr 15, 1850
& wife
Elizabeth Taylor
1807-Mar 23, 1873

Y. A. Taylor
Oct 7, 1826
Feb 11, 1899

Martha McClure Taylor
Apr 10, 1840
Jan 14, 1905
Married Y. A. Taylor
Mar 21, 1861

Lillie A., Daughter of
Y. A. & M. Taylor
Feb 9, 1876
Jan 23, 1879

Cora F. Taylor
Aug 25, 1872
Jul 10, 1908

Temple C. Taylor
Dec 14, 1861
Mar 3, 1924

Travis Hal Franklin
Jun 17, 1889
Jan 21, 1930

T. C. Taylor
Feb 4, 1825
Sep 23, 1894

Sarah Lavinia, Daughter of
J. W. & M. A. Solomon
Mar 8, 1861
Feb 14, 1862

Young, Son of
J. A. & Elizabeth Taylor
Mar 29, 1839
Oct 13, 1868

Joseph Stubblefield
Jun 12, 1819
Feb 12, 1890

Irene Stubblefield
May 10, 1829
Dec 11, 1904

J. H. Stubblefield
Jan 12, 1861
May 19, 1891
& wife
Mattie L. Stubblefield
Jan 24, 1864
(no date)

Julia Moriah, wife of
M. L. Spencer & Daughter
of J. M. & L. E. Dickey
Oct 17, 1867
Jan 1, 1902

Henry Naomi, Daughter of
J. H. & M. L. Stubblefield
Dec 18, 1890
Nov 18, 1891

Erastus Ward
Jan 29, 1886
Mar 18, 1940
&
Emma Lackey Ward
Aug 5, 1891
Aug 5, 1968

John R. Franklin
Feb 26, 1893
Jul 16, 1914

Middleton Benjamin
Franklin
Jul 26, 1861
Jul 31, 1946

Elizabeth C., wife of
M. B. Franklin
Aug 25, 1862
Jan 23, 1913

Della T., wife of
M. B. Franklin
Dec 1, 1873
Oct 31, 1957

Mary A. Taylor, wife of
J. C. Pylant
Nov 14, 1850
Feb 24, 1926

MULBERRY QUADRANGLE

Edmond Taylor
1786-Sep 1859 (broken)

Jane D. Taylor
1790-Dec 17, 1873
"A devoted Member of
the M. E. Church."

Andrew J. Taylor
1829-Apr 20, 1850

Martha J. Taylor
1831-1851

Jane McClure
Feb 11, 1820
Jun 30, 1891

Infant Son of
Mr. & Mrs. Tilman Moorehead
B&D Nov 10, 1917

Nannie Martin Nixon
Dec 19, 1842
Oct 3, 1910
&
Pop. Nixon
Jul 3, 1837
Jan 12, 1898

Freudelia A. Taylor, wife
of T. A. Eslick
Jan 10, 1861
Jan 2, 1910

Robert Edward Tucker
1869-1949
&
Ann Winford Tucker
1874-1934
Parents of Alex
Walton Tucker

E. T. Winford
Mar 5, 1902
Jan 4, 1919

Thomas J. Winford
Aug 21, 1863
Dec 2, 1943
&
Ida Taylor Winford
Oct 30, 1870
Jan 4, 1946

James Stiles *** & **
(no dates)
& wife
Mary A. Taylor Stiles
(no dates)

*** Family Records
** Court Records

Mary C.,* wife of
B. F. Tucker
Married May 8, 1862
Died Nov 25, 1909
Age: 69y, 10m.

Lula May, Daughter of
T. A. & F. A. Eslick
Oct 5, 1895
Oct 12, 1895

Thomas A. Eslick
Aug 27, 1862
Nov 23, 1947
&
Furdealia Ann Eslick
Jan 10, 1861
Jan 2, 1910

Ada F., Daughter of
W. R. & T. C. Taylor
Nov 24, 1882
Jun 6, 1895

W. R. Taylor
Dec 13, 1858
(no date)
&
Theresa C. Tucker Taylor
Oct 28, 1853
Jan 25, 1926

Mary Emma Norris Boyd
Apr 11, 1887
Jan 24, 1964

Hugh Rutledge Taylor
Dec 8, 1906
Jul 6, 1922

William Frank Taylor
Apr 22, 1866
Jun 28, 1932
&
Mary Pearl Taylor
Mar 13, 1877
May 4, 1937

James W. Tucker
1866-1936
&
Sarah A. Tucker
1877-1958

Ben L. Tucker
Aug 28, 1896
Aug 20, 1960
&
Mamie S. Tucker
Sep 17, 1897

Infant * of
Mr. & Mrs. J. A. Massey
Died Apr 28, 1914
Age: (not given)

Iva Pauline,* Daughter of
Pauline Etta Massey
Died Jul 6, 1902
Age: (not given)

William Dickey *
Died Aug 18, 1916
Age: 75 years.
C.S.A.

Mamie Sue Mills
Jan 30, 1930
Jan 30, 1930

Lucy Norris Mills
Sep 30, 1913
Nov 8, 1941

Luvina E. Eslick
Oct 19, 1855
Dec 8, 1862

Mary Jane Eslick
Jan 15, 1857
Aug 22, 1857

Infant Son of
Austin & Ann Eslick
B&D Sep 20, 1854

George R. Winford
Feb 23, 1838
Jun 8, 1879
Co K 32nd Tenn Inf
C.S.A.

Nicy P. Anderson, wife of
George R. Winford
Mar 14, 1844
May 22, 1922

D. R. Moorehead
Apr 21, 1870
Nov 17, 1947

Zilpha E. Moorehead
Jan 8, 1868
Aug 30, 1931

Andy W. Taylor
Jan 16, 1877
Nov 24, 1931
&
Emma D. Taylor
Dec 10, 1883

Berry W. Tucker
May 13, 1859
Mar 16, 1919
&
Mary E. Hoots Tucker
Mar 16, 1860
Feb 21, 1944

William Nixon *
Died Jan 20, 1892
Age: 54 years.

Thomas White *
Died Jul 11, 1890
Age: 34 years.

Ray,* Son of
Robert & Annie Tucker
Died Oct 21, 1897
Age: 4 years.

Elizabeth C. Styles,* wife of
Y. A. Taylor
Died Jul 21, 1860
Age: (not given)

Jane Winford
Feb 25, 1815
Jul 1, 1891

G. W. Winford
Jul 29, 1869
Dec 11, 1891

Mary C. Winford
Jan 7, 1857
Oct 12, 1882

B. F. Winford
1841-Feb 13, 1919

Mary M. Ward, wife of
B. F. Winford
Mar 15, 1835
Oct 22, 1900

Saphronia B. Renegar,
wife of
B. F. Winford
Jul 3, 1867
Jun 30, 1920

Daughter of
B. F. & S. B. Winford
Aug 21, 1902
(Date in ground)

Son of
B. F. & S. B. Winford
Dec 2, 1903
(no date)

John M. Gray
Apr 3, 1863
Feb 10, 1941
&
Ida Hoots Gray
Nov 25, 1869
Nov 17, 1958

John D., Son of
J. M. & Ida Gray
May 4, 1911
Jun 22, 1911

Tony Richard Parks
Jul 20, 1946
Apr 15, 1947

Mrs. Martha,* wife of
Samuel Nix
Died Jan 16, 1895
Age: 64 years.

Mrs. Sarah,*
Married in 1830 to
Simeon Nix
Died Aug 29, 1895
Age: 80y, 7m.

Mrs. Mattie,* widow of
William Taylor
Died Nov 29, 1897
Age: 47y, 6m, 3d.

Many unmarked graves.

* *

MULBERRY-PETERSBURG QUADRANGLE

WHITAKER CEMETERY

LOCATION: One and three fourth miles WSW of Mulberry on south side of Highway 50.

Susan, Daughter of
John J. & Sarah Whitaker
Feb 24, 1826
Aug 19, 1831

Rufus K., Son of
John J. & Sarah Whitaker
Aug 18, 1831
Jun 25, 1851

Isaac, Son of
John J. & Sarah Whitaker
Aug 12, 1815
Dec 3, 1853

Washington, Son of
John J. & Sarah Whitaker
Jan 25, 1828
May 20, 1854

John J. Whitaker
Dec 2, 1785
Apr 30, 1853
"Friend of the Poor."

Sally, Relict of
J. J. Whitaker &
Daughter of
Charles & Judith Hammonds
May   1791
Dec 1, 1863

John F., Son of
J. J. & Sally Whitaker
Dec 15, 1824
Aug 19, 1884

* *

PETERSBURG QUADRANGLE

MEDIUM CEMETERY

LOCATION: Three fourth mile SSW of Delina, located at the Marshall County line.

NOTE: This Cemetery began as the Hobbs Family Graveyard. Widow Nancy Hobbs owned this land and she is buried here. Nancy Hobbs, born 1785, died 1853. She was the widow of Joel C. Hobbs. Early members of the Dobbins Family are said to be buried here in unmarked graves. Some sources say that James Hobbs is buried here in an unmarked grave.

A. J. Wysong
1815-Jan 12, 1897

Elmira, wife of
A. J. Wysong
Jan 10, 1825
May 3, 1860

Sarah A. Wysong
Died Aug 31, 1901
Age: 75 years.

Carrie Wright
1882-1962

Rev. W. F. Wright
Nov 29, 1848
Oct 14, 1909
&
Josie Wright
Mar 8, 1846
(no date)

Joel C. Hunter
Aug 6, 1840
Dec 21, 1873
&
Mary L. Hunter Sanders
Aug 5, 1844
Mar 17, 1905

Verna Lou, Daughter of
G. T. & L. A. Eshman
Jun 1, 1894
Oct 28, 1897

Belva Elaine, Daughter of
G. T. & L. A. Eshman
B&D Sep 24, 1891

James H. Eshman
Nov 6, 1851
Nov 26, 1871

James L. Hendry
Jun 29, 1789
Jan 8, 1882

S. H. Hobbs
Sep 22, 1814
Oct 23, 1856

S. E., wife of
S. H. Hobbs
Nov 16, 1814
Mar 17, 1902

S. F. Barnes
Oct 17, 1823
Jul 30, 1860

Mary C., wife of
S. F. Barnes
Aug 16, 1825
Sep 28, 1905

Franklin Smith
Feb 14, 1802
Nov 2, 1862

Elizabeth, wife of
Franklin Smith
Jan 4, 1807
Jul 29, 1859

Marcus B. L., Son of
Franklin & Elizabeth Smith
Feb 28, 1838
Jul 22, 1864

B. L. Wright
Dec 29, 1849
Sep 4, 1905

Amanda Clift Wright
1853-1934

Peter Wright
Oct 1, 1822
Aug 6, 1854

Julia A., wife of
James Wright
Sep 20, 1827
Dec 11, 1913

W. O. Barnes
Oct 19, 1821
Jul 25, 1856
&
M. A. Barnes
Jun 26, 1825
Jul 24, 1918

Infant of
V. J. & A. E. McRee
Jan 6, 1868
Jan 21, 1868

Washington Hunter
May 15, 1807
Jan 26, 1873
Married Mar 17, 1836
& wife
Sarah Hunter
Sep 20, 1817
Jul 29, 1859

William Hunter
Dec 29, 1804
Apr 2, 1869

Margaret Hunter
Sep 22, 1809
Sep 1, 1864
Age: 55y, 11m, 10d.

Mariah S., Daughter of
V. J. & A. E. McRee
Jan 20, 1858
Nov 15, 1861

Virgil O., Son of
V. J. & A. E. McRee
Jan 28, 1860
Nov 20, 1861

Infant Daughter of
Mr. & Mrs. William W. Street
B&D Aug 20, 1940

Daughter of
Mr. & Mrs. Loyd Hobbs
B&D Jan 21, 1932

O. D. Clift
Feb 19, 1880
Aug 9, 1904

Paul Gilbert
1918-1948

James Isom Richardson
1867-1949
&
Sarah Dillie Richardson
1874-1935

PETERSBURG QUADRANGLE

Luther Richardson
Jun 24, 1880
Jul 17, 1896

Tennie Richardson
Jan 9, 1885
Oct 14, 1914

James Richardson
Jan 23, 1836
Oct 29, 1918

Mary J. Richardson
Dec 7, 1837
Aug 30, 1920

John Burgett
Sep 17, 1845
Oct 18, 1935
&
Net. Burgett
Sep 17, 1860
Sep 17, 1905

Mary B. Franklin
1881-1904

Alvarian Brewer
Oct 29, 1882
Feb 8, 1921

Woodrow Brewer
1918-1949

Rosa Brewer Callahan
1891-1948

Richard C. Hobbs
Co D. Tenn Calv.
C.S.A.

Infant Son of
W. F. & M. C. Hobbs
Oct 12, 1893
Oct 19, 1893

Floyd, Son of
W. F. & M. C. Hobbs
Sep 3, 1895
Sep 6, 1901

Buford, Son of
W. F. & M. C. Hobbs
Dec 1, 1901
Feb 10, 1904

Mecca C., wife of
W. F. Hobbs
Apr 12, 1872
Jan 17, 1925

James W. Hobbs
Oct 5, 1849
Apr 22, 1901
& wife
Amanda H. Hobbs
Aug 9, 1856
Oct 14, 1900

A. Shelby Collins
Mar 8, 1872
Mar 22, 1920

Sarah Collins Owen
Jun 18, 1879
Apr 9, 1951

D. V., wife of
J. W. Porch
Jun 20, 1860
May 6, 1904

J. S. Brewer
Jan 18, 1854
Sep 18, 1911

Louisa Josephine, wife of
J. S. Brewer
Feb 23, 1866
Nov 5, 1919

Sarah Catherine, wife of
A. H. Collins
May 30, 1830
Feb 3, 1902

Willie Meadows Reed
1888-1917

Boot Reed
Feb 3, 1867
Jun 23, 1939
&
Lizzie Reed
Mar 17, 1876
Jan 1, 1950

P. A. Edmondson
Jan 5, 1847
Jun 11, 1884

Lydia Jane Edmondson
Feb 8, 1848
Nov 24, 1919

James P. Graves
Apr 12, 1846
Feb 6, 1924
&
Rachel Hunter Graves
Aug 19, 1851
Jul 24, 1892

Mary A. Hunter
May 27, 1839
May 24, 1895

Rev. S. E. Hunter
Nov 17, 1853
May 6, 1891

Jennie Hunter
1859-1935

D. W. Hunter
1847-1931

Nannie C., Daughter of
Wash. & Sarah Hunter
Apr 2, 1842
Oct 24, 1881

Baby Son of
Burr. P. Smith & wife
Jul 3, 1907
Jul 10, 1907

Infant Son of
A. W. & M. A. Smith
B&D Aug 14, 1889

A. W. Smith
Apr 6, 1845
Jan 31, 1918
&
M. A. Smith
Feb 2, 1847
May 25, 1926

Nancy A., wife of
B. B. Muldin (Mauldin)
Jul 18, 1832
Feb 15, 1874
&
Sallie A., wife of
A. W. Smith
Jun 1, 1846
Feb 15, 1874

B. B. Mauldin
Mar 29, 1830
Feb 28, 1905

L. C., Son of
B. B. & Amanda Mauldin
Apr 11, 1870
May 22, 1905

W. H. Mauldin
Jul 14, 1857
Sep 15, 1910

Julia Mauldin
Nov 10, 1852
Nov 1, 1909

"Sister"
Eliza Mauldin
Feb 14, 1855
Nov 17, 1927

D. M. Caldwell
1821-1911
& wife
E. J. Caldwell
1832-1921

R. M. Swanner
1860-1899
& wife
N. A. Swanner
1861-1889

Martha J. Caldwell
Apr 13, 1863
Apr 28, 1884

W. H. Caldwell
Oct 30, 1853
Aug 19, 1878

Earnest, Son of
J. P. & R. A. Graves
Apr 12, 1869
Feb 13, 1909

E. L., Son of
J. P. & R. A. Graves
Jul 5, 1875
Sep 14, 1891

W. S., Son of
J. R. & B. A. Graves
Feb 7, 1873
Jul 21, 1892

James E., Son of
J. P. & R. A. Graves
Nov 15, 1880
Jul 22, 1908

J. W. Collins
Nov 11, 1868
Jul 22, 1892

Bert Caldwell
1909-1918
&
Sadie Caldwell
1890-1892

Dibrella J., Daughter of
Ben F. & M. J. Smith
May 2, 1865
Aug 14, 1883

Rev. J. H. Smith
Jul 13, 1861
Apr 6, 1883

W. F. "Boot" Smith
Jul 16, 1869
Aug 10, 1888

B. F. Smith
Aug 25, 1830
Nov 23, 1913

M. J. Hunter, wife of
B. F. Smith
Jan 23, 1837
Aug 27, 1899

Isaac A. Denham
1850-1893

Mary M. Denham
1858-1942

Esther Denham
1893-1893

Edna Denham
1892-1894

Lula M. Clark
Feb 10, 1878
Dec 28, 1908

PETERSBURG QUADRANGLE

Lizzie Wright
Feb 22, 1883
Aug 19, 1904
&
Mary T. Wright
Aug 6, 1859
Aug 31, 1900

P. L. Wright
Nov 29, 1854
Mar 17, 1925

Sallie Meadows
1865-1950

M. J. Sullivan
May 5, 1860
Oct 24, 1891

Infant Son of
John E. & L. E. Sullivan
Apr 16, 1913
May 3, 1913

Floyd J., Son of
John E. & Lessie Sullivan
Jul 5, 1915
Dec 14, 1921

Julia G. Endsley
1837-1927
"Erected by
J. E. Sullivan"

R. B. Gibson
Sep 6, 1817
Jul 26, 1893

Jane E. Gibson
Feb 8, 1832
Mar 5, 1921

Pleas, Son of
R. B. & R. J. Gibson
Apr 18, 1864
Oct 16, 1894

Daniel Taylor
Jan 8, 1813
Sep 29, 1895

Amaminta D., wife of
Daniel Taylor
Aug 27, 1816
Apr 15, 1895

Elizabeth Jane Taylor
Feb 6, 1843
Apr 3, 1920
&
Cornelia H. Taylor
May 20, 1850
Mar 18, 1923

Thomas H. March
1870-1898
&
Emma March
1870-1920

Cyrus A. March
1874-1898

Jessie, Son of
J. E. & Helen Ellis
Sep 23, 1896
Feb 15, 1897

Mary Lois Ellis
1900-1900

J. E. Ellis
1869-1939
&
Helen Ellis
1872-1929

Charles Homer Sowell
Dec 17, 1917
Jan 31, 1919

Jacob Eshman
Aug 12, 1815
Mar 16, 1894
& wife
Mary J. Eshman
Jun 24, 1827
Jan 28, 1903

Robert L. Wagster
Jun 18, 1868
Aug 20, 1899

Robbie Lee, Daughter of
R. L. & Minta Wagster
Dec 7, 1898
Aug 10, 1899

Felix Massey Mauldin
Feb 3, 1903
May 2, 1928
&
Dortha D. Mauldin
May 8, 1903
Nov 12, 1928

S. K. Caldwell
1860-1934
&
A. F. Caldwell
1854-1942

Infant Son of
A. F. & Kate Caldwell
B&D Jul 8, 1889

Infant Son of
J. W. & H. C. Caldwell
B&D Jun 30, 1897

Mary J., wife of
A. F. Caldwell
May 26, 1854
Mar 30, 1888

J. T. Benedict
Dec 2, 1853
Feb 6, 1912
&
A. J. Benedict
Aug 4, 1856
May 23, 1896

J. E. Caldwell
Feb 17, 1856
Dec 18, 1889

Claude Franklin
1882-1940
&
Stella Franklin
1884-1963

George W. Barnes
Nov 5, 1819
May 15, 1884
& wife
Melissa E. Barnes
Sep 15, 1829
(Date in ground)

Eliza Barnes
1870-1943

Leona R. Barnes
Aug 23, 1874
Oct 24, 1900

J. O. Barnes
Aug 7, 1858
Jul 19, 1893

Sterling C. Barnes
Sep 20, 1885
Feb 26, 1886

Henry Morgan, Son of
Mr. & Mrs. W. A. Ellis
Jun 31, 1884
Aug 10, 1884

Lizzie M., Daughter of
E. A. & M. W. Smith
Apr 2, 1881
Aug 17, 1881

Jane Stokes
1848-1908

Emily F., wife of
H. K. Street
Mar 11, 1832
Feb 2, 1904

S. B. Barnes
Feb 28, 1878
Dec 23, 1878
&
Mary E. Barnes
Dec 16, 1875
May 22, 1879
Children of
W. H. & L. E. Barnes

William H. Barnes
Jun 21, 1849
Apr 25, 1913
&
Lucinda E. Barnes
Aug 16, 1858
Nov 19, 1932

G. F. Barnes
Nov 19, 1878
Apr 24, 1897

Clarence N. Curry
1883-1956
&
Ozella B. Curry
1883-1962

William Alex Sanders
1883-1961

Grace T. Sanders
1896-1959

H. C. Sanders
Oct 2, 1843
Oct 2, 1916
&
L. A. Sanders
May 12, 1846
Nov 5, 1833

Margissie M., Daughter of
W. O. & M. A. Barnes
Jul 2, 1854
Sep 10, 1875

William Bailey Doggett
Died May 12, 1950
Age: 84y, 3m, 6d. (TM)

Jimmie, Son of
B. E. & Angie Burgess
(C. B. & Angie Burgett)
Jun 16, 1894
Nov 1, 1897

C. B. Burgett (Burgess)
Jun 7, 1855
Mar 13, 1925
& wife
Angie Burgett (Burgess)
Jan 7, 1861
(no date)

Lou Barnes, wife of
B. V. Darnell
1859-1833

W. M. Ray
Dec 30, 1844
Jan 13, 1923
&
M. S. Ray
Jan 11, 1854
Mar 1, 1923

Mrs. Jennie Wilson Ray ***
Died 1880
Age: (not given)

*** Family Records.

J. Wilburn Davis
1884-1960
&
Bernice H. Davis
1895-Jun 22, 1974

Sanford Glenn
Jul 6, 1924
Dec 2, 1967

PETERSBURG QUADRANGLE

V. Kate Haislip
Dec 7, 1901
Feb 20, 1964

G. Boliver Haislip
1872-1953
&
G. Leona Haislip
1875-1963

Jones Sullivan
1859-1941
&
Ida A. Sullivan
1869-1943

W. F. Jacobs
1855-1931
&
L. J. Jacobs
1865-1927

Billie M. Sullivan
1901-1919
&
Elizabeth Sullivan
1913-1931
&
Mildred Sullivan
1915-194-

Robbie, Daughter of
J. R. & Maggie Sanders
Apr 1, 1903
Apr 4, 1904

Rufus C. McAfee
Apr 9, 1859
Dec 21, 1936
&
Sarah A. McAfee
Feb 7, 1857
Feb 6, 1933
&
Annie D. McAfee
Jul 17, 1890
Jul 14, 1929

Joe M. McAfee
Oct 1, 1893
Apr 12, 1917
&
Henry J. McAfee
Dec 22, 1879
Sep 7, 1903

Kenneth B. Downing
1886-1898

Adrain M. Downing
1838-1910
&
Ella E. Downing
1849-1934

Lillie E. Downing
1872-1955

Adrain Burgett
1877-1944
&
Orah Burgett
1831-1951

Verna Lou, Daughter of
Adrain & Orah Burgett
Oct 4, 1899
Oct 8, 1902

Minta Taylor Wagster Crunk
1875-1952

Toker Franklin
1875-1904
&
Rilla Franklin
1874-1961

Una, Daughter of
Toker & Rilla Franklin
Feb 21, 1893
Sep 28, 1904

Delbert C. Franklin
Feb 26, 1901
Jul 5, 1921

J. H. Harper
1875-1955
&
Lou Harper
1878-1962

Leslie L. Haislip
1903-1936

B. M. Edwards
Mar 27, 1850
Mar 29, 1938

Lutishie M. Milton, wife
of B. M. Edwards
Oct 29, 1837
May 19, 1911

J. D. Edwards
Oct 15, 1849
May 18, 1939
&
S. B. Edwards
Jan 14, 1853
Sep 15, 1917

Willie Bert Haislip
Sep 6, 1901
Dec 31, 1965
&
Mattie Bell Haislip
Jan 16, 1904

Married May 30, 1920

Laura A., wife of
J. L. Sanders
Aug 7, 1885
Jul 29, 1908

Oma Mai, Daughter of
Mr. & Mrs. C. H. McCoy
Mar 9, 1927
Jun 28, 1929

Minnie, Daughter of
J. L. & M. A. Sanders
Sep 7, 1907
Sep 28, 1915

Martha Ann, wife of
J. M. Sanders
Sep 6, 1854
Jul 28, 1922

James M. Sanders
Myers Co 3 Tenn Cav
C.S.A.

Samuel D. Renegar
Mar 13, 1867
May 2, 1945
&
Fannie W. Renegar
May 27, 1870
Sep 16, 1923

"Our Baby"
Mariam Baucom
(no dates)

J. W. Caldwell
May 12, 1869
Aug 16, 1907

Safrona P., wife of
Sam Caldwell
Mar 12, 1832
Nov 11, 1911

Infant Son of
R. L. & O. M. Brock
B&D Jun 10, 1918

Robert L. Brock
1889-1931

Ossie M. Brock
1892-

J. A. Bigham
Feb 24, 1833
Mar 5, 1912

S. P. Bigham
Jan 1, 1836
May 14, 1916

Lee C. Bigham
1867-1953
&
Minnie Bigham
1879-1957

W. M. Bigham
Dec 8, 1850
Jan 13, 1923
&
M. E. Bigham
May 17, 1861
Mar 20, 1950

Anita Joyce Renegar
1957-1959

Mrs. M. F. Redden
Dec 24, 1878
Sep 18, 1958

Cornelius West
Dec 26, 1844
Sep 9, 1922

James Curry Stone
Aug 1, 1890

&
Esther May Stone
May 9, 1892
Apr 5, 1954

F. M. Stone
Nov 26, 1843
Mar 21, 1917
&
Mary A. Stone
Sep 1, 1848
Apr 15, 1932

B. Austin Haislip
Nov 19, 1895
Feb 16, 1963

Mrs. Austin Haislip
1890-1961

William Samuel Duckworth
Jun 2, 1870
Feb 26, 1929

K. L. Wakefield
Aug 11, 1896
Dec 2, 1919

T. J. Sullivan
Feb 26, 1861
Jun 15, 1928
&
Dona Sullivan
Nov 4, 1859
Mar 12, 1931

N. S. Finley
Aug 20, 1855
Dec 15, 1916

L. A. Finley
Mar 22, 1858
Aug 21, 1916

James L. Wilkerson
May 13, 1830
May 20, 1915

Lula May, wife of
James Wilkerson
May 12, 1879
Jan 29, 1923

PETERSBURG QUADRANGLE

D. B. Wells
Jun 26, 1871
Apr 23, 1964
&
Mollie D. Wells
Jun 7, 1879
Jun 17, 1919
&
Lula O. Wells
Sep 2, 1884
Dec 18, 1962

Earl Moyers
Jan 16, 1891
Jun 2, 1954
&
Janie Moyers
Sep 8, 1896

D. Cloy Gill
Apr 20, 1887
Nov 20, 1963
&
Edna C. Gill
Jul 8, 1889

Daughter of
D. C. & Edna Gill
Mar 20, 1930
Mar 23, 1930

Alex E. Caldwell
1885-1944

Nette B. Caldwell
1884-1965

Malvern Caldwell
Sep 29, 1898
Feb 21, 1967
&
Verna Caldwell
Dec 15, 1905

Will Caldwell
1875-1952
&
Hat Caldwell
1873-1941

D. A. Taylor
1854-1934
&
Jennie T. Taylor
1854-1932

J. S. March
1850-1935

Rosa L. March
1866-1951

Ross P. March
Jan 19, 1891
Feb 12, 1959

T. L. Bland
Feb 29, 1860
Mar 15, 1948
&
Ida Bland
Nov 28, 1864
Mar 14, 1939

Eddie Hobbs
1884-1933
&
Lillie B. Hobbs
1895-1936

Harold, Son of
Floyd & Nannie Richardson
1931-1931

Hubert J. Doggett
Nov 5, 1895

&
Mary Lou Doggett
Oct 12, 1901

Wendol Ray Stinson
Apr 23, 1935
Oct 22, 1936

Mrs. Bessie Haislip
1884-1952

Otalene H. Stinson
May 8, 1909
May 10, 1945

Charles H. Sullivan
Sep 10, 1890
Jun 29, 1963
&
Lucile T. Sullivan
May 15, 1885

Monroe Downing
1874-1945
&
Nannie Downing
1885-1950

Ben L. Talley
1907-1949

Oscar B. Doggett
Apr 30, 1902
Jun 29, 1968
&
Vera B. Doggett
Jun 5, 1905

Opha T. Doggett
1891-
&
Madie Doggett
1886-1959

Loyd Collins
1898-1948
&
Lola Collins
1897-1960

Earlie F. Roden
1891-
&
Lilla B. Roden
1894-1960

Mrs. Fannie J. Hughey
1884-1969

Norma Kay E. Hughey
1946-1949

Ross Carter
Jun 13, 1900

&
Irene Carter
Apr 16, 1898
Sep 28, 1968

Fannie F. Casteel
1876-1949

John W. Edwards
1874-1948
&
Ella M. Edwards
1881-1958

Shelby L. Short
Sep 3, 1894
Jun 5, 1965
&
Mary Lou Short
Aug 20, 1896

William M. Short
Kentucky
S2C U. S. Navy WW II
May 7, 1921
Jul 6, 1948

John O. Barnes
1880-1968
&
Jennie Maye Barnes
1878-1948

Clem McDaniel
1878-1957
&
Nora McDaniel
1882-1967

Athie R. Oliver
1898-1961

Robert E. Bigham
1893-1948
&
Allie D. Bigham
1892-

Audie I. Wilkerson
Jan 29, 1893
Jun 24, 1974
&
Veva M. Wilkerson
Sep 30, 1899
Jun 7, 1979

Cleburn Adams
1894-1953
&
Gothie Adams
1895-1964

A. L. "Lon" Wright
1884-1967

Dalton Lee Wilkerson
Jul 6, 1887
Mar 22, 1966
&
Bessie D. Wilkerson
Oct 26, 1896

Clyde Duckworth
Apr 24, 1903

&
Elizabeth L. Duckworth
Nov 16, 1906
Dec 4, 1964

Jesse M. Smith
Feb 3, 1898
Sep 28, 1965
&
Loutina D. Smith
Nov 30, 1906

Grady B. Welch
Nov 12, 1910
Jun 2, 1967
&
Notry Edwards Welch
Nov 17, 1916
Jun 29, 1951

Eddie L. Edwards
1880-1954
&
Estella Edwards
1884-1952

Mary E., wife of
J. W. Compton
1880-1965

Rollie W. McCoy
Nov 9, 1894

&
Georgie L. McCoy
Mar 30, 1900

PETERSBURG QUADRANGLE

Sallie Ann Cheatham
1859-1953

Jacob F. McCoy
1866-1950
&
Mary F. McCoy
1865-1947

Elwood D. McAfee
1877-1956
&
Nora B. McAfee
1877-1957

Albert J. McAfee
1882-1960
&
Gracie V. McAfee
1881-1953

William Walker Bradford
1892-1968

Edgar March
May 31, 1895
May 31, 1951

Neallie D. Wells
Jul 26, 1881
Aug 24, 1958
&
John T. Wells
Jun 18, 1875
(no date)
&
Minnie L. Wells
Aug 1, 1906
Jun 13, 1949

Billy Mauldin
Mar 28, 1920
Oct 18, 1936
&
Mary Mauldin
Dec 2, 1917
May 26, 1935

Walter L. Mauldin
Jun 27, 1889
Sep 5, 1940
&
Tula S. Mauldin
Sep 17, 1893
May 2, 1933

Adolphus Duckworth
1875-1951
&
Ella W. Duckworth
1874-1938

Charles Duckworth
Jul 28, 1879
Sep 27, 1962

Ann Margaret Reed
Nov 13, 1929
Jan 5, 1935

Nola B. Reed
Jun 6, 1890
Aug 23, 1913

Felix Haggard Liles
1869-1950
&
Lela Mae Liles
1876-1952

A. H. Caldwell
1854-1942

Mary Liles
Feb 15, 1898
Feb 1, 1923

Golie B. Adams
1900-
&
Gladys M. Adams
1906-1930
&
Mildred K. Adams
1908-

Carl Dee Renegar
Died Jul 2, 1974
Age: 74 years.

Ruby Clark Renegar
1904-1930

Ewell T. Franklin
Apr 10, 1910
Jun 21, 1968
&
Vivian H. Franklin
Apr 18, 1910

Lila Jean, Daughter of
E. T. & V. E. Franklin
Feb 16, 1931
Jun 18, 1930

Will Parks
Oct 29, 1865
Feb 3, 1939
&
Virgie Parks
Nov 20, 1870
(no date)

Claudie Dodd
1883-1950
&
Joel Thomas Dodd
1884-1944

James R. Smith
Age: 22 days
(no dates)

Billy Jerral Edwards
Mar 14, 1943
Mar 15, 1943

Mrs. W. B. Reed
1896-1920

William Henry Adams
1869-1946
&
Sarah Cordelia Adams
1875-1958

Alvie Lee Adams
Jan 1, 1903
Dec 30, 1954

Betty L. Jobe
1944

Mary Fay Liles
Jul 5, 1923
May 6, 1928

Mamie Reed
Jan 5, 1900
Apr 6, 1917

Tillman Finley
1874-1948
&
Rebecca Finley
1876-1959

G. B. Smith
Aug 12, 1882
Jan 12, 1940
&
Maxie Smith
Dec 31, 1891

Edd A. Smith
1854-1913
&
Mary Wash Smith
1863-1944

E. Claib Liggett
1878-1958
&
Ethel E. Liggett
1889-

Wiley A. Ellis
1856-1922
&
Margaret A. Ellis
1863-1940

Henry H. Hall
Nov 28, 1873
Mar 28, 1946

Laura J. Liles, wife of
H. H. Hall
Jul 6, 1874
Aug 24, 1936

Mary, Daughter of
H. H. & Laura J. Hall
Aug 22, 1916
Sep 9, 1916

Leota, Daughter of
H. H. & Laura J. Hall
Apr 27, 1907
Jul 8, 1907

Leora, Daughter of
H. H. & Laura J. Hall
Apr 27, 1907
Jun 20, 1907

Esther Mauldin, wife of
O. E. Sullivan
Jan 5, 1895
May 4, 1920

Blake B. Mauldin
Jun 24, 1891
Apr 27, 1914

Infant of
R. F. & C. C. Taylor
B&D Dec 13, 1908

Lafayette Taylor
Feb 14, 1841
Jan 3, 1923
&
Sarah B. Taylor
Apr 21, 1845
Feb 3, 1910

Henry Persis Jones
Oct 12, 1878
Apr 29, 1966
&
Beulah Benedict Jones

Lillian L. Jones
May 17, 1925
Jul 29, 1925

Ola G. Jones
Aug 3, 1893
Sep 10, 1917

George Allen Wakefield
1864-1929
&
Caldonia Wakefield
1870-(no date)

Albert Norwood
Oct 3, 1881
Oct 18, 1951
&
May Norwood
Dec 27, 1892

R. Eugene Taylor
Oct 20, 1879
Feb 25, 1957
&
Cora Caldwell Taylor
May 2, 1881
Nov 6, 1939

Rufus West
1860-1931

"Our Babies" of
J. M. & Stacy Clark
B&D Feb 23, 1915

PETERSBURG QUADRANGLE

James Monroe Clark
Feb 25, 1878
Sep 30, 1941
&
Stacy Louise Ellis Clark
Oct 25, 1879
Apr 13, 1945

John Finley
1882-(broken)
(Beasley FH)

William W. Finley
Jul 21, 1846
(no date)
&
Martha J. Finley
Jul 21, 1848
May 17, 1922

Charlie Franklin
1875-1912
&
Lutie West Franklin
1878-

R. Malvin Franklin
1907-1914
&
Infant Daughter (Franklin)
1905

Joe Haney
1828 (only date)
&
Joe Ann Haney
1828 (only date)

Mrs. Arminta D.,* wife of
Daniel Taylor
Married in 1838
Died Apr 15, 1895
Age: 78y, 8m.

George W. Mauldin
Oct 15, 1866
Dec 20, 1912

J. B. Mauldin
May 8, 1859
Jul 16, 1932
&
Bettie Mauldin
Jul 29, 1867
Jun 5, 1938

Little Georgie Mauldin
Jun 20, 1900
Jun 3, 1919

Mary E., Daughter of
J. B. & M. E. Mauldin
Feb 13, 1898
Apr 10, 1914

Minnie, Daughter of
J. B. & Bettie Mauldin
Nov 29, 1886
Jan 27, 1903

Ovid F. Avantaggio
Mass. Capt U.S.A.F.
Res WW I & WW II
Nov 3, 1896
Jul 14, 1967
Born in Newton, Mass.
&
Sophie Hopkins Avantaggio
born in Orleans, Mass.
Feb 5, 1894

D. C. Hall *
Died Oct 26, 1897
Age: "Old Age".

Mrs. W. J.,* wife of
James W. Dyer
Died Oct 19, 1902
Age: 69 years.

Rev. F. M. Liles
Mar 24, 1844
Jan 2, 1918

Margaret A., wife of
F. M. Liles
Sep 5, 1847
Sep 30, 1922

W. B. Liles
Jul 11, 1879
Feb 18, 1905

Dallas D. T., Son of
Rev. F. M. & M. A. Liles
Jul 11, 1882
Aug 7, 1895

J. T. Benedict
Dec 2, 1853
Feb 6, 1912
&
A. J. Benedict
Aug 4, 1856
May 23, 1896

Nancy Evira, wife of
J. G. Franklin
May 22, 1880
May 1, 1906

Many unmarked graves.

Several fieldstones,
no inscriptions.

Mrs. Tommie,* wife of
Richard Wright
Died Sep 1, 1900
Age: 41 years.

Alfred Granderson March *
Born in North Carolina
Nov 27, 1827
Came to Lincoln County, 1852,
Married in 1854 to
Rebecca Ann Childers, also
Married Nov 4, 1868 to
S. C. Cathey
Died Oct 16, 1895
Age: 67y, 10m, 19d.

J. W. Wright
Sep 25, 1871
Sep 30, 1918
&
M. S. Wright
Apr 25, 1868
Nov 14, 1940

Bob Wright
1901-1945

W. Hill Reed
1886-1961

Millard S. Reed
1913-1948

T. J. Lemond
May 26, 1829
Feb 4, 1903

Elizabeth J., wife of
T. J. Lemond
Nov 23, 1833
Apr 11, 1912

Ella Lemond
Sep 26, 1871
Aug 27, 1942

Phadure Carroll *
Died Oct 6, 1904
Age: 23 years.

Robert Denham *
Died Sep 19, 1906
Age: 28 years.

Miss Permelia Tooley *
Died Jul 31, 1893
Age: 50 years.

Mrs. S. M. McKinney *
Died May 8, 1915
Age: 73 years.
Left a Son,
J. D. Murray.

* *

HUDSON CEMETERY

LOCATION: One and one fourth miles SSE of Delina on the west side of Boonshill Road.

B. F. Hudson
1864-1917

Miss Ann Hudson
1858-1919

John Dobbins
Dec 21 1792
Sep 9, 1840
"War of 1812"

A. F. Dobbins
Apr 24, 1820
Jul 29, 1845

Mary Dobbins
Nov 14, 1821
Sep 19, 1839

Sadie, Daughter of
Dr. T. A. & Sarah E. Clark
B&D Sep 16, 1880

Sarah E., wife of
Dr. T. H. Clark
Jun 10, 1853
Nov 15, 1880

B. F. Hudson
1816-1884

Rebecca J., wife of
B. F. Hudson
1821-1870

E. C. Hudson
1851-1915

Eliza, Daughter of
B. F. & Rebecca Hudson
Jun 18, 1850
Jun 28, 1852

W. J., Son of
B. F. & C. M. Hudson
Nov 5, 1912
Nov 5, 1912

PETERSBURG QUADRANGLE

J. H. Hudson
Sep 9, 1855
Jan 28, 1912

Nancy Adaline, Consort of
Andrew M. Wilson
Nov 29, 1825
May 1, 1844

* *

TURNEY-JACOB CEMETERY

LOCATION: One and one half miles SE of Delina in woods on Turney Branch.

John Jacob
Born in
Amsterdam, Ger.
in 1790
Died Oct 28, 1865

NOTE: Next to the above grave is 4 Vaults, no inscriptions.

Mary E. Jacobs
Apr 29, 1855
Jun 3, 1897

G. L. Jacobs
Mar 27, 1881
May 24, 1889

L. E. Jacobs
Apr 3, 1886
Aug 30, 1888

E. M. Turney
Mar 3, 1841
Sep 17, 1917

W. R. Turney
Dec   1845
Feb 4, 1892

William Monroe Smith
Aug 4, 1857
Jan 14, 1938

Delia, wife of
W. M. Smith
Sep 30, 1867
Aug 7, 1907

Margaret M. Smith
Oct 5, 1893
Apr 4, 1924

Thomas H., Son of
W. R. & E. M. Turney
Jul 2, 1879
Sep 5, 1879

Lucinda Cora Turney,
wife of J. D. Scoggins
Jan 22, 1876
Sep 18, 1917

Mattie Dora Turney
Aug 22, 1869
Sep 21, 1917

Luisey, Daughter of
J. D. & L. C. Scoggins
B&D Jun 29, 1907

* *

PIGG CEMETERY

LOCATION: One and one fourth miles WSW of Blakeville on the west side of Morton Branch and Petersburg Road.

Rebecca Pigg Rucker
Mar 14, 1878
Dec 5, 1958

Henry Grady, Son of
J. & Isa Pigg
Nov 25, 1891
Apr 3, 1893

John K., Son of
John & Isa Pigg
Oct 8, 1895
Aug 9, 1897

John Pigg
Jun 9, 1847
Jan 16, 1937

Isa Dyer, wife of
John Pigg
1868-1953

Ida Bell, wife of
John Pigg
Nov 28, 1857
Mar 30, 1899
Age: 31y, 4m, 2d.

James Edmond, Son of
John & Ida Pigg
Oct 31, 1876
Sep 24, 1903

Ida May Pigg
1885-1967

Claiborn Pigg
Sep 9, 1831
Dec 15, 1901

Rebecca Pigg
Oct 20, 1808
Oct 12, 1876

Edmon Pigg
Jul 25, 1804
Dec 13, 1884

Mary Louisa, Daughter of
Edmon & Rebecca Pigg
Mar 10, 1837
Died in the year 1841

Elane Oneal
Oct 18, 1917
Nov 3, 1917

Infant Son of
Mr. & Mrs. Edd Tucker
1915-1915

Willie Boyd Cashion
Feb 24, 1923
Apr 6, 1923

John, Son of
T. & J. Morton
Died Nov 8, 1828
Age: 4m, 6d.

Isabella J., Daughter of
T. & J. Morton
Died Jul 24, 1832
Age: 2y, 10m.

ED NOTE: By the side of the above 2 graves are 2 large hewn stone vaults. We were told that they were man & wife by the name of Morton, could be T. & J. Morton.

A. G. Butler
Dec 23, 1858
Jan 26, 1914
&
Annie Butler
Nov 7, 1851
Jan 20, 1892

J. O. Butler
Oct 20, 1890
Oct 28, 1890

J. W. Butler
Aug 29, 1833
Dec 11, 1902

C. B. Butler
Dec 7, 1895
Sep 3, 1913

William H. Tucker
1862-1936
&
Martha E. Tucker
1868-1899
&
John R. Tucker
1894-1925

Willie J. Casteel
1874-1905
&
Lillie West Casteel
1880-1965

Willie J. Casteel
Jan 1, 1874
Sep 9, 1905

Oney C., wife of
John Patterson
Jan 13, 1820
Sep 12, 1838

PETERSBURG QUADRANGLE

J. W. Lemond
May 16, 1837
Apr 26, 1912
& wife
Martha C. Lemond
Nov 16, 1838
(no date)

Mary A. Pigg
Jan 22, 1825
Jan 19, 1912

J. C. Ellis
Jan 14, 1835
May 27, 1904

Nancy D., wife of
J. C. Ellis
Jan 14, 1836
Feb 28, 1911

Annie L., Daughter of
J. C. & N. D. Ellis
Aug 7, 1868
Sep 21, 1868

Sarah L., Daughter of
J. C. & N. D. Ellis
Mar 8, 1859
Mar 16, 1860

Nettie T. Scoggins
1889-1950

Espey E. B. Morrison
Tennessee
Pvt Btry D 17 Fld Arty
Dec 27, 1914
Aug 23, 1966

C. P. Morrison
Aug 11, 1886
Feb 3, 1929

Dona Lynn, Daughter of
Mr. & Mrs. J. R. Darnell
B&D Jul 19, 1960

John R. Dunman
Tennessee
Pfc 119th Inf 30 Div
WW I
Mar 31, 1894
Dec 12, 1948

Zula May Dunman
Apr 19, 1892
Jul 10, 1936

Mary L., Daughter of
R. J. & E. A. Luna
Nov 12, 1856
Aug 7, 1864
Age: 7y, 8m, 25d.

R. J. Luna
Jan 23, 1835
Apr 20, 1883
Married Jan 15, 1856
A. E. Pigg

Elizabeth Pigg Luna
Jan 17, 1833
Married to
R. J. Luna
Jan 15, 1858
Died May 11, 1907
Age: 74y, 3m, 24d.

Robert Tucker
1860-1941
&
Permellia Tucker
1865-1942

W. L. Welch
1881-1943

Icie T. Welch
1887-1935

Geneva Welch
1911-1931

E. C. Morrison
Nov 4, 1859
May 11, 1939
&
Icie N. Morrison
Apr 17, 1880
Mar 18, 1962

Fanny, wife of
E. C. Morrison
Nov 16, 1856
Oct 6, 1915

Several unmarked graves.

Several fieldstones,
no inscriptions.

Thomas J. Russell *
Died Apr 4, 1909
Age: 82 years.

Tranquella I. Tucker
1850-1932

"Father"
John Tucker
1891-1947
&
"Mother"
Mattie Lou Tucker
1897-19
&
"Daughter"
Ruby Tucker
1915-1941

C. W. Crabtree
Feb   1830
Sep 27, 1919
&
Mary Crabtree
Sep 6, 1835
Sep 5, 1920

Rosa Viola Crabtree
Jun 25, 1902
Jan 19, 1925

Ernest L. Crabtree
1881-1947

Rosa, wife of
E. L. Crabtree
Oct 7, 1883
Apr 24, 1919

Andrew Jobe
Nov 26, 1913
Feb 3, 1934

Ada Morrison, wife of
Eugene Jobe
Jun 22, 1883
Sep 5, 1938

Claibe Tucker
Mar 14, 1892
Apr 23, 1959

Mary E. Tucker
Mar 16, 1896
Mar 1, 1948

J. D. Tucker
Jan 16, 1908
Jul 28, 1933

Infant * of
Mrs. Philander Tucker
Died Apr 8, 1915
Age: (not given)

Luddie F. Smith
1877-1946

E. J. "Sis" Tucker
Jan 27, 1856
Feb 25, 1944

Emma N. Tucker
Sep 17, 1897
Oct 11, 1915

J. G. Poarch
Mar 14, 1862
May 6, 1911

M. M. Poarch
1874-1926

Buford, Son of
Mary J. Tucker
Feb 15, 1884
Oct 14, 1902

J. J. Fly
Died Jun 26, 1881
Age: 44 years.
&
Sarah J. Fly
Jul 24, 1840
Apr 29, 1911
&
Lula Fly
Apr 2, 1879
Mar 9, 1918

John R. Smith
Aug 3, 1828
Jun 15, 1902

Margrett, wife of
J. R. Smith
Apr 8, 1832
Jul 22, 1904

Dave Tucker
1867-1958
&
Dollie Fly Tucker
1868-1950

Albert Tucker
1875-19
&
Della Tucker
1873-1945

William Smith *
Died Jun 6, 1917
Age: 19 years.

* *

PETERSBURG QUADRANGLE

BUCHANAN CEMETERY

LOCATION: One half mile south of Blakeville on the west side of Craighead Creek, at Friendship Church.

Nancy A. Ellis
Jul 30, 1871
Feb 18, 1873

Stacy Brent
Aug 2, 1807
Jul 1, 1885

Mary Elizabeth Pigg
Feb 15, 1904
Sep 13, 1905

Mabel Pigg Barnes
1902-1918

Samuel Boone Pigg
1866-1929
&
Mattie Raney Pigg
1883-19

J. Taylor Pigg
Jan 21, 1848
Sep 30, 1924

Miss Delina A. Pigg
Oct 10, 1836
May 23, 1896

Mrs. Jane Foster *
Died Jul 21, 1902
Age: 80 years.

James Pigg
1835-1911
& wife
Lizzie Pigg
1840-1914

Miss Rausa J. Pigg
Sep 26, 1838
Aug 10, 1866

John Pigg
Jun 16, 1810
Dec 22, 1883
Age: 78y, 6m, 6d.

Dillie, wife of
John Pigg
Nov 24, 1813
Jun 15, 1889
Age: 75y, 6m, 21d.

J. D. Ramsey
Died Sep 10, 1849
Age: 26 years.
&
Eliza Ramsey
Died Jul 10, 1854
Age: 81 years.
&
James Ramsey
Died Oct 26, 1859
Age: 81 years.

Miss Jane Ramsey
Died Jan 14, 1890
Age: 66 years.

Eliza J., wife of
W. B. Moore & Daughter
of J. N. & Mary Pigg
Dec 7, 1854
Jun 20, 1879

Leonard Curtis, Son of
J. E. & Elpha B. Moore
Jul 23, 1901
Feb 21, 1903

Elpha B., wife of
J. E. Moore
Mar 17, 1881
Mar 9, 1903

Ida, wife of
J. E. Moore
Apr 22, 1882
Mar 11, 1918

John Buchanan
Jun 13, 1786
Feb 26, 1853
Age: 66y, 8m, 13d.
& Consort
Sarah Buchanan
Jul 7, 1795
Feb 3, 1860
Age: 64y, 6m, 26d.

Mary Pack
Age: 73 years.
(no dates)

J. H. Pack
Sep 25, 1847
(no date)
&
Finnetta J. Pack
Oct 20, 1851
Sep 10, 1899

Infant Daughter of
J. H. & F. J. Pack
B&D Aug 10, 1899

T. D. Pigg
Dec 5, 1856
Dec 30, 1912

Lillie Etta Pigg
Dec 2, 1862
Mar 7, 1925

Infant Daughter of
T. D. & L. E. Pigg
Feb 2, 1900
Apr 30, 1901

John N. Pigg
Died Mar 6, 1881
Age: 55 years.

Mary, wife of
John N. Pigg
Died May 2, 1896
Age: 77 years.

W. B. Moore
May 29, 1840
Jul 21, 1924

Martha A. Turney Pigg,
wife of W. B. Moore
Jul 1, 1851
Apr 3, 1901
Married Jan 13, 1881

Sophia Delilah, Daughter
of W. B. & M. A. Moore
Nov 7, 1881
Oct 5, 1883

* *

PIGG CEMETERY

LOCATION: One fourth mile NNE of Blakeville on the east side of Petersburg Road in pasture.

Joel T. Pigg
Apr 19, 1834
Sep 9, 1903
&
Martha E. Pigg
Sep 28, 1840
May 9, 1934

James G. Pigg
Nov 20, 1871
Apr 14, 1885

Jesse T. Pigg
Sep 8, 1873
Aug 2, 1883

* *

PETERSBURG QUADRANGLE

BUCHANAN CEMETERY

LOCATION: One fourth mile NNE of Blakeville on the east side of Petersburg Road, in pasture.

Samuel Buchanan Mar 13, 1778 Jan 30, 1852 Leaving a bereaved wife, 8 children and 25 Grand children. & Rachel Buchanan Jan 16, 1788 Nov 11, 1857 Thadus S. Buchanan Jan 2, 1849 Oct 7, 1867	John W. Buchanan Oct 18, 1822 Apr 16, 1857 Elder of C. P. Church. Cyntha Jane, Consort of John W. Buchanan Jun 20, 1830 Aug 13, 1850 Married Aug 13, 1846 "3 children: Sina Adeline, Thadeus Sylvester & Cyrus Jane." Almedia Buchanan Apr 20, 1819 May 4, 1856	Fletcher Worth Buchanan Jun 28, 1846 Jul 15, 1847 Infant Son of Thomas & Sarah A. Buchanan B&D Jun 13, 1856 Ina Adeline, Consort of Theo. Harris Mar 16, 1826 May 11, 1846 Marcus Y., Son of T. W. & Sarah A. Buchanan May 21, 1838 Jan 23, 1851	Nancy B. Rives 1843-1848 Elizabeth G. Buchanan Sep 18, 1845 Nov 8, 1845 Harriet V. Buchanan 1842-1844 Catharine V. Buchanan B&D 1856 Infant Daughter of W. & A. Buchanan B&D 1859

* *

CENTER POINT CEMETERY

LOCATION: One and one fourth miles east of Blakeville.

William D. Moore Aug 18, 1877 Jul 11, 1940 & Mary B. Moore Apr 23, 1882	Henry Turney Moore 1886-1956 Elma D. Moore Oct 11, 1892 May 16, 1970	NOTE: This was the site of Old Center Point School.

* *

CEMETERY

LOCATION: Two and one half miles NW of Howell on west side of Fishing Ford Road.

Here lies the Body of John D--- (Dean or Dunn) Died Dec 5, 1816 Age: (not given)	1840 (fieldstone) 3 large vaults, no inscriptions.	About 10 unmarked graves.

* *

BLAKE CEMETERY

LOCATION: At Old Bidwell, one fourth mile south of Cane Creek, on west side of Highway 431.

"Sister" Lucy H. Blake Mar 14, 1841 Jul 9, 1860 "Brother" John R. Blake Oct 6, 1829 Mar 7, 1882 "Brother" Stephen D. Blake Oct 25, 1830 Aug 7, 1884	John M. Blake Died Feb 8, 1862 Age: 70 years. & wife Mary A. Blake Died Apr 10, 1868 Age: 77 years. Emily V., Daughter of J. W. & M. A. Blake Died Mar 23, 1856 Age: 20 years.	William M. Blake Jan 1, 1798 May 7, 1850 & wife Della C. Blake Dec 18, 1805 Apr 1, 1879 William F. Blake Sep 29, 1813 Jul 28, 1858 & Marriett M. Blake May 27, 1819 Aug 2, 1855	Catharine D., wife of William C. Blackwell Jun 26, 1831 Feb 7, 1855 Clara Olivia, Daughter of B. F. & S. M. Bearden Nov 26, 1844 Feb 15, 1847 Mary A., wife of D. H. Bearden Nov 3, 1831 Feb 18, 1854

PETERSBURG QUADRANGLE

Sarah Ann, Daughter of
D. H. & M. A. Bearden
Aug 25, 1852
Apr 9, 1886

Martha D., wife of
George C. Gillespie
Sep 19, 1846
Aug 20, 1868

Many unmarked graves.

Mrs. Polly,* widow of
R. S. Woodard
Died Nov 10, 1897
Age: (not given)
Daughter of
---- Hatcher.

William, Son of
W. W. & Della E. Hampton
Jul 11, 1869
Dec 29, 1879

Mary C., Daughter of
W. W. & Della E. Hampton
Jul 25, 1872
Jun 25, 1874

Fannie Lou,* Daughter of
A. C. & S. A. Smith
Died Jul 24, 1896
Age: 11y, 8m, 5d.

George C. Carmack *
Died Sep 1908
Age: (not given)
Left a son, Sam C. Carmack.

Infant Son of
R. & S. A. Harris
B&D Oct 22, 1868

John B., Son of
T. K. & E. A. Warren
Feb 22, 1837
Aug 31, 1855

T. K. Warren
Died 1887
Age: (not given)

Elizabeth A., wife of
T. K. Warren
Apr 7, 1817
Jul 30, 1880

Charles Buvinger *
Died May 17, 1909
Age: 50 years.
His wife was the daughter
of George Carmack.

William Henry Warren
Jun 9, 1848
Oct 10, 1877
&
Lucetta Blanton Warren
Hanaway
Oct 16, 1848
Aug 31, 1937
&
William Henry Clinkscales
Warren
Jul 15, 1877
Dec 29, 1881

Mrs. Phenton Thornton *
Died May 5, 1899
Age: (not given)
Left a son, Matt, &
a daughter, Mrs. Saunders.

* *

COLLIER CEMETERY

LOCATION: Three fourth mile SSE of the point where the
Fishingford Road crosses the Boonshill Road, on the west
bank of Pleasant Valley Creek.

Richard R. Collier
Feb 4, 1845
Oct 2, 1894

Nannie M. Collier
Oct 12, 1849
Feb 26, 1903

* *

CHAPMAN CEMETERY

LOCATION: One half mile south of the Boonshill-Fishingford
Cross Roads, near Old Mt. Olivet P. B. Church.

Laura Brown
1862-1958

Ira L. Brown
1893-1921

Charlie M. Brown
1899-1920

A. Vann Brown
1864-1943
&
Martha E. Brown
1870-1910

Thomas Chapman
Died Jun 23, 1845
Age: 57 years.
&
Mary Chapman
Died Dec 17, 1881
Age: 91 years.

Della A. Lofton
Jun 12, 1815
May 18, 1865

Harriet Pickle
Apr 6, 1822
Jan 10, 1899
Age: 76y, 9m, 12d.

John A., Son of
L. & N. A. Marr
Apr 7, 1874
Feb 7, 1895

N. A. Marr
Oct 6, 1840
May 18, 1917
&
L. Marr
Feb 1, 1843
Jul 21, 1916

John Marr
Aug 12, 1800
Sep 13, 1891
&
Sallie Marr
Mar 12, 1802
Nov 26, 1897

John L. Scott
Jul 3, 1824
Oct 16, 1854
Age: 30y, 3m, 16d.

Mary I. Scott
Jun 7, 1853
Jul 18, 1855
(broken)

Thomas N. Scott
Dec 19, 1846
Jul 3, 1849

Harriet E., Daughter of
W. B. & A. O. Taylor
Aug 4, 1861
Aug 23, 1861

Several unmarked graves.

* *

PETERSBURG QUADRANGLE

ISOM CEMETERY

LOCATION: Two and one half miles NE of Delina on Dyer Branch, in Fuss Hollow on the east side of the road.

C. H. Isom Oct 19, 1819 Nov 14, 1887	Parthenia, wife of C. H. Isom Jan 17, 1820 May 14, 1877	2 graves with field-stones, no inscriptions.

* *

DANIEL CEMETERY

LOCATION: Two and one half miles NE of Delina on Dyer Branch, in Fuss Hollow on east side of road.

W. G. (no dates, fieldstone)	M. G. (no dates, fieldstone)	About 25 graves with fieldstones, no insc.

* *

CRABTREE CEMETERY

LOCATION: Two and three fourth miles NE of Delina on Dyer Branch and in Fuss Hollow, on the north side of Old Gregory Chapel.

H. Fate Crabtree 1865-1943 & Malindy J. Crabtree 1852-1918 Mrs. George Conwell * Died Aug 31, 1917 Age: 73 years.	James J. Crabtree Dec 25, 1844 Jan 3, 1892 Mary Lessie Crabtree Jan 14, 1892 Apr 16, 1968 Mrs. Lottie Crabtree * Died Aug 30, 1917 Age: 80 years Left a daughter, Mrs. Will Wright.	M. E., wife of D. K. Conwell Jan 14, 1845 Aug 24, 1917 Several fieldstones, no inscriptions. D. J. Franklin * Died Oct 24, 1912 Age: 75 years.	Clarence Jones, Son of W. C. Ervin Sep 16, 1894 Oct 9, 1895

* *

WAKEFIELD CEMETERY

LOCATION: Two miles NE of Delina on top of Ridge at the Marshall County line.

Tip Williams (no dates)	Samuel Wakefield 1775-Jan 1, 1865	Josiah Wakefield 1792-1817	Malissa Scott B&D Aug 13, 1846

About 12 unmarked graves.

* *

TULEY CEMETERY

LOCATION: One and one fourth miles NE of Delina, in mouth of Dyer Hollow.

Lucy A. Bland 1823-Oct 14, 1878 A. B. Collins Jul 5, 1843 Dec 12, 1910 Gedida E. Collins Feb 22, 1848 Sep 24, 1906	Adron Luna Sep 29, 1876 May 1, 1911 Sarah F. Pigg Nov 1, 1851 Feb 27, 1857	Eliza H. Pigg Mar 22, 1808 Sep 27, 1855 Thomas A. Pigg Feb 28, 1829 Jul 18, 1853	Henry Turney Aug 6, 1798 Jun 22, 1885 Delilah, wife of Henry Turney Jan 17, 1802 Aug 17, 1865

PETERSBURG QUADRANGLE

C. M. M. Tuley
Sep 1, 1834
May 20, 1914 *
C.S.A 1st Tenn Regt
Co K of Boonshill
Minute Men
    & wife
S. L. Tuley
Jun 2, 1847
Jul 9, 1912

J. T. Tucker
Jul 24, 1845
Oct 4, 1904

Many unmarked graves.

Many fieldstones,
no inscriptions.

Belzory Tucker
May 23, 1852
May 24, 1852

Dila O. Tucker
Nov 12, 1855
Sep 11, 1856

* *

CUMBERLAND PRESBYTERIAN CHURCH CEMETERY

LOCATION: At the side of the Cumberland Presbyterian Church in Petersburg.

Rena B., Daughter of
A. J. & M. D. Crunk
Jan 8, 1871
Feb 1, 1872

J. F. R. (Rives)
(no dates, fieldstone)

Henry T. Rives
Dec 22, 1862
Aug 12, 1864
    &
Dora Rives
Dec 22, 1862
Jan 17, 1864
Infant Son & Daughter of
R. C. & B. J. Rives

Nannie, Daughter of
F. C. A. & M. J. Troop
Jun 15, 1864
Aug 31, 1867

Lizzie, Daughter of
R. C. & R. J. Rives
May 14, 1864
Aug 1, 1867

James Blakemore
Sep 25, 1780
Sep 24, 1857

Sarah Blakemore
Mar 7, 1788
Apr 6, 1863

Virginia C. Blakemore
May 30, 1863
Sep 22, 1863

Hattie, Daughter of
R. C. & R. J. Rives
Apr 19, 1866
Feb 27, 1882
Age: 15y, 10m, 5d.

Lilla May, Daughter of
R. C. & R. J. Rives
Jun 13, 1868
Jul 13, 1883

Infant Son of
R. & S. A. Harris
Nov 1, 1869
Dec 19, 1869

Ida Belle, Daughter of
R. C. & R. J. Rives
Jan 1, 1875
Feb 10, 1876

Mary C., wife of
J. S. Johnson
May 10, 1870
Oct 24, 1892

John H. Chapman
Age: 47 years.
(no dates)

Robert S., Son of
J. H. & D. L. Chapman
Age: 6 months
(no dates)

John Winston Chapman
Oct 13, 1854
Jan 9, 1862

Augustus, Daughter of
Dr. W. R. & E. A. Smith
Mar 26, 1879
Jul 5, 1880

Infant Daughter of
J. M. & Amanda Brown
B&D Jun 11, 1862

J. E. Montgomery
Apr 23, 1871
Nov 14, 1891

A. C. S.
Died Jan 28, 1861

M. J. S.
(no dates, broken)

Infant Son of
C. B. & S. F. Metcalf
Dec 1862
Jan 1863

Infant Son of
C. B. & S. F. Metcalf
Sep 3, 1860
Sep 24, 1860

Charles M., Son of
M. H. & E. Husbands
Nov 9, 1857
Sep   1859

Cadie Metcalf Blake
Oct 18, 1855
Feb 19, 1861
Age: 5y, 4m, 1d.

Willie Robert Smith
Dec 14, 1872
Sep 4, 1875
Age: 2y, 8m, 24d.

Henrietta, Consort of
C. M. Blake
Aug 26, 1834
Sep 29, 1866

Johnie Allen, Son of
J. C. & Ida S. Street
Died Oct 7, 1878
Age: 4y, 1m, 26d.

Little Mary, First born of
J. C. & Ida Street
Died Sep 13, 1871
Age: 11 days.

Susan M. Bearden
Died Feb 4, 1875
Age: (not given)

B. F. Bearden
Died Jan 23, 1870
Age: 58 years.

Theo W. Bledsoe
Dec 16, 1838
Feb 21, 1867
Age: 28 years.

Mrs. E. Helen, wife of
Theo W. Bledsoe
Died Jan 15, 1883
Age: 44 years.

Amanda A. Blake
Died Aug 29, 1873
Age: (not given)

Dr. H. H. Rives
Born in Dinwiddie Co., Va.
Apr 13, 1817
Died of cholera
Dec 2, 1866

Rev. D. L. Mitchell
May 8, 1818
Oct 25, 1885

Mrs. M. A. Mitchell
Apr 13, 1828
Apr 30, 1885

----lis Green Rives
Sep 1, ----
Feb 1, 18-0 (broken)

W. M. Shofner
Mar 24, 1846
Sep 30, 1882

Martha M. Blakemore
May 24, 1824
--- --, 1861 (broken)

Daughter of
Dr. W. R. & Susan A.
Smith
May 13, 1864
Sep 12, 1867

Susan A., Consort of
Dr. W. R. Smith
Oct 11, 1838
Mar 13, 1867

Susan E., Infant of
B. W. & H. E. Rives
May 11, 1861
Jul 16, 1861

Many unmarked graves.

****

PETERSBURG QUADRANGLE

MARSH CEMETERY

LOCATION: Located in south Petersburg.

P. B. Marsh
Jan 18, 1828
Dec 20, 1909

Docia P., wife of
P. B. Marsh
Apr 15, 1828
Jan 26, 1892
Married Aug 15, 1850

Infant Son of
G. C. & Jennie Marsh
B&D Jan 10, 1892

Child of
G. C. & Jennie Marsh
(no dates)

Minnie, Infant of
J. D. & M. D. Hart
B&D May 18, 1901

W. C. Scott
Apr 7, 1881
Jul 9, 1904

Maggie J. Scott
Nov 1, 1880
Oct 6, 1904

Infant Son of
A. B. & M. E. Winford
B&D Jul 4, 1893

C. W. Wade
1847-1919

Mollie Catharine, wife
of C. W. Wade
1853-1893

W. P. Wade
1876-1931

* *

OLD ORCHARD CEMETERY

LOCATION: Petersburg, One fourth mile east of Petersburg, across Cane Creek.

Willie B. Pigg
1888-1946
&
Oma R. Pigg
1888-1968

Charlie H. Morton
1870-1953

James Berry Morton
1896-1968

Mary Ann Morton
1868-1930

William S. Morton
1905-1947

John J. Morton
Aug 20, 1900
Oct 25, 1969
&
Addie R. Morton
Jul 3, 1918

Will A. Gowan
Mar 15, 1862
Oct 17, 1950
&
Mattie Morton Gowan
Jun 6, 1870
Dec 6, 1929

N. S. A. Lambert
1846-1922

H. C. Lambert
1835-1923

Retta A. Lambert
1870-1935

T. J. Lambert
1870-1952

Maudie Lambert
1879-1956
&
J. K. "Bud" Lambert
1868-1939
&
Jemima Lambert
1857-1922

Charlie H. Davidson
1890-1895

Dr. Elijah A. Davidson
1845-1921
&
Lizzie M. Davidson
1861-1926

Isaac Marks Davidson
1886-1957

Ottie M. Sorrells
Jan 10, 1884
Dec 8, 1960

T. A. Sorrells
Jan 5, 1877
Oct 30, 1949

A. B. Sorrells
Jan 3, 1882
Jan 10, 1935

N. J. Sorrells
Oct 5, 1849
Aug 13, 1922

Elnorah H. Sorrells
May 27, 1853
Jun 20, 1923

Bernice Holloway
May 7, 1895
Nov 3, 1966

Minnie Lovings Tatum
Dec 25, 1877
Mar 25, 1918

J. W. Marsh
1835-1923
&
S. L. Marsh
1848-1918

Irene Sanders, wife of
W. E. Marsh
Aug 25, 1884
Feb 11, 1925

William E. Marsh
Jan 24, 1882
Oct 3, 1946

John L. Marsh
1889-1943
&
Sarah Marsh
1893-1968

Melba, Daughter of
John L. & Sarah Marsh
1915-1939

James B. Marsh
Mar 9, 1876
Sep 9, 1951

Effie N. Marsh
Oct 8, 1883
Feb 12, 1964

James B. Sowell
Mar 3, 1857
Aug 30, 1938

Susan J. Finley, wife of
J. B. Sowell
1863-1929

Charles A. Sowell
Aug 13, 1881
Aug 7, 1947

John Wilson Scott
Jan 29, 1871
Apr 3, 1943

Mrs. Ibby Delk Scott
Died Dec 8, 1969
Age: 97 years.
(Ralston FH)

Alva E. Barham
1906-
&
Sarah L. Barham
1904-1966

Eph L. Barham
1910-1929

C. E. Barham
1878-1941

Mabel L. Barham
1883-1945

A. T. Cordell, Jr.
Feb 11, 1935
Jan 28, 1938

Bill Bartlett
1892-1964

John Rainey
1878-1965

Myrtle Rainey
1875-1967

James Edward Bartlett
1921-1948

J. A. Bartlett
Sep 7, 1867
Jul 8, 1913

Robert W. Long
Feb 12, 1832
Feb 20, 1912
A Confederate Soldier
&
Tabitha Long
Nov 10, 1836
Dec 9, 1916

PETERSBURG QUADRANGLE

James L. Gilbert
1851-1923
&
Effie Gilbert
1861-1925

W. A. Morrison
Dec 21, 1853
Jul 22, 1930
&
Mary E. Morrison
May 26, 1857
Dec 31, 1912

Joe Stephenson
1864-1920

Frances E. Stephenson
1866-1946

Bessie D. Stephenson
1887-1903

A. F. Gilbert
Dec 20, 1843
Oct 8, 1921

Ticia, Daughter of
Golie & Ticia Scott
Sep 7, 1908
Jun 24, 1909

Golie E. Scott
Aug 25, 1875
Mar 23, 1934

Ticia, wife of
Golie E. Scott
Mar 3, 1878
Sep 9, 1908

Hattie Ramsey Scott
Mar 2, 1884
Aug 1, 1957

Fred L. Scott
Feb 22, 1906
Jul 4, 1939

Will Scott
Jul 30, 1870
Mar 1, 1923

Noah B. Scott
Jul 7, 1840
Oct 19, 1900
&
Rittie E. Scott
Mar 13, 1845
Jun 29, 1907

Virgil A. Scott
Jan 8, 1883
Jan 30, 1938

Elizabeth, wife of
V. A. Scott
Apr 27, 1886
Dec 6, 1917

G. Everett Stallings
1911-1964
&
Anita L. Stallings
1905-

Newsom Stallings
1847-1926
&
Rebecca Stallings
1855-1941

Ethel Stallings
Aug 5, 1867
May 28, 1924

Mabel G., wife of
P. L. Cunningham
Mar 2, 1883
Aug 9, 1907

Addie, wife of
Theo Sorrells &
Daughter of
J. N. & R. T. Stallings
Aug 29, 1878
May 9, 1906

S. E. Scott
Nov 17, 1867
Oct 27, 1940

Octa C. Scott
Sep 10, 1867
Jul 19, 1948

Aline R. Scott
Dec 22, 1893
Jun 24, 1949

T. Lindon Vaughn
Dec 27, 1893
Mar 9, 1962
&
Lucille S. Vaughn
Sep 8, 1893
Oct 11, 1967

J. F. Gilbert
1876-1929

Ethel F. Gilbert
1881-1970
(Mary Ethel Gilbert)
(Gowan-Smith FH)

Jesse P. Moore
Dec 30, 1893
Aug 19, 1967
&
Ruby P. Moore
Nov 5, 1907
Aug 25, 1969

Grady E. Whorley
Mar 5, 1898
May 16, 1959
&
Kathleen D. Whorley
May 11, 1905

Risa Kathleen Whorley
1961-1964

John C. Moore
Jun 23, 1848
Feb 4, 1932
&
Ava Long Moore
Apr 1, 1859
Jul 3, 1931

Kate Moore
1886-1948
(Beasley FH)

"Horris", Son of
J. C. & A. M. Moore
Feb 8, 1883
Sep 22, 1884

Charles Franklin Harrison, O.D.
1878-1919

Bertie Tate Harrison
1878-1962

Alice Rachel Harrison Pacque
1914-1969

Sebastian Z. Phlieger
West Virginia
Pvt U. S. Army WW I
Mar 17, 1896
Apr 23, 1969

G. W. Enochs
1846-1919
& wife
Mary Francis Enochs
1851-1919

Mecca E. Woosley
1869-1961

William F. Hart
1858-1925
&
Mattie E. Hart
1872-1927

James T. Crane
1864-1931
& wife
Naoma Crane
1875-1948

Archer B. Sanders
1872-1934
&
Louise E. Sanders
1879-1960

Robert T. Sanders
1877-1926
& wife
Landess Sanders
1888-

Mary Eleanor Vaughn
Dec 24, 1913
Oct 25, 1932

Ella Sowell Edwards
Jan 5, 1890
Mar 15, 1950

Comrade
George Bagley
Aug 2, 1876
May 5, 1948

Anna Sowell Bagley
1834-1926

George A. Bagley
1920-1920

Allen S. Bagley
1926-1926

Dora Ann Darnell
Apr 17, 1876
Jul 23, 1965

Beulah Darnell Sorrells
Aug 18, 1902
Nov 6, 1957

Oma G. Redd, wife of
Eugene Sorrells
1892-1924

Roy E. Lane
1889-1954

Florence Sorrells, wife
of Roy Lane
1898-1920
(picture)

Thurman B. Lane
Tennessee
M Sgt Armor WW II Korea
Nov 28, 1915
Jun 10, 1962

W. Ed Sorrells
Oct 30, 1875
Mar 17, 1951

Lilla Sorrells
Nov 24, 1881
Jan 18, 1969

Varda Sorrells
Oct 22, 1838
Feb 23, 1953

Frank A. Fowler
1870-1947

Beulah H. Fowler
1870-1947

Philip M. Harris
1866-1937

Theo F. Harris
1844-1922

Mary C. Harris
1846-1931

PETERSBURG QUADRANGLE

Robert F. Lambert
1877-1956

Mattie Lee Lambert
1903-1965

James T. Lambert
1912-1965

Ray Williams
1943-1967
(TM)

James W. Williams
1877-1953
&
Mattie P. Williams
1884-19

James W. Williams
Sep 24, 1916

&
Mary M. Williams
Dec 24, 1918
May 17, 1964

Carl M. Williams
1938-1940

Ernest W. Nichols
Feb 4, 1898
Dec 9, 1938
&
Jessie Lee Nichols
Nov 13, 1900
Jul 27, 1937

Robert G. Bills
1884-1950

Pat G. Bills
Died Feb 28, 1977
Age: (not given)

Ruth Bills

Ida Mae Williams
1911-1930

Everett E. Williams
Tennessee
S1 U.S.N.R. WW II
Jul 2, 1907
Mar 9, 1969

Thomas E. Sowell
1894-1964
&
Jennie Mai Sowell
1896-1951

George David Triplett, Jr.
Sep 10, 1947
Jan 13, 1950

Garland L. Franklin
Jul 9, 1894
Feb 12, 1962
&
Mamie B. Franklin
May 25, 1903

Thomas A. Franklin
Nov 12, 1870
Apr 16, 1934
&
Louella W. Franklin
Dec 25, 1861
Aug 14, 1948

Everett L. Franklin
Tennessee
Fl U.S.N. WW II
May 31, 1927
Oct 8, 1955

C. Bert Nichols
Nov 7, 1902

&
Lillian S. Nichols
Nov 10, 1902
Mar 10, 1967

Elbert Holt King
Apr 6, 1888
Nov 3, 1962
&
Lessie Lake McAdams King
Oct 15, 1890
Aug 10, 1951

Fred C. King
1910-1936

William A. King
Mar 19, 1855
May 23, 1945

Mary Dyer King
Dec 14, 1861
Apr 18, 1939

Abbie King Green
1893-1946

J. Owen Jones
1897-1955
&
Lucy K. Jones
1894-1956

Albert J. Conwell
Jan 11, 1880
Aug 20, 1964
&
Sally S. Conwell
Aug 3, 1885
Feb 28, 1965

Charlie N. Cole
1883-1923

Lela S. Cole
Jan 18, 1884
Dec 25, 1967

Walter Cole
1882-1940

Oren Fullerton
Jan 1, 1887
Sep 14, 1958

Ora B. Fullerton
Jul 10, 1882
Nov 7, 1964

William A. Morrison
Nov 7, 1853
Jan 1, 1928

Elizabeth C., wife of
William A. Morrison
May 13, 1854
Apr 13, 1922

Eric Alban Morrison
Dec 13, 1880
Mar 26, 1966

Lillie F. Morrison
Jul 13, 1884
Mar 9, 1964

Lee A. Morrison
Jun 23, 1879
Nov 25, 1942

W. T. Sorrells
1858-1939

Fannie Lee, wife of
W. T. Sorrells
1874-1948

Emily Ethel, Daughter of
W. T. & F. L. Sorrells
Nov 26, 1895
Sep 17, 1896

Fred E. Luna
1916-1920

Fronia O'Neal, wife of
Earn Luna
1879-1936

Earn Luna
1873-1934

C. A. Blakemore
1869-1945

Clemmie O'Neal, wife of
C. A. Blakemore
1877-1950

John Marsh Archer
1928-1932

M. R. A. Archer
1864-1959

J. W. Archer
1859-1945

Lucile F. Archer
1890-

Will M. Archer
1887-1065

Luther L. Hart
1882-1958

Edna A. Hart
1895-1927

Julius Phillips
1879-1954

Cana A. Phillips
1884-

Georgia Lee Fowler Scott
Jul 31, 1896
Jun 21, 1929

James Cecil Scott
Dec 11, 1889

Lena Hardin Scott
Oct 11, 1899
Aug 2, 1961

Golie Foster
1876-1955

Genie Foster
1884-1937

Oscar Davis
1881-1956

Clifford Davis
1908-1912
(Beasley FH)

"Brother"
William Robert Wright
Sep 9, 1855
Apr 14, 1911

"Sister"
Sarah Elender Wright
Apr 14, 1848
(no date)

James Henry Dunn
Oct 29, 1879
Apr 21, 1956
&
Ada Ann Dunn
Apr 22, 1883
Jun 18, 1939

T. W. Warren
Apr 20, 1858
(date gone)
&
Elizabeth Steelman Warren
Oct 30, 1861
Jun 20, 1935

Ola May, Daughter of
T. W. & Elizabeth Warren
Jun 17, 1896
Oct 17, 1917

J. Edgar Richardson
Jan 3, 1895
Dec 25, 1958

Pvt John H. Moore
May 16, 1894
Sep 18, 1918

Charles E. Whitsett
1896-1968
&
Annie Redd Whitsett
1897-1947
(Charles E. Whitsett
Tennessee
Pvt 11 Co AA Repl Dep.
C.A.C. WW I
May 13, 1896
Jan 23, 1968)

Clinton Whitsett
Oct 21, 1927
Aug 4, 1933

Pfc Walter E. Whitsett
Mar 20, 1930
Died in the Service
of his country
1950.

Thomas H. Redd
1887-1933
&
Ozelle Harkins Redd
1890-1954

Carl Dewitt Phillips
1882-1958

Mary Wilma Phillips
1884-1939

Infant Daughter of
Cowan Phillips & wife
B&D Sep 5, 1938

Infant Daughter of
Cowan Phillips & wife
B&D Dec 19, 1922

Infant Daughter of
Cowan Phillips & wife
B&D May 8, 1921

Sam N. Street
Oct 17, 1875
Mar 13, 1932

Cynthia E. Eslick, wife of
S. N. Street
Jan 14, 1876
Nov 1, 1921

Rufus C. Barham
1869-1950
&
Henrietta J. Barham
1873-1950

Mable Barham
1896-1922

Don Hastings
1898-
&
Gotha Hastings
1900-1957
&
Janet Hastings
1900-

James R. Bledsoe
1868-1951
&
Dillie Bell Bledsoe
1877-1968

Roy Lawson, Son of
J. R. & Dillie Bledsoe
Jun 4, 1905
Sep 20, 1921

William H. Touchstone
May 3, 1910
Dec 21, 1969
&
Elizabeth B. Touchstone
May 16, 1916

Allene Bledsoe
1905-1928

Della M. Bledsoe
May 29, 1883
Jan 5, 1968

W. A. Bledsoe
Sep 21, 1880
Jul 13, 1923

Clifford Murry Murdock
1902-1943

Alice Morgan Murdock
1904-1925

"Our Baby"(Murdock)
1924

Lynn Murdock Lumsden
1925-1947

J. N. Murdock
1873-1955

Elmer Hastings, wife of
J. N. Murdock
1877-1934

Dryden Murdock
1914-1957

Alexander Sanders
1846-1925

Margaret Holt Sanders
1852-1937

George W. Hunter
1872-1927

Lettie S. Hunter
1879-1949

John B. Wells
1868-1936
&
Fannie S. Wells
1867-1937

Little Billie, Son of W. E. &
Aug 20, 1925   M. L. Wells
Dec 12, 1927

Jessie Benton Wells
Jan 25, 1906
Feb 10, 1952
"Beloved husband of
Mary Lotz Wells".

Mrs. Minnie Wells Lee
1877-1957
(Beasley FH)

Charles F. Smith
Oct 20, 1893
Aug 16, 1960
&
Eva Ruth Smith
Dec 23, 1902
May 25, 1931

William Golie Freeman
1878-1959
&
Mary Fann Freeman
1881-1962

Walter E. Broadway
1881-1949
&
Maggie Luna Broadway
1885-1958

Henry E. Capley
1903-1949

Thomas D. Cashion
Jun 29, 1913
Oct 21, 1954
&
Murriel W. Cashion
Sep 19, 1916

Albert Davidson
1874-1949
&
Callie Davidson
1875-1960
&
Mamie Davidson
1900-

Mrs. David Adcock
1938-1962
(Beasley-Davis FH)

J. A. Warren
1884-1960
&
Lula Warren
1882-1950

Faye Crabtree
Jun 6, 1944
Apr 10, 1962

Howell B. Crabtree
1896-1963
&
Ouida S. Crabtree
1905-

A. Lois Wilson
1927-1965
(TM)

Jeanie Wilson
1958
(TM)

Mrs. C. D. Hunt
1904-1940
(Beasley FH)

C. D. Hunt
1904-1948
(Beasley FH)

T. H. Hunt
1881-1933

Ray Powers
Oct 21, 1949
Dec 14, 1950

William Roy Powers
1949-1951
(Beasley FH)

James E. Wilson
(no dates, TM)

Harvey Gibson
1867-1946
&
Ezella Gibson
1886-1967

Allen Gibson
1903-1962
&
Alla Mae Gibson
1900-

Allen Dalton Gibson
B&D Jan 7, 1931

Huff Nichols
1906-1940

PETERSBURG QUADRANGLE

George Crigler Hart, D.D.S.
Aug 4, 1879
Feb 11, 1934
&
Cora Shofner Hart
Jul 6, 1880

C. H. Davis
Sep 10, 1862
Nov 16, 1950
&
Annie McNeill Davis
Mar 27, 1872
Nov 2, 1926

Josie W. Davis
1877-1959

R. H. Hastings
Jul 3, 1870
Oct 9, 1926

Annie T. Hastings
Sep 17, 1875
Nov 15, 1950

Lee P. Hastings
Texas
Tec 5 Medical Dept WW II
May 30, 1902
Aug 19, 1964
(another marker)
Lee Pat Hastings
May 30, 1902
Aug 19, 1964

George L. Smith
1901-1947
&
Rosa Cole Smith
1903-

Carl Loyd Cole
Mar 20, 1903

&
Exie O. Gowan Cole
Nov 19, 1904
Apr 12, 1961

Henry Cole
Jan 3, 1881
Mar 18, 1945
&
May Cole
Feb 24, 1875
(no date)

W. Cyrus Carrigan
Dec 14, 1891
Jan 11, 1970
Military Stone:
William Carrigan
Tennessee
Pvt 135 Field Art WW I
&
Sara W. Carrigan
Jun 2, 1903

George W. Curtis
Tennessee
Pvt U. S. Army WW II
Sep 24, 1921
May 13, 1955

Mrs. G. W. Curtis
1923-1955
(Beasley FH)

Thomas B. Pierce
Tennessee
Pvt 1614 SVC Comd Unit
WW II
Apr 17, 1925
Feb 19, 1953

Jessie Whitsett
1893-1929
&
Bessie Whitsett
1889-1948

J. C. Conwell
1859-1934

Addie, wife of
J. C. Conwell
Aug 10, 1875
Dec 27, 1924

Karlene Brown
1895-1954

W. H. Redd, Jr.
1884-1924

Mrs. Mattie Dyer
1876-1963
(Bills-McGaugh FH)

A. A. Carrigan
1850-1935

Myrtle Carrigan
1875-1960

A. J. Carrigan
1880-1930

Horace Carrigan
1871-1947

Pearl S. Freeman
Aug 2, 1879
Jan 31, 1962

Lillian A. King
1915-1937

Kenneth Dodson
Tennessee
Pfc 23 Inf 2 Inf Div
Korea, PH
Apr 9, 1933
Feb 14, 1951

Damon A. Moore
1905-1967
(TM)

Robert P. Harkins
1879-1955
&
Anath R. Harkins
1879-19(no date)

Ollie F. Hazelwood
1896-19(no date)
&
Lillian A. Hazelwood
1894-1960

John A. Brown
Apr 24, 1895
Jan 3, 1968
&
Minnie Lou Brown
Sep 23, 1898
May 11, 1963

J. G. Fullerton
Jul 25, 1853
Dec 18, 1937
&
Mattie L. Fullerton
Aug 9, 1857
Oct 15, 1938

J. Henry Greer
1870-1940
&
Lillie J. Greer
1873-1957

John P. Welch
1856-1929
&
Mary E. Welch
1867-1936

Julius E. Welch
1903-1922

William O. Welch
1894-1953
&
Lizzie M. Welch
1889-1969

William Frederick Black
May 1, 1906
Apr 19, 1963

Samuel G. Haislip
1886-1962
&
Nora S. Haislip
1887-1955

George W. Fowler
1861-1950
&
Lola Luna Fowler
1870-1960

Paul D. Hurt
Oct 13, 1907
Jul 2, 1969
&
Mabel F. Hurt
Feb 7, 1902

J. E. Pyland
1876-1945

Minnie Pyland
1878-1959

Thomas Franklin Groce
Sep 2, 1861
Nov 24, 1927
&
Sue Ella Groce
Oct 6, 1863
Sep 12, 1940

William Thomas Groce
May 19, 1893
Mar 20, 1967
&
Gladys Grammer Groce
Jun 12, 1906

Imogene, Daughter of
Mr. & Mrs. P. O. Groce
B&D Aug 2, 1933

Billie Grammer, Son of
Mr. & Mrs. W. T. Groce
Sep 18, 1925
Apr 19, 1932

Gerald Groce
1930-1930

James Boone Moore
1838-1957
(Beasley FH)

Trixie Groce
1932-1932

Dixie Groce
1932-1933

Ollie E. "Doc" Moore
Sep 18, 1883
Jun 18, 1962

Beulah Lee Darnell
1911-1921

James T. Darnell
1874-1942
&
Mollie B. Darnell
1878-1963

Frankie A. McConnell
Feb 27, 1940
Aug 15, 1944

Pfc James H. Blacksher
Tennessee
Pfc 106 Inf 27 Div
WW II
Sep 19, 1916
Jun 23, 1944

Newsom Blacksher
1887-1949
& Flora Blacksher
1890-1954

PETERSBURG QUADRANGLE

Silas Leonard Bradford
Apr 23, 1915

Mary Elizabeth Bradford
Apr 26, 1918

Charles L. "Levon" Bradford
Tennessee
S/Sgt 6917 Scty GP A.F.
Sep 20, 1942
Apr 4, 1969
Age: 26 years.

T. Eugene Mitchell
Aug 13, 1910
Dec 10, 1968
&
Bertha B. Mitchell
Jul 5, 1915

Married Jun 25, 1932

W. Luther Williams
1883-1959
&
Ida Mae Williams
1877-1952

Eliza Edna Welch
Jul 4, 1883
May 19, 1962

Jim Thomas Welch
Jun 29, 1894
Jan 21, 1962
&
Oma Payton Welch
Nov 24, 1900

J. B. King
Mar 13, 1846
(no date)
&
Elizabeth King
Mar 17, 1842
Aug 23, 1919

Carl King Davis
Jul 29, 1896
Oct 18, 1918

Willie Ross Crane
Sep 13, 1901
Oct 11, 1959
&
Oma Thomas Crane
May 26, 1902

Bascom Davis
Oct 18, 1869
Oct 11, 1929
&
Emma Davis
Mar 24, 1871
(no date)

Francis McClenney
1881-1947

Walter Marion Morrison
1873-1951
&
Peggie Pylant Morrison
1876-1949

James Walter Pylant
Apr 3, 1872
Jul 22, 1897

Eugene Pylant
Jan 23, 1888
May 2, 1961

Lena H. Pylant
1887-1968

Samuel T. Scott
1870-1934

A. B. Scott
Sep 1, 1835
Oct 9, 1909
&
Martha A. Scott
Feb 15, 1840
Mar 12, 1914

Helen, Daughter of
S. T. & S. E. Scott
Nov 24, 1906
Mar 27, 1908

James M. Nelms
May 13, 1863
Feb 18, 1951

Hattie L. Nelms
Nov 24, 1880
Oct 9, 1942

Harriet E. Hastings
1843-1929

Alvie Thomas Conder
May 15, 1885
Jul 15, 1956
&
Lizzie Marsh Conder
Mar 7, 1891

Joseph Ross Conder
Aug 25, 1884
Dec 26, 1949
&
Gettie Davis Conder
Aug 31, 1883

Jim E., Son of
J. H. & N. E. Conder
Aug 21, 1901
Apr 13, 1913

J. H. Conder
Jul 5, 1858
Aug 27, 1916
&
N. E. Conder
Sep 14, 1858
Mar 10, 1943

Jessie R. Nelms
Aug 17, 1900
Aug 2, 1959

Charlie C. Crabtree
1895-1937
328 Inf 82 Div.
&
Lorene Ervin Crabtree
1903-1940

George A. Conder
1882-1964
&
Minnie Lee Conder
1896-

Twin Daughters of
A. & M. L. Conder
B&D May 22, 1916

Orline Scott Aderhold
Jan 27, 1911
Jun 22, 1953

Pfc Sam Scott
Jul 4, 1918
Wounded in the Invasion
of Guam
Died Aug 8, 1944

Margie Scott Lewis
Feb 4, 1916
Jul 11, 1952

F. G. G. Pylant
Dec 11, 1842
Apr 5, 1922
&
Canthus V. Pylant
Aug 21, 1851
Jun 10, 1910

William G. Pylant
Sep 4, 1837
Apr 7, 1919

Mattie Crane
Jan 29, 1869
Feb 3, 1940

Claytie Victoria Morrison
Dec 10, 1895
Feb 13, 1905

Robert Velva Morrison
May 1, 1894
Aug 7, 1894

Robert Amzia Morrison
May 20, 1830
May 24, 1903
& wife
Emily Jane Morrison
Feb 10, 1856
Aug 25, 1896

Novie Bell, wife of
J. T. Miller
Aug 6, 1869
Aug 8, 1912

Lonnie B. Miller
Jan 23, 1896
Jul 14, 1900

War'n
W. B. S.
1881-1901

Dr. W. R. Smith
1829-1895

Augusta E. Smith
1845-1909

Horace I. Crane
Nov 17, 1881
Jul 4, 1965
&
Maggie B. Crane
Apr 20, 1883

D. M. Holloway
Jan 24, 1867
Mar 10, 1952

Nolia N. Barnes, wife
of D. M. Holloway
Jun 9, 1868
Sep 17, 1953

Lynda Holloway Wagster
Aug 16, 1906
Mar 30, 1933

Pleas H. Holloway
Jul 26, 1891
Mar 4, 1953

John W. Massey
Sep 9, 1898
Jan 12, 1965
&
Callie O. Massey
Sep 11, 1901

Don Collier
Aug 21, 1832
(no date)
& wife
Martha Collier
Oct 15, 1831
Sep 7, 1900

H. A. Armstrong
Oct 17, 1867
Sep 3, 1934

Delia C., wife of
H. A. Armstrong
Mar 13, 1874
Mar 9, 1916

Lavoy L. Prosser
Dec 14, 1880
Aug 1, 1905

Leonore W. Prosser
Feb 9, 1856
Sep 15, 1937

James E. Prosser
Feb 25, 1858
Jul 12, 1934

Myrtle Prosser Landess
Mar 3, 1883
Oct 27, 1950

Charles I. Womack
Sep 25, 1892

&
Maida Foster Womack
Jul 25, 1892
Jul 2, 1968

Infant Son of
C. I. & Maida F. Womack
B&D Aug 17, 1927

Bettie Pack Davis
1865-1955

Ivie L. Freeman
1896-1953
&
Ruby M. Freeman
1901-

Alvis M. Bledsoe
1875-1937

Vada L. Bledsoe
Jan 20, 1886
Dec 22, 1961

William P. Bledsoe
1850-1939

J. Henry Hastings
1866-1949
&
Leona F. Hastings
1885-1957

T. A. Couch
Sep 17, 1884
Jun 4, 1947
&
Mary Etta Couch
Apr 4, 1888
May 12, 1941

Otis R. Couch
Jul 5, 1910
Mar 7, 1959
&
Geraldine F. Couch
Dec 12, 1918

R. Frank Reeves
Sep 1, 1883
Feb 23, 1957
&
Mattie Lee Reeves
Feb 5, 1893
Apr 8, 1940

Edward Reeves
Aug 23, 1911
Sep 3, 1963

Ottie J. Davis
Feb 23, 1892
Jan 11, 1962
&
Hattie W. Davis
Oct 25, 1892
Mar 24, 1963
Married Oct 12, 1913

Albert H. Rogers
May 20, 1905
Jan 18, 1970
&
Lucille P. Rogers
Mar 1, 1911

------ W. King
1879-1941
(Thompson FH)

Kittie King
1889-1962
(Howell-Thompson FH)

Henry C. King
Tennessee
Pvt Co C 104 Med. Tng Bn
WW II
Jul 1, 1917
Jul 18, 1955

Jim Owen
Mar 31, 1897

&
Maggie E. Owen
May 21, 1895
Sep 4, 1965

J. Marshall Owen
Jan 26, 1933
Oct 8, 1960

James R. Warren
1880-1935

Lenna Brown Warren
1893-1947

George F. Warren
1904-1933

Oliver Talley
1876-1954
&
Rhoda Sue Talley
1876-1966

N. E. Barham
1877-1933

John Bailey Eakin
1932-1933

Pearl Shofner Bailey
1872-1960

James B. Steelman
Nov 20, 1886
Jan 30, 1907
&
Fanny T. Steelman
Jan 30, 1860
(no date)
&
James L. Steelman
Jun 8, 1860
(no date)

N. A. Steelman
Jul 1, 1863
Jun 21, 1919

Lou, wife of
Naith Steelman
Mar 20, 1866
Nov 29, 1925

Bettie Steelman
Mar 7, 1895
Jan 17, 1914

Clarence Brown
Jan 21, 1901
Mar 4, 1970
&
Maggie G. Brown
Oct 18, 1902

Lizzie Marr Armstrong
1837-1916

Berry Sullivan
Jan 1, 1824
Oct 23, 1911

Emeline Sullivan
Nov 15, 1831
Jul 12, 1914

H. F. Leonard
1848-1913

Sarah J., wife of
H. F. Leonard
Feb 25, 1846
Apr 7, 1900

Ina Leonard
1888-1918

Coleman Leonard
Oct 22, 1914
Dec 13, 1929

Clarence A. Leonard
Nov 25, 1876
Feb 14, 1923

W. W. Leonard
Mar 19, 1882
Dec 19, 1951
&
Elizabeth Leonard
Oct 24, 1880

James T. Woodard
1870-1941

Nettie Brown Woodard
1869-1952

Willie A. Woodard
1894-1933

Joe R. Hastings
1898-1963
&
Ann W. Hastings
1892-

Paul Young
Oct 9, 1885
Jan 5, 1937
&
Margaret Neel Young
Aug 6, 1886
Oct 17, 1950

Wilburn Waid
1909-1933

Myrtis Sanders
1898-1936

Lula Crabtree
1872-1944

Oliver Davis
Tennessee
M/Sgt U. S. Army
Died Jan 24, 1937

Arthur Talley
Jan 8, 1874

&
Sally McRory Talley
Dec 26, 1875
Jul 23, 1951

Joe J. Hastings
1859-1939
&
Ella Foster Hastings
1868-1954

W. H. Hastings, Jr.
1925-1936

PETERSBURG QUADRANGLE

William H. Hastings
Tennessee
Pvt Co D 26 Machinegun
Bn   WW I
Apr 11, 1895
Jun 2, 1954

William F. Hudson
1868-1941
&
Bena Barnes Hudson
1878-1947

Bynyan W. Smith
Aug 11, 1918
Jan 5, 1967
&
Doris J. Smith
Aug 23, 1931

Baby
Joseph Lynn Cashion
B&D Sep 23, 1962

James Wilkerson
Feb 9, 1944
Nov 18, 1962

Henry B. Wiser
Mar 31, 1885
Jan 17, 1966
&
M. Elizabeth Wiser
Apr 28, 1889
Sep 1, 1963

Clyde B. Wiser
Tennessee
Pfc Co B 9 Arm'd Inf Bn
WW II   B.S.M.
Feb 18, 1923
Jul 9, 1934

J. Walter Swing
Sep 23, 1892

&
Annie Bell Swing
Sep 10, 1892
Oct 23, 1965

Joe W. Brewer
Jul 24, 1909
Dec 13, 1965
&
Wilma M. Brewer
Nov 25, 1911

Luther Hudson
Jul 9, 1915
Aug 1, 1936

Thomas E. Brown
1920-1937

Sarah Frances Talley
Nov 3, 1932
Dec 9, 1932

Minnie Hudson
Aug 13, 1871
Nov 15, 1943

Crawford Hart Talley
Dec 16, 1936
May 18, 1937

Dennis M. Farrar
Oct 9, 1890

&
Tonnie D. Farrar
Apr 5, 1881

"Teachers for 40 years."

J. Banks Bryant
1892-19
&
Eva L. McAdams Bryant
1897-1959

James W. Sullivan
Oct 28, 1909
Sep 12, 1968
&
Alice P. Sullivan
Feb 3, 1913

Jim Bolles
May 9, 1891
Feb 21, 1962
&
Leota Bolles
Jun 15, 1891

Oliver Davis
1880-1937

_. C. King
1870-1948
(Beasley FH)

Mrs. Susie Steed
1863-1934

John C. Holland
Feb 4, 1851
Oct   1918

Robert A. Holland
Mar 14, 1857
May 25, 1935

Jessie R. Holland
May 26, 1875
Dec 21, 1959

Annie Laurie, Daughter of
R. A. & J. R. Holland
May 31, 1911
May 8, 1916

Odelle Bolles Bell
Mar 20, 1927
Sep 11, 1961

Our Baby
Paul Beard, Jr.
B&D Jul 16, 1937

Mrs. J. R. Phifer
1846-1934

Clifford Walter Whorley
Nov 5, 1908
May 2, 1958
&
Lala Troop Whorley
Jul 21, 1909
Jun 23, 1942

J. W. Whorley
Jan 3, 1874
Dec 17, 1917
&
Maggie Whorley
Dec 6, 1885
(no date)

J. T. Hawkins
1888-
&
K. Modena Hawkins
1891-1958

W. A. Maultsby
Oct 2, 1914
Apr 15, 1965
&
Edith M. Maultsby
Apr 9, 1918

Leonard Hawkins
1914-1938

James Franklin Groce
1889-1939
&
Ada B. Brown Groce
1890-1962

Naomi Smith Conwell
Aug 21, 1919
Feb 2, 1963

Infant Daughter of
Naomi & L. D. Conwell
(no dates)

Infant Son of
Naomi & L. D. Conwell
(no dates)

Infant Son of
Naomi & L. D. Conwell
(no dates)

Infant Son of
Naomi & L. D. Conwell
(no dates)

Ola Doyle Conwell
Feb 10, 1875
Mar 4, 1937

Herbert Hastings
1900-1947

Robert Lee Richardson
Dec 25, 1890
Mar 17, 1948
&
Dollie Lee Richardson
Nov 5, 1892
Feb 28, 1968

Thomas S. Crabtree
Tennessee
Tec 5 102 Cav RCN Sq.
WW II
Mar 28, 1919
Oct 1, 1946

Blanche M. Crabtree
1897-

Will H. Crabtree
1894-1933

Will G. Hammonds
1893-1960

W. L. Hammonds
1874-1954
&
Lou Owen Hammonds
1874-1962

Timmy L. Phelps
1961-1963

Lester C. Ashby
Feb 12, 1910

&
Ola Mae Ashby
Mar 1, 1913
Jun 20, 1965

Timmy L. Sumners
Aug 23, 1964
1964

William V. Endsley (Virgil)
Tennessee
Pvt 351 AAA SLT Bn
CAC   WW II
Feb 18, 1920
Oct 3, 1944

Felix "Hop" Nichols
Mar 28, 1886
May 3, 1959
&
Susie King Nichols
Sep 9, 1890

Infant Whorley
1960
(Gowan-Smith FH)

Infant
W. A. Whorley
(no dates)
(Beasley FH)

PETERSBURG QUADRANGLE

Isiah Mills
1866-1938
&
Martha Davis Mills
1876-(no date)

Ollie T. Cole
1897-1943

Lizzie V. Cole
Aug 22, 1894

Angie V. Cole
1872-1961

Linda Marie Groce
May 14, 1940
Feb 21, 1941

Leroy Casteel
1916-1944

Mrs. Cl--a Casteel
1911-1944

Leanord Casteel
1912-1961

B. C. Casteel
1881-1953
&
Bartha F. Casteel
1887-1938

Roy C. Hutchison
1899-1938

Clarence P. Hazlett
1902-1968
(Bills-McGaugh FH)

Arthur Lee Hazlett
Oct 6, 1896
Jan 29, 1963
WW I

George O. Hazlett
1873-19(no date)
&
Hattie M. Hazlett
1878-1940

Carolyn Jene Wimberley
Jan 26, 1934
Aug 6, 1940

Mary Mills Sullivan
Oct 4, 1873
Jul 10, 1955

Mattie R. Brown
1901-1938

John F. Wise
1873-1951
&
Dora Conwell Wise
1879-1967

Mrs. M. W. Forrester
1905-1938

Homer Sullivan
1895-1970

Joyce Crabtree
1943-1943

George Albert Hastings
1865-1935
&
Donie Jane Hastings
1872-1921

James F. Brown
1876-1948
&
Lucy Ann Brown
1868-1943

F. M. Bledsoe
1857-1921

Mary Belle Bledsoe
1860-1895

Elma Carter Bledsoe
May 4, 1881
Jan 31, 1920

Roy Blake Bledsoe
1884-1916

T. H. Bledsoe
1808-1890
&
Elizabeth Bledsoe
1818-1891
(Newspaper states her
death date as
Jan 3, 1892.)

George W. Warren
Mar 13, 1866
May 16, 1948
&
Helen W. Warren
Oct 26, 1867
Nov 27, 1947

Rev. John B. Warren
Sep 28, 1819
Jan 12, 1896
&
Margaret B. Warren
Aug 12, 1832
Jun 24, 1911

William J. Warren
1871-1943

Nat Benedict
1852-1934

T. B. Scott
1875-1929

Alice L. Scott
1873-1956

Robert Walker Scott, Sr.
Jul 18, 1911
Jan 28, 1961

Lura Conwell Scott
May 22, 1876
Apr 2, 1953

Deneva Scott Steelman
Jul 21, 1899
May 4, 1939

Rufe Scott
Nov 3, 1872
Apr 28, 1926

Ethel White Scott
Oct 8, 1897
Jul 16, 1915

William S. Scott
Sep 23, 1868
Jun 11, 1937
&
Ellie C. Scott
Feb 8, 1871
Oct 31, 1930

Allen Scott
Jan 28, 1895
Jan 2, 1928
&
Willie Mae Scott
Feb 26, 1899

Howard Scott
1913-1925

Bernard Scott
1907-1931

Luther E. Scott
1886-1931
&
Mary B. Scott
1885-1967

J. K. Scott
Feb 1, 1845
Apr 29, 1913
&
R. A. Scott
Jun 18, 1843
Apr 21, 1919

Alonzo A. Holland
Jul 17, 1855
Apr 22, 1923

Anna E. Holland
Oct 15, 1856
Feb 7, 1950

Ida Marsh Holland
Aug 26, 1894
Apr 12, 1960

Tommie Holland
Died 1968
Age: (not given)

Judieth Chapman Reavis
Aug 20, 1845
Jun 15, 1933

Ben Franklin Wells
Jan 20, 1872
Nov 5, 1951

Dollie Lee Wells
Nov 6, 1865
Feb 16, 1948

Wynekta Barnes Ellis
May 8, 1913
Aug 9, 1955

Fred Lee Ellis
Aug 11, 1903
Jul 23, 1962

William Rufus Ellis
Jul 2, 1859
Apr 15, 1939

Maggie M. Ellis
Jun 4, 1861
Jan 31, 1927

Annie May Ellis
Aug 24, 1893
Oct 1, 1917

Roy Boone Ellis
Oct 29, 1887
Mar 31, 1935

Martha A. Smith
1853-1941

Lois Smith
1904-1918

James B. Smith
Nov 24, 1876
Jul 1, 1954

Elizabeth Pickle Smith
Sep 19, 1877
Jul 8, 1954

J. Raymond Adams
1895-1918

George Y. Ledford
Sep 17, 1861
Aug 1, 1933

Ida H. Ledford
Apr 4, 1867
Dec 7, 1944

Leon R. Hastings
Mar 17, 1893
Apr 30, 1906

Thomas D. Moore
1893-1953

Elizabeth M. Harness
1901-1945

Camilla Louise Harness
Dec 4, 1925
Feb 17, 1926

PETERSBURG QUADRANGLE

W. B. Moore
Oct 5, 1861
Nov 23, 1933

Louise, wife of
W. B. Moore
Jan 27, 1876
Dec 31, 1918

Emma Morgan Cunningham Moore
1869-1960

William C. Rodes
1868-1944

Laura W. Rodes
1868-1956

William Rodes, Jr.
Dec 30, 1895
Jan 10, 1922

Eva Douglas, wife of
J. E. Rodes
1901-1941

William J. Lynes
1904-1966

Margaret R. Lynes
1908-

Ann Brown
Jan 24, 1920
Aug 11, 1922

Joseph A. Green
Apr 21, 1864
Nov 15, 1937

Maggie L. Green
Aug 20, 1875
Feb 4, 1950

Sarah Louise, Daughter of
Earl & Jessie Green
1916-1919

John L. Pierce
1861-1941

Martha E. Pierce
1867-1937

Lessie Foster
1890-1936

Neely Foster
1885-1963
&
Fannie Foster
1888-1934

Ernest L. Foster
1909-1944

Alice Foster
1941-1942

John Brent Fishback
1865-1922
&
Florence S. Fishback
1878-1945

Jessamine Fishback
Feb 14, 1903
Oct 2, 1926

William W. Fishback
May 11, 1849
Apr 5, 1924

John Fishback Hathaway
Nov 12, 1899
Apr 16, 1968

George Parish Hathaway
Mar 6, 1856
Apr 14, 1923
&
Mollie Anna Hathaway
Mar 6, 1861
Nov 5, 1942

Isham H. Gill
May 14, 1849
Apr 8, 1925

Lucy H. Gill
May 17, 1855
May 20, 1930

Ed Sherwood
1886-1953

Mazie Davis Sherwood
1883-1952

Arby Sherwood Brown
1890-19(no date)

"Mother"
1858-1930

William F. Sherwood
1877-1944

Maude Barham Sherwood
1880-1937

James Walker Sherwood
1902-1964

Virginia Bryant Sherwood
1914-

Ada Cash Crane
1885-1953

Cordie L. Crane
1891-1964

Berry C. Morton
1859-1935

Ruth G. Morton
1865-1945

Mary Ann Morton
1869-1949

George H. Freeman
1879-1949
&
Margaret C. Freeman
1883-1964

Ethel Pearl Freeman
1892-1969

Mary Elizabeth Freeman
1871-1949

Harvey C. Freeman
1871-1943

William H. Freeman
1935-1936

Thomas H. Freeman
1914-1915

Roy N. Freeman
1890-1925

Willie Lee Davis
Jun 15, 1894
Jul 13, 1966

Robert Higgins
Feb 4, 1909

&
Bettie Higgins
Oct 13, 1914
Jul 14, 1962

Rev. Cart T.(Thomas) Ash
1908-1964
&
Mildred L. Ash
1919-

J. Mike Redd
Apr 16, 1881
Sep 9, 1965
&
Laura T. Redd
Dec 14, 1881
Jul 19, 1966

Floyd Daves
1892-1965

Anne Greer Price
1885-1935

Carrie Smythe Smith
1856-1929

Virginia Elizabeth Smythe
1844-1926

Mary Goldstone Smythe
1861-1920

Braxton Bragg Smythe
1863-1952

James Buchanan Smythe
1858-1927

Carrie Mae Smythe
1895-1948

Tate Goggin Smythe
1859-1946

John Greer Smythe
1848-1917

B. F. Dwiggins
Feb 1861
Jul 26, 1916

James P. Dwiggins
Nov 22, 1855
Dec 2, 1927

Elizabeth E. Dwiggins
Mar 18, 1856
Jan 7, 1926

Blanton Warren
1883-1917

W. Adron Warren
1877-1965
&
Mamie L. Warren
1878-1966

Infant
(no dates)

George C. London
1849-1923
&
Cornelia London
1850-1933

Lucile Cowden, wife of
C. B. Fox
Nov 2, 1881
Sep 9, 1914

Worth Cowden
Feb 17, 1849
Oct 29, 1910

Nannie Vance Cowden
May 11, 1862
Nov 25, 1922

James Cowden McKnight
1922-1923

Jennie Cowden McKnight
1878-1957

Robert McKnight
1870-1930

Charles L. McKnight
1833-1903

Adelaide McKnight
1847-1923

PETERSBURG QUADRANGLE

Pearl McKnight Gunn
1868-1927

Cecil McKnight
1879-1969

John C. McRady
Jul 13, 1867
Feb 20, 1948

Sallie Loyd, wife of
John C. McRady
Oct 1, 1866
Dec 4, 1952

Hugh Wilson, Son of
J. C. & Sallie McRady
Jan 3, 1907
May 19, 1938

Joe Loyd, Son of
J. C. & Sallie McRady
Jul 23, 1893
Oct 11, 1900

Dr. F. S. McRady
Nov 26, 1854
Dec 11, 1925

H. C. Dwiggins
Oct 8, 1844
Sep 13, 1914

M. G., wife of
H. C. Dwiggins
Aug 1, 1854
Feb 2, 1904

Charles Ivie Dwiggins
Jun 15, 1886
Mar 9, 1962

Harry C. Dwiggins
Husband of
Bessie B. Dwiggins
1884-1951

Nellie Dwiggins, wife of
Guy Fry
1897-1940

Mayme Dwiggins, wife of
Dr. E. O. Anderson
1882-1950

Ethel, Daughter of
H. C. & M. L. Dwiggins
Mar 17, 1877
Oct 12, 1899

Robbie Estelle, Daughter of
H. C. & M. L. Dwiggins
Jan 31, 1880
Dec 3, 1900

Charles M. Crawford
Dec 27, 1871
Jun 12, 1915

Cassie Crawford
1875-1960

E. M. Crawford
Mar 11, 1839
Apr 6, 1914

Mrs. M. J. Crawford
Apr 22, 1846
Mar 26, 1922

Quint L. Barham
Jul 19, 1891
Apr 16, 1961
&
Nola Mae Barham
Jul 26, 1892

Infant Son of
Mr. & Mrs. Q. L. Barham
1926

Baby Girl of
Quint & Nola Mae Barham
B&D Jan 22, 1913

Aunt Frances Sorrells
1858-1945

Frank W. Barham
1893-1928

Glydon Barham
1895-1923

Polly Womack, wife of
T. J. Barham
Mar 13, 1861
Feb 9, 1903

Thomas J. Barham
1866-1936
&
Cora Walker Barham
1877-1938

William Lyle Barham, Jr.
B&D Jul 12, 1966

Floyd D. Barham
Jul 27, 1913
Mar 14, 1923

Jessie J. Muse
Oct 28, 1872
Oct 21, 1961

William Asbury Prosser
1876-1956
(Gallant FH)

Fannie Prosser
Aug 9, 1878
Sep 5, 1940

James M. Prosser
Jul 15, 1844
(no date)
&
F. C. Prosser
Dec 23, 1843
Apr 28, 1917

J. P. Fox
Apr 11, 1839
Aug 29, 1925
& wife
Amelia Fox
Dec 15, 1843
May 20, 1905

Ernest S. Raby
1874-1949
&
Ola Fox Raby
1883-1907

Joe King
Aug 28, 1912
Jan 6, 1914

Arch P. Marsh
1872-1953

Esthma L. Marsh
1885-1954

J. T. Land
Sep 24, 1848
Sep 2, 1914

Mary Frances Land
Nov 7, 1847
Aug 18, 1922

Daniel Boone Land
Aug 28, 1882
Jan 25, 1919

John B. Land
Tennessee
Cpl Co A 316 Machine Gun
Bn   WW I
Sep 11, 1889
Mar 8, 1966

Dr. Charles N. Cowden
1864-1933

Ada May Dozier, wife of
Dr. Charles N. Cowden
1869-1918

Mary Cowden, wife of
Warren Gill
1887-1913

Will S. McAdams
1891-1966

Sarah Hart, wife of
W. S. McAdams
1891-1952

George Robert McAdams
1926-1929

Cecil N. Wilson
1899-1965
&
Willie Mae Wilson
1913-

Roy C. Powell
1912-1967
&
Frances E. Powell
1914-19

James Donald Wells
Died Jun 9, 1969
Age: 20y, 10m, 20d.
(Higgins FH)

Dr. J. W. Percy
1844-1925

Vedora A. Percy
1851-1928

Mamie L. Percy
1885-1962

Clara E. Percy
1873-1956

Ulric Wells
1882-1952

Martha E. Wells
1883-1959

L. I. Mills
May 24, 1886
May 8, 1956

N. O. Keith
1863-1925

Susie Robertson Keith
Died May 31, 1974
Age: 96 years.

Mary Bob Keith
Jul 28, 1904
Jul 16, 1930

George Lee Redd
1883-1964
&
Jessie F. Redd
1884-1965
&
Sarah E. Redd
1914-1915

Carl B. Ellis
Oct 24, 1892
Mar 10, 1960
&
Nina F. Ellis
Jan 20, 1895
Oct 21, 1969

W. H. "Dick" Davidson
Feb 7, 1887
Oct 18, 1968
&
Fannie F. Davidson
Oct 1, 1887

W. Sanford
Aug 16, 1892
Sep 2, 1966

Elsie I. Gilbert
Oct 3, 1893

Daisy Ann Gilbert
B&D May 4, 1930

Emmett Pearson
Feb 3, 1880
Feb 26, 1967
&
Ethel G. Pearson
Nov 29, 1887

Annie Catharine Pearson
Oct 24, 1903

R. Frank Moore
Mar 10, 1880
Nov 19, 1962

Georgie Nance Moore
Dec 10, 1888
Aug 25, 1931

Jessie E. Moore
Oct 28, 1878
Apr 20, 1951

Emma Nance Moore
Oct 29, 1876
Dec 29, 1955

Infants
Alfred & Mary Head
(no dates)

Carson Barham
1886-1957

Zolphus T. Barham
1884-1948

Willie Thomison
Aug 17, 1862
Jun 6, 1930
&
Belle Page Thomison
Jul 25, 1862
Oct 16, 1943

O. Hatcher Wells
Jun 3, 1889
May 14, 1968
&
Nannie M. Wells
Apr 21, 1898

Clark McGee
1874-1951
&
Dovia McGee
1878-1933

Charles H. McGee
1932-1933

Charlie L.(Lavoy) McGee
Jan 3, 1908
Jan 21, 1968
&
Katie B. McGee
Aug 26, 1903

Maggie Morrison
Nov 21, 1857
Apr 15, 1936

John S. Morrison
1864-1949
&
Ora B. Morrison
1884-1938

Clyde Watkins
Nov 13, 1902
Jul 25, 1925

Ruby Watkins
Sep 2, 1906
Sep 22, 1929

Vance Watkins
Feb 4, 1877
Sep 24, 1938

W. S. Watkins
Oct 26, 1870
(no date)

D. W. Mills
1926-1932

Walden Bradley Mills
Oct 10, 1890
Oct 14, 1967
&
Annie Lee Gleghorn Mills
Apr 11, 1902

Roy C. Mills
Aug 29, 1895
Oct 22, 1944
&
Sophia L. Hale Mills
Jan 24, 1898

Granville W. Mills
Jul 10, 1864
Feb 14, 1925
&
Maggie M. Mills
Nov 27, 1870
(no date)

A. G."Buddy" Howell
1897-1945
&
Fannie S. Howell
1898-(no date)

Infant Son of
A. G. & Fannie Howell
1928

Infant Daughter of
A. G. & Fannie Howell
1923

Robert R. Edmiston
1866-1920

Rebecca, wife of
R. R. Edmiston
1891-1956

William C. Edmiston
1854-1936

Ella Greer Edmiston
1861-1922

Clara Edmiston
1858-1945

William Sanders
1850-1926

Deborah Sanders
1855-1925

William E. Cowden
Nov 5, 1889
Feb 25, 1966

Cornelius C. London
Tennessee
Sfc 444 Co Trans. Corps
WW I
Aug 6, 1887
Feb 3, 1969

Zala Wakefield London
Jun 4, 1895

Ruby Wakefield Scott
Jun 15, 1904
Feb 14, 1925

Henry Smith Wakefield
Tennessee
Cpl Army Air Force
WW II
Feb 10, 1899
Nov 19, 1952

Jack Wakefield
May 11, 1902
Dec 10, 1924

Lula Dyer Wakefield
1866-1957

S. T. Wakefield
Nov 27, 1864
Mar 12, 1917

Dana Dyer
1859-1939

Narcissus Jane, wife of
J. W. Dyer
Mar 30, 1835
Oct 19, 1902

Jeremiah C. Pitts
Tennessee
Cpl 113 M.G.Bn 30 Div
WW I
Dec 4, 1890
Nov 30, 1951

J. C. Pitts
May 31, 1850
Sep 27, 1905
& wife
Mary F. Pitts
May 15, 1851
Jan 17, 1920

W. C. Dyer
1860-1939

Hallie Dyer
1870-1943

Eva Alta Dyer
1890-1945

Russell, Son of
W. C. & Hallie Dyer
May 30, 1903
Aug 3, 1903

Thelma L. Dyer
1908-1944

W. S. Albright
Oct 19, 1866
May 24, 1932

W. E. Ryals
Jan 5, 1822
Sep 22, 1880

S. E. Ryals
May 29, 1839
Sep 22, 1908

Manerva Albright
May 23, 1817
Jun 23, 1884

W. Rollin Loving
1873-1950
&
Grace M. Loving
1879-19

Mamie Loving
1873-1955

W. R. Loving
Sep 18, 1839
Feb 20, 1929

John Smith Loving
Sep 22, 1874
Feb 26, 1960

Mary E. Steele
Died Aug 6, 1966
Age: 82 years
(Laughlin Service,
Huntsville, Ala.)

PETERSBURG QUADRANGLE

George R. Russell
Tennessee
Pvt U. S. Marine Corp
WW I
Jun 29, 1897
Feb 22, 1958

John H. Russell
1842-1922
&
Mary Jane Russell
1845-1915

W. T. Russell
Feb 2, 1869
Oct 31, 1934

Eugenia H. Russell
Feb 15, 1870
May 10, 1944

Fannie E. Russell, wife of
Thomas H. White
1866-1887

Rutledge Smith
1867-1934

Joe Curtiss
1905-1966

James H. Curtiss
1854-1930

Beatrice S. Curtiss
1865-1940

Annie Curtiss
1888-1931

Mattie T. Curtiss
Nov 15, 1885
May 9, 1912

B. C. Dysart
1871-1914

Susie T. Dysart
1876-1968

Laura Clay Dysart
1899-1940

Edith Dysart
1905-1963

Addie Taylor Taylor
1889-1930

James Hubbard
1884-1943

John Diemer Gleghorn
Nov 18, 1909
Dec 17, 1926

Mary Wisdom Bradford
1898-1924
(Beasley FH)

Allen Wisdom
Jul 23, 1903
Nov 11, 1918

Will Wisdom
1876-1935

William C. Wisdom
1875-1935
&
Donie B. Wisdom
1878-1955

Thomas Deery Dryden
Tennessee
Sgt U. S. Army WW I
Jun 11, 1882
Dec 17, 1958

Lottie Cannon, wife of
Dr. D. M. Dryden
Nov 29, 1863
Apr 21, 1926

D. M. Dryden, Jr.
1898-1938

Cannon Duff Dryden
Dec 18, 1892
Dec 4, 1967

John L. Carlton
1860-1940

Agnes Carlton
1862-1936

Grace Carlton Winford
1886-1925

James E. Adams
1887-1935

J. T. Adams
1909-1932

Bettie Lou Murdock Finley
1868-1950

Howard K. Adams
Tennessee
S1 U. S. N. R. WW II
Aug 3, 1912
Aug 17, 1956

Dorothy Vance Kennedy
Oct 2, 1916
Sep 12, 1936

Frank Whorley
1876-1936
&
Daisy Whorley
1883-1957

Henry H. Boaz
1883-1964

Elizabeth Boaz, wife of
B. R. Stephens
Oct 5, 1872
Oct 15, 1934

Flora Elain Steelman
Jul 27, 1920
May 4, 1964

James Wayne Scott
1912-1961

J. A. Scott
1865-1928

Ada Boaz Scott
1878-1962

Mahlon William Scott
1910-1964

Hilda Scott
Apr 1, 1926
Jan 2, 1929
&
Norma Scott
Apr 11, 1924
Sep 6, 1935

Laura Estella Scott
Feb 13, 1895
Jan 24, 1970

James M. Beasley
Aug 17, 1894
Feb 8, 1929

Annie D. Beasley
Dec 21, 1900
Jun 5, 1938

T. J. Beasley
1848-1933

Ottie B. Warren
Oct 20, 1899
Feb 18, 1933

Joe Ellis Pigg
1924-1933

Louise Scott Pigg
1902-1953

Van D. Buntley
Jun 11, 1862
Jan 8, 1934

William Floyd Swing
Jan 21, 1900
Mar 11, 1967
&
Grace Buntley Swing
Aug 23, 1902

Jessie L. Muse
Oct 13, 1847
Oct 14, 1937

Sarah Elizabeth, wife of
J. L. Muse
Aug 1, 1846
Sep 28, 1905

William Blake Harris
Jun 16, 1902
Feb 15, 1960
&
Annie Lee Moore Harris
Dec 18, 1905

Oliver H. Moore
Nov 3, 1884
Mar 25, 1963
&
Minnie Archer Moore
Nov 9, 1882
Mar 26, 1935

Sallie Darnell
1871-1957
(Beasley FH)

Hugh Erwin Scott
Tennessee
Tec 4 102 Signal Co.
WW II
Jan 22, 1917
Sep 16, 1969

R. B. Scott
1879-1942

Daisy Armstrong
1881-1964

Leona Epps Sweeney
1881-1957
(Beasley FH)

Arch Sweeney
1887-1951
(R. H. Beasley FH)

Miss Liza Epps
1881-1953
(Beasley FH)

W. C. Epps
Jan 5, 1848
Aug 10, 1928

M. _. Epps
18??-193? (broken)
(Beasley FH)

W. T. Epps
1898-1962

J. C. Epps
1872-1940
(Beasley FH)

S. Hattie Epps
(Dates broken away)

C.(Charles) Clayton Scott
Jan 15, 1904
Jan 31, 1970

Lucille E. Scott
Jan 30, 1908

PETERSBURG QUADRANGLE

John Scales Evans
Mar 13, 1872
Feb 2, 1967

Mary L. Evans
1871-1942

Alfred Luna
Nov 8, 1880
Dec 27, 1936
&
Leona Luna
Apr 1, 1883
Mar 4, 1941

Joel T. Luna
Apr 18, 1858
Oct 1, 1940
&
Maud D. Luna
Sep 20, 1861
Jun 14, 1951

William R. Butler
Tennessee
Pvt 1Cl 315 Inf 79 Div
Died Sep 29, 1933
(no age given)

Kate Butler
1869-1934

Joe L. Butler
1869-1927

Robert L. Butler
1899-1956

Charles C. Butler
1890-1926

Charles, Son of
John & Mary Butler
Died Aug 19, 1930
Age: (not given)

Eva Wright, wife of
John Butler
1898-1927

John Butler
1897-1958

Eva Rebecca Butler
Dec 25, 1952
Dec 27, 1952

Ben F. Pack
1854-1943

Mary F. Pack
1858-1926

Joe Blacknall
1847-1924

Emma McCollum Hudson
Blacknall
1863-1926

James P. Wakefield
Jul 26, 1861
Nov 10, 1942

Molenda D. Wakefield
Nov 22, 1869
May 2, 1944

Mable A. Wakefield
Jan 9, 1900
Apr 9, 1953

Clive Clyde Collier
Tennessee
Cpl U. S. Army Dsc PH
WW I
Dec 30, 1890
May 28, 1957

Joe K. Russell
Aug 8, 1868
Jul 19, 1937

Olvia Russell
Feb 25, 1879
Oct 10, 1932

Maud Pack Collier
Oct 2, 1878
Mar 18, 1969

Richard Elerson Collier
Sep 30, 1871
Jun 11, 1963

W. Rudder Collier
Jul 3, 1887
Jan 15, 1919

Essie Foster Collier
1888-1966

Infant Son of
J. M. & E. S. Dyer
B&D Feb 2, 1915

James R. Dyer
Jul 23, 1858
May 24, 1933
&
Docia Ann Dyer
Oct 11, 1859
Jan 11, 1934

John M. Dyer
1894-1936
&
Elsie S. Dyer
1890-1936

Harry E. Dyer
Jul 23, 1884

Virgie Davis
Oct 24, 1885
Dec 24, 1965
&
Julia Davis
Oct 18, 1885

D. D. Helton, Jr.
Oct 24, 1860
Jun 17, 1912

P. A. Helton
Nov 14, 1853
May 17, 1924

W. N. Helton
Oct 4, 1851
Jan 27, 1932

B. N. Helton
Feb 28, 1858
Oct 9, 1938

J. W. Helton
Feb 16, 1862
Nov 2, 1953

J. C. Barrett
Nov 27, 1860
Jan 20, 1927

H. C., wife of
J. C. Barrett
May 15, 1859
(no date)

Mary J. Helton
Mar 13, 1855
Jan 4, 1935

J. Roy McRory
May 6, 1883
Sep 23, 1935

Robert H. Gaunt
Sep 3, 1857
Feb 16, 1939

Callie Marsh Gaunt
Feb 4, 1863
Jul 2, 1953

Mary McRory Hampton Gaunt
Mar 15, 1891
Oct 2, 1954

Elise McRory Porter
Jun 15, 1909
Jan 2, 1965

William G. Curlee
Feb 28, 1908
Sep 16, 1966
&
Sadie W. Curlee
Feb 23, 1906

Guelda Curlee
1933-1943

Calvin James Curlee
1880-1959
&
Cora Hickerson Curlee
1887-1969

Mamie M. McAdams
Oct 15, 1894
Aug 16, 1966
&
Bessie Ann McAdams
Feb 7, 1900
May 16, 1965

Walter McAdams
1865-1935
&
Ellen McAdams
1866-1938

Odie E. McAdams
Jun 5, 1893
Aug 1, 1943

Ocie Miller
1890-1964
&
Ida S. Miller
1885-1959

Claude Stacy
1898-19
&
Eva S. Stacy
1897-1959

Joe C. Wagster
1861-1937
&
Cordelia Wagster
1861-1935

John E. Sullivan
1887-1944
&
Lessie E. Sullivan
1892-1964

Mrs. S. O. McAdoo
1891-1943

Walter A. Barham
1867-1950

Permelia Barham
1869-1945

Sam D. Barham
1873-1951

Ossie B. Barham
1874-1956

R. K. Morgan, Sr.
1864-1935

Myrtle Morgan
1873-1946

R. K. Morgan, Jr.
1898-1967

G. R. Armstrong
1894-1962
&
Grace M. Armstrong
1905-

Orrin Parker King
1873-1950

Mary Etta King
1881-1936

H. Carlyle King, Jr.
Son of S/Sgt & Mrs.
H. Carlyle King
Feb 28, 1952
Mar 1, 1952

Allen B. King
Aug 27, 1902
Jul 17, 1969
&
Annie E. King
Mar 14, 1907

Married Oct 9, 1921

John I. Pierce, III
1946-1946

Eunice L. Pierce
1890-1970
(Lawrence FH)

Thomas Warren Mitchell
Sep 11, 1942
Jan 5, 1946

Sanford Solomon
Mar 15, 1865
Feb 14, 1936
&
Maybelle Solomon
Feb 28, 1883
Mar 21, 1948

Marshann Reavis
Died Sep 15, 1959
Age: (not given)

Charlie H. Troop
1867-1946
&
Maggie A. Troop
1872-1964

Goldie Moore
1890-1969
(Davis-Ralston FH)

Joe Richardson
1888-1951
&
Maggie Richardson
1892-(no date)

Will Powers
Sep 12, 1923
May 11, 1968

Denham Pigg
Dec 12, 1870
May 24, 1956
&
Alice M. Pigg
Feb 6, 1873
Sep 30, 1950

"Little Buddy"
Gary L. Richardson
1942-1945

Mary Frances Tate, wife
of Thomas A. Long
Mar 18, 1869
Feb 27, 1949

James W. Sanders
1889-1957
&
Vergie R. Sanders
1897-

James R. Roberts
1868-1929
&
Mary Belle Roberts
1874-1959

Floyd Roberts
1905-1926

Elizabeth Roberts
1909-1928

William Roberts
1912-1919

Allen & Mazie Roberts
1894-1895 & 1895-1896

Donnie Roberts Moore
1902-1936

Martha Dean Hastings
1925-1928

Cecil Hastings
1895-1969
&
Eula M. Roberts Hastings
1900-

William Rufus Hunter
Jun 26, 1867
Oct 6, 1948
    & his wife
Annie Lou Pigg Hunter
Feb 29, 1868
Jul 19, 1963

David R. Smith
Dec 17, 1889

Ola Long Smith
Nov 29, 1897

James B. Davis
Nov 19, 1932
May 5, 1968
&
Janice M. Davis
May 28, 1931

Married Mar 29, 1958

Frances Marie Partain
1920-1968

George A. Brown
Jul 8, 1908
Apr 12, 1969
&
Stella D. Brown
Nov 13, 1907
Apr 19, 1969
Married Dec 19, 1925

Ilda Vizola Brown
B&D Sep 15, 1968

Kelley Marie Jones
Oct 3, 1969
Oct 16, 1969

J. Harold Huffine
Jan 30, 1917
Dec 3, 1968
&
Marilyn W. Huffine
Apr 6, 1926

E. C. Maybrey
1909-1969
(Lawrence FH)

J. Ross Dyer
1898-1964
&
Louise C. Dyer
1909-

James Frank Cashion
Jan 27, 1937
Mar 5, 1970

Horace Smith
Feb 8, 1896
Nov 27, 1969
&
Mary A. Smith
Jul 13, 1904

Married Dec 26, 1923

Albert Horace Smith
Tennessee
Pvt Inf WW I
(no dates)

Donnie Ray Richardson
Jul 18, 1961
Jan 27, 1970

H. H. Bledsoe
1840-1907

Fannie Bledsoe
Apr 10, 1840
Feb 20, 1934

Ruth Rice
May 1, 1906
May 15, 1906

Louise Rice
Apr 17, 1895
Aug 12, 1896

Mary Haynes Rice
Sep 29, 1907
Nov 14, 1907

Ed C. Rice
1867-1933

Elma B. Rice
1870-1951

John R. Davidson
May 20, 1850
Feb 23, 1923

Ida B. Davidson
Aug 29, 1866
Jan 2, 1936

Mary Davidson
Jan 15, 1886
Feb 6, 1898

Billy Davidson
Jun 30, 1921
Jun 14, 1923

Sam Davidson
Jul 9, 1889
Apr 3, 1962

Robert C. Ogilvie
1842-1922
&
Mollie Y. Ogilvie
1844-1923
    & Daughter
Allie Ogilvie
Died 1890
Age: (not given)

Lola Sue Cowden, wife
of Ed C. Neil
Jul 30, 1872
Oct 19, 1902

Eugene Davis Neil
Apr 29, 1902
Nov 30, 1904

Sidney H. Allen
1870-1954

Julia Joplin Allen
1873-1958

Louis J. Allen
1898-1969

Lorena R. Allen
1901-

Jacob C. Greer
Tennessee
Sgt Btry B 318 field
Arty   WW I
Oct 8, 1890
Mar 1, 1966

Verna A. Greer
1894-

PETERSBURG QUADRANGLE

Martha R. Whitaker
Sep 18, 1923
Sep 20, 1923

Ed W. Reese
Jul 12, 1878
Jun 20, 1908

Bessilee E. Reese
Jun 24, 1882
Nov 27, 1934

Thomas B. Reese
Feb 21, 1850
Oct 18, 1926

Minnie J. Reese
May 22, 1855
Oct 12, 1940

John B. Foster
1852-1910
&
Ann Foster
1855-1933

Eva D. Foster
1889-1912

Dolphus G., Son of
W. B. & Lena Foster
Nov 18, 1909
Jan 3, 1910

Lena Bonner Foster
May 14, 1892
Dec 11, 1941

Felix W. Muse
Dec 5, 1876
May 1, 1969

Henry Freeman
Mar 1, 1885
Jul 7, 1959

Nancy Ann Freeman
Jul 1, 1891
Feb 13, 1969

Jody M. Pigg
1877-1962
&
Leila W. Pigg
1880-1959

John R. Freeman
1890-1967
(Davis-Ralston FH)

Edna Ethel Freeman
1895-1968

Estel Warren
Aug 13, 1908

&
Eunice B. Warren
Mar 27, 1898
Jun 8, 1969

Gladys Moore
1898-1957
&
Berta Moore
1889-1969

Ollie Hemphill
1877-1955
&
Jennie Hemphill
1892-

George Thomas Barnes
Tennessee
Cox U. S. N. R.
WW II
Jun 28, 1918
Nov 28, 1964

Betty Jean Barnes
1955-1955

John T. Sorrells
Sep 23, 1873
Jul 22, 1955
&
Ella King Sorrells
Sep 11, 1875
Aug 12, 1962

Elvert G. Barham
Nov 9, 1889
Nov 12, 1957

Josephine, wife of
E. G. Barham
Oct 19, 1893
Aug 13, 1913

James M. Eagin
Sep 11, 1901
Oct 4, 1961
&
Irene B. Eagin
Sep 19, 1907

C. Dyer
May 28, 1850
May 24, 1911

Lizzie Dyer
1850-1924

Gus Dyer
1873-1922

Mary H., wife of
J. A. Barham
Jul 12, 1859
May 12, 1918

Avon D. Barham
1903-1970

Ollie Barham
1874-1961

Edna Dyer Barham
1879-1935

Robert L. Davidson
Feb 20, 1866
May 8, 1946

Katie Clark Davidson
Jul 22, 1869
Feb 13, 1917

William F. Clark
Jan 29, 1833
Nov 1, 1907

Elizabeth T. Clark
Feb 10, 1840
May 4, 1917

Walter D., Son of
W. F. & E. T. Clark
May 7, 1867
Feb 25, 1888

Edd Cooper Gammill
1866-1911
&
Icy Armstrong Gammill
1865-1945

G. Edward Redd
1883-1950

Virgie G. Redd
1882-1964

Charles E. Redd
1921-1941

Charley Morton
Aug 4, 1834
Jul 17, 1904
&
Mary Elizabeth Morton
Jun 10, 1842
Mar 27, 1910

John H. Capley
1866-1933

Dr. William S. Joplin
Dec 25, 1875
Apr 11, 1960
&
Katherine G. Joplin
Aug 10, 1880

George C. Gillespie
Nov 30, 1846
Aug 1, 1915

Sallie Gill Gillespie
Mar 29, 1855
Jul 22, 1926

Angie Gillespie
Jul 28, 1882
Nov 23, 1910

John Jacob Gillespie
May 4, 1891
Sep 5, 1963

Joe Gill Gillespie
1886-1947
&
Margaret Dean Gillespie
1889-1966

W. Warren Gill
1886-1966

Cooper Rice Gill
1897-1966

Lucian Warren, Son of
W. W. & Cooper Gill
1916-1919

O. F. Gill
Oct 6, 1857
Oct 15, 1925

Mary W. Gill
Nov 16, 1860
Feb 8, 1951

James Sam Darnell
1889-
&
Willie B. Darnell
1897-1953

Robert E. Darnell
1929-1930

John Sam Darnell
1858-1913
&
Jennie V. Darnell
1876-1902

Leonard H. Darnell
1925-1928

J. F. Pack
Oct 9, 1822
Aug 28, 1895
&
E. A. Pack
Nov 25, 1828
Dec 25, 1902

Ida B. Tate, wife of
W. H. Pack
Jan 30, 1874
Jul 23, 1932

J. P. Pack
Nov 12, 1861
Nov 24, 1929

Charley M. Morrison
Jul 22, 1903
May 8, 1906

Jessie A. Morrison
Jun 12, 1906
Nov 3, 1906

Willie M. Morrison
Mar 16, 1890
May 21, 1905

James T. Morrison
1866-1939

Mary M. Morrison
Jul 4, 1864
Aug 22, 1909

Maude Morrison
1878-1932

Maybell Grammer
1888-1964

Daughter of
George & Mable Revin
B&D Mar 10, 1924

Earl Revin
Jun 9, 1889
Aug 30, 1907

William Ervin
1858-1943
(Beasley FH)

William R. Irvin
1891-1945
&
Emma L. Irvin
1895-1947

Birdell Endsley
Died Jun 17, 1974
Age: 75 years.

C. Bert Davidson
1893-1964
&
Bessie C. Davidson
1897-

Jim M. Davidson
1871-1947

G. H. Davidson
Feb 5, 1885
May 20, 1911

G. W. Davidson
Dec 10, 1843
Jan 30, 1912
&
S. A. Davidson
Oct 19, 1856
(no date)

J. B. Leftwich
1870-1942

Ermine Leftwich Muse
1871-1911

Elizabeth Leftwich
Sep 19, 1828
Mar 4, 1917

Jesse B. Leftwich
1869-1942

L. D. Leftwich
Jul 8, 1863
(no date)
&
W. J. Leftwich
Jul 8, 1863
Mar 10, 1922
"Leftwich Brothers"

Thomas C. Ellis
1860-1918
&
Anna Rives Ellis
1869-1937

Luther G. Rives
1876-1962
&
Blanche G. Rives
1876-1966

Sallie Rives
1873-1944

Robert C. Rives
1837-1914
&
Rebecca J. Rives
1839-1934

Mable Burton Smith
1878-1969 (TM)

Walter L. Troop
1875-1940
&
Kate Troop
1880-1965

Allen B. Shaddy
1902-1966
&
Cathryne Troop Shaddy
1905-

B. F. Hart
Jan 16, 1849
Apr 19, 1941
&
Hettie Wade Hart
Nov 19, 1852
Nov 26, 1938

Hugh Allen Marsh
May 7, 1889
Jan 25, 1914

Mamie Vivian Marsh
Jun 20, 1877
Jul 19, 1888

W. H. Marsh
Mar 28, 1852
Dec 6, 1921

Elizabeth Butler Marsh
Jan 18, 1859
Feb 2, 1941

William Lewis Marsh
Jun 13, 1884
Apr 10, 1916

Julia Marsh Hurt
Feb 3, 1879
Dec 3, 1923

Marion P. Marsh
Oct 3, 1886
Aug 16, 1936

Alberta Y. Marsh
Jan 2, 1904
Jan 26, 1950

Julia Fay Marsh
Jun 15, 1936
Apr 13, 1943

Harold Butler Marsh
May 20, 1894
Oct 10, 1951

Charley J. Gibson
Jan 26, 1890
Sep 9, 1955
&
Ethel W. Gibson
Jan 15, 1894
Jan 12, 1962

Olga Monteen Gibson
Oct 16, 1920
Oct 17, 1920

Elijah K. Williams
Nov 26, 1891
Nov 28, 1969
&
Maggie H. Williams
Sep 1, 1888
Jun 1, 1974

W. H. Williams
Jul 23, 1859
Mar 21, 1909
&
Bethany M. Williams
Feb 12, 1859
(no date)

S. Carson Foster
1886-1957
&
Helen Knight Foster
1891-1946

John W. Foster
Sep 19, 1883
Jun 3, 1960

Melba Jean, Daughter of
Mr. & Mrs. Odell Pack
B&D May 3, 1934

Frank Watson
1868-1953
&
Ellie Watson
1854-1956

J. Harris Glasscock
Jul 16, 1878
Nov 18, 1957
&
Vera F. Glasscock
Jun 23, 1879
May 10, 1954

James Monroe Crick
Dec 13, 1869
Aug 28, 1954

Mattie Lancaster Crick
Sep 5, 1875
Feb 26, 1942

Joe D. Hanaway
1863-1948

Jane Hanaway
1833-1920

Emma L. Hanaway
1877-1942

Willie T. Hanaway
Nov 30, 1859
Jun 9, 1861
&
Sallie L. Hanaway
Nov 17, 1856
Oct 12, 1870
Children of W. R. &
S. C. Hanaway.

S. C. Hanaway
Feb 28, 1831
Sep 22, 1834

Mollie E., wife of
W. C. Rice
Aug 13, 1856
Jun 16, 1892
Joined C. P. Church
Sept. 1891.

Joseph Marion Greer
1858-1940

Minnie Butler Greer
1868-1956

Callie C. Butler
Mar 7, 1834
May 29, 1907

Margaret Butler Green
(Greer)
1873-1955

Hugh Calvin Greer
Tennessee
M/M2 U. S. Navy WW I
Dec 25, 1892
Aug 4, 1958

Mary E. Dozier Hart
Oct 26, 1830
Jun 6, 1907

PETERSBURG QUADRANGLE

S. P. Hart
1856-1926

Thomas C. Hart
Jul 7, 1853
Jul 18, 1922

Mrs. Pearl S. Hart
1879-1960

James D. Hart
Jun 1, 1866
Jul 7, 1931

Minnie P. Marsh, wife of
J. D. Hart
May 13, 1873
Nov 16, 1941

John M. Thornton
Mar 23, 1849
May 27, 1907
&
Anna Hart Thornton
Aug 24, 1851
Apr 28, 1918
Married Mar 10, 1875

Mary Elizabeth Elzey
Oct 13, 1833
Jun 28, 1905

James "Macon" Hart
WW I Vet Med. Corps
Oct 14, 1895
Jun 1, 1976

Mary Docia Hart
Mar 7, 1898
Feb 11, 1974

M. C. Redd
Jun 16, 1856
Sep 28, 1904
(picture)
&
Emma E. Sorrells Redd
Nov 27, 1860
(no date, not here)

Grover C. Marsh
1883-1964
&
Fannie I. Marsh
1893-1963

James B. Marsh
May 13, 1916
May 17, 1957

Ben F. Redd
Apr 8, 1854
Jun 20, 1905

Sarah, wife of
Ben F. Redd
Sep 30, 1856
May 31, 1936

Jarred R. Taylor
1851-1928
&
Mary Ann Taylor
1855-1894

James F. Haynes
Nov 27, 1880
Jan 28, 1960

Pearle Cain Haynes
Jul 31, 1885
Mar 24, 1959

J. N. Haynes
Jun 17, 1845
Jun 12, 1925
& wife
Gartha Haynes
Jan 3, 1850
Aug 23, 1919

William Adel Taylor
1880-1901

G. W. Moore
Jun 8, 1856
Nov 12, 1940
&
Nancy J. Moore
Jun 15, 1860
Feb 25, 1930

W. Bon Moore
Oct 12, 1890
Feb 8, 1944

Lena May, wife of
W. Bon Moore
Feb 3, 1895
Dec 16, 1922

James Asbury Stephenson
Dec 16, 1828
Oct 1, 1902

Martha A. Moore, wife of
J. A. Stephenson
Sep 5, 1830
Nov 16, 1912

Thomas J. Rives
1838-1919
&
Alice Rives
1846-1932

Harry W. Rives
Dec 4, 1883
Apr 3, 1927

Dolly Rives
Apr 11, 1880
May 30, 1961

Ollin Moore
1896-1931

Guy Rives
Jul 4, 1869
Apr 29, 1902

Robbie Lynn, Daughter of
Robert & Mable Gaunt
May 15, 1909
Oct 25, 1918

Alfred E. Gaunt
Jul 25, 1878
Feb 18, 1906

Mollie Gaunt, wife of
W. P. Bledsoe
Dec 23, 1853
Mar 13, 1914

Lara Luna Fisher
Jul 16, 1895
Dec 30, 1956

W. T. Gaunt
Dec 27, 1859
May 18, 1935

L. B. Gaunt
Sep 10, 1864
Oct 22, 1922

Wilma B. Luna
May 2, 1898
Oct 25, 1916

"Peachy"
1914-Aug 6, 1925
"Wilma's pet cat"

James Davis Luna
1862-1945
&
Leona Gaunt Luna
1867-1960

Annie Martin, Daughter of
H. C. & Nannie Rives
Nov 16, 1892
Sep 18, 1920

Margie, Daughter of
H. C. & Nannie Rives
Apr 2, 1895
Jul 29, 1910

Nannie Meinert
Oct 5, 1872
Oct 22, 1930

Hugh C. Rives
Adopted Son of
B. W. & Catharine Rives
Died Feb 6, 1903
Age: 38y, 4m, 9d.
&
N. W. Rives
Jun 7, 1835
(no date)

James T. Bledsoe
1872-1959
&
Alberta G. Bledsoe
1878-1974 Age: 96 years.

James T. Bledsoe, Jr.
Tennessee
Tec 4 Medical Dept.
WW II
Aug 15, 1915
Sep 16, 1959

W. T. House
& wife
Henrietta House
1926
(all on stone)

J. M. Young
Feb 23, 1865
Nov 21, 1922
&
M. A. Young
Dec 20, 1866
(no date)

Martha A., wife of
J. L. Gibson
Jan 18, 1839
Dec 6, 1915

Mary Alice Wells, wife
of S. A. Morrison
Sep 7, 1894
May 5, 1916

Charles Edwin Morrison
Jan 1, 1915
Jul 24, 1915

John Manley Jones
North Carolina
Sgt Co M 119 Inf WW I
Jul 4, 1892
Dec 3, 1954
&
Ruth Adams Jones
1893-

Tom W. Duckworth
1871-1939
&
Florence Finley Duckworth
1868-19(no date)

Archie Ray Sorrells
Tennessee
S1 U. S. Navy   WW II
Aug 13, 1910
Feb 1, 1961

Allen Watson
1885-1948
&
Dallas Watson
1891-1941

Waldean Bevels
Nov 20, 1930
May 18, 1960

William C. Pearson
1873-(no date)
&
Mattie O'Neal Pearson
1874-1940

PETERSBURG QUADRANGLE

Mrs. Henry Blacksher
1857-1940

Robert A. Blacksher
Tennessee
Pfc Co C 117 Inf
WW I
Mar 22, 1895
Oct 27, 1954

Sallie Blacksher
1891-1959

Shirley A. Wells
Jul 24, 1892
Jul 19, 1938

Mrs. Blanche Wells
(no dates, Higgins FH)

Aubin Howard, Son of
S. A. & Blanche Wells
Aug 31, 1916
Sep 23, 1916

Robert Lee Foster
Jul 24, 1879
Nov 16, 1914

Virgie Lou Foster
Jan 4, 1883
Mar 6, 1938

W. R. Foster
1867-1940

Gotha E. Foster
Nov 1, 1871
Aug 20, 1899

Alva C., Son of
W. R. & G. E. Foster
Nov 29, 1897
Aug 24, 1899

Tula Smith Foster
1876-1967

Fred Foster Wallace
Feb 11, 1917
May 12, 1917

Infant of
W. L. & Essie Wallace
B&D May 2, 1918

Lonnie M. Nichols
1895-1968
&
Lona M. Nichols
1898-

Boyce Cummings
1877-1952

Joe S. Cummings
1883-1964

Joe H. Cummings
Aug 24, 1908
May 23, 1962

Jack B. Cummings
1885-1967

Robbie H. Cummings
1885-

J. B. Cummings, Jr.
1910-1943

Michael O. Gaffney, Sr.
May 20, 1924
Dec 22, 1967
&
Carmela G. Gaffney
Apr 28, 1924

Donald Ray, Son of
Thurman & Catharine Curlee
1942-1942

A. Richard Philpot
Jan 1, 1953

Mary J. Philpot
Feb 21, 1922

Joseph C. Roberts
Nov 14, 1883

Nora E. Roberts
Oct 24, 1879
Jul 10, 1963

Charles F. Roberts
Oct 28, 1919

Robert Davis
1938-1939

Oliver R. March
1912-1968

A. Oliver March
1885-1944

Margie R. March
1891-1955

Jake Burns
1898-1964

Mattie C. Burns
1904-1957

Frank F. Cashion
1877-1958
&
Fannie S. Cashion
1883-

J. W. Foster
1852-1936

L. V. Holland
(footstone, no dates)
&
John T. Holland
1851-1927
&
Mary G. Holland
1859-1898

E. T. Holland
(footstone, no dates)

C. C. Holland
(footstone, no dates)

E. A. Holland
(footstone, no dates)

John White Holland
Died Dec 19, 1969
Age: 80 years.
(Ralston FH)

J. Richard Holland
Apr 6, 1936
Jun 19, 1938

Willis Bonner Smith
Died Nov 11, 1966
Age: 79y, 9m, 23d.
(Higgins FH)

T. L. Foster
Nov 10, 1861
Jun 8, 1925

Kathryn "Kate" Hanaway
Foster
1876-1924

T. W. Hanaway
1867-1932

Sam Owen
1871-1938
&
Vera M. Owen
1886-1965

Irene Owen
Feb 20, 1907
May 20, 1966

Emmett Bedwell
May 1893
Feb 1938

Evert Bedwell
Aug 11, 1889
Mar 27, 1968

Lewis E. Bedwell
Jul 25, 1928
Jun 6, 1958

Margaret E. Bedwell
Dec 23, 1887
Mar 31, 1960

J. R. Muse
Apr 3, 1853
Dec 3, 1930

Mary F. Muse
Dec 20, 1853
Sep 17, 1917

Everett G. Foster,
Grandson of
J. R. & M. F. Muse
Dec 17, 1898
Feb 16, 1917

W. A. "Jase" Muse
Aug 8, 1880
Jul 21, 1946

Mary Talley Muse
Jun 4, 1881
Apr 19, 1963

Baby Son of
W. A. & Mary A. Muse
B&D Feb 15, 1916

T. B. Muse
Jun 8, 1857
Jul 3, 1928

Sarah E. Muse
Feb 13, 1857
Mar 7, 1934

Maud Muse
Oct 19, 1890
Jan 28, 1912

James A. Montgomery
Dec 21, 1875
Jul 29, 1959

Sarah Muse Montgomery
May 6, 1876
Apr 6, 1938

Fred Muse Montgomery
Oct 14, 1902
Jun 27, 1944

John Earl Marsh
Mar 19, 1878
Nov 14, 1949

Mabel Liggett, wife of
John Earl Marsh
Jun 27, 1895
Jul 31, 1964

John Davidson Marsh
Dec 20, 1853
Aug 27, 1911

May Belle Marsh
Nov 12, 1879
Aug 29, 1964

Dr. Charles P. Marsh
Nov 30, 1881
Jul 5, 1944

PETERSBURG QUADRANGLE

Viola Cowden Marsh
Jan 19, 1857
Jun 6, 1943

G. C. "Lum" Marsh
1857-1929

Jennie S. Marsh
1862-1937

George Everett Marsh
May 29, 1884
Apr 5, 1964

Theodotia Parthenia Marsh,
wife of S. B. Osteen
Nov 5, 1888
Oct 21, 1918
(picture)

Edwin D. Ashby
Sep 21, 1919
Nov 7, 1960

C. W. Mills
May 27, 1901
Aug 5, 1963
&
Mary J. Mills
May 15, 1909

Darnel Twins
B&D 1966
(Gowen-Smith FH)

Herbert Cashion
Aug 16, 1921
Mar 21, 1938

J. H. Leftwich
1867-1953
&
Gertie D. Leftwich
1880-1939

John G. Berry
1855-1926
&
Nettie Gaunt Berry
1862-1944

Berenice Luna Mason
Aug 20, 1892
Dec 7, 1954

Hugh McTier
Apr 20, 1813
Jun 3, 1878
&
Julia A. McTier
Oct 23, 1818
Jul 22, 1896

Mary E. McTier
Dec 8, 1851
Dec 17, 1928

J. R. McTier
Jun 12, 1857
Jun 7, 1933

Hugh McTier, Jr.
Dec 2, 1847
Aug 12, 1909

John W. McTier
of the 41 Regt Tenn Vols
Died Feb 7, 1862
Age: 20 years.

Adam McTier
Aug 15, 1854
Dec 27, 1897

A. J. McTier
Jan 8, 1860
Sep 17, 1925

John Clenny *
Died Feb 15, 1916
Age: 94 years.
Vet of Mexican &
C.S.A.

Jack Sorrells *
Died Sep 10, 1908
Age: 74 years.

Several unmarked graves.

Mrs. Susan Carmack *
Dec 4, 1843
Jun 23, 1905
Married Feb 27, 1868
to George C. Carmack
& Daughter of
Thomas K. Warren

* *

MERRITT CEMETERY

LOCATION: Two and one half miles SW of Petersburg at the
Marshall County line.

Olevid Merritt
Sep 25, 1842
May 23, 1845

J. H. Merritt
Dec 17, 1836
May 31, 1839

R. J. M.
(footstone, no dates)
Several unmarked graves.

* *

McEWEN CEMETERY

LOCATION: One mile SE of Petersburg at the forks of Cane
Creek and Little Cane Creek.

James N., Son of
W. R. & M. M. Ellis
Jan 6, 1886
Jul 5, 1896

W. B. Swing
Died 1918
Age: (not given)

T. W. Swing
Died 1916
Age: (not given)

Bettie V. Moore
Oct 27, 1862
Apr 7, 1890

John T. Greer
May 12, 1866
Oct 8, 1875

Thomas V. Greer
Jan 20, 1824
Dec 1, 1917
&
Elizabeth A. Greer
Jan 1, 1825
Jun 24, 1889

Annie P., Daughter of
J. W. & V. A. Percy
Died Feb 3, 1879
Age: 2 years.

J. G. Gillespie
Feb 5, 1851
Mar 27, 1911
&
Annie Wert Gillespie
Dec 25, 1849
Aug 7, 1887

Jacob Gillespie
Sep 21, 1814
Jul 30, 1892

Sarah Catharine, wife of
Jacob Gillespie
Jan 12, 1820
Sep 27, 1854

Catharine Jane, Daughter of
Jacob & Catharine S. Gillespie
Mar 16, 1849
Apr 6, 1850

Julia & Jennie, Twin Daughters
of Jacob & Letitia Gillespie
Born Oct 17, 1864
Julia died Jul 22, 1865
Jennie died Jun 26, 1868

Johnnie & Lena, Son &
Daughter of Jacob &
Letitia Gillespie
Johnnie born
Feb 21, 1866
Died Sep 7, 1867
Lena born
Aug 17, 1867
Died Jul 31, 1868

Fannie, Daughter of
Jacob & Catharine
Gillespie
Jan 23, 1842
Oct 10, 1867

John A., Son of
A. A. & E. R. Greer
Mar 5, 1853
Sep 14, 1867
Age: 14y, 6m, 9d.

PETERSBURG QUADRANGLE

A. A. Greer
Nov 21, 1817
Apr 10, 1883

Elzira, wife of
A. A. Greer
Jan 10, 1825
Aug 3, 1907

Little Buddie (Greer)
Dec 24, 1863
Sep 13, 1964

Ella & Babe
Ella Gillespie
Jul 25, 1857
Dec 27, 1858
&
Infant Son of
A. A. & E. R. Gillespie
B&D Jun 1, 1855
"Our Children"

George G., Son of
George & Sallie Gillespie
Jun 30, 1884
Oct 7, 1885

Jennie Cast Marshall
1859-1892

Elbert N. Street
Apr 24, 1878
(date broken away)

David R. Smythe
Jul 4, 1810
Jul 5, 1865
&
Jane G. Smythe
Dec 2, 1821
Jun 27, 1874
&
Sarah E. Smythe
Dec 12, 1846
Dec 20, 1867
&
Belle E. Smythe
May 31, 1859
Aug 13, 1867
&
Dixie M. Smythe
Aug 20, 1862
Aug 6, 1867
&
David R. Smythe, Jr.
Jan 25, 1853
1870

J. M. Menefee
Jan 28, 1844
Apr 11, 1913

Thomas Edward, Son of
J. M. & M. C. Memefee
May 28, 1888
Nov 13, 1890

Several unmarked graves.

Margaret, wife of
S. W. Carmack & Daughter
of Joseph & Mary Greer
Aug 8, 1813
Apr 1, 1857

Gustavus A. Jarvis
Jun 13, 1840
Feb 15, 1897
&
Lula M. Jarvis
Aug 12, 1847
Apr 14, 1892

Jonnie Greer, Son of
G. A. & L. M. Jarvis
Mar 5, 1872
Jan 8, 1874

E. G. McEwen
Nov 7, 1843
Fell at the Battle of
Franklin
Nov 30, 1864

Thomas J. Menefee
Dec 8, 1849
May 22, 1903

Miss Lizzie Walding *
Died Aug 27, 1894
Age: 50 years.

John W. Swing *
Died Nov 27, 1916
Age: 50 years.
Left wife & 7 children.

Reuben Thomas Redman
May 29, 1830
Apr 18, 1878
& wife
Margaret McEwen Redman
Aug 20, 1840
May 20, 1890

"Sisters"
Lititia Statum
1864-1942
&
Nannie Statum
1866-1935

A. A. McEwen
1846-1930

W. H. Cast
Aug 27, 1818
Sep 26, 1890

Mary E., wife of
W. H. Cast
Jul 25, 1831
Feb 7, 1899

Eddie H. Wells
Mar 22, 1887
Mar 20, 1890

Mrs. Elizabeth,* mother
of A. A., A. J., &
Campbell McEwen
Died Jan 13, 1897
Age: 82 years.

* *

WELCH CEMETERY

LOCATION: Two and one half miles SW of Petersburg, at the Marshall County line.

James L. Welch
Jan 20, 1851
Nov 9, 1924

Mrs. Neccie Welch
1861-1937

Sarah A., Daughter of
L. B. & M. A. Welch &
wife of J. H. Crabtree
Jun 15, 1838
May 5, 1881

Eslie, Son of
Mr. & Mrs. R. E. Welch
Jun 7, 1900
Sep 22, 1905

Erskine, Son of
Mr. & Mrs. R. E. Welch
May 31, 1902
Jan 27, 1903

Infant of
Mr. & Mrs. R. E. Welch
Apr 27, 1905
Apr 28, 1905

Robert E. Welch
Jan 10, 1873
Feb 23, 1934
&
Lula M. Welch
May 18, 1878
Apr 27, 1918

Martha E., wife of
W. S. Butler
Jul 4, 1841
May 24, 1900

R. M. Welch
Nov 17, 1844
Jan 18, 1913

Calvin, Son of
Mr. & Mrs. R. M. Welch
Nov 3, 1863
Jan 8, 1864

Theo, Son of
Mr. & Mrs. R. M. Welch
Feb 22, 1878
Aug 2, 1878

Several unmarked graves.

Kenneth E. Welch
Tennessee
Pfc Hq Co 31 Qm Bn WW II
Nov 6, 1917
Nov 17, 1962
&
Margaret C. Welch
Oct 10, 1928

Ida Crabtree
Jun 12, 1874
Oct 15, 1902

John L. Crabtree
1920-1940

Mrs. Effie Crabtree
1878-1947

M. O., Daughter of
F. F. & M. W. Crabtree
Dec 8, 1882
Jul 18, 1893

L. B. Welch *
Died May 29, 1891
Age: 81 years.

Roy L., Son of
J. A. & W. A. Crabtree
Mar 4, 1916
Oct 5, 1916

Nick Welch
1848-1886
&
Martha I. Welch
1850-1888

W. T. Welch
Oct 2, 1876
Jun 3, 1943

Jennie, wife of
W. T. Welch
Feb 28, 1873
Dec 28, 1905

Ida M., wife of
W. T. Welch
Jan 19, 1880
Sep 21, 1950

William Payton Welch
B&D Jun 11, 1931

TAFT QUADRANGLE

DUNLAP CEMETERY

LOCATION: One and three fourth miles NNW of Coldwater and One half mile north of Hobbs Bridge on west side of road.

James Dunlap and Died 1860 Age: about 65 years	Sarah Dunlap and Died Nov 13, 1839 Age: about 40 years.	Their three Sons & one daughter. "Erected by their Son from Georgia"

* *

CEMETERY

LOCATION: Two miles NNW of Coldwater, west of Hovis Bend of Elk River.

Old Graveyard, several graves with fieldstones, no inscriptions.

* *

BRIGHT-HASTINGS CEMETERY

LOCATION: One and one half miles NW of Molino, east of Summers Bend of Elk River.

Miss C. E. Bright (no dates)	W. D. Bright (no dates)	W. C. Bright (no dates)	Charles Thomas Bright * Died May 25, 1868 Age: 19 years.
William Bright 1769-Oct 23, 1858	James Bright Jan 15, 1798 Sep 2, 1873	Martha E. Dunlap (no dates)	Many unmarked graves.
Dorothy Bright 1773-Jul 30, 1844	R. C. Bright (no dates)	M. M. A. Hamlin (no dates)	

* *

PITTS CEMETERY

LOCATION: One and one fourth miles NW of Molino, south of Molino Creek and east of Summers Bend of Elk River.

Younger R., Son of P. A. & M. D. Deford Dec 2, 1884 Nov 6, 1885	Greenfield, Son of R. A. & E. P. Pitts Jun 11, 1893 Aug 14, 1896	Lettie E., Daughter of R. A. & E. P. Pitts Oct 27, 1890 Jul 15, 1891	David, Son of J. B. & Emma Sanders Dec 30, 1899 Nov 17, 1900
Infant Son of T. B. & R. E. Kilpatrick B&D Apr 18, 1881	R. W. Pitts Mar 5, 1830 Jun 2, 1898 & wife	Emma, wife of J. B. Sanders Apr 17, 1870 Dec 11, 1900	Several unmarked graves.
Rena E. Pitts, wife of T. B. Kilpatrick May 3, 1859 Dec 15, 1889	Finetti Pitts Feb 24, 1830 Oct 6, 1895		

* *

RAWLS CEMETERY

LOCATION: At Molino, Tennessee.

J. W. Rawls Died Jul 28, 1896 Age: 56 years. & Susan Griffis, wife of J. W. Rawls Died Oct 16, 1879 Age: 34 years.	A. F. Rawls Apr 18, 1871 Jun 14, 1872 J. E. Rawls Mar 1, 1873 Apr 16, 1874	Elizabeth, wife of J. J. Rawls Oct 18, 1840 Dec 9, 1867 Elbert B. Smith Oct 1, 1855 Aug 21, 1857	Baby Son of T. D. & M. E. Griffis B&D Feb 1, 1874 T. D. Griffis Aug 9, 1846 Feb 2, 1888

TAFT QUADRANGLE

W. R. Griffis
(no dates)

Dolly Griffis
(no dates)

Nancy Griffis
(no dates)

Several unmarked graves.

* *

PITTS CEMETERY

LOCATION: Three fourth mile south east of Molino on the west side of Camargo Road.

Samuel Hall
born ------------
died Oct 11, 1872
(broken away)

Rachel A., wife of
Samuel Hall
Dec 19, 1837
Aug 13, 1855

Samuel W., Son of
Samuel & S. A. Hall
Nov 7, 1869
Sep 22, 1887

J. Pitts
1784-1862
& wife
(no dates, no name)
(Rachel Young Pitts
1792-1867)

I. R. Pitts
May 9, 1829
Apr 23, 1887

Elvira, wife of
I. R. Pitts
Mar 11, 1829
Jan 16, 1888

Caroline, wife of
Terry Williamson
May 17, 1843
May 23, 1872

David Polk,* Son of
Bryson & Emma Sanders
Died Nov 17, 1900
Age: 10m, 17d.

J. V. Pitts *
Died Jul 15, 1917
Age: 61 years.

Mrs. M. R. Pitts
1830-Jun 15, 1853

Several unmarked graves.

* *

FIFE-GIVENS CEMETERY

LOCATION: One mile north of Camargo on the east side of the road.

Margaret Givens
Jan 15, 1791
Apr 28, 1861
(Vault)

William Givens
Died Jan 7, 1857
Age: 82y, 15d. (Vault)

William Fife
Jun 16, 1819
Feb 22, 1881
Age: 61y, 3m, 6d.

James Givens
Died Jun 1, 1840
Age: 61y, 1m, _d.
(day is chipped away)

Mary K. Fife, wife of
J. D. Wells
Dec 3, 1842
Mar 8, 1891

Clark,* Son of
W. B. Fife
Died Jun 26, 1895
Age: 1y, 11m.

* *

SANDLIN CEMETERY

LOCATION: One mile NNE of Camargo and one fourth mile north of Skinem Road.

J. E. Randolph
Oct 21, 1831
Jan 8, 1901

Louisa, wife of
J. E. Randolph
Oct 15, 1834
Jan 4, 1901

Mannie M., wife of
T. L. Randolph
Died Aug 12, 1909
Age: 33 years.

Amanda C., Consort of
D. M. Holloway
Jun 5, 1833
Jun 3, 1859

Sarah A. F., Daughter of
D. M. & A. C. Holloway
Dec 14, 1858
Jun 17, 1859

James Fuller
Died 1814
Age: about 50 years.
(2 unmarked graves
beside this grave.)

Mary Fuller
Died Oct 20, 1857
Age: 46 years.

Desdemona Meeks
Died Apr 8, 1855
Age: 55 years.

Nancy, wife of
James Fuller
Died Jun 14, 1870
Age: about 85 years.

A. J. Fuller
Died Apr 28, 1881
Age: 66 years.

Virginia A., wife of
A. J. Fuller
Died Nov 17, 1881
Age: 48 years.

John T. Fuller
Died Apr 21, 1884
Age: 79 years.

James H. Fuller
Feb 1, 1813
Sep 13, 1890

Anderson Ivey
1819-Jan 1895

J. R. Daniel
Aug 31, 1864
Nov 26, 1885

Sarah A. Danniel Pearson
Sep 1, 1852
Nov 1, 1916

Frances L. Taylor
May 6, 1840
Nov 30, 1888

TAFT QUADRANGLE

Hugh Randolph
Nov 28, 1814
Apr 30, 1900

L. I. Randolph
Dec 14, 1865
Sep 24, 1900

A. S. Randolph
1808-1893
&
Elizabeth Randolph
1812-1876

Tula Randolph, wife of
John James Rutledge
Jan 14, 1898
Jan 18, 1932

Martha Elizabeth Randolph
Dec 30, 1843
Dec 9, 1932

Albert C. Hutchinson
Jan 24, 1868
Jul 22, 1896

Jinnie Hutchinson
Aug 6, 1858
Sep 8, 1931

William A. Hutchinson
Jul 30, 1862
Oct 24, 1909

Margaret E., wife of
W. A. Hutchinson
May 30, 1874
Jul 26, 1895

James A. Hutchinson
Sep 28, 1856
Sep 8, 1895

John H. Hutchinson
Dec 29, 1823
Jan 14, 1892

Margaret E., wife of
J. H. Hutchinson
Feb 11, 1828
Feb 28, 1908

William G. Moore
May 7, 1864
Jul 16, 1929
& wife
Dessie E. Hutchinson Moore
Dec 19, 1865
Jun 9, 1895

Liddie Belle Watkins
May 18, 1874
Jul 13, 1895

W. C. Daniel
Apr 8, 1869
Nov 15, 1895

Robert Daniel
Died Jun 13, 1890
Age: about 55 years.

Martha Ann, wife of
R. Daniel
Died Jul 17, 1900
Age: about 55 years.

John Daniel
Died Sep 6, 1900
Age: 32 years.
&
Beulah Daniel
Died Nov 12, 1906
Age: 31 years.

Callie Womack
Died Sep 24, 1900
Age: 47 years.

Alpha Myrtle, Daughter of
W. J. & E. L. Malone
Apr 12, 1889
Aug 6, 1890

L. M. Price
1865-1936
&
Ada Price
1876-1954
(Wilson FH)

Clabe Womack
Sep 1, 1875
Jun 22, 1936

E. C. Womack
1875-1938

William H., Son of
J. P. & J. A. Bobo
Apr 12, 1893
Nov 27, 1897

George D., Son of
J. P. & J. A. Bobo
Feb 3, 1899
Oct 17, 1900

Mary D. Scruggs, wife of
T. D. Bobo
Dec 31, 1877
Feb 6, 1904

Starling Scruggs
(no dates)
&
Mary Scruggs
(no dates) *
(* Died Nov 21, 1900
Age: 55y, 3 weeks, 2d.

J. E. Mullins
1866-1935

Mrs. M. A. Mullins
1872-1944

Thomas H. Ivy
Jan 13, 1857
Apr 12, 1917

Janey Green
1855-1935

Jerry Mullins
1866-1935
&
Martha Mullins
1872-1944

Wesley, Son of
W. & M. E. T. Light
Mar 4, 1905
Jun 7, 1905

Elizabeth, Daughter of
G. W. J. & M. E. T. Kay
Jul 26, 1895
Mar 21, 1896

Mary, Daughter of
G. W. J. & M. E. T. Kay
May 19, 1894
Jun 28, 1895

Mackie, Daughter of
G. W. J. & M. E. T. Kay
Aug 15, 1891
Dec 13, 1893

Bettie Alburta, Daughter of
P. E. & D. S. Smith
Jun 29, 1906
Oct 16, 1906

May Pearl, Daughter of
P. E. & D. S. Smith
Sep 17, 1899
Jun 12, 1901

George Erwin
1867-1941

C. T. Harris
Died Dec 8, 1917
Age: 64 years.

Mrs. D. M. McMillin
1858-1943

Roy Clay McMillin
May 4, 1918
Jul 20, 1920
(picture)

Cowan L. McMillin
Mar 6, 1887
May 19, 1963
&
Mary B. McMillin
May 30, 1893
Jul 1, 1969

A. Ezell McMillin
Oct 12, 1865
Sep 3, 1928

Grady M., Son of
A. E. & Ida McMillin
Mar 27, 1912
Jan 7, 1919

Mary Loureen, Daughter
of A. E. & Ida McMillin
Feb 24, 1914
Sep 11, 1914

Shelby C. McMillin
Sep 23, 1881
Nov 22, 1925

John Robert McMillin
Jan 27, 1897
Feb 22, 1956

George A. McMillin
Jan 12, 1856
Oct 1, 1943

D. M. McMillin
Feb 15, 1856
Mar 5, 1928

Willie Ann Hargrove
1872-1946

Pearl Leona Wallace
Sep 21, 1893
Nov 9, 1935

Andrew Hargrove
1870-1953

Albert Pressley Wallace
Aug 15, 1920
Sep 14, 1922

Infant Son of
Oda & P. L. Wallace
B&D Oct 17, 1912

Mary Ireva, Daughter of
Leslie & Exie Reavis
Aug 4, 1924
Jan 22, 1929

L. B. McAlister
1881-1943

Nellie Lee, Daughter of
J. H. & Ella Spray
Mar 25, 1908
Sep 26, 1910

Hurley H. Spray
Oct 23, 1906
Apr 27, 1929

Clemmie M., Son of
J. H. & Ella Spray
Dec 3, 1886
Apr 16, 1912

Flossie Perl, Daughter
of J. H. & Ella Spray
Feb 13, 1902
Aug 19, 1909

TAFT QUADRANGLE

Annie Lucile, Daughter of
W. J. & M. S. Gattis
Dec 15, 1911
Jul 18, 1912

Charlie Locker
1868-1942
&
Sallie Locker
1872-1914

Wesley, Son of
S. V. & M. M. Beard
Sep 3, 1895
Nov 18, 1918

Martha M. Beard
Oct 10, 1878
Oct 7, 1909

Infant of
S. V. & M. M. Beard
B&D Feb 8, 1906

Boonie, Son of
S. V. & M. E. Beard
Oct 12, 1915
Apr 27, 1930

Sarah Lou, Daughter of
S. V. & M. E. Beard
Dec 10, 1913
Sep 17, 1917

Covie Finet Blankenship
Sep 26, 1902
Nov 5, 1904

A. V. Blankenship
Aug 16, 1860
May 9, 1903
&
E. C. Blankenship
1852
Apr 6, 1899

George Lee Bird
May 17, 1832
Jan 24, 1921

Wilda, Daughter of
Dock & Daisy Sandlin
Nov 8, 1893
Mar 3, 1909

Bonnie Beard
1915-1930

Ovel Haden, Son of
A. M. & F. E. Daniel
Oct 15, 1903
May 21, 1904

Infant Daughter of
W. A. & R. E. Fanning
Jan 3, 1899
Sep 4, 1899

L. A., Son of
B. F. & S. F. Fanning
Dec 14, 1875
Sep 26, 1898

S. F., wife of
B. F. Fanning
Sep 6, 1840
Apr 5, 1901

Ben F. Fanning
Oct 15, 1840
Jun 19, 1909

Joyce F. Spray
Jan 24, 1890
Sep 22, 1965

W. Wiley Spray
1856-1935

Dora Spray
1855-1933

Bertha, wife of
C. D. Spray
Sep 29, 1883
May 15, 1914

Infant of
Mr. & Mrs. W. W. Spray
B&D May 27, 1920

M. C. McMillin
Jun 26, 1826
Apr 20, 1900

Joseph William Mullins
Feb 11, 1843
Dec 5, 1906
&
Eliza M. Mullins
Jan 15, 1850
Dec 6, 1906

Infant Son of
J. K. & M. E. Clark
B&D Apr 25, 1890

William Jackson Smith
May 14, 1839
Aug 28, 1923
&
Sarah Jones Smith
Jan 16, 1842
Jan 3, 1897

Nancy Wells
1855-Apr 22, 1928

Sarah, wife of
W. J. Smith
Jan 16, 1842
Jan 3, 1897
(Same as above)

Infant Son of
J. F. & M. C. Smith
B&D July 1897
Age: 2 days.

Connie Spray
Apr 25, 1891
Sep 2, 1905

C. O. Smith
Jan 16, 1892
Jan 25, 1892

Claudie F., Son of
R. P. & N. J. Smith
Jun 23, 1889
Jan 9, 1891

Lena Bell, Daughter of
D. A. & J. V. Moyers
Mar 31, 1896
Sep 15, 1896

Jonathan, Son of
John & Jane Sandlin
Nov 23, 1832
Mar 3, 1906

Elizabeth M., wife of
Jonathan Sandlin
Aug 27, 1833
Jun 14, 1903
Age: 69y, 9m, 17d.

John Sandlin
Died Nov 21, 1868
Age: about 65 years.

Jane, wife of
John Sandlin
Sep 8, 1804
Mar 20, 1884

John Spray
Died Jun 1, 1905
Age: about 80 years.

Nancy, wife of
John Spray
Mar 6, 1830
Jul 14, 1901

Joseph Clark, Jr.
Apr 15, 1850
Nov 1, 1873

Joseph Clark, Sr.
Dec 6, 1798
Mar 11, 1863

Em Eliza, wife of
Joseph Clark, Sr.
Jun 12, 1822
Sep 2, 1854

James Clark
Aug 24, 1845
Oct 12, 1862

James Clark
Mar __, 1764
__ 10, 18_3
(broken)

M. Clark
(no date)

A. Clark
(no dates)

Em Elizabeth Clark
Jun 19, 1822
Sep 20, 1854
(second stone)

Robert M. Burton
Sep 25, 1845
Feb 21, 1895

Lowery D. Burton
Mar 27, 1882
Sep 3, 1883

James Burton
Jan 25, 1798
Sep 27, 1872

Nancy C., wife of
James Burton
Mar 9, 1814
Jan 3, 1887

James C. Burton
Jul 20, 1841
Feb 29, 1860

James A. Burton
Oct 10, 1903
Aug 3, 1930

Andrew J. Burton
Aug 19, 1852
Jan 4, 1929
&
Polina L. Burton
Nov 24, 1860
Aug 21, 1929

J. Price
(no dates)

J. Clark
(no dates)

M. A., Daughter of
John & Nancy Spray
Age: about 9 years.
(no dates)

Jonnie, Son of
John & Nancy Spray
Age: about 18 years.
(no dates)

Edward Moss Burton
1848-1932
&
Mary Ellice Burton
1877-1909

Malinda Walker, wife of
Samuel McAlister
Apr 31, 1832
Sep 4, 1870
Age: 38y, 4m, 3d.

W. M. Holt
Aug 20, 1821
Apr 23, 1857

Betty Smith
1929-1933

TAFT QUADRANGLE

Ada Phagan
Jun 21, 1885
Jan 22, 1910

Athie, Son of
W. W. & M. J. Spray
May 22, 1884
May 5, 1896

W. M. Daniel
Apr 2, 1860
Mar 26, 1918

Sarah Daniel, wife of
Samuel McAlister
Died Aug 29, 1888
Age: 48 years.

William Daniel
Died May 28, 1889
Age: 53 years.

N. D.
(no dates)

N. D.
(no dates)

T. D.
(no dates)

Mattie Randolph
Apr 3, 1848
Mar 9, 1920

Kelly Swinford
Apr 17, 1902
Feb 1, 1911
&
Jonnie A. Swinford
Jun 10, 1900
Oct 17, 1901
"Sons of J. P. &
Vena Swinford"

Johnie Swinford
Dec 6, 1874
Oct 1, 1898

T. D. S.
(no dates)

H. S.
(no dates)

J. H. Thrasher
May 29, 1863
Nov 22, 1921

Elizabeth McAlister
wife of
J. H. Thrasher
Sep 30, 1848
Apr 3, 1924

Ruth Ailene Tipps
1917-1917

Mary Tabitha Tipps
1921-1923

Moses Fisk
Jan   1818
Nov 22, 1888

Mary S. Jones, wife of
Moses Fisk
Jan 22, 1836
Mar 8, 1879

Thompson B., Son of
Moses & M. S. Fisk
Sep 16, 1862
Nov 18, 1883

Wallar Key
Jun 10, 1797
Jun 3, 1869

Hannah Key
May 3, 1799
Sep 8, 1875

Mrs. H. L. Key
Jun 18, 1845
Jan 3, 1930

C. S. Key
Dec 31, 1832
Sep 15, 1897

T. Y. Key
Apr 27, 1869
Mar 27, 1924
&
Mattie Land Key
Jan 18, 1871
Mar 28, 1913

Lenora McAlister
Nov 15, 1877
Dec 16, 1877

Naoma McAlister
Feb 6, 1879
Aug 8, 1879

Joseph McAlister
Jun 27, 1880
Jul 3, 1880

Virlina M., Daughter of
W. J. & M. T. McAlister
Sep 18, 1881
Oct 30, 1887

W. R. McAlister
Oct 27, 1874
Jun 26, 1894

Fred, Son of
W. J. & Tabitha McAlister
Jul 13, 1893
Dec 25, 1917

W. J. McAlister
Nov 4, 1853
Nov 12, 1929
&
Tabitha M. McAlister
Jul 22, 1858
Feb 6, 1921

Clarence McAlister
Aug 26, 1895
Apr 19, 1896
&
Lily McAlister
B&D May 30, 1903

Bertha, Daughter of
R. & I. McAlister
Jan 28, 1904
Oct 16, 1907

Richard, Son of
R. & I. McAlister
May 7, 1912
Oct 26, 1913

Paul, Son of
R. & I. McAlister
Mar 24, 1914
Sep 15, 1917

Arthur, Son of
William F. C. & T. A. Bates
Mar 7, 1889
Mar 14, 1889

William F. C. Bates
Nov 11, 1852
Apr 22, 1918

Tilda A. Powers, wife of
William F. C. Bates
Aug 14, 1854
May 27, 1890

Jeff A. Bates
May 10, 1878
Jan 30, 1902

Cora Higgins, wife of
Charlie F. Bates
May 15, 1884
Nov 6, 1909

Flossie V.(Viola) Puryear
Jul 17, 1897
Oct 5, 1955

Mary Belle Higgins
Dec 26, 1889
Nov 21, 1913

Mary B. Higgins
1889-1933

James M. Pylant
Sep 11, 1873
Apr 7, 1957
&
Annie D. Pylant
Feb 11, 1885

Marvin Pylant
Nov 28, 1909
Jan 4, 1911

James A. Moore
Jun 1, 1887
Mar 2, 1966

Alex N. Pearson
Jun 13, 1889
Oct 7, 1915

Alton H., Son of
A. N. & S. A. Pearson
May 3, 1909
Jan 28, 1911

F. N. McCown
1861-1930

Myrtle McCown, wife of
George Swinford
Aug 2, 1883
Mar 5, 1917

Essie L., Daughter of
J. D. & P. Key
Sep 10, 1904
Sep 17, 1911

R. E. Colbert
1878-1932

William Franklin Colbert
Apr 16, 1882
May 30, 1944

Della Simmons
1875-1912

Calline, wife of
L. N. Tribble
Feb 11, 1860
Jun 6, 1909

Lon B. McAlister
Jul 21, 1878
Mar 5, 1943

Sherlie, Daughter of
J. G. & A. L. McAlister
Oct 25, 1898
Sep 26, 1909

J. G. McAlister
May 4, 1860
Sep 12, 1926

Addie M. McAlister
Jul 22, 1867
Jul 21, 1948

Edna Katherine McAlister
Dec 8, 1906
Jul 30, 1927

Girtie May, Daughter of
J. G. & A. L. McAlister
& wife of I. B. Davis
Nov 30, 1888
Mar 17, 1925

J. A. Simmons
1866-1942

TAFT QUADRANGLE

Matthew W. McLemore
Jul 1, 1868
Apr 14, 1960
&
Velah A. McLemore
Mar 23, 1882
Jan 12, 1970

H. F. McLemore
Mar 11, 1921
Apr 22, 1925

Winnie McLemore
(no dates)

Winny McLemore
1912-1912

Jesse Hopkins
1877-1943

Annie Ruth Smith
Died Nov --, ----
Age: 19y, 9m.
(Laughlin FH)
(date gone)

_____ Smith (name gone)
Died Apr 23, ----
Age: 23 years.
(Galloway FH)
(date gone)

A. Jackson Swinford
Apr 23, 1870
Apr 12, 1912
&
Josephine Swinford
Nov 6, 1868
Sep 24, 1942

Nancy J., Daughter of
Willis & Mary Satterfield
Sep 14, 1865
May 2, 1909

Bill B. Reed
Tennessee
Pfc 50 Inftry
Died Aug 30, 1930

Wesley A. McAlister
Aug 21, 1925
Jun 21, 1942

John T. McAlister
Sep 10, 1872
Jan 16, 1927

Thurman D., Son of
J. T. & A. E. McAlister
Apr 14, 1903
Mar 7, 1921

Samuel McAlister
Dec 11, 1834
Dec 13, 1898

W. J. M. McAlister
Mar 3, 1912
(no date)
(fieldstone)

Youler Mc(Alister)
Born 1904
Died (no date)
(fieldstone)

Nora J., wife of
R. D. Boyd
Died May 15, 1912
Age: 58 years.
"Mother of C. C. &
L. A. Boyd".

S. M. Pitcock
Feb 5, 1830
Dec 6, 1906

Euphamy, wife of
S. M. Pitcock
Jul 30, 1830
Aug 10, 1904

S. B. Pitcock
Oct 23, 1869
Apr 12, 1905

Alice Lou, Daughter of
M. J. & Mary J. Bates
Sep 10, 1906
Oct 12, 1906

Milton J. Bates
1871-1937

Mary Beard Bates
1876-1962

Margaret R. Eakes
Aug 25, 1845
May 8, 1899
Age: 53y, 8m, 13d.

Ben A. Warren
Aug 20, 1871
Jan 3, 1899

James Cleveland Puryear
Died Apr 3, 1970
Age: 28 years.
(Gallant FH)

Infant Son of
R. L. & M. J. Askins
Dec 17, 1898
Jan 20, 1899

William H. McAlister
Feb 15, 1821
Apr 10, 1879
& wife
Virginia D. McWhirter
McAlister
Dec 30, 1831
Jun 27, 1901

Mrs. N. C. Stone, Daughter
of George A. McWhirter
Nov 21, 1826
Mar 13, 1879

Hugh McAlister
1888-1919
&
Daisy McAlister
1884-1942

Opal McAlister Duhon,
Daughter of
Hugh & Daisy McAlister
1911-1957

Billy Steger, Son of
Opal McAlister Duhon
1927-1934

Virginia May Spray
Sep 18, 1926
Jul 29, 1927

R. N., Son of
P. G. & N. E. Smith
Aug 27, 1883
Dec 29, 1883

J. C., Son of
P. G. & N. E. Smith
Nov 3, 1880
Oct 10, 1881

E. J., wife of
H. H. Floyd
Age: 75 years.
(no dates)

M. I. M.
(no dates, fieldstone)

W. D. Smith
Feb 3, 1873
Jun 7, 1896

P. G. Smith
Aug 9, 1841
Sep 3, 1897

Nancy E., wife of
P. G. Smith
Jun 10, 1844
Nov 16, 1908

John T. Davis
1887-1943

Katie Copeland Jacobs Davis
1891-1956
(Gallant FH)

Infant of
Mr. & Mrs. J. T. Davis
B&D Apr 26, 1923

Shomer ___ Davis
Oct 11, 1926
Mar 13, 1927
(stone in bad shape)

Allie Bunnd (Bunn)
1884-1939

T. W. Bunn
1879-1955

Lillie D. Parish
Jul 4, 1880
Mar 4, 1917

John Beard
1857-1936

Maudie A. Beard
1902-1936

Absolem Beard
1810-Jan 16, 1886
Age: 76 years.

Sarah E. Beard
Mar 11, 1829
Jan 3, 1911

Henry Spray
& his wife
Mary Ann Spray
(no dates)
&
W. J. Spray (no dates)
& his wife
Mary A. Spray
Dec 3, 1859
Jan 18, 1877
&
Mandy, wife of
Andy Kincade
(no dates)
&
William E. Kincade
Apr 30, 1874
Jun 11, 1894
&
Infant Daughter
(no dates)

Eli Spray
Feb 17, 1850
Mar 6, 1921
&
Milla J. Spray
Jan 9, 1858
(no date)

Sarah E. Spray
Died Jun 16, 1881
Age: (not given)

Robert Spray
(no dates)

J. W. Spray
Feb 16, 1881
Jun 10, 1912

Lucinda, wife of
James Spray
Dec 22, 1827
May 15, 1900

TAFT QUADRANGLE

Lydia H. Baker
Nov 25, 1843
May 19, 1907

L. D. Daniel
Died Oct 8, 1909
Age: 86 years.

Mary E., wife of
L. D. Daniel
May 14, 1834
Jun 21, 1906

Silas Swinford
1883-1952
(Wilson FH)

Tishie, wife of
S. S. Swinford
Feb   1881
Dec 20, 1909

James Chester L., Son of
J. E. & C. Daniel
Jul 11, 1905
Jun 16, 1907

George K. Turner
Aug 27, 1853
(no date)
&
Elizabeth J. Turner
Mar 24, 1854
Jan 20, 1916

Roy Jean
1909-1913

Edman F. Jean
1845-1909
&
Sinthe M. Jean
1854-(no date)

Jim Griffin
Died May 15, 1918
Age: about 41 years.

Orbern Noblin, Son of
A. M. & Fanny L. Jean
Jul 3, 1910
Apr 29, 1916

Thomas Grady, Son of
J. T. & F. L. Newbern
Aug 16, 1893
May 1, 1912

Dollie Wise, wife of
Arney M. Jean
1879-Feb 21, 1908

Joseph Herman, Son of
A. R. & Dollie Jean
Oct 4, 1904
Jan 8, 1906

Sallie May, Daughter of
S. A. & Gurtie Jean
Oct 12, 1903
Jun 23, 1905

Clara F. Olsen
1900-1952

Gordon Flynt
1903-1928

Pete Flynt
1868-1937
&
Ellen Flynt
1869-1945

Zelma Lee, Daughter of
Harry & Mamie Smith
Jul 5, 1913
Dec 14, 1918

Willie E. Scott
1870-1951
(Wilson FH)

Will Scruggs
1872-1933

Minnie W. Scruggs
1872-1955
(Gallant FH)

J. S. Sims
May 27, 1872
Feb 10, 1932

Margaret Coplin, wife of
J. S. Sims
Apr 16, 1876
Jul 10, 1923

William T. McAlister
Sep 9, 1916
Dec 7, 1931

J. Roy McAlister
Jun 10, 1886
Sep 14, 1920
&
L. Dona McAlister
Apr 7, 1885
Jan 10, 1932

Willa Beard Duckworth
1893-1934

Benjamin P. Beard
Died Apr 20, 1934
Age: 8? (gone)
(Huntsville, AL FH)

Thomas H. Beard
Sep 14, 1860
Dec 21, 1928

Nellie Owens
Jun 17, 1918
Jun 1, 1932

Lenard Gale Owens
Oct 17, 1915
Oct 11, 1916
&
Robert Anderson Owens
Nov 6, 1922
Feb 20, 1924

Robert C. Cowan
1865-1943
&
Effie J. Cowan
1865-1938

Alva Lee Flynt
1891-1932
& wife
Ella Mae Flynt
1894-1943

Silas M. Hopkins
Died Jan 26, 1918
Age: 63 years.

Lila McMillan Hopkins Moore
Jul 16, 1879
Apr 19, 1966

Claude Hopkins
1892-1932

Bill Scruggs
(no dates)
&
Clif Scruggs
(no dates)

J. E. Stephens
Sep 7, 1917
Mar 8, 1936

William L. Stephens
1886-1934
&
Emma H. Stephens
1890-1957

J. E. Stephens
Jun 27, 1882
Jan 26, 1931

Exie B. Stephens
1891-1963

Kenneth Stephens
May 18, 1853
Sep 10, 1913

Julia A. Stephens
Sep 20, 1855
Jul 26, 1934

Dan Swinford
1851-May 15, 1913

Mamie A. Swinford
1890-1917

Rena Daniel, wife of
Dan Swinford
1853-Jan 4, 1913

E. W. Daniel
1873-1935

Lue Dillions, wife of
E. W. Daniel
Nov 22, 1870
Feb 22, 1914

James P. Swinford
Jul 15, 1873
Dec 4, 1939

Vena Moyers, wife of
J. P. Swinford
Jun 30, 1874
Oct 7, 1926

Ernest Edward, Son of
Mr. & Mrs. J. W. Mullins
Apr 12, 1930
Mar 7, 1934

John R. Mullins
Oct 11, 1842
Jun 6, 1923
&
Florinda A. Mullins
Apr 1, 1866
Feb 11, 1934

J. D. Mullins
1934-1935

Billie Mullins
1936-1936

____ Ann Mullins
Apr 30, 1940
(dates gone)

Tera Daniel Swinford
1880-1925

Creamell, Daughter of
A. J. & Lucile Beech
Nov 5, 1927
Dec 27, 1927

Lucile, wife of
A. J. Beech
May 29, 1906
Jan 22, 1928

Barbria, wife of
Sam Jones
Aug 6, 1878
May 5, 1906

Mary Spray
May   1849
Apr 26, 1925
Age: 76y, 11m.

John Daniel
Nov 9, 1862
Jul 14, 1924

C. C. Pittman, wife of
John Daniel
Feb 1, 1841
Nov 30, 1914

Monie M., Daughter of
John & C. C. Daniel
Jan 30, 1892
Nov 9, 1905

TAFT QUADRANGLE

Lular P., Daughter of
John & C. C. Daniel
Mar 28, 1885
Jul 30, 1896

Alva C., Son of
John & C. C. Daniel
B&D Jan 20, 1890

Miss T. L. Watkins *
Died Jul 13, 1895
Age: 21 years.

Infant Son * of
William & Rainey Hambrick
Died Aug 8, 1895
Age: (not given)

Gladys Gertrude,* Daughter
of Mrs. Ella Mullins
Died May 25, 1896
Age: 1y, 4m.

Rutha Ethel,* Daughter of
Mr. & Mrs. B. F. Marshall
Died Jul 12, 1898
Age: 4m, 16d.

Infant * of
Thomas & Jennie Yell
Died Feb 13, 1906
Age: 6m.

Infant * of
Liggett & Piney Malone
Died Aug 6, 1898
Age: (not given)

Infant * of
Mr. & Mrs. B. F. Fannin
Died Feb 6, 1908
Age: (not given)

Miss Ella Abbott *
Died Jun 16, 1908
Age: 45 years.

Mary Lou,* Daughter of
Marion & Mollie Sims
Died Sep 16, 1898
Age: 1y, 10m.

Mrs. Martha Abbott *
Died Jan 2, 1900
Age: 65 years.

William Ratley *
Died Nov 27, 1909
Age: Old Age
Father of Mrs.
William Williams

Miss Tennie Bates *
Died Sep 15, 1908
Age: (not given)

Miss Mattie,* Daughter of
Isham Smith
Died Aug 10, 1891
Age: 28 years.

Mrs. F. A. Mullins
1866-1934

Gracie McConn Pearson
Mullins
Oct 10, 1885
Jan 8, 1929

Infant * of
Frank & Ellis Moyers
Died Feb 1897
Age: 3m.

Child * of
John Meeks
Died Sep 15, 1895
Age: 5m.

Mrs. Sarah Bond *
Died Apr 11, 1897
Age: 50y, 17d.

Joel Mullins *
Died Jan 11, 1896
Age: 24 years.

Infant * of
Mr. & Mrs. S. L. Daniel
Died Feb 2, 1911
Age: (not given)

Mrs. Charles R. Locker *
Died May 10, 1914
Age: 42 years.

Mrs. Rebecca McMillen *
Died Dec 15, 1910
Age: 74 years.
Left a Daughter,
Mrs. Rolfe Higgins.

Daughter * of
W. J. Bunn
Died May 12, 1907
Age: 9 years.

J. W. Billings *
Died Jul 29, 1916
Age: 65 years.

Dovie Ann,* Daughter of
Mr. & Mrs. William Hunter
Died Dec 3, 1898
Age: 3y, 11m.

Mrs. Lottie,* wife of
Will Baker
Born in Bedford Co., Tenn.
Oct 1872
Died Oct 12, 1908

George W. Colbert *
Died Aug 24, 1906
Age: 28 years.

Mrs. Netney Smith *
Married Isham Smith
Jun 22, 1837
Died Jul 17, 1900
Age: 78 years.

Mildred Harrison
1924-1930

Margaret M. Harrison
1885-1935

James M. Harrison
1881-1956

Monroe,* Son of
David Floyd
Died Aug 24, 1897
Age: (not given)

Mrs. Margaret,* wife of
Thomas Lock & mother of
B. F. Marshall
Died Sep 19, 1895
Age: 75 years.

Chester Marvin,* Son of
John & Martha Daniel
Died Sep 23, 1895
Age: 1y, 5m.

Mrs. L. P.,* wife of
T. L. Malone
Died Sep 21, 1898
Age: 19y, 10m.

Infant * of
Mrs. Ira Davis
Died Oct 16, 1914
Age: (not given)

A. M. Simmons *
Died Dec 24, 1915
Age: 83 years.

Mrs. Annie,* wife of
Fred Baker
Died Jan 8, 1916
Age: 18 years.

Mrs. Pearl,* wife of
C. A. Bird
Died Mar 9, 1916
Age: 32y, 1m, 19d.

Bradie Gray *
Died Apr 22, 1916
Age: 42 years.

Mrs. Amanda,* widow of
John H. Kay
Died Jun 7, 1916
Age: 77y, 5m, 19d.

John Ezell,* Son of
Mr. & Mrs. Claud Bird
Died Jun 17, 1916
Age: (not given)

Earl,* Son of
I. H. & Hester Smith
Died Jul 17, 1900
Age: 2 years & 3 months.

Barnie,* Son of
Mr. & Mrs. W. J. Smith
Died Jul 6, 1900
Age: 4 years.

Sallie Rhodes
Oct 17, 1879
Feb 17, 1946

J. W. Cannon
1878-1938

Nancy Cannon
1881-1949
(Raby FH)

Infant,* of
John & Sallie Rodes
Died Nov 20, 1897
Age: (not given)

Mrs. Sarah Wells *
Wife of A. Wells
Died Apr 17, 1898
Age: 78 years.

Mrs. Anderson Ivey *
Died Dec 5, 1895
Age: 67y, 6m.

Infant * of
Mr. & Mrs. A. L. Barnes
Died Jun 1, 1907
Age: 1 year.

Mrs. Manda Harris *
Died Jan 22, 1917
Age: 78 years.

Mrs. Douglas Burton *
Died Nov 12, 1906
Age: 30 years.

Infant Daughter * of
Wiley Bunn
Died Apr 30, 1907
Age: (not given)

Daughter * of
Mr. & Mrs. Doc Sandlin
Died Apr 1, 1909
Age: 10 years.

Infant * of
Mr. & Mrs. John Daniel
Died Oct 31, 1899
Age: (not given)

Annie May,* Daughter of
Mr. & Mrs. James J.
Bedwell
Died Jun 23, 1905
Age: 2 years.

Mrs. Susan A. *
Married in 1880 to
W. J. Lively
Died Sep 10, 1905
Age: 67 years.

May,* Daughter of
J. H. Smith
Died Jul 12, 1900
Age: 5 years.

TAFT QUADRANGLE

Alma Annie,* Daughter of
E. G. & E. B. Burton
Died Feb 11, 1901
Age: 10 months.

William K. Boyd *
Died Mar 9, 1901
Age: 76 years.

Nancy A. Colbert *
Died Aug 17, 1901
Age: 90 years.

Mrs. Tilda,* wife of
Robert McMillen
Died Apr 19, 1902
Age: 77 years.

John T. Sledge *
Married in 1863 to
Elizabeth Anderson
Died Apr 22, 1903
Age: 69 years.

Lewis Colbert *
Married in 1880 to
Jane Swinford
Died Jul 23, 1903
Age: (not given)

Mrs. Pearl,* wife of
C. A. Bird
Died Mar 9, 1916
Age: 32y, 1m, 19d.
Left Husband & 5 children.

Many unmarked graves.

Infant Son * of
John & Nancy Cannon
B&D Jun 28, 1904

Annie Lee,* Daughter of
J. M. & M. E. Fuller
Died Sep 18, 1904
Age: 3y, 11m, 23d.

Miss Effie,* Daughter of
W. J. Malone
Died Apr 27, 1905
Age: 14y, 1m, 1d.

Mrs. Mason *
Died Jul 26, 1905
Age: 56 years.

Rosco Hunter,* Son of
Mr. & Mrs. William Daniel
Died Oct 15, 1902
Age: 4 years.

Jesse Edgar,* Son of
E. G. & Alice Burton
Died Dec 27, 1902
Age: 6 years.

Moses Ivey *
Died Mar 4, 1903
Age: (not given)

Mrs. Charles R. Locker *
Died May 10, 1914
Age: 42 years.

Isham Smith *
Married Jimenter Olmer
in 1837
Died Jul 18, 1903
Age: 81y, 7m.

Mrs. Eliza Mathews *
Died Nov 13, 1890
Age: 52 years.

Loaton Cannon *
Died Mar 7, 1895
Age: 35 years.

Miss Amanda Jane Spray *
Died Oct 10, 1891
Age: 48 years.

Mr. Malone *
Died Jan 3, 1893
Age: Old Age.

Pryor,* Son of
Mrs. Collie Womack
Died Jan 4, 1895
Age: 8 years.

Mollie,* Daughter of
Sam & Ella Moyers
Died May 23, 1894
Age: 1y, 5m.

Mrs. Bertie,* wife of
O. F. Smith
Died May 15, 1914
Age: 24 years.
Left aged Father & Mother,
her husband & 3 brothers.

Mrs. Ollie Wells,* wife
of E. B. Taylor
Died Jun 8, 1893
Age: 22 years.

Infant * of
J. M. & Amanda Spray
Died Sep 7, 1895
Age: (not given)

Johnny,* Son of
T. Y. & Mattie Key
Died Feb 2, 1896
Age: 2y, 6m.

George Mason *
Died Apr 13, 1897
Age: 68 years.

Mrs. Myrtle Gray*
Married in 1898 to
Charles Spray
Died Apr 5, 1899
Age: 22y, 3m.

Miss Clarry Ann Fellow *
Died Mar 29, 1899
Age: 19y, 4m.

Miss Martha Land *
Died Jul 20, 1899
Age: 60 years.

Virgil Raymond,* Son of
I. H. Smith
Died Aug 24, 1914
Age: (not given)

* *

BUTLER CEMETERY

LOCATION: At Coldwater.

James R. Butler
Jul 15, 1831
Jan 11, 1863
A Confederate Soldier
Co I 8th Tenn Reg.

Nancy Ables, wife of
J. R. Butler
1833-1854

Infant of
J. R. & N. A. Butler
(no dates)

* *

BRYAN-HOVIS CEMETERY

LOCATION: One and one half miles NE of Coldwater on the
north side of a Dead End Road, east of Steadman Branch.

Willie E. Bryan
Dec 26, 1866
Aug 16, 1896

A. N. Bryan
Feb 7, 1832
Jul 10, 1917
&
F. A. Bryan
Aug 11, 1832
(no date)

Rufus H. Bryan
Jul 13, 1852
Oct 21, 1906

Tula May Bryan
May 14, 1892
Feb 8, 1904

Hallie Nora Bryan
Jan 13, 1887
Oct 26, 1890

A. B.
(no dates, fieldstone)

A. L. Bradley
Died Jun 20, 1909
Age: 41 years.

Nancy C. Childress
Died Aug 6, 1897
Age: about 100 years.

Dazy Elis (Ellis)
Died Mar 18, 1888
Age: (not given)

Mary Alas, Daughter of
J. C. & S. D. Cowen
Aug 13, 1894
Oct 16, 1898

W. L. Hicks
Nov 20, 1854
Aug 18, 1880

TAFT QUADRANGLE

Ernie, Son of
R. W. & Elizabeth Hicks
Sep 18, 1882
Nov 7, 1908

Martha C. Hodge
Aug 27, 1827
Sep 12, 1901

E. G. Hodge
Jan 5, 1853
Jul 4, 1917

Robbie Hardin
Nov 2, 1891
Jan 7, 1900

Mary L. Hardin
Dec 18, 1898
Jan 16, 1899

Bennie Hardin
Sep 25, 1888
Feb 28, 1890

Winnie Hardin
Died Nov 6, 1882
Age: (not given)

M. D. C. Hardin
Jan 5, 1850
Dec 25, 1904
Married Dec 9, 1873
to T. B. Hardin

Samuel H. Hovis
Feb 25, 1864
Oct 4, 1917

J. P. Hovis
Apr 1, 1849
Sep 16, 1894

Levi Hovis
Oct 15, 1807
Aug 7, 1896

Rachel Hovis
Jun 5, 1817
Sep 20, 1887

Robert Hovis
Jul 10, 1860
Feb 11, 1879

B. B. Bryan *
Married 1st Mary Hicks
in 1842, Married 2nd
Eliza Smith in 1881
Died Apr 16, 1895
Age: 74 years.

Louisana, wife of
E. D. Hicks
Jan 8, 1827
Mar 2, 1891

Edmond D. Hicks
Sep 4, 1825
Oct 3, 1900

Infant Daughter of
W. L. & N. A. Hicks
B&D Nov 6, 1880

R. L. Martin
Oct 1, 1810
Jan 22, 1881

L. L. C. Neece
Aug 22, 1840
Feb 20, 1916
& wife
Fannie A. Neece
Jun 20, 1847
Jan 28, 1888
Age: 35y, 2m, 8d.

Mrs. M. L., wife of
L. L. C. Neece
Jul 17, 1846
Nov 18, 1907

Nannie, Daughter of
L. L. C. & M. C.(L) Neece
Sep 1, 1885
Sep 20, 1885

Emma S. Laws, Daughter of
L. L. C. & Fannie A. Neece
Dec 12, 1866
Aug 2, 1893

F. E. Neece
May 15, 1873
Sep 23, 1905
Married Susie Martin
Jan 29, 1901

J. W. Pool
Jan 18, 1825
Jul 15, 1897
&
Mary Ann B. Pool
Sep 16, 1835
Mar 10, 1897

Thomas Hardin *
Died Nov 24, 1902
Age: (not given)

Ida May, Daughter of
J. S. & S. A. Rhodes
Apr 24, 1884
Feb 23, 1885

J. Y. Reynolds
May 12, 1846
Sep 22, 1916

Mary C. Strong
Apr 22, 1863
Oct 5, 1900

Mamie Strong
Oct 11, 1893
Oct 16, 1893
&
Lillie M. Strong
Mar 8, 1883
Jul 5, 1884
&
Brown Strong
May 17, 1886
Oct 2, 1890

Clark Bright, Son of
M. L. & A. E. Stedman
Aug 17, 1872
Apr 2, 1889

A. E., wife of
M. L. Stedman
Dec 22, 1839
Jun 25, 1901

M. L. Stedman
Jan 2, 1839
Dec 17, 1918

Pleasant G.(C) Smith
Aug 14, 1890
Jun 15, 1891

Mary E. Bryant, wife of
O. G. Smith
Dec 26, 1862
Jul 31, 1892

Roy C. Smith
Mar 4, 1886
Mar 20, 1891

Thomas Cowen *
Died Dec 19, 1916
Age: 60 years.

Henry Thornton *
Died Nov 30, 1914
Age: 25 years.

John J. Summerford
May 17, 1841
Sep 8, 1895

Mary E., wife of
John J. Summerford
Jul 13, 1832
Sep 19, 1905

Dock, Son of
W. T. & Allie Thornton
Feb 28, 1897
Died in France
Oct 13, 1918
Co G 57 Pioneer Inf

Jim C. Vaughn
Died Nov 22, 1961
Age: 93 years.

Cordie Vaughn
1872-1937

Robby Vaughn
1912-1931

Many unmarked graves.

William Turner *
Died Jun 21, 1901
Age: 80y, 6m.

Lucile,* Daughter of
J. H. & Maggie Campbell
Died Aug 5, 1907
Age: 1 year.

William Bryant *
Died Aug 16, 1896
Age: 28 years.

W. L. Hurlson *
Died Aug 21, 1911
Age: 76 years.

Clarence,* Son of
H. T. & Cynthia Woodard
Died Nov 12, 1898
Age: 1y, 10m, 2d.

Jack Cowen *
Died Mar 1914
Age: 14 years.

Esq. Rice W. Hicks *
Died Oct 29, 1916
Age: 62 years.

* *

TAFT QUADRANGLE

PITTS CEMETERY

LOCATION: One and one fourth miles SW of Molino on top of a ridge.

Several unmarked graves.   Several fieldstones, no insc.

* *

PITTS CEMETERY

LOCATION: One mile SW of Molino on the east side of Twitty Hollow Road.

R. K. Pitts
Jul 24, 1822
May 29, 1867
&
Elizabeth Ann Pitts
Oct 22, 1827
Dec 25, 1897

L. L. Pitts
Mar 14, 1852
Oct 16, 1869
Age: 17y, 7m, 2d.

Infant Son of
F. A. & M. F. Pitts
Nov 6, 1878
Dec 8, 1878

C. A. Pitts
(no dates)
Age: 7y, 3m, 4d.

T. J. Pitts
(no dates)
Age: 2y, 4m, 22d.

R. H. Pitts
(no dates)
Age: 1y, 3m, 15d.

C. A. McGee
May 24, 1849
Mar 29, 1873

------ McGee
1892-1893
(broken)

R. A. McGee
Oct 21, 1871
Mar 8, 1873

M. E. McGee
Feb 5, 1870
Feb 20, 1872

Several unmarked graves.

PITTS CEMETERY

LOCATION: Two miles SSE of Molino and one half mile NNW of Yukon.

Pamphilia A., wife of
J. C. Lincoln
Sep 11, 1850
May 7, 1884

Susan C. & Oscar M.,
Children of
J. C. & P. A. Lincoln
(no dates)
Age: 9 days & 1 year
respectively.

John M. Pitts
Sep 16, 1862
Mar 13, 1881

Many unmarked graves.

James L. Pitts
Mar 9, 1823
Feb 9, 1875

Many fieldstones,
no inscriptions.

* *

PROSPERITY CHURCH CEMETERY

LOCATION: At Prosperity A. R. P. Church at Yukon.

Lizzie A. Neece
Jun 7, 1869
Sep 11, 1880

C. L. H.
(no dates, fieldstone)

Martha E., Daughter of
W. W. & L. J. Templeton
May 25, 1853
Jan 7, 1876

Catharine T., Daughter of
James G. & Martha C.
Carithers
 Died Jul 15, 1853
Age: 5 years.

Martha L. Carithers
Jul 5, 1846
Dec 31, 1856

B. C.
(footstone)

William P., Son of
W. W. & L. J. Templeton
Nov 25, 1861
Jun 25, 1865

Lucinda J., wife of
W. W. Templeton
Apr 6, 1833
Mar 27, 1868

Mary M., Daughter of
W. W. & L. J. Templeton
Nov 7, 1856
Oct 6, 1857

Rachel, wife of
W. D. Good
1822-1862
Age: 40 years.

Mary E. Beech
May 1, 1837
Nov 9, 1891

H. T. Hayes
Oct 27, 1846
Jul 20, 1890
&
S. A. Hayes
Apr 23, 1853
Aug 21, 1897

John S. Foster
Apr 30, 1832
Feb 3, 1859

John D. Stewart
Apr 6, 1816
Sep 28, 1844
Age: 28y, 5m, 22d.

Robert Stewart
Mar 4, 1794
Oct 7, 1839
Age: 45y, 7m, 3d.

William Bryson Stewart
Apr 29, 1827
Sep 12, 1839
Age: 12y, 4m, 14d.

Mary L. Stewart
Mar 26, 1825
Sep 19, 1839
Age: 14y, 5m, 24d.

Jesse Morton
Jul 22, 1811
Aug 11, 1850

Samuel Sloan
Born in South Carolina
Aug 6, 1781
Died Oct 13, 1859

John A. Smith
Mar 6, 1850
May 23, 1858

TAFT QUADRANGLE

John Smith
Jun 3, 1804
Sep 23, 1884
Age: 80y, 3m, 20d.

Matilda, Consort of
John Smith
Mar 22, 1810
Sep 6, 1869

Columbus Smith
Mar 4, ----
Jun --, 1838
(dates gone)

Eliza Smith
Dec 22, 1847
Jul 26, 1849

Emaline Stephens
Mar 4, 1822
May   1834

John M. Stephens
Sep 4, 1818
Sep   1843

Catharine Stephens
Died Sep 4, 1833
Age: 46 years.

George H. Stephens
Jan 31, 1820
Sep   1843

Margaret Hodge
Died Jun 16, 1844
Age: 67 years.

William Caughran
Died Mar 14, 1840
Age: 54 years.

Iva Cordelia, Daughter of
W. P. & M. J. Galloway
Died Mar 26, 1878
Age: 1m, 7d.

Mary Etta, Daughter of
W. P. & M. J. Galloway
Died Jan 10, 1878
Age: 3y, 7m, 26d.

Infant Daughter of
J. T. & M. A. Kidd
Died Oct 26, 1868
Age: 24 years.

Joseph Calvin, Son of
W. J. & M. A. Galloway
Died Sep 23, 1864
Age: 3 years.

Eliza J., Daughter of
W. W. & Nancy Galloway
Jun 21, 1816
Oct 11, 1852

William W. Galloway
Died Jul 11, 1840
Age: 48 years

Nancy, Consort of
William W. Galloway
Died May 29, 1855
Age: 71y, 3m, 24d.

Samuel B. Galloway
Died Nov 28, 1854
Age: 30y, 1m, 19d.

Mrs. Jane C. Wilson
Died Mar 22, 1906
Age: 74y, 6m, 2d.

George K. Foster
May 4, 1806
Apr 4, 1837

Mary A. Massengale
Aug 2, 1846
Sep 22, 1846

Jonathan Smith
Died Jul 22, 1845
Age: 35 years.

R. Smith
Died 1845
Age: (not given)

Cyrena Smith
May 4, 1812
Apr 27, 1851

Ralph Smith
A Soldier of The
Revolutionary War
Aug 24, 1763
Nov 3, 1853

Elizabeth Smith
Jul 17, 1768
May 19, 1858

Elizabeth Stewart
Born in County Down,
Scotland, immigrated to
South Carolina at the age
of 12 years, removed to
Tenn. in 1827
Died 1844
Age: 68 years.

Mary, Consort of
George K. Foster
May 24, 1796
Dec 4, 1845

Margaret, wife of
Alexander Wiley
Died Dec 16, 1876
Age: 80 years.

Alexander Wiley
Died Jan 4, 1849
Age: 50 years.

Neil S. Brown
Nov 5, 1848
Oct 3, 1852

Harriet, wife of
R. A. Erwin & Daughter of
Samuel & Amanda Brown
Dec 15, 1828
Feb 25, 1851

Martha A., Daughter of
William & Nancy Stewart
Died Aug 22, 1852
Age: 3y, 8m, 28d.

Dr. William Stewart
Feb 13, 1809
Dec 22, 1895

Nancy, Consort of
Dr. William Stewart
Died Aug 28, 1869
Age: 58 years.

Sarah W. Wilson
Mar 11, 1828
Jun 25, 1906

James A. Wilson
May   1850
Dec 29, 1860

Margaret J. Wilson
Nov 18, 1858
Apr 1, 1860

Twin Babes (no name given)
Age: 9 days old
(Wilson FH)

Alexander W. Wilson
Mar 10, 1854
Jun 26, 1855

Katharine B., Consort of
Saly McCalla
Jan 4, 1826
May 17, 1862

Samuel T. McCalla
Dec 3, 1824
Sep 22, 1873

Manervy Jones, wife of
J. M. McFerran
Mar 30, 1847
Nov 20, 1873

Brown Parkerson, Jr.
Jul 26, 1830
Jul 16, 1863
Age: 32y, 11m, 20d.
C.S.A.

Manson A. S., Son of
O. A. & America Caughran
Jan 24, 1853
Feb 22, 1854
Age: 1y, 27d.

John T., Son of
O. A. & America Caughran
Jun 23, 1864
Aug 10, 1867
Age: 3y, 1m, 18d.

William H. Drennan
Age: 42 years.
(no dates)

Robert L. Drennan
Age: 59 years.
(no dates)

William Walter Burton
Jul 27, 1881
Mar 22, 1959
&
Frances Drennan Burton
Mar 31, 1910

Elizabeth, wife of
R. G. McAnn
May 4, 1804
May 17, 1882

Augustus, Consort of
Sarah Yeager
Oct 15, 1805
Jul 12, 1870
Age: 65y, 8m, 27d.

Mary Ella Stewart Foster
1873-1941

Eliza, wife of
J. P. Stewart
Jul 31, 1840
Oct 3, 1880

Jesse F., Son of
J. P. & Eliza Stewart
Nov 4, 1864
Aug 3, 1880

Hugh Parkinson
Sep 5, 1818
Feb 17, 1904
&
Lucinda Parkinson
Sep 20, 1820
Aug 12, 1910

Martha Bonner Parkinson
Jan 16, 1849
Aug 24, 1939

M. Alice, wife of
H. S. McCalla
Oct 18, 1856
Jan 3, 1884

H. Silas McCalla
1851-1922
&
Mary T. McCalla
1875-1931

Bessie Lou McCalla
1866-1953

John William Watson
May 16, 1907
May 23, 1907

TAFT QUADRANGLE

W. P. Watson
Aug 31, 1855
Nov 12, 1931
&
Ada B. Watson
Dec 23, 1866
May 29, 1952

Martha J., wife of
S. Y McCalla
Dec 16, 1839
Dec 3, 1886

Anna V., Daughter of
J. W. & M. J. Dandridge
Dec 16, 1875
Feb 14, 1888

J. W. Dandridge
Dec 2, 1843
Oct 6, 1883

Mary J., wife of
J. W. Dandridge
Nov 17, 1846
Dec 5, 1922

Ada Parkinson Moore,
Daughter of
James & Mary Parkinson
Nov 15, 1866
Nov 3, 1915

Mary Pinkerton, wife of
James Parkinson
Dec 31, 1838
Oct 20, 1906

James Parkinson
Jun 24, 1834
Sep 18, 1883
Age: 49y, 2m, 24d.

Dr. J. M. Stewart
1836-1929
&
Mary E. Stewart
1862-1933

J. L. Stewart
Co C 41st Tenn Reg.
C.S.A.
Died Dec 26, 1900
Age: 66 years.
& wife
Hattie Winburn Stewart
Apr 8, 1857
Sep 24, 1893

Henry M. Stewart
Aug 26, 1840
May 6, 1905 C.S.A.
& wife
Josephine Stewart
Mar 16, 1845
Sep 16, 1910

Elizabeth A. Stewart, wife
of A. J. Davis
May 4, 1842
Feb 4, 1907

O. Sidney Stewart
1851-1924

Sallie L. Stewart
1874-Jun 27, 1865

Oscar S. Stewart
Jul 31, 1877
Oct 20, 1923

J. Boyce Stewart
Dec 7, 1844
Apr 28, 1939
& wife
N. Josie Sloan Stewart
Nov 24, 1846
Mar 1, 1917

Samuel Moore Parkinson
Jan 28, 1853
Jan 14, 1909
&
Adelia Jamison Parkinson
Nov 25, 1855
Jun 2, 1938

M. Olevia Moore, wife of
John R. Bruce
Aug 18, 1882
May 15, 1903

Freddie Bryson Stewart
Dec 21, 1890
Mar 30, 1912

Clara Eslick Stewart
May 22, 1917
Jun 13, 1918

Amanda Sanders
Mar 23, 1877
Jul 23, 1898
Age: 21y, 4m.

Robert Harrison Bailey
Jun 18, 1874
Oct 29, 1939

Frances Blair Bailey
Dec 7, 1876
Mar 26, 1950

Terrell B. Bailey
Jul 8, 1903
Jun 10, 1936

Margaret Jane, wife of
Byers Blair
Jul 18, 1841
Jan 4, 1903

Palina E. Cole, wife of
J. C. Pepper
Oct 23, 1873
Nov 15, 1895

B. T. Cole
1842-1922
&
Mary R. Cole
1847-1907

Joseph Y. Lock
Born at Blanche, Tenn.
Jan 4, 1866
Died in Birmingham, Ala.
Feb 11, 1887
Age: 21y, 1m, 7d.

Joseph H. Lock
Died Jul 4, 1911
Age: 83 years.
&
Jennet Lock
Died Oct 26, 1911
Age: 88y, 11m, 8d.

James M. Locke
Apr 20, 1858
Apr 29, 1915

Theresa Robertson, wife of
M. A. Locke
Oct 24, 1861
Sep 8, 1887

Lillie, Daughter of
W. E. & Kate Bryan
May 25, 1895
Jul 15, 1898

Willa A., Son of
W. E. & Kate Bryan
May 12, 1896
Jul 20, 1898

Susan C., wife of
J. L. Robertson
May 26, 1855
Feb 23, 1884
Age: 23y, 8m, 27d.

Nora J. Cole, wife of
P. A. Robertson
Sep 10, 1870
Oct 27, 1896

Mary Cole Twitty
Jul 21, 1875
Apr 7, 1961

Mary B. Allen
Jun 17, 1901
Jul 18, 1922

Lillie A. Allen
Nov 19, 1896
Sep 20, 1964

Frances M. Allen
Jan 7, 1871
Mar 30, 1948

Minnie B. Allen
Nov 30, 1869
Sep 16, 1913

George E. Allen
Oct 17, 1897
Apr 20, 1900

Francis G. Allen
Aug 10, 1899
May 6, 1900

Alleen C. Allen
Jul 31, 1908
Apr 16, 1911

Annie Lee, Daughter of
D. C. & Emma Moore
Oct 24, 1898
Jun 23, 1900

Emma, wife of
D. C. Moore
Dec 25, 1878
Nov 17, 1915

D. Cowan Moore
Jan 22, 1871
Mar 3, 1926

Hiram Sandlin
Oct 18, 1865
Mar 17, 1918

Josie Moore, wife of
Hiram Sandlin
Sep 14, 1869
Mar 24, 1902

Isaac B. Moore
Jul 21, 1838
Apr 21, 1923

Culpernia Bearden, wife
of I. B. Moore
Sep 20, 1835
Aug 7, 1900

Martha Moore
May 18, 1833
Sep 20, 1901
Age: 68y, 4m, 2d.

John Neaves
Dec 25, 1813
Jan 2, 1896
Age: 82y, 7d.

Nancy, wife of
John Neaves
Feb 16, 1819
May 22, 1886
Age: 67y, 1m, 6d.

Docia, wife of
J. A. Hayes
Mar 10, 1857
Jul 29, 1891

Grady, Son of
J. A. & T. H. Hayes
Aug 21, 1890
Aug 13, 1891

Myrtle, Daughter of
R. C. & E. A. Templeton
Feb 23, 1893
Aug 24, 1896

Willie, Son of
R. C. & E. A. Templeton
Jul 27, 1896
Jun 18, 1898

TAFT QUADRANGLE

Robert Hayden Templeton
Oct 1, 1898
Sep 21, 1924
&
Calvin McCullough
Templeton
Oct 30, 1897

William Templeton
Died Mar 13, 1902
Age: 81 years.
C.S.A.

Rufus C. Templeton
1858-1932
&
Lizzie Pitts Templeton
1860-1935

Mamie Templeton
1887-1963
&
Beulah Templeton
1885-
&
Birdie Templeton
1891-

Milton N. Rowell
Jan 6, 1839
Oct 8, 1927
&
Nancy Martin Rowell
Aug 16, 1844
Dec 14, 1899

William H. Rowell
Aug 10, 1901
Feb 27, 1902

William H. Strong
Oct 30, 1898
Oct 23, 1899

John Monroe Strong
Nov 11, 1843
Jun 2, 1904

Louisa Gleghorn, wife of
J. M. Strong
Apr 20, 1856
Nov 15, 1909

James M. Strong
Aug 5, 1852
Jul 18, 1893

Isabella, wife of
G. R. Allen
Dec 11, 1835
Oct 16, 1894

G. R. Allen
Mar 2, 1833
Jan 9, 1907

Nora J., Daughter of
G. R. & I. Allen
Dec 25, 1859
Dec 27, 1897

Nina Estelle Allen
Jun 24, 1876
Jun 18, 1904
Age: 27y, 11m, 24d.

Sallie Elizabeth Allen
Jun 7, 1874
Feb 21, 1906
Age: 31y, 8m, 14d.

S. G. Allen
Oct 18, 1863
Sep 11, 1924
&
T. M. Allen
Aug 27, 1865
Jun 4, 1933
"Allen Brothers"

J. R. Allen
Jun 29, 1867
Dec 26, 1899

Asbury J. Wright
Died Sep 23, 1896
Age: 54 years.
&
James Witcher, Son of
A. J. & M. A. Wright
Died Aug 17, 1896
Age: 23 years.

L. C. McCowan
Mar 24, 1850
Sep 28, 1897

Beatrice, wife of
L. C. McCowan
Jan 23, 1856
Nov 10, 1937

Mary Bonnie, Daughter of
L. C. & B. O. McCowan
Apr 20, 1892
Jun 13, 1894

Ada, wife of
Andrew Hentz
Jan 1, 1871
Jun 13, 1899

Eula Ann Hentz
Feb 3, 1897
Oct 19, 1901

Cynthia C., Daughter of
M. N. & N. A. Rowell
Apr 8, 1879
Nov 29, 1890

Autie May, Daughter of
I. R. & N. A. Pitts
Feb 3, 1895
Jan 9, 1898

N. A., Daughter of
I. R. & N. A. Pitts
Jun 23, 1896
Aug 4, 1896

I. R. Pitts
May 1, 1865
Sep 29, 1930

N. A., wife of
I. R. Pitts
Aug 7, 1870
Jun 29, 1896

Nancy C., wife of
R. F. Pitts
Jun 15, 1874
Sep 29, 1890

Mary A. Hayes, wife of
R. G. Hayes & Daughter of
J. & M. Leatherwood
May 7, 1859
Oct 20, 1880

Lena Brown, Daughter of
R. G. & F. A. Hayes
Jul 6, 1895
May 20, 1896

John B. Hayes
Aug 16, 1859
Jan 31, 1895

Sarah E. Hayes
May 6, 1843
Oct 31, 1897

Minnie, wife of
Dr. L. Y. Hayes
Nov 23, 1876
Apr 23, 1901
& Daughter
Mary E. Hayes
Jul 5, 1900
May 7, 1901

Dr. L. Y. Hayes
Feb 12, 1867
May 18, 1909

Lawysm Nathaniel, Son of
Dr. L. Y. & L. J. Hayes
May 1, 1907
Aug 24, 1908

Jesse Leatherwood
Nov 7, 1820
Oct 8, 1901

Malinda G., wife of
Jesse Leatherwood
Oct 21, 1827
Aug 20, 1899

J. A. Leatherwood
Nov 8, 1847
Jul 31, 1923

Nancy A., wife of
J. A. Leatherwood
Dec 4, 1853
Feb 5, 1908

William Floyd McCowan
Feb 13, 1890
Apr 15, 1948

Lura Lee Twitty McCowan
Feb 23, 1892

Albert Lee McCowan
Born Mar 8, 1909
Homer Douglas McCowan
Born Sep 1, 1913
Floyd Ray McCowan
Born Nov 17, 1925
Children of William Floyd
& Lura Lee Twitty McCowan

Mary Pernie McFerrin
1879-1961

James Erskin McFerrin
May 14, 1903
Feb 20, 1904
&
Estella Pauline McFerrin
Nov 27, 1898
Feb 20, 1904

William Otie McFerrin
1871-1950
&
Henrietta McFerrin
1875-1904

C. Astor Moore
1889-1944
&
W. Brown Moore
1859-1938

Nannie A., wife of
Dr. J. D. Bryant
Died Jun 1, 1896
Age: 26y, 8m, 12d.

Clara Moore, Daughter of
Dr. J. D. & N. A. Bryant
Nov 8, 1895
Oct 30, 1896

Mary A., wife of
J. E. Watson
Sep 13, 1864
Aug 20, 1890
Age: 25y, 11m, 7d.

Cora, Daughter of
J. E. & M. A. Watson
Nov 1, 1884
Mar 23, 1905

J. E. Flynn
Oct 27, 1850
Dec 1, 1897

Mrs. Mary P. Flynn
Jan 16, 1849
Aug 1, 1914

TAFT QUADRANGLE

Exzene, Daughter of
H. A. & B. J. Flynn
Aug 6, 1871
Sep 2, 1888

Ada, Daughter of
H. A. & B. J. Flynn
Jul 1, 1886
Sep 29, 1890

Jones, Son of
H. A. & B. J. Flynn
Mar 10, 1876
Apr 10, 1895

Cary V. Summerford
Apr 2, 1861
Jun 22, 1888

C. T. Summerford
Nov 4, 1864
Dec 7, 1892

A. D. Summerford
Nov 4, 1864
Dec 7, 1892

C. A., wife of
A. D. Summerford
Oct 11, 1874
Mar 23, 1902

Celia A., wife of
James Erwin
Nov 1, 1840
Jul 13, 1899

Gilbert Girdayne, Son of
E. L. & M. A. England
Nov 17, 1899
Jan 9, 1923
Age: 23y, 1m, 22d.

E. L. England
1852-1931

Frances B., wife of
E. L. England
Jan 22, 1855
Dec 22, 1886

Martha Ann Rebecca Plexico,
wife of E. L. England
Dec 16, 1868
Jul 18, 1923
Age: 54y, 7m, 2d.

J. W. Watson
Husband of M. A. Watson
Sep 2, 1829
Oct 16, 1917

Sarah F., wife of
J. W. Watson
Oct 24, 1834
Oct 10, 1889
Age: 54y, 11m, 15d.

Emma C. Bishop
Dec 18, 1866
Dec 29, 1899

James H. Bishop
Jun 3, 1899
Aug 17, 1899

B. M. McCalla
Aug 16, 1847
Mar 26, 1927

Mary L., wife of
B. M. McCalla
Oct 21, 1850
Aug 12, 1901

Clara, Daughter of
B. M. & M. L. McCalla
Sep 19, 1873
Jun 26, 1889

W. C. McCalla
Nov 2, 1871
Aug 27, 1929

Logan Carpenter
Dec 22, 1828
Oct 18, 1902

Mary, wife of
Logan Carpenter
Dec 25, 1828
Mar 17, 1892
Age: 63y, 2m, 22d.

Rossie G. Forbes
1869-1934
&
J. R. Forbes
1858-1931
&
Amanda M. Forbes
1863-1903

Mary E., Infant of
J. R. & R. L. Forbes
Aug 27, 1905
Sep 5, 1905

Charlie, Son of
E. J. & M. M. Rodgers
Oct 30, 1895
May 22, 1897

J. A. Good
May 27, 1871
Nov 3, 1900
Age: 29y, 5m, 6d.

Ethridge, Son of
J. A. & M. E. Good
Jan 9, 1887
Sep 9, 1895

S. T. McCullough
Jul 22, 1824
Jan 6, 1892

Eliza McCullough
Sep 30, 1823
Oct 9, 1898

Mary, wife of
T. M. Sloan
Jun 20, 1848
Dec 25, 1906

Charlie B. Sloan
Jan 9, 1871
Jun 9, 1898

Robert H. Moore
Jul 13, 1865
May 28, 1893

Mary C. E. Jones, Daughter
of Rufus & M. A. Smith
Feb 23, 1865
Aug 20, 1888

John Wesley, Son of
Rufus & M. A. Smith
Aug 13, 1863
Jun 29, 1888

Thomas Clark, Son of
Rufus & M. A. Smith
Mar 10, 1876
Jul 28, 1888

Alma Lee, Son of
Rufus & M. A. Smith
Jun 29, 1871
Aug 18, 1888

Rufus Smith
Sep 27, 1839
Feb 28, 1914
&
Martha A. Smith
Sep 4, 1842
Apr 2, 1939

Sarah E. Henderson
Sep 5, 1860
Sep 19, 1913

Rena, wife of
J. R. Williams & Daughter
of D. M. & M. J. Sanders
Oct 10, 1869
Mar 8, 1897

J. R. Williams
May 7, 1863
Aug 10, 1898

Alice, wife of
J. R. Williams & Daughter
of H. P. & Mary Rowell
Sep 22, 1873
Nov 22, 1889
Age: 16y, 2m.

Allie May, Daughter of
J. R. & R. H. Williams
Dec 19, 1892
Jun 20, 1895

R. M. McLemore
Died Sep 7, 1893
Age: about 58 years.

J. I. Alexander
Jul 3, 1830
(no date)
& wife
Lou M. Alexander
Feb 1, 1836
Jan 15, 1906

J. T. Williams
May 14, 1861
Dec 5, 1913

"Sister"
Beattrice McMullen
Died Oct 24, 1900
Age: (not given)

"Brother"
Thomas Benton Jones
Jan 18, 1863
Jun 26, 1913
& "Sister"
Alice Jones
Jun 9, 1861
Dec 3, 1913

James Grider
Jan 28, 1825
May 14, 1893

Martha Grider
Aug 1, 1840
Mar 10, 1925

James Alexander Boggs
Oct 14, 1850
Oct 9, 1920
&
Anna Donaldson Boggs
Jan 10, 1865
Nov 18, 1898

Martha Jane, wife of
D. M. Sanders
Jan 16, 1841
Jul 4, 1895

S. W. Cole
Sep 23, 1866
Oct 4, 1935

M. L. Cole
Jan 4, 1862
Aug 28, 1943

Lila, wife of
M. L. Cole
Apr 20, 1862
Jun 19, 1889

S. E. Smith
Feb 25, 1864
Feb 2, 1906

Savilla, wife of
S. E. Smith
Jan 6, 1866
Dec 25, 1929

Infant Daughter of
S. E. & M. S. Smith
B&D Aug 2, 1889

TAFT QUADRANGLE

Arthur Washburn
1821-1901
& wife
Mary Hodges Washburn
1822-1901

W. P. Toole
Jan 3, 1821
Dec 19, 1906
Age: 85y, 11m, 16d.

Elizabeth M., wife of
W. P. Toole
May 7, 1827
Oct 31, 1898

Hugh Washington Sheffield
Jan 17, 1826
Mar 29, 1916
&
Elizabeth Bland Sheffield
May 22, 1827
Feb 23, 1899

James A. Hayes
Jan 22, 1853
Aug 6, 1900

M. B. Reynolds
Jan 27, 1877

Thomas A., Son of
G. N. & S. E. Porter
Died May 4, 1904
Age: 27 days.

Nancy Elizabeth, Daughter of
D. C. & D. A. Tucker
Apr 4, 1888
Aug 8, 1914

D. C. Tucker
Oct 18, 1845
Jul 1, 1922

Bessie Butler, wife of
D. C. Tucker
Aug 27, 1852
Jan 15, 1929

Modena, Daughter of
D. C. & D. A. Tucker
Apr 6, 1882
Oct 30, 1899

Nora Pearl, Daughter of
Rev. S. W. & F. O. Bruce
Apr 16, 1889
May 7, 1902

Rev. Silas Wright Bruce
Aug 13, 1844
Apr 22, 1913
& wife
Frances Octavia Pitts Bruce
Jan 2, 1856
Jun 10, 1910

Burr Ranson, Son of
Rev. S. W. & F. O. Bruce
Apr 16, 1893
Jul 24, 1902

W. S. Hayes
Sep 28, 1840
Jul 15, 1914
C.S.A.

Nancy P., wife of
W. S. Hayes
Oct 27, 1844
Nov 8, 1902

Maud P., Daughter of
W. S. & N. P. Hayes
Apr 7, 1881
Nov 12, 1904

Robert Clifford, Son of
W. M. & B. P. Hayes
Sep 15, 1898
Jul 13, 1899

Bulah Pearl, wife of
W. M. Hayes
Sep 27, 1879
Nov 18, 1898

Mary F., Daughter of
Otie & Bula Byers
Nov 10, 1902
Mar 7, 1904

Clarence Byers
Mar 10, 1905
Oct 24, 1905

O. H. Byers
Sep 11, 1874
Apr 7, 1906

Fannie A., wife of
J. E. Duckworth
Sep 23, 1876
Sep 30, 1901

Infant Daughter of
J. E. & Ida Duckworth
Mar 3, 1906
Apr 12, 1906

Infant Daughter of
A. R. & Essie Byers
B&D Oct 27, 1906

Buna May, Daughter of
A. R. & R. L. Commons
Oct 15, 1895
Mar 7, 1904

Afred R. Commons
Jul 15, 1864
Sep 1, 1909
& wife
Rossie Lee Stewart Commons
Oct 20, 1875
Feb 5, 1915

R. W. Stewart
Apr 11, 1842
Oct 18, 1919

Mary E., wife of
R. W. Stewart
Nov 7, 1852
Dec 26, 1903

Maggie, Daughter of
R. W. & M. E. Stewart
Jun 17, 1882
Feb 28, 1899

W. R. Tucker
Nov 18, 1870
Nov 14, 1949

Mary E., wife of
W. R. Tucker
Feb 13, 1879
Dec 12, 1907

Clay N., Son of
W. R. & Mary Tucker
Mar 3, 1901
Sep 5, 1901

Madge, Daughter of
W. M. & D. Reynolds
Mar 19, 1900
Sep 18, 1901

Rubin, Son of
W. M. & D. Reynolds
Mar 11, 1899
Mar 16, 1899

Mabel, Daughter of
W. M. & D. Reynolds
Jun 4, 1894
Oct 29, 1901

Jesse B., Son of
W. M. & D. Reynolds
Feb 11, 1904
Aug 18, 1904

Infant Son of
W. M. & D. Reynolds
B&D Aug 2, 1908

Murrell, Daughter of
W. M. & D. Reynolds
Jul 1, 1915
Sep 24, 1920

H. S. Reese
Oct 9, 1842
Nov 3, 1901

Josie, wife of
H. S. Reese
May 16, 1866
Apr 29, 1928

Minerva Ann Moore
Dec 11, 1839
Jun 7, 1907

Frances Marion Commons
Died Nov 17, 1909
Age: 74y, 1m, 23d.
& wife
Nancy Commons
Died Jun 27, 1915
Age: 71 years.

J. B. Cole
Mar 7, 1838
Jan 14, 1911
C.S.A.

Mary L. Cole
Jan 20, 1850
May 24, 1920

Elmina Cole
Aug 16, 1831
Nov 18, 1909

H. P. Rowell
Dec 23, 1844
Dec 1, 1915
&
M. C. Rowell
Jul 27, 1851
(no date)

J. L. Abbott
Aug 5, 1845
Jan 18, 1911

Thurza, wife of
J. L. Abbott
May 5, 1849
Jun 6, 1900

Bettie Moore, wife of
J. L. Abbott
Mar 7, 1862
Jun 20, 1924

W. T. Abbott
Died Sep 5, 1911
Age: 41 years.

Sallie B. Gleghorn, wife
of C. C. Carpenter
Died Dec 21, 1897
Age: 30 years.

Carrah, wife of
R. N. Bradford
Feb 13, 1878
Oct 21, 1903

Robert N. Bradford
Jul 24, 1876
Feb 17, 1907

Minervie Ann, wife of
J. B. Hays
Jul 7, 1854
Aug 16, 1906

Phillip W. Dunafon
(Dunnivan)
Apr 9, 1821
Dec 23, 1905

TAFT QUADRANGLE

Mary J., wife of
B. C. Debose
Died Sep 16, 1910
Age: 71y, 1m, 4d.

Riley C. Cowan
1865-1914
& wife
Nancy Ann Cowan
1867-1952

Thomas D. Davidson
Sep 17, 1850
Feb 6, 1913

Margaret E., wife of
Thomas D. Davidson
May 16, 1850
Aug 2, 1917

Margaret McFerran
Aug 15, 1820
May 26, 1849

Baby Bryson
Infant lived but
one hour.

William, Son of
Rev. Henry B. Bryson
Nov 4, 1829
Jan 5, 1830

Jane Bryson
Died Oct 12, 1874
Age: 35 years.

Rev. Henry B. Bryson, D.D.
Died Nov 8, 1874
Age: 75 years.
& wife
Hannah Bryson
Born in Abbeville District
South Carolina
Feb 21, 1809
Married Nov 28, 1828
Died May 21, 1886
Rev. Henry B. Bryson was
installed 1st Pastor of
Bethel & Prosperity Churches
May 10, 1828.

Henry, Son of
Rev. Henry Bryson
Jan 14, 1844
Aug 20, 1846

Robert, Son of
Rev. Henry Bryson
Aug 2, 1836
Sep 21, 1837

Erected by James McConnell
in Memory of his mother
Ann McConnell
Sep   1807
Jul 4, 1843

J. W. McCulloh
C.S.A.
(no dates)

Erected by Hugh P. Penny
in Memory of his mother
Margaret Penny
Jan 10, 1775
Jul 21, 1839

Nancy, wife of
Manson E. Rowell
Aug 1, 1833
Jun 29, 1889

Samuel DeHaven
Died Sep 8, 1895
Age: 76 years.

Margaret Patterson,
wife of
Samuel DeHaven
Died Sep 30, 1896
Age: 58 years.

Elizabeth, wife of
Samuel DeHaven
Nov 27, 1828
Jan 2, 1878

Ella D. Thompson,
Daughter of
Samuel & M. A. DeHaven
Mar 18, 1850
Oct 25, 1876

Lizzie J., Daughter of
G. W. & M. A. Crawford
Mar 6, 1875
Jul 7, 1876

Alta E., Daughter of
G. W. & M. A. Crawford
Apr 29, 1881
Nov 2, 1894

Willie G., Son of
G. W. & M. A. Crawford
Mar 15, 1873
Dec 27, 1891

Bertha I., Daughter of
G. W. & M. A. Crawford
Oct 4, 1885
Jun 3, 1909

Mrs. Mattie Dickey
1868-1960

G. J., Daughter of
A. P. & M. B. Hays
Oct 15, 1847
Jan 1, 1876

John Lindsay
Jun 28, 1800
Jan 14, 1884

Mrs. Martha Lindsay
Sep 5, 1802
Apr 2, 1882

James L. Spence
Jul 30, 1816
Dec --, 1873
(day gone)

Jane E. Spence
Oct 27, 1833
Feb 19, 1917

Mary E. Spence
Dec 24, 1869
Aug 4, 1871

Infant Son of
J. H. & E. C. Thompson
B&D Nov 9, 1872

Thomas Theron McFerrin
1885-1954
&
Anna Dale McFerrin
1890-

Beulah McFerrin, wife of
George W. Johnson, Jr.
Jul 6, 1873
Apr 2, 1938

Thomas McFerrin
Nov 7, 1842
Mar 17, 1925
A Confederate Soldier
Co C 41 Tenn Reg.
C.S.A.
& wife
Helen F. Dale McFerrin
Born in Wetumpka, Ala.
Jun 3, 1843
Oct 30, 1914

Charles Howard, Son of
Thomas & H. F. McFerrin
Dec 8, 1870
Jan 30, 1875

Mrs. Betsey McFerrin
Born in Chester, S. C.
Sep 22, 1807
Died Lincoln Co., Tenn.
Aug 31, 1871

John Moore
1767-Apr 5, 1850

Martha, Consort of
John Moore
1772-Mar 20, 1859
"A Mother in Isreal"

John McFerrin
Died Jan 28, 1853
Age: 19 years.
&
William G. McFerrin
Died Jun 27, 1853
Age: 23 years.

Nancy, Consort of
A. M. Galloway
Jul 15, 1821
Apr 27, 1852
Married Mar 13, 1838

John C., Son of
James & Mary Wiley
Aug 8, 1812
Apr 21, 1843

Rev. Thomas W. Parkinson
Minister of Associate
Reformed Church
Sep 3, 1823
Sep 6, 1857

Grisilda Sloan, wife of
Rev. T. W. Parkinson
Sep 22, 1824
Nov 29, 1905

Brown Parkinson
Jan 6, 1789
Feb 28, 1876

Mary, Consort of
Brown Parkinson
Feb 17, 1792
Apr 23, 1862

Martha Parkinson
May 20, 1829
Sep 2, 1848

James M. Moore
Mar 18, 1814
Oct 17, 1856
Son of John &
Martha Moore.

Sarah, Consort of
James M. Moore
Jan 1, 1807
Aug 27, 1866

James Stewart
Sep 11, 1798
Jan 19, 1885

Margery, wife of
James Stewart
Died May 26, 1885
Age: 90 years.

Thomas Wiley, Son of
James & Margery Stewart
Aug 24, 1825
Apr 26, 1859

Prof. John H. Stewart
Aug 31, 1823
Feb 1, 1865

M. A. Olevia, wife of
S. H. Sloan
Sep 13, 1825
Sep 27, 1892

J. T. W., Son of
J. H. & M. A. Stewart
Died Sep 14, 1861
Age: 5y, 11m, 15d.

TAFT QUADRANGLE

J. P. Caughran
Apr 1, 1818
Apr 9, 1862

Jane E. Caughran
Nov 13, 1824
Nov 18, 1905

Alexander McCaughran
Apr 5, 1853
Jun 16, 1855

Mary McMillen
1832-1905

W. B. McMillen
1832-1909
C.S.A.

Infant Daughter of
H. T. & N. J. Sloan
B&D Dec 27, 1888

Infants of
A. L. & S. Sloan
Jun 9, 1898
Jul 19, 1901

William G. Spence
1802-Aug 11, 1853
Age: 51 years.
&
Fanny Spence
Aug 20, 1806
May 3, 1871
Age: 64y, 8m, 20d.

Givins J. L. Caughran
Sep 21, 1848
Feb 24, 1855

Dan R. Holloway
May 22, 1837
Feb 22, 1862
C.S.A.

Sarah C., Daughter of
J. C. & E. M. Sloan
Oct 5, 1860
May 9, 1862

Mary C., Daughter of
J. C. & E. M. Sloan
Mar 3, 1855
Mar 23, 1857

Lettie L., Daughter of
J. C. & E. M. Sloan
Mar 4, 1852
Aug 31, 1853

Joseph Lindsay
Died Dec 13, 1860
Age: 29y, 11m, 6d.

Martha Lindsay
Oct 7, 1834
Mar 10, 1873

John J. Lindsay
Aug 4, 1843
Jun 9, 1907

Margaret J., Wife of
John C. Lindsay &
Daughter of
J. L. & M. T. Caughran
Jan 10, 1849
Jul 24, 1875

Mary F. Sloan, wife of
John Lindsay
Jan 1, 1853
Dec 12, 1924

Infant of
John & Mary Lindsay
B&D Apr 2, 1880

Minnie Louanna, Daughter of
John & M. Lindsay
Apr 2, 1880
Jun 21, 1880

Infant of
John & Mary Lindsay
Aug 28, 1881
Aug 29, 1881

Sarah, wife of
J. M. Good
Feb 12, 1836
Aug 26, 1881
Erected by her sons
S. M. & J. A. Good

W. A. Phagan
Oct 28, 1858
Feb 14, 1890

James H., Son of
John & Eliza C. Phagan
Died Jan 9, 1860
Age: 25y, 6m, 21d.

Eliza C., Consort of
John Phagan
Died Feb 7, 1860
Age: 43y, 11m, 10d.

Martha S., Daughter of
John & Margaret A. Phagan
Feb 11, 1863
Apr 26, 1864

James H., Son of
O. A. & America Caughran
Sep 22, 1846
Aug 9, 1867
Age: 20y, 11m, 14d.

Maj. John Moore
1802-1883
"A Charter Member of the
Prosperity Church at its
organization".
& wife
Mary Moore
1807-1865
"A Charter member of the
Prosperity church at its
organization".

Robert Moore
Died Dec 26, 1908
Age: 82y, 7m, 14d.

Margaret Moore
Died Nov 1, 1910
Age: 84y, 11m, 27d.

Malissa Moore
Apr 21, 1850
Oct 7, 1932

Sarah B. Strong
Mar 29, 1821
Dec 2, 1903

Infant Son of
J. P. & Eliza Stewart
(no dates)

Willie, Son of
W. A. & R. A. England
Jul 1, 1881
Oct 6, 1881

Walter Lee, Son of
J. R. & Maggie McMillen
Apr 11, 1880
Nov 1, 1880

Sarah J., Daughter of
W. B. & N. M. McMillen
Sep 9, 1868
Aug 30, 1876

Amanda R., wife of
D. C. Dollar
Nov 7, 1820
May 21, 1887

Guss Dollar
Sep 10, 1880
Jan 8, 1904

D. G. Dollar
Apr 8, 1817
May 25, 1899
C.S.A.

Robert A. Stewart
May 20, 1839
Mar 26, 1907
& wife
Mary E. J. Reid Stewart
May 8, 1842
Aug 24, 1890

Cascenia, wife of
L. C. McCowan
Jul 7, 1823
Jan 3, 1894

James F. McCowan
Jun 29, 1843
Jul 14, 1882

M. W. H.
1881
(fieldstone)

William Calvin, Son of
R. A. & E. J. Stewart
Jul 16, 1864
Jul 16, 1872

Samuel Sloan, Jr.
Sep 19, 1801
Mar 26, 1885

L. B. Stroud
Oct 15, 1825
Oct 28, 1904

Mattie E., wife of
John A. Dickson
Mar 8, 1857
Sep 22, 1880
Age: 23y, 6m, 14d.
&
Mattie E. L., Daughter
of J. A. & M. E. Dickson
Sep 14, 1880
Oct 4, 1880
Age: 20 days.

Samanta, wife of
L. B. Stroud
Mar 4, 1830
Aug 5, 1881
Age: 51y, 5m, 1d.

Eveline J. Stroud
Oct 13, 1849
Apr 4, 1902

Alonzo, Son of
W. L. & E. J. Stroud
Age: 12y, 6m, 27d.
(no dates)

J. H. Blair
Aug 20, 1845
Sep 1, 1908

Mary E. Blair
Nov 11, 1868
Mar 24, 1941
"A Mother"

A. L., Son of
W. L. & E. J. Stroud
Age: 17y, 2m, 17d.
(no dates)

Mattie, Daughter of
W. L. & E. J. Stroud
Age: 11m, 5d.
(no dates)

Calvin Lee, Son of
W. L. & E. J. Stroud
Died Jun 19, 1884
Age: 8y, 2m, 18d.

William G. Moore
Nov 22, 1853
Dec 23, 1912

Hettie A. Moore
Dec 2, 1855
Sep 20, 1920

TAFT QUADRANGLE

Eugene, Son of
W. G. & H. A. Moore
May 15, 1882
Jul 1, 1895

J. L., Son of
J. Lee & Louella Hayes
Aug 1, 1907
Sep 28, 1938

Evabell Reese, wife of
J. Lee Hayes
Jan 26, 1897

Louella Rees, wife of
J. Lee Hayes
Jan 20, 1873
Aug 12, 1912

J. Lee Hayes
Sep 6, 1878
Apr 30, 1954

Robert G. Hayes
Mar 14, 1852
Jan 13, 1930
&
Adelia Hayes
Jun 8, 1864
Jul 13, 1944

Phillip, Infant Son of
J. C. & Julia Moore
B&D Nov 16, 1915

Bobby Warren, Son of
Ralph & Julia Templeton
Oct 2, 1936
Oct 3, 1936

Ebbie C. Sloan
Died Aug 23, 1895
Age: 25 years.

G. A. Rogers
Dec 2, 1872
Oct 18, 1940

Ida Green Rogers
Jan 19, 1878
Feb 18, 1951

James Bonner Green
Feb 21, 1874
Oct 3, 1918

Rev. O. S. Sloan
Dec 8, 1821
Apr 27, 1893
&
Elizabeth J. Sloan
Nov 21, 1828
Dec 2, 1894

John C. Sloan
1813-1893
&
Elizabeth Morrow Sloan
1821-1908

Lt. Thompson Sloan
Sep 10, 1849
Oct 9, 1889
C.S.A.

Nora J. Sloan
Dec 15, 1850
Dec 10, 1900

Paul Neil, Son of
H. T. & M. J. Sloan
Apr 22, 1887
Oct 12, 1898

S. B. "Pap" Jones
Dec 2, 1818
Sep 22, 1907

Irena, wife of
S. B. Jones
Apr 16, 1822
May 6, 1883
Age: 61y, 20d.

Manerva E., wife of
S. B. Jones
Apr 9, 1842
Apr 3, 1892

Walter C. Templeton
Aug 12, 1880
Nov 30, 1943
&
Minnie C. Templeton
Dec 17, 1879
Apr 25, 1962

Will D. Hayes
1873-1961
&
Sallie B. Hayes
1881-1955

Dr. A. G. Hayes
1879-1922
&
Lola Sloan Hayes
1885-

J. T. Beech
Died Sep 19, 1903
Age: 20 years.

Nellie Gertrude Beech
Jan 14, 1899
Oct 14, 1904

A. P. Hayes
Mar 8, 1817
Apr 5, 1890
&
Mary B. Hayes
Mar 19, 1819
Aug 21, 1888

Infant Son of
J. A. & M. M. Good
(no dates)

Willie, Son of
J. A. & M. M. Good
Aug 20, 1888
Jul 8, 1889

Ernest, Son of
J. A. & M. M. Good
Oct 11, 1893
Mar 18, 1894

J. L. Stewart
Jul 11, 1840
Jun 12, 1881

S. A. Jobe
Nov 25, 1848
Oct 3, 1914
& wife
Nancy A. Jobe
Oct 3, 1849
Oct 15, 1915

David N., Son of
John & E. G. Good
Apr 14, 1859
Sep 15, 1887

Martha F., Daughter of
John & E. G. Good
Aug 22, 1869
Feb 1, 1889

Maggie L., Daughter of
John & E. G. Good
Feb 21, 1864
Jun 4, 1890

John Good
Jan 1, 1831
Jul 25, 1913

Elizabeth G., wife of
John Good
Aug 12, 1827
Jul 25, 1904

John Lapsley Good
Mar 24, 1857
Jan 20, 1928

John Pogue
Died Apr 24, 1903
Age: 79 years.

Samuel Walter Jobe
Dec 25, 1881
Jun 2, 1962

Gracie Jobe Baker
Apr 2, 1904
Nov 9, 1954

Nellie Jobe McMillin
1911-1940

Ethel McFerrin, wife of
S. W. Jobe
Sep 6, 1881
Feb 28, 1928

Varina, Daughter of
S. W. & Ethel Jobe
Jan 25, 1901
Sep 2, 1903

William G. Moore
Oct 6, 1829
May 20, 1900

Thomas G. Graham
Mar 14, 1858
Oct 15, 1927
&
Manerva E. Pitts Graham
Jul 1, 1863
Jan 4, 1938

Ila May, Daughter of
M. E. & T. G. Graham
Jun 25, 1887
Feb 7, 1888

Delia Bell, Daughter of
T. G. & M. E. Graham
Nov 29, 1896
Jun 5, 1904

Mrs. Delia Sheffield Smith
Mar 14, 1863
Sep 21, 1910

Walter Diemer Wright
Sep 11, 1878
Apr 19, 1963
&
Hallie Graham Wright
Feb 8, 1882
Jan 30, 1966

Arabella, Daughter of
J. W. & A. S. Smith
Feb 7, 1886
Jun 8, 1887

Charlie S., Son of
J. W. & Z. E. Blair
Jun 14, 1887
Jun 28, 1887

Hugh P. Moore
1861-1921
&
Fannie O. Moore
1861-1910
&
Leslie M. Moore
1884-1886

Arthur Leon Moore
Dec 16, 1911
Apr 24, 1933

John M. Moore
Apr 7, 1859
Jan 6, 1902

Walter Leslie, Son of
J. M. & Laura Moore
Mar 25, 1880
Oct 4, 1884
Age: 4y, 6m, 9d.

TAFT QUADRANGLE

W. B. Sanders
Jan 15, 1817
Mar 5, 1882
&
S. E. Sanders
Apr 22, 1820
Dec 30, 1907

W. C. Bland
Jun 27, 1807
Aug 9, 1876

Mary Gray, wife of
S. T. Bland
Died Jan 28, 1885
Age: 80 years.

Mary Bland
1780-Sep 11, 1868

Mary E. Stedman
Jan 27, 1811
Apr 10, 1884

William Jones
Oct 23, 1812
Sep 9, 1898

Mary L. Jones
Apr 23, 1825
Sep 15, 1867

George W. Jones
Aug 29, 1851
Sep 30, 1859
&
Columbus J. Jones
Dec 14, 1853
Apr 22, 1854

Manly C., Son of
J. & P. Shuffield
Nov 5, 1856
Oct 17, 1859

Permelia Shuffield, Daughter
of J. W. & R. Street
Nov 22, 1836
Sep 1, 1859

W. C. Sheffield
Oct 11, 1863
Jan 10, 1929

John W., Son of
J. J. & M. A. Sheffield
May 2, 1869
Mar 3, 1892

Dosie, Daughter of
J. J. & M. A. Sheffield
(no dates)

J. J. Sheffield
Aug 31, 1828
Sep 6, 1912
C.S.A.

Margaret, wife of
J. J. Sheffield
Apr 15, 1836
Jun 30, 1901

Arthur (B.) Sheffield
Aug 14, 1823
Jun 1, 1896

Mary V., wife of
A. B. Sheffield
Oct 12, 1837
May 7, 1887

Sarah J., wife of
A. B. Sheffield
Nov 3, 1826
Jul 26, 1869

Mary A. L., Daughter of
H. W. & E. M. Sheffield
Jul 8, 1860
Sep 12, 1879

Alphus A. Sheffield
Jun 4, 1855
Jan 9, 1859

Cordelia E., Daughter of
J. N. & Pernelia S. Bland
Jun 19, 1855
Nov 16, 1859
Age: 4y, 4m, 13d.

Samuel Brown
Apr 1, 1800
Aug 14, 1858

Amaranda Brown
Sep 3, 1804
May 22, 1856

Capt. John S. Brown
A Member of 8th Tenn Reg.
Infantry
Born Jun 20, 1840
Was killed at the Battle
of Resana, Ga.
May 14, 1864
C.S.A.

L. Ella, wife of
H. W. Wyatt
May 15, 1859
Jul 19, 1884

Rose Emma Sheffield
Aug 19, 1867
Nov 3, 1887

T. Hubberd McFerrin
Nov 4, 1873
Oct 5, 1889

Raymond B. McMillan
1914-19
&
Fannie B. McMillan
1907-1943

Frances L. Thompson
Jul 18, 1861
Oct 9, 1869

William, Son of
J. B. & Lee Moore
Dec 15, 1872
Jun 22, 1879
Age: 6y, 6m, 7d.

Infant of
Hiram & Josie Saddlin
(Sandlin)
Died 1893
Age: (not given)

Infant Daughter of
L. J. & M. J. Wiley
B&D Sep 30, 1873

Anna Lawrence
Feb 17, 1783
Sep 19, 1862

A. N. McClane
Died Feb 3, 1863
Age: 68 years.

R. G. Meann
Mar 27, 1800
Oct 18, 1868

C. N. Thompson
Jan 17, 1813
Feb 27, 1879

Mary A., wife of
C. N. Thompson
Sep 21, 1818
Aug 18, 1891

James M., Son of
Thomas & Martha Bovell
Jan 3, 1882
Feb 25, 1882
Age: 1m, 22d.

Mr. Gilbert H. England
Died Apr 5, 1969
Age: 81 years.

Miss Alice G. England
Nov 6, 1884
Dec 6, 1962
&
Rebecca A. Good, wife of
W. A. England
May 1, 1853
Aug 23, 1923
&
W. A. England
Jan 12, 1856
Jan 27, 1929

J. E. Green
Jan 5, 1837
Aug 3, 1879

Christianna, wife of
John Green & Daughter of
John & Jane Robertson
Apr 25, 1807
Aug 30, 1882

Fannie, wife of
J. E. Green
Oct 20, 1840
Jul 1, 1915

G. R. Denton
Jul 14, 1850
Apr 30, 1906

Dr. A. McDonald
Died Mar 9, 1884
Age: 55 years.

Orah H. Jones
1893-1953
&
Jennie B. Jones
1898-1958

Charlie J. Jones
Charlie James Jones
Tennessee
Pfc 60 Guard Co.
A. S. C.   WW I
1895-1960
&
Sallie Belle Jones
1896-

Pfc Douglas M. Jones
Jun 9, 1920
Died on Luzon, P.I.
Jun 30, 1942
U. S. Army A.F.
Tennessee
Pfc 27 AAF Bomb Gp
WW II

Leslie M. Jones
1886-1947
&
Etna Raby Jones
1890-1965

Greenberry Floyd Isom
Sep 15, 1866
Nov 28, 1936
&
Nancy Dandridge Isom
Aug 9, 1873
Jul 18, 1958

Lucy V. Jones
Aug 20, 1890
Feb 19, 1910
&
William R. Jones
1854-1929
&
Lee Ona Jones
1869-1942

Sallie J., wife of
Rev. J. A. Myers
May 19, 1834
Jan 14, 1884

TAFT QUADRANGLE

H. C. Sloan
1862-1885
&
Cordie Forbes Sloan
Also wife of
B. M. McCalla
1861-1930

John Pallace *
Died Apr 23, 1903
Age: 79 years.

Jimmie R.,* Son of
N. G. & N. J. Tucker
Died Jun 17, 1883
Age: 15m, 3d.
    also Mother
Nancy J.,* wife of
N. G. Tucker
Died Jun 19, 1833
Age: 34y, 7m.

Mrs. Mary I.,* Consort of
W. D. Taft
Dec 12, 1812
Jul 15, 1893

Mrs. Sarah,* wife of
Augustus Yeager
Died Mar 13, 1894
Age: 86 years.

J. H. Knox *
Married Emma Pogue
Dec 28, 1899
Died Mar 10, 1908
Age: 57 years.

Mrs. Emaline,* widow of
Harvey Gray
Married in 1836
Died Mar 16, 1908
Age: (not given)

Rebecca Hanks,* wife of
T. J. Jones
Died Nov 1897
Age: 50 years.

Mrs. Elizabeth Ann,*
wife of A. J. Davis
Died in Blum, Texas
Feb 4, 1907
Age: 65 years.

William T. Campbell *
Married in 1885 to
Lizzie Jean, a Daughter
of T. A. Jean
Died Mar 21, 1899
Age: 35 years.

M. Brooks *
Died Oct 11, 1897
Age: 53 years.

Infant * of
Sam & Josie Daniel
Died Apr 8, 1900
Age: 7 weeks

W. W. Poole *
Died Apr 16, 1900
Age: 52 years.

James M. Story *
Died Jul 17, 1893
Age: 34 years.

Robert Taylor,* Son of
Mr. & Mrs. A. J. Isom
Died Nov 2, 1910
Age: 4 years.

John P. Stewart *
Died Jan 23, 1911
Age: 79 years.
C.S.A.

Mrs. Mary Ann,*
Married Harrison Smith
about 1846
Died Jun 11, 1906
Age: 83 years.

Mrs. Katie J.,* wife of
J. C. McFerrin
Died Aug 19, 1914
Age: 32 years.

Duncan Dollar *
Died May 25, 1899
Age: 82 years.

Neil B.,* Son of
J. H. Good
Died Aug 14, 1914
Age: 23 years.

George Thomas *
Died Sep 25, 1905
Age: 65 years.

Mrs. Lizzie J.,* wife of
Dr. J. D. Bryant &
Daughter of
Mrs. M. E. Gray who is
83 years old.
Died Nov 21, 1902
Age: 40 years.

Mrs. Edna Joan,*
Married R. O. Pitts
Jan 15, 1900
Died Aug 27, 1903
Age: 20y, 8m.

James Beech *
Died Sep 23, 1903
Age: 72y, 11m.

Mrs. Judia A.,*
Married to Alex. Boggs
Oct 26, 1892
Died Sep 20, 1898
Age: 31 years.
Daughter of
Louis & Martha Donelson

J. P. Amos *
Born Aug 8, 1841
Died Jul 28, 1916
C.S.A.

Clyde,* Son of
Robert C. Drennan
Died Oct 2, 1908
Age: 7 years.

Robert H.,* Son of
Robert & Margaret Moore
Married in 1889 to
Emma C. McFerrin
Died May 28, 1893
Age: 28 years.

Mrs. Sarah Sims *
Died Sep 15, 1899
Age: 84 years.

Manda,* Daughter of
Mrs. Mary Sanders
Died Jul 23, 1898
Age: 21 years.

Robert Moore *
Died Jun 11, 1890
Age: 21 years.

Ivey,* Daughter of
Mr. & Mrs. A. P. Stephens
Died Nov 10, 1890
Age: 16 years.

John Toon *
Died Sep 25, 1891
Age: 36 years.

Mrs. Rachel,* wife of
G. R. Denton & Daughter
of D. C. & Amanda Dollar
Died Sep 1, 1891
Age: 35 years.

John C. Sloan *
Born in South Carolina
in 1830, Married
Elizabeth Morrow
Died Apr 24, 1893
Age: 82 years.

Mrs. Sam Dollar *
Died May 3, 1908
Age: (not given)

Mrs. Elizabeth,* widow
of John C. Sloan
Died Jul 12, 1908
Age: 86 years.
Grandmother of
A. L. Sloan.

Dollie L.,* wife of
James Dollar
Married in 1889
Died Jul 23, 1906
Age: (not given)

Evaline,* Daughter of
J. R. Whitaker
Died Apr 2, 1914
Age: 2 years.

Eunice,* Daughter of
Mr. & Mrs. J. A. Hayes
Died Sep 5, 1899
Age: 13y, 10m.

* **

McFERRIN CEMETERY

LOCATION: Three fourth mile WNW of Camargo on east side of
a lane to Old McFerrin Home.

Cordell Shuffield
Mar 13, 1778
Sep 25, 1850

Permilla Shuffield
Oct 13, 1787
Jul 27, 1870

Blakely McFerrin
Jul 12, 1886
Jul 25, 1900

Mary D. McFerrin
Nov 20, 1875
Nov 4, 1885

R. A. McFerrin
Dec 25, 1857
Feb 11, 1892
Age: 34y, 1m, 17d.

Amanda C., wife of
R. A. McFerrin
Aug 10, 1857-Nov 20, 1887
Age: 30y, 3m, 10d.

Susie R., wife of
R. H. White
Aug 26, 1877
Apr 30, 1905

James McFerrin
Died Mar 7, 1843
Age: 38 years.

TAFT QUADRANGLE

James McFerrin, Sr.
Died Mar 4, 1832
Age: (not given)

------ Mc(Ferrin)
---- the 21st ----

(Stone illegible)

W. S. McFerrin
Dec 5, 1854
May 25, 1903

Stilmon McFerrin
Nov 27, 1879
Jan 24, 1906

Octa Rogers, wife of
Samuel McFerrin
Mar 1, 1885
Jan 15, 1924

Samuel McFerrin
Mar 10, 1869
Jun 20, 1949

May, wife of
Samuel McFerrin
Jan 29, 1878
May 24, 1901

Mary Ann McFerrin
Feb 23, 1827
Jan 22, 1908

J. M. McFerrin
Nov 28, 1814
Mar 3, 1886

H. C. McFerrin
Mar 1, 1860
Nov 2, 1892

Archie Bonner, Son of
H. C. & S. J. McFerrin
Died Apr 16, 1894
Age: 3y, 10,m, 2d.

Ada Rogers McFerrin
1878-1932

Larah Agnes, Daughter of
M. L. & A. F. McFerrin
Nov 1, 1900
Oct 3, 1902

Garner Ranson, Son of
M. L. & L. B. McFerrin
Jun 13, 1895
Dec 16, 1895

Mary Pearl, Daughter of
M. L. & L. B. McFerrin
Dec 10, 1890
Oct 5, 1891

Infant Daughter of
M. L. & L. B. McFerrin
Oct 15, 1889
Mar 3, 1890

Martin Lee McFerrin
1864-1945

L. B., wife of
M. L. McFerrin
Dec 13, 1869
Dec 11, 1896

5 unmarked graves.

* *

SANDLIN CEMETERY

LOCATION: One half mile NW of Camargo in the woods.

Elisabeth Sandlin
J-- 9, 1808
Apr 13, 1816
(fence across her grave)

Lewis C. McDill *
died Dec 25, 1881
Age: 25 years.

Several unmarked graves.

* *

CEMETERY

LOCATION: Three fourth mile south of Camargo on the west
side of Kirkland Road.

Sprays are said to buried here.

Several unmarked grabes,
several fieldstones,
no inscriptions.

* *

BATES CEMETERY

LOCATION: One fourth mile south of Camargo on the east side
of road.

S. T. Bates
Mar 4, 1858
Feb 15, 1904

About 10 graves with
fieldstones, no inscriptions.

* *

TAFT QUADRANGLE

KIRKLAND CHAPEL CEMETERY

LOCATION: At Kirkland Chapel, Kirkland, Tennessee.

J. F. Young
Apr 22, 1881
Dec 14, 1965
&
Alice Young
Feb 7, 1891

Sidney J. Swinford
1886-1949

Robert Hayden White
Tennessee
Pvt 155 Infantry
WW II
Jan 30, 1920
Oct 4, 1951

Robert Henry White
Aug 7, 1878
Aug 20, 1961
&
Allie Swinford White
Feb 1, 1889

Everett J. Bradford
Tennessee
Sgt 117 Inf WW II
Jun 18, 1919
Jul 31, 1944

Herman L. Cowan
1902-1958
&
Elsie T. Cowan
1906-

H. L. Hopkins
1878-1947

William E. Hopkins
1877-1947
&
Jo Ann Hopkins
1881-1939

Robert R. Honea
1898-
&
Liza M. Honea
1900-

Hattie L. McMillin
Mar 12, 1881
Feb 5, 1961

William Prate Fults
Aug 19, 1874
Feb 21, 1941
&
Sarah Jane Fults
Sep 14, 1882
Nov 24, 1935

Robert F. Wilbanks
Mar 2, 1901
Dec 20, 1966
&
Naomi G. Wilbanks
Nov 27, 1899

Mose W. Jean
1888-1963
&
Ozemba F. Jean
1899-

Louis M. Maddox
1867-1953
&
Leeanner Maddox
1872-1948

Walter McAlister
Nov 27, 1895

&
Lelia McAlister
Feb 6, 1902

Harvey C. Gray
1884-1938
&
Ada B. Gray
1889-1962

William Howard Washburn
Jan 29, 1928
May 13, 1945
(picture)

William R. Washburn
Sep 13, 1887
Sep 26, 1957
&
Oma D. Washburn
Feb 6, 1889

Charles David Yarbrough
May 6, 1935
Jul 2, 1937

Edd Gray
1900-194-
(broken)

George David Dempsey
Died Oct 17, 1969
Age: 77 years. (Gallant FH)

William Albert Monks
Aug 20, 1940
Aug 21, 1940

Clarence L. Yarbrough
1895-1949

James W. Yarbrough
Jul 18, 1870
Sep 2, 1957
&
Mattie B. Yarbrough
Sep 30, 1875
Sep 4, 1966

Donald Yarbrough
Jul 19, 1874
May 30, 1947

Myra R. Bennett
Feb 7, 1956
Feb 8, 1956

Otto A. Jones
Died Jun 29, 1970
Age: 65 years.
(Gallant FH)

James Donald Isbell
Oct 22, 1915
Jan 11, 1965
&
Bertie P. Isbell
Aug 26, 1893

James Britton
Jul 7, 1887

Elve Harris, wife of
Thurston Ivey
Jun 22, 1915
May 18, 1941

Arney M. Jean
1874-1967

Fanny L. Jean
1872-1950

Greenfield Bryan
1891-1966
&
Ethel F. Bryan
1897-

Pfc. Harvey G. Harris
34520251
Co B 325th Glider Inf
Aug 31, 1922
Killed in Action
Jun 9, 1944 in
Normandy, France.

Richard S. Harris
Dec 22, 1877
Jul 5, 1952
&
Zenia Towry Harris
1897-

Hurley Berry Pitts
Apr 7, 1907
Oct 5, 1965

Janice Diane Jean
Feb 15, 1948
Apr 23, 1948

Allen George Payne
Ohio
S 2 U. S. Navy WW II
May 20, 1927
May 16, 1967

Rose C. Payne
Nov 18, 1894
Sep 19, 1963

P. Ed Smith
1875-1961
&
Della Abbott Smith
1880-1949

James A. Hill
Oct 31, 1885
Feb 20, 1961
&
Minnie S. Hill
Jul 23, 1888
(no date)

Tom Roland
Mar 31, 1893
Dec 14, 1952
&
Luaner Roland
Mar 4, 1893

Willis R. Moore
May 4, 1893
Jul 29, 1965
&
Mattie T. Moore
Apr 4, 1893

Billy Joe West
Aug 7, 1936
Apr 17, 1961

Oscar R. Hopkins
Jun 15, 1925
Jul 10, 1948

Mary Bradford
1903-1957

Thomas C. Honea
1876-1956
&
Nettie Bell Honea
1832-

TAFT QUADRANGLE

Isom Hambrick
1911-1961
&
Lucille Hambrick
1913-

Walter C. Hambrick
Kentucky
S2 U. S. N. R.
Mar 1, 1914
Jan 11, 1964

Rev. Oliver A. Honea
Jul 16, 1883

&
Iva Odell Honea
Mar 27, 1886
Feb 26, 1961

Wiley H. Smith
1919-1951

Charlie B. Beddingfield
1879-1955
&
Nova S. Beddingfield
1903-

Margaret Swinford
1906-1962

John Ashby
1881-1964

Molly Ashby
1879-1964

John H. Hopkins
1947-1961

Roy McKinney Jean
1905-1930
&
Bonnie Maddox Jean
1907-(no date)

Leathel William Hunter
Jun 2, 1921
Aug 7, 1965
&
Pauline B. Hunter
Sep 1, 1922

Ervie D. Mullins
Nov 6, 1886
Oct 27, 1960
&
Fannie P. Mullins
Dec 12, 1897

Floyd A. Rowell
1910-1969

Thomas G. Harrison
1886-1960
&
Ola Mai Harrison
1888-1961

Albert L. Flynn
Dec 1, 1879
Dec 22, 1947
&
Ora A. Flynn
Apr 16, 1886
(no date)

Leslie W. Good
1884-1966
&
Emma Ethel Good
1888-1957

Ranson A. Good
1896-1961

Ernie F. Hopkins
Nov 21, 1886
Dec 17, 1963
&
Phamie M. Hopkins
Oct 20, 1890
Oct 18, 1964

Artie H. Hopkins
Aug 13, 1884
Nov 3, 1964
&
Pearl T. Hopkins
Apr 30, 1884

Garner Hopkins
Aug 22, 1920

&
Bertha M. Hopkins
Jun 28, 1919
Jan 20, 1962

J. Dalton White
Mar 25, 1912
Jul 17, 1969
&
Grace H. White
Apr 4, 1918

Ben E. Drennon
1884-1945
&
Annie M. Drennon
1890-

Johnnie D. Sims
1927-1955
(Gallant FH)

Vida H. Sims
Oct 4, 1893
Apr 23, 1968

Jonnie D. Sims
Nov 14, 1927
Aug 23, 1955
(Same as above)

Mary Morgan Sims
May 11, 1894
Nov 26, 1939

Mrs. Mattie Bolden Hambrick
Sims
Died Jan 8, 1966
Age: 60y, 2m, 25d.
(Higgins FH)

Ray David, Son of
Willard & Margaret Jones
Mar 30, 1956
Apr 9, 1956

Retha Sims
Aug 24, 1909
Apr 7, 1956

James Robert McPhearson
Feb 24, 1901
Aug 27, 1955

Eddie Mat. Simms
1882-1953
&
Athie Lee Simms
1890-

Annie Sue Simms
1916-1940

D. C. Sims
(no dates)

Julie Ann Stephens
Mar 27, 1946
May 1, 1946

Tishie M. Stephens
Mar 29, 1903

Alvie R. Stephens
Oct 4, 1888
Apr 21, 1969

Vincent Edward Hargrove
Died May 24, 1970
Age: 3 days
(Gallant FH)

Nellie O. Winsett
1903-1942

Barbara Bevels
1938

Kirke Thomas McAlister
Jan 23, 1938
Aug 18, 1940

Sam V. Beard
1865-1949
&
Mary E. Beard
1882-1968

John B. Poole
1896-1962

H. A. Washburn
Aug 25, 1884
Jan 27, 1959
&
Fannie K. Washburn
Jun 11, 1884
Mar 18, 1960

Isom H. Smith
1868-1950
&
Hester A. Smith
1871-1948

Lawrence Smith
1902-1930

Melanie Ann Winsett
Nov 16, 1963
Nov 17, 1963

J. Arthur Washburn
1881-1953
&
Pearl C. Washburn
1881-1938

Thomas J. Tipps
Sep 11, 1861
Aug 15, 1959
&
Emma P. Tipps
Sep 14, 1864
(no date)

Shelby Tipps
1883-1966
&
Oleen Tipps
1913-1965

Gail, Daughter of
W. S. & Oleen Tipps
Mar 28, 1949
Mar 30, 1949

A. Thomas Moffett
May 11, 1907
May 16, 1966
&
Nettie I. Moffett
Oct 1, 1905
Mar 12, 1966

James Chesley Childress
1888-1947

Beedie Childress
1894-1957

Mrs. Clara Elizabeth
Rhoden Phillips
Died Jun 15, 1970
Age: 73y, 5d.
(Higgins FH)

Infant of
Bonnie Phillips
1930

TAFT QUADRANGLE

Roy Clay Mathis, Jr.
Died Sep 26, 1969
Age: 1 day
(Gallant FH)

Walter Lee Broadrick
1885-1961
(Gallant FH)

Nina Smartt Broadrick
Died Jun 19, 1966
Age: 80y, 5m.
(Gallant FH)

William G. Posey
Apr 12, 1919
Jun 15, 1952

Brenda Sue Whitman
Jan 5, 1963
Sep 13, 1965

Linda G. Butler
1951-1969

James M. Beard
1912-1969
&
Carinne G. Beard
1929-

William "Dock" Smith
Aug 6, 1930
Jul 18, 1958

David Arthur Childress
Aug 21, 1945
Feb 18, 1946
(picture)

Emma Jean Childress
1943-1949
(picture)

W. C. "Jack" Bates
May 23, 1903
Dec 12, 1959
&
Eunice Spray Bates
Jun 28, 1909

Samuel Kenneth Bates
Feb 24, 1926

&
Nellie Darene Bates
Feb 1, 1930
Aug 7, 1964
(color picture)

John D. Dubois
1878-(no date)
&
Fannie C. Dubois
1880-1951

Robert B. Dubois
Oct 21, 1917
Aug 30, 1966
&
Sadie E. Dubois
Apr 9, 1916

Minnie Rice Dubois
1900-19(no date)

Ernie C. Jones
Jul 9, 1899
Jan 8, 1962
&
Lonna L. Jones
Oct 9, 1902

Waymon B. Aldridge
Sep 6, 1897
Jul 20, 1960
&
Sallie Posey Aldridge
Aug 1, 1903

John W. Beddingfield
1901-(no date)
&
Annie R. Beddingfield
1899-1961

Bobbie Dwyer Poole
Sep 13, 1900
Mar 12, 1962
&
Mary Broadrick Poole
Jul 24, 1906

Cleveland Smith
Dec 30, 1921

&
Ozella R. Smith
Apr 18, 1920

Married Jan 4, 1941

* *

MOYERS CEMETERY

LOCATION: One half mile SW of Kirkland on south side of Ardmore Highway.

S. H. Moyers
Aug 9, 1835
Jan 22, 1907
& wife
Rena Moyers
Nov 14, 1846
Jan 7, 1928

8 unmarked graves.

Dana M., Daughter of
S. H. & Rena Moyers
Jan 29, 1889
Oct 20, 1895

John W., Son of
S. H. & Rena Moyers
Oct 13, 1878
Died in Infancy

Sylva, Daughter of
Tabitha Stephens
May 26, 1885
Mar 17, 1888

Myrtle,* Daughter of
Mr. & Mrs. S. H. Moyers
Died Oct 20, 1895
Age: 6y, 8m.

* *

MARY'S GROVE CEMETERY

LOCATION: Three fourth mile SW of Kirkland on the south side of Ardmore Highway.

Samuel Wallace
Jan 19, 1795
Jul 13, 1861
He was a Regular Soldier
through the War of 1812
and had an Honorable
from his Officers.

Mrs. Hannah Wallace *
Relict of
Samuel Wallace
Died Nov 19, 1879
Age: 78 years.

Sara A. Bates
(no dates)

Hanah C. Bates
Died Jul.the
....(not finished)

Wesley M. Bates
Aug 10, 1855
Nov 10, 1855

James F.(E.) Bates
Mar 22, 1859
Oct 3, 1863

Infant of
L. W. Cale
(no dates)

Robbert D. Cale
May 30, 1864
Nov 14, 1864

Caroline Cale
Feb 16, 1841
Dec 8, 1864

Margaret Simmons
May 16, 1823
Oct 24, 1896

J. C. Stephens
(no dates)

David Watson
Jan 20, 1783
Oct 31, 1867

Erwin Stephens *
Died Nov 7, 1895
Age: 80 years.

Cora,* Granddaughter of
Erwin Stephens
Died Apr 25, 1893
Age: 7 years.

Hurley,* Son of
C. C. & Mary Sanders
Died Mar 23, 1896
Age: 40y, 2m, 7d.

TAFT QUADRANGLE

Hettie,* wife of
John Sanders
Died Nov 24, 1897
Age: 24 years.

Mrs. Lucy Burk,* wife of
Robert Bates
Died Jan 3, 1907
Age: 58 years.

Lora Stephens ***
(no dates)

*** Family Records.

Jim B. Stephens ***
(no dates)

* *

COLE CEMETERY

LOCATION: One half mile SSE of Kirkland on south side of road.

James M. Cole
Jun 1, 1854
Sep 7, 1887

2 fieldstones,
no inscriptions.

* *

CARPENTER CEMETERY

LOCATION: Two and one half miles NNW of Taft on the west side of Taft-Coldwater Road.

Sarah Carpenter
Jun 20, 1846
Oct 12, 1873

Theophilus Pepper
Oct 12, 1837
Apr 9, 1901

Jane Parthenia, wife of
Theo. Pepper
Dec 30, 1842
Sep 13, 1887

W. E., Son of
Theo & J. P. Pepper
Apr 1, 1871
Sep 25, 1888
Age: 17y, 5m, 24d.

Infant of
J. E. & F. A. Duckworth
B&D Sep 9, 1901

* *

ABERNATHY CEMETERY

LOCATION: Two miles NW of Taft on the north side of the Ardmore Highway.

No markers remain.

* *

CARPENTER CEMETERY

LOCATION: One and one fourth miles NW of Taft on the north side of Ardmore Highway.

Several fieldstones,
no inscriptions.

* *

SULSER CEMETERY

LOCATION: Three fourth mile NNW of Taft on the east side of Coldwater Road.

Henry Sulser
Nov 2, 1818
Jan 10, 1880
&
Narcissus E. Sulser
Apr 15, 1839
Apr 29, 1918

Sarah Salser (Sulser)
Feb 24, 1791
May 4, 1864

John Sulser
Aug 7, 1816
Sep 12, 1886

Lizzie B.,* Daughter of
Henry Bryant
Died Jan 19, 1907
Age: 8 years.

Jas. Gilliland
May 13, 1825
Sep 4, 1848

John Thomas Powell
May 16, 1842
Aug 6, 1906

Many unmarked graves.

James G. Tafts
Sep 30, 1837
Mar 5, 1909

M. E., wife of
J. G. Tafts
Sep 26, 1837
Mar 29, 1900

* *

TAFT QUADRANGLE

BAGGERLY CEMETERY

LOCATION: One and one fourth miles NE of Taft on west side of Robinson Hollow Road.

James A. Smith
Mar 2, 1854
Jul 21, 1922
&
Laura E. Smith
Oct 28, 1864
Oct 30, 1899

Esther H. Beggerly,
wife of J. M. Biles
Apr 2, 1859
Oct 12, 1899

J. S. Bland
Jan 23, 1859
Oct 27, 1889

John B. Cole
Nov 25, 1833
Mar 18, 1884
& wife
Emily Cole
1832-1911

Huston Hathcoat
Apr 6, 1886
Aug 11, 1922

John Marion Haythcoat
Mar 25, 1885
Oct 30, 1902

Mrs. Julia Haithcoat *
Died Mar 13, 1909
Age: 45 years.

Lillie I. Rowell
Aug 11, 1879
Sep 20, 1899

William Hoytt, Son of
W. T. & M. G. Blair
Nov 16, 1894
Mar 27, 1896

E. Cornelia, Daughter of
J. B. & F. A. Baggerly
Feb 3, 1873
Aug 10, 1888

William R. Cole
1856-1879
&
Mary A. Cole
1868-1881

Calvin Street
Apr 15, 1827
Jul 18, 1890
Age: 63y, 3m, 3d.

Catharine Street
Nov 9, 1829
Jan 11, 1900
Age: 70y, 2m, 3d.

Mrs. Elizabeth Honey *
Died Jan 21, 1904
Age: 90 years.

Mrs. Willie,* wife of
Henry Lee
Died May 11, 1903
Age: 33 years.

Mattie R., wife of
W. T. Blair
Oct 30, 1861
Oct 3, 1889

Frances A., wife of
J. B. Baggerly
1848-1899

David L. Baggerly
Aug 5, 1821
Sep 28, 1901
& wife
Caroline Baggerly
Nov 12, 1825
Dec 26, 1901

Martha A. H., Daughter of
Calvin & Sarah C. Street
Mar 11, 1858
Oct 17, 1861

Annie D., wife of
Davy Jones
Dec 16, 1835
May 24, 1925

W. E. Smith
(no dates, fieldstone)

Mrs. Ada Winston Hanna *
Died Apr 26, 1909 by Cyclone
Age: 21 years

Miss Atlas,* Daughter of
J. M. Phillips
Died Oct 11, 1901
Age: 18 years.

Elmina Catharine,
Daughter of
W. S. & M. A. Cole
Jul 13, 1880
Mar 2, 1885

Infant Son of
W. B. & M. D. Cole
Died Aug 31 (no year)
Age: 1 day

Mary Rawls, Daughter of
W. S. & M. A. Cole
Aug 18, 1874
Jan 15, 1896

J. M. Phillips
1859-1939

Eliza Phillips
1839-1935

R. A. Phillips
(no dates, fieldstone)

J. A. Neely
Feb 3, 1871
Nov 24, 1917

Mrs. J. T. Moffatt *
Died Nov 13, 1911
Age: (not given)

* *

ROBINSON CEMETERY

LOCATION: One and three fourth miles NE of Taft and east of Robinson Hollow Road.

No markers remain.

Michael Robinson home place.

* *

COLE CEMETERY

LOCATION: One and one half miles east of Taft on the north side of Ardmore Highway and west side of a lane.

No signs of this cemetery remain today.

Informed sources states the following being buried here: Mr. & Mrs. Charles Dozier and their children, Emaline Baggerly, Becky Baggerly and the McAnally family. Eds.

* *

TAFT QUADRANGLE

CEMETERY

LOCATION: Two miles East of Taft and west of curve of Ardmore Highway.

Fieldstones, no inscriptions.

Informed sourses states that the following are buried here: Sanders, Stewarts, Satterfields and others. Eds.

* *

NEELY CEMETERY

LOCATION: Two and three fourth miles ENE of Taft on the north side of Ardmore Highway.

Alex. Boggs
Sep 28, 1896
Jun 9, 1964
&
Zella Neely Boggs
Oct 3, 1898

Maggie, wife of
G. B. Hopkins
Jul 21, 1879
May 1, 1915

Thomas F. Hopkins
May 22, 1932
Mar 19, 1935

Iliff Thomas Moffett
Aug 11, 1883
Aug 14, 1956

Mattie Moffett
Jul 15, 1882
Jan 1, 1913

Thelma Katharine Moffett
1910-1911

Rufus D. Neely
Jan 31, 1875
Nov 13, 1923
&
Mary E. Neely
Sep 2, 1883
Jun 17, 1952

Mrs. N. E. Neely *
Died Oct 17, 1907
Age: 83 years.

Lelar, Daughter of
R. D. & M. E. Neely
Feb 28, 1901
Feb 24, 1902

Elius H. Neely
Jan 10, 1812
Jan 18, 1889

Sarah Jane Neely
Nov 17, 1854
Jun 23, 1956

E. A. Neely
Sep 6, 1854
Jun 11, 1933

Thomas McKinley Scott
Pvt Co F 1 Regt Ala Inf
Spanish American War
Oct 31, 1877
Jan 23, 1956
&
Viola A. Scott
1881-1964

Joseph N. Neely
Jul 12, 1845
Apr 5, 1929
&
M. Angeline Neely
Nov 16, 1838
Feb 7, 1926

Sarah Lula, wife of
S. N. Neely
Jul 26, 1876
May 1, 1930

Alie E. Pearson
Jun 17, 1881
Aug 11, 1901

Alva Thrasher
1880-1951

Erskin Thrasher
1902-1944

Gertie Thrasher
1903-1951

* *

MILAM CEMETERY

LOCATION: Two and one half miles ENE of Taft, north of Ardmore at end of a long lane.

E. T. Leatherwood
Sep   1848
Dec 17, 1883
&
Ann C. Leatherwood
May 21, 1848
Oct 20, 1887
&
Frankie W. Leatherwood
Jan 5, 1879
Jun 16, 1887

B. E. Hopkins *
Died Mar 1, 1902
Age: 40 years.

Cora Lee Honea *
Died Nov 2, 1906
Age: 16 days.

Samuel R. Leatherwood
Sep 26, 1876
Nov 21, 1876
&
John R. Leatherwood
Aug 25, 1874
Sep 12, 1874

Culpernia S. Hobb
Oct 10, 1850
Oct 20, 1874

Sarah A. P. Neely
Mar 24, 1847
Aug 14, 1887

J. P. Dennis *
Died Sep 24, 1896
Age: 73 years.

James Wesslie Milam
Jul 26, 1862
Aug 24, 1921

Mary E. Thrasher Milam
Mar 8, 1872
Sep 13, 1957

Wiley C. Milam
Jan 15, 1825
Aug 19, 1894

Martha E. Milam
May 1, 1831
Jan 23, 1900

I. B.,* Son of
J. B. & Piney Stalcup
Died Oct 27, 1909
Age: 7 months.

Bedford Hopkins
Died Oct 22, 1886
Age: 76 years.

Nancy Hopkins
Died Nov 17, 1881
Age: 60 years.

James W. Wheeler
1852-1930

Hettie S., wife of
J. W. Wheeler
Oct 9, 1851
Jan 12, 1899

Mrs. Bell,* wife of
Silas Hopkins
Died Mar 3, 1900
Age: 37 years.

* *

TAFT QUADRANGLE

BEARDEN CEMETERY

LOCATION: Two and one half miles SW of Kirkland on the east side of Ardmore Highway.

Alfred Bearden Born in Spartenburg, S.C. Feb 16, 1811 Dec 14, 1888 & Margaret Downing Bearden Born in Williamson Co., Tennessee Jul 3, 1807 Jun 20, 1890 Married Feb 24, 1831	Capt. N. Monroe, Son of Alfred & Margaret Bearden Feb 8, 1837 Jan 22, 1863 Died from wounds received at the Battle of Stones River. Co E 8th Tenn C.S.A. 1 unmarked grave.	Robinson M. Brown 1837-1864 Killed at the Battle of Atlanta Co E 8th Tenn C.S.A.	Mary E. V., Daughter of Alfred & Margaret Bearden Mother of Lileon M. & Margaret Brown Mar 21, 1839 Sep 11, 1864 Alfred Bearden Jul 29, 1852 Nov 17, 1852

* *

BLAIR CEMETERY

LOCATION: Three miles SW of Kirkland and three miles NE of Taft on the north side of Coldwater Road, across creek from Potato Hill.

Thomas Blair Nov 8, 178? Jun 20, 18?? (broken) & Milly Blair Oct 15, 1790 Aug 5, 1846 Age: 56y, 9m. John W. Blair Oct 22, 1846 Jan 2, 1888 Anna H. Blair Nov 4, 1873 Oct 16, 1874 Collins A., Son of J. W. & Z. E. Blair Apr 1, 1875 Aug 24, 1889 Harrison Blair Apr 9, 1816 Aug 10, 1859 Jane M., wife of Harrison Blair Apr 4, 1820 Mar 19, 1888 Married Jan 25, 1838 James Smith Jan 18, 1802 Feb 6, 1896 & Gincy Smith Oct 16, 1808 Aug 15, 1874 William Smith * Died Jan 15, 1891 Age: 63 years.	Martha E., Daughter of Harrison & Jane M. Blair Aug 23, 1848 Sep 11, 1879 L. C. Blair Jul 2, 1827 Jun 10, 1896 Addie A. X., wife of J. F. Blair Apr 4, 1861 Sep 10, 1885 J. W. Blair Apr 7, 1819 Jan 20, 1891 Eliza Jane Blair Jan 9, 1820 Apr 20, 1862 Age: 42y, 2m, 29d. James Brown Died Oct 13, 1832 Age: 57y, 4m. & Jane Brown Died Apr 11, 1840 Age: 67y, 10m. William Smith Jan 8, 1777 Apr 16, 1857 & Sarah Smith Dec 25, 1784 Sep 7, 1860 Mijaman Smith Mar 18, 1800 Apr 7, 1886 Mrs. Betsey Smith * Died Feb 11, 1891 Age: 88 years.	Josiah R. Brown Died Jan 5, 1834 Age: 1y, 10m. Mary Brown Died Jan 24, 1834 Age: 24y, 8m. Infant Daughter of John & Lucretia Brown B&D Oct 8, 1844 John Fowler Apr 20, 1808 Dec 14, 1858 & Susannah Fowler Nov 22, 1809 Nov 9, 1873 William N. Hicks Dec 22, 1819 Nov 17, 1879 S. B. McLemore Nov 10, 1857 Dec 27, 1916 & J. W. McLemore Mar 16, 1856 (no date) W. L. Thompson 1900-1935 James N. Yarbrough Sep 13, 1831 Mar 5, 1905 Member of the M. E. Church, South. L. C. Martin * Died Oct 11, 1900 Age: 40y, 9m.	Mary E., wife of J. N. Yarbrough Sep 2, 1841 --- --, 1884 (broken) Lucy J., wife of J. S. Yarbrough Mar 12, 1860 Oct 25, 1884 Mrs. Sarah Moore Nov 21, 1799 Oct 30, 1887 John W. Rowell Died Sep 5, 1844 Age: 30y, 10m. Lucinda, wife of J. W. Rowell Died Mar 17, 1844 Age: 29y, 11m. Samuel M. Rowell Jan 6, 1818 Sep 9, 1885 & wife Matilda W. Rowell Aug 29, 1813 Aug 15, 1894 W. Gidion Rowell Aug 30, 1841 Nov 24, 1854 & M. Alice Rowell Oct 1, 1851 Apr 27, 1853 Children of S. M. & M. Alice Rowell Jonathan W. Rowell Nov 26, 1834 Apr 12, 1859

TAFT QUADRANGLE

Mrs. Lavina,* wife of
James Blair
Died Dec 9, 1878
Age: about 70 years.

Mrs. Martha J.,* wife of
the late S. B. Smith
Died Jun 28, 1899
Age: 71y, 4m, 4d.

J. W. Blair *
Died in Normandy, Tenn.
Jan 19, 1894
Age: 75 years.

Mrs. Louisa C.,* wife of
J. J. Martin
Married in 1831
Died Aug 9, 1897
Age: 53y, 7m.

Several unmarked graves.

Jesse Hawkins *
Died Jun 19, 1890
Age: 85 years.

Lt. William Robinson *
Died 1813
(Soldier of the Revolution)

Capt. Andrew Caruthers *
Died 1811
(Soldier of the Revolution)

Levi Rodgers *
Died Oct 20, 1895
Age: 80 years.

Flora,* Daughter of
David & Fannie Rogers
Died Jan 19, 1900
Age: (not given)

Infant * of
Mr. & Mrs. Russell
Died Aug 19, 1899
Age: (not given)

* *

PETTY CEMETERY

LOCATION: One half mile east of Blanche Store on Old Blanche-Coldwater Road. Copied in October 1975 by Martha Ann and Bobby Lewter.

Sarah Ann, wife of
W. W. Pettey, Daughter
of Madison & Malinda
Porter
Aug 30, 1830
Feb 16, 1856

Mary Elizabeth Pettey
Sep 18, 1845
Mar 8, 1853

Richard Albert Pettey
Mar 11, 1854
Dec 27, 1854

1 Slate Rock, no
inscription.

NOTE: W. W. Pettey was the first storekeeper in Blanche, (about 1850), after his wife and children died, he moved to Fayetteville. He and his brother Richard later ran the Pettey House in Fayetteville. - Martha Ann and Bobby Lewter, 1975.

* *

END OF LINCOLN

MOORE COUNTY CEMETERY RECORDS

BELLEVILLE QUADRANGLE

PROSSER CEMETERY

LOCATION: In Bartlett Hollow, two miles west of Charity.

James Prosser Died Oct 22, 1854 Age: 63 years.	Frances Prosser Died Oct 2, 1858 Age: 56 years.	Several fieldstones, no inscriptions.

* *

PROSSER CEMETERY

LOCATION: Near Chestnut Ridge Community on Highway 231.

T. N. Bledsoe Sep 27, 1843 (no date)	Mary Gowen Oct 22, 1842 Dec 28, 1918	R. W. Prosser Feb 1, 1832 Feb 28, 1898	John F., Son of M. W. & Frances Redd Feb 25, 1874 Sep 15, 1876
M. F. Bledsoe Mar 25, 1849 Dec 8, 1911	Mattie E., wife of S. H. Gowen Aug 8, 1858 Nov 14, 1892	America Prosser Apr 18, 1836 (no date)	Mary E., Daughter of M. W. & Frances Redd Aug 12, 1871 Sep 6, 1876
Infant of J. T. & Bertie Bledsoe B&D Jul 26, 1899	Elmer, Daughter of W. B. & Mattie Hudson Apr 18, 1878 Oct 20, 1879	Permelia Prosser Apr 20, 1814 Jun 21, 1896	Lee Richardson Mar 8, 1876 Sep 16, 1892
Pauline, Daughter of J. T. & Bertie Bledsoe May 23, 1904 Sep 1, 1904	J. A. Prosser Oct 5, 1824 May 24, 1885	John N. Prosser Dec 17, 1818 Mar 16, 1898 Many unmarked graves.	Annie Richardson May 14, 1874 Apr 15, 1891

* *

WARREN CEMETERY

LOCATION: In Bartlett Hollow, near Chestnut Ridge Community.

Marah Bartlett Oct 7, 1846 Oct 19, 1888	Elijah Warren Jun 25, 1826 Feb 21, 1913 & Elizabeth Warren 1825-Aug 22, 1901	"Wash" C. Wagster 1856-1900 & Pollie W. Wagster 1862-1956	Mrs. Lige Warren 1875-1931 A. P., Daughter of E. & E. S. Warren Jul 28, 1899 Jul 26, 1900
D. N. Bartlett Dec 29, 1835 Oct 15, 1899	John C. Warren 1890-1965 & Nettie P. Warren 1895-1965	W. M. Burrow 1858-1944 & Malinda Burrow 1879-1958	R. C. Burrow Aug 24, 1852 Jan 15, 1922
John Bartlett (no dates)			
Joseph J. Jernigan 1973-1973 (Gowen-Smith FH)	Julius B. Williams Jul 9, 1851 May 25, 1919	Daniel Warren Mar 6, 1791 Jan 8, 1876 "Father"	Thomas L. Moseley 1867-1944 & Sallie W. Moseley 1880-1963
Elijah Warren 1867-1956 & Elizabeth Warren 1875-1931	Nancy E. Williams Feb 2, 1854 Nov 3, 1935	Lecil Bartlett 1878-1938 & "Mother"	Nancy, 1st wife of Daniel Warren Died Dec 1859 (no marker)
E., Son of E. & S. E. Warren Jul 4, 1897 Jan 18, 1900	Michael J. Powell Died Dec 21, 1962 Age: (Infant) (TM)	Frances W. Bartlett 1876-1951 & "Son" Leonard Bartlett 1904-1952	Pricilla Newsom Jackson, 2nd wife of Daniel Warren Apr 2, 1821 Apr 22, 1884 (May be buried here, no marker)
Elijah, Son of T. W. & Lizzie Warren Mar 6, 1890 Dec 29, 1892	Infant Son of E. & S. E. Warren B&D Sep 4, 1896	Infant of T. W. & Lizzie Warren B&D Jun 12, 1893	Many unmarked graves.

* *

BOONEVILLE QUADRANGLE

ALLEN CEMETERY

LOCATION: Near the Bedford County line, south of New Herman.

Emily J. Brown
Died Feb 12, 1912
Age: about 84 years.

Pinkney Mizell Allen
Jun 3, 1864
Jan 20, 1888
&
Maude Idella Allen
Apr 24, 1870
Oct 30, 1873
Children of
J. F. & M. E. Allen.

John Stone
Jan 1, 1814
Jun 22, 1884

James Hawkins Womack
1844-1883
&
Sophia Allen Womack
1849-1895

Elizabeth, wife of
Calvin Stone
Dec 21, 1821
Dec 9, 1891

James N. Stone
Jan 11, 1844
May 29, 1899

Margret Tennessee, Daughter
of John & Sarah Stone
Dec 16, 1866
Sep 9, 1884

Sarah Ann, wife of
John Stone
Dec 29, 1826
Dec 8, 1877
Married Jun 29, 1846
Age: 50y, 1m, 10d.

Minnoe O., wife of
J. G. Woodard
Oct 18, 1874
Oct 30, 1903

Margret J., wife of
J. F. Wiseman
(dates broken away)

Several unmarked graves.

Nancy Jane, wife of
J. N. Stone
Dec 13, 1847
Dec 12, 1905

Mrs. M. J., wife of
T. A. Edens
Aug 22, 1853
Sep 30, 1891
Age: 38y, 1m, 8d.

10 Rock Vaults, no
inscriptions.

* *

BAXTER CEMETERY

LOCATION: In Robertson Hollow, NW of Lynchburg.

Infant of
J. F. & H. Baxter
B&D Apr 10, 1864

and

Infant of
J. F. & H. Baxter
B&D Apr 10, 1864

5 graves with no
markers.

* *

BUCKEYE CEMETERY

LOCATION: About two miles NW of Lynchburg, at Buckeye Hollow and Hobbs Hill.

Newton Foster
1864-1866
& wife
Minnie Foster
(no dates)
&
Marion Foster
1862-1904

Ella Woodard
Jan 5, 1874
Jan 15, 1896

William H. Locke
May 19, 1808
Sep 30, 1885

Cyntha, wife of
William H. Locke
Mar 10, 1810
Jun 15, 1887

Martha P. Locke
Dec 12, 1844
Mar 10, 1864

Ollie Wood
1888-1895
&
Mattie Wood
1876-1883
Children of
N. H. & Sadie Wood

William Woodard
Jul 30, 1830
Sep 5, 1902

Washington M. Foster
1822-1897
&
Janie Allen Foster
1820-1902

Nannie Wood
1867-1906

Minerva Woodard
May 25, 1830
Jul 20, 1909

About 15 graves marked with fieldstones, no inscriptions.

* *

BROWN CEMETERY

LOCATION: On the Fayetteville Road, One and one half miles SW of Lynchburg on Douglas Tipps Farm. This is one of the oldest graveyards in Moore County.

William Brown
Feb 15, 1773
May 6, 1844
Married May 15, 1804

Elizabeth Brown
Married May 15, 1804
Died Jan 26, 1826
Age: (not given)

Ann Brown
Born Feb 4, 1822
Died in the year 1847(?)

Several fieldstones, no
inscriptions.

Polly Brown
Born Jan 28, 1813
Died in the year 1817

M. E. Hinkle
(no dates, fieldstone)

* *

BOONEVILLE QUADRANGLE

CEMETERY

LOCATION: Two and one half miles west of Lynchburg in Buckeye Hollow on the Old John Keller Farm.

Several fieldstones, no inscriptions. Information supplied by Mr. Klyne Jack Keller.

* *

CHARITY CEMETERY

LOCATION: Three miles north of Booneville, at Bagley Hollow and West Fork of Mulberry Creek.

Rev. J. L. Leftwich
May 8, 1787
Jun 13, 1847

James Edde, Son of
Joel & Patience Rees
May 26, 1842
May 3, 1845

James S. Bryant
Oct 9, 1822
Oct 19, 1854

Francis Kincannon, Son of
Joel & Patience Rees
Jan 3, 1832
May 19, 1843

Mattie A., Daughter of
J. L. & F. B. Bryant
Mar 6, 1823
Jan 25, 1865

Polly Rees
Jan 9, 1814
Aug 27, 1839

Jack L., Son of
Rebecca & A. G. Gill
Nov 1, 1832
Sep 15, 1837

Alanson G., Son of
Rebecca & A. G. Gill
May   1844
May 18, 1844

W. W., Son of
Rebecca & A. G. Gill
Jan 17, 1836
Jan 30, 1853

William H. H., Son of
A. G. & Rebecca Gill
Jun 10, 1840
Jan 25, 1855

Ermin Katharine, Daughter
of Alanson & Rebecca Gill
Aug 19, 1851
Dec 9, 1853

Rebecca S., Consort of
A. G. Gill & Daughter of
Jack H. & Jane Leftwich
Mar 13, 1812
Nov 23, 1855

Gabriel Pylant
Oct 18, 1821
Jun 18, 1905
&
Nancy B. Bryant
Sep 15, 1820
Jul 21, 1905

Fanny H., wife of
John Bryant
Aug 16, 1810
Aug 19, 1839

W. L. Rees
Sep 26, 1820
Mar 5, 1839

Susan, wife of
W. L. Rees
Nov 24, 1824
Mar 23, 1896

T. J. Rees
Dec 1, 1829
Dec 2, 1852

Mildred Rees
Oct 17, 1846
Dec 29, 1854

William M. Rees
Feb 18, 1849
Dec 29, 1854

Nancy J. Rees
Sep 27, 1844
Dec 27, 1854

William Minor, Son of
T. M. & C. A. Rees
Mar 5, 1868
Jan 18, 1874

Infant Daughter of
J. C. & M. H. Bryant
B&D Jun 22, 1874

Robert, Son of
Mark & V. C. Collier
Oct 22, 1852
Jan 3, 1855

John, Son of
Mark & V. C. Collier
Jan 22, 1854
Jan 14, 1855

Laura, Daughter of
Mark & V. C. Collier
Nov 9, 1855
Oct 21, 1857

Billie, Son of
Mark & V. C. Collier
Sep 26, 1857
Mar 3, 1868

Infant Son of
B. L. & S. E. Collier
B&D Dec 18, 1894

Infant of
B. L. & S. E. Collier
B&D Jan 16, 1890

Infant Daughter of
B. L. & S. E. Collier
B&D Nov 23, 1887

Joel Rees
Born in Bedford Co., Va.
Feb 4, 1804
Oct 31, 1861

Patience, wife of
Joel Rees
May 17, 1817
Mar 23, 1883

Nathaniel S. Rees
Dec 24, 1836
Jun 5, 1866

Mary B. Roughton
Jan 15, 1863
(only date on stone)

Eugene G. Smith
Jun 23, 1864
Jan 1, 1901

Rev. Samuel D. Sims
Oct 20, 1830
Dec 11, 1861
Age: 31y, 2m, 9d.

Infant of
T. R. & E. H. Morris
B&D Jul 4, 1884

Mary Jane Raby
Aug 19, 1853
Oct 16, 1892

M. A., wife of
W. H. Bagley
Sep 6, 1832
Apr 10, 1900

A. R. Smith
Jul 4, 1827
Mar 24, 1913
& wife
Nancy J. Rees Smith
Sep 6, 1830
May 13, 1880

Nettie, Daughter of
J. A. & Nannie Richardson
Oct 1, 1884
Apr 13, 1900

Edgar, Son of
J. A. & N. C. Richardson
May 2, 1892
Jul 22, 1893

Dempsey Sullivan
Jan 6, 1811
Feb 12, 1888
& wife
Naoma Sullivan
May 22, 1812
Sep 18, 1884

J. T. Smith
Jun 17, 1852
Jan 13, 1918
&
Dottie Smith
Feb 16, 1850
Oct 22, 1890

Dottie, Daughter of
J. T. & Donie Smith
Died Jun 27, 1894
Age: 10m, 25d.
&
Jones Douglas, Son of
W. O. & Willie Smith
Mar 17, 1893
Jul 10, 1893

William Richardson
Jan 5, 1826
Oct 17, 1908
& wife
Nancy Richardson
Mar 2, 1823
May 2, 1895

George W. Heath
Jul 4, 1842
Jun 17, 1917

Martha Heath
Oct 14, 1849
Feb 2, 1892

Maggie A., wife of
T. B. Bryant
Mar 6, 1860
Oct 29, 1880

Nannie A. Dean
Jul 7, 1844
Jun 18, 1869

James Neece
Jul 23, 1872
Apr 21, 1891

Mary, wife of
Dr. J. R. Carroll
Jun 26, 1846
Mar 10, 1896

Clara, Daughter of
Dr. J. T. & Mary Carroll
Feb 26, 1890
Nov 30, 1896

Jones M., Son of
S. D. & F. W. Renegar
Aug 18, 1893
Oct 16, 1896

Infant Son of
S. D. & F. W. Renegar
Aug 4, 1896
Aug 12, 1896

Infant Son of
S. D. & F. W. Renegar
B&D Mar 23, 1895

John R. Bagley
Nov 10, 1804
Jun 15, 1871

Robert Lee Smith
Sep 17, 1861
Apr 29, 1880

Mrs. Dorothy Lentini
1923-1967

Sarah Elizabeth, Daughter of
Thomas O. & Ettie Allen
B&D Aug 10, 1925

William Michael Richardson
Died Sep 13, 1968
Age: 42 years.

Bessie Richardson
1906-1910

Berry F. Richardson
1859-1935
&
Annie R. Richardson
1871-1961

J. Edwin Richardson
Tennessee
Pfc Co M 350 Inf
WW II B.S.M.
Jan 6, 1921
Jun 27, 1957

Mil Roy Lee Richardson
Tennessee
Pfc Co F 117 Inf
WW I PH
Dec 23, 1893
Jan 9, 1959

Rolen Newsom
1838-1898
&
Susan R. Newsom
1868-1942

Roy Edward Collier
1902-1928
&
Charlie Isom Collier
1894-1922
&
Theophilus J. Collier
1870-1912
&
M. Etta Gill Collier
1873-1954

Laura B. Collier
1904-1905

Infant Son of
T. J. & Etta Collier
1906

George L., Son of
T. M. & C. A. Rees
Apr 3, 1875
Nov 28, 1897

Robert T., Son of
R. O. & N. I. Reese
Mar 9, 1911
Mar 22, 1911

William Evans Reese
Feb 6, 1871
Oct 1, 1916

Mandy Reese
1880-1946

John A. Richardson
1857-1932
&
Nannie B. Richardson
1860-1939

May Ola, Daughter of
T. M. & M. T. Rees
Mar 27, 1895
Dec 22, 1895

Rob. Cleveland, Son of
T. M. & Ella Rees
Died Nov 3, 1900
Age: (not given)

Catharine A., wife of
T. M. Rees
Oct 10, 1846
Feb 16, 1896

Malnua Rees
Nov 22, 1873
Dec 4, 1904

Myrtle Richardson
1890-1921

James D., Son of
B. E. & S. M. Richardson
Apr 20, 1914
Jul 30, 1914

Mark Collier
May 20, 1824
Aug 14, 1900
&
Virginia Collier
Feb 1, 1826
Mar 31, 1902

Laton, Son of
M. D. & S. E. Collier
Dec 5, 1897
Sep 12, 1902

Mark Collier
May 18, 1851
Jun 15, 1918

Sallie, wife of
M. D. Collier
Aug 21, 1866
Aug 12, 1906

Claud E. Collier
Feb 17, 1885
Oct 30, 1957

Lorene, Daughter of
M. D. & Fannie Collier
Jan 21, 1913
Jan 28, 1913

Charles W. Gill
Died Aug 16, 1906
Age: (not given)

W. N. Gill
Mar 3, 1862
Aug 23, 1906

O. C. Gill, Jr.
Oct 21, 1910
Jan 8, 1914

W. H. Robinson
1879-1923
&
Lois Robinson
1885-1923

Almar J. Collier
Aug 16, 1906
Sep 30, 1907

Alice E., Daughter of
A. M. & Day. Partain
1919-1926

McGruder Phelps
1870-1946
&
Ida Alice Phelps
1873-1948

H. K. Raney
1827-1908
&
M. E. Raney
1838-(no date)

Infant Son of
H. P. & M. E. Collier
Mar 24, 1919
Mar 27, 1919

T. B. Rees
1862-(no date)
&
Sallie E. Rees
1864-1935

James E. Rees
Aug 25, 1849
Apr 3, 1927
&
Fannie A. Rees
Oct 18, 1848
Feb 13, 1920

John H. Broadway
Died Feb 5, 1912
Age: 34y, 11m, 19d.

P. L. Bryant, Jr.
Apr 28, 1895
Aug 14, 1895

Tommie H. Bryant
Nov 21, 1896
Mar 15, 1911

Virginia E. Runnels,
wife of P. L. Bryant
Feb 19, 1865
Dec 27, 1906

Henry Runnels
1867-1938
&
Etta Runnels
1873-1947

J. E. Runnels
May 27, 1835
Sep 15, 1894
& wife
Mary F. Rees Runnels
Mar 1, 1825
Jun 26, 1898

John H. Smith
1860-1941

Susie Gill Smith
1867-1923

BOONEVILLE QUADRANGLE

Ethel, Daughter of
J. H. & Susie Smith
(no dates)

Coleman T., Infant of
J. H. & Susie Smith
(no dates)

R. Gill Smith
Mar 19, 1901
Mar 18, 1955

William P. Petty
1876-(no date)
&
Josie Reese Petty
1882-1929

Andrew C. Petty
1884-1960
&
Mary R. Petty
1884-

Ben O. Petty
1883-1944
&
Fannie M. Petty
1890-

Willie Benny Petty
1946-1946

Albertia Petty
1909-1927

Irene P. Moore
Feb 28, 1916
Nov 3, 1955

Lee B. McNatt
1870-1943
&
Mattie McNatt
1870-1963

Callie McNott(McNatt)
1872-1937

Sybil P. Williams
Mar 31, 1903
Oct 31, 1958

J. T. Richardson
1854-1937
&
Nannie Richardson
1859-1934

Infant Daughter of
O. C. & Daisy Richardson
B&D Mar 5, 1910

C. W. Bagley
1863-1929
&
Laura Bagley
1868-1936

Several unmarked graves.

* *

COX CEMETERY

LOCATION: On the West Fork of Mulberry Creek, near Warren
Hollow, about one and one half miles SW of Charity Church.

J. L. Cox
1830-1894

A. W. Cox
1895-1921

Sallie Cox
1826-1906

Joseph W. Cox
1861-1929

N. L. Cox
Oct 4, 1857
Aug 25, 1933

Several unmarked graves.

* *

CRESON CEMETERY

LOCATION: Two miles west of Charity Church, on the West
Fork of Mulberry Creek, near Warren Hollow.

James Creson
1810-1852

3 graves with fieldstones,
no inscriptions.

Rebecca, wife of
James Creson
Nov 8, 1813
Feb 25, 1891

Louisa C., Daughter of
J. & R. Creson
Dec 20, 1835
Feb 22, 1858

Sarah A., Daughter of
J. & R. Creson
Aug 14, 1832
Aug 31, 1857

* *

DANIEL CEMETERY

LOCATION: Two and one half miles SW of Lynchburg and north
of Highway # 55.

Calaway Daniel
Died Jan 21, 1864
Age: 63 years.
&
Lucinda Daniel
Died Jan 29, 1847
Age: 48 years.

L. D.
(no dates)

William Butler Heath
Apr 15, 1877
Apr 2, 1878

Belle T., wife of
J. W. T. Heath
Apr 24, 1857
May 26, 1902

Many unmarked graves.

James S. Connor
Jun 1, 1828
Feb 20, 1902

M. E., Daughter of
J. S. & M. E. Connor
B&D Nov 30, 1860

Matilda, wife of
Wilson Hinkle
Jan 15, 1818
Mar 16, 1878

Aldin J., wife of
W.T. Baldwin
Jan 15, 1838
May 27, 1877

Fanie L., Daughter of
W.T. & A.J. Baldwin
1862-1863

* *

BOONEVILLE QUADRANGLE

DAWDY CEMETERY

LOCATION: This cemetery is located where Dogtail Creek strikes Eden Hollow.

Thomas Blythe
Mar 4, 1783
Aug 28, 1829
&
Pheby, Consort of
Thomas Blythe
Aug 9, 1793
Jan 3, 1860

Howel Dawdy
Died Dec 20, 1830
Age: 84 years.
&
Phebe, His wife
Died Dec 10, 1831
Age: 81 years.

Ahena Myrtle, Daughter of
F. M. & P. S. Edns (Edens)
Mar 28, 1872
Feb 11, 1875
Age: 2y, 11m, 17d.

Bolen Clark
Apr 4, 1817
Mar 12, 1885

Sarah, wife of
Bolen Clark
Mar 7, 1820
Feb 16, 1868

Many fieldstones, no inscriptions.

Sonie, Daughter of
C. C. & S. E. Cox
Nov 19, 1886
Apr 13, 1888

Thos. Bevehon
Aug 28, 1820 (Died)
Age: 46y, 5m, 24d.

Many unmarked graves.

* *

EATON CEMETERY

LOCATION: One and one half miles SW of Lynchburg on the East Fork of Mulberry Creek.

William Spencer and
Mar 14, 1798
Jan 21, 1878
Age: 80y, 10m, 7d.

Nancy, wife of
William Spencer
May 11, 1799
Aug 24, 1869
Age: 70y, 3m, 13d.

Susan, Consort of
Alfred Eaton
Sep 5, 1810
Jul 12, 1866
Age: 55y, 9m, 27d.

* *

EDEN CEMETERY

LOCATION: One and one half miles north of Lynchburg near Price Creek and Enochs Hollow.

Andrew Wagner
Oct 12, 1826
Jan 16, 1868
&
J. E. Wagner
Oct 16, 1867
Mar 12, 1870
&
Infant Daughter of
Andrew & Emily Wagner
1859

Acy Oliver
Oct 15, 1827
Mar 4, 1876

Mary, wife of
Acy Oliver
Sep 13, 1833
Dec 10, 1883

Elisabeth A., wife of
M. L. Parks
Mar 17, 1831
Sep 29, 1867
Age: 36y, 6m, 12d.

Alexander Edens
Jun 25, 1799
Apr 13, 1871

Cincinnati, wife of
Alexander Edens
Dec 12, 1803
Jun 20, 1887
Age: 83y, 1m, 10d.

About 20 graves with fieldstones, no inscriptions.

Joseph T. Edens
Aug 28, 1839
Jan 14, 1857

Amanda M., wife of
W. A. Hobbs
May 26, 1826
Sep 22, 1864
Age: 38y, 3m, 26d.

* *

GATTIS CEMETERY

LOCATION: This cemetery is located SW of Lynchburg, on Raymond Spencer Farm, this graveyard is almost gone, it was a large graveyard at one time.

William Gattis
Died Feb 12, 1855
Age:(not given)
(fieldstone)

Elizabeth Gattis
Died Oct 10, 1854
Age: (not given)
(fieldstone)

Marracia R., Consort of
W. A. Hobbs
Oct 28, 1816
Aug 29, 1852
Age: 35y, 10m, 1d.

G. G. Burton
Sep --, 1827
Oct --, 1861
(fieldstone)

J. M. Whitlock
Aug --, 1831
Feb 1, 1863
(fieldstone)

Mary Marilda Whitlock
Mar 26, 1861
Mar 6, 1863
(fieldstone)

D.
A. P. S.
1868
(fieldstone)

Many graves marked with fieldstones, no inscriptions.

* *

BOONEVILLE QUADRANGLE

GOWEN CEMETERY

LOCATION: This cemetery is about four and one half miles north of Lynchburg, on Wiseman Road between Anderson Hollow and Bedford Hollow, on top of hill.

James J. Gowen
Dec 29, 1847
Feb 4, 1922
&
Permelia E. Gowen
Jul 24, 1843
Jun 15, 1934

Albert Parks Gowen
Nov 26, 1879
Aug 17, 1956

Isaac Franklin Gowen
Oct 8, 1882
Jul 3, 1949

James Gowen
Pvt. Tennessee Vols
War of 1812
Died May 14, 1880
Age: (not given)

Elenor Merrill, widow
of Isaac Wiseman
Died Mar 3, 1891
Age: 100y, 5m.
(Family Record)

Sarah M., wife of
Thomas J. Baxter
Sep 20, 1849
Nov 28, 1882

Mattie, Daughter of
Thomas J. & Sarah M.
Baxter
Jan 24, 1874
Jun 7, 1875

Billie, Son of
L. W. & Rebecca Gowan
Apr 6, 1872
May 12, 1874

L. W. Gowan
Oct 30, 1847
Nov 12, 1923

Rebecca N. Gowan
Mar 25, 1846
Feb 29, 1876

Ora Gowen
Apr 29, 1890
Apr 6, 1892
&
Ola Gowen
Apr 29, 1890
Jun 29, 1890

B. F. Bedford
Mar 10, 1828
Oct 25, 1902

Nancy Ann Bedford
Oct --, 1839
Aug 22, 1885

Lucy Beatrice Bedford
Aug 26, 1874
Oct 17, 1878

Sydney Pauline Jane Bedford
Dec 12, 1887 *
Feb 20, 1870
(* we believe these dates
are reversed on the stone)

Several unmarked graves.

James Stone
Sep 5, 1799
Jun 27, 1876

Margaret Stone
Nov 19, 1804
Oct 8, 1882

T. R. Cunningham
Jul 3, 1858
Feb 14, 1880

Earnest L., Son of
T. N. & S. J. Driver
May 2, 1878
Mar 12, 1882

William Floyd
Feb 13, 1820
Jul 11, 1906
&
Sallie Floyd
May 22, 1823
Oct 25, 1889

* *

HICKS CEMETERY

LOCATION: Two miles north of Booneville, where Spankem Branch runs into Mulberry Creek.

Marker:
"The Family of
Elisha Hicks".

Clarence Hicks
Oct 21, 1890
Nov 1, 1910

Clyde Hicks
Aug 12, 1896
Oct 14, 1910

Toxie Florence Hicks
Jan 7, 1901
Oct 30, 1905

About 4 unmarked graves.

* *

HIGHVIEW CEMETERY

LOCATION: This cemetery is located in Lynchburg. This is a Colored Cemetery.

Dena Whitaker
1863-1969
(Harrison FH)

James Wesley Smith
May 2, 1848
Feb 27, 1931

Hattie Robinson
Nov 13, 1895
Aug 30, 1920

Mary Jane Smith Robinson
Nov 13, 1871
Aug 11, 1904

Philip Reese
Sep 21, 1828
Feb 24, 1904
& wife
Loueza Timmons Reese
Aug 26, 1845
May 3, 1903

Pvt, Harold Eady
Jul 2, 1952
Aug 2, 1972
&
Gertrude Eady
Jun 17, 1951

Mary Lenetta Reese
1972-1972
(Harrison FH)

Harriet A. Womack, wife
of J. W. Smith
Aug 16, 1851
Mar 6, 1915

Nancy Kelsaw
Died Jan 12, 1894
Age: (not given)

Bennie P. Reese
1876-1955
(Harrison FH)

Emma F. Reese
Jun 7, 1885
Nov 22, 1925

John Horton
1914-1972
(Harrison FH)

Annett Vance
1962-1962
(Harrison FH)

Berry B. Smith
May 20, 1887
Mar 9, 1910

Ella Smith
Aug 28, 1892
May 29, 1898

Charlie Lee Reese
1957-1958
(Harrison FH)

Sp 4 Freddie L. Daniel
Tennessee
  Sp 4 Btry C 1 Bn
44 Art. Vietnam, B.S.M.
PH
Jun 18, 1945
Jun 27, 1965

Morth, wife of
Ike Womack
(no dates)

Anner C. Burgess
1874-1964

J. F. D.(Daniel)
(no dates)

Eliza Lee Daniel
1891-1957
(Harrison FH)

Edith Lee Ingle
1885-1957
(Harrison FH)

Lillian B. Waggoner
1923-1955
(Harrison FH)

Hiram L. Waggoner, Jr.
1937-1959

Robert L. Daniel
1908-1963
(Harrison FH)

Mary Jane Hudson
1871-Sep 25, 1901

William E. Green
Mar 1, 1864
Sep 4, 1950
&
Rosie A. Green
Apr 1, 1867
Mar 20, 1939

Elizzia Green
May 29, 1890
Sep 13, 1908
Age: 18y, 8m, 6d.

Wallace Henderson
1955-1955
(Harrison FH)

Infant Word
1961-1961
(Harrison FH)

Gorge Daniel
1826-1906

Scott Thomison
1885-1957
(Gregory-Howard FH)

Cordelia Thomison
1891-1968
(TM)

Reak H. Green
1898-1959
(Harrison FH)

Oscar Green
Tennessee
  Pvt U. S. Army WW I
Jul 24, 1972 (died)
&
Della J. Green
Jan 8, 1895
Sep 2, 1967

Willie O. Daniel
1937-1940

Minnie, wife of
T. H. Hiles
1876-May 7, 1918

Emiline Hiles
1859-Feb 3, 1907

Laurie Smith
1873-May 26, 1900

Christ Grizzard
1870-1952

Tom Green
Oct 11, 1892
Feb 7, 1971
&
Gurtrude Green
May 12, 1892

Henry Bailey
Tennessee
  Corp 418 Res Labor Bn
Feb 3, 1934 (died)

Vivianne Henderson
1964-1964
(Harrison FH)

Nathaniel Ingle
1876-1963
(Harrison FH)

Katie S. Ingle
1885-1969
(Harrison FH)

Alma Fay Peppers
1930-1959
(Harrison FH)

George Green
Jun 13, 1866
(no date)
&
Missie Green
Mar 12, 1872
Mar 23, 1931

Charlie Green
1874-1962
(Harrison FH)

Mary E. Green
1872-(gone)(Harrison FH)

Susan F. Overbey
Dec 25, 1865
Jul 10, 1916

L. B. McGowen, Jr.
1965-1965
(Harrison FH)

_____ --derson
born (date gone)
died 1966
(Harrison FH)

William Jessie Eady
May 15, 1874
Dec 27, 1941

Henry Green
1901-1974
(Harrison FH)

Parthenia Green
Dec 2, 1869
Jul 29, 1948

Timothy Wade Reese
1966-1966
(J. A. Welton FH)

Hosea Parker
1889-1969
(Harrison FH)

Nannie Parker
1887-1974
(Harrison FH)

Billy Norman Trollinger
Tennessee
  Pvt U. S. Army
Aug 9, 1951
Oct 28, 1971

John Wesley Green
Tennessee
  A2C U. S. Air Force
Jul 24, 1925
Jan 14, 1970

Milton J. Green
Tennessee
  Pvt Co F 6 Pioneer Inf
WW I
Sep 5, 1893
Apr 1, 1960

Reak H. Green
Tennessee
  Pvt 6 Co Recruit Camp
WW I
Jul 3, 1897
Mar 20, 1959

Ethel Green
1954-1954
(Harrison FH)

Nancy Green
1953-1953
(Harrison FH)

Coy White
Nov 25, 1888
Sep 17, 1968
&
Sadie White
Dec 22, 1895
Jan 8, 1943

Irene G. Carter
1876-1955
(Harrison FH)

Lucy Parks
Died Jan 11, 1951
Age: (not given)

Dick Show (Shaw)
Feb 24, 1858
Mar 2, 1913

Fan Shaw
Age: 88 years
(no dates)

Ethel C., wife of
Joe Dance
Jul 24, 1887
Oct 7, 1913

Annie Garmon
1873-1963
(Harrison FH)

Ed Hart
1867-(no date)
&
Fannie Hart
1868-1947

Annie Eady Ingle
Sep 8, 1915
Jul 10, 1932

Sarah May, Daughter of
Lee Voy & Annie Ingle
Jun 14, 1932
Jul 15, 1932

Morris Eady
Jul 7, 1893
Nov 20, 1970
&
Ella Eady
Oct 23, 1893

Mary Sue Eady
Jun 18, 1932
Feb 24, 1933

George White
1886-1961
(Harrison FH)

Maria Anne White
1901-1973
(J. A. Welton FH)

Dora B. Whitaker
1900-1956

BOONEVILLE QUADRANGLE

Jessie G. Green
Aug 9, 1889
Mar 17, 1972
&
Mattie Green
May 10, 1889

Henry Baxter
1875-1959

Arthur Green
Tennessee
Pvt Co C 324 SVC Bn
QMC WW I
Nov 20, 1896
Jan 2, 1969

Fannie P. Green
1901-1965
(Harrison FH)

Bobby L. Phelps
May 7, 1938
May 31, 1964

Tom Bonner
1888-1969
(J. A. Welton FH)

Lillie S. Bonner
1888-1966

Beverly Word
1959-1965
(Harrison FH)

Mahaley Allen
1866-1905

Robert Ingle
1922-1952
(Harrison FH)

Many unmarked graves.

* *

LYNCHBURG CEMETERY

LOCATION: This cemetery is located within the City limits of Lynchburg, sometimes called Masonic & Odd Fellow Cemetery.

North-East Section

William Brady Gattis
Aug 16, 1894

&
Laura May Tipps Gattis
Mar 12, 1898
Apr 24, 1968

Tracy Eugene Painter
1973-1973
(Harrison FH)

Teddy P. Vaughan
Tennessee
AT1 U. S. Navy, Korea
Sep 20, 1931
Feb 17, 1973

James M. Turpin
1947-1969
(Harrison FH)

Edwin Lester Burton
Tennessee
AMN U. S. Air Force,
Korea
Nov 19, 1932
Sep 21, 1972

Effie V. Evans
1895-1929
&
Cordellia Evans
1856-1947

James William Prater
Cunningham
Jul 13, 1925
Aug 25, 1970

Emmett Martin
Jul 12, 1897

&
Teresa P. Martin
Feb 4, 1901
Dec 13, 1967

J. W. Hazelwood
Jul 13, 1917
Jul 14, 1970
&
Frances Hazelwood
Jan 5, 1921

James Albert Deal
1913-1968
(Gowen-Smith FH)

Douglas E. McNeil
Aug 18, 1917

Evelyn S. McNeil
Feb 2, 1917
Aug 12, 1967

Jim W. Wagoner
1885-1950
(Harrison FH)

Ben T. Kight
Mar 13, 1898
Dec 29, 1971
&
Nettie H. Kight
May 4, 1900
May 8, 1973

Belinda Faye Tucker
B&D Jun 19, 1971

Edward Earl Horton
Aug 24, 1965
Sep 4, 1965

William P. Stone
1895-1974
(Harrison FH)

Lon Burton
1885-1971
&
Carrie Burton
1893-1971

Robert D. Wiseman
Aug 18, 1903

&
Beatrice Wiseman
Feb 22, 1905
Apr 18, 1966

Ernest Eugene Locke
Tennessee
SK3 U. S. N. R. F.
WW I
Dec 1, 1890
Aug 8, 1966

A. Leo Sanders
Jun 22, 1916
Nov 25, 1968
&
Virginia W. Sanders
Jun 7, 1916

Jake Evans
Aug 20, 1898
Dec 17, 1967
&
Annie Simpson Evans
Feb 11, 1894

Ernest L. Riddle
Jul 27, 1905

&
Crysta Lee A. Riddle
Dec 1, 1901
Dec 12, 1927
Married Nov 1927

Jack Henry Chapman
Dec 15, 1952
Sep 9, 1966

Amy Henry Chapman
Jun 30, 1919

Everett A. Chapman
Jun 15, 1919

John Leonard Chapman
Jun 11, 1894
Feb 29, 1972

Stella Massey Chapman
Apr 1, 1898

Thomas J. Lesley
Jul 11, 1849
Mar 8, 1937
&
Manervia C. Lesley
Feb 25, 1873
Jun 9, 1948

Robert W. Lesley
Nov 29, 1900
Mar 30, 1934

Ruth Hudgins Ward
Oct 7, 1912
Feb 21, 1971

Otis Henry Templeton
Oct 18, 1905

Mary D. Fanning Templeton
May 23, 1910
May 22, 1973

Elijah Ward Stone
Oct 7, 1887
Nov 16, 1966

Lema Price Stone
Jul 6, 1889
Jul 18, 1972

Huston L. Burton
Jan 12, 1935
Aug 22, 1965

BOONEVILLE QUADRANGLE

Horace W. Ervin
Tennessee
Tec 5 469 AA AW Bn
WW II
Dec 15, 1922
Jul 1, 1970
&
Ruby T. Ervin
Jan 2, 1924

Clifford W. Bearden
Dec 5, 1894
Jul 20, 1965
&
Ireva Spencer Bearden
Oct 5, 1899

Married Dec 12, 1921

William Emmett Stone
Tennessee
MAM 2 U. S. N. R.
WW II
Sep 29, 1915
Apr 10, 1964

Ruth Poe Stone
Mar 19, 1918

Thomas Z. Haslett
Jan 16, 1873
Jan 22, 1938
&
Floy B. Haslett
Aug 27, 1890
Jun 13, 1966

Howard C. Collins
Tennessee
Tec 3 3108 Ordnance Co
WW II
Jun 19, 1920
Aug 12, 1963

Mattie Glenn Travis Collins
May 19, 1890
Jan 6, 1971

R. Milton Bates
Sep 17, 1908
Dec 24, 1964
&
Karona G. Bates
Apr 14, 1917

Sammie Dewane Haslett
Dec 7, 1952
Dec 9, 1952

Billy Haslett
Sep 21, 1927
Apr 8, 1934

G. A. Massey
1873-1932

Bettie Massey
1874-1934

Daniel C. Gray
Oct 18, 1860
Apr 18, 1944
&
Sallie E. Gray
Jan 28, 1862
Dec 8, 1931

Charles Dillard Gray
Sep 15, 1884
Apr 3, 1954
&
Myrtle Wanslow Gray
Aug 2, 1887
Apr 28, 1965

Robert W. Smith
1859-1938
&
Mollie C. Smith
1864-1960

William B. Smith
May 1, 1901

&
Mary L. Smith
Nov 1, 1906
Feb 5, 1953

Curtis Sawyer
1895-1956
&
Esther Sawyer
1894-1942

Lodger Burton
Jun 18, 1905
Jan 8, 1970
&
Nell Haslett Burton
May 26, 1910

Ray L. Rhoton
Feb 24, 1896
Feb 8, 1965
&
Lula Mae Rhoton
Dec 23, 1901
Aug 27, 1964

George R. Collins
1952-1971
(Daves-Culbertson FH)

Matthew R. Noles
Tennessee
Cpl H. V. Mort. Co.
21 Inf, Korea
Aug 15, 1927
Jan 2, 1964

Mattie Noles
1895-1973
(Moore-Cortner FH)

Ollie R. Edde
Sep 18, 1882
Dec 30, 1965

William Cliff Deal
Jul 30, 1904
Sep 6, 1964
&
Leona Evans Deal
Jan 28, 1903

Charles F. Johnston
Apr 10, 1911

&
Hazel Fae Johnston
Mar 17, 1912
May 27, 1964

Jesse G. Fanning
Jul 11, 1891
Dec 12, 1968
&
Vannie C. Fanning
Oct 18, 1897
Sep 6, 1969

William Bobo "Bill" Majors, Sr.
Nov 7, 1938
Oct 18, 1965

Samuel W. Parks
May 22, 1894

&
Katie R. Parks
May 16, 1898
Aug 28, 1966

Infant Twin Daughters of
Billy J. & Helen Henshaw
B&D Jun 15, 1964

Don V. Snyder
Sep 24, 1918

&
Kate F. Snyder
Oct 30, 1888

Hayden Alton Brazier
1895-1946

Sam Ransom Sawyer
Feb 19, 1900
Jun 22, 1956

Thomas G. Riddle
Jan 14, 1870
Jan 9, 1945

Emma Hinkle Riddle
Jul 9, 1877
Dec 21, 1955

James Edde, Jr.
1889-1972
&
Mattie C. Edde
1892-1941

Carlis H. Edde, Jr.
Oct 2, 1922
Jan 26, 1946

Frank Walker
Jun 10, 1913

&
N. Kathleen Walker
Nov 25, 1918
Mar 14, 1971

Carlis H. Eddie
Oct 11, 1899
Aug 1, 1956
&
Mattie Lou Eddie
Dec 22, 1893

Florence Lee
Jun 28, 1896
Nov 5, 1951

Essie Olena Lee
Jan 20, 1892
Nov 24, 1941
&
Marion R. Lee
Dec 1, 1891
Aug 19, 1959

Fred W. Durham
1914-
&
Nelle E. Durham
1921-1971
Married Feb 15, 1941

Chaney L. Fanning
Jul 10, 1894

William D. Bailey
Apr 30, 1869
Oct 14, 1946
&
Ora Belle Bailey
Nov 12, 1888
Jun 15, 1957

Buford Henry Price
Dec 24, 1896
Apr 5, 1946
&
Pauline W. Price
Jan 20, 1905

Dena Page Price
Oct 16, 1860
Oct 22, 1960

Charles Leo Harrison
Nov 27, 1900
Oct 7, 1969
&
Christine Ervin Harrison
Jun 22, 1908

Married Dec 20, 1930

Mary Della Fanning
Apr 17, 1895
Jun 5, 1972
(on same stone as C. L.)

BOONEVILLE QUADRANGLE

James Clarence Rhoton and Agnes Ruth Eddins Rhoton
Tennessee   Apr 21, 1897
Sgt Quarter Master Corps ------------
WW I
Jan 27, 1894
Dec 2, 1968

Middle-North Section

Estill Crocker
May 12, 1916
 Aug 17, 1972
&
Hattie D. Crocker
Jun 24, 1917

Married Jun 22, 1935

Clyde C. Armstrong
Feb 27, 1901

&
Lyndal D. Armstrong
Dec 24, 1908
Oct 19, 1967

Lloyd T. Waggoner, Sr.
May 26, 1913
Sep 17, 1965
&
Catherine A. Waggoner
Apr 24, 1912
Mar 19, 1972

Thomas A. Bean
Jan 14, 1875
Feb 4, 1969

Marion Alvis Bean
1874-1961
&
Delia Brooks Bean
1890-1925

Louis Edward Martin
May 5, 1906

&
Annie Eleanor Martin
Feb 20, 1915
Jun 4, 1972

Jesse C. Gamble
Dec 21, 1901

&
Lenous D. Gamble
Sep 19, 1906

Madison E. Tripp
Aug 21, 1892
Jul 18, 1968
&
Ollye W. Tripp
Nov 28, 1895

Unknown Boy
1970-1970
(Harrison FH)

Billie R. Capps
May 22, 1926

&
Otis B. Capps, Jr.
Jun 7, 1918

Married Jul 12, 1947

John C. Woosley
Nov 29, 1899
Feb 14, 1963
&
Mattie L. Woosley
Sep 13, 1901

Billie Joe Finney
Dec 4, 1938
Dec 8, 1938

Ruby Walker Finney
Oct 1, 1913
Aug 10, 1955

Charlie O. Sawyer
1898-1970
&
Clara E. Sawyer
1897-1971

G. Tom Noblitt
1875-1949
&
Ada J. Noblitt
1878-1946

D. P. Smoot
Nov 8, 1858
Jan 6, 1904

Bettie, wife of
D. P. Smoot
Apr 16, 1869
Sep 15, 1899

Infant Daughter of
D. P. & Bettie Smoot
Sep 14, 1899
Mar 16, 1900

Ann T., wife of
Daniel Smoot
Jan 1, 1827
Jun 15, 1885

Fred M. Raby
1867-1920
(Gowen-Smith FH)

Nannie E. Raby
1867-1951
(Gowen-Smith FH)

P. A. Raby
Dec 30, 1837
Jan 17, 1916
&
Anna H. Raby
Jun 12, 1837
May 13, 1905

J. Eggleston Raby
Dec 23, 1873
Jan 21, 1902

Pink M. Allen
1882-1947

Candace S. Allen
1882-1957

Errett Mullins
1838-1944
&
Florence Mullins
1895-19(no date)

Parks Lyle Hays
Tennessee
Sgt Co E 119 Inf WW I
Feb 15, 1895
May 20, 1966

Lucile H. Hays
1894-1951

May L. Hays
1870-1948

Thomas A. Hays
1865-1947

Davie Danuel, Son of
Mr. & Mrs. M. G. Osborn
Sep 14, 1887
Oct 16, 1888

M. G. Osborne
Oct 20, 1833
Jan 30, 1897

Martha J., wife of
M. G. Osborn
Oct 20, 1830
Aug 24, 1877

James Wilson Byrom
Mar 12, 1838
Apr 27, 1919
&
Katherine Millsaps Byrom
Aug 17, 1851
Apr 25, 1922

Emmett Stone
1891-1948
&
Nell Stone
1895-1967

John W. Stone
Sep 17, 1919
Jul 9, 1939

Bill Clark
Jun 30, 1887

&
Mary Clark
Jun 6, 1887
Apr 21, 1969
&
Jack Clark
May 7, 1931
Jun 12, 1933

John W. Clark
May 6, 1945
Nov 29, 1967

John Lawrence Haston
Mar 28, 1890
Jul 25, 1918

C. W. Wiggins
Nov 28, 1884

& wife
Annie Lee Wiggins
Nov 1, 1886
Sep 27, 1924

Jose Peal
Oct 15, 1830
Jun 7, 1911
&
Mary Peal
Apr 9, 1833
Aug 8, 1909

John W. Tipps
1871-1937
&
Cora Evans Tipps
1880-1961

Raybella, Daughter of
J. W. & Cora Tipps
May 15, 1913
Oct 24, 1918

James W. Evans
1921-1941
&
F. Carl Evans
1893-1940

BOONEVILLE QUADRANGLE

Rufus W. Sweeney
1884-

Beulah Snow Sweeney
1890-1971

Thelma, Daughter of
R. W. & B. A. Sweeney
1911-1924

Alvis F. Cobb
Aug 16, 1894

&
Ruth Wanslow Cobb
Aug 19, 1899
Jul 4, 1966

Thomas G. Hardy
1871-1962
&
Sarah Hardy
1881-1957

Enciel L. Daniel
Feb 10, 1883
Dec 3, 1970
&
Maggie D. Daniel
Nov 11, 1880
May 26, 1965

Elon L. Robertson
Oct 11, 1904

&
Shirley J. Robertson
Dec 22, 1896
Jul 2, 1973
Married Oct 30, 1921

Lurene Rhoton Robert
Dec 15, 1913
Feb 2, 1968

Eldie Rhoton
Mar 6, 1889
Mar 22, 1962
&
Nannie Rhoton
Jan 26, 1885
May 25, 1963

Lawrence T. Hise
Tennessee
Pfc Btry A 197 Field Arty
WW II
Jul 28, 1918
Oct 14, 1961
&
Doris B. Hise
Jul 31, 1929

Henry P. Millsaps
Jul 16, 1885
Jul 30, 1925
&
Beulah B. Millsaps
Sep 23, 1887
Jun 30, 1968

John M. Walker
Oct 23, 1872
Apr 29, 1947
&
Leah M. Walker
Apr 11, 1881
Jun 12, 1965

Charles M. Smith
Apr 6, 1891
Dec 19, 1959
&
Eunice Smith
Apr 14, 1903
Jan 3, 1956

Jack Gray Harrison
Tennessee
AMM 1 U. S. N. R.
WW II
Nov 13, 1914
Dec 5, 1962

Charles L. Price
Oct 7, 1889
Dec 26, 1960

Laura M. Price
Nov 3, 1891

Rufus W. Price
Nov 1, 1901
Sep 17, 1960

Clemmie V. Price
May 17, 1907

Michael Stephen Ashby
Jan 19, 1958
Jan 20, 1958

P. H. Wanslow
Mar 31, 1869
Feb 11, 1941

Lula S. Wanslow
Sep 18, 1873
Jan 8, 1938

W. M. Rhoton
Nov 10, 1848
Oct 7, 1929

Dorris M., wife of
Marvin C. Foster
1901-1945

Georgia Walker Armstrong
Nov 4, 1904
Jul 24, 1954

Elizabeth (Walker) Evans
Nov 11, 1874
Mar 22, 1957

Maria Hobbs Bobo
Nov 3, 1902
Dec 7, 1965

Collis Evans
Aug 6, 1906

Annie B. Evans
Oct 18, 1910

Martha Ann Evans
May 12, 1944
Feb 8, 1962

T. J. (Thomas J.) Hise
Sep 16, 1886
1974 (TM)
&
Estill Hise
Jul 3, 1903
1972 (TM)

Bettie F. Burton
1930-1968
(Harrison FH)

Edna K. Allen
Sep 2, 1900
Jun 24, 1972

J. D. Allen
Tennessee
Pfc U. S. Marine Corps
WW II
Mar 26, 1920
Feb 4, 1968
&
Nell Allen
Mar 1, 1923

Thelma Tipps Walker
Aug 13, 1905
Nov 18, 1964

John N. Walker
1904-1967
(Harrison FH)

Sallie Simpson Parks
Sep 22, 1902
Aug 11, 1943
&
Samuel Prater Parks
Sep 16, 1898

&
Julia Smith Parks
Aug 18, 1902
Mar 13, 1964

Robert Rorax
Feb 7, 1879
Jun 17, 1951
&
Nora Rorax
Oct 23, 1879
Jul 28, 1965

Sallie Lillian, Daughter of
W. A. & C. B. Menges
Jan 13, 1909
Aug 14, 1909

Frank Gentry
May 22, 1861
Dec 25, 1920
&
Mary Gentry
Dec 8, 1866
Jun 21, 1957

J. V. Leftwich
1868-1951
&
Mary Leftwich
1878-1949

Cassie Warren
May 15, 1899

Fannie Warren
Dec 27, 1874
Oct 17, 1890

Maggie Warren
Jun 7, 1852
Dec 17, 1872

Roscoe "Doc" Reese
Aug 11, 1910
Nov 23, 1969
&
Odell Allen Reese
Sep 15, 1918
Aug 3, 1970
Married Feb 27, 1936

James Thomas Tipps
Feb 5, 1878
May 25, 1960
&
Minnie Painter Tipps
Mar 3, 1888
Jul 23, 1955

Beulah C. Bell
1893-1969

O. H. P. Bell
1853-1897
&
Jane E. Warren Bell
1853-1930

Robert Leon, Son of
C. R. & E. O. Tipps
Feb 25, 1926
Mar 27, 1926

Clumms Preston
Tennessee
Pfc U. S. Marine Corps
R. E. S.   WW II
Oct 21, 1911
Sep 12, 1958
&
Ruby S. Preston
Apr 12, 1917

Charles Allen
Jul 29, 1935

Frank Allen
1854-1967

BOONEVILLE QUADRANGLE

"Mother"
Catherine Leftwich
1848-1906
& "Daughter"
Lorena Leftwich
1864-1938

John C. Wagoner
1928-1972
&
Mildred I. Wagoner
1929-
Married Oct 25, 1947

John E. Waggoner
1904-1956
&
Ethel Waggoner
1907-

Gloria Carol Waggoner
Jul 2, 1955
Jul 3, 1955

Guy Waggoner
1885-1932
&
Mamie Waggoner
1887-1938

Infant Waggoner
(no date)
&
Nell E. Waggoner
1919-1920
&
Hilda J. Waggoner
1925-1925

Hubert Ike Vanzant
1903-1967

"Father"
G. H. Warren
Feb 4, 1826
Jan 16, 1906
& "Mother"
S. C. Warren
Nov 7, 1833
Feb 12, 1884

James Phillips Parks, Jr.
Feb 16, 1956
Feb 19, 1956

William H. Waggoner
Feb 19, 1864
Jun 7, 1931
&
Mary F. Waggoner
Apr 3, 1873
Sep 10, 1934

Marion A. Pitts
Jan 13, 1888
Apr 6, 1967
&
Thomas W. Pitts
Oct 5, 1880
Jun 11, 1971

Sue Frances, Daughter of
Tom & Marion Pitts
Sep 23, 1912
Mar 17, 1915

William R. Pitts
Nov 19, 1908
May 25, 1871

Oscar G. Conwell
Sep 5, 1883

&
Ethel M. Conwell
Oct 30, 1886
Jun 12, 1966

Clyde P. Codie
Oct 3, 1903

&
Onuf L. Codie
Oct 5, 1897
Oct 3, 1958

Thomas Frank Bobo
Oct 27, 1903
Feb 12, 1909

Sam L. Bobo
Jul 21, 1915
Sep 10, 1957

George D. Bobo
Oct 4, 1878
Jul 28, 1961

Pearl P. Bobo
Jul 30, 1878
Apr 7, 1967

Chanie S. Bobo
Apr 28, 1852
Dec 23, 1915
&
Laura Bobo
Jan 27, 1854
Feb 16, 1926

James T.(Thomas) Daniel
Mar 11, 1887
Sep 30, 1973
&
Kathryn S. Daniel
Mar 29, 1892

Married Feb 28, 1912

Argie Agnes Daniel
Sep 15, 1896
Dec 24, 1930

Infant of
Mr. & Mrs. C. E. Daniel
(no dates)

Nettie Sue Daniel
Sep 17, 1916
Sep 19, 1916

Charles Newton White
Jul 17, 1906
Mar 30, 1963
&
Adell Riddle White
Jan 6, 1912

William Colsher
1837-1921
&
Susan Colsher
1848-1927

Roy H. Parks, Sr.
1876-1948
&
Eva C. Parks
1879-1973

Lee C. Bobo
Tennessee
Pvt Field Arty
Jan 21, 1881
Sep 26, 1938
&
Nora Wiseman Bobo
Dec 24, 1880
Jul 2, 1960

Hogan C. Bobo
Apr 30, 1919
Feb 8, 1949

Ellie K. Pitts
Jul 17, 1867
May 19, 1939

George F. Waggoner
1877-1935

Lissie Waggoner
1897-1926

Charles R. Waggoner
1906-1916

Ernest White
1884-1949
&
Sarah E. White
1868-1924
&
John S. White
1910-1941

Charles A. Spann
Sep 13, 1868
Mar 28, 1941
&
Millia O. Spann
Oct 15, 1858
Jun 13, 1956

Ernest Floyd Sigmon
North Carolina
Pfc U. S. Army
WW I
Jul 14, 1895
Jul 3, 1955
&
Myrtle Parks Sigmon
Mar 3, 1897

Charlie L. Smith
Tennessee
Pfc Co D 46 Inf
WW I
Aug 17, 1888
Sep 8, 1965
&
Ova Rolman Smith
Sep 7, 1894

"Father"
R. C. Spann
Oct 22, 1874
Apr 10, 1926
"Mother"
M. E. Spann
Dec 19, 1873
(no date)

Mollie E. Spann
1874-1953
(Harrison FH)

Jimmy Sullivan
1958-1958
(Harrison FH)

Horace T. Ashby
Jul 15, 1900
Sep 16, 1970
&
Mary P. Ashby
Mar 6, 1909

Florida F. Smith
Sep 23, 1906
Aug 31, 1968

BOONEVILLE QUADRANGLE

North-West Section

Michael Alan Spray
Jan 17, 1954
Oct 5, 1972

Shela Ann, Daughter of
Glenn & Betty Ervin
Dec 12, 1946
Dec 15, 1946

Glenn O. Ervin
Tennessee
CSP U. S. Navy
WW II
Dec 23, 1901
Nov 26, 1971

J. Kermit Hill
Feb 7, 1907
Sep 22, 1968

Carrie Ann Shelton
1969-1969
(Harrison FH)

Theron V. Teeters
1890-1965
(Harrison FH)

E. E. "Gene" Allbritton
Mar 24, 1918
Dec 29, 1971
&
B. Lorene Allbritton
Nov 18, 1917

William Franklin Driver
Nov 30, 1945
Oct 20, 1966
(color picture)

George W. Burton
Aug 15, 1875
Jan 3, 1956
&
Lillie V. Burton
Dec 2, 1879
Nov 10, 1963

Gordon Alexander Jared
Jan 6, 1904
Oct 18, 1951
&
Rilda Copeland Jared
Jan 21, 1906

Willie Richard Womack
1948-1955
(Harrison FH)

Michie Sawyer
1889-1953
(Harrison FH)

Ben L. Sawyer
1882-1955
(Harrison FH)

Leonard Newton Smith
Dec 3, 1897
May 26, 1965
&
Eva Harding Smith
Dec 20, 1897
Feb 2, 1957
Married Sep 1, 1918

Marion C. Holt
Jan 17, 1907
Oct 21, 1965

Shederick L. Holt
Jan 31, 1916
Dec 31, 1955

John F. Simpson
Tennessee
Pvt Co G 6 Inf
WW I PH
Aug 14, 1895
Feb 9, 1964

J. L. Simpson
Sep 9, 1909
Mar 10, 1956

Sam L. Simpson
1900-1955

Lacy Simpson
1886-19
&
Donie Simpson
1886-1971

Thomas Turley Bedford
Jan 19, 1898

&
Mary Frances Bedford
Mar 6, 1897
Jan 27, 1963

Charles Ray Bedford
1928-1971

Riggs S. Bedford
Oct 31, 1870
Jul 29, 1959
&
Laura Stone Bedford
Jul 8, 1877
May 22, 1955

C. Lloyd Inlow
Oct 21, 1895
Mar 24, 1954

Elizabeth W. Inlow
May 28, 1918
Jun 22, 1967

Lillian Parks Bowen
1917-1960

Earl R. Bobo
1903-1952
&
Larue Bobo
1903-

John Thomas Stone
Oct 10, 1905
Nov 30, 1955

L. G. "Bud" Grant
Jul 30, 1864
Aug 2, 1958
&
Mollie Gray Grant
Sep 20, 1870
Dec 17, 1919

Robert Elam Bobo
Tennessee
SFC Arty WW II B.S.M.
Mar 24, 1913
Apr 15, 1968

Nora Dance Bobo
Sep 25, 1882
Oct 22, 1971

Landry C. Bobo
Aug 13, 1881
Jan 24, 1958

Walter Sawyer
Mar 16, 1874
Mar 20, 1952
&
Della Sawyer
Jul 4, 1876
Sep 13, 1952

Samuel Wilson Burton, Jr.
Jan 25, 1934
Dec 16, 1934

Jessie Lawrence Waggoner
Aug 3, 1890

Sallie Morris Waggoner
Aug 26, 1894

Christine Parks Sullivan
Dec 17, 1921
Feb 17, 1970

George W. Burrow
Jul 13, 1875
Jan 31, 1948
&
Eliza W. Burrow
Jan 19, 1875
May 3, 1962

Charlie C. Burrow
Aug 23, 1910
Feb 7, 1969

Thomas E. Simpson, Sr.
Oct 6, 1890
Feb 28, 1953

Tommy Simpson, Jr.
Feb 1, 1930
Feb 13, 1948

James Elmer Gore
Sep 30, 1890
Jun 26, 1965
&
Barshie Fears Gore
Apr 18, 1898

Elmer Gore
1935-1950

James D. "Red" Gore
Feb 11, 1920

&
Clara M. Gibbs Gore
Mar 27, 1917
Mar 19, 1964

Hollis Esco Turner
Feb 22, 1921
Nov 2, 1950
&
Mary Ellen Turner
Jun 17, 1910

Grady Reese
Oct 8, 1903
Jun 8, 1971
&
Evalene Reese
Apr 13, 1914

Married Sep 22, 1930

Gilford R. Parks
Oct 21, 1901
Oct 6, 1953
&
Siddie C. Parks
Nov 20, 1900
Apr 11, 1972

Alexander Huskey
1862-1933
&
Margaret S. Huskey
1867-1956

Clarence T. Huskey
Jul 17, 1894
Aug 7, 1959
&
Lillie Gattis Huskey
Jul 19, 1890

BOONEVILLE QUADRANGLE

John E. Bobo
Mar 18, 1869
Nov 13, 1928
&
Bessie L. Bobo
Jul 31, 1884
Dec 11, 1959

Anita, Daughter of
William D. &
Mary F. Copeland
Apr 15, 1936
May 5, 1936

Dr. J. D. McCord
1881-1941
&
Alice O. McCord
1890-1936

Infant Son of
Dr. & Mrs. J. D. McCord
B&D Oct 23, 1924

Anthony Floyd
1866-1942
&
Tennie Floyd
1873-1957

John D. Floyd
Oct 30, 1901
Mar 26, 1924

Stephen "T." Bobo
1875-1945
&
Jonnie Bobo
1878-1941

Ollie P. Sawyer
Dec 16, 1886
Dec 26, 1946
&
Minnie M. Sawyer
Mar 3, 1886
Jun 14, 1936

Imogene Sawyer
Nov 7, 1935
Jun 15, 1939

George F. Gray
Aug 21, 1899

&
Bessie Bobo Gray
Aug 11, 1898
Apr 6, 1971

Nora Rogers Gray
Jan 19, 1906

Carl F. Gray
Dec 27, 1888
Oct 23, 1960

Dorothy Jean, Daughter of
C. F. & Nora R. Gray
Jun 6, 1925
Jun 14, 1925

Elijah Dyer Moore
Sep 12, 1856
Sep 2, 1932
&
Sallie Stone Moore
Apr 16, 1858
May 2, 1931

Lillian, Daughter of
E. D. & Sallie Moore
Mar 25, 1900
Jan 7, 1913

John D. Solomon
May 18, 1873
Mar 27, 1947
&
Annie Joe Solomon
Jan 27, 1881
Dec 1, 1938

Mattie Leona Solomon
Jan 15, 1904
Aug 15, 1953

Reagor Motlow Garner
Jul 17, 1926
Jan 11, 1928

Henry Garner
1873-1967
(Motlow-Moore FH)

Elza B. Jenkins, Sr.
Feb 7, 1896
Oct 15, 1969
&
Clara Mae Jenkins
Oct 14, 1900
Jan 13, 1958

Margaret, Daughter of
Elza & Clara Jenkins
1924-1925

James P. Gray
Nov 14, 1865
Oct 4, 1952
&
Elizabeth Rogans Gray
Nov 29, 1867
Aug 18, 1958

James G. Gray
May 1, 1900
Oct 26, 1970
&
Frances F. Gray
Aug 6, 1912

Jesse Neece
1847-1924
&
Mattie Ann Neece
1848-1929

William Rees Neece
Aug 24, 1883
Aug 9, 1953

Daniel Lester Wheeler
Sep 19, 1898

&
Hazel Ervin Wheeler
Nov 18, 1901
Aug 6, 1964

James Barbee Brandon
Dec 18, 1892
(no date)

Josephine Rives Brandon
Jul 5, 1893
May 27, 1952

Jas. Reva, Daughter of
J. B. & F. J. Brandon
Aug 29, 1921
Sep 25, 1926

John G. Waggoner
Aug 8, 1847
Jan 9, 1930
&
Mary A. Waggoner
Dec 27, 1844
Nov 5, 1929

H. Clinton Levan
Oct 3, 1879
Sep 12, 1949
&
Clara L. Levan
Dec 1, 1893

John W. Evans
1872-1919
&
Sallie C. Evans
1872-1956

James S. Harrison
1880-1947
&
Virgie M. Harrison
1882-

Scott A. Ervin
Oct 10, 1872
Jul 28, 1954
&
Bettie M. Ervin
Jun 14, 1873
Sep 10, 1932

G. Alvin Ervin
1875-1923
&
Maggie M. Ervin
1880-

James W. Grammer
1877-1952
&
Nannie J. Grammer
1887-

John Henry Grammer
1869-1939
&
Mary Arreva Grammer
1876-1940

D. Rhoton Wanslow
Jan 6, 1859
Jul 11, 1897
&
Nancy E. Silvertooth
Wanslow
Jan 22, 1862
Sep 29, 1910
"Erected by Daughter
Connie W. Gray."

Roy M. Gray
Oct 28, 1889
Jul 3, 1953
&
Connie D. Gray
Jul 19, 1896

Elton E. Gray
1896-
&
D. Floyd Gray
1893-1970

Annie Cobble Allen Smith
Mar 16, 1873
Apr 7, 1949

James G. Price
1862-1924
&
Tennie Price
1861-1932

Hugh Price
1898-1938

Eula Mae Price Mitchell
Apr 22, 1903
Jan 1, 1970

Mary Ann, Daughter of
Billy Dance & Nora S.
Fanning
B&D Mar 28, 1955

Lee L. Dance
1875-1934
&
Mary A. Dance
1874-1940

Claude Harrison
1910-
&
Rosie Beatrice Harrison
1911-1971

James Leland Harrison
Nov 13, 1901
Oct 3, 1957

BOONEVILLE QUADRANGLE

J. Frank Harrison
Oct 1, 1868
Mar 19, 1929

Lillie Cowley Harrison
Mar 12, 1888
Nov 13, 1945

Ira Richard Wilkes
Feb 2, 1902

&
Josie Lou Wilkes
Dec 10, 1904
May 15, 1967

W. A. Allen
Aug 25, 1889
Jul 16, 1926

W. H. Scivally
1846-1928
&
Avo Harrison Scivally
1860-1932

Alice Maud Scivally
Dec 4, 1879
Jan 16, 1880
&
Maggie May Scivally
Dec 4, 1879
Aug 10, 1910
"Twin Sisters"

Henry Frank Scivally
Tennessee
Pvt Co 1 131 Inf WW I
Sep 21, 1893
Feb 26, 1966
&
Ruby Woodard Scivally
1899-

P. O. Harrison
1866-1934

Nannie V. Harrison
1880-1969

George Moseley Harrison
1914-

Mary Gordon Boone
Dec 19, 1841
Apr 24, 1913
&
Rosalie Amzi Gordon Boone
Mar 3, 1854
Jun 27, 1904
&
Susanna Harriet Overby
Aug 30, 1821
Jun 26, 1902

Lant Russell Wood
Feb 28, 1881
Sep 27, 1973
Elma Enochs Wood
Mar 19, 1885
Jan 16, 1974

Homer Hilton Tipps
Oct 10, 1900

&
Ola Renegar Tipps
Jun 20, 1903

William J. Renegar
Jul 6, 1876
Oct 30, 1961
Dolus E. Renegar
Apr 7, 1885
Aug 3, 1967

L. Clifton Millsap
Jun 11, 1905
Dec 4, 1952
&
Laurine Tipps Millsap
Mar 17, 1910

Elmer Lee Cashion
Aug 16, 1890
Dec 6, 1962
&
Bernice Harrison Cashion
Aug 2, 1889

William W. Gordon
May 20, 1848
Aug 1, 1906
&
Mary E. Gordon
Aug 13, 1848
Oct 28, 1942

Russell Gordon
Sep 23, 1871
Apr 9, 1900

Anna Lois Smoot
Jan 14, 1887
Nov 19, 1892
Age: 5y, 10m, 5d.

Henry J. Evans
1855-1941
&
Sallie E. Evans
1863-1950

Ben W. Tipps
Aug 18, 1867
May 12, 1941
&
Donie Massey Tipps
Sep 30, 1877
Oct 18, 1957

Daniel Clifford Tipps
Dec 19, 1887
Mar 4, 1969
"Mason, Farris Creek
50 years."

D. H. Tipps
Jul 29, 1898
Jun 20, 1923

D. W. Tipps, Jr., Son of
D. W. & Donie Tipps
Sep 13, 1917
Oct 7, 1921

Louis Otis, Son of
D. W. & Donie Tipps
Oct 29, 1899
Sep 28, 1900

J. E. M. Enochs
Jan 3, 1848
Jul 5, 1925
&
Nancy Enochs
Dec 13, 1855
May 17, 1926

J. H. Enochs
Jan 5, 1850
Jul 31, 1925

Raymond A. Massey
1904-1961
(Harrison FH)

James Wade Smoot
Sep 17, 1855
Jan 17, 1942
&
Minnie Boyers Smoot
Apr 9, 1859
May 30, 1922

South-West Section

John D. Preston
1863-1938
&
Emma Preston
1869-1937

Jesse Preston
Jun 9, 1893
May 6, 1963
&
Laura Preston
May 31, 1913

Lawson S., Son of
Jesse & Laura Preston
1936-1936

John Willie Tolley
Jun 22, 1878
Nov 23, 1893

Jim Connor Tolley
Jan 16, 1910
Apr 7, 1971
&
Margaret Templeton Tolley
Aug 6, 1917

Daisy, Daughter of
John D. & Jennie P. Tolley
Feb 27, 1876
Jan 19, 1879

Infant Daughter of
John D. & Jennie P. Tolley
Nov 21, 1879
Dec 5, 1879

Tolley, Son of
W. M. & F. E. Tipton
Jun 13, 1875
Sep 3, 1879

John D. Tolley
1837-1912
&
Jennie P. Tolley
1851-1912

Lillie Nell, Daughter of
John & Julia Allen
Oct 5, 1921
Dec 1, 1940

Pvt John Wiseman Allen
Nov 1, 1893
Oct 14, 1970
Co G 117 Inf 30 Div

Julia Gore Allen
Oct 22, 1896

Jack Daniel
1850-1911

Dick Daniel
1868-1932

Irene Motlow Daniel
1872-1941

John T. Daniel
1901-1904

Robert L., Son of
W. P. & S. E. Daniel
Oct 26, 1881
Jan 26, 1903

Elizabeth Daniel, wife
of James S. Connor
1839-1926

373

BOONEVILLE QUADRANGLE

Clyde Wilson Wilkes
Oct 1, 1908
Jun 15, 1966

Ida Mae Call Wilkes
Feb 5, 1888
Apr 20, 1963

Lemuel Augustus Waggoner
Jul 18, 1892
Mar 19, 1970

Margaret Sory Waggoner
Oct 16, 1896
Dec 14, 1968

B. F. Tipps
Nov 16, 1891
Mar 4, 1922
&
Jonnye Waggoner Tipps
Nov 10, 1894

J. H. Waggoner
Nov 19, 1863
Jun 2, 1934
&
Amanda Grammer Waggoner
Apr 16, 1867
May 1, 1957

Daniel Roy Massey
Jul 28, 1891
May 17, 1954
&
Beulah Clark Massey
Sep 23, 1890

George L. Massey
1866-1941
&
Martha Ann Massey
1866-1956

James O. Massey
Jun 4, 1889
Mar 5, 1957

Dwight L. Wilkes
Jul 7, 1880
Apr 14, 1954

James William Simpson
1883-1946
&
Ethel Waggoner Simpson
1888-1959

Nancy E. Allen
Sep 23, 1864
Nov 11, 1923

Grady Tucker
Jan 31, 1915
Nov 25, 1917
&
J. W. Tucker
Feb 20, 1936
Feb 22, 1936
"Brothers"

Ernest M. Tucker
Dec 29, 1890
Aug 26, 1952
&
Annie B. Tucker
Nov 9, 1894
Mar 27, 1971

Walten W. Holt
Jul 19, 1848
Jul 29, 1925

Sue Motlow, wife of
W. W. Holt
1843-1909

James B. Holt
Nov 7, 1875
Jan 4, 1903

Robert Burns, Son of
James B. & Nora E. Holt
Jun 27, 1899
Nov 3, 1899

W. W., Jr., Son of
Tull & Bessie Holt
1909
Age: 3 months.

Ora Agness Atwood
May 29, 1894
Nov 17, 1895
&
Dovie Evelyn Atwood
Sep 27, 1873
Mar 13, 1941
&
John W. Atwood
Sep 3, 1866
Dec 27, 1941

Jno. Thomas Anderton
Sep 2, 1887
Mar 18, 1964
&
Lillie V. Anderton
Sep 2, 1894
Jun 1, 1954

James N. Daniel
Sep 9, 1876
Apr 2, 1941

Emma Parks, wife of
James N. Daniel
Aug 21, 1879
Dec 25, 1946

Annie E. Motlow, wife of
W. C. Sugg
Apr 9, 1874
Sep 19, 1902

Sarah Motlow Floyd
Mar 4, 1854
May 30, 1941

John Clarence Motlow
Sep 3, 1888
Jul 26, 1961

Tull A. Holt
1878-1940

Jas. Burns Motlow
1846-1907

Azpell A., Son of
D. B. & Sallie Holt
(no dates)

Alexander Raby
May 12, 1885

&
Barshie Raby
Aug 3, 1887
Jan 13, 1958
(color picture)

Alfred Eaton
Jul 7, 1807
Feb 28, 1886

T. J. Eaton
Jun 7, 1840
Dec 19, 1892

A. F. Eaton
1837-1910

Susie Eaton
Age: 10 years
Died May 11, 1889

F. W. Motlow
Oct 7, 1840
Mar 30, 1892

Mrs. Birdie Lou Bobo
May 13, 1868
Nov 8, 1893
&
Infant Son
Still-born
Sep 3, 1892
"Wife & Child of
S. L. Bobo".

Dale Holt Gowen
1899-1949

Maggie Holt, wife of
Charles Gowen
1873-1933

Eleise, Daughter of
C. E. & M. O. Gowen
Feb 27, 1892
Apr 25, 1896

Infant Daughter of
Mr. & Mrs. Parks L. Hayes
B&D Jul 1, 1934

Lodwick Holt
Dec 28, 1810
Jan 9, 1873
&
Eliza Holt
Nov 18, 1822
Jan 5, 1896

George P. Holt
Dec 30, 1870
Jul 29, 1938

Lula Bobo Holt
Aug 14, 1874
Sep 22, 1967

Herby M. Fanning
(no dates)

Nell Holt Fanning
(no dates)

F. W. Waggoner
Jan 16, 1849
Jun 21, 1913
&
Mary J. Waggoner
Jun 1, 1851
May 4, 1926

Allen Roughton Waggoner
Oct 13, 1882
Dec 29, 1948

Huldah Maurine, Daughter
of F. W. & M. J. Waggoner
Feb 1, 1891
Jul 8, 1891

William Horace, Son of
F. W. & M. J. Waggoner
Feb 12, 1880
Jul 8, 1889

Daniel J. Waggoner
1852-1929
&
Egland B. Waggoner
1859-1943

Emma Parks
Jan 17, 1870
Oct 17, 1931

W. K. Cobb
1876-1953
(Wilson FH)

W. A. H.
(no dates, fieldstone)

William H. Taylor
1878-1940
&
Bertha M. Taylor
1886- (TM: 1972, Mary B.)

William Dan Taylor
Dec 25, 1939
Mar 1, 1940

Johnnie A. Taylor
Sep 20, 1908

&
Laura May Taylor
Oct 10, 1918
Apr 3, 1970

BOONEVILLE QUADRANGLE

Bobby Joe Bedford
Apr 9, 1933
Nov 3, 1934

Rufus Rhoton Bedford
Sep 13, 1889
Apr 9, 1946

Nora Bedford Anderton
Sep 19, 1889
Nov 10, 1966

James S. Bedford
1858-1929
&
Ella D. Bedford
1875-1931

Joe Parker, Son of
Mr. & Mrs. E. R. Bedford
Mar 12, 1936
Aug 27, 1937

David R. Bedford, 1st
Sep 13, 1839
Jul 14, 1895
    & wife
Anna Elizabeth Moore
Bedford
Nov 13, 1842
Jul 12, 1924
Married Feb 13, 1866
"Erected by Daughter
Pearl Bedford Pfoetner,
Walnut Springs, Texas."

Dan N. Tipps
Aug 26, 1892
Jul 24, 1939
&
Viola Tipps
Jul 13, 1871
Sep 5, 1943

W. N. Simpson
Oct 1, 1861
Feb 7, 1920
&
Sophie Simpson
May 25, 1868
(no date)

Luther N. Simpson
Nov 1, 1886
Mar 20, 1941

Emma Evans, wife of
William H. Mitchell
Aug 2, 1874
Nov 25, 1957

Lucy E. McKenzie
1878-1953

Stanley Evans
Nov 28, 1821
Nov 21, 1905
&
Elizabeth Evans
Mar 25, 1823
Apr 9, 1902

Baby B. Bedford
Oct 7, 1875
Nov 8, 1875

Fannie Beth Bedford
Jul 13, 1871
Aug 1, 1871

John W. Bedford
Jul 12, 1848
Jan 11, 1917
"Father of John W., Jr.
& D. R., & James S."

Homer H. Bean
May 23, 1895
Jun 5, 1938

Emma Holt Bean
Jan 3, 1869
Aug 28, 1959

James J. Bean
Oct 16, 1864
Oct 19, 1940

Sarah Janice Riddle
1941-1942
(Harrison FH)

William R. Riddle
1918-1952
(Daves-Culbertson FH)

Lewis R. Riddle, Sr.
Mar 20, 1891
May 22, 1971
&
Sular S. Riddle
Sep 19, 1895
(no date)

Orville Riddle
Tennessee
A2C U. S. Air Force
Feb 11, 1932
Sep 26, 1967

Worley Riddle
May 3, 1916
Jun 30, 1930

Louise Riddle
Sep 26, 1927
Nov 14, 1930

Helen G. Huffmaster Baxter
Jul 12, 1904
Nov 28, 1972

Justion L. Baxter
Aug 18, 1903

J. E. Baxter
Apr 30, 1883
Jun 13, 1936

Louetta Dean Baxter
Aug 16, 1883
Dec 22, 1938

David R. Allen
Tennessee
Pvt 2 Co Div Bn WW I
Dec 28, 1891
Jun 12, 1955

James W. Allen
1888-1952
(Harrison FH)

Marvin Allen
1885-1957
(Harrison FH)

Henry J. Allen
1864-1931
&
Sarah E. Allen
1866-1929

George E. Allen
Nov 15, 1889
Jun 2, 1937

Mary A., wife of
James E. Gore
1843-1899

Luther E. Allen
1901-1928

O. J. Allen
1925-1928

Clarence W. Allen
Aug 12, 1897
Nov 21, 1971

Walter W. Shofner
May 29, 1877
Aug 7, 1955
    & wife
Ella Shofner
Feb 9, 1878
Sep 8, 1905

W. A. Hobbs
Feb 4, 1818
Oct 17, 1894
&
Amanda Hobbs
Apr 14, 1837
Mar 10, 1920

George H. Hobbs
Oct 5, 1871
Apr 12, 1927

Oliver J. Hobbs
1867-1932
&
Pearl L. Hobbs
1879-1971

Lizzie, Daughter of
Joe S. & M. C. Hobbs
Dec 12, 1886
Jul 6, 1888

Martha C., wife of
Joe S. Hobbs
May 29, 1860
Apr 24, 1889

Joseph S. Hobbs
Nov 1, 1838
Feb 12, 1893

Bettie J., wife of
Joe S. Hobbs
Feb 3, 1854
Jun 24, 1894

D. O. Allen
Mar 31, 1857
Apr 2, 1928
    & wife
Nannie A. Rainey Allen
Jan 11, 1861
Jul 12, 1928

John C. Billingsley
Oct 28, 1865
Aug 17, 1898

Jessie Morgan Billingsley
Nov 2, 1871
Apr 30, 1951

James W. Waggoner
Tennessee
Sgt 335 Base Unit
A. A. F. WW II
Apr 22, 1914
Oct 7, 1967

Davis Wilson Waggoner
Mar 8, 1875
Feb 18, 1945
&
Carrie Waggoner
Mar 12, 1888

C. Clifford Frame
Tennessee
Pvt Btry C 2 field Arty
WW I
Oct 22, 1900
Jul 14, 1942
&
Etta M. Frame
Apr 23, 1908

Married Jul 16, 1925

Stella, wife of
H. Rees Blythe
Died Dec 16, 1911
Age: 27y, 4m, 7d.

Mary Blythe
B&D Oct 30, 1879
&
Mattie Blythe
Oct 30, 1879
Nov 17, 1879
"Children of
H. R. & B. W. Blythe".

BOONEVILLE QUADRANGLE

James Blythe
1823-1878
&
Sarah Blythe
1827-1878

Ernest Andrew Tong
1890-1966

J. G. Woodard
Nov 1, 1869
Dec 14, 1910

Orrie Toch Holt
Mar 27, 1883
Jan 2, 1966

Clayton Lee Tosh
Feb 6, 1914

&
Nancy Motlow Tosh
Mar 15, 1914

Willard Paul Tosh
Feb 15, 1917
Nov 7, 1966

D. B. A.
(no dates, fieldstone)

D. P. C. Allen
Jan 21, 1832
Mar 14, 1894
&
Emaline Allen
Apr 9, 1833
Feb 19, 1907

Thomas Null
May 24, 1877
Sep 20, 1877
&
Sarah H. Null
May 24, 1877
Jul 20, 1877
Children of
J. R. & N. E. Null.

H. R. Blythe
Dec 8, 1850
Feb 2, 1936
&
Bettie W. Blythe
Died Jun 25, 1910
Age: 57 years.

Clemmie M., Daughter of
H. R. & B. W. Blythe
Oct 20, 1877
Sep 21, 1879

J. A. Bruce
Oct 3, 1840
Aug 7, 1929
&
Mary Bruce
Oct 5, 1844
Sep 3, 1925

Josephine Bruce
Dec 14, 1874
Mar 13, 1932

Fannie, wife of
Frank Motlow
Feb 7, 1880
Oct 24, 1900

Charles Motlow
Dec 11, 1870
Mar 4, 1910

James A. Motlow
Sep 5, 1867
Jun 3, 1909

Zadock, Son of
Felix & Margaret Motlow
Nov 26, 1831
Aug 18, 1889

Nancy H., wife of
Z. Motlow
Jan 8, 1844
Oct 30, 1875

D. D. Blythe
Jun 17, 1856
(no date)
&
Mary F. Blythe
Apr 6, 1854
Jan 6, 1926

J. L., Son of
D. D. & M. F. Blythe
Mar 21, 1883
Mar 19, 1883

Frances Blythe Enoch
Jul 31, 1884
Jan 23, 1952

Mabel Blythe Holt
Aug 2, 1880
Mar 7, 1968

J. E. Bobo
Nov 23, 1834
Feb 4, 1914
& wife
E. A. Bobo
May 15, 1836
Sep 28, 1896

Hester Bobo
Jun 21, 1900
Aug 22, 1901

Sallie E. Bobo
Jun 30, 1863
Sep 27, 1939

Charlie, Son of
J. E. & E. A. Bobo
Jul 1, 1876
Jan 14, 1889

W. P. Bobo
Apr 9, 1865
Aug 17, 1904

Otis Pratt, Son of
W. P. & Musa Bobo
Apr 24, 1893
Jul 28, 1897

Ruth Bobo Smith
1902-1929

Ellar F. Womble
Sep 25, 1868
Sep 19, 1911

Homer Lafayette Laws
Dec 30, 1900

&
Laura G. Hobbs Laws
Dec 4, 1905

Infant Daughter of
Mr. & Mrs. Homer Laws
1939

Loine Burton
Sep 25, 1903
Dec 15, 1972

Jas. M. Frame
Jun 22, 1829
Jun 17, 1891

Erritte F. Acuff
1871-1941
&
Ellen Bobo Acuff
1879-1948

Mrs. N. J., wife of
J. S. Acuff
Jul 6, 1846
Jan 18, 1898

J. Eugene Bobo
May 7, 1885
Apr 6, 1951
&
Dolores R. Bobo
Jan 15, 1894
Feb 15, 1970

Henry Reeves Melson
1859-1939
&
Martha Edens Melson
1859-1946

Mildred Melson
1893-1958

Bennie Melson Branaman
1901-1949

Infant Daughter of
E. R. & J. L. Burton
B&D Jan 12, 1898

Rufus L. Laws
Jun 19, 1877
Nov 27, 1911

Annie W. Laws
Sep 24, 1872
Jun 11, 1955

Lannie N. Burton
May 3, 1893
Dec 15, 1971
&
Emma Stocstill Burton
Apr 22, 1897

William A., Husband of
Mollie S. Sutton
Died Jul 7, 1890
Age: 31y, 8m, 1d.

Lillian Sutton
Died Mar 17, 1894
Age: 6y, 3m, 21d.

Luther F. Edens
Oct 3, 1857
Jul 16, 1916
&
Bettie Edens
Jan 29, 1859
Jun 7, 1938

Benjamin Marshall Edens
Jul 13, 1822
Oct 20, 1909
&
Pauline Blythe Edens
Aug 18, 1827
Dec 30, 1915

Lillian Bryant
Jan 5, 1896
Apr 20, 1898

Essie Florence, Daughter
of James & Nannie Ferguson
Oct 24, 1881
Sep 10, 1897
Age: 15y, 10m, 18d.

Albert H. Timmons
Sep 21, 1911
Sep 18, 1961

Charles Aldon Tipps
Apr 15, 1898
Apr 15, 1973

Nell Laws Tipps
Mar 9, 1903

Jack Burton
(no dates)
&
Sallie Burton
(no dates)
(Harrison FH)

BOONEVILLE QUADRANGLE

Benjamin F. Burton
Dec 19, 1889
May 19, 1965
&
Daisy C. Burton
Sep 29, 1895

&
Ollie R. Burton
Apr 8, 1920

Marvin Lee, Son of
Lannie & Emma Burton
(no dates)

Dan D. Riley
May 17, 1883
Feb 7, 1915

James B. Hardy
1885-1955

John A. Stocstill
Jul 6, 1861
Mar 30, 1922

Amanda Stocstill
Mar 12, 1853
Jun 13, 1931

Amanda Lorene Hardy
Jan 2, 1922
Oct 10, 1926

T. M. Spriggs
Nov 10, 1854
Dec 5, 1925

V. A. Williams, Wife of
T. M. Spriggs
Jan 13, 1861
Nov 29, 1911

Edna M. Spriggs
Nov 3, 1883
Feb 9, 1965

South-Middle Section

C. M. Wilson
Jul 22, 1826
Apr 6, 1909
&
Elizabeth Ann Wilson
Sep 9, 1835
Feb 13, 1903

John G. Wilson
May 31, 1825
Nov 15, 1903

C. M. Wilson, Jr.
1863-1925

Doll Wilson
1870-1930

Berry Wilson
1874-1945

Alice W. Wilson
1883-1962

W. Clyde Wilson
1878-1948

Lauriett, wife of
E. H. Womack
Jan 1, 1814
Dec 12, 1888
Age: 74y, 11m, 19d.

E. H. Womack
Jul 4, 1799
Jul 15, 1878
Age: 79y, 11d.

B. W. A.
(no dates)

Lucus Philpot
Dec 23, 1881
Apr 17, 1972
&
Florence Philpot
Feb 16, 1884
Jan 5, 1962

G. B. Campbell
Nov 8, 1860
Aug 18, 1913
&
Anna L. Campbell
Apr 24, 1868
Feb 27, 1935

B. F. Womack
1832-1907
&
Mildred G. Womack
1842-1930
&
Elisha H. Womack
1874-1892
&
Aubrey L. Womack
1880-1905
&
Clatie N. Womack
1872-1872
&
Grace Womack
1863-1926

Stephen M. Dance
1854-1930

Effie W. Dance
1867-1928

Frieda K. Dance
1892-1928

Townsend P. Dance
1908-1936

J. Frank Dance
1898-1934

James Cecil Dance
Apr 10, 1869
Oct 16, 1913

Hayden M. Dance
Sep 20, 1873
Apr 9, 1931

Lulan A. Dance
1895-1967

John Harmon Womack
Jul 13, 1860
Apr 1, 1929

George W. Burton
1857-1935
&
Martha Jane Burton
1848-1909
"Brother & Sister".

J. F. Burton
Jul 12, 1828
Apr 3, 1900
&
Susan Burton
Died Sep 5, 1899
Age: about 70 years.

William J. Burton
1870-1948
&
Willie L. Burton
1872-1928

C. C. McLemore
Jul 22, 1847
Sep 30, 1872
& wife
Mary Green McLemore
Oct 7, 1846
May 30, 1879
& Daughter
Mary C. McLemore
Jul 20, 1872
Sep 27, 1872

J. F. Baxter
Jan 12, 1831
Sep 7, 1902

Hannah Elizabeth, wife of
J. F. Baxter
Mar 5, 1827
Jan 30, 1913

Mary C. Baxter
Mar 5, 1857
Feb 16, 1941

Wiley A. Baxter
Apr 13, 1865
Sep 7, 1935
&
Nancy C. Baxter
Aug 31, 1877
May 19, 1965

Martha E., wife of
G. W. Clark
Feb 8, 1853
Jul 7, 1914

Billy B. Wiseman
Tennessee
Pvt 30 Inf 3 Inf Div
WW II
Mar 21, 1924
Jan 25, 1944

Infant Daughter of
Lem & Clara Motlow
B&D Oct 14, 1896

Lem Motlow
1869-1947

Clara Reagor, wife of
Lem Motlow
Nov 10, 1872
Nov 14, 1901
Age: 29y, 4d.

W. D. L. Record
Jan 3, 1849
Jan 28, 1897

Sue Dance Record
Feb 25, 1859
Apr 10, 1945

James Dance Record
Jan 5, 1883
Nov 23, 1920

Sion T. Record
Nov 17, 1877
Feb 15, 1912

Eula Record
Died Oct 16, 1953
Age: (not given)

Finettie Record
(no dates)

Rev. W. R. Waggoner
Feb 23, 1827
May 20, 1889
&
Nancy A. Waggoner
Sep 12, 1824
Mar 3, 1900

D. W. Waggoner
Sep 16, 1862
Apr 2, 1895

BOONEVILLE QUADRANGLE

William Green
1840-1864

Minnie Green
1856-1880

Townsend P. Green
1813-1886
&
Mary A. Green
1813-1897

John L. Green
1854-1886

Stanton J. Green
1838-1885

Nancy Green
1843-1910

Wesley Green
1845-1847

Julia Evans
Feb 9, 1855
Feb 11, 1877

Dan Evans
Jun 7, 1851
May 29, 1890

Bird Evans
Jun 25, 1856
Jun 18, 1950

Charlie Evans
Oct 2, 1885
Aug 4, 1955

Olivia Evans
Jan 5, 1879
Sep 26, 1879

W. A. Waggoner
Dec 11, 1865
Feb 27, 1920

Hettie Agness, wife of
W. A. Waggoner
Feb 27, 1872
Apr 26, 1905

F. M. Waggoner
1875-1946

Fannie W. Waggoner
1872-1950

James R. Waggoner
Jan 6, 1852
Aug 9, 1907
&
Laura A. Waggoner
Oct 20, 1855
Jan 22, 1932

Oscar, Son of
Albert & Fannie Friedman
Mar 7, 1892
Jun 25, 1892

Maud, Daughter of
E. M. & L. H. Dance
Mar 26, 1881
Aug 12, 1881

T. B. Manning
Mar 13, 1850
Jan 5, 1890

Fannie Manning
1851-1935

Hattie, Daughter of
T. B. & S. F. Manning
Jul 16, 1876
Feb 27, 1876

Mollie E., Daughter of
John T. & Finettie Motlow
May 20, 1849
May 16, 1922

Bettie Broadway, wife of
R. B. Parkes
Oct 4, 1846
Jul 24, 1931
"Aunt Bet".

Bessie B. Little
Oct 28, 1889
Jun 13, 1954

Ben A. Spencer
1859-1930
&
Josie Spencer
1861-1936

Nannie S., wife of
Walton Hiles &
Daughter of
William & Jane Thomison
Jul 26, 1846
Nov 11, 1881

Walton Hiles
Feb 6, 1831
Jul 10, 1894

Joe Lee, Son of
W. & N. S. Hiles
Jul 12, 1873
Apr 4, 1875

Samuel Hinkle
Jun 6, 1818
Jul 4, 1880

Tommy G., Son of
R. E. & Frank Hinkle
Feb 26, 1917
Sep 11, 1917

Eva, Daughter of
A. R. & M. E. Hinkle
Jul 18, 1879
Jun 19, 1890

Arthur R. Hinkle
Nov 6, 1847
May 14, 1942
&
Mary Elon Hinkle
Jul 19, 1852
Oct 21, 1942

Harry W. Hinkle
Apr 17, 1875
Sep 15, 1954

"Father"
Richard E. "Dick" Hinkle
Oct 11, 1885
1974 (TM)
& wife
Frank Silvertooth Hinkle
Jun 3, 1887
Jul 31, 1956

Mary Fern Bryant
1913-1973
(Harrison FH)

William H. Dance
Sep 8, 1863
May 18, 1938
&
Mary Ann Dance
Oct 9, 1867
Jan 29, 1954

Mark E. Dance
1909-1974
(Harrison FH)

Nancy Louise Dance
Apr 1, 1918
Aug 16, 1918

S. E. H. Dance
Mar 30, 1834
Mar 20, 1900
& wife
Miami A. Dance
Jul 29, 1839
Mar 26, 1900

Harry Dance
Apr 12, 1878
Aug 25, 1965

Charles Stephen, Son of
Harry & Nancy L. Dance
Mar 9, 1902
Sep 24, 1902

Henry, Son of
Harry & Nancy L. Dance
Mar 14, 1914
Oct 8, 1915

Robert Roy Dance
1898-1922

Fannie Ingle Berry
1869-1941

Mae Berry
1866-1948

Benjamin H. Berry
Sep 18, 1841
Dec 9, 1904
&
Mary T. Berry
Jun 22, 1845
Jun 18, 1889

Clifford Taylor
1883-1954
&
Era Taylor
1881-1967

Lula H., wife of
Hayden M. Dance
Apr 11, 1877
Aug 24, 1911

J. T. S., Son of
Hayden & Lula Dance
Oct 29, 1903
Nov 30, 1911

T. H. Parks
Oct 19, 1840
Apr 27, 1891

Emily Taylor, wife of
T. H. Parks
Oct 10, 1846
Aug 13, 1922

Nellie B., Daughter of
T. H. & Emily T. Parks
Apr 14, 1886
Apr 23, 1894

Will K. Parks
Mar 7, 1878
Oct 4, 1941

Emily Record, wife of
Will K. Parks
(no dates)

Eugene & Irene, Infants
of T. H. & Emily T. Parks
Jul 16, 1882
Jul 17 & 18, 1882

Harry T. Parks
1883-1937

Nova P. Parks
1887-1970

J. Lee Parks
1873-1929

Meeks Spencer
Sep 26, 1884
Jan 16, 1912

Evelyn Evans
1885-1958

Dr. Charles W. Evans
1849-1907
&
Sue Taylor Evans
1854-1887

BOONEVILLE QUADRANGLE

Daughter of
C. W. & Sue Evans
1881-1881

Daughter of
C. W. & Sue Evans
1887-1887

A. M. Spencer
Jan 15, 1826
Aug 18, 1893
&
Nancy A. Spencer
Mar 9, 1827
Aug 13, 1894

Dance, Son of
T. L. & Tera Spencer
Jan 25, 1890
Dec 2, 1891

Jasper N. Taylor
Mar 8, 1838
Mar 27, 1907
&
Caroline McClelland Taylor
Jan 7, 1853
Mar 18, 1936

Nancy S. Whipple
Feb 25, 1872
Feb 17, 1961

H. E., wife of
William G. McClelland
Mar 17, 1832
Jun 22, 1890

Woody B. Taylor
Mar 15, 1829
Jun 7, 1889

Griffieth B. Moorhead
1884-1923

Charles W. Estill
1863-1890
&
Lura M. Estill
1864-1909

O. D. "Boss" Harrison
1874-1940
&
Lillie E. Harrison
1875-1963

Infant Son of
B. J. & Mary Waggoner
(no dates)

Leone Waggoner
Nov 27, 1899
Oct 16, 1900

Susan Temple, wife of
J. S. Maupin
Died Feb 7, 1907
Age: 67y, 4m, 15d.

John S. Taylor
Feb 28, 1831
Jan 21, 1916
&
F. M. (Marion) Taylor
Oct 18, 1840
Jul 6, 1914

Elizabeth Ford, wife of
John H. Taylor
Mar 24, 1808
Sep 5, 1890

John H. Taylor
Feb 26, 1801
Jun 21, 1890

Pinkney R. Bobo
Jun 11, 1836
Nov 20, 1907
&
Martha J. Bobo
Jan 24, 1841
Jun 15, 1920

Saline M. Sebastian
Feb 25, 1873
Jun 25, 1952

Daniel J. Waggoner
Oct 1, 1832
May 31, 1911
& wife
Silena J. Bobo Waggoner
May 25, 1845
Mar 24, 1927

Joseph M. Sebastian
Sep 4, 1841
Mar 19, 1906
& wife
Emma V. Sebastian
Jan 9, 1856
Jan 11, 1902
Age: 40y, 6m, 2d.

E---- W. Sebastian
Died Dec --, 194-
Age: 66 years.
(Lynchburg FH)

John R. Sebastian
Feb 22, 1877
May 26, 1909

Victor H. Paulk
1898-1961
&
Sue Parkes Paulk
1909-1968

Charles M. Parkes
1875-1941
&
Mamie Evans Parkes
1882-1954

John Webb Parkes
Jun 27, 1904

&
Marion Francis Parkes
Jul 9, 1903
Sep 6, 1966

Son of
Charles & Mamie Parks
1913-1913

D. H. Allen
Jul 22, 1818
Jan 15, 1892
&
Mary F. Allen
Feb 6, 1825
Nov 19, 1904

George W., Son of
D. H. & M. F. Allen
Feb 11, 1861
Apr 7, 1879

"Mother"
S. E. N. Nobletts
1836-1925
& "Sister"
N. A. N. Nobletts
1886-1919

Frank Motlow
Dec 7, 1868
Oct 10, 1925

Floy Sebastian, wife of
Frank Motlow
Jul 20, 1884
Feb 2, 1920

Clara Sue, Daughter of
Frank & Floy Motlow
Sep 27, 1916
Mar 8, 1918

Felix Evans
Mar 4, 1888
Sep 1, 1967

Lillian Ward Evans
Jan 28, 1888
Feb 23, 1960

George E. Raby
1872-1930
&
Lena Parks Raby
1877-1924

James B. Parks
1884-1952

Ella Parks
Aug 13, 1882
Jun 26, 1888

Milton C., Son of
M. L. & S. V. Parks
Oct 21, 1874
Jan 7, 1877

R. A. Parks
Oct 21, 1849
Jun 11, 1937
&
Susan Ann Holt Parks
Jul 5, 1851
May 30, 1930

Annie May, Daughter of
R. A. & S. A. Parks
Aug 21, 1886
Sep 7, 1886

Albert H. Parks
1879-1949

Laura Moore Parkes
Apr 21, 1873
Feb 3, 1927
&
Susan Bird Parkes
Oct 8, 1876
Sep 1, 1958
Daughters of
Dr. A. H. &
Elizabeth Keller Parkes.

Dr. Albert H. Parkes
Oct 11, 1836
Mar 6, 1890

Mary Elizabeth Parkes
Nov 26, 1844
Nov 14, 1908

M. L. Parks
May 17, 1831
Mar 5, 1917
&
S. V. Parks
Sep 11, 1845
Apr 17, 1913

M. N. Parkes
Jan 19, 1839
Mar 4, 1916

Fannie, wife of
M. N. Parkes
Jul 10, 1846
Jun 12, 1910

John Jefferson Allen
Jan 12, 1895
Mar 20, 1967
&
Pearl Smith Allen
May 31, 1899

Fred B. Hobbs
Jan 7, 1892
Jan 29, 1906

A. D. Hobbs
Apr 24, 1855
Feb 16, 1921

Cora Lee, Daughter of
A. D. Hobbs
Mar 12, 1866
Jun 18, 1904

Bessie, Daughter of
A. D. & C. L. Hobbs
Dec 21, 1889
Dec 26, 1893

Jack D. Motlow, Jr.
Tennessee
Captain U. S. Army
WW II
Jan 14, 1918
Jul 30, 1973

Mary Jane Thayer Motlow
Aug 20, 1921

Jack Daniel Motlow, III
Aug 24, 1947

Jack Daniel Motlow
1889-1953
&
Ella Smith Motlow
1895-1969

Buford & Bunie Bobo
Twin Son & Daughter of
Isaac F. & Mariam Bobo
Feb 16, 1874
Nov 11, 1876

Harry T. Burton
Tennessee
Tec 4 Co B 69 Inf Tng Bn
WW II
May 9, 1913
Mar 11, 1970

Henry B. Morgan
Oct 14, 1843
Jun 24, 1923
& wife
Mary J. Morgan
Oct 25, 1847
Sep 5, 1921

J. B. Warren
Nov 9, 1863
Sep 25, 1906

Harriett Shaw Warren
Sep 14, 1868
Oct 1, 1942

Dr. Edwin L. Barber
Born Meridian, Miss.
Mar 14, 1926
Married Viva Josephine
Motlow, Lynchburg, Tenn.
Jun 30, 1954
Died Tullahoma, Tenn.
Oct 2, 1964
"One Daughter,
Laura Jo Barber."

Susan M., Daughter of
W. L. & M. E. C. Bobo
May 6, 1868
Nov 25, 1873

Myrtle, Daughter of
W. L. & M. E. C. Bobo
Mar 7, 1875
Oct 24, 1877

Isaac Franklin Bobo
Jul 14, 1848
Jun 25, 1927

Mariam, wife of
Isaac Franklin Bobo
Feb 10, 1852
May 20, 1915

I. N. Ballard
1842-May 3, 1912
&
Anna Eliza Ballard
1836-Jun 15, 1908

Jonnie Rees Norton
1864-1943

L. N. Norton
Dec 5, 1855
Nov 12, 1893

George Sweeney
Jun 26, 1886

&
Ida Mills Sweeney
Oct 8, 1895
Jul 2, 1968

J. J. Sweeney
1848-1929

Ruby, Daughter of
C. M. & W. W. Solomon
Nov 3, 1896
Nov 5, 1896

Edgar P. Bobo
Sep 19, 1880
Jul 18, 1911

W. L. Bobo
Jun 29, 1840
Jun 4, 1905
&
M. E. C. Bobo
Jun 28, 1847
Jan 22, 1911

Calvin A., Son of
I. F. & M. Bobo
Nov 14, 1880
Nov 18, 1881

Nannie Eva, Daughter of
I. F. & Mariam Bobo
Sep 28, 1877
Jul 18, 1892

Floy Ida, Daughter of
I. F. & Mariam Bobo
Oct 22, 1878
Dec 13, 1900

William Townsend Roughton
Oct 29, 1864
Jan 1, 1943
&
Adelaide Dusenberry Roughton
Jun 15, 1867
Nov 13, 1943

Claude Roughton
Oct 9, 1888
May 9, 1943

Ida Roughton Rutledge
1858-1919

James Henry Rutledge
1858-1919

J. M. Roughton
Dec 2, 1826
Aug 11, 1878
Age: 51y, 8m, 9d.

N. C., wife of
J. M. Roughton
Nov 8, 1829
Feb 17, 1901

Don B. Rutledge
Aug 9, 1895
Feb 24, 1935

James Lodrick Baxter
Aug 9, 1853
Oct 20, 1939

Mary R. Baxter
Jan 19, 1856
Mar 2, 1901

Infant Daughter of
J. L. & Mary L. Baxter
B&D Jan 9, 1898

William F. Baxter
Mar 4, 1874
Jul 20, 1890
Age: 16y, 4m, 26d.

Nannie J. Bickley
Aug 23, 1848
Jun 3, 1899
Age: 50y, 9m, 10d.
Married 1875 to
John A. Norman &
Married 1894 to
James T. Bickley

Thomas Gregory Motlow
May 19, 1877
Mar 21, 1969

Ethel Motlow Edmonds
Mar 4, 1885
Jul 29, 1954

John L. Tolley
1870-1930

Lillie B. Tolley
1872-1945

Jess B. Motlow
Feb 4, 1875
Oct 28, 1957

Alice Shofner Motlow
Aug 7, 1881
Aug 28, 1954

R. B. Parkes
May 5, 1827
Sep 21, 1897

Emily J., wife of
R. B. Parkes
Apr 7, 1827
Nov 30, 1884
Age: 57y, 7m, 23d.

Infant Son of
T. A. & M. L. Hays
Oct 6, 1890
Oct 7, 1890

F. M. Shaw
Aug 19, 1850
Jan 2, 1891

J. A. Norman
Jul 18, 1835
Jun 30, 1880
Age: 44y, 11m, 12d.

Eliza A., wife of
John A. Norman
Nov 24, 1844
Jul 6, 1874

John Thomas
Apr 28, 1880
May 7, 1946
&
Mamie M. Thomas
Nov 20, 1883
Apr 14, 1959

Edwin Lee Parks
Feb 9, 1864
Mar 26, 1944

Nannie R., wife of
Edwin L. Parks
Jan 4, 1867
Sep 15, 1893

Ermine Foster, wife of
Edwin L. Parks
Aug 21, 1867
Aug 5, 1932

Nell Parks Ingram
Jul 1, 1905
Oct 16, 1972

Wallace Ingram
Dec 4, 1891
Jun 17, 1937

A. W. Parkes
Mar 18, 1797
Nov 18, 1884

BOONEVILLE QUADRANGLE

Fannie Parkes
May 17, 1802
Jan 6, 1877

Mrs. A. M. Piant
Born at Lynchburg, Tenn.
Oct 3, 1833
Died at Nashville, Tenn.
Nov 7, 1899
Age: 66y, 1m, 4d.

James M. Mansfield
1872-1958
&
Mamie N. Mansfield
1874-1936

Ralph B., Son of
J. L. & Hattie Norman
Oct 12, 1897
Oct 17, 1897

Frankie Parks
Dec 20, 1889
Jan 7, 1896

Sue E., wife of
M. N. Parks, Jr.
Jan 25, 1867
Feb 27, 1903

M. N. "Brad" Parkes
Feb 25, 1866
Oct 31, 1934
&
Minnie Bobo Parkes
Feb 3, 1873
Mar 14, 1957

Thomas J. Shaw
Aug 28, 1825
Jan 19, 1892
& wife
Susan M. Shaw
Oct 16, 1831
Nov 15, 1832

Laura Shaw Meyer
Apr 10, 1866
Sep 12, 1932

Kate Shaw Neece
Feb 17, 1854
Mar 11, 1888

M. E., Consort of
M. F. McGregor
Dec 23, 1853
Mar 14, 1882

A. J. Setliff
1867-1955

Infant Daughter of
W. W. & M. A. Setliff
B&D Mar 12, 1902

Leta, Daughter of
W. W. & M. A. Setliff
(no dates)

Francis Marion Milton
Nov 10, 1846
Mar 13, 1899
&
Nettie Smoot Milton
Jul 25, 1847
Aug 14, 1900

J. A. Silvertooth
Mar 19, 1818
Jan 13, 1892

M. E., wife of
J. A. Silvertooth
May 29, 1837
Mar 3, 1880
Age: 42y, 9m, 4d.

Amelia A., wife of
John A. Silvertooth
Feb 21, 1842
Dec 3, 1909

James Silvertooth
Dec 21, 1857
Jan 23, 1917
&
Vinie Silvertooth
Jul 22, 1861
Mar 12, 1929

James T. Bickley
Oct 12, 1841
Sep 14, 1915
& wife
Josie Bickley
Nov 14, 1846
Apr 28, 1893
& wife
Mollie Bickley
Jan 6, 1854
(no date)

Alice G. Setliff
Died Jan 15, 1876
Age: 24 years.

Mary C. Shaw
Nov 21, 1839
Jan 6, 1902

J. L. Moore
1862-1937

Mamie H. Moore
1868-1943

James Harvey Moore
1864-1954

Ida Mai Moore
1879-1946

M. N. Moore
Mar 10, 1829
Jan 5, 1906
& wife
E. L. Moore
Sep 12, 1832
May 31, 1896

William L. Moore
Jul 18, 1877
Jan 12, 1912

Infant Son of
M. N. & E. L. Moore
Died Jun 22, 1876
Age: Less than one day.

Samuel McDowell
Mar 20, 1839
Feb 9, 1923
& wife
Agness Andrews McDowell
Nov 12, 1839
Mar 4, 1897

Samuel G., Son of
E. H. & G. B. McDowell
Aug 19, 1889
Feb 18, 1898

Georgie Brown, wife of
E. H. McDowell
Aug 12, 1870
Sep 7, 1889

Mattie Edwards McDowell
Mar 16, 1854
Dec 13, 1933

Brownie, Daughter of
W. W. & M. A. Setliff
Jun 27, 1894
Oct 2, 1894

Dr. Abram Setliff
1817-1875
&
Nancy Shaw Setliff
1837-1921

William W. Setliff
Sep 18, 1862
Dec 26, 1909
& wife
Mattie Alice Setliff
Nov 18, 1873
Feb 4, 1949

Daisye Setliff
1872-1969

R. B. Setliff
1874-1932

Mary B. Setliff
1875-1913

Infant Daughter of
R. B. & Belle Setliff
B&D Sep 28, 1893

Lou A. Dillon, wife of
J. J. Harrison
Jan 21, 1836
Jan 11, 1922

Mary Norton Hix
Jan 18, 1886
Nov 27, 1968

Sarah G., wife of
J. M. Hughes
Dec 30, 1835
Aug 27, 1874

Etna Motlow McCormack
1885-1971

Ailleene Motlow
1889-1944

Bryant Motlow
May 9, 1883
Sep 4, 1884

James Wilson Motlow
1851-1921
&
Willie Bryant Motlow
1858-1915

Infant Daughter of
C. C. & Nora Stone
(no dates)

Fidelia Martin
Jul 1, 1823
Jun 11, 1894

Joseph C. Martin
1864-1921
&
Jennie M. Martin
1867-(no date)

Harry Martin
Tennessee
Blacksmith 2 Cl
U. S. N. R. F.
Nov 9, 1886
Jun 25, 1945
&
Eliza Martin
1891-19(1974 - TM)

Charley, Son of
N. R. & Nannie Martin
Dec 14, 1889
Jun 7, 1890

George, Son of
J. C. & J. M. Martin
Jan 11, 1895
Feb 27, 1895

Clemmie E., Daughter of
J. C. & Jennie Martin
Jan 1, 1898
Oct 27, 1898

Thomas P. Alston
Aug 1, 1861
Feb 11, 1882

E. J. Alston
Jun 8, 1830
Aug 7, 1895

Jimmy Clark
B&D Mar 29, 1944

BOONEVILLE QUADRANGLE

Leo Hughes Harrison
1877-1948
&
Lena Maud Harrison
1889-1946

Jessee L. Bryant
Sep 25, 1824
Apr 5, 1883
&
Finetty Leftwich Bryant
1830-1910

Myrtle Gardiner, Daughter of
J. L. & F. B. Bryant
Feb 11, 1857
Oct 8, 1874

Jesse, Son of
J. W. & N. M. Gardiner
B&D Sep 21, 1874

William Mortimer Colsher
1880-1939

Maggie Hughes Colsher
1858-1936

Sadie Louise, Daughter of
J. N. & Maggie H. Colsher
Mar 28, 1892
Dec 25, 1924

J. H. Jones
1864-1921
&
Mary Jones
1862-1941

Margie Jones
Mar 11, 1892
Jun 15, 1903

Matthew B. Sims
1841-1907
&
Lucinda G. Sims
1851-1946

Inda Sims
1875-1960

Myrtle Sims Kimmins
Jan 25, 1878
Jul 14, 1955

Ruble (Sims)
(no dates)

Eva Sue Hobbs
B&D May 31, 1932

Joe Thomas Hobbs
B&D Jan 30, 1931

"Father"
Lacy L. Hobbs
May 10, 1901
Jun 17, 1955

"Mother"
Nell Parks Hobbs
Feb 22, 1901

Abe Frizzell
Mar 20, 1837
Jun 17, 1877
Age: 40y, 2m, 17d.

William L. Haslett
1868-1955
&
Mary Shaw Haslett
1881-1953

William Shaw Haslett
Tennessee
Pvt 119 Inf 30 Div
Jun 15, 1901
Nov 28, 1932

Inza H. Strain
1900-1957

Mrs. N. K., wife of
E. D. Moore
Oct 9, 1860
Aug 22, 1886

Infant of
E. D. & N. K. Moore
B&D Aug 7, 1886

Mamie Alice, Daughter of
E. D. & N. K. Moore
Sep 26, 1881
Feb 3, 1882
Age: 4m, 7d.

O. J. Bailey
(no dates)
&
M. Bailey
(no dates)
&
N. Bailey
(no dates)
&
S. Bailey
(no dates)
&
W. Bailey
(no dates)

Edna Mae, Daughter of
J. C. & L. M. Burton
1935-1942

J. C. Burton
1901-1967
(Harrison FH)

Lillian M. Burton
1903-1967
(Harrison FH)

J. Wilson Burton
1848-1929
&
Mary B. Burton
1843-1898

Claude A. Prince
Mar 15, 1882
Dec 7, 1965

T. J. L. Shaw
1850-1915
&
Martha J. Shaw
1849-1933
&
George M. Shaw
1875-1944

Maggie, Daughter of
T. J. L. & M. J. Shaw
Dec 13, 1878
Jan 19, 1879

Carl, Son of
J. F. & R. E. Shaw
Feb 22, 1910
Sep 18, 1910

John P. Huffman
Aug 24, 1865
Feb 11, 1934
&
Silena C. Huffman
Feb 3, 1875
Dec 16, 1962

Hugh P. Stafford
Aug 8, 1874
Jan 15, 1875
&
Charles A. Stafford
Jul 31, 1876
Dec 18, 1876
Sons of J. W. &
Anna Stafford.
&
John W. Stafford
Nov 25, 1837
Sep 5, 1912
&
Anna Stafford
Jan 12, 1849
Oct 25, 1881

South-East Section

Harwell L. Tipps, Sr.
May 5, 1901
Feb 5, 1971

Clara Ashby Tipps
Nov 17, 1902
Dec 30, 1959

Harwell L. Tipps, Jr.
Mar 16, 1927

Virginia P. Tipps
Sep 2, 1928

Glendon B. Campbell
1897-1963

Annie M. Campbell
1904-1930

Robert M. Tipps
Dec 23, 1870
Jan 14, 1948
&
Alice Clark Tipps
Aug 17, 1876
Dec 17, 1960

BOONEVILLE QUADRANGLE

Hayden E. Robertson
Apr 14, 1887
Apr 18, 1957

Mary T. Robertson
Sep 12, 1895

Guy F. Price
1897-1974
(Harrison FH)

Robert D. Robertson
Jul 16, 1915
Aug 18, 1938

Paul E. Robertson
Jan 22, 1913

Frances S. Robertson
Aug 15, 1916

Ada Gore Davis
Aug 20, 1870
Feb 21, 1956

James Lafayette Gore
Jul 6, 1902
Oct 27, 1941

Lillian Lucile Gore
Aug 29, 1896

Thomas Herman Dance
Jan 14, 1885
Dec 4, 1941
&
Jessie Millsap Dance
Aug 17, 1891

Jodie H. Morris
1893-1972
(Harrison FH)

Jesse A. Hobbs
Feb 6, 1889
Aug 4, 1958

Lucile Moore Hobbs
Dec 21, 1892
Jul 12, 1949

Jesse L. Hobbs
Apr 28, 1875
Nov 21, 1931
&
Carrie Bearden Hobbs
Feb 2, 1869
Mar 4, 1956

Arthur G. Thompson
1877-1941
&
Ary Saviller Thompson
1861-1954

James A. Millsap
Jul 7, 1867
Dec 16, 1944
&
Alice Huffman Millsap
Sep 18, 1867
Apr 4, 1941

William R. Millsap
Jun 13, 1866
Sep 7, 1944

John Wesley Owens
Aug 16, 1883
Aug 11, 1970
&
Nancy Elizabeth Owens
Dec 22, 1886

Flossie Brown
1915-1948
(Raby FH)

Dorris E. Cooper
Apr 10, 1933
Apr 11, 1971

Mary Alice Cooper
May 4, 1934

F. P Enochs
Jul 14, 1857
Apr 21, 1938
&
Fannie E. Enochs
Mar 16, 1864
Aug 16, 1934

William A. Gore
1867-1935
&
Mary Alice Gore
1867-1943

Jim Gore
1879-1962

"Aunt"
Sarah Morris Gore
1849-1934

Charlie Wilson Cashion
Aug 19, 1880
Nov 27, 1932
&
Jennie Elizabeth Cashion
Oct 30, 1890
Nov 6, 1951

Alfred Cashion
1917-1960
&
Mary Ruth Cashion
1924-

George M. Smith
Jan 23, 1871
Aug 19, 1940
&
Emma Smith
Jan 10, 1871
Mar 15, 1958

James W. Huffman
Mar 29, 1870
Nov 15, 1946
&
Ella Millsap Huffman
Jan 17, 1872
Feb 12, 1948

Charles Floyd Millsap
Jan 12, 1895
Sep 3, 1958
&
Viola Norman Millsap
Aug 27, 1911

Boone Morris
Nov 13, 1891

Auldred Morris
Jun 3, 1914
Mar 20, 1972

Frances S. Morris
Apr 13, 1920

Frank Morris
Mar 5, 1950

Mrs. Margaret Matilda Owen
Died Dec 17, 1971
Age: 64 years.
(Gallant FH)

William Thomas Webb
1935-1952

Jessie H. Owen
Oct 11, 1883
Nov 14, 1947
&
Leota F. Owen
Nov 14, 1885
Nov 29, 1945

Mary Lou Dance

Paul P. Dance
Nov 15, 1890
Feb 19, 1956

W. G. "Billy" Dance
Jun 24, 1915
Nov 27, 1970

James Holman Copeland
Aug 27, 1871
May 13, 1943
&
Lily Pearl Copeland
Jul 11, 1879
Jun 25, 1934

James Roy Copeland
Apr 17, 1904
Jan 1, 1968

Pete Golden
May 12, 1870
Jan 8, 1946
&
Della C. Golden
Feb 10, 1883
1970
(Harrison FH)

Clarence Golden
1901-1952

Lawrence W. Golden
1904-1968
(Harrison FH)

Trixie Gray Harrison
1892-1966

Jack Harrison
1890-1945

Essie F. Harrison
1904-1957

Horace E. Harrison
1897-1934

Nancy Glene, Daughter of
Jack & Trixie Harrison
Oct 25, 1927
Dec 16, 1933

George W. Forrester
Sep 18, 1863
Sep 10, 1943

G. G. Grant
Sep 2, 1858
Sep 17, 1931

Sallie Grant
Aug 31, 1877
Nov 6, 1961

Charles M. Matlock
1862-1937
&
Bettie M. Matlock
1864-1948

James Elam Matlock
1889-1951

Adah Lacy Matlock
1900-

BOONEVILLE QUADRANGLE

Jonnie Mae Snow
1896-1967
George Snow
Jun 16, 1894
Nov 15, 1944
&
May Snow
Jun 17, 1896

Pfc Morris Reese
Oct 21, 1922
May 8, 1947
(picture)
"Decorations & Citations
3rd Army 87th Division
Foreign Service 1 year
8 months & 10 days
Eamet Ribbon, WW II
Victory Ribbon, Purple
Heart, American Theater
Ribbon."

John T. Snow
Oct 21, 1861
Sep 24, 1896
&
Margaret C. Smith Snow
Sep 27, 1865
Jul 24, 1950

Felix William Parks
Tennessee
Pvt MG Co 125 Inf WW I
May 4, 1896
Sep 2, 1961

Boyce A. Waggoner
Aug 29, 1904
Apr 3, 1936

Hattie Matlock Counts
Nov 5, 1894
Oct 2, 1955

Jim Sawyer Parkes
Jun 24, 1933
Aug 6, 1936

Donald Ray Parks
Jul 22, 1934
Feb 17, 1936
&
Medisa Fay Parks
May 31, 1908

&
Marion Ray Parks
Jun 15, 1903
Jan 24, 1962

Bernice W. Horton
1902-1970
(Harrison FH)

Clarence T. Waggoner
Tennessee
Sgt 1Cl Air Service
WW I
Nov 20, 1888
Mar 8, 1946

William B. Smith
Mar 24, 1901

&
Arah A. Smith
Jul 29, 1901
Sep 1, 1972

Albert McGee
Aug 22, 1887
Sep 21, 1958
&
Cora McGee
Jun 16, 1890

Lee McGee
Mar 2, 1891
Feb 1, 1956
&
Levert White McGee
Oct 26, 1890

Tillman A. McGee
1881-1942
&
Ruby Woodard McGee
1879-1950

Addie A. Gray
1892-1972
(Harrison FH)

Jean Cashion
1935-1936

C. Rufus Cashion
1910-1967

John K. Spencer
1873-1964
&
Minnoe O. Spencer
1873-1937

Infant Son of
Robert & Yvonne Daniel
B&D Mar 14, 1942

Mitchell Lafayette Spencer
Apr 9, 1852
Jul 3, 1907
&
Mary E. Smith Spencer
May 1, 1859
Dec 14, 1940

Charles M. Spencer
Feb 7, 1884
Mar 17, 1955
&
Elma W. Spencer
Oct 13, 1892

Bobbie McFarrar
1899-1947
(Harrison FH)

Horace Sullivan
Jun 2, 1892

&
Mattie M. Sullivan
Sep 23, 1888
Oct 20, 1961

Robert L. Smith
1907-1950
&
Olena G. Smith
1913-

James E. Smith
Sep 8, 1919
Mar 21, 1943

Robert Farrar
1900-1965
(Harrison FH)

Ella Waggoner Spencer
Jan 4, 1902
Jul 17, 1939
"Wife of
John G. Spencer."

Walter Waggoner
Mar 13, 1872
Feb 2, 1944
&
Attie S. Waggoner
Nov 17, 1873
May 27, 1962

Nathan Ashby
Oct 24, 1859
Jun 28, 1926
&
Bettie Ashby
Jul 28, 1863
Apr 8, 1941

William R. Ashby
Jan 13, 1899

&
Lena W. Ashby
Jan 1, 1901
Mar 26, 1961

Roy Clinton Ashby
Feb 17, 1889
Sep 1, 1962
&
Dottie Ruth Logan Ashby
Mar 12, 1905

Sam Darnell
Sep 10, 1901
Apr 11, 1964
&
Grace Darnell
May 13, 1901

Nore E. Althauser
Mar 3, 1876
Jan 4, 1951

Ottie B. McGee
Tennessee
Pvt QMC WW I
Aug 10, 1896
Aug 20, 1950

Mabel Thompson McGee
Aug 25, 1904
Apr 7, 1966

Callie Bobo
Jun 15, 1852
Jul 16, 1933

Thomas L. Bobo
Aug 22, 1878
Oct 28, 1934

Eli Byrom
Jan 26, 1863
Sep 28, 1941
&
Fannie Byrom
May 25, 1866
Apr 28, 1947

Lawrence Matlock
Sep 16, 1892
Feb 16, 1961

Mattie Matlock
Jan 5, 1897

Crawford Matlock
Oct 4, 1918

Nell Matlock
Nov 12, 1919

Roy Matlock
Sep 9, 1900
Dec 14, 1972

Mrs. Roy Matlock
Jun 10, 1906

Sammie R. Cashion
1890-1966

Samuel L. Haslett
1854-1937
&
Evelyn P. Haslett
1856-1937

Hattie Dickey Rogers
1886-19

Mattie Felps
1845-1930

Harry Richmond
1890-1970
&
Ellie Richmond
1892-1964

BOONEVILLE QUADRANGLE

William J. Majors
1878-1939
&
Ella Majors
1881-1955

William Newman
1841-1875
&
Henry Newman
Sep 13, 1877
Nov 5, 1949
&
Elizabeth Newman
Apr 29, 1847
May 13, 1924

Ernest Floyd Tipps
1893-1944
&
Lillie Brown Tipps
1903-19

Johnnie Levoy Tipps
Mar 11, 1904

Katherine Cashion Grant
Feb 27, 1918
Mar 6, 1963

Bessie Tipps Tucker
Mar 7, 1896
Nov 20, 1973

Pearl Grammer Dickey
1889-19

Luther C. Dickey
1890-1957

Willie Alice Dickey
1888-1934

T. Oscar Travis
1887-1939

Rev. John S. Rice
1867-1940

Belle B. Rice
1878-1959

Nancy Rice
1888-1971

James E. Ervin
1910-1971

Samuel Prater Ervin
Sep 16, 1870
Mar 26, 1940

Fannie S., wife of
S. P. Ervin
Mar 14, 1869
Mar 24, 1938

John Luther Darnell
1911-1944

Walker Ashby
Jan 2, 1867
Jul 20, 1943
&
Mary N. Ashby
Mar 16, 1874
Oct 25, 1908

James J. Hill
Jul 23, 1876
Sep 23, 1959
&
Lillie Mai Hill
May 16, 1880
Oct 24, 1962

William G. Cashion
1885-1946

Roy E. Spencer
Sep 4, 1895

&
Martha E. Spencer
Apr 3, 1892
Oct 12, 1971
Married Sep 2, 1914

D. Reed Spencer
Dec 31, 1915

Lucille S. Spencer
Jan 10, 1925

Rhonda E. Spencer
Sep 24, 1951
Jun 21, 1972

John "Cliff" Parks
Feb 2, 1894

&
Elma May Parks
Apr 9, 1895
Jun 25, 1960

Leonard E. Bennett
Jul 16, 1896
Oct 13, 1971
&
Lara Bess Bennett
Jul 7, 1897

Carl L. Ingle
1894-1973
(Harrison FH)

Benjamin L. Waggoner
1875-1959
&
Priscilla Waggoner
1871-1940

Ruby B. Waggoner
1911-1960
(Harrison FH)

Bill Henry Call
Jul 20, 1913
Feb 27, 1968

Frank M. Finney
Apr 19, 1916
Oct 24, 1944
"Missing in Action in
Burma."

James A. Finney
Jun 3, 1920
Aug 10, 1944
"Killed in Action on
Guam."

Walter C. Finney
1877-1952
&
Huldah L. Finney
1884-1967

Infant of
Mr. & Mrs. James E. Hise
B&D Apr 30, 1949

Estill Sanders
Nov 21, 1892
May 21, 1972
&
Lila A. Sanders
May 26, 1893

Edgar Lee Ward
1867-1956
&
Jane Stone Ward
1869-1939

Ruth Ervin Moore
Dec 2, 1894
Jan 7, 1957

Earl D. Moore
1895-1966
(Moore FH)

V. Hulon Haddon
Apr 20, 1905
Aug 12, 1972
&
Ruth Call Haddon
Jun 6, 1908

Ruby A. Norman
Sep 8, 1911
Aug 18, 1972

Alton Wiseman
Aug 6, 1916
Jun 22, 1968
&
Alda Wiseman
Sep 22, 1902

Maud Lee Smith
Jul 7, 1888
Jan 16, 1947

Chaney B. Smith
Mar 13, 1885
Dec 7, 1957
&
Cora Ann Smith
Mar 20, 1885
Aug 17, 1972

Felix Boyd Smith
Tennessee
Pfc 32 Inftry WW II
Sep 17, 1907
Oct 24, 1944

Lanny H. Wiseman
1887-(TM: 1973)
&
Della A. Wiseman
1895-1971

Walter Wiseman
1910-1939
&
Frankie Wiseman
1892-19(no date)
&
Horace Wiseman
1885-1955

Matt Falls Neill
Mar 13, 1870
Dec 10, 1934
&
Mamie Brown Neill
Dec 28, 1874
Mar 1, 1953

Benjamin H. Berry
1806-1869
&
Ann Roundtree Berry
1819-1963

Fate Anderson
1868-1940
&
Narsia Anderson
1873-1947

Ernest Wiseman Stone
Feb 11, 1889
Mar 29, 1944
"Staff Sgt Radio Gunner
Flying Fortress, missing
in action over Perleberg,
Germany"
&
Berdye Byrom Stone
Nov 13, 1896

Ernest Stone, Jr.
Aug 31, 1922
May 8, 1944

J. H. Byrom
May 26, 1850
Nov 7, 1927
&
Cincinnati Byrom
Jul 12, 1854
Sep 14, 1916

BOONEVILLE QUADRANGLE

Infant Daughter of
James & Clara Logan
B&D Sep 11, 1944

Nelda Laverne, Daughter of
James & Clara Logan
B&D Mar 6, 1952

Leonard D. Cunningham
Jun 1, 1906
Jan 7, 1967
&
Jessie M. Cunningham
Oct 20, 1907

Amanda R. Sipes
Jan 26, 1885

Leonard C. Robertson
Nov 11, 1895

James B. Huskey
1870-1941
&
Vista Call Huskey
1884-1956

J. B. Huskey
Jun 29, 1904
Aug 16, 1968

George W. Miles
1874-1946
&
Hester Norvell Miles
1876-1953

Robert Golden
Tennessee
Pvt Co B 117 Inf
30 Div WW I
Mar 27, 1892
Dec 25, 1960

Reagor Waggoner
1912-1948

Joe Waggoner
Jan 18, 1887
Jul 22, 1959
&
Ollye A. Waggoner
Nov 11, 1892

R. Gordon Moorhead
May 10, 1904
Nov 12, 1973
&
Annie J. Moorhead
Aug 18, 1913

Wylie L. Robertson
Tennessee
Jorseshoer Sup Co
129 Inf WW I
Jan 7, 1894
Jan 12, 1954

J. Carson Reese
Nov 23, 1898
Apr 6, 1967

Henry Clay Travis
Tec 5 Med Det
399 Inf Regt WW II BSM
Dec 16, 1919
Sep 26, 1970
&
Donna Ray Travis
Apr 26, 1928

Betty Sue, Daughter of
Mr. & Mrs. Henry C. Travis
B&D Sep 11, 1942

Dale Travis, Sr.
Apr 14, 1882
Aug 15, 1946
&
Elizabeth Travis
Jun 8, 1887
Feb 3, 1966

Willie Joe Spriggs
Nov 2, 1881
Nov 3, 1967
&
Rena Pitts Spriggs
Oct 1, 1884

Thomas Dale Travis, Jr.
Apr 16, 1913
Oct 29, 1968
&
Enza Lee S. Travis
Aug 30, 1914

William E. Conwell
Tennessee
SC1 U.S.N.R.F. WW I
Mar 2, 1891
May 22, 1970
&
Betty R. Conwell
Aug 31, 1888
Feb 22, 1972
Married Jul 20, 1940

Jim H. Bean
1868-1947
&
Ova L. Bean
1871-1946

Claude Logan
Jun 23, 1878
May 8, 1960
&
Nancy Smith Logan
Feb 10, 1882
Oct 13, 1953

Nancy Faye Logan
Jul 14, 1953
Apr 13, 1955

W. A. Brown
1865-1947
&
Lillie Brown
1872-1955

Ida Belle Spencer
1875-1962
&
Clair E. Spencer
1867-1946

Ervin C. Crutcher
1899-1974
(Harrison FH)

Fred Edison Collins
Tennessee
MM1 U. S. N. R.
WW II
Dec 24, 1908
May 2, 1951

Mary Spencer Collins
Mar 15, 1908

Elizabeth Diane Damron
1974-1974
(Harrison FH)

Guy (Guy) Golden
Feb 28, 1894
Jul 7, 1960
&
Bessie Golden
Oct 25, 1906

Jim Golden
Sep 7, 1862
Feb 11, 1947

William A. Flippo
Dec 6, 1868
Feb 5, 1955
&
Mattie M. Flippo
Aug 15, 1880
Oct 16, 1963

John W. Stone
1872-1946
&
Lula E. Stone
1877-1955

James Horace Stone
Mar 4, 1900
Feb 10, 1951

Horace Bedford Wiseman, Sr.
Dec 17, 1924
Jan 29, 1967

Sarah Helene W. Wiseman
Feb 8, 1928

Jack Bobo
Feb 10, 1881
May 27, 1948

R. K. "Bob" Massey
Nov 24, 1885
Apr 10, 1958
&
Mollie G. Massey
Mar 28, 1879
Jul 25, 1954

Eldridge W. "Bill"
Huffman
Feb 25, 1919
Oct 15, 1967
&
R. B. Golden Huffman

Jessie L. Chapman
1898-1971
(Harrison FH)

Reuben Edward Cobble
1889-1954
&
Elizabeth Norvell Cobble
1906-

Herman Haynes
Aug 18, 1903
Mar 1, 1965
&
Maggie Haynes
Nov 4, 1906

Bryan Woodard
Nov 14, 1902

Loise White Woodard
Aug 6, 1904

Wiley M. Damron
Mar 12, 1888
Mar 30, 1963

Frank M. Tucker
Oct 2, 1875
Jun 2, 1959
&
Beatrice Tucker
Feb 11, 1886
Jan 18, 1972

Dorothy Jean, Daughter
of Glendon & Georgia
Rogers
Dec 20, 1944
Feb 13, 1947

James Clinton Simmons
Jul 4, 1904

&
Roxie Dillard Simmons
Nov 9, 1903

BOONEVILLE QUADRANGLE

Buford Moorhead
1888-1956
&
Myrtle M. Moorhead
1887-1965

Morris Nute Branch
Tennessee
Pvt U. S. Army WW I
Jun 9, 1891
May 26, 1972
&
Lodar G. Branch
Mar 2, 1897
Oct 14, 1969

Gary Wayne Branch
Jul 2, 1950
Dec 31, 1969
(color picture)

Robert L. Edens
1919-1963

Margie Brown, wife of
Floyd Driver
Jul 12, 1897
Nov 21, 1948

Floyd Driver
Jun 26, 1893
Oct 16, 1959

Coba Bailey, wife of
Floyd Driver
Nov 8, 1908

Annie Darnell
1912-1953
(Harrison FH)

James W. Norman
1884-1952
&
Ida H. Norman
1881-

Marion Burton
1900-1954
(Harrison FH)

George R. Bobo
1881-1949
&
Dora Parks Bobo
1883-1967

Frank "Pete" Hinkle
1907-1968
(Moore-Cortner FH)

Nellie Mae Damron
Apr 12, 1912
Jan 6, 1970

Roy Joseph Byrom
Jan 14, 1884
May 25, 1948

James A. Andrews
Aug 16, 1865
Oct 17, 1949
&
Mima E. Andrews
Dec 20, 1874
Jan 12, 1956

Charles A. Andrews
Dec 20, 1898

&
Clara Lee Andrews
Mar 20, 1902
May 31, 1952

Charles Harlan, Son of
Charles & Helen Hobbs
Jul 18, 1955
Jul 19, 1955

Charles Edwin Hobbs
May 10, 1921
Feb 22, 1955
&
Helen Counts Hobbs
Sep 20, 1924

F. M. Counts
Sep 25, 1875
Oct 9, 1952
&
Mary S. Counts
Jan 20, 1878
Aug 1, 1958

Cornice S. T. Golden
Nov 19, 1901
Sep 24, 1957
&
Flossie May Golden
Nov 18, 1907

Addie L. Golden
1895-1951
&
Susie M. Golden
1899-19

John Dillon Harrison
Dec 13, 1892
Jan 29, 1955
&
Maude Wilkes Harrison
Sep 30, 1896
Mar 28, 1970

Otho Grady Harrison
Sep 15, 1902
Jun 23, 1962
&
Estelle H. Harrison
Jun 19, 1908

&   Willie Allen Byrom
Feb 4, 1885
Jan 21, 1960

John Henry Hasty
Apr 10, 1884
Jun 24, 1964
&
Loda Hasty
Jun 26, 1884
May 30, 1948

David M. Smith
Apr 9, 1893
Sep 29, 1961
&
Ellen C. Smith
May 6, 1899

Dillard Gray Tucker
Aug 1, 1915
Feb 22, 1973

Robert F. Tucker
May 31, 1877
Dec 26, 1965
&
Luella S. Tucker
Nov 19, 1879
May 5, 1964

Hugh D. Smith
Mar 22, 1914
Oct 27, 1951
&
Catherine E. Smith
Apr 11, 1917

Maudalyne Bobo Hinkle
1913-1961

Walter P. Murray
Tennessee
S1 U. S. N. R. WW II
Feb 5, 1927
Oct 11, 1949

Rachel Ann Murray
1963-1963
(Harrison FH)

William Frank Parks
Jan 18, 1890
Dec 11, 1959

Mamie Dora Parks
Dec 25, 1890

Frank Wilburn Parks
Pfc 172 Inf
Jul 27, 1921
Mar 19, 1945
"Lost his life fighting
for Liberty in South
Pacific."

Cleo Tipps Waggoner
Apr 6, 1880
Aug 24, 1948

Roy Allen, Jr., Son of
Roy & Willie Byrom
Dec 7, 1915-Mar 10, 1916

Benjamin A. Baits
Tennessee
Cpl Co M 117 Inf WW I
Feb 7, 1891
Jan 7, 1968
&
Gracie W. Baits
May 25, 1902

Julia Y. Cook
1899-1962
(Howell-Thompson FH)

Fred Wiseman
1901-1963
&
Mavis Wiseman
1905-

Lawson Wilson Norman
Apr 14, 1913
Dec 3, 1965

Clara Parks Norman
Oct 9, 1918

J. D. Sawyer
May 14, 1911
Dec 15, 1970
&
Frances Pierce Sawyer
Jul 30, 1911

James O. Pierce
Nov 10, 1880
Sep 9, 1952
&
Addie May Pierce
Dec 4, 1889
Feb 17, 1970

Plummer S. Parks
Sep 2, 1877
Jan 18, 1949

Bettie C. Parks
Sep 10, 1883
Aug 30, 1971

Roy E. Parks
Jan 8, 1913

Juanita M. Parks
Sep 3, 1908
Nov 8, 1972

W. T. "Bill" Simpson
1881-1956
&
Mary Simpson
1885-1963

James A.(Albert Byrom
Tennessee
Sgt U. S. Army WW II
Jul 21, 1919
Sep 19, 1972

BOONEVILLE QUADRANGLE

Berdye Nell, Daughter of
Roy & Willie Byrom
Mar 11, 1918
Dec 5, 1919

James M. Philpot
1905-
&
Purnie J. Philpot
1907-1946

------ Philpot
Died Nov 25, 1948
Age: ---
(Gowen-Smith FH)

* *

MARTIN CEMETERY

LOCATION: Located at the North end of Buckeye Hollow, near the head of Buckeye Creek.

Thomas C. Martin &
Oct 8, 1828
Aug 9, 1896

Lavina King Martin
Jun 19, 1820
Oct 12, 1894

Loise Stone
Jan 30, 1900
Feb 2, 1900

Mattie, wife of
J. F. Horsley
May 26, 1855
Sep 18, 1885

Charley W. White
Apr 8, 1878
Aug 1, 1900

* *

MENNONITE BROTHERHOOD CEMETERY

LOCATION: Two miles south of New Herman.

James Mahlon Weaver
Jul 13, 1973
Jul 20, 1973

* *

MOTLOW CEMETERY

LOCATION: One mile NW of Lynchburg, on Price Branch.

Zadok Motlow
Sep 6, 1787
Oct   1863
(old marker)

Zadock Motlow
Sep 6, 1789
Oct   1863
&
Mary G. Motlow
Nov 24, 1796
Aug   1883
(New marker)

Andy, Son of
Ewin & Nancy Moore
Died 1852
Age: 2 years.

NOTE: Outside of fenced-in area, in pasture, about 20 or more graves with no markers, condition of the graves and fieldstones indicates that this part of the cemetery was established first. Eds.

3 unmarked graves, all in Iron-fence enclosure.

* *

McNATT CEMETERY

LOCATION: Two miles NW of Charity Church, in McNatt Hollow.

Jas. McNatt
Jun 3, 1827
Mar 28, 1899
&
Eliza McNatt
Sep 25, 1826
(no date)

Johnnie McNatt
Died Sep 2, 1872
Age: 19y, 5m, 26d.

N. B. McNatt
Jan 1, 1856
Jul 27, 1897

Johnnie Jodie McNatt
Died Aug 6, 1887
Age: 12y, 4m, 3d.

Mollie J. McNatt
Oct 26, 1859
Oct 19, 1889

Ermine Rees, Daughter of
James & Elisa McNatt
Jul 12, 1854
Mar 30, 1882

About 12 graves with fieldstones, no inscriptions.

Mildred, Daughter of
Carl & Mary McNatt
B&D Sep 22, 1917

Dempsey McNatt
Mar 6, 1870
Apr 15, 1928

C. L. M.
(This is a footstone and next to Dempsey McNatt)

* *

BOONEVILLE QUADRANGLE

NEECE CEMETERY

LOCATION: Three and one half miles NW of Charity Church, in Bartlett Hollow.

Several unmarked graves.

J. E. Neece
Oct 20, 1834
Jan 24, 1906
Age: 71y, 3m, 4d.

Elizabeth A., wife of
J. E. Neece
Aug 12, 1831
Aug 13, 1898

Gertie, Daughter of
J. M. & O. F. Owen
Aug 2, 1894
Oct 1, 1895

* *

PEARSON CEMETERY

LOCATION: On Wiseman Road in Bedford Hollow, in the Northern part of Moore County.

In Memory of
William Pearson, who was
born the 10th day of
April 1761 and died the
10 day of October 1844
Age: 83y, 6m, 10d.
(Soldier of the
Revolution)

Dixon A., Son of
P. A. & L. E. Noblett
Jul 20, 1884
Dec 9, 1890

Washington P. Bobo
Jun 23, 1812
Apr 11, 1883
Age: 69y, 9m, 18d.
Marker made by
N. J. Calhoon,
Shelbyville, Tenn.

Silena Alice Noblett
Jun 23, 1869
Aug 19, 1887

Georgia, Daughter of
J. M. & M. E. Green
Dec 5, 1888
May 3, 1889

Large marker with
C. E. Bobo (footmarker)
(buried in ground)

NOTE: This was a large
cemetery at one time,
now destroyed by cattle.
                    Eds.

* *

RABY CEMETERY

LOCATION: In Warren Hollow, about one mile south of the Bedford County line, and two miles NW of Charity.

Thomas L. Cummings
1960-1966
(Gowen-Smith FH)

Kate P. Cummings
Feb 9, 1906
Oct 11, 1946

James Forrest Redd, Jr.
Died Dec 13, 1971
Age: 25y, 10m, 13d.
(Manchester FH)

William D. Warren
1858-1945

Lou Settie Warren
1863-1945

Edgar Warren
Jun 11, 1899
Nov 2, 1918

Jim P. Warren
1873-1957
&
Bess A. Warren
1880-1957

Neil Grant Redd
B&D Jul 4, 1943

Mock W. Redd
Oct 16, 1837
Aug 22, 1918
&
Frances P. Redd
Apr 6, 1844
Jan 5, 1927

Carl, Son of
R. W. & B. B. Redd
Jun 15, 1910
Nov 13, 1912

Prudie Redd, Daughter of
W. A. & Josie E. Pamplin
1899-1918

Wynemo Caschigonos
Apr 27, 1907
(TM: 1972)

Louis James Phelps
Tennessee
Pvt 374 Escort Guard Co MP
Aug 24, 1903
Feb 3, 1945

N. Phelps
1901-1953
(Thompson FH)

W. A. P.(Phelps)
(no dates)

Ray W. Miles
Oct 2, 1938
Aug 18, 1953

George H.(Henry) Redd
Mar 3, 1881
Dec 17, 1966
&
Laura W. Redd
Mar 2, 1881
Nov 16, 1916

Rufus W. Redd
1876-19(no date)
&
Bell Redd
1881-1932

Flora L. Redd
Jul 27, 1899
Feb 27, 1916

Flora, Daughter of
W. A. & Josie Pamplin
May 27, 1903
Nov 13, 1918

William A. Pamplin
Apr 15, 1867
Nov 15, 1918
&
Josie R. Pamplin
Dec 28, 1879
Mar 14, 1960

Floyd Laws
1907-1934

J. T.(John Turner) Redd
Jul 5, 1875
Apr 27, 1923

Ollie Lee Redd
Oct 27, 1890
Jun 14, 1969
&
Nessie R. Redd
Nov 23, 1904

Lee Athel Redd
Dec 2, 1882

&
Bessie D. Wagster Redd
May 8, 1889

Harold Addison Redd
Tennessee
Tec 5 8 Air Force WW II
Jan 19, 1918
Oct 23, 1969

William Athol Redd
Tennessee
Sgt U. S. Air Force,
Vietnam
Sep 22, 1947
Dec 27, 1970

BOONEVILLE QUADRANGLE

James F. Redd
Aug 11, 1912
Jun 28, 1970
&
Katherine H. Redd
Jul 10, 1917

Mildred, Daughter of
W. A. & Josie Pamplin
Dec 9, 1916
Mar 1, 1919

Nora O., Daughter of
W. A. & Josie E. Pamplin
1904-1945

C. W. Marr
1945-1945

Charles Mount
Apr 6, 1911
Jul 19, 1968

J. J. Thomas
Oct 6, 1889
Jul 14, 1914

Lee Hazelwood
Nov 16, 1890
Feb 4, 1950

Albert Hazelwood
Aug 28, 1868
Aug 10, 1928
&
Katherine Hazelwood
Oct 4, 1871
Apr 24, 1939

A. H. & Ola
(fieldstone)

Mary Victoria Rutledge,
wife of
Hayes Bartlett
Jul 29, 1880
Nov 27, 1905

D. F. (David Floyd)
Warren
Feb 28, 1884
Jul 20, 1918
&
Annie Ethel (Wagster)
Warren
Feb 20, 1889
Oct 12, 1965

Thomas J. Richardson
1849-1904
&
Louisa Richardson
1853-1946

Cleophus Warren
May 14, 1907
Jul 8, 1907

Deavor Warren
Oct 20, 1913
Oct 27, 1913

A. B. & B. B.
(fieldstone)

Alvis Warren
1886-(date gone)

Alice Thomas, wife of
Alvis Warren
Jun 19, 1900
Jun 28, 1925

Nola Warren
1884-1968
(Gowen-Smith FH)

Janie May Marr
1905-1949

J. Henry Marr
1879-1948
&
Mattie W. Marr
1884-(TM: 1967)

B. A. Marler
Mar 4, 1837
Apr 2, 1914

"Father"
J. C. Warren
May 2, 1858
Jan 24, 1945
&
"Mother"
S. M.(Susan M. Grazier)
Warren
Mar 24, 1861
Apr 3, 1916

Lillie F., Daughter of
J. C. & S. M. Warren
Dec 26, 1890
Sep 5, 1896

Infant Daughter of
J. C. & S. M. Warren
B&D Feb 11, 1899

"Father"
D. W. Sanders
Aug 19, 1823
May 12, 1911
& wife
Jane Sanders
Sep 2, 1825
Jan 18, 1905

M. H. Sanders
Oct 18, 1855
Oct 30, 1919

Henry E. Lowe
1888-1962

Mattie M. Lowe
1891-1935

E. Leona Lowe
1922-1924

George H. Bartlett
1870-1948
&
S. Pink Bartlett
1867-1939

J. R.(John Rufus) McNatt
Jan 17, 1867
(TM: 1945)
&
E. A. McNatt
Jul 28, 1865
Nov 21, 1927

S. C. Glazier
Mar 25, 1828
Feb 10, 1905

S. M. Woosley
Jun 26, 1883
Jul 24, 1899
&
Infant Daughter of
J. F. & S. M. Woosley
B&D Jul 22, 1899
&
J. F. Woosley
May 23, 1877
Mar 30, 1912

J. C., Son of
J. F. & S. M. Woosley
Jul 13, 1898
Oct 9, 1898

William G.(Grant) Thomas
1869-1934
&
Dora M. Thomas
1881-1953

Julia Catherine, Daughter
of Marion & Fannie Sanders
Aug 3, 1878
Jul 13, 1888

Joshua C. Woosley
Oct 20, 1854
May 31, 1945
&
Sarah E. Woosley
Jun 12, 1866
Aug 12, 1957

J. C. Raney
Jun 29, 1837
Jan 2, 1911
& wife
Mollie Raney
Dec 2, 1843
Jun 16, 1902

Infant Son of
C. H. & A. Gammill
B&D Mar 9, 1915

Robert L. Marr
1886-1944
&
Mattie Marr
1893-1926

Timothy C. Marr
Died Dec 18, 1889
Age: 1 month.

John W. Warren
Feb 8, 1864
Jul 31, 1940

Sallie F. (Thomas), wife
of J. W. Warren
Mar 3, 1865
Jan 18, 1915

Cleveland, Son of
J. W. & Sallie Warren
Jun 9, 1888
Jun 25, 1901

Ottie L. Warren
1903-1938

Janie Warren
Jun 18, 1895
Apr 16, 1906

N. A. Redd
Mar 31, 1856
Sep 17, 1898
&
M. A. Redd
Dec 24, 1882
Sep 9, 1893

Oliver Sanders
Apr 1, 1894
Nov 26, 1894
&
Andy Sanders
Feb 21, 1901
Apr 8, 1902
&
Clara Sanders
Jun 15, 1904
Jan 31, 1905
Children of
R. J. & E. C. Sanders.

J. M. Casteel
Mar 29, 1853
Jun 30, 1923
&
Mary Ellen Casteel
Dec 25, 1854
(no date)

J. T. Marr
1876-1930

Sarah Jane Marr
1881-1953

Sarah Warren
Dec 17, 1823
Sep 20, 1900

John Warren, Sr.
Nov 15, 1813
Jul 14, 1889

BOONEVILLE QUADRANGLE

Leizzie, wife of
F. B. Warren
Dec 26, 1892
Jan 21, 1950

2 Infants of
J. E. & V. S. Warren
Jan 3, 1891
Nov 5, 1891

Infant Son of
J. H. & N. A. Redd
B&D Sep 1, 1886
&
T. H. Redd
Sep 1, 1886
Sep 15, 1887

Dolph, Son of
T. J. & Louisa Richardson
Oct 13, 1884
Jul 29, 1893

S. F. Richardson
May 17, 1852
Oct 20, 1866

Albert, Son of
T. J. & Louisa Richardson
Aug 22, 1891
Jul 24, 1893

Lillard, Son of
T. J. & Louisa Richardson
Jun 11, 1889
Nov 17, 1890

Alta, Daughter of
T. J. & Louisa Richardson
Jan 21, 1881
Feb 15, 1881

John Warren
Apr 18, 1859
Sep 6, 1922
&
Mellie S.(Permelia) Warren
May 12, 1869
Apr 3, 1954

W. D., Son of
J. & M. C. Warren
Dec 1, 1897
Dec 5, 1897

John W. Marr
Nov 16, 1855
Sep 18, 1918

Slina C. Marr
Mar 17, 1854
Apr 5, 1920

J. C. McNatt
Dec 12, 1882
Feb 7, 1911

Ida Ruth McNatt
Oct 4, 1908
Oct 20, 1911

Bell Raby, wife of
Newell McNatt
1852-1930

Thomas T. Warren
1897-1963
&
Sadie May Warren
1907-1950

James Raby
Sep 8, 1814
Nov 11, 1892
& wife
Isabella Phillips Raby
Aug 2, 1810
(no date)

George W. Jones, Son of
James & Isabella Raby
Oct 4, 1855
Oct 12, 1855
Age: 8 days.

A. E., wife of
J. B. McNatt
Sep 12, 1848
Mar 4, 1892

D. C., Son of
J. B. & A. E. McNatt
Sep 7, 1878
Apr 4, 1880

Many unmarked graves.

E. B. Raby
May 25, 1825
Feb 24, 1895

Elizabeth, wife of
E. B. Raby
Oct 19, 1822
May 31, 1887
Age: 64y, 6m, 12d.

T. R.
(fieldstone)

G. L. Thomas
Oct 15, 1862
Apr 18, 1896
&
N. B. Thomas
Jul 21, 1861
(no date)

Susan A., wife of
George L. Thomas
Aug 3, 1861
Apr 13, 1886

Ida Belle, Daughter of
George L. & S. A. Thomas
Jan   1885
Aug 4, 1884

Martha E. Gammill
May 19, 1845
Mar 14, 1863

T. W. Crane
Aug 17, 1848
Apr 25, 1901

Elizabeth Belle, wife of
T. W. Crane
Feb 27, 1840
Feb 19, 1880

D. C.
(fieldstone)

J. W. Moore
Died Jan 8, 1897
Age: 41 years.
&
Sarah E. (Warren) Moore
Died Apr 14, 1920
Age: 63 years.

Allie C. Womble
Aug 9, 1895
Oct 12, 1901

Mrs. J. F. Prosser
Nov 5, 1869
Feb 14, 1902
"Our beloved wife &
Mother."

William C. Sharp
1848-1924
&
Mary J. Sharp
1856-1924
&
Samuel Sharp
1880-1900

Johnie Layton Rees
1904-1904
&
Thomas Clayton Rees
1904-1906

Attie Rees
1870-1944
&
Sarah Phine Rees
1872-1965

Daniel Warren
Oct 22, 1829
Mar 28, 1883
&
Elizabeth (Felps) Warren
Oct 18, 1827
Mar 28, 1906

Twin Sons of
J. C. & S. M. Warren
B&D Mar 29, 1880

Buddie Warren
B&D Jan 19, 1852

Willie Moore
1887-19
&
R. C. Moore
1884-1932

* *

RUDD CEMETERY

LOCATION: Three miles NE of Booneville, on Rudd Branch.

Mandy Jane Rudd
May 29, 1871
Sep 18, 1872

20 or more graves with fieldstones, no inscriptions.

Some of the Old Rudd Family   buried here.

* *

BOONEVILLE QUADRANGLE

WAGGONER-BUCKEYE CHURCH CEMETERY

LOCATION: Three miles west of Lynchburg on the Booneville Road.

Wilson F. Wagoner
Aug 27, 1862
Dec 11, 1922

Susan A. Forrester, wife
of W. F. Wagoner
Sep 13, 1856
Dec 2, 1917

Willie Wagoner
Oct 21, 1890
Feb 3, 1906

Charlie Wagoner
Aug 23, 1889
Sep 28, 1905

Nancy Ann Wagoner
Jan 30, 1888
Aug 6, 1888

Annie B., Daughter of
B. F. & Sallie Wagoner
Jul 21, 1891
Oct 11, 1894

Infant Son of
B. F. & Sallie Wagoner
B&D Sep 4, 1896

Ben F. Wagoner
1861-1941
&
Sallie J. Wagoner
1862-1931

Margaret, wife of
Frederick Wagoner
Dec 30, 1811
Jul 12, 1905

Infant Daughter of
G. B. & M. C. Felps
Sep 30, 1883
Jan 5, 1884

Ellen Gault, wife of
T. J. Russell
1858-19(no date)

T. J. Russell
1854-1932

Clee Woodard
Jun 30, 1862
Nov 30, 1901

Mollie, wife of
J. W. Morris
Aug 18, 1860
Jun 16, 1891

William A. Horton
Sep 26, 1833
Jul 25, 1858

Mary A. Buchanan
Aug 29, 1838
Apr 16, 1862

Boy Phillips
May 20, 1873
May 3, 1871
(These dates must be
reversed)

Joshua Phillips
Oct 28, 1863
Sep 19, 1876

Cooper Phillips
May 11, 1866
Sep 20, 1876

Candis, wife of
J. W. Morris
Oct 12, 1854
Jul 6, 1879

Infant of
J. W. & Candis Morris
(no dates)

Elizabeth A. Wagoner,
wife of J. H. Phillips
Oct 13, 1832
Mar 18, 1884

Bill Russell
1875-1889

Infant Daughter of
L. & V. Robertson
Feb 26, 1867
Feb 27, 1867

Malinda H. Wagoner
Jun 13, 1840
Mar 11, 1863
&
Frederick Wagoner
May 12, 1795
Aug 23, 1866
&
Mary Wagoner
Jun 20, 1797
Jul 7, 1863

Infant Son of
K. J. & Susan Bobo
B&D Jan 29, 1877

Louis M., Son of
K. J. & Susan Bobo
Dec 15, 1875
Oct 17, 1876
Age: 10m, 2d.

William D. Allen
Oct 2, 1886
May 31, 1941

Lodrick Robertson
May 6, 1817
Nov 23, 1893

Nancy, wife of
L. Robertson
Feb 3, 1823
Feb 28, 1863

Vienna, wife of
L. Robertson
Jun 14, 1829
Jun 1, 1910

John J., Son of
L. & N. Robertson
Mar 3, 1843
Dec 18, 1866

Mary C., Daughter of
L. & N. Robertson
May 3, 1855
Jun 10, 1864

Malinda E., Daughter of
L. & N. Robertson
Jun 24, 1860
Jan 22, 1863

William F. Robertson
Oct 3, 1844
Jan 18, 1923
& wife
Sallie Morris Robertson
Sep 12, 1845
Aug 22, 1923

Ella Ward Pierce
Mar 30, 1874
May 20, 1905

Mary C., wife of
E. W. Gentery
Mar 29, 1844
Mar 12, 1897

Margaret Crenshaw
Aug 10, 1795
Aug 8, 1881

Jacob Waggoner
Oct 15, 1828
Oct 23, 1874

Cyntha, wife of
Jacob Wagoner
May 19, 1830
Jan 22, 1885

J. N. A. Waggoner
Nov 2, 1865
Mar 23, 1876

Mary Stephens, wife of
Clyde Elliott
May 1, 1901
Sep 8, 1959

Alexander Forrester
Sep 29, 1820
Jan 1, 1909

J. H., wife of
J. B. Forrester
Aug 6, 1870
Mar 17, 1897

Ellen, wife of
J. B. Forrester
May 25, 1886
Jun 16, 1909

Manerva, wife of
Alex. Forrester
Nov 11, 1820
Aug 26, 1892

Leona Ruth Farr
1911-1966

Mollie Robertson Askins
May 14, 1865
Jun 18, 1939

James A. Stone
Oct 2, 1886
Aug 1, 1953
&
Maggie J. Stone
Jul 4, 1888

Ireney Stephens
Aug 29, 1822
Dec 3, 1893
Age: 71y, 3m, 4d.

Infant Daughter of
J. & Fannie Stephens
(no dates)

William M. Stephens
Nov 18, 1888
May 21, 1889

Barnett R. Stephens
Aug 22, 1883
Oct 15, 1908

Lee Stephens
Mar 27, 1887
Apr 4, 1909

J. R. Stephens
Aug 2, 1859
Dec 21, 1924
&
Fannie Stephens
Dec 4, 1864
Apr 6, 1953

Andy C. Stephens
Feb 21, 1891
Apr 22, 1911

BOONEVILLE QUADRANGLE

J. C. Bartlett
Dec 31, 1928
Sep 5, 1964
&
Mittie Bartlett
Sep 3, 1907

&
Earl Bartlett
Apr 28, 1905

Johnie, Son of
W. M. & Cyntha Green
Dec 23, 1878
Dec 24, 1878

Mittie A., Daughter of
W. M. & Cyntha Green
Aug 28, 1876
Jul 30, 1884

Myrtle, Daughter of
W. M. & Cyntha Green
Jun 20, 1885
Aug 17, 1885

W. M. Green
Aug 11, 1852
Feb 12, 1928
& wife
Cynthia Forrester Green
Nov 17, 1851
Jul 18, 1929

K. J. Bobo
Jun 16, 1840
May 9, 1914
&
Susan Bobo
Nov 8, 1840
Dec 4, 1924

William P. Bobo
Feb 10, 1874
Nov 4, 1903

Samuel L. Bobo
Apr 2, 1871
Apr 30, 1911

W. D. Allen, Jr.
Aug 25, 1916
Aug 8, 1937

Hensley A. Locke
Apr 22, 1851
Sep 19, 1929
&
Louisa Locke
Jan 25, 1852
Mar --, 1943

Hubert Locke
1885-1969
(TM)

Bertie Locke
Aug 5, 1882
Mar 12, 1907

Mai Locke
Feb 10, 1875
Jan 19, 1961

Cora M., Daughter of
H. A. & Lou Locke
Aug 11, 1877
Oct 17, 1899

Boone Smith
(no dates)

Mary Thompson Smith
(no dates)

Ollie Smith
Mar 11, 1882
Oct 24, 1903

Samuel Carl Smith
Jun 4, 1907
Oct 5, 1908

S. C. Woodard
Jul 4, 1836
May 6, 1901

E. L. Woodard
Jan 3, 1841
Jun 30, 1903

Nannie, wife of
J. W. Woodard
Apr 19, 1857
Jun 6, 1899

2 enclosures with
Robertsons, no markers.

Boley Baxter
1866-1953
&
Amandy Baxter
1866-1934

Infant Daughter of
B. R. & Amanda Baxter
B&D Mar 19, 1891

Andy Franklin, Son of
B. R. & Amanda Baxter
Dec 14, 1889
Aug 29, 1890

Clarence Evans
1895-1963
&
Floy O. Evans
1895-1936

Elbert & Albert Evans
1925

E. C. Hix
Jun 30, 1852
Jan 23, 1909

Julia A., wife of
E. C. Hix
Mar 11, 1856
Aug 26, 1906

Josh M. Pierce
1869-1958
&
Annie C. Pierce
1872-1901

J. D. Morris
May 6, 1814
Apr 26, 1895

Sarah, wife of
Jas. D. Morris
Jun 29, 1819
Oct 26, 1890
Age: 71y, 3m, 27d.

Lod J. Morris
1861-1936
&
Emma Morris
1872-1898

Fannie B. Simpson
1897-1961

E. Clark
Jul 27, 1849
Nov 27, 1917

Emily J. Edens, wife of
E. Clark
Jan 1, 1842
Dec 21, 1899

George T. Clark
Nov 17, 1877
Aug 6, 1922

Mary Lee, Daughter of
E. & Emily J. Clark
Jun 19, 1876
Jul 14, 1890

George B. Wagoner
Sep 17, 1873
Feb 5, 1958
&
Martha J. Allen Wagoner
Jan 1, 1877
Nov 10, 1966

Allen, Son of
G. B. & M. J. Wagoner
B&D Jul 7, 1911

Thomas N. Allen
Jun 28, 1870
Jul 18, 1901

Joe A. Wagoner
1885-1886
&
A. F. Wagoner
1860-1936
&
Mattie Wagoner
1854-1927

F. A. Wagoner
1863-1933
&
Fannie Wagoner
1868-1957
&
Elijah B. Wagoner
1887-1888

William F. Locke
1848-1922
&
Sarah E. Locke
1849-1905
&
Maggie E. Locke
1866-19(no date)

Infant Son of
Clyde & Mary Elliott
B&D May 15, 1923

Clyde Logan
1878-1933
&
Sarah Wagoner Logan
1879-1939

Tallman C., Son of
Mr. & Mrs. Clyde Logan
Jun 3, 1903
Feb 8, 1904

David O. Logan
1881-1952

Joe F. Baxter
Jul 17, 1877
Jul 4, 1957

Mary W. Baxter
Dec 10, 1882
Mar 20, 1957

Edgar H. Davis
Apr 13, 1875
May 17, 1938

Nannie J. Davis
May 2, 1888
Dec 30, 1926

C. W. Felps
Mar 3, 1838
Aug 31, 1912

Elizabeth R., wife of
C. W. Felps
Jul 21, 1842
Feb 21, 1903

Wiley C. Murray
Dec 19, 1903
May 16, 1904

J. N. Hobbs
1849-1920
&
Sue A. Hobbs
1855-1934

BOONEVILLE QUADRANGLE

Mary M. Stephens, wife
of J. N. Hobbs
Aug 16, 1853
May 1, 1910

G. C. Stephens
Mar 4, 1885
Sep 10, 1912
& wife
Sallie Stephens
Feb 17, 1886
(no date)

Infant Son of
G. C. & Sallie Stephens
Jan 1, 1909
Jan 7, 1909

Tom B. Smith
1873-1961
&
Allie Stacy Smith
1876-1936

Charlie B. Smith
Feb 22, 1900
Jul 25, 1920

Wilson L. Smith
Mar 10, 1910
Jun 10, 1970

E. Stone
Dec 20, 1842
Mar 8, 1924
&
Fanny Jane Stone
Jan 26, 1843
Sep 10, 1912

Charlie Stone
1873-1930
&
Lucy Stone
1876-1949

A. D. Robertson
Sep 15, 1857
Oct 28, 1940
&
Mattie Robertson
Jan 7, 1863
Oct 7, 1920

J. B. Forrester
Apr 1, 1859
Jan 24, 1928

Minnie H., Daughter of
J. B. & J. H. Forrester
Died Jun 7, 1911
Age: 21y, 8m.

Robert David Stacy
Sep 21, 1874
Aug 14, 1938
&
Mary Jane Stacy
Mar 14, 1877
Sep 29, 1956

Edd C. Woodard
1867-1957
&
Collie Jones Woodard
1882-1948

Alva E. Woodard
Jan 2, 1903
Jan 4, 1903

Ola Lee, Daughter of
Earl & Mettie Bartlett
B&D Dec 24, 1927

Zelma Stone
Jun 23, 1897
Nob 5, 1905

J. E. Stone
1913-1913

George E. Felps
Nov 20, 1881
Sep 27, 1904

Roy T. Phelps
1876-1953

Nannie C. Phelps
1883-1949

William Noah Ward
Jul 23, 1903

&
Nellie Geraldine Ward
Aug 10, 1904
Jan 4, 1945

G. H. Wagoner
Sep 15, 1836
Mar 10, 1905
&
Ann Wagoner
Feb 13, 1841
Aug 16, 1921

R. L. Wiggins
Dec 19, 1868
May 19, 1927

Betty Waggoner Wiggins
Mar 24, 1868
Jun 8, 1934

Frank, Son of
Joe F. & Mary S. Baxter
Oct 6, 1911
Nov 16, 1913

William Andrews
1860-1933
&
Sallie Andrews
1862-19(no date)

Ollie Smith
1876-1943
&
Lizzie Smith
1875-1960

W. Arthur Ward
Aug 6, 1882
May 21, 1958
&
Loncie B. Ward
Apr 5, 1889
Jul 1, 1959

James Franklin Moore
Mar 14, 1941
Mar 15, 1951

Douthard Massey
1877-1938
&
Savanna Massey
1883-1964

Ephraim H. Allen
Sep 28, 1846
Feb 13, 1926

Mimia, wife of
Ephraim Allen
Nov 3, 1846
Sep 5, 1911

Luther Ephraim, Son of
E. H. Allen
Oct 1, 1887
Jan 16, 1900

Ida McNatt, wife of
Thomas N. Allen
Oct 17, 1876
Jul 11, 1901

Florence Christine,
Daughter of
Mr. & Mrs. D. C. Gray
Jul 2, 1920
Sep 13, 1927

Don W. Gray
Aug 6, 1931
Jun 26, 1935

Thomas A. Chapman
Aug 13, 1863
Jun 22, 1941
&
Nanie E. Chapman
May 12, 1866
Apr 29, 1925

Floyd Ray Russell
Jun 14, 1928
Jul 9, 1930

Floy Mae Russell
Jun 14, 1928
Jun 14, 1930

Walter Clay Logan
B&D Feb 16, 1920

Roy W. Parks
Dec 3, 1903
Oct 28, 1957

Layton L. Morris
Nov 2, 1897
May 19, 1960 (6)
&
Thelma O. Morris
Mar 3, 1902
Jun 18, 1967

Thomas R. Morris
1858-1927
&
Finettie H. Morris
1858-1905
&
Martha B. Morris
1877-1951

J. W. Morris
1859-1929
&
Mattie Morris
1872-1952

Maud, wife of
W. D. Bailey
Feb 19, 1878
Sep 1, 1905

Owen J. Bailey
Aug 29, 1905
Sep 2, 1905
&
Infant Sons of
Mr. & Mrs. W. D. Bailey
B&D Jun 8, 1904

James M. Burrow
1865-1942
&
Lula Davis Burrow
1871-1946

Joe L. Russell
Jan 17, 1895
Feb 17, 1959
&
Ozell B. Russell
Sep 6, 1893

Burnice Lucille Hill
Mar 7, 1920
Jul 8, 1930

Will J. Smith
Mar 11, 1885
Apr 12, 1931
&
Ida M. Parks Smith
May 19, 1890

Joseph G. Nichols
Aug 17, 1915
May 10, 1916

Josephine M. Nichols
Apr 3, 1878
Nov 9, 1916

BOONEVILLE QUADRANGLE

Joe Fred Wiggins and
Jul 7, 1894

&
Bettye Snow Wiggins
Aug 16, 1898
Aug 4, 1929

Bettye Louise Wiggins
Jul 24, 1923
Jul 4, 1946

Bobby Wayne, Son of
Mr. & Mrs. W. P. Smith
Mar 24, 1932
Dec 27, 1932

Will Ashby
1893-1962
(TM)

Martha Ashby
1922-1968
(TM)

John Ashby
Dec 1, 1850
Mar 2, 1935
&
Mollie Ashby
Mar 22, 1851
Jan 31, 1943

Henry Ashby
Feb 1, 1884
Dec 24, 1911

* *

WHITMAN CEMETERY

LOCATION: On Jack Waggoner farm, on West Mulberry Creek, one mile SE of Charity Church, on Charity road.

Information submitted by
Mrs. Jack Waggoner.

A. Whitman
Jan 11, 1815
Oct 18, 1852

D. P. Whitman
Feb 6, 1837
Jul 2, 1852

1 fieldstone, no inscription.

* *

WOMACK CEMETERY

LOCATION: This cemetery is at the head of Dogtail Creek, in the northern section of the County.

Lizzie Carter, wife of
Peyton Womack
Oct 8, 1853
Jan 11, 1895

Willie M. Lowe, wife of
Peyton Womack
Jan 8, 1873
Sep 12, 1899

Martha E. Womack
Feb 13, 1873
Dec 21, 1887

Thomas W., Son of
B. A. & S. J. Womack
Jun 28, 1878
Nov 8, 1878

Solomon Womack ***
Jun 25, 1826
Aug 12, 1868

Lucinda Ervin, 1st wife of
Solomon Womack ***
1829-1961

Margaret Jones,*** 2nd
wife of Solomon Womack
Died Aug 16, 1912

*** Family Records.

* *

CUMBERLAND SPRINGS/LYNCHBURG EAST QUADRANGLE

BAXTER CEMETERY

LOCATION: NE of Lynchburg, in Baxter Hollow.

Martha E., Daughter of
J. T. & Na. Baxter
Aug 8, 1869
Oct 17, 1872

Joseph H. Moore
Sep 13, 1868
Jun 18, 1901
Age: 33y, 9m, 17d.

May Bee Byrom
May 20, 1898
Nov 28, 1898

Leona L. Moore
Mar 8, 1873
Sep 10, 1878

D. H. Byrom
Mar 14, 1865
Nov 3, 1893

Several graves with
fieldstones, no inscriptions.

Several unmarked graves.

P. H. Wanslow
Nov 22, 1822
Apr 27, 1907

Annie, wife of
P. H. Wanslow
Nov 22, 1824
Sep 29, 1897

* *

BENNETT CEMETERY

LOCATION: Three miles south of Cumberland Springs, on Hurricane Creek.

John Bennett and
Feb 28, 1830
Oct 11, 1890

Martha Bennett
May 6, 1831
Jul 10, 1899

Sarah F. Hanson
Jan 4, 1850
Dec   1904

Several graves with
fieldstones, no inscript.
Several unmarked graves.

* *

CUMBERLAND SPRINGS QUADRANGLE

BENNETT CEMETERY

LOCATION: This cemetery is located near Motlow College on the road to Raus, Bedford County.

Hezekiah Bennett and his wife Mymie Bennett are buried in this cemetery, there are no markers left in this graveyard, as it is completely gone.

* *

BETHEL CEMETERY

LOCATION: At Jack Daniel's Distillery in Lynchburg.

Joseph T. Walker May 7, 1818 Oct 18, 1840	Benjamin Berry, Sr. Jan 17, 1806 Jun 30, 1869	Col. G. W. S. Hart Mar 5, 1805 Jul 26, 1850	Mary Hart Sep 13, 1779 Nov 3, 1850
Infant Daughter of A. W. & Elizabeth Walker (no dates)	Andrew W. Walker Oct 25, 1778 Sep 16, 1850	Ann, Consort of Benjamin H. Berry Aug 30, 1819 Aug 19, 1863	Elizabeth Walker May 15, 1784 Dec 18, 1853
(name gone) Died Jun 17, 1842 Age: (age gone)	Mary Walker Anthony 1807-1837 Many unmarked graves.	J. K. 1839 (fieldstone, John M. Keller)	Several Rock Vaults. Several fieldstones, no inscriptions.

* *

BOBO CEMETERY

LOCATION: Two and one half miles NE of Lynchburg on the Highway # 55, toward Tullahoma.

Samuel Bobo Sep 28, 1815 Jun 18, 1891 & Simmer Bobo Dec 31, 1818 Jan 29, 1892	L. M. Bobo Jan 28, 1861 Feb 17, 1909 & Addie Bobo Jan 28, 1864 Dec 11, 1886 & Clemmie Bobo Sep 26, 1863 (no date)	Ella, Daughter of Mr. & Mrs. C. S. Bobo Dec 19, 1876 Mar 1, 1890 Infant Son of L. M. & Addie Bobo (no dates)	Adie, wife of L. M. Bobo & Daughter of G. W. & M. A. Gardner Jan 28, 1864 Dec 11, 1886 Married Jul 29, 1880 (Same as Addie Bobo)
Thomas Bobo Dec 15, 1855 Dec 22, 1882	Clarence S., Son of Mr. & Mrs. C. S. Bobo Nov 15, 1884 Jun 16, 1886	Chaney Simpson, Son of L. M. & M. C. Bobo Jun 12, 1888 Jun 18, 1888	Ellen E. Darnaby Feb 22, 1842 Aug 30, 1890 Age: 48y, 6m, 8d.

* *

COUNTY LINE CEMETERY

LOCATION: Three miles north of Lynchburg, off Highway # 82.

W. A. Stone Feb 14, 1862 Sep 11, 1889 & Nora Ann Stone Aug 16, 1864 Jun 24, 1906	J. N. Felps Feb 23, 1863 Dec 6, 1889 Essie Felps Sep 20, 1885 Dec 18, 1897	J. L. Ervin Mar 15, 1867 Feb 24, 1901 & Mary J. Stephenson Ervin Oct 13, 1866 Oct 17, 1913	Lema Jane, Daughter of W. T. & Nan Hice Nov 12, 1901 Aug 11, 1902 William Homer Hice Dec 1, 1913 Jul 15, 1918
Annie M., Daughter of W. A. & N. A. Stone Feb 27, 1889 May 27, 1889	Martha J. Conwell Dec 4, 1865 Jan 9, 1897	Ellen Hice Sep 14, 1871 Mar 1, 1893	Buford G., Son of E. F. & N. E. Hice Nov 28, 1903 Jul 24, 1904

CUMBERLAND SPRINGS QUADRANGLE

W. B. Hice
Jan 1, 1825
Jun 2, 1913
&
S. J Abbott Hice
Feb 13, 1835
Oct 22, 1918

Nancy Ervin Hice
1879-1932

E. F. Hice
Jan 30, 1874
Aug 11, 1949

Ben Duckworth
Apr 18, 1863
Apr 23, 1908

William N. Price
Feb 1, 1886
Jun 1, 1965

James H., Son of
M. P. & Millie Duckworth
Oct 22, 1860
Jun 24, 1897
Age: 36y, 8m, 2d.

T. F. Price
1856-1927
&
Sarah E. Ward Price
1862-1911

Edward Price
1900
&
Nora Price
1906

Martin C., Son of
M. P. & Milly Duckworth
Apr 29, 1858
Oct 29, 1888

Robert Cunningham
1823-1906
&
Nancy Cunningham
1831-1906

J. I. Cunningham
Nov 16, 1860
May 24, 1902

Mary M., wife of
Elisha Gore
Aug 7, 1841
Sep 8, 1888
Age: 47y, 1m, 1d.

Infant Son of
J. C. & S. E. Byrom
B&D Jul 8, 1898

Amanda, wife of
G. W. Woodard
Mar 18, 1866
Mar 1, 1892

Thomas N. Driver
May 22, 1842
Jul 2, 1922
&
Sidney I. Driver
Mar 16, 1854
Dec 25, 1926

Emet E. Driver
Jul 6, 1873
Feb 15, 1898

Ollie Clinton Ervin
1881-1956
&
Flossie Driver Ervin
1888-1934

Willie Lavoyd, Son of
S. M. & E. J. Williams
May 20, 1887
Aug 4, 1888

Jonnie Byrd
1901-

Net Price Byrd
1866-1922

Albert Lee Price
Oct 29, 1883
Feb 1, 1947
&
Mary Jane Gore Price
Aug 24, 1887
Oct 28, 1963

William S. Price
Oct 19, 1854
Dec 24, 1917
&
Sallie F. Price
Oct 22, 1860
Oct 15, 1937
"Parents of Georgia,
Albert & Lema."

Infant Son of
Ed & Maggie Martin
Aug 15, 1900
Aug 17, 1900

Infant Son of
Ed & Maggie Martin
Jun 13, 1899
Jun 14, 1899

James F. Stone
Jan 10, 1860
Dec 5, 1887

M. A., wife of
J. F. Stone
Nov 13, 1864
Oct 8, 1886

Mary A., wife of
Elisha W. Stone
May 11, 1839
Apr 4, 1908

Elizabeth Gore Hix
Apr 18, 1850
Nov 23, 1935

Elisha Gore
Jan 29, 1842
Jul 27, 1908

Jno. E. Gore
Apr 4, 1826
May 11, 1904
&
Jane M. Gore
Jun 1, 1828
Sep 8, 1899

J. N. Duckworth
Feb 10, 1856
Nov 13, 1908
&
Eliza R. Duckworth
Aug 3, 1858
Aug 25, 1913

P. F. Ervin
Aug 22, 1838
Dec 26, 1912
&
F. J. Ervin
Jan 11, 1845
Feb 22, 1915

Sterling Wiseman
Oct 29, 1816
Mar 21, 1894

Eliza M., wife of
Sterling Wiseman
Jul 26, 1820
Apr 9, 1886

Emma Lee Wiseman
Jan 20, 1884
Aug 16, 1884

Albert Wiseman
(no dates)

Infant Wiseman
(no dates)

Infant Wiseman
(no dates)

Charles B. Wiseman
May 1882
May 1941

Eldridge Whitworth
May 5, 1903
Mar 17, 1966

Grace Whitworth
May 29, 1901

Arthur J. Hice
1882-1926
&
Eliza J. Hice
1873-1937

Frank Gore
Sep 16, 1907
May 30, 1915

Robert Elisha Gore
1861-1940
&
Alice Floyd Gore
1867-1959

Eaf Woodard
Pvt U. S. Army
Jul 10, 1897
Dec 28, 1974
&
Sallie Lois Woodard
1898-

Edward Hice
May 11, 1890
Aug 15, 1969
&
Mary Hice
Jan 7, 1895
(no date)

George Wiseman
Feb 2, 1847
Aug 10, 1882
Age: 35y, 6m, 8d.

Willie Price Wiseman
Sep 10, 1886
Jul 16, 1887

Infant Son of
J. R. & P. A. Wiseman
Born Jul 29, 1879

James Riley Wiseman
1857-1936
&
Polly Ann Wiseman
1861-1937

J. Frank Wiseman
1903-1959

Jesse Ewell Ervin
Jun 24, 1887
May 29, 1967
&
Lena Gore Ervin
Jan 10, 1891
Nov 4, 1972

Mica Ervin
Mar 28, 1915
Jul 24, 1915
&
Myra Ervin
Mar 28, 1915
Jul 28, 1915
Children of
J. E. & M. L. Ervin.

Annie Gore, wife of
Dr. S. E. Parrott
Dec 21, 1889
Jan 19, 1922

CUMBERLAND SPRINGS QUADRANGLE

W. T. Hice
Feb 20, 1864
May 17, 1938
&
N. A. Pylant Hice
Dec 7, 1866
May 11, 1943

S. L. Wiseman
1860-1927

Jim Bill, Son of
S. L. & F. C. Wiseman
Sep 21, 1892
Aug 27, 1894

Horace W., Son of
T. S. & S. T. Holt
Aug 3, 1890
Jul 10, 1891

Bobbie Lee, Son of
J. R. & M. A. Wiseman
Nov 22, 1886
Mar 6, 1890

Sarah Alma Wiseman
Sep 29, 1884
Apr 26, 1954
&
Cora Ida Wiseman
Jun 19, 1878
Jun 5, 1967

----on Ervin
---- - 1968
(Harrison FH)

Wade Williams, Son of
J. E. & L. M. Ervin
1924-1937

Wayne Thomas, Son of
J. E. & L. M. Ervin
Dec 20, 1923
Dec 21, 1924

Jennie Womack
Age: 83 years
(no dates)

D. Cliff Crutcher
1856-1922
&
Lucinda Ervin Crutcher
1863-1913

Infant Daughter of
J. F. & Mary Ervin
(no dates)

Ward, Son of
W. W. & Lorena Brown
Feb 4, 1892
Sep 21, 1924

William Ware Brown
Sep 28, 1870
Aug 1, 1954
&
Tacie Ervin Brown
Nov 29, 1871-Aug 4, 1960

W. S. Ervin
1859-1932
&
Maggie Ervin
1861-1947

Allice, Daughter of
W. S. & Maggie Ervin
Jan 30, 1896
Aug 3, 1896

Tilitha C., wife of
B. S. Hinkle & Daughter
of J. S. & C. J. Ervin
Mar 15, 1865
Aug 26, 1888

G. R. Hice
1909-1942

Lee Cashion
Nov 26, 1906
Jul 28, 1976
&
Mamie Cashion
Jul 8, 1910

Robert Duncan Taylor
Feb 22, 1914
Jan 6, 1915

Eld. J. S. Ervin
Apr 4, 1832
Jul 10, 1908

Catharine, wife of
J. S. Ervin
Oct 2, 1833
Apr 5, 1880

Alma, wife of
J. B. Ervin
Nov 3, 1869
Oct 29, 1910

Julian P. Jacoway
1932-1937
(Harrison FH)

Harold Wade Hix
May 9, 1920
Dec 6, 1921

Ollie C. Hix
Aug 20, 1887
Apr 20, 1924
&
Annie L. Hix
Jan 19, 1890

Bessie, Daughter of
Wm. S. & Maggie Ervin
Sep 17, 1885
Aug 4, 1886

Omer L. Hice
1901-1962
&
Louise T. Hice
1908-

B. A. Womack
1855-1910
&
Jane Womack
1856-1962

Pless Marvin Bohannon
Jan 31, 1892
Jan 5, 1969
&
Olive Gladys Byrom Bohannon
Aug 7, 1901
Aug 29, 1967
Married Jun 29, 1929

Rebecca Dillingham, wife
of J. S. Ervin
Jan 13, 1835
Mar 10, 1915

Infant Son of
J. S. & C. Ervin
(no dates)

Eva L., Daughter of
W. W. & Lorena Brown
Dec 12, 1890
Feb 13, 1926

Joseph B. Ervin
1869-1953
&
Myrtle M. Ervin
1886-(no date)

Robert Lynn Jacoway
Jun 7, 1898
Jul 26, 1960
&
Floy Brown Jacoway
Apr 23, 1893
Sep 5, 1977

Kattie Pearl Ervin
Jul 1, 1893
Nov 30, 1932

G. J. Pylant
Mar 5, 1880
Jun 6, 1904

Ann Eliza Pylant
Oct 14, 1828
Jun 13, 1899

James S. Ervin
Jun 19, 1804
Nov 7, 1881

Jemimah, wife of
J. S. Ervin
Apr 8, 1804
Nov 9, 1881

George Hice
1857-1930
&
Mary Ann Hice
1866-1944

John Calvin Byrom
Apr 5, 1865
Sep 23, 1951
&
Siddie E. Gore Byrom
Jan 1, 1868
Feb 8, 1933

D. S. Womack
Jun 8, 1849
Oct 8, 1888
&
Ruth Womack
May 24, 1850
(no dates)

J. H. Steed
Aug 31, 1859
Mar 1, 1931
& wife
S. J. Steed
Nov 24, 1879
Aug 22, 1928

Amanda Ervin Taylor
Apr 25, 1863
Jul 3, 1903

John Edward, Jr., Son of
John & Sallie Steed
Mar 13, 1910
Aug 19, 1926

James S. Deal
1936-1939

Nannie B., Daughter of
W. F. & M. C. Taylor
Sep 5, 1887
Jan 17, 1889

J. Herby Deal
Aug 9, 1909
May 18, 1970
&
Bell S. Deal
Mar 14, 1912

Married Jul 16, 1932

"Father"
T. Frank Hice
Dec 25, 1912
Mar 17, 1981
&
"Mother"
Mattie Lou Hice
Apr 14, 1913

Several unmarked graves.

CUMBERLAND SPRINGS QUADRANGLE

COUSER CEMETERY

LOCATION: One half mile west of Smith Chapel on the Old Lynchburg Road.

No markers remain in this cemetery. Descendants say the following to be buried here:

John F. Couser 1780-1860/63	Rebecca Couser 1778-before 1860	Robert M. Couser 1816-1867/70	Amos Gore Nov 25, 1789 May 17, 1871 & Mary A. (Couser) Gore Nov 20, 1802 Oct 10, 1881

Probably other members of the Couser family buried here.

Info. by Mrs. Maybee, now deceased.

* *

DANCE CEMETERY

LOCATION: One and one fourth mile north of Lynchburg, on the East Fork of Mulberry Creek.

J. T. S. Dance Jun 28, 1822 Jul 24, 1897 & wife Susan Finetta Boon Dance Aug 5, 1828 Apr 19, 1900	Infant Son of S. E. N. & M. A. Dance B&D Jul 20, 1859	James P. Baxter Apr 14, 1792 Sep 9, 1859	Infant Son of Abram & Minnie Setliff B&D Aug 27, 1873
	Rev. S. M. Dance Mar 8, 1788 Aug 23, 1853	Elizabeth C., wife of James P. Baxter Sep 12, 1800 Aug 30, 1880	Edward Setliff Mar 30, 1855 Dec 19, 1856
Luther, Son of J. T. S. & S. F. Dance May 3, 1864 Nov 20, 1871	Sarah, wife of S. M. Dance Mar 5, 1793 Jun 8, 1863	Samuel P., Son of Dr. S. H. & N. C. McWhirter Died Aug 3, 1852 Age: (not given)	Lilian A. Setliff Oct 5, 1856 Jun 22, 1858
Fannie N. Stacy, wife of J. E. Dance Oct 9, 1856 Aug 12, 1878	David L. Enochs Feb 8, 1820 Jun 4, 1894 Age: 74y, 4m, 26d.	George M., Son of Dr. S. H. & N. C. McWhirter Died Sep 23, 1852 Age: (not given)	Frances R. Setliff Died Jul 22, 1855 Age: 8 hours.
Hosea Anthony Dec 15, 1816 Nov 25, 1898	Martha A. E., wife of D. L. Enochs Jan 31, 1818 Aug 29, 1876	In Memory of James Clack Born June 1756 Died Oct 1834 "A Revolutionary Soldier".	Daisy I. Setliff Died Nov 3, 1871 Age: 2 years.
Madora, Daughter of J. T. S. & S. F. Dance Nov 9, 1856 Jan 13, 1859	Sarah M. S., Daughter of D. L. & M. A. Enochs Mar 12, 1860 Aug 9, 1860		Mary E. Setliff Died Jul 21, 1873 Age: 24 years.
Infant Son of J. T. S. & S. F. Dance Still born Jul 1, 1861	William S. I. Enochs Oct 24, 1854 Mar 20, 1859	James Clack Smith Dec 4, 1837 Jul 1, 1839	Georgiana B. Setliff Mar 24, 1858 Aug 11, 1858
Sarah, Daughter of J. T. S. & S. F. Dance Feb 6, 1851 Dec 31, 1858	William Flournoy Smith Martin Mar 27, 1845 Jan 2, 1846	Mary Kennon Brown Smith Aug 27, 1805 Dec 20, 1840	Margaret E. Setliff Dec 1, 1829 Jul 12, 1859
Infant Son of J. T. S. & S. F. Dance Still born Sep 6, 1862		Mrs. H. L. S. Waggonner Apr 6, 1837 Sep 1856	Mary Waggonner Sep 2, 1856 Jan 20, 1857
Benjamin, Son of S. E. N. & M. A. Dance May 26, 1860 Jun 3, 1862			

Many graves with fieldstones, no inscriptions.

Many unmarked graves.

* *

CUMBERLAND SPRINGS QUADRANGLE

GRAMMER-WAGGONER CEMETERY

LOCATION: Three miles SE of Lynchburg, on Highway # 50 and road to Hickory Hill School and Lois Road.

Brice A. Chapman
Jul 17, 1874
Mar 29, 1935
&
Mary A. Chapman
Oct 29, 1879
(Date gone, Harrison FH)

Bernice Chapman Brown
Died May 9, 1939
Age:(Not given)

Charlotta Ann Brown
B&D May 3, 1939

Dillard R., Son of
A. E. & J. H. Waggoner
Apr 19, 1905
Nov 20, 1909

Marion Grammer
1853-1909
&
Fannie Grammer
1861-1941

W. N., Son of
C. M. & M. F. Matlock
Jul 2, 1891
Aug 30, 1893

Nealy A. Grammer
Jan 15, 1870
Nov   1870

Lemer L. Grammer
May 14, 1886
Nov 14, 1887

William Floyd, Son of
A. G. & A. M. Waggoner
Aug 22, 1894 (born)
Age: 1y, 1m, 28d.

Finis Daffron, Son of
A. G. & A. M. Waggoner
Died Dec 9, 1909
Age: 3m, 7d.

Jimmie Era, Daughter of
A. G. & A. M. Waggoner
Born Feb 22, 1898
Age: 2y, 4m, 19d.

Allen Green Waggoner
1861-1928
&
Alis Almeta Waggoner
1869-1924

J. A. Waggoner
1882-1950
(Raby FH)

Minnie J. Grammer, wife of
Joe A. Waggoner
Feb 16, 1884
Oct 29, 1921

Seller M., Daughter of
J. L. & C. N. Codie
Jul 24, 1894
Aug 23, 1894

Infant Daughter of
J. W. & Hattie M. Counts
B&D Apr 19, 1918

Emma E. Parks
1899-1923

Many unmarked graves.

Infant Son of
Charlie & Elma Spencer
Nov 17, 1914
Nov 23, 1914

John Grammer
Dec 11, 1837
May 31, 1917
&
Mary A. Grammer
Feb 7, 1841
Jun 10, 1924

B. C. Grammer
Sep 7, 1856
Dec 17, 1938

"Father"
W. M. Grammer
Oct 28, 1828
Aug 17, 1908

"Mother"
Francis Grammer
Nov 16, 1830
Feb 13, 1911

M. A. Grammer
Oct 7, 1846
Sep 22, 1909

Grace, Daughter of
J. F. & N. F. Grammer
Aug 13, 1903
Oct 12, 1907

James M. Grammer
Nov 17, 1843
Jul 19, 1920

Susan E. Grammer
Mar   1846
May 2, 1904

Pearl E. Grammer
May 16, 1899
Sep 23, 1900

Cora Bell Grammer
Mar 27, 1881
Sep 10, 1919

Dillon Waggoner
Dec 14, 1898
Nov 29, 1903

Fannie M. Grammer
Nov 27, 1876
Feb 16, 1881

Margaret Fern, Daughter
of B. F. & E. C. Grammer
Feb 3, 1920
Jul 3, 1920

Mary A. Wise
Oct 11, 1837
Dec 1, 1911

Samuel L. Mathis
(no dates)
&
Earl Mathis
(no dates)
&
Ruby E. Mathis
(no dates)
&
Brownie Mullins Mathis
(no dates)
&
Lemuel Mathis
Mar 1, 1903
Feb 2, 1922

* *

HOOVER GROVE CHURCH CEMETERY

LOCATION: One mile west of Turkey Creek School.

Ruth A. Cleek
Nov 24, 1929
Mar 11, 1944

William J. Cleek
1850-1937
&
Zora Jane Cleek
1863-1940

Floyd D. Cleek
Tennessee
Pvt 1Cl 17 Inf 11 Div
Mar 8, 1934

George Lecil Cleek
Jan 11, 1898
Oct 24, 1930

William Hord Smith
1885-1973
(Daves-Culbertson FH)

Elmore Eggleston
Tennessee
Sgt Co D 34 Inf
Jun 14, 1893
Jan 30, 1956

George Tankersly
May 12, 1897
Feb 14, 1925

Donald W. Tankersley
Apr 16, 1943
Jul 16, 1972
&
Sandra H. Tankersley
Oct 22, 1948

Married Jun 29, 1968

Jimmie Tankersley
B&D Apr 28, 1948

Willis Hoss Tankersley
Dec 13, 1874
Apr 29, 1935
&
Nancy J. Vibbart
Tankersley
Oct 11, 1876
Sep 2, 1946
Age: 69y, 1m, 15d.

G. F. T.
(fieldstone)

G. F. T.
(fieldstone)

CUMBERLAND SPRINGS QUADRANGLE

Frank Mullins, Jr.
1925-1927
(Daves-Culbertson FH)

Mary Katharine Mullins
1930-1930
(Daves-Culbertson FH)

Donald Wayne Tankersley
B&D Jul 5, 1934

Norma Cobb Eggleston
Sep 10, 1895

Herman L. Tankersley
Tennessee
Pvt Co A 216 Inf Tng Bn
WW II
Jul 6, 1917
Jun 13, 1959

"Father"
Frazier Tankersley
Jul 28, 1902
Aug 6, 1971
&
"Mother"
Elijah B. Tankersley
Oct 6, 1903
Mar 14, 1972

Norma Cobb
Sep 10, 1895

W. Thomas Eggleston
1918-1928
(Harrison FH)

Clifford Cleek
Jun 13, 1906
Mar 4, 1930

Herbert L. Smith
Tennessee
Tec 5 457 Engr Depot Co
WW II
Oct 16, 1910
Feb 11, 1973

Edith Wilma Smith
Dec 17, 1922
Jun 2, 1943

Julia Fay Smith
May 8, 1942
Jun 10, 1946
&
Laura Kay Smith
May 8, 1942
Jun 10, 1946
"Twins of Ralph &
Elizabeth Smith".

J. W. Martin
Aug 13, 1828
Aug 22, 1920

Mary Kirkland Martin
Apr 15, 1849
Apr 24, 1936

John W. Martin
Nov 9, 1878
Jul 28, 1952
&
Ida Tankersley Martin
Jun 5, 1882
Apr 10, 1966

Lillian Martin
1890-1973
(Tullahoma FH)

Bettie Gail Smith
1953-1953
(Gowen-Smith FH)

Loyd E. Stroisch
Ohio
Sgt Co B 2 Bn 32 Inf
Vietnam SS BSM PH
Sep 4, 1945
Apr 12, 1968

Terry L. Stroisch
Jul 26, 1946
Sep 3, 1946

Frances S. Stroisch
Sep 5, 1918
May 31, 1962

Louis Wilson Troxler
Sep 18, 1862
Dec 23, 1928

Minerva E. Coop
Aug 24, 1887
Jun 22, 1939

Taylor Lynch
Jun 14, 1849
Jun 2, 1916

David A. Burt
Nov 8, 1888

&
Clara Burt
Aug 12, 1893
Jun 14, 1948

Johnie Mae, Daughter of
D. A. & Clara Burt
Mar 12, 1915
Mar 5, 1935

William J. Russell
Sep 22, 1884
Feb 23, 1968
&
Dennie I. Russell
May 24, 1889
Nov 8, 1965

Calvin Russell
Jun 20, 1911
Mar 7, 1940

Mary Jane Miley
1832-1926

Infant Son of
W. J. & Dennie Russell
Jun 10, 1914
May 16, 1915

Edna F. Sharpe
Jan 7, 1906
Jun 6, 1932

Billy, Son of
Noel & Edna Sharpe
Jul 6, 1930
Oct 13, 1930

Homer Luther Casteel
Died Feb 3, 1961
Age: 52 years.
(Buckner FH,
  Cleveland, Tenn.)

William Pink Casteel
Died Jul 31, 1925
Age: 83y, 11m, 8d.
(Bomar Shrader & D----,
 Tullahoma, Tenn.)

Ethel T. Finney
May 28, 1915
Dec 18, 1972

Barar Ann, Daughter of
J. H. & Ethel Finney
Apr 18, 1938
Apr 21, 1938

Marion Federic Brown
Nov 26, 1865
Jan 15, 1940
&
Laura Ann Brown
Nov 30, 1870
Dec 20, 1938

Hugh R. Brown
1901-1967
(TM)

Anderson Clark
Tennessee
Pvt 358 Inf 90 Div WW I
Dec 24, 1895
Apr 15, 1948

Mary Ann Clark
1859-1950

Samuel Andrew Clark
1893-1961
(Daves-Culbertson FH)

Gertrude E Randall
1903-1950

Will Cleek
Tennessee
Cpl Co E 53 Inf WW I
Mar 3, 1889
Sep 26, 1953
&
Essie Brown Cleek
Apr 7, 1890

Carroll M. Tankersley
May 18, 1845
Jan 31, 1939
&
Melvina Tankersley
Dec 9, 1852
Jan 4, 1941

George Thomas Eggleston
Jun 10, 1860
Mar 7, 1939
&
Mary Jane Eggleston
Aug 31, 1866
Mar 17, 1945

Walter Reavis
1869-1935
&
Mary Reavis
1868-1947

Lucile, Daughter of
Walter & Mary Reavis
Mar 10, 1893
May 30, 1914

Elam L. Reavis
1898-1968

George Lynch
Sep 17, 1897
Mar 8, 1946
&
Myrtle Lynch
Jan 29, 1893

Joise M. Hunter
Oct 1, 1881
Apr 20, 1970

Clarence E., Son of
Mr. & Mrs. George H.
Hunter
B&D Nov 6, 1946

Frances J. Holder
B&D May 18, 1933

Frank Fulmer
Jan 9, 1859
Jan 29, 1941
&
Mary Fulmer
Mar 3, 1862
Jun 29, 1952

Joseph A. Smith
1880-1955
&
Minnie (Lawson) Smith
1883-1955

Orbin C. Smith
Jun 16, 1914
Mar 10, 1972

Idumea Holt Smith
Nov 24, 1879
Feb 6, 1930

CUMBERLAND SPRINGS QUADRANGLE

Pauline Smith
(no dates)
&
Infant Smith
(no dates)
&
Infant Smith
(no dates)

Jim Smith
1908-1936

Robert M. Bennett
Nov 17, 1876
Apr 3, 1950
&
Maude Holt Smith Bennett
Jul 28, 1877
Aug 5, 1955

Elizabeth T. Couser
Aug 16, 1858
Feb 2, 1950

Sarah A. Mullins
Mar 29, 1869
Jan 17, 1942

------- Mullins
(no dates, Harrison FH)

Alexander R. -----
(TM, all dates gone)

Graham Pollock
1885-1968
&
Ada P. Graham
1888-19

David W. Smith
Jan 27, 1883
Apr 3, 1864
&
Johnnie C. Smith
May 5, 1894
May 18, 1967

George W. H. Packard
1854-1940

Vester McEwen
1907-1967
(Motlow-Moore FH)

Thomas Stewart
1938-1973
(Tullahoma FH)

Danny W. Tankersley
Oct 7, 1950
Mar 9, 1951

M. F. Tankersley
1898-1961
(Motlow-Moore FH)

Joy L. Tankersley
1967
(Motlow-Moore FH)

William M. Tankersley
Tennessee
Pfc U. S. Army WW II
May 13, 1912
Dec 7, 1958

Nova Leona (Buchanan)
Tankersley
Mar 19, 1901
Jun 3, 1967

Robert E. Tankersley
Tennessee
Pfc 1843 SVC Unit WW II
Jul 2, 1914
Jun 27, 1967

Thomas M. Tankersley
Oct 22, 1868
Apr 8, 1928
&
Josie Tankersley
Oct 30, 1876
May 6, 1950

Albert F. Montgomery
May 22, 1910
May 18, 1970
&
Annie Ruth Montgomery
Nov 2, 1919

William Ray Sanders
1972-1972
(Tullahoma FH)

Baby Martin
1963
(Motlow-Moore FH)

Martha Jane Lawson
Aug 7, 1879
Nov 5, 1962

William Hord Smith
1885-1973
(Daves-Culbertson FH)

Many unmarked graves.

John W. Smith
Jun 27, 1899
Feb 26, 1940

John Smith
Feb 2, 1862
Jan 9, 1931
&
Nannie Smith
Nov 19, 1867
Aug 27, 1952

William T. Leach
Dec 3, 1872
Jan 23, 1953
&
Lucy Idelia Leach
Jun 1, 1873
Mar 5, 1953

J. Loyd Smith
Mar 15, 1895

&
Mattie E. Smith
Jun 13, 1896
Apr 7, 1971
Married Dec 25, 1912

Henry Lawson
1883-1957
&
Sheba Lawson
1883-(no date)

Treda Gail Ray
Feb 8, 1967
Mar 22, 1967

W. H. "Bill" Weddington
Jul 29, 1924

&
Wanda Faye Weddington
Jan 27, 1928
Apr 17, 1971

William Luther Brown
Oct 11, 1891

&
Lema D. Cleek Brown
Nov 8, 1891
Jan 24, 1969

Dessie E. Smith
1885-1973
(Daves-Culbertson FH)

Howard Eugene Farrar
B&D Dec 5, 1964

Arthur L. Coop
Aug 8, 1891
Feb 27, 1943
&
Myrtle L. Coop
Mar 30, 1893

Lura Vivian Stewart
1889-1973
(Daves-Culbertson FH)

Herbert L. Smith
Tennessee
Tec 5 457 Engr Depot Co
WW II
Oct 16, 1910
Feb 11, 1973

Luther Stewart
Nov 7, 1906
Sep 29, 1969
&
Louella T. Stewart
Jun 15, 1910

Billy J. Stewart
1936-1937

Edna G. Stewart
1942-1942

Jewel E. Stewart
1945-1945

Lyndia D. Stewart
1948-1948

Jim F. Stewart
1901-1969
(Tullahoma FH)

Grace Stewart
1923-1969
(Tullahoma FH)

Patricia Joan Mueller
Aug 17, 1941
Nov 8, 1965

Homer P. Womack
Feb 17, 1899

&
Ethel C. Womack
Oct 11, 1896
Mar 12, 1973
Married Mar 12, 1922

* *

CUMBERLAND SPRINGS QUADRANGLE

HURRICANE CHURCH CEMETERY

LOCATION: Six miles NE of Lynchburg, off Highway # 55, near Fire Tower.

Benjamin F. Cates
1852-1936
&
Sarah C. Cates
1854-1935

Moses Lee Cates
Apr 2, 1891
Sep 15, 1970

Argie Cates Stephens
May 5, 1891
Mar 11, 1966

Delphia Malinda Cates
Nov 29, 1877
Nov 6, 1914
&
James Henry Cates
Apr 29, 1868
Oct 16, 1928
&
Lula Cates
Nov 7, 1880
Oct 6, 1946

Charles M. Cates
Mar 12, 1869
Apr 21, 1958
&
Millie Elizabeth Cates
"Betty"
Oct 15, 1873
Sep 18, 1956
Married Dec 25, 1889

Luddy, Son of
J. H. & D. M. Cates
Oct 26, 1904
Nov 4, 1906

Everett J., Son of
Mr. & Mrs. Alvis Woosley
Jan 16, 1923
Jan 19, 1923

Ewin Woosley
(no dates)

Jessie Woosley
(no dates)

D. A. Woosley
Jan 7, 1864
Mar 17, 1938
&
Mahalie A. Woosley
Jul 22, 1866
(no date)

Oscar L. Brandon
1883-1951
&
Jennie H. Holt Brandon
1877-1945

Clarence Brandon
1913-1973
(Harrison FH)

Roy Lee Williams
Oct 15, 1903
(no date)
&
Myrtle Williams
Jul 7, 1901
Nov 3, 1951

Harriet I. Allen
"Hattie"
1881-1964

Thomas A. Nelson
Feb 18, 1898
Jul 11, 1972
&
Carol Ann Nelson
Mar 12, 1935
Nov 19, 1935

Enoch T. Nelson
Mar 25, 1915
Apr 25, 1954
&
Myrtle Nelson
May 27, 1921

John D. Ray
Feb 10, 1902
Mar 22, 1967
&
Juanita Ray
Jun 30, 1926

Jeff Thorn
Tennessee
S1 U. S. Navy WW II
Dec 9, 1913
Dec 8, 1968

Thomas Oliver Tankersley
1906-1973
(Tullahoma FH)

Bertha Tankersley
1917-1969
(Tullahoma FH)

Walter Lee Thorn
Feb 15, 1943
Jul 20, 1943

Wanda Ellen Wiser
Jul 1, 1960
May 31, 1962

Infant Howard
1933

Charles Cates
May 10, 1827
Dec 31, 1904
&
Jane Cates
Jun 28, 1835
Aug 7, 1909

Edward Brandon
1916-1969
(Harrison FH)

Elise M. Brandon
1917-1971
(Tullahoma FH)

Thomas E. Tankersley
1949-1967
&
Helen C. Tankersley
Apr 1948-Aug 1948

Murray G. Nicholson
1896-1933

Samuel P. Sells
Mar 1, 1875
Apr 22, 1929
&
Lanora A. Sells
Jul 15, 1881
Oct 15, 1926

Infant Son of
Willie & Wilma Sells
B&D Aug 4, 1940

Hester Sells
Nov 25, 1907
Apr 14, 1931

Myrtle Sells
May 19, 1910
Jan 24, 1936

John Edgeman
Sep 22, 1895
(TM: 1971)
&
Sallie Edgeman
Sep 16, 1898
Jan 14, 1967

Mary Edgeman
B&D Sep 1930

Martha C. Lee
1863-1932

M. J. Smith
1858-1928
&
Mary Smith
1882-19

Baby Smith
(no dates, TM)

Baby Smith
1962-1962
(Motlow-Moore FH)

Baby Smith
1961
(Motlow-Moore FH)

Baby Boy Smith
1959-1959
(Motlow-Moore FH)

William M. Smith
1958-1958
(Motlow-Moore FH)

Billy Ray Weddington
Sep 29, 1962
May 5, 1964

Houston J. Adams
Tennessee
Pvt 109 Engr Combt Bn
34 Inf Div WW II
May 4, 1919
Jul 16, 1944

Mary N. Adams
1886-1953

L. D. Holder
Apr 15, 1872
Aug 2, 1930

Mary Holder
Dec 29, 1871
Nov 23, 1946

Ewin Howard
1909-1970
(Tullahoma FH)

Bertice, Daughter of
Hascul & Josie Prince
1906-1921

Jabel Martin Ray
Dec 5, 1847
May 20, 1896
&
Nancy L. Ray
Feb 1, 1849
Jun 22, 1924

Bob Cyree
Nov 24, 1887
Aug 6, 1968
&
Nora Cyree
Dec 16, 1885
Apr 4, 1970

J. B. Austin
1908-1949

CUMBERLAND SPRINGS QUADRANGLE

Edgar T. Pollard
Feb 4, 1905
Mar 3, 1960

Baby Partin
1968 (TM)

James F. Thorneberry
1873-1951
(Thompson FH)

Dolly Thorneberry
1884-1963
(Motlow-Moore FH)

Alvis Ernest Cates
Dec 9, 1881
Dec 8, 1951
&
Arie Maud Cates
Jun 9, 1883
Jun 17, 1934

Ivison Ezra Ray
Jun 28, 1881
Mar 19, 1939
&
Clara Mae Ray
Apr 3, 1885
Aug 21, 1965

Thelma Jaunita, Daughter of
Randon & Loretta Ray
B&D Jul 9, 1927

Tyron Quay, Son of
Walter & Altaloma Ray
Nov 12, 1927
Feb 13, 1928

Charles T. Anderton
1867-Jan 29, 1941
&
Lue Ener Anderton
1875-Jul 3, 1942

Henry Stephens
"Shorty"
Sep 23, 1899
Jul 7, 1969
&
Pearl H. Stephens
Jul 12, 1918
(TM: 1974)

Finis R. Simmons
Feb 13, 1891
Nov 6, 1969

Nora S. Simmons
Mar 21, 1901
Mar 18, 1949

Eula E. Simmons
Oct 24, 1893
Aug 16, 1919

Frank Malone
Jul 11, 1885
Feb 14, 1955
&
Nettie Malone
Sep 10, 1893
Mar 10, 1968

Nannie Damrel
Oct 7, 1867
Mar 3, 1928

George B. Damrel
Apr 30, 1839
May 26, 1918
&
Elizabeth Damrel
Jul 7, 1837
Jan 7, 1920

Ben Damrel
1878-1932
& wife
Ovena Damrel
1902-(no date)

Marion Williams
Apr 6, 1867
Aug 20, 1946
&
Sarah C. Williams
Oct 10, 1873
Nov 27, 1944

Lula Byrom West
Dec 15, 1882
Sep 12, 1928

Hubert Lee, Son of
Albert & Mae Byrom
Apr 20, 1912
Sep 28, 1919

Johnie, Son of
M. W. & Nerva Byrom
Oct 28, 1889
Aug 20, 1899

M. W. Byrom
Feb 12, 1856
Oct 8, 1936
&
Minerva Ann Byrom
May 9, 1862
Jul 8, 1929

Wilburn Huelette, Son of
Laster & Ethel Byrom
May 18, 1922
Nov 3, 1926

J. Laster Byrom
Sep 27, 1880
Mar 4, 1967
&
Ethel Cobb Byrom
Nov 13, 1896
Jan 4, 1960

Anna Mae, wife of
Arthur Gordon
Sep 13, 1888
Oct 21, 1921

David Reavis
Jul 7, 1829
Feb 10, 1907

Elizabeth E. Reavis
Jun 2, 1833
Nov 21, 1908

A. W. Reavis
Jun 9, 1825
Jan 30, 1879

Beecher Powers
1903-1973
(Tullahoma FH)

Mary Weeks
1885-1963
(Howell-Thompson FH)

Victoria B. Brown
1878-1930
(Tullahoma FH)

Ada Brown
(Tullahoma FH)

Earl G. Brown
Tennessee
Pvt U. S. Army WW II
Feb 29, 1903
May 3, 1973

Jeffie Holt
Oct 4, 1886
Jun 7, 1902

Infant Son of
Thomas J. & Ellen Holt
1896

Infant of
Thomas J. & Nora E. Holt
B&D Feb 22, 1912
"Twin Sister of
Ophelia"

Ophelia W. Holt
Feb 22, 1912
Nov 6, 1962

Ellen Blake Holt
1865-Sep 6, 1908

Nora E. Holt
Apr 8, 1880
(no date)

Thomas J. Holt
Jun 14, 1862
Oct 23, 1931

Lottie Lorene Holt
B&D Jan 28, 1916

George W. West
1868-1950
&
Annie S. West
1875-(no date)

Isom F. West
Aug 31, 1909
Aug 11, 1935
&
Mamie West
Dec 23, 1911

G. W. West
1830-1916

Mary Jane Stephens
Died Feb 18, 194?
Age: 42y, 10m, 25d.
(Moore FH)

Charles Howard
1920-1967
(Motlow-Moore FH)

H. H. Howard
(no dates, fieldstone)

Gale Howard
Died 194?

John Howard Smith
Feb 14, 1899
Oct 30, 1932
"Father"
&
"Mother"
Cathern Howard Smith
Mar 10, 1887
Nov 1, 1957
&
Step-Father
W. W. Smith
Mar 10, 1876
Sep 12, 1957

Samuel J. Adams
1883-1963

Tennie Adams
1882-1969
(Tullahoma FH)

Will Anderton
1892-1961
(Motlow-Moore FH)

Susie Austin
1877-1964
(Motlow-Moore FH)

------ Austin
Died Nov 10, 192?
Age: --y, 5m, 16d.
(TM)

CUMBERLAND SPRINGS QUADRANGLE

Charlie Ladd
1896-1973
(Harrison FH)

Mary P. Ladd
1882-19-4
(Motlow-Moore FH)

Malissa Shofner, wife of
T. S. Ladd
Aug 31, 1855
Jun 22, 1916

Lee Roy Ladd
Apr 2, 1889
Jan 28, 1970
&
Virgie Holt Ladd
May 30, 1896
Nov 30, 1955

Ola Ladd
(no dates)

Robert Ladd
(no dates)

Roy Ladd, Jr.
(no dates)

Billy Joe Nelson
Sep --, ----
(dates gone)

Annie Mae Ray
Sep 21, 1912

James Wyley Ray
Nov 12, 1867
(no date)
&
Mattie Alice Ray
Jun 3, 1869
Oct 30, 1929

Roy Phillip Farrar
1941-1941
(Harrison FH)

J. Price McArthur
Aug 16, 1885
Oct 31, 1966
&
Alma Lee McArthur
Aug 8, 1901

Douglas McArthur
B&D Jan 24, 1942

Pricie Lee, Daughter of
J. P. & Alma Lee McArthur
Nov 16, 1919
Nov 18, 1919

Infant Anderton
    1908

John Rogers
(no dates, Thompson FH)

Albert B. Ray
Sep 9, 1895
Nov 22, 1928

Leona Mae Ray
Sep 5, 1901
Jul 10, 1926

Gordon D., Son of
W. R. & M. J. Ray
Sep 28, 1897
Feb 4, 1900

Vesta Ray
Mar 26, 1897
Oct 8, 1898

W. M. Ray
1844-(no date)
&
M. J. Ray
1845-1915

James Harvey Spry
Died Sep 20, 1973
Age: 96y, 5m, 26d.
(Manchester FH)

Treda D. Ray
1958-1958
(Motlow-Moore FH)

James W. Pollock
1921-1962
(Motlow-Moore FH)

Claud E. Pollock
1856-1960
(Motlow-Moore FH)

Mrs. Lucy Carter
(no dates, Thompson FH)

Arthur Carter
(no dates, Thompson FH)

Sarah E. Ray
Mar 8, 1896
Jan 5, 1895
(these dates could be
reversed)

Ella, wife of
J. H. Ray
1868-1918

Jennie Ether, wife of
W. E. Sanders
Dec 24, 1884
Sep 12, 1914

J. M. Byrom
Mar 10, 1825
Sep 16, 1914
&
Sarah Ann Byrom
Apr 25, 1829
Apr 15, 1904

Thirsia Anderton Harbin
Jun 13, 1902
Aug 22, 1928

Vester, Daughter of
C. T. & L. E. Anderton
Jul 10, 1908
Oct 12, 1912

Henry Anthony Anderton
Apr 4, 1894
Dec 11, 1917

H. R. Allmon
1852-1926
& wife
Mary Ann Dean Allmon
1854-1915

Enoch Nelson
Mar 23, 1869
Apr 28, 1939
&
Lizzie Nelson
Mar 29, 1869
(no date)

Osker Nelson
Tennessee
Pvt 318 Field Arty 81 Div
Born 1894
Died May 22, 1938

Mae A. Keaton
1918-1966
(Motlow-Moore FH)

Mary Ruth Anderton
Dec 8, 1926
Jan 31, 1928
&
Helen Anderton
B&D Nov 31, 1937

John Washington Anderton
Oct 26, 1859
Mar 5, 1923

Dora Louise Shelton
B&D May 24, 1936

Nanie B. Mullins
Oct 4, 1935
Oct 5, 1935
&
Emma Fay Mullins
Aug 7, 1939
Jan 26, 1940
&
Annie Lee Mullins
Oct 4, 1935
Oct 12, 1935

Luther Neal Anderton
Feb 15, 1893
May 8, 1935

Katie Pearl Anderton
Aug 7, 1915
Mar 24, 1951

Mary C. Anderton
Apr 22, 1858
Aug 20, 1939

Bulah Mai, Daughter of
J. H. & Rebecca E.
Anderton
Nov 13, 1916
Dec 7, 1919

J. W. Anderton
Mar 14, 1839
Sep 3, 1913

Omey, wife of
J. W. Anderton
Dec 17, 1841
Apr 7, 1910

Ugene Anderton
Dec 27, 1871
May 28, 1901

J. H. Anderton
Aug 13, 1873
May 17, 1934
&
Rebecca Anderton
Dec 5, 1880
(no date)

James Franklin Anderton
1878-1958

Infant of
J. B. & M. C. Byrom
B&D Apr 28, 1896

James B. Byrom
Jul 16, 1861
Apr 20, 1926
&
Cann C. Byrom
Oct 25, 1861
Aug 13, 1934

Infant Daughter of
J. B. & M. C. Byrom
B&D Jan 28, 1902

Rev. I. M. Coop
Dec 24, 1842
Oct 25, 1897
& wife
Sarah C. Coop
Dec 24, 1857
May 26, 1885

James E. Coop
Aug 9, 1875
Apr 24, 1914
&
Lula L. Coop
Feb 1, 1876
Feb 17, 1929

Sarah L., Daughter of
J. E. & L. L. Coop
Dec 9, 1906
Sep 10, 1909

Edwin C., Son of
J. E. & L. L. Coop
Apr 4, 1910
Mar 27, 1913

CUMBERLAND SPRINGS QUADRANGLE

John W. Scivally
1872-1961
&
Hattie B. Scivally
1892-

Annie West
1872-1967
(Motloe-Moore FH)

Esmond Foster
Jun 10, 1924
Jun 27, 1924
&
Kenith Foster
B&D Dec 22, 1925
&
Edward Foster
Mar 5, 1922
Sep 28, 1926

Marion A. Smith
Mar 27, 1906
May 23, 1957

Rosa Bates Smith
Jul 31, 1881
Mar 23, 1947

John D. Bates
Jan 28, 1861
Oct 24, 1936
&
Mary J. Bates
Jul 13, 1865
Mar 2, 1956

George R. Bates
Jun 8, 1874
Feb 27, 1915

Leutana Bates
Dec 21, 1847
Apr 5, 1917
&
M. N. Bates
May 29, 1850
(no dates)

Infant Son of
Dave & Maggie Bates
B&D Aug 4, 1910

Sally Ann Farrar
1971-1971
(Tullahoma FH)

Randy Farrar
1953-1953
(Howell FH)

Joe Farrar, Jr.
1971-1972
(Gowen-Smith FH)

Eldie Farrar
Sep 19, 1898
Jun 23, 1969

Jack & Mary Allen
(no dates)

Porter A. Messingill
Jul 29, 1886
(Motlow-Moore FH, 1968)
&
Ethel Neely Messingill
Feb 9, 1903
Jul 16, 1965

Mary E., wife of
Morgan Minor
May 15, 1844
Oct 15, 1897

Alvis J. Woosley
1885-1940
&
Lena Woosley
1884-1955

Alton S. McEwen
1957-1957
(Motlow-Shasteen FH)

Patricia A. McEwen
1954-1954
(Motlow-Shasteen FH)

Tracy L. Prince
1970-1970
(Tullahoma FH)

Martha Cates
Aug 30, 1856
May 6, 1886

Sonie C. Ford
Jan 16, 1901
May 29, 1950

Mary Lora Cyree
Feb 21, 1900
Jul 24, 1959
&
James Logan Cyree
Mar 18, 1878
Jul 4, 1923
&
J. E. Cyree
Oct 3, 1923
Jan 1, 1929

Forrest J. Cyree
May 6, 1894
Sep 13, 1963
&
Annie W. Cyree
Nov 5, 1895

John Cyree
1868-1924
&
Mary Cyree
1870-1935

Lillian Louella, wife of
S. B. Foster
Nov 5, 1905
Nov 28, 1927

Jerry Lee Smith
1969-1969
(Gowen-Smith FH)

Raleigh H. Smith
Aug 8, 1917
Nov 18, 1918

Baby Smith
Jan 29, 1914
Jan 30, 1914

Harvey E. Smith
May 6, 1887
Oct 6, 1964
&
Dora B. Smith
Dec 19, 1888
Oct 14, 1966

Mary Smith
Jun 10, 1889
Jan 29, 1914

Louise Elizabeth Sawyers
1862-1904

Rufus B. Cobb
Mar 9, 1884
Jul 15, 1923

Irene Bohanan
1907-1972
(Tullahoma FH)

George Cunningham
1843-1912
&
Sallie Cunningham
1854-(no date)

Sallie Hargrove
1927-1965
(Motlow-Moore FH)

Pauline Corvin
(Tullahoma FH)

Robert Helton, Jr.
B&D Apr 1921

Richard Nelson
Aug 2, 1920
May 19, 1921

R. E. Helton
Apr 1933
May 1934

Major Helton
May 1925
May 1925

Doris Helton
Apr 1935
Apr 1935

Oscar Helton
Aug 1943
Dec 1943

George W. Carter
(no dates)

John C. Adams
May 15, 1870
May 19, 1915

James Bates
1889-1944
(Thompson FH)

Jennie Elizabeth Wadkins
Died Feb 18, 1947
Age: 1y, 4m, 31d.
(Daves-Culbertson FH)

Will E. Steed
1865-1935
&
Emma Ray Steed
1871-1914

M. M. Mitty Steed
B&D Nov 15, 1895

Jable Dean
Tennessee
Corp 162 Inf 41 Div
Nov 4, 1936

"Father"
Thomas Adams
Mar 28, 1880
Aug 21, 1928
& Son
Elijah Adams
1910-1912
& Daughter
Infant Adams
B&D May 12, 1908

James Clay Ferrell
Jan 26, 1962
Feb 22, 1962

Angela Ferrell
B&D Apr 26, 1960

Robert W. Helton
Jan 21, 1899
Sep 5, 1972
&
Dovie N. Helton
Jun 16, 1902

Laney Scot Helton
1973-1973
(Tullahoma FH)

Tina L. Helton
1969-1969
(Tullahoma FH)

Johnnie Shields Helton
Tennessee
Pfc Btry B 745 AAA Gun Bn
CAC WW II
Jan 27, 1923
Jun 20, 1964

CUMBERLAND SPRINGS QUADRANGLE

Claude N. Jones, Jr.
Tennessee
Pvt Co B 728 Mil Pol Bn
WW II
Apr 10, 1922
Sep 23, 1971

Willie P. Jones
1919-1956
(Daves-Culbertson FH)

Claud Newton Jones
Oct 14, 1894

&
Ola Molene Jones
Feb 2, 1894
Mar 12, 1969

William Donnell
1962-1962
(Howell FH)

Lannie Ray Cates
1908-1973
(Daves-Culbertson FH)

Gladys Cates
1910-1964
(Daves-Culbertson FH)

Howell Timothy Ray
B&D May 29, 1956

Joe Howard
1887-1956
(Motlow-Moore FH)

Christopher A. Anderton
Oct 8, 1962
Nov 5, 1962

John Aaron McBride
1904-1960
(Daves-Culbertson FH)

Beverly D. Howard
Nov 3, 1961
Dec 10, 1961

Charles E. Lewis
Tennessee
Pvt U. S. Army Korea
Aug 12, 1929
Aug 30, 1973

Essie Carter
1875-1957
(Cothron-Thompson FH)

Skippy Larandy Dulin
Aug 11, 1953
Oct 18, 1953

John L. Stephens
1879-1951
(Harrison FH)

Boyd Brooks
1896-1954
&
Florence Brooks
1894-

Katherine Byford
1960-1960
(Motlow-Moore FH)

David Henry Bates
Jun 12, 1879
Jan 13, 1962
&
Maggie Anderton Bates
Dec 24, 1890

Lonnie Reagor Mullins
Mar 7, 1892
May 25, 1964

Fannie Smith Mullins
Jul 21, 1891
Dec 21, 1867

Melody Grogan
1966-1966
(Harrison FH)

Joyce Ann Nippers
Sep 25, 1944
Jul 23, 1964

John Henry Williams
Aug 16, 1891
Jun 1, 1960

Thomas Wesley Williams
Dec 2, 1898
Sep 30, 1958

Many unmarked graves.

Andrea Michele Spry
1968-1968
(Daves-Culbertson FH)

Charline Cates
Died 1964
Age: (not given)
(TM)

William E. Adams
Feb 5, 1913
Apr 14, 1971

Madie (Adams) Ray
May 1, 1883
Mar 7, 1963

Connie J. Foster
Feb 5, 1962
(Motlow-Moore FH)

Randall Lee Street
(no dates, Tullahoma FH)

Herbert Thompson
Jun 17, 1907
Apr 15, 1967
&
Mildred H. Thompson
Oct 1, 1907
Jan 5, 1963

Glendon Woosley
Tennessee
Pvs Co D 145 Inf Korea
Jul 30, 1929
Aug 28, 1955

Grady Lynn Henley
&
Jackson Lynn Henley
B&D Dec 6, 1970

Joseph Fred Burt
1908-1961
(Daves-Culbertson FH)

Isaac W. Cyree
May 14, 1898

&
Ethel H. Cyree
Feb 7, 1903
May 8, 1968

Annie Hazel, wife of
S. B. Foster
Mar 5, 1908
Mar 25, 1955

Sylvester Foster
1899-1972
(Tullahoma FH)

William Thomas Lee
May 10, 1912

&
Minnie Pearl Lee
Mar 27, 1914
May 20, 1965

Infant Cunningham
1961-1961
(Harrison FH)

Shelia Jane Cunningham
1955-1955
(Harrison FH)

Walter E. Simmons
Jan 8, 1903
Jun 19, 1967
&
Viney A. Simmons
May 2, 1901

Lem D. Cunningham
Tennessee
Pvt U. S. Army WW II
Jun 4, 1902
Oct 2, 1972

Myrtle Kennemer
1900-1952
(Motlow-Moore FH)

Juanita Lynn Moore
B&D Dec 5, 1964

John O. Presley
May 27, 1905
Aug 31, 1971
&
Mary H. Presley
Mar 8, 1926

Married Aug 9, 1949

* *

PIONEER CEMETERY

LOCATION: NE of Lynchburg about one mile.

Margaret Boone
Died Oct 25, 1872
Age: 74y, 5m.

T. H. Shaw
Feb 23, 1793
Feb 23, 1871
Age: 73y, 5m, 4d.

K. C. Shaw
Jun 10, 1803
Jun 10, 1867
Age: 64 years.

George W. J., Son of
T. J. & S. M. Shaw
Apr 15, 1860
Jan 27, 1861

Anna Glaser
Died Apr 3, 1874
Age: 7y, 5m, 14d.

T. L. D. Parks
Sep 27, 1823
Nov 30, 1900

Martin L., Son of
T. L. D. & Rebecca Parks
Apr 2, 1864
Sep 22, 1865
Age: 1y, 5m, 2d.

Susan B., Daughter of
T. L. D. & Rebecca Parks
Dec 23, 1848   Age: 12y,
Ayg 5, 1861   7m, 13d.

CUMBERLAND SPRINGS QUADRANGLE

John Motlow
1st Lieut. 5th S. C. Inf
Rev. War
Jul 28, 1757
May 25, 1812
"John Motlow
1757-1812 His remains
were removed to this grave,
1952, from his graveyard
at Lima, Greenville Co.,
S. C., 250 yards north of
Hwy 11 & 100 yards east
of Hwy along west side of
Saluda River."

Agnes McElhaney Motlow
1760-1825
"Widow of Rev. War
Soldier John Motlow,
1757-1812."

Felix Motlow
Jun 13, 1801
Feb 23, 1872
Age: 70y, 8m, 10d.

Margaret, wife of
Felix Motlow
Died Nov 7, 1855
Age: 48y, 27d.

J. W. M. Parks
Feb 18, 1875
Sep 12, 1875

James B., Son of
R. B. & E. J. Parks
Feb 4, 1855
Sep 4, 1857

Francis M., Daughter of
R. B. & E. J. Parks
Jul 2, 1851
Aug 18, 1858

Martin L. Parkes
Aug 1793
Dec 1845
&
Susan B. Parkes
Aug 1803
Aug 1881

Mary M., Daughter of
T. D. L. & Rebecca Parks
Jan 6, 1827
Jul 18, 1840

Infant Daughter Parks
Stillborn
Aug 31, 1873
&
Infant Daughter Parks
B&D Sep 19, 1874
"Infant Daughters of
R. A. & S. A. Parks."

Emma, Daughter of
R. B. & S. A. Parks
Aug 21, 1858
Dec 29, 1859

Olivia, Daughter of
R. B. & E. J. Parks
Nov 27, 1856
Aug 16, 1862

Laura, Daughter of
R. B. & E. J. Parks
Aug 25, 1853
Oct 30, 1853

Daniel Smoot
Sep 6, 1814
Apr 17, 1863

Callie, Daughter of
Feliz & Margaret Motlow
Died Oct 25, 1851
Age: 3y, 2m, 15d.

W. W. Motlow
Mar 25, 1824
Aug --, 1853

Mary Motlow
Sep 4, 1804
Dec 11, 1854

John Motlow
Oct 17, 1797
Dec 18, 1854

Louisa M. Motlow
Dec 17, 1838
Nov 29, 1858

George T. Motlow
Died May 27, 1869
Age: 15y, 4m, 29d.

Many graves with no markers, also many graves with fieldstones, no inscriptions.
This Cemetery is marked with a Tennessee Historical Marker that states land
given by William S. Smith, a Revolutionary Soldier.

* *

PLEASANT HILL CHURCH CEMETERY

LOCATION: Two and one half miles south of Raysville.

Ross Huffman
Apr 19, 1889

&
Florence Huffman
Feb 17, 1893

&
Coleene Huffman
May 4, 1927
Aug 18, 1964
(picture of all three)

Dora Lee Rhoton Mitchell
Dec 8, 1890
Jun 28, 1963

Ronald Edward Womble
B&D Feb 19, 1943

Tommie Litchford
1898-1962
(Harrison FH)

William Charles Litchford
Tennessee
Pvt Infantry WW I
Jul 20, 1888
May 12, 1966

William Franklin Parker
1888-1956
(Daves-Culbertson FH)

James J. Sanders
Tennessee
Pfc 109 Inf 28 Inf Div
WW II
Sep 26, 1919
Sep 13, 1944

Lela J. Neal
Oct 30, 1904
Jan 10, 1945

W. L. Rhoton
Sep 3, 1865
Feb 21, 1934
& wife
Mary E. Baker Rhoton
Jan 22, 1870
Mar 14, 1944

_____ Smith
194_
(Daves-Ramsey FH)

Leon Millsap
1884-1963
(Motlow-Moore FH)

Paul Millsap
1899-1972
(Tullahoma FH)

Infant Thompson
1959-1959
(Harrison FH)

Mary Neoma Hatfield
1940-1942

Clennie A. Hatfield
1901-1958
&
Zelma R. Hatfield
1913-

Harvey T. Hatfield
Apr 4, 1938
Mar 27, 1971

George B. Rhoton
Jan 15, 1878
Aug 27, 1939
&
Elizabeth Rhoton
Feb 10, 1884
Mar 5, 1943

Clayton Rhoton
1914-1935
&
Esther Rhoton
1910-

Kenneth Stein, Son of
E. C. & Lula Mae Huffman
Aug 15, 1950
Nov 23, 1950

Tom Marion Stewart
Dec 1, 1850
Oct 27, 1933
&
Sarah C. Stewart
Sep 3, 1870
Jan 19, 1929

Buford E. Downum
Apr 24, 1903
Aug 15, 1933
&
Elmer J. Downum
Aug 20, 1921
Jun 3, 1929

Mother
Silena Hall
Jul 16, 1886
Dec 19, 1937

Dan N. Hill
May 19, 1861
Feb 22, 1924
&
Jennie Hill
Aug 7, 1867
(no date)

L. B.
(fieldstone)

L. B.
(fieldstone)

CUMBERLAND SPRINGS QUADRANGLE

Newt Patterson
Dec 5, 1883
Apr 7, 1962

Tom Patterson
1882-1959

Charley Patterson
Jan 30, 1879
May 23, 1939
&
Annie Patterson
Dec 16, 1883
(TM: 1968)

Mae Elizabeth Chapman
1900-1948

Tom D. Chapman
May 24, 1895
(no date)
&
Ida Neal Chapman
Jun 19, 1884
Jan 17, 1947

Lucy Chapman
Oct 2, 1885
Jul 23, 1938

Edna Chapman
Dec 2, 1862
Jul 5, 1941

Burrel Chapman
Aug 27, 1855
Dec 21, 1934

Charlie E. Hall
Jan 31, 1905

&
Mary L. Hall
Jul 15, 1905
Mar 2, 1965

Horace Greely Sanders
Mar 19, 1886
Oct 6, 1951
&
Sallie Ann Sanders
Sep 11, 1890

Jack Bennett Greenwood
Apr 17, 1870
Apr 1, 1951
&
Fannie Mae Greenwood
Aug 4, 1867
May 21, 1940

David M. Hix
Jan 23, 1870
Jan 22, 1937
&
Rosa Ann Hix
Mar 21, 1836
Nov 2, 1928

J. M. Sanders
Feb 1, 1876
Jun 26, 1949
& wife
Ida Damron Sanders
Jan 8, 1874
Dec 26, 1945

Infant Spencer
1950-1950
(Harrison FH)

Mary Lee Spencer
1952-1952
(Harrison FH)

Dollie, wife of
Roy Burton
Aug 16, 1900

Roy Burton
Aug 27, 1890
Oct 23, 1951

Richard R. Burton
Mar 9, 1923
Sep 24, 1929

Hubert Hill
Jun 13, 1888
Oct 14, 1949
&
Carrie Hill
Feb 22, 1890

Opal Jaunita Patterson
Jun 11, 1937
Jun 23, 1941

Mary Dell Scroggins
Jan 8, 1939
Jan 28, 1939
&
Martha Nell Scroggins
Jan 8, 1939
Jan 10, 1939

A. P. Patterson
Sep 18, 1875
Jun 5, 1961
&
Ida Leona Patterson
Apr 23, 1876
Feb 25, 1940

Bernice Ov Patterson
Nov 19, 1901
Jul 11, 1927

Frank G. Burton
(no dates)

William J. Hazelwood
Aug 27, 1890
Dec 18, 1940
&
Fannie Lou Hazelwood
Apr 30, 1893
Mar 12, 1947

Henry Lee Preston
Mar 28, 1874
Sep 2, 1945
&
Ada L. Hill Preston
Mar 5, 1884
May 8, 1921

C. D. Hasty
Dec 11, 1880
May 11, 1962
&
Lema L. Hasty
Aug 21, 1893
Jan 22, 1928

Wallace L. Hasty
Jan 6, 1919
Aug 31, 1919

Annie Sanders
Apr 15, 1911
Nov 8, 1960
&
Roy Sanders
Dec 20, 1892

&
Ida Sanders
Mar 12, 1893
Jul 22, 1935

Polemlia P. McKinney
1867-1955

M. L. Pollock
Jun 19, 1862
Feb 23, 1923
&
T. A. Pollock
Apr 17, 1847
May 1928

"Father"
Charlie Wilhoite
Oct 3, 1881
Jan 29, 1941
&
"Mother"
Vera Wilhoite
Nov 26, 1882
(no date)
& Son
Clifton Wilhoite
Jan 9, 1910
Nov 14, 1928

Sally, wife of
J. W. Wilhoite
Mar 4, 1851
Aug 23, 1921
Age: 70y, 7m, 19d.

John A. Reese
Tennessee
Pvt 62 Pioneer Inf WW I
Mar 2, 1897
Sep 16, 1971
&
Callie Mae Reese
Apr 6, 1906
Nov 8, 1922

Fred Reece
1877-1932
&
Terry Reece
1876-1958

Johnnie H. Branch
Nov 3, 1887
Jan 18, 1944
&
Annie May Branch
Feb 15, 1897

Branch
(fieldstone)

Branch
(fieldstone)

Jeff Flippo
Dec 19, 1872
Dec 9, 1956
&
Fannie Flippo
Apr 5, 1872
Apr 13, 1969

James T., Son of
L. T. & Roxie Coop
Oct 26, 1917
Sep 21, 1920

David C., Son of
M. C. & Pearl Scroggins
1937-1938

Mack C. Scroggins
Dec 29, 1888
Dec 22, 1960
&
Pearl R. Scroggins
Jun 19, 1914

Joe Woosley
Apr 8, 1883
May 19, 1921
&
Betty Woosley
Jan 25, 1896
Jul 21, 1941

Frank Downum
1849-1932
&
Nancy Downum
1846-1929
&
Lizzie Downum
1878-1945

Danny Glen Stewart
Apr 25, 1954
Oct 24, 1957

Clara Cenora, Daughter of
R. S. & M. A. B. Anthony
Aug 30, 1832
Feb 1, 1896

CUMBERLAND SPRINGS QUADRANGLE

A. M. Tims
Aug 8, 1825
Feb 14, 1905

William Thomas Hazelwood
Died Nov 24, 1923
Age:(not given) (TM)
&
Mary Margaret Hazelwood
(no dates)

G. J. Anderton
May 5, 1864
Sep 23, 1896
Age: 32y, 4m, 18d.

John Anderton
Jul 29, 1837
May 3, 1908
&
Mary Anderton
May 9, 1839
(no date)

Henry Stewart
Jun 9, 1886
Oct 28, 1940
&
Etta Stewart
Jan 29, 1890
Dec 2, 1951

Docia Cunningham
1882-1966
(TM)

Spencer Cunningham
1886-1938

Lora Bell Cunningham
1879-1945

Willie Tom Cunningham
1907-1963

W. S. Cobble
Nov 25, 1855
Jun 14, 1933

N. J., wife of
W. S. Cobble
Oct 31, 1866
Sep 12, 1893

Robert E. Cobble
Jun 6, 1884
Oct 28, 1901

Annie Lee Jean
Jul 16, 1910
Mar 13, 1943

Luke, Son of
J. F. & E. L. Jean
Jul 20, 1903
Aug 28, 1917

Robert, Son of
J. F. & E. L. Jean
Feb 3, 1897
Oct 3, 1918

John Jean
Oct 25, 1864
Jan 9, 1929
&
Ella Jean
Mar 26, 1887
Apr 26, 1959

Jemima Price
Dec 12, 1823
Mar 2, 1896
Age: 72y, 2m, 20d.

Mollie Burton Goosby
"erected 1970"
(no dates)

W. R. Burton
1849-1926

Nancy R., wife of
W. R. Burton
Jan 14, 1849
Jan 21, 1905

Henry B. Burton
Jan 22, 1873
Apr 24, 1897

Octavia, wife of
R. W. Burton
Nov 22, 1827
Aug 22, 1894

Robert W. Burton
Jun 9, 1823
Feb 4, 1909

Roberta Burton
May 21, 1889
Feb 24, 1914

Rev. John F. Neal
Nov 29, 1850
Feb 17, 1898
&
Rachel M. Neal
May 3, 1857
Oct 31, 1893

"Son"
W. G. Neal
Mar 11, 1880
Feb 25, 1881

"Daughter"
Tobitha Neal
May 4, 1891
May 8, 1891

Sarah Gordor(n)
Mar 22, 1862
May 21, 1905

John Thomas Stewart
Jan 11, 1878
Apr 24, 1967

Zora Tennessee Stewart
Sep 18, 1887
Jun 1, 1973

Marthy Ann Patterson
Jul 14, 1822
Mar 21, 1905

J. W. Patterson
Feb 16, 1846
Feb 19, 1934

Lizy Jane, wife of
J. W. Patterson
Feb 25, 1846
Aug 23, 1920

James E. Evans
Oct 12, 1834
Oct 12, 1896
Age: 62 years.
&
Nancy C. Evans
May 28, 1831
Sep 12, 1910
Age: 79y, 3m, 14d.

D. C. Baker
Sep 22, 1865
Oct 12, 1938
&
Fannie (Marildria) Baker
Oct 10, 1876
(TM: 1956)

Charles R. Burrum
Co A 37 Regt Tenn Vols
C.S.A.
Oct 28, 1841
Mar 27, 1930

Mary Magdalene Rogers Burrum
1861-1922

Alien Cunningham
Oct 3, 1909
Oct 14, 1909

Mary Jane Cunningham
Mar 15, 1855
Jan 29, 1889

Ernest O. Cunningham
May 3, 1904
Jun 13, 1909

Ora Lee, Daughter of
J. R. & E. J. Massey
Jul 11, 1891
Nov 5, 1891

John R. Massey
Dec 4, 1857
Mar 25, 1901

Eliza Massey Parks
Mar 21, 1861
Dec 31, 1937

Floyd, Son of
Ed & Lizzie Anderton
Dec 17, 1897
May 2, 1900

W. M. Cobb
Oct 3, 1851
Apr 24, 1910
&
J. E. Cobb
Jun 26, 1865
Aug 28, 1939

Patrick Lee, Son of
Mr. & Mrs. Eddie Mears
Jan 1, 1971
Jan 15, 1971

Lizzie Ozell Baker
Mar 6, 1930
Nov 27, 1955

Albert H. Timmons
1868-1918
&
Nannie Myrtle Timmons
1881-1921

Elvy Bennett
Jun 3, 1894
Oct 28, 1895

Fannie Ruth Bennett
Sep 25, 1900
Apr 11, 1939

William H. Bennett
Sep 17, 1871
Jan 18, 1952
&
Daisy Brown Bennett
Jul 9, 1875
Jul 23, 1948

James M. Neal
Oct 19, 1876
Dec 27, 1951
&
Pearl N. Neal
Mar 4, 1883
(no date)

Easter E. W., wife of
Rev. W. H. Neal
Aug 28, 1845
Oct 8, 1896

Mattie, wife of
T. J. Gore
Jun 27, 1866
Feb 27, 1899

Lillie
(no dates, fieldstone)

W. J. Johnson
1853-1908
& wife
(no name given)
1853-1930

Lannie Baker
1918-1953
(Harrison FH)

CUMBERLAND SPRINGS QUADRANGLE

Horace E. Sanders
Mar 25, 1885
Sep 22, 1958
&
Zena S. Sanders
Apr 1, 1889
Feb 16, 1959

Edna Pearl, Daughter of
H. E. & Zena Sanders
Mar 22, 1908
May 8, 1918

Sam M. Neal
Jul 11, 1880
Mar 15, 1965
&
Eula May Neal
Feb 3, 1886

Vivian Void Neal
Nov 11, 1910
Sep 19, 1913

R. E. Neal
1917-1938

L. E. Neal
Jul 1, 1856
Mar 23, 1926

T. J. Neal
Mar 6, 1855
Jan 12, 1924

Chaney Shasteen, Daughter
of J. P. & S. E. Damron
Feb 26, 1891
Nov 12, 1892

Lucy O. Dell, Daughter
of J. P. & S. E. Damron
Jul 27, 1881
Aug 28, 1881

Callie Harp
(no dates, fieldstone)

W. F. Grammer
Feb 20, 1860
May 6, 1898

Fred Timmons
1914-1954

Jeff Bennett
1886-1966
(Howell-Thompson FH)

Mrs. Clemmie Bennett
1886-1950
(Thompson FH)

Everett H. Bennett
Mar 9, 1922
Aug 16, 1944

Alfred Marion Huffman
Oct 15, 1827
Feb 7, 1903
Age: 75y, 3m, 23d.

Emila, wife of
A. M. Huffman
Feb 23, 1832
Jul 17, 1894

Lena P., Daughter of
George & L. P. Scivally
& wife of
W. M. Damron
Oct 25, 1889
Jan 4, 1913

Martha E., Daughter of
J. P. & S. E. Damron
Oct 8, 1869
May 6, 1912

"Father"
J. P. Damron
Jul 27, 1843
Jul 9, 1896
&
"Mother"
S. E. Damron
Aug 11, 1851
Mar 10, 1930

Hazel M. Damron
May 24, 1916
Dec 1, 1917

Amanda E. Damron
Oct 27, 1883
Jun 8, 1917

George D. Damron
1879-1957

Lou Adah Bruce Damron
Jul 23, 1878
Feb 4, 1946

Abbie, wife of
J. A. Baxter
Apr 10, 1870
Apr 11, 1893

Edmon Ross Baxter
Oct 7, 1881
Nov 25, 1887

W. A. J. Baxter
May 30, 1841
Mar 18, 1886

Albert J. Baxter
Jan 11, 1909
Jun 23, 1909
&
Lillian Lucille Baxter
B&D Mar 6, 1895
Children of
J. A. & Anna Baxter.

Deborah K. Grant
1958-1958
(Motlow-Moore FH)

Thelma Baker
Oct 3, 1909
Jul 9, 1931

William Baker
(no dates)

William Robert Smith
Jun 24, 1892
Jan 14, 1942

Joe A. Smith
1854-1932

Josie Smith
May 23, 1853
Jun 1, 1945

J. W. Cunningham
Nov 29, 1851
Mar 24, 1908
&
S. C. Cunningham
Feb 16, 1858
(no date)
&
M. L. Cunningham
Mar 17, 1881
Nov 14, 1881
&
N. C. Cunningham
Jul 31, 1893
Sep 17, 1893

James B. Baker
Jan 8, 1870
Sep 13, 1953
&
Jannie S. Baker
Sep 2, 1875
Sep 27, 1962

Ernest Floyd Baker
Nov 12, 1920
Apr 12, 1924

Martha J. Baker
Feb 18, 1939
Sep 18, 1939

Loyd Baker
Died 1939

Charles Richard Baker
Oct 18, 1964
Mar 17, 1968

Leonard Baker
May 10, 1900
Feb 5, 1974
&
Pearlie Baker
Mar 9, 1903

Married May 12, 1921

Herman Lester Coop
1913-1969
(Daves-Culbertson FH)

William Henry Coop
1872-1960
(Daves-Culbertson FH)

Jefferson Flippo
Tennessee
Pvt Co E Tenn Inf C.S.A.
Oct 14, 1824
Sep 10, 1891

S. J. Flippo
Jul 1839
Nov 1907

Arah, Daughter of
S. E. & S. F. Flippo
Feb 10, 1900
Jun 24, 1904

William Moulder
Oct 19, 1911
Aug 29, 1949
&
Ola Moulder

Mary Lee Moulder
Aug 13, 1888
Dec 11, 1959

Jack Hardy
Jun 4, 1876
Mar 2, 1956
&
Lula Hardy
May 9, 1881
Jan 29, 1926

Argie Mai Murray
1901-1932

J. H. Ray
1868-(no date)
&
Blanche Ray
1881-1928

W. F. Steed
1825-1913

Nannie Mable, Daughter
of W. P. & Mantie Davis
Apr 7, 1901
Jul 17, 1901

W. R. Smith
Mar 2, 1844
Mar 25, 1928

Mary M., wife of
W. R. Smith
Apr 9, 1850
Mar 11, 1912

D. C. B.
(no dates, fieldstone)

CUMBERLAND SPRINGS QUADRANGLE

Eugene Branch
1940-1940
(Harrison FH)

Christine Branch
1941-1941
(Harrison FH)

Jessie William Branch
Oct 10, 1904
Nov 27, 1955
&
Johnnie Maude Branch
Nov 25, 1914

Harwell Branch
1943-1943
(Harrison FH)

Elain Branch
1944-1945
(Harrison FH)

Charles T. Reynolds
Sep 23, 1903
Jun 1, 1973
&
Nina Mae Reynolds
Mar 2, 1905

Married Dec 28, 1927

W. N. E.
(no dates, fieldstone)

Lawrence E. Huffman
Nov 26, 1885
May 12, 1949
&
Maggie "Oma" Huffman
Apr 18, 1888
Jun 25, 1971

G. A. Huffman
Jun 27, 1854
Sep 30, 1932

Nancy, wife of
G. A. Huffman
Jul 27, 1862
Oct 10, 1904

Nina P., Daughter of
G. A. & N. P. Huffman
Sep 12, 1904
Nov 18, 1904

Edward E. Huffman
1903-1972
(Harrison FH)

Douglas Harper
1821-1904
& wife
Martha Brown Harper
1827-1900

John C. Harper
1859-1936

L. J. Harper
Oct 6, 1862
Aug 10, 1894

Pamela Ann Baker
1962-1962
(Harrison FH)

Mrs. Elsie Baker
Died Mar --, 1970
Age: 61 years.
(Spry FH)

Bell F. Spencer
1886-1919
&
Elgie F. Spencer
1881-1918
&
James "Billie" Spencer
1881-1921

Georgie Minnie Hall
1885-1966
(Daves-Culbertson FH)

Minnie Ruth, Daughter of
Marion & Bernice Hall
B&D Jan 5, 1936

John T. Gore
May 4, 1873
Jul 30, 1915

W. L. Gore
Apr 20, 1851
Mar 12, 1917

Sallie E. Baxter, wife of
W. L. Gore
Jan 22, 1857
Dec 26, 1907
Age: 50y, 11m, 4d.

Sammy L., Son of
W. L. & S. E. Gore
Mar 6, 1894
Sep 20, 1899

M. A. R.
(no dates, fieldstone)

J. W. R.
(no dates, fieldstone)

"Grandfather"
Tom Reese
(no dates)
&
"Grandmother"
Linda Reese
(no dates)

J. W. Reese
Sep 3, 1874
Jul 6, 1936
&
Mollie Reese
Sep 3, 1876
Apr 24, 1904

Joe Reece
Mar 7, 1944
Apr 20, 1947
&
Fred Reece
Jan 19, 1947
Apr 20, 1947

Raymon Sanders
Jan 8, 1899
Aug 11, 1901

Sarah Alice Sanders Parker
Nov 29, 1891
Jul 22, 1941

Rev. J. T. Baxter
Mar 4, 1829
Dec 24, 1902

Nancy, wife of
James T. Baxter
Oct 25, 1837
Nov 30, 1892

Lunar W., Daughter of J.T. &
Feb 14, 1877   Na. Baxter
Sep 16, 1881

J. H. Parker
Oct 5, 1835
Aug 16, 1921

S. J. Baxter
Sep 5, 1855
Aug 22, 1887
Age: 31y, 11m, 17d.

Amanda E. Smith
Mar 29, 1860
Aug 15, 1921

Gregory Wayne Painter
1959-1959
(TM)

J. R. Painter
1875-1963
(Motlow-Moore FH)

John Fredrick Painter
1962-1962
(Daves-Culbertson FH)

Elma B. Branch
1910-1969
(Harrison FH)

Johnie T. Branch
1869-1958
(Harrison FH)

Ed Sanders
Jan 20, 1874
Feb 8, 1955
&
Callie Damron Sanders
Jun 9, 1876
Sep 17, 1964

"Mother"
Lucy Hall
Feb 4, 1869
Oct 25, 1904
&
"Father"
Marion Riley "Dulch" Hall
May 6, 1860
May 7, 1951
&
"Mother"
Jennie Hall
Apr 12, 1875
Jun 8, 1950

Mary Louisa Hall
1858-1952
(Daves-Culbertson FH)

J. T. Simpson
Jul 3, 1856
Dec 11, 1919
&
Florence N. Haslett
Simpson
Jun 27, 1860
Aug 11, 1919

Leonard Simpson
1893-1963
&
Naoma G. Simpson
1895-1927

Lucy Reece
(no dates)

William M. Sanders
Sep 11, 1864
Feb 6, 1936
&
Nancy E. Sanders
Nov 2, 1866
Sep 12, 1896
& Daughter
Lillie Sanders
Jul 31, 1893
Oct 6, 1895

John Felix Harp Sanders
Feb 26, 1867
Jan 23, 1941
&
Mary Ann Branch Sanders
Mar 10, 1868
Jul 25, 1956

Margaret Ann Sanders
1869-1894

F. H. Sanders
Oct 22, 1825
Mar 26, 1897

Andrew Cunningham
(no dates)

Meacy Cunningham
(no dates)

CUMBERLAND SPRINGS QUADRANGLE

Jessie Rhoton
May 5, 1892
Feb 12, 1893

Sammie Reynolds
Mar 6, 1881
May 15, 1882
&
Alice Reynolds
Jun 15, 1877
Sep 12, 1878

R. F. Reynolds
Jul 19, 1849
Oct 6, 1912

A. L. Reynolds
Mar 9, 1852
Mar 23, 1927

Eddie, Son of
J. E. & M. C. Timmins
B&D Nov 21, 1882

Sallie F., wife of
R. F. Reynolds
Nov 6, 1855
Dec 26, 1922

Myrtle D. Chapman
May 19, 1888
Sep 4, 1905

Jim Mathis
1866-1931

Martha Elizabeth, wife
of J. C. Mathes
Mar 4, 1857
Apr 11, 1898

* *

POLLOCK CEMETERY

LOCATION: Three fourth mile SW of Turkey Creek School.

T. B. Pollock
1857-1902
&
Ellen Pollock
1864-1934

Vinnie P. Pollock
Aug 22, 1900
May 19, 1915

Joseph Henry Pollock
Co E 23 Bn Tenn Inf C.S.A.
1836-1867

Pricilla Dillingham Pollock
1839-1916

W. A. Leigh
Jul 22, 1903
Aug 24, 1926

Rollie C. Burt, Jr.
Nov 4, 1929
Jan 9, 1933

Lula V. Burt
Mar 19, 1884
Jul 23, 1915

"Father"
J. J. Pollock
Mar 13, 1859
Aug 25, 1911
&
"Mother"
R. E. Pollock
Jun 29, 1862
(no date)

* *

PRICE CEMETERY

LOCATION: In Baxter Hollow, NE of Lynchburg.

Mary Catharine Price
Died Aug 17, 1873
Age: 36y, 14d.

1 unmarked grave.

* *

RAYSVILLE CHURCH CEMETERY

LOCATION: At Raysville.

William R. Ray
May 31, 1871
Jan 1, 1944
&
Jennie Ray
Dec 26, 1873
Jul 14, 1957

James Edgar Horton
Apr 14, 1886
     1964
&
Annie Bell Horton
May 12, 1892
Feb 17, 1964

Harold B. Anderton
Dec 13, 1871
Feb 29, 1960
&
Arrie Ray Anderton
Oct 18, 1878
Oct 17, 1956

Krispin Nichol, Daughter
of Gary & Ophelia McCowell
Ray
Apr 11, 1972
May 26, 1972

Sam A. Haynes
Sep 6, 1876
Dec 3, 1951

Alma L. Haynes
Jan 16, 1907

Doyle Tallent
Mar 17, 1946
Apr 5, 1946

Several unmarked graves.

"Mother"
Elizabeth Stockton
Jan 13, 1907

& "Daughter"
Margaret Abercrombie
Dec 25, 1925
Nov 30, 1950

Erlene F. Jeffery
1923-1955
(Motlow-Moore FH)

* *

CUMBERLAND SPRINGS QUADRANGLE

RIDGEVILLE CEMETERY

LOCATION: At the Chestnut Ridge Baptist Church, at Ridgeville.

Lilly M. Edwards
Oct 11, 1885
Nov 28, 1970

Bassil Neal
Feb 10, 1906
Sep 22, 1968
&
Grace Neal
May 5, 1908

Sallie Stewart, wife of
R. J. Gaut
Oct 9, 1884
Jan 21, 1911

M. R. Stewart
(no dates, fieldstone)

J. Floyd Stewart
Apr 18, 1889
Jun 9, 1970
&
Pettie A. Stewart
Jun 2, 1894

Johnny Hall
Aug 23, 1918

&
Emmie Hall
Oct 15, 1904

Mary B., Daughter of
J. & A. Rolman
Dec 31, 1899
Nov 21, 1911

Lavon Burt
Dec 27, 1921

&
Ruby Lee Burt
Dec 3, 1919
Jul 31, 1973
Married Nov 16, 1945

J. H. Tankersley
May 12, 1882
Mar 29, 1931
& wife
Cora Weaver Tankersley
Dec 13, 1887
(TM: 1965)

Willie Pearl, Daughter of
J. M. & Zelma Rolman
Oct 17, 1918
Dec 2, 1921

Joe Rolman
Mar 20, 1867
Feb 24, 1951
&
Nancy A. Bean Rolman
Dec 31, 1874
Jan 27, 1919

John W. Smith
Apr 17, 1818
Jul 16, 1899
"Erected by
Jennie Smith, wife of
John W. Smith".

Jennie, wife of
Capt. John W. Smith
Jul 22, 1832
Professed faith in
Christ 1857
Died Jun 24, 1902

Mary Ann, wife of
J. W. Smith
Mar 29, 1828
Dec 23, 1883

Stephen E. Huffman
Jan 11, 1873
Sep 13, 1876

Bl-gy Adams
(fieldstone, no dates)

E. L. Majors
Mar 26, 1852
May 29, 1929
&
Mary Majors
Oct 21, 1859
Oct 14, 1938

"Daughter"
Louise Hall
(no dates)

Jim Hall
(no dates)
&
Renzie Hall
(no dates)

Baby Hall
(no dates)

J. H. Reavis
Jan 5, 1870
Oct 29, 1921
& wife
Fannie A. Shasteen Reavis
Feb 28, 1870
Feb 2, 1922

Eld. J. A. Reavis
Jun 19, 1849
Apr 4, 1910

Anna L., wife of
J. A. Reavis
May 8, 1849
Dec 14, 1897
Age: 48y, 7m, 6d.

Simion S. Reavis
Jul 7, 1827
Apr 3, 1899
Age: 71y, 8m, 26d.
&
Sarah Ann Reavis
Dec 2, 1826
Apr 17, 1907
Age: 80y, 4m, 15d.

Sarah E. Reavis
Dec 28, 1874
Aug 4, 1894

Jessie Emmett, Son of
J. A. & A. L. Reavis
Apr 17, 1892
Sep 26, 1908

R. E. L. Smith
Apr 15, 1867
Apr 4, 1912

Willie Adams
(no dates, fieldstone)

J. W. Parham
Feb 12, 1854
Jul 9, 1911

Theadore, Son of
E. M. & F. J. Leech
Jun 6, 1874
Sep 13, 1874

Horace Leaon, Son of
J. M. & R. C. Shasteen
Oct 19, 1903
Nov 5, 1908

Jim W. Rolman
Apr 20, 1864
Nov 23, 1944
&
Anner A. Rolman
Dec 14, 1868
Feb 16, 1933

Millard Rolman
Oct 1, 1891
Mar 10, 1937
&
Zelma Hatchett Rolman
Dec 1, 1893

Nollie Lee "Hut" Rolman
Oct 16, 1903
Apr 1, 1940

Nancy Jones
Apr 10, 1836
Sep 12, 1882

Martha L., Daughter of
W. C. & Nancy Jones
Sep 10, 1869
Jul 24, 1893

Marilda Hasty Limbaugh
1882-1950

George W. Hasty
Jul 24, 1882
Mar 21, 1916

Charley S. T., Son of
G. W. & M. R. Hasty
Jun 6, 1906
Jan 19, 1910

J. A. Simpson
Apr 9, 1852
Dec 23, 1918

Georgeann C., Daughter of
G. W. & V. V. P. Byrom
Sep 4, 1862
Oct 19, 1863
Age: 1y, 1m, 15d.

Victoria V. P., wife of
G. W. Byrom
May 22, 1840
Jan 28, 1891
&
Mollie O., wife of
J. A. Simpson
Jul 8, 1859
Mar 20, 1886

Waid M. Sanders
Nov 16, 1875
Sep 3, 1954
&
Vera I. Sanders
Aug 8, 1881
Dec 25, 1955

Susan Mashburn
Feb 25, 1811
Sep 27, 1888

Nancy L. J., Daughter of
J. B. & S. W. Muse
Aug 13, 1864
Nov 2, 1864
Age: 2m, 20d.

CUMBERLAND SPRINGS QUADRANGLE

John P. M., Son of
Joab B. & Sopia H. Muse
Mar 2, 1863
Aug 11, 1863
Age: 5m, 9d.

Daniel P., Son of
Alison & Omega Muse
Nov 1, 1841
Aug 13, 1863
Age: 21y, 10m, 12d.

James D., Son of
Alison & Omega Muse
Nov 17, 1854
May 4, 1855
Age: 5m, 17d.

W. D., Son of
Alison & Omega Muse
May 7, 1852
Sep 28, 1852
Age: 4m, 21d.

Delila J., Daughter of
Alison & Omega Muse
Jun 21, 1848
Nov 22, 1864
Age: 16y, 5m, 1d.

Eli B., Son of
Alison & Omega Muse
Oct 15, 1832
Dec 6, 1857
Age: 25y, 1m, 21d.

Abner L., Son of
Alison & Omega Muse
Oct 30, 1847
Mar 6, 1863
Age: 16y, 4m, 6d.

Omega C. Ivy, Daughter of
Alison & Omega Muse &
Consort of J. H. Ivy
Jun 19, 1834
Dec 29, 1858
Married Dec 30, 1852
Age: 24y, 6m, 10d.

Sarah A., Daughter of
Alison & Omega Muse, &
Consort of Rise Simpson
Oct 20, 1839
Aug 20, 1860
Married Dec 18, 1856
Age: 20y, 9m, 24d.

Alison Muse, Consort of
Omega Muse
May 28, 1811
Apr 5, 1857
Married Dec 9, 1830
Age: 45y, 10m, 7d.

Omega, wife of
A. Muse
Aug 30, 1811
Jun 1, 1861
Married Dec 9, 1830
Age: 49y, 8m, 1d.

"Daddy"
Lois Edward Tankersley
Oct 1, 1896
Jan 28, 1972
&
"Mother"
Gracie Sanders Tankersley
Jun 11, 1899

James W. Simpson
Nov 9, 1850
Dec 11, 1928
& wife
Jane Simpson
Feb 15, 1856
Nov 1, 1934

H. M. Spann
Jan 9, 1835
Aug 11, 1911
&
M. H. Spann
Jan 28, 1832
Jan 26, 1907

N. A. Spann
Feb 12, 1859
(no date)
&
Z. E. Spann
Sep 12, 1861
Jul 28, 1927

Denis Holt
Mar 1, 1848
May 13, 1906

Nancy Hardy, wife of
Bill Hall
(no dates)

L. Y Sanders
Nov 22, 1864
(fieldstone)

Annie D. Sanders
1793-1862

Elizabeth C. Daniel
1757-1853

-------- Neal
Nov 1, 1856
--- 31, 1857
(fieldstone, broken)

-------- Neal
Dec 21, 1839
Feb 22, 1857
(fieldstone, broken)

Rev. William H. Neal
Sep 1818
Sep 1882

Baby Son of
J. W. Majors & wife
Nov 29, 1901
Dec 1, 1901

Johnnie Ruth Neal
Nov 23, 1911
Mar 19, 1931

John Neal
1878-1950
&
Ella Neal
1882-1970
(Mattie L.)

Byrd M. Neal
Sep 2, 1901
Sep 8, 1962
&
Lonnie Neal
Aug 5, 1900
Sep 29, 1968
& Son
Aubrey Neal
Apr 7, 1919

Buford Hall
Oct 9, 1905
Oct 6, 1918

Maria Millsap
Died Apr 4, 1914
(fieldstone)

Mike Millsap
Apr 20, 1845
Oct 17, 1926

Vinettie Sanders
1878-1878

Eli Sanders
Oct 2, 1853
Nov 18, 1882

W. B. Sanders
Mar 31, 1818
Mar 28, 1900

Martha Sanders
Dec 28, 1821
Jun 25, 1900

George W. Sanders
Feb 15, 1838
Apr 13, 1905

Martha J., wife of
George W. Sanders
Feb 25, 1840
Feb 27, 1897

Dellah P. Sanders
Nov 20, 1871
Sep 3, 1872

William A. Sanders
Oct 21, 1867
Sep 6, 1868

Sarah An, Daughter of
T. H. & M. J. Baget
Nov 3, 1859
Jan 13, 1860

----- M. Shasteen
(info gone, fieldstone)

Willie May Hall
1914-1918
&
Gracie Hall
1910-1918

Florence Hall
May 2, 1913
Oct 8, 1918

W. H. "Bill" Hall
Sep 21, 1851
Nov 6, 1933

George Meakens Harper
1887-1890

Seliena Harper
Nov 6, 1855
Oct 27, 1937

J. W. Miles
Mar 12, 1855
Apr 11, 1926

Mary L. Miles
Aug 21, 1847
Jan 26, 1928

Willie P., Son of
J. W. & M. L. Miles
Oct 21, 1878
May 30, 1910

A. F. C. Browning
Dec 27, 1859
May 7, 1861
Age: 1y, 4m, 10d.
Son of W. M. &
R. M. Browning.

John W., Son of
W. M. & R. M. Browning
Feb 26, 1858
Jul 26, 1859

Luther Walter Millsap
Apr 23, 1909
Oct 25, 1912

Thomas Edward Millsap
May 17, 1912
Sep 7, 1912

L. W. Millsap
Nov 3, 1847
Jan 7, 1885
Age: 37y, 2m, 4d.

Lewis O. Hall
Feb 22, 1881
Jan 13, 1960
&
Lucy May Hall
May 1, 1889

CUMBERLAND SPRINGS QUADRANGLE

Bulh B. Grammer
Nov 4, 1836
Sep 3, 1918

Nancy, wife of
Mike Millsap
Mar 2, 1845
Dec 22, 1886

G. W., Son of
Mr. & Mrs. Unos Hasty
Oct 24, 1932
Jan 9, 1933

Jessie Maie Golden
May 8, 1913
Nov 21, 1949

------ Stewart, wife of
A. A. Simpson
1849-1924

Arthur Lee "Buster" Gore
Nov 14, 1896
Jan 16, 1959
&
Nancy Ann Gore
Jun 26, 1907

& Daughter
Infant Daughter Gore
B&D Oct 18, 1929

Marvin Henry Hall
Tennessee
Pvt Med Det 1975 SVC Unit
WW II
Dec 8, 1899
Feb 26, 1966

John M. Hall
Jan 12, 1877
Jun 20, 1970
&
Alpha B. Hall
Apr 18, 1881
Oct 9, 1961

Roy Hall
(no dates, fieldstone)

Hall
(no dates, fieldstone)

Media Simpson
Jan 20, 1869
Apr 19, 1909

Alma Simpson
Died Oct 30, 1894
Age: (not given)

J. H. Ivey
Apr 12, 1855
Aug 19, 1900

Sarah Jane Stewart
Nov 17, 1864
Jun 5, 1921

Newman Stewart
1858-1921
&
Sallie M. Stewart
1867-1950

Eller E. Stewart
Oct 10, 1875
May 14, 1940

William Thomas Stewart
Jun 9, 1871
May 23, 1938

C. H. Stewart
1846-1934
& wife
A. A. Simpson Stewart
1849-1924

W. H. Anderton
Feb 7, 1826
Oct 11, 1896
& wife
M. E. Anderton
Nov 12, 1834
Mar 9, 1902

W. H., Son of
W. H. & M. Anderton
Apr 17, 1862
Jan 10, 1878
"Little Willie Sleeps".

F. R. Woodard
Nov 27, 1846
Nov 12, 1912

Infant Smith
1963-1963
(TM)

L. M. Smith
(TM: no dates)

Henry J. Crowell
1899-1961

"Father"
Joe Nelson
1885-1968
&
"Mother"
Ida Hall Nelson
1884-1973
& Daughter
Georgia Nelson
Age: 13 months
(no dates)

Cilla Hardy
(no dates)
&
Susie Hardy
(no dates)
&
Mollie Hardy
(no dates)

Jim "Shelt" Hardy
1845-1934
&
Sarah "Sack" Hardy
1850-1929

Sarah W. Simpson, wife of
T. C. Warren
Jan 26, 1868
Aug 15, 1895
Age: 27y, 6m, 19d.

Cora A. Simpson
Feb 19, 1877
Mar 3, 1896
Age: 19y, 0m, 14d.

Rice Simpson
Dec 21, 1836
Aug 1, 1903

Charity Sanders
Feb 23, 1879
Jul 16, 1897

Nancy M. Sanders
Oct 29, 1857
Aug 22, 1897

George Sanders
Nov 28, 1894
Apr 22, 1911

Rollie Clifton, Son of
J. P. & Minnie Sanders
Oct 16, 1904
Oct 17, 1914

William R. Sanders
Dec 22, 1851
Jun 1, 1920

J. P. "Pink" Sanders
1877-1942
&
Minnie Sanders
1881-1952

Mary E. Sanders
Sep 28, 1883
Aug 5, 1961

Henry A. Sanders
Jan 28, 1881
Jul 18, 1961
&
Elsie W. Sanders
Jul 13, 1893
Nov 19, 1928

Johnny P., Son of
C. A. & T. A. Majors
May 10, 1867
Feb 27, 1885

Francis A., Daughter of
G. & E. Lewis
May 25, 1864
Oct 4, 1868
Age: 4y, 4m, 9d.

Allen T., Son of
G. L. & E. Lewis
Aug 20, 1873
May 1, 1874
Age: 8m, 1d.

Giles M. Searcy
1889-1952
(Thompson FH)

Lula S. Searcy
1889-1963
(Howell-Thompson FH)

J. F. Hasty
Dec 11, 1853
(no date)
&
Adline Hasty
Mar 10, 1842
Jul 1, 1918

Sarah Elizabeth, Daughter
of Jas. W. &
Catharine Byrom
Mar 29, 1876
Aug 12, 1876

Mary, Daughter of
Jas. W. & Catharine Byrom
Jan 8, 1882
Feb 27, 1885
Age: 3y, 24d.

Charles W. Byrom
Nov 13, 1888
Oct 3, 1894

Clatie, Daughter of
R. L. & Lucy Byrom
Jul 21, 1892
Oct 27, 1894
&
Lucy LoRenzie, Daughter
of R. L. & Lucy Byrom
Oct 13, 1900
Sep 10, 1901

Infant Daughter of
E. & Gabrel Lewis
Stillborn
Apr 10, 1875

Martha A., Daughter of
G. & E. Lewis
Jul 29, 1871
May 25, 1876
Age: 4y, 10m, 21d.

"Father"
T. E. Turner
Jun 29, 1824
Jun 18, 1906
&
"Mother"
M. E. Turner
Nov 30, 1838
Mar 8, 1921

CUMBERLAND SPRINGS QUADRANGLE

S. A. Millsap
(no dates, fieldstone)

Mar Mil (Millsap)
(no dates, fieldstone)

S. M. Mill (Millsap)
(no dates, fieldstone)

Essie Hardy
1887-1959

Isaiah Hardy
Died 1944
Age: (not given)

Jep Hardy
(no dates)

Polly A., wife of
W. J. Hardy
1848-1893

Dolly, Daughter of
J. W. & S. A. Hardy
1873-1894

Jeffery C. Deaton
May 25, 1961
May 27, 1961

Elisabeth, wife of
G. Lewis
Mar 17, 1835
Jan 18, 1877

S. E., wife of
J. W. Anderton &
Daughter of
R. B. & Margaret
Mashburn
Dec 20, 1861
Apr 27, 1884

Essie Anderton
Jul 17, 1892
Jan 4, 1894

R. B. Mashburn
Jun 25, 1834
Dec 4, 1906
& wife
Margaret Mashburn
May 19, 1836
Aug 8, 1909

Many unmarked graves.

W. T. Mashburn
Mar 23, 1866
Oct 10, 1893
Age: 27y, 6m, 17d.

Lillie M. Mashburn
Mar 21, 1892
Mar 7, 1894

Marilda, Daughter of
R. B. & Margaret Mashburn
Jul 22, 1869
Dec 11, 1903
Age: 34y, 4m, 19d.

John R. Mashburn
Dec 16, 1863
Jun 28, 1912

T. L. D. Simpson
Oct 9, 1876
Jun 21, 1905

L. C. Davis
Aug 1, 1830
Jun 31, 1885
(fieldstone)

E. A. Davis
Dec 1, 1875
Aug 1, 1884
(fieldstone)

M. E. Davis
Feb 26, 1823
Aug 1, 1900
(fieldstone)

James Poe
Nov 8, 1803
Nov 12, 1868
Age: 65y, 4d.

Polly, wife of
James Poe
Nov 7, 1801
Mar 12, 1890

Thomas B. Poe
Sep 3, 1827
Jun 30, 1888
&
Winnie A. Poe
Jan 11, 1834
May 1, 1897

Elda, Son of
Samuel J. &
Susan I. Shasteen
Sep 13, 1891
Sep 24, 1892

* *

SAWYER CEMETERY

LOCATION: At Bakertown.

Carrol Evans
May 27, 1824
May 27, 1908
&
Millie Evans
Mar 29, 1822
May 22, 1909

Emma Lee Painter
1907-1965
(Harrison FH)

Luther M. Huskey
Died Apr 7, 1910
Age: 24 years.

Majorie, Daughter of
L. M. & Stella Huskey
Died Sep 4, 1910
Age: 15 months.

Lacy M. Huskey
May 14, 1891
Sep 15, 1891

Roy P. Huskey
Apr 22, 1890
Feb 21, 1920

Fred R. Huskey
Aug 6, 1895
Jan 14, 1919

W. C.(William) Sawyer
Aug 7, 1872
Dec 30, 1952

Cynthia, wife of
J. B. Huskey
Sep 2, 1865
May 28, 1918

Jim Sawyer
Mar 10, 1849
Dec 24, 1911
&
Mattie Sawyer
Oct 1, 1854
Oct 11, 1934

Donnie B. Huskey
Nov 14, 1887
Dec 7, 1908

Carl L., Son of
Joe & Katie McKinney
Jan 19, 1910
Jun 4, 1911

Dock Branch
Nov 11, 1890
Dec 15, 1917

Several unmarked graves.
Several graves with fieldstones, no inscriptions.

Grandmothers:
Harden & Whitlock
(no other information)

Morrison, Jr., Son of
M. N. & L. L. Branch
Sep 21, 1918
Jan 13, 1927

Sallie Waggoner, wife of
Jim Golden
Mar 15, 1881
Mar 21, 1920

Alfred L. Chapman
1867-1950
&
Emma W. Chapman
1868-1925

Annie Gladys Chapman
1900-

* *

CUMBERLAND SPRINGS QUADRANGLE

SMITH CHAPEL CEMETERY

LOCATION: Five miles NE of Lynchburg on Highway # 55.

George Dodson
1890-1966
(Motlow-Moore FH)

Infant Dodson
1966-1966
(Howell-Thompson FH)

J. W. Sawyer
Oct 12, 1847
Mar 27, 1901

John Albert Simmons
1884-1947

Margaret D. Pollock
1863-1956
(Daves-Culbertson FH)

John William Pollock
1866-1961
(Daves-Culbertson FH)

Porter D. Emeritt
1938-1956
(Gowen FH)

John O. Ray
Nov 29, 1828
May 5, 1893

Zella, Daughter of
J. M. & Sallie A. Lee
Oct 10, 1878
Mar 22, 1896

Ellen, wife of
J S. Smith
Died Jun 9, 1898
Age: 18y, 5m, 13d.

Joseph M Lee
Feb 14, 1837
Sep 12, 1918
&
Sallie A Lee
Nov 24, 1856
Oct 24, 1896

Ethel, Daughter of
J. M. & Sallie A. Lee
Nov 13, 1894
Oct 29, 1894
(We believe these dates
are reversed)

O. G. Steagall
Husband of
Mary Steagall
Jun 10, 1806
Feb 14, 1892

Mary, wife of
O. G. Steagall
Feb 16, 1807
Aug 31, 1885

J. D. Burgess
Jul 24, 1894

&
Ola Burgess
Sep 16, 1898
Jun 30, 1960

Lee J., Son of
J. D. & Ola Burgess
Oct 30, 1920
Jan 14, 1922

Marie S., Daughter of
J. D. & Ola Burgess
1923-1924
Age: 16 months.

L. F. Frame
1911-1956
&
May Frame
1907-1948

Ernest W. Frame
1886-1954
&
Mary E. Frame
1878-1951

Percy M. Miller
May 15, 1902
Nov 25, 1962
&
Gladys O. Miller
Nov 28, 1903
Feb 20, 1939

Ollie Milton Miller
Mar 19, 1929
Dec 10, 1931

Sam Dillingham
May 11, 1836
Dec 23, 1917
&
Mary Dillingham
Apr 12, 1837
Dec 10, 1903

James M. Mullins
Mar 11, 1861
Mar 30, 1924
&
Annie Lee Mullins
Nov 27, 1865
Aug 7, 1922

Hubert Mullins
1902-1944
&
Bettie Mullins
1905-

Floyd Mullins
1895-1973
(Daves-Culbertson FH)

John Hollis Mullins
Jan 1, 1899
Feb 24, 1938
&
Hattie Lee Mullins
Oct 23, 1900
Feb 8, 1954

Freddy Martin
1969-1969
(Tullahoma FH)

Willie Lee McNutt
1881-1957
(Daves-Culbertson FH)

Ollie Reed
1866-1928
&
Fannie Reed
1871-19(no date)

Alex. Buchanan
Jan 24, 1848
Apr 7, 1926
&
Josie Buchanan
Apr 30, 1854
Jan 9, 1922

Ogia Buchanan
Jul 31, 1874
Aug 10, 1900
&
Lula Buchanan
May 15, 1884
Aug 7, 1900

Ara, Daughter of
M. A. & Josie Buchanan
Aug 17, 1890
Nov 26, 1890

Minnie, Daughter of
M. A. & Josie Buchanan
Aug 25, 1879
Dec 17, 1882

Thomas Raymond Reed
Jul 2, 1919

&
Christine Marie Reed
May 15, 1923
Jan 7, 1973

Lawrence Reed
1896-1959
&
Edna L. Reed
1903-1937

Margorie Cunningham
1918-1935

David H. Cunningham
1882-1939
&
Mary J. Cunningham
1899-19

James R. McNutt
1855-1925
&
Pearl F. McNutt
1888-1970

J. P. Locke
1835-1910

Terry Raney
May 1, 1919
Jul 23, 1919

Robert Lee Raney
Jan 11, 1878
Sep 4, 1929
&
Onie L. Raney
Aug 11, 1888

Brenda Gayle Raney
Feb 23, 1955
Mar 11, 1955

John R. Burgess
Dec 19, 1857
Apr 28, 1930
&
Polly Burgess
Jan 19, 1858
Apr 16, 1945

Ollie B. Bateman
1900-1962
(Harrison FH)

Connie Bateman
1952-1952
(Harrison FH)

Charlie L. Bryant
1863-1943
&
Fronie W. Bryant
1872-1950

Mary J. Bryant
Sep 5, 1951
Sep 9, 1951

John Henry Allen
1848-1924
&
Sue Hobbs Allen
1854-1933

Mary McNabb Bryant
Dec 11, 1831
Nov 9, 1904

CUMBERLAND SPRINGS QUADRANGLE

Allie G., Son of
R. A. & Mertie Reed
Jan 13, 1903
Dec 18, 1905

Samuel J. Burt
Oct 26, 1853
Jan 24, 1923
  & wife
Mary L. Ray Burt
Apr 9, 1854
Aug 11, 1909

Infant Son of
S. J. & M. L. Burt
B&D May 14, 1896

Juda, wife of
A. J. Burt
Jan 2, 1820
Sep 12, 1886

George R. Petty
Tennessee
Pvt 7 Receiving Co WW I
May 25, 1894
Oct 6, 1967
(Family marker has
born Mar 15, 1894)
&
Florence E. Petty
Jun 19, 1898
(TM: 1972)

George Douglass Petty
Nov 13, 1894
Jan 14, 1972
&
Vernie Cheshire Petty
May 6, 1893
Oct 26, 1969

William Allen
1824-1875
&
Elizabeth Allen
1827-1920

Joe R.(Richard) Frame
1862-1952
&
Cordie Frame
1868-1935

Bettie Dillingham, wife of
Watt Ray & Mother of
Pauline Cooper &
Bob Lacy.
Apr 28, 1872
Oct 1, 1908

Infant Son of
Watt & Bettie Ray
Died Apr 1894
Age: (not given)

John C. Ray
1828-1893
&
A. Jane Ray
1833-1915

William C. Ray
Feb 15, 1831
Nov 14, 1900
&
Elizabeth M. Ray
Mar 14, 1835
Jun 30, 1913

Mary Ray
Mar 30, 1869
Dec 18, 1900

Jennie Myrtle, Daughter of
J. C. & Jane Ray
Jun 9, 1879
Mar 10, 1888

Roy "Bud" Sullenger
Aug 13, 1893
May 23, 1965
&
Lucy Jean Sullenger
Aug 17, 1898

Sallie A. Allen, wife of
J. C. Kimbro
Feb 17, 1852
Jul 6, 1905

John Enoch Pearson
Apr 23, 1826
Jul 18, 1910
&
Jane Newsom Pearson
Apr 6, 1834
Aug 9, 1908

George T. Pearson
1854-1944

Almeda, Daughter of
J. H. & M. S. Cur
Died May 2, 1868
Age: (deep in ground)

William Franklin Wooten
Sep 30, 1870
Oct 20, 1946
&
Dora Fuller Wooten
Aug 14, 1873
Jul 21, 1958

Leona, Daughter of
Dora & Frank Wooten
Nov 8, 1898
Oct 21, 1902

E. J. Nutt, wife of
J. W. Wooten
Apr 14, 1853
Dec 29, 1903

J. W. Wooten
1837-1934

Jessie Mai Wooten
May 11, 1903
Mar 22, 1907

Felix Z. Wooten
Mar 1, 1884
Nov 8, 1915

Bettie Wooten
1881-1947

Jesse Wooten
1874-1952

Fannie Wooten Wiggs
1876-1906

Willie Wiggs
1898-1914

William Stone
May 2, 1825
Sep 25, 1905
&
Sarah Stone
May 9, 1830
Nov 24, 1897

Here lies
W. A. & M. A. Nix
(no dates)

Perlina, wife of
W. P. Floyd & Daughter
of William & Sarah Stone
Dec 19, 1861
Apr 21, 1886

Thomas Henry Wooten
Dec 12, 1878
Jun 29, 1933
&
Lydia Caroline Wooten
Apr 3, 1880
May 9, 1970

C. J. High
Oct 2, 1846
Nov 20, 1923
&
Martha L. High
Mar 23, 1854
Nov 23, 1944

G. A. High
Feb 23, 1885
Jun 23, 1915

Mary Holland High
Jun 20, 1925
Oct 24, 1927

William C. High
1881-1960
&
Irene T. High
1893-
Married Oct 19, 1909

Mildred M. High, wife of
Anthony T. Angelone
Nov 29, 1914
Sep 1, 1952

Joseph W. Bennett
1859-1936
&
Tennie Nix Bennett
1875-1954

Joe William Bennett, Jr.
May 14, 1909
Jan 15, 1970

Charlie, Son of
W. L. & N. S. Anderson
Sep 14, 1894
Nov 24, 1895

Harold Cyree
Feb 10, 1923
Jun 1, 1924

J. Luther Cyree
Jul 9, 1889
Mar 20, 1957
&
Margaret H. Cyree
Jul 21, 1893

Walter T. Womble
Nov 5, 1911
Feb 11, 1973
&
Cova H. Womble
Jan 30, 1914

Married Jun 3, 1938

Lizzie Tucker
1896-1963
(Motlow-Moore FH)

Martha Ward
Jul 28, 1916
May 24, 1937

Billie Davis
Oct 27, 1900
Dec 6, 1920
&
J. W. Davis
Dec 26, 1871
(no date)
&
Lula Davis
Feb 20, 1867
Feb 27, 1943

Donie Prince
May 4, 1868
Sep 19, 1939
& Sister
Irene Prince Cunningham
Mar 23, 1871
Jan 28, 1940

Ben Prince
May 20, 1837
Apr 23, 1919
&
Mary Prince
Nov 9, 1840
Dec 22, 1930

CUMBERLAND SPRINGS QUADRANGLE

W. M. Gentry
Aug 10, 1869
Dec 29, 1924
&
Ellen Gentry
Nov 16, 1873
Dec 20, 1915

Emory T. Gentry
1866-1943
&
Laura B. Gentry
1867-1953

Nora Gentry
Aug 27, 1867
Jul 27, 1909

Benton Bell Templeton
Jun 5, 1844
Apr 13, 1929
&
Martha E. Templeton
Nov 16, 1844
May 17, 1912

John Harvey Templeton
Nov 16, 1882
Jan 20, 1887

Mary Katie Templeton
Feb 18, 1880
Dec 13, 1880

Infant Son of
W. P. & Ann Floyd
Died Jan 27, 1891
Age: (not given)

Vernon L. Stewart
Mar 18, 1908
Apr 12, 1971
&
Connie C. Stewart
Oct 27, 1910
(TM: 1973)
(Tullahoma FH)

Jasper N. Gibbs
May 2, 1878
Oct 7, 1964
&
Mary T. Gibbs
Jun 1, 1881
Jul 4, 1967

"Mother"
Carmie Couser
Jan 31, 1895

& Daughter
Colleen Couser
Apr 5, 1931
Jun 10, 1948

W. B. Stephens
May 25, 1865
Sep 2, 1927
&
Dora B. Stephens
Jan 8, 1873
Oct 7, 1964

T. J. Stephens
Mar 3, 1846
Apr 21, 1910
&
Louisa Hix Stephens
Sep 19, 1846
May 4, 1910

Samuel Leander Fariss
Dec 2, 1887
Sep 2, 1902

Joshua Y. Price
May 8, 1835
Jan 17, 1914

James Frank "Shug" Womble
Aug 8, 1913
Sep 15, 1971
&
Maude Stewart Womble
Nov 18, 1922

Henry Clinton Womble
Tennessee
Pfc Ord Dept WW I
Aug 7, 1891
May 13, 1960

Lota Mae Brinkley Womble
Aug 23, 1896
Jun 10, 1964

Jim W. Womble
Apr 13, 1885
Jan 8, 1956
&
Georgia Burgess Womble
Jan 15, 1887
Oct 14, 1972

Wilson Womble
Apr 6, 1940
May 23, 1955

Granville Womble
Jan 5, 1856
May 15, 1936
&
Mary Ellen Womble
Aug 28, 1851
Jan 12, 1932

Carroll M., Son of
Joseph S. & Nancy Evaline
Hurdlow
Oct 11, 1882
Nov 2, 1884

Joseph S. Hurdlow
Jun 5, 1844
Jun 1, 1888
&
Nancy Evaline Hurdlow
Sep 25, 1848
Jul 24, 1897

Samuel K. Fariss
Sep 25, 1822
Dec 28, 1899
&
Katharine M. Fariss
Sep 6, 1822
Mar 22, 1891

Infant Son of
C. J. & Annie Enochs
Died Sep 26, 1895
Age: (not given)

John B. Fariss
Mar 21, 1860
Nov 7, 1917
&
Tennie Fariss
Sep 25, 1865
Sep 15, 1931

Fletcher M. Fariss
1855-1929
&
Mary V. Fariss
1858-1929
"Brother & Sister".

Thomas J. Fariss
1862-1949
&
Esther E. Fariss
1874-1964

Hollis D. Reed
Sep 3, 1908

&
Grace P. Reed
Aug 31, 1909

G. L. Reed
Aug 7, 1904

&
Georgia M. Reed
May 1, 1908

Marvin E. Gambill
1880-1934
&
Lillian M. Gambill
1887-1963

Elijah Thomas Floyd
1848-1887
&
Mary Pearson Floyd
1850-1940

William P. "Cage" Floyd
Dec 12, 1855
Nov 22, 1937
&
Ann Price Floyd
Sep 29, 1869
Feb 11, 1940

Sallie P., wife of
J. Y. Price
Sep 15, 1843
Sep 20, 1903

Emma Holt Pinkerton
Apr 9, 1899
Jul 30, 1970

John T. Kelly
Nov 19, 1873
Jan 8, 1963
&
Ida L. Kelly
Feb 14, 1881
Jul 24, 1967

Johnnie Maude Kelly
Aug 29, 1901

John A. Parks
Oct 13, 1893
Nov 6, 1952
&
Essie G. Parks
Feb 29, 1886
Feb 12, 1951

John B. Price
Jul 2, 1875
Jun 30, 1938
&
Finettie Holt Price
Apr 23, 1873
Aug 29, 1932

Effie Thorne
1885-1964
(Harrison FH)

J. L. Holt
Feb 19, 1834
Mar 18, 1903
&
Angeline Davis Holt
Oct 12, 1838
Feb 2, 1889

William Felix, Son of
J. L. & Angeline Holt
Feb 16, 1860
Nov 17, 1878

Mary D., wife of
H. H. Holt
Aug 10, 1866
Jul 30, 1899

CUMBERLAND SPRINGS QUADRANGLE

Henry H. Holt
1862-1938
&
Odell Neece Holt
1873-1936

Finettie Angeline, Daughter
of H. H. & Mary Holt
Feb 25, 1897
Jun 23, 1897

Will P. Holt
Apr 30, 1884
Jan 13, 1932

Sarah E. Holt
Feb 5, 1884
Dec 5, 1937

James L. Holt
1868-1934
&
Janie Holt
1872-1946

Thomas F. Parks
Apr 9, 1868
Sep 24, 1944
&
Fannie H. Parks
Jul 17, 1871
Sep 3, 1950

Isaac Parks
1867-1938
&
Bena Parks
1868-1924

Hiram Warner
Dec 25, 1852
Jun 17, 1908

Bettie P. Hix
Apr 16, 1856
Jan 1, 1918

Joshua W. Hix
Nov 7, 1854
May 1, 1902

J. Holt, Son of
Josh & Bettie Holt Hix
Apr 4, 1894
Oct 7, 1894

Albert H. Davis
Sep 30, 1875
Jan 28, 1950
&
Mary Ray Davis
Jun 28, 1879
Jan 18, 1937

William M. Davis
Jan 11, 1847
(no date)
&
Perlina E. Davis
May 3, 1847
Aug 24, 1915

Mary F. Davis
Mar 7, 1867
Sep 30, 1953

John V. Davis
Apr 12, 1857
Feb 5, 1935

Miss Lizzie Davis,
Apr 10, 1879
She was married to
Mr. E. D. Morgan
Mrs. Lizzie Morgan
Married Jul 24, 1902
Died Jul 30, 1904

N. J., wife of
John V. Davis
May 5, 1857
Feb 1, 1884

Annie P., wife of
Felix T. Davis
Feb 2, 1817
Feb 28, 1900

Sarah R., wife of
J. W. M. Dance
Dec 18, 1826
Mar 25, 1887

J. W. M. Dance
May 5, 1826
Nov 30, 1902

S. M. Dance
Dec 9, 1854
Apr 6, 1915
&
Mary Dance
Aug 14, 1860
Apr 23, 1929

George W. Hurdlow
Co E 4th Ark. Cal.
Mar 9, 1832
Apr 28, 1922

Lucy Hurdlow
Nov 2, 1807
Feb 11, 1892

James P., Son of
J. W. & N. B. Weaver
Dec 5, 1904
Dec 19, 1904

James W. Weaver
Jul 10, 1875
Mar 31, 1956

Nora B. Silvertooth, wife
of J. W. Weaver
Jul 27, 1881
Oct 24, 1914

Joseph M. Silvertooth
1870-1937
&
Minnie A. Silvertooth
1878-1953

Robert B. Huskey
1870-1932
&
Cora E. Huskey
1882-1967

John Addison Holt
Apr 30, 1858
Jun 16, 1940
&
Sonie Dillingham Holt
May 18, 1858
May 16, 1921

Infant Daughter of
J. L. & Angeline Holt
B&D Jul 12, 1879

William D. Anthony
Mar 14, 1866
Oct 4, 1956

Susan E. Anthony
Oct 7, 1865
Jan 29, 1936

Johnie Bob, Son of
W. D. & S. E. Anthony
Feb 1, 1898
Nov 7, 1898

J. H. Silvertooth
Feb 3, 1846
Apr 11, 1902
&
Fannie Silvertooth
Oct 15, 1842
Feb 23, 1916

Cora E., Daughter of
J. H. & Fannie Silvertooth
Mar 28, 1878
Mar 14, 1888

H. W. Silvertooth
Jun 28, 1875
Oct 27, 1937

Bessie Boyd Silvertooth
Jun 7, 1884
Jan 23, 1959

James Silvertooth
B&D Mar 8, 1908

Walter Hooper Silvertooth
1910-1963
(Motlow-Moore FH)

S. Holt Bennett
Feb 28, 1922
Jun 22, 1973
&
Arlene W. Bennett
Feb 8, 1923

Married Jul 31, 1942

Charles U. Dillingham
Dec 22, 1880
Nov 10, 1959
&
Lena Ladd Dillingham
Aug 6, 1883
Nov 10, 1952

Infant of
H. B. & M. A. Dillingham
May 18, 1887
Jun 17, 1887

Britt Dillingham
Dec 3, 1844
Feb 24, 1926
&
Millie Dillingham
Oct 10, 1853
Aug 13, 1904

T. W. Dance
1891-1964
&
Maggie Dance
1861-1940
&
W. S. Dance
1859-1929

Della Anderson
1877-1966
(Daves-Culbertson FH)

Elizabeth A., wife of
R. M. Couser
May 18, 1818
Dec 25, 1885

Infant Son of
Mr. & Mrs. S. A. Mullins
B&D Dec 24, 1899

K. L. Hamlin
Mar 12, 1827
Dec 27, 1904

Thomas C. Couser
Mar 12, 1891
May 8, 1948

Marion T. Brown
Aug 5, 1866
Jul 12, 1940

Elijah N. Bobo
Aug 30, 1870
May 17, 1928
&
Annie Bobo
Aug 12, 1878
May 9, 1930

Infant Son of
L. C. & Nora Bobo
Jul 18, 1920

CUMBERLAND SPRINGS QUADRANGLE

L. L. Bobo
Feb 8, 1850
Oct 16, 1920
&
Sarah J., wife of
L. L. Bobo & Daughter of
Thomas Gore & wife
Mar 20, 1849
Jun 8, 1904
Married Lacy L. Bobo
Nov 18, 1869

Bular, Daughter of
Lacy L. & Sarah Bobo
Mar 1, 1879
Jan 3, 1881

Infant Daughter of
L. L. & S. J. Bobo
Sep 10, 1888
Sep 17, 1888

Manon P. Couser
Dec 25, 1852
Feb 22, 1917
&
Mollie A. Couser
Apr 20, 1851
Sep 19, 1907

Marion L. Couser
Mar 24, 1878
Apr 6, 1926

Joseph F. Daniel
Sep 30, 1857
Dec 1, 1915
&
Susan D. Daniel
Mar 15, 1856
Jul 23, 1942

Charlie U. Daniel
Jun 10, 1890
Aug 1, 1970

Thomas Gore
Aug 8, 1811
May 21, 1890

Elvira, wife of
Thomas Gore
Jun 17, 1817
Sep 25, 1886

Thomas J. Gore
May 31, 1858
Sep 29, 1923
Age: 65y, 5m.

Infants,
Son & Daughter of
T. J. & Lula Gore
Jan 6, 1903
Sep 17, 1904

Elva Couser Richter
Feb 9, 1907
Sep 19, 1936

Estle Weaver
1891-1945
Tenn Pvt Inf
&
Effie Weaver
1888-19

Robert Kenneth Couser
Feb 3, 1884
Feb 21, 1929
&
Sallie May Couser
Jan 24, 1883
Oct 22, 1956

Infant Son of
M. P. & Mollie Couser
Sep 23, 1888

Thomas Bennett
Apr 29, 1847
Feb 10, 1889

Sarah Couser Bennett
Sep 16, 1848
May 1, 1878

Mary Bennett
Jul 15, 1876
May 18, 1881

James T. Martin
1885-1960
&
Mollie B. Martin
1889-19

Noah A. Martin
1889-1956
(Harrison FH)

William C. Martin
Aug 21, 1871
Jun 2, 1947
&
Mary Louetta Martin
Jun 25, 1878
(no date)

Robert Taylor Martin
Dec 28, 1905
Apr 29, 1913

M. L. Couser
Mar 22, 1856
Feb 25, 1922
&
Martha J. Couser
Jul 22, 1860
Jun 18, 1932

Newt Cates
1854-1930
&
Rebecca Cates
1859-1934

Fannie E. Cates
1887-1941

Wyatt T. Woodruff
Jul 31, 1853
Sep 17, 1907

Newton Dillingham
Sep 22, 1848
Dec 23, 1921
&
Nannie Dillingham
Feb 22, 1850
Apr 25, 1932

Margaret Dillingham
Oct 10, 1833
Nov 24, 1919

Martha K. Pierce
1877-1954

Rhoda Auston
Aug 13, 1833
May 30, 1900

James T. Riddle
Jun 12, 1875
Jul 18, 1952
&
Nora L. Riddle
Mar 11, 1877
(no date)

Mary E., wife of
J. M. Green
Dec 20, 1857
Nov 8, 1917

Norman Leslie, Son of
Gustus & Dora Green
Jun 28, 1908
Nov 1, 1913

William G. Green
Tennessee
Sgt 60 Inf WW II
Feb 13, 1916
Aug 11, 1944

Gustus L. Green
Nov 20, 1880
Oct 20, 1966
&
Dora I. Green
Aug 11, 1884
Jul 15, 1960

Ronnie Harold Green
1946-1946

Cecil Haynes
Tennessee
Cpl U. S. Army WW II
Feb 4, 1919
Dec 29, 1969

Wilburn A. Haynes
Aug 12, 1874
Oct 22, 1950
&
Nancy C. Haynes
Mar 19, 1882
Nov 1, 1963

Tommie E. Haynes
Jun 26, 1906
Dec 7, 1948

Lacy Gowen Mullins
Apr 17, 1909
Apr 27, 1972

Manon G. Pearson
Dec 12, 1820
Oct 30, 1900

A. J. Parks
Feb 19, 1844
Oct 10, 1890
&
Elizabeth Parks
Mar 22, 1847
Jul 22, 1905

T. Anderson
Jul 29, 1849
Jun 29, 1929
&
Margaret A. Anderson
Feb 2, 1849
Apr 15, 1929

Harry Woosley
1896-1961
(Tullahoma FH)

Mamie Woosley
1896-1967
(Tullahoma FH)

Willie Womble
Dec 28, 1899
Mar 10, 1913

E. B. Malone
Died Oct 31, 1930
Age: (not given)

Jane Malone
Died Nov 13, 1943
Age: (not given)

Mary Horsefield
Oct 23, 1869
Jul 18, 1912

Linda B. Casteel
1914-1962
(Motlow-Moore FH)

Joseph E. Boyd
1891-(TM: 1974)
(Tullahoma FH)
&
Annie B. Boyd
1896-1964

Lissie E. Ray
1907-1969
(Tullahoma FH)

Annie M. Hicks
1900-1967
(Motlow-Moore FH)

CUMBERLAND SPRINGS QUADRANGLE

Infant Son of
T. J. & L. B. Hicks
B&D Jun 22, 1913

Samuel Mitchell
Feb 14, 1811
Apr 24, 1899
Age: 88y, 2m, 10d.
&
Susan C. Mitchell
Dec 17, 1841
Sep 19, 1886
Age: 45y, 9m, 2d.

Mamie M. Chapman
1893-1967
(Motlow-Moore FH)

Infant Son of
T. J. & L. B. Hicks
Mar 13, 1908

Lessie Mae Carter Farrar
Feb 22, 1913
May 5, 1971

Don Griffin
1943-1974
(Tullahoma FH)

Pvt Claude Hicks
Feb 15, 1917
Oct 29, 1944

T. J. Hicks
1879-1955

Laura Bell Hicks
Feb 18, 1879
Mar 15, 1921

Infant Hicks
Jan 23, 190-
(broken)

W. Charlie Ward
Jan 4, 1879
Oct 11, 1936
&
Annie Davis Ward
Jul 13, 1881

Robert W. Daniel
1886-1950
&
Vesta S. Daniel
1895-1969
Married Feb 12, 1912

Haywood Daniel
1914-1972
(Tullahoma FH)

Floyd Mullins
1895-1973
(Daves-Culbertson FH)

Nannie Smith Reese
1886-1952

Stanley Keith Sons
1974-1974
(Daves-Culbertson FH)

James Hulan Sons
1918-1970
(Daves-Culbertson FH)

Lillie D. Sons
1900-1968
(Harrison FH)

Joe L. Sons
1889-1970
(Harrison FH)

Several unmarked graves.

* *

TURKEY CREEK CHURCH CEMETERY

LOCATION: Two and one half miles SE of Cumberland Springs, between Hurricane Creek and Turkey Creek.

Infant Daughter of
J. H. & C. Byrom
Born Feb 8, 1878
Age: 2 days.

Henry A., Son of
J. H. & C. Byrom
Jan 30, 1876
Jul 17, 1877

Winnie, Daughter of
J. H. & C. Byrom
Dec 15, 1871
Jul 4, 1873

William Smith
Co F 4 Tenn Cav C.S.A.
Jan 2, 1834
Mar 30, 1882

I. G. Cobb
Mar 15, 1858
Mar 9, 1941
& wife
Mary R. Burt Cobb
Jan 21, 1859
Jun 21, 1935

Riggs Monroe Cobb
Tennessee
Pvt Btry E 138 field Arty
WW I
Aug 3, 1892
Dec 6, 1960

Richard Rogers Davis
Mar 3, 1904
Apr 17, 1964

Larkin Burt
Jan 28, 1892

&
Leona S. Burt
Dev 17, 1892
May 8, 1969
Married Dec 24, 1912

Tennessee, Daughter of
J. W. & E. Byrom
Sep 3, 1875
Drowned
Apr 6, 1877

Virginia Frances,
Daughter of
J. E. & A. E. Byrom
Jun 20, 1877
Apr 14, 1878

Mary A. J. Burt
May 13, 1874
Aug 15, 1874
Age: 2m, 2d.

Emily J. Burt
Jun 23, 1875
Aug 20, 1875

J. J. Burt
Oct 26, 1823
May 20, 1873

Thomas Albert Byrom
Oct 28, 1893

&
Fannie Mae Byrom
Aug 2, 1898
Feb 10, 1971

Walter Prince
Feb 28, 1873
Sep 7, 1952
&
Lula Prince
Dec 23, 1878
Sep 25, 1954

H. L. Byrom
Feb 18, 1824
Aug 7, 1889
&
W. C. Byrom
Jul 8, 1826
Aug 27, 1868

Elzira C. Cobb
Jul 5, 1857
Feb 28, 1923

J. W. Leach
Mar 12, 1843
Apr 9, 1925
& wife
Nancy E. Leach
May 7, 1850
Nov 20, 1927

Lucy F., Daughter of
J. W. & N. F. Leach
Aug 20, 1879
Feb 20, 1900

Charlie L. Edens
Oct 2, 1890
Jun 22, 1967
&
Lula Burt Edens
Nov 19, 1893

Married Jun 25, 1911

Roy E. Tankersley
Jun 25, 1895
Jan 13, 1972
&
Evelyn B. Tankersley
Jul 26, 1898

Married Dec 24, 1916

Jackson K. Cobb
Jan 18, 1855
Aug 25, 1943

Mary Almedia Cobb
Jan 6, 1868
May 24, 1954

Bessie Burt Cobb
Apr 28, 1900
Oct 29, 1952

Mary L. Bolin
Oct 4, 1873
Dec 28, 1877

Mary A. E. Chasteen
Nov 19, 1837
Feb 20, 1902

William Chasteen
Co C 4 Tenn Inf
C.S.A.

V. M.
(no dates)

M. M.
(no dates)

M. M.
(no dates)

CUMBERLAND SPRINGS QUADRANGLE

Edward Nichols Thomas
Tennessee
WT 2 U. S. Navy WW I
Sep 17, 1898
Mar 21, 1964
&
Goldie Coop Thomas
1902-

Mary E. Eggleston, wife of
C. F. Burt
Oct 17, 1839
Mar 29, 1890
Married Oct 14, 1855

William D. Burt
Aug 1, 1852
Jul 12, 1934
&
Ella Burt
Apr 13, 1860
Feb 16, 1953

Seth Lawson
(no dates)

Adelia, wife of
J. F. Burt
Mar 31, 1863
Jun 15, 1891

James T. Coop
Jan 22, 1838
Jun 12, 1904

Virginia A. Coop
Jun 3, 1840
Feb 9, 1918

William M. Coop
Aug 11, 1861
Mar 8, 1903

Sylvia Coop
Feb 26, 1902

J. Henry Coop
Jan 21, 1868
May 1, 1960

"Mother"
Martha Freeman
1869-1937
& "Son"
Frank Freeman
1889-1937
& "Son"
John Freeman
1898-1919

Infant Daughter of
Martha & Daniel Freeman
1903

Buan B. Smith
1907-1971

Dessie Mae Smith
Jul 30, 1898
Nov 4, 1964

Joe R. Smith
Mar 17, 1857
Feb 23, 1927
&
Ellen Smith
Nov 15, 1866
(no date)

Mary A., Daughter of
William & M. S. Tankersley
Aug 18, 1871
Dec 1, 1884

Erastus Tankersley
Aug 2, 1907
Jan 6, 1910

William Tankersley
Jul 8, 1840
Aug 26, 1904

Martha S. Tankersley
Mar 9, 1849
Jul 21, 1928

Joseph Fred Leach
1867-1956
(Daves-Culbertson FH)

Eddie Leach
1871-1951
(Harrison FH)

Maudie, Daughter of
J. F. & Eddie Leach
Nov 29, 1904
Aug 13, 1909

"Father"
Daniel Marshall Freeman
Nov 4, 1866
Jun 30, 1942
& "Daughter"
Lizzie Mae Freeman
Mar 12, 1901

Elizabeth Freeman Dyer
Jan 22, 1834
Mar 9, 1888

Alex H. Lynch
Apr 6, 1878
Aug 13, 1948
&
Sarah E. Lynch
Aug 20, 1880
Dec 20, 1953

Jack Wiley Kizziah
May 8, 1889
Dec 25, 1960

Jim A. Smith
Jan 12, 1858
Oct 29, 1943
&
Sarah Jane Smith
Jul 2, 1860
Jun 26, 1939

Mrs. W. B. Smith
Feb 11, 1840
Dec 14, 1924

Bettie Smith
1870-1888

Jack Finney
1833-1918

Nancy Finney
1837-1910

Burl W. Holder
1878-1948
&
Fannie B. Holder
1876-1948
(TM: F. B. Smith Holder)

Mammie Holder
Jun 3, 1900
May 24, 1914

Lois Thomas Prince
Mar 18, 1899
Dec 22, 1963
&
Offie Burt Prince
Dec 1, 1903

Married Dec 25, 1920

Garvin S. Bennett
Jan 13, 1897

&
Stella Burt Bennett
Feb 14, 1895
May 29, 1954

Leonard Burt
(no dates)
&
Clyde Burt
(no dates)
&
Oliver Burt
(no dates)
&
Idona Burt
(no dates)
Children of Joe Smith &
Mary Virginia Burt.

Isom A. Burt
Tennessee
Sgt 44 Inf 13 Div
Jun 4, 1890
Sep 1, 1945

David W. Burt
1857-1904
&
Mollie Burt
1864-1949

Infant Son of
J. H. & Kate Burt
Mar 25, 1922

Asbury Burt
1868-1946
&
Fannie Burt
1873-1923

Nannie Lawson
1874-1917

Wallace & Nancy, Son &
Daughter of
Larkin & Leona Burt
(no dates)

John Henry Burt
Aug 30, 1878
Jan 11, 1954
&
Kate Allen Burt
Aug 24, 1879
Oct 28, 1955

Henry H. Burt
Feb 14, 1904
Jan 17, 1955
&
Mary A. Burt
Nov 10, 1918

Joe Smith Burt
Nov 21, 1871
Apr 30, 1938
&
Mary Virginia Burt
Nov 9, 1875
Jul 23, 1955

Larry Randel, Son of
Clarence & Irene Burt
May 23, 1939

Beverly Dawn Burt
Oct 26, 1952

Alvin Burt
1916-1974
(Tullahoma FH)

Ola Burt Richardson
1894-1938

Joe W. Tankersley
Dec 7, 1877
Jun 24, 1913
&
Virginia T. Tankersley
Mar 11, 1880
Mar 30, 1971

William H. Tankersley
Feb 17, 1855
Mar 6, 1923

Mary Tankersley
Mar 12, 1859
Jun 12, 1938

J. Richard Tankersley
Mar 19, 1880
Jul 10, 1938

CUMBERLAND SPRINGS QUADRANGLE

"Brother"
Edward Smith
Jul 17, 1911
Mar 3, 1917
&
"Sister"
Daisy D. Smith
Oct 30, 1911
Feb 28, 1921
"Children of
Mr. & Mrs. W. H. Smith".
(we believe the birth
date on one of the above
children is incorrect)

J. R. Pogue
Sep 28, 1850
Jun 9, 1913

John William Tankersley
Mar 11, 1873
Feb 19, 1964
&
Annie Lou Tankersley
Jan 20, 1877
Jan 15, 1953

Walter Freeman
Died Sep 7, 1938
Age: (not given)
(Bomar-Shrader-Davis FH)

Dora M. Osborne Damrel
Jul 30, 1863
Oct 18, 1952

Herbert R. Davies
1904-
&
Virgie A. Dunn Davies
1908-1972

Felix E. Dunn
Oct 5, 1910

&
Dorothy C. Dunn
Aug 18, 1911

Alexander R. Burt
Dec 29, 1868
Oct 30, 1947
Age: 78y, 10m, 1d.

John R. Majors
Oct 21, 1881
Oct 9, 1956
&
Virginia T. Majors
Feb 2, 1885
Jul 1, 1968

Charles, Daughter of
J. R. & J. L. Majors
May 30, 1916
Jun 8, 1916

Virginia I. Burt
May 25, 1936
May 27, 1936

Sam E. Burt
Tennessee
Pvt Co M 46 Inf WW I
Nov 16, 1893
Dec 25, 1968
&
Odessa C. Burt
Aug 5, 1901

Author Taylor Lawson
Aug 1, 1927
Jan 11, 1953

Richard Lawson
1895-1967
(Motlow-Moore FH)

Dovie B. Lawson
Sep 18, 1895
May 3, 1954

W. (Woods) Dunn
1885-1958
&
Nancy B. Dunn
1882-1952

Martha E. Eggleston
Apr 12, 1863
Jul 5, 1892
Married in 1879 to
G. F. Eggleston

Jonathan C. Harris
Feb 18, 1815
Aug 5, 1884
Age: 69y, 5m, 17d.

John M. Smith
1881-1949
&
Lizzie L. Smith
1889-1914

Ewin Smith
1909-1931

S. E. Hasty
(no dates, fieldstone)

Wiley G. Lawson
Feb 3, 1857
May 29, 1918

A. L. L.
Died Sep 14, 1896
Age: (not given)
(fieldstone)

Martin Lynch
1922-1943

H. M. Lynch
1881-1961
&
Mollie Lynch
1889-(no date)

Taylor W. Lynch
May 22, 1908
Feb 11, 1972
&
Viola T. Lynch
Apr 26, 1912

Lee Allen
Aug 26, 1876
Jan 16, 1961
&
Cynthia Allen
Aug 12, 1879
Oct 1, 1963

Joseph Frazier, Son of
Lee & Cynthia Allen
Apr 14, 1921
Apr 14, 1924

James B. Eggleston
1894-1936
&
Stella Eggleston
1900-

Marry E. Burt
Dec 7, 1861
Dec 28, 1931
Age: 70y, 0m, 21d.

Johnnie Burt
Feb 11, 1878
Aug 19, 1908

Sgt James J. Burt
Co K 17 Inf Tenn Inf
C.S.A.

Ed Nelson
Jul 31, 1876
Apr 30, 1917

Rev. W. H. Anthony
Aug 8, 1819
May 1, 1884

Elizabeth, Consort of
Rev. W. H. Anthony
May 31, 1811
Jun 8, 1888

Cleek Infants
3 graves
(no dates)

Fannie B. Nelson
May 21, 1876
Oct 27, 1900
Age: 24y, 5m, 6d.

J. W. Eggleston
Dec 22, 1818
Nov 23, 1886
&
Anne Eggleston
Feb 7, 1818
Aug 18, 1895

J. A. Nelson
Nov 7, 1848
Aug 7, 1917
&
Mary Nelson
Feb 22, 1844
(no date)

Selinda Odear
1965-1965

Several unmarked graves.

* *

WILLIAMS CEMETERY

LOCATION: Near Cumberland Springs.

Martha Jane Johnson
was born the 30 day &
died (this stone was never
finished by the stone cutter.)

Williams Family says that some Williams are buried here
with no markers.

Many graves with fieldstones, no inscriptions.

* *

CUMBERLAND SPRINGS QUADRANGLE

WISEMAN CEMETERY

LOCATION: Three miles north of Lynchburg on Highway # 82, to Shelbyville.

Clarence S. Wiseman
1890-1958
&
Ruby Bedford Wiseman
1894-19

Ben Fate Wiseman
Jan 1, 1919
Jul 25, 1921

Jesse Gordon Moore
Nov 28, 1845
Apr 25, 1921
&
Catharine Shipman Moore
Jun 1, 1848
Feb 25, 1937

Mack C. Mullins
Jul 19, 1838
Nov 18, 1878
&
Marilda Mullins
Sep 13, 1844
Jan 29, 1909

Cleo, wife of
J. C. Mullins
Mar 4, 1886
Apr 7, 1915

Nannie Bedford
Feb 15, 1855
Jun 23, 1933

Callie F. Wiseman
Dec 9, 1864
Oct 1, 1937

Wilson Carroll Tims
Jul 18, 1869
Jan 22, 1936
&
Mary Ellen Tims
Dec 24, 1874
Mar 11, 1958

Horace A. Tims
Apr 26, 1894
Oct 3, 1918
"Soldier- WW I"

Ayleen, Daughter of
Edd & Carrie Bedford
1907-1923

Onie Mullins
Aug 11, 1896
Aug 26, 1912

Dick Mullins
Dec 16, 1887
Dec 10, 1966

Will Noblett
Feb 20, 1872
Aug 16, 1911

Callie B., wife of
William Noblett
May 7, 1866
Nov 30, 1931

Baby Noblett
(no dates)

Elizabeth, wife of
Josh Noblett
Oct 24, 1845
Aug 28, 1914

Edd Bedford
1877-1925
& wife
Carrie Bedford
1879-1937

Buna, wife of
Edd Mullins
Jul 4, 1892
Sep 6, 1918

Ella Mullins
Apr 2, 1930
May 22, 1930

Louisa, wife of
J. W. Mullins
Jun 16, 1863
Aug 4, 1918

Peter L. Shofner
Jun 11, 1834
Dec 27, 1909
&
Harried M. Shofner
Feb 1, 1843
Jan 23, 1912

Nancy C., Daughter of
J. M. Wanslee
Mar 22, 1817
Jan 24, 1848

William Burch Clark
1887-1945

Glendon E. Norvell
1900-1916

J. Burnie Clark
1881-1904

Thomas Wiley Clark
1854-1934
&
Fannie Gowen Clark
1856-1902

William T. Murray
Jun 19, 1868
Oct 3, 1935
&
Nancy E. Murray
Aug 4, 1881
Sep 16, 1943

W. T. Mullins
Jun 8, 1863
Oct 3, 1936
&
Laura Gowen Mullins
May 28, 1859
Jul 4, 1910

Orbin Mullins
Sep 28, 1896
Jun 22, 1931

Pauline I., wife of
W. S. Howard
Mar 10, 1848
Jun 23, 1871

Elbert Brown
Feb 14, 1835
Feb 8, 1907
&
Finettie Brown
Jan 15, 1852
(no date)

F. M. Edens
Sep 9, 1832
Dec 25, 1912

G. W. Pyrdam
Aug 1, 1879
Mar 25, 1911

Jessie B. Pyrdam
Nov 21, 1853
Jan 29, 1908
& wife
Cynthia A. Pyrdam
Aug 26, 1858
Apr 10, 1934

Arthur F. Martin
Sep 13, 1884
Jul 26, 1939
&
Floy Tims Martin
Oct 7, 1891
Jul 10, 1951

Earnest C. Martin
Sep 24, 1906
Aug 14, 1908

John Bartlett
1892-1936
&
Minnie Bartlett
1901-

J. N. Cluverius
Aug 26, 1854
Apr 17, 1930
& wife
Minnie Gowen Cluverius
Jul 28, 1868
1940

Lillie, wife of
J. T. Daniel
Sep 21, 1887
Jun 15, 1908

Elijah W. Stone
Mar 27, 1832
Feb 1, 1870

John F. Stone
Mar 4, 1840
Nov 29, 1863

George R. Stone
Jan 12, 1837
Sep 29, 1860

Baby Stone
(no dates)

Joshua Stone
Feb 23, 1834
Feb 1, 1853

Stone (Adult)
(no dates)

Wilmuth Stone
Mar 26, 1821
Jan 19, 1840

Grace Mullins
Jan 27, 1888
1972
& "Sister"
Maude G. Mullins
Feb 22, 1890
Jan 28, 1959

Infant Son of
William & Rebecca Price
B&D Sep 22, 1851

William Price
Jul 18, 1817
Aug 21, 1853

Rebecca Price
Nov 30, 1821
Aug 8, 1900

Alice Stone
1867-1924
&
John Stone
1859-1917

John F. Wiseman
Aug 19, 1869
Oct 27, 1870
&
Edward L. Wiseman
Apr 16, 1875
Mar 8, 1877
Children of W. R. &
S. E. Wiseman

CUMBERLAND SPRINGS QUADRANGLE

Elisha Wiseman
Sep 12, 1842
Feb 6, 1914
&
Mary J. Wiseman
Sep 25, 1848
Dec 21, 1911

Infant Daughter of
J. W. & Shaw Irvin
Jun 24, 1919

Nancy, Daughter of
J. W. & Shaw Irvin
Jul 8, 1936
Mar 8, 1937

Charlie Jackson, Son of
Horace & Ruby Irvin
Dec 23, 1946
Dec 24, 1946

Walden Jackson Irvin
Mar 19, 1899
Apr 1, 1968
&
Tommie Shaw Irvin
Jan 5, 1902
Mar 31, 1960

Many unmarked graves.

Mary Frances, Daughter of
Pearl & M. T. Gowen
Feb 25, 1923
Mar 12, 1923

Infant Daughter of
Mr. & Mrs. F. M. Allen
Died Aug 2, 1919
Age: (not given)

Francis Anderson
Jul 3, 1916
Nov 25, 1919

Thomas Shaw Holt
Jun 24, 1866
Jul 9, 1901
&
Sarah Tennessee Holt
Apr 14, 1869
Feb 15, 1942

Matthew Price & wife
Elizabeth Price, natives
of South Carolina are
buried here. (Info from
Family Records)

* *

LOIS QUADRANGLE

BEAN CEMETERY

LOCATION: South-east of Marble Hill, on River.

Sarah, wife of
William Bean
Sep 10, 1808
Dec 16, 1842
Age: 34y, 3m, 6d.

W. A. Marshals
Dec 26, 1878

M. Awalt
Died 1885
Age: (not given)

Many graves without
markers, some marked
with fieldstones, no
inscriptions.

* ** *

BEAN CEMETERY

LOCATION: One mile east of Marble Hill.

Pattie Bean
Dec 2, 1877
Dec 7, 1909

Infant Son of
M. A. & Pattie Bean
(no dates)

E. M. Bean
Aug 31, 1835
Jan 24, 1898

Infant Son of
M. A. & Pattie Bean
(no dates)

Mabel Clara Lee
Jul 2, 1887
Mar 20, 1888

Arthur A. Lee
Feb 16, 1847
Dec 27, 1911

Ada Pearl, Daughter of
E. M. & L. E. Bean
Aug 30, 1879
Mar 13, 1911

Dollie McKinzie
Oct 2, 1873
Apr 14, 1917

Rosa A. Lee
May 2, 1860
Jan 20, 1899

Hattie L. Bean
Dec 19, 1872
Sep 23, 1894

Many unmarked graves.

R. M. W.
Died Sep 15, 1887
Age: (not given)
(fieldstone)

Nathan Limbaugh
Nov 27, 1859
Nov 19, 1897

Mollie E. Limbaugh
Dec 29, 1861
Dec 18, 1916

* *

BRANDON CEMETERY

LOCATION: On hill across the road from Brandon Methodist Church.

"Father" &
Lemual Brandon
Jul 10, 1849
Jun 4, 1894
    & "Mother"
Callie Cruse Brandon
Apr 10, 1849
Oct 10, 1889

"Daughter"
Mary Kathran Brandon
Oct 18, 1873
Sep 29, 1891

Willi Chapman
Jan 30, 1890
May 9, 1890

W. F. Bruce
Feb 26, 1817
Apr 11, 1897
 & wife
Sarah A. Bruce
Apr 27, 1822
Jul 28, 1892

Rev. Lemuel Brandon
Aug 24, 1790
Jul 21, 1860

Mary Beall, wife of
Rev. Lemuel Brandon
1807-Nov 18, 1885

LOIS QUADRANGLE

F. W.
(no dates, fieldstone)

Taylor, Son of
L. & M. Brandon
Mar 23, 1847
Apr 21, 1864

W. M. Chapman
Jul 13, 1834
Feb 14, 1909

James C. Chapman
Mar 15, 1865
May 10, 1889

NOTE: This was community cemetery. Many unmarked graves.

* *

COBBLE CEMETERY

LOCATION: Two and one half miles north of Marble Hill on Bull Run Creek.

Rubbin, Son of
A. & Olar Baker
Nov 19, 1910
Nov 26, 1911

Dr. E. A. Cobble
Sep 3, 1841
Feb 29, 1904

Mary E. Ivy, Daughter of
Dr. E. A. & Adeline Cobble
Sep 19, 1866
Aug 2, 1894

Thomas D. Allen
1867-1933

Annie M., wife of
A. C. Cobble
Oct 1, 1819
Sep 25, 1906

Thomas Jefferson Cobble
Nov 5, 1849
Apr 5, 1873

E. L. T. Cobble
Aug 10, 1871
Oct 20, 1889

A. W. Cobble
Aug 31, 1844
Jun 17, 1906
& wife
Nancy C. Cobble
Jun 15, 1846
Feb 3, 1904

A. C. Cobble
Jun 22, 1815
Apr 15, 1891

Mollie, wife of
Thomas D. Allen
Nov 7, 1870
Jul 16, 1901

M. M. E. Tipps
Dec 4, 1839
Dec 1, 1884

Ellen M., wife of
David Wood
Mar 17, 1867
Jan 29, 1919

Roy E., Son of
W. T. & W. B. Cobble
Nov 2, 1896
Jan 6, 1897

Rilda E., wife of
J. F. Stone
Aug 13, 1864
Sep 11, 1887

E. J., Son of
P. D. & Annie Allen
Jun 13, 1911
Oct 24, 1911

Infant Twin Daughters of
Henry & Shadden Garner
Aug 20, 1921

J. D. Wood
Dec 12, 1862
Dec 1, 1934
& wife
Josie Cobble Wood
Dec 24, 1859
Nov 7, 1922

* *

COPELAND CEMETERY

LOCATION: Near Fuga Community.

John Copeland
Mar 1793
Feb 1865
"A Primitive Baptist
Elder for 35 years."

Mrs. Sarah, wife of
Rev. Jno. Copeland
1786-May 1857
"Member of the Primitive
Baptist Church 37 years."

Permelia Tucker
Nov 1, 1852
Dec 18, 1907

Lee Ova, wife of
W. T. Copeland
Mar 16, 1877
Jul 26, 1902

William Thomas Copeland
Dec 29, 1879
Feb 7, 1920

W. M. Smith
Nov 11, 1833
Dec 10, 1908

Mary E. Smith
Died Mar 25, 1910
Age: 76y, 8m.

Hairman Claudie, Son of
W. T. & L. O. Copeland
Jun 19, 1902
Sep 12, 1902

Amanda M., wife of
H. L. Brown
Mar 1, 1862
Oct 3, 1899

James Alton Smith
Nov 11, 1921
Sep 30, 1926

Harvey C., Son of
H. L. & A. M. Brown
Dec 8, 1898
Apr 3, 1899

Ruffus B. Smith
Feb 26, 1860
Jun 21, 1917

Cordelia Smith
May 27, 1868
Jul 26, 1934

Siota Ella Tucker
Jul 17, 1885
Nov 19, 1902

* *

ERVIN CEMETERY

LOCATION: One mile west of Liberty Hill, on Robinson Creek.

S. G. Ervin
Dec 15, 1813
Dec 28, 1891

Martha G. Gray, wife of
S. G. Ervin
Sep 28, 1825
Apr 23, 1909

W. H. Ervin
Mar 24, 1858
Jun 2, 1914

Pamelia Kate Ervin
Sep 25, 1862
Jun 6, 1939

Infant Son of
S. P. & F. S. Ervin
B&D Dec 22, 1906

* *

LOIS QUADRANGLE

EVANS CEMETERY

LOCATION: Three fourth mile NW of Brandon Chapel Church.

Jimmie Evans (no dates)	Edd Evans (no dates)	M. E. Evans (no dates)	W. M. Evans (no dates)
	4 unmarked graves.	Wall erected Apr 21, 1921.	

* *

FRAME CEMETERY

LOCATION: One mile north of Hurdlow, on the west side of Wet Prong of Farris Creek.

Houston M. McKenzie
1903-1952
&
Donie Walker McKenzie
1900-19

James R. Taylor
1891-1955
&
Mary Taylor
1895-

Infant Son of
A. L. & M. K. Lewis
B&D Mar 1, 1935

Susan I. Galloway
May 13, 1833
Jan 21, 1916

Infant Son of
S. I. & T. K. Galloway
Oct 2, 1875
Oct 30, 1875

Susan A. Mitchell
Aug 18, 1798
May 6, 1865

Ibebey Tripp
May 23, 1807
Sep 9, 1848
&
Infant
Sep 2, 1848
Sep 8, 1848

Aaron Wesley Tripp
Oct 24, 1831
Oct 4, 1922
& wife
Susan Elizabeth Tripp
Oct 14, 1839
Apr 15, 1918

Margaret E., Daughter of
A. W. & S. E. Tripp
Jun 20, 1860
Mar 24, 1863

Sarah C., Daughter of
Ely & I. Tripp
Feb 14, 1846
Oct 19, 1855
Age: 9y, 7m, 29d.

William --------
Feb --, ----
(TM)

John W. Walker
Mar 22, 1895
Apr 1, 1967
&
Gracie R. Walker
May 7, 1899

T. J. Spencer
Apr 3, 1836
Jun 17, 1920

Eli Tripp
Oct 17, 1807
Sep 4, 1864

Annis Vernetta Tripp
Jul 8, 1843
Jan 4, 1922

Thomas Wells
Sep 6, 1796
Jan 17, 1873
Age: 76y, 4m, 11d.

Polly, wife of
Thomas Wells
Dec 8, 1800
Dec 28, 1882

Mary A., Daughter of
A. W. & S. E. Tripp
Oct 14, 1867
Mar 31, 1893

Martha E., Daughter of
A. W. & S. E. Tripp
Aug 8, 1870
Mar 30, 1890

Sarah S., Daughter of
A. W. & S. E. Tripp
Jan 1, 1859
Jun 24, 1861

Infant Son of
A. W. & S. E. Tripp
B&D Oct 14, 1875

Mary A. Smith, Daughter
of Eli & I. Tripp
Jun 18, 1829
Oct 30, 1855

Infant of
Ely & Ibbey Tripp
B&D Sep 17, 1830

Mary, wife of
J. C. Crabtree
Feb 16, 1839
Nov 21, 1912

James F. Spencer
Mar 23, 1841
Jun 14, 1866

Sarah Spencer
Dec 11, 1833
Jul 13, 1909

Oscar Deal
Nov 4, 1902
Aug 12, 1942
&
Susie Deal
Sep 3, 1905

C. C. Lewis
Feb 8, 1885
Apr 24, 1928
&
Hattie Evans Lewis
Jan 14, 1896

James T. Wade
1861-1929
&
Sara J. Wade
1878-1956

J. R. Solomon
Mar 1872
Aug 1955

Lillie Viola Deal
1902-1961

Arthur G. McKenzie
1880-1948
&
Lula M. McKenzie
1883-1956

Ernest Fanning
1910-
&
Johnnie B. Fanning
1912-1945

J. C. Crabtree
Sep 22, 1832
Nov 29, 1887

James R. Frame
Jan 19, 1865
Nov 5, 1902
&
Mary C. Frame
Oct 18, 1866
Dec 31, 1933

Martha V., wife of
S. J. Walker
Dec 12, 1878
Sep 27, 1937

John C. Lewis
Aug 18, 1895
Jan 5, 1934

Caldonia Lewis
May 2, 1867
Jan 15, 1943

John H. Lewis
Jan 10, 1837
Jan 4, 1903

Caineth Marion Lewis
1824-1900
&
Louise Jane Lewis
1848-1932

Della Lewis
Aug 16, 1878
Aug 17, 1944
&
Alice Lewis
Oct 19, 1868
Apr 2, 1966

S. M. Walker
Husband of Martha Frame
Died Sep 30, 1880
Age: (not given)

429

LOIS QUADRANGLE

Clara Frances Frame
Jul 28, 1928
Aug 30, 1928

T. H. Frame
Oct 8, 1894
Nov 4, 1915

Arle P. Eslick
Nov 20, 1891
Jan 24, 1946
&
Bettie Eslick
Mar 16, 1898
May 5, 1967

James F. Deal
1872-1939
&
Elizabeth Deal
1880-1934

S. J. Walker
Died Sep 7, 1949
Age: about 78 years.

Boss Walker
1881-1962

Vonie Walker
1885-1931

Cyntha Jane Marlow, wife
of John H. Lewis
Aug 30, 1839
Jun 16, 1925

Willmer, Daughter of
C. C. & Hattie Lewis
Oct 30, 1916
Nov 14, 1916

Several unmarked graves.

George R. Lewis
Jan 5, 1872
May 11, 1936
& wife
Lou A. Brazier Lewis
Feb 18, 1875
Aug 8, 1961

Maude Walker
1901-1910

Guston Walker
1903-1919

* *

GRABLE CEMETERY

LOCATION: Three fourth mile SE of Brandon Chapel Church.

B. F. Grable
Feb 29, 1846
May 4, 1924
Age: 78y, 2m, 5d.
& wife
Virginia M. Grable
Feb 11, 1856
(no date)

Ruthy L., wife of
D. F. Grable
Jan 30, 1845
Jan 31, 1894

William R., Son of
Rutha L. & D. F. Grable
May 12, 1871
May 13, 1871

Lucinda, wife of
R. M. Stephens
Mar 1, 1815
Jan 28, 1892

Several unmarked graves.

Infant Son of
James & Cumi Hill
1895

* *

DAVID GRAY CEMETERY

LOCATION: One and one half miles SE of Brandon Chapel Church.

Infant of
J. F. & L. L. Harrison
Aug 29, 1900
Sep 22, 1900

Brice Gray, Son of
J. F. & L. L. Harrison
Jun 7, 1895
Jul 6, 1896

Infant of
J. F. & L. L. Harrison
Aug 12, 1893
Aug 14, 1893

Brice P. Gray
Nov 16, 1815
Feb 10, 1882
Age: 36y, 2m, 24d.

Carrie Lee Gray
May 13, 1875
Mar 15, 1896

Joe R. Johnston, wife of
Brice P. Gray
1851-1926

Thomas Elijah Cunningham
Apr 25, 1871
Oct 1, 1931
&
Edna Gray Cunningham
Jan 3, 1874-Aug 5, 1903

Allen D., Son of
B. P. & J. R. Gray
Jun 23, 1881
Oct 28, 1903

Mary Gray, wife of
J. M. Damron
Dec 30, 1876
Jun 1, 1906

Lena L., wife of
J. F. Harrison
Nov 16, 1872
Jun 23, 1917

Clarar Harrison, wife of
J. H. Osborne
May 28, 1898
Jun 13, 1921

George W., Son of
D. S. & M. G. Gray
Sep 2, 1854
Jan 15, 1880

M. J., Daughter of
D. S. & M. J. Gray
Sep 14, 1852
May 29, 1854
Age: 1y, 8m, 15d.

Three Infants of
J. W. & Mary E. Bedford
(no dates)

D. S. (David) Gray
Aug 1, 1817
Dec 14, 1854
Age: 37y, 4m, 10d.

Mary G., wife of
D. S. Gray
Mar 6, 1820
Sep 2, 1900

James E. Gray
May 14, 1848
Aug 12, 1892
Age: 44y, 2m, 28d.

Molly R., Daughter of
J. E. & M. E. Gray
Feb 24, 1879
Dec 22, 1879

Bettie Gray
Mar 8, 1860
Mar 9, 1920

Lucy J. Gray, wife of
O. H. Grant
Sep 8, 1884
Jan 9, 1909

Lillian L. Cunningham, wife
of J. W. Webb
Jan 26, 1900
Jan 3, 1920

James Gray
Aug 13, 1898
Jan 21, 1920

Jesse Lee Gray
Oct 15, 1889
Jan 17, 1922

Maron, Son of
J. L. & Adaie M. Gray
May 30, 1919
Jun 6, 1919

David N. Gray
1850-1930

Maggie A. Bowers, wife
of D. N. Gray
Feb 2, 1850
May 21, 1907

Maud M., Daughter of
D. N. & M. A. Gray
Dec 23, 1878
Jun 28, 1887

George W., Son of
D. N. & M. A. Gray
Feb 12, 1880
Oct 10, 1881

Several unmarked graves.

* *

LOIS QUADRANGLE

JOHN GRAY CEMETERY

LOCATION: Near Marble Hill and Ebenezer Church.

John D. Gray
Sep 2, 1818
Jul 15, 1903
&
Mary Gray
Apr 12, 1828
Dec 6, 1903

J. W. G. (Gray)
(footmarker)

J. D. Gray
Jan 1, 1849
Jan 7, 1944
&
Jennie Gray
Jan 26, 1856
Sep 13, 1928

Several unmarked graves.

Doris, Daughter of
C. D. & Myrtle Gray
Oct 20, 1912
Apr 30, 1913

Hannah, Daughter of
J. D. & Mary Gray
Mar 1, 1858
Aug 7, 1875

Molly Gray, wife of
L. G. Grant
Sep 20, 1872
Dec 17, 1919

Sallie, wife of
J. C. Tipps & Daughter
of J. & P. Gray
Feb 11, 1868
Jul 26, 1896

* *

JENKINS CEMETERY

LOCATION: Across from Brandon Chapel Church on a very high hill. 4 or 5 graves with no markers.

* *

LOIS CEMETERY

LOCATION: Main cemetery for the Community of Lois.

Houston O. Perry
1913-1972
&
Ellen H. Perry
1904-(1973:Tullahoma FH)

William E. Perry
(no dates)
(Tullahoma FH)

Alfred L. Evans
1867-1945
&
Sallie D. Evans
1864-1943

William Henry Darnell
Oct 20, 1864
Aug 11, 1956
&
Marilda Agnes Darnell
Oct 12, 1870
Apr 16, 1942

Don H., Son of
J. L. & Louise Darnell
1936-1937

Robert R. Evans
Aug 30, 1890
Mar 22, 1959
&
Della A. Evans
Sep 23, 1891
Mar 18, 1936

Thomas Jefferson Copeland
1861-1934
&
Martha Jane Copeland
1861-1934

Joseph Robert Sullenger
1885-1949
&
Sarah Frances Sullenger
1882-1954

William T. Wiseman
1857-1937
&
Sarah J. Wiseman
1858-1939

Charlie H. Eslick
1878-1947
&
Mary E. Eslick
1882-1965

John T. Parks
Age: 27 years.
(no dates)

Mrs. Ada O. Hinkle
1888-1936

Byrd Alice Sawyer
Feb 23, 1891
Mar 7, 1961
&
Zery Norman Sawyer
Feb 1, 1891
Jan 1, 1934

James Eslick
1876-(no date)
&
Lucy Eslick
1881-1944

Roy W. Evans
Apr 5, 1898
Feb 11, 1951
&
Ozell C. Evans
Jan 1, 1902

Ernest Mitchell
Apr 7, 1910
Jul 29, 1968
&
Virginia S. Mitchell
Feb 5, 1915

QM Sgt William H. Mitchell
Co L 10 U. S. Inf
Sp. Am. War
Jun 18, 1873
Sep 14, 1930

Thomas W. Wiseman
1882-1971
(Harrison FH)

Vivian, Daughter of
Raymond & Ruth Sweeney
May 22, 1936

J. L. (John) Mitchell
Aug 13, 1861
May 16, 1930

Rickey Robin Brown
Died Oct 6, 1965
Age: (not given)
(Higgins FH)

James H. Counts
1866-1941
&
Alice M. Counts
1871-1944

George Washington Counts
Apr 21, 1871
Apr 9, 1955
&
Minnie L. Brown Counts
Jul 21, 1875
Mar 1, 1934

John W. Counts
Tennessee
Pvt 324 Inf 81 Div
Aug 12, 1939

James Gary Mitchell
Nov 14, 1950
Dec 28, 1954

Ina M. Gattis
Dec 5, 1874
Jul 15, 1960

John T. Gattis
1845-1932
&
Donie S. Gattis
1858-1938

Dr. James L. Cody
Mar 28, 1863
Jun 20, 1919

Cassie Ann Cody
Apr 30, 1865
Jul 25, 1930

Arthur Homer Eslick
Mar 3, 1911
Jan 29, 1939

Sallie S. Mitchell
Aug 17, 1883
Feb 1, 1969

William Edgar Marshall
Dec 10, 1872
Mar 10, 1947
&
Ella Jane Marshall
Jul 28, 1875
Jul 2, 1955

LOIS QUADRANGLE

Calvin Evans
1868-1928
&
M. Josie Evans
1874-1948

B. W. Hunt
1933-1944
&
Glenn M. Hunt
1942-1942

James "Dillon" Evans
Feb 10, 1915
Sep 27, 1920

Pinkney E. Evans
Apr 28, 1892
Jul 16, 1952
&
Georgia M. Evans
Aug 13, 1897

William L. Chapman
1887-1954
&
Eliza E. Chapman
1884-1928

Barbara Jean Preston
Jun 8, 1952
Oct 12, 1970

Willie N. Preston
1899-1967
&
Oma P. Preston
1902-19

Bobby Ralph Preston
May 27, 1936
Jul 17, 1936

Delta Evans
1902-1955

Joan & Judy Eslick
1951-1951

Florence Sweeney
1897-1946

Floyd L. Sweeney
Sep 10, 1903
Dec 3, 1940

J. E. Owens
Feb 11, 1888
Dec 22, 1961
&
Amanda C. Owens
Sep 11, 1884
Mar 22, 1959

Ella P. Ashby
1891-1973
(Harrison FH)

Mary E. Ashby
1935-1940

Horace H. Eslick
Nov 25, 1898
Jul 2, 1964
&
Levonia S. Eslick
Mar 8, 1903

Lucy F. Mitchell
1891-19
&
J. Grace Mitchell
1882-1947
&
Joe G. Mitchell
1930-1931

Wanda Diane Fuller
B&D Nov 11, 1954

Knox A. Fuller, Jr.
B&D May 22, 1953

John D. Preston
1888-1949
&
Eunice A. Preston
1891-19

John S. Sweeney
1873-19(no date)
&
Mary C. Sweeney
1877-1950

Roy Isaac Gattis
Aug 10, 1906
Oct 8, 1955
&
Lorena Thelma Gattis
May 12, 1913

W. F. Philpot
Oct 24, 1845
Mar 6, 1917
"Buried Oak Grove Cemetery, Moore County."

Frances, wife of
W. F. Philpot
Mar 6, 1850
Jan 19, 1929

C. Richard Evans
Jun 11, 1944
Jun 19, 1944

Ralph W. Limbaugh
1952

John Cary Spencer
Feb 11, 1949
Nov 27, 1966

Pamela Jane Spencer
Mar 18, 1953
Nov 27, 1966

Aurelia Jane Spencer
Jun 13, 1925
Nov 27, 1966

John Parks Spencer
Sep 25, 1920

Betty Russell
(no dates)

James W. Patton
Died Oct 1901
Age: (not given)
&
Allie Counts Patton
Died Nov 30, 1931
Age: (not given)

Lena May Evans
Jan 24, 1892
Dec 5, 1939

W. C. Evans
1866-1932

Mattie Evans
1869-1950

Charles H. Casey
Jun 11, 1909
Nov 3, 1958
&
Betty Lee Casey
Apr 23, 1882
Oct 16, 1948
&
Jim L. Casey
Mar 5, 1880
Dec 23, 1968

Earnest R. Casey
Tennessee
Pfc Medical Dept WW II
Jan 12, 1911
Jun 6, 1966

Rufe L. Preston
Jul 19, 1894

&
Louella Y. Preston
Jan 18, 1900
(TM: 1973)
Married Dec 24, 1916

Frank Riddle
Dec 6, 1879
Feb 10, 1959
&
Ida Hill Riddle
Oct 5, 1882
Apr 10, 1961

Michael Eugene Baker
1964-1966

James N. Walker
Tennessee Pvt
Co E 306 Inf WW I
Jul 6, 1894
May 18, 1970

Edwin Cunningham, Jr.
Mar 9, 1931
Mar 18, 1931

T. F. Casey
Jul 31, 1912
Jan 27, 1964
&
Virgie E. Casey
Dec 17, 1918

Ernest C. Evans
Sep 23, 1910
Jan 10, 1969

Wilse R. Ashby
Aug 13, 1885

&
Ella P. Ashby
Apr 8, 1891
Apr 4, 1973

James W. Grammer
1882-1953
&
Leona M. Grammer
1880-19

James D. Brazier
Oct 6, 1951
Stillborn

Ross E. George
Jul 13, 1902
Sep 16, 1958

James Asberry Ashby
1876-1949
&
Nora Warden Ashby
1887-1938

Jeff S. Casey
1888-1972

Margaret E. Snow
1891-1970

Mollie Copeland
Jul 24, 1877
Feb 10, 1957

William Donald Copeland
Jun 29, 1939
Jul 31, 1963

Charles Alton Tripp
Tennessee
SP5 Hq Co 12 Engr
Const. Bn Korea
Dec 11, 1927
Aug 16, 1966

Emily Ruth Walker
May 25, 1955
Feb 1, 1956

Edwin H. Cunningham
May 23, 1900
Apr 21, 1958
&
Nancy Ermine Cunningham
Sep 17, 1895

LOIS QUADRANGLE

Isaac Thurston Preston
Jan 18, 1907

&
Bernice Smith Preston
Jun 1, 1913

Audrey G. Hunt
Mar 27, 1911
Oct 25, 1961

Monnie Tripp Walker
Feb 11, 1884
May 16, 1955

William M. Spencer
Feb 12, 1895
Feb 12, 1957
&
Clara C. Spencer
Sep 27, 1902

C. Wilford Evans
Mar 25, 1924
Nov 14, 1969
&
Mary Lee Evans
Aug 2, 1925

Curtis W. Patton
Mar 30, 1894
Oct 19, 1941
&
Julia W. Patton
Aug 21, 1896

Emmet E. Sullenger
Nov 30, 1908

&
Mattie W. Sullenger
Dec 5, 1917
Jan 7, 1969

Carl Ulman Parks
May 2, 1892
Nov 25, 1966
&
Lala Ashby Parks
Jul 6, 1906

Luther M. Spencer
1879-1958
&
Gracie D. Spencer
1899-19

* *

MOOREHEAD CEMETERY

LOCATION: Near Hurdlow Community.

George Moorehead
Age: 47 years.
(no dates)
&
Ann Moorehead
Age: 79 years.
(no dates)

Lawrence Moorehead
Age: 7 years.
(no dates)
&
Baker Moorehead
Age: 7 years.
(no dates)

Thomas E. Moorehead
Apr 27, 1877
Oct 5, 1895

Several fieldstones.

Nannie I., Daughter of
Frank & Mary Moorhead
Nov 27, 1897
Oct 10, 1900

Infant Son of
W. F. & M. C. Moorhead
Jun 1, 1907
Jun 8, 1907

J. N. Moorhead
Dec 26, 1825
Sep 28, 1903
& wife
Mary E. Moorhead
Aug 23, 1834
May 12, 1919

Ellie A., Daughter of
A. W. & Ida Spencer
Jul 10, 1888
Sep 3, 1888

James Read
Feb 24, 1850
Jan 3, 1931
& wife
Jacyntha E. Read
Nov 11, 1852
Dec 3, 1881

Virginia C. Wiseman
Mar 16, 1882
Feb 27, 1929
&
5 Infant Babies.

William F. Wiseman
Feb 14, 1846
Feb 24, 1907

Nancy J. Wiseman
Nov 25, 1856
Jan 24, 1919

S. T. Read
Aug 8, 1876
Nov 14, 1894

Charlie Dillon Gore
Feb 11, 1893
Jun 15, 1915

Ether G., Daughter of
T. N. & D. A. Gore
Nov 20, 1909
Oct 21, 1911

Tollie, Son of
J. T. & N. E. Gore
Jul 5, 1880
Mar 2, 1906

Thomas N. Gore
1876-1961
(Harrison FH)

* *

OAK GROVE CEMETERY

LOCATION: Two miles NW of Hurdlow, on Dry Prong of Farris Creek. This cemetery is also known as Moores Chapel.

Josha, Daughter of
J. H. & Winey Fears
Mar 4, 1883
Nov 1, 1904

W. I. Young
Aug 20, 1861
Mar 24, 1927
&
Sarah A. Young
Mar 2, 1867
1940

Susan Lavonia Spencer
1871-1899

Emeline G. Waggoner
Feb 28, 1834
Jan 1, 1906

Massey Copeland
Mar 21, 1824
Nov 3, 1901
&
Eady E. Copeland
Apr 18, 1832
Mar 16, 1921

Catherine Tucker
1802-1886
& Son
Ezekiel Tucker
1846-1884

W. D. Young
May 10, 1834
Apr 28, 1900

Martha E., wife of
W. D. Young
Jul 29, 1836
Oct 4, 1892

William Tucker
1843-1918
& wife
Martha J. Copeland Tucker
1843-1910

Charley, Son of
John & Ruth Copeland
Jun 18, 1859
Apr 2, 1924

Susan E., wife of
Charley Copeland
Feb 14, 1863
Jun 2, 1900

Fannie Tucker Copeland
Apr 5, 1867
Nov 11, 1940

James Scott
1861-1952
&
Mary Elizabeth Scott
1861-1952

Nathan McClure
Jul 9, 1806
Aug 9, 1890

LOIS QUADRANGLE

Sarah, wife of
Nathan McClure & Daughter
of T. & E. Gore
Dec 9, 1806
May 1, 1876
Age: 69y, 4m, 22d.

William B., Son of
F. M. & Susan Copeland
Jun 9, 1882
Feb 3, 1883

Aurora Riddle
Dec 11, 1875
Jan 17, 1876
&
Victoria Riddle
Dec 11, 1875
Jan 18, 1876

Twin Sons of
James & Mary Scott
(no dates)

Muriel Scott
1883-1884

Fenton Scott
1878-1878

Several unmarked graves.

Otis B., Son of
B. N. & Myrtle Eslick
Jan 1910

Mary B., Daughter of
F. M. & Susan Copeland
May 31, 1881
Jul 4, 1881

* *

PLEASANT HILL CEMETERY

LOCATION: One mile north of Hurdlow, on hill between Wet Prong and Dry Prong of Farris Creek.

Cora Lee, Daughter of
J. H. & L. P. Copeland
Oct 2, 1900
Nov 10, 1905

Mrs. M. A. Bates
Mar 1, 1836
Dec 13, 1905
Age: 69y, 9m, 13d.

Travis A. Bates
Dec 17, 1845
Dec 9, 1900

T. P. Baits
Aug 11, 1849
Apr 16, 1906

Rachel, wife of
T. P. Baits
Oct 29, 1853
Mar 19, 1926

Ruthie A. J. Baits
May 12, 1887
Jun 16, 1889

Infant Daughter of
J. H. & L. P. Copeland
B&D Jun 30, 1899

Infant Son of
J. H. & L. P. Copeland
Sep 15, 1908
Sep 17, 1908

I. M., of
N. L. Hinkle
Dec 23, 1855
Sep 2, 1880
Age: 49y, 8m, 9d.

Alexander Baits
Nov 16, 1816
Oct 16, 1884

Mary, wife of
Alexander Baits
May 30, 1820
Jun 16, 1883

Robert L. Gillespie
Sep 9, 1828
Feb 7, 1888

* *

PORTER CEMETERY

LOCATION: This cemetery is a colored cemetery and located near the mouth of Robinson Creek and Elk River.

Joe Porter
Jun 1, 1852
Mar 24, 1929
& wife
Ann Scott Porter
Jun 20, 1851
May 15, 1921

Boss, Son of
Joe & Ann Porter
Died May 18, 1907
Age: 15 years.

Several unmarked graves.

Emma Porter, wife of
Sam Tate
Oct 20, 1885
Mar 19, 1917

Myrtle Porter, wife of
Aron Smart
Sep 10, 1888
Mar 2, 1928

* *

REED CEMETERY

LOCATION: Near Fuga Community.

J. M. Eslick
May 18, 1850
Sep 12, 1907

Emma Della, wife of
E. C. Spencer
Jun 2, 1869
Feb 6, 1892

I. V. Gattis
Feb 28, 1844
Aug 25, 1910

Oma Smith, wife of
James Hensley
1865-1941

J. Roy Hensley
1898-1942

"Father"
M. Hensley
Jun 1840
Jun 26, 1913

Emma G., Daughter of
John C. & Mary F. Riddle
(no dates)

George W. Lesley
1866-1925
&
Mary Lou Lesley
1883-1952

James W. Smith
Jul 26, 1891
Apr 24, 1894

James R. Smith
Sep 7, 1828
Sep 25, 1907

Rebecca J., wife of
James R. Smith
Jun 26, 1833
Jun 15, 1911

Amanda F., wife of
W. M. Smith
Jan 8, 1831
Dec 6, 1886

Martha A. Smith
Feb 15, 1862
Nov 16, 1886

Thomas J. Smith
Dec 13, 1860
Oct 23, 1878

Oma A. Smith
Nov 19, 1862
Sep 29, 1880

Eliza Smith
Aug 3, 1856
Aug 30, 1890

LOIS QUADRANGLE

Emily Smith
Jun 30, 1889
May 2, 1891

Birdy Lois, Daughter of
Wilson & Jenety Ashby
May 22, 1888
Oct 4, 1894
Age: 6y, 4m, 12d.

Robert Lee Fears
1873-1945
(Thompson FH)

Mrs. Ida Mae Fears
1882-1952
(Thompson FH)

M. A., wife of
G. W. Fanning
1832-1886

L. M., Son of
G. & M. J. Fanning
May 14, 1883
Aug 14, 1883

Mary F., wife of
B. M. G. Forsyth
Dec 25, 1859
Aug 1, 1888

Ann M. Hensley
1919-1940
(Harrison FH)

Sue Eva Hensley
1889-1948
(Harrison FH)

John C. Hensley
1877-1938
(Harrison FH)

James R. Hensley
1879-1964
(Harrison FH)

E. Y. "Sam" Grammer
Dec 10, 1874
Dec 27, 1947
&
Frances Grammer
Nov 25, 1889

Sam P. Cowley
Jul 3, 1893
Mar 30, 1941

Anita Ruth Cowley
May 11, 1927
Jun 17, 1940

Lillie Kathrine Cowley
Apr 9, 1937

J. B., Son of
Jeffie & Ozell Sawyers
Jan 16, 1922
Mar 19, 1922

Billie Sawyer
1857-1914
&
Sarah Sawyer
1857-1930

Chaney Smith
Jan 28, 1806
Dec 5, 1886

Lusinda, wife of
Chaney Smith
Died Oct 27, 1897
Age: (not given)

Lizzie Tripp, wife of
Henry Sullenger
May 28, 1892
Nov 5, 1918

J. W. Alton Wise
Nov 16, 1895
Nov 2, 1918

Johnnie William, Son of
W. A. & Della Wise
Jan 13, 1917
Nov 11, 1918

Emmy Gattis
1882-1913

Lon Gattis
1878-1918

Riley Gattis
1901-1918

Katie Gattis
1912-1924

W. Mc. Smith
Dec 30, 1858
Jan 9, 1918
& wife
Mollie M. Snow Gattis
May 17, 1860
(no date)

Elizabeth Gattis
May 10, 1857
Dec 21, 1927

Infant Son of
C. W. & M. G. Tripp
B&D Apr 1, 1919

T. J. Tripp
1862-1944

Mary L. Tripp
1869-1928

Margerlette Tucker
Apr 26, 1929
Oct 6, 1929

Infant Sons of
Elmer (A.) & Ina Tucker
Mar 9, 1925
Jul 7, 1927

W. Ballard Preston
1865-1926
&
Mattie J. Preston
1871-1940

Leroy Preston
Feb 1, 1891
Sep 6, 1919

John Read
Mar 2, 1820
Feb 15, 1890

Elizabeth, wife of
John Read
Sep 5, 1819
Jan 29, 1898

Josie, Daughter of
John & Elizabeth Read
Apr 28, 1853
Jan 20, 1910

Martha, Daughter of
John & Elizabeth Read
Feb 1, 1844
Jul 24, 1914

Huldah Read, wife of
J. C. Tipps
May 3, 1860
Sep 25, 1912

W. L. Baits
Jun 3, 1880
Dec 27, 1968
& wife
Sue Ella Smith Baits
Mar 24, 1886
Oct 24, 1918

Susan B. Baits
Jan 13, 1883
Sep 8, 1954

Dorthy R. Baits
Jan 29, 1922
Sep 27, 1926

Rufus Reed
Feb 3, 1862
Dec 30, 1927
&
Julia D. Reed
Apr 9, 1866
(no date)

Henry J. Brown
Jul 18, 1900
Mar 17, 1969
&
Vianna A. Brown
Sep 2, 1894

Essie B., Daughter of
Henry & Vianna Brown
Oct 23, 1927
Nov 9, 1928

Myra Hilda Moorehead
Sep 23, 1946
Nov 14, 1946

Ollie May Ashby
1920-1925

Lafayette Tripp
1873-1933
&
Martha C. Tripp
1882-1947

Sue Glendon, Daughter of
Roy E. & Mattie B. Spencer
1918-1926

Hitie Robert Snow
Sep 5, 1891
Nov 18, 1918

Ethel Wise, wife of
H. R. Snow
Jan 1, 1894
Nov 23, 1918

William Henry Snow
Feb 14, 1888
May 25, 1957

Williard Thurmon Snow
Mar 9, 1912
Jul 13, 1937

Oscar Tripp
1883-1938
&
Mamie A.(Sawyer) Tripp
1894-1958

Many graves unmarked.

Several fieldstones,
no inscriptions.

LOIS QUADRANGLE

SCIVALLY CEMETERY

LOCATION: One mile NW of Marble Hill on Short Creek.

George W. Scivally
Apr 8, 1804
Apr 6, 1876

Joel Z., Son of
Z. M. & S. U. Scivally
Dec 9, 1868
Aug 22, 1869

Several unmarked graves.

* *

SHELTON-PORTER CEMETERY

LOCATION: South of Liberty Hill, on top of ridge.

Esop Shelton
Born 1777
Died Apr 22, 1861

Jerman Porter
Died Nov 23, 1894
Age: 81 years.

More than 25 graves with fieldstones, no inscriptions.

* *

SNOW CEMETERY

LOCATION: Two miles NW of Hurdlow.

Henry Snow
Feb 8, 1813
Feb 10, 1892

Martha Ann Snow
Nov 5, 1821
Aug 19, 1897

John Titus Snow
Oct 21, 1861
Sep 24, 1895

8 or more graves with fieldstones, no inscriptions.

* * * * * * * * * * * * * * * * * ** * * * * * * * * * * * *

TIPPS CEMETERY

LOCATION: One fourth mile south of Marble Hill.

Doda L. M., wife of
J. E. Woodard
Apr 18, 1865
Feb 1, 1893

Roy Calvin L., Son of
J. E. & Loda Woodard
Aug 13, 1886
Jul 15, 1887

Michael Tipps
Jul 15, 1809
Jan 25, 1883
Age: 73y, 9m, 10d.

Several unmarked graves.

Mary, wife of
J. C. Tipps
Aug 25, 1840
Feb 29, 1888

John Calvin, Son of
J. C. & Hulda Tipps
Oct 17, 1880
Nov 5, 1881

* *

TRAVIS CEMETERY

LOCATION: One mile SE of Marble Hill, where Coffee Creek empties into Elk River.

William Grant
Oct   1812
Apr 6, 1869
    & wife
Elizabeth Grant
Jun 1, 1820
Apr 13, 1897

Andrew J. Travis
May 30, 1842
Mar 25, 1888

Mary Elizabeth, wife of
A. J. Travis
Aug 17, 1842
Oct 3, 1881

Many unmarked graves.

Sallie E., Daughter of
A. J. & M. E. Travis
Aug 4, 1878
Sep 19, 1880

Joel E., Son of
A. J. & M. E. Travis
Oct 1, 1870
Apr 12, 1877

Attie, Daughter of
J. P. & N. P. Travis
Jan 13, 1871
Jan 29, 1873
Age: 2y, 16d.

D. S., Son of
J. E. & E. A. Travis
Mar 26, 1844
Nov 22, 1868
Age: 24y, 7m, 3d.

J. J. Harrison
May 5, 1836
Feb 3, 1899

H. C. Embrey
Oct 23, 1870
Dec 27, 1900

Elizabeth Philips, Consort
of Z. H. Murrell
May 18, 1797
Sep 14, 1824

J. W. Ballard
Jul 22, 1826
Dec 31, 1907

Many graves with fieldstones, no inscriptions.

J. P. Cole
May 6, 1822
Feb 20, 1873

Soota D. Browning, Consort
of Allen Johnston
Jun 28, 1822
Mar 4, 1857
Age: 34y, 8m, 6d.

Idah Y., Daughter of
A. & S. D. Johnston
Dec 6, 1855
Feb 15, 1857
Age: 1y, 2m, 9d.

Infant Son of
A. & S. D. Johnston
B&D Feb 28, 1857

* *

LOIS QUADRANGLE

UNION CHURCH CEMETERY

LOCATION: Near Lois Community.

J. M. Spencer
Jan 21, 1857
Feb 22, 1915
Married Nov 4, 1880
   & wife
Ruthie M. Spencer
Jun 5, 1859
(no date)

W. B. Parks
Nov 13, 1823
Mar 11, 1893
   & wife
Adaline Parks
Dec 25, 1833
Mar 1, 1918

Rev. L. R. Massey
Feb 7, 1848
Mar 4, 1921
   & wife
Callie Brazier Massey
Mar 22, 1847
Oct 9, 1920

Charlie W. Parks
May 7, 1866
Sep 6, 1910

* *

WAGGONER CEMETERY

LOCATION: One mile north of Hurdlow on Wet Prong of Farris Creek.

A. W.
1878
(fieldstone)

C. L. Waggoner
Jul 18, 1829
Nov 21, 1897
&
E. M. Waggoner
Mar 24, 1836
Mar 28, 1881

Beulah S. Waggoner
Apr 26, 1891
Nov 14, 1929
&
Vera Laurene Waggoner
Sep 2, 1915
Nov 5, 1922
&
Bettie W. Waggoner
Dec 12, 1848
Dec 21, 1926

E. W. Mitchell
Jan 6, 1890
Feb 11, 1920

Willard W. Marshall
1900-1919

James F. Spencer
1849-1918
&
Bettie Copeland Spencer
1853-1926

Charles Franklin, Son of
J. F. & S. E. Spencer
Feb 7, 1881
Jul 25, 1907
Age: 26 years.

Martha A. Butler
Aug 30, 1859
Oct 28, 1915

Lou Mitchell Grammer
Feb 24, 1890
Nov 5, 1952

Annie Stacy Spencer
1897-1918

"Father"
J. H. Higginbotham
Mar 6, 1844
Mar 16, 1916
   & "Mother"
Lavina E. Higginbotham
Aug 10, 1843
Jun 27, 1907

Daisy May, Daughter of
H. T. & M. L. Waggoner
Feb 20, 1897
Aug 28, 1898

J. M. Waggoner
Mar 5, 1837
Mar 2, 1893
"A Confederate Soldier"
Co G 41st Tenn
&
M. A. Waggoner
Apr 10, 1837
(no date)

Laura C., wife of
D. N. Hill
Aug 11, 1860
Apr 20, 1881

Houston Gattis
Died Jul 28, 1900
Age: (not given)

Kate, wife of
W. H. Clark
Feb 19, 1876
Jan 11, 1912

Several unmarked graves.

James W. Gattis
1876-1933
&
Ruthy E. Gattis
1871-1934

J. H. Wilks
Jan 8, 1857
Dec 30, 1903
   & wife
M. E. Horsley Wilks
Jun 26, 1875
Mar 30, 1904

"Brother"
Jessie L. Higginbotham
May 12, 1881
Jul 18, 1900
   & "Sister"
Emily Higginbotham
Jul 5, 1865
Jun 23, 1896

Infant Son of
H. J. & Floy Boles
(no dates)

Benjamin E. Spencer
Apr 24, 1822
Nov 28, 1900
&
Mary S. Spencer
Dec 16, 1825
Apr 18, 1876

W. A. S. (Spencer)
1830-1887
(fieldstone)

Annie B. Spencer
Oct 2, 1888
Jul 7, 1889
Age: 9m, 5d.
&
Mary Short Spencer
Sep 4, 1890
Mar 28, 1892
Age: 1y, 6m, 24d.
Children of
J. W. & E. E. Spencer.

Will Gattis
Mar 9, 1862
Married Nannie Wiseman
Jul 25, 1883
Died Aug 7, 1892

Ellie Gattis
Died Oct 24, 1880
Age: (not given)

Felix M. Waggoner
Co K Tenn Inf
C.S.A.

J. F. Horsley
Sep 1, 1851
Jul 18, 1913
   & wife
Mary F. Horsley
Jan 6, 1859
Apr 27, 1942

John C. Owens
1873-1917

Nina Owens Counts
1878-(no date)
&
Floy Owens Hoots
1900-1928

George W. Owens
Nov 6, 1859
Dec 12, 1900

Louisa Ann Owens
Jan 25, 1862
Jan 18, 1888

J. E. Spencer
Mar 20, 1830
May 15, 1892
"A Confederate Soldier"
Capt. Co C 44 Tenn

John T. Spencer
May 29, 1861
Nov 3, 1863

* *

LOIS QUADRANGLE

WALKER CEMETERY

LOCATION: One and one half miles west of Liberty Hill, on Copeland Hill.

Sue Latham 1871-1896 & Levi Latham 1820-1895 & Tilda Latham 1869-1890 & Bettie Latham 1840-1884	George Latham 1893-1912 & Rubin Walker 1867-1892	Matt Walker 1865-1891 & Moses Walker 1845-1937 & Francis Walker 1849-1887	40-50 graves, with fieldstones, no inscriptions & unmarked graves.

* *

WALLER CEMETERY

LOCATION: One mile south of Liberty Hill, on Ridge.

Zack Busbee Dec 13, 1884 Oct 14, 1935	Lora, wife of W. C. Crabtree Feb 20, 1874 Sep 7, 1889	Jasper Z. Walker 1862-1948 & Mary V. Walker 1876-19(no date)	Bettie, wife of F. T. Cashion Apr 15, 1884 Aug 3, 1907
John Busbee Feb 29, 1856 Apr 17, 1936	G. W. Grant (no dates, fieldstone)	Joseph Floyd Walker Aug 10, 1909 Jun 23, 1968	Mack, Son of J. P. & Mary Cashion Dec 10, 1903 Dec 18, 1903
Julia Ann, wife of J. A. Busbee Dec 25, 1856 Feb 14, 1917	F. M. Tripp Feb 21, 1861 Feb 13, 1922	Josie E. Syler Nov 5, 1878 Jan 17, 1902	Jessie Grady, Son of R. B. & E. Cashion Oct 2, 1905 Aug 17, 1917
Infant of John & Julia Busbee B&D Oct 1, 1894	W. H. Waller Sep 30, 1835 Mar 11, 1901	Wilson B., Son of D. H. & M. J. Call Jan 27, 1862 Apr 1, 1900	Ella, wife of R. B. Cashion Mar 17, 1870 Aug 2, 1897
Ema Pearl Busbee Dec 23, 1899 Aug 4, 1901	Martha A. Waller Dec 21, 1841 Jul 14, 1929	Mollie, wife of W. B. Call Feb 27, 1868 Feb 24, 1888	G. L. Cashion Sep 8, 1844 Apr 20, 1902
William Jefferson, Son of J. Z. & Mary Walker --- 17, 1887 Mar 30, 1909	Pansie M. E., Daughter of W. T. & M. D. Richardson Nov 18, 1891 Jan 18, 1892	Holland L., Son of G. W. & J. M. Fanning Aug 21, 1903 Dec 3, 1903	Sarah A., wife of G. L. Cashion Mar 2, 1848 Jul 28, 1909
Roy, Son of J. Z. & M. B. Walker Spr 28, 1906 Dec 7, 1911	Betty Noles Eslick 1854-1913 John M. Fanning Oct 31, 1890 Feb 7, 1919	Infant Daughter of H. H. & J. E. Heath B&D Jun 28, 1898	Brice D. Shelton Dec 10, 1810 May 15, 1879
Mary, wife of J. Z. Walker Oct 1, 1864 Jan 23, 1899	I. F. E. (no dates, fieldstone)	N. L. (no dates, fieldstone)	Margret J., wife of B. D. Shelton Jul 30, 1824 Aug 28, 1879
Infant Daughter of Mr. & Mrs. Ben McCormick (no dates)	Newton "Bud" Eslick 1845-1899 L. (no dates, fieldstone)	Felix, Son of May & John Fanning Aug 4, 1910 Aug 18, 1910	------ Hill (no dates, fieldstone)
Barshia Walker McCormick Nov 29, 1900 Oct 3, 1943	Otis Alton, Son of C. B. & C. A. Smith Jan 13, 1910 Apr 5, 1910	F. N. Noles Dec 26, 1855 (buried at another place in this cemetery)	Evadean Walker Noles Dec 4, 1859 Dec 5, 1929
Maggie B. Cashion, wife of J. S. Bedford Apr 27, 1866 Apr 16, 1908	Cavin (fieldstone)	Gladys Edde (no dates, no marker)	Mrs. John Fanning (no dates, no marker)

LOIS QUADRANGLE

C. L. Smith
Jun 9, 1854
May 16, 1923

Lunas E., Son of
James & N. A. Edde
Jan 30, 1897
Jan 7, 1912

F. R. Noles
Dec 26, 1855
Nov 30, 1940

Infant Daughter of
Jasper & Lizzie Noles
Oct 28, 1930

James Edde
Dec 21, 1859
Oct 30, 1935
&
Nancy Ann Edde
Feb 27, 1867
Feb 14, 1954

William H. Thronesberry
Oct 5, 1907
Dec 18, 1919
&
Roy L. Thronesberry
Mar 23, 1909
Dec 18, 1919

Our thanks to Mr. Paul Ray Cashion and his daughter Paulette for their help with this cemetery.

* *

WISEMAN CEMETERY

LOCATION: On hill behind Gore's Store, near Hurdlow.

J. B. Wiseman
Feb 27, 1858
Mar 31, 1911
Married Nov 4, 1888
&
Mary O. Wiseman
Apr 22, 1867
(no date)

John C. Wiseman   and
Husband of
Sopha A. Hickman
Feb 7, 1810
Apr 7, 1894
Married Apr 1, 1841

Sophia A. Hickman Wiseman
Apr 23, 1817
Jan 2, 1900

Many graves with no markers.

Several graves with fieldstones, no inscriptions.

* *

MULBERRY QUADRANGLE

BRAZIER CEMETERY

LOCATION: This Cemetery was ommitted in 1st Edition. A small Family Cemetery located two miles east of Highway # 50 on the north side of Lois Road. On site search failed to locate this cemetery.

* *

SMITH CEMETERY

LOCATION: Three and one half miles SW of Lynchburg, on the west side of Highway # 50.

Hardy H. Smith
Oct 9, 1815
Jul 12, 1864

"Father"
T. B. Smith
Jul 19, 1850
Aug 8, 1907

Signs of older graves, no markers.

* *

NAME INDEX

A

ABBOTT: 22, 41, 43, 44, 45, 46, 48, 115, 194, 211, 237, 241, 333, 341
ABERCROMBIE: 413
ABERNATHY: 64, 351
ABLES: 23, 42, 44, 47, 48, 185, 234, 235
ACUFF: 266, 376
ADAIR: 271, 280, 282
ADAMS: 51, 115, 295, 296, 313, 317, 403, 404, 406, 407, 414
ADCOCK: 308
ADCOX: 87
ADERHOLD: 310
ADLES: 48
AKIN: 115
ALBRIGHT: 115, 237, 316
ALDRIDGE: 350
ALEXANDER: 97, 98, 109, 114, 115, 177, 179, 265, 340
ALFORD: 110, 115
ALFRED: 112
ALLBRITTON: 371
ALLEN: 56, 115, 171, 176, 249, 269, 319, 338, 339, 359, 361, 366, 368, 369, 373, 374, 375, 376, 379, 392, 393, 394, 403, 406, 418, 419, 425, 428
ALLEY: 222
ALLISON: 79, 214, 264, 270, 271
ALLMON: 405
ALSTON: 381
ALSUP (ALLSUP): 192, 193, 194
ALTHAUSER: 384
AMASON: 179
AMOS: 346
ANDERSON: 37, 38, 39, 68, 73, 78, 103, 115, 175, 217, 283, 315, 334, 385, 419, 421, 422, 427
ANDERTON: 374, 375, 404, 405, 407, 410, 413, 416, 417
ANDREWS: 11, 178, 262, 387, 394
ANGELONE: 419
ANTHONY: 115, 396, 399, 409, 421, 425
ARCHER: 115, 307
ARMSTRONG: 13, 14, 71, 87, 88, 92, 93, 174, 209, 210, 311, 317, 318, 368, 369
ARNEY: 25, 30, 208, 211
ARNOLD: 168, 169, 198, 204, 205, 207, 212, 214, 222, 224, 225, 226, 268
ASH: 314

ASHBY: 16, 18, 52, 56, 57, 95, 104, 114, 115, 116, 181, 225, 261, 263, 267, 311, 324, 349, 369, 370, 384, 385, 395, 432, 435
ASHWORTH: 244, 245, 246, 247, 282
ASKEY: 279
ASKINS (ADKINS): 36, 39, 40, 42, 46, 47, 48, 114, 115, 116, 227, 331, 392
ASKINSON: 114
ATWOOD: 374
AUSTIN (AUSTON): 71, 73, 85, 218, 219, 220, 284, 403, 404, 422
AYERS: 65, 92, 271
AVANTAGGIO: 297
AWALT: 426

B

BABER: 118
BADGETT: 97
BAFFORD: 252
BAGGERLY (BEGGERLY): 352
BAGGETT (BAGET): 111, 415
BAGLEY: 7, 10, 109, 119, 130, 306, 360, 361, 362
BAILEY: 44, 51, 54, 117, 119, 262, 264, 311, 338, 365, 367, 382, 394
BAIN: 258
BAIRD: 82, 83
BAKER: 188, 189, 253, 332, 333, 344, 410, 411, 412, 428, 432
BALDWIN: 266, 267, 268, 362
BALLARD: 225, 380, 436
BANISTER: 110
BANKSTON: 243, 245, 246
BARBER: 380
BARHAM: 3, 8, 80, 305, 308, 311, 315, 316, 318, 320
BARKER: 170, 175, 176, 231
BARNES: 24, 29, 31, 32, 37, 116, 117, 118, 198, 237, 271, 291, 293, 295, 300, 320, 333
BARNETT (BARNETTE): 82, 83, 116, 118, 178, 256
BARRETT: 116, 117, 118, 318
BARROW: 192
BARTLETT (BARTLETTE): 3, 4, 52, 55, 116, 305, 358, 390, 393, 394, 426
BARZ: 119

BASS: 194
BASTER: 194
BATEMAN: 56, 262, 264, 271, 418
BATES (BAITS, BAITES): 47, 75, 81, 117, 118, 172, 179, 183, 187, 188, 207, 234, 235, 236, 240, 243, 245, 251, 252, 253, 256, 283, 330, 331, 333, 347, 350, 351, 367, 387, 406, 407, 434, 435
BATTLE: 118
BATTSON: 117
BAUCOM: 294
BAXTER: 153, 180, 188, 189, 203, 205, 208, 215, 221, 265, 359, 364, 366, 375, 377, 380, 393, 394, 395, 399, 411, 412
BAYLES: 107
BEAL: 201
BEAN: 83, 368, 375, 386, 426, 427
BEANLAND: 9
BEARD: 82, 194, 227, 228, 241, 312, 329, 331, 332, 349, 350
BEARDEN: 23, 24, 30, 38, 54, 79, 80, 118, 204, 227, 301, 302, 304, 354, 367
BEASLEY: 117, 193, 317
BEATIE (BEATY): 86, 86, 87, 91, 92
BEAVERS: 120, 184, 185, 257
BECK: 4
BEDDINGFIELD: 40, 84, 118, 198, 202, 205, 238, 349, 350
BEDFORD: 364, 371, 375, 426, 430, 438
BEDWELL (BIDWELL): 20, 56, 94, 95, 116, 117, 323, 333
BEECH: 43, 46, 251, 332, 336, 344, 346
BELL: 15, 16, 116, 118, 119, 120, 192, 255, 312, 369
BENDERMAN: 116
BENEDICT: 293, 297, 313
BENJAMIN: 117
BENNETT: 169, 177, 209, 348, 385, 395, 396, 402, 410, 411, 419, 421, 422, 424
BENSON: 59, 117, 166, 174, 175, 180, 190, 222, 223, 225, 282
BERCHEEN: 116
BERRIER: 181
BERRY: 111, 167, 262, 324, 378, 385, 396
BERRYHILL: 81

BERRYMAN: 48
BEVEHON: 363
BEVERLY: 81, 260
BEVILS (BEVELS): 118, 198, 202, 204, 246, 322, 349
BICKLEY: 380, 381
BIGHAM: 116, 294, 295
BILES: 532
BILLINGS: 75, 236, 333
BILLINGSLEY: 375
BILLIONS (BILLONS): 49, 66, 72, 75, 76
BILLS: 68, 307
BINGHAM: 117, 174
BINKLEY: 288
BINTZLER: 117
BIRD: 329, 333, 334
BIRDSONG: 206
BIRMINGHAM: 220
BISHOP: 21, 80, 235, 340
BLACK: 309
BLACKBURN: 266
BLACKNALL: 318
BLACKSHER: 309, 323
BLACKWELL: 265, 268, 301
BLAIR: 32, 33, 76, 78, 117, 120, 172, 224, 338, 343, 344, 352, 354, 355
BLAKE: 118, 301, 304
BLAKELY: 118
BLAKEMORE: 117, 118, 304, 307
BLAND: 79, 80, 210, 250, 295, 303, 345, 352
BLANKENSHIP: 56, 103, 118, 172, 329
BLAYLOCK: 245, 246
BLEDSOE: 2, 4, 5, 6, 26, 64, 69, 91, 181, 304, 308, 311, 313, 319, 322, 358
BLUNT: 199
BLYTHE: 363, 375, 376
BOAZ: 19, 20, 90, 97, 98, 103, 109, 117, 119, 317
BOBO: 12, 250, 328, 369, 370, 371, 372, 374, 379, 380, 384, 386, 387, 389, 392, 393, 396, 421, 422
BOGGS: 39, 44, 116, 340, 346, 353
BOGLE: 117
BOHANNON (BOHANAN): 398, 406
BOLANDER: 81, 244, 246
BOLDIN: 81
BOLES: 260, 437
BOLING (BOLIN): 48, 83, 226, 423
BOLLES: 10, 312
BOLTON: 69, 71
BOND: 74, 82, 116, 333
BONNER: 3, 5, 8, 109, 116, 118, 123, 177, 366

BOONE: 51, 52, 53, 108, 271, 373, 407
BORDINARO: 116
BOSTICK (BOSTIC): 169, 216, 221, 224, 240, 289
BOULDIN: 80, 117
BOVELL: 345
BOWEN: 116, 221, 222, 224, 371
BOWERS: 63
BOWLING: 78
BOYCE: 109, 117
BOYD: 110, 111, 118, 290, 331, 334, 422
BOYLES: 109, 116
BRADEN: 174, 197, 209, 210, 211, 213
BRADFORD: 11, 36, 44, 45, 46, 47, 48, 72, 93, 98, 118, 175, 179, 186, 296, 310, 317, 341, 348
BRADLEY: 46, 47, 116, 169, 204, 222, 226, 334
BRADSHAW: 102, 109, 117
BRADY (BREADY, BRADLEY): 29, 59, 193, 208, 212, 226, 267, 272, 278, 281
BRAGG: 237
BRANAMAN: 376
BRANCH: 387, 409, 412, 417
BRANDON: 117, 119, 372, 403, 427, 428
BRANNON: 23
BRANSON: 99
BRAY: 169, 182, 282
BRAZELL: 243
BRAZELTON: 48, 225, 234
BRAZIER: 367, 432, 439
BRENTS (BRENT): 116, 118, 217, 300
BREWER: 43, 105, 180, 194, 195, 205, 206, 209, 210, 211, 292, 312
BRIDGES: 248
BRIGGS: 117
BRIGHT: 108, 111, 112, 118, 170, 326
BRITTON: 280, 282, 348
BROADRICK: 24, 25, 350
BROADAWAY (BROADWAY): 70, 103, 116, 120, 308, 361
BROCK: 64, 75, 227, 294
BROGAN: 120
BROOK (BROOKS): 117, 118, 119, 169, 170, 183, 215, 226, 346, 407
BROSSARD: 117
BROTHERTON: 198, 202
BROWN: 10, 11, 19, 20, 42, 43, 53, 66, 68, 71, 75, 82, 87, 90, 91, 92, 94, 95, 96,

BROWN: 116, 117, 118, 120, 172, 174, 176, 177, 188, 215, 222, 226, 232, 239, 253, 254, 264, 267, 268, 269, 270, 273, 289, 302, 304, 309, 311, 312, 313, 314, 319, 337, 345, 354, 359, 383, 386, 398, 400, 401, 402, 404, 421, 426, 428, 431, 435
BROWNING: 415
BROWNLOW: 207
BROWSON: 120
BROYLES: 114, 116, 117, 275
BRUCE: 61, 118, 173, 212, 338, 341, 376, 427
BRUMITT: 251
BRYAN: 75, 334, 335, 338, 348
BRYANT: 25, 54, 64, 66, 79, 83, 89, 90, 91, 92, 100, 117, 119, 170, 171, 172, 173, 175, 176, 179, 194, 200, 203, 204, 223, 224, 228, 281, 285, 312, 335, 339, 346, 351, 360, 361, 376, 378, 382, 418
BRYSON: 117, 172, 342
BUCHANAN: 27, 78, 87, 91, 100, 101, 106, 107, 116, 117, 118, 119, 217, 277, 300, 301, 392, 418
BUCK: 251
BUCKNER: 117
BUFFALOE (BUFFALO): 67, 78, 192
BULLARD: 248
BUMPAS: 107
BUNN (BUNND): 116, 118, 119, 251, 253, 256, 331, 333
BUNTLEY: 16, 17, 20, 56, 94, 116, 117, 317
BURCHFIELD: 190
BURDEN: 177
BURFORD: 69
BURGESS: 77, 119, 120, 206, 235, 293, 365, 418
BURGETT: 292, 293, 294
BURKE: 110
BURNAM: 118
BURNS: 3, 7, 51, 72, 116, 117, 205, 275, 323
BURRAS: 119
BURROUGH: 110, 112
BURROW (BURROWS): 6, 9, 252, 358, 371, 394
BURRUM: 410
BURT: 401, 407, 413, 414, 419, 423, 424, 425

BURTON: 236, 329, 333, 334, 337, 363, 366, 367, 369, 371, 376, 377, 380, 382, 387, 409, 410
BUSBEE: 438
BUTLER: 246, 250, 298, 318, 321, 325, 334, 350, 437
BUVINGER: 302
BYERS: 64, 78, 79, 186, 216, 341
BYFORD: 407
BYNUM: 177, 182, 188, 189
BYRD: 218, 397
BYROM: 368, 384, 387, 388, 395, 397, 498, 404, 405, 414, 416, 423

C

CAGLE: 169
CAHELA: 169
CALDWELL: 11, 21, 120, 121, 123, 175, 186, 187, 208, 212, 218, 268, 271, 272, 279, 280, 282, 292, 293, 294, 295, 296
CALE: 350
CALHOUN: 40
CALL: 265, 267, 385, 438
CALLAHAN: 292
CAMBRON: 120, 172, 173, 179, 216, 220, 226
CAMP: 219, 235
CAMPBELL: 23, 25, 30, 47, 48, 52, 54, 64, 70, 85, 124, 178, 208, 215, 234, 263, 266, 269, 271, 273, 274, 281, 282, 285, 335, 346, 377, 382
CANANT: 216
CANNON (CANNAN): 14, 54, 57, 124, 227, 252, 253, 262, 333, 334
CANTRELL: 218, 230, 232, 234, 248
CAPERTON: 84
CAPLEY: 120, 124, 173, 308, 320
CAPPS: 368
CARDIN: 199
CARITHERS: 336
CARLISLE: 176, 178
CARLOSS: 109, 123
CARLTON: 317
CARMACK: 120, 302, 324
CARPENTER: 33, 77, 79, 81, 111, 121, 123, 198, 207, 208, 340, 341, 351
CARRIGAN: 120, 309
CARRIGER: 53, 54
CARROLL: 54, 55, 57, 121, 297, 361
CARTER: 38, 66, 71,

CARTER: 120, 121, 122, 124, 170, 217, 225, 231, 235, 248, 273, 279, 282, 284, 285, 295, 365, 405, 406, 407
CARTWRIGHT: 190, 269, 273
CARTY: 111
CARUTHERS: 355
CARVER: 123
CARY: 39, 122
CASAWAY: 284
CASCHIGONES: 389
CASEY: 269, 432
CASH: 235
CASHION: 90, 94, 120, 121, 123, 167, 170, 254, 256, 276, 281, 282, 288, 298, 308, 312, 319, 323, 324, 373, 383, 384, 385, 398, 438
CASSEL: 234
CAST: 325
CASTEEL: 6, 295, 298, 313, 390, 401, 422
CASTLEMAN: 89, 254
CATES: 52, 54, 55, 56, 190, 218, 240, 403, 404, 406, 407, 422
CATHCART: 22, 78, 121, 193, 210
CATHEY: 21, 24, 33, 297
CAUDLE: 104, 120, 284
CAUGHRAN: 40, 41, 42, 43, 45, 47, 101, 120, 121, 123, 124, 215, 265, 337, 343
CERTAIN: 274, 284
CHADICK: 108
CHAFIN: 120, 121
CHANDLER: 73, 74
CHAPMAN: 88, 92, 208, 209, 302, 304, 366, 386, 394, 400, 409, 413, 417, 423, 428, 432
CHEATHAM: 60, 61, 121, 296
CHESSER: 80
CHICK: 122
CHILCOAT: 110, 112
CHILDERS: 98, 122, 267, 297
CHILDRESS: 22, 29, 198, 212, 237, 238, 239, 240, 269, 334, 349, 350
CHILDS: 26, 53, 91
CHITWOOD: 28
CHOCKLEY: 153
CHRISTA: 178
CHRISTIAN: 78, 122, 123
CHRISTOPHER: 199
CHURCH: 87, 224
CLACK: 399
CLARDY: 124
CLARK: 22, 23, 24, 25, 27, 28, 43, 46, 55,

CLARK: 86, 87, 88, 90, 91, 93, 102, 120, 121, 122, 123, 183, 186, 195, 197, 201, 204, 205, 206, 209, 225, 237, 241, 249, 253, 292, 296, 297, 320, 329, 363, 368, 377, 381, 393, 401, 426, 437
CLARKE: 21, 26, 108, 123
CLAYTON: 34, 123, 257
CLEEK: 6, 400, 401, 425
CLEGHORN: 37
CLEM: 75
CLENNY: 324
CLEVENGER: 178
CLICK: 104
CLIFFORD: 5
CLIFT: 23, 92, 99, 122, 291
CLINE: 218
CLOYD: 120
COATS: 76, 77, 79
COBB: 109, 369, 374, 401, 406, 410, 423
COBBLE: 255, 386, 410, 428
COBLE: 25, 59, 193, 198, 206
CODIE (CODY): 370, 400, 431
COFFE: 36
COGGIN (COGGINS): 25, 212, 238
COLBERT: 78, 80, 174, 227, 234, 236, 237, 240, 330, 333, 334
COLDWELL: 8
COLE: 13, 14, 15, 16, 78, 81, 104, 120, 171, 204, 205, 238, 259, 307, 309, 313, 338, 340, 341, 351, 352, 436, 86
COLEMAN: 25, 38, 39, 41, 43, 120, 122
COLGROVE: 123
COLLETT: 171
COLLIER: 121, 302, 310, 318, 360, 361
COLLINS: 22, 24, 25, 28, 31, 32, 52, 72, 73, 122, 124, 174, 192, 194, 201, 206, 207, 208, 211, 212, 249, 255, 263, 292, 295, 303, 367, 386
COLSHER: 370, 382
COLSTON: 123, 204
COLTER: 14, 19, 89, 124
COMBS: 75
COMMONS: 28, 51, 65, 109, 341
COMPTON: 193, 295
CONAWAY (CONOWAY): 87, 103, 104, 121, 122
CONDER: 310
CONGER: 96, 121, 122, 132

CONINE: 62
CONNER: 33, 267
CONNOR: 362, 373
CONRAD: 92, 121
CONWAY: 261
CONWELL: 8, 52, 88, 91, 102, 303, 307, 309, 312, 370 386, 396
COOK: 175, 242, 273, 387
COOLEY: 283
COOP (COOPE): 6, 401, 402, 405, 409, 411, 424
COOPER: 67, 80, 123, 171, 185, 223, 259, 268, 271, 373
COPE: 249
COPELAND: 169, 172, 174, 175, 176, 177, 286, 287, 288, 289, 372, 383, 428, 431, 432, 433, 434
CORBIN: 63, 65
CORDELL: 305
CORDER: 51, 53, 81, 93, 121, 171, 180, 212, 228, 259, 287
CORNELIUS: 189
CORNELL: 248
COPIER: 74
CORVIN: 406
COSSEY: 187
COSTON: 123, 282
COTHRAN (COTHRUM, COTHREN, COTHRUM): 7, 8, 61, 121, 179, 249, 251, 252, 254
COTNER: 181
COTTON: 248
COUCH: 123, 218, 222, 223, 311
COUNTS: 169, 172, 173, 174, 175, 177, 178, 179, 181, 190, 191, 215, 251, 384, 387, 400, 431, 437
COUSER: 399, 402, 420, 421, 422
COWAN: 8, 58, 66, 103, 107, 120, 122, 172, 179, 183, 184, 185, 232, 233, 253, 259, 332, 342, 348
COWDEN: 101, 314, 315, 316
COWEN: 102, 334, 335
COWLEY: 225, 279, 280, 435
COWN: 169
COX: 34, 51, 53, 56, 187, 189, 362, 363
CRABTREE: 25, 90, 122, 124, 190, 245, 254, 299, 303, 308, 310, 311, 312, 313, 325, 429, 438
CRAIG: 120, 216, 218
CRAIN: 25
CRAMSIE: 41, 122

CRANE: 12, 24, 93, 122, 261, 306, 310, 314, 391
CRANFORD: 175, 178
CRAWFORD: 27, 81, 86, 90, 100, 102, 122, 123, 174, 179, 184, 221, 239, 245, 246, 265, 315, 342
CRAWLEY: 122, 219
CREASON (CRESON): 11, 18, 50, 52, 54, 55, 56, 57, 122, 271, 362
CRENSHAW: 392
CRICK: 120, 321
CROCKER: 368
CRONEY: 121
CROSS: 74, 83
CROUCH: 225
CROWDER: 123, 185
CROWELL: 224, 416
CRUMBLEY: 177
CRUMLEY: 234
CRUNK: 120, 234, 294, 304
CRUTCHER: 277, 386, 398
CULVERIUS: 426
CUMMINGS (CUMMINS): 87, 111, 121, 122, 123, 185, 253, 323, 389
CUNNINGHAM: 16, 17, 24, 26, 29, 30, 32, 103, 104, 113, 120, 121, 122, 123, 171, 205, 206, 258, 279, 282, 306, 364, 386, 397, 406, 407, 410, 411, 412, 418, 419, 430, 432
CUR: 419
CURLEE: 104, 121, 123, 318, 323
CURREY (CURRY): 173, 176, 177, 293
CURRIN: 70, 121
CURTIS (CURTISS): 83, 199, 200, 211, 309, 317
CUZZORT: 170, 178
CYREE: 403, 406, 407, 419

D

DALE: 45, 49, 124
DALY: 124
DAMRON (DAMERON, DAMREL): 41, 220, 221, 253, 254, 256, 259, 386, 387, 404, 411, 425, 430
DANCE: 365, 372, 377, 378, 399, 421
DANDRIDGE: 338
DANIEL (DANIELS): 125, 126, 178, 217, 219, 237, 251, 266, 303, 327, 328, 329, 330, 332, 333, 334, 346, 362, 365, 369, 370,

DANIEL: 373, 374, 384, 415, 422, 423, 426
DANLEY: 82
DARNABY: 396
DARNELL (DARNEL): 125, 293, 299, 306, 309, 317, 320, 324, 384, 385, 387, 431
DAVENPORT: 124
DAVES: 89, 92, 102, 126, 314
DAVIDSON: 50, 92, 124, 126, 244, 271, 285, 305, 308, 315, 319, 320, 321, 342
DAVIES: 425
DAVIS: 30, 43, 59, 64, 66, 71, 86, 99, 104, 122, 124, 125, 126, 190, 192, 194, 204, 205, 206, 208, 210, 211, 212, 213, 225, 226, 232, 233, 234, 242, 249, 250, 252, 293, 307, 309, 310, 311, 312, 314, 318, 319, 323, 330, 331, 333, 338, 346, 383, 393, 411, 417, 419, 421, 423
DAWDY: 363
DAY: 188
DEAILY: 174
DEAL: 92, 366, 367, 398, 429, 430
DEAN: 124, 125, 301, 361, 406
DEATON: 417
DEBOSE: 198, 342
DECKER: 186
DEFORD: 36, 126, 326
DeHAVEN: 124, 342
DELAP: 252, 254
DELK: 8
DEMASTERS: 113
DEMPSEY (DEMSY): 34, 67, 93, 251, 348
DENHAM: 30, 292, 297
DENNIS: 250, 353
DENTON: 235, 240, 345, 346
DERRICK: 26, 125, 221
DERROR: 270
DEVER (DEVERS): 75, 205
DEWVOICE: 191
DICKENS: 126
DICKEY: 27, 36, 37, 40, 41, 45, 47, 125, 169, 234, 254, 255, 256, 280, 283, 289, 290, 342, 385
DICKSON: 110, 343
DIEMER: 111, 125
DIETZ: 125
DILLINGHAM: 418, 421, 422
DILLWORTH: 124
DIMOCH: 125
DINWIDDIE (DENWIDDIE): 124, 125

DISMUKES: 125
DIXON: 208
DOBBINS: 63, 124, 125, 291, 297
DODD: 24, 296
DODSON: 124, 126, 178, 309, 418
DOGGETT: 293, 295
DOLLAR: 63, 64, 65, 82, 245, 343, 346
DOLLINS: 14, 15
DONAHEW: 209
DONALDSON: 203, 218, 222
DONELSON: 346
DONNELL: 407
DOOLEY: 15, 125
DOTSON: 72, 190, 217
DOUGLAS: 108, 111
DOUTHIT (DOUTHAT): 125, 126, 202, 203, 230
DOWDA: 125
DOWDY: 124
DOWNING: 80, 82, 124, 125, 126, 227, 294, 295
DOWNUM: 408, 409
DOZIER: 124, 352
DRAKE: 108, 125
DRENNAN (DRENNON): 41, 124, 179, 337, 346, 349
DRIVER: 200, 364, 371, 387, 397
DRYDEN: 125, 317
DUBOIS: 350
DUCKWORTH: 294, 295, 296, 322, 332, 341, 351, 397
DUDLEY: 15
DUFF: 226, 271
DUGGER: 73
DUHON: 331
DUKE: 272, 273, 285, 287
DULIN: 407
DUNCAN: 8, 16, 18, 232, 240, 243
DUNDAS: 280
DUNIVAN (DONOVAN, DUNAFON): 124, 126, 341
DUNLAP: 326
DUNMAN: 44, 47, 48, 299
DUNN: 52, 54, 57, 67, 124, 125, 301, 307, 425
DUNNAVANT: 70, 76, 206, 207, 209
DUNSTON: 188
DURHAM: 124, 173, 177, 221, 254, 367
DUSENBERRY: 261, 265
DWIGGINS: 314
DYE: 186
DYER: 9, 10, 125, 126, 200, 297, 309, 316, 318, 319, 320, 424
DYSART: 317

E

EADY: 364, 365
EAGIN: 63, 320
EAKES (EAKS): 87, 91, 126, 331
EAKIN: 311
EASLEY: 127
EASTLAND: 27, 183
EATON: 262, 363, 374
ECHOLS: 185, 250
EDDE (EDDIE): 367, 426, 438, 439
EDDINS (EDDINGS): 43, 45, 106
EDENS (EDNS): 359, 363, 376, 387, 423, 426
EDGEMAN: 56, 403
EDMISTON (EDMINSON, EDMISON): 29, 47, 54, 86, 87, 94, 99, 127, 222, 316
EDMONDS (EDMON): 235, 380
EDMONDSON (EDMONSON, EDMISON, EDMASTON): 19, 26, 35, 94, 111, 126, 189, 282, 292
EDWARDS: 51, 82, 83, 126, 127, 167, 194, 270, 294, 295, 296, 306, 414
EGGLESTON (EGLESTON): 400, 401, 425
ELERSON: 201
ELEY: 126, 224, 251
ELKINS: 98
ELLIOTT: 72, 126, 392, 393
ELLIS (ELIS): 10, 66, 89, 106, 126, 204, 293, 296, 299, 300, 313, 315, 321, 324, 334
ELMORE: 47, 72, 127, 266
ELZEY: 322
EMBREY: 436
EMERITT: 418
EMERSON: 63
EMMONS: 208, 209, 212
ENDSLEY: 126, 212, 256, 293, 312, 321
ENGLAND: 340, 343, 345
ENGLISH: 37, 46, 253
ENGLMAN: 126
ENNIS: 176
ENOCH (ENOCHS): 306, 373, 376, 399, 420
EPPS: 13, 43, 87, 88, 92, 259, 317
ERVIN: 303, 321, 367, 371, 372, 385, 396, 397, 398, 428
ERWIN: 23, 24, 25, 126, 249, 328, 337, 340
ESHMAN: 92, 131, 291, 293
ESLICK: 126, 127, 170, 172, 183, 281, 285, 288, 290, 430, 431, 432, 434, 438

ESTILL: 265, 379
EVANS: 41, 67, 104, 126, 127, 128, 175, 176, 189, 207, 213, 266, 271, 284, 318, 366, 368, 369, 373, 375, 378, 379, 393, 410, 417, 429, 431, 432, 433
EWING: 68
EZELL: 199

F

FANNING (FANNIN): 48, 49, 117, 127, 166, 187, 218, 285, 288, 329, 333, 367, 372, 374, 429, 435, 438
FARISS: 420
FARLEY: 223
FARMER: 187, 188, 217
FARQUHARSON: 128
FARR: 392
FARRAR (FARER, FARRER): 34, 42, 60, 79, 109, 127, 128, 172, 201, 203, 269, 270, 312, 384, 402, 405, 406, 423
FARRIS (FARIS): 224, 233, 271, 285
FATE: 186
FAULKINBERRY: 75
FAULKNER: 16, 17, 51, 52, 54, 55, 56, 168, 174, 225, 262, 263, 269
FEARS: 433, 435
FEENEY: 127, 128
FELLOW: 334
FELPS: 53, 384, 392, 393, 394, 396
FENNER: 11
FERGUSON (FERGASON): 7, 8, 16, 72, 73, 77, 79, 80, 85, 171, 176, 376
FERRELL: 406
FEW: 127
FIFE: 42, 327
FINCH: 187
FINLEY: 294, 296, 297, 317
FINN: 127
FINNEY: 368, 385, 401, 424
FISHBACK: 314
FISHER: 175, 322
FISK (FISKE): 71, 270, 330
FITCH: 179
FITZSIMMONS: 25, 65, 178, 206, 237
FLACK: 7
FLANAGAN: 78
FLAUTT: 24
FLEMING: 97, 110, 112, 127, 134
FLIPPO: 386, 409, 411
FLOWERS: 217

FLOYD: 331, 333, 364, 372, 374, 419, 420
FLY: 299
FLYNN (FLYN): 107, 176, 339, 340, 349
FLYNT (FLINT, FLYNTT): 14, 230, 231, 250, 281, 282, 332
FORBES (FORBS): 76, 78, 340
FORD: 35, 47, 245, 406
FOREST: 88, 127
FORGEY: 248
FORMWALT: 127, 128
FORRESTER (FORESTER, FORRESTOR): 17, 19, 52, 55, 57, 95, 127, 263, 313, 383, 392, 394
FORSYTH: 435
FOSTER: 2, 3, 4, 5, 127, 175, 222, 226, 249, 279, 300, 307, 314, 320, 321, 323, 336, 337, 359, 369, 406, 407
FOWLER: 71, 128, 174, 176, 187, 259, 306, 309, 354
FOX: 14, 90, 314, 315
FRAME: 181, 252, 256, 375, 376, 418, 419, 429, 430
FRANCH: 112
FRANCIS: 127
FRANKLIN: 67, 75, 81, 84, 85, 109, 112, 123, 127, 128, 171, 172, 238, 286, 288, 289, 292, 293, 294, 296, 297, 303, 307
FRASIER: 176
FREEMAN: 4, 5, 6, 7, 8, 64, 75, 127, 264, 265, 268, 269, 280, 282, 308, 309, 311, 314, 320, 424, 425
FRENCH: 127
FRIEDMAN: 378
FRIEND: 120
FRIZZELL: 382
FROST: 53, 57
FRY: 280, 315
FULLER: 15, 57, 176, 251, 258, 327, 334, 432
FULLERTON: 33, 35, 38, 40, 128, 307, 309
FULMER: 401
FULTON: 46, 109, 110, 112, 127, 157
FULTS: 348

G

GAFFNEY: 323
GAGE: 57
GALLOWAY (GALLAWAY): 38, 40, 42, 45, 46, 128, 129, 337, 342, 429

GAMBILL (GAMBRILL, GAMBRELL): 88, 89
GAMBLE: 368, 420
GAMMILL: 8, 320, 390, 391
GAMMON: 130, 174, 244, 282
GANT: 111, 129
GARDNER (GARDINER): 185, 187, 189, 382, 396
GARMON: 365
GARNER: 111, 218, 372, 428
GARRETT: 212
GARY: 81, 130, 207, 213
GASKILL: 129
GATLIN: 24, 51, 78, 84, 206
GATTIS: 129, 168, 169, 177, 178, 215, 216, 219, 223, 267, 269, 272, 273, 283, 288, 329, 363, 366, 431, 432, 434, 435, 437
GAULT: 36, 37, 38, 44, 46, 179, 205, 233
GAUNT: 39, 318, 322
GAUT: 414
GAUTNEY: 46, 253
GENTRY (GENTERY): 43, 202, 369, 392, 420
GEORGE: 15, 60, 61, 62, 63, 70, 71, 75, 87, 89, 94, 102, 128, 129, 130, 172, 174, 178, 179, 188, 201, 202, 204, 225, 230, 234, 256, 260, 286, 287, 288, 432
GEOWEN: 94
GIBBS: 61, 81, 420
GIBSON (GIPSON): 1, 10, 11, 101, 178, 185, 232, 233, 293, 308, 321, 322
GILBERT: 2, 7, 8, 291, 306, 316
GILES: 92
GILL: 54, 55, 130, 194, 197, 201, 202, 203, 206, 243, 269, 271, 295, 314, 315, 320, 360, 361
GILLESPIE: 111, 130, 302, 320, 324, 325, 434
GILLIAM (GILLHAM, GILHAM): 176, 211, 223, 256, 259, 280
GILLILAND: 109, 129, 249, 258, 351
GIPSON: 248
(see Gibson)
GIVENS: 129, 327
GLASER: 407
GLASS: 129
GLASSCO: 176
GLASSCOCK: 321
GLAZE: 63

GLAZIER: 130, 390
GLEGG: 36
GLEGHORN: 38, 39, 79, 128, 205, 317
GLENN: 25, 293
GODBEY: 248
GOLDEN: 166, 184, 187, 383, 386, 387, 416, 417
GOOD: 336, 340, 343, 344, 346, 349
GOODMAN: 173
GOOCH: 249
GOODNER: 280
GOODRICH: 12, 110, 111, 129, 130, 151
GOODWIN: 167
GOOLSBY: 65
GOOSBY: 51, 54, 57, 129, 266, 269, 273, 410
GORDON (GORDEN, GORDIN, GORDOR): 65, 109, 128, 129, 130, 373, 404, 410
GORE: 128, 371, 375, 383, 397, 410, 412, 416, 422, 433, 434
GOTCHER: 129
GOUGH: 111, 112
GOWAN: 56, 305, 364
GOWDER: 128
GOWEN: 29, 358, 364, 374, 427
GRABLE: 430
GRACY: 102, 107
GRAHAM: 4, 5, 7, 52, 172, 181, 344, 402
GRAMMER: 6, 128, 223, 321, 372, 400, 411, 416, 432, 435, 437
GRANT: 371, 383, 385, 411, 430, 436, 438
GRANTLAND: 79, 248
GRAVES: 81, 237, 252, 255, 292
GRAY: 48, 103, 111, 128, 129, 130, 165, 168, 169, 171, 177, 178, 182, 187, 188, 228, 229, 230, 231, 232, 236, 237, 257, 268, 278, 281, 282, 288, 290, 333, 346, 348, 367, 372, 384, 394, 430, 431
GREEN: 114, 128, 129, 160, 221, 238, 246, 253, 256, 307, 314, 328, 344, 345, 365, 366, 378, 389, 393, 422
GREENFIELD: 243
GREENWOOD: 409
GREER: 1, 4, 10, 86, 110, 112, 128, 309, 319, 321, 324, 325
GREGORY: 128, 198, 278
GRIDER: 129, 340
GRIFFIN: 25, 71, 73, 75, 85, 130, 170,

GRIFFIN: 216, 223, 224, 226, 282, 332
GRIFFIS: 41, 109, 205, 206, 326, 327
GRIGGS: 217
GRIGSBY (GRIGBY): 103, 104
GRILLS: 129, 229
GRIMES: 211
GRISARD: 111, 264
GRISSOM: 248, 258
GRISWELL: 130
GRIZZARD: 128, 365
GRIZZELL: 174
GROCE: 18, 19, 20, 55, 56, 130, 277, 309, 312, 313
GROGAN: 407
GROOVES: 177
GROVES (GROVE): 270, 284
GRUBBS: 64, 65, 66
GULLEY: 65
GULLET: 112
GULLEY: 180, 223, 282
GUNN: 287, 315
GUNTER: 22, 23, 25, 29, 37, 128, 130, 195, 207, 208, 209, 211
GURLEY: 238
GUTHRIE: 288
GUY: 30
GUYNN: 129

H

HADDON: 385
HAGUE: 110, 266, 268, 271
HAIRSTON (HARISTON): 227, 244
HAISLIP: 132, 193, 195, 205, 210, 294, 295, 309
HALBERT: 33, 34, 100, 107, 134, 207
HALCOMB: 174, 180
HALE: 10, 11, 185
HALEY: 133, 245
HALL: 14, 44, 64, 65, 67, 69, 72, 73, 131, 132, 134, 185, 201, 218, 223, 224, 225, 296, 297, 327, 408, 409, 412, 414, 415, 416
HAMBRICK (HAMBRIC): 186, 218, 233, 235, 258, 333, 349
HAMILTON: 30, 33, 36, 37, 38, 39, 40, 42, 48, 68, 71, 72, 91, 110, 130, 131, 132, 133, 134, 201, 215, 216, 218, 219, 220, 223, 226, 280, 282
HAMLIN: 24, 25, 57, 134, 205, 210, 326, 421
HAMMONS (HAMMONDS): 238, 291, 312

HAMPTON: 27, 91, 132, 201, 202, 203, 265, 266, 279, 302
HANAWAY: 321, 323
HANCOCK: 132, 133, 243, 245, 246, 248
HANEY: 183, 297
HANKS: 89, 95, 241
HANNAH (HANNA): 247, 352
HANSELL: 109
HANSON: 395
HANVEY: 235
HARBIN: 131, 134, 172, 177, 178, 254, 259, 279, 281, 282, 405
HARDIMAN: 25
HARDIN (HARDEN, HARDING): 66, 67, 68, 81, 105, 132, 169, 192, 219, 221, 244, 335, 417
HARDY: 369, 377, 411, 416, 417
HARGRAVE (HARGRAVES): 72, 74, 83
HARGROVE: 71, 79, 83, 328, 349, 406
HARKINS: 7, 8, 309
HARMENING: 171, 176, 190, 222, 226
HARMS: 42, 133
HARNESS: 313
HARNEY: 200
HARP: 411
HARPER: 192, 207, 212, 216, 294, 412, 415
HARRELL: 171
HARRIS: 27, 32, 88, 92, 100, 130, 131, 132, 133, 167, 175, 179, 181, 198, 207, 226, 227, 235, 236, 241, 249, 264, 301, 302, 304, 306, 317, 328, 333, 348, 425
HARRISON: 31, 113, 201, 202, 203, 225, 265, 271, 306, 333, 349, 367, 369, 372, 373, 379, 381, 382, 383, 387, 430, 436
HART: 86, 133, 305, 306, 307, 309, 321, 322, 365, 396
HARTER: 133
HARTON: 249, 250
HARWELL: 39, 43, 48, 131, 132, 134, 194, 197, 205, 206, 210, 211, 249
HASLETT: 382, 384
HASTEN: 80
HASTINGS: 130, 131, 134, 308, 309, 310, 311, 312, 313, 319
HASTON: 368
HASTY: 19, 54, 55, 131, 387, 409, 414, 416, 425
HATCHER: 131, 132, 133, 134, 302

444

HATCHETT: 80
HATFIELD: 194, 408
HATHAWAY: 314
HATHCOAT (HAYTHCOAT, HAITHCOAT): 352
HATHCOCK: 42
HATLEY: 174, 217
HAWKINS: 64, 173, 191, 312, 355
HAYES: 59, 218, 235, 287, 336, 338, 339, 341, 344, 346, 374
HAYNES: 322, 386, 413, 422
HAYNIE: 56, 89, 90, 95
HAYS: 44, 134, 341, 342, 368, 380
HAZELWOOD (HASELWOOD, HAZLEWOOD): 88, 178, 189, 256, 264, 266, 309, 366, 390, 409, 410
HAZLETT: 91, 92, 313, 367
HEAD: 316
HEARD: 73
HEARLSTON: 184
HEATH: 3, 255, 361, 362, 438
HEDGEPETH: 198
HELM (HELMS): 52, 63, 178, 179, 243, 267, 285
HELTON: 318, 406
HEMPHILL: 80, 320
HENDERSON: 27, 42, 44, 134, 189, 230, 231, 232, 233, 234, 235, 246, 253, 254, 255, 257, 258, 259, 260, 340, 365
HENDRIX: 130, 132
HENDRY: 291
HENLEY: 133, 407
HENRY: 237
HENSHAW: 367
HENSLEY: 2, 435
HENSON: 131, 134, 172
HENTZ: 170, 246, 339
HEREFORD: 131, 132, 199, 200
HERNDON: 277
HESS: 8
HESTER: 9, 104, 132, 172, 176, 182
HICE: 396, 397, 398
HICKLEN: 65, 66, 75
HICKS: 34, 64, 133, 334, 335, 354, 364, 422, 423
HICKSON: 132, 189
HIGGINBOTHAM: 437
HIGGINS: 98, 102, 131, 132, 133, 216, 314, 330, 333
HIGGS: 211
HIGH: 419
HILES: 365, 378
HILL: 43, 45, 85, 103, 108, 131, 133, 170, 178, 188, 208, 216,

HILL: 232, 234, 247, 248, 255, 265, 267, 272, 278, 348, 371, 385, 394, 408, 409, 429, 437, 438
HILLER: 133
HILLIARD: 134, 221
HILLIS: 189
HILLYARD: 196
HIMEBAUGH: 16, 131
HINES: 86, 87, 88, 96, 132, 133
HINKLE: 359, 362, 378, 387, 398, 431
HINTON: 75, 238
HIRLSTON: 254
HISE: 369, 385
HIX: 381, 393, 397, 409, 421
HOBBS (HOBB): 23, 60, 61, 72, 110, 132, 193, 201, 202, 204, 205, 263, 264, 291, 292, 295, 353, 363, 375, 379, 380, 382, 383, 387, 393, 394
HODGE: 222, 249, 335, 337
HOGAN: 207
HOLDER: 251, 283, 401, 403, 424
HOLDING: 109
HOLLAND: 45, 62, 65, 66, 67, 76, 79, 104, 131, 269, 312, 313, 323
HOLLIS: 252
HOLLOW: 212
HOLLOWAY: 305, 310, 327, 343
HOLLY (HOLLEY): 6, 7, 132, 209, 211
HOLMAN: 22, 70, 72, 84, 110, 131, 132, 133, 134, 214, 226, 235, 252, 262, 264
HOLMES: 174
HOLT: 63, 64, 66, 172, 174, 186, 189, 211, 252, 329, 371, 374, 376, 398, 404, 415, 420, 421, 427
HONE: 189
HONEA: 216, 348, 349, 353
HONEY: 190, 228, 232, 352
HOOPER: 132
HOOTS: 55, 98, 131, 133, 134, 178, 217, 255, 277, 437
HOPKINS: 238, 239, 240, 241, 244, 245, 246, 251, 252, 257, 282, 331, 332, 348, 349, 353
HOPPER: 23, 30, 38, 88, 131, 203, 204, 205, 209
HORNE: 133
HORSEFIELD: 422

HORSLEY: 388, 437
HORTON: 184, 216, 259, 364, 366, 384, 392, 413
HOSSE: 76
HOUCH: 131
HOUCHIN: 134
HOUSE: 322
HOVIS: 133, 134, 198, 335
HOWARD: 5, 130, 132, 216, 246, 252, 270, 274, 275, 403, 404, 407, 426
HOWE: 132
HOWELL: 207, 228, 234, 235, 255, 257, 258, 316
HUBBARD: 317
HUDGINS: 174, 229
HUDSON: 19, 53, 58, 88, 93, 172, 187, 188, 215, 221, 259, 297, 298, 312, 318, 358, 365
HUFF: 268
HUFFINE: 319
HUFFMAN: 382, 383, 386, 408, 411, 412, 414
HUGHES: 32, 211, 381
HUGHEY: 23, 24, 25, 32, 134, 201, 204, 295
HULSEY: 86, 105, 131, 217
HUMPHREYS: 132
HUNT: 179, 308, 432, 433
HUNTER: 23, 99, 110, 131, 133, 168, 182, 234, 238, 240, 241, 245, 251, 254, 264, 291, 292, 308, 319, 333, 349, 401
HURDLOW: 420, 421
HURLEY: 208, 212
HURLSTON: 104, 335
HURT: 309, 321
HUSBANDS: 304
HUSCH: 179
HUSKEY: 371, 386, 417, 421
HUTCHINSON: 79, 235, 328
HUTCHISON: 29, 313
HYATT: 252

I

INGLE: 17, 53, 134, 267, 365, 366, 385
INGRAM: 380
INLOW: 371
IRVIN: 427
ISAACS: 110
ISBELL: 348
ISOM: 43, 94, 95, 97, 98, 134, 135, 303, 345, 346
IVEY (IVY): 67, 84, 183, 222, 240, 327, 328, 333, 334, 348, 415, 416
IVIE: 135

J

JACKS: 215, 217, 218
JACKSON: 17, 179, 205, 210, 217, 358
JACOBS (JACOB): 36, 43, 47, 97, 135, 194, 294, 298
JACOWAY: 398
JAMES: 23, 67, 135
JANSON: 135
JARED: 285, 371
JARVIS: 136, 325
JEAN (JEANS): 103, 135, 136, 167, 180, 202, 203, 224, 225, 226, 227, 233, 241, 243, 244, 245, 249, 279, 287, 332, 346, 348, 349, 410
JEFFERY: 413
JEFFRIES: 238, 240
JENKINS (JINKINS): 22, 33, 91, 92, 103, 104, 135, 241, 248, 282, 372, 430
JENNINGS: 135, 166, 168, 214, 268, 286, 287
JERNIGAN: 358
JEROME: 136
JETTON: 184
JESTER: 67
JEWELL: 103
JOBE: 37, 39, 75, 136, 296, 299, 344
JOHNS: 249, 259
JOHNSON: 17, 24, 29, 56, 76, 77, 79, 82, 91, 92, 95, 134, 135, 136, 169, 170, 198, 199, 206, 208, 209, 211, 212, 217, 266, 267, 304, 342, 410, 425
JOHNSTON: 54, 55, 57, 135, 136, 367, 436
JOINS (JOINES): 194, 206, 211, 237, 239
JONES: 3, 22, 24, 30, 61, 65, 72, 73, 81, 103, 113, 135, 136, 186, 188, 200, 216, 217, 219, 221, 224, 225, 231, 236, 239, 243, 255, 262, 265, 267, 269, 296, 307, 319, 322, 332, 340, 344, 345, 346, 348, 349, 350, 352, 382, 407, 414
JOPLIN: 320
JORDAN (JORDON): 19, 67, 82, 90, 135
JUDD: 135
JUDIA: 42
JUDSON: 8, 263

K

KAY: 241, 328, 333
KEATON: 405
KEBNELL: 81
KEELING: 137, 168
KEEN: 64

KEITH: 19, 21, 96, 104, 223, 225, 255, 279, 315
KELLER: 187, 188, 226, 234, 396
KELLY (KELLEY): 172, 420
KELSO (KELSAW): 136, 137, 229, 263, 280, 364
KENNAIRD: 257
KENNEDY: 44, 46, 103, 136, 137, 184, 185, 219, 258, 278, 317
KENNEMER: 407
KENNEY: 247
KENT: 28, 136, 137, 210, 274, 283, 284
KERBO: 182, 232, 233, 257
KERCHEVAL: 103, 111
KERR: 137
KEY: 236, 251, 256, 330, 334
KIDD: 37, 38, 40, 41, 47, 137, 216, 337
KIGHT: 366
KILGORE: 137
KILMARTIN: 30, 137
KILPATRICK: 46, 172, 179, 183, 190, 217, 326
KIMBRO: 419
KIMBROUGH: 132, 187, 264
KIMES (KIME): 86, 86, 269
KIMMINS: 382
KINCAID (KINCADE): 122, 331
KINCANNON: 109, 111
KINESS: 107
KING: 4, 7, 8, 109, 185, 191, 245, 254, 307, 309, 310, 311, 312, 315, 319
KINNINGHAM: 123
KINTCHEN: 36, 213
KIRBY: 136
KIRKLAND: 136
KIRKPATRICK: 136
KIZZIAH: 424
KNIGHT: 137
KNOWLES: 172, 249
KNOX: 44, 64, 67
KOONCE: 111, 136, 137, 228, 229, 231, 232, 255
KRAUSS: 137

L

LACKEY (LACKY): 109, 138, 181, 202, 228, 259, 289
LADD: 93, 138, 405
LAMB: 137, 138, 139
LAMBERT: 2, 3, 4, 305, 307
LAND: 171, 181, 232, 259, 261, 315, 334
LANDESS: 12, 137, 138, 139, 311
LANE: 16, 18, 19, 55, 56, 57, 94, 95, 97, 138, 139, 258, 270, 271, 306
LANGFORD: 174, 177, 178, 182
LANGSTON: 226
LANIER: 109, 206
LARGEN: 95, 138, 139, 255
LASATER: 138, 248
LASEBY: 33
LATEN: 137, 230, 231, 232, 233
LATHAM: 438
LATSON: 235
LAUDERDALE: 138, 139
LAUGHLIN: 255
LAWLER: 138
LAWRENCE: 345
LAWS: 11, 16, 138, 376, 389
LAWSON: 402, 424, 425
LAXON: 246
LAY: 35, 113
LAYMAN: 172, 218
LEACH (LEECH): 402, 414, 423, 424
LEATHERWOOD: 80, 82, 166, 232, 339, 353
LEDFORD: 313
LEE: 176, 194, 223, 308, 352, 367, 403, 407, 418, 427
LEFTWICH: 321, 324, 360, 369, 370
LEGG: 139
LEIGH: 413
LEMING: 139
LEMMONS (LEMONS): 81
LEMOND: 29, 297, 299
LENTINI: 361
LEONARD: 167, 170, 311
LESLEY: 286, 366, 434
LESTER: 29
LEVAN: 372
LEVY: 138
LEWIS: 170, 248, 249, 286, 310, 407, 416, 417, 429, 430
LEWTER: 41, 43, 64, 65, 66, 69, 71, 72, 73, 83, 84, 85
LIACEAH: 113
LIGGETT: 296
LIGHT: 139, 328
LILES: 296, 297
LIMBAUGH: 414, 427, 432
LINCOLN: 46, 336
LINDSAY: 29, 42, 138, 139, 342, 343
LINEBERGER: 17, 23, 137, 139
LINK: 54
LITCHFORD: 408
LITTLE: 97, 137, 138, 139, 166, 225, 282, 378
LIVELY: 280, 333
LOCKE (LOCK): 66, 67, 75, 333, 338, 359, 366, 393, 418
LOCKER: 229, 230, 231, 329, 333, 334
LOFTON: 302
LLOYD (LOYD): 138
LOCKER: 139, 232, 259
LOGAN: 55, 56, 57, 271, 386, 393, 394
LONDON: 314, 316
LONG: 88, 211, 277, 305, 319
LOTTS: 138
LOVE: 250
LOVETT: 3, 193, 205
LOVING: 9, 316
LOWE: 49, 248, 390
LOYD (LLOYD): 188, 264, 274, 277, 285
LUCAS: 222
LUMPKIN: 138
LUMSDEN: 308
LUNA: 65, 70, 139, 206, 207, 208, 209, 213, 299, 303, 307, 318, 322
LUSK: 139
LUTTRELL (LITTRELL): 169, 171, 173, 174, 223, 224, 225, 226, 251
LYNCH: 277, 401, 424, 425
LYNES: 314
LYONS: 90

M

MADDEN: 139
MADDOX: 43, 64, 66, 78, 79, 80, 82, 142, 348
MAGNESS: 231
MAJORS: 367, 385, 414, 415, 416, 425
MALLORY: 64
MALONE: 64, 65, 66, 70, 71, 72, 74, 80, 139, 172, 180, 181, 197, 208, 328, 333, 334, 404, 422
MANDERSON: 189
MANGRUM: 22
MANLEY: 112, 245
MANN: 171, 224
MANNING: 236, 259, 378
MANSFIELD: 17, 55, 56, 98, 141, 143, 252, 253, 254, 258, 274, 381
MARCH: 21, 28, 86, 100, 140, 143, 196, 293, 295, 296, 297, 323
MARKHAM: 143, 194, 209, 212
MARKS: 139
MARLER: 6, 390
MARQUESS: 145
MARR (MARRS): 97, 98, 107, 140, 141, 142, 143, 144, 172, 174, 176, 231, 269, 302, 390, 391
MARSH: 1, 141, 142, 230, 254, 305, 315, 321, 322, 323, 324
MARSHALL (MARSHALS): 21, 64, 65, 66, 81, 142, 145, 196, 227, 236, 253, 259, 278, 325, 333, 426, 427, 431, 437
MARTAIN: 142
MARTIN: 28, 52, 53, 54, 56, 77, 82, 101, 108, 112, 125, 140, 141, 142, 143, 188, 235, 262, 335, 354, 355, 366, 368, 381, 388, 397, 399, 401, 402, 418, 422, 426
MARTY: 177, 178
MASHBURN: 414, 417
MASON: 144, 172, 178, 184, 187, 222, 248, 249, 250, 259, 324, 334
MASSENGALE: 337
MASSEY: 32, 84, 110, 112, 200, 288, 290, 310, 367, 373, 374, 386, 394, 410, 437
MATHIS (MATHES): 43, 45, 48, 51, 350, 400, 413
MATLOCK: 69, 70, 84, 140, 143, 383, 384, 400
MATTHEWS (MATHEWS): 141, 170, 334
MATTOX: 197
MAULDIN (MULDIN): 27, 28, 292, 293, 296, 297
MAULTSBY: 312
MAUPIN: 379
MAY (MAYS, MAYES): 189, 204, 215, 230, 251, 254, 256, 259
MAYBREY: 319
MEAD: 269, 271, 276
MEADOWS: 293
MEANN: 345
MEARSE (MEARS): 186, 224, 225, 226, 410
MEDEARIS: 141
MEDLEY: 73, 142, 143
MEEKS: 143, 204, 327, 333
MEINERT: 322
MELSON: 2, 4, 7, 10, 376
MELTON: 193, 205
MENEFEE: 139, 209, 325
MENGES: 369
MERRELL (MERRILL): 69, 70, 72, 73, 80, 199, 218
MERRITT: 142, 324
MESSINGILL: 406
METCALF (METCALFE, MITCALF): 60, 109, 143, 170, 201, 204, 235, 251, 253, 255, 257, 304
MEYER: 381
MIDDLETON: 179, 266
MILAM: 353

MILES: 17, 109, 144, 249, 259, 273, 274, 285, 386, 389, 415
MILEY: 401
MILHOUS: 141
MILLARD: 54, 86, 89, 142
MILLER: 53, 109, 140, 144, 188, 217, 244, 260, 310, 318, 418
MILLIGAN: 33
MILLIKEN (MILLIKIN): 32, 33, 37, 39, 208
MILLS: 5, 17, 43, 47, 94, 96, 97, 140, 141, 142, 143, 144, 217, 245, 258, 290, 313, 315, 316, 324
MILLSAP (MILLSAPS): 369, 373, 383, 408, 415, 416, 417
MILNER: 237
MILSTEAD: 17, 115, 142, 261
MILTON: 194, 205, 381
MIMS: 171
MINATREE: 23, 32
MINOR: 67, 406
MIRES: 185, 252, 260
MITCHELL: 43, 44, 61, 64, 65, 66, 67, 70, 72, 78, 79, 80, 140, 142, 143, 144, 172, 198, 201, 202, 203, 205, 206, 207, 208, 210, 255, 258, 264, 265, 269, 271, 273, 304, 310, 319, 372, 375, 408, 423, 429, 432, 437
MOCKBEE: 140
MOFFETT (MOFFITT, MOFFATT): 99, 240, 241, 349, 352, 353
MONDAY: 91, 141
MONKS: 236, 237, 238, 240, 248
MONTGOMERY: 40, 42, 48, 49, 144, 145, 304, 323, 402
MOONEY: 25, 193
MOONEYHAM: 249, 258
MOORE (MOOR): 4. 20, 52, 54, 55, 58, 66, 70, 88, 90, 92, 93, 96, 97, 101, 107, 140, 141, 142, 143, 144, 145, 187, 190, 192, 194, 209, 217, 218, 224, 229, 231, 232, 234, 235, 239, 249, 250, 251, 261, 262, 263, 265, 266, 271, 300, 301, 306, 308, 309, 313, 314, 316, 317, 319, 320, 322, 324, 328, 330, 332, 338, 339, 340, 341, 342, 343, 344, 345, 346, 348, 354, 362, 372, 381, 382,

MOORE: 385, 388, 391, 394, 395, 407, 426
MOOREHEAD (MOORHEAD): 143, 174, 257, 258, 269, 279, 282, 284, 288, 290, 379, 386, 387, 433, 435
MOORES: 34, 35, 96, 108, 140, 142, 144
MORAN: 67
MORGAN: 108, 109, 119, 141, 143, 144, 190, 191, 215, 216, 218, 276, 318, 380, 421
MORRIS: 2, 142, 143, 218, 360, 383, 392, 393, 394
MORRISON: 3, 88, 113, 141, 299, 306, 307, 310, 316, 320, 321, 322
MORROW: 179, 346
MORTON: 4, 7, 66, 140, 298, 305, 314, 320, 336
MOSELEY: 35, 358
MOSS: 243
MOTLOW: 103, 140, 141, 269, 271, 374, 376, 377, 378, 379, 380, 381, 388, 408
MOULDER: 411
MOUNT: 390
MOYERS (MOYER): 110, 111, 112, 139, 140, 142, 143, 144, 145, 185, 204, 236, 239, 240, 277, 281, 282, 295, 329, 333, 334, 350
MUELLER: 402
MULLIKIN: 172
MULLINS (MULLENS): 67, 73, 81, 113, 144, 204, 230, 237, 239, 240, 241, 268, 328, 329, 332, 333, 349, 368, 401, 402, 405, 407, 418, 421, 422, 423, 426
MUNTZ: 110
MURDOCK: 308
MURPHEY (MURPHY): 36, 145, 248
MURRAY (MURRAH): 6, 68, 143, 224, 297, 387, 393, 411, 426
MURRELL (MURELL, MORELL): 68, 436
MUSE: 2, 5, 139, 140, 144, 315, 317, 320, 321, 323, 414, 415
MYERS: 41, 44, 208, 345
MYRICK: 176, 240

Mc

McADAMS: 1, 2, 9, 315, 318
McADOO: 318
McAFEE: 19, 25, 28, 52, 62, 208, 209, 262, 263, 294, 296

McALISTER: 48, 70, 236, 239, 240, 328, 329, 330, 331, 332, 348, 349
McANALLY: 185, 187, 352
McANN: 78, 80, 337
McARTHUR: 405
McBAY: 142, 181, 234
McBRIDE: 48, 243, 249, 407
McCALLA: 81, 140, 337, 338, 340
McCALLUM: 86
McCANLESS: 284
McCARTNEY: 229, 278
McCAULY: 144
McCLAIN (McCLANE): 97, 143, 345
McCLELLAN (McCLELLAND): 86, 119, 140, 142, 165, 228, 280, 379
McCLENNEY: 310
McCLURE: 54, 222, 226, 286, 290, 433, 434
McCLURKIN: 32
McCLUSKY (McCLUSKEY): 140, 236, 247
McCOLLUM: 101, 141
McCONNELL: 309, 342
McCOOL: 47, 49, 68
McCORD: 109, 139, 372
McCORMICK: 221, 438
McCOWN (McGOWN, McCOWAN): 33, 38, 41, 42, 44, 46, 66, 76, 141, 142, 143, 145, 245, 255, 257, 258, 259, 330, 339, 343
McCOY: 63, 217, 294, 295, 296
McCRACKEN: 194, 199, 200, 208, 212
McCREARY: 187
McCRELESS: 178
McCRORY: 249, 252, 253, 256
McCULLOUGH (McCULLOH, McCULLOCK, MACCULIC): 104, 139, 140, 142, 181, 194, 227, 232, 281, 339, 340, 342
McCURDY: 52
McDANIEL: 21, 23, 30, 43, 47, 75, 77, 78, 80, 106, 107, 141, 143, 144, 169, 202, 242, 295
McDILL: 44, 141, 347
McDONALD: 77, 111, 140, 174, 345
McDOUGAL: 233, 234
McDOWELL: 381
McELDERRY: 215
McELROY: 106, 142, 144
McELYEA: 217
McEWEN: 140, 325, 402, 406
McFARRAR: 384
McFERRIN (McFERRAN): 46, 141, 145, 337, 339, 342, 345, 346, 347
McGAHA: 143

McGAUGH: 39
McGEE (McGHEE): 4, 15, 17, 20, 51, 55, 56, 58, 64, 93, 144, 188, 229, 254, 262, 316, 336, 384
McGEEHON (McGEEHAN): 246, 270
McGEHEE: 20, 178, 188, 218, 277, 285
McGHIA: 143
McGOWN (McGOWEN): 143, 365
McGREGOR: 381
McGUIRE: 61, 62, 140
McKAY: 123, 143, 202
McKEE: 191, 248
McKELVIE (McKELVY): 187, 191
McKENZIE (McKINZIE): 17, 139, 140, 375, 426, 427, 429
McKEOVE: 144
McKIN: 251, 253, 257
McKINNEY (McKINEY): 16, 69, 110, 112, 139, 140, 141, 142, 143, 207, 209, 228, 241, 297, 409, 417
McKNIGHT: 140, 197, 314, 315
McLAIN: 97, 266
McLANE: 265
McLAUGHLIN: 75, 131, 140, 141, 143, 168, 176, 223, 270
McLAURINE: 145
McLEAN: 49
McLEMORE: 76, 331, 340, 354, 377
McLIN: 212
McMILLEN (McMILLIN, McMILLAN): 86, 86, 143, 144, 328, 329, 333, 334, 343, 344, 345, 348
McMULLEN: 37, 340
McNATT (McNOTT): 52, 58, 139, 142, 362, 388, 390, 391
McNEAL: 140, 184, 185
McNEECE: 270, 274
McNEILL: 92
McNEIL: 366
McNELLEY (McNELLY): 112
McNUTT: 418
McPHAIL: 141, 142, 145
McPHERSON (McPHEASRON): 256, 349
McRADY: 315
McREE: 291
McRORY: 318
McTIER: 324
McWHORTER (McWHIRTER): 28, 140, 267, 280, 284, 331, 399
McWILLIAMS: 141, 144

N

NANCE: 82, 263
NATION: 200
NAYLOR: 145

NEAL: 235, 408, 410, 411, 414, 415
NEAVES: 81, 338
NEECE: 43, 50, 145, 335, 336, 361, 372, 381, 389
NEEL: 146
NEELD: 109, 110, 111, 112, 145, 264
NEELY: 16, 352, 353
NEIL (NEILL): 319, 385
NELMS: 310
NELSON: 61, 146, 204, 213, 233, 403, 405, 406, 416, 425
NERREN: 28, 29
NEVILL (NEVILLS): 145, 208
NEWBERN: 332
NEWBOURN: 235
NEWBY: 240
NEWGENT: 184
NEWMAN: 145, 146, 222, 254, 385
NEWSOM: 103, 145, 267, 361
NEWTON: 36, 38, 39, 40, 185
NICHOLS: 2, 3, 4, 92, 145, 212, 307, 308, 312, 323, 394
NICHOLSON: 403
NICKS: 109, 241, 264
NIPPERS: 407
NIX (NICK): 288, 289, 290, 419
NIXON: 187, 189, 290
NOAH: 145, 146, 202, 213
NOBLIN: 146
NOBLITT (NOBLETTS, NOBLETT): 19, 52, 53, 54, 146, 254, 368, 379, 389, 426
NOE: 170, 172
NOLAND: 4
NOLES: 145, 171, 274, 285, 367, 426, 438, 439
NORED: 145
NORMAN: 52, 145, 146, 165, 169, 177, 180, 222, 223, 224, 270, 271, 282, 380, 381, 385, 387
NORRIS: 112
NORTON: 380
NORVELL: 426
NORWOOD: 14, 296
NULL: 376
NUNLEY: 4, 185

O

OAKLEY: 264
ODEAR: 425
ODELL: 179
ODEM: 174, 177
OGILVIE: 319
OGLE: 48
OGLESBY: 22
OLD: 9
OLDHAM: 22, 35, 179, 231, 233
OLMER: 334
OLIVER (OLLIVER): 21, 295, 363
OLSEN: 332
O'NEAL (ONEAL): 62, 72, 172, 298
ORR: 169
ORRICK: 15, 88
ORTNER: 11
OSBORNE (OSBORN): 219, 272, 368, 430
OSTEEN: 324
OUSLEY: 117, 271
OVERBEY (OVERBY): 365, 373
OWEN (OWENS): 22, 23, 24, 29, 31, 32, 76, 108, 202, 211, 215, 224, 234, 236, 272, 273, 287, 292, 311, 323, 332, 383, 389, 432, 437

P

PACK: 10, 146, 147, 148, 217, 300, 318, 320, 321
PACKARD: 402
PACQUE: 306
PAINTER: 366, 412, 417
PALLACE: 346
PAMPLIN: 16, 20, 94, 95, 96, 97, 98, 106, 147, 256, 389, 390
PANTER: 188, 218
PARHAM: 414
PARISH: 331
PARK: 56, 213, 220
PARKER: 42, 98, 148, 197, 207, 219, 222, 365, 408, 412
PARKERSON: 217, 337
PARKINSON: 147, 148, 337, 338, 342
PARKS (PARKES): 16, 54, 74, 95, 105, 146, 147, 148, 223, 264, 266, 270, 271, 276, 290, 296, 363, 365, 367, 369, 370, 371, 374, 378, 379, 400, 407, 408, 410, 420, 421, 422, 431, 433, 437
PARM: 250
PARR: 204, 205, 208
PARRILL: 147
PARROTT: 397
PARTAIN (PARTIN): 17, 52, 146, 147, 207, 208, 210, 319, 361, 404
PARYEAR: 147
PASSON: 243
PATE: 170, 223
PATRICK: 146, 177, 215, 230, 234, 255
PATTERSON: 2, 15, 61, 62, 66, 85, 148, 171, 185, 188, 230, 249, 298, 342, 409, 410
PATTON (PATTEN): 2, 29, 86, 87, 92, 146, 147, 216, 219, 432, 433
PAULK: 379
PAYNE: 81, 148, 170, 206, 217, 233, 234, 237, 271, 348
PAYSINGER: 62, 68
PAYTON: 146
PEACH: 148
PEAKE: 146
PEAL: 368
PEARCE: 147, 204
PEARSON: 20, 44, 93, 147, 251, 264, 316, 322, 327, 330, 333, 353, 389, 419, 422
PENDERGRASS: 177, 188
PENNINGTON: 237
PENNY: 342
PEOPLES: 66
PEPPER (PEPPERS): 81, 177, 188, 189, 219, 338, 351, 365
PEARCY: 315, 324
PERKINS: 266
PERRY: 39, 49, 93, 146, 204, 218, 251, 274, 431
PETTY (PETTEY): 147, 180, 260, 355, 362, 419
PFOETNER: 375
PHAGAN: 36, 38, 41, 43, 46, 147, 148, 330, 343
PHELPS: 51, 53, 54, 55, 56, 57, 312, 361, 366, 389, 394
PHIFER: 312
PHILLIPS (PHILIPS): 6, 7, 146, 148, 189, 203, 204, 236, 242, 245, 246, 247, 307, 308, 349, 352, 392
PHILPOTT (PHILPOT): 68, 77, 78, 80, 148, 323, 377, 388, 432
PHLIEGER: 306
PIANT: 381
PIERCE: 309, 314, 319, 387, 392, 393, 422
PIERSON: 246
PICKETT: 169, 170, 221, 223, 224, 230, 257
PICKLE: 100, 302
PIGG: 146, 148, 177, 249, 281, 298, 299, 300, 303, 305, 317, 319, 320
PIKE: 148
PINKERTON: 420
PINKSTAFF: 89
PIRTLE: 89, 92, 181, 255, 258
PITCOCK: 170, 191, 331
PITTS: 36, 51, 55, 66, 89, 93, 94, 95, 98, 104, 105, 146, 147, 148, 174, 178, 179, 181, 183, 189, 263, 266, 268, 269, 271, 279, 316, 326, 327, 336, 339, 346, 348, 370
PLEXICO: 340
PLUNKETT: 186
POARCH: 208, 299
POE: 417
POGUE: 226, 344, 346, 425
POINDEXTER: 86, 146
POLLARD: 404
POLLOCK: 148, 205, 402, 405, 409, 413, 418
POLLY (POLLEY): 64, 66
POOL (POOLE): 66, 75, 335, 346, 349, 350
POOR: 248
POPE: 146
PORCH: 25, 29, 292
PORTER: 27, 75, 146, 147, 207, 227, 230, 232, 243, 244, 250, 253, 318, 341, 355, 434, 436
PORTERFIELD: 108
POSEY: 26, 87, 90, 147, 148, 247, 248, 249, 350
POST: 62
POSTON: 77
POWELL: 6, 37, 90, 181, 186, 188, 216, 315, 351, 358
POWERS: 287, 308, 319, 404
PRATER: 187, 366
PRESLEY: 407
PRESTON: 179, 223, 225, 272, 369, 373, 409, 432, 433, 435
PRICE: 56, 70, 88, 147, 230, 233, 235, 248, 251, 254, 256, 268, 314, 328, 329, 367, 369, 372, 383, 397, 410, 413, 420, 426, 427
PRINCE: 382, 403, 406, 419, 423, 424
PROSSER: 6, 13, 86, 147, 148, 206, 311, 315, 358, 391
PRUETT (PRUITT): 174, 175, 178, 185, 189, 207, 211, 223, 224, 251, 252, 254, 258, 260
PRYOR: 167, 250, 259
PUCKETT (PUCKETTE): 80, 148
PULLEY: 283
PULLIAM: 224
PURDY: 184
PURTLE: 148
PURYEAR: 330, 331
PUTMAN: 75, 146

PYBAS: 16
PYLANT (PYLAND): 13, 53, 89, 147, 215, 216, 219, 289, 309, 310, 330, 360, 398
PYRDAM: 426

Q

QUARLES: 27, 271
QUICK: 233, 236, 238, 251, 253, 255, 256, 258, 259, 260
QUIMBY: 148

R

RABY: 6, 50, 51, 52, 149, 151, 268, 269, 315, 360, 368, 374, 379, 391
RAINES: 175
RAINEY: 79, 81, 305
RALSTON: 150
RAMBO: 23, 149, 150, 195
RAMSEY: 23, 25, 31, 49, 111, 149, 150, 206, 217, 274, 284, 300
RAMY: 249
RANDALL: 401
RANDOLPH: 151, 327, 328, 330
RANEY: 3, 5, 361, 390, 418
RATLEY: 65, 333
RATLIFF: 284
RAWLS: 42, 44, 77, 80, 149, 150, 326
RAY: 149, 150, 175, 181, 188, 293, 402, 403, 404, 405, 407, 411, 413, 418, 419, 422
READ: 433, 435
READY: 149, 151
REAGAN: 218
REAGOR: 54, 55
REAVIS: 234, 313, 319, 328, 401, 404, 414
RECORD (RECARD): 235, 249, 377
REDD: 1, 3, 4, 149, 308, 309, 314, 315, 320, 322, 358, 389, 390, 391
REDDEN: 294
REDMAN: 325
REED: 69, 111, 150, 151, 175, 192, 205, 208, 210, 211, 218, 244, 285, 292, 296, 297, 331, 418, 419, 420, 435
REES: 50, 103, 150, 151, 266, 360, 361, 391
REESE (REECE): 5, 37, 43, 44, 48, 49, 51, 93, 105, 113, 149, 150, 238, 271, 320, 341, 361, 364, 365,

REESE: 369, 371, 384, 386, 409, 412, 423
REEVES: 71, 220, 221, 245, 311
REID: 188, 220
RENEGAR: 110, 149, 150, 151, 180, 214, 264, 268, 271, 273, 276, 278, 285, 290, 294, 296, 361, 373
RENFROW (RENFRO): 13, 103, 148
REVIN: 321
REVIS: 181
REYNOLDS (RAYNOLDS, RENOLDS, RENNOLDS): 20, 80, 149, 150, 151, 178, 215, 219, 277, 335, 341, 412, 413
RHEA: 114, 148, 149, 269
RHODES: 75, 100, 148, 333, 335
RHOTEN (RHOTON): 266, 367, 368, 369, 408, 413
RICE: 151, 186, 319, 321, 385
RICH: 172, 221, 222, 281
RICHARDSON: 24, 46, 55, 148, 150, 207, 238, 269, 291, 292, 295, 308, 312, 319, 358, 360, 361, 362, 390, 391, 424, 438
RICHMOND: 34, 384
RICHTER: 422
RIDDLE: 270, 272, 273, 366, 367, 375, 422, 432, 434
RIEMER: 25
RIGSBY: 217
RILEY: 74, 78, 80, 90, 222, 225, 248, 377
RINER: 208
RINGO: 205
RIVES: 11, 50, 55, 149, 150, 270, 301, 304, 321, 322
ROACH: 115, 149, 151
ROBERTS (ROBERT): 111, 257, 319, 323, 369
ROBERTSON: 78, 81, 108, 149, 150, 216, 220, 221, 338, 345, 369, 383, 386, 392, 394
ROBINSON: 185, 186, 192, 202, 203, 206, 210, 212, 352, 355, 361, 364
ROBISON: 149, 184, 195, 210
RODEN: 23, 192, 194, 295
RODES: 149, 150, 314, 333
RODGERS: 69, 70, 151, 202, 340, 355
ROE: 19, 90, 151, 262

ROGERS: 5, 43, 47, 70, 81, 150, 215, 226, 239, 240, 243, 246, 247, 311, 344, 355, 384, 386, 405
ROLAND: 48, 49, 190, 233, 348
ROLMAN: 414
ROOKS: 174
ROPER: 71, 72, 74, 83, 84, 175
RORAX: 57, 369
ROSEBOROUGH (ROSBOROUGH): 86, 86, 91
ROSS: 149, 202, 204, 217
ROTEN: 194
ROUGHTON: 360, 380
ROUSE: 149
ROUTT (ROUTTE): 149, 199, 227, 229, 238, 278
ROWE: 227
ROWELL: 39, 82, 85, 339, 340, 341, 342, 349, 352, 354
ROWZEE: 111, 151
ROWLAND: 258
ROZAR: 54, 55
ROZELL (ROZAL): 187, 188, 259
ROZIER: 20
RUBERT: 151
RUCKER: 151, 298
RUDD: 31, 148, 180
RUNNELS: 361
RUSH: 253
RUSSELL (RUSSEL, REUSSELL): 4, 15, 21, 54, 108, 110, 151, 170, 199, 202, 299, 317, 318, 355, 392, 394, 432
RUTH: 22, 150
RUTLEDGE: 50, 54, 58, 94, 150, 151, 178, 243, 249, 251, 253, 262, 263, 265, 328, 380, 390
RUTHERFORD: 60
RYALS: 316

S

SAMPLES: 208
SANDERS: 24, 39, 45, 65, 67, 78, 80, 153, 155, 186, 187, 196, 202, 203, 204, 207, 213, 252, 253, 258, 274, 282, 291, 293, 294, 306, 308, 311, 316, 319, 326, 327, 338, 340, 345, 346, 350, 351, 353, 366, 385, 390, 402, 405, 408, 409, 411, 412, 414, 415, 416
SANDERSON: 73
SANDLIN (SADDLIN): 44, 154, 329, 333, 338, 345, 347
SANFORD: 315
SATTERFIELD: 100, 233,

SATTERFIELD: 331, 353
SAUNDERS: 153, 302
SAVAGE: 6
SAWYERS (SAWYER): 22, 27, 87, 90, 92, 93, 111, 205, 209, 210, 213, 239, 259, 367, 368, 371, 372, 387, 406, 417, 418, 431, 435
SCARBROUGH: 218
SCHNETZLER: 243, 246
SCHOENBERGER: 156
SCIVALLY: 217, 218, 373, 406, 411, 436
SCOGGINS: 298, 299
SCOTT (SCOT): 9, 22, 24, 74, 87, 89, 91, 92, 108, 109, 112, 151, 153, 154, 217, 227, 270, 284, 302, 303, 305, 306, 307, 310, 313, 316, 317, 332, 353, 433, 434
SCREWS: 177
SCRIMSHER: 248
SCROGGINS: 409
SCRUGGS: 328, 332
SEARCY: 416
SEATON: 180, 181, 234, 238
SEBASTIAN (SEBASTAIN): 265, 379
SELF: 191
SELLS: 403
SETLIFF: 381, 399
SHACKLEFORD: 155
SHADDEN: 268
SHADDY: 3, 4, 321
SHAND: 67
SHANNON: 84
SHARP (SHARPE): 102, 188, 391, 401
SHASTEEN (CHASTEEN): 182, 414, 415, 417, 423
SHAW (SHOW): 49, 153, 208, 365, 380, 381, 382, 407
SHEARRON: 77
SHEFFIELD (SHUFFIELD): 43, 341, 345, 346
SHELTON: 10, 44, 151, 152, 153, 156, 179, 182, 212, 218, 251, 252, 254, 257, 258, 260, 283, 284, 371, 405, 436, 438
SHEPARD (SHEPPARD): 173
SHERRELL: 61, 62, 63, 85, 98, 153, 156, 170, 203
SHERWOOD: 13, 233, 252, 314
SHIPP: 30, 154, 155
SHIELDS: 17, 51, 177
SHIREY: 171
SHOCKLEY: 243, 244, 249
SHOFNER: 58, 152, 154, 156, 262, 265, 266, 268, 269, 304, 375, 426

SHOOK: 231
SHORES: 118
SHORT: 87, 112, 151, 155, 282, 295
SHRADER: 173, 176, 217
SHUBERT: 175, 177, 178
SHUGART: 86
SHULL: 99
SIGMON: 370
SILVERTOOTH: 381, 421
SILVESTER: 60
SIMMONS: 2, 151, 152, 156, 168, 169, 170, 173, 174, 175, 178, 234, 235, 239, 244, 245, 274, 281, 282, 283, 289, 330, 333, 350, 386, 404, 407, 418
SIMPSON: 156, 252, 259, 266, 371, 374, 375, 387, 393, 412, 414, 415, 416, 417
SIMS (SIMMS): 19, 49, 63, 72, 76, 89, 95, 153, 155, 171, 176, 184, 217, 252, 254, 255, 256, 257, 258, 259, 260, 332, 333, 346, 349, 360, 382
SIPES: 386
SISCO: 237
SISK: 40, 45, 47, 73, 170
SLAGLE: 235
SLATER: 112
SLAUGHTER: 85
SLAYTON (SLATON): 65, 67, 244, 245
SLEDGE: 334
SLOAN: 151, 153, 156, 336, 340, 342, 343, 344, 346
SMALL: 15, 152, 263, 266
SMART: 33, 34, 434
SMITH: 1, 6, 10, 11, 19, 22, 23, 25, 26, 27, 29, 32, 46, 47, 55, 56, 61, 64, 65, 67, 69, 70, 71, 72, 73, 74, 75, 76, 77, 78, 79, 81, 86, 89, 90, 91, 92, 93, 95, 97, 98, 99, 106, 108, 109, 111, 112, 151, 152, 153, 154, 155, 156, 168, 169, 170, 173, 174, 175, 176, 178, 179, 183, 184, 187, 188, 192, 197, 198, 203, 205, 206, 208, 209, 210, 211, 212, 216, 218, 219, 221, 222, 223, 225, 226, 227, 228, 229, 230, 231, 232, 241, 244, 245, 247, 253, 264, 279, 285, 287, 291, 292, 293, 295, 296, 298, 299,

SMITH: 302, 304, 308, 309, 310, 312, 313, 314, 317, 319, 321, 323, 326, 328, 329, 331, 332, 333, 334, 335, 336, 337, 340, 344, 346, 348, 349, 350, 352, 354, 355, 360, 361, 362, 364, 365, 367, 369, 370, 371, 372, 376, 383, 384, 385, 387, 393, 394, 395, 399, 400, 401, 402, 403, 404, 406, 408, 411, 412, 414, 416, 418, 423, 424, 425, 428, 434, 435, 438, 439
SMOOT: 368, 373, 408
SMYTHE: 155, 314, 325
SNELL: 152
SNODDY: 151, 166, 278
SNOW: 63, 65, 176, 178, 384, 432, 435, 436
SNYDER: 367
SOLOMON: 85, 113, 114, 153, 155, 264, 265, 266, 276, 278, 279, 280, 281, 289, 319, 372, 380, 429
SOLTERS: 248
SONS: 423
SORRELL (SORRELLS): 1, 7, 8, 12, 13, 153, 305, 306, 307, 315, 320, 322, 324
SORROW: 30, 203
SOUTH: 155
SOUTHERLAN: 223
SOUTHWORTH: 27, 165, 182
SOWELL: 25, 153, 293, 307
SPANN: 370, 415
SPARKS: 103
SPECK: 170, 179, 186, 224
SPEER: 205
SPENCE: 38, 342, 343
SPENCER: 151, 152, 156, 176, 266, 267, 271, 286, 287, 289, 363, 378, 379, 384, 385, 386, 400, 409, 412, 429, 432, 433, 434, 435, 437
SPIVY: 192
SPRAY: 24, 47, 152, 251, 254, 328, 329, 330, 331, 332, 334, 347, 371
SPRIGGS: 377, 386
SPRY: 405, 407
SPURLOCK: 152, 155
STACY: 57, 262, 318, 394
STAFFORD: 244, 252, 258, 382
STALCUP: 75, 78, 353
STALLINGS: 306

STATON: 81, 190
STATUM: 325
STEADMAN: 65, 66, 76
STEAGALL: 418
STEDMAN: 151, 335, 345
STEED (STEEDE): 15, 93, 312, 398, 406, 411
STEELE: 111, 155, 191, 216, 219, 316
STEELMAN: 6, 18, 19, 50, 51, 56, 57, 92, 152, 154, 229, 234, 311, 313, 317
STEGALL: 154
STEPHENS (STEPENS): 36, 67, 237, 238, 241, 283, 317, 332, 337, 346, 349, 350, 351, 392, 394, 403, 404, 407, 420, 429
STEPHENSON: 5, 102, 123, 151, 154, 156, 228, 283, 306, 322
STEVENSON: 61, 154, 179, 182, 183, 188, 189, 252, 254, 255, 256, 259, 260
STEWART: 41, 44, 47, 152, 153, 154, 155, 173, 190, 201, 202, 203, 219, 220, 229, 230, 237, 238, 252, 256, 336, 337, 338, 341, 342, 343, 344, 346, 353, 402, 408, 409, 410, 414, 416, 420
STEWMAN (STEWMON): 153, 156, 251, 287
STILES (STYLES): 172, 173, 174, 177, 179, 188, 189, 190, 214, 221, 290
STINSON: 295
STOCKTON: 413
STOCSTILL (STOGSTILL): 152, 155, 377
STOKES: 293
STONE: 12, 15, 49, 51, 63, 98, 105, 151, 152, 153, 154, 155, 185, 190, 191, 235, 294, 359, 364, 366, 367, 368, 371, 381, 385, 386, 388, 392, 394, 396, 397, 419, 426, 428
STONEBREAKER (STONEBRAKER): 155, 165
STOREY (STORY): 30, 154, 197, 199, 203, 204, 207, 210, 212
STORMENT: 41
STOUT: 11
STOVALL: 74, 75, 215, 218, 221
STOWERS: 154, 156
STRAIN (STRANE): 33, 59, 63, 382
STRAISCH: 401

STRATTON: 65
STREET: 17, 151, 152, 166, 179, 181, 231, 262, 268, 282, 291, 293, 304, 308, 325, 345, 352, 407
STRONG: 153, 154, 155, 156, 335, 339, 343
STROUD: 343
STUART: 201, 202
STUBBLEFIELD: 151, 152, 154, 155, 214, 269, 279, 289
SUGG (SUGGS): 34, 153, 156, 252, 374
SULLENGER (SULLINGER): 179, 234, 279, 285, 286, 288, 419, 431, 433, 435
SULLIVAN: 17, 19, 28, 55, 155, 179, 255, 261, 263, 270, 285, 293, 294, 295, 296, 311, 312, 313, 318, 360, 370, 371, 384
SULSER (SALSER): 77, 81, 351
SUMMARELL: 216
SUMMERFORD: 90, 91, 93, 335, 340
SUMMERS: 172, 185
SUMNERS (SUMNER): 22, 36, 48, 49, 59, 154, 192, 208, 209, 312
SUTHERLAND: 227
SUTTLE: 196
SUTTON: 197, 216, 376
SWAFFORD: 215
SWAIN: 16
SWANNER (SWANER): 151, 192, 203, 208, 292
SWEENEY: 151, 152, 317, 369, 380, 431, 432
SWEESY: 152
SWINDELL: 173
SWINDLE (SWINDELL): 13, 155
SWINEBROAD: 196
SWINEY (SWINNEY): 21, 152, 273
SWINFORD: 187, 232, 239, 240, 330, 331, 332, 334, 348, 349
SWING: 312, 317, 324, 325
SYLER: 177, 222, 223, 224, 225, 226, 438

T

TAFT (TAFTS): 77, 78, 81, 233, 346, 351
TALLENT (TALENT): 80, 233, 413
TALLEY: 87, 89, 222, 233, 295, 311, 312
TALLMAN: 91, 92, 206
TANKERSLEY (TANKERSLY): 400, 401, 402, 403, 414, 415, 423, 424, 425
TANNER: 238

TARKINGTON: 279
TATE: 36, 37, 39, 89, 90, 97, 156, 157, 158, 434
TATUM: 305
TAYLOR: 12, 27, 32, 37, 41, 42, 46, 88, 99, 156, 157, 158, 165, 167, 168, 172, 174, 176, 180, 181, 206, 223, 224, 225, 226, 251, 254, 255, 262, 269, 270, 272, 278, 279, 280, 282, 287, 289, 290, 293, 295, 296, 297, 302, 317, 322, 327, 334, 374, 378, 379, 398, 429
TEEL (TEAL): 157, 176
TEEPLES: 72
TEETERS: 371
TEMPLETON: 22, 23, 40, 157, 222, 224, 246, 336, 338, 339, 344, 366, 420
TERRY: 54, 157, 158, 186, 266
THANE: 88
THOMAS: 14, 51, 56, 82, 86, 87, 89, 90, 156, 157, 246, 264, 346, 380, 390, 391, 424
THOMASON: 249
THOMISON: 103, 104, 156, 157, 158, 228, 264, 316, 365, 378
THOMPSON: 22, 25, 32, 42, 43, 47, 54, 57, 65, 66, 67, 68, 73, 77, 78, 156, 157, 158, 178, 190, 231, 235, 275, 279, 280, 282, 283, 284, 285, 287, 288, 342, 345, 354, 383, 407, 408
THOMSON: 15
THORN (THORNE): 403, 420
THORNBROUGH: 157
THORNEBERRY: 404
THORNTON: 14, 16, 46, 71, 156, 157, 158, 280, 302, 322, 335
THORPE: 197, 200
THRASHER: 187, 330, 353
THRONESBERRY: 426, 439
TIDWELL: 288
TIELKING: 243, 244, 251, 255, 257
TIGERT: 27, 157
TILERY: 71
TILLER: 20, 64
TILLERY: 83
TILMAN: 158
TIMMONS (TIMMINS): 39, 376, 410, 411, 413
TIPPS: 158, 224, 239, 240, 241, 266, 267, 268, 269, 272, 273, 330, 349, 368, 369,

TIPPS: 373, 374, 375, 376, 382, 385, 431, 435, 436
TIMS: 410, 426
TIPTON: 187, 373
TODD: 73, 111, 158, 177, 178
TOLLEY: 267, 268, 272, 373, 380
TOM: 158
TOMLINSON: 157
TONG: 376
TOOLE: 37, 86, 86, 341
TOOLEY: 297
TOON (TOONE): 43, 72, 158, 346
TOSH: 66, 376
TOUCHSTONE: 39, 308
TOWERY (TOWRY): 157, 184, 185, 236, 237, 238, 239, 240, 242, 244, 249, 252, 253, 254, 256, 257, 260, 287
TRANTHAM (TRATHAM): 158, 208, 210, 211, 212, 213
TRAVIS: 250, 385, 386, 436
TREECE: 73
TRENTHAM: 252
TRIBBLE: 72, 158, 330
TRIGG: 156, 158
TRIPLETT: 307
TRIPP: 158, 272, 273, 368, 429, 432, 435, 438
TROLLINGER: 365
TROOP: 223, 304, 319, 321
TROXLER: 194, 401
TRYLING: 158
TUCKER: 24, 30, 31, 34, 56, 57, 79, 96, 99, 110, 157, 170, 175, 180, 181, 202, 205, 212, 218, 233, 235, 236, 240, 253, 255, 256, 257, 259, 269, 270, 273, 277, 280, 285, 286, 287, 288, 289, 290, 298, 299, 304, 341, 346, 366, 374, 385, 386, 387, 419, 428, 433, 435
TULEY (TULLEY, TULLY): 156, 210, 211, 257, 304
TUNSTILL: 186
TUREMAN: 158
TURLEY: 35, 157
TURNER: 22, 25, 31, 66, 78, 104, 190, 191, 203, 239, 248, 332, 335, 371, 416
TURNEY: 23, 30, 91,158, 298, 303
TURPIN: 366
TWITTY: 77, 78, 338

U
UNDERWOOD: 240
UPTON: 215

V
VANCE: 158, 364
VANN (VAN): 186, 234, 243
VAN SAUN: 54
VANZANT: 370
VAUGHN (VAUGHAN): 43, 47, 133, 158, 186, 237, 306, 335, 366
VENTRESS: 229, 230, 232, 276, 277
VICKERS: 64, 65, 72, 79, 158
VINES: 189
VINING: 158, 247, 248
VINZANT: 283

W
WADDELL: 162
WADDING: 249
WADDLE: 110, 112, 161, 162
WADE (WAID): 8, 11, 88, 90, 95, 99, 159, 162, 163, 205, 261, 287, 305, 429
WADKINS: 406
WAGGONER (WAGGONNER, WAGONER): 20, 52, 54, 55, 56, 158,159, 160, 163, 263, 264, 267, 268, 270, 365, 366, 368, 370, 371, 372, 374, 375, 377, 378, 379, 384, 385, 386, 387, 392, 393, 394, 399, 400, 433, 437
WAGNER: 363
WAGSTER: 3, 4, 160, 293, 310, 318, 358
WAID: 8, 311(see WADE)
WAITE: 46, 48
WAKEFIELD: 39, 107, 159, 220, 221, 294, 296, 303, 316, 318
WALDEN: 185, 203, 325
WALDREP: 48
WALKER: 64, 66, 82, 89, 105, 106, 182, 219, 221, 223, 225, 226, 229, 230, 231, 236, 237, 238, 239, 241, 242, 244, 245, 246, 251, 260, 272, 287, 367, 369, 396, 429, 430, 432, 433, 438
WALL: 22
WALLACE: 68, 79, 110, 159, 160, 241, 323, 328, 350
WALLER: 438
WANSLEE: 426
WANSLOW: 369, 372, 395
WARD: 52, 100, 159, 160, 161, 172, 277,

WARD: 287, 288, 289, 366, 385, 394, 419, 423
WARDEN: 18, 19, 53, 95, 96, 97, 103, 104, 159, 160, 161, 162, 163, 251
WARNER: 421
WARREN (WAR'N): 10, 17, 102, 159, 160, 162, 163, 169, 170, 175, 177, 206, 224, 230, 251, 267, 270, 277, 281, 302, 307, 308, 310, 311, 313, 314, 317, 320, 331, 358, 369, 370, 380, 389, 390, 391, 416
WASHBURN: 10, 15, 246, 341, 348, 349
WATERS: 191
WATKINS: 79, 159, 316, 328, 333
WATSON: 22, 77, 79, 80, 87, 176, 204, 211, 212, 321, 322, 337, 338, 339, 340, 350
WATT: 24, 30
WEAR: 109
WEAVER: 388, 421, 422
WEBB: 26, 39, 44, 112, 159, 162, 259, 271, 278, 279, 280, 282, 284, 383, 430
WEBSTER: 81, 248
WEDDINGTON: 402, 403
WEEKS: 404
WEGOLD: 161
WEIR: 176
WEISS: 161, 179, 279
WELCH (WELSH): 63, 90, 159, 161, 253, 254, 258, 295, 299, 309, 310, 325
WELLER: 159
WELLS: 8, 158, 159, 161, 162, 163, 175, 177, 196, 215, 227, 228, 241, 257, 295, 296, 308, 313, 315, 316, 323, 325, 327, 329, 333, 429
WEST: 28, 41, 43, 44, 45, 47, 48, 159, 161, 203, 206, 209, 210, 211, 212, 294, 296, 348, 404, 406
WHALEY: 69, 70
WHEELER: 353, 372
WHERLY: 66
WHIPPLE: 379
WHITAKER (WHITTAKER): 23, 25, 34, 35, 61, 96, 98, 108, 158, 159, 161, 162, 163, 187, 193, 234, 252, 263, 264, 265, 267, 268, 270, 271, 272, 291, 320, 346, 364, 365

WHITE: 32, 37, 45, 84, 89, 159, 160, 162, 163, 166, 184, 217, 233, 268, 274, 275, 290, 317, 346, 348, 349, 365, 370, 388
WHITEHEAD: 34, 211, 217
WHITFIELD: 174, 191
WHITLOCK: 363, 417
WHITMAN: 66, 350, 395
WHITSETT: 308, 309
WHITT: 69, 70, 71, 77, 79, 83, 173
WHITTINGTON: 163
WHITWORTH: 13, 95, 175, 177, 181, 230, 397
WHORLEY: 30, 161, 306, 312, 317
WICKS: 183, 228, 253, 259
WIDNER: 159, 163
WIGGINS: 368, 394, 395
WIGGS: 419
WILBANKS (WILLBANKS): 41, 66, 204, 217, 348
WILBURN: 169
WILES: 50, 55
WILEY: 16, 40, 41, 42, 49, 104, 146, 159, 160, 161, 337, 342, 345
WILHOITE: 409
WILKERSON: 294, 295, 312
WILKES (WILKS): 56, 163, 373, 374, 437
WILLIAMS: 22, 24, 40, 66, 75, 78, 159, 160, 161, 162, 186, 187, 222, 224, 225, 229, 230, 234, 237, 252, 267, 277, 279, 282, 303, 307, 310, 321, 333, 340, 358, 362, 397, 403, 404, 407, 425
WILLIAMSON: 31, 32, 86, 163, 173, 174, 240, 254, 282, 327
WILSON: 21, 22, 25, 32, 33, 34, 38, 44, 45, 46, 56, 70, 77, 110, 111, 159, 160, 161, 162, 163, 192, 195, 196, 238, 298, 308, 315, 337, 377
WIMBERLEY: 248, 313
WINE: 179
WINFORD: 80, 161, 290, 305, 317
WINN: 111, 175, 179
WINSETT: 43, 44, 87, 92, 163, 187, 188, 189, 231, 349
WISDOM: 317
WISE: 313, 400, 435
WISEMAN: 226, 267, 359, 364, 366, 377, 385, 386, 387, 397, 398, 426, 427, 431, 433, 437, 439

WISENER: 22, 54, 171
WISER: 312, 403
WITT: 244, 245, 246
WOLAVER: 185, 254, 257, 258
WOMACK: 167, 274, 311, 328, 334, 359, 365, 371, 377, 395, 398, 402
WOMBLE: 7, 376, 391, 408, 419, 420, 422
WOOD: 22, 48, 57, 89, 161, 163, 266, 271, 359, 373, 428
WOODALF: 66
WOODALL: 182
WOODARD: 9, 51, 76, 103, 107, 159, 160, 161, 162, 163, 197, 199, 201, 202, 255, 302, 311, 335, 359, 376, 386, 392, 393, 394, 397, 416, 436
WOODFIN: 81
WOODROOF: 114
WOODRUFF: 224, 422
WOODS: 85, 109, 160, 161, 163, 185, 186
WOODWARD: 202
WOOSLEY: 53, 306, 368, 390, 403, 406, 407, 409, 422
WOOTEN: 419
WORKMAN: 46
WORD: 365, 366
WORLEY (WORLDLY): 259
WORSHAM: 110, 111, 186
WRIGHT: 7, 15, 16, 25, 35, 38, 44, 87, 159, 161, 162, 163, 174, 192, 206, 207, 208, 209, 210, 211, 212, 213, 215, 221, 245, 256, 291, 293, 295, 297, 303, 307, 339, 344
WRITCH: 64
WYATT: 33, 42, 43, 49, 159, 160, 162, 345
WYMAN: 160
WYNN (WYNNE): 66, 178
WYSONG: 291

Y

YANT: 104, 111
YARBROUGH: 163, 215, 217, 219, 348, 354
YATES: 163, 164
YEAGER: 337, 346
YEARWOOD: 163, 164
YELL: 263, 333
YORK: 41, 207
YOST: 172
YOUNG: 61, 62, 80, 92, 163, 164, 171, 177, 179, 182, 218, 225, 257, 287, 311, 322, 348, 433
YOWELL: 34

Z

ZIMMERMAN: 35, 86
ZINIMON: 200
ZIVELEY (ZIVLEY): 109